EDUCATION POLICY AND THE LAW

EDUCATION POLICY AND THE LAW

Cases and Commentary

Second Edition

Bernard James
Pepperdine University School of Law
Malibu, California

Vandeplas Publishing

United States of America

Published by Vandeplas Publishing LLC - August 2020
801 International Parkway, 5th Floor
Lake Mary, FL 32746

Library of Congress Cataloging-in-Publication Data
James, Bernard
Education Policy and the Law: Cases and Commentary
Includes index
ISBN 978-1-60042-518-9 (paperback)
1. Education Law- United States-States-Cases

DEDICATIONS

To My Family in Whom I Find Redemption

Constance Rhetta

Catherine Irene

Michael Bernard

Michael Robert

Rory Anjali

PREFACE

Since the first edition, waves of reform have broken on the shores of education jurisprudence. Most of the landscape swept away is the result of swells of positive law from state legislatures and state courts. To say that comparatively fewer changes have been brought about by federal law is simply to recognize that education policy is primarily the enterprise of state governments. Despite the federal constitutional constraints on state policymakers, the themes, structures, and developments that shape the education mission are distinctly the product of federalism, state constitutional law, and local autonomy.

The second edition is a snapshot of these singular reforms to challenges to the education mission that did not exist a decade ago. The debate over whether education should be deemed a fundamental right is shifting to discussions about school safety and the search for a rubric for maintaining a learning environment that balances restorative justice with the right to be free from victimization. Student rights continue to evolve in ways separately from claims asserted by citizens outside of education, but with an emphasis on identity politics and "me too" claims to fairness. Even so, no one appears to have foreseen the resurgence of *in loco parentis* or the manner in which the rising authority of school officials is blunting the traditional limitations framed by the First, Fourth, and Fifth Amendments to the U.S. Constitution. Perhaps this explains the single most unforeseen wave of reform, the rigorous liability standards directed toward educators who abuse their authority.

The claim that education policy is shifting away from federal influence is a difficult, contentious endeavor. Constraints on school officials in this era of local empowerment do emerge primarily from state legislatures and state courts. But Congress has labored tacitly around the questions of curricular reform, antidiscrimination, and special needs education and continue to do so through tangible conditions on federal educational funding.

Although many of its cases are new, the objective and focus of the book is the same, to look beneath the surface of the case holdings to examine insofar as possible what educators are thinking. The book still addresses all of the main topics, including the right of parents to direct the education of their children through an increasing range of choices. Yet, all of this remains shaped by the hope that a student who systematically studies these materials will formulate their own views. As before, I have indicated my restatement of the facts or other passages in these materials by square brackets around the text. I have omitted footnotes without specifically indicating this fact. The footnotes that appear retain their original numbering. A special note of thanks to my colleague Jared Padgett, by whose hands the formidable tasks of preparing the manuscript were accomplished with aplomb.

BERNARD JAMES
MALIBU, CALIFORNIA
April 7, 2020

TABLE OF CONTENTS

PART I: Public Education, Institutional Framework, and Parental Rights

Chapter One: Overview of Public Education: The Institutional Interests 1

I. The Judicial Interest

Epperson v. Arkansas 2
Grutter v. Bollinger 4
Board of Education v. Rowley 4
Bethel School District No. 403 v. Fraser 7
Cross County School District v. Spencer 11
Tinker in the Era of Judicial Deference: The Search for Bad Faith 14
Rethinking the Narrative on Judicial Deference in Student Speech Cases 17

II. The Legislative and Executive Interests

A. State Constitutional and Statutory Provisions

Constitution of the State of Arkansas 19
Constitution of the State of California 19
Constitution of the State of Colorado 19
Colorado Revised Statutes 20
Constitution of the State of Nevada 21
Nevada Revised Statutes 21
Constitution of West Virginia 22
West Virginia Statutes 22

B. State Separation of Powers Issues

Rogers v. Helena-West Helena School District 24
West Virginia Board of Education v. Hechler 26
Notes and Comments 28
Mendoza v. State 30
Cobb v. O'Connell 35
Utah School Boards Association v. Utah State Board of Education 37
Notes and Comments 39

C. The Federal Government and Public Education

1. Federal Statutory Provisions

43 U.S.C. § 2000d (Title IV) 43

2. Role of the Federal Government in Education
Brown v. Board of Education 46
San Antonio Independent School District v. Rodriguez 48
United States v. Lopez 48
Notes and Comments 50
Rumsfeld v. Forum for Academic & Institutional Rights, Inc. 52
Notes and Comments 55

Chapter Two: Public Education, Parental Rights and School Choice 58

I. The Constitutional Rights of Parents
The Trustees of Schools v. People *ex rel.* Van Allen 58
Pierce v. Society of Sisters 60
Wisconsin v. Yoder 63
Wofford v. Evans 70
Changing the Face of Parents' Rights 74

II. Parental Rights and the Education Mission
Parents United v. Philadelphia Board of Education 77
Parents for Privacy v. Barr 81
On Educating Children: A Parentalist Manifesto 94
Notes and Comments 98

III. Parental Choice through Education Reform
A. Home Schools
People v. Bennett 101
Murphy v. State 106
For God or Grades? States Imposing Fewer Requirements on Religious Home Schoolers and the Religion Clauses of the First Amendment 112
Homeschooling in Germany and the United States 118

B. Charter Schools
Utah School Boards Association v. Utah State Board of Education 121
Catapult Learning, L.L.C. v. Board of Education 122
Racine Charter One, Inc. v. Racine Unified School District 124
Charting the Court: Challenges to Charter Schools 131

C. Voucher Programs
Zelman v. Simmons-Harris 133
Why the Decisions in Zelman Makes So Much Sense 136
Cain v Horne 138
The Past Should Not Shackle the Present: The Revival of a Legacy of Religious Bigotry by Opponents of School Choice 143
Notes and Comments 145

Chapter Three: Education as a Fundamental Right 147
I. Education under the Federal Constitution
San Antonio Independent School District v. Rodriguez 148
Notes and Comments 161
Rethinking Judicial Activism and Restraint in State School Finance Litigation 161
Plyler v. Doe 164
Kadrmas v. Dickenson Public Schools 170

II. Education under State Constitutions
Brown in State Hands: State Policymaking and Educational Equality After *Freeman v. Pitts* 173
Serrano v. Priest (1971) 174
Serrano v. Priest (1976) 177
Notes and Comments 178
Kukor v. Grover 180
Rose v. Council for Better Education, Inc. 188
Hootch v. Alaska State-Operated School System 195
James v. Alabama Coalition for Equity, Inc. 198
Notes and Comments 199
Woonsocket School Committee v. Chafee 202

PART II: Due Process, Discipline, and School Safety

Chapter Four: Constitutional Safeguards and Procedural Due Process 211
I. Students and Procedural Due Process
Goss v. Lopez 212
Fuller *ex rel.* Fuller v. Decatur Public School Board 218
Zero Tolerance or (In)Tolerance Policies? Weaponless School Violence, Due Process, and the Law of Student Suspensions and Expulsions: An Examination of Fuller v. Decatur Public School Board of Education School District 220
Zell v. Ricci 221
Doe. v. Washington County Department of Education 225
School Discipline Reform & Restorative Justice: A Policy Analysis 232
Notes and Comments 238

II. Procedural Due Process and the Scope of Discipline: The "Off-Campus" Cases
Doe v. Superintendent of Schools of Stoughton 245
C.R. v. Eugene School District 41 247
J.C. v. Beverly Hills School District 252
Suspending and Expelling Children from Educational Opportunity: Time to Reevaluate Zero Tolerance Policies 260

III. Faculty, Staff, and Procedural Due Process
Board of Regents v. Roth 263
Cleveland Board of Education v. Loudermill 267
Segal v. City of New York 271
Determining the Appropriate Level of Judicial Deference to Public School Board Determinations of Cause in Wrongful Termination Cases 276
Notes and Comments 280

Chapter Five: The Right to Privacy and Freedom from Unreasonable 281
I. The Fourth Amendment and Students
A. "Pat-downs," Book Bags, and Strip Searches
New Jersey v. T.L.O. 282
Safford Unified School District v. Redding 286
In the Matter of T.A.S. 291
T.S. v. State 296
Notes and Comments 299
B. Drug Testing
Vernonia School District 47J v. Acton 304
Board of Education v. Earls 307
C. Suspicionless Student Searches
Jane Doe v. Little Rock School District 311
The Doctrine of Deference: Shifting Constitutional Presumptions and The Supreme Court's Restatement of Student Rights After *Board of Education v. Earls* 316
Notes and Comments 319
Theodore v. Delaware Valley School District 322
Notes and Comments 327
University of Colorado v. Derdeyn 332

II. Faculty, Staff and the Fourth Amendment
Hearn v. Board of Public Education 337
Friedenberg v. School Board of Palm Beach County 341
School Board Control Over Education and a Teacher's Right to Privacy 352

III. The Family Educational Rights and Privacy Act (FERPA)
A. Remedies under FERPA
Gonzaga University v. Doe 357
Notes and Comments 361

B. Defining the "Education Record" under FERPA
Owasso Independent School District No. 1-011 v. Falvo 361
BRV, Inc. v. Superior Court 365
Notes and Comments 370

C. Disclosure of Information under FERPA
Connecticut Office v. Hartford Board of Education 373
Jensen v. Reeves 375
FERPA Regulations: A Response to Campus Shootings, 9/11-Terrorism and New Technology 376
Notes and Comments 378

IV. The Health Insurance Portability and Accountability Act (HIPAA)
Protection and Advocacy v. Freudenthal 383
Lex-Praxis of Education Informational Privacy for Public School Children 391
Notes and Comments 395

Chapter Six: Safe Schools, Criminal Procedure and Law Enforcement on Campus 401
I. Educators as Guarantors of Student Safety
A. The Problem of Unsafe Schools
U.S. Secret Service & Dep't of Educ., The Final Report and Findings of the Safe School Initiative 402
Bullying in Schools: The Disconnect Between Empirical Research and Constitutional, Statutory, and Tort Duties to Supervise 403

B. Statutory Reform for Safe Schools
U.S. Congress - Safe and Drug Free Schools and Communities 407
Washington, DC - Establishment of the Metropolitan Police Department School Safety Division 409
Florida - School Resource Officers and School Safety Officers 410
Pennsylvania - Office for Safe Schools 411

C. Judicial Expansion of Educators' Authority to Maintain Safe Schools
New Jersey v. T.L.O. 412
In re F.B. 413
T.S. v. State 416
Notes and Comments 416

II. The Fifth Amendment and Student Interrogations
J.D.B. v. North Carolina 419
B.A. v. State 426
D.Z. v. State 431
Miranda, Please Report to the Principal's Office 433
State v. Pablo 435
State v. Daniell 438
Farewell *Michael C.*, Hello *Gault*: Considering the Miranda Rights of Learning Disabled Children 440
Notes and Comments 442

III. Campus Policing and Excessive Force
E.W. v. Dolgos 449
K.W.P. v. Kansas City Public Schools 457
Carter v. Pointe Coupee Parish School Board 466
Notes and Comments 469

PART III: Equality, Discrimination, and Special Education

Chapter Seven: Equal Protection of the Laws 471
I. Racial Discrimination
Brown v. Board of Education 471
Freeman v. Pitts 471
Villanueva v. Carere 482
Notes and Comments 487
American Public Schools Fifty Years After Brown: A Separate and Unequal Reality 490
Grutter v. Bollinger 492
Parents Involved in Community Schools v. Seattle School District No. 1 498
Notes and Comments 503

II. Alienage Discrimination
Plyler v. Doe 504
The Wisdom of *Plyler v. Doe* 504
Martinez v. Bynum 509
Notes and Comments 509
Ambach v. Norwick 509

III. Gender Discrimination
U.S. v. Virginia 511
Mississippi University for Women v. Hogan 519
A.N.A. *ex rel.* S.F.A. v. Breckinridge Board of Education 525
Notes and Comments 531

IV. Emerging Categories of Discrimination in Public Schools
Acevedo v. Monsignor Donovan High School 531
National Law Center on Homelessness and Poverty v. New York 534
Balancing the Books: The Stewart B. McKinney Homeless Assistance Act and Separate Schools for Homeless Children in Arizona 538
Racine Charter One, Inc. v. Racine Unified School District 539
Equal Protection Theory and the Harvey Milk High School: Why Anti-Subordination Alone Is Not Enough 540

Chapter Eight: Title IX of the Educational Amendments of 1972 545
Bernice R. Sandler: Too Strong for a Woman 545
I. Private Remedies under Title IX
Cannon v. University of Chicago 549
Franklin v. Gwinnett County Public Schools 553
Notes and Comments 555

II. Sexual Assaults and Harassment under Title IX
Gebser v. Lago Vista Independent School District 557
Davis *ex rel.* Lashonda D. v. Monroe County Board of Education 561
Murrell v. School District No. 1 568
Fitzgerald v. Barnstable School Committee 573
Notes and Comments 577

III. Expanded Scope of Title IX: Discrimination in Athletics
McCormick *ex rel.* McCormick v. School District of Mamaroneck 582
Equity in Athletics, Inc. v. U.S. Department of Education 592
Structure Versus Effect: Revealing the Unconstitutional Operation of Title IX's Athletics Provisions 595
Notes and Comments 598

Chapter Nine: Special Needs Education 599
I. Historical Exclusion of the Disabled
Pennsylvania Ass'n v. Pennsylvania 600

II. Section 504 of the Rehabilitation Act and the ADA
School Board of Nassau County v. Arline 603
Knapp v. Northwestern University 608
Martinez v. Hillsborough County 612

Notes and Comments ... 618
Indiana Area School District v. H.H. ... 622

III. The Individuals with Disabilities Education Act: Affirmative Duties and an "Appropriate Education"
Board of Education v. Rowley ... 624
Endrew F. v. Douglas County School District ... 631
Cedar Rapids Community School District v. Garret F. ... 636
Independent School District No. 283 v. E.M.D.H. ... 641
Individuals with Disabilities Education Act—The Right 'IDEA' for All Children's Education ... 648
Notes and Comments ... 650

IV. Special Education and Procedural Safeguards: Manifestation Hearings, "Staying-Put," and Mainstreaming
Honig v. Doe ... 654
M.C. v. Antelope Valley Union High School ... 661
Notes and Comments ... 666

PART IV: Free Speech, Religion and the Right of Association

Chapter Ten: The First Amendment and Freedom of Speech ... 671
I. The Origins of Student Free Speech Rights
West Virginia Board of Education v. Barnette ... 672
Tinker v. Des Moines Independent Community School District ... 674
Notes and Comments ... 678

II. Current Doctrine on the Protection of Student Expression
Bethel School District No. 403 v. Fraser ... 679
Hazelwood School District v. Kuhlmeier ... 682
Morse v. Frederick ... 685
Griggs *ex rel.* Griggs v. Ft. Wayne School Board ... 688
Valuing Student Speech: The Work of the Schools as Conceptual Development ... 693
Notes and Comments ... 695

III. Student Expression in Higher Education
Christian Legal Society v. Martinez ... 701
Christian Legal Society v. Walker ... 710
Young America's Foundation v. Kaler ... 714

IV. Faculty, Staff and Free Speech
Mt. Healthy City School District Board of Education v. Doyle ... 721
Givhan v. Western Line Consolidated School District ... 725

Mayer v. Monroe County Community School Corp. 727
Kluge v. Brownsburg Community Schools 729
Notes and Comments 734
Public Employee Speech, Categorical Balancing and § 1983: A Critique of *Garcetti v. Ceballos* 736

Chapter Eleven: The First Amendment and the Right of Association 741
I. Intimate Association
Chi Iota Colony of Alpha Epsilon Pi Fraternity v. CUNY 742
Notes and Comments 747

II. Expressive Association
Christian Legal Society v. Walker 748
Christian Legal Society v. Martinez 751
Notes and Comments 752

III. Compelled Association
Board of Regents v. Southworth 752
Southworth v. Board of Regents 756
Striking the Balance Between Anti-Discrimination Laws and First Amendment Freedoms: An Alternative Proposal to Preserve Diversity 758

Chapter Twelve: The First Amendment and Religious Expression 761
I. The Free Exercise Clause
Chalifoux v. New Caney School District 761
Littlefield v. Forney Independent School District 767
Axson-Flynn v. Johnson 770
The Free Exercise of Religion and Public Schools: The Implications of Hybrid Rights on the Religious Upbringing of Children 775
Notes and Comments 777

II. The Establishment Clause
Everson v. Board of Education 778
Zorach v. Clauson 782
Edwards v. Aguillard 784
Zelman v. Simmons-Harris 786
Access to Public School Facilities for Religious Expression by Students, Student Groups and Community Organizations: Extending the Reach of the Free Speech Clause 786
Good News Club v. Milford Central School 788
Santa Fe Independent School District v. Doe 790
Newdow v. Rio Linda Union School District 796
Notes and Comments 803

PART V: Liability, Affirmative Duties and Educational Accountability

Chapter Thirteen: Constitutional Liability and Substantive Due Process ... 807

I. Substantive Due Process and Intentionally or Maliciously Inflicted Injuries

Ingraham v. Wright ... 808
Saylor v. Board of Education ... 813
Notes and Comments ... 818
Banning Corporal Punishment: A Constitutional Analysis ... 820
Meeker v. Edmundson ... 823
Doe *ex rel.* Doe v. Hawaii Department of Education ... 826
Out on a Limb: *Doe v. State of Hawaii Department of Education* (with apologies to Joyce Kilmer) ... 829

II. Substantive Due Process, Affirmative Duties and Deliberate Indifference

Johnson v. Dallas Independent School District ... 830
Notes and Comments ... 834
The Lessons of *Deshaney*: Special Relationships, Schools & the Fifth Circuit ... 835
Doe. v. Hillsboro Independent School District ... 840
L.R. v. School District of Philadelphia ... 843
Keeping Schools Safe: Why Schools Should Have an Affirmative Duty to Protect Students from Harm by Other Students ... 850
Notes and Comments ... 854

Chapter Fourteen: Common Law Torts and Statutory Approaches to Liability ... 855

I. Liability in K-12 Institutions

A. Common Law Torts

Broward County School Board v. Ruiz ... 855
Gibbons v. Orleans Parish School Board ... 859
Simonetti *ex rel.* Simonetti v. School District of Philadelphia ... 860
Notes and Comments ... 865
Fallon v. Indian Trail School ... 869
Levie v. Orleans Parish School Board ... 871
Cory v. Stroudsburg Area School Authority ... 875
Seal v. Carlsbad Independent School District ... 878
Notes and Comments ... 880

B. Statutory Remedies for Injuries

Fitzgerald v. Barnstable School Committee ... 884
Stevenson *ex rel.* Stevenson v. Martin County Board of Education ... 884
S.S. v. Eastern Kentucky University ... 887
Clausing v. San Francisco Unified School District ... 891
Snethen v. Board of Education ... 893

King v. Northeast Security, Inc. 894
Notes and Comments 901

II. Liability in Higher Education: Colleges and Universities
McClure v. Fairfield University 903
The Doctrine of In Loco Parentis, Tort Liability and the Student-College Relationship 908
Freeman v. Busch 910
Notes and Comments 913

III. Educational Malpractice
Miller v. Loyola University 914
Hunter v. Board of Education 920
Donohue v. Copiague Union Free School District 921
Educational Malpractice: If Our Children Aren't Learning Who Should be Held Responsible? 922
Newark Parents Ass'n v. Newark Schools 923
Using the Courts to Influence the Implementation of No Child Left Behind 926
Notes and Comments 932

Table of Cases 935
Index 939

Part I
Public Education, Institutional Framework, and Parental Rights

Chapter One
Overview of Public Education: The Institutional Interests

> [P]eople elect school boards, who in turn select administrators, who select the teachers, and these are the individuals best able to determine the substance of that policy....[L]ocal control of education involves democracy in a microcosm. In most public schools in the United States the parents have a large voice in running the school. Through participation in the election of school board members, the parents influence, if not control, the direction of their children's education. A school board is not a giant bureaucracy far removed from accountability for its actions; it is truly "of the people and by the people." *Board of Education v. Pico*, 457 U.S. 853, 891-92 (1982) (Burger, J., dissenting).

Policymaking in education is unique in a number of ways. It is viewed most accurately as a local enterprise. A community of parents combines their common interest in educating their children through the creation and operation of a local campus dedicated to implementing an education plan. The education mission represents a contract of sorts. School officials serve as representatives of the community in providing a vision for clarifying the nuts and bolts of the education mission as well as its daily management. It is in this light that the phrase "democracy in a microcosm" best captures the theme of public education.

Conflict resolution in public education is equally distinctive. The competing interests of the various stakeholders are animated by democratic principles. Stakeholders often attempt to define and control the components of the education mission, or its implementation, or both. The public school district is often under immense pressure to accommodate the interests of parents, state and federal courts, legislatures and local officials. The dynamics of these legitimate, competing interests raise fascinating and difficult issues of law and policy. For example, the judiciary often brings a suspicious attitude to reviewing education policy, but more often prefers to defer to the "democracy in a microcosm." Nevertheless, consider how many seminal areas of constitutional civil rights come out of public education litigation. Federalism concerns are also prominent, creating the possibility that neither parents nor local officials will control the outcome of a policy dispute that is taken over by state or federal officials. Moreover, issues of taxation, contracts, family law and international law are occasionally featured in a conflict over education policy. Therefore, the law-as-law in public education is something of a misnomer. Education law and the process of policymaking are interdependent. Each must be given serious consideration as forces that shape the educational enterprise for better or for something more complex.

This chapter presents an overview of the institutional structure of public education. You will meet judges, legislators, and school officials from state and federal governments who compete to shape local policy decisions. There is a surprising predictability to local policymaking in education. Local autonomy appears to control until evidence of imbalance, disparity, inequality or abuse prompts an intervention. The competing stakeholders discover that the ability to control outcomes on specific issues of education policy create foreseeable consequences when the natural order of policymaking shifts away from local officials to other decision-makers.

I. The Judicial Interest

Perhaps the most unusual facet of public education is the deference given to educators' decisions by the courts in the ordinary course of dispute resolution. The education mission is frequently viewed as a compelling interest by judges, effectively allowing school officials greater freedom from interference in the absence of abuse of authority or a clear violation of clearly established law. When applying the precedent in regard to the education mission, courts typically recite the mantra of "[t]he broad authority to control the conduct of students granted to school official permits a good deal of latitude in determining which policies will best serve educational and disciplinary goals."[1]

As you read the cases think about why this judicial deference is necessary. Also consider the consequences and limits of this restraint. How would you summarize the role of courts in reviewing and resolving lawsuits challenging school policies? The cases present a view that many consider dominant—judges should defer to educators' decisions that are made in good faith and further the educational mission. Assuming you agree with this approach, try to articulate a rule that will balance judicial deference to school officials against the rights of students, faculty and staff to fair, effective implementation of the education mission.

EPPERSON v. ARKANSAS
393 U.S. 97 (1968)

OPINION BY: FORTAS, Justice

I.

This appeal challenges the constitutionality of the 'anti-evolution' statute which the State of Arkansas adopted in 1928 to prohibit the teaching in its public schools and universities of the theory that man evolved from other species of life. The statute was a product of the upsurge of 'fundamentalist' religious fervor of the twenties. The Arkansas statute was an adaption of the

---

[1] *Sypniewski v. Warren Hills Reg'l Bd. of Educ.*, 307 F.3d 243, 259 (3d Cir. 2002), *cert denied,* 538 U.S. 1033; 155 L. Ed. 2d 1062 (2003). This mantra can be traced back to *Epperson v. Arkansas*, 393 U.S. 97, 104 (1968), when the Court, while resolving a conflict over the teaching of evolution, noted: "Judicial interposition in the operation of the public school system of the Nation raises problems requiring care and restraint.... By and large, public education in our Nation is committed to the control of state and local authorities."

famous Tennessee 'monkey law' which that State adopted in 1925. The constitutionality of the Tennessee law was upheld by the Tennessee Supreme Court in the celebrated *Scopes* case in 1927.

The Arkansas law makes it unlawful for a teacher in any state-supported school or university 'to teach the theory or doctrine that mankind ascended or descended from a lower order of animals,' or 'to adopt or use in any such institution a textbook that teaches' this theory. Violation is a misdemeanor and subjects the violator to dismissal from his position.

The present case concerns the teaching of biology in a high school in Little Rock. According to the testimony, until the events here in litigation, the official textbook furnished for the high school biology course did not have a section on the Darwinian Theory. Then, for the academic year 1965-1966, the school administration, on recommendation of the teachers of biology in the school system, adopted and prescribed a textbook which contained a chapter setting forth 'the theory about the origin * * * of man from a lower form of animal.

Susan Epperson, a young woman who graduated from Arkansas' school system and then obtained her master's degree in zoology at the University of Illinois, was employed by the Little Rock school system in the fall of 1964 to teach 10th grade biology at Central High School. At the start of the next academic year, 1965, she was confronted by the new textbook (which one surmises from the record was not unwelcome to her). She faced at least a literal dilemma because she was supposed to use the new textbook for classroom instruction and presumably to teach the statutorily condemned chapter; but to do so would be a criminal offense and subject her to dismissal.

III.

The antecedents of today's decision are many and unmistakable. They are rooted in the foundation soil of our Nation. They are fundamental to freedom.

...

Judicial interposition in the operation of the public school system of the Nation raises problems requiring care and restraint. Our courts, however, have not failed to apply the First Amendment's mandate in our educational system where essential to safeguard the fundamental values of freedom of speech and inquiry and of belief. By and large, public education in our Nation is committed to the control of state and local authorities. Courts do not and cannot intervene in the resolution of conflicts which arise in the daily operation of school systems and which do not directly and sharply implicate basic constitutional values. On the other hand, the vigilant protection of constitutional freedoms is nowhere more vital than in the community of American schools.

.....

There is and can be no doubt that the First Amendment does not permit the State to require that teaching and learning must be tailored to the principles or prohibitions of any religious sect or dogma. In Everson v. Board of Education, this Court, in upholding a state law to provide free bus service to school children, including those attending parochial schools, said: 'Neither (a State nor the Federal Government) can pass laws which aid one religion, aid all religions, or prefer one religion over another.' 330 U.S. 1, 15, 67 S.Ct. 504, 511, 91 L.Ed. 711 (1947). ...While study of religions and of the Bible from a literary and historic viewpoint, presented objectively as part of a secular program of education, need not collide with the First Amendment's prohibition, the State may not adopt programs or practices in its public schools or colleges which 'aid or oppose' any religion. Id., at 225, 83 S.Ct., at 1573. This prohibition is absolute. It forbids alike the preference of a religious doctrine or the prohibition of theory which is deemed antagonistic to a particular dogma. ...These precedents inevitably determine the result in the present case. The State's undoubted right to prescribe the curriculum for its public schools does not carry with it the right to prohibit, on pain of criminal penalty, the teaching of a scientific theory or doctrine where that prohibition is based upon reasons that violate the First Amendment. It is much too late to argue that the State may impose upon the teachers in its schools any conditions that it chooses, however restrictive they may be of constitutional guarantees.

In the present case, there can be no doubt that Arkansas has sought to prevent its teachers from discussing the theory of evolution because it is contrary to the belief of some that the Book of Genesis must be the exclusive source of doctrine as to the origin of man. No suggestion has been made that Arkansas' law may be justified by considerations of state policy other than the religious views of some of its citizens.

The judgment of the Supreme Court of Arkansas is reversed.

GRUTTER v. BOLLINGER
539 U.S. 306 (2003)

[This Case appears in the textbook in Chapter Seven on page 492.]

BOARD OF EDUCATION v. ROWLEY
458 U.S. 176 (1982)

[NOTE: This Case appears in in full in Chapter Nine on page 624. The U.S. Supreme Court in *Rowley* reversed the ruling of the lower courts, whose interpretation given to a federal special education law would have required a public school to hire an interpreter for a deaf student. The Court held that the federal statute required educators only to provide access to competent instruction, but not instruction that would, in the words of the lower courts, "maximize each child's potential." Section IV and VI below, discuss the role of judicial review in the interpretation of federal education statutes.]

IV

A

As mentioned in Part I, the Act permits "[a]ny party aggrieved by the findings and decision" of the state administrative hearings "to bring a civil action" in "any State court of competent jurisdiction or in a district court of the United States without regard to the amount in controversy." § 1415(e)(2). The complaint, and therefore the civil action, may concern "any matter relating to the identification, evaluation, or educational placement of the child, or the provision of a free appropriate public education to such child." § 1415(b)(1)(E). In reviewing the complaint, the Act provides that a court "shall receive the record of the [state] administrative proceedings, shall hear additional evidence at the request of a party, and, basing its decision on the preponderance of the evidence, shall grant such relief as the court determines is appropriate." § 1415(e)(2).

The parties disagree sharply over the meaning of these provisions, petitioners contending that courts are given only limited authority to review for state compliance with the Act's procedural requirements and no power to review the substance of the state program, and respondents contending that the Act requires courts to exercise *de novo* review over state educational decisions and policies. We find petitioners' contention unpersuasive, for Congress expressly rejected provisions that would have so severely restricted the role of reviewing courts. In substituting the current language of the statute for language that would have made state administrative findings conclusive if supported by substantial evidence, the Conference Committee explained that courts were to make "independent decision[s] based on a preponderance of the evidence."

But although we find that this grant of authority is broader than claimed by petitioners, we think the fact that it is found in § 1415, which is entitled "Procedural safeguards," is not without significance. When the elaborate and highly specific procedural safeguards embodied in § 1415 are contrasted with the general and somewhat imprecise substantive admonitions contained in the Act, we think that the importance Congress attached to these procedural safeguards cannot be gainsaid. It seems to us no exaggeration to say that Congress placed every bit as much emphasis upon compliance with procedures giving parents and guardians a large measure of participation at every stage of the administrative process, see, *e.g.*, §§ 1415(a)-(d), as it did upon the measurement of the resulting IEP [individualized education plan], against a substantive standard. We think that the congressional emphasis upon full participation of concerned parties throughout the development of the IEP, as well as the requirements that state and local plans be submitted to the Secretary for approval, demonstrates the legislative conviction that adequate compliance with the procedures prescribed would in most cases assure much if not all of what Congress wished in the way of substantive content in an IEP.

Thus the provision that a reviewing court base its decision on the "preponderance of the evidence" is by no means an invitation to the courts to substitute their own notions of sound educational policy for those of the school authorities which they review. The very importance which Congress has attached to compliance with certain procedures in the preparation of an IEP would be frustrated if a court were permitted simply to set state decisions at nought. The fact that § 1415(e) requires that the reviewing court "receive the records of the [state] administrative proceedings" carries with it the implied requirement that due weight shall be given to these proceedings. And we find nothing in the Act to suggest that merely because Congress was rather sketchy in establishing substantive requirements, as opposed to procedural requirements for the preparation of an IEP, it intended that reviewing courts should have a free hand to impose substantive standards of review which cannot be derived from the Act itself. In short, the statutory authorization to grant "such relief as the court determines is appropriate" cannot be read without reference to the obligations, largely procedural in nature, which are imposed upon recipient States by Congress.

Therefore, a court's inquiry in suits brought under § 1415(e)(2) is twofold. First, has the State complied with the procedures set forth in the Act?[27] And second, is the individualized educational program developed through the Act's procedures reasonably calculated to enable the child to receive educational benefits?[283] If these requirements are met, the State has complied with the obligations imposed by Congress and the courts can require no more.

B

In assuring that the requirements of the Act have been met, courts must be careful to avoid imposing their view of preferable educational methods upon the States.[294] The primary responsibility for formulating the education to be accorded a handicapped child, and for choosing the educational method most suitable to the child's needs, was left by the Act to state and local educational agencies in cooperation with the parents or guardian of the child. The Act expressly charges States with the responsibility of "acquiring and disseminating to teachers and administrators of programs for handicapped children significant information derived from educational research, demonstration, and similar projects, and [of] adopting, where appropriate, promising educational practices and materials." § 1413(a)(3). In the face of such a clear statutory directive, it seems highly unlikely that Congress intended courts to overturn a State's choice of appropriate educational theories in a proceeding conducted pursuant to § 1415(e)(2).[305]

We previously have cautioned that courts lack the "specialized knowledge and experience" necessary to resolve "persistent and difficult questions of educational policy." *San Antonio*

---

[27] This inquiry will require a court not only to satisfy itself that the State has adopted the state plan, policies, and assurances required by the Act, but also to determine that the State has created an IEP for the child in question which conforms with the requirements of § 1401(19) .

[28] When the handicapped child is being educated in the regular classrooms of a public school system, the achievement of passing marks and advancement from grade to grade will be one important factor in determining educational benefit.

[29] In this case, for example, both the state hearing officer and the District Court were presented with evidence as to the best method for educating the deaf, a question long debated among scholars. See Large, Special Problems of the Deaf Under the Education for All Handicapped Children Act of 1975, 58 Wash.U.L.Q. 213, 229 (1980). The District Court accepted the testimony of respondents' experts that there was "a trend supported by studies showing the greater degree of success of students brought up in deaf households using [the method of communication used by the Rowleys]." 483 F.Supp., at 535.

[30] It is clear that Congress was aware of the States' traditional role in the formulation and execution of educational policy. "Historically, the States have had the primary responsibility for the education of children at the elementary and secondary level." 121 Cong.Rec. 19498 (1975) (remarks of Sen. Dole). See also *Epperson v. Arkansas*, 393 U.S. 97, 104, 89 S.Ct. 266, 270, 21 L.Ed.2d 228 (1968) ("By and large, public education in our Nation is committed to the control of state and local authorities").

Independent School Dist. v. Rodriguez, 411 U.S., at 42, 93 S.Ct., at 1301. We think that Congress shared that view when it passed the Act. As already demonstrated, Congress' intention was not that the Act displace the primacy of States in the field of education, but that States receive funds to assist them in extending their educational systems to the handicapped. Therefore, once a court determines that the requirements of the Act have been met, questions of methodology are for resolution by the States.

.....

VI

Applying these principles to the facts of this case, we conclude that the Court of Appeals erred in affirming the decision of the District Court. Neither the District Court nor the Court of Appeals found that petitioners had failed to comply with the procedures of the Act, and the findings of neither court would support a conclusion that Amy's educational program failed to comply with the substantive requirements of the Act. On the contrary, the District Court found that the "evidence firmly establishes that Amy is receiving an 'adequate' education, since she performs better than the average child in her class and is advancing easily from grade to grade." 483 F.Supp., at 534. In light of this finding, and of the fact that Amy was receiving personalized instruction and related services calculated by the Furnace Woods school administrators to meet her educational needs, the lower courts should not have concluded that the Act requires the provision of a sign-language interpreter. Accordingly, the decision of the Court of Appeals is reversed, and the case is remanded for further proceedings consistent with this opinion.

BETHEL SCHOOL DISTRICT NO. 403 v. FRASER
478 U.S. 675 (1986)

CHIEF JUSTICE BURGER delivered the opinion of the Court.

We granted certiorari to decide whether the First Amendment prevents a school district from disciplining a high school student for giving a lewd speech at a school assembly.

On April 26, 1983, respondent Matthew N. Fraser, a student at Bethel High School in Pierce County, Washington, delivered a speech nominating a fellow student for student elective office. Approximately 600 high school students, many of whom were 14-year-olds, attended the assembly. Students were required to attend the assembly or to report to the study hall. The assembly was part of a school-sponsored educational program in self-government. Students who elected not to attend the assembly were required to report to study hall. During the entire speech, Fraser referred to his candidate in terms of an elaborate, graphic, and explicit sexual metaphor.

Two of Fraser's teachers, with whom he discussed the contents of his speech in advance, informed him that the speech was "inappropriate and that he probably should not deliver it," App. 30, and that his delivery of the speech might have "severe consequences." *Id.* at 61. During Fraser's delivery of the speech, a school counselor observed the reaction of students to the speech. Some students hooted and yelled; some by gestures graphically simulated the sexual activities pointedly alluded to in respondent's speech. Other students appeared to be bewildered and embarrassed by the speech. One teacher reported that on the day following the speech, she found it necessary to forgo a portion of the scheduled class lesson in order to discuss the speech with the class. *Id.* at 41-44.

A Bethel High School disciplinary rule prohibiting the use of obscene language in the school provides: "Conduct which materially and substantially interferes with the educational process is prohibited, including the use of obscene, profane language or gestures."

The morning after the assembly, the Assistant Principal called Fraser into her office and notified him that the school considered his speech to have been a violation of this rule. Fraser was presented with copies of five letters submitted by teachers, describing his conduct at the assembly; he was given a chance to explain his conduct, and he admitted to having given the speech described and that he deliberately used sexual innuendo in the speech. Fraser was then informed that he would be suspended for three days, and that his name would be removed from the list of candidates for graduation speaker at the school's commencement exercises.

****

Respondent, by his father as guardian ad litem, then brought this action in the United States District Court for the Western District of Washington. Respondent alleged a violation of his First Amendment right to freedom of speech and sought both injunctive relief and monetary damages under 42 U. S. C. § 1983. The District Court held that the school's sanctions violated respondent's right to freedom of speech under the First Amendment to the United States Constitution, that the school's disruptive-conduct rule is unconstitutionally vague and overbroad, and that the removal of respondent's name from the graduation speaker's list violated the Due Process Clause of the Fourteenth Amendment because the disciplinary rule makes no mention of such removal as a possible sanction. The District Court awarded respondent $ 278 in damages, $ 12,750 in litigation costs and attorney's fees, and enjoined the School District from preventing respondent from speaking at the commencement ceremonies. Respondent, who had been elected graduation speaker by a write-in vote of his classmates, delivered a speech at the commencement ceremonies on June 8, 1983.

The Court of Appeals for the Ninth Circuit affirmed the judgment of the District Court

We granted *certiorari*, 474 U.S. 814 (1985). We reverse.

II

This Court acknowledged in *Tinker* v. *Des Moines Independent Community School Dist., supra,* that students do not "shed their constitutional rights to freedom of speech or expression at the schoolhouse gate." *Id.* at 506. The Court of Appeals read that case as precluding any discipline of Fraser for indecent speech and lewd conduct in the school assembly. That court appears to have proceeded on the theory that the use of lewd and obscene speech in order to make what the speaker considered to be a point in a nominating speech for a fellow student was essentially the same as the wearing of an armband in *Tinker* as a form of protest or the expression of a political position. The marked distinction between the political "message" of the armbands in *Tinker* and the sexual content of respondent's speech in this case seems to have been given little weight by the Court of Appeals. In upholding the students' right to engage in a nondisruptive, passive expression of a political viewpoint in *Tinker*, this Court was careful to note that the case did "not concern speech or action that intrudes upon the work of the schools or the rights of other students." *Id.* at 508.

It is against this background that we turn to consider the level of First Amendment protection accorded to Fraser's utterances and actions before an official high school assembly attended by 600 students.

III

The role and purpose of the American public school system were well described by two historians, who stated: "[Public] education must prepare pupils for citizenship in the Republic. . . . It must inculcate the habits and manners of civility as values in themselves conducive to happiness and as indispensable to the practice of self-government in the community and the nation." C. Beard & M. Beard, New Basic History of the United States 228 (1968). In *Ambach* v. *Norwick*, 441 U.S. 68, 76-77 (1979), we echoed the essence of this statement of the objectives of public education as the "[inculcation of] fundamental values necessary to the maintenance of a democratic political system."

These fundamental values of "habits and manners of civility" essential to a democratic society must, of course, include tolerance of divergent political and religious views, even when the views expressed may be unpopular. But these "fundamental values" must also take into account consideration of the sensibilities of others, and, in the case of a school, the sensibilities of fellow students. ...It does not follow, however, that simply because the use of an offensive form of expression may not be prohibited to adults making what the speaker considers a political point, the same latitude must be permitted to children in a public school. In *New Jersey* v. *T. L. O.*, 469 U.S. 325, 340-42 (1985), we reaffirmed that the constitutional rights of students in public school are not automatically coextensive with the rights of adults in other settings. As cogently expressed by Judge Newman, "the First Amendment gives a high school student the classroom right to wear Tinker's armband, but not Cohen's jacket." *Thomas v. Bd. of Educ., Granville Central Sch. Dist.*, 607 F.2d 1043, 1057 (CA2 1979) (opinion concurring in result).

Surely it is a highly appropriate function of public school education to prohibit the use of vulgar and offensive terms in public discourse. Indeed, the "fundamental values necessary to the maintenance of a democratic political system" disfavor the use of terms of debate highly offensive or highly threatening to others. Nothing in the Constitution prohibits the states from insisting that certain modes of expression are inappropriate and subject to sanctions. The inculcation of these values is truly the "work of the schools." *Tinker*, 393 U.S. at 508; *see Ambach Norwick, supra.* The determination of what manner of speech in the classroom or in school assembly is inappropriate properly rests with the school board.

The process of educating our youth for citizenship in public schools is not confined to books, the curriculum, and the civics class; schools must teach by example the shared values of a civilized social order. Consciously or otherwise, teachers—and indeed the older students—demonstrate the appropriate form of civil discourse and political expression by their conduct and deportment in and out of class. Inescapably, like parents, they are role models. The schools, as instruments of the state, may determine that the essential lessons of civil, mature conduct cannot be conveyed in

a school that tolerates lewd, indecent, or offensive speech and conduct such as that indulged in by this confused boy.

The pervasive sexual innuendo in Fraser's speech was plainly offensive to both teachers and students—indeed to any mature person. By glorifying male sexuality, and in its verbal content, the speech was acutely insulting to teenage girl students. *See* App. 77-81. The speech could well be seriously damaging to its less mature audience, many of whom were only 14 years old and on the threshold of awareness of human sexuality. Some students were reported as bewildered by the speech and the reaction of mimicry it provoked.

This Court's First Amendment jurisprudence has acknowledged limitations on the otherwise absolute interest of the speaker in reaching an unlimited audience where the speech is sexually explicit and the audience may include children. ... These cases recognize the obvious concern on the part of parents, and school authorities acting *in loco parentis*, to protect children—especially in a captive audience—from exposure to sexually explicit, indecent, or lewd speech.

****

We hold that petitioner School District acted entirely within its permissible authority in imposing sanctions upon Fraser in response to his offensively lewd and indecent speech. Unlike the sanctions imposed on the students wearing armbands in *Tinker*, the penalties imposed in this case were unrelated to any political viewpoint. The First Amendment does not prevent the school officials from determining that to permit a vulgar and lewd speech such as respondent's would undermine the school's basic educational mission. A high school assembly or classroom is no place for a sexually explicit monologue directed towards an unsuspecting audience of teenage students. Accordingly, it was perfectly appropriate for the school to disassociate itself to make the point to the pupils that vulgar speech and lewd conduct is wholly inconsistent with the "fundamental values" of school education. Justice Black, dissenting in *Tinker*, made a point that is especially relevant in this case: "I wish therefore, . . . to disclaim any purpose . . . to hold that the Federal Constitution compels the teachers, parents, and elected school officials to surrender control of the American public school system to public school students." 393 U.S. at 526.

CROSS COUNTY SCHOOL DISTRICT v. SPENCER
58 S.W.3d 406 (Ark. Ct. App. 2001)

OPINION BY: TERRY CRABTREE

The appellants, Cross County School District, the school's principal, superintendent, and school board members, appeal from an order of the Cross County Chancery Court in which the court reversed the school board's decision to expel Hannah Spencer Moran, the daughter of Naomi Spencer and Roger Spencer. We reverse.

Hannah Spencer was in the eighth grade of the Cross County School District when the facts of this case arose. Hannah and another student, Leslie Headley, had been close friends, but the friendship had ended. On Monday, February 21, 2000, a teacher observed Hannah, near the cafeteria, loudly and angrily shouting Leslie's name while approaching Leslie with her fists tightly clinched and her arms extended to her sides. The teacher intervened and separated the two girls. No violence occurred. Subsequent to this altercation, a student told the principal, Mr. David Hopkins, that she had something he needed to see. Principal Hopkins was then given a handwritten, two-page note, addressed to a student named Calvin. The note contained considerable profanity and threats, including death threats against Leslie. The note was signed by Hannah. The note outlined Hannah's plans to fight with Leslie at lunch on Monday. In fact, the incident took place on Monday at lunch. Leslie had not seen the note.

Principal Hopkins took Hannah into his office, asked her about the note, and she admitted writing the note. Principal Hopkins then suspended Hannah and recommended to the school board that she be expelled for the remainder of the 1999–2000 school year. A hearing was held before the school board on March 2, 2000, in which the school board was presented with the note, and accepted the expulsion recommendation. On March 7, 2000, Hannah through her parents, Naomi Spencer and Roger Spencer, filed a Petition for Temporary Restraining Order to have appellee reinstated to school. A hearing was held on March 8, 2000, in which the court granted the petition. A trial on the merits was held on April 6, 2000. On June 27, 2000, the court filed its opinion making the injunction permanent. It is from this order that appellants bring this appeal.

We agree with appellants' contention that the trial court ignored its proper role in reviewing the school board's decision and substituted its judgment for that of the board. Such an act is prohibited by law and is a flagrant abuse of discretion. Arkansas Code Annotated § 6–18–506(c) (Repl.1999) requires school boards to hold pupils strictly accountable for disorderly conduct in school and on the school grounds. There is a general policy against intervention by the courts in matters left to school authorities. "Judicial interposition in the operation of the public school system of the Nation raises problems requiring care and restraint.... By and large, public education in our Nation is committed to the control of state and local authorities." *Goss v. Lopez,* 419 U.S. 565, 577–78, 95 S.Ct. 729, 42 L.Ed.2d 725 (1975), citing *Epperson v. Arkansas,* 393 U.S. 97, 89 S.Ct. 266, 21 L.Ed.2d 228 (1968)). The courts have been reluctant to interfere with the authority of local school boards to handle local problems. A chancery court has no power to interfere with school district boards in the exercise of their discretion when directing the operation of the schools unless the boards clearly abuse their discretion. The burden is upon those charging such an abuse to prove it by clear and convincing evidence.

In this case, Hannah was expelled from school pursuant to Rule 23 of the Cross County High School Handbook, entitled "Threatening Another Student," which states "A student shall not threaten another student." Rule 23 then cites Ark.Code Ann. § 5–13–301, the statute covering terroristic threatening. The trial court found that there was no indication that Hannah "set in motion any chain of events reasonably calculated to communicate the contents of the note beyond the person to whom it was addressed, *i.e.,* Calvin." Also, the court found that it cannot be held that Hannah intended to terrorize the other student referenced in the letter; *i.e.,* Leslie. Based on this, the court reversed the school board's decision to expel Hannah. Appellants point out that although Rule 23 contains a statutory reference to the crime of terroristic threatening, the text of the statue is not set out in the policy.

As stated earlier, our supreme court, in acknowledging a school board's power to expel a student, has held it does not have the power to substitute its judgment for that of such a board, and will do so only when the court determines the board's judgment was arbitrary, capricious, or contrary to law. From our careful examination of the record before us, we cannot say that the Board abused its discretion or acted arbitrarily, capriciously, or in any way contrary to law. The Board found that Rule 23 is not limited to threats that are communicated to the target of the threat. It is conclusive that the letter written by Hannah contained threatening language toward Leslie. As such, we hold that the appellants acted reasonably in enforcing its policy against a student threatening another student under Rule 23. The trial court improperly substituted its own judgment for that of the Board. Accordingly, we reverse the trial court's decision, and reinstate the Board's decision.

WENDELL L. GRIFFEN, Judge, concurring.

I concur in the decision to reverse and remand the chancellor's decision. While I agree that the school board did not abuse its discretion when it voted to expel Hannah Moran because she clearly violated Rule 23 by threatening a student, I suspect that the litigation in this case might have been avoided had parents and school officials acted more responsively.

First, it is regrettable that the families in this case could not resolve this matter privately so that it never became an issue for the school board to consider. Hannah's mother admittedly knew about the tension between Hannah and Leslie Heady. Even if she was dissatisfied with the school's response, she was nonetheless responsible for her daughter's compliance with the school rules. Likewise, Leslie's family was responsible for her compliance with the school rules. We should not be surprised when school officials seem challenged to address behavioral problems that parents are either unwilling or unable to address.

Second, this litigation may have been avoided if school administrators had made a more energetic attempt to determine the source of the problem and had disciplined both girls. Although the record shows that the school board acted within its discretion to impose that discipline upon Hannah, the fact that Leslie was not also disciplined leaves the appearance of favoritism. The record is clear that both Ms. Greene (the counselor) and Mr. Hopkins (the principal) were aware that there were problems between Hannah and Leslie. Greene testified that Hannah came to her office and told her that she was having problems with Leslie and that she had tried to talk to Hopkins about it, but he was out of his office. She further testified that Hannah told her that other students told Hannah that Leslie had placed a note in her locker. Greene testified that she asked Hannah later if her "problem" had "cleared up," and Hannah indicated that she wanted to talk to Hopkins.

Hopkins testified that on the morning of the incident, Hannah's mother telephoned him and indicated there was a problem between Hannah and Leslie. Hopkins thereafter separately called each girl into his office. He told the girls that he "didn't know exactly what was going on," informed the girls of the consequences of breaking the school's rules, and warned the girls to stay away from each other. He further testified that "[t]hey apparently have problems with each other and I didn't probe into why they have problems.... I didn't feel like it was necessary at the time."

In addition, the school board received an unsigned noted addressed to Hannah, that was found in her locker, which stated in part that "if we got into a fight, I would kill you!" Hopkins testified that he had not seen that note prior to the school board meeting, and that if he had discovered who wrote the note, "the same thing I did in this case I would do in that case."

As the majority correctly notes, our function is to determine whether the school board's decision was an abuse of discretion. However, if we were reviewing the chancellor's order, I would affirm.

Given Hopkins's admitted failure to even attempt to determine "exactly what was going on" and the undisputed evidence that Hannah was having problems with Leslie and vice versa, the chancellor was understandably concerned about the appearance of partiality when the record contained evidence that both girls engaged in threatening behavior, but only Hannah was disciplined. In her letter opinion, the chancellor stated:

> It is also significant, as Ms. Greene substantiates, that Hannah was the object of objectionable missives from the other student and sought out the assistance of the school authorities. Hannah could not obtain redress through appropriate channels. Her mother sought to address the issue on two separate occasions, without success.
>
> The punishment meted out to Hannah is not only disproportionate given the totality of the circumstances, it is disparate as between the girls involved. There is no discernable reason why the one girl's actions would be ignored while another, whose situations appears to be precisely the same, is expelled for the balance of the school year. This is particularly so when the girl who has gone unpunished might very well have been the instigator.

Parenting and school administration are functions that ought to complement each other. In this case, an adversarial posture developed between a parent and school administrators over an issue that no sensible parent or administrator should discount or disregard—the threat of school violence. Unfortunately, this issue became a legal controversy because the parents failed to insist that their children obey school rules, and because school administrators failed to investigate promptly and thoroughly, and failed to discipline both students.

Bernard James: Tinker in The Era of Judicial Deference: The Search for Bad Faith, 81 UMKC L. Rev. 601 (2013)

In the context of public education, judicial review has proven to be a daunting task because in the American Republic education policymaking is set apart from other government functions. It is correctly viewed by anyone who studies it seriously as a nearly intimate democratic enterprise. A community combines their common interest in educating their children through a board of neighbors who stand in loco parentis while carrying out the mandate. These representatives function within the tutelary framework, providing the nuts, bolts, and implementation of the education mission, ostensibly under the accountability of the community. The current experimentation with charter schools is a tacit acknowledgment of the challenges of reform through variations on the theme of local control. Chief Justice Warren Burger was correct when he characterized education policymaking as a "democracy in a microcosm":

> [P]eople elect school boards, who in turn select administrators, who select the teachers, and these are the individuals best able to determine the substance of that policy...[L]ocal control of education involves democracy in a microcosm...A school board is not a giant bureaucracy far removed from accountability for its actions; it is truly "of the people and by the people."[6]

These observations help explain, in part, how it is that conflict resolution in education is unique. There is a surprising level of judicial deference to school officials. When talking about this deference in regard to the education mission, courts frequently observe that, "[t]he broad authority [of school officials] to control the conduct of students . . . permits a good deal of latitude in determining which policies will best serve educational and disciplinary goals." This thinking runs back to a spate of early Twentieth Century education-mission decisions in which both federal and state courts began raising the bar on judicial intervention to good-faith actions in support of the education mission. In Meyer v. Nebraska, where the Court upheld the right of parents to teach a foreign language to their children, nevertheless the justices made it clear that the state could "do much, go very far," in its pursuit of the education mission. In Pierce v. Society of Sisters, while upholding the right of parents to elect to place their children in a private school, the justices made it plain that,

> No question is raised concerning the power of the state reasonably to regulate all schools, to inspect, supervise and examine them, their teachers and pupils; to require that all children of proper age attend some school, that teachers shall be of good moral character and patriotic disposition, that certain studies plainly essential to good citizenship must be taught, and that nothing be taught which is manifestly inimical to the public welfare. [7]

---

[6] Bd. of Educ., Island Trees Union Free Sch. Dist. No. 26 v. Pico, 457 U.S. 853, 891-92 (1982) (Burger, J., dissenting).
[7] Pierce v. Society of the Sisters of the Holy Names of Jesus & Mary, 268 U.S. 510, 534 (1925).

State court decisions were in accord with the emerging view on the police power on matters of education policy.

By 1968, this notion of judicial deference had flourished to its current form. In Epperson v. Arkansas, the Court, while resolving a conflict over the teaching of evolution, summarized education policy disputes as an area which judges could not be too careful in avoiding:

> Judicial interposition in the operation of the public school system of the Nation raises problems requiring care and restraint. . . . By and large, public education in our Nation is committed to the control of state and local authorities. [8]

In the decades since Epperson, the U.S. Supreme Court and scholars have advanced this characterization of public education in a manner that induces a more forgiving standard of judicial review. In 1988, in Hazelwood School District v. Kuhlmeier, one of the featured cases in this symposium, the Court upheld the administrative censorship of articles in a high-school student newspaper with the following statement:

> [T]he determination of what manner of speech in the classroom or in school assembly is inappropriate properly rests with the school board," rather than with the federal courts. [9]

In the higher education case featured in this symposium, Widmar v. Vincent, the Court observed that:

> [W]e [do not] question the right of the University to make academic judgments as to how best to allocate scarce resources or to determine for itself on academic grounds who may teach, what may be taught, how it shall be taught, and who may be admitted to study. [10]

Today, with few exceptions, lower courts in both state and federal judicial systems, have applied this deference to the complete range of school law related litigation. The sound bites are noteworthy. For example, the Eleventh Circuit, upholding campus restrictions on student political speech, stated that:

> The central justification for a student government organization is that it supports the educational mission of the University. This deference to the educational mission . . . has resulted in the recognition of [an educator's] right to exclude even

---

[8] Epperson v. Arkansas, 393 U.S. 97, 104 (1968).
[9] Hazelwood Sch. Dist. v. Kuhlmeier, 484 U.S. 260, 266 (1988).

[10] Widmar v. Vincient, 454 U.S. 263, 276 (1981).

> First Amendment activities that violate reasonable campus rules or substantially interfere with the opportunity of other students to obtain an education.[11]

...

These statements confirm what our instinct already tells us-a shift has taken place in the judicial attitude about the rights of students in school. Anyone who sets out to analyze an education law dispute ignores the implications of this state of judicial affairs at their peril, for deference is often the best explanation for the outcome. School officials seeking to place their policies on the constitutional side of the line and the students for whose benefit the line exists deserve to be released from the opacity of current judicial review.

...

It is enough now to observe that this deference may have run its course. In the last decade, seven justices on the Supreme Court have expressed an interest in returning rigor to the judicial review of student rights disputes. The [affirmative action case] Grutter dissents round up many of these sentiments.- For example, Chief Justice Rehnquist, rather than deferring, examines the factual record and arrives at a very Tinker-like conclusion:

> Although the Court recites the language of our strict scrutiny analysis, its application of that review is unprecedented in its deference. . . . "[M]ore than good motives should be required when government seeks to allocate its resources by way of an explicit racial classification system." . . . [The] actual program bears no relation to [its] asserted goal. Stripped of its . . . veil, the Law School's program is revealed as a naked effort to achieve racial balancing.[12]

Moreover, Justice Kennedy stated in his [Grutter] dissent: "The Court confuses deference to a university's definition of its educational objective with deference to the implementation of this goal. . . . The safeguard [is] rigorous judicial review."[13] Justice Scalia noted that: "Deference does not imply abandonment or abdication of judicial review."[14]

In another case featured in this symposium, Morse v. Frederick, the Court deferred and upheld school discipline in response to Joseph Frederick's curious message "BONG HiTS 4 JESUS." Justice Stevens' dissenting opinion said this of the deference standard:

> To the extent the Court defers to the principal's ostensibly reasonable judgment, it abdicates its constitutional responsibility. . . . When [[government officials] are entitled to no deference as to whether particular speech amounts to a "clear and

---

[11] Alabama Student Party v. Student Gov't Assn of the Univ. of Alabama, 867 F.2d 1344, 1345 (11th Cir.1989).
[12] Grutter v. Bollinger, 539 U.S. 306, 379-380. (2003), (Rehnquist, J., dissenting).

[13] Id. at 388, (Kennedy, J., dissenting).

[14] Id. at 348-349, (Scalia, J., dissenting)

> present danger," it is hard to understand why the Court would so blithely defer to the judgment of a single school principal.[15]

Finally, in Earls, a Fourth Amendment case in which the Court deferred to suspcionless searches in the form of drug testing, Justice Ginsberg observed in her dissent that the "'[T]he legality of a search of a student' . . . should depend on the reasonableness of

---

Sean R. Nuttall: Rethinking the Narrative on Judicial Deference in Student Speech Cases, 83 N.Y.U. L. Rev. 1282 (2008)

Judicial deference to the reasonable judgments of decisionmakers is justified when applying [a] type of outcome-focused test. Both the decisionmaker's choice… and the judge's evaluation of that choice necessarily involve complex fact- and context-dependent judgments. Judicial deference to reasonable decisions acknowledges the difficulty that decisionmakers face in predicting ex ante the likely consequences of speech and recognizes the problems inherent in judges' ex post, counterfactual second-guessing of these decisions, especially because judges have no more expertise predicting the future than anyone else.

…

Of course, deferring to the reasonable judgments of decisionmakers may exacerbate the inherent susceptibility of such tests to inconsistent application and manipulation. However, the increased malleability is at least partially counterbalanced by these tests' requirement of a showing of likely harm. Demanding that there be a clear and present danger of a substantive evil, or that there be the possibility of a substantial and material disruption to school activities, means that there remains at least some check on judicial discretion and censorship. There may also be countervailing interests at play, such as those present in the public school system, that support deference to reasonable decisions to restrict speech.

…

This deference is based on two related rationales: first, that school boards and teachers have the requisite experience, expertise, and familiarity with local culture and values to determine how best to instruct students, and second, that education policy is primarily the responsibility of the states. Therefore, federal judges, who have little experience or expertise in this regard, should not indiscriminately overrule educators' decisions. In the Supreme Court's oft-quoted words,

---

15 Morse v. Frederick, 551 U.S. 393, 441-443 (2007) n.6 (Stevens, J., dissenting) (Justices Souter and Ginsburg also joined the dissenting opinion).

> It is not the role of the federal courts to set aside decisions of school administrators which the court may view as lacking a basis in wisdom or compassion. . . . The system of public education that has evolved in this Nation relies necessarily upon the discretion and judgment of school administrators and school board members.[16]

Making an accurate prediction about whether a particular type of speech is likely to cause a substantial disruption involves a complex judgment based on a number of factors, including "past experience in the school, current events influencing student activities and behavior, and instances of actual or threatened disruption relating to the speech in question." Given the difficulty of making this type of decision, judges--who do not share the educators' knowledge or experience--should accord considerable respect to teachers' predictions of disruption. Similarly, judicial deference serves federalism values by allowing room for states, local school boards, and teachers to set educational policy, control the classroom environment, and inculcate community values.

...

The question of how coextensive the speech rights of children, both in and out of schools, should be with those of adults sits atop a deep tension in liberalism between the commitment to personal liberty and the need for society to educate its young.

II. The Legislative and Executive Interests

A. State Constitutional and Statutory Provisions

Public education is a unique function of state government. Although the federal government occasionally influences policymaking through the receipt of federal funds on the local implementation of certain policies, it is clear that the education mission is a product of the sovereignty of each state. The U.S. Supreme Court has acknowledged, "Education is perhaps the most important function of state and local governments." *Brown v. Bd. of Educ.*, 347 U.S. 483 (1954). Later, as though to underscore public education as a state enterprise, the Court noted; "[e]ducation, of course, is not among the rights afforded explicit protection under [the federal] constitution. Nor do we find any basis for saying it is implicitly protected." *San Antonio Ind. Sch. Dist. v. Rodriguez*, 411 U.S. 980 (1973).

States bring a range of themes to public education, all organized around notions of control, accountability, uniformity, efficiency and access without cost. Note the diversity of both language and vision in the following state constitutional and statutory provisions.

---

[16] Wood v. Strickland, 420 U.S. 308, 326 (1975).

CONSTITUTION OF THE STATE OF ARKANSAS

Art. 14, § 1
Section 1. Free school system

Intelligence and virtue being the safeguards of liberty and the bulwark of a free and good government, the State shall ever maintain a general, suitable and efficient system of free public schools and shall adopt all suitable means to secure to the people the advantages and opportunities of education.

CONSTITUTION OF THE STATE OF CALIFORNIA

Art. IX
§ 1. Legislative policy

A general diffusion of knowledge and intelligence being essential to the preservation of the rights and liberties of the people, the Legislature shall encourage by all suitable means the promotion of intellectual, scientific, moral, and agricultural improvement.

§ 5. Common school system

The Legislature shall provide for a system of common schools by which a free school shall be kept up and supported in each district at least six months in every year, after the first year in which a school has been established.

§ 28

(Right to Safe Schools). All students and staff of public primary, elementary, junior high and senior high schools have the inalienable right to attend campuses, which are safe, secure and peaceful.

CONSTITUTION OF THE STATE OF COLORADO

Art. IX, Section 2
Establishment and Maintenance of Public Schools

The general assembly shall, as soon as practicable, provide for the establishment and maintenance of a thorough and uniform system of free public schools throughout the state, wherein all residents of the state, between the ages of six and twenty-one years, may be educated gratuitously. One or more public schools shall be maintained in each school district within the state, at least three months in each year; any school district failing to have such school shall not be entitled to receive any portion of the school fund for that year.

COLORADO REVISED STATUTES
C.R.S. 22-7-601
22-7-601. Legislative Declaration

(1) The general assembly hereby finds that:

(a) While section 2 of article IX of the state constitution directs the general assembly to establish and maintain a thorough and uniform system of free public schools throughout the state, the wide variety of practices and curriculum among school districts and public schools throughout the state make it increasingly difficult to measure whether there is a thorough and uniform system of schools throughout the state;

(b) It is difficult for most parents to determine whether the public schools in which their children are enrolled are providing quality academic instruction in an environment that is conducive to learning;

(c) Business owners and other taxpayers in each school district have a right to know whether their tax dollars are being appropriately spent by the school district to provide students within the district with an opportunity for a quality education;

(d) Directing the department of education to compile objective indicators of every public school's academic performance and making those compilations readily available will assist the general assembly, parents, and taxpayers in making choices that will enable all children to have an opportunity for a quality education;

(e) Giving each public school an accountability report on its performance and improvement in academic achievement will assist the general assembly, parents, and taxpayers in identifying those public schools that are providing students with an opportunity for a quality education; and

(f) By requiring annual accountability reports, the general assembly, parents, and taxpayers will be able to monitor the progress that schools make toward providing students with an opportunity for a quality education in a safe learning environment

(2) The general assembly recognizes that the rating of public schools will be controversial. Therefore, the general assembly finds that it is important that objective indicators be used in a manner that will ensure consistent application throughout the state in rating public schools. It is the intent of the general assembly that, in calculating a school's academic performance rating, the department of education shall use, except for limited statutory exceptions, the scores and other objective indicators of all students enrolled in the school.

CONSTITUTION OF THE STATE OF NEVADA
Article 11, Section 1
EDUCATION

1. Legislature to encourage education; appointment, term and duties of superintendent of public instruction.

The legislature shall encourage by all suitable means the promotion of intellectual, literary, scientific, mining, mechanical, agricultural, and moral improvements, and also provide for a superintendent of public instruction and by law prescribe the manner of appointment, term of office and the duties thereof.

2. Uniform system of common schools.

The legislature shall provide for a uniform system of common schools, by which a school shall be established and maintained in each school district at least six months in every year, and any school district which shall allow instruction of a sectarian character therein may be deprived of its proportion of the interest of the public school fund during such neglect or infraction, and the legislature may pass such laws as will tend to secure a general attendance of the children in each school district upon said public schools.

NEVADA REVISED STATUTES
385.005
Declaration of legislative intent; policies of integration or desegregation of public schools; recommendations to legislature for equality of educational opportunity.

1. The legislature reaffirms its intent that public education in the State of Nevada is essentially a matter for local control by local school districts. The provisions of this Title are intended to reserve to the boards of trustees of local school districts within this state such rights and powers as are necessary to maintain control of the education of the children within their respective districts. These rights and powers may only be limited by other specific provisions of law.

2. The responsibility of establishing a statewide policy of integration or desegregation of public schools is reserved to the legislature. The responsibility for establishing a local policy of integration or desegregation of public schools consistent with the statewide policy established by the legislature is delegated to the respective boards of trustees of local school districts and to the governing body of each charter school.

3. The state board shall, and each board of trustees of a local school district, the governing body of each charter school and any other school officer may, advise the legislature at each regular session of any recommended legislative action to ensure high standards of equality of educational opportunity for all children in the State of Nevada.

CONSTITUTION OF WEST VIRGINIA
W. Va. Const. Art. XII

§ 1. Education

The legislature shall provide, by general law, for a thorough and efficient system of free schools.

§ 2. Supervision of Free Schools

The general supervision of the free schools of the State shall be vested in the West Virginia board of education which shall perform such duties as may be prescribed by law. The board shall consist of nine members to be appointed by the governor, by and with the advice and consent of the senate, for overlapping terms of nine years, except that the original appointments shall be for terms of one, two, three, four, five, six, seven, eight, and nine years, respectively. No more than five members of the board shall belong to the same political party, and in addition to the general qualifications otherwise required by the Constitution, the legislature may require other specific qualifications for membership on the board. No member of the board may be removed from office by the governor except for official misconduct, incompetence, neglect of duty, or gross immorality, and then only in the manner prescribed by law for the removal by the governor of state elective officers.

The West Virginia board of education shall in the manner prescribed by law, select the state superintendent of free schools who shall serve at its will and pleasure. He shall be the chief school officer of the State and shall have such powers and shall perform such duties as may be prescribed by law.

WEST VIRGINIA STATUTES
W. Va. Code § 18-1-4
§ 18-1-4. Education improvement plan.

(a) The governor, the Legislature, the state board and the people of West Virginia agree that the education of their children is of utmost importance to the future well-being of the state and that the purpose of enacting education laws and providing funding to support a system of free schools is to assure that all of our children have every opportunity to secure an education which is thorough and is provided in an efficient manner. The governor, the Legislature, the state board and the people of West Virginia further agree that improvements are needed in the education system of West Virginia if these objectives are to be met.

(b) Therefore, the governor, the Legislature, the state board and the people of West Virginia have established goals for themselves which are measurable and achievable through the combined efforts of the government, the school system and the people through an increased focus on the needs of children. These goals are:

(1) All children entering the first grade will be ready for the first grade;

(2) All students will have equal education opportunity;

(3) Student performance on national measures of student performance will equal or exceed national averages and the performance of students falling in the lowest quartile will improve by fifty percent;

(4) Ninety percent of ninth graders will graduate from high school;

(5) High school graduates will be fully prepared for college, other post-secondary education or gainful employment. The number of high school graduates entering post-secondary education will increase by fifty percent; and

(6) All working age adults will be functionally literate.

The intent of the governor, the Legislature and the state board is to pursue the accomplishment of these goals through strategies which focus on: (i) Early childhood development; (ii) improving the quality of teaching; (iii) technology and learning; (iv) helping at-risk students; (v) work force preparation; and (vi) restructuring and accountability in the education system.

(c) The state board shall report progress toward meeting and achieving the goals, as set forth in subsection (b) of this section, to the governor and the Legislature at the beginning of the legislative session in each of the next four years, beginning in the year one thousand nine hundred ninety-seven, and shall include in such report how the legislative priorities of the board address attainment of the goals.

B. State Separation of Powers Issues

It might at first seem odd to discuss the concept of separation of powers in the public school context. But it would be naïve to ignore the manner in which preemption affects education policymaking. Disputes between local school officials and state policymakers beg the question of whether the education mission is really a local enterprise. It may well be that few degrees of separation exist between local school educators and state officials. As you read the cases the below try to think strategically about the matter of local control. Is it better for there to be a strict wall of separation that preserves local autonomy? When should state legislative preferences preempt local decision-making? The cases below present just a few of the difficult issues surrounding the matter. Note that some of the justifications for local school autonomy are substantive matters of state constitutional law, while others are matters of public policy as to which branch of state government should control the education mission.

ROGERS v. HELENA-WEST HELENA SCHOOL DISTRICT
No. 2:06CV00160 SWW, 2006 U.S. Dist. LEXIS 72790 (E. D. Ark. Oct. 4, 2006)

JUDGE: Susan Webber Wright

Plaintiffs are all residents of Phillips County, Arkansas, and were employed by separate defendant Helena-West Helena School District in non-certified positions. They are all African-Americans. According to the State Defendants, on April 11, 2005, the Arkansas State Board of Education declared that the District was in "fiscal distress," and on September 8, 2005, pursuant to § 6-20-1909 (Supp. 2005), the Arkansas State Board of Education suspended the District's School Board. The Arkansas Department of Education took over the operation of the District, and plaintiffs subsequently were fired by defendant Rudolph Howard, the State-appointed superintendent of the District.

.....

Plaintiffs allege their rights to due process and equal protection were violated when the State Defendants "usurped control of their school district without the input participation notice to the true operators of the Helena-West Helena School District, i.e. the voters." ...The control of the public school system is a State matter delegated and lodged in the State Legislature by the Arkansas Constitution. *See* Ark. Const. Art. 14, § 1. The Arkansas Legislature vested general supervision over all State public schools in the Arkansas State Board of Education.

.....

Pertinent provisions of the Act provide: "The purpose of this subchapter shall be to establish and implement a program by which the Department of Education shall identify, assess, and address school districts in fiscal distress." Ark. Code Ann. § 6-20-1902 (Supp. 2005). "Any school district meeting any of the following criteria may be identified by the Department of Education to be a school district in financial distress upon final approval by the State Board of Education: (1) A declining balance determined to jeopardize the fiscal integrity of a school district; (2) Any act or violation determined to jeopardize the fiscal integrity of a school district . . . ; or (3) Any other fiscal condition of a school district deemed to have a detrimental negative impact on the continuation of educational services by that school district." Ark. Code Ann. § 6-20-1904 (Supp. 2005).

Plaintiffs appear to assert that the Act violates their right to equal protection because it denies them the right to vote for their school board, prohibits former school board members from serving on the board and thus deprives plaintiffs of the right to retain their elected representatives, and treats them differently than other school district on account of their race...

Just as there is no fundamental right to vote for members of a school board, there is no fundamental right to retain an elected official. Where offices are created by statute, the Legislature may abolish the offices even during an incumbent's term. *Robinson v. White*, 26 Ark. 139, 141 (1870) ("The Legislature has absolute control over all statutory offices, and may abolish them at pleasure; and in doing so no vested right is being invaded.") The school board offices were created by statute. *See*

Ark. Code Ann. § 6-13-634 (Supp. 2005). Thus, the Arkansas Legislature has the authority to modify their authority, vest in the Arkansas State Board of Education the power to suspend it, or even abolish the District School Board altogether.

The Seventh Circuit rejected an equal protection challenge to similar school reform in Chicago, Illinois. In *Hearne v. Chicago Bd. of Educ.*, 185 F.3d 770 (7th Cir. 1999), the plaintiffs challenged the constitutionality of a state statute that applied only to the Chicago public school system which the legislature had found was in an educational crisis. School district employees claimed the legislation which restricted their bargaining rights had a racially disparate impact. In dismissing plaintiffs' equal protection claim, the court said:

> [T]here is nothing here to indicate that the Illinois General Assembly structured the Chicago school reform legislation specifically because it wanted to disadvantage African Americans. There are substantial numbers of African Americans in many other cities in the state, and it is simply too great a stretch to say that the population represented by the Chicago school system is such a good proxy for African Americans that the ostensibly neutral classification is 'an obvious pretext for racial discrimination.' The plaintiffs' saying this is so in their pleadings is not enough to survive a Rule 12(b)(6) motion, when the legislation itself contains not a hint of an impermissible racial classification.

Id. at 776; *see also Moore v. Detroit Sch. Reform Bd.*, 293 F.3d 352 (6th Cir. 2002) (Michigan School Reform Act establishing new school board for Detroit did not violate equal protection; in absence of showing race discrimination was motivating factor, Act was rationally related to legislature's attempt to experiment with different techniques to advance public education).

A court must reject an equal protection challenge to a statutory classification if there is any reasonably conceivable state of facts that could provide a rational basis for the classification. …

Legislative bodies are given broad latitude in their legislative determinations, and it is not the province of the courts to monitor the inputs into each legislative decision. … A review of the Act shows that it is racially neutral on its face and applies to all school districts regardless of racial composition. Plaintiffs cite no factual basis for their allegations of racial bias or motive. Because there are no facts to support the conclusory allegation of purposeful discrimination, and their claims do not otherwise involve a fundamental right, plaintiffs' equal protection claims should be dismissed.

WEST VIRGINIA BOARD OF EDUCATION v. HECHLER
376 S.E.2d 839 (W. Va. 1988)

OPINION BY: McHugh, Chief Justice.

In this original proceeding, the petitioners, the West Virginia Board of Education (hereinafter the "Board") and Tom McNeel, State Superintendent of Schools, seek a writ of mandamus directing the respondent, Ken Hechler, Secretary of State, to file rules approved by the Board. This Court has reviewed the petition, the response, and all arguments and exhibits attached thereto. We are of the opinion that the relief requested by the petitioners should be granted.

In June, 1988, the West Virginia legislature amended the State Administrative Procedures Act, W. Va. Code, 29A-1-1 to 29A-7-4, as amended, by adding to it a new article, namely, article 3A. The new article, inter alia, establishes a "legislative oversight commission on education accountability." The oversight commission is to be comprised of eight members: three from the House of Delegates; three from the Senate; and the Speaker of the House and Senate President as ex officio, nonvoting members.

Pursuant to the provisions of this new article, the Board must submit its approved legislative rules to the oversight commission for review. After review of a rule approved by the Board, the oversight commission is required to recommend that the legislature either promulgate the rule in whole or in part, or recommend that the rule be withdrawn. If the legislature fails to act on a rule submitted to it by the oversight commission, then the Board is prohibited from taking any action on the rule "unless and until otherwise authorized to do so." W. Va. Code, 29A-3A-13(b) [1988].

In August, 1988, the Board adopted a rule entitled "West Virginia Minimum Requirements for Design and Equipment of School Buses," to be effective October 22, 1988. The rule was filed with the respondent Secretary of State in order to be placed in the West Virginia State Register. The respondent, however, refused to file the rule, basing his refusal on the Board's failure to comply with the newly enacted provisions of the Administrative Procedures Act.

II

We begin by discussing the constitutionally preferred status of public education in West Virginia. "The provisions of Article XII, Section 1, et seq., as well as Article X, Section 5 of the West Virginia Constitution, when construed in light of our prior cases, gives a constitutionally preferred status to public education in this State." *State ex rel. Bd. of Educ. v. Rockefeller*, 167 W. Va. 72, 281 S.E.2d 131 (1981).

Article XII, § 1 of the West Virginia Constitution states: "The legislature shall provide, by general law, for a thorough and efficient system of free schools." Article XII, § 2 of the State Constitution, however, provides in pertinent part: "The general supervision of the free schools of the State shall be vested in the West Virginia board of education which shall perform such duties as may be prescribed by law." The petitioners contend that this general supervisory provision implies rule-making power, and by enacting W. Va. Code, 29A-3A-12 and -13 [1988], the legislature has effectively diminished article XII, § 2 of the State Constitution. The Board's rule-making power is viewed by the respondent as being derived primarily from W. Va. Code, 18-2-5 [1983], which states in part:

> Subject to and in conformity with the constitution and laws of this State, the state board of education shall determine the educational policies of the State and shall make rules for carrying into effect the laws and policies of the State relating to education, including rules relating to the physical welfare of pupils, the education of feeble-minded and physically disabled or crippled children of school age, school attendance, evening and continuation or part-time day schools, school extension work, the classification of schools, the issuing of certificates upon credentials, the distribution and care of free textbooks by the county boards of education, the general powers and duties of county boards of education, and of teachers, principals, supervisors and superintendents, and such other matters pertaining to the public schools of the State as may seem to the state board to be necessary and expedient.

See Pauley v. Bailey, 174 W. Va. 167, 324 S.E.2d 128, 133-34 (1984). Referring to this statutory provision, this Court has stated that "although this grant of rule-making authority is tempered by a requirement that it be exercised in conformance with other statutory provisions, it is indicative of the broad power of the State Board of Education over county boards of education, particularly in the area of state educational policy." *Bailey v. Truby*, 174 W. Va. 8, 321, S.E.2d 302, 311-12 (1984).

The Board has traditionally been exempt from legislative rule-making review pursuant to W. Va. Code, 29A-1-3 [1986]. The legislature, however, amended this provision in 1988 by removing the Board's exemption, thus allowing enactment of W. Va. Code, 29A-3A-12 and -13, requiring the Board to submit its legislative rules to the legislature for approval.

In accordance with W. Va. Code, 18-2-5 [1983], the Board adopted a rule governing the design and operation of school buses. This rule is clearly within the purview of "general supervision" of state schools pursuant to art. XII, § 2 of the West Virginia Constitution. 5 In *Bailey v. Truby*, 174 W. Va. 8, 321 S.E.2d 302 (1984), we concluded that "any statutory provision that interferes with the State Board of Education's 'general supervision of the free schools of the State' under article XII, § 2 of the West Virginia Constitution is void." *Id.* at 19, 321 S.E.2d at 312. Rules proposed by the Board, like the rule in this case, are integral to the day-to-day operation of schools. An attempt to impede this process is not consistent with the general supervisory powers conferred upon the Board by art. XII, § 2 of the State Constitution.

"General supervision" is not an axiomatic blend of words designed to fill the pages of our State Constitution, but it is a meaningful concept to the governance of schools and education in this state. Decisions that pertain to education must be faced by those who possess expertise in the educational area. These issues are critical to the progress of schools in this state, and, ultimately,

the welfare of its citizens. In 1957, the citizens of this state conferred general supervisory powers over education and one need not look further than art. XII, § 2 of the State Constitution to see that the "general supervision" of state schools is vested in the State Board of Education. Unlike most other administrative agencies which are constituents of the executive branch, the Board enjoys a special standing because such a constitutional provision exists.

The rule-making power prescribed by W. Va. Code, 18-2-5 [1983] is a provision that has aided the Board's general supervisory functions. The newly enacted provisions of the State Administrative Procedures Act, however, namely, W. Va. Code, 29A-3A-12 and -13 [1988], pose an interference with the Board's rule-making power, and consequently, the Board's general supervisory functions.

Therefore, we hold that rule-making by the State Board of Education is within the meaning of "general supervision" of state schools pursuant to art. XII, § 2 of the West Virginia Constitution, and any statutory provision that interferes with such rule-making is unconstitutional. Consequently, W. Va. Code, 29A-3A-12 and -13 [1988] are hereby declared to be unconstitutional.

Article XII, § 1 of the State Constitution, granting the legislature the authority to establish "a thorough and efficient system of free schools," does not entail the exclusive delegation of rule-making functions that are part of the Board's general supervisory powers pursuant to art. XII, § 2. An attempt to undertake the Board's general supervisory powers violates the provision of art. V, § 1 of the State Constitution which states: "The legislative, executive and judicial departments shall be separate and distinct, so that neither shall exercise the powers properly belonging to either of the others[.]" Hence, such an attempt is unconstitutional.

Consistent with the foregoing, a rule adopted by the State Board of Education, setting forth minimum requirements for the design and equipment of school buses, is within the meaning of "general supervision" of state schools pursuant to art. XII, § 2 of the West Virginia Constitution. W. Va. Code, 29A-3A-12 and -13 [1988] interfere with such "general supervision," and, therefore, are unconstitutional.

Notes and Comments

1. Local Challenges to State Legislative Reform

The decision in *Rogers* describes the degree of control that State legislatures possess over public education. In the absence of a traditional constitutional claim (or a claim of total arbitrariness—*see* Chapter 4 on Substantive Due Process), courts presume the validity of state laws regulating public education. The court in *Rogers* relies on *Hearne v. Chicago Bd. of Educ.*, 185 F.3d 770 (7th Cir. 1999), where the seventh circuit upheld Illinois reform legislation that only applied to the Chicago school system. The court noted:

> The plaintiffs concede that the proper test… for their geographical discrimination argument is whether the legislature had a rational basis for devising a separate system for Chicago. They are right and we agree with the district court that the
>
> sections of this legislation now before us pass that minimal hurdle… The legislature was entitled to take the position that the optimal way to assure

> accountability of teaching and non-teaching staff members would be different because of the scale of operations in Chicago. The crisis it perceived in Chicago also was a legitimate reason to take immediate action there, leaving open the possibility of extending similar measures to other places. *Id.* at 774-75.

See also Moore v. Detroit Sch. Reform Bd., 293 F.3d 352 (6th Cir. 2002) (upholding legislation that called for the state take-over of the Detroit Public School System).

2. State versus Local Control of Public Education

All states have provisions that seek to protect local control in counties and cities. The logic behind such laws is to allow local decision-makers to resolve uniquely local issues free of interference by the state government. Such a system makes sense where a generally applicable state law would not make good policy for all local governments within a particular state.

As *Rogers* and *Hearne* illustrate, there is a natural tension between the goal of "home rule" laws and the education reform preferences of the state legislature. Courts have been reluctant to rule against state legislatures, primarily because of the long-standing declaration of interest in educational matters by the states.

When "home rule" provisions are not in conflict with state legislative preferences, these local control laws effectively cede legislative authority over local matters to cities and municipalities. In so doing the principle of local self-government is given meaning and communities more directly control policy outcomes. In public education, variations on the home rule theme result in local school boards having the last word in addressing issues of local concern in the K-12 setting.

Rogers and *Hearne* do not adequately address the question of whether a state take-over of a local school district makes good policy. A school board is specifically accountable to its community and (so one would think) more responsive to the need to correct failures. One would also think that as the size of the city or county increases, the state legislature would be reluctant to interfere with attempts by local officials to solve the problem. This issue usually turns on whether the local matter at issue can also be characterized as a statewide concern, triggering the corrective police powers of the legislature. Courts tend to resolve these collisions of institutional interests in favor of state police power. Professor Briffault observes

> The tension between home rule and state power to respond to local citizen demands is particularly poignant—indeed, paradoxical—when the demand is for local self-government. Considerable regulatory and fiscal authority, responsibility for the provision of public goods and services, and the power to deliberate and determine a wide range of public policy questions has been delegated to local governments accountable primarily to local electorates and subject to little active state oversight. There must be some legitimate and substantial state interest in the [Staten Island] government arrangements for 379,000 people—a population large enough to constitute the second largest city in the state [of New York]. Regardless of the number of people involved, it must be that just as the state can act to promote

> public health or civil rights at the local level, so too it may act to promote local self-government. If, because of political, economic, or social developments, sharp differences emerge within a municipality, it may become apparent to the state that the residents of a portion of the municipality will be better served if their community is carved out of the existing municipality and given local independence.

Briffault, Voting Rights, Home Rule, and Metropolitan Governance, 92 COLUM. L. REV. 775, 816 (1992).

MENDOZA v. STATE
57 Cal. Rptr. 3d 505 (Ct. App. 2007)

OPINION BY: Croskey, J.

Mayors in certain large cities around the country have been granted control of the school districts in those cities. Antonio Villaraigosa, the Mayor of the City of Los Angeles (the Mayor), sought similar control over the Los Angeles Unified School District (LAUSD) through state legislation. The California Constitution grants to the voters within the LAUSD the right to determine whether their board of education is to be elected or appointed. Therefore, the Legislature could not simply enact a statute granting the Mayor authority to appoint the members of the LAUSD Board of Education (the Board). Moreover, the California Constitution also prohibits the transfer of authority over any part of the school system to entities outside of the public school system. Therefore, the Legislature could not simply enact a statute transferring control over the LAUSD to the Mayor. The Legislature attempted to avoid these prohibitions with the enactment of Assembly Bill No. 1381 known as the "Romero Act."

At issue in this appeal is the constitutionality of the Romero Act. At the heart of that statute are two main provisions: (1) the transfer of substantial power from the Board to the LAUSD District Superintendent (the District Superintendent), and the grant to the Mayor of authority to ratify the appointment of the District Superintendent; and (2) the transfer of complete control of three low-performing high schools (and their feeder schools) from the Board to a partnership led by the Mayor.

We conclude that the Romero Act is an unconstitutional attempt to do indirectly what the Legislature is prohibited from doing directly. The Legislature cannot overrule the LAUSD's voters' determination that their Board is to be elected rather than appointed, nor may it transfer authority over part of the school system to entities outside of the public school system. We will therefore affirm the trial court's issuance of a writ of mandate preventing the enforcement of the Romero Act.

****

The controlling constitutional provisions are found in article IX of the California Constitution. Section 1 provides that "the Legislature shall encourage by all suitable means" the promotion of education. The Constitution provides for three different types of agencies to govern education in California: state, county, and district.

At the statewide level, the Constitution provides for the election of a statewide Superintendent of Public Instruction. (Cal. Const., art. IX, § 2.) The Constitution also provides for a State Board of Education, and requires that the Legislature provide for its election or appointment. (Cal. Const., art. IX, § 7.)

At the county level, there is to be a county superintendent of schools and county board of education. (Cal. Const., art. IX, §§ 3, 7.) A county's charter may provide for an elected county board of education (Cal. Const., art. IX, § 3.3); in the absence of such a provision, the Legislature is to provide whether the county board of education is elected or appointed (Cal. Const., art. IX, § 7). The Constitution leaves it to the voters of each county to determine whether the superintendent of schools is to be elected by the voters or appointed by the county board of education (Cal. Const., art. IX, § 3).

At the district level, the state is to be organized, by the Legislature, into school districts. "The Legislature shall have power, by general law, to provide for the incorporation and organization of school districts, high school districts, and community college districts, of every kind and class, and may classify such districts." (Cal. Const., art. IX, § 14.) The Constitution references the "governing boards" of school districts without specifically defining them. (*Ibid.*) The gap is filled by the Education Code, which provides that "[e]very school district shall be under the control of a board of school trustees or a board of education." (Ed. Code, § 35010, subd. (a).). The Constitution permits charter cities to establish, in their charters, "for the manner in which, the times at which, and the terms for which the members of boards of education shall be elected or appointed, for their qualifications, compensation and removal, and for the number which shall constitute any one of such boards." (Cal. Const., art. IX, § 16.) Therefore, the board of education provided for in a city charter is the "governing board" of the relevant school district. The Legislature has provided that the governing board of any school district may "employ" a district superintendent. (Ed. Code, § 35026.) The Legislature has imposed certain recordkeeping and reporting duties on the governing boards of school districts (Ed. Code, § 35250); the governing board is permitted to delegate any of these duties to the district superintendent (Ed. Code, § 35026). Governing boards of larger school districts may also appoint a director of school building planning, to be responsible "for the coordination of the building program of the district." (Ed. Code, § 35045.)

Under the Constitution, the public schools themselves exist at the district level and are governed by the school districts. Section 5 of article IX provides, "The Legislature shall provide for a system of common schools by which a free school shall be kept up and supported in each district at least six months in every year …." (Cal. Const., art. IX, § 5.) "The Public School System shall include all kindergarten schools, elementary schools, secondary schools, technical schools, and State colleges, established in accordance with law and, in addition, the school districts and the other agencies authorized to maintain them. No school or college or any other part of the Public School

System shall be, directly or indirectly, transferred from the Public School System or placed under the jurisdiction of any authority other than one included within the Public School System." (Cal. Const., art. IX, § 6.) Section 8 of article IX confirms that "[n]o public money shall ever be appropriated for the support of any sectarian or denominational school, or any school not under the exclusive control of the officers of the public schools … ." (Italics added.)

"The Legislature may authorize the governing boards of all school districts to initiate and carry on any programs, activities, or to otherwise act in any manner which is not in conflict with the laws and purposes for which school districts are established." (Cal. Const., art. IX, § 14.) The

Legislature has done so. Education Code section 35160 provides, "On and after January 1, 1976, the governing board of any school district may initiate and carry on any program, activity, or may otherwise act in any manner which is not in conflict with or inconsistent with, or preempted by, any law and which is not in conflict with the purposes for which school districts are established."

****

In some large cities across the country, mayors have sought and obtained authority over their local school districts. In the 2005 Los Angeles mayoral runoff election, the two candidates, then Mayor James Hahn and then Councilmember Villaraigosa, each announced that they would seek some measure of control over the LAUSD. Villaraigosa stated that, if elected, he would seek ultimate authority over the LAUSD, as in some other major cities. Villaraigosa was elected mayor on May 17, 2005.

****

[T]he Legislature was considering legislation to give the Mayor power over the LAUSD. On August 18, 2005, the Legislative Counsel issued an opinion on a then pending Senate bill which would have authorized the Mayor of Los Angeles, upon making a finding of "educational failure," to fill by appointment any vacancies on the LAUSD Board of Education (and continue to fill such vacancies by appointment upon the expiration of the terms of incumbent board members). The Legislative Counsel concluded that the bill would be unconstitutional, in that it would violate Los Angeles's right under California Constitution, article IX, section 16, to choose whether its board of education members are elected or appointed.

The Legislative Counsel was then asked "whether authority or control over educational functions currently performed by a school district may be transferred by statute to the mayor of a charter city." On July 17, 2006, the Legislative Counsel issued its opinion that such a statute would be unconstitutional, in that it would violate California Constitution, article IX, section 6's prohibition against the transfer of any part of the public school system from the authority of the public school system to any authority outside the public school system. Finally, the Legislative Counsel was asked whether transferring control over the educational functions of a school district to the mayor of a charter city would be permissible if the county superintendent of schools were given authority to oversee the mayor's performance. The Legislative Counsel concluded this would still be an unconstitutional transfer of power. (Ops. Cal. Legis. Counsel, No. 0620862 (Aug. 21, 2006) School District: Transfer of Authority to Mayor of Charter City, pp. 1, 4.)

On September 8, 2006, the Romero Act was enacted into law. The Romero Act, which is called the "Los Angeles Unified School District: Gloria Romero Educational Reform Act of 2006," makes, by statute, several key changes in the governance of the LAUSD. Specifically, it adds a new chapter to the Education Code entitled, "Los Angeles Unified School District Administration." Section 35900 is added to the Education Code and sets forth the legislative findings that the Legislature believed justified the Romero Act. These findings include that the LAUSD "has unique challenges and resources that require and deserve special attention to ensure that all pupils are given the opportunity to reach their full potential." (Ed. Code, § 35900, subd. (a)(1).) The Legislature also found that "[t]he freedom to deviate from the strictures of generally applicable education statutes and regulations while maintaining the constant commitment to fairness and equity, and to increasing academic achievement among all pupils regardless of background, is central to the success of quality schools in California and is appropriate, as a concept, for the unique circumstances of the Los Angeles Unified School District." (Ed. Code, § 35900, subd. (a)(2).) The Legislature made no findings that LAUSD was failing in its obligation to deliver a constitutionally adequate education to its students.

****

In short, after the Legislative Counsel had indicated its belief that it would be unconstitutional for the Mayor to be statutorily granted appointment power over the Board, and that it would likewise be unconstitutional for the powers over education possessed by the Board to be statutorily transferred to the Mayor, the Romero Act transferred many of the powers over education possessed by the Board to the District Superintendent, and effectively gave the Mayor veto power over the appointment of the District Superintendent.

****

We are concerned solely with the constitutionality of the Romero Act. We first consider whether the Romero Act violates article IX, section 16 of the California Constitution, which grants charter cities the right to determine whether their boards of education are to be elected or appointed. We conclude that it does. We next consider whether the Romero Act violates article IX, section 6 of the California Constitution, which prohibits the transfer of control of any part of the public school system to any authority not included within the public school system. We conclude that it does. As we conclude that the Romero Act is unconstitutional on two separate bases, we see no need to consider the further challenges to its constitutionality. We next consider whether the unconstitutional provisions of the Romero Act can be severed and the remainder of the Romero Act allowed to stand. We conclude the Romero Act is not severable. We will therefore affirm the trial court's judgment issuing a writ of mandate prohibiting the implementation or enforcement of the Romero Act in its entirety.

****

"[T]he Legislature's power over the public school system [is] 'exclusive, plenary, absolute, entire, and comprehensive, subject only to constitutional constraints.'" (*State Bd. of Educ. v. Honig,* 13

Cal. App. 4th at p. 754.) "Public education is an obligation which the State assumed by the adoption of the Constitution. The system of public schools, although administered through local districts created by the Legislature, is 'one system ... applicable to all the common schools...'" (*Butt v. State of Cal.* (1992) 4 Cal. 4th 668, 680). Management and control of the public schools is a matter of state care and supervision; local districts are the state's agents for local operation of the common school system.

However, certain powers of local districts are enshrined in the California Constitution. Thus, California Constitution, article IX, section 16 guarantees to charter cities the right to provide "for the manner in which, the time at which, and the terms for which members of boards of education shall be elected or appointed, for their qualifications, compensation and removal, and for the number which shall constitute any one of such boards." Moreover, article IX, section 14 provides that "[t]he Legislature may authorize the *governing boards of all school districts* to initiate and carry on any program, activities, or to otherwise act in any manner which is not in conflict with the laws and purposes for which school districts are established." (Italics added.) In other words, while the Constitution does not *require* that the Legislature delegate any powers to the governing boards of local school districts, the *only entities* to which the Constitution *expressly permits* the

Legislature to delegate powers regarding education are the very same governing boards that the Constitution mandates charter cities have the right to elect.

....

It would be a clear violation of the plain language of article IX, section 16, if the Legislature passed a law giving the Mayor the right to appoint the members of the Board. But the constitutional provision would be annulled if the Legislature could simply bypass it by taking the powers of the Board away from that entity and giving them to the Mayor, or the Mayor's appointee. This is nothing more than an end run around the Constitution. If article IX, section 16 is to mean anything, it must mean that charter cities can not only choose the composition of their boards of education, but that charter cities are guaranteed freedom from legislative interference even when the Legislature is of the opinion that they have made the wrong choice.

Article IX of the California Constitution governs education in California. It provides for a State Superintendent and Board of Education; county superintendents and boards of education; and local school districts with governing boards. These are the entities constitutionally authorized to maintain public schools, and we conclude they are, therefore, the only entities referred to in article IX, section 6. (*See Wilson v. State Bd. of Educ.*, 75 Cal. App. 4th 1125, 1142 [each entity provided for in art. IX is an entity authorized to maintain schools in our public school system and is therefore part of the public school system].) As the Council of Mayors and the Mayor's Partnership 22 are not article IX entities, they are not part of the public school system.

[T]he Romero Act transfers all authority "exercised by the [LAUSD Board of Education] and the district superintendent" to the Mayor's Partnership. ... No public school system authority is authorized to demand responses to inquiries concerning financial or other matters. There is no unlimited access to inspect or observe any part of the demonstration project schools at any time. There is no provision for public school system authorities to terminate the demonstration project for a violation of law. There is no provision for public school system authorities to demand steps be taken to cure problems as they occur. There is no provision for the State Board of Education to take corrective action (or terminate the program) in the face of grave breaches of financial, fiduciary, or educational responsibilities. While the clusters of schools in the demonstration project are still subject to the governing statutes, when waivers have not been obtained, it is apparent that the very purpose of the demonstration project is to give complete operational control over these schools, for six years, to the Mayor's Partnership. In the absence of any real oversight by public school system authorities, this is unconstitutional.

With respect to the provisions of the Romero Act regarding the Council of Mayors, the question is somewhat closer. The Romero Act transfers many elements of management and control over the schools in the LAUSD from the Board to the District Superintendent. Standing alone, these provisions do not work a violation of article IX, section 6 of the Constitution, in that the District Superintendent, as a Board employee, is a part of the public school system. However, the Romero Act goes further and gives the Council of Mayors the power to ratify the "appointment, contract term, contract renewal, refusal to renew a contract, or removal of the district superintendent." (Ed. Code, § 35921, subd. (b).) The cases construing article IX, section 6 are concerned with ultimate control being in the hands of the public school system. ...Here, ultimate control is with the Council of Mayors. While the Board can make the initial selection of the District Superintendent (or whether to fire, or retain an individual in that position), that act is for naught without the approval of the Council of Mayors. As such, control over the very crucial selection of the District Superintendent is out of the hands of the public school system. This is a violation of article IX, section 6 of the Constitution.

CONCLUSION

The citizens of Los Angeles have the constitutional right to decide whether their school board is to be appointed or elected. If the citizens of Los Angeles choose to amend their charter to allow the Mayor to appoint the members of the Board, such amendment would indisputably be proper. What is not permissible is for the Legislature to ignore that constitutional right and to bypass the will of the citizens of Los Angeles and effectively transfer many of the powers of the Board to the Mayor, based on its belief, hope, or assumption that he could do a better job. The trial court's order granting the writ prohibiting the enforcement of the Romero Act in its entirety must be affirmed.

COBB v. O'CONNELL

36 Cal. Rptr. 3d 170 (Ct. App. 2005)

[Oakland city residents and taxpayers filed this lawsuit to challenge the state takeover of the school district. The plaintiffs claimed the California Legislature's passage of the takeover legislation, to save the school district from insolvency, violated the "home rule" provisions of the California Constitution and the Oakland City Charter. Both the trial court and the appellate court disagreed with this contention].

II.

……

Our analysis starts with the "home rule" provisions of the California Constitution.

As a charter city recognized in the California Constitution (Cal. Const., art. XI, §§ 2, 3), Oakland is empowered to govern its own "municipal affairs." In this regard, article XI, section 5, subdivision (a), reads in relevant part: "It shall be competent in any city charter to provide that the city governed thereunder may make and enforce all ordinances and regulations in respect to municipal affairs, subject only to restrictions and limitations provided in their several charters and in respect to other matters they shall be subject to general laws." This constitutional "home rule" doctrine reserves to charter cities the right to adopt and enforce ordinances, provided the subject of the regulation is a "'municipal affair'" rather than being a subject of "'statewide concern.'" *Johnson v. Bradley* 4 Cal. 4th 389, 399; (1992), *accord, Traders Sports, Inc. v. City of San Leandro*, 93 Cal. App. 4th 37, 45 (2001).

Appellants maintain that [the state takeover legislation's] requirement that a state-appointed administrator temporarily manage the Oakland schools conflicts with the "home rule" doctrine, as well as with provisions of the Oakland City Charter providing for the election of a local school board.

……

[C]harter cities have been specifically granted the power to manage certain of their own affairs without interference from the state Legislature. (Cal. Const., art. XI, § 5.) In particular, subdivision (b) of this constitutional provision directly grants to charter cities the power and authority to legislate in four "core" areas "that are by definition, 'municipal affairs.'" (*Johnson*, at 398.) When a charter city's enactment falls within one of these core areas, it supersedes any conflicting state statute. (*See, e.g., Ector v. City of Torrance*, 10 Cal.3d 129, 132-33 (1973) [109 Cal. Rptr. 849, 514 P.2d 433].) The "conduct of city elections" is one of the few specifically enumerated core areas of autonomy for home-rule cities. (Cal. Const., art. XI, § 5, subd. (b).) Additionally, Article IX section 16, subdivision (a) authorizes a charter city to provide for "the manner in which ... and the terms for which the members of boards of education shall be elected or appointed ... ."

[The state takeover legislation] does provide that the management of the school district is, temporarily, in the hands of a state appointed administrator until the present fiscal crisis may be dealt with and the district may be returned to definite solvency. But this temporary administration and goal of solvency does not conflict with any provision of the Oakland charter, or prevent the election of a local school board in the manner specified by the Oakland charter. *Cf. Traders*, at 45. We find no genuine conflict between [the state takeover legislation] and the text of the Oakland charter regarding city elections. *Id.* at 45.

…..

It is well established, and even appellants do not dispute, that education is a matter of statewide concern, as is the need to rescue school districts from insolvency in order to continue the education of students. *Butt v. State of California*, 4 Cal. 4th 668, 691-92 (Cal. 1992). Our high court has specifically referred to the "state's plenary power over education" as affording an adequate basis for the complete takeover of an insolvent local school district which requires an emergency state appropriation. *Id.* at 692. Consideration of this factor does not support appellants' challenge to [the state takeover legislation].

.....

Appellants urge that there was a more narrow option available to the Legislature. The Legislature could have funded Oakland's debt, without insisting on new fiscal oversight measures that gave temporary control of the district to a state appointed administrator. We cannot say that the option appellants propose would have sufficiently dealt with the fiscal problems facing the Oakland school district. We are unable to second-guess the Legislature's judgment in this regard, especially where the Legislature is exercising the state's "plenary power" to rescue a local school district experiencing a self-induced financial emergency.

UTAH SCHOOL BOARDS ASSOCIATION v. UTAH STATE BOARD OF EDUCATION
17 P.3d 1125 (UT 2001)

[In 1998, the Utah Legislature passed the Utah Charter Schools Act. The legislation authorized the creation of "up to eight charter schools [in Utah] for a three-year pilot program." The legislation authorized the State Board to act in a supervisory role, specifically to review applications for charter schools, grant charters and terminate or renew charter schools. The Utah School Boards Association filed suit arguing that the Utah Constitution limited the scope of authority the legislature could grant to the State Board. The Boards Association position was that because the state constitution vested the State Board with the "general control and supervision of the public education system," Utah Const. art. X, § 3, the legislature could authorize the State Board to act only for the whole system, not grant local and specific controls to the State Board.]

.....

[T]he essential question before us is whether the legislature had authority to pass the Act giving the State Board the designated supervisory powers.

The Utah Constitution is not one of grant, but one of limitation. "'The state having thus committed its whole lawmaking power to the legislature, excepting such as is expressly or impliedly withheld by the state or federal constitution, it has plenary power for all purposes of civil government.'" *Univ. of Utah v. Bd. of Examiners*, 4 Utah 2d 408, 426 (1956) (quoting *Kimball v. Grantsville*, 19 Utah 368, 383 (1899)); *see also Spence v. Utah State Agric. Coll.*, 119 Utah 104, 112 (1950); 16 C.J.S. Constitutional Law § 58, at 150 (1984) ("As a general rule, the legislature possesses and may exercise all legislative power, or power to enact statutes, of the state or people of the state, subject only to the limitations or prohibitions imposed by the state constitution."). Therefore, if the legislature is to be "restricted in educational as well as all other matters, it is imperative that the Legislature be restricted expressly or by necessary implication by the Constitution itself. As a result, the Act at issue must be deemed constitutional unless an examination of the Utah Constitution reveals limitations upon the legislature with respect thereto.

The Utah Constitution provides in relevant part:

> The Legislature shall make laws for the establishment and maintenance of a system of public schools, which shall be open to all the children of the State and be free from sectarian control.

Utah Const. art. III, ord. 4. Accordingly, article X, which provides for Utah's system of education, states:

> The Legislature shall provide for the establishment and maintenance of the state's education systems including: (a) a public education system, which shall be open to all children of the state; and (b) a higher education system. Both systems shall be free from sectarian control. *Id.* art. X, § 1. In addition,
>
> The public education system shall include all public elementary and secondary schools and such other schools and programs as the Legislature may designate. The higher education system shall include all public universities and colleges and
>
> such other institutions and programs as the Legislature may designate. Public elementary and secondary schools shall be free, except the Legislature may authorize the imposition of fees in the secondary schools. *Id.* § 2 (emphasis added).

The legislature has plenary authority to create laws that provide for the establishment and maintenance of the Utah public education system. This includes any other schools and programs the legislature may designate to be included in the system. However, its authority is not unlimited. The legislature, for instance, cannot establish schools and programs that are not open to all the children of Utah or free from sectarian control, and it cannot establish public elementary and secondary schools that are not free of charge, for such would be a violation of articles III and X of the Utah Constitution.

However, the Boards Association argues that it is another provision of the constitution that serves as a restriction on the powers of the legislature as applied to this case. That provision states:

> The *general control* and *supervision* of the public education system shall be vested in the State Board of Education. The membership of the board shall be established and elected as provided by statute. The State Board of Education shall appoint a State Superintendent of Public Instruction who shall be the executive officer of the board.

Utah Const. art. X, § 3 (emphasis added). The Boards Association contends that the phrase "general control and supervision" restricts the legislature by limiting the authority the legislature may grant to the State Board.

The Boards Association argues that the term "general control and supervision" means that the State Board may be granted authority only to manage the public education system uniformly and universally as a whole. This is unreasonable. It is beyond question that the State Board has always been able to manage separate types of schools and programs differently. For example, the accreditation rules propagated by the State Board for elementary schools are different from those for junior high and middle schools, and the accreditation rules propagated for junior high and middle schools are different from those for secondary schools and special schools. *See* Utah Admin. Code R277-411 to -413. In addition, it is beyond doubt that the State Board can manage vocational programs differently from athletic programs differently from educational programs. *See, e.g., id.* R277-502, -517, -518...From the common and ordinary understanding of the plain language of the Utah Constitution, it is clear that the State Board has been vested with the authority to direct and manage all aspects of the public education system in accordance with the laws made by the legislature. This must include not only the laws regarding the public elementary and secondary schools, but also the laws regarding any other schools and programs that the legislature designates as part of the public education system.

Accordingly, the legislature has used its plenary authority to establish charter schools as a means of pursuing the goal of continually improving and customizing public educational programs. The charter school program is part of the public education system, and the State Board has been given authority to supervise the charter school program in accordance with the Act. Article X, section 3 of the Utah Constitution does not prohibit the legislature from authorizing the State Board to exercise the control and supervision provided in the Act. We affirm the district court's decision that the Act is constitutional.

Notes and Comments

1. Local Control and Separation of Powers

Should school districts be considered part of the state? The U.S. Supreme Court has noted that "no single tradition in public education is more deeply rooted than local control over the operation of schools," *Milliken v. Bradley*, 418 U.S. 717, 741 (1974). But, should this mean that state legislators should stay away? What arguments can be made for the position that local school districts should be autonomous from state control?

A general "yes" or "no" may be unwise; the cases above suggest that the answer may vary with the context of the dispute. It is enough for now to acknowledge that states have an interest in tinkering with the education mission from time-to-time however imprecise the line of local autonomy.

2. Local School Districts and Sovereign Immunity

Legal scholarship has largely ignored the question of separation of powers at the state constitutional level. The author of the article below suggests that the default position should be that subdivisions in general, and school districts in particular, should be considered arms of the state. The author uses the school funding debate as the context for his view. As you read the excerpt below, do you see any holes in the reasoning of the author?

Christofferson, Rodriguez Reexamined: The Misnomer of "Local Control" and a Constitutional Case for Equitable Public School Funding, 90 Geo. L.J. 2553 (2002).

> Despite the vast attention paid to the subject, one topic has been conspicuously absent from the cases and from the literature: local governments.
>
> Whether in a city, town, county or special irrigation district, almost every one of us lives within the category of governmental spheres known as local governments. Indeed, for most of us, the political entity with which we have the most contact is local government; yet, local governmental entities have escaped any substantial treatment or definition in our federal system.
>
> ************
>
> The legal status of local governments is rooted in the colonial history of this country. Prior to 1789, the colonies were chartered and given legal standing by the King. The sovereignty of the colonies, which eventually would evolve into the various sovereign states, was founded on an amalgam of the King's grants, the laws of God, and popular will. These colonies were autonomous, as well as socially, culturally, and politically independent of each other. Townships within the original colonies, however, were not wholly autonomous. Specifically, the colonies ruled over all people residing within their borders without interference from local townships, and this sovereignty persisted up to and through the founding of the country. In this time period, towns and cities became truly subservient to states functionally, if not formally.
>
> This functional relationship between states and local governments has important implications for any discussion of federalism. The United States is founded on a constitutional system of dual sovereignty in which states and the federal government share a bifurcated power structure.
>
> ************
>
> The Founders, however, did not include local governments in the constitutional firmament. At the Constitutional Convention, debate focused on the sovereignty of the states in a new national government, with little or no attention paid to the role of local cities and towns. As a result, there is no reference to local governments in the text of the Constitution. Even those who argue that local governments should retain greater autonomy concede that it was not part of the original compact. Of course, the Founders likely envisioned the states as comprised of political

subdivisions, but the form and substance of the subdivisions would be the sole province of individual states, not the federal system. In this way, the constitutional text seemingly does not envision local governments as distinct from the states.

****

Unlike the Court's federalism jurisprudence, the Supreme Court's Eleventh Amendment jurisprudence treats local governments as entities separate from the state. The Eleventh Amendment provides states with immunity from suits by United States citizens. The Supreme Court, however, has clearly stated that to receive the cloak of immunity, the entity invoking immunity must be an arm of the state. What constitutes an arm of the state, however, is far from clear. While the Court has attempted to delineate various factors relevant to determining whether an entity is an arm of the state, the result has been confusion among the Circuits and greater, if not exclusive, weight given to whether a damage claim against the entity would be paid from the state coffers rather than another private or public source.

Despite the confusion enveloping the arm-of-the-state doctrine, the Supreme Court has held explicitly that Eleventh Amendment immunity does not extend to counties and similar municipal corporations.

****

Unlike the United States Constitution, which is a document of grant, state constitutions are documents of limitation; so long as a state is not acting contrary to the Federal Constitution, one should assume that a state has the power to act unless prohibited by the state constitution.

****

Under traditional state law, municipalities are arms of the state and can exercise only that power granted to them by the state. This is described in "Dillon's Rule":

It is a general and undisputed proposition of law that a municipal corporation possesses and can exercise the following powers, and no others: First, those granted in express words; second, those necessarily and fairly implied or incident to the powers expressly granted; third, those essential to the accomplishment of the declared objects and purposes of the corporation—not simply convenient, but indispensable.

Thus, a local government has no power independent of that granted by the state. Such reasoning is prevalent in many jurisdictions, and Dillon's Rule remains a significant maxim of state statutory construction. Some states have passed laws granting localities greater autonomy to make law, and some state courts have a looser interpretation of Dillon's Rule. These jurisdictions, however, are in the minority. Most jurisdictions are still founded on the idea that the state, in this case through statutory law, grants some of its sovereign power to localities.

Proponents of local control make the mistake of conflating local control of education, which would include control of the purse strings, with local supervision of education. Arguably, because local school districts are in the best position to measure the educational needs of their populations and to devise strategies and develop curricula to meet those needs, local control is an important state interest in education. However, this argument fails in light of the Dillon's Rule analysis, which suggests that localities are mere arms of the state. Dillon's Rule suggests that local control, as it relates to funding, is not a true interest. Even assuming that localities are in the best position to do these things, it does not necessarily follow that inequity in funding between districts is a necessary component of, or even an unavoidable byproduct of, local supervision.

****

Thus, while local supervision may be an important interest, a state educational system that allows such wide funding disparities cannot be justified as being substantially related to the achievement of that objective. Indeed, for poorer districts, increased and equalized funding will no doubt provide substantially greater flexibility for those districts to supervise and implement core educational policies. With respect to those wealthier districts whose funds might be reduced with a more equitable distribution of funding (assuming a fixed level of statewide funding), any funding cuts in those districts might well come from expensive educational luxuries that are not part of the core curricula in those districts. Equitable funding, therefore, will not necessarily restrict local supervision.

Quite simply, local control cannot justify unequal funding. Under Dillon's Rule, local control is not a legitimate objective as it relates to funding because the ability to raise funds locally is sanctioned and regulated by the state. And, even if local supervision is a legitimate objective, an inequitable system of public school funding is not substantially related to that objective. All of this suggests that a constitutional reexamination of our public school funding systems is necessary.

C. The Federal Government and Public Education

The role of the federal government in public education is as much about form as it is about substance. The legislative powers enumerated in the Constitution do not directly equip the federal government to preempt or control state education policy. When Congress does succeed in implementing positive regulations in education it is usually due to a creative use of the spending power. The power of federal law to negate state law is a different story. Federal law automatically preempts state laws that violate constitutional rights of students, faculty or members of the staff. The cases below provide an overview into range of options and challenges Congress faces when it attempts to advance federal interests in public education.

1. Federal Statutory Provisions

42 U.S.C. §§ 2000b-2000c (Title IV)
§ 2000b. Civil actions by the Attorney General

(a) Whenever the Attorney General receives a complaint in writing signed by an individual to the effect that he is being deprived of or threatened with the loss of his right to the equal protection of the laws, on account of his race, color, religion, or national origin, by being denied equal utilization of any public facility which is owned, operated, or managed by or on behalf of any State or subdivision thereof, other than a public school or public college as defined in section 401 of title IV hereof [42 USCS § 2000c], and the Attorney General believes the complaint is meritorious and certifies that the signer or signers of such complaint are unable, in his judgment, to initiate and maintain appropriate legal proceedings for relief and that the institution of an action will materially further the orderly progress of desegregation in public facilities, the Attorney General is authorized to institute for or in the name of the United States a civil action in any appropriate district court of the United States against such parties and for such relief as may be appropriate, and such court shall have and shall exercise jurisdiction of proceedings instituted pursuant to this section. The Attorney General may implead as defendants such additional parties as are or become necessary to the grant of effective relief hereunder.

42 U.S.C. § 2000d (Title VI)
§ 2000d.

No person in the United States shall, on the ground of race, color, or national origin, be excluded from participation in, be denied the benefits of, or be subjected to discrimination under any program or activity receiving Federal financial assistance.

42 U.S.C. § 2000e-2 (Title VII)
§ 2000e-2. Unlawful employment practices

It shall be an unlawful employment practice for an employer—

(1) to fail or refuse to hire or to discharge any individual, or otherwise to discriminate against any individual with respect to his compensation, terms, conditions, or privileges of employment, because of such individual's race, color, religion, sex, or national origin; or

(2) to limit, segregate, or classify his employees or applicants for employment in any way which would deprive or tend to deprive any individual of employment opportunities or otherwise adversely affect his status as an employee, because of such individual's race, color, religion, sex, or national origin.

(b) Employment agency practices. It shall be an unlawful employment practice for an employment agency to fail or refuse to refer for employment, or otherwise to discriminate against, any individual because of his race, color, religion, sex, or national origin, or to classify or refer for employment any individual on the basis of his race, color, religion, sex, or national origin.

20 U.S.C. § 1681 (Title IX)

(a) No person in the United States shall, on the basis of sex, be excluded from participation in, be denied the benefits of, or be subjected to discrimination under any education program or activity receiving Federal financial assistance.

****

(b) Nothing contained in subsection (a) of this section shall be interpreted to require any educational institution to grant preferential or disparate treatment to the members of one sex on account of an imbalance which may exist with respect to the total number or percentage of persons of that sex participating in or receiving the benefits of any federally supported program or activity, in comparison with the total number or percentage of persons of that sex in any community, State, section, or other area: Provided, That this subsection shall not be construed to prevent the consideration in any hearing or proceeding under this title of statistical evidence tending to show that such an imbalance exists with respect to the participation in, or receipt of the benefits of, any such program or activity by the members of one sex.

(c) “Educational institution” defined. For purposes of this title an educational institution means any public or private preschool, elementary, or secondary school, or any institution of vocational, professional, or higher education, except that in the case of an educational institution composed of more than one school, college, or department which are administratively separate units, such term means each such school, college, or department.

20 U.S.C. § 1232g (FERPA)

§ 1232g. Family Educational and Privacy Rights

(A) No funds shall be made available under any applicable program to any educational agency or institution which has a policy of denying, or which effectively prevents, the parents of students who are or have been in attendance at a school of such agency or at such institution, as the case may be, the right to inspect and review the education records of their children. If any material or document in the education record of a student includes information on more than one student, the parents of one of such students shall have the right to inspect and review only such part of such material or document as relates to such student or to be informed of the specific information contained in such part of such material. Each educational agency or institution shall establish appropriate procedures for the granting of a request by parents for access to the education records of their children within a reasonable period of time, but in no case more than forty-five days after the request has been made.

(B) No funds under any applicable program shall be made available to any State educational agency (whether or not that agency is an educational agency or institution under this section) that has a policy of denying, or effectively prevents, the parents of students the right to inspect and review the education records maintained by the State educational agency on their children who are or have been in attendance at any school of an educational agency or institution that is subject to the provisions of this section.

10 U.S.C. § 983 (Solomon Amendment)

§ 983. Institutions of higher education that prevent ROTC access or military recruiting on campus: denial of grants and contracts from Department of Defense, Department of Education, and certain other departments and agencies

(a) Denial of funds for preventing ROTC access to campus. No funds described in subsection (d)(1) may be provided by contract or by grant to an institution of higher education (including any subelement of such institution) if the Secretary of Defense determines that that institution (or any subelement of that institution) has a policy or practice (regardless of when implemented) that either prohibits, or in effect prevents—

(1) the Secretary of a military department from maintaining, establishing, or operating a unit of the Senior Reserve Officer Training Corps (in accordance with section 654 of this title [10 USCS § 654] and other applicable Federal laws) at that institution (or any subelement of that institution); or

(2) a student at that institution (or any subelement of that institution) from enrolling in a unit of the Senior Reserve Officer Training Corps at another institution of higher education.

(b) Denial of funds for preventing military recruiting on campus. No funds described in subsection (d)(1) may be provided by contract or by grant to an institution of higher education (including any subelement of such institution) if the Secretary of Defense determines that that institution (or any subelement of that institution) has a policy or practice (regardless of when implemented) that either prohibits, or in effect prevents—

(1) the Secretary of a military department or Secretary of Homeland Security from gaining access to campuses, or access to students (who are 17 years of age or older) on campuses, for purposes of military recruiting in a manner that is at least equal in quality and scope to the access to campuses and to students that is provided to any other employer; or

(2) access by military recruiters for purposes of military recruiting to the following information pertaining to students (who are 17 years of age or older) enrolled at that institution (or any subelement of that institution):

(A) Names, addresses, and telephone listings.

(B) Date and place of birth, levels of education, academic majors, degrees received, and the most recent educational institution enrolled in by the student.

---

2. Role of the Federal Government in Education

BROWN v. BOARD OF EDUCATION
347 U.S. 483 (1954)

OPINION: MR. CHIEF JUSTICE WARREN delivered the opinion of the Court.

These cases come to us from the States of Kansas, South Carolina, Virginia, and Delaware. They are premised on different facts and different local conditions, but a common legal question justifies their consideration together in this consolidated opinion.

In each of the cases, minors of the Negro race, through their legal representatives, seek the aid of the courts in obtaining admission to the public schools of their community on a nonsegregated basis. In each instance, they had been denied admission to schools attended by white children under laws requiring or permitting segregation according to race. This segregation was alleged to deprive the plaintiffs of the equal protection of the laws under the Fourteenth Amendment. In each of the cases other than the Delaware case, a three-judge federal district court denied relief to the plaintiffs on the so-called "separate but equal" doctrine announced by this Court in *Plessy v. Ferguson*, 163 U.S. 537. Under that doctrine, equality of treatment is accorded when the races are provided substantially equal facilities, even though these facilities be separate. In the Delaware case, the Supreme Court of Delaware adhered to that doctrine, but ordered that the plaintiffs be admitted to the white schools because of their superiority to the Negro schools.

The plaintiffs contend that segregated public schools are not "equal" and cannot be made "equal," and that hence they are deprived of the equal protection of the laws. Because of the obvious importance of the question presented, the Court took jurisdiction.

****

In the first cases in this Court construing the Fourteenth Amendment, decided shortly after its adoption, the Court interpreted it as proscribing all state-imposed discriminations against the Negro race. The doctrine of "separate but equal" did not make its appearance in this Court until 1896 in the case of *Plessy v. Ferguson*, *supra*, involving not education but transportation. American courts have since labored with the doctrine for over half a century. In this Court, there have been six cases involving the "separate but equal" doctrine in the field of public education. In *Cumming v. County Board of Education*, 175 U.S. 528, and *Gong Lum v. Rice*, 275 U.S. 78, the validity of the doctrine itself was not challenged. In more recent cases, all on the graduate school level, inequality was found in that specific benefits enjoyed by white students were denied to Negro students of the same educational qualifications. *Missouri ex rel. Gaines v. Canada*, 305 U.S. 337; *Sipuel v. Oklahoma*, 332 U.S. 631; *Sweatt v. Painter*, 339 U.S. 629; *McLaurin v. Oklahoma State Regents*, 339 U.S. 637. In none of these cases was it necessary to re-examine the doctrine to grant relief to the Negro plaintiff. And in *Sweatt v. Painter*, supra, the Court expressly reserved decision on the question whether *Plessy v. Ferguson* should be held inapplicable to public education.

In approaching this problem, we cannot turn the clock back to 1868 when the Amendment was adopted, or even to 1896 when *Plessy v. Ferguson* was written. We must consider public education in the light of its full development and its present place in American life throughout the Nation. Only in this way can it be determined if segregation in public schools deprives these plaintiffs of the equal protection of the laws.

Today, education is perhaps the most important function of state and local governments. Compulsory school attendance laws and the great expenditures for education both demonstrate our recognition of the importance of education to our democratic society. It is required in the performance of our most basic public responsibilities, even service in the armed forces. It is the very foundation of good citizenship. Today it is a principal instrument in awakening the child to cultural values, in preparing him for later professional training, and in helping him to adjust normally to his environment. In these days, it is doubtful that any child may reasonably be expected to succeed in life if he is denied the opportunity of an education. Such an opportunity, where the state has undertaken to provide it, is a right which must be made available to all on equal terms.

We come then to the question presented: Does segregation of children in public schools solely on the basis of race, even though the physical facilities and other "tangible" factors may be equal, deprive the children of the minority group of equal educational opportunities? We believe that it does.

In *Sweatt v. Painter*, *supra*, in finding that a segregated law school for Negroes could not provide them equal educational opportunities, this Court relied in large part on "those qualities which are incapable of objective measurement but which make for greatness in a law school." In *McLaurin v. Oklahoma State Regents*, *supra*, the Court, in requiring that a Negro admitted to a white graduate school be treated like all other students, again resorted to intangible considerations: ". . . his ability to study, to engage in discussions and exchange views with other students, and, in general, to learn his profession." Such considerations apply with added force to children in grade and high schools. To separate them from others of similar age and qualifications solely because of their race generates a feeling of inferiority as to their status in the community that may affect their hearts and minds in a way unlikely ever to be undone. The effect of this separation on their educational opportunities was well stated by a finding in the Kansas case by a court which nevertheless felt compelled to rule against the Negro plaintiffs:

> Segregation of white and colored children in public schools has a detrimental effect upon the colored children. The impact is greater when it has the sanction of the law; for the policy of separating the races is usually interpreted as denoting the inferiority of the negro group. A sense of inferiority affects the motivation of a child to learn. Segregation with the sanction of law, therefore, has a tendency to [retard] the educational and mental development of negro children and to deprive them of some of the benefits they would receive in a racial[ly] integrated school system.

Whatever may have been the extent of psychological knowledge at the time of *Plessy v. Ferguson*, this finding is amply supported by modern authority. Any language in *Plessy v. Ferguson* contrary to this finding is rejected.

We conclude that in the field of public education the doctrine of "separate but equal" has no place. Separate educational facilities are inherently unequal. Therefore, we hold that the plaintiffs and others similarly situated for whom the actions have been brought are, by reason of the segregation complained of, deprived of the equal protection of the laws guaranteed by the Fourteenth Amendment.

SAN ANTONIO INDEPENDENT SCHOOL DISTRICT v. RODRIGUEZ
411 U.S. 1 (1973)

[This Case is Reported in Chapter Three on Page 148]

UNITED STATES v. LOPEZ
514 U.S. 549 (1995)

CHIEF JUSTICE REHNQUIST delivered the opinion of the Court.

In the Gun-Free School Zones Act of 1990, Congress made it a federal offense "for any individual knowingly to possess a firearm at a place that the individual knows, or has reasonable cause to believe, is a school zone." 18 U.S.C. § 922 (q)(1)(A) (1988 ed., Supp. V). The Act neither regulates a commercial activity nor contains a requirement that the possession be connected in any way to interstate commerce. We hold that the Act exceeds the authority of Congress "to regulate Commerce . . . among the several States . . . ." U.S. Const., Art. I, § 8, cl. 3.

On March 10, 1992, respondent, who was then a 12th-grade student, arrived at Edison High School in San Antonio, Texas, carrying a concealed .38 caliber handgun and five bullets. Acting upon an anonymous tip, school authorities confronted respondent, who admitted that he was carrying the weapon. He was arrested and charged under Texas law with firearm possession on school premises. The next day, the state charges were dismissed after federal agents charged respondent by complaint with violating the Gun-Free School Zones Act of 1990. A federal grand jury indicted respondent on one count of knowing possession of a firearm at a school zone, in violation of § 922(q). The District Court conducted a bench trial, found him guilty of violating § 922(q), and sentenced him to six months' imprisonment and two years' supervised release.

We start with first principles. The Constitution creates a Federal Government of enumerated powers. *See* Art. I, § 8. As James Madison wrote, "the powers delegated by the proposed Constitution to the federal government are few and defined. Those which are to remain in the State governments are numerous and indefinite." The Federalist No. 45, pp. 292-293 (C. Rossiter ed. 1961). This constitutionally mandated division of authority "was adopted by the Framers to ensure protection of our fundamental liberties." *Gregory v. Ashcroft*, 501 U.S. 452, 458 (1991) (internal quotation marks omitted). "Just as the separation and independence of the coordinate branches of the Federal Government serve to prevent the accumulation of excessive power in any one branch, a healthy balance of power between the States and the Federal Government will reduce the risk of tyranny and abuse from either front." *Ibid.*

The Constitution delegates to Congress the power. "to regulate Commerce with foreign Nations, and among the several States, and with the Indian Tribes." Art. I, § 8, cl. 3. The Court, through Chief Justice Marshall, first defined the nature of Congress' commerce power in *Gibbons v. Ogden*, 22 U.S. 1, 9 Wheat. 1 (1824):

> Commerce, undoubtedly, is traffic, but it is something more: it is intercourse. It describes the commercial intercourse between nations, and parts of nations, in all its branches, and is regulated by prescribing rules for carrying on that intercourse.

The commerce power "is the power to regulate; that is, to prescribe the rule by which commerce is to be governed. This power, like all others vested in congress, is complete in itself, may be exercised to its utmost extent, and acknowledges no limitations, other than are prescribed in the constitution." *Id.* at 196. The *Gibbons* Court, however, acknowledged that limitations on the commerce power are inherent in the very language of the Commerce Clause. Consistent with this structure, we have identified. three broad categories of activity that Congress may regulate under its commerce power. First, Congress may regulate the use of the channels of interstate commerce. Second, Congress is empowered to regulate and protect the instrumentalities of interstate commerce, or persons or things in interstate commerce, even though the threat may come only from intrastate activities. Finally, Congress' commerce authority includes the power to regulate those activities having a relation to interstate commerce, i.e., those activities that substantially affect interstate commerce.

We now turn to consider the power of Congress, in the light of this framework, to enact § 922(q). The first two categories of authority may be quickly disposed of: § 922(q) is not a regulation of the use of the channels of interstate commerce, nor is it an attempt to prohibit the interstate transportation of a commodity through the channels of commerce; nor can § 922(q) be justified as a regulation by which Congress has sought to protect an instrumentality of interstate commerce or a thing in interstate commerce. Thus, if § 922(q) is to be sustained, it must be under the third category as a regulation of an activity that substantially affects interstate commerce.

....

Section 922(q) is a criminal statute that by its terms has nothing to do with "commerce" or any sort of economic enterprise, however broadly one might define those terms. Section 922(q) is not an essential part of a larger regulation of economic activity, in which the regulatory scheme could be undercut unless the intrastate activities were regulated. It cannot, therefore, be sustained under our cases upholding regulations of activities that arise out of or are connected with a commercial transaction, which viewed in the aggregate, substantially affects interstate commerce.

Second, § 922(q) contains no jurisdictional element which would ensure, through case-by-case inquiry, that the firearm possession in question affects interstate commerce. For example, in *United States v. Bass*, 404 U.S. 336 (1971), the Court interpreted former 18 U.S.C. § 1202(a), which made it a crime for a felon to "receive, posses[s], or transport in commerce or affecting commerce . . . any firearm." 404 U.S. at 337. …Unlike the statute in *Bass*, § 922(q) has no express jurisdictional element which might limit its reach to a discrete set of firearm possessions that additionally have an explicit connection with or effect on interstate commerce.

The Government's essential contention, in fine, is that we may determine here that § 922(q) is valid because possession of a firearm in a local school zone does indeed substantially affect interstate commerce. The Government argues that possession of a firearm in a school zone may result in violent crime and that violent crime can be expected to affect the functioning of the national economy in two ways. First, the costs of violent crime are substantial, and, through the mechanism of insurance, those costs are spread throughout the population. Second, violent crime reduces the willingness of individuals to travel to areas within the country that are perceived to be unsafe. The Government also argues that the presence of guns in schools poses a substantial threat to the educational process by threatening the learning environment. A handicapped educational process, in turn, will result in a less productive citizenry. That, in turn, would have an adverse effect on the Nation's economic well-being. As a result, the Government argues that Congress could rationally have concluded that § 922(q) substantially affects interstate commerce.

We pause to consider the implications of the Government's arguments. The Government admits, under its "costs of crime" reasoning, that Congress could regulate not only all violent crime, but all activities that might lead to violent crime, regardless of how tenuously they relate to interstate commerce. Similarly, under the Government's "national productivity" reasoning, Congress could regulate any activity that it found was related to the economic productivity of individual citizens: family law (including marriage, divorce, and child custody), for example. Under the theories that the Government presents in support of § 922(q), it is difficult to perceive any limitation on federal power, even in areas such as criminal law enforcement or education where States historically have been sovereign. Thus, if we were to accept the Government's arguments, we are hard pressed to posit any activity by an individual that Congress is without power to regulate.

****

To uphold the Government's contentions here, we would have to pile inference upon inference in a manner that would bid fair to convert congressional authority under the Commerce Clause to a general police power of the sort retained by the States. … To do so would require us to conclude that the Constitution's enumeration of powers does not presuppose something not enumerated, and that there never will be a distinction between what is truly national and what is truly local, *cf. Jones & Laughlin Steel*, *supra*, at 30. This we are unwilling to do.

Notes and Comments

1. *U.S. v. Lopez* and Gun-Free School Zones

Following the ruling in *U.S. v. Lopez*, Congress amended the law to add a jurisdictional requirement. The Act now provides, "It shall be unlawful for any individual knowingly to possess *a firearm that has moved in or that otherwise affects interstate or foreign commerce* at a place that the individual knows, or has reasonable cause to believe, is a school zone." 18 U.S.C. § 922(q)(2)(A) (emphasis added). The law has been upheld by the courts. *See United States v. Danks*, 221 F.3d 1037 (8th Cir. 1999), *cert. denied*, 528 U.S. 1091 (2000). For a thorough history of the policy impact of the Gun-Free Schools Act of 1994 on state law see, Christina L. Anderson, Double Jeopardy: The Modern Dilemma for Juvenile Justice, 152 U. Pa. L. Rev. 1181, 1185-1186 (2004) ("After the passage of the Gun-Free Schools Act of 1994, all fifty states introduced zero-tolerance legislation."). Congress also enacted the Drug-free School Zone Act, 21 USCS § 860, which doubles the usual sentence for a person convicted of a drug offense, "by distributing, possessing with the intent to distribute, or manufacturing a controlled substance ... within one thousand feet of, the real property comprising a public or private elementary, vocational or secondary school." 21 U.S.C. § 860(a). The courts have upheld the validity of this law based on the Commerce Clause, ruling that "[d]rug trafficking is an inherently commercial activity." *Kuromiya v. United States*, 37 F. Supp. 2d 717, 724 (E.D. Pa. 1999)

2. Federal Spending Power Legislation and Safe Schools Policies

Title II of the *Comprehensive Drug Abuse Prevention and Control Act of 1970*, made it a Federal crime to sell drugs in or near a public or private elementary, secondary, vocational, or post-secondary school. Pub. L. 91–513. In 1984, President Reagan created the *National School Safety Center* using a Presidential directive authorizing the Department of Justice and its partner institution Pepperdine University to, "inform teachers and other officials of their legal rights and to provide a computerized national clearinghouse for school safety resources...that would help principals and others reestablish good order in our schools." See, *Public Papers of the Presidents of the United States: Ronald Reagan*, page 181, February 7, 1984. *The Safe and Drug-Free Schools and Communities Act* was established in 1986 by the *Anti-Drug Abuse Act*. Public Law 101-226. It provides grants to the states and national programs to provide substance abuse education and violence prevention activities. Programs funded by the Act include: (1) drug education and prevention which emphasize individual responsibility; (2) education about the consequences of disruptive and violent behavior; (3) instruction on prejudice and tolerance; (4) violence prevention programs which focus on individual responsibility; (5) model programs for training of school personnel, parents, and members of the community; (6) Drug Abuse Resistance Education (DARE) programs; and (7) direct services to school districts with particularly severe drug and violence problems. With the support of over $5.1 billion in federal aid from the Safe and Drug-Free Schools and Communities Act, school districts in all states have been able to promote school safety, reduce violence, and create disciplined, orderly environments conducive to teaching and learning.

RUMSFELD v. FORUM FOR ACADEMIC & INSTITUTIONAL RIGHTS, INC.

547 U.S. 47 (2006)

OPINION: Chief Justice Roberts delivered the opinion of the Court.

When law schools began restricting the access of military recruiters to their students because of disagreement with the Government's policy on homosexuals in the military, Congress responded by enacting the Solomon Amendment. *See* 10 U.S.C.A. § 983 (Supp. 2005). That provision specifies that if any part of an institution of higher education denies military recruiters access equal to that provided other recruiters, the entire institution would lose certain federal funds. The law schools responded by suing, alleging that the Solomon Amendment infringed their First Amendment freedoms of speech and association. The District Court disagreed but was reversed by a divided panel of the Court of Appeals for the Third Circuit, which ordered the District Court to enter a preliminary injunction against enforcement of the Solomon Amendment. We granted certiorari.

I

Respondent Forum for Academic and Institutional Rights, Inc. (FAIR), is an association of law schools and law faculties. Its declared mission is "to promote academic freedom, support educational institutions in opposing discrimination and vindicate the rights of institutions of higher education." FAIR members have adopted policies expressing their opposition to discrimination based on, among other factors, sexual orientation. They would like to restrict military recruiting on their campuses because they object to the policy Congress has adopted with respect to homosexuals in the military. *See* 10 U.S.C. § 654. The Solomon Amendment, however, forces institutions to choose between enforcing their nondiscrimination policy against military recruiters in this way and continuing to receive specified federal funding.

II

The Solomon Amendment denies federal funding to an institution of higher education that "has a policy or practice . . . that either prohibits, or in effect prevents" the military "from gaining access to campuses, or access to students . . . on campuses, for purposes of military recruiting in a manner that is at least equal in quality and scope to the access to campuses and to students that is provided to any other employer." 10 U.S.C.A. § 983(b) (Supp. 2005). The statute provides an exception for an institution with "a longstanding policy of pacifism based on historical religious affiliation." § 983(c)(2). The Government and FAIR agree on what this statute requires: In order for a law school and its university to receive federal funding, the law school must offer military recruiters the same access to its campus and students that it provides to the nonmilitary recruiter receiving the most favorable access.

****

We think it appropriate in the present case to consider whether institutions can comply with the Solomon Amendment by applying a general nondiscrimination policy to exclude military recruiters.

We conclude that they cannot and that the Government and FAIR correctly interpret the Solomon Amendment. ...The Solomon Amendment does not focus on the content of a school's recruiting policy.... Instead, it looks to the result achieved by the policy and compares the "access . . . provided" military recruiters to that provided other recruiters. Applying the same policy to all recruiters is therefore insufficient to comply with the statute if it results in a greater level of access for other recruiters than for the military. Law schools must ensure that their recruiting

policy operates in such a way that military recruiters are given access to students at least equal to that "provided to any other employer." (Emphasis added).

III

The Constitution grants Congress the power to "provide for the common Defence," "[t]o raise and support Armies, "and "[t]o provide and maintain a Navy." Art. I, § 8, cls. 1, 12-13. Congress' power in this area is broad and sweeping, and there is no dispute in this case that it includes the authority to require campus access for military recruiters. That is, of course, unless Congress exceeds constitutional limitations on its power in enacting such legislation. *See Rostker v. Goldberg*, 453 U.S. 57, 67 (1981). But the fact that legislation that raises armies is subject to First Amendment constraints does not mean that we ignore the purpose of this legislation when determining its constitutionality; as we recognized in *Rostker*, "judicial deference . . . is at its apogee" when Congress legislates under its authority to raise and support armies. *Id.* at 70.

Although Congress has broad authority to legislate on matters of military recruiting, it nonetheless chose to secure campus access for military recruiters indirectly, through its Spending Clause power. The Solomon Amendment gives universities a choice: Either allow military recruiters the same access to students afforded any other recruiter or forgo certain federal funds. Congress' decision to proceed indirectly does not reduce the deference given to Congress in the area of military affairs. Congress' choice to promote its goal by creating a funding condition deserves at least as deferential treatment as if Congress had imposed a mandate on universities.

Congress' power to regulate military recruiting under the Solomon Amendment is arguably greater because universities are free to decline the federal funds. In *Grove City College v. Bell*, 465 U.S. 555, 575-576, (1984), we rejected a private college's claim that conditioning federal funds on its compliance with Title IX of the Education Amendments of 1972 violated the First Amendment. We thought this argument "warrant[ed] only brief consideration" because "Congress is free to attach reasonable and unambiguous conditions to federal financial assistance that educational institutions are not obligated to accept." *Id.* at 575. We concluded that no First Amendment violation had occurred—without reviewing the substance of the First Amendment claims—because Grove City could decline the Government's funds. *Id.* at 575-576.

Other decisions, however, recognize a limit on Congress' ability to place conditions on the receipt of funds. We recently held that, "'the government may not deny a benefit to a person on a basis that infringes his constitutionally protected . . . freedom of speech even if he has no entitlement to

that benefit.'" *United States v. Am. Library Ass'n*, 539 U.S. 194, 210 (2003). Under this principle, known as the unconstitutional conditions doctrine, the Solomon Amendment would be unconstitutional if Congress could not directly require universities to provide military recruiters equal access to their students.

This case does not require us to determine when a condition placed on university funding goes beyond the "reasonable" choice offered in Grove City and becomes an unconstitutional condition. It is clear that a funding condition cannot be unconstitutional if it could be constitutionally imposed directly. Because the First Amendment would not prevent Congress from directly imposing the Solomon Amendment's access requirement, the statute does not place an unconstitutional condition on the receipt of federal funds.

A

The Solomon Amendment neither limits what law schools may say nor requires them to say anything. Law schools remain free under the statute to express whatever views they may have on the military's congressionally mandated employment policy, all the while retaining eligibility for federal funds. *See* Tr. of Oral Arg. 25 (Solicitor General acknowledging that law schools "could put signs on the bulletin board next to the door, they could engage in speech, they could help organize student protests"). As a general matter, the Solomon Amendment regulates conduct, not speech. It affects what law schools must do—afford equal access to military recruiters—not what they may or may not say.

****

In this case, accommodating the military's message does not affect the law schools' speech, because the schools are not speaking when they host interviews and recruiting receptions. Unlike a parade organizer's choice of parade contingents, a law school's decision to allow recruiters on campus is not inherently expressive. Law schools facilitate recruiting to assist their students in obtaining jobs. A law school's recruiting services lack the expressive quality of a parade, a newsletter, or the editorial page of a newspaper; its accommodation of a military recruiter's message is not compelled speech because the accommodation does not sufficiently interfere with any message of the school.

... Nothing about recruiting suggests that law schools agree with any speech by recruiters, and nothing in the Solomon Amendment restricts what the law schools may say about the military's policies. We have held that high school students can appreciate the difference between speech a school sponsors and speech the school permits because legally required to do so, pursuant to an equal access policy. *Bd. of Educ. of Westside Community Schools v. Mergens*, 496 U.S. 226, 250 (1990) (plurality opinion); *accord Id.* at 268, (Marshall, J., concurring in judgment); *see also Rosenberger v. Rector and Visitors of Univ. of Va.*, 515 U.S. 819, 841 (1995) (attribution concern "not a plausible fear"). Surely students have not lost that ability by the time they get to law school.

****

Because Congress could require law schools to provide equal access to military recruiters without violating the schools' freedoms of speech or association, the Court of Appeals erred in holding

that the Solomon Amendment likely violates the First Amendment. We therefore reverse the judgment of the Third Circuit and remand the case for further proceedings consistent with this opinion.

Notes and Comments

1. Federal Law and Public Education

The role of the federal government in public education has proven to be a controversial topic. The Constitution of the United States does not speak to public education, nor does it enumerate any power to Congress on this subject. When Congress implements federal education policy, it engages in a hazardous enterprise. In the 1996 Presidential campaign, the republican candidate, Kansas Senator Bob Dole, ran on a party platform that included the promise to eliminate the U.S. Department of Education. The idea behind the proposal was that public education should be left to the several States. On the other side of this debate is the view that the federal government should supervise public education and influence state and local education reform from time-to-time.

The use of federal law to affect state education policy is of relatively recent vintage. Little attention was paid to public education by federal officials until a spate of events beginning after World War II. Federal laws were applied to negate a variety of state policies that were held to violate individual rights guaranteed under the U.S. Constitution. The Equal Protection Clause (*see* Chapter Seven, the First Amendment (*see* Chapter Ten), and the Due Process Clauses (*see* Chapter Four), were used to shape state education policy by establishing boundaries for state educators on matters involving the curriculum and student rights.

At the same time, Congress began experimenting with its enumerated powers to find tools to influence state policy makers. President Eisenhower and Congress enacted the National Defense Education Act of 1958, which allocated federal funding to supplement instruction in math and science programs in public schools. With each reauthorization of this funding law, Congress has added additional conditions to the receipt of federal educational funding. President Johnson and Congress used this approach to enact the Elementary and Secondary Education Act ("ESEA"). Title I of ESEA provides supplemental federal aid to disadvantaged children and provided the statutory basis for early special education funding. In 1994, Congress and President Clinton reauthorized the ESEA as the Improving America's Schools Act. For the first time, schools accepting Title I funds were required to adopt proficiency standards and assessments to measure whether students receiving Title I services were achieving those standards. Most recently, Congress and President Bush reauthorized the ESEA as the No Child Left Behind Act of 2001.

Thus, the primary tools for federal involvement in public education have consistently been provided by the provisions of the Fourteenth Amendment which give Congress authority to protect civil rights and the provisions of Article I, section 8 which contain fiscal powers and the right to regulate interstate commerce.

2. Federal Power over Education Policy and the Spending Power

How would you characterize the interest of the federal government in influencing education policy? What does the *Brown* decision suggest about the need for federal supervision of state education policy? How might the federal government get around the outcome in *Lopez*? Can you suggest ways in which state education officials should respond to spending power legislation after *Rumsfeld*?

Professor Engdahl offers this view on the use of federal funding as a means of influencing state policy makers,

> Congress today probably [regulates] more human behavior by conditions accompanying federal funding than by any exercise of its legislative powers. Roughly two-thirds of the federal budget in recent years has been spent on social security, social and economic assistance, education, and other aid and development programs—few of which had any counterpart in practice before the New Deal. Virtually all of these (as well as procurements and other federal
>
> activities involving expenditures) involve eligibility conditions to which aspirants, to succeed, must conform, as well as conditions that must be agreed to as consideration for receiving federal funds. Many of these conditions, including the several anti-discrimination mandates sweepingly employed today, are peripheral or unrelated to the basic purposes of most such expenditures. And, at least with regard to private recipients, most are unrelated to any objective the federal government has legislative power to attain. David E. Engdahl, *The Contract Thesis of The Federal Spending Power*, 52 S.D. L. Rev. 496, 535 (2007).

Chapter Two
Public Education, Parental Rights and School Choice

> There is no doubt as to the power of a State, having a high responsibility for education of its citizens, to impose reasonable regulations for the control and duration of basic education. …A State's interest in universal education, however highly we rank it, is not totally free from a balancing process when it impinges on fundamental rights and interests, such as … the traditional interest of parents with respect to the religious upbringing of their children."
> *Wisconsin v. Yoder*, 406 U.S. 205 (1972).

> As with all constitutional rights, the right of parents to make decisions concerning the care, custody, and control of their children is not without limitations. [P]arents' liberty interest in the custody, care, and nurture of their children resides "first" in the parents, but does not reside there exclusively, nor is it beyond regulation [by the state] in the public interest. *Fields v. Palmdale School*, 427 F.3d 1197 (9th Cir. 2005).

The model presented in Chapter One of a "democracy in a microcosm" leaves a wide range of questions to consider about the rights and the roles of parents in public education. Education policy has always assumed some kind of relationship between the educators and parents through notions of *parens patriae* and *in loco parentis*. However, these concepts, at best, beg the underlying questions of how to balance legitimate, but competing interests. For example, if parents have a fundamental right to educate their children, then when and how should school officials accommodate this interest in their policymaking? Should an educator stand in the shoes of the parents? If so, then when should the interests of the real parents override the preferences of school officials or the community at-large?

Section I presents the landmark cases, *Van Allen*, *Pierce* and *Yoder* that establish and define parental rights. Section II presents recent decisions that describe judicial approaches for resolving conflicts involving the rights of parents. Section III examines current "school choice" reform designed to give parents alternatives in educating their children: charter schools, voucher programs and home schooling.

I. The Constitutional Rights of Parents

THE TRUSTEES OF SCHOOLS v. PEOPLE EX REL. VAN ALLEN
87 Ill. 303 (1877)

Mr. CHIEF JUSTICE SCHOLFIELD delivered the opinion of the Court:

This was a proceeding by mandamus to compel the trustees of schools of the town of Lake View to admit the realtor's son, Frank Van Allen, as a pupil in the high school of that town....The material question is, were the respondents authorized, for the cause by them alleged, to deny to relator's son admission to the high school?

The facts stated in the petition, which the demurrer admits, are, the relator, being a citizen and tax-payer of the township, applied to the respondents to have his son admitted as a pupil in the high school. The son passed a satisfactory examination and was sufficiently proficient in all branches of study, except that of grammar, to entitle him, under the regulations prescribed by respondents, to admission to the high school. The realtor had forbidden his son to study grammar, and desired that he should pursue no study which necessitated a previous knowledge of grammar—and asked that he be admitted to pursue only those studies in which he was sufficiently proficient to entitle him to admission to the high school. The respondents denied the son admission to the high school, solely because of his inability to pass satisfactory [an] examination in grammar.

The high school was established under the fourth clause of section 35 of the school law, which is as follows:

> Upon petition of fifty voters of any school township, filed with the township treasurer at least fifteen days preceding a regular election of trustees, it shall be the duty of said treasurer to notify the voters of the township that an election "For" and "Against" a high school will be held at the next ensuing election of trustees, and the ballots to such effect shall be received and canvassed at such election; and if the majority of the voters at such election shall be found to be in favor of a high school, it shall be the duty of the trustees of the township to establish at some central point, most convenient for a majority of the pupils of the township, a high school for the education of the more advanced pupils. (Rev. Stat. 1874, p. 957.)

The next clause provides, "For the purpose of building a school house, supporting the school, and other necessary expenses, the town shall be regarded as a school district, and the trustees shall have the power and discharge the duties of directors for such district in all respects."

It is apparent the object of the legislature was simply to increase the facilities for acquiring a good education in free schools. The high school thus established can no more be controlled for the benefit of some to the exclusion of others, than can the district school. All children in the township, within the prescribed ages for admission to the public schools, have equal rights of admission to the high school when they are sufficiently advanced to need its instruction. It would be contrary to natural right and the manifest purpose of the legislature, to hold that the high school, by arbitrary and unreasonable regulations of the trustees, should be practically closed to all but a favored few. Every tax payer contributes to its maintenance, and there should be no arbitrary regulation to prohibit the enjoyment of its benefits, in equal degree by all.

It is, of course, to be kept in view that its purpose is the teaching of more advanced branches than those taught in the district school, and that to insist that precisely the same studies should be pursued there as in the district school, would be to defeat the purpose of its creation.

The powers and duties of the trustees being, with respect to the high school, the same as those of directors with respect to the district school, it becomes necessary to ascertain what are the powers and duties of directors with respect to district schools. So far as they affect the question before us, they are "to adopt and enforce all necessary rules and regulations for the management and government of the schools; to direct what branches of study shall be taught, and what text-books and apparatus shall be used, and to enforce uniformity of textbooks." (Rev. Stat. 1874, p. 962-3, § 48.)

Here, then, is power to decide what branches of study shall be taught in the high school, what text-books shall be used, and to prescribe necessary rules and regulations for the management and government of the school; but not to decide what particular branches of study, of those decided to be taught, shall be pursued by each pupil. Under the power to prescribe necessary rules and regulations for the management and government of the school, they may, undoubtedly, require classification of the pupils with respect to the branches of study they are respectively pursuing, and with respect to proficiency or degree of advancement in the same branches; that there shall be prompt attendance, diligence in study, and proper deportment. All regulations or rules to these ends are for the benefit of all, and, presumptively, promotive of the interests of all. No parent has the right to demand that the interests of the children of others shall be sacrificed for the interests of his child; and he can not, consequently, insist that his child shall be placed or kept in particular classes, when by so doing others will be retarded in the advancement they would otherwise make; or that his child shall be taught studies not in the prescribed course of the school, or be allowed to use a text-book different from that decided to be used in the school, or that he shall be allowed to adopt methods of study that interfere with others in their studies. The rights of each are to be enjoyed and exercised only with reference to the equal rights of all others.

But no attempt has hitherto been made in this State to deny, by law, all control by the parent over the education of his child. Upon the contrary, the policy of our law has ever been to recognize the right of the parent to determine to what extent his child shall be educated, during minority—presuming that his natural affections and superior opportunities of knowing the physical and mental capabilities and future prospects of his child, will insure the adoption of that course which will most effectually promote the child's welfare. The policy of the school law is only to withdraw from the parent the right to select the branches to be studied by the child, to the extent that the exercise of that right would interfere with the system of instruction prescribed for the school, and its efficiency in imparting education to all entitled to share in its benefits. No particular branch of study is compulsory upon those who attend school, but schools are simply provided by the public in which prescribed branches are taught, which are free to all within the district between certain ages. In most primary schools it would be both absurd and impracticable to require every pupil to pursue the same study at the same time. Discrimination and preference between different branches of study, until some degree of advancement is attained, is inevitable—and, afterwards, a due regard for the interests of the child will always require it, in greater or less degree.

It is not claimed that every pupil attending the high school must pursue every study taught therein, and manifestly, in the absence of legislation expressly requiring this, a regulation to that effect would be regarded as arbitrary and unreasonable, and could not, therefore, receive the sanction of the courts. Conceding that all the branches of study decided to be taught in the school shall not necessarily be pursued by every pupil, we are unable to perceive how it can, in anywise, prejudice the school, if one branch rather than another be omitted from the course of study of a particular pupil.

If the relator's son had possessed the required knowledge of grammar, but would not have been compelled to further pursue that branch of study or to pursue any other branch of study to which a knowledge of grammar was essential, it is impossible to perceive how his position in the high school, so far as it might affect teachers and pupils, would be different from that he now occupies. He is qualified to pursue, as a pupil, every branch of study that the relator desires that he shall pursue in the high school. If he is qualified to go on with the studies selected by the relator, of what consequence is it that he is ignorant of some branch of study in no manner connected with those branches? This may, possibly, be a misfortune to Frank Van Allen—it surely can not affect the government of the school or incommode the other students or the teachers. Whether fortunate or unfortunate to him, however, it is for the parent, not the trustees, to direct the branches of education he shall pursue, so far as they are taught, and he is by necessary preliminary education qualified to pursue them, in the high school.

It is possible that a father may have very satisfactory reasons for having his son perfected in certain branches of education to the entire exclusion of others; and so long as, in exercising his parental authority in making the selection of the branches he shall pursue, none others are affected, it can be of no practical concern to those having the public schools in charge.

We think the exclusion of the relator's son from the high school, upon the ground alleged, by the respondents, unauthorized by the statute. The regulation requiring it is arbitrary and unreasonable, and can not be enforced, but must be disregarded.

PIERCE v. SOCIETY OF SISTERS
268 U.S. 510(1925)

MR. JUSTICE McREYNOLDS delivered the opinion of the Court.

These appeals are from decrees, based upon undenied allegations, which granted preliminary orders restraining appellants from threatening or attempting to enforce the Compulsory Education Act adopted November 7, 1922, under the initiative provision of her Constitution by the voters of Oregon. Jud. Code, § 266. They present the same points of law; there are no controverted questions of fact. Rights said to be guaranteed by the federal Constitution were specially set up, and appropriate prayers asked for their protection.

The challenged Act...requires every parent, guardian or other person having control or charge or custody of a child between eight and sixteen years to send him "to a public school for the period of time a public school shall be held during the current year" in the district where the child resides; and failure so to do is declared a misdemeanor. There are exemptions—not specially important here—for children who are not normal, or who have completed the eighth grade, or who reside at considerable distances from any public school, or whose parents or guardians hold special permits from the County Superintendent. The manifest purpose is to compel general attendance at public schools by normal children, between eight and sixteen, who have not completed the eighth grade. And without doubt enforcement of the statute would seriously impair, perhaps destroy, the profitable features of appellees' business and greatly diminish the value of their property.

Appellee, the Society of Sisters, is an Oregon corporation, organized in 1880, with power to care for orphans, educate and instruct the youth, establish and maintain academies or schools, and acquire necessary real and personal property. It has long devoted its property and effort to the secular and religious education and care of children, and has acquired the valuable good will of many parents and guardians. It conducts interdependent primary and high schools and junior colleges, and maintains orphanages for the custody and control of children between eight and sixteen. In its primary schools many children between those ages are taught the subjects usually pursued in Oregon public schools during the first eight years. Systematic religious instruction and moral training according to the tenets of the Roman Catholic Church are also regularly provided. All courses of study, both temporal and religious, contemplate continuity of training under appellee's charge; the primary schools are essential to the system and the most profitable. It owns valuable buildings, especially constructed and equipped for school purposes. The business is remunerative—the annual income from primary schools exceeds thirty thousand dollars—and the successful conduct of this requires long time contracts with teachers and parents. The Compulsory Education Act of 1922 has already caused the withdrawal from its schools of children who would otherwise continue, and their income has steadily declined. The appellants, public officers, have proclaimed their purpose strictly to enforce the statute.

After setting out the above facts the Society's bill alleges that the enactment conflicts with the right of parents to choose schools where their children will receive appropriate mental and religious training, the right of the child to influence the parents' choice of a school, the right of schools and teachers therein to engage in a useful business or profession, and is accordingly repugnant to the Constitution and void. And, further, that unless enforcement of the measure is enjoined the corporation's business and property will suffer irreparable injury.

Appellee, Hill Military Academy, is a private corporation organized in 1908 under the laws of Oregon, engaged in owning, operating and conducting for profit an elementary, college preparatory and military training school for boys between the ages of five and twenty-one years. The average attendance is one hundred, and the annual fees received for each student amount to some eight hundred dollars. The elementary department is divided into eight grades, as in the public schools;

the college preparatory department has four grades, similar to those of the public high schools; the courses of study conform to the requirements of the State Board of Education. Military instruction and training are also given, under the supervision of an Army officer. It owns considerable real and personal property, some useful only for school purposes. The business and incident good will are very valuable. In order to conduct its affairs long time contracts must be made for supplies, equipment, teachers and pupils. Appellants, law officers of the State and County, have publicly announced that the Act of November 7, 1922, is valid and have declared their intention to enforce it. By reason of the statute and threat of enforcement appellee's business is being destroyed and its property depreciated; parents and guardians are refusing to make contracts for the future instruction of their sons, and some are being withdrawn.

No question is raised concerning the power of the State reasonably to regulate all schools, to inspect, supervise and examine them, their teachers and pupils; to require that all children of proper age attend some school, that teachers shall be of good moral character and patriotic disposition, that certain studies plainly essential to good citizenship must be taught, and that nothing be taught which is manifestly inimical to the public welfare.

The inevitable practical result of enforcing the Act under consideration would be destruction of appellees' primary schools, and perhaps all other private primary schools for normal children within the State of Oregon. These parties are engaged in a kind of undertaking not inherently harmful, but long regarded as useful and meritorious. Certainly there is nothing in the present records to indicate that they have failed to discharge their obligations to patrons, students or the State. And there are no peculiar circumstances or present emergencies which demand extraordinary measures relative to primary education.

Under the doctrine of *Meyer v. Nebraska*, 262 U.S. 390 (1923), we think it entirely plain that the Act of 1922 unreasonably interferes with the liberty of parents and guardians to direct the upbringing and education of children under their control. As often heretofore pointed out, rights guaranteed by the Constitution may not be abridged by legislation which has no reasonable relation to some purpose within the competency of the State. The fundamental theory of liberty upon which all governments in this Union repose excludes any general power of the State to standardize its children by forcing them to accept instruction from public teachers only. The child

is not the mere creature of the State; those who nurture him and direct his destiny have the right, coupled with the high duty, to recognize and prepare him for additional obligations.

The courts of the State have not construed the Act, and we must determine its meaning for ourselves. Evidently it was expected to have general application and cannot be construed as though merely intended to amend the charters of certain private corporations, as in *Berea College v. Kentucky*, 211 U.S. 45. No argument in favor of such view has been advanced.

Generally it is entirely true, as urged by counsel, that no person in any business has such an interest in possible customers as to enable him to restrain exercise of proper power of the State upon the ground that he will be deprived of patronage. But the injunctions here sought are not against the exercise of any proper power. Plaintiffs asked protection against arbitrary, unreasonable and unlawful interference with their patrons and the consequent destruction of their business and property.

....

The decrees below are Affirmed.

WISCONSIN v. YODER
406 U.S. 205 (1972)

MR. CHIEF JUSTICE BURGER delivered the opinion of the Court.

On petition of the State of Wisconsin, we granted the writ of certiorari in this case to review a decision of the Wisconsin Supreme Court holding that respondents' convictions of violating the State's compulsory school-attendance law were invalid under the Free Exercise Clause of the First Amendment to the United States Constitution made applicable to the States by the Fourteenth Amendment. For the reasons hereafter stated we affirm the judgment of the Supreme Court of Wisconsin.

Respondents Jonas Yoder and Wallace Miller are members of the Old Order Amish religion, and respondent Adin Yutzy is a member of the Conservative Amish Mennonite Church. They and their families are residents of Green County, Wisconsin. Wisconsin's compulsory school-attendance law required them to cause their children to attend public or private school until reaching age 16 but the respondents declined to send their children, ages 14 and 15, to public school after they completed the eighth grade. The children were not enrolled in any private school, or within any recognized exception to the compulsory-attendance law, and they are conceded to be subject to the Wisconsin statute.[3]

On complaint of the school district administrator for the public schools, respondents were charged, tried, and convicted of violating the compulsory-attendance law in Green County Court and were fined the sum of $5 each. Respondents defended on the ground that the application of the compulsory-attendance law violated their rights under the First and Fourteenth Amendments. The

---

[3] Prior to trial, the attorney for respondents wrote the State Superintendent of Public Instruction in an effort to explore the possibilities for a compromise settlement. Among other possibilities, he suggested that perhaps the State Superintendent could administratively determine that the Amish could satisfy the compulsory-attendance law by establishing their own vocational training plan similar to one that has been established in Pennsylvania. Supp. App. 6. Under the Pennsylvania plan, Amish children of high school age are required to attend an Amish vocational school for three hours a week, during which time they are taught such subjects as English, mathematics, health, and social studies by an Amish teacher. For the balance of the week, the children perform farm and household duties under parental supervision, and keep a journal of their daily activities. The major portion of the curriculum is home projects in agriculture and homemaking. *See generally* J. Hostetler & G. Huntington, Children in Amish Society: Socialization and Community Education, c. 5 (1971). A similar program has been instituted in Indiana. *Ibid. See also* Iowa Code § 299.24 (1971); Kan. Stat. Ann. § 72-1111 (Supp. 1971).
The Superintendent rejected this proposal on the ground that it would not afford Amish children "substantially equivalent education" to that offered in the schools of the area.

trial testimony showed that respondents believed, in accordance with the tenets of Old Order Amish communities generally, that their children's attendance at high school, public or private, was contrary to the Amish religion and way of life. They believed that by sending their children to high school, they would not only expose themselves to the danger of the censure of the church community, but, as found by the county court, also endanger their own salvation and that of their children. The State stipulated that respondents' religious beliefs were sincere.

In support of their position, respondents presented as expert witnesses scholars on religion and education whose testimony is uncontradicted. They expressed their opinions on the relationship of the Amish belief concerning school attendance to the more general tenets of their religion, and described the impact that compulsory high school attendance could have on the continued survival of Amish communities as they exist in the United States today. The history of the Amish sect was given in some detail, beginning with the Swiss Anabaptists of the 16th century who rejected institutionalized churches and sought to return to the early, simple, Christian life de-emphasizing material success, rejecting the competitive spirit, and seeking to insulate themselves from the modern world. As a result of their common heritage, Old Order Amish communities today are characterized by a fundamental belief that salvation requires life in a church community separate and apart from the world and worldly influence. This concept of life aloof from the world and its values is central to their faith.

Amish objection to formal education beyond the eighth grade is firmly grounded in these central religious concepts. They object to the high school, and higher education generally, because the values they teach are in marked variance with Amish values and the Amish way of life; they view secondary school education as an impermissible exposure of their children to a "worldly" influence in conflict with their beliefs. The high school tends to emphasize intellectual and scientific accomplishments, self-distinction, competitiveness, worldly success, and social life with other students. Amish society emphasizes informal learning-through-doing; a life of "goodness," rather than a life of intellect; wisdom, rather than technical knowledge; community welfare, rather than competition; and separation from, rather than integration with, contemporary worldly society.

....

The Amish do not object to elementary education through the first eight grades as a general proposition because they agree that their children must have basic skills in the "three R's" in order to read the Bible, to be good farmers and citizens, and to be able to deal with non-Amish people when necessary in the course of daily affairs. They view such a basic education as acceptable because it does not significantly expose their children to worldly values or interfere with their development in the Amish community during the crucial adolescent period. While Amish accept compulsory elementary education generally, wherever possible they have established their own elementary schools in many respects like the small local schools of the past. In the Amish belief higher learning tends to develop values they reject as influences that alienate man from God.

On the basis of such considerations, Dr. Hostetler testified that compulsory high school attendance could not only result in great psychological harm to Amish children, because of the conflicts it would produce, but would also, in his opinion, ultimately result in the destruction of the Old Order Amish church community as it exists in the United States today. The testimony of Dr. Donald A.

Erickson, an expert witness on education, also showed that the Amish succeed in preparing their high school age children to be productive members of the Amish community. He described their system of learning through doing the skills directly relevant to their adult roles in the Amish community as "ideal" and perhaps superior to ordinary high school education. The evidence also showed that the Amish have an excellent record as law-abiding and generally self-sufficient members of society.

....

There is no doubt as to the power of a State, having a high responsibility for education of its citizens, to impose reasonable regulations for the control and duration of basic education. *See, e.g., Pierce v. Society of Sisters*, 268 U.S. 510, 534 (1925). Providing public schools ranks at the very apex of the function of a State. Yet even this paramount responsibility was, in *Pierce*, made to yield to the right of parents to provide an equivalent education in a privately operated system. There the Court held that Oregon's statute compelling attendance in a public school from age eight to age 16 unreasonably interfered with the interest of parents in directing the rearing of their offspring, including their education in church-operated schools. As that case suggests, the values of parental direction of the religious upbringing and education of their children in their early and formative years have a high place in our society. *See also Ginsberg v. New York*, 390 U.S. 629, 639 (1968); *Meyer v. Nebraska*, 262 U.S. 390 (1923); *cf. Rowan v. Post Office Dept.*, 397 U.S. 728 (1970). A State's interest in universal education, however highly we rank it, is not totally free from a balancing process when it impinges on fundamental rights and interests, such as those specifically protected by the Free Exercise Clause of the First Amendment, and the traditional interest of parents with respect to the religious upbringing of their children so long as they, in the words of *Pierce*, "prepare [them] for additional obligations." 268 U.S. at 535.

It follows that in order for Wisconsin to compel school attendance beyond the eighth grade against a claim that such attendance interferes with the practice of a legitimate religious belief, it must appear either that the State does not deny the free exercise of religious belief by its requirement, or that there is a state interest of sufficient magnitude to override the interest claiming protection under the Free Exercise Clause. Long before there was general acknowledgment of the need for universal formal education, the Religion Clauses had specifically and firmly fixed the right to free exercise of religious beliefs, and buttressing this fundamental right was an equally firm, even if less explicit, prohibition against the establishment of any religion by government. The values underlying these two provisions relating to religion have been zealously protected, sometimes even at the expense of other interests of admittedly high social importance.

....

The essence of all that has been said and written on the subject is that only those interests of the highest order and those not otherwise served can overbalance legitimate claims to the free exercise of religion. We can accept it as settled, therefore, that, however strong the State's interest in universal compulsory education, it is by no means absolute to the exclusion or subordination of all other interests.

II

In evaluating those claims we must be careful to determine whether the Amish religious faith and their mode of life are, as they claim, inseparable and interdependent. A way of life, however virtuous and admirable, may not be interposed as a barrier to reasonable state regulation of education if it is based on purely secular considerations; to have the protection of the Religion Clauses, the claims must be rooted in religious belief.

....

[T]he record in this case abundantly supports the claim that the traditional way of life of the Amish is not merely a matter of personal preference, but one of deep religious conviction, shared by an organized group, and intimately related to daily living.

****

As the record so strongly shows, the values and programs of the modern secondary school are in sharp conflict with the fundamental mode of life mandated by the Amish religion; modern laws requiring compulsory secondary education have accordingly engendered great concern and conflict. The conclusion is inescapable that secondary schooling, by exposing Amish children to worldly influences in terms of attitudes, goals, and values contrary to beliefs, and by substantially interfering with the religious development of the Amish child and his integration into the way of life of the Amish faith community at the crucial adolescent stage of development, contravenes the basic religious tenets and practice of the Amish faith, both as to the parent and the child.

In sum, the unchallenged testimony of acknowledged experts in education and religious history, almost 300 years of consistent practice, and strong evidence of a sustained faith pervading and regulating respondents' entire mode of life support the claim that enforcement of the State's requirement of compulsory formal education after the eighth grade would gravely endanger if not destroy the free exercise of respondents' religious beliefs.

III

Neither the findings of the trial court nor the Amish claims as to the nature of their faith are challenged in this Court by the State of Wisconsin. Its position is that the State's interest in universal compulsory formal secondary education to age 16 is so great that it is paramount to the undisputed claims of respondents that their mode of preparing their youth for Amish life, after the traditional elementary education, is an essential part of their religious belief and practice. Nor does the State undertake to meet the claim that the Amish mode of life and education is inseparable from and a part of the basic tenets of their religion—indeed, as much a part of their religious belief and practices as baptism, the confessional, or a sabbath may be for others.

****

We turn, then, to the State's broader contention that its interest in its system of compulsory education is so compelling that even the established religious practices of the Amish must give way. Where fundamental claims of religious freedom are at stake, however, we cannot accept such a sweeping claim; despite its admitted validity in the generality of cases, we must searchingly examine the interests that the State seeks to promote by its requirement for compulsory education to age 16, and the impediment to those objectives that would flow from recognizing the claimed Amish exemption. *See, e.g., Sherbert v. Verner, supra*; *Martin v. City of Struthers*, 319 U.S. 141 (1943); *Schneider v. State*, 308 U.S. 147 (1939).

The State advances two primary arguments in support of its system of compulsory education. It notes, as Thomas Jefferson pointed out early in our history, that some degree of education is necessary to prepare citizens to participate effectively and intelligently in our open political system if we are to preserve freedom and independence. Further, education prepares individuals to be self-reliant and self-sufficient participants in society. We accept these propositions.

However, the evidence adduced by the Amish in this case is persuasively to the effect that an additional one or two years of formal high school for Amish children in place of their long-established program of informal vocational education would do little to serve those interests. Respondents' experts testified at trial, without challenge, that the value of all education must be assessed in terms of its capacity to prepare the child for life. It is one thing to say that compulsory education for a year or two beyond the eighth grade may be necessary when its goal is the preparation of the child for life in modern society as the majority live, but it is quite another if the goal of education be viewed as the preparation of the child for life in the separated agrarian community that is the keystone of the Amish faith. *See Meyer v. Nebraska*, 262 U.S. at 400.

****

There is nothing in this record to suggest that the Amish qualities of reliability, self-reliance, and dedication to work would fail to find ready markets in today's society. Absent some contrary evidence supporting the State's position, we are unwilling to assume that persons possessing such valuable vocational skills and habits are doomed to become burdens on society should they determine to leave the Amish faith, nor is there any basis in the record to warrant a finding that an additional one or two years of formal school education beyond the eighth grade would serve to eliminate any such problem that might exist.

....

The requirement for compulsory education beyond the eighth grade is a relatively recent development in our history. Less than 60 years ago, the educational requirements of almost all of the States were satisfied by completion of the elementary grades, at least where the child was regularly and lawfully employed.[15] The independence and successful social functioning of the

---

[15] *See* Dept. of Interior, Bureau of Education, Bulletin No. 47, Digest of State Laws Relating to Public Education 527-559 (1916); Joint Hearings on S. 2475 and H. R. 7200 before the Senate Committee on Education and Labor and the House Committee on Labor, 75th Cong., 1st Sess., pt. 2, p. 416.
Even today, an eighth grade education fully satisfies the educational requirements of at least six States. *See* Ariz. Rev. Stat. Ann. § 15-321 (B)(4) (1956); Ark. Stat. Ann. § 80-1504 (1947); Iowa Code § 299.2 (1971); S. D. Comp. Laws Ann.

Amish community for a period approaching almost three centuries and more than 200 years in this country are strong evidence that there is at best a speculative gain, in terms of meeting the duties of citizenship, from an additional one or two years of compulsory formal education. Against this background it would require a more particularized showing from the State on this point to justify the severe interference with religious freedom such additional compulsory attendance would entail.

....

IV

Finally, the State, on authority of *Prince v. Massachusetts*, 321 U.S. 804 (1944) argues that a decision exempting Amish children from the State's requirement fails to recognize the substantive right of the Amish child to a secondary education, and fails to give due regard to the power of the State as parens patriae to extend the benefit of secondary education to children regardless of the wishes of their parents.

....

This case, of course, is not one in which any harm to the physical or mental health of the child or to the public safety, peace, order, or welfare has been demonstrated or may be properly inferred. The record is to the contrary, and any reliance on that theory would find no support in the evidence.

....

Our holding in no way determines the proper resolution of possible competing interests of parents, children, and the State in an appropriate state court proceeding in which the power of the State is asserted on the theory that Amish parents are preventing their minor children from attending high school despite their expressed desires to the contrary. Recognition of the claim of the State in such a proceeding would, of course, call into question traditional concepts of parental control over the religious upbringing and education of their minor children recognized in this Court's past decisions. It is clear that such an intrusion by a State into family decisions in the area of religious training would give rise to grave questions of religious freedom comparable to those raised here and those presented in *Pierce v. Society of Sisters*, 268 U.S. 510 (1925). On this record we neither reach nor decide those issues.

---

§ 13-27-1 (1967); Wyo. Stat. Ann. § 21.1-48 (Supp. 1971). (Mississippi has no compulsory education law.) A number of other States have flexible provisions permitting children aged 14 or having completed the eighth grade to be excused from school in order to engage in lawful employment. E. g., Colo. Rev. Stat. Ann. §§ 123-20-5, 80-6-1 to 80-6-12 (1963); Conn. Gen. Stat. Rev. §§ 10-184, 10-189 (1964); D. C. Code Ann. §§ 31-202, 36-201 to 36-228 (1967); Ind. Ann. Stat. §§ 28-505 to 28-506, 28-519 (1948); Mass. Gen. Laws Ann., c. 76, § 1 (Supp. 1972) and c. 149, § 86 (1971); Mo. Rev. Stat. §§ 167.031, 294.051 (1969); Nev. Rev. Stat. § 392.110 (1968); N. M. Stat. Ann. § 77-10-6 (1968).

An eighth grade education satisfied Wisconsin's formal education requirements until 1933. *See* Wis. Laws 1927, c. 425, § 97; Laws 1933, c. 143. (Prior to 1933, provision was made for attendance at continuation or vocational schools by working children past the eighth grade, but only if one was maintained by the community in question.) For a general discussion of the early development of Wisconsin's compulsory education and child labor laws, see F. Ensign, Compulsory School Attendance and Child Labor 203-230 (1921).

.....

Indeed it seems clear that if the State is empowered, as *parens patriae*, to "save" a child from himself or his Amish parents by requiring an additional two years of compulsory formal high school education, the State will in large measure influence, if not determine, the religious future of the child. Even more markedly than in Prince, therefore, this case involves the fundamental interest of parents, as contrasted with that of the State, to guide the religious future and education of their children. The history and culture of Western civilization reflect a strong tradition of parental concern for the nurture and upbringing of their children. This primary role of the parents in the upbringing of their children is now established beyond debate as an enduring American tradition. If not the first, perhaps the most significant statements of the Court in this area are found in *Pierce v. Society of Sisters*, in which the Court observed:

> Under the doctrine of *Meyer v. Nebraska*, 262 U.S. 390, we think it entirely plain that the Act of 1922 unreasonably interferes with the liberty of parents and guardians to direct the upbringing and education of children under their control. As often heretofore pointed out rights guaranteed by the Constitution may not be abridged by legislation which has no reasonable relation to some purpose within the competency of the State. The fundamental theory of liberty upon which all governments in this Union repose excludes any general power of the State to standardize its children by forcing them to accept instruction from public teachers only. The child is not the mere creature of the State; those who nurture him and direct his destiny have the right, coupled with the high duty, to recognize and prepare him for additional obligations. 268 U.S., at 534-35.

.....

V

For the reasons stated we hold, with the Supreme Court of Wisconsin, that the First and Fourteenth Amendments prevent the State from compelling respondents to cause their children to attend formal high school to age 16. Our disposition of this case, however, in no way alters our recognition of the obvious fact that courts are not school boards or legislatures, and are ill-equipped to determine the "necessity" of discrete aspects of a State's program of compulsory education. This should suggest that courts must move with great circumspection in performing the sensitive and delicate task of weighing a State's legitimate social concern when faced with religious claims for exemption from generally applicable educational requirements. It cannot be overemphasized that we are not dealing with a way of life and mode of education by a group claiming to have recently discovered some "progressive" or more enlightened process for rearing children for modern life.

.....

Nothing we hold is intended to undermine the general applicability of the State's compulsory school-attendance statutes or to limit the power of the State to promulgate reasonable standards that, while not impairing the free exercise of religion, provide for continuing agricultural vocational education under parental and church guidance by the Old Order Amish or others similarly situated. The States have had a long history of amicable and effective relationships with church-sponsored schools, and there is no basis for assuming that, in this related context, reasonable standards cannot be established concerning the content of the continuing vocational education of Amish children under parental guidance, provided always that state regulations are not inconsistent with what we have said in this opinion.[23]

WOFFORD v. EVANS
390 F.3D 318 (4th Cir. 2009)

OPINION

One Wednesday afternoon, several students at Colonial Elementary School reported to their teacher that M.D., a ten-year-old classmate, had brought a gun to school. During the ensuing investigation, school administrators twice held M.D. in the principal's office for questioning. During the second detention, law enforcement officers also quizzed the child. M.D.'s mother, Jennifer Wofford, was not contacted until the police had departed.

Wofford claims that the school's failure to notify her violated her rights to due process under the Fourteenth Amendment. She also alleges that the detainments violated M.D.'s Fourth Amendment right to be free from unlawful seizures. The district court dismissed these claims.

We now affirm. School officials must have the leeway to maintain order on school premises and secure a safe environment in which learning can flourish. Over-constitutionalizing disciplinary procedures can undermine educators' ability to best attain these goals. Imposing a rigid duty of parental notification or a per se rule against detentions of a specified duration would eviscerate the ability of administrators to meet the remedial exigencies of the moment. The Constitution does not require such a result.

I

.....

On the eve of Thanksgiving in 2001, a teacher at Colonial Elementary School in Botetourt County, Virginia, called Assistant Principal Rosa with some disquieting news. Several students had reported that their classmate M.D. had brought a gun to school. Rosa immediately located the accused pupil and escorted her to the assistant principal's office. In the office, Rosa repeatedly questioned M.D.

---

[23] Several States have now adopted plans to accommodate Amish religious beliefs through the establishment of an "Amish vocational school." *See* n. 3, *supra*. These are not schools in the traditional sense of the word. As previously noted, respondents attempted to reach a compromise with the State of Wisconsin patterned after the Pennsylvania plan, but those efforts were not productive. There is no basis to assume that Wisconsin will be unable to reach a satisfactory accommodation with the Amish in light of what we now hold, so as to serve its interests without impinging on respondents' protected free exercise of their religion.

about the allegation. M.D. permitted Rosa to search her book bag and her classroom desk. Finding no weapon, Rosa escorted M.D. to the school bus that was waiting for her.

On the Monday following Thanksgiving, the assistant principal, now accompanied by Principal Evans, continued to investigate the incident. The two principals spoke with the children who had initially made the allegation. Several of them maintained that M.D. had brought a weapon to school the week before. One of these pupils, Josh Bane, said he had seen M.D. throw a black handgun into the woods adjoining the school. Their concerns rekindled, the school officials contacted the police. Rosa and Evans summoned M.D. to the office once more and renewed their inquiries about the weapon. During the questioning, M.D. complained of nausea and requested the presence of her mother. Neither school official obliged, however, and the investigation continued.

Three detectives arrived at the school in the middle of the morning. They spoke with M.D.'s four accusers before interviewing the student herself in the assistant principal's office. In the presence of the school officials, they quizzed M.D. about the allegation once more. In response to the officers' inquiries, the pupil repeatedly denied bringing a gun to school. On several occasions she asked for her mother, but the officers and school officials did not contact Wofford. M.D. even alleges that her interviewers ignored her request to visit the restroom. While two officers continued their interrogation, Detective Markham sought out Josh Bane. Bane showed the officer and Rosa where he saw M.D. discard the gun. Markham swept the school grounds for a weapon, but found nothing.

Rosa, Evans, and Markham recall the questioning lasting about fifteen minutes. M.D., by contrast, claims to have been with the police for at least an hour and a half. Despite M.D.'s requests, her mother was not contacted while the police were at the school. On his way back to the station, Markham called Wofford to inform her that her daughter had spoken to the police. M.D.'s mother arrived at the school shortly after receiving this news. She waited a further forty minutes before retrieving her daughter from the principal's office.

.....

II

It is now a commonplace that students do not "shed their constitutional rights ... at the schoolhouse gate." *Tinker v. Des Moines Ind. Cmty. Sch. Dist.*, 393 U.S. 503, 506 (1969). But the Supreme Court has never held that the "full panoply of constitutional rules applies with the same force and effect in the schoolhouse as its does in the enforcement of criminal laws." *New Jersey v. T.L.O.*, 469 U.S. 325, 350 (1985)(Powell, J., concurring). Indeed, school officials have been afforded substantial leeway to depart from the prohibitions and procedures that the Constitution provides for society at large. See, e.g., *Bethel Sch. Dist. v. Fraser*, 478 U.S. 675, 683 (1986) (permitting the punishment of a public school student for using lewd speech); T.L.O., 469 U.S. at 340-42 (declining to require a warrant supported by probable cause for searches of students by school officials); *Ingraham v. Wright*, 430 U.S. 651, 678-80 (1977)(finding no constitutional requirement of notice or a hearing prior to the administration of corporal punishment).

Such leeway is particularly necessary when school discipline is involved. The Court has noted the "substantial interest of teachers and administrators in maintaining discipline in the classroom." *T.L.O.*, 469 U.S. at 339, 105 S.Ct. 733. Educators must be able to respond effectively to the disciplinary exigencies of the moment. They must also be able to tailor these responses to the peculiar remedial needs that exist in particular schools. The Supreme Court has long recognized that educators are best situated to identify those needs and optimize their implementation. The "education of the Nation's youth is primarily the responsibility of parents, teachers, and state and local officials, and not of federal judges." *Hazelwood Sch. Dist. v. Kuhlmeier*, 484 U.S. 260, 273 (1988).

With these injunctions in mind, we decline to announce a requirement of parental notification or a ban on detentions of a certain length when school officials are investigating a serious allegation of student misconduct. Such strictures would be particularly inappropriate when, as here, several students corroborate the accusation and an eyewitness shows the investigators where the transgression occurred.

The appellants' proposed rules would force educators to choose between abandoning their preferred method of discipline altogether or complying with burdensome procedures decreed by federal courts. The consequences of inaction in the face of dangerous conditions can be grave. Teachers and administrators might face liability for omissions that lead to student injury. *See generally Johnson v. Dallas Indep. Sch. Dist.*, 38 F.3d 198, 201-02 (5th Cir.1994)(discussing the circumstances under which school officials may be liable for shooting deaths of students). And under appellants' proposed rule, the consequences of action would be as serious for educators as the consequences of inaction. An administrator contemplating discipline would face the threat of a lawsuit with all its attendant diversion of energy and resources from educational pursuits.

Appellants protest that, in the age of cell phones and e-mail, a bright-line rule requiring parental notification would hardly burden school officials. They also suggest that student welfare would be improved if parents were present during questioning. But these rejoinders miss the mark. When faced with imminent danger to the safety of their students, school officials may well find an immediate inquiry in the absence of a parent a necessary investigatory step. Federal courts should be wary of removing such devices from the disciplinary tool-box with the blunt instrument of constitutional decree. It would be a misfortune to exchange the informality of the school setting for the adversarial atmosphere of formalized procedure. Although the rule appellants urge may appear clear, it invites a series of derivative questions: What efforts must school officials make to contact parents? Must both parents be alerted? May officials proceed if the parents cannot be reached? At what stage in an investigation must notification occur? Must parents be present at an interrogation or is notice alone sufficient? If their presence is required, how long do parents have to arrive before questioning can continue? And what exactly are the permissible limits on parents' roles once they appear? Expository litigation to answer such questions would stretch out and out.

We are not unsympathetic to appellants' claim that parental notification might maximize pupils' well-being. But a federal court is not the best forum to address such concerns. Appellants note that state law and school board rules provide rights and remedies that bear on this question. The Virginia Code states that "the principal or his designee shall ... notify the parent of any student involved in an incident ... [including] ... the illegal carrying of a firearm ... onto school property." *Va.Code Ann.*

§ 22.1-279.3:1 (Michie 2003). A school board rule requires the principal or his designee to make a "reasonable effort to contact the parent or guardian" before a law enforcement officer interrogates a student. J.A. 492. Wofford and M.D. might have pressed their grievances with the school board. Had they still been dissatisfied, they could have sought state judicial review of an adverse decision. *See Va.Code Ann.* § 22.1-87 (Michie 2003).

In the final analysis, the balance of rights and interests to be struck in the disciplinary process is a task best left to local school systems, operating, as they do, within the parameters of state law. The Supreme Court has recognized as much. *See Kuhlmeier,* 484 U.S. at 273, 108 S.Ct. 562. We are also mindful of the Court's warning that § 1983 should not become "a font of tort law to be superimposed upon whatever systems may already be administered by the States." *Paul v. Davis,* 424 U.S. 693, 701 (1976). Notifying parents may be a good idea in many situations. But it is the province of legislation to embody good ideas, and it is not beyond the purview of state courts to apply state law as individual cases arise. A constitutional ruling, by contrast, preempts both legislative processes and state governance. By declining to extend the law in the manner that appellants urge, we respect the important democratic axiom that disputes should be resolved by those most intimately affected by them.

III

A

With these principles established, we proceed to address appellants' particular claims. Wofford alleges that the school officials' failure to contact her infringed her rights to due process. She notes that the Supreme Court has recognized a parental interest in the "care, custody, and control of their children." *Troxel v. Granville,* 530 U.S. 57, 65, 120 S.Ct. 2054, 147 L.Ed.2d 49 (2000). The Court has also required the state to comply with the procedural strictures of the Due Process Clause when it interferes with these interests. *See Lassiter v. Dep't of Soc. Servs.,* 452 U.S. 18, 27-28, 101 S.Ct. 2153, 68 L.Ed.2d 640 (1981).

Appellants find an interference with their liberty interests in the violations of school board policies and police regulations that they say occurred here. The Supreme Court has cautioned, however, that "the range of interests protected by procedural due process is not infinite." *Bd. of Regents v. Roth,* 408 U.S. 564, 570, 92 S.Ct. 2701, 33 L.Ed.2d 548 (1972). The Constitution requires such protection "only when a decision of the State implicates an interest within the protection of the Fourteenth Amendment." *Ingraham,* 430 U.S. at 672, 97 S.Ct. 1401. In this regard, we have held that violations of state law are insufficient by themselves to implicate the interests that trigger a due process claim. *See Weller v. Dep't of Soc. Servs.,* 901 F.2d 387, 392 (4th Cir.1990). State school board policies and police department regulations derive the basic legal authority they possess from state law. Appellants' suggestion that the putative violations of these local rules should dictate our due process analysis is thus without merit.

Certainly, state social services cannot deny parents custody of their children without notice and an adequate hearing. *See Stanley v. Illinois,* 405 U.S. 645, 658, 92 S.Ct. 1208, 31 L.Ed.2d 551 (1972);

Jordan v. Jackson, 15 F.3d 333, 343 (4th Cir.1994). But the cases to which appellants point to establish their liberty interest all involve a change in the physical custody of the child. They evince an unquestioned familial interest in a child's general supervision and well-being, an interest most directly implicated in domestic custody disputes. Contrary to appellants' suggestion, *Stanley* and its progeny do not establish a parental stake in a child's freedom from temporary detention at school for disciplinary purposes. Consequently, the procedures mandated by these decisions do not apply here. At all times during the investigation, M.D. remained on school property, under the auspices of school administrators. The Constitution does not impose a duty of parental notification before the pupil's disciplinary detainment while such school guardianship persists.

Our conclusion is strengthened by the absence of parental notification from the Supreme Court's discussion of students' due process rights. Referring to the procedures preceding a suspension of up to ten days, the Court indicated that "[t]here need be no delay between the time 'notice' is given and the time of the hearing. In the great majority of cases the disciplinarian may informally discuss the alleged misconduct with the student minutes after it has occurred." *Goss,* 419 U.S. at 582, 95 S.Ct. 729. Of course, students' rights are conceptually distinct from parental interests in their children's liberty while at school. But if these latter concerns were expansive enough to require parental notification here, it would be odd for the Supreme Court to endorse a disciplinary procedure that ignores such appraisal before the student's suspension. *Accord Zehner v. Cent. Berkshire Reg'l Sch. Dist.,* 921 F.Supp. 850, 859 (D.Mass.1995)("Plaintiffs have cited no law, and the Court has found none, which would indicate that notice to a student in such circumstances is inadequate unless it is provided to the student's parents as well.")

……

[Fourth Amendment claim, also dismissed, is omitted here. This subject is taken up in Chapter Five]

Ralph D. Mawdsley: The Changing Face of Parents' Rights
2003 B.Y.U. Educ. & L. J. 165 (2003)*

Since the latter part of the nineteenth century, courts have recognized the right of parents to make educational decisions for their children. Courts and legislatures have sought to balance the states' authority to educate students with the parents' natural authority to raise their children. However, the legal basis for such balancing of interests has changed. Parents' rights have evolved over four historical periods and have been influenced in the past thirty years by changing perspectives concerning the rights of students, school boards, and justiciable causes of action.

During the first of the four historical periods, spanning the nineteenth century and the early twentieth century, various state courts fashioned common law to determine whether parents could make decisions contrary to the rules of local school boards. During the second period, beginning with the end of World War I, state legislatures took a more active role in designing compulsory attendance laws. Two prominent United States Supreme Court decisions during this period facially challenged the authority of states to prohibit the operation of nonpublic schools. In the third period, courts wrestled with the rights of parents to direct their children's education for religious reasons. This followed a prominent Supreme Court decision addressing the authority of states to apply facially neutral compulsory attendance laws to religious-based nonpublic schools. Finally, in the current and fourth period, Congress and state legislatures have attempted to restore some authority to parents. However, parents, frequently frustrated with such legislative efforts, have tried to assert a variety of legal claims against public schools.

With the demise of the free exercise clause as an effective restriction on government regulation of parent educational choices, only the liberty clause of the Fourteenth Amendment remained as a constitutional limitation on states and local school districts. However, parents' efforts since [*Oregon v. Smith*] to invoke the *Meyer* and *Pierce* liberty clause right to direct their children's education have been generally ineffective.

Does the lack of success using the liberty clause mean that parents no longer have any legal basis for asserting their educational claims against school districts? With the exception of an emerging but generally unsuccessful effort by parents to assert free speech claims against public schools on behalf of their children, parents have looked to Congress and state legislatures to protect their interests.

The two most prominent federal statutes asserting parental authority have been the Family Rights and Privacy Act of 1974 (FERPA) and the Education for All Handicapped Children Act of 1975 (hereinafter referred to under its current title, IDEA). For the first time under FERPA, Congress created a national right of unrestricted access by parents to the education records of their children, as well as a more limited right to control disclosure of their children's education records. Under FERPA, parents have "the right to inspect and review the education records of their children," the right "to challenge the content of such student's education records," and the right to prevent disclosure of students' records (with specified exceptions) "without the written consent of their parents."

IDEA went even further, declaring parents of special education students to be equal partners with public schools in determining the educational program for their children and the services necessary to achieve that program. Congress declared as one of its findings in enacting IDEA that the "education of children with disabilities can be more effective by ... strengthening the role of parents and ensuring that families of such children have meaningful opportunities to participate in the education of their children at school and at home."

State legislatures have also strengthened parents' rights. For example, state statutes contributed to parents' selection of nonpublic school venues for their children by restricting the number of regulations. Extensive litigation in the 1970s and 1980s regarding the application of state compulsory attendance regulations to nonpublic schools has given way to statutory exemptions from many of these regulations. State legislatures have found ways to minimize state intrusion into curriculum, personnel, and student matters in nonpublic schools. Although not all of these legislative accommodations come with a legislative history, the overall effect has been to facilitate parents' direction of their children's education by making the operation of nonpublic schools less onerous. All states now recognize home schooling as a permissible parent option, although some states exert more regulatory control than others. For, some states permit students participating in nonpublic schools (including home schools) to take part in public school courses and extracurricular activities, including athletics.

However, the accommodations made by states regarding parents' direction of their children's education apply largely to the choice of the place where the child will be taught. Most states do not permit parents to intrude into curricular matters in public schools. One prominent exception is the comprehensive Parents Rights and Responsibilities Act passed in Texas in 2000. This act provides a parent access "to all written records of a school district concerning the parent's child." In addition, parents can petition the school principal to add a course, to permit their child "to attend a class for credit above the child's grade level", and to permit the child to graduate early if all courses required for graduation have been completed. The Texas statute states explicitly that such "requests will not be unreasonably denied." Finally, parents are entitled to review all teaching and test materials to be used by their children and "to remove [their children] temporarily from a class or other school activity that conflicts with the parent's religious or moral beliefs."

****

At least one other state, Michigan, has declared that "it is [a] natural, fundamental right of parents and legal guardians to determine and direct the care, teaching, and education of their children." However, the extent of parent rights is not nearly as great as in Texas and parent rights to affect curriculum are limited only to courses dealing with "sex education."

****

Even though parents have not been successful in facing changes within public schools through litigation, parents have achieved many of their goals to select the educational venue for their children. Many of the purposes that parents sought to achieve using the *Meyer-Pierce-Yoder* trilogy have been achieved, not in the courtroom, but in the assemblies of state legislatures and Congress. Parents have greater freedom today in choosing nonpublic venues for their children with state relaxation of regulatory control over those schools. At least one state, Texas, has given parents considerable legislative authority within schools. The extent to which other states will follow remains to be seen.

Comparing the rights of parents today to those under common law in the nineteenth century is not easy. How one views the current status of rights of parents to direct the education of their children depends on where the children are being educated. For those who choose to educate their children outside public schools, the authority of parents is probably greater today if only because state statutory changes have limited the regulation of nonpublic schools. With fewer regulations of nonpublic schools, parents have more opportunities to select nonpublic school options for their children. For those children who stay within the public schools, the parents' rights to direct education are not as protected as under common law. This lack of protection is largely due to the greater authority that the Supreme Court has given to school officials in controlling curriculum.

II. Parental Rights and the Education Mission

PARENTS UNITED v. PHILADELPHIA BOARD OF EDUCATION
148 F.3d 260 (3d Cir. 1998)

SCIRICA, Circuit Judge.

The issue on appeal is whether a board of education exceeded its authority by implementing a consensual program to distribute condoms in public schools in order to prevent disease. Because the Philadelphia School Board acted within its statutory and regulatory authority, and because the policy neither coerces parental or student participation nor offends the rights of parents to direct the care and custody of their children, we will affirm.

……

On June 24, 1991, acting under the School Code and the Philadelphia Home Rule Charter, the Board adopted Policy Number 123, entitled "Adolescent Sexuality." According to the Board "adolescent pregnancy, sexually transmitted diseases, and HIV infection are epidemic among school age youth . . . . The Board recognizes that schools, in concert with all segments of the Philadelphia community, have an obligation to promote a healthy lifestyle for all adolescents." The Board enunciated a broad purpose:

> 1.1 The Board of Education reaffirms its policy to provide comprehensive human growth and development instruction to all public school students. In accordance with School District policy and state law, such instruction should be part of the public school program and should be shared by the public schools, home, and community. The primary purposes of such instruction are to promote more wholesome family and interpersonal relationships; to help young people understand their sexuality at all levels of development; and to develop healthy habits and moral values regarding human sexuality.
>
> 1.2 The Board recognizes that the expression of human sexual behavior can be the source of many of life's most meaningful experiences as well as its most painful problems; and the Board of Education firmly asserts that abstinence from sexual activity during adolescence promotes good health and a healthy lifestyle.
>
> 1.3 The Board of Education firmly believes that successful pursuit of the mission of promoting a healthy lifestyle for all adolescents depends upon the cooperation of a broad spectrum of the Philadelphia community, including schools, families, religious institutions, health care providers, social service agencies, businesses, government, and media.

The Board described the Policy's objectives as follows:

> 2.1.a. To enable and encourage students to abstain from sexual intercourse until ready to enter marriage or another mutually monogamous relationship.
>
> 2.1.b. To reduce high risk sexual behavior leading to teen pregnancy, sexually transmitted diseases and HIV infection.
>
> 2.1.c. To assure a safe, equitable and positive school experience for lesbian and gay students.
>
> 2.1.d. To assure that all programs and activities take into consideration the broad spectrum of ethnic and cultural diversities, as well as mental and physical disabilities.

To effectuate the aforementioned objectives, the Board prescribed specific curricula:

> 3.1 The Superintendent shall direct the development and acquisition of curricula which comprehensively promote healthy behavior and which shall be taught in all grade levels, pre-kindergarten through grade twelve. Such curricula shall focus on behavioral outcomes and effective methods to convey the message that abstinence is the most effective way of preventing pregnancy, sexually transmitted diseases and HIV infection; a voluntary parental education component, designed to enhance the frequency and effectiveness of parents' communication with their children; and a mechanism for monitoring the efficacy of the curricula.

The policy also empowers the Superintendent "to develop additional partnerships with health care providers that expand and maximize access to in-school comprehensive health care for all children." The cornerstone of the policy, and its most controversial provision, is its directive to facilitate student access to condoms:

> 3.4 The Board believes that the effectiveness of the curricula to promote healthy lifestyles and to prevent pregnancy, sexually transmitted diseases and HIV infection is enhanced for sexually active students by facilitating their access to condoms outside of school. Toward that end, the Board supports the School District's involvement in city wide efforts to maximize access to condoms.
>
> 3.5 The Board of Education directs the Superintendent to immediately initiate the design of a pilot, educationally-based program, permitting in-school availability of condoms and the counseling of students in the use of same, utilizing established non-School District health care and social service providers, in partnership with participating schools. Such programs shall commence not later than the Fall of 1991.
>
> 3.6 The phased-in pilot program of condom availability in schools shall apply only to students in grades nine through twelve.

> ***
>
> 3.7 A component of the phase in pilot program shall be specifically for the education of parents, designed to enhance the frequency and effectiveness of parents' communication with their children about sexuality.

Schools employ two models for condom distribution:

One model, which shall be referred to as the comprehensive School Based Clinic model, has professionally-trained health educators and clinicians provide health and sexuality information as well as condoms through existing school health clinics... The second model, Health Resource Centers, establishes separate centers inside high schools, staffed by experienced counselors or social workers, where teens can go to receive condoms with counseling and health and sexuality information. No health care services are provided in these Centers. Rather, students are referred to services in the community.

The condom distribution program specifically gives parents the option of refusing to let their child participate:

> 4.1 Parents or guardians of students in schools taking part in the phase-in pilot program shall have the absolute right to veto their child's or children's participation in the program.

****

The condom distribution program began on December 21, 1991 when letters were mass-mailed to parents by the principals of schools with pilot programs advising them of the availability of condoms to students as part of the "health services" program

.... Plaintiffs filed a complaint in the Philadelphia County Court of Common Pleas seeking a permanent injunction and declaratory relief.

****

Plaintiffs maintain the Board only enjoys that authority explicitly granted by the legislature. In the absence of express statutory authorization to provide a new health service, plaintiffs contend the Board exceeded its powers by implementing a program operated exclusively by non-school district personnel who provide a service never before offered by any school district in Pennsylvania. Plaintiffs also characterize the health services offered as too remote from education, the primary function of the Board. We believe plaintiffs have too restrictive a view of Board authority. The General Assembly delegated broad powers to the Board to execute the School Code and effectuate its underlying policies. School authorities must be given broad discretionary powers to ensure a better education for the children of this Commonwealth and any restrictions on the exercise of these powers must be strictly construed.

.....

An examination of considerable statutory and regulatory authority granted to the Board by the General Assembly supports the conclusion that the Board acted within its broad discretionary powers when implementing the condom distribution program.

......

B.

Plaintiffs argue the Board's policy violates their fundamental right to remain free from unnecessary governmental interference with bringing up their children. According to plaintiffs, because the Board's policy not only educates students about safe sex, but also provides the condoms needed to accomplish the activity, the state supplants parental authority. Plaintiffs take issue with the opt out provision because it apparently "requires parents to take action to reclaim their authority and prevent the state from distributing condoms to their children." Plaintiffs maintain "requiring consent before distributing condoms leaves parental authority intact unless the parent takes action to give his authority to state officials."

The Supreme Court has long recognized the right of parents to the care, custody and nurture of their children as a liberty interest protected by the Fourteenth Amendment. Equally honored is the principal that parental consent must be secured before medical treatment is obtained...

We recognize the strong parental interest in deciding what is proper for the preservation of their children's health. But we do not believe the Board's policy intrudes on this right. Participation in the program is voluntary. The program specifically reserves to parents the option of refusing their child's participation. Once parents return the opt out form, their child will not be able to receive either counseling or condoms.

The Board's policy contains adequate notice provisions designed to effectively inform parents. ... Although the notice provision requires parents to affirmatively object to their child's participation, it specifically advises (1) that any student who asks for a condom at school may receive one and (2) that students will receive counseling on the importance of abstinence. Students are not required to seek out or obtain condoms or counseling and may furthermore refuse condoms after counseling.

We find the policy coerces neither parents nor students.

.....

We hold the Philadelphia School Board, by implementing the policy, acted within its statutory and regulatory authority and effectuated its educational mandate. In enacting a voluntary program, the Board did not offend parental rights regarding the custody and care of their children. In light of parents' ability to opt out of the program, we need neither assess the privacy rights of minors to contraceptives, nor balance this privacy right, if any, against the interests of parents and the Commonwealth in the health and welfare of children. Therefore, we need not reach this constitutional issue addressed by the district court.

PARENTS FOR PRIVACY v. BARR
949 F.3d 1210 (9th Cir. 2020)

TASHIMA, Circuit Judge:

This case concerns whether an Oregon public school district may allow transgender students to use school bathrooms, locker rooms, and showers that match their gender identity rather than the biological sex they were assigned at birth. Plaintiffs oppose the school district's policy, asserting that it violates Title IX, as well as the constitutional rights—including the right to privacy, the parental right to direct the education and upbringing of one's children, and the right to freely exercise one's religion—of students and of parents of students in the school district. Defendants and many amici highlight the importance of the policy for creating a safe, non-discriminatory school environment for transgender students that avoids the detrimental physical and mental health effects that have been shown to result from transgender students' exclusion from privacy facilities that match their gender identities.

It is clear that this case touches on deeply personal issues about which many have strong feelings and beliefs. Moreover, adolescence and the bodily and mental changes it brings can be difficult for students, making bodily exposure to other students in locker rooms a potential source of anxiety—and this is particularly true for transgender students who experience gender dysphoria. School districts face the difficult task of navigating varying student (and parent) beliefs and interests in order to foster a safe and productive learning environment, free from discrimination, that accommodates the needs of all students. At the outset, we note that it is not our role to pass judgment on the school district's policy or on how the school district can best fulfill its duty as a public educational institution. We are asked only to resolve whether the school district's policy violates Title IX or Plaintiffs' constitutional rights.

In a thorough and well-reasoned opinion, the district court dismissed the federal causes of action against the school district for failure to state a claim upon which relief can be granted.1 Parents for Privacy v. Dallas Sch. Dist. No. 2, 326 F. Supp. 3d 1075 (D. Or. 2018). We agree with the district court and hold that there is no Fourteenth Amendment fundamental privacy right to avoid all risk of intimate exposure to or by a transgender person who was assigned the opposite biological sex at birth. We also hold that a policy that treats all students equally does not discriminate based on sex in violation of Title IX, and that the normal use of privacy facilities does not constitute actionable sexual harassment under Title IX just because a person is transgender. We hold further that the Fourteenth Amendment does not provide a fundamental parental right to determine the bathroom policies of the public schools to which parents may send their children, either independent of the parental right to direct the upbringing and education of their children or encompassed by it. Finally, we hold that the school district's policy is rationally related to a legitimate state purpose, and does not infringe Plaintiffs' First Amendment free exercise rights because it does not target religious conduct. Accordingly, we affirm the district court's dismissal with prejudice of the action.

I.

In September 2015, a student at Dallas High School who had been born and who remained biologically female publicly identified as a boy, and he asked school officials to allow him to use the boys' bathroom and locker room. Defendant-Appellee Dallas School District No. 2 (the "District") responded by creating and implementing a "Student Safety Plan" for the transgender boy ("Student A") and any other transgender student who might make a similar request in the future, in order to ensure that transgender persons like Student A could safely participate in school activities.

The Plan acknowledged Student A as a "transgender male" and permitted him to use the boys' locker room and bathroom facilities with his peers at Dallas High School.[3] The Plan also provided that, while Student A had not indicated "which bathroom he feels comfortable using," Student A could "use any of the bathrooms in the building to which he identifies sexually." In addition, to ensure Student A's safety, the Student Safety Plan provided that all staff would receive training and instruction regarding Title IX, that teachers would teach about anti-bullying and harassment, that the Physical Education ("PE") teacher would be first to enter and last to leave the locker room, and that Student A's locker would be in direct line of sight of the PE teacher in the coach's office. The Student Safety Plan also listed several "Safe Adults" with whom Student A could share any concerns.

[3] The District also planned to spend between $200,000 and $500,000 upgrading the high school's bathrooms and locker rooms to better accommodate their use by transgender students.

Student A began using the boys' locker room and changing clothes "while male students were present." This caused several cisgender boys "embarrassment, humiliation, anxiety, intimidation, fear, apprehension, and stress," because they had to change clothes for their PE class and attend to their needs while someone who had been assigned the opposite sex at birth was present. Although privacy stalls were available in the bathrooms, these were insufficient to alleviate the cisgender boys' fear of exposing themselves to Student A, because the stalls had gaps through which "partially unclothed bodies" could "inadvertently" be seen. And an available single-user bathroom was often inconvenient or was considered inferior because it lacked a shower. As a consequence of their fear of exposure to Student A, some cisgender boys began using the restroom as little as possible while at school, and others risked tardiness by using distant restrooms during passing periods in order to try to find a restroom in which Student A was unlikely to be present.

When parents and other students in the Dallas community became aware of the Student Safety Plan, many opposed it publicly at successive school board meetings, in an effort to dissuade the District from implementing the policy. Some parents in the District are concerned and anxious about the prospect of their children using locker rooms or bathrooms together with a student who was assigned the opposite biological sex at birth. The Student Safety Plan also interferes with some parents' preferred moral and/or religious teaching of their children concerning modesty and nudity. In addition, several cisgender girls suffered from stress and anxiety as a result of their fear that a transgender girl student who remains biologically male would be allowed to use the girls' locker room and bathroom. Girls had the option of changing in the nurse's office, but it was on the other side of the school.

Students who opposed the Student Safety Plan attempted to circulate a petition opposing the policy, but the high school principal confiscated the petitions and ordered students to discontinue doing so or face disciplinary action. Despite the objections raised by several parents and students, the District continued to allow Student A to use the bathroom and locker room that matched the gender with which he identified.

II.

In November 2017, Plaintiffs-Appellants Parents for Privacy, Parents' Rights in Education, and several individuals (collectively, "Plaintiffs") sued the District, the Oregon Department of Education, the Governor of Oregon, and various federal officials and agencies (collectively, the "Federal Defendants"), arguing that the Student Safety Plan violates the Constitution and numerous other laws.

……

III.

We have jurisdiction under 28 U.S.C. § 1291, and we review de novo the grant of a Rule 12(b)(6) motion to dismiss for failure to state a claim upon which relief may be granted.

……

IV.

A.

First, Plaintiffs challenge the district court's dismissal of their claim for violation of a fundamental right to privacy under the Fourteenth Amendment.

The district court dismissed this claim on the ground that the complaint did not allege infringement of any constitutionally protected right. It concluded that the Fourteenth Amendment does not provide high school students with a constitutional privacy right not to share restrooms or locker rooms with transgender students whose sex assigned at birth is different than theirs. Parents for Privacy, 326 F. Supp. 3d at 1099.

In reaching this conclusion, the district court examined the authorities on which Plaintiffs relied, but rejected those cases as inapposite because, unlike the scenario presented in this case, those cases "involve[d] egregious state-compelled intrusions into one's personal privacy," such as "government officials"—often law enforcement or correctional officers—"viewing or touching the naked bodies of persons of the opposite sex against their will."…Because "none of these cases support[ed] the proposition that high school students have a fundamental right not to share restrooms and locker rooms with transgender students who have a different assigned sex than theirs," the district court concluded that "Plaintiffs have failed to sufficiently allege a fundamental right to privacy cognizable under the Fourteenth Amendment." Id. at 1096–99. It explained that "[t]o hold otherwise would sweepingly expand the right to privacy beyond what any court has recognized," in contravention of the Supreme Court's reluctance to expand the "short list" of liberty rights protected by the Due Process Clause, including "the rights to marry, to have children, to direct the education and upbringing of one's children, to marital privacy, to use contraception, to bodily integrity, and to abortion." Id. at 1099 (quoting Glucksberg, 521 U.S. at 720, 117 S.Ct. 2258). Thus, because "[t]he potential threat that a high school student might see or be seen by someone of the opposite biological sex while either are undressing or performing bodily functions in a restroom, shower, or locker room does not give rise to a constitutional violation," the district court concluded that Plaintiffs failed to state a claim for violation of the Fourteenth Amendment. See id.

On appeal, Plaintiffs make several ultimately unavailing arguments about why the district court erred in dismissing their privacy rights claim under the Fourteenth Amendment...Plaintiffs do not allege that transgender students are taking nude photographs of them or purposefully taking overt steps to invade their privacy for no legitimate reason...Plaintiffs fail to show that the contours of the privacy right protected by the Fourteenth Amendment are so broad as to protect against the District's implementation of the Student Safety Plan. This conclusion is supported by the fact that the Student Safety Plan provides alternative options and privacy protections to those who do not want to share facilities with a transgender student, even though those alternative options admittedly appear inferior and less convenient. See Caribbean Marine Servs. Co. v. Baldrige, 844 F.2d 668, 678 (9th Cir. 1988) (suggesting that in cases in which privacy interests must be weighed against governmental interests, inconvenience and slight discomfort that results from attempting to accommodate both interests are not enough to establish a privacy violation)...Accordingly, we affirm the district court's dismissal with prejudice of Plaintiffs' claim for violation of privacy under the Fourteenth Amendment's Due Process Clause.

B.

Next, Plaintiffs contend that the district court erred in failing to recognize that the District's policy violates Title IX by turning locker rooms, showers, and multi-user restrooms into sexually harassing environments and by forcing students to forgo use of such facilities as the solution to harassment.

Title IX provides that "[n]o person in the United States shall, on the basis of sex, be excluded from participation in, be denied the benefits of, or be subjected to discrimination under any education program or activity receiving Federal financial assistance ...." 20 U.S.C. § 1681(a). Plaintiffs allege that the Student Safety Plan violates Title IX because it "produces unwelcome sexual harassment and create[s] a hostile environment on the basis of sex." They allege that the Plan "needlessly subjects Student Plaintiffs to the risk that their partially or fully unclothed bodies will be exposed to students of the opposite sex and that they will be exposed to opposite-sex nudity, causing the Student Plaintiffs to experience embarrassment, humiliation, anxiety, intimidation, fear, apprehension, stress, degradation, and loss of dignity." According to Plaintiffs, "[a]llowing people to use restrooms, locker rooms or showers designated for the opposite biological sex violates privacy and creates a sexually harassing environment," in part because "[e]xposure to opposite-sex nudity creates a sexually harassing hostile environment." As a result of this allegedly harassing environment, "all Student Plaintiffs find that school has become intimidating and stressful," and some of them "are avoiding the restroom" and "are not able to concentrate as well in school."

Stating a Title IX hostile environment claim requires alleging that the school district: (1) had actual knowledge of; (2) and was deliberately indifferent to; (3) harassment because of sex that was; (4) "so severe, pervasive, and objectively offensive that it can be said to deprive the victims of access to the educational opportunities or benefits provided by the school." Davis ex rel. LaShonda D. v. Monroe Cty. Bd. of Educ., 526 U.S. 629, 650, 119 S.Ct. 1661, 143 L.Ed.2d 839 (1999); see also Reese v. Jefferson Sch. Dist. No. 14J, 208 F.3d 736, 738–39 (9th Cir. 2000). The district court ruled that Plaintiffs had failed to establish the third and fourth elements and, on that basis, dismissed Plaintiffs' Title IX hostile environment claim. Parents for Privacy, 326 F. Supp. 3d at 1104.

The district court concluded that the alleged harassment was not discrimination on the basis of sex within the meaning of Title IX, because the "District's plan does not target any Student Plaintiff because of their sex." Id. at 1102. Rather, the Student Safety Plan applies to all students regardless of their sex, and therefore "Student Plaintiffs have not demonstrated that they are being treated any differently from other students at Dallas High School."

......

Again, we agree with the district court's analysis and find Plaintiffs' contrary arguments unpersuasive. First, Plaintiffs argue broadly that Title IX "unequivocally uphold[s] the right to bodily privacy" and therefore requires that facilities be segregated based on "biological" sex rather than "gender identity." To support this argument, Plaintiffs point out that the statute provides that it should not be construed to "prohibit any educational institution ... from maintaining separate living facilities for the different sexes," 20 U.S.C. § 1686, and that Title IX's implementing regulations specifically authorize providing separate but comparable "toilet, locker room, and shower facilities on the basis of sex," 34 C.F.R. § 106.33. Plaintiffs further argue that Title IX's text and its legislative history make clear that the permitted basis on which such "separate" facilities may be segregated—"sex"— refers to "biological sex" as assigned at birth, and cannot encompass gender identity.

But just because Title IX authorizes sex-segregated facilities does not mean that they are required, let alone that they must be segregated based only on biological sex and cannot accommodate gender identity...Nowhere does the statute explicitly state, or even suggest, that schools may not allow transgender students to use the facilities that are most consistent with their gender identity. That is, Title IX does not specifically make actionable a school's decision not to provide facilities segregated by "biological sex"; contrary to Plaintiffs' suggestion, the statute does not create distinct "bodily privacy rights" that may be vindicated through suit. Instead, Title IX provides recourse for discriminatory treatment "on the basis of sex." 20 U.S.C. § 1681(a). Thus, even if Plaintiffs are correct that "Congress intended to preserve distinct privacy facilities based on biological sex" and that the District chose not to do so, that fact alone is insufficient to state a legally cognizable claim under Title IX. Rather, to show that the District violated Title IX, Plaintiffs must establish that the District had actual knowledge of and was deliberately indifferent to harassment because of sex that was "so severe, pervasive, and objectively offensive that it can be said to deprive the victims of access to the educational opportunities or benefits provided by the school." Davis, 526 U.S. at 650, 119 S.Ct. 1661; see also Reese, 208 F.3d at 739.

Plaintiffs focus on the third and fourth elements of a Title IX hostile environment claim, as did the district court, namely whether there was harassment because of sex that was so severe, pervasive, and objectively offensive that it deprived Plaintiffs of access to the educational opportunities or benefits provided by Dallas High School. First, Plaintiffs assert that the Student Safety Plan created harassment on the basis of sex "because the only way to achieve the policy's purpose of opposite-sex affirmation is to select facilities based on the sex (or gender identity) of users." But just because the Student Safety Plan implicitly addresses the topics of sex and gender by seeking to accommodate a transgender student's gender identity, or because it segregates facilities by gender identity, does not mean that the Plan harasses other students on the basis of their sex. As the district court explained, the Plan does not target students or discriminate against them on the basis of their sex; the Student Safety Plan treats all students—male and female—the same. See Parents for Privacy, 326 F. Supp. 3d at 1096–97.

......

[T]reating both male and female students the same suggests an absence of gender/sex animus, while Title IX is aimed at addressing discrimination based on sex or gender stereotypes. Numerous courts have ruled that a Title IX sexual harassment hostile environment claim fails where the alleged harassment is inflicted without regard to gender or sex, i.e., where there is no discrimination.

......

The district court also correctly ruled that Plaintiffs failed to establish the fourth element of their Title IX claim. See id. at 1104. Plaintiffs argue that they satisfy the fourth element of a hostile environment claim because the alleged harassment is both viewed subjectively as harassment by the victims and is, objectively, sufficiently severe or pervasive that a reasonable person would agree that it is harassment. However, even crediting Plaintiffs' subjective perceptions, under the totality of the circumstances, the alleged harassment is not so severe, pervasive, and objectively offensive to rise to the level of a Title IX violation. Plaintiffs do not allege that transgender students are making inappropriate comments, threatening them, deliberately flaunting nudity, or physically touching them. Rather, Plaintiffs allegedly feel harassed by the mere presence of transgender students in locker and bathroom facilities. This cannot be enough. The use of facilities for their intended purpose, without more, does not constitute an act of harassment simply because a person is transgender...Accordingly, we affirm the district court's dismissal with prejudice of Plaintiffs' Title IX hostile environment claim. Because the Student Safety Plan does not discriminate on the basis of sex, amendment would be futile.

C.

Next, Plaintiffs challenge the dismissal of their Fourteenth Amendment claim for violation of Parent Plaintiffs' fundamental rights to direct the care, education, and upbringing of their children.

As discussed above, the Fourteenth Amendment's Due Process Clause "specially protects those fundamental rights and liberties which are, objectively, deeply rooted in this Nation's history and tradition, and implicit in the concept of ordered liberty." Glucksberg, 521 U.S. at 720–21, 117 S.Ct. 2258 (internal quotation marks and citations omitted). The Supreme Court has held that one such fundamental liberty interest protected by the Due Process Clause is "the fundamental right of parents to make decisions concerning the care, custody, and control of their children."[14] Troxel v. Granville, 530 U.S. 57, 66, 120 S.Ct. 2054, 147 L.Ed.2d 49 (2000); see also Fields, 427 F.3d at 1204. Among other things, this right means that

> the state cannot prevent parents from choosing a specific educational program—whether it be religious instruction at a private school or instruction in a foreign language. That is, the state does not have the power to "standardize its children" or "foster a homogenous people" by completely foreclosing the opportunity of individuals and groups to choose a different path of education.
> Id. at 1205 (quoting Brown v. Hot, Sexy & Safer Prods., Inc., 68 F.3d 525, 533–34 (1st Cir.1995), abrogated on other grounds by Martinez v. Cui, 608 F.3d 54 (1st Cir. 2010)).

This freedom, however, does not "encompass[ ] a fundamental constitutional right to dictate the curriculum at the public school to which [parents] have chosen to send their children." Id.

[14] This right is commonly referred to as the Meyer– Pierce right because it finds its origin in two Supreme Court cases, Meyer v. Nebraska, 262 U.S. 390, 43 S.Ct. 625, 67 L.Ed. 1042 (1923), and Pierce v. Society of Sisters, 268 U.S. 510, 45 S.Ct. 571, 69 L.Ed. 1070 (1925).

Parent Plaintiffs allege that the fundamental parental right to make decisions concerning the care, custody, and control of their children also encompasses the following rights: (1) "the power to direct the education and upbringing of [their] children"; (2) the right to "instill moral standards and values in their children"; (3) the "right to determine whether and when their children will have to risk being exposed to opposite sex nudity at school"; and (4) the "right to determine whether their children, while at school, will have to risk exposing their own undressed or partially unclothed bodies to members of the opposite sex" in "intimate, vulnerable settings like restrooms, locker rooms and showers." Parent Plaintiffs claim that the District's implementation of the Student Safety Plan violates these rights, and therefore the Fourteenth Amendment, because Parent Plaintiffs "do not want their minor children to endure the risk of being exposed to the opposite sex ... nor do they want their minor children to attend to their personal, private bodily needs in the presence of members of the opposite sex." They explain that they "desire to raise their children with a respect for traditional modesty, which requires that one not undress or use the restroom in the presence of the opposite sex," and that some parents also object to the Student Safety Plan because of "sincerely-held religious beliefs."

The district court disposed of this claim on the ground that the fundamental parental right protected by the Fourteenth Amendment's Due Process Clause is narrower than Plaintiffs assert. See Parents for Privacy, 326 F. Supp. 3d at 1108–09. The district court reasoned that although Parent Plaintiffs have the right to choose where their children obtain an education, meaning that they have a right to remove their children from Dallas High School if they disapprove of transgender student access to facilities, binding Ninth Circuit authority makes clear that "Parent Plaintiffs' Fourteenth Amendment liberty interest in the education and upbringing of their children 'does not extend beyond the threshold of the school door.' " Id. at 1109 (quoting Fields, 427 F.3d at 1207). The district court thus disagreed with Plaintiffs' unsupported proposition that parents "retain the right to prevent transgender students from sharing school facilities with their children." Id.

On appeal, Parent Plaintiffs argue that the district court erroneously limited their fundamental parental rights. They challenge in particular the district court's conclusion that their parental rights do not "extend beyond the threshold of the school door." Plaintiffs, relying on Troxel, 530 U.S. at 65–66, 120 S.Ct. 2054 (quoting Prince v. Massachusetts, 321 U.S. 158, 166, 64 S.Ct. 438, 88 L.Ed. 645 (1944)), note that "the custody, care, and nurture of the child reside first in the parents, whose primary function and freedom include preparation for obligations the state can neither supply nor hinder." But other than affirming that parents have a long-recognized constitutional right to "make decisions concerning the care, custody, and control of their children," Troxel lends no concrete support to Plaintiffs' specific argument in this case. Id. at 66, 120 S.Ct. 2054. Troxel concerned a state government's interference with a mother's decision about the amount of visitation with her daughters' paternal grandparents that was in her daughters' best interests; it did not address the extent of parents' rights to direct the policies of the public schools that their children attend.[16] See id. at 67–73, 120 S.Ct. 2054. Moreover, we have previously explained that although the Supreme Court "recognized that parents' liberty interest in the custody, care, and nurture of their children resides 'first' in the parents, [it] does not reside there exclusively, nor is it 'beyond regulation [by the state] in the public interest.' " Fields, 427 F.3d at 1204 (second alteration in original) (quoting Prince, 321 U.S. at 166, 64 S.Ct. 438).

[16] Similarly, Plaintiffs' reliance on Wisconsin v. Yoder, 406 U.S. 205, 92 S.Ct. 1526, 32 L.Ed.2d 15 (1972), in their reply brief is unavailing. In that case, the Supreme Court held that the state of Wisconsin could not compel Amish parents to send their children to formal high school up to the age of 16, because as applied to the Amish parents in that case, doing so violated the Free Exercise Clause of the First Amendment, and also interfered with "the traditional interest of parents with respect to the religious upbringing of their children." Id. at 214, 92 S.Ct. 1526; see also id. at 232–36, 92 S.Ct. 1526. Yoder supports the district court's recognition that parents have the right to remove their children from Dallas High School, but it does not support Plaintiffs' assertion that their parental rights go beyond that decision and extend to a right to require a particular bathroom access policy for transgender students.

Next, Plaintiffs attempt to distinguish Fields, the Ninth Circuit case on which the district court relied, by pointing out that the instant case is not about curriculum, but rather "about conduct authorized by the school allowing opposite-sex students into privacy facilities." Fields involved conduct authorized by the school allowing a researcher to administer a survey that included questions about sexual topics. Fields, 427 F.3d at 1200–01. We held that although "[p]arents have a right to inform their children when and as they wish on the subject of sex," they "have no constitutional right ... to prevent a public school from providing its students with whatever information it wishes to provide, sexual or otherwise, when and as the school determines that it is appropriate to do so." Id. at 1206. While the purported risk of Parent Plaintiffs' children being exposed to the unclothed bodies of students who were assigned the opposite sex at birth does not involve the provision of information, as did Fields, it similarly involves students being exposed to things of which their parents disapprove.

In any case, in Fields we adopted the Sixth Circuit's view that parents not only lack a constitutional right to direct the curriculum that is taught to their children, but that they also lack constitutionally protected rights to direct school administration more generally. See id. at 1206 (rejecting a "curriculum exception"). Specifically, we endorsed the Sixth Circuit's explanation that:

> While parents may have a fundamental right to decide whether to send their child to a public school, they do not have a fundamental right generally to direct how a public school teaches their child. Whether it is the school curriculum, the hours of the school day, school discipline, the timing and content of examinations, the individuals hired to teach at the school, the extracurricular activities offered at the school or ... a dress code, these issues of public education are generally committed to the control of state and local authorities.
> Id. (internal quotation marks omitted) (quoting Blau v. Fort Thomas Pub. Sch. Dist., 401 F.3d 381, 395–96 (6th Cir. 2005)).

This binding precedent thus directly supports the district court's conclusion that Parent Plaintiffs lack a fundamental right to direct Dallas High School's bathroom and locker room policy...Plaintiffs nonetheless argue that, contrary to Fields, the Supreme Court has extended parental rights into the classroom. Specifically, they argue that the Supreme Court has ruled that students from Jehovah's Witness families could not be compelled to recite the Pledge of Allegiance at school. See W. Va. State Bd. of Educ. v. Barnette, 319 U.S. 624, 642, 63 S.Ct. 1178, 87 L.Ed. 1628 (1943). But that Supreme Court decision rested on the First Amendment; nowhere did the Supreme Court reference the fundamental rights of parents to direct their children's upbringing. See Barnette, 319 U.S. at 639, 642, 63 S.Ct. 1178. Thus, Plaintiffs fail to cite any Supreme Court authority showing that parents' substantive due process rights under the Fourteenth Amendment encompass a right to direct the curriculum, administration, or policies of public schools.

……

In sum, Plaintiffs fail to cite any authority that supports their asserted fundamental Fourteenth Amendment parental right to "determine whether and when their children will have to risk being exposed to opposite sex nudity at school" and "whether their children, while at school, will have to risk exposing their own undressed or partially unclothed bodies to members of the opposite sex" in "intimate, vulnerable settings like restrooms, locker rooms and showers." In fact, Fields makes clear that the fundamental right to control the upbringing of one's children does not extend so far as Plaintiffs' hypothesize. See Fields, 427 F.3d at 1206–07. Plaintiffs neither distinguish this precedent nor address the practical issue raised by Fields: that accommodating the different "personal, moral, or religious concerns of every parent" would be "impossible" for public schools, because different parents would often likely, as in this case, prefer opposite and contradictory outcomes. Id. at 1206. As a result, Plaintiffs' legal theory fails. Considering that Supreme Court and Ninth Circuit case law not only have not recognized the specific rights asserted by Plaintiffs, but further forecloses recognizing such rights as being encompassed by the fundamental parental rights protected by the Fourteenth Amendment's Due Process Clause, amendment of this claim would be futile.

For the foregoing reasons, we affirm the district court's dismissal with prejudice of this claim.

D.

Fourth, Plaintiffs contend that the district court erred in dismissing their claim for violation of their First Amendment free exercise rights.

The First Amendment provides that "Congress shall make no law respecting an establishment of religion, or prohibiting the free exercise thereof ...." U.S. Const., amend. I. "The free exercise of religion means, first and foremost, the right to believe and profess whatever religious doctrine one desires." Emp't Div., Dep't of Human Res. of Or. v. Smith, 494 U.S. 872 877, 110 S.Ct. 1595, 108 L.Ed.2d 876 (1990), superseded by statute in other contexts as stated in Holt, 135 S. Ct. at 859–60. The Supreme Court has explained that the First Amendment "obviously excludes all 'governmental regulation of religious beliefs as such,' " meaning that "[t]he government may not compel affirmation of religious belief, punish the expression of religious doctrines it believes to be false, impose special disabilities on the basis of religious views or religious status, or lend its power to one or the other side in controversies over religious authority or dogma." Id. (citations omitted) (quoting Sherbert v. Verner, 374 U.S. 398, 402, 83 S.Ct. 1790, 10 L.Ed.2d 965 (1963)). The Supreme Court has also suggested that the government would interfere with the free exercise of religion impermissibly if it sought to ban the performance of or abstention from certain physical acts, but "only when [those acts] are engaged in for religious reasons, or only because of the religious belief that they display." Id. Nevertheless, the "freedom to act" pursuant to one's religious beliefs "cannot be" absolute; "[c]onduct remains subject to regulation for the protection of society." Stormans, Inc. v. Selecky, 586 F.3d 1109, 1128 (9th Cir. 2009) (citing Cantwell v. Connecticut, 310 U.S. 296, 303–04, 60 S.Ct. 900, 84 L.Ed. 1213 (1940)). Thus, "[t]he Cantwell right to freely exercise one's religion ... 'does not relieve an individual of the obligation to comply with a "valid and neutral law of general applicability on the ground that the law proscribes (or prescribes) conduct that his [or her] religion prescribes (or proscribes)." ' " Id. at 1127 (quoting Smith, 494 U.S. at 879, 110 S.Ct. 1595).

Here, Plaintiffs claim that the Student Safety Plan violates their First Amendment rights to freely exercise their religion because the Student Safety Plan forces them to be exposed to an environment in school bathrooms and locker facilities that conflicts with, and prevents them from fully practicing, their religious beliefs. Specifically, the complaint alleges that many Student Plaintiffs and some Parent Plaintiffs "have the sincere religious belief" that children "must not undress, or use the restroom, in the presence of a member of the opposite biological sex, and also that they must not be in the presence of the opposite biological sex while the opposite biological sex is undressing or using the restroom." Because the Student Safety Plan permits transgender students who were assigned the opposite biological sex at birth into their locker rooms, the Plan "prevents Student Plaintiffs from practicing the modesty that their faith requires of them, and it further interferes with Parent Plaintiffs teaching their children traditional modesty and insisting that their children practice modesty, as their faith requires." Plaintiffs further assert that, as a result, "[c]omplying with the requirements of the Student Safety Plan ... places a substantial burden on the Plaintiffs' exercise of religion by requiring Plaintiffs to choose between the benefit of a free public education and violating their religious beliefs."

The district court dismissed this claim on the basis that the Student Safety Plan was neutral and generally applicable with respect to religion, noting that "neutral, generally applicable laws that incidentally burden the exercise of religion usually do not violate the Free Exercise Clause of the First Amendment" because they need only be "rationally related to a legitimate government interest." Parents for Privacy, 326 F. Supp. 3d at 1110 (quoting Holt, 135 S. Ct. at 859) (citing Church of the Lukumi Babalu Aye, Inc. v. City of Hialeah, 508 U.S. 520, 531, 113 S.Ct. 2217, 124 L.Ed.2d 472 (1993)). The district court rejected Plaintiffs' assertion that, because the Plan pertains specifically to Student A, the Plan is not generally applicable. Id. The court, citing Lukumi, 508 U.S. at 532–33, 113 S.Ct. 2217, explained that "Plaintiffs misunderstand the law," because neutrality and general applicability are "considered with respect to religion" rather than with respect to the person or groups to which the law most directly pertains. Parents for Privacy, 326 F. Supp. 3d at 1110. Because the District's Plan did not force any Plaintiff to embrace a religious belief and did not punish anyone for expressing their religious beliefs, the district court concluded that the Plan is "neutral and generally applicable with respect to religion," and therefore did not violate Plaintiffs' First Amendment rights. Id.

On appeal, Plaintiffs argue that the district court should have applied strict scrutiny because, contrary to the district court's conclusion, the Student Safety Plan is not neutral or generally applicable. Plaintiffs point out that the Student Safety Plan was implemented to benefit one student in particular, and they claim, without any supporting citation, that "a policy implemented for a single student is not generally applicable." Plaintiffs do not address the district court's reasoning that neutrality and general applicability are considered with respect to religion. Nor does their argument acknowledge that the Plan applies to all transgender students, not just to Student A; that is, the argument does not distinguish between an event that triggered development of a policy and the breadth of the resulting policy itself.

In assessing neutrality and general applicability, courts evaluate both "the text of the challenged law as well as the effect ... in its real operation." Stormans, Inc. v. Wiesman, 794 F.3d 1064, 1076 (9th Cir. 2015) (ellipsis in original) (internal quotation marks omitted). As the district court correctly explained, the two tests for whether a law is neutral and generally applicable focus on whether a law specifically targets or singles out religion. See Parents for Privacy, 326 F. Supp. 3d at 1110; Lukumi, 508 U.S. at 532, 113 S.Ct. 2217 ("[T]he protections of the Free Exercise Clause pertain if the law at issue discriminates against some or all religious beliefs or regulates or prohibits conduct because it is undertaken for religious reasons.").

First, "if the object of a law is to infringe upon or restrict practices because of their religious motivation, the law is not neutral." Selecky, 586 F.3d at 1130 (emphasis added) (quoting Lukumi, 508 U.S. at 533, 113 S.Ct. 2217). For example, "[a] law lacks facial neutrality if it refers to a religious practice without a secular meaning discernable from the language or context." Lukumi, 508 U.S. at 533, 113 S.Ct. 2217. Even if a law is facially neutral, it may nonetheless fail the neutrality test if "[t]he record ... compels the conclusion that suppression of [a religion or religious practice] was the object of the ordinances." Id. at 534, 542, 113 S.Ct. 2217. Thus, in Lukumi, the Supreme Court concluded that an animal ordinance that in its operation effectively banned only the ritual animal sacrifice performed by practitioners of the Santeria religion, was not neutral because it accomplished a "religious gerrymander," i.e., an impermissible attempt to target religious practices through careful legislative drafting. See id. at 535–37, 113 S.Ct. 2217.

Here, on the other hand, Plaintiffs' complaint contains no allegation suggesting that the Student Safety Plan was adopted with the object of suppressing the exercise of religion. To the contrary, Plaintiffs allege that the District developed and implemented the Student Safety Plan in "response to the threat of [federal] enforcement action" and in "response to Student A's complaints for accommodation." Moreover, the Student Safety Plan "make[s] no reference to any religious practice, conduct, belief, or motivation." See Wiesman, 794 F.3d at 1076. Instead, the Plan itself states that it was "created to support a transgender male expressing the right to access the boy's locker room at Dallas High School." Plaintiffs do not counter this evidence or point to anything in the record suggesting that the Student Safety Plan was adopted with the specific purpose of infringing on Plaintiffs' religious practices or suppressing Plaintiffs' religion. Accordingly, the district court correctly concluded that the Student Safety Plan is neutral for purposes of analyzing the free exercise claim.

Second, the question of general applicability addresses whether a law treats religious observers unequally. See Lukumi, 508 U.S. at 542, 113 S.Ct. 2217. For example, "inequality results when a legislature decides that the governmental interests it seeks to advance are worthy of being pursued only against conduct with a religious motivation." Id. at 542–43, 113 S.Ct. 2217. Thus, "[a] law is not generally applicable if its prohibitions substantially underinclude non-religiously motivated conduct that might endanger the same governmental interest that the law is designed to protect." Wiesman, 794 F.3d at 1079 (citing Lukumi, 508 U.S. at 542–46, 113 S.Ct. 2217). "In other words, if a law pursues the government's interest 'only against conduct motivated by religious belief,' but fails to include in its prohibitions substantial, comparable secular conduct that would similarly threaten the government's interest, then the law is not generally applicable." Id. (quoting Lukumi, 508 U.S. at 545, 113 S.Ct. 2217). For example, in Lukumi, the Court concluded that the challenged ordinances were not generally applicable because they "pursue[d] the city's governmental interests only against *1236 conduct motivated by religious belief" and "fail[ed] to prohibit nonreligious conduct that endanger[ed] these interests in a similar or greater degree than Santeria sacrifice does." Lukumi, 508 U.S. at 543, 545, 113 S.Ct. 2217; see also Selecky, 586 F.3d at 1134.

Here, the Student Safety Plan is not underinclusive, because it does not require only religious students to share a locker room with a transgender student who was assigned the opposite sex at birth, nor does the Plan require only religious teachers and staff to receive training or to teach about anti-bullying and harassment. In other words, the Student Safety Plan affects all students and staff—it does not place demands on exclusively religious persons or conduct. Plaintiffs' singular argument that the Student Safety Plan is underinclusive because it was aimed at a particular student and does not allow every student to use the facilities of their choosing regardless of biological sex or self-identified gender misses the mark because it misunderstands the applicable test. Underinclusiveness is determined with respect to the burdens on religious and non-religious conduct and the interests sought to be advanced by the policy. That the Student Safety Plan focuses on transgender students rather than allowing all students to claim a right to use whichever facility they wish regardless of gender is irrelevant because that alleged underinclusion is not related to the interests furthered by the plan, and Plaintiffs have not tied it to burdens on secular versus religious conduct. The correct inquiry here is whether, in seeking to create a safe, non-discriminatory school environment for transgender students, the Student Safety Plan selectively imposes certain conditions or restrictions only on religious conduct. Because Plaintiffs have not made any showing that the Plan does so, the district court correctly determined that the Plan is generally applicable for purposes of the free exercise analysis. See Parents for Privacy, 326 F. Supp. 3d at 1110.

Because the Student Safety Plan qualifies as neutral and generally applicable, it is not subject to strict scrutiny. See Selecky, 586 F.3d at 1129 ("[A] neutral law of general applicability will not be subject to strict scrutiny review."); see also Smith, 494 U.S. at 888, 110 S.Ct. 1595 ("Precisely because we are a cosmopolitan nation made up of people of almost every conceivable religious preference, and precisely because we value and protect that religious divergence, we cannot afford the luxury of deeming presumptively invalid, as applied to the religious objector, every regulation of conduct that does not protect an interest of the highest order." (citation and internal quotation marks omitted)).

Plaintiffs argue that strict scrutiny should nevertheless apply because this suit concerns the alleged infringement of multiple constitutional rights. Relying on Smith, 494 U.S. at 882, 110 S.Ct. 1595, they argue that "[w]here, as here, plaintiffs allege multiple fundamental rights arising under the First and Fourteenth Amendments (bodily privacy, parental rights and free exercise rights), hybrid rights analysis requires strict scrutiny as well." The district court rejected this argument because it had already dismissed Plaintiffs' other constitutional claims. See Parents for Privacy, 326 F. Supp. 3d at 1110 n.10. For the following reasons, we agree with the district court that Plaintiffs' argument—that strict scrutiny is required simply because Plaintiffs alleged multiple constitutional claims concerning fundamental rights—fails here.

The extent to which the hybrid rights exception truly exists, and what standard applies to it, is unclear. In Smith, the Court noted that "[t]he only decisions in which we have held that the First Amendment bars application of a neutral, generally applicable law to religiously motivated action have involved not the Free Exercise Clause alone, but the Free Exercise Clause in conjunction with other constitutional protections." Smith, 494 U.S. at 881, 110 S.Ct. 1595. However, Smith did "not present such a hybrid situation," and thus the Court did not further explain how a hybrid rights scenario should be scrutinized. See id. at 882, 110 S.Ct. 1595. The Ninth Circuit subsequently discussed the nature of "hybrid rights" at length, and a three-judge panel majority concluded that, "[i]n order to trigger strict scrutiny, a hybrid-rights plaintiff must show a 'fair probability'—a 'likelihood'—of success on the merits of his companion claim." Thomas v. Anchorage Equal Rights Comm'n, 165 F.3d 692, 706 (9th Cir.), reh'g granted, opinion withdrawn, 192 F.3d 1208 (9th Cir. 1999). The dissent, however, noted that "there is real doubt whether the hybrid-rights exception even exists" because "the Supreme Court itself has never explicitly held that it exists." Id. at 722–23 (Hawkins, J., dissenting). "[T]he paragraph in Smith purporting to carve out a hybrid-rights exception is dicta," "the Supreme Court in Smith did not announce a different test for hybrid-rights cases," and "[e]ven the cases which the Supreme Court cited as involving 'hybrid rights' did not explicitly refer to or invoke strict scrutiny or a compelling government interest test." Id. at 723–24.

……

Nonetheless, we need not resolve that question now, because even if a hybrid rights exception does exist, it would not apply in this case... As explained earlier in this opinion, Plaintiffs have not established colorable companion claims—they have not shown even a likelihood of success, which is why their claims were all dismissed with prejudice. Thus, even if the hybrid rights exception does exist, it would not apply to require strict scrutiny in this case. Alternatively, if the hybrid rights exception does not actually exist, then, of course, it cannot apply to this case to require strict scrutiny of Plaintiffs' purported hybrid claims.

……

Instead, we review the Plan for a rational basis, which means that the Plan must be upheld if it is rationally related to a legitimate governmental purpose...For the foregoing reasons, we affirm the dismissal with prejudice of Plaintiffs' First Amendment free exercise claim.

Stephen Giles: On Educating Children: A Parentalist Manifesto,
63 U. Chi. L. Rev. 937 (1996)*

In a liberal society, who should decide which values children are taught to live by? Many contemporary political and constitutional theorists answer this question by subordinating the authority of individual parents to overriding conceptions of liberal democratic values or to the decisions of political majorities. Other theorists seek to give the child primary responsibility for developing his or her own values by requiring both parents and the state to expose children to diverse values and beliefs. For its part, the Supreme Court has adhered to its *Lochner*-era pronouncement in *Pierce v. Society of Sisters* that parents have a constitutional right to direct and control the education of their children. But the Court has never developed a theory to explain this result. Nor has it clarified the terms on which this right coexists with what the Court has also declared to be the state's fundamental interest in ensuring that children are educated to be productive individuals and responsible citizens. Consequently, parental educational rights are both ill defined and vulnerable to unduly deferential judicial review of state educational regulation.

……….

I. The Case for Parental Educational Authority

Liberal societies are committed to treating adults as self- governing persons entitled to choose and pursue their own conceptions of the good life. Liberal constitutions therefore refrain from requiring citizens to conform to any one conception of the good life, and prohibit political majorities from using state power for that purpose absent some overriding justification. ... Consequently, no one in a liberal society may coerce another's choice of values or beliefs unless somehow privileged to do so. ...These widely held principles provide an initial fix on the problem of liberal educational authority. The root difficulty is that human beings are not born into the world as self-governing, reasoning individuals. If they were, education might still be necessary, but it would not be problematic. By hypothesis these persons would, from birth, be capable of deciding for themselves what values and conception of the good life to adopt. Consequently, neither the liberal state nor their parents could legitimately assert the right to choose on their behalf.

Most academic writing about education proceeds on the assumption that the combined authority of parents, schools, and the state over the child's education is quite extensive. Parents and teachers cannot abuse or imprison a child, but as educators they may decide what values to teach the child, even if the child resists or disagrees. On this view, the crucial question is how to apportion the broad grant of educational authority between parents and the state (with teachers as agents of one or the other).

... We can all agree that children need an education, and that this education must both be consistent with, and prepare them for, their future autonomy as adults. But the fact of ineradicable pluralism must be reckoned with. We cannot agree on the good life, and consequently we cannot agree on the good education. This deadlock makes the problem of allocating educational authority all the more urgent: what is at stake is who decides what kind of education the child shall receive. Yet if we cannot agree on the good education, how can we hope ever to agree on the good educator?

1. The child's best interest as a neutral principle.

The solution to this quandary derives from the familiar liberal proposition that educational authority must be justified primarily in terms of the child's best interest. ... A basic education that equips the child to speak, read, write, calculate, and reason is, I shall assume, among the minimum human goods necessary for normal human flourishing in our society.

Now, if this modest assumption about the child's best interest is correct, we have converted an allocation issue into an affirmative limit (indeed, an obligation) on the child's educators—whoever they turn out to be. We have a consensus that every normal child's education should aim at equipping the child with these basic skills. That, in turn, gives us a benchmark with which every child's education must, in principle, comply. A law making that benchmark binding is therefore plainly legitimate.

3. Parents' and teachers' incentives compared.

[I]s it not clear that teachers' incentives to act in the child's educational best interest are far weaker than those of individual parents? The teacher will spend a fraction of each school day with the child for perhaps a year. The teacher will have many pupils to care for, and in any event professional caring preserves a certain distance from the child. The teacher will have personal or family commitments of his or her own. Although teachers individually may assign intrinsic value to teaching, teachers collectively may structure school rules to reduce their workloads and responsibilities. Moreover, society cannot hold teachers accountable, either individually or collectively, in the ways that it can parents. As compared to parents, individual teachers bear far less of the costs associated with a badly educated child and far less of the benefits associated with a well educated one. Consequently, their incentives to act in the child's best educational interest are plainly inferior.

But what about teachers' educational expertise? [L]et us assume that many teachers bring significant expertise to educating children. All the more reason to follow the usual model of professionalism, which would place educational decision-making authority in the hands of the party with the best incentives to demand and make use of that expertise: the consumer, or in the case of child consumers, parents. Let parents choose teachers, and the demand for expert teachers will increase.

....

Nature provides us with parents for children, and by regulating the parent-child relationship we can at low administrative cost enhance the natural incentives parents have to act in their child's best interest. Thus, parental educational authority yields better incentives at lower cost. Where incentives and administrative costs point in the same direction, we have what ought to be an easy case.

....

4. Majoritarian control of the child's values is unjust.

Most parents would presumably find themselves in the political majority. These majority parents would of course remain free to educate their children in accord with their basic values. Beyond that, their efforts would be reinforced by the state's endorsement of those values. Minority parents, by contrast, would continue to have general custody of their children, and with it the responsibility for nurturing them. But insofar as their conception of the good clashed with the majority's, they would be compelled to teach contrary to—or, at least, to refrain from teaching in accord with—their beliefs.

Dissenting parents would find themselves in an impossible predicament. The state expects them to love and care for their children, yet forbids raising them by the parents' own best lights. ...It is also unjust, as against the baseline of liberal toleration for the reasonable comprehensive views of others. Why should the mere fact that some parents are in the majority entitle them to teach their children as they think best, while using the state's coercive powers to prevent minority parents from doing the same?

5. Majoritarian interference with parental transmission of values is likewise unjust.

[T]he more fundamental problem is that the paradigm of the state battling with minority parents to win the child's allegiance is both subversive of parental nurturing and authority, and counter to the widely held and reasonable judgment (explicated below) that the child needs to receive a coherent education shaped by some controlling conception of the good.... Day in, day out, in the context of formal schooling, the children of dissenting parents are to be taught the state's established wisdom concerning the human good, and made aware (either explicitly or by implication) that this authoritative teaching clashes with the values they have been taught at home.

…………..

IV. Translating Parentalist Theory into Constitutional Law

The political theory of parental educational rights developed so far may be summarized as follows: so long as they remain parents in good standing, individuals should enjoy the authority to educate their children in accord with their own conceptions of the good and the right. The liberal state may insist that parents provide their children with an education that will develop the basic skills and competences necessary for normal human development and liberal citizenship. State regulation of education must, however, remain neutral among competing reasonable conceptions of the good life and of liberal virtues. Consequently, provided that parental educational choices are consistent with reasonable conceptions of the good life and of liberal citizenship, the state may not use coercive means to promote the majority's preferred conceptions in the domain of formal schooling. In sum, the state may not ordinarily override parental educational choices at home or in school unless those choices are plainly unreasonable.

There are three plausible sources of federal constitutional protection for parental educational authority: substantive due process, free exercise of religion, and freedom of speech and expression. …Substantive due process protection entails some form of "reasonableness" review. Government does not act reasonably when it coercively overrules the judgments of dissenting parents as applied to their own children unless the parents' stance is unreasonable in terms of the child's best interest or society's legitimate interest in the child as future citizen.

It might be better, then, to look to the Free Exercise Clause of the First Amendment as the source of parental constitutional rights. These rights necessarily imply that the state may not seek to win children away from the religious convictions of their parents through coercive means. Thus, the most important holding in *Yoder* incorporates the idea at the core of *Pierce*: that parental educational rights trump even legitimate state purposes unless "harm to the physical or mental health of the child or to the public safety, peace, order, or welfare has been demonstrated or may be properly inferred." [As to] freedom of speech… I argue that parents have a free speech right to communicate their values to their children both directly and through the speech of teachers and schools as their chosen agents. Consequently, state educational regulation that coerces or pressures parents to conform their child's education to the state's preferred values constitutes viewpoint-based interference with parental speech. As such, it is presumptively unconstitutional.

[T]he tradition of parental educational authority should be respected and enlarged, not subordinated to contestable norms of democratic education. This tradition is rooted in liberalism's commitment to tolerating competing reasonable conceptions of the good, and especially in its commitment to promoting the human flourishing of parents and children, both of which depend on parents' ability to nurture and educate their children by their own best lights. Provided their educational choices are reasonable (that is, do not violate the core notions of the human good and of social responsibility on which there is liberal consensus), individual parents should be free to pass on their values to their children and to reject state efforts to try to inculcate contrary values through mandatory public schooling, curriculum regulation, selective funding, or other coercive means. Arguments from parental incentives and parental ideals furnish a powerful theoretical basis for recognizing broad parental educational authority as a matter of substantive due process. But the best constitutional locus for implementing this theory of parental educational rights may be the First Amendment's guarantee of free speech and expression. Rightly interpreted, the First Amendment protects parental educative speech against viewpoint-based and content-based state regulation; and the category of parental educative speech should be understood to include both direct parental communication in the home and indirect parental communication, through parents' agents, in the schools that parents choose.

Notes and Comments

1. Parental Rights and the History of Public Education
Retracing the history of public education law helps one understand the uniqueness of the state interest in education as well as the delicate balance modern law maintains between the rights of parents and the education mission (see discussion in note two below).

The patriots of the American Revolution were early proponents for a public education system. George Washington, William Penn, John Adam and Thomas Jefferson, among others spoke often of the connection between the health of the new republic and an educated citizenry. George Washington spoke of this connection in his last official address as President;

> Promote then, as an object of primary importance, institutions for the general diffusion of knowledge. . . . In proportion as the structure of a government gives force to public opinion, it is essential that public opinion should be enlightened. Washington's Farewell Address 1796.

Massachusetts was the first colony to enact a compulsory education law in 1642. Connecticut followed in 1650, Pennsylvania was next in 1682, and the other colonies quickly followed suit. The early period of public education balanced instruction against the agrarian culture of the day. Students of middle or lower class were lucky to experience education beyond primary grades. Primary education then consisted of little more than spelling, reading and writing, arithmetic, and some science and history.

Beyond the basic education, vocation-based learning was a necessity well into the industrial age. Indeed, parents would frequently need to interrupt school in order to add their children to the labor force for crop planting, weeding or harvesting. Upper class students were favored with opportunities to apprentice in a profession or to continue higher education at one of the many new colleges in the new republic. For more in the history of public education, *see* Symposium, *Civic Education: Recent History, Current Status, and the Future*, 62 Alb. L. Rev. 1425 (1999); Note: *Education and the Court: The Supreme Court's Educational Ideology*, 40 Vand. L. Rev. 939 (1987); and Martin D. Carcieri, *Democracy and Education in the Thought of Jefferson and Madison*, 26 J.L. & Educ. 1 (1997). *See also* Ellwood P. Cubberley, PUBLIC EDUCATION IN THE UNITED STATES 101-15 (1919); R. Freeman Butts & Lawrence A. Cremin, A HISTORY OF EDUCATION IN AMERICAN CULTURE 141-50 (1953).

2. Parental Rights and *In Loco Parentis*

Most modern discussions of parental rights are forced to acknowledge the role of the educator as the surrogate parent under the notion of *in loco parentis*. Unfortunately, discussions concerning *in loco parentis* can be daunting in many respects; modern use of the term is often symbolic rather than precise, making it a difficult concept to navigate. Three distinct notions remain in play in determining the degree to which educators stand *in loco parentis*.

The first is historical and rooted in the common law. At common law, educators stood *in loco parentis* in an absolute sense. This carried with it two important corollaries. First, students had no rights on campus unless parents and educators agreed. Second, school officials were subject to few, if any legal limits, because they were acting on behalf of parents. This branch of *in loco parentis* was repudiated in *New Jersey v. T.L.O.*, 469 U.S. 325 (1985), where the Court expanded the authority of school officials to conduct searches of students without probable cause. Justice Blackman summarized the common law notion as inconsistent with the Bill of Rights. "In carrying out searches and other disciplinary functions pursuant to such policies, school officials act as representatives of the State, not merely as surrogates for the parents, and they cannot claim the parents' immunity from the strictures of the Fourth Amendment." *Id.* at 336-37.

A second branch of *in loco parentis* which survived *T.L.O.* involves special functions performed or assumed by public educators which raise exceptional care and safety concerns. School trips and off-campus events are said to invoke *in loco parentis* in a form that conveys greater authority to educators. Considering that parental permission is required for a trip that may not involve curriculum, additional challenges to safety, supervision and liability, "create a need for a greater range of intervention by an administrator than is the case when a student is only active within the relatively orderly confines of a school." *Webb v. McCullough*, 828 F.2d 1151, 1157 (6th Cir. 1987) (upheld power of school officials to search hotel room of a student on sponsored field trip). *See also Rhodes v. Guarricino*, 54 F. Supp. 2d 186 (S.D.N.Y. 1999) (same holding); *Hassan v. Lubbock Indep. Sch. Dist.*, 55 F.3d 1075 (5th Cir. 1995) (upheld power of school officials to punish students while on sponsored road trip). The legal justification for this branch of *in loco parentis* appears to be based on liability. "To expose administrators and school districts to increased tort liability while denying them the authority necessary to lessen the likelihood of student injury would be inequitable." *Webb*, 828 F.2d at 1157.

The third branch is the quasi-*in loco parentis*, articulated in the *Vernonia—Earls* decisions which give educators the power to enforce suspicionless search policies on campus. *See Bd. of Educ. v. Earls*, 536 U.S. 822 (2002); *Vernonia Sch. Dist. v. Acton*, 515 U.S. 646 (1995). Careful to link the notion with the *T.L.O.* rejection of common law *in loco parentis* the Court asserts: "[a]lthough public school officials do not stand entirely [*in loco parentis*] with respect to the students, they do exercise a "custodial and tutelary" authority that permits "a degree of supervision and control that could not be exercised over free adults" and that cannot be ignored in conducting a "reasonableness" inquiry. *Vernonia*, at 655-56. This language is best understood as a refusal by the Court to return to the common law notion, which would effectively immunize educators from liability. For more, *see* Brian Jackson, *The Lingering Legacy of In Loco Parentis: An Historical Survey and Proposal for Reform*, 44 Vand. L. Rev. 1135, 1136 (1991). *See also* Stephen R.

Goldstein, *The Scope and Sources of School Board Authority to Regulate Student Conduct and Status: A Nonconstitutional Analysis*, 117 U. Pa. L. Rev. 373, 377-84 (1969); and Todd A. DeMitchell, *The Duty to Protect: Blackstone's Doctrine of In Loco Parentis: A Lens for Viewing the Sexual Abuse of Students*, 2002 B.Y.U. Educ. & L.J. 17 (2002).

3. Parental Rights, Codes of Conduct and School Discipline

In loco parentis is a two-edged sword for school officials. At one edge, educators are expected to consider the best interests of children generally when implementing the education mission. The other contains a duty to protect a specific child when any risk of harm arises. The two sides are usually in harmony except when educators enforce the code of conduct or collaborate with local law enforcement officials. Two states have examined the conflict that arises in school discipline cases and have decided that parents should be more involved in protecting the rights of their child.

Colorado law provides for more direct involvement of parents in school discipline cases.

> A public school employee shall not use a student's statement concerning an act alleged to have been committed by the student that results in mandatory expulsion …unless the statement is signed by the student and a parent, guardian, or legal or physical custodian is present when the student signs the statement or admission or a reasonable attempt was made to contact the parent, guardian, or legal or physical custodian to have the parent, guardian, or legal or physical custodian present when the student signed the statement. The school shall be deemed to have made a reasonable attempt to contact the parent, guardian, or legal or physical custodian if the school calls each of the phone numbers the parent, guardian, or legal or physical custodian provides to the school and all phone numbers the student provides to the school for the parent, guardian, or legal or physical custodian. C.R.S. 22-33-106.3(1).

Indiana law triggers greater parental involvement when law enforcement officials come onto campus to interrogate a student.

> If a student who is at least eighteen (18) years of age is interrogated by a law enforcement officer:
>
> (1) on school property; and
>
> (2) regarding an investigation in which the student may be a suspect;
>
> the school principal must make an effort to immediately notify the student's parent of the interrogation, or if immediate notification is not possible, the school principal must notify the student's parent not later than twelve (12) hours after the interrogation occurs. Ind. Code Ann. § 20-33-11-3(b).

Can you think of other scenarios that may call for educators to be sensitive to the need to involve parents more directly? See Chapter Four for more materials on codes of conduct and student rights.

III. Parental Choice through Education Reform

A. Home Schools

PEOPLE v. BENNETT
501 N.W.2d 106 (Mich. 1993)

OPINION BY: BRICKLEY

The issue before us is whether, in a challenge not involving religious convictions, a teacher certification requirement for home schools violates a parent's right to direct a child's education under the Fourteenth Amendment. The Bennetts, in challenging the requirements, are claiming that their Fourteenth Amendment right to direct the education of their children should be classified as a "fundamental right," thus making it impervious to the minimal scrutiny due process test. The state contends that the Court of Appeals properly applied the minimal scrutiny test and that the requirement was constitutionally justifiable. The defendants also claim that Michigan's compulsory education law, as applied, violated their statutory and due process rights because they were prosecuted without an administrative hearing to determine whether they were in compliance with the private and parochial schools act.

For the reasons that follow, we hold that a parent's Fourteenth Amendment right to direct a child's education is not one of those rights described by the United States Supreme Court as fundamental, and, thus, the strict scrutiny test is unwarranted. We further hold that the defendants were entitled under the statute, as administrators of a private home school, to the hearing provided by the private and parochial schools act before they could be prosecuted as parents who failed to send their children to school in violation of the compulsory education laws. As a result, we vacate the defendants' convictions and order the state superintendent to conduct a hearing to determine if the defendants' home school satisfies Michigan law.

I

John and Sandra Bennett and their four children, Scott, Erika, Jason, and Krista, live in Wayne County. In 1986, the defendants were charged with four counts of failing to send their children to school during the 1985-86 school year. After a trial before the 35th District Court, the defendants were found guilty and fined $50 for each count. The Wayne Circuit Court affirmed the defendants' convictions.

****

The crux of the defendants' convictions concerns their decision to withdraw their four children from public school. Dissatisfaction with the public school system was their stated reason for their action, not any religious belief. Defendants believed that they could provide their children a better education than the local public school, even though neither defendant is a certified teacher.

Defendants enrolled their children in the home based education program (HBEP) sponsored by Clonlara, Inc., of Ann Arbor, Michigan. The HBEP provides parents with a home instruction program, and allows parents to utilize the services of certified teachers and classrooms on the Ann Arbor campus. Defendants maintained that their children were often brought to the Ann Arbor campus and were instructed by certified teachers for a total of four to six hours per month. Even more frequent contact between the children and the Clonlara teachers was maintained through the use of conference telephone calls from the defendants' home.

Defendants stated that they held classes for their children approximately five hours per day, five days per week, for the entire school year and made monthly attendance reports to Clonlara. The children studied math, English, spelling, reading, writing, science, social studies, history, and art. At the beginning of the school year, defendants submitted proposals for four individualized curricula to the superintendent of the Plymouth-Canton School District, the district in which the children had been attending school. At the end of the school year, standardized achievement test results indicated that three of the four children were either at or above their grade level.

Despite their attempts to teach their children at home, defendants were convicted of failing to send their children to school in violation of Michigan's compulsory education laws. The trial court found that the children were not being properly taught at home because the parents were not in compliance with Department of Education guidelines for educating children in the home. Specifically, the court found that 1) defendants failed to utilize the services of a certified teacher for at least a substantial portion of the school day, 2) there was no proof of use of a curriculum that was comparable to that used in the public school, 3) there was no evidence that the children were instructed for at least 180 days and 900 hours, and 4) there were no attendance records offered to substantiate the claims of the hours and days the children received instruction.

The trial court paid particular attention to the defendants' claim that their children received instruction from certified teachers. Defendants asserted that two women, Pearl Wander and Julie

Kuhar, provided instruction to the children. The court found, however, that the instruction provided by these women did not satisfy the state's requirements. Ms. Wander, for example, while certified to teach, was never shown to have actually visited the Bennett home. Instead, Ms. Wander had contact with the children through the occasional use of a speaker phone and the family's occasional visits to the Clonlara campus for a total of four to six hours per month. This contact, the court found, was not sufficient to meet the state's requirements. Rather, the court concluded, Ms. Wander's role with respect to the children was that of a supervisor, not a teacher. With regard to Ms. Kuhar, the court noted that she was not in fact certified to teach at the time of her contact with the Bennett children.

The fact that defendants were not substantially utilizing the services of a certified teacher and were not themselves certified to teach was sufficient for the trial court to find them guilty of failing to send their children to school. As a result, the trial court 1) required defendants to contact the local public school and arrange to have their children tested for the purposes of academic achievement and grade placement, 2) required defendants to immediately arrange for their children to be taught by certified teachers, and 3) fined each of the defendants $50.

On appeal in the Court of Appeals, defendants raised five issues for review, two of which are now before this Court. The Court of Appeals first addressed the defendants' contention that the teacher certification requirement violated the Fourteenth Amendment right of parents to direct their children's education. It recognized the existence of the right and that the right was protected under the personal substantive due process guarantees of the Fourteenth Amendment. However, it found that where the requirement was rationally related to some legitimate state purpose, the law would be upheld. The Court was satisfied that the state's purpose was legitimate.

[The Court of Appeals affirmed the trial court].

……

II

Defendants argue that there is state and federal case law in support of their contention that, as parents, they have a fundamental right to direct their children's education. We do not, however, find that the cited cases should be so interpreted. Indeed, we have not found and defendants have not presented any case that finds the existence of a Fourteenth Amendment fundamental right of parents to direct their children's secular education free of reasonable regulation. We conclude that parents do not have such a constitutional right requiring a strict scrutiny standard. On the contrary, the state may reasonably regulate education, including the imposition of teacher certification and curricula requirements on home-school programs, in order to advance the legitimate interest of compulsory education.

Defendants contend that the Fourteenth Amendment guarantees them the fundamental right to direct the education of their children, even when the desire to direct education does not stem from any religious belief. Defendants cite *Pierce v. Society of Sisters*, 268 U.S. 510 (1925), for the proposition that it is beyond a state's authority to interfere with parents' choice of private education for their children. Similarly, defendants argue, the State of Michigan is telling parents that their children may be taught only by state-certified teachers, the same type of teachers who teach in public schools. Without explicitly so stating, defendants infer that because the state requires the same type of teachers for both private and public schools, it is blurring the distinction between these schools and thus interfering with a parent's right to choose private schools for their children.

Defendants also quote at length from *Wisconsin v. Yoder*, 406 U.S. 205 (1972), which held that parents have the right to take their children out of high school and give them informal vocational training in order to protect sincerely held religious beliefs. The defendants noted in *Yoder* that the Supreme Court emphasized the case involved the "fundamental interest of parents, as contrasted with that of the State, to guide the *religious* future and education of their children. The history and culture of Western civilization reflect a strong tradition of parental concern for the nurture and upbringing of their children." *Id.* at 232 (emphasis added).

The defendants' reliance on most of the cases cited is misplaced because those cases deal with religious issues under the First Amendment. This case is specifically not about religion and must be so considered. For example, in a broad sense, *Pierce* stands for the proposition that parents have a right to choose either public or private education for their children. In a narrow sense, *Pierce* has been interpreted as providing parents the right to direct the religious education of their children. In no sense, however, has *Pierce* been interpreted to mean that parents have a fundamental right to direct all of their children's education decisions. *Pierce* does not, therefore, stand for the position that parents have a fundamental right to direct their children's education under all circumstances, and so the defendants' reliance on *Pierce* for this reason is mistaken.

The defendants' misplaced reliance on *Yoder* is even more obvious. Hardly a page of that opinion can be read without seeing at least one reference to the parents' religious beliefs. Indeed, the Court discussed the case in terms of having to balance the state's interest in universal education with the First Amendment and "the traditional interest of parents with respect to the religious upbringing of their children…" *Yoder*, 406 U.S. 214 (citing *Pierce*, 268 U.S. 535). In determining that the parents in *Yoder* could remove their children from school after the eighth grade in spite of the compulsory education laws, the Court specifically noted that it was dealing with a "centuries-old religious society," and not "with a way of life and mode of education by a group claiming to have recently discovered some 'progressive' or more enlightened process for rearing children for modern life." The defendants' argument that *Yoder* lends support to the claim that parents have any rights to remove their children from school for nonreligious reasons is completely without merit.

In further support of their contention that the Fourteenth Amendment provides a fundamental right to direct the education of their children, defendants cite *Meyer v. Nebraska*, 262 U.S. 390 (1923), in which the state tried to prohibit private, denominational, parochial, or public schools from teaching in any language other than English to students who had not reached the eighth grade. Defendants contend that this case stands for the proposition that the state could not interfere in parental choices for children's education in this manner because it interfered "with the power of parents to control the education of their own children." *Meyer*, 262 U.S. 401.

The defendants' reliance on *Meyer* is misplaced partially for the same reason that reliance upon *Pierce* is misplaced. At issue in *Meyer* was whether a statute that prohibited teaching foreign languages denied the defendant teacher his liberty as guaranteed by the Fourteenth Amendment. 262 U.S. 399. The only reference to parental rights in the entire opinion consists of one sentence noting that the ban on languages had the effect of interfering with "the calling of modern language teachers, with the opportunities of pupils to acquire knowledge, and with the power of parents to control the education of their own." *Id.* at 401. While *Meyer* may have made one general statement concerning parental rights to control their children's education, it certainly does not stand for the proposition that the Fourteenth Amendment guarantees parents the fundamental right to direct their children's education free from reasonable regulation.

Defendants contend that the Supreme Court's most recent affirmation of this fundamental right is found in *Employment Div, Dep't of Human Resources v. Smith*, 494 U.S. 872 (1990). *Smith* recognizes this parental right as fundamental, defendants contend, because it held that strict scrutiny must be applied when evaluating state actions that interfere with the rights of parents to direct their children's education. In support of this contention, defendants quote *Smith*:

> *Yoder* said that "the Court's holding in *Pierce* stands as a charter of the rights of parents to direct the religious upbringing of their children. And, when the interests of parenthood are combined with a free exercise claim... more than merely a 'reasonable relationship to some purpose within the competency of the State' is required to sustain the validity of the State's requirement under the First Amendment." *Id.* at 881, n. 1 (quoting *Yoder*, 406 U.S. 233).

This, defendants conclude, "reaffirms the applicability of the compelling interest test to a claim of Fourteenth Amendment parental rights standing alone."

Perhaps the defendants' most creative interpretation is of the *Smith* decision. The quotation above explicitly states that it is only when the interests of parenthood are combined with the Free Exercise Clause (a claim defendants are not making) that parents are entitled to constitutional protection of a fundamental right. Nowhere in the opinion does the Court make as bald a statement as the defendants' reading of *Smith*. Rather, as the state pointed out, defendants ignored *Smith*'s clear language and persistently maintain their position despite a directly contradictory holding.

These cases, defendants are convinced, exemplify the United States Supreme Court's recognition of a Fourteenth Amendment fundamental right in parents to direct the education of their children. When considered with other cases that defendants argue apply the fundamental rights of parents found in *Pierce* to home-school situations, they are convinced that the constitution guarantees them the fundamental right to educate their children at home. They may teach their children on their own, defendants conclude, because if the Fourteenth Amendment allows them to direct their children's education, they ought to be able to provide that education themselves.

****

Having found strict scrutiny unnecessary because of the absence of a fundamental right, the state's teacher certification requirement need only satisfy the minimal scrutiny test....

In general, it can be assumed the state has an interest in seeing that all children within its borders are properly educated. Specifically, in a previous case in federal court, the same Michigan teacher certification requirements were recognized as a reasonable means to a legitimate state interest. *Hanson, supra* at 115. We also find that ensuring the minimum competence of those entrusted to teach to be, at the very least, a legitimate state interest. Under the second part of the minimal scrutiny test, a state law prevails if it is in any way reasonably related to the state's interest. Such a relationship is not difficult to establish because a challenge fails if the relationship is "'at least debatable.'" *Metropolitan Life Ins. Co. v. Ward*, 470 U.S. 869, 881 (1985)..... Across the country, state and federal courts have upheld home-school regulations simply on the ground that they were reasonable state actions.

****

While we [disagree] with defendants regarding the first issue, we agree that they were entitled to a hearing before being prosecuted under the compulsory education laws. This conclusion is complicated, however, by the absence of any Michigan statute relating specifically to home schools. While all may agree that such schools are not illegal per se, there is no agreement about how they should be run. The compulsory education laws require parents to send their children to public school, unless the children are attending "state approved nonpublic school[s]." Thus, a home school is valid only if it can be considered a state-approved nonpublic school. The School Code defines a "state approved nonpublic school" as one that meets the requirements of the private and parochial schools act. Therefore, to be valid, a home school must meet the requirements of the private and parochial schools act. Indeed, the state prosecuted defendants, *inter alia*, because their home-school program did not utilize the services of a certified teacher, nor did they provide proof of a curriculum comparable to that offered by the public school. These requirements are the same as those required by the private and parochial schools act. If defendants can be prosecuted for failing to comply with certain provisions of the private and parochial schools act, it would seem that there is no reason why all of the act's provisions should not apply to defendants, including the provision requiring a hearing before the state may close a nonpublic school.

In essence, what defendants argue is correct: before home-school parents can be prosecuted under the compulsory education laws for failing to send their children to "school," it must first be determined that the involved home school does not meet the requirements of the private and parochial schools act.

****

IV

We conclude that the Fourteenth Amendment does not provide parents a fundamental right to direct their children's secular education, and, thus, the state regulation need only be judged by a rational relationship test. We further conclude that the defendants have not met the burden of establishing that teacher certification is not reasonably related to the state's legitimate interest. Moreover, defendants were entitled, under the statute, as administrators of a private home school, to the hearing provided by the private and parochial schools act before they could be prosecuted as parents who failed to send their children to school in violation of the compulsory education laws.

MURPHY v. STATE
852 F.2d 1039 (8th Cir. 2007)

OPINION BY: HEANEY, Circuit Judge

Appellants challenge the decision of the district court upholding the constitutionality of the Arkansas Home School Act, Ark.Code Ann. §§ 6-15-501-6-15-507. We affirm the decision of the district court.

I. Facts

Doty and Phyllis Murphy are evangelical Christians who believe that "Christian Scriptures require parents to take personal responsibility for every aspect of their children's training and education."[17] They have six children, ages four through eighteen. The Murphys educate their children at home, providing an "education that is pervasively religious in nature and which does not conflict with the religious beliefs they hold, based upon their understanding of the scriptures."

Under Arkansas law, a parent must educate her children through the age of sixteen. This requirement may be satisfied by sending the child to public, private, or parochial school or by educating the child at home. The Arkansas Home School Act, Ark.Code Ann. §§ 6-15-501-6-15-507, requires parents intending to school their children at home to notify in writing the superintendent of their local school district prior to the commencement of each school year. The notice must provide information concerning the name, age, and grade of each student, the core curriculum to be offered, the schedule of instruction and the qualifications of the person teaching. The parent must also agree to submit the children to standardized achievement tests each year and, when the children reach the age of fourteen, to a minimum performance test. All of these tests are administered, interpreted, and acted upon by the Arkansas Department of Education. Finally, the parent must provide any information to the superintendent which might indicate the need for special educational services for the children.

The achievement test administered to a student schooled at home is chosen by the parent from a list of nationally recognized tests provided by the director of the State Department of Education or the director's designee. The parent may be present when the standardized test is administered, but both parent and student are under the supervision of a test administrator. The results of the standardized tests are used for several purposes. Most significantly, if a home school student does not achieve a composite score within eight months of grade level in designated subjects, the student must be placed in a public, private, or parochial school. No such annual testing is required for

[17] Appellants' brief asserts, "[t]heir belief that they are ultimately and solely responsible for every aspect of the education of their children is based upon their understanding and interpretation of the Bible and based upon such scriptures as Proverbs 22:6:
'Train a child on the way he should go, and when he is old he will not depart from it.'

and Deuteronomy 6:4-9:
'Hear, Oh Israel; The Lord our God, the Lord is one. Love the Lord your God with all your strength. These commandments that I give you today are to be upon your hearts. Impress them on your children. Talk about them when you sit at home and when you lie down and when you get up. Tie them as cymbals to your hands and bind them on your foreheads. Write them on the doorframe of your houses and on your gates.'

and Deuteronomy 11:19-12a:
'Teach them to your children talking about them when you sit at home and when you walk along the road, when you lie down and when you get up ... so that your days and the days of your children may be many in the land and that the Lord swore to give your forefathers.' "

Brief for Appellants at 12.

students in public, private, or parochial schools. If children not schooled at home are, for some reason, tested, no remedial placement is required for those who do not achieve certain scores.

The Murphys allege that the Arkansas statutory scheme deprives them of the right to free exercise of religion, the right of due process of law, the right of equal protection of the laws, and the right of privacy and parental liberty in violation of the United States Constitution. The Murphys brought an action for a declaratory judgment in federal district court. That court awarded judgment to the state.

II. Discussion

A. The Free Exercise Clause

The Murphys assert that Ark.Code Ann. § 6-15-504, requiring that a standardized test be given to their children under the supervision of a test administrator deprives them of the right to free exercise of religion as guaranteed by the first amendment. They argue that their religious beliefs require they must be *completely* responsible for *every* aspect of their children's education. In contrast, the Arkansas Home School Act places responsibility for testing and interpreting test results with the State of Arkansas, rather than with the parents.

To determine whether governmental conduct infringes upon an individual's first amendment free exercise rights, a court must first inquire whether the challenged governmental action interferes with the claimant's "sincerely held religious beliefs."[18] Second, if such a belief is interfered with, the court must determine whether the governmental action is the least restrictive means of achieving some compelling governmental interest. *Wisconsin v. Yoder,* 406 U.S. 205, 214-15, 92 S.Ct. 1526, 1532-33, 32 L.Ed.2d 15 (1972).

In the case before us, the parties have stipulated that the testing requirements of the Arkansas law interfere with the Murphys' sincerely held religious beliefs. Thus, we will go no further in examining the subtleties of the Murphys' beliefs. Consequently, the resolution of the free exercise claim involves answering two related questions: First, does the state have a compelling interest in the education of all children? Second, if so, is the Arkansas statutory scheme the least restrictive means of achieving that objective? We believe that the answer to both of these questions is yes.

The government has a compelling interest in educating all of its citizens. Education of the citizenry is and always has been a preeminent goal of American society.[19] Reaching back through the

---

[18] In determining whether the religious beliefs are sincerely held, the court will not second-guess the acceptability, logic, consistency, or comprehensibility of these beliefs, for "[c]ourts are not arbiters of scriptural interpretation." *Thomas v. Review Board of the Indiana Employment Security Division,* 450 U.S. 707, 714, 716, 101 S.Ct. 1425, 1430, 1431, 67 L.Ed.2d 624 (1981).

[19] Philip Kurland has written, "It has long been an American dream that education affords a means for upward mobility in an open society. The Supreme Court * * * has framed much of the country's constitutional law on the unstated premise that formal education is the means by which American society remains fluid yet cohesive, pluralistic yet unitary, aspiring to be a democracy while being governed by a meritocracy." P. Kurland, *The Supreme Court, Compulsory Education, and the First Amendment Religion Clauses,* 75 W.Va.L.Rev. 213 (1973).

collective memory of the Republic, the fundamental importance of education in the design of our system of government rapidly becomes clear. Article III of the Northwest Ordinance states in part: “Religion, morality, and knowledge being necessary to good government and the happiness of mankind, schools and the means of education shall forever be encouraged.” In *Yoder,* the Supreme Court adopted Thomas Jefferson's often expressed belief that education was a “bulwark” against tyranny. Specifically, the Court stated:

> Thomas Jefferson pointed out early in our history, that some degree of education is necessary to prepare citizens to participate effectively and intelligently in our open political system if we are to preserve freedom and independence. Further, education prepares individuals to be self-reliant and self-sufficient participants in society.

406 U.S. at 221, 92 S.Ct. at 1536.

The fundamental importance of education in terms of access and achievement in American society was further underscored by the Court in *Brown v. Board of Education,* 347 U.S. 483, 493, 74 S.Ct. 686, 691, 98 L.Ed. 873 (1954), where it stated:

Today, education is perhaps the most important function of state and local governments. Compulsory school attendance laws and the great expenditures for education both demonstrate our recognition of the importance of education to our democratic society. It is required in the performance of our most basic public responsibilities, even service in the armed force. It is the very foundation of good citizenship. Today it is a principal instrument in awakening the child to cultural values, in preparing him for later professional training, and in helping him to adjust normally to his environment. In these days, it is doubtful that any child may reasonably be expected to succeed in life if he is denied the opportunity of an education. Such an opportunity, where the state has undertaken to provide it, is a right which must be made available to all on equal terms.

Following from these recognized concerns, the Supreme Court has observed that

> a substantial body of case law has confirmed the power of the States to insist that attendance at private schools, if it is to satisfy state compulsory-attendance laws, be at institutions which provide minimum hours of instruction, employ teachers of specified training, and cover prescribed subjects of instruction.

Board of Education v. Allen, 392 U.S. 236, 245-46, 88 S.Ct. 1923, 1927-28, 20 L.Ed.2d 1060 (1968) (footnote omitted).[20]

---

[20] In relevant dicta, the Court continued:

> Indeed, the State's interest in assuring that these standards are being met has been considered a sufficient reason for refusing to accept instruction at home as compliance with compulsory education statutes. These cases were a sensible corollary of *Pierce v. Society of Sisters,* [268 U.S. 510, 45 S.Ct.

Thus, as the district court correctly noted, it is "settled beyond dispute, as a legal matter, that the state has a compelling interest in ensuring that all its citizens are being adequately educated."

Given the existence of a compelling governmental interest, we must next inquire whether Arkansas' home testing system is the least restrictive means to achieve that purpose. In doing so, we recognize that the state must have a mechanism by which it can confidently and objectively be assured that its citizens are being adequately educated.

Upon examination, it would appear that Arkansas has created the least restrictive system possible to assure its goal. By providing the option of home schooling, Arkansas allows parents vast responsibility and accountability in terms of their children's education-control far in excess of limitations on religious rights that have been previously upheld. For example, in *Fellowship Baptist Church v. Benton,* 815 F.2d 485 (8th Cir.1987), this Court upheld the power of the State of Iowa to require teachers in "church schools" to be certified by the state for basic competence. On remand, the district court upheld regulations prescribing curriculum in such schools. *Fellowship Baptist Church v. Benton,* 678 F.Supp. 213 (S.D.Iowa 1988). In contrast, Arkansas requires neither that the parent instructing the home-schooled child be a certified teacher nor that the parent follow a mandated curriculum. The state's only safeguard to ensure adequate training of the home-schooled student is the standardized achievement test.[21] Even regarding this test, the state allows wide latitude to the parents. The parent may choose a test administered from a list of nationally recognized standard achievement tests and may be present while the test is administered.

Finally, the Murphys make no showing, as made by the Amish in *Yoder,* that the state can be assured its interest will be attained if appellants' religious beliefs are accommodated. We reject the Murphys' argument that parental "testing" of children provides a sufficient safeguard to assure the state's interest in education is protected. Likewise, parental affidavits concerning the children's progress would also be insufficient. In the end, we believe that the state has no means less restrictive than its administration of achievement tests to ensure that its citizens are being properly educated.

B. Equal Protection

The Murphys argue that the Arkansas Home School Act violates the equal protection clause of the fourteenth amendment. Specifically, they claim that those who school their children at home for religious reasons are a suspect class or that parental control over a child's education involves a fundamental right. Further, they argue that, because the Home School Act discriminates against this class or burdens this right, it fails the strict scrutiny test of the equal protection clause. Alternatively, the Murphys assert that the Home School Act requires various filings with the local superintendent, testing by the state, and remedial action for unsatisfactory test results, while no such requirements are imposed on persons who educate their children in public or private schools.

> 571, 69 L.Ed. 1070 (1925)]: if the State must satisfy its interest in secular education through the instrument of private schools, it has a proper interest in the manner in which those schools perform their secular function.

Id. at 246-47, 88 S.Ct. at 1928.

[21] We note with interest that the Murphys state they "have tested their children using nationally recognized standardized tests in order to determine if their [children's] progress was sufficient." Brief for Appellants at 21.

Moreover, although the public schools are subject to pervasive regulation, the Murphys point out that private schools are virtually free of any such supervision. Thus, the Murphys contend that the state appears irrationally to allow parents to educate their children in religious private schools without any state regulatory supervision but subjects children schooled at home to the various requirements of the Home School Act.

While home school families impelled by deep-seated religious convictions might be the type of "discrete and insular minorit[y]" to which Justice Stone referred in footnote four of *United States v. Carolene Products Co.,* 304 U.S. 144, 58 S.Ct. 778, 82 L.Ed. 1234 (1938), the broad secular category of individuals who prefer to school their children at home is not. Clearly, the statute is aimed at this second category of individuals.

It could be argued that the statute, while superficially neutral, has a discriminatory impact on the category of deeply religious individuals impelled by their convictions to school their children at home. Yet, even if such discriminatory impact were shown-which it has not been-this would not be sufficient to invoke strict scrutiny. The Murphys would still bear the burden of proving discriminatory purpose or intent. *Washington v. Davis,* 426 U.S. 229, 96 S.Ct. 2040, 48 L.Ed.2d 597 (1976). Because no such showing of either discriminatory impact or discriminatory intent has been made, strict scrutiny analysis is inappropriate here.

Second, we find no persuasive arguments advanced that there is a fundamental right of parents to supervise their children's education to the extent that the Murphys contend. The recognition of such a right would fly directly in the face of those cases in which the Supreme Court has recognized the broad power of the state to compel school attendance and regulate curriculum and teacher certification. *See Board of Education v. Allen,* 392 U.S. at 245-46, 88 S.Ct. at 1927-28; *Pierce v. Society of Sisters,* 268 U.S. 510, 534, 45 S.Ct. 571, 573, 69 L.Ed. 1070 (1925). Thus, again, strict scrutiny cannot be invoked in this case.

Given that strict scrutiny analysis does not apply, we move to the question of whether Arkansas has a rational reason to subject home schooling to regulatory requirements, while at the same time freeing private schools from virtually any regulation. This step by the legislature in Arkansas may at first glance offend common sense, and, sitting as a legislature, we might not have made this same decision. However, our job is *not* to sit as a legislature and the constitutional standard of rationality under the equal protection clause is a relaxed one. In this area of the law, the Supreme Court has declared its willingness to uphold any classification based "upon [any] state of facts that reasonably can be conceived to constitute a distinction, or difference in state policy * * *." *Allied Stores v. Bowers,* 358 U.S. 522, 530, 79 S.Ct. 437, 443, 3 L.Ed.2d 480 (1959).

We believe that such a state of facts exists here. First, it could be argued that the notion of an actual independent school, away from home, implies more formality and structure than a home school. This could lead the state to believe that more serious instruction would be occurring there than in the relaxed atmosphere of a child and parents in their own home. Second, the notion that more than one family is likely to be sending their children to the private school may provide an additional objective indication of the private school's quality that is not present in the context of individual home schools. Finally, unlike a home-school, parents sending a child to a private school have to pay money for education and, hence, would be more likely to demand their money's worth of instructional quality from the private school. All these possibilities together could provide Arkansas with a passable reason for the challenged distinction under the minimum rationality standards of the equal protection clause.

C. Right of Privacy

The Murphys argue that the right of privacy should be extended to protect parental decisions concerning the direction of a child's education from state interference.

In *Runyon v. McCrary,* 427 U.S. 160, 96 S.Ct. 2586, 49 L.Ed.2d 415 (1976), the Supreme Court specifically rejected this contention, stating:

> A person's decision whether to bear a child and a parent's decision concerning the manner in which his child is to be educated may fairly be characterized as exercises of familial rights and responsibilities. But it does not follow that because the government is largely or even entirely precluded from regulating the child-bearing decision, it is similarly restricted by the Constitution from regulating the implementation of parental decisions concerning a child's education.
>
> The Court has repeatedly stressed that while parents have a constitutional right to send their children to private schools and a constitutional right to select private schools that offer specialized instruction, they have no constitutional right to provide their children with private school education unfettered by reasonable government regulation. * * * Indeed, the Court in *Pierce* expressly acknowledged "the power of the State reasonably to regulate all schools, to inspect, supervise and examine them, their teachers and pupils."

427 U.S. at 178, 96 S.Ct. at 2598 (citations omitted).
The Supreme Court has spoken clearly on this issue, and we are bound by its decision. Moreover, we agree with the Court's reasoning and its conclusion. We thus decline to extend the right of privacy to this situation.

Laura J. Bach: For God or Grades? States Imposing Fewer Requirements on Religious Home Schoolers and the Religion Clauses of the First Amendment, 38 Val. U.L. Rev. 1337 (2004)*

Picture a neighborhood including three families: the Joneses, the Smiths, and the Does. Mr. and Mrs. Jones and Mr. and Mrs. Smith have all completed high school, but have no additional education. Mr. and Mrs. Doe each have bachelor's degrees. The Jones family is religious and their church encourages home education of children. The other two families are not religious. All three families want to home school their children. In many states, the requirements each family must meet to home school their children are the same. A unique situation arises if their neighborhood is located in Alabama, Virginia, or Wyoming. In these three states, the Joneses would be subject to fewer state home schooling requirements because they are religious.

If located in Alabama, the Joneses could home school as a church school by filing a one-time attendance form, keeping an attendance record, and obtaining sponsorship from their church. In contrast, the Smith and Doe families face fewer choices and greater obstacles in Alabama. The only home education option for the Smiths and the Does in Alabama is under the private tutor statute. Under the private tutor statute, the families would be required to provide instruction 140 days a year including three hours a day between 8:00 a.m. and 4:00 p.m., include specific subjects in their curriculum, file annual notice, and keep records of attendance and academic progress. In addition, the private tutor statute requires teacher certification.

If located in Virginia, the Joneses would be able to home school under the religious exemption statute. The Jones family would merely have to provide one-time notice to the local school board or superintendent claiming the religious exemption, and may wish to include statements from their pastor and friends to vouch for the sincerity of their beliefs. The Smiths and the Does could not use the religious exemption statute and would have to comply with one of the options under the home school statute. The Smith family could not use option one because neither parent has a baccalaureate degree. They could home school under option three, approved correspondence course, or option four, submission of evidence of parent's ability to teach. The Does could also home school under option three or four, but would likely choose option one, requiring a baccalaureate degree. Under any of the options available to them, the Smith and Doe families would have to submit a curriculum description including subjects taught and textbooks used, file annual notice, submit standardized test scores to the local superintendent every other year, and hold classes a minimum of one hundred eighty days a year. However, the Jones family would not be subject to those requirements under the religious exemption.

If located in Wyoming, all three could home school under the state's home school statute. The home school statute requires annual notice that the required subjects are being taught. However, this requirement may be reduced or eliminated for the Jones family. Under the home school statute, the Jones family can exclude from the required subjects any topic or concept not in conformity with their religious beliefs. The Jones family also has the option of home schooling without any state regulation as a church school, if their church or denomination sponsors them.

The modern home schooling movement began in the 1960s from two very different groups. One group came from the "New Left" and turned to home schooling due to dissatisfaction with the restrictions of public education. The other group began home schooling for religious reasons. The number of home schoolers in the United States is difficult to determine, but all estimates indicate a steady growth in the movement. It is estimated there may be as many as 1.7 million children currently being home schooled. When considering the turnover rate, the percentage of children home schooled at some point in their education could be somewhere between six and twelve percent....

Although many home schoolers are religious, religion is just one reason parents choose to home school. Those Christians who educate their children at home for religious reasons generally believe that "parents have a duty to provide [their] child with a godly education." Some religious home schoolers also see public education as destructive to their beliefs. Others believe that education that ignores religion is incomplete and fails to teach children essential moral values.

However, there are many other reasons parents choose to educate their children at home. Some common reasons parents choose to home school include: the belief that their children will receive a better education, poor performance and dangerous environment of public schools, and dissatisfaction with and inability to afford private school. Other parents choose to home school because they have children that are exceptionally bright or children with special learning needs.

The two main criticisms of home schooling are inferiority of education and lack of socialization. The first criticism boils down to concern that home schooled children receive a substandard education since parents are not qualified to educate their children. However, home schoolers consistently score above average on standardized tests. In addition, many home schoolers successfully make the transition to college. Also, if home schooling parents want their children's curriculum to include subjects they are not qualified to teach, they have several options. One option is to join a home school co-op or group offering certain classes by either other home schooling parents or another person qualified to teach the subject. Another option is to use video, online, or correspondence courses. In addition, some public and private schools permit home schoolers to attend school part-time, and at some colleges and universities, home schoolers can earn credit by taking classes while they are still in high school. Another resource for home schoolers may be extended family members willing to teach certain subjects in which they have some expertise.

Those who criticize home schooling because of socialization concerns argue that children who are home schooled will not develop necessary social skills. However, studies of home schoolers do not support this position. The average home schooler participates in 5.2 activities outside the home per week, and ninety-eight percent of home schoolers are involved in at least two activities outside the home a week.

1. State Regulation of Home Schooling

Thirty-six states have home schooling statutes. Thirteen states and the District of Columbia allow home schooling under private tutor, private school, or religious school statutes. Connecticut has no statute, but allows home schooling under the state's Department of Education procedures. States also vary in the amount of regulation imposed on home schooling. While most constitutional challenges to the regulation of home schooling have been unsuccessful, the trend in most states is to impose fewer requirements on home schoolers. In fact two states, Alaska and Idaho, allow home schooling to remain virtually unregulated. Of those states that do regulate, common types of requirements include: notice, curriculum, attendance, standardized testing, record keeping, and parent education. Another type of requirement, teacher certification, is only used in a few states.

Thirty-nine states impose notice requirements on home schoolers. These requirements typically require parents to provide some type of written notification to educational officials of their intent to home school at specified times. Some states require a one-time notice, while others require annual notice. Notice requirements are viewed by courts as minimal and have survived constitutional challenges. However, in one case a notice requirement also requiring local school superintendent approval was struck down as unconstitutionally vague.

Another way some states regulate home schooling is to impose a curriculum requirement. Curriculum requirements generally consist of a broad description of subjects that must be taught. In some states a curriculum requirement simply specifies the subjects that must be taught or requires parents to submit a list of texts that will be used. In other states more detailed descriptions and lesson plans must be submitted.

Thirty-one states and the District of Columbia have attendance requirements. Attendance requirements generally dictate either a specific number of days or hours. However, some states require a period of time substantially equivalent to public schools.

Standardized testing is required in some states and has survived constitutional challenge. Some states require minimum scores on standardized testing, while others merely require they be taken. Some states requiring testing allow alternative methods of evaluating academic progress to be used in place of standardized testing. Some have criticized standardized testing as a poor indicator of academic performance. Also, standardized testing requirements may raise issues of equal protection and due process.

Another type of requirement is record keeping. In some states the requirement is only maintenance, and not submission, of records. In other states, records must be submitted on a regular basis, typically every year. The type of records that must be kept can vary from attendance and standardized testing records to immunization records. However, only twenty-two states and the District of Columbia have imposed record keeping requirements.

Some states have parental education level requirements. In some states the requirement is that the teaching parent have a high school diploma or equivalent ("GED"). Other states require a baccalaureate degree. However, the requirement of a baccalaureate degree is usually one of several options for meeting an instructor qualification requirement, although meeting the requirement with a baccalaureate degree, rather than other options, may exempt the home schooler from other requirements. Although there is an increase in standardized test scores among children home schooled by a parent with a baccalaureate degree, those home schooled by parents without a baccalaureate degree, even those who had not completed high school, still average standardized test scores between the 80th and 90th percentile. In addition, in comparing standardized test scores of students with parents who have not completed high school, home schooled students averaged fifty-five percentile points higher than public school students. Based on standardized testing, lack of parental education appears to have a less significant negative effect on student academic performance for home school students than public school students. Also, the fact that thirty-nine states and the District of Columbia do not impose any parental education requirements may be an indication that many states do not see the requirement as an accurate indicator of parental ability to supervise a home education program.

Teacher certification is also a type of home school requirement. Requiring teacher certification is likely the heaviest burden the state can impose on home schoolers because it disqualifies virtually all parents. Even courts have acknowledged the heavy burden teacher certification requirements place on home schoolers. Teacher certification has not been shown to improve academic performance. In fact, some states do not require teacher certification for public and private school teachers. In addition, some have questioned the effectiveness of teacher certification requirements in promoting the state's interest in educating its citizens. In the few states still using teacher certification as a requirement, it is usually one of several options for parents to meet the state requirements to home school; however, in Alabama, teacher certification is a requirement for all home schoolers who do not qualify as a church school. In Michigan, a teacher certification requirement was found unconstitutional when applied to religious home schoolers, but not unconstitutional when applied to secular home schoolers. However, in Alabama, Iowa, and North Dakota, teacher certification requirements survived Free Exercise challenges.

Although the requirements imposed on home schoolers vary from state to state, in most states the regulation of home schooling is religion-neutral. However, in some states religious home schoolers are not subjected to the same requirements imposed on other home schoolers.

2. States Favoring Religious Home Schoolers

Alabama, Virginia, and Wyoming impose fewer regulations on religious home schoolers. Alabama does not have a home school statute, but permits home schooling under its statutes for church schools and private tutors. Under the private tutor statute, parents who educate their children at home are required to obtain teacher certification. In addition, parents home schooling under the private tutor statute must hold classes a specified number of days between specified hours, include specified subjects in their curriculum, file a statement with the local superintendent, and maintain records of their children's work and attendance. However, under Alabama's church school statute, religious parents may home school by filing a one-time attendance form, keeping an attendance record, and obtaining sponsorship from their church or a similar religious organization.

In Virginia, home schooling is permitted under the state's home school statute. The statute provides four options under which parents may home school their children: (1) if the parent has a baccalaureate degree, (2) if the parent is a certified teacher, (3) if the parent uses an approved correspondence course, or (4) if evidence is submitted of the parent's ability to teach curriculum meeting the state's objectives. In addition, parents are required to hold classes 180 days a year, file annual notice, submit annual standardized test results, and provide a description of the curriculum that will be used. However, Virginia also has a religious exemption statute. Under the religious exemption, parents may home school by providing a one-time notice of intent, and without meeting the requirements other home schoolers must meet.

Wyoming allows home schooling under a home school statute. Under the statute, parents home schooling their children must provide annual notice that specific subjects are included in their curriculum. However, Wyoming statutes create two religion-based exemptions for home schoolers. One exemption allows religious home schools to be considered a church school if they are sponsored or controlled by a church or denomination. If a home school is considered a church school, it is exempt from state regulation and does not have to submit notice of compliance with curriculum requirements. The other religion-based exemption allows those home schooling under the home school statute to exclude from their curriculum any "topic, concept or practice" inconsistent with the home schooler's religious beliefs. Under this curriculum exemption, the home schooler is not exempt from the entire requirement, only those topics that conflict with his or her religious beliefs, and the home schooler is not required to obtain church sponsorship. Like the statutes in Alabama and Virginia, the Wyoming statutes impose fewer requirements on religious home schoolers. These religion-based exemptions may conflict with the First Amendment religion clauses.

....

IV. PROPOSED MODEL HOME SCHOOL STATUTE

Proposed Home-Based Educational Program Statute

Section 1: Parental rights in general

Parents have the natural and fundamental right to guide the upbringing of their children. This right includes the choice of educational program for children in the parent's charge. There shall be a rebuttable presumption that parents act in the best interests of children in their charge when making decisions regarding education. Home-based educational programs are recognized as a legitimate alternative to the compulsory school attendance requirement [insert state code section].

Section 2: Definitions

As used in this statute:

(A) "Home-based educational program" is defined as a program of education primarily conducted by parents for the children in their charge.

(B) "Parent" is defined for the purpose of this statute as a parent or legal guardian of a child subject to the compulsory school attendance requirements of [insert state code section].

Section 3: Requirements

(A) Notice:

A parent providing a home-based educational program must submit a one-time notice of intent to his or her local school superintendent. Notice must also be submitted to the local school superintendent if a home-based educational program is discontinued and the student is still subject to the compulsory education requirements of [insert state code section].

(B) Curriculum:

A home-based educational program must provide a basic academic program. A basic academic program may, but is not required to, include instruction in science, mathematics, history, government, writing, reading, grammar, health, geography, and physical education.

(C) Attendance:

Students in a home-based educational program shall be required to complete a period of instruction substantially equivalent in duration to that of public school students of the same age or grade level.

(D) Disqualification for residence of a registered sex offender:

A home-based educational program may not be operated in the residence of a person required to register as a sex offender under [insert state code section].

Aaron T. Martin: Homeschooling in Germany and the United States,
27 Ariz. J. Int'l & Comp. Law 225 (2010)*

On March 30, 2009, the Georgia House of Representatives took an unprecedented move and passed a resolution exhorting the German government to legalize homeschooling. The Tennessee Legislature followed suit two months later on May 26, 2009.

Georgia and Tennessee took such an unprecedented stand because currently, homeschooling is illegal in Germany. German students must attend school beginning at six years old and continue for at least nine years. This compulsory schooling involves regular attendance of lessons and other compulsory school events. In the mind of state legislators in the United States, the German system prioritizing state control over individual liberty is an infringement on the most basic liberties of German citizens. ... [T]his note argues that any infringement on parental rights to homeschool is inconsistent with the principles of a robust liberal political democracy. The note concludes by acknowledging the current problems in educational policy as well as future threats to homeschooling in the United States and Germany.

......

B. A Brief History of Homeschooling in Germany

The homeschooling "movement" began at the turn of the 20th century when Berthold Otto, a private tutor and educational leader, started the movement by educating his own children at home. After some time, other families brought their children to Otto's home to be educated. As a result, a "homeschool" developed that addressed individual students' needs. Prior to 1920, Germany allowed homeschooling as a valid exception to compulsory attendance requirements in certain instances. The Constitution of the Weimar Republic *(Reichsgrundschulgesetz)* (1919-33) required obligatory school attendance as an effort to create an "equality of opportunities" among members of different social classes in Germany. ...By 1938, Nazi law was in effect and specifically outlawed homeschooling under *Reichsschulpflichtgesetz,* the first general regulation in the German Reich without exceptions and with criminal consequences in case of contraventions." ...

Not until the 1980s, however, did German parents make the first real attempts to homeschool. In one case, Helmut Stucher, an accountant, removed his children from the public school because he thought that the curriculum was "incompatible with his Christian belief and moral values." This action led Stucher through several years of legal disputes with fines, loss of child custody and a five-day prison sentence. In 1989, Stucher was given back "full child custody" after nine years of trying to homeschool. In another case, a couple, teachers by training, did not send their son to school because he did not want to attend the local public school. The couple faced "several fines and penalty payment" for keeping their son out of school and when they challenged the constitutionality of the State's action, their complaint was dismissed. This family, as others have done, moved to Austria, where homeschooling is legal.

.....

B. The Current State of Homeschooling in America

Homeschooled students in the United States today number about 2 million. As homeschooling enters the 21st century, parents' motivations for homeschooling are varied: over 70% of homeschooling parents cite a non-religious reason for choosing to homeschool. Increasing numbers of professionals and highly educated parents are choosing homeschooling over traditional schools. Many parents cite failing public schools-or a failed educational method in general-for why they homeschool. In one candid interview, a public school administrator admitted that the school "had to teach to the 40th percentile" while researchers note that "public schools have suffered at least since the mid-seventies from watered-down assignments and exams, politically correct textbooks, incompetent or lazy teachers who can't be fired because of union protection, and trendy educational fads like 'New Math' that have pushed aside the three Rs."

The swell of parental involvement in grassroots advocacy movements brought homeschooling into mainstream society. It is now a big business, and supporters have developed a broad and powerful lobby in Congress and all fifty states. This movement led state legislatures to enact laws allowing homeschooling in some form.

.....

IV. PART THREE: PUBLIC POLICY, PARENTAL RIGHTS, AND THE FUTURE OF HOMESCHOOLING

The normative question of what rights parents should exercise over their children and how that question should influence discussions about education and homeschooling baffles scholars, courts, and legislatures today in Germany and the United States alike. Although the United States has a far more developed body of law on the subject, the future of homeschooling is as uncertain in the

United States as it is in Germany. Courts and legislators in both countries are hesitant to draw clear and distinct lines demarcating where parental rights end and state interests begin. Scholars writing about homeschooling in the United States ... agree [that] as long as government regulation of homeschooling is "reasonable," that regulation should withstand challenges from parents seeking to circumvent those regulations.

.....

B. Emerging Public Policy on Homeschooling

The family is widely regarded "as a training ground for democratic values, where children first learn lessons of cooperation, sacrifice and submission to legitimate authority." Further, as part of its fundamental mission, the family serves as the filter through which children experience the world and society. In this capacity, the most critical function of the family is the transmission of fundamental moral, religious and cultural values between the generations. In free societies like the United States and Germany, however, some argue that democratic government itself has the task of forming its citizens, including forming the moral and social dimensions of each person. Such formation in democracy, it is thought, is essential to the preservation of individual liberty. Thus, many will not respect the rights of families unless there is some showing that the asserted liberty interest of parental rights over the education of children]must be critical, or central, to the preservation of liberty. Prior to the twentieth century, there was general worldwide consensus that the family played a pivotal role in educating children and educating them *for* citizenship and participation in a civil society. Families that were able to maintain their own set of core values contributed to pluralism in society, adding to the diverse set of viewpoints that sustains a healthy democracy. But when these parental rights confronted state-run public education systems, the clash between the two interests required policy makers to create a hierarchical structure in which they situated these values

The United Nations' Special Rapporteur's recommendations to Germany focus on such parental rights and on individualized education.[22] The State, because it recognizes a basic human right to education, needs to settle issues plaguing the German educational system. One such issue is the seemingly tense relation between the state and federal governments. The [Special Rapporteur's recommendations state that the] clash between state and federal educational interests "has often led to policy debates, while the need for national coordination resulted in the creation of various federal level bodies." ... [T]he Special Rapporteur suggests

> that the educational system should be structured in such a way as to render it more permeable-in other words, more responsive to the needs and rights of the pupils, bearing in mind that children develop in different ways and come from different cultural backgrounds and, most important, that any educational system should proceed from the principle of diversity as the cornerstone of its operation.

---

[22] See, Vernor Munoz, Special Rapporteur on the Right to Education, Implementation of General Assembly Resolution 60/251 of 15 March 2006 Entitled "Human Rights Council," P 8, delivered to the General Assembly, U.N. Soc. A/HRC/4/29/Add.3 (Mar. 9, 2008).

This individualized approach to education is at the heart of homeschooling.

And to ensure these individualized approaches, the Special Rapporteur suggests more active parental involvement in the educational decisions over their children: "[m]others and fathers, together with the pupils themselves, should have a real possibility to participate in the adoption of decisions relating to classification and other essential aspects of the educational system. This possibility should be established in law." This suggestion sounds largely like an endorsement of homeschooling, or at least a support for stronger parental rights over the education of children. And if it were not clear enough, the Special Rapporteur ends this part of his discussion by saying:

> According to reports received, it is possible that, in some Lander, *education is understood exclusively to mean school attendance.* Even though the Special Rapporteur is a strong advocate of public, free and compulsory education, it should be noted that *education may not be reduced to mere school attendance* and that educational processes should be strengthened to ensure that they always and primarily serve the best interests of the child. Distance learning methods and *home schooling* represent valid options which could be developed in certain circumstances, bearing in mind that *parents have the right to choose the appropriate type of education for their children,* as stipulated in article 13 of the International Covenant on Economic, Social and Cultural Rights. The promotion and development of a system of public, government-funded education *should not entail the suppression of forms of education that do not require attendance at a school.* In this context, the Special Rapporteur received complaints about threats to withdraw the parental rights of parents who chose home-schooling methods for their children.

These same suggestions are distilled in the Rapporteur's final set of recommendations: "[N]ecessary measures should be adopted to ensure that the home schooling system is properly supervised by the State, thereby upholding the right of parents to employ this form of education when necessary and appropriate, bearing in mind the best interests of the child." Although the Special Rapporteur is clear in his suggestions to German officials, it is still very uncertain whether Germany will move to tolerate, much less embrace, homeschooling.

B. Charter Schools

UTAH SCHOOL BOARDS ASSOCIATION v. UTAH STATE BOARD OF EDUCATION

17 P.3d 1125 (Utah 2001)

[This Case appears in Chapter One on Page 37]

CATAPULT LEARNING, L.L.C. v. BOARD OF EDUCATION

2008 U.S. Dist. LEXIS 10306 (E.D. Mo. Feb. 12, 2008)

JUDGES: Donald J. Stohr, UNITED STATES DISTRICT JUDGE.

On November 12, 2007, plaintiff filed a second amended complaint against defendant Board of Education of the City of St. Louis, defendant Special Administrative Board for the Transitional School District of the City of St. Louis, and Charter. Plaintiff alleges that it is owed $220,014.00 for educational services provided to Charter during the 2005-06 school year. Plaintiff's second amended complaint asserts two counts against Charter. Count I asserts a claim of breach of contract, and Count II asserts a claim of unjust enrichment. On November 29, 2007, Charter filed its second motion to dismiss Count II of plaintiff's complaint, arguing that Charter should be regarded as a school district or municipal corporation and, under Missouri law, cannot be sued for unjust enrichment.

For purposes of these motions, the Court finds the following facts. Charter is a "charter school" located in St. Louis, Missouri. Pursuant to a written contract, Education Station, LLC provided supplemental educational services to Charter students during the 2005-06 school year, and was to receive $220,014.00 for such services. Plaintiff is a successor in interest to Education Station with respect to Education Station's right to receive and collect payments for the supplemental educational services that Education Station provided at Charter during the 2005-06 school year.

Plaintiff alleges that it is the successor of an entity that had an express contract with Charter, that services were provided to Charter pursuant to the contract, and that Charter has failed to pay for those services. However, in its motion to dismiss, Charter argues that under Missouri law plaintiff cannot maintain a claim of unjust enrichment against Charter, and that the Court should dismiss Count II of plaintiff's second amended complaint.

Missouri law controls this diversity case. Under Missouri law:

> No county, city, town, village, school township, school district or other municipal corporation shall make any contract, unless the same... including the consideration, shall be in writing...and shall be subscribed by the parties thereto.... Mo. Rev. Stat. § 432.070.

The purpose of this statute "is to protect the governmental entity upon which another seeks to impose or enforce some claimed contractual obligation or agreement... [and] is not for the protection of the person seeking to impose the contractual agreement upon the governmental entity." *Pub. Water Supply Dist. No. 16 v. City of Buckner*, 44 S.W.3d 860, 864 (Mo. App. 2001). Specific to the case at hand, the statute has been interpreted by Missouri courts "to preclude recovery against a school district on any theory of implied contract." *Mays-Maune & Assocs. v. Werner Bros., Inc.*, 139 S.W.3d 201, 208 (Mo. App. 2004).... Accordingly, the Court must determine whether Charter, a "charter school," is a "county, city, town, village, school township, school district or other municipal corporation" as contemplated by Mo. Rev. Stat. § 432.070.

In general, a charter school is a school that "is a cross between a public and a private school." James E. Ryan and Michael Heise, *The Political Economy of School Choice*, 111 Yale L.J. 2043, 2073 (2002). Typically, such schools are "publicly funded, tuition-free, nonsectarian... [and] operate pursuant to a contract between the school and the chartering agency...." *Id.* In a recent Missouri Court of Appeals decision, the court described Missouri charter schools as follows:

> Charter schools, which [can] operate without traditional bureaucratic and legal constraints and [can], perhaps, make more innovative and responsive curriculum changes, [are] seen as a possible benefit and a possible middle ground to traditional public schools and purely private schools. *State ex rel. Sch. Dist. of Kansas City*, 141 S.W.3d 418, 422, 424 (Mo. App. 2004).

Charter schools are authorized by the Missouri Charter Schools Act ("MCSA"), Mo. Rev. Stat. § 160.400 *et seq.* Pursuant to the MCSA, a charter school is "an independent public school," and "may be sponsored by...[t]he school board of the district" in which the charter school is operated. Mo. Rev. Stat. § 160.400 (1), (2). Missouri case law dictates that the MCSA "must be *narrowly* construed." *State ex rel. Sch. Dist. of Kansas City*, 141 S.W.3d at 425 (emphasis added).

Under the MCSA, a charter school "shall be a Missouri *nonprofit corporation....*" Mo. Rev. Stat. § 160.400 (5) (emphasis added). Nevertheless, the MCSA further states that "[a]ny entity, either public or private, operating, administering, or otherwise managing a charter school shall be considered a *quasi-public governmental body*" subject to the provisions of Missouri's open meetings laws, and that "members of the governing board of the charter school shall be considered decision-making public servants...for the purposes of [] financial disclosure requirements...." Mo. Rev. Stat. § 160.405 (12); Mo. Rev. Stat. § 160.400 (12) (emphasis added). Further, the MCSA provides that charter schools "shall... [e]xcept as provided in [the MCSA], be exempt from all laws and rules relating to schools, governing boards and school districts." Mo. Rev. Stat. § 160.405 (5).

Charter argues that, because charter schools are subject to Missouri's open meeting laws, and because members of the boards of charter schools are considered public servants for limited purposes, charter schools fall within the ambit of Mo. Rev. Stat. § 432.070. The Court disagrees. By statute, charter schools are entities that are exempt from *all* laws and rules relating to schools, governing boards, and school districts—*except those provided for in the MCSA*. While the MCSA explicitly contemplates subjecting charter schools to Missouri's open meeting laws and certain board members to the disclosure requirements of a public servant, the MCSA does not contemplate charter schools having the burden of complying with, or receiving the benefit of, Mo. Rev. Stat. § 432.070. Narrowly construing the MCSA, the Court finds that Mo. Rev. Stat. § 432.070 does not apply to Charter in this case, and plaintiff may maintain an unjust enrichment claim against Charter.

RACINE CHARTER ONE, INC. v. RACINE UNIFIED SCHOOL DISTRICT

424 F.3d 677 (7th Cir. 2005)

WILLIAMS, Circuit Judge.

Wisconsin law provides for two kinds of charter schools: those sponsored by local school districts, Wis. Stat. § 118.40, and those sponsored by other entities explicitly authorized by the state legislature, Wis. Stat. § 118.40(2r) (hereinafter, "(2r) charter schools"). Charter One falls within the latter category, established by the University of Wisconsin-Parkside pursuant to authority granted on a pilot basis by Wisconsin Statute § 118.40(2r)(b)(1)(c). The plaintiff school is located in Racine County, Wisconsin, and falls within the geographical boundaries of the RUSD.

The charter school, which is open and free to all who seek to enroll, is the only (2r) charter school located within the RUSD. The school operates independently from the defendant, as the district does not govern or exert any control whatsoever over the (2r) charter school. Charter One currently teaches grades K-6, and enrolls approximately 305 students. Its school year is longer than the ordinary RUSD public school year, and even includes a mandatory three-week summer session. Its students reside throughout Racine County.

In addition to providing for the establishment of charter schools, Wisconsin law also obliges local school districts to provide transportation to certain students residing within their districts. Wisconsin Statute § 121.54 requires each local school district to transport public, private, and parochial school students who (1) reside within the district; (2) attend a school within the geographical boundaries of that district; (3) attend a school within their designated attendance area; and (4) (a) reside two miles or more from that school or (b) would otherwise encounter unusual hazards in walking to and from that school. Wis. Stat. §§ 121.54(2)(a), 121.54(2)(b), & 121.54(9). RUSD's written transportation policy closely tracks the requirements of Section 121.54, with one exception. In contrast to the state-required minimum radius of two miles, the RUSD policy provides transportation for all otherwise qualifying K-5 students who live only one and one-half miles or more from their respective schools. Thus, at least in this one respect, RUSD has extended the busing benefit to more students than Wisconsin state law would require.

Before opening in September 2002, Charter One requested that RUSD bus its students. In response to this request, RUSD sought legal advice from various sources—including its own counsel and Chief Legal Counsel to the Wisconsin Department of Public Instruction (DPI)—as to whether the district was legally obliged to provide transportation to Charter One. All agreed that Wisconsin Statute § 121.54 did not require public school districts to transport students of independent charter schools established pursuant to Wisconsin Statute § 118.40(2r). The DPI further concluded that such an interpretation of the statute did not violate the Equal Protection Clause of the Fourteenth Amendment to the United States Constitution. Based on this understanding of Wisconsin law, the RUSD school board, by a vote of 5-4, denied Charter One's request for transportation service in February 2003.

In May 2003, Charter One brought this action against RUSD, asserting that its refusal to bus Charter One students violated the Equal Protection Clause of the Fourteenth Amendment and 42 U.S.C. §

1983. The district court granted RUSD's motion for summary judgment, finding that Charter One students were not "similarly situated" to those students who did receive the RUSD busing benefit, and that RUSD had a rational basis for its decision not to bus Charter One students—namely, avoiding the "unique and additional costs" that such busing would present. Charter One appeals.

....

Here, the district court properly construed Charter One's complaint as alleging a class of one equal protection claim. ("Whether the complaint alleges a class of one or of [more] is of no consequence because we conclude that the number of individuals in a class is immaterial for equal protection analysis."). Charter One argues that local government officials within the RUSD denied the school and its students the benefit of busing otherwise provided to all others similarly situated without a rational basis for distinction. Accordingly, we review the merits of Charter One's claim under the *Olech* standard, examining first whether the plaintiff's students are indeed similarly situated to those students within the RUSD who do receive busing.

A. Charter One Students Are Not Similarly Situated

To be considered "similarly situated," comparators must be "prima facie identical in all relevant respects," *Purze v. Vill. of Winthrop Harbor*, 286 F.3d 452, 455-56 (7th Cir. 2004), or "directly comparable to [plaintiff] in all material respects," *Ajayi v. Aramark Bus Servs., Inc.*, 336 F.3d 520, 532 (7th Cir. 2003). Here, the pertinent comparison must be made between those students within the RUSD who receive busing, and those Charter One students who do not. More accurately, the comparison pits RUSD public and private school students who reside within the RUSD, who live one and one-half miles or more from their school or encounter hazardous conditions along the school route, and who do receive busing, against Charter One students who reside within the RUSD, who live one and one-half miles or more from their school or encounter hazardous conditions along the school route, and who do not receive busing.

But there is some controversy as to whether the comparison should end there. Charter One thinks so, contending that we should look only to—and see patent similarities in—both class' residence and attendance within the district, and their distance from school or their proximity to hazardous conditions along the way. Indeed, if this were all to our comparison, the students of both classes would clearly be similarly situated, as the James family illustrates. Two of the James children attend Charter One, and one attends an RUSD public school. All live in the same house and face the same hazardous condition in getting to school (there is no sidewalk on their road). But while the RUSD student gets free busing, the Charter One students do not.

****

We begin by noting that the Wisconsin laws defining public schools and public school districts were passed well before the legal conception of charter schools. For that reason, much of the operative law on which our analysis must focus fails to account for these charter schools, or, more importantly, the Unified School Districts' obligations with respect to them. Thus, as we broach this uncertain area of Wisconsin law, we must make clear that our opinion extends only to the narrow issue before us: whether RUSD's decision not to bus (2r) charter school students violates equal protection.

Wisconsin Statute § 121.54(2) requires school districts like RUSD to transport "public" school students. That Charter One is a public school, no one contests. But while Charter One contends that its public status entitles it to Section 121.54 busing at RUSD's expense, RUSD insists that the statute's reach does not extend so far. While it is true that Section 121.54 does require RUSD to transport public school students, it does not mandate the transportation of all such students. Rather, it obliges the district to transport only those public school students who reside within its geographical boundaries. Certainly, no party would argue that Section 121.54 requires the RUSD to bus the residents of other school districts to public schools located in other districts. Wis. Stat. § 121.54(10) ("[A] school board may not provide transportation under this subsection for a nonresident pupil to or from a location within the boundaries of the school district in which the pupil resides."). Nor, with irrelevant exceptions, would the district be required to bus the residents of other school districts who attend RUSD public schools. Furthermore, and again with exceptions not pertinent here, the RUSD would not be required to bus its own residents to schools located in other school districts.

With these limitations in mind, RUSD contends that Charter One is the functional equivalent of an independent school district, and as such responsible for its own busing. By RUSD's measure, while Charter One is a public school, its students would be no more entitled to RUSD-funded busing than students attending adjacent school districts such as Kenosha Unified School District, Oak Creek School District, or Raymond School District. While Charter One would at first blush appear to fall within the geographical boundaries of the RUSD, it is, according to the defendant, in fact its own administrative island—an independent school district surrounded on all sides, though not subsumed, by the RUSD.

Charter One is a unique statutory creation. Unlike other public schools within the RUSD (or private and parochial schools for that matter), Charter One came to being through a charter granted by the University of Wisconsin-Parkside. The University was specifically vested with the authority to do so by the Wisconsin state legislature pursuant to Wisconsin Statute § 118.40(2r)(b). Charter One has its own board, its own faculty, and its own staff. As an administrative matter, the school operates wholly independent of RUSD. RUSD governs neither the charter school nor its board. Indeed, the district may not exert any control whatsoever over Charter One, and Charter One cannot exert any control over the district. The two entities simply enjoy no legal relationship.

This autonomy in administration goes a long way to suggest that Charter One is not just an independent public school, but also an independent public school district. Wisconsin law defines "school district" as "the territorial unit for school administration." Wis. Stat. § 115.01(3). And while this provision does not explicitly include the word "charter," it does not exclude the term from its definition either. To the contrary, Charter One's independence and sole responsibility for its own administration would suggest that the otherwise unmentioned entity falls squarely within Section 115.01(3)'s definition.

Charter One's administrative autonomy—particularly with reference to busing obligations—is further demonstrated by its own charter. Section 4.8 of the Charter School Contract Between the Board of Regents of the University of Wisconsin System and Charter One, entitled "Transportation Contracts," vests Charter One with the authority to "enter into contracts with *other school districts* or persons, including municipal and county governments, for the transportation of Charter School students *to and from school* and for field trips." (emphasis added). This language, along with signaling the charter school's administrative autonomy, also suggests that contracting for—as opposed to stark entitlement to—busing from school districts was contemplated from the outset. Charter One, however, insists that its ability to contract for transportation services does not set it apart from other schools within the RUSD. First, it notes that RUSD itself possesses such authority. But such a comparison is self-defeating, as Charter One's effort here to liken itself to an independent school district only reinforces the view that the school is an autonomous district as well.

In addition, we think it worthy to note, though not dispositive to our analysis of the current state of Wisconsin law, that the Wisconsin legislature has twice attempted—and failed pursuant to gubernatorial veto—to pass legislation that would provide charter schools like Charter One the busing to which the plaintiff here claims a present entitlement. A.B. 261, Assem., 2003 Reg. Sess. (Wis. 2003); S.B. 44, Senate, 2003 Reg. Sess. (Wis. 2003). These attempts suggest that even the body entrusted with providing the busing benefit does not believe that it has yet been conferred to charter schools.

Accordingly, we affirm the district court's finding that Charter One has failed to show that its students are similarly situated to those students who do receive the busing benefit.

B. RUSD Has A Rational Basis for its Decision to Deny the Busing Benefit

But even assuming that Charter One's students are similarly situated to other students within the RUSD, the school's challenge fails nonetheless in light of the plaintiffs' failure to meet the class of one claim's second prong.

The exact contours of the second prong of the class of one equal protection claim are not quite clear. As we noted above, the Supreme Court in *Olech* held that it has "recognized successful equal protection claims brought by a 'class of one,' where the plaintiff alleges that she has been intentionally treated differently from others similarly situated and that there is no rational basis *for the difference in treatment*." 528 U.S. at 564 (emphasis added). However, since *Olech* was decided, the standard for such class of one claims has been muddled in this circuit by two divergent lines of cases. *Tuffendsam v. Dearborn County Bd. of Health*, 385 F.3d 1124, 1127 (7th Cir. 2004) (recognizing divergent lines); *Indiana Land Co. v. City of Greenwood*, 378 F.3d 705, 713 (7th Cir. 2001) (same). In one line of cases, panels of this court have held that a class of one equal protection claim is established where the defendant has intentionally treated the plaintiff differently than others similarly situated either without any rational basis for doing so or out of some "totally illegitimate animus." *See Lunini v. Grayeb*, 395 F.3d 761, 768 (7th Cir. 2005); *Levenstein v. Salafsky*, 414 F.3d 767, 775-76 (7th Cir. 2005); *McDonald v. Vill. of Winnetka*, 371 F.3d 992, 1001

(7th Cir. 2004) (citing *inter alia, Olech*, 528 U.S. at 564); *Nevel v. Vill. of Schaumburg*, 297 F.3d 673, 681 (7th Cir. 2002); *Albiero v. City of Kankakee*, 246 F.3d 927, 932 (7th Cir. 2001). In another line, however, we have held that the mere absence of a rational basis is not enough to sustain the class of one claim, and that instead the plaintiff must prove illegitimate animus in order to succeed. *See Hilton v. City of Wheeling*, 209 F.3d 1005, 1008 (7th Cir. 2000); *see also Crowley v. McKinney*, 400 F.3d 965, 972 (7th Cir. 2005); *Purze v. Vill. of Winthrop Harbor*, 286 F.3d 452, 455 (7th Cir. 2002); *Cruz v. Town of Cicero*, 275 F.3d 579, 587 (7th Cir. 2001); *Bartell v. Aurora Public Schools*, 263 F.3d 1143, 1149 (10th Cir. 2001); *Bell v. Duperrault*, 367 F.3d 703, 709-13 (7th Cir. 2004) (Posner, J., concurring).

....

Indeed, it appears our court may have created a "tension" with *Olech* and established national law where previously none existed. *Indiana Land Co.*, 378 F.3d at 714 (Ripple, J., concurring). True, sound reasons have been advanced for grafting the animus requirement onto the class of one claim—without such a requirement, "breathtaking vistas of liability" might be opened, *Tuffendsam*, 385 F.3d at 1127, and ordinary state law disputes might become the subject of constitutional challenge, Bell, 367 F.3d at 712 (Posner, J., concurring). That said, the appearance of the animus requirement on the class of one stage is no less jarring. However, we need not decide under which standard the class of one plaintiff must proceed, as here Charter One fails under both. Because the plaintiff has failed to allege, let alone show, any subjective ill will on the part of the RUSD in denying the busing benefit, Charter One's class of one claim would clearly fail under the animus standard.

Under the rational basis test, the court "will uphold the legislative enactment (or classification) so long as it bears a rational relation to some legitimate end." *Eby-Brown Co., LLC v. Wis. Dep't of Agric., Trade & Consumer Prot.*, 295 F.3d 749, 754 (7th Cir. 2002). A court will not strike down a state policy merely because it "may be unwise, improvident, or out of harmony with a particular school of thought." *Id.* Rather, this inquiry requires the court to "consider only whether any state of facts reasonably may be conceived to justify the classification," *Rabbi Abraham Grossbaum and Lubavitch of Indiana, Inc. v. Indianapolis-Marion County Bldg. Auth.*, 100 F.3d 1287, 1292 (7th Cir. 1996), and it is enough that "a purpose may conceivably or may reasonably have been the purpose and policy of the relevant governmental decisionmaker," even if the decisionmaker never articulated that rationale, *Nordlinger v. Hahn*, 505 U.S. 1, 15 (1992). Here, the unique and independent nature of Charter One not only suggests that the school's students are not similarly situated to those who do receive RUSD busing, but also provides a rational basis for denying the benefit to those students.

Again, the unique and autonomous nature of Charter One—a seeming functional equivalent of an independent school district—provides one such rational basis for RUSD's decision not to bus the charter school's students. According to RUSD, its goal is to provide busing only to those students whom it is required to transport by law—namely, students of its own schools and resident students of private and parochial schools located within the district. Were we to view Charter One as its own school district, RUSD would be no more required to transport the charter school's students than it would be required to transport resident students who attend adjacent school districts. Indeed, as Charter One concedes, RUSD's policy is consistent with that of school districts throughout

Wisconsin, which uniformly exclude independent charter schools from their busing schemes. And the mere fact that Charter One is the only independent charter school within the geographic boundaries of the RUSD does not render its exclusion discriminatory. Based on the administrative autonomy afforded (2r) charter schools under Wisconsin law, it seems that they do exist beyond the pale of local school district transport obligations—an independence that would serve as a rational basis to deny such schools Section 121.54 busing.

But we need not find that Wisconsin charter schools established under Wisconsin Statute § 118.40(2r) in general, or Charter One in particular, constitute independent schools districts of their own right in order to reveal the deficiency in the plaintiff's class of one equal protection claim here. Rather, we need only recognize the unique and additional costs that RUSD would incur were it to provide such service to Charter One.

As RUSD expressed at oral argument, "Cost is the issue; cost is everything here." This Court has already recognized cost as a rational basis for differential treatment. *Irizarry v. Bd. of Educ. of City of Chicago*, 251 F.3d 604, 610 (7th Cir. 2001); *see also Bankers Life & Casualty Co. v. Crenshaw*, 486 U.S. 71, 83-84. The record does not provide a hard number on exactly how much more it would cost RUSD to bus Charter One students. It does afford an estimate of how much it would cost to implement from scratch an independent busing scheme devoted solely to Charter One students—$124,000 per year for 257 students—a quote Charter One obtained from a bus company as a result of its own research into potential transportation costs. But this figure is in all likelihood overinflated. For one, the estimate assumed that nearly the entire Charter One student body at the time would require busing—an unlikely assumption (though we do note that the size of the student body has since expanded to over 300, and is designed to reach at least 400 in the future). Furthermore, the extension of the RUSD busing benefit to Charter One students would not require the wholesale implementation of new busing schedules and routes, but rather could be accomplished, at least in part, by taking advantage of the busing scheme already in place.

.....

But the defendant's financial straits need not be dire for us to find its refusal to extend transportation services to Charter One rational. We need only recognize that extending the busing benefit will come at a significant enough expense to RUSD, and that is rational basis enough to justify its transportation policy decision. For now, it suffices to say that Charter One is not entitled to a free ride.

III. CONCLUSION

For the reasons stated above, we AFFIRM the district court's grant of summary judgment in the defendant's favor.

CUDAHY, Circuit Judge, concurring in part and concurring in the judgment.

While I concur in the affirmance of the district court, I would follow a different course of reasoning. Specifically, although I agree that Charter One, as a unique statutory creation with distinct sources of funding, is not similarly situated to other schools located in the RUSD (and thus may be subject to disparate treatment), I believe that the children of the two individual plaintiffs, who are Charter One students, are similarly situated to at least some of the students furnished busing by the RUSD. Accordingly, RUSD's refusal to bus Charter One students based solely on their school affiliation seems irrational.

Purely as a matter of logic, the RUSD policy does not hold up. Of course, as a general matter it is rational to base government policies on considerations of cost. [But] since there is no indication in the record that Charter One students are somehow inherently more costly to transport per mile than other students that RUSD has chosen to bus, a per se policy excluding them on cost grounds is not rational.

RUSD (and the district court) point out that Charter One students have a longer school year than students at other public schools and a mandatory summer session, both of which, it is claimed, will make Charter One students uniquely costly to transport on an annual basis. Yet it is undisputed that RUSD already buses students of at least one year-round elementary school (James Elementary School) and provides busing for RUSD summer school students. (App. D. at 44.) Thus cost considerations related to the length of the Charter One school year do not explain why RUSD refuses to bus Charter One students but is willing to transport these other year-round students.

Yet the claims of the student plaintiffs still must fail for one simple reason: they have not alleged or introduced evidence suggesting that RUSD acted out of hostility or illegitimate animus toward them.

Contrary to the majority's framing of the class of one inquiry, we have held quite recently that "'to make out a prima facie case [of a 'class of one' denial of equal protection] the plaintiff must present evidence that the defendant deliberately sought to deprive him of the equal protection of the laws for reasons of a personal nature unrelated to the duties of the defendant's position.'" That is, the plaintiffs must demonstrate that the defendant's actions were not merely arbitrary and irrational, but motivated by "animosity" or "personal hostility"—a desire to make the plaintiff worse off than others similarly situated. *Crowley v. McKinney*, 400 F.3d 965, 972 (7th Cir. 2005).

Yet at least two of the cases upholding an animus requirement actually post-date authorities relied upon by the majority, comprising some of this Court's most recent pronouncements on the issue. Additionally, while the Supreme Court's cursory treatment of the class of one theory in *Village of Willowbrook v. Olech*, 528 U.S. 562, 564-65 (2000), does not reach this animus requirement, the Court also does not disavow it, and over the last year we have concluded that some level of animus is implied in the requirement that any adverse treatment be "intentional": "We don't think the Supreme Court in *Olech* intended to overrule *Personnel Administrator of Massachusetts v. Feeney*, 442 U.S. 256 (1979), which holds that an official 'intends' a consequence when he acts because rather than in spite of it." *Tuffendsam*, 385 F.3d at 1127.

More fundamentally, as long as the cases recognizing the animus requirement have not been overruled or otherwise authoritatively rejected, I think it preferable in cases like this to rely on a lack of animus rather than, with all respect, to have recourse to rather tortured analyses of irrationality. The present case is an excellent example of the need for a sensible limiting principle less elusive than the sometimes will-of-the-wisp of irrationality.

This animus requirement was introduced out of concern that, in its broader formulations, the class of one theory opens up "breathtaking vistas of liability," *Tuffendsam*, 385 F.3d at 1127, and threatens to transform ordinary state law disputes—or even previously unreviewable acts of police discretion—into fodder for constitutional lawsuits. *See Bell v. Duperrault*, 367 F.3d 703, 712 (7th Cir. 2004) (Posner, J., concurring) (noting that since "irrational differences in treatment having nothing to do with discrimination against a vulnerable class abound at the bottom rung of law enforcement . . . . the federal courts will be swamped with 'class of one' cases remote from the purpose, and beyond the feasible scope, of the equal protection clause"); *Olech*, 528 U.S. 562, 566 (2000) (Breyer, J., concurring) (registering "concern about transforming run-of-the-mill zoning cases into cases of constitutional right"); *Hilton*, 209 F.3d at 1008 (rejecting the "no rational basis" approach because "if a merely unexplained difference in police treatment of similar complaints made by different people established a prima facie case of denial of equal protection of the laws, the federal courts would be drawn deep into the local enforcement of petty state and local laws").

Indeed in the case before us one can certainly glimpse the enormous new areas of potential liability opened up by the "class of one" theory, as well as the corresponding need for a limiting animus requirement. If elementary school students may resort to a federal constitutional lawsuit to challenge any irrational misallocation of school district resources—even ones that implicate no fundamental right and involve no suspect classification—what else might be covered by the Equal Protection Clause? Absent some restriction on the doctrine, Judge Posner's nightmare scenario, outlined in *Bell v. Duperrault*, 367 F.3d at 709-10, of citizens bringing constitutional challenges against the uneven issuance of speeding tickets may not be hyperbole after all. Certainly RUSD's policy here, as applied to the individual plaintiffs, is no more arbitrary or irrational than the decision of a traffic cop to ticket one particular speeding car while refusing to ticket other cars traveling at similar speeds.

Robert J. Martin: Charting the Court: Challenges to Charter Schools,
109 Penn St. L. Rev. 43 (2004)*

One of the most controversial developments in public education during the past decade has been the establishment of charter schools. By their establishment, charter schools provide families an opportunity to choose an education for their children in public schools that are individually chartered and separated from the local public school system. This type of choice is especially geared for families who believe that the traditional public schools are not well suited for their children but who lack the means to afford private schools or the ability to relocate to more highly regarded school districts. If families are dissatisfied with the assignment of their children within

---

the traditional public schools of their local school district, they may seek placement of their children in available public charter schools, space permitting.

Because the establishment of charter schools constitutes an implicit criticism of and challenge to the existing public school system, however, charter school proponents have often encountered fierce resistance from organized groups associated with traditional public schools.

....

In so doing, adversaries have raised a wide variety of legal claims. Such claims have included state constitutional challenges based on requirements to provide a thorough and efficient education; state statutory challenges based on eligibility qualifications for the issuance of charters and the criteria of funding formula for distribution of state aid; federal constitutional challenges based on the First Amendment and the Equal Protection Clause of the Fourteenth Amendment; and federal statutory challenges based on Title VI of the Individuals with Disabilities in Education Act. Moreover, the adversaries' proposed remedies for alleged violations have included orders declaring that state charter school programs be abolished on grounds that their enabling acts are unconstitutional, that funding for charter schools be terminated because the methods for obtaining revenue are impermissible, and that individual charter schools be suspended or closed for failure to comply with mandatory statutes.

....

Unfortunately, policymakers have sometimes failed to appreciate the ramifications of their charter school enabling acts, especially the ways in which they may conflict with goals mandated by state constitutions Thus the charting of legal challenges to charter schools in the state and federal courts, as presented here, may provide a general roadmap to policymakers as well as school officials to help guide them through relatively unexplored legal terrain so that they may be more fully cognizant of potential pitfalls.

....

My review and analysis of the of challenges to charter schools in state courts during the first decade of their existence demonstrates that such challenges have not proven to be a significant impediment to the growth of the charter school movement. None of the state court decisions - including five state supreme court decisions - held that their respective states' charter school enabling acts was unconstitutional. The courts held that such acts provided reasonable safeguards, including sufficient public accountability, appropriate allocation of control and adequate state supervision, to withstand challenges alleging an improper delegation of authority. Thus, so far, these courts have determined that one of the central characteristics of charter schools, their relative freedom from traditional regulations, is not problematic from a legal perspective.

....

In general, the decisions of state courts have demonstrated two tendencies: (1) the state courts' inclination to uphold prior decisions of their state boards of education; and (2) the state courts' inclination to uphold their charter school enabling acts. By their actions, the state courts have thus helped to sustain and promote the development of the charter school movement and to lend support to the view that charter schools represent a legitimate means of pursuing improvement in public school systems.

As with the state court cases, the charter school cases decided by federal courts have followed similar tendencies. In federal cases plaintiffs have consistently proven unsuccessful in their attempts to establish that state charter school programs have violated constitutional provisions or other federal laws. The results of these cases suggest that future broad-based federal challenges to charter schools will not have a high likelihood of success and, therefore, will probably not alter the status quo of most states' charter school programs.

Thus, apparently, the charter school movement has successfully survived the initial legal challenges to its right of operation and continued expansion during the first decade of its existence. The legal battles, however, may be far from over. To the extent that the movement continues to grow and leads to the creation of still more charter schools, especially in districts with high concentrations of historically disadvantaged students, the concern regarding the movement's fiscal impact on traditional public schools will probably increase in significance. This may likely produce further court challenges, regarding fundamental issues of public school financing that the courts up to now have tended to avoid. Failure on the part of individual charter schools to comply with federal laws specifically designed to assist historically disadvantaged students may also lead to additional court challenges, especially students with disabilities.

Yet, during their brief history, charter schools have obtained the consistent backing of state and federal court systems in their legal battles to open and remain in operation. Whether they provide the rich learning environments for students that their proponents have predicted, of course, is well beyond the scope of this article. Nevertheless, charter schools have at least proven overwhelmingly successful in overcoming court cases challenging their status as a legitimate component within the public school framework.

C. Voucher Programs

ZELMAN v. SIMMONS-HARRIS
536 U.S. 639 (2002)

CHIEF JUSTICE REHNQUIST delivered the opinion of the Court.

The State of Ohio has established a pilot program designed to provide educational choices to families with children who reside in the Cleveland City School District. The question presented is whether this program offends the Establishment Clause of the United States Constitution. We hold that it does not.

Ohio enacted, among other initiatives, its Pilot Project Scholarship Program, Ohio Rev. Code Ann. ... The program provides financial assistance to families in any Ohio school district that is or has been "under federal court order requiring supervision and operational management of the district by the state superintendent." ... Cleveland is the only Ohio school district to fall within that category.

The program provides two basic kinds of assistance to parents of children in a covered district. First, the program provides tuition aid for students in kindergarten through third grade, expanding each year through eighth grade, to attend a participating public or private school of their parent's choosing. ... Second, the program provides tutorial aid for students who choose to remain enrolled in public school. ...

The tuition aid portion of the program is designed to provide educational choices to parents who reside in a covered district. Any private school, whether religious or nonreligious, may participate in the program and accept program students so long as the school is located within the boundaries of a covered district and meets statewide educational standards. ... Participating private schools must agree not to discriminate on the basis of race, religion, or ethnic background, or to "advocate or foster unlawful behavior or teach hatred of any person or group on the basis of race, ethnicity, national origin, or religion." ... Any public school located in a school district adjacent to the covered district may also participate in the program. ...Adjacent public schools are eligible to receive a $ 2,250 tuition grant for each program student accepted in addition to the full amount of per-pupil state funding attributable to each additional student. ...All participating schools, whether public or private, are required to accept students in accordance with rules and procedures established by the state superintendent.

****

The program has been in operation within the Cleveland City School District since the 1996-1997 school year. In the 1999-2000 school year, 56 private schools participated in the program, 46 (or 82%) of which had a religious affiliation. None of the public schools in districts adjacent to Cleveland have elected to participate. More than 3,700 students participated in the scholarship program, most of whom (96%) enrolled in religiously affiliated schools. Sixty percent of these students were from families at or below the poverty line. In the 1998-1999 school year, approximately 1,400 Cleveland public school students received tutorial aid. This number was expected to double during the 1999-2000 school year.

The Establishment Clause of the First Amendment, applied to the States through the Fourteenth Amendment, prevents a State from enacting laws that have the "purpose" or "effect" of advancing or inhibiting religion. *Agostini v. Felton*, 521 U.S. 203, 222-23 (1997)... There is no dispute that the program challenged here was enacted for the valid secular purpose of providing educational assistance to poor children in a demonstrably failing public school system. Thus, the question presented is whether the Ohio program nonetheless has the forbidden "effect" of advancing or inhibiting religion.

To answer that question, our decisions have drawn a consistent distinction between government programs that provide aid directly to religious schools, ... and programs of true private choice, in which government aid reaches religious schools only as a result of the genuine and independent choices of private individuals, *Mueller v. Allen*, 463 U.S. 388 (1983); *Witters v. Washington Dept. of Servs. for Blind*, 474 U.S. 481 (1986); *Zobrest v. Catalina Foothills Sch. Dist.*, 509 U.S. 1 (1993). While our jurisprudence with respect to the constitutionality of direct aid programs has "changed significantly" over the past two decades, … our jurisprudence with respect to true private choice programs has remained consistent and unbroken. Three times we have confronted Establishment Clause challenges to neutral government programs that provide aid directly to a broad class of individuals, who, in turn, direct the aid to religious schools or institutions of their own choosing. Three times we have rejected such challenges.

In *Mueller*, we rejected an Establishment Clause challenge to a Minnesota program authorizing tax deductions for various educational expenses, including private school tuition costs, even though the great majority of the program's beneficiaries (96%) were parents of children in religious schools.

In *Witters*, we used identical reasoning to reject an Establishment Clause challenge to a vocational scholarship program that provided tuition aid to a student studying at a religious institution to become a pastor.

[I]n *Zobrest*, we applied *Mueller* and *Witters* to reject an Establishment Clause challenge to a federal program that permitted sign-language interpreters to assist deaf children enrolled in religious schools.

Mueller, *Witters*, and *Zobrest* thus make clear that where a government aid program is neutral with respect to religion, and provides assistance directly to a broad class of citizens who, in turn, direct government aid to religious schools wholly as a result of their own genuine and independent private choice, the program is not readily subject to challenge under the Establishment Clause. A program that shares these features permits government aid to reach religious institutions only by way of the deliberate choices of numerous individual recipients. The incidental advancement of a religious mission, or the perceived endorsement of a religious message, is reasonably attributable to the individual recipient, not to the government, whose role ends with the disbursement of benefits. … [W]e have never found a program of true private choice to offend the Establishment Clause.

It is true that 82% of Cleveland's participating private schools are religious schools, but it is also true that 81% of private schools in Ohio are religious schools. To attribute constitutional significance to this figure, moreover, would lead to the absurd result that a neutral school-choice program might be permissible in some parts of Ohio, such as Columbus, where a lower percentage of private schools are religious schools, … but not in inner-city Cleveland, where Ohio has deemed such programs most sorely needed, but where the preponderance of religious schools happens to be greater. … Likewise, an identical private choice program might be constitutional in some States, such as Maine or Utah, where less than 45% of private schools are religious schools, but not in other States, such as Nebraska or Kansas, where over 90% of private schools are religious schools.

... The constitutionality of a neutral educational aid program simply does not turn on whether and why, in a particular area, at a particular time, most private schools are run by religious organizations, or most recipients choose to use the aid at a religious school. As we said in *Mueller*, "such an approach would scarcely provide the certainty that this field stands in need of, nor can we perceive principled standards by which such statistical evidence might be evaluated."

...

In sum, the Ohio program is entirely neutral with respect to religion. It provides benefits directly to a wide spectrum of individuals, defined only by financial need and residence in a particular school district. It permits such individuals to exercise genuine choice among options public and private, secular and religious. The program is therefore a program of true private choice. In keeping with an unbroken line of decisions rejecting challenges to similar programs, we hold that the program does not offend the Establishment Clause.

JUSTICE STEVENS, dissenting.

Is a law that authorizes the use of public funds to pay for the indoctrination of thousands of grammar school children in particular religious faiths a "law respecting an establishment of religion" within the meaning of the First Amendment? In answering that question, I think we should ignore three factual matters that are discussed at length by my colleagues.

First, the severe educational crisis that confronted the Cleveland City School District when Ohio enacted its voucher program is not a matter that should affect our appraisal of its constitutionality.

Second, the wide range of choices that have been made available to students within the public school system has no bearing on the question whether the State may pay the tuition for students who wish to reject public education entirely and attend private schools that will provide them with a sectarian education.

Third, the voluntary character of the private choice to prefer a parochial education over an education in the public school system seems to me quite irrelevant to the question whether the government's choice to pay for religious indoctrination is constitutionally permissible.

I have been influenced by my understanding of the impact of religious strife on the decisions of our forbears to migrate to this continent, and on the decisions of neighbors in the Balkans, Northern Ireland, and the Middle East to mistrust one another. Whenever we remove a brick from the wall that was designed to separate religion and government, we increase the risk of religious strife and weaken the foundation of our democracy.

I respectfully dissent.

JUSTICE SOUTER, with whom JUSTICE STEVENS, JUSTICE GINSBURG, and JUSTICE BREYER join, dissenting.

The occasion for the legislation thus upheld is the condition of public education in the city of Cleveland. The record indicates that the schools are failing to serve their objective, and the vouchers in issue here are said to be needed to provide adequate alternatives to them. If there were an excuse for giving short shrift to the Establishment Clause, it would probably apply here. But there is no excuse. Constitutional limitations are placed on government to preserve constitutional values in hard cases, like these. "Constitutional lines have to be drawn, and on one side of every one of them is an otherwise sympathetic case that provokes impatience with the Constitution and with the line. But constitutional lines are the price of constitutional government." *Agostini v. Felton*, 521 U.S. 203, 254.

JUSTICE BREYER, with whom JUSTICE STEVENS and JUSTICE SOUTER join, dissenting.

I write separately, however, to emphasize the risk that publicly financed voucher programs pose in terms of religiously based social conflict. I do so because I believe that the Establishment Clause concern for protecting the Nation's social fabric from religious conflict poses an overriding obstacle to the implementation of this well-intentioned school voucher program. "[P]arental choice" cannot significantly alleviate the constitutional problem.

Frank J. Macchiarola: Why the Decisions in Zelman Makes So much Sense, 59 N.Y.U. Ann. Surv. Am. L. 459 (2003)*

The Supreme Court's decision in *Zelman v. Simmons-Harris* came to the relief of two age-old victims of political discrimination in America, Catholics and Blacks. One class of victims, the Catholics, had been forced in the nineteenth century to found their own religious schools because they would not send their children to public schools where Protestantism served as the unofficial but actual state-sponsored religion. For long before the Supreme Court had found school prayer to be unconstitutional, Catholic parents and their leaders had refused to submit their children to education in schools that demeaned their beliefs by making them worship in ways that were heretical.

The discrimination by political leaders in places like Boston, New York and Philadelphia during the period of immigration of the Catholic Irish and Catholic Germans was the primary cause of the creation of a Catholic parochial system in the United States. But the hate mongers who set convents, churches and schools afire were not content just to drive Catholics from the public schools. They also unleashed at the state and federal levels an era of nativism which sought to deny any aid, direct or indirect, to the religious schools that were set up in response to the Protestant-run public schools. The fear of foreign influence, or popery as it was called, put into place laws and practices that were blatantly anti-Catholic. The nativists tried to make permanent their political advantage by enacting a constitutional amendment barring direct or indirect aid to religious schools, an effort that barely failed. They were more successful with constitutional provisions at the state level as many states, including New York, adopted these so-called "Blaine Amendments." These efforts were effective in preventing the admission of territories into the Union if they did not enact these provisions. As a result, there are significant numbers of states that enacted these amendments, the tenor of which is to inhibit the rights of citizens to the full exercise of their religious freedoms.

. . . . .

After states and localities prevented Catholics from attending public schools without being forced to worship in alien ways, the United States Constitution was used to deny them any forms of state aid. This was done by a blatant misreading of the First Amendment's Establishment Clause, where at its extreme the Supreme Court fashioned a "wall of separation" between church and state. Beyond misstating the framers' intent and corrupting the language of the Constitution itself, the characterization of "a wall" strongly suggested that religion had no place in the public square. Left unnoticed were years in our early history where public funding for the support of religious institutions was a common practice. The erection of a wall reflected judicial hostility toward religion rather than the tolerance and encouragement that characterized the early American republic's movement toward freedom for religious exercise. The fear of a state religion had been replaced by hostility toward all religious aid.

It is only in modern times that the Supreme Court has begun the task of reexamining the relationship of state and church and taken a much more tolerant attitude toward the freedom of religion guarantees that seemed to be underappreciated for so long.

There are many reasons, beyond the service to the children who attend them, that can justify direct public support to these schools. They do, after all, save taxpayers more money than they cost, given the considerable per student cost disparity that exists between parochial and public schools. Additionally, they provide a quality education which compares favorably with public schools, particularly in the inner-cities. In addition, these parochial schools admit students who are not Catholic and thus in many respects are public schools.

There is a further benefit, not generally mentioned, when considering the public benefit Catholic schools confer. Today, many suburban public school systems, with seats available, do not make their schools available to students from adjacent communities. As in the *Zelman* case, where every suburban district was invited to participate in Cleveland's program and refused to do so, good public schools are not really universally available. Entitlements to these schools are closely guarded, and segregation in public education is a way of life in America almost as extensive as it was before *Brown v. Board of Education*. Thus *Zelman* provided an opportunity for the Court not only to examine the limited rights of Catholic schools, it also gave the Court the chance to consider the effects of inadequate public schooling on the largely minority students taking advantage of the opportunity to opt out of those poorly performing public schools.

CAIN v. HORNE

183 P.3d 1269 (Ariz. Ct. App. 2008)

VASQUEZ, Judge.

In 2006, the Arizona legislature enacted House Bill 2676 and Senate Bill 1164, establishing respectively the Arizona Scholarships for Pupils with Disabilities Program (the "scholarship program"), and the Arizona Displaced Pupils Choice Grant Program (the "grant program"). Under the scholarship program, public-school students with a disability may transfer to a public or private, primary or secondary school, and the state will pay a scholarship up to the amount of basic state aid the student would generate for a public school district. Under the grant program, the state will pay $5,000 or the cost of tuition and fees, whichever is less, for children who have been placed in foster care to attend a private primary or secondary school. Under both programs (collectively, the "school voucher programs"), parents or legal guardians select the school their child will attend. The state then disburses grant funds to the parent or guardian, who must "restrictively endorse" the check or warrant for payment to the school. Both sectarian and nonsectarian schools may participate in the school voucher programs, and schools are not required to alter their "creed, practices or curriculum" in order to receive the funding.

In February 2007, Cain filed a complaint in Maricopa County Superior Court, challenging the constitutionality of the school voucher programs and seeking to enjoin Horne [State Superintendent of Public Instruction] from implementing them. ... The trial court granted Horne's motion, finding the school voucher programs did not violate the provisions of the Arizona Constitution cited by Cain, and dismissed all of Cain's claims with prejudice.

Here, Cain argues the school voucher statutes violate two distinct provisions of the Arizona Constitution. First, he contends the statutes violate article II, § 12 of the Arizona Constitution (the "Religion Clause"), which provides: "No public money or property shall be appropriated for or applied to any religious worship, exercise, or instruction, or to the support of any religious establishment." Second, he maintains the statutes are unconstitutional pursuant to the prohibitions in article IX, § 10 of the Arizona Constitution (the "Aid Clause"), read either alone or in conjunction with other constitutional provisions establishing a system of public education. The Aid Clause provides: "No tax shall be laid or appropriation of public money made in aid of any church, or private or sectarian school, or any public service corporation." We note that although there may be some overlap between these clauses, the Religion Clause—Arizona's analog to the federal Establishment Clause—was intended to ensure the separation of church and state, whereas the Aid Clause—which has no equivalent in the United States Constitution—was aimed at placing restrictions on the disbursement of public funds to specified institutions, both religious and secular. ...And, while we analyze Cain's Religion Clause challenge according to Arizona precedent and in the light of federal Establishment Clause jurisprudence, the question of whether or when a program that directs state funds to private schools violates the Aid Clause is an issue of first impression.

The parties devote a significant portion of their briefs discussing the question whether the constitutional provisions at issue in this case are so-called "Blaine amendments." In 1875, Congressman James Blaine introduced an amendment to the United States Constitution prohibiting states from using public funds for the benefit of any religious sect. See *Kotterman v. Killian*, 193 Ariz. 273, 972 P.2d 606, 624 (1999). It failed to pass, but similar amendments were subsequently made to a number of state constitutions. *Id.* Although the original Blaine amendment, and the amendments made to state constitutions in its immediate aftermath, may have been motivated by anti-Catholic bigotry, there is "no recorded history directly linking the amendment with Arizona's constitutional convention" thirty-five years later. *Id.* Furthermore, the Aid Clause does not discriminate between secular and religious private schools. And, in any event, none of the parties has produced any authority suggesting we may disregard constitutional provisions merely because we suspect they may have been tainted by questionable motives. We thus agree with the position of the National School Boards Association, expressed in its amicus brief, that this question "is irrelevant to the resolution of this case."

Religion Clause

However, our supreme ... court's analysis of Arizona's constitution suggests a position virtually indistinguishable from the United States Supreme Court's interpretation of the federal Establishment Clause.

[O]ur supreme court considered the constitutionality of state payments partially reimbursing the Salvation Army, a religious organization, for emergency welfare services it had provided to individuals and families under a contract with the Arizona Department of Public Welfare. *Community Council v. Jordan,* 102 Ariz. at 450, 432 P.2d at 462. In upholding the payments, the court noted that the purpose of the Religion Clause was "to provide for the historical doctrine of separation of church and state, the thrust of which was to insure that there would be no state supported religious institutions." *Id.* at 451, 432 P.2d at 463. It thus concluded the Religion Clause was not intended to place a blanket prohibition on the channeling of public funds to religious institutions, but rather to prohibit "assistance in any form whatsoever which would encourage or tend to encourage the preference of one religion over another, or religion per se over no religion." *Id.* at 454, 432 P.2d at 466.

More recently, in *Kotterman v. Killian*, the court considered a constitutional challenge, under both the United States and Arizona Constitutions, to a statute authorizing a state tax credit for donations to school tuition organizations. 193 Ariz. 273, 972 P.2d at 609-10. There the court stopped short of explicitly declaring that Arizona's Religion Clause is no more restrictive than the federal Establishment Clause. But it expressed skepticism that any historical analysis would show the framers had intended Arizona's provision to be more restrictive. *Id.* at 53-54. Emphasizing "the range of choices reserved to taxpayers, parents, and children, [and] the neutrality built into the system," it found the tax credit did not violate Arizona's Religion Clause. *Id.* at 46.

Furthermore, we note that the United States Supreme Court applied similar reasoning to an Establishment Clause challenge to Ohio's school voucher program:

> [W]here a government aid program is neutral with respect to religion, and provides assistance directly to a broad class of citizens who, in turn, direct government aid to religious schools wholly as a result of their own genuine and independent private choice, the program is not readily subject to challenge under the Establishment Clause. A program that shares these features permits government aid to reach religious institutions only by way of the deliberate choices of numerous individual recipients. The incidental advancement of a religious mission, or the perceived endorsement of a religious message, is reasonably attributable to the individual recipient, not to the government, whose role ends with the disbursement of benefits.

Zelman v. Simmons-Harris, 536 U.S. 639, 652 (2002). Like the Ohio program and the measures challenged in *Jordan* and *Kotterman*, the statutes at issue here are facially neutral and favor neither one religion over another nor religion over nonreligion. And, as in *Kotterman*, parents and children make an independent, personal choice to direct the funds to a particular school, which may be either religious or secular. We therefore concur with the trial court's finding that, "[a]s enacted, the State's school voucher programs do not result in an appropriation of public money for, or an application of public money to, any religious worship, exercise or instruction or to the support of any religious establishment in violation of Article 2, Section 12 of the Arizona Constitution."

Arizona Constitution's Aid Clause

However, as noted above, Arizona has another constitutional provision relevant to the disposition of this case. The Aid Clause prohibits any "appropriation of public money made in aid of . . . private or sectarian school[s]." Ariz. Const. art. IX, § 10. And Cain argues the state's "disbursement of benefits" under the school voucher programs here does "precisely what [the Aid Clause] forbids," and contends the trial court erred in finding otherwise. The plain language of our state constitution requires us to agree. As Cain suggests, the best guide to what the Aid Clause means is what is says.

[S]tates with constitutional provisions similar to ours have uniformly rejected the notion that schools are not aided by tuition payments:

> Assuming, but not deciding, the soundness of the view that the private institutions involved receive no direct benefit from the transportation of pupils or the furnishing of textbooks to them, the same cannot be said of provisions for the payment of tuition and institutional fees at such schools. Tuition and institutional fees go directly to the institution and are its very life blood. Such items are the main support of private schools which are not sufficiently endowed to insure their maintenance. Surely a payment by the State of the tuition and fees of the pupils of a private school begun on the strength of a contract by the State to do so would be an appropriation to that school. *Almond v. Day*, 197 Va. 419 (1955).

And, in *Hartness v. Patterson*, 255 S.C. 503 (1971), the South Carolina Supreme Court, applying a South Carolina constitutional provision that contains "in aid of" language similar to that in our Aid Clause, explained:

> We reject the argument that the tuition grants provided under the Act do not constitute aid to the participating schools. Students must pay tuition fees to attend [these schools] and the institutions depend upon the payment of such fees to aid in financing their operations. *While it is true that the tuition grant aids the student, it is also of material aid to the institution to which it is paid.*

(Emphasis added.) *See also Sheldon Jackson Coll. v. State*, 599 P.2d 127, 130-31 (Alaska 1979) (tuition payments are substantial, and unconstitutional, benefit to school even when paid indirectly); *State ex rel. Gallwey v. Grimm*, 146 Wn.2d 445, 48 P.3d 274, 279 (Wash. 2002) (tuition grants support educational institutions with public funds).

.....

Indirect Aid Prohibited

Courts have also been reluctant to uphold otherwise unconstitutional legislation that channels state funds for private-school tuition payments through students, parents, or other intermediaries: "[T]he Legislature cannot circumvent an express provision of the Constitution by doing indirectly what it may not do directly. Here the grant is not directly to a private school but rather to a student, but it must be used for tuition at a private school." *State ex rel. Rogers v. Swanson*, 192 Neb. 125, 219 N.W.2d 726, 730 (Neb. 1974). Even Alaska, whose constitution prohibits only "direct" aid to private schools, has concluded that "while a direct transfer of funds from the state to a private school will of course render a program constitutionally suspect, merely channeling the funds through an intermediary will not save an otherwise improper expenditure of public monies." *Sheldon Jackson Coll.*, 599 P.2d at 130-31.

In the present case, our legislature apparently intended to foreclose the argument that the school voucher programs give unconstitutional aid to private schools by including statutory language, such as that in § 15-817.01(B), stating that the public funds are a "grant of aid to a qualifying pupil through the qualifying pupil's respective custodian and not to the grant school in which the qualifying pupil is enrolled." However, we have an affirmative duty to independently review and interpret legislation and rule on its constitutionality. *See Martin v. Moore*, 61 Ariz. 92, 95, 143 P.2d 334, 335 (1943). Horne concedes that, under the school voucher programs, state funds are sent directly to participating schools, albeit in the form of checks or warrants made payable to students' parents or legal guardians who must endorse them in favor of the school. But even if the mechanism for disbursing tuition payments were more circuitous, it would still transfer state-appropriated funds to private schools. *See Crozier v. Frohmiller*, 65 Ariz. 296, 299, 179 P.2d 445, 447 (1947) (legislature may not do indirectly what it cannot do directly). And the fact that public schools are included with private schools under the scholarship program does not change our conclusion.

We conclude, therefore, that the school voucher programs provide aid to private schools in violation of the Aid Clause, article IX, § 10, of the Arizona Constitution. We recognize that when "the legislature has clearly spoken on a matter within its domain, its word constitutes public policy on that subject and controls, assuming no constitutional impediments exist." *See Taylor v. Graham County Chamber of Commerce*, 201 Ariz. 184, P27, 33 P.3d 518, 525 (App. 2001). But where our constitution has spoken, it is our duty to uphold it, ... regardless of the "wisdom, necessity, propriety or expediency of the legislation in question," *Indus. Dev. Auth. v. Nelson*, 109 Ariz. 368, 371, 509 P.2d 705, 708 (1973). ... Only by ignoring the plain text of the Arizona Constitution prohibiting state aid to private schools could we find the aid represented by the payment of tuition fees to such schools in this case constitutional. Of course, "if legislators wish to revive what is foreclosed by our constitutional . . . text, they may propose a constitutional amendment. Should Arizona's citizens want to repeal our constitutional prohibitions, they may adopt such an amendment." *Kotterman*, 193 Ariz. 273, P132, 972 P.2d at 639 (Feldman, J., dissenting).

Disposition

For the foregoing reasons, we vacate the trial court's judgment and remand with direction to enter judgment for Cain, enjoining Horne from expending public funds pursuant to the school voucher statutes.

Robert Gall: The Past Should not Shackle the Present: The Revival of A Legacy of Religious Bigotry by Opponents of School Choice, 59 N.Y.U. Ann. Surv. Am. L. 413 (2003)*

Zelman did not end the legal battles over school choice. Opponents of school choice had based their attacks on these programs not only on the Establishment Clause, but also on state constitutional provisions known as "Blaine amendments." In the wake of *Zelman*, these amendments have become their most prominent weapon. Generally, school choice opponents argue that these amendments provide greater protection against religious establishment than that provided by the Establishment Clause. The problem with this argument is (at least) two-fold. First, …the Blaine amendments were not rooted in a noble desire to supplement the protection against religious establishment provided by the First Amendment; rather, they were the product of the political triumph of anti-Catholic bigotry in the resolution of the great "School Question" of the nineteenth century… Second… the Blaine amendments, rather than provide greater protection against the establishment of religion, run afoul of the First Amendment when they are interpreted in such a manner as to discriminate against religion. [T]he battle over school choice should focus on providing educational opportunity to all of America's children; it should not be waged with weapons of bigotry forged in the fires of nineteenth century anti-Catholicism.

****

In the 1870s, Catholics mounted a renewed challenge to the Protestant answers to the "School Question," which was really a two-part question concerning the consolidation and protection of Protestants' common-school monopoly over public education. The questions were: (1) whether public funding could go to private Catholic schools and (2) whether students would read the King James Bible in public schools. The first question concerned preserving a monopoly over public funds so that Catholic schools would not undermine the universality of the common school system; the second concerned ensuring that the monopoly was worth preserving, i.e., that Protestant morality would continue to be taught within that system. By the Civil War, Protestants had secured the answers they wanted to both of the question: "no" to the former, and "yes" to the latter.

In the war's aftermath, however, Catholics had modest success in challenging the Protestant majority's answers to the "School Question." By the 1870s, they had succeeded in eliminating

---

Bible reading from some public school systems. Moreover, as Catholics gained majority status in many northern cities, they succeeded in obtaining public funding for Catholic schools. The "School Question" again became an important, highly charged political issue.

The Protestant backlash to this "Catholic menace" was swift and powerful. Protestant churches joined with nativist groups to take up the battle, fighting to preserve both Bible reading in the common school and the common school's monopoly on public funding. They found an important and willing ally in President Ulysses S. Grant, who sensed that the enormous popularity of an anti-Catholic movement might divert attention from the scandals of his administration and boost the electoral prospects of the Republican Party by casting it as the party of "reform." In 1875, he made a speech in which he proclaimed that Americans should "encourage free schools, and resolve that not one dollar, appropriated for their support, shall be appropriated to the support of any sectarian schools." He later proposed that Congress pass a constitutional amendment that would block such appropriations.

James G. Blaine, then a Republican congressman with serious presidential ambitions, recognized that Grant had given him an opening to use anti-Catholic sentiment to realize those ambitions. He quickly submitted to the House of Representatives his draft of the amendment Grant had asked Congress to pass. Most political observers recognized Blaine's amendment for what it was: an instrument of political opportunism that was directed against Catholics.

The original text of the amendment that Blaine submitted to the House read as follows:

> No State shall make any law respecting an establishment of religion, or prohibiting the free exercise thereof; and no money raised by taxation in any State for the support of public schools, or derived from any public fund therefor, nor any public lands devoted thereto, shall ever be under the control of any religious sect; nor shall any money so raised or lands so devoted be divided between religious sects or denominations.

The Blaine Amendment passed the House by a vote of 180 to 7, and the vote in the Senate was 28 to 16 in favor of its passage. However, the Senate vote fell short of the supermajority requirement necessary to amend the Constitution.

Not all states had a choice as to whether anti-Catholicism would become a permanent part of their constitutional fabric. Congress forced new states, including Washington, Montana, New Mexico, Utah, North Dakota, South Dakota, Oklahoma, Arizona, and others to include versions of the Blaine Amendment in their constitutions in order to gain admission into the Union. Today, thirty-seven states have constitutional provisions with Blaine-like language that forbid public aid to religious schools.

****

School choice programs, like Medicaid and Social Security, are general welfare programs designed to address the needs of the public—in this case, the need for a quality education. No one would seriously contend that a Jewish or Catholic person should be excluded from participation in a program like Medicaid because she might choose to receive treatment at a religious hospital, or be disallowed her monthly Social Security check because she might give a portion of the check's proceeds to her synagogue or church. However, opponents of school choice, by latching on to Blaine amendments, are employing that same line of reasoning within the context of school choice programs.

****

The Blaine amendments were passed in order to prevent state governments from appropriating public money to sectarian, i.e., Catholic, schools. By contrast, school choice programs such as vouchers are appropriations to parents, who make genuine and independent choices from a host of options - including religious and non-religious private schools, as well as public schools - as to where their children are educated. Religious schools benefit from this aid only as a result of the genuine and independent choices of parents; parents, not state governments, determine where public funds go.

.....

The promise of *Brown v. Board of Education*, that all children have the opportunity to receive a quality education, remains unfulfilled so long as a single child remains trapped in a school that consistently fails to provide him with that opportunity. School choice programs provide real educational opportunity where it did not previously exist. Thus, interpreting Blaine amendments to strike down such programs because they allow the participation of religious schools permits a shameful legacy of bigotry to thwart the realization of Brown's promise. Opponents of school choice should deal honestly with this irony. Fortunately, the principle of religious neutrality, if vindicated by the courts confronted with these amendments and the real interest that lurks behind them, will keep the legacy of James Blaine where it belongs—in a part of the past that most Americans disavow without hesitation.

Notes and Comments

1. Parental Choice and Bigotry

There is a natural link between the growing pains of the charter school reform movement and the controversy emerging over voucher programs. An examination of the two approaches is often distracted by church/state issues that refocus the debate on the question of whether or not public educators violate the Establishment Clause when implementing voucher programs. *See* discussion in chapter twelve on the First Amendment and Religious Expression.

Zelman, for the moment, has left the examination of the virtues of voucher programs free of this distraction. The public policy debate regarding vouchers appears to revolve around at least three branches of inquiry. Consider the relative merit of each branch.

> A. Do voucher programs offer a realistic "school choice" for children who are trapped in underperforming schools? Should school choice be seen as a "civil rights" issue?

B. Does direct public support for vouchers serve to hasten the demise of the public education system instead of prompting meaningful incentive for reform?

C. Does opposition to school choice mask a form of religious bigotry?

Chapter Three
Education as a Fundamental Right

> Education, of course, is not among the rights afforded explicit protection under our Federal Constitution. Nor do we find any basis for saying it is implicitly so protected. As we have said, the undisputed importance of education will not alone cause this Court to depart from the usual [deference] standard for reviewing a State's social and economic legislation. *San Antonio Indep. Sch. Dist. v. Rodriguez,* 411 U.S. 1 (1973).

> This Court, in defining efficiency must, at least in part, be guided by these clearly expressed purposes. The framers of Section 183 emphasized that education is essential to the welfare of the citizens of the Commonwealth. By this... we recognize that education is a fundamental right in Kentucky. *Rose. v. Council for A Better Education,* 790 S.W.2d 186 (1989).

The study of fundamental rights presents perhaps the most important aspect of the checks and balances in the American democracy. The rights guaranteed in the Bill of Rights of the Constitution of the United States function as limitations on the policy preferences of communities and policy-makers. So deeply rooted is the notion of fundamental rights in American culture that often educators and students assume rights that do not exist.

The *Rose* and *Rodriguez* decisions, quoted above, serve to frame the issue of fundamental rights as to a public education. Should a public education be a fundamental right? If so, then what are the implications of this as a matter of public policy? To state it in another way, what affirmative duties should government officials acknowledge if education is a fundamental right? Similarly, if education is not deemed fundamental, then how should state officials view their role as providers of knowledge within a formal system of learning? Moreover, if education is not a fundamental right, then what role, if any, is there for the courts in protecting the interests of students, faculty and staff?

This chapter examines the status of education as a fundamental right from both a federal and a state law perspective. The role of federalism will become clearer as you move through the sections. Section I summarizes the current position of federal law on the subject of education as a fundamental right. Section II provides an overview of the response of the States using their constitutions to address the issue of education as a fundamental right.

How do you account for the different conclusions in state and federal law as to the importance of public education? What role, if any, does the federal constitution play in protecting the rights of students to a pubic education? How would you summarize the role of state law in this regard?

I. Education under the Federal Constitution

SAN ANTONIO INDEPENDENT SCHOOL DISTRICT v. RODRIGUEZ
411 U.S. 1 (1973)

OPINION: MR. JUSTICE POWELL delivered the opinion of the Court.

This suit attacking the Texas system of financing public education was initiated by Mexican-American parents whose children attend the elementary and secondary schools in the Edgewood Independent School District, an urban school district in San Antonio, Texas. They brought a class action on behalf of school children throughout the State who are members of minority groups or who are poor and reside in school districts having a low property tax base. [A] three-judge court ...rendered its judgment ... holding the Texas school finance system unconstitutional under the Equal Protection Clause of the Fourteenth Amendment. For the reasons stated in this opinion, we reverse the decision of the District Court.

I.

The first Texas State Constitution, promulgated upon Texas' entry into the Union in 1845, provided for the establishment of a system of free schools.[6] Early in its history, Texas adopted a dual approach to the financing of its schools, relying on mutual participation by the local school districts and the State. As early as 1883, the state constitution was amended to provide for the creation of local school districts empowered to levy ad valorem taxes with the consent of local taxpayers for the "erection . . . of school buildings" and for the "further maintenance of public free schools." Such local funds as were raised were supplemented by funds distributed to each district from the State's Permanent and Available School Funds. The Permanent School Fund, its predecessor established in 1854 with $ 2,000,000 realized from an annexation settlement, was thereafter endowed with millions of acres of public land set aside to assure a continued source of income for school support. The Available School Fund, which received income from the Permanent School Fund as well as from a state ad valorem property tax and other designated taxes, served as the disbursing arm for most state educational funds throughout the late 1800's and first half of this century. Additionally, in 1918 an increase in state property taxes was used to finance a program providing free textbooks throughout the State.

****

The Program calls for state and local contributions to a fund earmarked specifically for teacher salaries, operating expenses, and transportation costs. The State, supplying funds from its general revenues, finances approximately 80% of the Program, and the school districts are responsible—as

---

[6] Tex. Const., Art. X, § 1 (1845):
"A general diffusion of knowledge being essential to the preservation of the rights and liberties of the people, it shall be the duty of the Legislature of this State to make suitable provision for the support and maintenance of public schools."
Id. § 2:
"The Legislature shall as early as practicable establish free schools throughout the State, and shall furnish means for their support, by taxation on property ..."

a unit—for providing the remaining 20%. The districts' share, known as the Local Fund Assignment, is apportioned among the school districts under a formula designed to reflect each district's relative taxpaying ability. The Assignment is first divided among Texas' 254 counties pursuant to a complicated economic index that takes into account the relative value of each county's contribution to the State's total income from manufacturing, mining, and agricultural activities. It also considers each county's relative share of all payrolls paid within the State and, to a lesser extent, considers each county's share of all property in the State. Each county's assignment is then divided among its school districts on the basis of each district's share of assessable property within the county. The district, in turn, finances its share of the Assignment out of revenues from local property taxation.

The design of this complex system was twofold. First, it was an attempt to assure that the Foundation Program would have an equalizing influence on expenditure levels between school districts by placing the heaviest burden on the school districts most capable of paying. Second, the Program's architects sought to establish a Local Fund Assignment that would force every school district to contribute to the education of its children but that would not by itself exhaust any district's resources. Today every school district does impose a property tax from which it derives locally expendable funds in excess of the amount necessary to satisfy its Local Fund Assignment under the Foundation Program.

In the years since this program went into operation in 1949, expenditures for education—from state as well as local sources—have increased steadily. Between 1949 and 1967, expenditures increased approximately 500%. In the last decade alone the total public school budget rose from $750 million to $2.1 billion and these increases have been reflected in consistently rising per-pupil expenditures throughout the State. Teacher salaries, by far the largest item in any school's budget, have increased dramatically-the state-supported minimum salary for teachers possessing college degrees has risen from $2,400 to $6,000 over the last 20 years.

****

The school district, in which appellees reside, the Edgewood Independent School District, has been compared throughout this litigation with the Alamo Heights Independent School District. This comparison between the least and most affluent districts in the San Antonio area serves to illustrate the manner in which the dual system of finance operates and to indicate the extent to which substantial disparities exist despite the State's impressive progress in recent years. Edgewood is one of seven public school districts in the metropolitan area. Approximately 22,000 students are enrolled in its 25 elementary and secondary schools. The district is situated in the core-city sector of San Antonio in a residential neighborhood that has little commercial or industrial property. The residents are predominantly of Mexican-American descent: approximately 90% of the student population is Mexican-American and over 6% is Negro. The average assessed property value per pupil is $5,960 - the lowest in the metropolitan area—and the median family income ($4,686) is also the lowest. At an equalized tax rate of $1.05 per $100 of assessed property—the highest in the metropolitan area—the district contributed $26 to the education of each child for the 1967-1968 school year above its Local Fund Assignment for the Minimum Foundation Program. The

Foundation Program contributed $222 per pupil for a state-local total of $248 Federal funds added another $108 for a total of $356 per pupil.

Alamo Heights is the most affluent school district in San Antonio. Its six schools, housing approximately 5,000 students, are situated in a residential community quite unlike the Edgewood District. The school population is predominantly "Anglo," having only 18% Mexican-Americans and less than 1% Negroes. The assessed property value per pupil exceeds $49,000, n33 and the median family income is $8,001. In 1967-1968, the local tax rate of $ .85 per $100 of valuation yielded $333 per pupil over $225 provided from that Program, the district was able to supply $ 558 per student. Supplemented by a $36 per-pupil grant from federal sources, Alamo Heights spent $594 per pupil.

Although the 1967-1968 school year figures provide the only complete statistical breakdown for each category of aid, more recent partial statistics indicate that the previously noted trend of increasing state aid has been significant. For the 1970-1971 school year, the Foundation School Program allotment for Edgewood was $356 per pupil, a 62% increase over the 1967-1968 school year. Indeed, state aid alone in 1970-1971 equaled Edgewood's entire 1967-1968 school budget from local, state, and federal sources. Alamo Heights enjoyed a similar increase under the Foundation Program, netting $491 per pupil in 1970-1971. These recent figures also reveal the extent to which these two districts' allotments were funded from their own required contributions to the Local Fund Assignment. Alamo Heights, because of its relative wealth, was required to contribute out of its local property tax collections approximately $100 per pupil, or about 20% of its Foundation grant. Edgewood, on the other hand, paid only $8.46 per pupil, which is about 2.4% of its grant. It appears then that, at least as to these two districts, the Local Fund Assignment does reflect a rough approximation of the relative taxpaying potential of each.

Despite these recent increases, substantial interdistrict disparities in school expenditures found by the District Court to prevail in San Antonio and in varying degrees throughout the State still exist. And it was these disparities, largely attributable to differences in the amounts of money collected through local property taxation that led the District Court to conclude that Texas' dual system of public school financing violated the Equal Protection Clause. The District Court held that the Texas system discriminates on the basis of wealth in the manner in which education is provided for its people. Finding that wealth is a "suspect" classification and that education is a "fundamental" interest, the District Court held that the Texas system could be sustained only if the State could show that it was premised upon some compelling state interest. On this issue the court concluded that "[n]ot only are defendants unable to demonstrate compelling state interests . . . they fail even to establish a reasonable basis for these classifications."

Texas virtually concedes that its historically rooted dual system of financing education could not withstand the strict judicial scrutiny that this Court has found appropriate in reviewing legislative judgments that interfere with fundamental constitutional rights or that involve suspect classifications. If, as previous decisions have indicated, strict scrutiny means that the State's system is not entitled to the usual presumption of validity, that the State rather than the complainants must carry a "heavy burden of justification," that the State must demonstrate that its educational system has been structured with "precision," and is "tailored" narrowly to serve legitimate objectives and that it has selected the "less drastic means" for effectuating its objectives, the Texas financing system and its counterpart in virtually every other State will not pass muster. The State candidly admits that "[n]o one familiar with the Texas system would contend that it has yet achieved perfection." Apart from its concession that educational financing in Texas has "defects" and "imperfections," the State defends the system's rationality with vigor and disputes the District Court's finding that it lacks a "reasonable basis."

This, then, establishes the framework for our analysis. We must decide, first, whether the Texas system of financing public education operates to the disadvantage of some suspect class or impinges upon a fundamental right explicitly or implicitly protected by the Constitution, thereby requiring strict judicial scrutiny. If so, the judgment of the District Court should be affirmed. If not, the Texas scheme must still be examined to determine whether it rationally furthers some legitimate, articulated state purpose and therefore does not constitute an invidious discrimination in violation of the Equal Protection Clause of the Fourteenth Amendment.

II

The District Court's opinion does not reflect the novelty and complexity of the constitutional questions posed by appellees' challenge to Texas' system of school financing. In concluding that strict judicial scrutiny was required, that court relied on decisions dealing with the rights of indigents to equal treatment in the criminal trial and appellate processes, and on cases disapproving wealth restrictions on the right to vote. Those cases, the District Court concluded, established wealth as a suspect classification. Finding that the local property tax system discriminated on the basis of wealth, it regarded those precedents as controlling. It then reasoned, based on decisions of this Court affirming the undeniable importance of education, that there is a fundamental right to education and that, absent some compelling state justification, the Texas system could not stand.

We are unable to agree that this case, which in significant aspects is sui generis, may be so neatly fitted into the conventional mosaic of constitutional analysis under the Equal Protection Clause. Indeed, for the several reasons that follow, we find neither the suspect-classification nor the fundamental-interest analysis persuasive.

A

The wealth discrimination discovered by the District Court in this case, and by several other courts that have recently struck down school-financing laws in other States, is quite unlike any of the forms of wealth discrimination heretofore reviewed by this Court. Rather than focusing on the unique features of the alleged discrimination, the courts in these cases have virtually assumed their findings of a suspect classification through a simplistic process of analysis: since, under the traditional systems of financing public schools, some poorer people receive less expensive educations than other more affluent people, these systems discriminate on the basis of wealth. This approach largely ignores the hard threshold questions, including whether it makes a difference for purposes of consideration under the Constitution that the class of disadvantaged "poor" cannot be identified or defined in customary equal protection terms, and whether the relative—rather than absolute—nature of the asserted deprivation is of significant consequence. Before a State's laws and the justifications for the classifications they create are subjected to strict judicial scrutiny, we think these threshold considerations must be analyzed more closely than they were in the court below.

The case comes to us with no definitive description of the classifying facts or delineation of the disfavored class. Examination of the District Court's opinion and of appellees' complaint, briefs, and contentions at oral argument suggests, however, at least three ways in which the discrimination claimed here might be described. The Texas system of school financing might be regarded as discriminating (1) against "poor" persons whose incomes fall below some identifiable level of poverty or who might be characterized as functionally "indigent," or (2) against those who are relatively poorer than other, or (3) against all those who, irrespective of their personal incomes, happen to reside in relatively poorer school districts. Our task must be to ascertain whether, in fact, the Texas system has been shown to discriminate on any of these possible bases and, if so, whether the resulting classification may be regarded as suspect.

****

However described, it is clear that appellees' suit asks this Court to extend its most exacting scrutiny to review a system that allegedly discriminates against a large, diverse, and amorphous class, unified only by the common factor of residence in districts that happen to have less taxable wealth than other districts. The system of alleged discrimination and the class it defines have none of the traditional indicia of suspectness: the class is not saddled with such disabilities, or subjected to such a history of purposeful unequal treatment, or relegated to such a position of political powerlessness as to command extraordinary protection from the majoritarian political process.

We thus conclude that the Texas system does not operate to the peculiar disadvantage of any suspect class. But in recognition of the fact that this Court has never heretofore held that wealth discrimination alone provides an adequate basis for invoking strict scrutiny, appellees have not relied solely on this contention. They also assert that the State's system impermissibly interferes with the exercise of a "fundamental" right and that accordingly the prior decisions of this Court require the application of the strict standard of judicial review. It is this question—whether education is a fundamental right, in the sense that it is among the rights and liberties protected by the Constitution—which has so consumed the attention of courts and commentators in recent years n68.

B

In *Brown v. Board of Education*, 347 U.S. 483 (1954), a unanimous Court recognized that "education is perhaps the most important function of state and local governments." *Id.* at 493. What was said there in the context of racial discrimination has lost none of its vitality with the passage of time: "Compulsory school attendance laws and the great expenditures for education both demonstrate our recognition of the importance of education to our democratic society. It is required in the performance of our most basic public responsibilities, even service in the armed forces. It is the very foundation of good citizenship. Today it is a principal instrument in awakening the child to cultural values, in preparing him for later professional training, and in helping him to adjust normally to his environment. In these days, it is doubtful that any child may reasonably be expected to succeed in life if he is denied the opportunity of an education. Such an opportunity, where the state has undertaken to provide it, is a right which must be made available to all on equal terms." *Ibid.*

Nothing this Court holds today in any way detracts from our historic dedication to public education. We are in complete agreement with the conclusion of the three-judge panel below that "the grave significance of education both to the individual and to our society" cannot be doubted. But, the importance of a service performed by the State does not determine whether it must be regarded as fundamental for purposes of examination under the Equal Protection Clause. Mr. Justice Harlan, dissenting from the Court's application of strict scrutiny to a law impinging upon the right of interstate travel, admonished that "[v]irtually every state statute affects important rights." *Shapiro v. Thompson*, 394 U.S., at 655, 661. In his view, if the degree of judicial scrutiny of state legislation fluctuated depending on a majority's view of the importance of the interest affected, we would have gone "far toward making this Court a 'super-legislature.'" *Ibid.* We would, indeed, then be assuming a legislative role and one for which the Court lacks both authority and competence. But Mr. Justice Stewart's response in *Shapiro* to Mr. Justice Harlan's concern correctly articulates the limits of the fundamental-rights rationale employed in the Court's equal protection decisions:

> The Court today does not 'pick out particular human activities, characterize them as "fundamental," and give them added protection ...' To the contrary, the Court simply recognizes, as it must, an established constitutional right, and gives to that right no less protection than the Constitution itself demands." *Id.* at 642.

****

The lesson of these cases in addressing the question now before the Court is plain. It is not the province of this Court to create substantive constitutional rights in the name of guaranteeing equal protection of the laws. Thus, the key to discovering whether education is "fundamental" is not to be found in comparisons of the relative societal significance of education as opposed to subsistence or housing. Nor is it to be found by weighing whether education is as important as the right to travel. Rather, the answer lies in assessing whether there is a right to education explicitly or implicitly guaranteed by the Constitution.

Education, of course, is not among the rights afforded explicit protection under our Federal Constitution. Nor do we find any basis for saying it is implicitly so protected. As we have said, the undisputed importance of education will not alone cause this Court to depart from the usual standard for reviewing a State's social and economic legislation. It is appellees' contention, however, that education is distinguishable from other services and benefits provided by the State because it bears a peculiarly close relationship to other rights and liberties accorded protection under the Constitution. Specifically, they insist that education is itself a fundamental personal right because it is essential to the effective exercise of First Amendment freedoms and to intelligent utilization of the right to vote. In asserting a nexus between speech and education, appellees urge that the right to speak is meaningless unless the speaker is capable of articulating his thoughts intelligently and persuasively. The "marketplace of ideas" is an empty forum for those lacking basic communicative tools. Likewise, they argue that the corollary right to receive information becomes little more than a hollow privilege when the recipient has not been taught to read, assimilate, and utilize available knowledge.

A similar line of reasoning is pursued with respect to the right to vote. Exercise of the franchise, it is contended, cannot be divorced from the educational Foundation of the voter. The electoral process, if reality is to conform to the democratic ideal, depends on an informed electorate: a voter cannot cast his ballot intelligently unless his reading skills and thought processes have been adequately developed.

We need not dispute any of these propositions. The Court has long afforded zealous protection against unjustifiable governmental interference with the individual's rights to speak and to vote. Yet we have never presumed to possess either the ability or the authority to guarantee to the citizenry the most effective speech or the most informed electoral choice. That these may be desirable goals of a system of freedom of expression and of a representative form of government is not to be doubted. These are indeed goals to be pursued by a people whose thoughts and beliefs are freed from governmental interference. But they are not values to be implemented by judicial intrusion into otherwise legitimate state activities.

Even if it were conceded that some identifiable quantum of education is a constitutionally protected prerequisite to the meaningful exercise of either right, we have no indication that the present levels of educational expenditure in Texas provide an education that falls short. Whatever merit appellees' argument might have if a State's financing system occasioned an absolute denial of educational opportunities to any of its children, that argument provides no basis for finding an interference with fundamental rights where only relative differences in spending levels are involved and where—as is true in the present case—no charge fairly could be made that the system fails to provide each child with an opportunity to acquire the basic minimal skills necessary for the enjoyment of the rights of speech and of full participation in the political process.

Furthermore, the logical limitations on appellees' nexus theory are difficult to perceive. How, for instance, is education to be distinguished from the significant personal interests in the basics of decent food and shelter? Empirical examination might well buttress an assumption that the ill-fed, ill-clothed, and ill-housed are among the most ineffective participants in the political process, and that they derive the least enjoyment from the benefits of the First Amendment.

****

We have carefully considered each of the arguments supportive of the District Court's finding that education is a fundamental right or liberty and have found those arguments unpersuasive. In one further respect we find this a particularly inappropriate case in which to subject state action to strict judicial scrutiny. The present case, in another basic sense, is significantly different from any of the cases in which the Court has applied strict scrutiny to state or federal legislation touching upon constitutionally protected rights. Each of our prior cases involved legislation which "deprived," "infringed," or "interfered" with the free exercise of some such fundamental personal right or liberty. ... A critical distinction between those cases and the one now before us lies in what Texas is endeavoring to do with respect to education.

****

Every step leading to the establishment of the system Texas utilizes today—including the decisions permitting localities to tax and expend locally, and creating and continuously expanding state aid—was implemented in an effort to extend public education and to improve its quality. Of course, every reform that benefits some more than others may be criticized for what it fails to accomplish. But we think it plain that, in substance, the thrust of the Texas system is affirmative and reformatory and, therefore, should be scrutinized under judicial principles sensitive to the nature of the State's efforts and to the rights reserved to the States under the Constitution.

C

It should be clear, for the reasons stated above and in accord with the prior decisions of this Court, that this is not a case in which the challenged state action must be subjected to the searching judicial scrutiny reserved for laws that create suspect classifications or impinge upon constitutionally protected rights.

We need not rest our decision, however, solely on the inappropriateness of the strict-scrutiny test. A century of Supreme Court adjudication under the Equal Protection Clause affirmatively supports the application of the traditional standard of review, which requires only that the State's system be shown to bear some rational relationship to legitimate state purposes. This case represents far more than a challenge to the manner in which Texas provides for the education of its children. We have here nothing less than a direct attack on the way in which Texas has chosen to raise and disburse state and local tax revenues. We are asked to condemn the State's judgment in conferring on political subdivisions the power to tax local property to supply revenues for local interests. In so doing, appellees would have the Court intrude in an area in which it has traditionally deferred to state legislatures. This Court has often admonished against such interferences with the State's fiscal policies under the Equal Protection Clause:

> The broad discretion as to classification possessed by a legislature in the field of taxation has long been recognized. . . . [The] passage of time has only served to underscore the wisdom of that recognition of the large area of discretion which is needed by a legislature in formulating sound tax policies. ...It has . . . been pointed out that in taxation, even more than in other fields, legislatures possess the greatest freedom in classification.
>
> Since the members of a legislature necessarily enjoy a familiarity with local conditions, which this Court cannot have, the presumption of constitutionality can be overcome only by the most explicit demonstration that a classification is a hostile and oppressive discrimination against particular persons and classes.... *Madden v. Kentucky*, 309 U.S. 83, 87-88 (1940).

Thus, we stand on familiar ground when we continue to acknowledge that the Justices of this Court lack both the expertise and the familiarity with local problems so necessary to the making of wise decisions with respect to the raising and disposition of public revenues. Yet, we are urged to direct the States either to alter drastically the present system or to throw out the property tax altogether in favor of some other form of taxation. No scheme of taxation, whether the tax is imposed on property, income, or purchases of goods and services, has yet been devised which is free of all discriminatory impact. In such a complex arena in which no perfect alternatives exist, the Court does well not to impose too rigorous a standard of scrutiny lest all local fiscal schemes become subjects of criticism under the Equal Protection Clause.

In addition to matters of fiscal policy, this case also involves the most persistent and difficult questions of educational policy, another area in which this Court's lack of specialized knowledge and experience counsels against premature interference with the informed judgments made at the state and local levels. Education, perhaps even more than welfare assistance, presents a myriad of "intractable economic, social, and even philosophical problems." *Dandridge v. Williams*, 397 U.S. at 487. The very complexity of the problems of financing and managing a statewide public school system suggests, "there will be more than one constitutionally permissible method of solving them," and that, within the limits of rationality, "the legislature's efforts to tackle the problems" should be entitled to respect. *Jefferson v. Hackney*, 406 U.S. at 546-547. On even the most basic questions in this area, the scholars and educational experts are divided. Indeed, one of the major sources of controversy concerns the extent to which there is a demonstrable correlation between educational expenditures and the quality of education— an assumed correlation underlying virtually every legal conclusion drawn by the District Court in this case. Related to the questioned relationship between cost and quality is the equally unsettled controversy as to the proper goals of a system of public education. And the question regarding the most effective relationship between state boards of education and local school boards, in terms of their respective responsibilities and degrees of control, is now undergoing searching re-examination. The ultimate wisdom as to these and related problems of education is not likely to be divined for all time even by the scholars who now so earnestly debate the issues. In such circumstances, the judiciary is well advised to refrain from imposing on the States inflexible constitutional restraints that could circumscribe or handicap the continued research and experimentation so vital to finding even partial solutions to educational problems and to keeping abreast of ever-changing conditions.

It must be remembered, also, that every claim arising under the Equal Protection Clause has implications for the relationship between national and state power under our federal system. Questions of federalism are always inherent in the process of determining whether a State's laws are to be accorded the traditional presumption of constitutionality, or are to be subjected instead to rigorous judicial scrutiny. While "[t]he maintenance of the principles of federalism is a foremost consideration in interpreting any of the pertinent constitutional provisions under which this Court examines state action," it would be difficult to imagine a case having a greater potential impact on our federal system than the one now before us, in which we are urged to abrogate systems of financing public education presently in existence in virtually every State.

The foregoing considerations buttress our conclusion that Texas' system of public school finance is an inappropriate candidate for strict judicial scrutiny. These same considerations are relevant to the determination whether that system, with its conceded imperfections, nevertheless bears some rational relationship to a legitimate state purpose. It is to this question that we next turn our attention.

III

The basic contours of the Texas school finance system have been traced at the outset of this opinion. We will now describe in more detail that system and how it operates, as these facts bear directly upon the demands of the Equal Protection Clause.

Apart from federal assistance, each Texas school receives its funds from the State and from its local school district. On a statewide average, a roughly comparable amount of funds is derived from each source. The State's contribution, under the Minimum Foundation Program, was designed to provide an adequate minimum educational offering in every school in the State. Funds are distributed to assure that there will be one teacher—compensated at the state-supported minimum salary—for every 25 students. Each school district's other supportive personnel are provided for: one principal for every 30 teachers; one "special service" teacher—librarian, nurse, doctor, etc.—for every 20 teachers; superintendents, vocational instructors, counselors, and educators for exceptional children are also provided. Additional funds are earmarked for current operating expenses, for student transportation, and for free textbooks.

****

In its reliance on state as well as local resources, the Texas system is comparable to the systems employed in virtually every other State. The power to tax local property for educational purposes has been recognized in Texas at least since 1883. When the growth of commercial and industrial centers and accompanying shifts in population began to create disparities in local resources, Texas undertook a program calling for a considerable investment of state funds.

****

Appellees do not question the propriety of Texas' dedication to local control of education. To the contrary, they attack the school-financing system precisely because, in their view, it does not provide the same level of local control and fiscal flexibility in all districts. Appellees suggest that local control could be preserved and promoted under other financing systems that resulted in more equality in educational expenditures. While it is no doubt true that reliance on local property taxation for school revenues provides less freedom of choice with respect to expenditures for some districts than for others, the existence of "some inequality " in the manner in which the State's rationale is achieved is not alone a sufficient basis for striking down the entire system. *McGowan v. Maryland*, 366 U.S. 420, 425-426 (1961). It may not be condemned simply because it imperfectly effectuates the State's goals. *Dandridge v. Williams*, 397 U.S. at 485. Nor must the financing system fail because, as appellees suggest, other methods of satisfying the State's interest, which occasion "less drastic" disparities in expenditures, might be conceived. Only where state action impinges on the exercise of fundamental constitutional rights or liberties must it be found to have chosen the least restrictive alternative. *Cf. Dunn v. Blumstein*, 405 U.S. at 343; *Shelton v. Tucker*, 364 U.S. 479, 488 (1960). It is also well to remember that even those districts that have reduced ability to make free decisions with respect to how much they spend on education still retain under the present system a large measure of authority as to how available funds will be allocated. They further enjoy the power to make numerous other decisions with respect to the operation of the schools. The people of Texas may be justified in believing that other systems of school financing, which place more of the financial responsibility in the hands of the State, will result in a comparable lessening of desired local autonomy. That is, they may believe that along with increased control of the purse strings at the state level will go increased control over local policies.

****

These practical considerations, of course, play no role in the adjudication of the constitutional issues presented here. But they serve to highlight the wisdom of the traditional limitations on this Court's function. The consideration and initiation of fundamental reforms with respect to state taxation and education are matters reserved for the legislative processes of the various States, and we do no violence to the values of federalism and separation of powers by staying our hand. We hardly need add that this Court's action today is not to be viewed as placing its judicial imprimatur on the status quo. The need is apparent for reform in tax systems which may well have relied too long and too heavily on the local property tax. And certainly innovative thinking as to public education, its methods, and its funding is necessary to assure both a higher level of quality and greater uniformity of opportunity. These matters merit the continued attention of the scholars who already have contributed much by their challenges. But the ultimate solutions must come from the lawmakers and from the democratic pressures of those who elect them.

Reversed .

CONCUR: MR. JUSTICE STEWART, concurring.

The method of financing public schools in Texas, as in almost every other State, has resulted in a system of public education that can fairly be described as chaotic and unjust. It does not follow, however, and I cannot find, that this system violates the Constitution of the United States…..

Unlike other provisions of the Constitution, the Equal Protection Clause confers no substantive rights and creates no substantive liberties. The function of the Equal Protection Clause, rather, is simply to measure the validity of classifications created by state laws.[2]

DISSENT: MR. JUSTICE BRENNAN, dissenting.

Although I agree with my Brother WHITE that the Texas statutory scheme is devoid of any rational basis, and for that reason is violative of the Equal Protection Clause, I also record my disagreement with the Court's rather distressing assertion that a right may be deemed "fundamental" for the purposes of equal protection analysis only if it is "explicitly or implicitly guaranteed by the Constitution." *Ante*, at 33-34. As my Brother MARSHALL convincingly demonstrates, our prior cases stand for the proposition that "fundamentality" is, in large measure, a function of the right's importance in terms of the effectuation of those rights which are in fact constitutionally guaranteed.

---

[2] There is one notable exception to the above statement: It has been established in recent years that the Equal Protection Clause confers the substantive right to participate on an equal basis with other qualified voters whenever the State has adopted an electoral process for determining who will represent any segment of the State's population. *See, e.g., Reynolds v. Sims* , 377 U.S. 533; *Kramer v. Union School District*, 395 U.S. 621; *Dunn v. Blumstein*, 405 U.S. 330, 336. But there is no constitutional right to vote, as such. *Minor v. Happersett*, 21 Wall. 162. If there were such a right, both the Fifteenth Amendment and the Nineteenth Amendment would have been wholly unnecessary.

Thus, "[a]s the nexus between the specific constitutional guarantee and the nonconstitutional interest draws closer, the nonconstitutional interest becomes more fundamental and the degree of judicial scrutiny applied when the interest is infringed on a discriminatory basis must be adjusted accordingly."

Here, there can be no doubt that education is inextricably linked to the right to participate in the electoral process and to the rights of free speech and association guaranteed by the First Amendment. See post, at 111-15. This being so, any classification affecting education must be subjected to strict judicial scrutiny, and since even the State concedes that the statutory scheme now before us cannot pass constitutional muster under this stricter standard of review, I can only conclude that the Texas school-financing scheme is constitutionally invalid.

MR. JUSTICE WHITE, with whom MR. JUSTICE DOUGLAS and MR. JUSTICE BRENNAN join, dissenting.

The difficulty with the Texas system, however, is that it provides a meaningful option to Alamo Heights and like school districts but almost none to Edgewood and those other districts with a low per-pupil real estate tax base. In these latter districts, no matter how desirous parents are of supporting their schools with greater revenues, it is impossible to do so through the use of the real estate property tax. In these districts, the Texas system utterly fails to extend a realistic choice to parents because the property tax, which is the only revenue-raising mechanism extended to school districts, is practically and legally unavailable. That this is the situation may be readily demonstrated.

The Equal Protection Clause permits discriminations between classes but requires that the classification bear some rational relationship to a permissible object sought to be attained by the statute. It is not enough that the Texas system before us seeks to achieve the valid, rational purpose of maximizing local initiative; the means chosen by the State must also be rationally related to the end sought to be achieved.

Neither Texas nor the majority heeds this rule.

MR. JUSTICE MARSHALL, with whom MR. JUSTICE DOUGLAS concurs, dissenting.

The Court today decides, in effect, that a State may constitutionally vary the quality of education which it offers its children in accordance with the amount of taxable wealth located in the school districts within which they reside. The majority's decision represents an abrupt departure from the mainstream of recent state and federal court decisions concerning the unconstitutionality of state educational financing schemes dependent upon taxable local wealth. More unfortunately, though, the majority's holding can only be seen as a retreat from our historic commitment to equality of educational opportunity and as unsupportable acquiescence in a system which deprives children in their earliest years of the chance to reach their full potential as citizens. The Court does this despite the absence of any substantial justification for a scheme which arbitrarily channels educational resources in accordance with the fortuity of the amount of taxable wealth within each district.

In my judgment, the right of every American to an equal start in life, so far as the provision of a state service as important as education is concerned, is far too vital to permit state discrimination on grounds as tenuous as those presented by this record. Nor can I accept the notion that it is sufficient to remit these appellees to the vagaries of the political process, which contrary to the majority's suggestion, has proved singularly unsuited to the task of providing a remedy for this discrimination. I, for one, am unsatisfied with the hope of an ultimate "political" solution sometime in the indefinite future while, in the meantime, countless children unjustifiably receive inferior educations that "may affect their hearts and minds in a way unlikely ever to be undone." *Brown v. Board of Education*, 347 U.S. 483, 494 (1954). I must therefore respectfully dissent.

.....

Authorities concerned with educational quality no doubt disagree as to the significance of variations in per-pupil spending. Indeed, conflicting expert testimony was presented to the District Court in this case concerning the effect of spending variations on educational achievement. We sit, however, not to resolve disputes over educational theory but to enforce our Constitution. It is an inescapable fact that if one district has more funds available per pupil than another district, the former will have greater choice in educational planning than will the latter. In this regard, I believe the question of discrimination in educational quality must be deemed to be an objective one that looks to what the State provides its children, not to what the children are able to do with what they receive. That a child forced to attend an underfunded school with poorer physical facilities, less experienced teachers, larger classes, and a narrower range of courses than a school with substantially more funds—and thus with greater choice in educational planning—may nevertheless excel is to the credit of the child, not the State, *cf. Missouri ex rel. Gaines v. Canada*, 305 U.S. 337, 349 (1938). Indeed, who can ever measure for such a child the opportunities lost and the talents wasted for want of a broader, more enriched education? Discrimination in the opportunity to learn that is afforded a child must be our standard.

.....

I would like to know where the Constitution guarantees the right to procreate, *Skinner v. Oklahoma*, 316 U.S. 535, 541 (1942), or the right to vote in state elections, e.g., *Reynolds v. Sims*, 377 U.S. 533 (1964), or the right to an appeal from a criminal conviction, e.g., *Griffin v. Illinois*, 351 U.S. 12 (1956). These are instances in which, due to the importance of the interests at stake, the Court has displayed a strong concern with the existence of discriminatory state treatment. But the Court has never said or indicated that these are interests which independently enjoy full-blown constitutional protection.

.....

The task in every case should be to determine the extent to which constitutionally guaranteed rights are dependent on interests not mentioned in the Constitution. As the nexus between the specific constitutional guarantee and the nonconstitutional interest draws closer, the nonconstitutional interest becomes more fundamental and the degree of judicial scrutiny applied when the interest is infringed on a discriminatory basis must be adjusted accordingly. Thus, it cannot be denied that interests such as procreation, the exercise of the state franchise, and access to criminal appellate processes are not fully guaranteed to the citizen by our Constitution. But these interests have nonetheless been afforded special judicial consideration in the face of discrimination because they are, to some extent, interrelated with constitutional guarantees. Procreation is now understood to be important because of its interaction with the established constitutional right of privacy. The exercise of the state franchise is closely tied to basic civil and political rights inherent in the First Amendment. And access to criminal appellate processes enhances the integrity of the range of rights implicit in the Fourteenth Amendment guarantee of due process of law. Only if we closely protect the related interests from state discrimination do we ultimately ensure the integrity of the constitutional guarantee itself. This is the real lesson that must be taken from our previous decisions involving interests deemed to be fundamental.

Notes and Comments

1. Is it clear why education is not deemed a fundamental right under the federal Constitution? What is the primary concern of the Court in its reluctance to deny fundamental status to education? Does the dissent offer a compromise method of protecting education under the Equal Protection Clause?

2. Try to draft an outline of an opinion that rewrites the *Rodriguez* decision that makes education a fundamental right. What affirmative duties does your opinion place on the states? What limits do you place on the power of school officials? What other constitution arguments can you think of that justify making education fundamental?

3. There is a rich database of comment and criticism of the *Rodriguez* decision. The school finance issue and the ruling on the status of education as a fundamental right have attracted equal attention. For several thoughtful articles on these subjects, *see* Paula J. Lundberg, State Courts and School Funding: A Fifty-State Analysis, 63 Alb. L. Rev. 1101 (2000); Roger J.R. Levesque: The Right to Education in the United States: Beyond the Limits of the Lore and Lure of Law, 4 Ann. Surv. Int'l & Comp. L. 205 (1997); Note: What Happens to A Dream Deferred?: Cleansing *The Taint Of San Antonio Independent School District V. Rodriguez*, 55 Duke L.J. 405 (2005); Timothy D. Lynch: Education as a Fundamental Right: Challenging the Supreme Court's Jurisprudence, 26 Hofstra L. Rev. 953 (1998).

Larry J. Obhof: Rethinking Judicial Activism and Restraint in State School Finance Litigation, 27 Harv. J.L. & Pub. Pol'y 569 (2004)*

It is obvious that policymakers and voters recognize education as one of the most important functions of state and local governments. Why, then, would school finance litigation ever be necessary? Could we not expect that elected officials would adequately fund schools, even if only to protect their own electoral careers? There are in fact strong disincentives for governors and legislators to make comprehensive changes to school finance systems. First—and perhaps most important—is the fear of being associated with the introduction of new taxes. A related problem stems from the nature of legislative representation. Individual legislators represent individual districts, whose goals (and need for increased spending) may differ from that of the state as a whole. Legislators who raise taxes that are likely to improve schools primarily in other districts may draw the ire of voters at home. These factors are amplified by the fact that representatives from poor districts, who are likely to support reform, tend to be outnumbered by the representatives of middle class and wealthy districts combined, who often oppose it.

For their part, governors are accountable to the entire state and are therefore less likely to be constrained by local interests. Governors have a limited amount of political capital, however, and are generally reluctant to expend it on a single issue. Like legislators, they must also be careful not to spend too much of a state's resources only on education. Thus, while governors are often more willing than legislators to support education reform, they are unlikely to do so without an outside catalyst such as pressure from the courts.

Many states have had a need for such a catalyst. The debates about the importance of money notwithstanding, educational opportunity is typically defined in terms of resource inputs, such as funding levels, as well as the number and quality of teachers, texts, and other quantifiable factors. Variations on these measures, including per pupil expenditures, are significant both within and among states. In any system where local property taxes account for a significant portion of the school finance system, a basic, inescapable problem remains: property values are unequally distributed across school districts and across states. Inequalities in revenues per pupil therefore exist within and among school districts; these inequalities "are primarily the result of differences among districts in per pupil taxable property base."

As Jonathan Kozol so aptly stated in the seminal book *Savage Inequalities*, "the shock of going from one of the poorest schools to one of the wealthiest cannot be overstated." Indeed, this author has visited public schools that have "Astroturf football fields, larger and better kept than those of many colleges; indoor track and field facilities; Olympic-sized swimming pools; and weight rooms that surpass the quality of most private clubs. At the same time, and in some cases only a few miles away, children attend schools that do not have enough money to purchase textbooks or provide students adequate or even safe school facilities.

****

Some have argued that finding a statewide system of school finance unconstitutional is the "quintessential example of judicial activism." It involves the least accountable branch of government overruling policies set not only by state and local legislative bodies, but also by voters themselves. School finance cases also typically rely on novel legal precedent. Furthermore, such cases inevitably lead to court involvement in taxation issues, which even the courts themselves are often wary to do.

There are a number of other reasons why state judiciaries should be, and often are, reluctant to get involved in school finance litigation. Courts generally lack the institutional competence to act in an area as complex as school funding. Indeed, determining what constitutes an "adequate" education often requires judges to go beyond what even educators and social scientists can determine. This has in turn "spawned a huge industry of competing expert witnesses, traveling from state to state, from one adequacy' hearing to another."

Even the courts themselves often emphasize why courts should defer to the legislature in such situations. This is consistent with the traditional view of separation of powers. It is not the purpose of judicial review to make sure that "fundamental values" are respected. The role of the judiciary is to "say what the law is and to direct the popularly elected officials back to the proper course." These facts have been key to defendants' arguments and may play an even more important role in the public sphere than the legal one.

****

How can courts achieve a proper balance between their responsibilities and those of the legislature? William Thro has suggested an approach to school finance litigation that balances the principles of judicial review and judicial restraint. First, courts should emphasize the importance of the constitutional text. The courts should examine the text and determine: (1) whether the state constitution sets a quality standard at all, and if so (2) what that standard is. Courts should not discard this approach in order to substitute their own opinions for the wording of the state's education clause. Doing so oversteps a court's authority to interpret—but not make—the law.

Second, courts should acknowledge that they are not "omnicompetent in educational matters." What is "adequate" often comes down to a court's judgment. Judges, however, are trained and work in the interpretation of law—not in the formation of public policy. School finance is not—nor should it be—a judge's area of expertise. Separation of powers arguments aside, the judiciary is simply the least equipped branch to decide the means to enforce education standards.

A third and related issue stems from this. Courts should defer to the other branches of government in the making of public policy. Some have argued that most legislators are no more expert in the area of school finance than the courts. Perhaps this is true. The basic fact remains, however, that it is a legislator's job, indeed his or her responsibility, to formulate public policy. Those policies, furthermore, must take into account the scarcity of resources and the other goals and functions for which the state is responsible. A court that focuses solely on school finance is not capable of making policy judgments that will invariably affect other areas.

In a world of scarce resources, legislators and governors are called upon to determine which distribution of resources will benefit society the most. That is what they—and only they—are elected to do.

PLYLER v. DOE
457 U.S. 202 (1982)

JUSTICE BRENNAN delivered the opinion of the Court.

The question presented by these cases is whether, consistent with the Equal Protection Clause of the Fourteenth Amendment, Texas may deny to undocumented school-age children the free public education that it provides to children who are citizens of the United States or legally admitted aliens.

I

Since the late 19th century, the United States has restricted immigration into this country. Unsanctioned entry into the United States is a crime, 8 U. S. C. § 1325, and those who have entered unlawfully are subject to deportation, 8 U. S. C. §§ 1251, 1252 (1976 ed. and Supp. IV). But despite the existence of these legal restrictions, a substantial number of persons have succeeded in unlawfully entering the United States, and now live within various States, including the State of Texas.

In May 1975, the Texas Legislature revised its education laws to withhold from local school districts any state funds for the education of children who were not "legally admitted" into the United States. The 1975 revision also authorized local school districts to deny enrollment in their public schools to children not "legally admitted" to the country. Tex. Educ. Code Ann. § 21.031 (Vernon Supp. 1981). These cases involve constitutional challenges to those provisions.

.....

II

The Fourteenth Amendment provides that "[no] State shall . . . deprive any person of life, liberty, or property, without due process of law; nor deny to *any person within its jurisdiction* the equal protection of the laws." (Emphasis added.) Appellants argue at the outset that undocumented aliens, because of their immigration status, are not "persons within the jurisdiction" of the State of Texas, and that they therefore have no right to the equal protection of Texas law. We reject this argument. Whatever his status under the immigration laws, an alien is surely a "person" in any ordinary sense of that term. Aliens, even aliens whose presence in this country is unlawful, have long been recognized as "persons" guaranteed due process of law by the Fifth and Fourteenth Amendments. Shaughnessy v. Mezei, 345 U.S. 206, 212 (1953); *Wong Wing v. United States*, 163 U.S. 228, 238 (1896); *Yick Wo v. Hopkins*, 118 U.S. 356, 369 (1886). Indeed, we have clearly held that the Fifth Amendment protects aliens whose presence in this country is unlawful from invidious discrimination by the Federal Government. *Mathews v. Diaz*, 426 U.S. 67, 77 (1976).[9]

---

[9] It would be incongruous to hold that the United States, to which the Constitution assigns a broad authority over both naturalization and foreign affairs, is barred from invidious discrimination with respect to unlawful aliens, while exempting the States from a similar limitation. *See* 426 U.S. at 84-86.

In concluding that "all persons within the territory of the United States," including aliens unlawfully present, may invoke the Fifth and Sixth Amendments to challenge actions of the Federal Government, we reasoned from the understanding that the Fourteenth Amendment was designed to afford its protection to all within the boundaries of a State.

III

In applying the Equal Protection Clause to most forms of state action, we thus seek only the assurance that the classification at issue bears some fair relationship to a legitimate public purpose.

But we would not be faithful to our obligations under the Fourteenth Amendment if we applied so deferential a standard to every classification. The Equal Protection Clause was intended as a restriction on state legislative action inconsistent with elemental constitutional premises. Thus we have treated as presumptively invidious those classifications that disadvantage a "suspect class,"[14] or that impinge upon the exercise of a "fundamental right."[15] With respect to such classifications, it is appropriate to enforce the mandate of equal protection by requiring the State to demonstrate that its classification has been precisely tailored to serve a compelling governmental interest. In addition, we have recognized that certain forms of legislative classification, while not facially invidious, nonetheless give rise to recurring constitutional difficulties; in these limited circumstances we have sought the assurance that the classification reflects a reasoned judgment consistent with the ideal of equal protection by inquiring whether it may fairly be viewed as

---

[14] Several formulations might explain our treatment of certain classifications as "suspect." Some classifications are more likely than others to reflect deep-seated prejudice rather than legislative rationality in pursuit of some legitimate objective. Legislation predicated on such prejudice is easily recognized as incompatible with the constitutional understanding that each person is to be judged individually and is entitled to equal justice under the law. Classifications treated as suspect tend to be irrelevant to any proper legislative goal. *See McLaughlin v. Florida*, 379 U.S. 184, 192 (1964); *Hirabayashi v. United States*, 320 U.S. 81, 100 (1943). Finally, certain groups, indeed largely the same groups, have historically been "relegated to such a position of political powerlessness as to command extraordinary protection from the majoritarian political process." *San Antonio Ind. Sch. Dist.* v. *Rodriguez*, 411 U.S. 1, 28 (1973); *Graham* v. *Richardson*, 403 U.S. 365, 372 (1971); *see United States v. Carolene Products Co.*, 304 U.S. 144, 152-53, n. 4 (1938). The experience of our Nation has shown that prejudice may manifest itself in the treatment of some groups. Our response to that experience is reflected in the Equal Protection Clause of the Fourteenth Amendment. Legislation imposing special disabilities upon groups disfavored by virtue of circumstances beyond their control suggests the kind of "class or caste" treatment that the Fourteenth Amendment was designed to abolish.

[15] In determining whether a class-based denial of a particular right is deserving of strict scrutiny under the Equal Protection Clause, we look to the Constitution to see if the right infringed has its source, explicitly or implicitly, therein. But we have also recognized the fundamentality of participation in state "elections on an equal basis with other citizens in the jurisdiction," *Dunn v. Blumstein*, 405 U.S. 330, 336 (1972), even though "the right to vote, *per se*, is not a constitutionally protected right." *San Antonio Ind. Sch. Dist., supra*, at 35, n. 78. With respect to suffrage, we have explained the need for strict scrutiny as arising from the significance of the franchise as the guardian of all other rights. *See Harper* v. *Virginia Bd. of Elections*, 383 U.S. 663, 667 (1966); *Reynolds* v. *Sims*, 377 U.S. 533, 562 (1964); *Yick Wo v. Hopkins*, 118 U.S. 356, 370 (1886).

furthering a substantial interest of the State.[16] We turn to a consideration of the standard appropriate for the evaluation of § 21.031.

A

Sheer incapability or lax enforcement of the laws barring entry into this country, coupled with the failure to establish an effective bar to the employment of undocumented aliens, has resulted in the creation of a substantial "shadow population" of illegal migrants—numbering in the millions—within our borders. This situation raises the specter of a permanent caste of undocumented resident aliens, encouraged by some to remain here as a source of cheap labor, but nevertheless denied the benefits that our society makes available to citizens and lawful residents. The existence of such an underclass presents most difficult problems for a Nation that prides itself on adherence to principles of equality under law.[19]

The children who are plaintiffs in these cases are special members of this underclass. Persuasive arguments support the view that a State may withhold its beneficience [sic] from those whose very presence within the United States is the product of their own unlawful conduct. These arguments do not apply with the same force to classifications imposing disabilities on the minor *children* of such illegal entrants. At the least, those who elect to enter our territory by stealth and in violation of our law should be prepared to bear the consequences, including, but not limited to, deportation. But the children of those illegal entrants are not comparably situated. Their "parents have the ability to conform their conduct to societal norms," and presumably the ability to remove themselves from the State's jurisdiction; but the children who are plaintiffs in these cases "can affect neither their parents' conduct nor their own status." *Trimble* v. *Gordon*, 430 U.S. 762, 770 (1977). Even if the State found it expedient to control the conduct of adults by acting against their children, legislation directing the onus of a parent's misconduct against his children does not comport with fundamental conceptions of justice.

---

[6] See *Craig v. Boren*, 429 U.S. 190 (1976); *Lalli v. Lalli*, 439 U.S. 259 (1978). This technique of "intermediate" scrutiny permits us to evaluate the rationality of the legislative judgment with reference to well-settled constitutional principles. "In expounding the Constitution, the Court's role is to discern 'principles sufficiently absolute to give them roots throughout the community and continuity over significant periods of time, and to lift them above the level of the pragmatic political judgments of a particular time and place.'" *University of California Regents v. Bakke*, 438 U.S. 265, 299 (1978) (opinion of Powell, J.), quoting A. Cox, The Role of the Supreme Court in American Government 114 (1976). Only when concerns sufficiently absolute and enduring can be clearly ascertained from the Constitution and our cases do we employ this standard to aid us in determining the rationality of the legislative choice.

[19] We reject the claim that "illegal aliens" are a "suspect class." No case in which we have attempted to define a suspect class, *see, e. g.*, n. 14, *supra*, has addressed the status of persons unlawfully in our country. Unlike most of the classifications that we have recognized as suspect, entry into this class, by virtue of entry into this country, is the product of voluntary action. Indeed, entry into the class is itself a crime. In addition, it could hardly be suggested that undocumented status is a "constitutional irrelevancy." With respect to the actions of the Federal Government, alienage classifications may be intimately related to the conduct of foreign policy, to the federal prerogative to control access to the United States, and to the plenary federal power to determine who has sufficiently manifested his allegiance to become a citizen of the Nation. No State may independently exercise a like power. But if the Federal Government has by uniform rule prescribed what it believes to be appropriate standards for the treatment of an alien subclass, the States may, of course, follow the federal direction. *See De Canas v. Bica*, 424 U.S. 351 (1976).

Of course, undocumented status is not irrelevant to any proper legislative goal. Nor is undocumented status an absolutely immutable characteristic since it is the product of conscious, indeed unlawful, action. But § 21.031 is directed against children, and imposes its discriminatory burden on the basis of a legal characteristic over which children can have little control. It is thus difficult to conceive of a rational justification for penalizing these children for their presence within the United States. Yet that appears to be precisely the effect of § 21.031.

.....

In addition to the pivotal role of education in sustaining our political and cultural heritage, denial of education to some isolated group of children poses an affront to one of the goals of the Equal Protection Clause: the abolition of governmental barriers presenting unreasonable obstacles to advancement on the basis of individual merit. Paradoxically, by depriving the children of any disfavored group of an education, we foreclose the means by which that group might raise the level of esteem in which it is held by the majority. But more directly, "education prepares individuals to be self-reliant and self-sufficient participants in society." *Wisconsin v. Yoder, supra,* at 221. Illiteracy is an enduring disability. The inability to read and write will handicap the individual deprived of a basic education each and every day of his life. The inestimable toll of that deprivation on the social, economic, intellectual, and psychological well-being of the individual, and the obstacle it poses to individual achievement, make it most difficult to reconcile the cost or the principle of a status-based denial of basic education with the framework of equality embodied in the Equal Protection Clause. What we said 28 years ago in *Brown v. Board of Education*, 347 U.S. 483 (1954), still holds true: "Today, education is perhaps the most important function of state and local governments. ...

B

These well-settled principles allow us to determine the proper level of deference to be afforded § 21.031. Undocumented aliens cannot be treated as a suspect class because their presence in this country in violation of federal law is not a "constitutional irrelevancy." Nor is education a fundamental right; a State need not justify by compelling necessity every variation in the manner in which education is provided to its population. ... But more is involved in these cases than the abstract question whether § 21.031 discriminates against a suspect class, or whether education is a fundamental right. Section 21.031 imposes a lifetime hardship on a discrete class of children not accountable for their disabling status. The stigma of illiteracy will mark them for the rest of their lives. By denying these children a basic education, we deny them the ability to live within the structure of our civic institutions, and foreclose any realistic possibility that they will contribute in even the smallest way to the progress of our Nation. In determining the rationality of § 21.031, we may appropriately take into account its costs to the Nation and to the innocent children who are its victims. In light of these countervailing costs, the discrimination contained in § 21.031 can hardly be considered rational unless it furthers some substantial goal of the State.

IV

.....

The Constitution grants Congress the power to "establish an uniform Rule of Naturalization." Art. I., § 8, cl. 4. Drawing upon this power, upon its plenary authority with respect to foreign relations and international commerce, and upon the inherent power of a sovereign to close its borders, Congress has developed a complex scheme governing admission to our Nation and status within our borders. ... The States enjoy no power with respect to the classification of aliens. This power is "committed to the political branches of the Federal Government." ...

.....

We are reluctant to impute to Congress the intention to withhold from these children, for so long as they are present in this country through no fault of their own, access to a basic education. In other contexts, undocumented status, coupled with some articulable federal policy, might enhance state authority with respect to the treatment of undocumented aliens. But in the area of special constitutional sensitivity presented by these cases, and in the absence of any contrary indication fairly discernible in the present legislative record, we perceive no national policy that supports the State in denying these children an elementary education. The State may borrow the federal classification. But to justify its use as a criterion for its own discriminatory policy, the State must demonstrate that the classification is reasonably adapted to *"the purposes for which the state desires to use it." Oyama v. California*, 332 U.S. 633, 664-65 (1948) (Murphy, J., concurring) (emphasis added). We therefore turn to the state objectives that are said to support § 21.031.

V

Appellants argue that the classification at issue furthers an interest in the "preservation of the state's limited resources for the education of its lawful residents." ... First, appellants appear to suggest that the State may seek to protect itself from an influx of illegal immigrants. While a State might have an interest in mitigating the potentially harsh economic effects of sudden shifts in population, § 21.031 hardly offers an effective method of dealing with an urgent demographic or economic problem. There is no evidence in the record suggesting that illegal entrants impose any significant burden on the State's economy. ...Thus, even making the doubtful assumption that the net impact of illegal aliens on the economy of the State is negative, we think it clear that "[charging] tuition to undocumented children constitutes a ludicrously ineffectual attempt to stem the tide of illegal immigration," at least when compared with the alternative of prohibiting the employment of illegal aliens. 458 F.Supp., at 585. *See* 628 F.2d, at 461; 501 F.Supp., at 579, and n. 88.

Second, while it is apparent that a State may "not . . . reduce expenditures for education by barring [some arbitrarily chosen class of] children from its schools," *Shapiro v. Thompson*, 394 U.S. 618, 633 (1969), appellants suggest that undocumented children are appropriately singled out for exclusion because of the special burdens they impose on the State's ability to provide high-quality public education. But the record in no way supports the claim that exclusion of undocumented children is likely to improve the overall quality of education in the State. ... Finally, appellants suggest that undocumented children are appropriately singled out because their unlawful presence within the United States renders them less likely than other children to remain within the boundaries of the State, and to put their education to productive social or political use within the State. Even assuming that such an interest is legitimate, it is an interest that is most difficult to quantify. The State has no assurance that any child, citizen or not, will employ the education provided by the State within the confines of the State's borders. In any event, the record is clear that many of the undocumented children disabled by this classification will remain in this country indefinitely, and that some will become lawful residents or citizens of the United States. It is difficult to understand precisely what the State hopes to achieve by promoting the creation and perpetuation of a subclass of illiterates within our boundaries, surely adding to the problems and costs of unemployment, welfare, and crime. It is thus clear that whatever savings might be achieved by denying these children an education, they are wholly insubstantial in light of the costs involved to these children, the State, and the Nation.

VI

If the State is to deny a discrete group of innocent children the free public education that it offers to other children residing within its borders, that denial must be justified by a showing that it furthers some substantial state interest. No such showing was made here. Accordingly, the judgment of the Court of Appeals in each of these cases is

Affirmed.

Chief Justice Burger, with whom Justice White, Justice Rehnquist, and Justice O'Connor join, dissenting.

Were it our business to set the Nation's social policy, I would agree without hesitation that it is senseless for an enlightened society to deprive any children—including illegal aliens—of an elementary education. I fully agree that it would be folly—and wrong—to tolerate creation of a segment of society made up of illiterate persons, many having a limited or no command of our language. However, the Constitution does not constitute us as "Platonic Guardians" nor does it vest in this Court the authority to strike down laws because they do not meet our standards of desirable social policy, "wisdom," or "common sense."

The Court makes no attempt to disguise that it is acting to make up for Congress' lack of "effective leadership" in dealing with the serious national problems caused by the influx of uncountable millions of illegal aliens across our borders. ... However, it is not the function of the Judiciary to provide "effective leadership" simply because the political branches of government fail to do so... The Court's holding today manifests the justly criticized judicial tendency to attempt speedy and wholesale formulation of "remedies" for the failures—or simply the laggard pace—of the political processes of our system of government. The Court employs, and in my view abuses, the Fourteenth Amendment in an effort to become an omnipotent and omniscient problem solver. That the motives for doing so are noble and compassionate does not alter the fact that the Court distorts our constitutional function to make amends for the defaults of others.

KADRMAS v. DICKINSON PUBLIC SCHOOLS
487 U.S. 450 (1988)

[The Kadrmas family filed suit to challenge a decision by their local school board to charge a fee for bus transportation to and from school. The family lived 16 miles from the nearest school and lived in poverty. Their lawsuit claimed that the policy interfered with the fundamental right to a public education and discriminated against the poor. Justice O'Connor, writing for a five-member majority disagreed].

.....

We have previously rejected the suggestion that statutes having different effects on the wealthy and the poor should on that account alone be subjected to strict equal protection scrutiny. *See, e. g., Harris v. McRae*, 448 U.S. 297, 322-23 (1980); *Ortwein v. Schwab*, 410 U.S. 656, 660 (1973). Nor have we accepted the proposition that education is a "fundamental right," like equality of the franchise, which should trigger strict scrutiny when government interferes with an individual's access to it. *See Papasan v. Allain*, 478 U.S. 265, 284 (1986); *Plyler v. Doe, supra*, at 223; *San Antonio Ind. Sch. Dist. v. Rodriguez, supra.*

Relying primarily on *Plyler v. Doe, supra*, however, appellants suggest that North Dakota's 1979 statute should be subjected to "heightened" scrutiny. This standard of review, which is less demanding than "strict scrutiny" but more demanding than the standard rational relation test, has generally been applied only in cases that involved discriminatory classifications based on sex or illegitimacy. In *Plyler*, which did not fit this pattern, the State of Texas had denied to the children of illegal aliens the free public education that it made available to other residents. Applying a heightened level of equal protection scrutiny, the Court concluded that the State had failed to show that its classification advanced a substantial state interest. We have not extended this holding beyond the "unique circumstances," that provoked its "unique confluence of theories and rationales." Nor do we think that the case before us today is governed by the holding in *Plyler*. Unlike the children in that case, Sarita Kadrmas has not been penalized by the government for illegal conduct by her parents. On the contrary, Sarita was denied access to the school bus only because her parents would not agree to pay the same user fee charged to all other families that took advantage of the service. Nor do we see any reason to suppose that this user fee will "promot[e] the creation and perpetuation of a subclass of illiterates within our boundaries, surely adding to the problems and costs of unemployment, welfare, and crime." ... The case before us does not resemble *Plyler*, and we decline to extend the rationale of that decision to cover this case.

Appellants contend, finally, that whatever label is placed on the standard of review, this case is analogous to decisions in which we have held that government may not withhold certain especially important services from those who are unable to pay for them. Appellants cite *Griffin v. Illinois*, 351 U.S. 12 (1956) (right to appellate review of a criminal conviction conditioned on the purchase of a trial transcript); *Smith v. Bennett*, 365 U.S. 708 (1961) (application for writ of habeas corpus accepted only when accompanied by a filing fee); *Boddie v. Connecicut*, 401 U.S. 371 (1971) (action for dissolution of marriage could be pursued only upon payment of court fees and costs for service of process); *Lindsey v. Normet*, 405 U.S. 56 (1972) (appeal from civil judgments in certain landlord-tenant disputes conditioned on the posting of a bond for twice the amount of rent expected to accrue during the appellate process); and *Little v. Streater*, 452 U.S. 1 (1981) (fee for blood test in quasi-criminal paternity action brought against the putative father of a child receiving public assistance).

Leaving aside other distinctions that might be found between these cases and the one before us today, each involved a rule that barred indigent litigants from using the judicial process in circumstances where they had no alternative to that process. Decisions invalidating such rules are inapposite here. In contrast to the "utter exclusiveness of court access and court remedy," *United States v. Kras*, 409 U.S. 434, 445 (1973), North Dakota does not maintain a legal or a practical monopoly on the means of transporting children to school. Thus, unlike the complaining parties in all the cases cited by appellants, the Kadrmas family could and did find a private alternative to the public school bus service for which Dickinson charged a fee. That alternative was more expensive, to be sure, and we have no reason to doubt that genuine hardships were endured by the Kadrmas family when Sarita was denied access to the bus. Such facts, however, do not imply that the Equal Protection Clause has been violated.

Applying the appropriate test—under which a statute is upheld if it bears a rational relation to a legitimate government objective—we think it is quite clear that a State's decision to allow local school boards the option of charging patrons a user fee for bus service is constitutionally permissible. The Constitution does not require that such service be provided at all, and it is difficult to imagine why choosing to offer the service should entail a constitutional obligation to offer it for free. No one denies that encouraging local school districts to provide school bus service is a legitimate state purpose or that such encouragement would be undermined by a rule requiring that general revenues be used to subsidize an optional service that will benefit a minority of the district's families. It is manifestly rational for the State to refrain from undermining its legitimate objective with such a rule.

.....

In sum, the statute challenged in this case discriminates against no suspect class and interferes with no fundamental right. Appellants have failed to carry the heavy burden of demonstrating that the statute is arbitrary and irrational. The Supreme Court of North Dakota correctly concluded that the statute does not violate the Equal Protection Clause of the Fourteenth Amendment, and its judgment is affirmed.

DISSENT: JUSTICE MARSHALL, with whom JUSTICE BRENNAN joins, dissenting.

In *San Antonio Ind. Sch. Dist. v. Rodriguez*, 411 U.S. 1 (1973), I wrote that the Court's holding was a "retreat from our historic commitment to equality of educational opportunity and [an] unsupportable acquiescence in a system which deprives children in their earliest years of the chance to reach their full potential." *Id.* at 71 (dissenting). Today, the Court continues the retreat from the promise of equal educational opportunity by holding that a school district's refusal to allow an indigent child who lives 16 miles from the nearest school to use a school-bus service without paying a fee does not violate the Fourteenth Amendment's Equal Protection Clause. Because I do not believe that this Court should sanction discrimination against the poor with respect to "perhaps the most important function of state and local governments," *Brown v. Board of Education*, 347 U.S. 483, 493 (1954), I dissent.

.....

Since *Brown*, we frequently have called attention to the vital role of education in our society. We have noted that "education is necessary to prepare citizens to participate effectively and intelligently in our open political system . . . ." *Wisconsin v. Yoder*, 406 U.S. 205, 221 (1972); *see San Antonio Ind. Sch. Dist. v. Rodriguez*, 411 U.S., at 112-15 (Marshall, J., dissenting). We also have recognized that education prepares individuals to become self-reliant participants in our economy. *See Plyler v. Doe, supra*, at 221-22; *Wisconsin v. Yoder, supra*, at 221. A statute that erects special obstacles to education in the path of the poor naturally tends to consign such persons to their current disadvantaged status. By denying equal opportunity to exactly those who need it most, the law not only militates against the ability of each poor child to advance herself or himself, but also increases the likelihood of the creation of a discrete and permanent underclass. Such a statute is difficult to reconcile with the framework of equality embodied in the Equal Protection Clause.

JUSTICE STEVENS, with whom JUSTICE BLACKMUN joins, dissenting.

When the sovereign applies different rules to different segments of its jurisdiction, it must have a rational basis for doing so. "The term 'rational,' of course, includes a requirement that an impartial lawmaker could logically believe that the classification would serve a legitimate public purpose that transcends the harm to the members of the disadvantaged class." In this case, JUSTICE MARSHALL accurately explicates the harm to certain members of the disadvantaged class. And since the Supreme Court of the State of North Dakota has unequivocally identified the actual purpose of the geographic discrimination, I would not second-guess that conclusion and presume that the harm JUSTICE MARSHALL describes has been imposed for other reasons.

.....

This explanation of the state legislative purpose makes two propositions perfectly clear. First, free bus transportation is an important component of public education in a sparsely populated State; otherwise the alleviation of parental concerns regarding the cost of student transportation in a reorganized district could not have been expected to motivate a significant number of voters. Second, after the voters in a school district have had a fair opportunity to decide whether or not to reorganize, there is no longer any justification at all for allowing the nonreorganized districts to place an obstacle in the paths of poor children seeking an education in some parts of the State that has been removed in other parts of the State. *Cf. G. D. Searle & Co. v. Cohn*, 455 U.S. 404, 420 (1982) (Stevens, J., dissenting) ("[T]he Constitution requires a rational basis for the special burden imposed on the disfavored class as well as a reason for treating that class differently").

Thus, the State Supreme Court's explanation of the purpose of this discrimination does not include the "elements of legitimacy and neutrality that must always characterize the performance of the sovereign's duty to govern impartially." Cleburne, supra, at 452 (footnote omitted). Accordingly, I respectfully dissent.

II. Education under State Constitutions

Bernard James and Julie M. Hoffman: Brown in State Hands: State Policymaking and Educational Equality After *Freeman v. Pitts*, 20 Hastings Const. L.Q. 521 (1993)*

On the constitutional Richter scale, *Brown v. Board of Education* has proven to be one of the few truly high magnitude tremors. Its aftershocks continue to provide a jolt to equal protection jurisprudence. It is fair to add that the impact of *Brown* jurisprudence extends even to contemporary areas of law not usually associated with notions of suspect classifications and discrimination.

Most attention is directed to notions of equality and federalism—*Brown*'s rule that race is an invalid classification for policymaking and the constitutional principle that states as sovereigns are free to enact laws that further policies distinct from those of the central government. With this focus, one discovers the contradictions of the *Brown* era and their impact on public education: supremacy versus autonomy, delegation versus accountability, liberty versus equality. Point and counterpoint.

The initial impact of the *Brown* decision on public education not only shattered the idea of racial classifications, but also dismissed what remained of the concept of states rights, particularly as that label was used for the notion that federal policies could be acknowledged or ignored. An interesting and often problematical state-federal relationship evolved after *Brown*—*Brown II* in particular—and its emphasis on a deliberate dismantling of local school systems that had been built on invidious classifications and inequitable programs. States either did nothing at all in the way of formulating new educational policies or acted defensively in response to supervised federal orders and coercive federal spending programs. While the evolution of this relationship clarified much of what we now associate with modern federal supremacy, it has created a new set of problems concerning the ultimate accountability for formulating educational policies to address inequalities arising out of race, wealth, and other classifications.

....

If one limits the characterization of *Brown* to the proposition that educational policies based on racial classifications are per se invalid, this goal has been accomplished. No state would consider using race as a criterion for furthering an otherwise legitimate policy. But beyond racial classifications, the question becomes how much official resistance remains to the moral influence of *Brown*, which postures education as "perhaps the most important function of state and local governments." As it becomes more difficult to characterize disparity in public education in constitutional terms (so as to trigger the safeguards of federal equal protection rules), states will

---

again find themselves in charge of formulating policies to address the remaining facets of inequality.

The equality principle will, in effect, revert to state hands. This, in some ways, will be a return to normalcy. Public education has been one of the essential responsibilities of state and local governments. It is the constitutions of the states, after all, that provide for a "uniform" education, a "thorough and efficient" education, and a "right to safe schools." The school desegregation jurisprudence of the *Brown* era is in this respect something of an anomaly developed out of the urgency to prompt reluctant elected officials to "come forward with a plan that promises realistically to work ... now."

The state constitutions are good reference points for speculation about notions of equality in public education after *Brown*. The growth of the state lawmaking machinery—particularly on constitutional issues—has been unprecedented over the last two decades. Whatever one may think of the phenomenon of modern state constitutional law in the abstract, it is now clear beyond quibble that these documents have become the cloth out of which modern social compacts are woven. On matters of taxation, spending, crime and punishment, the environment, and substantive due process, state constitutions are being used to provide a forum for both discussion and resolution of the major issues of the day.

A closer examination of the capacity of state policymakers to use these tools to direct the future of public education now seems essential in the twilight of the *Brown* era. The inquiry highlights a dire prognosis. Since *Brown*, state policymaking on education issues has been unimaginative and reactive. State educational policy generally reflects the fear that meaningful equality—when defined as merely an equal opportunity to succeed-is undesirable, too costly, or both. Any movement toward public school reform is boilerplate, reflecting the spirit, and reluctantly, the letter of federal law.

SERRANO v. PRIEST
487 P.2d 1241 (Cal. 1971)

OPINION BY: SULLIVAN

We are called upon to determine whether the California public school financing system, with its substantial dependence on local property taxes and resultant wide disparities in school revenue, violates the equal protection clause of the Fourteenth Amendment. We have determined that this funding scheme invidiously discriminates against the poor because it makes the quality of a child's education a function of the wealth of his parents and neighbors. Recognizing as we must that the right to an education in our public schools is a fundamental interest which cannot be conditioned on wealth, we can discern no compelling state purpose necessitating the present method of financing. We have concluded, therefore, that such a system cannot withstand constitutional challenge and must fall before the equal protection clause.

The complaint sets forth three causes of action. The first cause alleges in substance as follows: Plaintiff children attend public elementary and secondary schools located in specified school districts in Los Angeles County. This public school system is maintained throughout California by a financing plan or scheme which relies heavily on local property taxes and causes substantial disparities among individual school districts in the amount of revenue available per pupil for the districts' educational programs. Consequently, districts with smaller tax bases are not able to spend as much money per child for education as districts with larger assessed valuations.

.....

I

We begin our task by examining the California public school financing system, which is the focal point of the complaint's allegations. At the threshold, we find a fundamental statistic—over 90 percent of our public school funds derive from two basic sources: (a) local district taxes on real property and (b) aid from the State School Fund.

By far the major source of school revenue is the local real property tax. Pursuant to article IX, section 6 of the California Constitution, the Legislature has authorized the governing body of each county, and city and county, to levy taxes on the real property within a school district at a rate necessary to meet the district's annual education budget. The amount of revenue which a district can raise in this manner thus depends largely on its tax base—i.e., the assessed valuation of real property within its borders. Tax bases vary widely throughout the state; in 1969-1970, for example, the assessed valuation per unit of average daily attendance of elementary school children ranged from a low of $103 to a peak of $952,156—a ratio of nearly 1 to 10,000.

The other factor determining local school revenue is the rate of taxation within the district. Although the Legislature has placed ceilings on permissible district tax rates (§ 20751 et seq.), these statutory maxima may be surpassed in a "tax override" election if a majority of the district's voters approve a higher rate. (§ 20803 et seq.) Nearly all districts have voted to override the statutory limits. Thus the locally raised funds which constitute the largest portion of school revenue are primarily a function of the value of the realty within a particular school district, coupled with the willingness of the district's residents to tax themselves for education.

Most of the remaining revenue comes from the State School Fund pursuant to the "foundation program," through which the state undertakes to supplement local taxes in order to provide a "minimum amount of guaranteed support to all districts . . . ." (§ 17300.) With certain minor exceptions, n6 the foundation program ensures that each school district will receive annually, from state or local funds, $ 355 for each elementary school pupil (§§ 17656, 17660) and $ 488 for each high school student. (§ 17665.)

III

B

.....

The fundamental importance of education has been recognized in other contexts by the United States Supreme Court and by this court. These decisions—while not legally controlling on the exact issue before us—are persuasive in their accurate factual description of the significance of learning.

The classic expression of this position came in *Brown v. Board of Education* (1954) 347 U.S. 483, which invalidated de jure segregation by race in public schools. The high court declared: "Today, education is perhaps the most important function of state and local governments. Compulsory school attendance laws and the great expenditures for education both demonstrate our recognition of the importance of education to our democratic society. It is required in the performance of our most basic public responsibilities, even service in the armed forces. It is the very foundation of good citizenship. Today it is a principal instrument in awakening the child to cultural values, in preparing him for later professional training, and in helping him to adjust normally to his environment. In these days, it is doubtful that any child may reasonably be expected to succeed in life if he is denied the opportunity of an education. Such an opportunity, where the state has undertaken to provide it, is a right which must be made available to all on equal terms." (*Id.* at p. 493.)

.....

Finally, education is so important that the state has made it compulsory—not only in the requirement of attendance but also by assignment to a particular district and school. Although a child of wealthy parents has the opportunity to attend a private school, this freedom is seldom available to the indigent. In this context, it has been suggested that "a child of the poor assigned willy-nilly to an inferior state school takes on the complexion of a prisoner, complete with a minimum sentence of 12 years." (*Coons, Clune & Sugarman, supra*, 57 Cal. L. Rev. at p. 388.)

C

The Financing System Is Not Necessary to Accomplish a Compelling State Interest

We now reach the final step in the application of the "strict scrutiny" equal protection standard-the determination of whether the California school financing system, as presently structured, is necessary to achieve a compelling state interest.

.....

We need not decide whether such decentralized financial decision-making is a compelling state interest, since under the present financing system, such fiscal freewill is a cruel illusion for the poor school districts. We cannot agree that Baldwin Park residents care less about education than those in Beverly Hills solely because Baldwin Park spends less than $600 per child while Beverly Hills spends over $1,200. As defendants themselves recognize, perhaps the most accurate reflection of a community's commitment to education is the rate at which its citizens are willing to tax themselves to support their schools. Yet by that standard, Baldwin Park should be deemed far more devoted to learning than Beverly Hills, for Baldwin Park citizens levied a school tax of well over $5 per $100 of assessed valuation, while residents of Beverly Hills paid only slightly more than $2.

In summary, so long as the assessed valuation within a district's boundaries is a major determinant of how much it can spend for its schools, only a district with a large tax base will be truly able to decide how much it really cares about education. The poor district cannot freely choose to tax itself into an excellence which its tax rolls cannot provide. Far from being necessary to promote local fiscal choice, the present financing system actually deprives the less wealthy districts of that option.

.....

We, therefore, arrive at these conclusions. The California public school financing system, as presented to us by plaintiffs' complaint supplemented by matters judicially noticed, since it deals intimately with education, obviously touches upon a fundamental interest. For the reasons we have explained in detail, this system conditions the full entitlement to such interest on wealth, classifies its recipients on the basis of their collective affluence and makes the quality of a child's education depend upon the resources of his school district and ultimately upon the pocketbook of his parents. We find that such financing system as presently constituted is not necessary to the attainment of any compelling state interest. Since it does not withstand the requisite "strict scrutiny," it denies to the plaintiffs and others similarly situated the equal protection of the laws. If the allegations of the complaint are sustained, the financial system must fall and the statutes comprising it must be found unconstitutional.

SERRANO v. PRIEST

557 P.2d 929 (Cal. 1976)

Our decision in *Serrano I*, which due to the then legal posture of the proceeding directed itself only to the sufficiency of allegations of the complaint to state a cause of action and contemplated full trial proceedings for the proof of such allegations, nevertheless attracted the immediate attention of the California Legislature. As a result the lawmakers passed two bills—Senate Bill No. 90 (S.B. 90) and Assembly Bill No. 1267 (A.B. 1267) —which, upon becoming law during the pendency of trial proceedings, brought about certain significant changes in the public school financing system then under judicial scrutiny....

In Serrano I, we described the prior financing system as follows:

> We begin our task by examining the California public school financing system, which is the focal point of the complaint's allegations. At the threshold, we find a fundamental statistic—over 90 percent of our public school funds derive from two

> basic sources: (a) local district taxes on real property and (b) aid from the State School Fund.

……

If, we held, the allegations of the complaint upon trial were found to be true, thus establishing that the system described was the one actually existing in California, that system would be invalid as in violation of state and federal equal protection provisions. The Legislature, apparently recognizing the likelihood of such a finding, decided not to await the outcome of such proceedings but to address itself immediately to the problem....

[I]t is clear that substantial disparities in expenditures per pupil resulting from differences in local taxable wealth will continue to exist under S.B. 90 and A.B. 1267. The reason for this is that essentially local wealth is the principal determinant of revenue, that high wealth districts do not need to make the same tax effort as low wealth districts in order to reach, let alone exceed, the level of the foundation program and that in this setting, basic aid becomes antiequalizing and "convergence" of doubtful achievement....

We—along with the trial court and the parties—think it is clear that *Rodriguez* undercuts our decision in *Serrano I* to the extent that we held the California public school financing system (if proved to be as alleged) to be invalid as in violation of the equal protection clause of the Fourteenth Amendment to the United States Constitution. However, as we made clear in footnote 11, our decision in *Serrano I* was based not only on the provisions of the federal Constitution but on the provisions of our own state Constitution as well....... [Because of *Rodriguez*], we now adhere to our determinations, made in *Serrano I*, that our state public school financing system [is invalid] in light of our state constitutional provisions guaranteeing equal protection of the laws (1) discrimination in educational opportunity on the basis of district wealth involves a suspect classification, and (2) education is a fundamental interest.

Notes and Comments

1. State Constitutions and Education as a Fundamental Right

After the decision by the California Supreme Court in *Serrano*, the courts of 14 other states—Alabama, Connecticut, Kentucky, Minnesota, New Hampshire, New Jersey, North Carolina, North Dakota, Vermont, Virginia, Washington, West Virginia, Wisconsin, and Wyoming—have declared education to be a fundamental right. *See* Opinion of the Justices, 624 So. 2d 107, 157 (Ala. 1993); *Horton v. Meskill* (*Horton I*), 172 Conn. 615, 646, 376 A.2d 359 (1977); *Rose v. Council for Better Educ., Inc.*, 790 S.W.2d 186, 206 (Ky. 1989); *Skeen v. State*, 505 N.W.2d 299, 313 (Minn. 1993); *Claremont Sch. Dist. v. Governor*, 142 N.H. 462, 473, 703 A.2d 1353 (1997); *Robinson v. Cahill*, 69 N.J. 133, 147, 351 A.2d 713 (1975), cert. denied sub nom. *Klein v. Robinson*, 423 U.S. 913 (1975); *Leandro v. State of North Carolina*, 346 N.C. 336, 348, 488 S.E.2d 249 (1997); *Bismarck Pub. Sch. Dist. 1 v. State*, 511 N.W.2d 247, 256 (N.D. 1994); *Brigham v. State*, 166 Vt. 246, 262, 692 A.2d 384 (1997); *Scott v. Commonwealth*, 247 Va. 379, 386, 443 S.E.2d 138, 10 Va. Law Rep. 1192 (1994); *Seattle Sch. Dist. v. State*, 90 Wn. 2d 476, 511, 585 P.2d 71 (1978); *Pauley v. Kelly*,

162 W. Va. 672, 707, 255 S.E.2d 859 (1979); *Kukor v. Grover*, 148 Wis. 2d 469, 496, 436 N.W.2d 568 (1989); *Washakie Co. Sch. Dist. No. One v. Herschler*, 606 P.2d 310, 333 (Wyo. 1980) *cert. denied* 449 U.S. 824 (1980).

One state court has avoided the question on the status of education but has invalidated state policies using the equal protection provision of the state constitution. *See Dupree v. Alma Sch. Dist. No. 30*, 279 Ark. 340, 651 S.W.2d 90 (1983). Another state court has avoided the issue by invalidating a state education policy using the free instruction clause. *See Tennessee Small Sch. Sys. v. McWherter*, 851 S.W.2d 139 (Tenn. 1993).

Six States—Colorado, Georgia, Idaho, Maryland, New York, and Ohio—have ruled that education is not a fundamental right under the state constitution. *See Lujan v. Colorado State Bd. of Education*, 649 P.2d 1005 (Colo. 1982); *Bd. of Educ. v. Nyquist*, 57 N.Y.2d 27, 43, 439 N.E.2d 359 (1982); *Bd. of Educ. v. Walter*, 58 Ohio St. 2d 368, 390 N.E.2d 813, (1979); *Hornbeck v. Somerset County Bd. of Educ.*, 295 Md. 597, 458 A.2d 758 (1983); *McDaniel v. Thomas*, 248 Ga. 632, 285 S.E.2d 156 (1981); *Idaho Sch. for Equal Educ. Opportunity v. Evans*, 123 Idaho 573, 850 P.2d 724 (Idaho 1993).

Two additional states have ruled that education is fundamental as a matter of state constitutional law:

- Michigan – *Lintz v. Alpena Public Schools of Alpena and Presque Isle Counties*, 119 Mich. App. 32 (1982). The court interpreted Michigan's Constitution to include a fundamental right to a free public education. *Id.* at 37.

- Pennsylvania – *Lisa H. v. State Bd. of Educ.*, 67 Pa. Commw. 350 (1982). The right of entitlement to public education in Pennsylvania is a property interest constitutionally created and statutorily established. *Id.* at 357.

One additional state has used the education clause to impose higher duties on educators:

- Florida – *Bush v. Holmes*, 919 So. 2d 392 (Fla. 2006). The court interpreted Florida's education clauses to impose a "maximum duty on the state to provide for public education that is uniform and of high quality." *Id.* at 404.

2. Education and "Free Instruction" Clauses under State Constitutions

The California Supreme Court in *Serrano* ruled that under the state constitution education was a fundamental right despite that fact that the education provision made mention only of a free public school system. North Dakota courts have also determined their state constitutions provide a fundamental right to equal educational funding despite education clauses that required only a free public school system. *See Bismarck Public School Dist. 1 v. State*, 511 N.W.2d 247 (N.D. 1994). The *Bismark* court presents a unique argument in its rationale.

> The education provisions of our state constitution have "at least equal standing" with the guarantees of freedom of religion and freedom of speech and press, and the State has a compelling interest in establishing minimum standards of education to ensure that our children receive an adequate education. Funding of education promotes "[a] high degree of intelligence, patriotism, integrity and morality on the part of every voter in a government by the people . . . to insure the continuance of that government and the prosperity and happiness of the people" [Art. VIII, § 1, N.D. Const.] and is essential to the practical realization of the fundamental right enumerated in our state constitution: the right to a "uniform system of free public schools throughout the state" which "shall be open to all children of the state of North Dakota." Art. VIII, §§ 1 & 2, N.D. Const. In order to meet those state constitutional requirements, the funding of education must be at least on par with the right to bring a personal injury lawsuit and homestead rights.
> *Bismarck Public Schools*, 511 N.W.2d 247, at 259 (citations omitted).

KUKOR v. GROVER
436 N.W.2d 568 (Wis. 1989)

OPINION BY: CECI

The appellants maintain that the unconstitutional deficiency in the system is that the school finance program fails to take into account the fact that children have differing educational needs, some of which may, as a result of socioeconomic factors, require greater financial resources to achieve the same level of educational opportunity. It is further argued that those districts with the greatest educational burden are the least capable of raising sufficient financing from property taxation as a result of lower property valuations or "municipal overburden" placing greater tax demands upon the property.

The deficiencies presented by appellants in support of the argument that the method of school finance is unconstitutional specifically include the following. First, appellants discuss the failure of the finance system to compensate for the "educational overburden" resulting from a high concentration of poverty students and concomitant financial burden of providing for the following services more greatly needed in poverty districts: early childhood education; compensatory education; dropout prevention programs; vocational education; and supportive services, including the provision of social workers and psychologists. It is asserted that the need to provide programs to compensate for poverty effects on education has required the redirection of funds from regular programs and, consequently, an inability to provide regular programs of instruction equal to those of higher expenditure districts. Additionally, appellants allege deficiency in the system's failure to compensate for "municipal overburden." Municipal overburden is a term used to describe the circumstances of high municipal service needs and costs and resultant high property tax rates which preclude increases in revenue for school purposes. Related to the general argument regarding municipal overburden is the more specific factor of high costs of education in metropolitan districts due to higher labor costs; security and vandalism costs; and high maintenance and energy costs because of older school buildings. Finally, appellants argue that the disparities in per-pupil expenditures among districts are demonstrative of the deficiency in the operation of the current school finance system.

This court, in reviewing the trial court's findings of evidentiary or historical fact, will uphold those findings unless they are clearly erroneous. *Treiber v. Knoll*, 135 Wis. 2d 58, 64, 398 N.W.2d 756 (1987). We heed to this deferential standard in the present case and uphold the following findings of the circuit court. We note, however, that subsequently enacted legislation may have alleviated certain burdens.

1. "The record in this case clearly shows that districts with a high concentration of poverty students face an educational overburden in the area of early childhood education."

2. "The evidence also shows that districts with a high concentration of poverty students face an extraordinary educational burden in the important area of compensatory education."

3. "The record does show that districts with a high concentration of poverty students face an educational overburden in the area of dropout prevention programs for high-risk youth."

4. "Districts with a high concentration of poverty students unquestionably face an educational overburden in the area of vocational education."

5. "While districts may deploy various personnel in different ways to attempt to meet the needs of poverty students, the evidence presented at trial particularly emphasized the supportive services overburden as it impacts upon social workers, psychologists and nurses."

6. "The results of insufficient categorical aids is that local revenues absorb much of the costs of these programs and acts as a drain on local district resources."

7. "There are wide disparities in operating expenditures among Wisconsin school districts."

8. "[N]on-school tax burdens make it difficult for Milwaukee taxpayers and those in other municipally overburdened jurisdictions to increase property taxes to provide appropriate educational programs for pupils . . . ."

9. "[T]he cost of education is higher in the metropolitan districts in the state." In this regard, the trial court discussed high salary costs, security and vandalism costs, and high costs due to the operation of school in old structures.

I. *Uniformity Provision of art. X, sec. 3*

Article X, sec. 3 of the Wisconsin Constitution provides in part as follows:

> The legislature shall provide by law for the establishment of district schools, which shall be as nearly uniform as practicable; and such schools shall be free and without charge for tuition to all children between the ages of 4 and 20 years . . . .

. . . . .

We have reviewed the constitutional debates and are convinced, upon such readings and upon consideration of art. X, sec. 3 in the context of the related provisions of art. X, that the present system of school finance is not inconsistent with the uniformity provision of art. X. The analysis applied to arrive at this conclusion regarding the interpretation of art. X, sec. 3 is structured upon a framework previously established and applied in *Buse*. 74 Wis. 2d at 568. This court will consider the following in a question of constitutional interpretation:

(1) The plain meaning of the words in the context used;

(2) The historical analysis of the constitutional debates and of what practices were in existence in 1848, which the court may reasonably presume were also known to the framers of the 1848 constitution, *see State ex rel. Zimmerman v. Dammann* (1930), 201 Wis. 84, 88, 89, 228 N.W. 593, and *State ex rel. Comstock* [*v. Joint School District*, 65 Wis. 631, 636, 27 N.W. 829 (1886)]; and

(3) The earliest interpretation of this section by the legislature as manifested in the first law passed following the adoption of the constitution. *Payne v. Racine* (1935), 217 Wis. 550, 259 N.W. 437. *Id.*

Having determined that the plain meaning of the constitutional uniformity provision is not evident and that this court's previous decisions have not resolved the precise question as to this provision before the court today, we turn to debates of the constitutional convention for guidance. ...There is no question that the adoption of art. X of the 1948 Wisconsin Constitution represented recognition by the framers that public education was a function of the state. During the constitutional convention of 1847-48, more debate attended the issue of the extent of, as opposed to the question of, the state's participation in the funding of public schools. In a debate regarding whether the funds from the land grants from the United States government should be applied to the establishment of a school fund, it was stated by a member of the general committee on education that appropriation of the fund to public schools was necessary, since "[a] general system of education was the only system on which we could depend for the preservation of our liberties." Journal and Debates, Constitutional Convention, at 238 (1847-48) [hereinafter Journal and Debates]. While the state's role of supporting schools by means of the school fund was deemed crucial, at no point was the state's function regarded as requiring the complete support of public schools:

> The committee on education and school funds . . . had not, in any of the plans which had received favorable consideration at their frequent consultations, contemplated providing a fund, the revenues of which would afford the whole means of educating the children and youth of the state. On the contrary, they proposed to give the people a direct pecuniary interest in the support of their schools by calling upon them to contribute at least one third of the amount required for their sustenance, by direct taxation.

Id. at 236. More specifically, it was observed:

> It was intended that whatever the amount of the school fund might be, one-third of the expense of supporting schools, should be borne by each town. If a sufficient sum was not contributed by the school fund, the towns should have power to raise more. This provision was directly for the advantage of the poor. The gentleman who had last spoken, might not appreciate this; but a poor man with a family of children, and no fancy lots to dispose of, could understand the advantage. Experience had shown that if nothing was contributed by the town, the common schools languished, and select schools rose on their ruins. The school fund of Connecticut was so large as to be sufficient to defray the expenses of the education of every child within the limits of the state. Yet there, until a year or two, the district school system had declined. No adequate interest was felt by the people, in common schools, unless they contributed to their support. To obviate this danger, the committee had inserted the section.

Id. at 335. Interestingly, the framers expressed no concern as to the adequacy of the school fund to support the schools, and in fact it was opined that "there would be an excess above the wants of the primary and common schools." *Id.* at 342. Since the framers believed the school fund would be more than adequate to support the state's share of the educational cost burden, the provisions made as to the distribution of these funds is conclusively indicative of the framers' view of that which would constitute an equitable division of the state's resources to the districts.

The present equalization system far exceeds the degree of uniformity which might be accomplished under the constitutional provision: whereas the constitution provides only for each district to receive an equal amount of state resources per pupil, Ch. 121, Stats. provides a greater amount of state funds per pupil to districts with lower equalized property valuations. The general aid formula operates to assure that all districts will be able to provide for the basic education of its pupils, regardless of property wealth, at a cost slightly higher than the average state cost per pupil of the previous year. As explained above, to the extent that the needs of a district exceed that cost ceiling, in addition to categorical grants, supplemental "secondary aid" may be available to districts with relatively low property valuation.

Consequently, while greater uniformity in educational opportunities is, in the opinion of both parties, desirable and necessary, it is not something which is constitutionally mandated under the uniformity provision.

****

II. *Equal Protection Under art. I, sec. 1*

We now proceed to examine the scheme of financing under the constitutional provision for equal protection. Wisconsin Constitution art. I, sec. 1 provides:

> All people are born equally free and independent, and have certain inherent rights; among these are life, liberty and the pursuit of happiness; to secure these rights, governments are instituted, deriving their just powers from the consent of the governed.

Recently, this court restated the basis for determining the standard to be applied to equal protection challenges as follows: "'[U]nless a statute may be said to affect a "fundamental right" or to create a classification based on a "suspect" criterion, the standard this court uses in reviewing the constitutionality of a statutory classification is the "rational basis" test.'" *Treiber*, 135 Wis. 2d at 70. Appellants have not asserted that the alleged discrimination affects a "suspect" class. We would, furthermore, have rejected a claim of wealth discrimination constituting a suspect criterion had such a claim been made.

However, we do agree with appellants that "equal opportunity for education" is a fundamental right: "The involvement of the legislature from the framing of the constitution to the present and the many cases which have come before this court, emphasize that the equal opportunity for education *as defined by* art. X, sec. 3, is a fundamental right." *Buse*, 74 Wis. 2d at 567 (emphasis added). We qualify this finding by emphasizing that "equal opportunity for education" does not mandate absolute equality in districts' per-pupil expenditures. In fact, such complete equalization is constitutionally prohibited to the extent that it would necessarily inhibit local control. *Id.* at 570-72.

Moreover, to the extent that art. X delineates state distribution of resources on an equal per-pupil basis, to assert that equal opportunity for education mandates an entirely different scheme of financing requiring the state to distribute resources unequally among students to respond to the particularized needs of each student is inconsistent with the intent evidenced in the express language of art. X. Accordingly, since the deficiency allegedly exists not in the denial of a right to attend a public school free of charge, nor in the less affluent districts' failure to meet the educational standards delineated under sec. 121.02, Stats., nor in the state's failure to distribute state resources to the less affluent districts on at least an equal per-pupil basis as distribution is made to wealthier districts, no fundamental right is implicated in the challenged spending disparity.

.....

Therefore, notwithstanding our recognition that education is, to a certain degree, a fundamental right, we apply, as did the United States Supreme Court in *Rodriguez*, a rational basis standard because the rights at issue in the case before the court are premised upon spending disparities and not upon a complete denial of educational opportunity within the scope of art. X.

.....

While our deference would abruptly cease should the legislature determine that it was "impracticable" to provide to each student a right to attend a public school at which a basic education could be obtained, or if funds were discriminatorily disbursed and there existed no rational basis for such finance system, we will otherwise defer to the legislature's determination of the degree to which fiscal policy can be applied to achieve uniformity. Consequently, we hold, for the reasons discussed above that in the present case there is a rational basis justifying any disparities in per-pupil expenditures resulting from the operation of Ch. 121, Stats., the rational basis being the preservation of local control over education as mandated by art. X of the Wisconsin Constitution.

Because issues such as equality in education are peppered with political perceptions and emotionally laden views, we have carefully restrained our consideration of the constitutional issues before us from becoming so flavored. Therefore, our approach to the case at bar has been with a "'disciplined perception of the proper role of the courts in the resolution of our State's educational problems, and to that end, more specifically, judicial discernment of the reach of the mandates of our State Constitution in this regard.'" *Hornbeck v. Somerset County Bd. of Ed.*, 295 Md. 597, 658, 458 A.2d 758, 790 (1983). "To do otherwise would be an unwise and unwarranted entry into the controversial area of public school financing, whereby this Court would convene as a 'super-legislature,' legislating in a turbulent field of social, economic and political policy." *McDaniel v. Thomas*, 248 Ga. 632, 644, 285 S.E.2d 156, 165 (1981). ...

More recently, additional legislation was enacted and was targeted to respond to the problems of educationally and economically disadvantaged students. This legislation, which amended Ch. 119, Stats., was contained within the budget bill, 1987 Wis. act 399. Those provisions of 1987 Wis. act 399 which addressed educational problems associated with poverty included the following: (1) Section 371d, creating sec. 119.71, Stats., which provided grants to Milwaukee public schools for expansion of the half-day five-year-old kindergarten program to a full-day program for children who meet federal income eligibility standards for free lunch; (2) sec. 371h, creating sec. 119.72, Stats., which provided aid to Milwaukee public schools for early childhood education for four- and five-year-olds, targeting educationally disadvantaged pupils; (3) sec. 371mp, creating sec. 119.74, Stats., which provided for the establishment of mentor programs for economically or educationally disadvantaged pupils. The sum appropriated to finance the kindergarten and early childhood education programs for Milwaukee public schools provided under secs. 371d and 371h, respectively, is 3.1 million dollars. 1987 Wis. act 399, sec. 20.255(2)(ec). Thus, the legislature has been responsive to the problems before the court.

What has been challenged in the case at bar is not that less affluent schools have insufficient funds to provide for basic education, but that they have inadequate funds to provide specialized programs and to meet the particularized needs of students related to the effects of poverty. We recognize that more and improved programs are needed in the less affluent or overburdened districts but find that these legitimate demands may not be correctly described as claims for uniformity under Wis. Const. art. X, sec. 3 or equal treatment under Wis. Const. art. I, sec. 1, but rather constitute demands for that amount of resources necessary to meet the additional costs imposed by the student constituency of these districts. Such demands cannot be remedied by claims of constitutional discrepancies, but rather must be made to the legislature and, perhaps, also to the community.

By the Court. —The judgment of the circuit court is affirmed.

DISSENT: WILLIAM A. BABLITCH, J. (dissenting).

The majority characterizes this case as one of "spending disparities." That is not at all the focus of this case. The primary issue is whether the state, through its system of school financing, has met its constitutional obligation to provide an equal opportunity for education to all children of this state, rich and poor alike. As the record amply demonstrates, it has not.

Every member of this court agrees on four basic points:

1) that it is a fundamental right of every child in this state to have an equal opportunity for education;

2) that the state is constitutionally mandated to provide that opportunity;

3) that the method the state has chosen to fulfill its constitutional responsibility is the statutorily created system of financing K-12 public education;

4) that the trial record clearly establishes that the educational needs of a significant number of school children in this state, primarily those from high poverty districts, are very great, and these needs are not being met. These children come to school unready to learn. Compensatory education programs are unavailable to remedy their learning deficiencies. Supportive services and exceptional educational needs are insufficient to assist them. The little money that is channeled into these programs comes at the expense of the regular educational programs, thereby "shorting" the regular programs. The result, as one educator at trial stated, is that "until you meet those (social and emotional) needs, you're not going to be doing much educating. . . ." Circuit Court dec. at 18.

The reason these educational needs are not being met was established beyond any doubt in the trial court: the state system of financing K-12 public education is fundamentally flawed.

The fundamental flaw of the state formula is that it distributes dollars without regard to educational needs. It assumes that every child in this state begins his or her educational journey from the same starting point. If all children began that journey from the same starting point, then the formula would provide no constitutional objection: every child would start with the same opportunity. That may well have been the reality, with few exceptions, in 1848. It is not even close to reality today. The result is that a significant number of school children in this state are denied an equal opportunity to become educated people.

To use an analogy, which everyone can understand, while a majority of our children are handed the "educational ball" on the twenty-yard line, a significant number are handed this ball on the one-yard line with a three-hundred pound lineman on their back. Unquestionably, both groups of youngsters have the "opportunity" to score an educational touchdown. The opportunity, however, is far from equal.

I conclude that the uniformity clause of art. X, sec. 3, of the Wisconsin Constitution mandates that the state provide a character of instruction in the state schools such that each child is provided with a uniform opportunity to become an educated person. Neither absolute uniformity nor absolute equality is required. The funding may come in part from the state and part from local government, or in whole from the state. However it comes, the opportunity to become an educated person must be relatively equal across the state. To use the analogy once more, the uniformity clause does not mandate that the character of instruction be such that everyone must score a touchdown; it does mandate that everyone on the playing field have an equal opportunity to do so. Because the state has the constitutional responsibility to provide this equal opportunity, and because it has failed to do so, I respectfully dissent.

.....

I would hold that the uniformity clause of art. X, sec. 3 of the Wisconsin Constitution mandates that the state provide a character of instruction in the state schools such that each child is provided with a uniform opportunity to become an educated person. I would further hold that the school finance formula, which is the state's only effort that is before us to fulfill its constitutional mandate, fails to do so.

Does this mean there must be absolute uniformity, absolute equality? Clearly not. The constitution does not require absolute uniformity of educational opportunity nor an equal expenditure per district. ...To achieve reasonable equality in educational opportunity for those districts having disproportionately high concentrations of children with special needs (primarily the high poverty districts), there must be adequate funding allowing a district to provide not only basic courses of instruction but special needs programs to properly prepare these children for receiving such instruction, as well as other programs designed to give these children an equal opportunity to become educated citizens. The challenged school financing scheme is not designed to meet these objectives. As one school district superintendent testified, "[the financing formula is] not a system which is in any way directly cognizant of educational needs and tasks. It's a system designed to create taxpayer equity . . . [the formula] doesn't guarantee anything to school children. It's not a mechanism designed to insure adequate levels of resources that are commensurate with the task districts face."

.....

While I do not dismiss the legislature's recent effort to address the deficiencies in the school financing formula, this court is simply unable to conclude, absent specific findings of fact, what effect, if any, this legislation has on the problems noted.

I am authorized to state that CHIEF JUSTICE NATHAN S. HEFFERNAN and JUSTICE SHIRLEY S. ABRAHAMSON join in this dissent.

ROSE v. COUNCIL FOR BETTER EDUCATION, INC.
790 S.W.2d 186 (Ky. 1989)

OPINION BY: STEPHENS

The issue we decide on this appeal is whether the Kentucky General Assembly has complied with its constitutional mandate to "provide an efficient system of common schools throughout the state." [Ky. Const. Sec. 183.].

In deciding that it has not, we intend no criticism of the substantial efforts made by the present General Assembly and by its predecessors, nor do we intend to substitute our judicial authority for the authority and discretion of the General Assembly. We are, rather, exercising our constitutional duty in declaring that, when we consider the evidence in the record, and when we apply the constitutional requirement of Section 183 to that evidence, it is crystal clear that the General Assembly has fallen short of its duty to enact legislation to provide for an efficient system of common schools throughout the state. In a word, the present system of common schools in Kentucky is not an "efficient" one in our view of the clear mandate of Section 183. The common school system in Kentucky is constitutionally deficient.

In reaching this decision, we are ever mindful of the immeasurable worth of education to our state and its citizens, especially to its young people. The framers of our constitution intended that each and every child in this state should receive a proper and an adequate education, to be provided for by the General Assembly. This opinion dutifully applies the constitutional test of Section 183 to the existing system of common schools. We do no more, nor may we do any less.

The goal of the framers of our constitution, and the polestar of this opinion, is eloquently and movingly stated in the landmark case of *Brown v. Board of Education*:

> education is perhaps the most important function of state and local governments. Compulsory school attendance laws and the great expenditures for education both demonstrate our recognition of the importance of education to our democratic society. It is required in the performance of our most basic public responsibilities, even service in the armed forces. It is the very foundation of good citizenship. Today it is a principal instrument in awakening the child to cultural values, in preparing him for later professional training, and in helping him to adjust normally to his environment. In these days, it is doubtful that any child may reasonably be expected to succeed in life if he is denied the opportunity of an education. Such an opportunity, where the state has undertaken to provide it, is a right, which must be made available to all on equal terms. *Id.*, 347 U.S. 483, 493, 74 S. Ct. 686, 691, 98 L. Ed. 873 (1954) (emphasis added).

These thoughts were as applicable in 1891 when Section 183 was adopted as they are today and the goals they express reflect the goals set out by the framers of our Kentucky Constitution.

.....

Following the trial of this case, the circuit judge, in three separate documents, prepared extensive findings of fact, conclusions of law and judgment(s). Because of the length of these documents, we feel it important to analyze them in some detail.

The trial judge identified four issues before him: (1) The necessity for defining the phrase "an efficient system of common schools" as contained in Section 183 of the Kentucky Constitution; (2) Whether education is a "fundamental right" under our Constitution; (3) Whether Kentucky's current method of financing its common schools violates Section 183, and (4) Whether students in the so-called "poor" school districts are denied equal protection of the laws.

"Efficient," in the Kentucky constitutional sense was defined as a system which required "substantial uniformity, substantial equality of financial resources and substantial equal educational opportunity for all students." Efficient was also interpreted to require that the educational system must be adequate, uniform and unitary.

Because of the language of Section 183, the trial court ruled that education, indeed, is a fundamental right in Kentucky.

In ruling on the issue of whether Kentucky's method of school financing violates Section 183 and underpinning the point with extensive findings of fact, the trial court declared that students in property poor school districts are offered a minimal level of educational opportunities, which is inferior to those offered to students in more affluent districts. Such "invidious" discrimination, based on the place of a student's residence, was determined to be unconstitutional. The trial court ruled that the school finance system violates the equal protection guarantees of Section 1 and 3 of the Kentucky Constitution.

.....

Ever broadening the definition and setting non-instructional standards, the trial court required an efficient school system to provide sufficient physical facilities, teachers, support personnel, and instructional materials to enhance the educational process. An adequate school system must also include careful and comprehensive supervision at all levels to monitor personnel performance and minimize waste. If and where waste and mismanagement exist, including but not limited to improper nepotism, favoritism, and misallocation of school monies, they must be eliminated, through state intervention if necessary. The General Assembly has all the power necessary to guarantee that the resources provided by Kentucky taxpayers for schools are spent wisely.

The trial court thus, with a very broad brush, included in its constitutional definition of "efficient" goals to be met by an education and requirements as to school financing, curriculum, personnel, accessibility to all children, physical facilities, instructional materials and management of the schools.

Moreover, the trial court made it clear that the duty—the absolute, unequivocal duty—to provide this system is solely the responsibility of the General Assembly. The court reiterated that its judicial power did not extend to specifying to the General Assembly the methods by which to implement and maintain this efficient system of education.

.....

If one were to summarize the history of school funding in Kentucky, one might well say that every forward step taken to provide funds to local districts and to equalize money spent for the poor districts has been countered by one backward step.

It is certainly true that the General Assembly, over the years, has made substantial efforts to infuse money into the system to improve and equalize the educational efforts in the common schools of Kentucky. What we must decide, based solely on the evidence in the record as tested by the Kentucky Constitution, Section 183, is whether the trial court was correct in declaring that those efforts have failed to create an efficient system of common schools in this Commonwealth.

V. THE EVIDENCE

Students in property poor districts receive inadequate and inferior educational opportunities as compared to those offered to those students in the more affluent districts.

That Kentucky's overall effort and resulting achievement in the area of primary and secondary education are comparatively low, nationally, is not in dispute. Thirty-five percent of our adult populations are high school drop-outs. Eighty percent of Kentucky's local school districts are identified as being "poor," in terms of taxable property. The other twenty percent remain under the national average. Thirty percent of our local school districts are "functionally bankrupt."

Evidence relative to educational performance was introduced by appellees to make a comparison of Kentucky with its neighbors—Ohio, Indiana, Illinois, Missouri, Tennessee, Virginia, and West Virginia. It also ranked Kentucky, nationally in the same areas.

In the area of per pupil expenditures, Kentucky ranks 6th among the 8 states and ranks 40th, nationally. With respect to the average annual salary of instructional staff, Kentucky again ranks 6th among its neighbors and 37th nationally. In the area of classroom teacher compensation, Kentucky is 7th and 37th. Our classroom teacher average salary is 84.68% of the national average and our per pupil expenditure is 78.20% of the national average.

When one considers the use of property taxes as a percent of sources of school revenue, Kentucky is 7th among our neighboring states and 43rd nationally. The national average is 30.1% while Kentucky's rate is 18.2%. If any more evidence is needed to show the inadequacy of our overall effort, consider that only 68.2% of ninth grade students eventually graduate from high school in Kentucky. That ranks us 7th among our eight adjacent sister states. Among the 6 of our neighboring states that use the ACT scholastic achievement test, our high school graduates average score is 18.1, which ranks us 4th. Kentucky's ratio of pupil-teacher is 19.2, which ranks us 7th in this region. In spite of the appellants' claim, at both the trial level and on appeal, that appellees' statistics are not current, all the above figures are based on a 1986 study, which was published in 1987.

Numerous well-qualified educators and school administrators testified before the trial court and all described Kentucky's educational effort as being inadequate and well below the national effort.

.....

Can anyone seriously argue that these disparities do not affect the basic educational opportunities of those children in the poorer districts? To ask the question is to answer it. Children in 80% of local school districts in this Commonwealth are not as well-educated as those in the other 20%.

It is argued by the appellants that the so-called permissive taxes, are at least part of the solution to equalizing local financial efforts. There are two easy answers that dispose of this argument. First, the taxes are permissive. Responding to obvious voter resistance to the imposition of taxes, 89 districts have enacted the tax on gross utility receipts; 5 districts have enacted the occupational tax; 82 districts have also enacted a special building tax, normally for a specific project for one time only, and not affecting teacher pay, instructional equipment, or any of the specific needs of educational opportunity. As the nature of the taxes is permissive, in many districts they are not adopted and therefore do not produce one cent in additional local revenue.

Secondly, according to the testimony of the expert witnesses, even if all the permissive taxes were enacted, the financial effort would still be inadequate, and because the population of the districts is in direct proportion to the amount of money that could and is raised by these taxes, the overall problem of an unequal local effort would be exacerbated by such action. Clearly, the permissive taxes are not the solution to the problems. Rather, they contribute to the disparity of per pupil expenditures.

Additionally, because the assessable and taxable real and personal property in the 177 districts is so varied, and because of a lack of uniformity in tax rates, the local school boards' tax effort is not only lacking in uniformity but is also lacking in adequate effort. The history of school financing in Kentucky certainly corroborates the trial court's finding as to the lack of uniformity and the lack of adequacy of local and state funding of education in the state. Based on the record before us, it is beyond cavil that the trial court's finding was correct.

.....

X. WHAT IS AN "EFFICIENT SYSTEM OF COMMON SCHOOLS?"

In a few simple, but direct words, the framers of our present Constitution set forth the will of the people with regard to the importance of providing public education in the Commonwealth.

.....

It serves no purpose to further lengthen this opinion with more verbiage from the Constitutional debates. Delegates Beckner and Moore told their fellow delegates and have told us, what this section means.

- The providing of public education through a system of common schools by the General Assembly is the most "vital question" presented to them.

- Education of children must not be minimized to the "slightest degree."

- Education must be provided to the children of the rich and poor alike.

- Education of children is essential to the prosperity of our state.

- Education of children should be supervised by the State.

- There must be a constant and continuing effort to make our schools more efficient.

- We must not finance our schools in a de minimis fashion.

- All schools and children stand upon one level in their entitlement to equal state support.

This Court, in defining efficiency must, at least in part, be guided by these clearly expressed purposes. The framers of Section 183 emphasized that education is essential to the welfare of the citizens of the Commonwealth. By this animus to Section 183, we recognize that education is a fundamental right in Kentucky.

.....

As can be seen, this Court, since the adoption of the present Constitution, has, in reflecting on Section 183, drawn several conclusions:

1) The General Assembly is mandated, is duty bound, to create and maintain a system of common schools - throughout the state.

2) The expressed purpose of providing such service is vital and critical to the well being of the state.

3) The system of common schools must be efficient.

4) The system of common schools must be free.

5) The system of common schools must provide equal educational opportunities for all students in the Commonwealth.

6) The state must control and administer the system.

7) The system must be, if not uniform, "substantially uniform," with respect to the state as a whole.

8) The system must be equal to and for all students.

.....

It is textbook law that enactments of the General Assembly have a strong presumption of constitutionality. It is also a textbook law that where legislative discretion is present, the judiciary will be reluctant to interfere. The separation of powers doctrine of the Kentucky Constitution underpins and buttresses these legal theories. Ky. Const. Sec. 27, 28, 29; *Legislative Research Commission v. Brown*, Ky., 664 S.W.2d 907 (1984).

In this context, we review the question before us. The ultimate issue is whether the system of common schools in the Commonwealth established by the General Assembly, with respect to the mandate of Section 183, is in compliance with the constitution. Specifically, we are asked—based solely on the evidence in the record before us—if the present system of common schools in Kentucky is "efficient" in the constitutional sense. It is our sworn duty, to decide such questions when they are before us by applying the constitution. The duty of the judiciary in Kentucky was so determined when the citizens of Kentucky enacted the social compact called the Constitution and in it provided for the existence of a third equal branch of government, the judiciary.

The issue before us—the constitutionality of the system of statutes that created the common schools—is the only issue. To avoid deciding the case because of "legislative discretion," "legislative function," etc., would be a denigration of our own constitutional duty. To allow the General Assembly (or, in point of fact, the Executive) to decide whether its actions are constitutional is literally unthinkable.

We believe that what these several cases cited as controlling by appellants mean is that great weight should be given to the decision of the General Assembly. We believe they mean that the presumption of constitutionality is substantial. We believe that they mean that legislative discretion—in this specific matter of common schools—is to be given great weight and, we do so in this decision. We do not question the wisdom of the General Assembly's decision, only its failure to comply with its constitutional mandate. In so doing, we give deference and weight to the General Assembly's enactments; however, we find them constitutionally deficient.

The judiciary has the ultimate power, and the duty, to apply, interpret, define, construe all words, phrases, sentences and sections of the Kentucky Constitution as necessitated by the controversies before it. It is solely the function of the judiciary to so do. This duty must be exercised even when such action serves as a check on the activities of another branch of government or when the court's view of the constitution is contrary to that of other branches, or even that of the public.

.....

The essential, and minimal, characteristics of an "efficient" system of common schools, may be summarized as follows:

1) The establishment, maintenance and funding of common schools in Kentucky is the sole responsibility of the General Assembly.

2) Common schools shall be free to all.

3) Common schools shall be available to all Kentucky children.

4) Common schools shall be substantially uniform throughout the state.

5) Common schools shall provide equal educational opportunities to all Kentucky children, regardless of place of residence or economic circumstances.

6) Common schools shall be monitored by the General Assembly to assure that they are operated with no waste, no duplication, no mismanagement, and with no political influence.

7) The premise for the existence of common schools is that all children in Kentucky have a constitutional right to an adequate education.

8) The General Assembly shall provide funding which is sufficient to provide each child in Kentucky an adequate education.

9) An adequate education is one which has as its goal the development of the seven capacities recited previously.

XI. IS THE PRESENT SYSTEM "EFFICIENT"?

We have described, infra, in some detail, the present system of common schools. We have noted the overall inadequacy of our system of education, when compared to national standards and to the standards of our adjacent states. We have recognized the great disparity that exists in educational opportunities throughout the state. We have noted the great disparity and inadequacy, of financial effort throughout the state.

In spite of the past and present efforts of the General Assembly, Kentucky's present system of common schools falls short of the mark of the constitutional mandate of "efficient." When one juxtaposes the standards of efficiency as derived from our Constitution, the cases decided thereunder, the persuasive authority from our sister states and the opinion of experts, with the virtually unchallenged evidence in the record, no other decision is possible.

Lest there be any doubt, the result of our decision is that Kentucky's entire system of common schools is unconstitutional. There is no allegation that only part of the common school system is invalid, and we find no such circumstance. This decision applies to the entire sweep of the system—all its parts and parcels. This decision applies to the statutes creating, implementing and financing the system and to all regulations, etc., pertaining thereto. This decision covers the creation of local school districts, school boards, and the Kentucky Department of Education to the Minimum Foundation Program and Power Equalization Program. It covers school construction and maintenance, teacher certification—the whole gamut of the common school system in Kentucky.

HOOTCH v. ALASKA STATE-OPERATED SCHOOL SYSTEM
536 P.2d 793 (Alaska 1975)

[28 students of school age filed suit to challenge an Alaska policy that forced them to leave their villages to attend school. Their homes were in inaccessible, rural parts of the State. The under State law each student attended school at state expense (including transportation, room and board) away from home in state-operated regional schools. The students, relying on provisions of the Alaska Constitution, argued that they has a right to attend secondary schools in their communities of residence.]

.....

Art. VII, § 1 of the Alaska Constitution provides in part:

The legislature shall by general law establish and maintain a system of public schools open to all children of the State . . . .

We have construed art. VII, § 1 on two previous occasions. In *Macauley v. Hildebrand*, we noted that art. VII, § 1 was a "constitutional mandate for pervasive state authority in the field of education". Then, in *Breese v. Smith*, a case involving the constitutionality of a junior high school grooming regulation under which a student was suspended because his hair was too long, we stated that "article VII, section 1 . . . . guarantees all children of Alaska a right to public education". Thus, this court has recognized the dual aspect of the constitutional provision. It imposes a duty upon the state legislature, and it confers upon Alaska school age children a right to education.

We are now called upon to ascertain whether the constitutional right to education includes the right to attend secondary school in one's community of residence.

.....

Appellants seek a definition of the constitutional provision in terms of a particular set of asserted facts. They seek to demonstrate that the right to education includes a right to local secondary schools because the right to education is unduly burdened and rendered hollow without the subsidiary right.

In determining the scope of a constitutional right, the focus of the court's inquiry is not, however, on the question of whether there is a burden on the exercise of that right. We must look to the intent of the framers of the constitution concerning the nature of the right itself, the problems which they were addressing and the remedies they sought. While prior practice and the framers' purposes are not necessarily conclusive, an historical perspective is essential to an enlightened contemporary interpretation of our constitution.

The pre-statehood pattern of high school locations, which is reflected in the current system of secondary education, was generated by the dual school system. High schools in incorporated cities enrolled both Native and non-Native students who lived in these populated areas. Secondary education for students living in rural areas of the state was limited or nonexistent. Rural Native students were presented with the choice of either staying at home and foregoing secondary education or leaving home and attending Mr. Edgecumbe, a BIA boarding school established for Native students. When enrollment at Mt. Edgecumbe eventually exceeded the school's capacity, the BIA began admitting Native Alaskans to Indian boarding schools in other states. Hundreds of Alaska Natives entered boarding schools in Chemawa, Oregon and Chilocco, Oklahoma.

.....

In view of this history, we conclude that art. VII, § 1 was intended to ensure that the legislature established a system of education designed to serve children of all racial backgrounds....

Comparison of the education provision in the Alaska Constitution with those in other states is also instructive in interpreting art. VII, § 1. The phrase "public schools open to all children of the State" in art. VII, § 1 is rarely found or paraphrased in other state constitutions....Unlike most state constitutions, the Constitution of Alaska does not require uniformity in the school system. The phrase "open to all" appears in lieu of the customary uniformity requirements. It seems likely that the drafters of the constitution had in mind the vast expanses of Alaska, its many isolated small communities which lack effective transportation and communication systems, and the diverse culture and heritage of its citizens. Since educational programs may well require special design to confront the divergent problems presented, a uniformity requirement in the Alaska education system might well prove unworkable. Thus, in art. VII, § 1, the Alaska Constitution appears to contemplate different types of educational opportunities including boarding, correspondence and other programs without requiring that all options be available to all students.

We have previously noted that different approaches are appropriate to meet the educational needs in the diverse areas of the state..... We conclude that art. VII, § 1 permits some differences in the manner of providing education. Reference to the events preceding the ratification of the Alaska Constitution further bolsters our conclusion. The delegates to the constitutional convention were aware that the principal Alaska opposition to statehood was based on arguments that the territory could not afford the costs of a state government. While endeavoring to draft the best possible constitution for the new state, the practical considerations of securing ratification of that document had also to be considered. To have proposed that the new constitution mandate secondary schools in all rural communities having eight school children would have been considered preposterous at that time in view of the grave financial problems which confronted the new state. Moreover, if the delegates had intended that secondary education be provided in each rural community, they certainly would have expressed themselves more directly and clearly than by use of the phrase "open to all".

We subscribe to the doctrine that our constitution is not a static document and that its provisions must be construed in light of changing social conditions. Here, however, we are being asked to insert into the constitution a concept not present in the original document and departing so far from its original terms and meaning as to constitute a radical invasion by the judiciary into an area specifically delegated by the very provision in question to the legislature. To do so is beyond our powers.

The nonjudicial nature of this problem is emphasized by appellants' concession that the right to local education is not absolute, and that when less than eight school age children reside in a community, the right to attend school locally must yield to the reality that there are too few children present to constitute a school. The decision as to when it is feasible to establish local secondary schools is peculiarly legislative and executive in nature.

The question of the desirability of local secondary schools is related not only to the number of students residing in a community, but also to complex policy questions bearing on the quality of education afforded children by small local secondary schools as opposed to larger regional schools n46 or urban schools attended while boarding in private homes. These issues are also inappropriate for judicial resolution.

It may well be that the exercise of the right to education is burdened by certain disadvantages. The existence of disadvantages is not, however, tantamount to a violation of the constitutional provision dictating that the right to education be open to all. The contemplation in art. VII, § 1 of some differences in the manner of providing education sanctions some disadvantages. So long as they are not violative of equal protection, the nature and proper means of overcoming the disadvantages present questions for the legislature. Appellants have been afforded a right to education, although they are not furnished a right to attend secondary schools in their communities of residence. We cannot find this latter right mandated by the constitution, absent a valid equal protection claim.

Affirmed and remanded.

DISSENT: RABINOWITZ, Chief Justice (dissenting).

Article VII, section 1 of the Alaska Constitution provides in pertinent part:

> The legislature shall by general law establish and maintain a system of public schools open to all children of the State . . . .

I read this constitutional mandate as imposing upon appellees the obligation to supply secondary schools to the rural communities of Alaska.

.....

Appellees have forcefully argued throughout this litigation that under article VII, section 1 of the Alaska Constitution, it is the legislature that is given complete authority to regulate the nature of Alaska's public education system, either directly or through delegated powers. Appellees further argue that since the legislature has not mandated that the public school system include secondary schools in appellants' communities, it is not the proper role of the courts to usurp the legislative prerogative. While I am mindful of the limited judicial expertise in the field of public education, appellees' concept of judicial deference is so broad that, if adopted, it would cause this court to abdicate its constitutional role. Under article IV, section 1 of the Alaska Constitution, the "judicial power" of the State is vested in Alaska's courts. The courts are charged with the solemn responsibility for interpreting and construing Alaska's laws, including our constitution, by which we are all bound. Under Alaska's constitution, as the highest court of the State of Alaska, the Supreme Court of Alaska is the final arbiter of the meaning of Alaska's constitution. Rather than a "radical invasion by the judiciary into an area specifically delegated by" article VII, section 1, to the legislature, I believe and would characterize our task as one of delineation of the constitutional perimeters of the educational delegation to Alaska's legislature. To illustrate the point, assume that the legislature decreed that all school age children in Alaska must, for nine months a year, attend public schools located only in Fairbanks, Alaska. Is there any doubt that such a legislative enactment is violative of article VII, section 1 of Alaska's constitution?

JAMES v. ALABAMA COALITION FOR EQUITY, INC.
836 So. 2d 813 (Ala. 2002)

[Alabama citizens successfully sued the state 10 years earlier and its courts found that the state's public education financing system was unconstitutional. Over the intervening years, court-ordered remedies to reform education in the state were met with political resistance, delay and judicial debate over the role of the state courts in fashioning a remedy for education reform.]

PER CURIAM.

This Court "shall never exercise the legislative and executive powers, or either of them; to the end that it may be a government of laws and not of men." Ala. Const. 1901 § 43. In Alabama, separation of powers is not merely an implicit "doctrine" but rather an express command; a command stated with a forcefulness rivaled by few, if any, similar provisions in constitutions of other sovereigns. Amendment 582 to the Alabama Constitution of 1901 reflects this State's adherence to this command by effectively nullifying any "order of a state court, which requires disbursement of state funds … until the order has been approved by a simple majority of both houses of the Legislature." Compelled by the weight of this command and a concern for judicial restraint, we hold (1) that this Court's review of the merits of the still pending cases commonly and collectively known in this State, and hereinafter referred to, as the "Equity Funding Case," has reached its end, and (2) that, because the duty to fund Alabama's public schools is a duty that—for over 125 years—the people of this State have rested squarely upon the shoulders of the Legislature, it is the Legislature, not the courts, from which any further redress should be sought. Accordingly, we hold that the Equity Funding Case is due to be dismissed.

…..

As the various opinions attached to this and other decisions of this Court stemming from the Equity Funding Case demonstrate, members of this Court have expressed serious concerns regarding the underlying foundations of this case and the trial court's actions and legal conclusions leading up to and included in its [holding that the state system of financing public education was illegal].

Given our ultimate holding in this opinion, we deem it judicially imprudent now - after issuing four decisions in this case over the past nine years—to test the bounds of judicial restraint in such a manner. …

…..

Our consideration of this issue stems from our June 29, 2001, order vacating the remand in *Ex parte James*… In *Ex parte James*, the Court recognized the serious difficulties implicated by judicial involvement in the administrative details of school funding. 713 So. 2d at 880-82. …

Our conclusion that the time has come to return the Equity Funding Case *in toto* to its proper forum seems a proper and inevitable end, foreshadowed not only by the obvious impracticalities of judicial oversight… Continuing the descent from the abstract to the concrete, we now recognize that any specific remedy that the judiciary could impose would, in order to be effective, necessarily involve a usurpation of that power entrusted exclusively to the Legislature. Accordingly, … we complete our judicially prudent retreat from this province of the legislative branch in order that we may remain obedient to the command of the people of the State of Alabama that we "never exercise the legislative and executive powers, or either of them; to the end that it may be a government of laws and not of men." Ala. Const. 1901, § 43.

Cases dismissed.

Notes and Comments

1. Role of State Courts in Education Reform

In the decision of the U.S. Supreme Court in *San Antonio Independent School District v. Rodriguez*, 411 U.S. 1 (1973), the justices commented on the difficulty of assigning a role to the judiciary in education reform debates.

> [T]his case also involves the most persistent and difficult questions of educational policy, another area in which this Court's lack of specialized knowledge and experience counsels against premature interference with the informed judgments made at the state and local levels. Education, perhaps even more than welfare assistance, presents a myriad of intractable economic, social, and even philosophical problems. The very complexity of the problems of financing and managing a statewide public school system suggests that there will be more than one constitutionally permissible method of solving them, and that, within the limits of rationality, the legislature's efforts to tackle the problems should be entitled to respect….. [T]he judiciary is well advised to refrain from imposing on the States inflexible constitutional restraints that could circumscribe or handicap the continued research and experimentation so vital to finding even partial solutions

> to educational problems and to keeping abreast of ever-changing conditions. 411 U.S. at 42-43.

These views on the role of court have understandably affected lower court decisions in federal courts that must follow the lead of the Supreme Court. Surprisingly, the *Kukor*, *Hootch*, and *James* cases also convey a degree of judicial discomfort over the role of state courts in resolving disputes over the meaning and enforcement of state constitutional provisions on education.

Two separate issues surface in these discussions. First, there is the interpretive issue of how to interpret what the state constitutional provision on public education. State court judges find themselves with the same basic choices for this task, as do federal judges. They can approach the provision conservatively by limiting inquiry to the intent of the framers or they can breath life into the provision by interpreting it in light of changes in state policy and philosophies since its inception. Second, there is the standard of review issue. On this matter, state courts also unwittingly follow the federal courts. State courts may defer to the legislature by applying the rational basis test—the lowest level of judicial scrutiny that essentially presumes the validity of a legislative policy. Or state judges case apply strict scrutiny. Under strict scrutiny, a state policy affecting rights in public education is presumed to be invalid unless state officials have an extraordinary justification.

One state court judge writes about the discomfort in this manner.

> [S]tates in recent years have avoided proclaiming that an adequate education is a fundamental right because that carries with it the obligation of the courts to examine and scrutinize all legislation respecting education strictly. We must admit to some apprehension about using a strict-scrutiny standard, because it has never been this court's constitutional function to micromanage the public schools of this state or even to retain jurisdiction over the public school system until, in our judgment, an adequacy standard has been achieved. *Lake View Sch. Dist. No. 25 v. Huckabee*, 351 Ark. 31, 55; 91 S.W.3d 472, (Ark. 2002).

The Arkansas courts in the Lakeview case found the public school financing scheme unconstitutional. After the legislature did not pass satisfactory legislation, the courts decided to supervise the state legislature. It appointed a special master to monitor legislation toward a remedy. In 2007, the legislature enacted a new school funding approach that was approved by the court. *See Lake View Sch. Dist. No. 25 v. Huckabee*, 370 Ark. 139 (Ark. 2007).

Other state courts have agreed with the Alabama courts in *James* and ruled that judicial interference with the legislative is a violation of separation of powers. *See Labato v. State*, 2008 Colo. App. LEXIS 69 (Colo. Ct. App., Jan. 24, 2008); *Coalition for Adequacy & Fairness in School Funding, Inc. v. Chiles*, 680 So.2d 400, 406-07 (Fla. 1996); *Lewis E. v. Spagnolo*, 186 Ill. 2d 198, 710 N.E.2d 798, 802, (Ill. 1992); *Nebraska Coalition for Educational Equity & Adequacy v. Heineman*, 273 Neb. 531, 731 N.W.2d 164, 183 (Neb. 2007); *Oklahoma Education Ass'n v. State*, 2007 OK 30, 158 P.3d 1058, 1066 (Okla. 2007); *Marrero v. Commonwealth*, 559 Pa. 14, 739 A.2d 110, 111-113 (Pa. 1999); *City of Pawtucket v. Sundlun*, 662 A.2d 40, 58-59 (R.I. 1995).

2. Education and "Uniformity" Clauses under State Constitutions

As the *Kukor* decision above suggests, states may limit the reach of the "uniformity" clauses in their state constitutions. Several state courts have held that "uniform" merely applies to the general system of education, and not to equality in funding. *See Skeen v. State*, 505 N.W.2d 299, 310 (Minn. 1993) (constitutional requirement met so long as all state schools provide "adequate level of basic education"); *Shofstall v. Hollins*, 110 Ariz. 88, 515 P.2d 590, 592 (Ariz. 1973) ("general and uniform" requirement met since Arizona's system assures every child a basic education); *Thompson v. Engelking*, 96 Idaho 793, 537 P.2d 635, 648 (Idaho 1975); *Idaho Schools for Equal Educ. v. Evans*, 123 Idaho 573, 850 P.2d 724 (Idaho 1993) ("The uniformity requirement in the education clause requires only uniformity in curriculum, not uniformity in funding."); *Olsen v. State*, 276 Ore. 9, 554 P.2d 139, 148 (Or. 1976) (Constitution is "complied with if the state requires and provides for a minimum of educational opportunities in the district and permits the districts to exercise local control over what they desire, and can furnish, over the minimum."); *Coalition for Equit. Sch. Fund. v. State*, 311 Ore. 300, 811 P.2d 116 (Or. 1991); *Lujan v. Colorado State Bd. of Educ.*, 649 P.2d 1005, 1018-19 (Colo. 1982), (Colorado General Assembly must provide each school age child the opportunity to receive a free education, and must establish guidelines); *Britt v. North Carolina State Bd. of Educ.*, 86 N.C. App. 282, 357 S.E.2d 432, 433-37 (N.C.App. 1987); *St. Johns County v. N.E. Fla. Builders*, 583 So. 2d 635, 641 (Fla. 1991). But *see Seattle Sch. Dist. No. 1 of King Cty. v. State*, 90 Wash. 2d 476, 585 P.2d 71 (Wash. 1978) (school funding system found unconstitutional based on requirement making it the "paramount" duty of the state to make "ample" provision for education); *Washakie Co. Sch. Dist. No. One v. Herschler*, 606 P.2d 310 (Wyo. 1980) (funding based on county wealth violates equal protection). *Bismarck Pub. Sch. Dist. #1 v. State*, 511 N.W.2d 247, 1994 N.D. LEXIS 26 (N.D. 1994) (the statutory method for distributing funding did not totally deprive any student of access to the fundamental right to education, the method of distribution involved important substantive matters which required intermediate level scrutiny. The court held that the effect of the statutory method did not bear a close correspondence to the goals of providing an equal educational opportunity and of supporting education from state funds based on the educational cost per pupil.)

3. Judicial Activism, Separation of Powers, and the *Rose* decisions as a Template for Education Reform

The *Rose* decision has been influential in the debate over education as a fundamental right. Courts in several states apply its rationale when addressing the question of how to interpret and enforce the education clauses in a state constitution. *See Lake View School No. 25 v. Huckabee*, 91 S.W.3d 472, 487-488 (Ark. 2002); *Opinion of the Justices*, 624 So.2d 107, 155 (Ala. 1993); *Claremont School District v. Governor*, 703 A.2d 1353, 1359 (N.H. 1997); *McDuffy v. Sec'y of the Executive Office of Educ.*, 615 N.E.2d 516, (Mass. 1993); and *Abbeville Co. School District v. State*, 515 S.E.2d 535, 540 (S.C. 1999).

The court in *Huckabee* said the following about *Rose* and separation of powers.

> The State devotes a substantial portion of its opening brief to its argument that the constitutionality of the school-funding system is a nonjusticiable issue for the courts. In the State's view, the courts unduly interfere and even usurp legislative

> and executive branch functions when they declare school-funding systems unconstitutional. Moreover, the State contends that the funding of our public schools is a political question involving public policy and the interplay between the State and local school districts, which is best left to the General Assembly to resolve.
>
> [T]he two branches do not operate at cross purposes in the school-funding context..... This court's refusal to review school funding under our state constitution would be a complete abrogation of our judicial responsibility and would work a severe disservice to the people of this state. We refuse to close our eyes or turn a deaf ear to claims of a dereliction of duty in the field of education.... The Supreme Court of Kentucky [in *Rose*] has emphasized the need for judicial review in school-funding matters. The language of that court summarizes our position on the matter, both eloquently and forcefully, and, we adopt it. *Lake View School No. 25 v. Huckabee*, 91 S.W.3d 472, 483-85.

WOONSOCKET SCHOOL COMMITTEE V. CHAFEE
89 A.3d 778 (R.I. 2014)

OPINION

Chief Justice SUTTELL, for the Court.

Few responsibilities of government are as important as providing for the education of children; few issues are as passionately debated by citizens as the appropriate way to meet that responsibility. This case concerns the parameters of the General Assembly's duty to promote public education, which is set forth in the Education Clause, article 12, section 1 of the Rhode Island Constitution. Specifically, the plaintiffs challenge the legislatively enacted school funding formula, which, they allege, fails to allocate adequate resources to less affluent communities. These plaintiffs maintain that said formula, together with a confluence of statutory mandates, Rhode Island Department of Education regulations, educational standards, and the low tax capacity of certain urban municipalities, operate to inhibit students in their respective cities from obtaining a quality education.

The plaintiffs in this case are the Woonsocket and Pawtucket School Committees and their respective Superintendents, and unnamed students enrolled in Woonsocket and Pawtucket public schools, as well as their unnamed parents (collectively, plaintiffs). These various plaintiffs brought suit against the legislative and executive branches of Rhode Island's state government, specifically: the Governor, the Senate President, the Speaker of the House of Representatives, the General Assembly, and the State Treasurer (collectively, defendants). The plaintiffs sought injunctive and declaratory relief, alleging violations of the Education Clause as well as of their substantive due process and equal protection rights. The plaintiffs now appeal from the Superior Court's order granting defendants' motion to dismiss the complaint. For the reasons set forth herein, we affirm the order of the Superior Court.

...

The complaint begins with a summary of the origins of public education in Rhode Island. The plaintiffs assert that each city and town in Rhode Island contained at least one public school by the end of the eighteenth century and that the General Assembly began legislating in this arena in 1828. The plaintiffs note that Rhode Island's Constitution of 1842[2] included an education clause, article 12, section 1, which read as follows:

> [2] The 1842 Constitution replaced the Royal Charter of 1663, granted by Charles II, as the state's organic law. The Constitution was ratified in November 1842, in the aftermath of the Don–Rebellion, and it became effective in May 1843. We shall refer to it as the 1842 Constitution.

> "The diffusion of knowledge, as well as of virtue among the people, being essential to the preservation of their rights and liberties, it shall be the duty of the general assembly to promote public schools, and to adopt all means which they may deem necessary and proper to secure to the people the advantages and opportunities of education."

……

[P]laintiffs address the lack of parity between educational standards and funding. The plaintiffs express support for the policies of RIDE and the Board of Regents aimed at "enact[ing] minimum education program standards for all of Rhode Island's children"; plaintiffs' claim for judicial relief centers on "the General Assembly's failure to allocate adequate resources to permit the realization of those standards." The plaintiffs assert that, beginning in 1991, the General Assembly's funding policy has "lack[ed] a rational relationship to community need, and ha[s] increased the burdens on urban communities to an unsustainable level, depriving them of the resources needed to educate their children to the minimum level mandated by the State."

The plaintiffs begin this portion of the complaint with a discussion of the "1960 funding formula," which provided for school districts to set their own budgets, with the state paying a proportion (the "share ratio") of these budgets based on each district's relative property-tax wealth per student. This funding formula was titled the "operations aid" program. The formula was amended in 1967 and 1988 to increase the state's share of funding; in 1991, however, the state failed to provide full funding for the operations aid program and imposed a reduction of $26.3 million pro rata among the districts.[3] The plaintiffs assert that the operations aid funding from 1997 through 2005 "was not proportionate to a district's student population, relative wealth, or any measurable criterion" and that, "[b]y 2004–5, the state share for education remained at 43%, one of the seven lowest in the country."

[3] In response to this reduction, the municipalities of Pawtucket, Woonsocket, and West Warwick brought suit against the state, seeking to remedy disparities in the school funding system. The plaintiffs in that case prevailed in the Superior Court, but the judgment was reversed on appeal. *See City of Pawtucket v. Sundlun,* 662 A.2d 40 (R.I.1995), discussed *infra.*

…..

The plaintiffs devote the next portion of their complaint to a description of the educational consequences of the General Assembly's inadequate funding formulas. They assert that "[a]s a result of the General Assembly's commendable action to establish minimum standards, the Woonsocket and Pawtucket school committees are faced with increasing funding requirements," and yet they "lack the resources to meet these standards." Specifically, plaintiffs assert that the 2008–2009 NECAP scores for Woonsocket's and Pawtucket's elementary, middle, and high-school students were woefully below state averages and showed extremely low levels of proficiency in reading, writing, mathematics, and science. The NECAP scores also showed an achievement gap between white and nonwhite students, and the schools were unable to comply with the Board of Regents' regulations governing educational programs for students learning English as a second language. The state has classified some of these schools as making "insufficient progress" for failing to meet academic targets in core subject areas.

The plaintiffs assert that all schools in Woonsocket and Pawtucket are mandated pursuant to state regulations to provide additional support for students whose reading and mathematics proficiency is below grade level; however, the schools lack the funding necessary to comply with these mandates. The schools also suffer from inferior facilities and a lack of adequate materials. For example, plaintiffs assert that Pawtucket's Shea High School has unmanageable climate control, mold problems, leaks, broken windows, and science labs lacking running water or gas. While the school enrolls children from fifty different countries who speak twenty-five different languages, it has only one translator. The school's social studies textbooks end with the Clinton presidency, and the school runs out of paper part way through the academic year. The plaintiffs assert that if the Board of Regents' regulations come into effect, imposing NECAP scores of partially proficient as a graduation requirement, 64 percent of Shea High School's students will not qualify for a diploma.

The plaintiffs assert that "[t]he lack of educational opportunities available to children in Rhode Island's urban communities, including Woonsocket and Pawtucket, contribute significantly to the State's position of having some of the lowest performing public schools in the country."

Count 1 of plaintiffs' complaint alleges a violation of the Education Clause, article 12, section 1 of the Rhode Island Constitution. The plaintiffs assert that the General Assembly has "enacted minimum academic standards that apply to all children in Rhode Island" pursuant to its constitutional duty to promote public schools. According to plaintiffs, "the General Assembly has repeatedly failed to provide adequate resources to implement those standards, even while recognizing this inadequacy and articulating many viable solutions."

Count 2 sets forth the language of article 1, section 2 of the Rhode Island Constitution[4] and alleges that "[p]laintiffs have a substantive due process right to public education," which has "been denied * * * due to the General Assembly's failure to provide adequate school aid." This count also sets forth the language of article 1, section 5 of the Rhode Island Constitution.[5] Although count 2 is titled "Substantive Due Process," the hearing justice found that plaintiffs were "also alleging violations of equal protection," because article 1, section 2 refers to both due process and equal protection, and because plaintiffs' prayer for relief states a deprivation of the right to equal treatment under the law.

[4] Article 1, section 2 of the Rhode Island Constitution provides:

> "Laws for good of whole—Burdens to be equally distributed—Due process—Equal protection—Discrimination—No right to abortion granted.—All free governments are instituted for the protection, safety, and happiness of the people. All laws, therefore, should be made for the good of the whole; and the burdens of the state ought to be fairly distributed among its citizens. No person shall be deprived of life, liberty or property without due process of law, nor shall any person be denied equal protection of the laws. No otherwise qualified person shall, solely by reason of race, gender or handicap be subject to discrimination by the state, its agents or any person or entity doing business with the state. Nothing in this section shall be construed to grant or secure any right relating to abortion or the funding thereof."

[5] Article 1, section 5 of the Rhode Island Constitution provides:

> "Entitlement to remedies for injuries and wrongs—Right to justice.—Every person within this state ought to find a certain remedy, by having recourse to the laws, for all injuries or wrongs which may be received in one's person, property, or character. Every person ought to obtain right and justice freely, and without purchase, completely and without denial; promptly and without delay; conformably to the laws."

……

In their prayer for relief, plaintiffs seek: (1) a declaration that the student plaintiffs have a right to receive an adequate education pursuant to article 12 and the Rhode Island General Laws; (2) a finding that the present system of education financing deprives plaintiffs of their right to an adequate education; (3) a finding that the present system of education financing systematically deprives plaintiffs of their right to equal treatment under the law in violation of article 1, section 2; (4) a finding that the Paiva–Weed Act places unconstitutional restrictions on the ability of communities to raise local taxes for public education; (5) a declaration that the 2010–2011 through 2016–2017 allocations of aid to Pawtucket and Woonsocket are inadequate according to the 2010 funding formula; (6) an injunction against further constitutional violations; (7) an injunction directing defendants to devise and implement a funding program that complies with constitutional standards; and (8) attorneys' fees and costs.

…………..

III

The outcome of this case largely depends on our interpretation of the Education Clause, article 12, section 1 of the Rhode Island Constitution, which reads as follows:

> "Duty of general assembly to promote schools and libraries.—The diffusion of knowledge, as well as of virtue among the people, being essential to the preservation of their rights and liberties, it shall be the duty of the general assembly to promote public schools and public libraries, and to adopt all means which it may deem necessary and proper to secure to the people the advantages and opportunities of education and public library services."

When confronted with an issue of constitutional interpretation, "this Court's 'chief purpose is to give effect to the intent of the framers.' " *Viveiros v. Town of Middletown,* 973 A.2d 607, 610 (R.I.2009) (quoting *Riley v. Rhode Island Department* ***788** *of Environmental Management,* 941 A.2d 198, 205 (R.I.2008)). "We 'employ the well-established rule of construction that when words in the constitution are free of ambiguity, they must be given their plain, ordinary, and usually accepted meaning.' " *Id.* (quoting *Riley,* 941 A.2d at 205). Furthermore, " '[e]very clause must be given its due force,' meaning 'no word or section must be assumed to have been unnecessarily used or needlessly added.' " *Id.* at 610–11 (quoting *Riley,* 941 A.2d at 205). "[W]e must 'presume the language was carefully weighed and its terms imply a definite meaning.' " *Id.* at 611 (quoting *Riley,* 941 A.2d at 205).

We will also look to the "historical context of a constitutional provision" when "ascertaining its meaning, scope and effect." *Viveiros,* 973 A.2d at 611. "Thus, this Court may properly consult extrinsic sources, including 'the history of the times' and the 'state of affairs as they existed' when the constitutional provision in question was adopted, as well as the proceedings of constitutional conventions." *Id.* (quoting *Sundlun,* 662 A.2d at 45).

…………..

The portion of the Education Clause concerning education was not substantively revised during the constitutional convention of 1986, despite numerous efforts to amend the language in order to provide what was thought to be a more equitable school funding system. *Sundlun,* 662 A.2d at 49. We noted in *Sundlun:*

> "The convention's adoption of article 12, section 1, signifies that the framers of the 1986 Constitution did not intend to alter the state's approach to funding education or to impose new constitutional requirements upon the General Assembly in respect to education. * * * The framers * * * had the opportunity to radically alter the nature of the state's role in public education. They chose not to do so." *Sundlun,* 662 A.2d at 50.

Thus, in *Sundlun* we addressed the issue of whether the General Assembly is constitutionally obligated to establish a system of public schools that provides the opportunity for an equitable, adequate education for all children in the state. After expounding on the history of the constitutional treatment of public education, we determined that the General Assembly is not constitutionally required to provide for such a system. Having made this determination, however, we were left to define the substantive rights, if any, created by the language of article 12, section 1. After examining the meaning of the word "promote" in its historical and contemporary contexts, we concluded:

> "[T]he word 'promote' in article 12, section 1, does not mean 'found' or 'establish.' The meaning of the word in its historical context clearly precludes such a definition, first, because the towns themselves 'founded' or 'established' their public schools, not the General Assembly, and, second, because the State Constitution of 1842 did not require the founding or establishing of a public school in every town. The historical evidence demonstrates that since the time article 12 was adopted, the establishment of schools has been left to the local communities

> although financial and other assistance were provided by the state." *Sundlun,* 662 A.2d at 56.

We then went on to discuss the remaining language of article 12, section 1, which states that it shall be the duty of the General Assembly "to adopt all means which it may deem necessary and proper to secure to the people the advantages and opportunities of education * * *." We determined that this portion of the Education Clause vested the General Assembly with plenary power in the realm of public education: "We concur with plaintiffs that the right to an education is a constitutional right in this state, but we stress that article 12 assigns to the General Assembly the responsibility for that right." *Sundlun,* 662 A.2d at 57.

2. Repeal of the Continuing Powers Clause

We also cited in *Sundlun* to the now-repealed article 6, section 10 of the Rhode Island Constitution—the so-called "Continuing Powers Clause," which read as follows: "The general assembly shall continue to exercise the powers it has heretofore exercised, unless prohibited in this Constitution." *See Sundlun,* 662 A.2d at 50. We stated:

> "Among the powers the General Assembly had exercised prior to the adoption of the 1986 Constitution was the power to promote public education through a statutory funding scheme and through reliance on local property taxation. The ratification of article 6, section 10, of the Rhode Island Constitution of 1986 represented a knowing and an express endorsement of the Legislature's primacy over education. * * * It is thus clear that the General Assembly's plenary and exclusive power over public education in Rhode Island has not changed since the adoption of the State Constitution in 1842." *Sundlun,* 662 A.2d at 50.

The plaintiffs' main contention on appeal is that, because the Rhode Island electorate has since repealed article 6, section 10 of the Rhode Island Constitution, this Court now has "the Constitutional responsibility to review legislative action more closely" than we did when we decided *Sundlun.* ... The plaintiffs are correct in their assertion that our state government has undergone significant changes since we decided *Sundlun.* In 2004, Rhode Island's electorate approved four amendments to the state constitution, commonly referred to as the "separation of powers amendments." These amendments clearly established, for the first time in Rhode Island's history, three separate and distinct departments of government. One of these amendments consisted of repealing the Continuing Powers Clause, article 6, section 10.

……

Our prior case law reveals that the Education Clause has always been interpreted in a manner that grants the General Assembly broad discretion in carrying out its constitutional duty to promote public education in Rhode Island, and this interpretation has not been based on the Continuing Powers Clause. necessary and proper to secure to the people the advantages and opportunities of education * * *." R.I. Const. art. 12, sec. 1 (emphasis added). …..This is not to say, however, that there could not be a situation in which the General Assembly violates its "constitutional mandate to support and promote education so as to warrant a judicial response." *Sundlun,* 662 A.2d at 57. We agree with our prior holding in *Sundlun* that the Rhode Island Constitution imposes an affirmative duty upon the General Assembly to promote public schools. It is not our function, however, to explore hypothetical scenarios beyond the facts that are currently before us on review.

B

Separation of Powers

Here, plaintiffs have focused their argument on the "duty to promote" portion of the Education Clause, and they have framed their appeal "in terms of whether this Court has any role whatever in reviewing the General Assembly's duty to promote public schools under [article 12, section 1]." Instead of asking us to formulate a new system of educational funding, plaintiffs have asked us to declare that the legal framework established by the General Assembly for regulating and funding public education creates unattainable mandates and, therefore, fails to "promote" public schools. Functionally, however, these two claims represent a request for the same impermissible goal: imposing our own judgment over that of the Legislature in order to determine whether a particular policy benefits public education. We decline to interfere with the General Assembly's prerogative to fashion the policies that it, as a collective representative of the people, deems most appropriate for the establishment and maintenance of the state's public schools.[9]

[9] Indeed, the arena of education policy presents many difficult dilemmas that are not easily resolved. Reasonable minds could reach many different conclusions regarding how best to accomplish the goal of educating our state's children. For example, South Korea and Finland are known to produce some of the best educational outcomes in the world; they accomplish these outcomes, however, through two entirely different educational frameworks. *See* Best Education In the World: Finland, South Korea Top Country Rankings, U.S. Rated Average, http://www.huffingtonpost.com/2012/11/27/best-education-in-the-wor_n_2199795.html?view=print&comm_ ref=false (last visited March 4, 2014). We, the unelected judiciary, are not suited to make these difficult policy decisions for the people of Rhode Island.

We emphasize that we are deeply concerned by the conditions of the schools in Pawtucket and Woonsocket as alleged by plaintiffs, as well as by the alleged predicaments of those municipalities regarding their inabilities to allocate the funding required to meet state mandates. Installing a means of providing adequate educational opportunities to every child in the state is not only an admirable goal; it is "perhaps the most important function of state and local governments." *San Antonio Independent School District v. Rodriguez,* 411 U.S. 1, 29, 93 S.Ct. 1278, 36 L.Ed.2d 16 (1973) (quoting *Brown v. Board of Education,* 347 U.S. 483, 493, 74 S.Ct. 686, 98 L.Ed. 873 (1954)). An educated populace is an essential element of our system of government, necessary for the continued protection of our rights and liberties. The framers of our constitution clearly reflected these ideas when they drafted article 12, section 1. We, however, are not the branch of government that the framers charged with implementing a system of education. The plaintiffs' complaint is more appropriately addressed to the General Assembly, which has been charged with both the power and the duty to address their concerns.[10]

[10] The plaintiffs and defendants also raised the issue of whether this case presents a nonjusticiable political question. Because we have decided the matter on the grounds of our previous precedent and the separation of powers doctrine, we decline to address the political question issue.

C

Substantive Due Process

The plaintiffs also argue that the 2010 funding formula violates substantive due process because it "is an arbitrary and capricious political solution" that impairs plaintiffs' "fundamental right to adequately funded education in the basic core subjects." Substantive due process is found in article 1, section 2 of the Rhode Island Constitution, which provides in pertinent part: "No person shall be deprived of life, liberty or property without due process of law, nor shall any person be denied equal protection of the laws."

The first inquiry in a substantive due process analysis is whether the challenged government action affects a fundamental right. *Riley,* 941 A.2d at 205–06. We have previously held that the Rhode Island Constitution does not provide a fundamental right to education, and we do not presently perceive any reason to question this holding. Thus, when no fundamental right is at issue, a party seeking to establish a substantive due process violation must show that the challenged statute or action is "clearly arbitrary and unreasonable, having no substantial relation to the public health, safety, morals, or general welfare." *Id.* (quoting *Cherenzia v. Lynch,* 847 A.2d 818, 826 (R.I.2004)).... Although the plaintiffs spare no ink in outlining the alleged inadequacies of the 2010 funding formula, they do not present facts to suggest that this legislative enactment is devoid of any "substantial relation to the public health, safety, morals, or general welfare." *See East Bay Community Development Corp.,* 901 A.2d at 1150 (quoting *Cherenzia,* 847 A.2d at 826).

....

For the reasons stated herein, we affirm the order of the Superior Court. The record shall be returned to the Superior Court.

Part II
Due Process, Discipline, and School Safety

Chapter Four
Constitutional Safeguards and Procedural Due Process

> Judicial interference with discretionary exercise of a school board power is permissible where the action of the board was based on a misconception of law, ignorance through lack of inquiry into the facts necessary to form an intelligent judgment, or the result of arbitrary will or caprice.... An abuse of discretion is not merely an error of judgment, but if in reaching a conclusion, the law is overridden or misapplied, or the judgment exercised is manifestly unreasonable, or the result of partiality, prejudice, bias or ill will, as shown by the evidence of record, discretion is abused.
> Parents United for Better Schools v. Board of Education, 148 F.3d 260 (1998).

Court decisions that invalidate educational policies are extraordinary in several respects. These decisions represent a departure from the judicial deference ordinarily accorded school officials. The courts enforce constitutional rights designed to safeguard students, faculty and staff from flawed decision-making. A different judicial attitude emerges from a study of constitutional cases lost by educators. Its elements succinctly set forth above in the *Parents United* case, explain in precise terms what the Constitution requires and permits of educators. Essentially, the education mission is illegitimate when its implementation infringes on clearly defined civil rights. And the result of the invalidation of a school policy forces educators to abolish the policy or to try another, more lawful approach to it implementation.

Remember, that although access to a public education is not deemed a fundamental right, the rights contained in the Bill of Rights of the Untied States Constitution are designed to apply to government officials, which includes public educators. The materials presented in the next three chapters present an essential part of the constitutional short list of limitations on educators that are immutable in the sense that no judge should resolve doubts in favor of a policy that fails to satisfy minimum standards in each of the respective areas. Procedural fairness, the right to privacy, the right to be free from unreasonable searches, seizures and interrogations are important civil rights.

I. Students and Procedural Due Process

Generally speaking the United States Constitution does not consider education to be a fundamental right. *See San Antonio Indep. Sch. Dist. v. Rodriguez*, 411 U.S. 1 (1973). As a result, the Due Process Clauses provide little fire to which the feet of educators can be held and few student rights emerge. Procedural Due Process does apply when students are faced with the deprivation of education as a "property interest." Procedural due process is often misunderstood in this regard. It creates, at best, a methodology for determining unfairness in the application of discipline by educators. Its rules are also useful in highlighting of presence of illegitimate educational concerns as a motivating factor in a suspension or expulsion.

GOSS v. LOPEZ
419 U.S. 565 (1975)

MR. JUSTICE WHITE delivered the opinion of the Court.

Ohio law, Rev. Code Ann. § 3313.64 (1972), provides for free education to all children between the ages of six and 21. Section 3313.66 of the Code empowers the principal of an Ohio public school to suspend a pupil for misconduct for up to 10 days or to expel him. In either case, he must notify the student's parents within 24 hours and state the reasons for his action. A pupil who is expelled, or his parents, may appeal the decision to the Board of Education and in connection therewith shall be permitted to be heard at the board meeting. The Board may reinstate the pupil following the hearing. No similar procedure is provided in § 3313.66 or any other provision of state law for a suspended student. Aside from a regulation tracking the statute, at the time of the imposition of the suspensions in this case the CPSS itself had not issued any written procedure applicable to suspensions.[1] Nor, so far as the record reflects, had any of the individual high schools involved in this case.[2] Each, however, had formally or informally described the conduct for which suspension could be imposed.

The nine named appellees, each of whom alleged that he or she had been suspended from public high school in Columbus for up to 10 days without a hearing pursuant to § 3313.66, filed an action under 42 U.S.C. § 1983 against the Columbus Board of Education and various administrators of the CPSS. The complaint sought a declaration that § 3313.66 was unconstitutional in that it permitted public school administrators to deprive plaintiffs of their rights to an education without a hearing of any kind, in violation of the procedural due process component of the Fourteenth Amendment. It also sought to enjoin the public school officials from issuing future suspensions pursuant to § 3313.66 and to require them to remove references to the past suspensions from the records of the students in question.

The proof below established that the suspensions arose out of a period of widespread student unrest in the CPSS during February and March 1971. Six of the named plaintiffs, Rudolph Sutton, Tyrone

---

[1] At the time of the events involved in this case, the only administrative regulation on this subject was § 1010.04 of the Administrative Guide of the Columbus Public Schools which provided: "Pupils may be suspended or expelled from school in accordance with the provisions of Section 3313.66 of the Revised Code."

[2] According to the testimony of Phillip Fulton, the principal of one of the high schools involved in this case, there was an informal procedure applicable at the Marion-Franklin High School. It provided that in the routine case of misconduct, occurring in the presence of a teacher, the teacher would describe the misconduct on a form provided for that purpose and would send the student, with the form, to the principal's office. There, the principal would obtain the student's version of the story, and, if it conflicted with the teacher's written version, would send for the teacher to obtain the teacher's oral version—apparently in the presence of the student. Mr. Fulton testified that, if a discrepancy still existed, the teacher's version would be believed and the principal would arrive at a disciplinary decision based on it.

Washington, Susan Cooper, Deborah Fox, Clarence Byars, and Bruce Harris, were students at the Marion-Franklin High School and were each suspended for 10 days on account of disruptive or disobedient conduct committed in the presence of the school administrator who ordered the suspension. One of these, Tyrone Washington, was among a group of students demonstrating in the school auditorium while a class was being conducted there. He was ordered by the school principal to leave, refused to do so, and was suspended. Rudolph Sutton, in the presence of the principal, physically attacked a police officer who was attempting to remove Tyrone Washington from the auditorium. He was immediately suspended. The other four Marion-Franklin students were suspended for similar conduct. None was given a hearing to determine the operative facts underlying the suspension, but each, together with his or her parents, was offered the opportunity to attend a conference, subsequent to the effective date of the suspension, to discuss the student's future.

Two named plaintiffs, Dwight Lopez and Betty Crome, were students at the Central High School and McGuffey Junior High School, respectively. The former was suspended in connection with a disturbance in the lunchroom which involved some physical damage to school property. Lopez testified that at least 75 other students were suspended from his school on the same day. He also testified below that he was not a party to the destructive conduct but was instead an innocent bystander. Because no one from the school testified with regard to this incident, there is no evidence in the record indicating the official basis for concluding otherwise. Lopez never had a hearing.

Betty Crome was present at a demonstration at a high school other than the one she was attending. There she was arrested together with others, taken to the police station, and released without being formally charged. Before she went to school on the following day, she was notified that she had been suspended for a 10-day period. Because no one from the school testified with respect to this incident, the record does not disclose how the McGuffey Junior High School principal went about making the decision to suspend Crome, nor does it disclose on what information the decision was based. It is clear from the record that no hearing was ever held.

There was no testimony with respect to the suspension of the ninth named plaintiff, Carl Smith. The school files were also silent as to his suspension, although as to some, but not all, of the other named plaintiffs the files contained either direct references to their suspensions or copies of letters sent to their parents advising them of the suspension.

On the basis of this evidence, the three-judge court declared that plaintiffs were denied due process of law because they were "suspended without hearing prior to suspension or within a reasonable time thereafter," and that Ohio Rev. Code Ann. § 3313.66 (1972) and regulations issued pursuant thereto were unconstitutional in permitting such suspensions. It was ordered that all references to plaintiffs' suspensions be removed from school files.

****

The defendant school administrators have appealed the three-judge court's decision. Because the order below granted plaintiffs' request for an injunction—ordering defendants to expunge their records—this Court has jurisdiction of the appeal pursuant to 28 U.S.C. § 1253. We affirm.

II

At the outset, appellants contend that because there is no constitutional right to an education at public expense, the Due Process Clause does not protect against expulsions from the public school system. This position misconceives the nature of the issue and is refuted by prior decisions. The Fourteenth Amendment forbids the State to deprive any person of life, liberty, or property without due process of law. Protected interests in property are normally "not created by the Constitution. Rather, they are created and their dimensions are defined" by an independent source such as state statutes or rules entitling the citizen to certain benefits. *Board of Regents v. Roth*, 408 U.S. 564, 577 (1972).

.....

Here, on the basis of state law, appellees plainly had legitimate claims of entitlement to a public education. Ohio Rev. Code Ann. §§ 3313.48 and 3313.64 (1972 and Supp. 1973) direct local authorities to provide a free education to all residents between five and 21 years of age, and a compulsory-attendance law requires attendance for a school year of not less than 32 weeks. Ohio Rev. Code Ann. § 3321.04 (1972). It is true that § 3313.66 of the Code permits school principals to suspend students for up to 10 days; but suspensions may not be imposed without any grounds whatsoever. All of the schools had their own rules specifying the grounds for expulsion or suspension. Having chosen to extend the right to an education to people of appellees' class generally, Ohio may not withdraw that right on grounds of misconduct, absent fundamentally fair procedures to determine whether the misconduct has occurred.

Although Ohio may not be constitutionally obligated to establish and maintain a public school system, it has nevertheless done so and has required its children to attend. Those young people do not "shed their constitutional rights" at the schoolhouse door. *Tinker* v. *Des Moines School Dist.*, 393 U.S. 503, 506 (1969). "The Fourteenth Amendment, as now applied to the States, protects the citizen against the State itself and all of its creatures—Boards of Education not excepted." *West Virginia Board of Education v. Barnette*, 319 U.S. 624, 637 (1943). The authority possessed by the State to prescribe and enforce standards of conduct in its schools although concededly very broad, must be exercised consistently with constitutional safeguards. Among other things, the State is constrained to recognize a student's legitimate entitlement to a public education as a property interest which is protected by the Due Process Clause and which may not be taken away for misconduct without adherence to the minimum procedures required by that Clause.

The Due Process Clause also forbids arbitrary deprivations of liberty. "Where a person's good name, reputation, honor, or integrity is at stake because of what the government is doing to him," the minimal requirements of the Clause must be satisfied. *Wisconsin v. Constantineau*, 400 U.S. 433, 437 (1971); *Board of Regents v. Roth, supra*, at 573. School authorities here suspended appellees from school for periods of up to 10 days based on charges of misconduct. If sustained and recorded, those charges could seriously damage the students' standing with their fellow pupils and their teachers as well as interfere with later opportunities for higher education and employment.

It is apparent that the claimed right of the State to determine unilaterally and without process whether that misconduct has occurred immediately collides with the requirements of the Constitution.

[I]n determining "whether due process requirements apply in the first place, we must look not to the 'weight' but to the *nature* of the interest at stake." *Board of Regents v. Roth, supra,* at 570-571. Appellees were excluded from school only temporarily, it is true, but the length and consequent severity of a deprivation, while another factor to weigh in determining the appropriate form of hearing, "is not decisive of the basic right" to a hearing of some kind. *Fuentes v. Shevin*, 407 U.S. 67, 86 (1972). The Court's view has been that as long as a property deprivation is not *de minimis*, its gravity is irrelevant to the question whether account must be taken of the Due Process Clause. *Sniadach v. Family Finance Corp.*, 395 U.S. 337, 342 (1969) (Harlan, J., concurring); *Boddie v. Connecticut*, 401 U.S. 371, 378-379 (1971); *Board of Regents v. Roth, supra*, at 570 n. 8. A 10-day suspension from school is not *de minimis* in our view and may not be imposed in complete disregard of the Due Process Clause.

A short suspension is, of course, a far milder deprivation than expulsion. But, "education is perhaps the most important function of state and local governments," *Brown v. Board of Education*, 347 U.S. 483, 493 (1954), and the total exclusion from the educational process for more than a trivial period, and certainly if the suspension is for 10 days, is a serious event in the life of the suspended child. Neither the property interest in educational benefits temporarily denied nor the liberty interest in reputation, which is also implicated, is so insubstantial that suspensions may constitutionally be imposed by any procedure the school chooses, no matter how arbitrary.

****

III

"Once it is determined that due process applies, the question remains what process is due." *Morrissey v. Brewer*, 408 U.S., at 481. We turn to that question, fully realizing as our cases regularly do that the interpretation and application of the Due Process Clause are intensely practical matters and that "[the] very nature of due process negates any concept of inflexible procedures universally applicable to every imaginable situation." *Cafeteria Workers v. McElroy*, 367 U.S. 886, 895 (1961). We are also mindful of our own admonition:

> Judicial interposition in the operation of the public school system of the Nation raises problems requiring care and restraint. . . . By and large, public education in our Nation is committed to the control of state and local authorities. *Epperson v. Arkansas*, 393 U.S. 97, 104 (1968).

.....

The student's interest is to avoid unfair or mistaken exclusion from the educational process, with all of its unfortunate consequences. The Due Process Clause will not shield him from suspensions properly imposed, but it disserves both his interest and the interest of the State if his suspension is in fact unwarranted. The concern would be mostly academic if the disciplinary process were a totally accurate, unerring process, never mistaken and never unfair. Unfortunately, that is not the case, and no one suggests that it is. Disciplinarians, although proceeding in utmost good faith, frequently act on the reports and advice of others; and the controlling facts and the nature of the conduct under challenge are often disputed. The risk of error is not at all trivial, and it should be guarded against if that may be done without prohibitive cost or interference with the educational process.

The difficulty is that our schools are vast and complex. Some modicum of discipline and order is essential if the educational function is to be performed. Events calling for discipline are frequent occurrences and sometimes require immediate, effective action. Suspension is considered not only to be a necessary tool to maintain order but a valuable educational device. The prospect of imposing elaborate hearing requirements in every suspension case is viewed with great concern, and many school authorities may well prefer the untrammeled power to act unilaterally, unhampered by rules about notice and hearing. But it would be a strange disciplinary system in an educational institution if no communication was sought by the disciplinarian with the student in an effort to inform him of his dereliction and to let him tell his side of the story in order to make sure that an injustice is not done. "[Fairness] can rarely be obtained by secret, one-sided determination of facts decisive of rights. . . ." "Secrecy is not congenial to truth-seeking and self-righteousness gives too slender an assurance of rightness. No better instrument has been devised for arriving at truth than to give a person in jeopardy of serious loss notice of the case against him and opportunity to meet it." *Anti-Fascist Committee v. McGrath, supra*, at 170, 171-172 (Frankfurter, J., concurring).[9]

We do not believe that school authorities must be totally free from notice and hearing requirements if their schools are to operate with efficiency. Students facing temporary suspension have interests qualifying for protection of the Due Process Clause, and due process requires, in connection with a suspension of 10 days or less, that the student be given oral or written notice of the charges against him and, if he denies them, an explanation of the evidence the authorities have and an opportunity to present his side of the story. The Clause requires at least these rudimentary precautions against unfair or mistaken findings of misconduct and arbitrary exclusion from school.

---

[9] The facts involved in this case illustrate the point. Betty Crome was suspended for conduct which did not occur on school grounds, and for which mass arrests were made—hardly guaranteeing careful individualized factfinding by the police or by the school principal. She claims to have been involved in no misconduct. However, she was suspended for 10 days without ever being told what she was accused of doing or being given an opportunity to explain her presence among those arrested. Similarly, Dwight Lopez was suspended, along with many others, in connection with a disturbance in the lunchroom. Lopez says he was not one of those in the lunchroom who was involved. However, he was never told the basis for the principal's belief that he was involved, nor was he ever given an opportunity to explain his presence in the lunchroom. The school principals who suspended Crome and Lopez may have been correct on the merits, but it is inconsistent with the Due Process Clause to have made the decision that misconduct had occurred without at some meaningful time giving Crome or Lopez an opportunity to persuade the principals otherwise.

We recognize that both suspensions were imposed during a time of great difficulty for the school administrations involved. At least in Lopez' case there may have been an immediate need to send home everyone in the lunchroom in order to preserve school order and property; and the administrative burden of providing 75 "hearings" of any kind is considerable. However, neither factor justifies a disciplinary suspension without *at any time* gathering facts relating to Lopez specifically, confronting him with them, and giving him an opportunity to explain.

There need be no delay between the time "notice" is given and the time of the hearing. In the great majority of cases the disciplinarian may informally discuss the alleged misconduct with the student minutes after it has occurred. We hold only that, in being given an opportunity to explain his version of the facts at this discussion, the student first be told what he is accused of doing and what the basis of the accusation is. Lower courts which have addressed the question of the *nature* of the procedures required in short suspension cases have reached the same conclusion. *Tate v. Board of Education*, 453 F.2d 975, 979 (CA8 1972); *Vail v. Board of Education*, 354 F.Supp. 592, 603 (NH 1973). Since the hearing may occur almost immediately following the misconduct, it follows that as a general rule notice and hearing should precede removal of the student from school. We agree with the District Court, however, that there are recurring situations in which prior notice and hearing cannot be insisted upon. Students whose presence poses a continuing danger to persons or property or an ongoing threat of disrupting the academic process may be immediately removed from school. In such cases, the necessary notice and rudimentary hearing should follow as soon as practicable, as the District Court indicated.

In holding as we do, we do not believe that we have imposed procedures on school disciplinarians which are inappropriate in a classroom setting. Instead we have imposed requirements which are, if anything, less than a fair-minded school principal would impose upon himself in order to avoid unfair suspensions. Indeed, according to the testimony of the principal of Marion-Franklin High School, that school had an informal procedure, remarkably similar to that which we now require, applicable to suspensions generally but which was not followed in this case. Similarly, according to the most recent memorandum applicable to the entire CPSS, *see* n. 1, *supra*, school principals in the CPSS are now required by local rule to provide at least as much as the constitutional minimum which we have described.

. . . . .

We should also make it clear that we have addressed ourselves solely to the short suspension, not exceeding 10 days. Longer suspensions or expulsions for the remainder of the school term, or permanently, may require more formal procedures. Nor do we put aside the possibility that in unusual situations, although involving only a short suspension, something more than the rudimentary procedures will be required.

IV

]The District Court found each of the suspensions involved here to have occurred without a hearing, either before or after the suspension, and that each suspension was therefore invalid and the statute unconstitutional insofar as it permits such suspensions without notice or hearing. Accordingly, the judgment is *Affirmed*.

FULLER ex rel. FULLER v. DECATUR PUBLIC SCHOOL BOARD
251 F.3d 662 (7th Cir. 2001)

EVANS, Circuit Judge.

On September 17, 1999, a violent fight broke out in the bleachers at a high school football game in Decatur, Illinois, leaving spectators scrambling to escape the melee. The students involved in the fight were members of rival street gangs—the Vice Lords and the Gangster Disciples. As so often happens these days, a bystander caught the fight on videotape. It showed participants punching and kicking each other without concern for the safety of others in the stands. Six students who attended three different high schools in the Decatur Public School District were expelled from school for 2 years for their roles in the fight. The fight and the expulsions received considerable media attention as well as the attention of the Reverend Jesse Jackson and Illinois Governor George Ryan. When the dust settled, the original 2-year expulsions were reduced to expulsions for the remainder of the school year with the students being given the opportunity to attend an alternative high school. Nevertheless unsatisfied, some of the students, by their parents, brought this action pursuant to 42 U.S.C. § 1983, alleging that their constitutional rights were violated because one of the three school disciplinary rules they were found to have violated was void for vagueness. At trial, the district court ruled for the School District, denying the students' request for declaratory relief. The students appeal.

The students expelled were Roosevelt Fuller and Errol Bond, who attended Stephen Decatur High School; Gregory Howell and Shawn Honorable, who were students at Eisenhower High School; and Terence Jarrett and Courtney Carson, who were students at MacArthur High School. The fight in which the students were involved began on one end of the bleachers and traveled all the way to the other end. Fans were jumping over the railing, trying to get onto the track which surrounds the football field, to escape the fight. The principal at MacArthur said he had never seen a fight as bad as this one in his 27 years in education.

Each of the students had a separate hearing before Dr. David O. Cooprider, who had been the regional superintendent for Macon and Piatt Counties and who at the time was a hearing officer under contract to conduct expulsion hearings. Evidence at the hearings showed that each student was an active participant in the fight. It also showed that the students were members of the rival gangs, the Vice Lords and the Gangster Disciples that fought that night.

……

In this court the students seek a ruling that the prohibition against "gang-like activity" is facially unconstitutional because it lacks clear definitions of what the prohibited conduct is. Because the expulsions were based at least in part on this rule, the students—including Howell, who claims to have standing despite withdrawing from school—contend that their due process rights were denied. Because the period of expulsion has ended, the students recognize that any remedy is necessarily limited, but they seek an order sending the case back to the district court for a determination whether expungement of the disciplinary records is an appropriate remedy. …If the students' constitutional rights were violated, expungement might very well be an appropriate equitable remedy…. The problem for the students, however, is convincing us that their rights were, in fact, violated.

Rule 10, in place when the trouble started, prohibits students from engaging in "gang-like activities." It provides:

> As used herein, the phrase "gang-like activity" shall mean any conduct engaged in by a student 1) on behalf of any gang, 2) to perpetuate the existence of any gang, 3) to effect the common purpose and design of any gang and 4) or to represent a gang affiliation, loyalty or membership in any way while on school grounds or while attending a school function. These activities include recruiting students for membership in any gang and threatening or intimidating other students or employees to commit acts or omissions against his/her will in furtherance of the common purpose and design of any gang.
>
> A violation of the rule is grounds for suspension or expulsion from school.

Whatever is true of other rules, rule 10 is not devoid of standards. It delineates specific activities which are covered by the rule: recruiting students for membership in a gang, threatening or intimidating other students to commit acts or omissions against their will in furtherance of the purpose of the gang. It is different from the rule in *Stephenson v. Davenport Community School District*, 110 F.3d 1303 (8th Cir. 1997), which is directed at gang-related activities such as "display of 'colors', symbols, signals, signs, etc."—activities more likely to implicate First Amendment rights. Similarly, the rule in another case the students cite, *West v. Derby Unified School District No. 260*, 206 F.3d 1358 (10th Cir. 2000), goes primarily to speech-related activities. On the other hand, in our case, the rule on its face and certainly as applied to these students prohibits threatening and intimidating actions taken in the name of a gang. With that in mind, we turn to the students' constitutional challenge.

A rule, regulation, or law can be facially unconstitutional under two different theories. First, laws that inhibit the exercise of First Amendment rights can be invalidated under the overbreadth doctrine. *Broadrick v. Oklahoma*, 413 U.S. 601 (1973). The students do not proceed under this theory. Rather, they rely on the second, which is that even if a law does not reach a substantial amount of constitutionally protected conduct, it can be found to be impermissibly void if it fails to define the offense with sufficient definiteness that ordinary people can understand what conduct is prohibited and it fails to establish standards to permit enforcement in a nonarbitrary, nondiscriminatory manner. *Kolender v. Lawson*, 461 U.S. 352 (1983).

Furthermore, the nature of the law affects the analysis. An enactment imposing criminal sanctions demands more definiteness than one which regulates economic behavior, Hoffman Estates, or as is relevant in our case, one which regulates the conduct of students in the school setting. In *Bethel School District No. 403 v. Fraser*, 478 U.S. 675, 686 (1986), the Supreme Court said:

> Given the school's need to be able to impose disciplinary sanctions for a wide range of unanticipated conduct disruptive of the educational process, the school disciplinary rules need not be as detailed as a criminal code which imposes criminal sanctions.

For a number of reasons, we conclude that no facial challenge can be made to rule 10. It is doubtful whether rule 10 proscribes behavior which is protected under any constitutional provision. It is questionable whether it involves free speech rights. In addition, gang membership seems not to implicate the right of association:

Is the rule unconstitutional as applied to these students? The phrase the students contend is vague is "gang-like activity." The rule goes on to say that "gang-like activity" is conduct engaged in "on behalf of any gang," "to perpetuate the existence of any gang," "to effect the common purpose" of a gang, or "to represent a gang affiliation, loyalty or membership . . . ." Fighting in support of one's gang falls under more than one of these definitions.

That any persons charged with keeping the peace—e.g., police officers or school officials—have an obligation to break up a violent fight in the stands at a high school football game cannot be disputed. Then later, when a careful investigation reveals that the fight was between well-known rival street gangs, it is reasonable for school officials to see the fight as "gang-like activity." In fact, the students do not say that the fight was not gang-related. As applied in this case, the school disciplinary rule, even before it was changed, was sufficiently definite to withstand this constitutional challenge.

The decision of the district court is AFFIRMED.

Kevin P. Brady: Zero Tolerance or (In)Tolerance Policies? Weaponless School Violence, Due Process, and the Law of Student Suspensions and Expulsions: An Examination of *Fuller v. Decatur* Public School Board of Education School District, 2002 BYU Educ. & L.J. 159 (2002)*

Today, states and school districts have the great authority and flexibility to monitor and control student behavior on school property and at school-sponsored activities through the adoption and use of reasonable school disciplinary suspensions and expulsions. Reasonable disciplinary rules and regulations, even those that may encroach upon students' constitutionally protected rights, have been upheld in court if the disciplinary actions are "justified by a legitimate educational interest." This heightened level of school district discretion relating to disciplinary suspensions and expulsions is justified largely by the school's responsibility to protect students while in school as well as to ensure that school environments are conducive to learning. Indeed, the courts have "exercised limited review of student disciplinary regulations, and pupils were seldom successful in challenging policies governing their behavior."

Historically, public schools have exercised broad authority in disciplining students, largely unrestricted by due process requirements. Moreover, the common law embraced the principal of in loco parentis, or "in the place of the parent," whereby teachers and principals have "the authority and the duty to guide, correct, and punish the child in the accomplishment of educational objectives." However, beginning in the 1960s, federal courts began to rule in favor of requiring some due process for students expelled from school. By the late 1960s and early 1970s, most federal courts were applying, albeit to varying degrees, the Due Process Clause to school expulsions. It appears unclear, however, as to whether a student's education was a property interest and whether due process should apply to school suspensions of a short duration.

Despite the growing popularity of zero tolerance policies and their use in public schools across the country, students who are disciplined under zero tolerance policies do not "shed their constitutional rights ... at the schoolhouse gate". Indeed, students have basic legal rights under the U.S. Constitution, as well as under a variety of federal and state statutes. Thus, one of the deeply entrenched issues associated with implementing and enforcing student discipline policies is the inherent tension between the school administrators' need to develop and maintain an orderly school environment, especially given the special status of students, and the need to protect student rights.

At a minimum, students enrolled in public schools who are subject to either suspensions or expulsions are entitled to:

(1) Due process under the Fourteenth Amendment;

(2) Constitutional and federal civil rights protections that prohibit inherently discriminatory policies based on race, class, or national origin;

(3) Additional protection by federal statutes, such as Section 504 of the Rehabilitation Act of 1973 and the Individuals with Disabilities Education Act (IDEA) if the student is classified as special needs.

As applied to abuses of zero tolerance policies, school administrators, students, and their advocates need to be aware of these federal protections as well as state constitutions and statutes that provide comparable or additional restrictions on zero tolerance policies.

Zell v. Ricci

957 F.3d 1 (1st Cir. 2020)

THOMPSON, Circuit Judge.

High school is not without its unique challenges, this much we know; we also know that the same can be said for bringing a civil lawsuit and navigating the rigors associated with contentious litigation. Each of these dynamics comes together in the case now before us: Kelsey Zell ("Zell") appeals the United States District Court for the District of Rhode Island's dismissal of her case. Zell advanced a slew of claims against the various defendants below, but of the many claims dismissed, she has whittled down her appellate challenges to a select few (as we'll momentarily discuss).

……

Incident, Suspension, and Immediate Aftermath

The event that served as the springboard for this litigation took place at Rhode Island's Chariho High School (CHS) on October 16, 2015, which was the Friday of CHS's "Spirit Week," a day historically marked by "mayhem," "increased risk for students," and "school-sponsored bad decisions," as well as "lighthearted and not-so-lighthearted bantering or even aggression." The day began as it always did, with toga-clad seniors processing into school through a shower of silly string, sprayed both by the seniors themselves and the surrounding underclassmen. Students were allegedly vandalizing lockers and throwing streamers and litter around in the hallway. And in addition to the aforementioned "lighthearted and some not-so-lighthearted bantering," there were also "shows of aggressive bantering."

In the midst of this scene, then-junior Zell was on the sidelines of the procession sporting her field hockey uniform as a display of school spirit -- like everyone else, she was "indiscriminately" spraying silly string in the air at student passers-by, and some of that silly string landed on then-senior McGinley. Then, while chatting idly with friends and with her back turned towards McGinley, Zell, out of the blue, was attacked. Using her cell phone as a weapon, McGinley sprinted towards Zell and with the "hard edge" of her phone, delivered several "hammer blows" to Zell's head. Zell fell forward, and McGinley ran away laughing.

Zell went to class in pain and confused, then was summoned to Dean Bridgham's office. Once there, Zell had "trouble comprehending" what Dean Bridgham was saying to her, but she did register that McGinley had self-reported hitting Zell. Dean Bridgham sent Zell back to class after asking her a few questions -- not about her wellbeing, though -- then she was called back down to Dean Bridgham's office a little while later, this time with Principal Weber present. The two questioned Zell, after which Dean Bridgham made an unexpected announcement. He informed Zell that she would face a one-day suspension for "fighting (or instigating a fight)" because the school had found out that she supposedly called McGinley a bitch and sprayed McGinley in the face with silly string. Same punishment to befall McGinley.

……

The Suspension Appeals

So began the Zells' challenge to the school's suspension decision. With Zell at home recovering for six days, her father first appealed to Superintendent Ricci, providing to him a detailed account of the events as told by Zell and her friends, and corroborated by the surveillance video of the incident. At first, Superintendent Ricci asked to speak with Zell, but ended up upholding the suspension without talking to her directly. The Zells appealed Superintendent Ricci's decision to the Committee… As Zell tells it, Chairperson Louzon signed the Committee's decision to uphold the suspension "without review or input," and so the suspension stood.

Still aggrieved, the Zells, now represented by counsel, appealed that decision to RIDE, where a two-day hearing ensued with over ten witnesses (all of whom were subjected to direct and cross examination), and which yielded "nearly a foot of transcripts." During that proceeding, Dean

Bridgham acknowledged "there was a lack of some needed policy or some related failure by the school district to handle the situation, including [Zell]'s concussion." ...Ultimately, RIDE issued a decision with "two-and-half pages" of analysis upholding the suspension, causing the Zells to take issue with such a "shockingly short" decision, which cited to literally none of their evidence....Undeterred, the Zells pressed on, appealing RIDE's decision to the Council...[T]he Council upheld the suspension, and later followed up with a May 9, 2017 written five-page decision rejecting the Zells' claims of error and affirming the suspension with, as the Zells tell it, "no reasoning whatsoever."

Count I: Procedural Due Process

On appeal, Zell challenges the dismissal of her procedural due process claims against RIDE and the Council. Before we lay out the particulars of her challenge, we spell out some due process basics. "The threshold question in any claim for denial of procedural due process is whether [a plaintiff was] deprived of a liberty or property interest protected by the United States Constitution." Aponte-Rosario v. Acevedo-Vilá, 617 F.3d 1, 9 (1st Cir. 2010) (citing Lowe v. Scott, 959 F.2d 323, 334 (1st Cir. 1992)). And when a protected interest exists, the analysis turns to a determination of "what process was due." Id. (citing Goss v. López, 419 U.S. 565, 577, 95 S.Ct. 729, 42 L.Ed.2d 725 (1975) (explaining that "[n]either the property interest in educational benefits temporarily denied nor the liberty interest in reputation, which is also implicated, is so insubstantial that suspensions may constitutionally be imposed by any procedure the school chooses, no matter how arbitrary")). As we make that determination, we observe that "due process is flexible and calls for such procedural protections as the particular situation demands." Morrissey v. Brewer, 408 U.S. 471, 481, 92 S.Ct. 2593, 33 L.Ed.2d 484 (1972).

Homing in on Zell's claims, her complaint describes her protected interests as the "right and liberty interest in not being deprived of her reputation" as well as a "right to not endure 'stigma' plus a right to not be deprived of present or future educational, scholarship, and job opportunities" because of the blight on her record (the mention of educational opportunity loss smacks of an alleged property interest, though Zell never explicitly says as much). As for Zell's denial of due process allegations, she contends, in Count I, that she was deprived of her protected liberty interests as a result of the actions of RIDE and the Council, particularly when they did not afford her proper notice, opportunity to be heard, and a fair hearing with an impartial decisionmaker. These assertions culminate in the allegation that RIDE and the Council "deprived [Zell] of her liberty interests without due process of law."

......

Before us Zell narrows her focus. Her procedural due process contention solely takes aim at the written decisions issued by RIDE and the Council which she seems to be arguing are unconstitutionally reasoned. The decisions, she posits, are so deficient in character and content as to constitute insufficient due process. She says that because the RIDE hearing lasted two days, involved ten witnesses, and generated a foot-high pile of transcripts, "the written decision should have been comprehensive and balanced, more in sync with the hearing it was based on." But alas, she bemoans, the analysis in the decision is too short, "cited to virtually no evidence, and only cited to evidence presented by the school district." Further trampling her due process rights, the Council, as Zell tells it, also erred in affirming RIDE's decision with similarly legally insufficient analysis and reasoning to support its adverse ruling. And Zell continues, the district court doubly erred in its own ruling. Had it reviewed her complaint more comprehensively, it would have seen that her due process allegation had been adequately pled. Then, maintaining her fixation on the purported deficiency of the written decisions, Zell argues that the district court applied the wrong legal framework to its scrutiny of her arguments.

……

But even giving Zell the benefit of the doubt that her complaint should be read as she now contends, we conclude, as RIDE and the Council argue, that Zell's Count I "insufficiently-reasoned-decision" theory was properly dismissed. We so conclude because Zell primarily advances only one legal argument in support of her claim -- one which widely misses the mark…Zell points to Goldberg v. Kelly, 397 U.S. 254, 271, 90 S.Ct. 1011, 25 L.Ed.2d 287 (1970), the Supreme Court's landmark case setting forth the fundamental requisites of procedural due process law. According to Zell, Goldberg explains that "the decision maker should state the reasons for his determination and indicate the evidence he relied on," and, importantly, she has received neither. Id. But here's the rub: even using Zell's preferred case to review her contention, it must be noted that the Goldberg language she emphasizes is only a snippet of the guidance offered by the Court, which went on to add "though his statement need not amount to a full opinion or even formal findings of fact and conclusions of law."

With the complete Goldberg standard in mind, we look at the RIDE and Council decisions about which Zell complains (too short, not enough evidence cited, lack of reasoning) and consider whether she has sufficiently alleged in her complaint that they were so inadequate as to constitute a deprivation of her due process rights…And even applying Goldberg to the information we have, we know that the written decision by RIDE included two-and-a-half pages of analysis and the Council's decision was a five-pager; both decisions provide reasoning, and both cite evidence. Zell fails to explain why the length of these administrative opinions should matter. Nor is it apparent to us how the decisions' failure to address every plausible reason for upholding the suspension decision, or failure to reference every bit of evidence submitted by Zell, makes these opinions constitutionally infirm when, according to Goldberg, the decision maker's decision, though it need be reasoned and make reference to the evidence, nonetheless, "need not amount to a full opinion or even formal findings of fact and conclusions of law."

Moreover, the Supreme Court has specifically addressed what fundamentally fair procedures are generally required for school suspensions of less than ten days. Goss, 419 U.S. at 581-82, 95 S.Ct. 729.10 It has indicated that the student must first "be told what [s]he is accused of doing and what the basis of the accusation is." Id. at 582, 95 S.Ct. 729. Then, she must be given "an opportunity to explain [her] version of the facts" at an informal hearing. Id. Absent an unusual situation, school officials are not obligated to generate any written opinion, much less hold a trial-like proceeding followed by a multi-page refutation of arguments and evidence. Id. at 583, 95 S.Ct. 729 (remarking that "hearings in connection with short [ten-day] suspensions" need not "afford the student the opportunity to secure counsel, to confront and cross-examine witnesses supporting the charge, or to call his own witnesses," and cautioning against "further formalizing the suspension process and escalating its formality and adversary nature"). Accordingly, we note our agreement with the district court that Zell "received [from these defendants] significantly more process than she was due." As such, Zell failed to "plausibly narrate a claim for relief," Schatz, 669 F.3d at 55, and the district court did not err when it dismissed her complaint.

Doe v. Washington County Department of Education
__ F.Supp. 3d. __, 2020 WL 2479337 (E.D. Tenn. 2020)

Cynthia Richardson Wyrick, United States Magistrate Judge

This case is before the undersigned pursuant to 28 U.S.C. § 636(c), Rule 73(b) of the Federal Rules of Civil Procedure, and the consent of the parties, for all further proceedings, including entry of judgment [Doc. 13].

I. BACKGROUND

The Complaint at issue was filed after Plaintiff John Doe and several other students were disciplined by the Washington County Department of Education ("school board") following a reported hazing incident at a Fellowship of Christian Athletes Football Camp which Plaintiff attended with the David Crockett High School ("DCHS") football team on or about July 14-16, 2015 at Tennessee Technical University in Cookeville, Tennessee. Shortly after the team returned from the camp, an anonymous email was sent to several of Defendant's agents, including DCHS principal Peggy Wright and Director of Schools Ron Dykes, as well as to local media outlets alleging that underclassmen football players had been "hazed in a sexual manner" at the football camp. After receiving the email, school officials investigated the allegations by interviewing a number of students who attended the camp. After this investigation, Defendant dismissed Plaintiff and three (3) other students from the football team and required them to attend alternative school for the entire upcoming academic year. Plaintiff alleges that the manner in which Defendant conducted the disciplinary process violated his due process rights and that he received an unreasonably harsh punishment because he was treated in the same manner as the other three students who participated in the hazing event despite having played a diminished role. Plaintiff asserts that as a result of Defendant's conduct, he is entitled to money damages.

Defendant takes the overarching position that the disciplinary proceedings complied with all due process requirements and did not violate any of Plaintiff's constitutional rights. ...Defendant takes the position that Plaintiff lost any right to take issue with Defendant's actions when he transferred to another school system during the disciplinary process; that Plaintiff had sufficient state remedies; and that Plaintiff had no liberty interest and failed to request a name-clearing hearing. Defendant lastly notes that punitive damages may not be awarded against a governmental entity, that Plaintiff was not denied access to the educational process because he was offered an equivalent education at an alternative school, and that Plaintiff is not entitled to injunctive relief given that he has already been awarded a high school diploma.

……

IV. ANALYSIS

There is little on which the parties agree in this case, but the Court will first outline the few relevant facts which are undisputed. Plaintiff began attending David Crockett High School ("DCHS") in the 2014-2015 academic year as a freshman and was a member of the football team throughout his time at the school. Plaintiff was a standout football player but struggled academically. In the summer immediately preceding Plaintiff's sophomore year, the DCHS football team attended a camp at Tennessee Tech (the "camp") which was sponsored by the Fellowship of Christian Athletes. Upon the team's return from camp, an unidentified person sent an anonymous email to members of the Washington County School Board and certain local media outlets claiming that some of the freshman football players had been hazed during the camp and demanding the perpetrators be punished. Plaintiff ultimately admitted that he played a role in this hazing event by holding the feet of a certain freshman while fellow members of the football team placed their genitals on the face of the freshman football player. Plaintiff was initially sent to the alternative school for ten days and was advised that he could not play football during the coming school year; however, after a disciplinary board hearing Plaintiff's punishment was increased to a full school year at the alternative school.

While it was clear during trial that Plaintiff and his family believe his punishment was too harsh given the role that he played in the hazing, as referenced above, the issue before the Court is whether Plaintiff was provided with due process during the disciplinary process and, if not, whether Plaintiff suffered a compensable injury as a result.

The Court acknowledges the difficulties Defendant likely experienced in addressing this matter while facing intense scrutiny from the media at a time when hazing incidents such as the one at issue were a media focus across the country. Undoubtedly, Defendant would have felt significant pressure to quickly investigate this matter and punish those it found to have been involved in any hazing incident that may have taken place. No one can dispute Defendant's duty to fully investigate the allegations and appropriately punish any student who hazed a fellow student at a school-sponsored event. As the Washington County Department of Education High School Handbook aptly notes in the "Conduct" section, for a school environment to be conducive to learning it must be safe. Defendant must balance the responsibility to maintain that safe environment with its duty to ensure that no student is disciplined without first being provided with due process protections to ensure that the student is in fact guilty of the act of which he or she has been accused because of the significant harm removing a student from the regular classroom environment can have on the student's reputation and educational opportunities. When a notation of discipline is entered onto a student's permanent record, he or she carries that throughout life.

……

Due Process

Plaintiff's Claims Under the Due Process Clause of the Fourteenth Amendment

Plaintiff alleges Defendant deprived him of procedural due process by each of the following acts or omissions, or, in the alternative, by the sum of these acts or omissions:

1) Failure to provide advanced noticed and/or written notice of intent to increase Plaintiff's suspension to more than ten days;

2) Failure to provide Plaintiff/parent written notification of the time and place of any review;

3) Failure to inform Plaintiff of the specific actions he was alleged to have taken;

4) Failure to provide Plaintiff with an opportunity to be heard; and

5) Failure to review Plaintiff's written arguments in lieu of permitting Plaintiff to make oral arguments.

Property Interest

The Fourteenth Amendment guarantees that no person will be deprived of life, liberty, or property without due process of law. U.S. Const., amend. XIV; Goss v. Lopez, 419 U.S. 565, 572 (1975). In order to succeed on a due process claim, Plaintiff must first establish a property or liberty interest that entitles him to due process protection. See Goss, 419 U.S. at 572-73. Children in Tennessee are statutorily entitled to a free public education, and a compulsory attendance law requires children in Tennessee between the ages of six (6) and seventeen (17) years to attend either public or non-public school. Tenn. Code Ann. § 49-6-3001. Although Tennessee is not constitutionally obligated to establish and maintain a public-school system, because it has chosen to do so and to require attendance by law, "the State is constrained to recognize a student's legitimate entitlement to a public education as a property interest which is protected by the Due Process Clause and which may not be taken away for misconduct without adherence to the minimum procedures required by that Clause." Id. at 574.

Suspension to Alternative School as Deprivation of Property Interest[11]

[11] Part of Plaintiff's punishment also prevented him from playing football or attending school activities. "In Tennessee, like the majority of jurisdictions, the right to participate in athletics is considered to be a mere privilege. Because there is no legal right to participate in sports, participation in interscholastic athletics is deemed to fall outside the protection of the due process clause of the Fourteenth Amendment." Bean v. Wilson Cty. School Sys., 488 S.W.3d 782, 790 (Tenn. Ct. App. 2015).

Defendant makes a two-fold argument as to why Plaintiff was not deprived of any property interest. Defendant first takes the position that Plaintiff was not actually suspended from school but was simply relocated to the alternative school where he was provided an education of substantially similar quality. The Sixth Circuit has previously held that a student is not entitled to procedural due process for the sanction of attending an alternative school "absent some showing that the education received at the alternative school is significantly different from or inferior to that received at his regular public school." Buchanan v. City of Bolivar, Tenn., 99 F.3d 1352, 1359 (6th Cir. 1996). At the same time, the Sixth Circuit has found that under certain circumstances in-school suspension could constitute as much educational deprivation as an actual suspension or expulsion. Laney v. Farley, 501 F.3d 577, 581-82 (6th Cir. 2007).

> The primary thrust of the educational process is classroom instruction; in both situations the student is excluded from the classroom. This is not to say that any in-school detention would necessarily be equivalent to a suspension; it would depend on the extent to which to student was deprived of instruction of the opportunity to learn.
> Id. at 582.

This same reasoning could be applied to attending alternative school. But see Jahn v. Farnsworth, 617 F. App'x 453, 461 (6th Cir. 2015) (holding that imposition of a suspension for the remainder of the school year during which the student would have been allowed to finish classes from home and obtain his high school diploma as scheduled did not merit characterization as expulsion).

While Defendant claims that the alternative school education was substantially similar to that provided by DCHS, the proof demonstrated that students in the alternative school were primarily parked in front of a computer and received no classroom instruction. Both Plaintiff and Michael Moffitt credibly testified as to the lack of instruction provided by the alternative school. While Defendant offered testimony through at least two of its witnesses that sometimes students did better in the regular school population after attending the alternative school and that there were licensed teachers and teacher's assistants available to students as a resource, Defendant provided no proof to contradict the testimony of Plaintiff and Moffitt that they were primarily left to learn on their own without educational instruction. The Court does not find that Defendant provided an education of similar quality to students at the alternative school; thus, Defendant's initial suspension of ten days and subsequent suspension of one year to the alternative school were the type of property-interest deprivation that compelled the School System to provide Plaintiff with due process before the discipline was imposed.

Impact of Plaintiff's Transfer on Property Interest

Defendant also argues that when Plaintiff transferred to another school district prior to the conclusion of Defendant's disciplinary process he waived any property interest he might have otherwise had. Defendant's claim overlooks the fact that Plaintiff remained enrolled in the Tennessee public school system and the school system into which Plaintiff transferred enforced the disciplinary action that Defendant imposed against Plaintiff in its district as well. T.C.A. § 49-6-3401(f) makes it clear that the discipline a student receives in one Tennessee school district can adversely impact that student in another district. In fact, a Tennessee school district may deny admission altogether to a student under suspension or expulsion from another school district inside or outside of the state. Id. Additionally, Mr. Dyke's testimony demonstrated that Plaintiff would have been permitted to transfer back to the Washington County School System had he chosen to do so; therefore, the Washington County School System's decision continued to impact his educational opportunities in that school district as well. For these reasons, the Court cannot find that Plaintiff's transfer constituted a waiver of his property interest.

Liberty Interest

The minimal requirements of the Due Process Clause must be satisfied "[w]here a person's good name, reputation, honor, or integrity is at stake because of what the government is doing to him." Goss, 419 U.S. at 574 (quoting Wisconsin v. Constanineau, 400 U.S. 433, 437 (1971)). In Goss, the Court held that charges of misconduct against a student by school officials that led to a suspension "could seriously damage the students' standing with their fellow pupils and their teachers as well as interfere with later opportunities for higher education and employment." Id. at 575. But see Paul v. Davis, 424 U.S. 693, 710 (1976) ("[A]ny harm or injury to that interest [of reputation], even where as here inflicted by an officer of the State, does not result in a deprivation of any liberty or property recognized by state or federal law, nor has it worked any change of respondent's status as theretofore recognized under the State's laws."). The proof offered at trial established that Plaintiff's reputation suffered as a result of the disciplinary proceedings related to the hazing incident. Therefore, the Court finds that Plaintiff also has a valid liberty interest upon which to base his claim.

Minimal Due Process Required

When a student is suspended from public school for disciplinary reasons, due process requires that "the student be given oral or written notice of the charges against him and, if he denies them, and explanation of the evidence the authorities have and an opportunity to present his side of the story." Bd. of Curators of Univ. of Mo. v. Horowitz, 435 U.S. 78, 85 (1978) (quoting Goss, 419 U.S. at 584); see also Jahn v. Farnsworth, 617 F. App'x 453, 460 (6th Cir. 2015) (holding that due process requires that the school system or administrator explain the evidence of the student's wrongdoing and give the student an opportunity to present his version of the facts.). Goss describes the minimal requirement of "an informal give and take between the student and the administrative body dismissing him that would, at least, give the student the opportunity to characterize his conduct and put it in what he deems the proper context." Id. at 86 (citing Goss, 419 U.S. at 584 (internal quotations omitted)). The Supreme Court has frequently emphasized that the very nature of due process requires a certain degree of flexibility and does not lend itself to a rigid structure with universal applicability. Id.; Cafeteria Workers v. McElroy, 367 U.S. 886, 895 (1961). While the Supreme Court has stopped short of requiring a formal hearing in the context of every school suspension, reasoning that further formalizing the suspension process could escalate the adversarial nature of a suspension making it too costly to use as a form of regular discipline and also "destroy its effectiveness as part of the teaching process," the Court also noted that "[l]onger suspensions or expulsions for the remainder of the school term, or permanently, may require more formal procedures." Id. at 583-84.

Throughout the trial of this cause, Defendant's witnesses repeatedly referred to the "Due Process packet" that was utilized in relation to Plaintiff's discipline and asserted that by use of this packet

Plaintiff was automatically provided with due process; however, the mere labeling of a set of documents with the phrase "due process" does not ensure that the information contained therein comports with due process requirements. As the Supreme Court made clear in Goss, a student is only to be disciplined after first being provided with "notice of the charges against him and, if he denies them, an explanation of the evidence the authorities have and an opportunity to present his side of the story." 419 U.S. at 581. That information can be provided orally or in writing, but it must be provided. Id. Plaintiff testified that he was not told what he was alleged to have done wrong either time that he was questioned about the hazing incident. While Principal Wright testified that she was confident Plaintiff knew what he was accused of doing, she also testified that she could not remember what she told Plaintiff about the allegations against him. Plaintiff was provided with a copy of the "Due Process" form, but in looking to that form, the only information it contains under the nature of offense portion is: "Hazing incident at Football Camp, Cookeville, Tenn. July 14-16." Ex. 8. The document contains no information about what hazing was alleged to have taken place or what part Plaintiff was alleged to have played in the incident. Additionally, the disciplinary hearing notes from Plaintiffs' board hearing state for the first time that the charge against him was "conduct prejudicial to good order and discipline in that he was involved in a hazing incident. This incident is a violation of Title 9 and is viewed to be reprehensible behavior and sexual assault."

Plaintiff may well have had some idea of what part he was alleged to have played in the hazing incident and who he was accused of hazing but that is not a substitute for Defendant informing him of the role he was accused of playing and the evidence of his conduct for the purposes of imposing discipline against him. The Court finds that Defendant did not meet its constitutional obligations to Plaintiff in terms of advising him of the allegations against him, including the evidence Defendant had in support of those allegations such that Plaintiff could effectively respond to them.

……

Despite the finding of multiple due process violations, it should be noted all such issues could have easily been remedied had the school board simply provided Plaintiff with a full and fair closed hearing. While Defendant correctly notes that the school board was not obligated by law to provide such a hearing because it was not increasing the punishment handed down by the disciplinary board, given the circumstances it would have been the prudent thing to do and likely would have allowed Defendant to avoid the lawsuit at issue altogether. Defendant contends that the hearing requested by Plaintiff was unnecessary because the process utilized by the school board allowed Plaintiff's voice to be heard. Defendant notes that Plaintiff was permitted to present a packet of information for the school board's consideration containing any information that Plaintiff deemed pertinent to the disciplinary issue; however, this position overlooks the fact that Plaintiff had never been provided with any specifics regarding the conduct in which he was alleged to have engaged nor information about the evidence the School System had demonstrating his culpability.

While the school board was provided with a packet of information which included the statements of those who had been hazed, at least one of which indicated that Plaintiff had played an active role in the hazing incident, once again the record reflects that the school board did not meet its obligation to independently review the disciplinary board's ruling. School board member David Hammond testified at trial that there was nothing that Plaintiff could have presented that would have caused him to disapprove of Principal Wright's recommended punishment despite her being in her first year on the job. He further testified that he believed Plaintiff had engaged in sexual assault and didn't know much of anything about Title IX. While the Court appreciated Mr. Hammond's candor, his testimony also made it clear that he did not independently review and consider the actions of the disciplinary board. School board member Annette Buchanan was asked about her understanding of Title IX. She could not articulate an appropriate understanding of the law nor did she remember that Plaintiff had been accused of violating it. She also testified that she did not seek clarification of what constituted sexual assault despite Plaintiff being alleged to have committed sexual assault… When the testimony of the school board members who appeared at trial is coupled with this lack of deliberation or discussion, it becomes clear that once again Plaintiff was deprived of due process because the school board did not independently review the disciplinary board's decision.

……

V. CONCLUSION

The Court finds that defendant Washington County Department of Education deprived Plaintiff of his right to due process by the manner in which the disciplinary proceedings as to Plaintiff's suspension from school were conducted. Defendant never advised Plaintiff of the specific acts he was alleged to have committed. Those involved in the disciplinary process simply "rubber-stamped" Principal Wright's recommendation as to Defendant's punishment. However, the procedure by which Defendant suspended Plaintiff from the football team for one year did not violate Plaintiff's due process rights because he was not entitled to due process in relation to that suspension. The Court also notes that because Plaintiff ultimately admitted to playing an active role in the hazing incident, although to a lesser degree than the others involved, Defendant's policies provided Defendant with the authority to discipline Plaintiff by imposing a one-year suspension had Defendant simply provided Plaintiff with proper due process. The fact that Plaintiff was likely subjected to the same hazing the year before and perhaps even at the same camp where he hazed others, while concerning and perhaps worthy of some consideration as a mitigating factor, did not deprive Defendant of the right to impose the recommended punishment upon Plaintiff for his participation in the hazing of other students.

As a result of Defendant's due process violations, Plaintiff asserted that he was entitled to have his permanent record modified to remove the discipline imposed and was further entitled to monetary damages; however, at trial Plaintiff's proof of damages was very limited. While it was clear that Plaintiff was emotionally impacted to a significant degree by the discipline he received, given that Defendant would have been entitled to impose the same level of discipline had Plaintiff simply been provided with due process, it is difficult to see how Plaintiff would have been emotionally impacted to a significantly lesser degree if he had received the same discipline after receiving due process. Plaintiff was ultimately able to return to regular classes and to his new high school's football team prior to the end of the 2015-2016 school year and to graduate on time. Plaintiff provided no testimony to indicate that the discipline imposed has negatively impacted his ability to attend college or serve in the military.

Still, the fact that Plaintiff was deprived of due process left him to wonder if things might have been different if his side of the story had been fully heard. The Court finds it appropriate to award nominal damages of $1.00 because, while Plaintiff has failed to prove with sufficient specificity how he was impacted by Defendant's failure to provide him with due process, it is clear that he was in fact impacted by this deprivation.

Because Plaintiff's ten-day and one-year suspensions were imposed without the benefit of due process, the Court also finds that Plaintiff is entitled to have any reference to this discipline removed from his permanent record, except that any reference as to his suspension from the football team which currently exists may remain. Any reference to Plaintiff's suspension from the football team must not indicate that Plaintiff committed sexual assault or violated Title IX, as Defendant's actions do not meet the definition of sexual assault under Tennessee law and, as Defendant concedes, Plaintiff as an individual could not have violated Title IX.

Bernard James and Kameron Johnston: School Discipline Reform & Restorative Justice: A Policy Analysis, 2017 Journal of School Safety 14*

For nearly a decade, educators in the United States have been experimenting with new forms of discipline policies. The goal appears to be to strike a balance in the outcomes of student discipline decision-making. The need for balance is obvious from the data that suggests that school policies that mandate predetermined consequences for specific offenses are more harmful than imagined or intended. These "zero tolerance" policies have fallen under suspicion in nearly all research studies of school incidents, but especially for incidents that do not involve serious crimes involving drugs or guns.

> "Zero tolerance policies were formulated with the best of intentions...However...in a desire to be tough, no-nonsense, and scrupulously equal in punishment, schools have sacrificed measured and proportional responses for mechanical, non-discretionary decision-making...[that] is derailing the educational process."
> Kim Fries and Todd A. DeMitchell, Zero Tolerance and the Paradox of Fairness: Viewpoints from the Classroom, 36 J.L. & Educ. 211, 214 (2007).

It is out of this body of scholarship that the call for more measured and proportional responses to student discipline is emerging. Phrases, slogans, and watchwords now animate the search for a balanced approach to student discipline. Most often, one hears that emerging school discipline reform constitutes "restorative justice," a theory that is designed to change the approach to criminal justice and juvenile justice - and which has done so in New Zealand, Canada, the United States and other countries. However, this is not an accurate description of what is taking place in public schools. At best, the current school discipline reform incorporates a mild version of restorative justice, but that is still animated by strict accountability for serious disruptions. Nearly all educators

---

continue to operate from the belief that as the nature of the campus incident becomes more serious, discipline policies should mandate predetermined consequences for specific offenses. Hence, the elements of the education version of restorative justice are more distinctive and variable.

.....

Restorative Justice: Outside the School Environment

The most frequent statement about restorative justice theory is that it is "a process of bringing together the individuals who have been affected by an offense and having them agree on how to repair the harm caused by the crime." Howard Zehr, *The Little Book of Restorative Justice* 36 (2002). See also, Tina S. Ikpa, *Note, Balancing Restorative Justice Principles and Due Process Rights in Order to Reform the Criminal Justice System*, 24 Wash. U. J.L. & Pol'y 302, (2007).

> "a restorative justice process that seeks to empower stakeholders to repair the harm of an injustice will produce outcomes that are more distributively satisfying to [individuals who have been affected by an offense] than a process that seeks to deliver equal punishments to equal wrongs. If we put the problem in the center of the circle, as opposed to putting the person in the center, we are more likely to come up with a solution to the problem that is perceived by the participants to deliver just distributive benefits." J. Braithwaite (2006) *Doing Justice Intelligently in Civil Society,* Journal of Social Issues 62(2), at page 398.

This point takes on added significance when one recognizes that the elements of the restorative justice theory are organized around collaboration in the same way that interagency child welfare systems shape positive outcomes with collaborative risk-factor and protective-factor analysis. Modern educators are familiar with the collaborative culture as well as the benefits it produces for decision-making.

Outside the school environment, restorative justice theory expands upon the traditional penal theory that crime and wrongdoing are an offence against an individual, the community, and the state. (See, Marty Price, Personalizing Crime: Mediation Produces Restorative Justice for Victims and Offenders (2001), http://vorp.com/articles). When its elements are used in problem-solving, the theory helps officials improve the process by personalizing the individual injury, measuring community harm, and assessing the needs of the offender in a more tangible way. Four ideals shape this focus:

> (1) Encounter: creating opportunities for victims, offenders, their families and community members to meet to discuss the crime and its impact on them;
> (2) Amends: expecting wrongdoers to take steps to repair the harm they have caused;
> (3) Reintegration: seeking to restore victims and offenders to wholeness, to become contributing members to the community; and

> (4) Inclusion: providing opportunities for parties with a stake in a specific crime or incident to participate in its resolution.
> See, John Braithwaite, Principles of Restorative Justice, in Restorative Justice & Criminal Justice (2003).

When correctly put into practice, the elements of restorative justice, described above, provide a meaningful language for a more effective assessment of a problem in light of existing policy. Decision-makers are not allowed to look at solutions to a problem in the same old way until examining the causes that led to the problem in the first place. The goal of restorative justice is not to produce a new mechanical approach for implementing a necessary policy, but to equip decision-makers with a means for producing outcomes that will be personally suited to the conditions that created the problem in the first place.

In its original intended application - in the criminal justice system - restorative justice theory alters traditional criminal procedure to include conversations between a victim, an offender, and the community. This encounter or "mediation," has been shown to produce high rates of victim satisfaction and offender accountability. This feature of restorative justice has a range of applications, each capable of increasing the number of participants to the conversation as necessary: victim offender conferences, family group conferences, mediation circles, diversionary programs, and transitional programs.

Restorative justice theory is heavily documented with positive assessments. It is enough for now to cite a few typical examples.

> Systemic use of restorative justice processes will lead to general deterrence and to a decrease in the crime rate. The alliance between victims and community members that is created through restorative processes produces greater satisfaction and trust, consequently increasing the percentages of reported new crimes. The rise in the reporting rates increases the risk of being caught and hence the reluctance of potential offenders to commit offenses. See, Dancig-Rosenberg and Gal, *Extent or Effect of Victim's Injuries*, 34 Cardozo L. Rev. 2313, 2327-2328 (2013).

***

> [O]ffender satisfaction with both corporate and traditional individual restorative justice programs has been extremely high. The evidence of offenders being restored in the sense of desisting from criminal conduct is encouraging with victim-offender mediation, conferencing, restorative business regulatory programs, and whole-school antibullying programs, though not peer mediation programs for bullying. See, John Braithwaite, Restorative *Justice: Assessing Optimistic and Pessimistic Accounts*, 25 Crime & Just. 1, 26 (1999).

***

> The opportunity restorative justice allows to come face-to-face with an offender clearly enhances the likelihood of an apology being offered: indeed, apology is

> usually seen as central to the process of restoration. Furthermore, it appears that the expression of remorse and a genuine desire for reconciliation on the part of the offender is a significant predictor of offenders' desistance from future offending. Heather Strang & Lawrence W. Sherman, *Repairing the Harm: Victims and Restorative Justice*, 2003 Utah L. Rev. 15, 27 (2003) (citing Gabrielle M. Maxwell & Allison Morris, *Family, Victims and Culture: Youth Justice in New Zealand* (1993).

In analyzing the scholarship on satisfaction with the theory, the principal questions are: are there *limits to its application* in the criminal justice system? Does restorative justice theory produce praiseworthy results *for all crimes*? Are there some offences for which the *theory is unsuitable*? The answer appears to be that restorative justice theory loses its effectiveness inversely to the severity of the crime. In other words, its impact on the decision-making process in the area of criminal justice is strongest in the area of its initial focus - minor criminal offenses. Dr. Howard Zehr, one of the creators of the theory, emphasizes that "restorative justice began as an effort to deal with burglary and other property crimes that are usually viewed (often incorrectly) as relatively minor offenses." Zehr, *The Little Book of Restorative Justice* 3 (2002). It important to note that Dr. Zehr believes that restorative justice theory is more important in the cases involving serious crime. "Restorative justice is not primarily intended for "minor" offenses or first-time offenders. It may be easier to get community support for programs that address such cases. However, experience has shown that restorative approaches may have the greatest impact in more severe cases. Moreover, if the principles of restorative justice are taken seriously, the need for restorative approaches is especially clear in severe cases." Id, at page 9.

This assessment is readily apparent in the school environment. It explains why most educators continue to operate from the belief that as the nature of the campus incident becomes more serious, discipline policies should mandate predetermined consequences for specific offenses.

The single most frequent error by those who seek to apply the theory is to confuse restorative justice with actual policy. (For examples of wayward thinking about restorative justice theory, see, Jennifer Lim, *Arguing for Restorative Justice as an Alternative to Mass Incarceration*, 37 Los Angeles Lawyer 36 (2014). See also, Joan W. Howarth, Toward *the Restorative Constitution: A Restorative Justice Critique of Anti-Gang Public Nuisance Injunctions*, 27 Hastings Const. L.Q. 717 (2000). See, Nils Jareborg, *Criminalization as Last Resort (Ultima Ratio),* 2 Ohio St. J. Crim. L. 521 (2005)).

Dr. Zehr notes:

> Like all change efforts, as restorative justice has developed and spread, it has sometimes lost its way. With more and more programs being termed "restorative justice," its meaning often has been diluted or confused. Under the inevitable pressures of working in the real world, restorative justice has sometimes been subtly co-opted or diverted from its principles.
> Zehr, The Little Book of Restorative Justice, at page 4.

Restorative justice is not substantive policy. Rather, social scientists call it "meta-strategy"- a theory whose principles make more effective an existing policy. Its primary benefit is twofold. First, it helps to improve the process of decision-making through a collaborative framework that includes the actual stakeholders. Second, it discourages shortcuts to problem-solving by resisting mechanical, non-discretionary decision-making that tends to quickly move toward a predetermined solution. The irony of its application in the school environment, discussed below, is that school officials who misunderstand restorative justice theory tend to stumble in their decision-making by wrongly substituting the new predetermined solution (extreme tolerance) for the disfavored old mechanical solution (zero tolerance). The reasons for this misunderstanding are extraordinarily complex. No simple explanation can be given that will account for all or even most of the misapplications of the restorative justice theory. To date, the most important opinion is offered by one of its creators, Dr. Zehr.

> 1. Restorative justice is not primarily about forgiveness or reconciliation. Reconciliation is the prerogative of the victim, as is forgiveness. Offenders are usually required to complete their punishment even if forgiven.
>
> 2. Restorative justice is not mediation. An encounter is not always chosen or appropriate. No meeting between a victim and the offender is appropriate unless the parties are assumed to be on a level moral playing field, often with responsibilities that may need to be shared on all sides as a result of the incident.
>
> 3. Moreover, to participate in most restorative justice encounters, a wrongdoer must admit to some level of responsibility for the offense, and an important component of such programs is to name and acknowledge the wrongdoing. The neutral language of mediation may be misleading and even offensive in such cases.
>
> 4. Restorative justice is not primarily designed to reduce recidivism. Reduced recidivism is an expected byproduct, but restorative justice is done first of all because it is the right thing to do: victims' needs should be addressed, offenders should be encouraged to take responsibility, those affected by an offense should be involved in the process, regardless of whether offenders "get it" and reduce their offending.
>
> 5. Restorative justice is not a particular program or a blueprint. Restorative justice is not a map but the principles of restorative justice can be seen as a compass pointing a direction. At minimum, restorative justice is an invitation for dialogue and exploration in the context of victim-offender encounters.
> Zehr, The Little Book of Restorative Justice, at pages 6-9.

Restorative Justice: Inside the School Environment

Once one has a grasp of the basic terrain of the restorative justice theory, he must step back and reflect on how it is being applied in the school environment. In regard to the zero tolerance/restorative justice distinction, school officials maintain an almost uncompromising insistence on keeping both in play as tools for maintaining a safe campus. To be sure, elements of restorative justice are recognizable in current policies and the best examples of this are found in the provisions of revisions to school disciplinary policies. Nevertheless, current school policies retain a surprising variety of predetermined consequences for specific offenses. The zero tolerance/restorative justice distinction is not obliterated, and critics of zero tolerance need to take note of this. While it is still to be taken note of in the wider range of frequent and foreseeable violations of the code of conduct, the difference is irrelevant as the gravity of the offence increases.

Among the things that need to be said about the education environment is that it comes tailor-made for the application of the elements of restorative justice. There is simply too much scholarship to accept any suggestion that restorative justice theory is incompatible with school safety. (See, Seitz, J., *Rethinking school discipline* (2014). See also, Sumner, D., Silverman, C., & Frampton, M., *School-based Restorative Justice as an Alternative to Zero-Tolerance Policies: Lessons from West Oakland.* (2010). See also, Mirsky, L., & Wachtel, T. *The Worst School I've Ever Been To: Empirical Evaluations of a Restorative School and Treatment Milieu.* (2007). See also, Ashworth, J., Van Bockern, S., et. al., *An Alternative to School Detention.* (2008). See, Coldren, J., Haring, *School-Based Restorative Justice Data Template Final Report.* (2011). See also, Evans, K., & Lester, J., *Restorative Justice in Education: What We Know So Far* (2013). See, McMorris, B. J., Beckman, K. J., Shea, G., Baumgartner, J., & Eggert, R. C., *Applying Restorative Justice Practices to Minneapolis Public Schools Students Recommended for Possible Expulsion.* (2014)).

***

Three research studies illustrate this compatibility.

> The Family and Youth Restorative Conference Program has a positive impact on at-risk students. The evaluation demonstrates evidence of positive changes in behavior, attitudes, and opinions for both students and family members who participate. Given that temporary exclusion from school and involuntary school transfers can be a precursor to disengagement from school, the RCP appears to interrupt downward trajectories and return students to a path of academic progress. McMorris, B. J., Beckman, K. J., Shea, G., Baumgartner, J., & Eggert, R. C., Applying Restorative Justice Practices to Minneapolis Public Schools Students Recommended for Possible Expulsion (2014). http://www.legalrightscenter.org/uploads/2/5/7/3/25735760/lrc_exec_summ-final.pdf.

***

> [P]ositive school culture (focusing on the positive, creating leaders, and stressing consequences) is important in establishing a safe environment, and that restorative Justice practices can assist in this endeavor…[T]he administrators and teachers have already begun implementing mediation and other informal techniques to peacefully reconcile conflicts. Although they noted that this process consumes time and energy of all involved, it alleviates stress by addressing the root causes of the conflict. Many times, all parties come to an

> agreement, thereby reducing future conflicts. Coldren, J., Haring, School-Based Restorative Justice Data Template Final Report, 64 (2011). http://www.ibarj.org/docs/SchoolRJFinalReport.pdf.
>
> ***
>
> Although we cannot definitively say that restorative justice was the cause of the suspension and expulsion reductions, the steep decline in suspensions and expulsions in the year the program was fully implemented at the school and the maintenance of these reductions in its second year provide strong supporting evidence that restorative justice did indeed reduce suspensions and expulsions. Sumner, D., Silverman, C., & Frampton, M., *School-based Restorative Justice as an Alternative to Zero-Tolerance Policies: Lessons from West Oakland, 31* (2010). https://www.law.berkeley.edu/files/thcsj/10-2010_Schoolbased_Restorative_Justice_As_an_Alternative_to_Zero-Tolerance_Policies.pdf.

Nevertheless, the insistence on keeping both in play as tools for maintaining a safe campus is clearly evident in a convenience sample of the current discipline policies of school districts of various sizes in the United States. The compilation gathers the discipline policy for 60 U.S. school districts: the 21 largest; 20 moderate sized; and 20 small or rural public school districts. In addition to selecting policies that included provisions on "restorative justice," the compilation took policies that made references to referrals to law enforcement, expulsion standards, suspension standards, and alternative school transfer standards.

Conclusion

In singling out actual school district policies for analysis, the most important conclusion that emerges is that school discipline reform reflects the politics of the jurisdiction as a whole. School discipline reform cannot be understood solely in terms of the restorative justice philosophy. Indeed, only a few school districts appear to embrace restorative justice in its classic form. Instead, the experiments over discipline policy will continue to be shaped by the nature of the campus incidents themselves and their impact on the community. School discipline policies will change in this wave of reform, but it will be an incremental change, in response to specific outcome failures attributable to the traditional decision-making model.

Notes and Comments

1. *In loco Parentis* Doctrine and the Authority of Educators

Since the time of Blackstone, the common wisdom has been that school officials are cloaked in a form of parental authority to the students they inherit each day and that this is particularly true in matters relating to conduct and discipline. See, 1 William Blackstone, *Commentaries on the Laws of England*,s 441 (1765) ("[the father] may also delegate part of his parental authority, during his life, to the tutor or schoolmaster of his child; who is then in loco parentis, and has such a portion of the power of the parent committed to his charge, viz. that of restraint and correction, as may be necessary to answer the purposes for which he is employed."). The notion of in loco parentis first appears in American jurisprudence in 1837. In the case of *State v. Pendergrass*, involving corporal punishment (an educator whipped as student with a switch), the court notes, "One of the most sacred duties of parents, is to train up and qualify their children, for becoming useful and virtuous members of society; this duty cannot be effectually performed without the ability to command obedience, to control stubbornness, to quicken diligence, and to reform bad habits .... The teacher is the substitute of the parent; ... and in the exercise of these delegated duties, is invested with his power." State v. Pendergrass, 19 N.C. 365, 365–366 (1837).

Three recent cases illustrate the modern application of *in loco parentis*.

• In *Orr v. Ferebee*, (2017 WL 1509309 (S.D. Ind. Apr. 27, 2017)), a federal court is asked to resolve a dispute over the use of force by a teacher. The student claimed that the teacher, "choked him, hit his head against a wall, and dragged him down a hallway by the neck" in an effort to break up a fight with another student. The student argues that the school policy on the use of force was invalid as was the training based on the policy. The student also challenged the validity of the Indiana Education Code authorizing the use of force. (Indiana Code § 20-33-8-8(b), "In all matters relating to the discipline and conduct of students, school corporation personnel: (1) stand in the relation of parents to the students of the school corporation."). The court applies the plain meaning rule, to uphold the provisions of the statute that authorizes educators to "take any disciplinary action necessary to promote student conduct that conforms with an orderly and effective educational system." The court rejected the student's challenge to the teacher's use of force by echoing the statute, "[in] regarding matters of discipline and the conduct of students, public schools stand in the relation of parents and guardians." (2017 WL 1509309 at page 1).

• In *Lujan v. Carranza*, (63 Misc. 3d 235, 91 N.Y.S.3d 869 (N.Y. Sup. Ct. 2019)), a state court is asked to adjudicate a claim by a parent that restrictions placed on his access to the school were unlawful. The parent had been convicted for the rape of a juvenile with a deadly weapon in 1988. He was released from prison and discharged from parole supervision in 1998. In 2015, educators at his son's school placed restrictions on his access to the school based on his Level III sex offender status and the fact that his victim was a juvenile. The restrictions were not a complete prohibition from entering the school but prevented the parent from coming within 1000 feet of school grounds without prior approval and supervision by school personnel. The parent argued that the, "crime took place long ago and there was no rational connection between the facts underlying his conviction and the restrictions." (63 Misc.3d at page 237). The court dismissed the parent's challenge to the school policy declaring, "schools stand *in loco parentis* to their students and have a duty to protect them. The precautionary measures and restrictions here address the particular concerns [the father] presents and are rationally related to the school's *in loco parentis* duty." (63 Misc.3d at page 243).

• In *Friedenberg v. School Board of Palm Beach County*, (257 F. Supp. 3d 1295 (S.D. Fla. 2017), aff'd, 911 F.3d 1084 (11th Cir. 2018).)), a federal appeals court affirms the validity of drug testing as part of the screening process for substitute teachers. An applicant with a conditional offer to become a substitute teacher refused to submit to the testing, claiming that suspicionless drug testing for a teaching job was a violation of the Fourth Amendment. The lower court upheld the policy on the basis that urinalysis was not unduly intrusive and that it furthered the compelling interest of the school to protect "children under a substitute teacher's charge." (257 F. Supp. 3d at 1313). The appellate court affirms this ruling, first noting that ordinarily, "[a] suspicionless search by the government is presumptively unconstitutional. So goes the basic hornbook law of the Fourth Amendment. The details are a bit more complex." (911 F.3d. at 1087). The court then proceeds to rebut the presumption in a case-by-case summary of *in loco parentis* authority with the following conclusion:

> The *in loco parentis* status of school administrators does not give rise to a constitutional duty to protect, but it has a protective element nonetheless, especially insofar as that protection relates to influences that are seen as immoral. Whether we view it as a matter of physical protection or a matter of value-inculcation, we think that schools have a meaningful interest in keeping active drug users—including teachers—away from their students." 911 F.3d. at 1103. (quotations and citations omitted).

What is important here is that i*n loco parentis* has made a deep imprint on the development of education law. Under its influence, the concept of the authority of educators has shifted from referring simply to the power to tutor children and to compel school attendance for this purpose. Instead, it has become a way of referring to a generalized power to make decisions in the best interest of students that might conceivably have something to do with schooling. For informative scholarship on this, see Perry A. Zirkel & Henry F. Reichner, *Is the In Loco Parentis Doctrine Dead*?, 15 J.L. & Educ. 271 (1986); Susan Stuart, *In Loco Parentis in the Public Schools: Abused, Confused and in Need of Change*, 78 U. Cin. L. Rev. 969 (2010); Tyler Stoehr, Comment, *Letting the Legislature Decide: Why the Court's Use of In Loco Parentis Ought to be Praised, Not Condemned*, 2011 BYU L. Rev. 1695.

What do you make of the following applications of the doctrine of *in loco parentis*?

-- In Washington State, the United States Court of Appeals affirmed the dismissal of a lawsuit filed by a parent who argued that a school policy limiting his communications with school district employees was a violation of his First Amendment rights. The appellate court ruled that the policy was a reasonable, content neutral, and viewpoint neutral effort to manage the father's relentless and unproductive communications with school officials. *L. F. v. Lake Washington Sch. Dist. #414*, 947 F.3d 621 (9th Cir. 2020).

-- In New York, the New York Supreme Court ruled that school officials were not liable for a student's death by suicide on the basis of the allegation that the educators failed to act to stop bullying. The court reasoned that the duty of care exists *in loco parentis* but operates within the limited zone of an educator's physical custody of and control over a student. The student's death occurred after school hours and off school premises, where district had no control over student, and there was no allegation that school officials were on notice of possibility of student's suicide. *Collazo v. Hicksville Union Free Sch. Dist.*, 65 Misc. 3d 268, 108 N.Y.S.3d 708 (N.Y. Sup. Ct. 2019).

2. Procedural Due Process and "Zero Tolerance" Policies

What would you tell school officials about so-called "zero tolerance" policies in light of the material above? Assume that a school district wants to address the problem of cell phones on campus. Write a zero tolerance policy that you believe would pass muster under these cases.

3. School Discipline and Extra-Curricular Activities

The question of whether or not a student has a property interest in extra-curricular activities has been litigated a surprising number of times. The courts do not agree on the answer. The vast majority of state and federal courts have concluded that students do not have a property interest in extra-curricular activities. These courts routinely uphold temporary and permanent suspensions of privileges to which *Goss* does not apply.

For examples, see *Herbert v. Ventetuolo*, 638 F.2d 5 (1st Cir. 1981) (high school hockey); *Angstadt v. Midd-West School Dist.*, 377 F.3d 338 (3d Cir. 2004) (high school basketball); *Hardy v. University Interscholastic League*, 759 F. 2d 1233 (5th Cir. 1985) (high school football); *Poling v. Murphy*, 872 F.2d 757 (6th Cir. 1989) (student counsel elections); *McFarlin v. Newport Special School Dist.*, 980 F.2d 1208 (8th Cir. 1992) (high school basketball); *Rutledge v. Arizona Bd. of Regents*, 660 F.2d 1345 (9th Cir. 1981) (college football); *Seamons v. Snow*, 84 F.3d 1226 (10th Cir. 1996) (high school football); *Davenport v. Randolph County Board of Education*, 730 F. 2d 1395 (11th Cir. 1984) (high school football); *James By and Through Singleton v. Tallassee High School*, 907 F. Supp. 364 (M.D. Ala. 1995) (high school cheerleading); *Tiffany By and Through Tiffany v. Arizona Interscholastic Ass'n, Inc.*, 726 P.2d 231 (Ariz. Ct. App. Div. 1. 1986) (all high school interscholastic sports); *Giannattasio v. Stamford Youth Hockey Ass'n*, 621 F. Supp. 825 (D. Conn. 1985) (high school hockey); *Stewart v. Bibb County Bd. of Educ.*, 2006 WL 449197 (M.D. Ga. 2006) (high school football); *Florida High School Athletic Ass'n v. Melbourne Central Catholic High School*, 867 So. 2d 1281 (Fla. Dist. Ct. App. 5th Dist. 2004) (high school football); *Bryant v. Oak Forest High School Dist., 228 Bd. of Educ.*, 2007 U.S. Dist. LEXIS 67292 (N.D. Ill. 2007) (high school football); *D.N. ex rel. Huff v. Penn Harris Madison School Corp.*, 2006 U.S. Dist. LEXIS 9217 (N.D. Ind. 2006) (high school football and track); *Hysaw v. Washburn University of Topeka*, 690 F. Supp. 940 (D. Kan. 1987) (university athletic scholarships); *Brands v. Sheldon Community School*, 671 F. Supp. 627 (N.D. Iowa 1987) (high school wrestling); *Havenkampv. Unified School District*, 689 F. Supp. 1055) (D. Kansas 1986) (high school cheerleading); *S.B. ex rel. Brown v. Ballard County Bd. of Educ.*, 780 F. Supp. 2d 560 (W.D. Ky. 2011) (high school softball); *Peterson v. Independent School Dist. No. 811*, 999 F. Supp. 665 (D. Minn. 1998) (extra-curricular activities generally); *Davis v. Churchill County School Board of Trustees*, 616 F. Supp. 1310 (D. Nev. 1985) (junior varsity basketball); *Palmer v. Merluzzi*, 689 F. Supp. 400, 1988 U.S. Dist. LEXIS 9857 (D.N.J. 1988) (high school football); *Mazevski v. Horseheads Cent. School Dist.*, 950 F. Supp. 69 (W.D. N.Y. 1997) (high school marching band); *Dziewa v. Pennsylvania Interscholastic Athletic Ass'n, Inc.*, 2009 U.S. Dist. LEXIS 3062 (E.D. Pa. 2009) (high school wrestling); *Bundick v. Bay City Independent School Dist.*, 140 F. Supp. 2d 735 (S.D. Tex. 2001) (extra-curricular activities generally and graduation); *Taylor v. Enumclaw School Dist. No. 216*, 133 P.3d 492 (Wash. App. Div. 1 2006) (all high school interscholastic sports); *Sisson v. Virginia High School League, Inc.*, 801 F. Supp. 2d 526 (W.D. Va. 2010) (extra-curricular activities generally); *Longoria Next Friend of M.L. v. San Benito Indep. Consol. Sch. Dist.*, 942 F.3d 258

(5th Cir. 2019) (removal from the cheerleading squad due to off-campus social media activity); *Johnson v. Cache Cty. Sch. Dist.*, 323 F. Supp. 3d 1301 (D. Utah 2018) (same).

A minority of courts have held that students have a property interest in extra-curricular activities. The rationale of these cases appears to be that extra-curricular activities – especially interscholastic athletics – serve as a means to college scholarships and lucrative professional careers. For examples, see *Boyd v. Board of Education of McGehee School District No. 17*, 612 F. Supp. 86, 93 (D. Ark. 1985) (high school football); *Behagen v. Intercollegiate Conference of Faculty Representatives*, 346 F. Supp. 602, 604 (D. Minn. 1972) (college basketball); *Duffley v. N.H. Interscholastic Athletic Assoc.*, 122 N.H. 484, 446 A.2d 462 (N.H. 1982) (using the state constitution to find a property interest in high school basketball).

Still, some courts are undecided on the issue. While many of these courts have chosen to follow the various state and federal decisions that reject the notion of students' property interest in extra-curricular activities, some courts are undecided, citing the lack of clarity and established law. For examples, see *Farver v. Board of Education Carroll County*, 40 F. Supp. 2d 323, 324-25 (D. Md. 1999) (recognizing that Maryland may protect students' right to extracurricular activities, but no law has yet been established); *Braesch v. DePasquale*, 265 N.W.2d 842 (Neb. 1978) (acknowledging the uncertainty as to whether participation in extracurricular activities is a constitutionally protected right)

4. Procedural Due Process in Higher Education

Do the protections of procedural due process follow a student into college? The courts have not resolved this question. Perhaps, because of the status of the student as an adult, or the contractual nature of the college environment, there has been reluctance to apply *Goss v. Lopez* to the higher education setting.

In *Gomes v. University of Maine System* 304 F. Supp. 2d 117 (D. Me. 2004), who was suspended for one year by university officials for alleged sexual assault on another student, brought suit claiming that the disciplinary process violated substantive due process. The court decided that this right did not apply at the college level, as the student did not have a property interest in higher education.

Some courts have found that a student at a public university has a property or liberty interest in continuing studies at the institution. *See, e.g.*, *Stoller v. College of Medicine*, 562 F. Supp. 403 (3d Cir. 1983) (holding that a medical student has a property interest in continuing his studies); *Ross v. Pennsylvania State Univ.*, 445 F. Supp. 147 (M.D. Pa. 1978) (holding that a graduate student has a property interest in continuing his studies); *Reilly v. Daly*, 666 N.E.2d 439, 444 (Ind. Ct. App. 1996) (acknowledging that expulsion could threaten a student's liberty interest in pursuing education); *Hall v. University of Minnesota*, 530 F. Supp. 104, 107 (D. Minn. 1982) (holding that due process protects a university student's property right); *Thomas v. Gee*, 850 F. Supp. 665 (S.D. Ohio 1994) (finding a liberty interest in a student's freedom to pursue an education free of governmental discrimination). A student may have a contractual interest in higher education as well. *See Branum v. Clark*, 927 F.2d 698, 705 (2d Cir. 1991) (implying a contractual agreement between a university and its students providing a basis for property interest that would be entitled to constitutional protection). Ultimately, some courts have held that college students have some type of interest, thus entitling students to due process.

However, other courts have held differently, recognizing no definite decision by the Supreme Court as to the matter. In *Lee v. University of Michigan* (2007 U.S. Dist. LEXIS 72236 (2007)), the court held that an expelled student did not have a procedural due process right. In the decision, the court recognized inconsistencies in decisions throughout the U.S., particularly in the Sixth Circuit.

Other courts have not followed this line of reasoning. *See, e.g., Lee v. Board of Trustees of Western Illinois University*, No. 98-4038, 2000 U.S. App. LEXIS 418, 2000 WL 14419 (7th Cir. Jan. 5, 2000) ("The plaintiffs conclude, without analysis, that children have a property interest in attending elementary and secondary public schools and so necessarily there is a similar interest in attending public universities. But we have never decided this question, and there are obvious differences between compulsory education and post-secondary programs") (citation omitted); *Osteen v. Henley*, 13 F.3d 221, 223 (7th Cir. 1993) ("it is an open question in this circuit whether a college student as distinct from attendance"); *Tigrett v. Rector and Visitors of University of Virginia*, 290 F.3d 620, 627 (4th Cir. 2002) ("[t]he Supreme Court has assumed, without actually deciding, that university students posses a 'constitutionally protected property right' in their continued enrollment in a university").

There is even disagreement over this matter within this circuit. Some courts have cited the opinion in *Regents of the University of Michigan v. Ewing*, 474 U.S. 214, 106 S. Ct. 507, 88 L. Ed. 2d 523 (1985), as establishing that a public university student has an interest in continued enrollment. *See, e.g., Picozzi v. Sandalow*, 623 F. Supp. 1571, 1576 (E.D. Mich. 1986) (citing *Ewing* for the proposition that "[a] public university student has a protected interest in continuing his studies"). However, the Supreme Court's opinion in *Ewing* is itself based upon the assumption that a university had a property interest, which "gave rise to a substantive right under the Due Process Clause to continued enrollment from arbitrary state action." *Ewing*, 474 U.S. at 223. Given the Supreme Court's reasoning in *Ewing*, one district court attempted to read the underlying Sixth Circuit decision in *Ewing v. Board of Regents of University of Michigan*, 742 F.2d 913 (6th Cir. 1984), rev'd, 474 U.S. 214 [see above](1985), as establishing that a state university student has both a substantive and procedural due process right in continuing his studies. *Megenity v. Stenger*, 27 F.3d 1120, 1123 (6th Cir. 1994). But the Sixth Circuit itself has backed away from this approach, concluding that although the Supreme Court "did not necessarily reject the central holding of our decision" the trial court's reliance on the Sixth Circuit's Ewing opinion was "misplaced" and "tenuous authority." *Id.* The Sixth Circuit concluded that, "[the] plaintiff had no clearly established constitutional right to substantive or procedural due process in her disciplinary proceeding at the University based upon her expectation of continued enrollment, much less her expectation of a certain type of due process itself." *Id.*

Do you agree? Can an argument be made that procedural due process should apply with equal rigor in public colleges and universities?

II. Procedural Due Process and the Scope of Discipline: The "Off-Campus" Cases

An emerging group of cases that raise fairness issues involve the so-call "off-campus" codes of conduct. Courts are understandably concerned about the reach of the long arm of school officials when school discipline is applied to misconduct that occurs away from school. The easy cases involve school-sponsored activities. Courts always uphold the power of school officials in such cases as a logical extension of the power to manage events for which educators are responsible. The school is seen as literally being "on the road" with no change in the relationship between tutor and student. *See Ette v. Linn-Mar Cmty. Sch. Dist.*, 656 N.W.2d 62 (Iowa 2002) (smoking on a field trip); *Fuller v. Decatur Pub. Sch. Bd. of Educ. Sch. Dist. 61*, 251 F.3d 662 (7th Cir. Ill. 2001) (gang activity at a football game); and *Katchak v. Glasgow Independent School System*, 690 F. Supp. 580 (W.D. Ky. 1988) (drinking on a field trip); *Webb v. McCullough*, 828 F.2d 1151 (6th Cir.1987) (search of students' hotel room during band field trip); *Rhodes v. Guarricino* 54 F.Supp.2d 186 (S.D.N.Y.1999) (search of student's hotel room during class trip to Disney World); *Shade v. City of Farmington*, 309 F.3d 1054 (8th Cir.2002) (search of student during class held off campus).

The more difficult cases involve policies that permit school discipline for off-campus behavior that is not related to a class activity nor to a school-sponsored event. Two examples appear below.

"Any local or regional board of education…may expel, subject to the provisions of this subsection, any pupil in grades three to twelve, inclusive, whose conduct on school grounds or at a school-sponsored activity is violative of a publicized policy of such board and is seriously disruptive of the educational process or endangers persons or property or whose conduct off school grounds is violative of such policy and is seriously disruptive of the educational process."

Conn. Gen. Stat. Ann. § 10-233d.

"A student may be removed from class and placed in a disciplinary alternative education program under Section 37.008 based on conduct occurring off campus and while the student is not in attendance at a school-sponsored or school-related activity if: (1) the superintendent or the superintendent's designee has a reasonable belief that the student has engaged in conduct defined as a felony offense other than aggravated robbery under Section 29.03, Penal Code, or those offenses defined in Title 5, Penal Code; and (2) the continued presence of the student in the regular classroom threatens the safety of other students or teachers or will be detrimental to the educational process." Tex. Educ. Code Ann. § 37.006.

How much of a pupil's out-of-school life should be the concern of public school officials? And should educators be allowed to punish students for activity for which the school faces no exposure to liability (since most field trips require the signing of waivers)? Do the cases below provide clear guidelines on the matter?

DOE v. SUPERINTENDENT OF SCHOOLS OF STOUGHTON
767 N.E.2d 1054 (Mass. 2002)

JUDGES: Present: Marshall, C.J., Greaney, Ireland, Spina, Cowin, Sosman, & Cordy, JJ.

COWIN, J.

This is an appeal from the Superior Court's determination that Stoughton school authorities acted arbitrarily and capriciously in suspending a student pursuant to G. L. c. 71, § 37H1/2, the statute providing for the suspension of students who have been charged with felonies. The principal of Stoughton High School suspended John Doe after learning that he had been charged with indecent assault and battery on a child under the age of fourteen years, and rape and abuse of a child. The principal's decision was based on these felony charges and his determination that John's attendance at school posed a threat to the safety, security and welfare of the students at Stoughton High School. The superintendent of Stoughton public schools upheld the principal's determination, and John's parents sought judicial review of that decision in the Superior Court. A judge in the Superior Court concluded that the superintendent's decision was an abuse of discretion, and permanently enjoined school authorities from prohibiting John's attendance at Stoughton High School. We reverse. Judgment is to enter for the defendants.

John Doe, a fifteen year old freshman student at Stoughton High School, was charged with sexually assaulting a six year old child in a garage during the prior summer. On learning of the charges, the principal of Stoughton High School sent John's parents a letter notifying them that he would hold a hearing to consider John's possible expulsion based on the felony charges that had been filed against him by the Stoughton police department.

In addition, the principal considered John's first quarter grade report and disciplinary record. Although John's grades were poor, his record did not indicate prior disciplinary problems during his brief time at Stoughton High School. The principal notified the parents by letter of his decision to exclude John from school pending the resolution of the charges, stating that "[John] poses a threat to the safety, security and welfare of the Stoughton High School community," and that he could not "risk the possibility that a similar occurrence might take place within the High School" by allowing him to return.

.....

General Laws c. 71, § 37H1/2, authorizes the suspension of students who have been charged with felonies. G. L. c. 71, § 37H1/2 (1996). The statute specifies that the principal or headmaster makes the initial decision to suspend, and must provide the student with written notification and a hearing before any suspension may take effect. A felony charge alone is not sufficient basis for imposing suspension; the statute also requires a determination that "the student's continued presence in school would have a substantial detrimental effect on the general welfare of the school." The student has the right to appeal from the principal's determination to the superintendent.

Although we have yet to decide the appropriate standard of review of a superintendent's decision to suspend a student under G. L. c. 71, § 37H1/2, we have always accorded school officials substantial deference in matters of discipline. Students have an important interest in public education, but we have recognized that "educational opportunities can be lost by students as a result of their actions." *Doe v. Superintendent of Schs. of Worcester, supra* 421 Mass. at 130-131. School officials have a duty to "provide a safe and secure environment in which all children can learn." *Id.* 421 Mass. at 131. Because school officials are in the best position to determine when a student's actions threaten the safety and welfare of other students, we must grant school officials substantial deference in their disciplinary choices. Thus, we will overturn a superintendent's decision to suspend a student only if it is arbitrary and capricious, so as to constitute an abuse of discretion. Although this is an appeal from a Superior Court determination, we review the record before the superintendent to determine whether the decision is arbitrary or capricious without giving the view of the Superior Court judge any special weight.

Reversal of the superintendent's decision is warranted only if it "lacks any rational explanation that reasonable persons might support." *Fire Chief of E. Bridgewater v. Plymouth County Retirement Bd.*, 47 Mass. App. Ct. 66, 69, 710 N.E.2d 644 (1999). A decision is not arbitrary and capricious if "reasonable minds could differ" on the proper outcome. *Kinchla v. Board of Appeals of Falmouth,* 11 Mass. App. Ct. 927, 927, 415 N.E.2d 882 (1981). It is not the place of a reviewing court to substitute its own opinion for that of the superintendent. *Id.* We will affirm the superintendent's decision if it is rational.

The plaintiffs argue that, in reviewing the propriety of the suspension, we may not consider an affidavit by the superintendent stating, inter alia, that Stoughton High School is located on the same premises as the elementary and middle schools. ... The superintendent could have been cognizant of the location of the schools to support a concern that younger children will be endangered by John's presence at the high school. We need not consider that he made no mention of this factor because his decision is fully supported.

[T]he superintendent's determination is within his discretion. We agree with the Superior Court judge's interpretation of G. L. c. 71, § 37H1/2: more than a felony charge is required to impose suspension. The superintendent, however, made the necessary finding that John's attendance at school "would have a substantial detrimental effect on the general welfare of the school," G. L. c. 71, § 37H1/2, and this finding is supported by the evidence in the record. The statute does not prohibit the principal from drawing an inference of detrimental effect based on the nature of the crime alone. The crime at issue in this case is particularly troublesome. The police reports provide evidence that John engaged in deviant sexual conduct with a young child. Further, not only did John fail to express remorse for his conduct; he sought to explain the incident as "a joke." Given the nature and seriousness of the allegations, John's admitted participation in the crime, and his lack of remorse or appreciation for the gravity of his actions, the principal reasonably concluded that there was a danger John may attempt to engage in similar behavior with his fellow students.

John's parents argue cursorily that the notice and statement of reasons provided by the principal was insufficient to meet the requirements of G. L. c. 71, § 37H1/2. The parents' claim that the principal's letter informing them of his decision to suspend is defective because it "is silent as to the required determination of the substantial detrimental effect of [John's] presence at school."

However, in his letter, the principal explicitly states that his determination was based on the police reports that led him to the conclusion "that [John] poses a threat to the safety, security and welfare of the Stoughton High School community." General Laws c. 71, § 37H1/2, requires only that "the student . . . receive written notification of the charges and the reasons for such suspension prior to such suspension taking effect." The procedures followed in this case clearly meet the statute's requirements.

C.R. v. EUGENE SCHOOL DISTRICT 4J

835 F.3d 1142 (9th Cir. 2017)

TASHIMA, Circuit Judge:

C.R., a student in the Defendant Eugene School District 4J (the "School District"), was twelve years old when he was suspended from Monroe Middle School for sexually harassing two younger students. The incident that led to his suspension was the last in an escalating series of encounters with two younger students at the school. It occurred about five minutes after school let out, a few hundred feet from campus. C.R. challenged his suspension in district court under the First Amendment, arguing that because the harassment occurred off-campus, in a public park, the school lacked the authority to discipline him. C.R. also challenged his suspension on due process grounds. The district court rejected C.R.'s claims and granted the School District's motion for summary judgment.

We have jurisdiction under 28 U.S.C. § 1291, and we affirm.

I.

C.R. was a seventh-grade student at Monroe Middle School when the incident at issue occurred. In October 2011, C.R., along with a few other seventh-grade boys, began following two sixth-grade students home. The two sixth-graders, a girl (A.I.) and a boy (J.R.), were both disabled. All of the children took the same route home: a bike path leading from the school, across a public park, to a neighboring street. The park borders the school's athletic fields, but there is no visible boundary to indicate where school property ends and the park begins. On the far side of the park, across from the school, is a track belonging to the School District. The school's administrators casually refer to the park, track, and fields collectively as "the back field."

Over the course of several days, the older boys engaged in teasing behavior, which quickly escalated. The boys began by giving the younger students vulgar fake names, like "Ass-Julio," and insisting the sixth-graders repeat them. Soon, the boys' jokes became sexual in nature. On the day in question, the group of older boys circled the younger students. The boys asked the younger students if they watched pornography. The boys asked if A.I. and J.R. were dating, and one boy suggested that J.R. take A.I. to the local B.J.'s Restaurant. This set off a series of comments—puns—on the similarity between the restaurant's name and an abbreviation for the slang term "blowjob," referring to oral sex. One boy told the younger students that there was a "really good" sandwich at B.J.'s that "takes two to eat." He suggested J.R. and A.I. try it together.

Tracy Parks, an instructional aide in the School District, was biking home from school with her daughters when she rode past the group of students. Parks was a friend of C.R.'s mother and had known C.R. since he was in kindergarten. Concerned by the group's posture, Parks approached. She noticed that A.I. looked "a little scared." Parks asked both A.I. and J.R. if they felt comfortable, and although J.R. said "yes," A.I. said "no." Parks told the boys to leave and walked the two younger students home. Along the way, A.I. recounted what had happened, telling Parks that the boys "were talking about [B.J.'s] restaurant, but she thought it was [actually] something else." A.I. repeated to Parks that she was uncomfortable with what had happened.

On Monday, Parks called the school to report what she had seen. Parks spoke with Katherine Kiraly, the school's vice principal. Although she did not know the other boys, Parks told Kiraly that she knew C.R. and could identify him as a participant. Kiraly conferred with then-principal Peter Tromba about Parks' report. She then began an informal investigation.

Kiraly met first with A.I. and J.R. A.I. recounted the series of encounters with the older boys, including their use of vulgar fake names, increasingly sexual comments, and the B.J.'s puns. She told Kiraly that the final encounter made her feel unsafe. Kiraly also interviewed J.R., who did not report feeling uncomfortable during the encounter. Tromba recalled later overhearing the students discussing the incident at lunch with their friends, who *1147 were upset to hear how A.I. and J.R. had been treated.

Kiraly next interviewed the boys she suspected had been involved in the incident, including C.R. C.R. denied any involvement and insisted that nothing inappropriate had happened. The administrators asked C.R. not to tell the other boys about the interview. C.R. ignored their request and discussed his interview at lunch that same day.

The other boys involved in the incident confirmed A.I.'s story. They admitted making inappropriate comments, including the B.J.'s puns. The boys were clear that they intended their comments about B.J.'s to refer to oral sex. The boys also confirmed that C.R. had participated in the incident, and at least one indicated that C.R. was the ringleader. Called in for a second interview, C.R. admitted that he had made a comment about B.J.'s and that his behavior was inappropriate. Based on these interviews, administrators determined that the incident fell within the School District's definition of sexual harassment and that C.R. had participated in that harassment.

Tromba and Kiraly disciplined all of the boys involved in the incident, including C.R. In an email, the administrators informed C.R.'s parents of the basis of that decision: Not only had C.R. participated in the incident, he also lied to administrators in his first interview and disobeyed their request to refrain from discussing the interview with his friends. Under the School District's "door-to-door" policy, the administrators determined that they had the power to discipline C.R. for his off-campus speech. Accordingly, the school imposed a two-day, out-of-school suspension.

II.

The parties do not dispute the basic facts of the case, as outlined above. Both parties generally agree that a group of boys, including C.R., surrounded A.I. and J.R. in a public park, several hundred feet from the school's property line, and made a series of comments to the younger students about B.J.'s Restaurant. Where, as here, the underlying facts are not in dispute, the only question is whether the district court correctly applied the law.

.....

III.

We begin by summarizing the framework for analyzing school regulation of student speech under the First Amendment...We conclude that C.R.'s suspension was permissible under the First Amendment.

A. First Amendment Framework: School Regulation of Student Speech

......

The Supreme Court has outlined four types of student speech that schools may restrict, each governed by its own lead case: "(1) vulgar, lewd, obscene, and plainly offensive speech is governed by Fraser; (2) school-sponsored speech is governed by Hazelwood [School District v. Kuhlmeier, 484 U.S. 260, 108 S.Ct. 562, 98 L.Ed.2d 592 (1988)];" (3) "speech promoting illegal drug use" is governed by Morse v. Frederick, 551 U.S. 393, 127 S.Ct. 2618, 168 L.Ed.2d 290 (2007); and (4) "speech that falls into [none] of these categories' is governed by Tinker." Wynar v. Douglas Cty. Sch. Dist., 728 F.3d 1062, 1067 (9th Cir. 2013) (internal citations and quotation marks omitted). Each of these leading cases, however, concerns only a school's ability to regulate students' on-campus speech. Whether and how these precedents apply to off-campus speech are questions the Supreme Court has yet to answer. See Morse, 551 U.S. at 401, 127 S.Ct. 2618.

We have twice considered whether schools may regulate students' off-campus speech. Both times, we concluded that the school's regulation was permissible. Wynar, 728 F.3d at 1072; LaVine, 257 F.3d at 989...Wynar identified two tests used by our sister circuits to determine when a school may regulate off-campus speech. In Kowalski v. Berkeley County Schools, 652 F.3d 565 (4th Cir. 2011), the Fourth Circuit applied a "nexus" test, asking whether a student's off-campus speech was tied closely enough to the school to permit its regulation. Id. at 573. In S.J.W. v. Lee's Summit R–7 School District, 696 F.3d 771 (8th Cir. 2012), the Eighth Circuit applied a test asking whether it was "reasonably foreseeable" that off-campus speech would reach the school. Id. at 777. "[R]eluctant to try and craft a one-size fits all approach," Wynar declined to choose between these tests, holding that both were satisfied in the case of a threatened school shooting. Wynar, 728 F.3d at 1069.

More recently, the Fifth Circuit en banc also held that schools may sometimes discipline students for off-campus speech. See Bell v. Itawamba Cty. Sch. Bd., 799 F.3d 379 (5th Cir. 2015) (en banc). In Bell...the court declined "to adopt or reject approaches advocated by other circuits," instead holding that a school may regulate students' off-campus speech "when a student intentionally directs at the school community speech reasonably understood by school officials to threaten, harass, and intimidate a teacher...." Id. at 396. Whatever the legal test ultimately applied, courts consistently engage in a circumstance-specific inquiry to determine whether a school permissibly can discipline a student for off-campus speech.

……

B. The School District Had the Authority to Discipline C.R. for His Off-Campus, Sexually Harassing Speech

……

We follow Wynar in applying both the nexus and reasonable foreseeability tests to C.R.'s speech. We conclude that under either test, the School District had the authority to discipline C.R. for his off-campus speech.

1. Nexus

Although the harassment at issue in this case took place off school property, it was closely tied to the school. First, all of the individuals involved were students, a fact that typically counsels in favor of finding that a student's speech was susceptible to school discipline. Next, the incident took place on a path that begins at the schoolhouse door. The path then runs from the school's fields across a public park that shares a boundary with school property, before eventually meeting a neighboring street. A.I. and J.R. had not yet reached the street when the older boys caught up to them. As a result, the students were only a few hundred feet from the school door when the harassment began. Moreover, while the park is technically city property, it is referred to by school administrators as part of "the back field." There is no visual marker (i.e., a fence or other boundary) to indicate where school property ends and the city park begins; it is therefore unclear whether the students even recognized that they had left school property.

Furthermore, all of the students had been let out of school just minutes before the incident. The school's schedule thus brought the students together on the bike path. Had all of the students not been released from school at the same time and walked home along the same path, the older students would not have had the same opportunity to sexually harass the younger students. The record does not reflect whether there were alternative routes home available to the younger students, but it is clear that it was school itself that brought the children together on the path. Moreover, it is a reasonable exercise of the School District's in loco parentis authority to be concerned with its students' well being as they begin their homeward journey at the end of the school day. See Fraser, 478 U.S. at 684, 106 S.Ct. 3159; Veronica Sch. Dist. 47J v. Acton, 515 U.S. 646, 654–56, 115 S.Ct. 2386, 132 L.Ed.2d 564 (1995) (collecting cases).

2. Reasonable Foreseeability

Because the harassment happened in such close proximity to the school, administrators could reasonably expect the harassment's effects to spill over into the school environment. Simply seeing their harassers in the hallway could well be disruptive for affected students. Similarly, a student who is routinely subject to harassment while walking home from school may be distracted during school hours by the prospect of the impending harassment. A student's ability to focus during the day could be impaired by intrusive worries about whether she or he would once again face uncomfortable and sexually intimidating comments immediately after school lets out.

Administrators could also reasonably expect students to discuss the harassment in school. Indeed, A.I. was upset enough about the incident to discuss it with her friends in the lunch room. And administrators likely could not disregard the possibility that the older students would continue to harass their targets if they encountered one another in the hallways or the school yard. Because the harassment in this case was so closely connected to campus—on the students' walk home, a few hundred feet from the school, immediately after school let out—administrators could reasonably expect that the effects of the speech would extend to the students' in-school experience. Under either the nexus test or the reasonable foreseeability test, the School District could take reasonable disciplinary action against C.R.'s off-campus speech.

……

Our decision is necessarily restricted to the unique facts presented by this case: The speech at issue occurred exclusively between students, in close temporal and physical proximity to the school, on property that is not obviously demarcated from the campus itself. A school may act to ensure students are able to leave the school safely without implicating the rights of students to speak freely in the broader community. In short, the School District's actions were reasonable under Wynar. For all of the foregoing reasons, we conclude that the School District had the authority to discipline C.R. for his off-campus, sexually harassing speech.

C. C.R.'s Suspension Was Permissible Under Tinker

Tinker permits schools to restrict student speech in two broad sets of circumstances: if the speech "might reasonably lead school authorities to forecast substantial disruption of or material interference with school activities," or, alternatively, if the speech "collides 'with the rights of other students to be secure and to be let alone.' " Wynar, 728 F.3d at 1070 (quoting Tinker, 393 U.S. at 508, 514, 89 S.Ct. 733). The School District's decision to discipline C.R. falls squarely within Tinker's second set of circumstances.

……

The facts of this case illustrate the point. Both of the targeted students were unable to return home after school without being subjected to questions about sex acts and whether they were dating—inappropriate and unsettling questions for students just out of elementary school. Unsurprisingly,

A.I. reported feeling scared and uncomfortable after the encounter. The school could therefore reasonably expect that those feelings would cause A.I. to feel less secure in school, affecting her ability to perform as a student and engage appropriately with her peers. Moreover, the harassment had already begun to escalate from the repetition of curse words to sexual comments directed at the victims. The school could reasonably expect the harassment to escalate further if allowed to continue unchecked. Without intervening administrative action, the younger students would be deprived of their right to be secure at school.

AFFIRMED

J.C. v. BEVERLY HILLS SCHOOL DISTRICT
711 F. Supp. 2d 1094 (C.D. Cal. 2010)

The following material facts are undisputed. Plaintiff J.C. was a student at Beverly Vista High School ("the School") in May 2008. Individual Defendant Erik Warren ("Warren") is, and at all relevant times was, the principal of the School. Individual Defendants Cherryne Lue-Sang ("Lue Sang") and Janice Hart ("Hart") are, and at all relevant times, were the administrative principal and counselor at the School, respectively.

On the afternoon of Tuesday, May 27, 2008, after the students had been dismissed from the School for the day, Plaintiff and several other students gathered at a local restaurant. While at the restaurant, Plaintiff recorded a four-minute and thirty-six second video of her friends talking. The video was recorded on Plaintiff's personal video-recording device. The video shows Plaintiff's friends talking about a classmate of theirs, C.C. One of Plaintiff's friends, R.S., calls C.C. a "slut," says that C.C. is "spoiled," talks about "boners," and uses profanity during the recording. R.S. also says that C.C. is "the ugliest piece of shit I've ever seen in my whole life." During the video, J.C. is heard encouraging R.S. to continue to talk about C.C., telling her to "continue with the Carina rant."

In the evening on the same day, Plaintiff posted the video on the website "YouTube" from her home computer. While at home that evening, Plaintiff contacted 5 to 10 students from the School and told them to look at the video on YouTube. She also contacted C.C. and informed her of the video. C.C. told Plaintiff that she thought the video was mean. Plaintiff asked C.C. whether she would like Plaintiff to take the video off the website, but C.C. asked her to keep the video up. C.C.'s mother told C.C. to tell Plaintiff to keep the video on the website so that they could present the video to the School the next day. Plaintiff estimates that about 15 people saw the video the night it was posted. The video itself received 90 "hits" on the evening of May 27, 2008, many from Plaintiff herself.

On May 28, 2008, at the start of the school day, Plaintiff overheard 10 students discussing the video on campus. C.C. was very upset about the video and came to the School with her mother on the morning of May 28, 2008 so they could make the School aware of the video. C.C. spoke with school counselor Hart about the video. She was crying and told Hart that she did not want to go to class. C.C. said she faced "humiliation" and had "hurt feelings." Hart spent roughly 20-25 minutes counseling C.C. and convincing her to go to class. C.C. did return to class, and the record indicates that she likely missed only part of a single class that morning.

School administrators then investigated the making of the video. Lue-Sang viewed the video while on the school campus. She called Plaintiff to the administrative office to write a statement about the video. Lue-Sang and Hart also demanded that Plaintiff delete the video from YouTube, and from her home computer. School administrators questioned the other students in the video, including R.S., V.G., and A.B., and asked each of them to make a written statement about the video. R.S.'s father came to the School and watched the video with R.S. on campus. He then took R.S. home for the rest of the day.

Lue-Sang and Hart also contacted principal Warren regarding the video. Warren then contacted Amy Lambert, the Director of Pupil Personnel for the District, regarding whether the School could take disciplinary action against Plaintiff for posting the video on the Internet. Lambert discussed the situation with attorneys and advised Warren that Plaintiff could be suspended. Plaintiff was suspended from school for two days. No disciplinary action was taken against the other students in the video.

Plaintiff had a prior history of videotaping teachers at the School. In April 2008, Plaintiff was suspended for secretly videotaping her teachers, and was told not to make further videotapes on campus. During the investigation about the YouTube video on May 28, 2008, school administrators also discovered another video posted by Plaintiff on YouTube of two friends talking on campus. It is unclear when this video was recorded or posted on the Internet, but it clearly was made while J.C. was at School.[23]

Students at the School cannot access YouTube or other social networking websites on the School's computers, as those websites are blocked by means of a filter. Certain cell phones can access the Internet, including the YouTube website, and allow the user to view videos. However, the School is not aware of how many students have cell phones with that capability. Students at the School are prohibited from using their cell phones on campus in any manner. There is no evidence that any student viewed the YouTube video on his or her cell phone while at School. The only instances the video was viewed on campus, to the parties' knowledge, were during the school administrator's investigation of the video.

……

III. ANALYSIS

B. Violation of First Amendment Rights

Plaintiff contends that the School District and the school administrators, Hart, Lue-Sang, and Warren, violated her First Amendment rights by punishing her for making the YouTube video and

---

[23] These videos are not of the same variety of the YouTube video that is the subject of this lawsuit.

posting it on the Internet. Plaintiff argues that the School had no authority to discipline her because her conduct took place entirely outside of school. To resolve this issue, the Court must first determine the scope of a school's authority to regulate speech by its students that occurs off campus but has an effect on campus.

1. The Supreme Court Student Speech Precedents

In 1969, the Supreme Court held in Tinker v. DesMoines Independent Community School District that a school may regulate a student's speech or expression if such speech causes or is reasonably likely to cause a "material and substantial" disruption to school activities or to the work of the school. 393 U.S. 503, 89 S. Ct. 733, 21 L. Ed. 2d 731 (1969). ...In an oft-quoted passage, the Court noted: "It can hardly be argued that either students or teachers shed their constitutional rights to freedom of speech or expression at the schoolhouse gate." Id. at 506. ... The Court held that a student may express his opinions, even on controversial subjects, so long as doing so does not materially and substantially "interfer[e] with the requirements of appropriate discipline in the operation of the school" or "collid[e] with the rights of others." Id. at 513. Conversely, school discipline is appropriate where the facts "reasonably [lead] school authorities to forecast substantial disruption of or material interference with school activities" as a result of the student's speech. Id. at 514.

The Supreme Court decided three cases after Tinker. ... First, in Bethel School District v. Fraser, the Court held that there is no First Amendment protection for lewd, vulgar or "patently offensive" speech that occurs in school. ...[Second], [i]n 1988, the Court carved out another exception from Tinker for school-sponsored speech. Hazelwood School District v. Kuhlmeier, 484 U.S. 260, 108 S. Ct. 562, 98 L. Ed. 2d 592 (1988). ...Distinguishing Tinker, the Court explained that the issue of whether a school must tolerate particular student speech is different from whether the school must affirmatively promote particular speech. Id. at 270. In sum, "educators are entitled to exercise greater control" over speech that might reasonably be perceived to "bear the imprimatur of the school." Id. at 271. [Third], in the Supreme Court's most recent decision addressing student speech, Morse v. Frederick, the Court held that a school may restrict "student speech at a school event, when that speech is reasonably viewed as promoting illegal drug use." 551 U.S. 393, 403, 127 S. Ct. 2618, 168 L. Ed. 2d 290 (2007). ...The Court noted that neither Hazelwood nor Fraser governed its decision, as the student's banner did not bear "the school's imprimatur" nor was it lewd, vulgar, or "plainly offensive." Id. at 405-06, 409. Instead, the Court focused on the special characteristics of the school environment and the "governmental interest in stopping student drug abuse" and concluded that schools may restrict student expression at a school-sponsored event that they reasonably regard as promoting illegal drug use. Id. at 408.[24]

---

[24] Justice Thomas, in his concurring opinion, expressed concern about the Court's creation of a third carve-out from the rule in Tinker. Thomas insightfully noted: "[W]e continue to distance ourselves from Tinker, but we neither overrule it nor offer an explanation of when it operates and when it does not. I am afraid that our jurisprudence now says that students have a right to speak in schools except when they don't - a standard continuously developed through litigation against local schools and their administrators." 551 U.S. at 418-19. Given the difficulty with which this Court has decided Plaintiff's motion, and the variety of divergent applications of Tinker in the lower courts, the Court shares Justice Thomas' concerns.

2. Application of the Student Speech Precedents by Lower Courts

The Supreme Court has yet to address the factual situation presented by the case at hand - that is, whether a school can regulate student speech or expression that occurs outside the school gates, and is not connected to a school-sponsored event, but that subsequently makes its way onto campus, either by the speaker or by other means. Several lower courts, including the Ninth Circuit, however, have held that a school may regulate such speech under Tinker, if the speech causes or is reasonably likely to cause a material and substantial disruption of school activities.

In LaVine v. Blaine School District, the Ninth Circuit upheld a school's emergency expulsion of a student, James, who wrote a graphic and violent poem about killing his classmates. 257 F.3d 981 (9th Cir. 2000). The poem was written off campus, in the evening, and not as part of any school project. Id. at 983. James later brought the poem to campus to show one of his teachers. The teacher was disturbed by the poem and brought it to the school counselor and eventually to the principal. After an investigation regarding the poem and James' history, James was expelled. Id. at 986. ... [T]he court applied the substantial disruption test from Tinker. Id. at 989. The Ninth Circuit ultimately concluded that the school was reasonable to portend a substantial disruption and upheld James's expulsion. Id. at 992.

Like LaVine, many other courts analyzing off-campus speech that subsequently is brought to campus or to the attention of school authorities apply the substantial disruption test from Tinker without regard to the location where the speech originated (off campus or on campus). ...In these cases, the courts have directly applied the Tinker substantial disruption test to determine if a First Amendment violation occurred, without first considering the geographic origin of the speech. As the district court for the Central District of California recently explained in O.Z. v. Board of Trustees: "[T]he fact that Plaintiff's creation and transmission of the [speech or expression] occurred away from school property does not necessarily insulate her from school discipline. . . . [O]ff-campus conduct can create a foreseeable risk of substantial disruption within a school." 2008 U.S. Dist. LEXIS 110409, 2008 WL 4396895, *4. In sum, the substantial weight of authority indicates that geographic boundaries generally carry little weight in the student-speech analysis. Where the foreseeable risk of a substantial disruption is established, discipline for such speech is permissible.

Some courts (primarily the Second Circuit), however, have considered the location of the speech to be an important threshold issue for the court to resolve before applying the Supreme Court's student speech precedents. For example, in a recent case involving communication over the Internet, the Second Circuit considered the nexus between the speech and the school campus. Wisniewski ex rel. Wisniewski v. Bd. of Educ., 494 F.3d 34 (2d. Cir. 2007). In Wisniewski, a middle school student, Aaron, was using AOL Instant Messaging ("IM") software on his home computer. Aaron created an icon used to identify himself when sending instant messages to his friends. The icon was a small drawing of a pistol firing a bullet at a man's head above which were dots indicating splattered blood. Beneath the drawing were the words "Kill Mr. Vander-Molen." Mr. Vander-Molen was Aaron's English teacher. Id. at 35-36. Another student printed a copy of the icon and gave it to Mr. Vander-Molen at school, who later brought the matter to the school

principal. Id. at 36. After disciplinary hearings, Aaron was suspended.
The Second Circuit applied Tinker to the school's decision, but first discussed the nexus between Aaron's icon and the school campus. The court noted that "the panel is divided as to whether it must be shown that it was reasonably foreseeable that Aaron's IM icon would reach the school property or whether the undisputed fact that it did reach the school pretermits any [such] inquiry." Id. at 39. Ultimately, however, the court concluded that the violent nature of the icon and the fact that Aaron transmitted it via the Internet to 15 of his friends over a three week period made it foreseeable that the icon would eventually come to the attention of the school authorities and Mr. Vander-Molen. Id. at 39-40. Thus, Tinker applied.

Similarly, in *Doninger v. Niehoff*, cited by Defendants here, the Second Circuit again considered the location of a student's speech. 527 F.3d 41 (2d. Cir. 2008). The student in Doninger, Avery, sent an email to students and parents affiliated with the school and posted a message on her personal blog criticizing the school for cancelling a school event. Avery's email and blog posting encouraged the recipients to contact the school officials and complain about the cancellation of the event. Id. at 44-46. Applying the rule from Wisniewski to Avery's speech, the court concluded that it was reasonably foreseeable that Avery's message would reach the school campus. Id. at 50. Indeed, the message was purposefully designed to come to campus - it encouraged readers to contact the school and voice their dissatisfaction regarding the cancelled event. Id. Moreover, after the message was posted, the school received numerous calls and emails from persons concerned about the event. Id. at 44. Thus, there was no dispute that the speech had its desired effect. The court concluded that Avery's message was governed by Tinker, and found that the substantial disruption test was met. Id. at 50-52.

Finally, in *J.S. v. Bethlehem Area School District*, the Supreme Court of Pennsylvania analyzed whether J.S. could be disciplined for a website he created, which contained violent and derogatory comments about school officials. 569 Pa. 638, 807 A.2d 847 (Pa. 2002). In deciding whether school discipline was appropriate, the court noted that the "location" of the speech is the first inquiry. That is, the court must determine if the speech was on-campus speech subject to Tinker, or purely off-campus speech, "which would arguably be subject to some higher level of First Amendment protection." Id. at 864.

Applying the facts of the specific case, the court in Bethlehem concluded that there was "a sufficient nexus" between the website and the school campus to warrant application of the Supreme Court's student speech precedents. Id. at 865. Notably, J.S. had accessed the website during class and informed other students about it. Also, members of the faculty accessed the website at school, and school officials were the subjects of the website. Id. In light of these facts, "it was inevitable that the contents of the website would pass from students to teachers." Id. The court therefore applied Tinker and found that the website created a substantial disruption. Id. at 869.

Given this background, the Court can draw several general conclusions regarding the application of the Supreme Court's precedents to student expression originating off campus.[25] First, the majority of courts will apply Tinker where speech originating off campus is brought to school or to the attention of school authorities, whether by the author himself or some other means. The end result established by these cases is that any speech, regardless of its geographic origin, which causes or is foreseeably likely to cause a substantial disruption of school activities can be regulated by the school. Second, some courts will apply the Supreme Court's student speech precedents, including Tinker, only where there is a sufficient nexus between the off-campus speech and the school. It is unclear, however, when such a nexus exists. The Second Circuit has held that a sufficient nexus exists where it is "reasonably foreseeable" that the speech would reach campus. The mere fact that the speech was brought on campus may or may not be sufficient. Third, in unique cases where the speaker took specific efforts to keep the speech off campus (Thomas), or clearly did not intend the speech to reach campus and publicized it in such a manner that it was unlikely to do so (Porter), the student speech precedents likely should not apply. In these latter scenarios, school officials have no authority, beyond the general principles governing speech in a public arena, to regulate such speech.

.....

Thus, the Court concludes that the Supreme Court precedents apply to Plaintiff's YouTube video, and that Tinker governs the present dispute. Clearly, Hazelwood and Morse do not apply. No one could argue that the YouTube video bore the "imprimatur" of the School, like the school newspaper in Hazelwood. Further, the YouTube video was not made or transmitted in connection with a school-sponsored event and does not condone illegal drug use; thus, Morse does not apply.

Fraser is also inapplicable. Although J.C.'s video certainly contains language that is lewd, vulgar, and plainly offensive, the rule in Fraser is limited to speech that occurs in school. [26] Indeed, the Supreme Court in Hazelwood expressly interpreted the holding in Fraser as follows:

A school need not tolerate student speech that is inconsistent with its 'basic educational mission,' even though the government *could not sensor similar speech outside the school.* Accordingly, we held in Fraser that a student could be disciplined for having delivered a speech that was 'sexually explicit' but not legally obscene at an official school assembly, because the school was entitled to

---

[25] Notably, even the Supreme Court itself has expressed some confusion over when its precedents should apply. Morse, 551 U.S. at 401 ("There is some uncertainty at the outer boundaries as to when courts should apply school speech precedents.").

[26] Neither party argues that Fraser should apply to this case.

'disassociate itself' from the speech in a manner that would demonstrate to others that such vulgarity is 'wholly inconsistent with the 'fundamental values' of public school education.[27]

Hazelwood, 484 U.S. at 266-67 (emphasis added) (internal citations omitted); see also Hedges v. Wauconda Community Unit Sch. Dist. No. 118, 9 F.3d 1295, 1300-01 (7th Cir. 1993) (Easterbrook, J.) ("We know from Bethel School District No. 403 v. Fraser, that a high school may insist on civility when students speak, even though government has no such power outside school doors.") (internal citation omitted); Saxe v. State College Area Sch. Dist., 240 F.3d 200, 213 (3d. Cir. 2001) (Alito, J.) ("According to Fraser, then, there is no First Amendment protection for 'lewd,' 'vulgar,' 'indecent,' and 'plainly offensive' speech *in school.*) (emphasis added); J.S. ex rel. Snyder v. Blue Mountain School Dist., 593 F.3d 286, 317 (3d Cir. 2010) (Chagares, J., concurring in part and dissenting in part) ("Fraser does not apply to off-campus speech."). The Court is not aware of any authority from the circuit courts applying Fraser to speech that takes place off campus. [8] Moreover, the reasoning of Fraser, which is anchored in the school's duty to teach norms of civility to its students, does not support extending Fraser to lewd or offensive speech occurring off campus. For these reasons, the Court will not apply Fraser to Plaintiff's YouTube video.

In sum, the Court finds that the YouTube video clearly falls into the "all other speech" category, governed by Tinker. See LaVine, 257 F.3d at 989. The final issue for the Court to resolve, therefore, is whether J.C.'s speech created, or was reasonably likely to have created, a substantial disruption of school activities.

3. Substantial Disruption

.....

---

[27] The Court is aware of an unreported case from the Middle District of Pennsylvania that applied Fraser to off-campus speech that was posted on the Internet. J.S. v. Blue Mountain Sch. Dist., No. 3:07cv585, 2008 U.S. Dist. LEXIS 72685, 2008 WL 4279517 (M.D. Pa., Sept. 11, 2008) (discussed further infra section III.B.3.a.). The court in J.S. relied, in part, on a 1976 case from the same district in which the court upheld a student's suspension where the student saw a teacher at a shopping mall on a Sunday afternoon and told a friend "He's [the teacher] a prick." 2008 U.S. Dist. LEXIS 72685, [WL] at *7 (discussing Fenton v. Stear, 423 F. Supp. 767 (W.D. Pa. 1976)). This Court finds the reasoning in J.S. unpersuasive. Furthermore, the holding in Fenton demonstrates the precise danger of extending Fraser to allow schools to regulate student speech occurring off campus simply because it is lewd, vulgar or offensive, and without regard to the effect that speech has on school activities. This Court does not wish to see school administrators become censors of students' speech at all times, in all places, and under all circumstances. See Thomas v. Board of Educ., Granville Central Sch. Dist., 607 F.2d 1043, 1052 (2d. Cir. 1979). Such broad authority would clearly intrude upon the rights of parents to "direct the rearing of their children." Reno v. ACLU, 521 U.S. 844, 865, 117 S. Ct. 2329, 138 L. Ed. 2d 874 (1997).

Furthermore, when Blue Mountain School District was reviewed on appeal, the Third Circuit declined to apply Fraser to the student's off-campus speech. 593 F.3d 286, 298 (3d Cir. 2010). While the Third Circuit did not go so far as to hold that Fraser could never apply to off-campus speech, the court distanced itself considerably from the district court's analysis. Id. at 301 ("Since we are expressly not applying Fraser to conduct off school grounds, there is no risk that a vulgar comment made outside the school environment will result in school discipline absent a significant risk of substantial disruption at the school.") The Third Circuit ultimately analyzed the case under Tinker, and concluded that the speech caused no actual substantial disruption, but that a substantial disruption was reasonably foreseeable. Id. at 300-01.

The substantial disruption inquiry is highly fact-intensive. Perhaps for that reason, existing case law has not provided clear guidelines as to when a substantial disruption is reasonably foreseeable. There is, for example, no magic number of students or classrooms that must be affected by the speech. One court has held that a substantial disruption requires something more than "a mild distraction or curiosity created by the speech" but need not rise to the level of "complete chaos." J.S. ex rel. H.S. v. Bethlehem Area Sch. Dist., 569 Pa. 638, 807 A.2d 847, 868 (Pa. 2002). Not surprisingly, however, the gulf between those two concepts swallows the vast majority of factual scenarios. Further complicating matters is the fact that the Court has not uncovered any cases, in this Circuit or otherwise, that address speech targeted at a particular student, as is the case here. That being said, the Court has observed from the case law that certain factors are relevant to the substantial disruption analysis.
First, the fact that students are discussing the speech at issue is not sufficient to create a substantial disruption, at least where there is no evidence that classroom activities were substantially disrupted. [Second], [w]here a student's speech is violent or threatening to members of the school, several courts have found that a school can reasonably portend substantial disruption. ...[T]he content of the speech alone may be a sufficient basis upon which to reasonably predict a substantial disruption, at least where the speech is violent or threatens harm to a person affiliated with the school. [Third], [a]nother factor relevant to the substantial disruption inquiry is whether school administrators are pulled away from their ordinary tasks to respond to or mitigate the effects of a student's speech. ...Finally, the Court must consider whether the school's decision to discipline is based on evidence or facts indicating a foreseeable risk of disruption, rather than undifferentiated fears or mere disapproval of the speech. .....

In contrast, where "a school can point to a well-founded expectation of disruption - especially one based on past incidents arising out of similar speech - the restriction may pass constitutional muster." Saxe, 240 F.3d at 212. For example, in West v. Derby Unified School District No. 260, the Tenth Circuit upheld a student's suspension for drawing a Confederate flag in violation of the school's policy against racial harassment. 206 F.3d 1358 (10th Cir. 2000). In so doing, the Tenth Circuit adopted the following reasoning from the district court:

School officials in Derby had evidence from which they could reasonably conclude that possession and display of Confederate flag images, when unconnected with any legitimate educational purpose, would likely lead to a material and substantial disruption of school discipline. The district experienced a series of racial incidents or confrontations in 1995, some of which were related to the Confederate flag. The incidents included hostile confrontations between a group of white and black students at school and at least one fight at a high school football game. . . . The history of racial tension in the district had made administrators' and parents' concerns about future substantial disruptions from possession of Confederate flag symbols at school reasonable.

Based on the undisputed facts, and viewing all reasonable inferences in favor of the Defendants, the Court finds that no reasonable jury could conclude that J.C.'s YouTube video caused a substantial disruption to school activities, or that there was a reasonably foreseeable risk of substantial disruption as a result of the YouTube video. ...First, what the Defendants contend was an actual disruption is entirely too *de minimis* as a matter of law to constitute a substantial disruption. …J.C.'s video was not violent or threatening. There was no reason for the School to believe that C.C.'s safety was in jeopardy or that any student would try to harm C.C. as a result of the video. Certainly, C.C. never testified that she feared any type of physical attack as a result of the video. Instead, C.C. felt embarrassed, her feelings were hurt, and she temporarily did not want to go to class. These concerns cannot, without more, warrant school discipline. The Court does not take issue with Defendants' argument that young students often say hurtful things to each other, and that students with limited maturity may have emotional conflicts over even minor comments. However, to allow the School to cast this wide a net and suspend a student simply because another student takes offense to her speech, without any evidence that such speech caused a substantial disruption of the school's activities, runs afoul of Tinker.

Alicia C. Insley: Suspending and Expelling Children from Educational Opportunity: Time to Reevaluate Zero Tolerance Policies, 50 Am. U.L. Rev. 1039 (2001)*

1. Disciplinary methods from the 1960s to the 1990s

Zero tolerance policies employed in schools throughout the United States are predetermined, nondiscretionary, disciplinary consequences for certain actions. Although such policies have existed for a relatively short time period, understanding the greater evolution of such harsh disciplinary measures aids in comprehending the notion that current school violence and disciplinary issues "do not exist in a vacuum but are part of the developing sociological landscape."

Between 1946 and 1964, eighty million people were born in the United States. This baby-boom generation led to tremendous growth in school populations in the 1960s, coinciding with instability caused by the civil rights, women's rights, and Vietnam protest movements. School administrators soon realized they needed a new approach to discipline, concluding that antiquated disciplinary techniques such as corporal punishment lacked the effectiveness they once had in less populated schools. From the Puritan settlement of the Massachusetts Bay Colony in the seventeenth century through the nineteenth century in the United States, schoolhouses and classrooms often contained whipping posts and paddling devices. When a student misbehaved, the teacher whipped or paddled him in front of other students to show them the consequences of misconduct. Administrators used these techniques as deterrents for other students in the classroom. This function of corporal punishment lost its effectiveness, however, in the larger schools of the 1960s where students were less likely to observe disciplinary measures that more often occurred in the principal's office. Instead, in the 1960s and 1970s, school systems began to frequently use out-of-school suspensions and expulsions as a way to remove disruptive students from school.

By the late 1970s and early 1980s, school districts changed their approach and began to use in-school suspensions as an alternative to exclusionary policies following lawsuits such as Goss v. Lopez, which challenged expulsions and suspensions on due process grounds. Schools also

---

responded to social pressure to develop more humane disciplinary methods for youth through in-school suspensions. In-school suspensions provided an alternative to out-of-school suspensions by removing disruptive children from the classroom, but keeping them in school and working on academic assignments during the period of their punishment.

The now prevalent and even stricter approach to school discipline known as zero tolerance policies did not emerge until the late 1980s and early 1990s. At this time, schools began to abandon the rehabilitative model and instead employ rigid, "get-tough" policies in response to the public's perception of increasing violence in schools. Throughout the 1990s, as the public became increasingly disturbed and outraged by violence in American schools, federal and state policymakers and school officials worked to strengthen and expand zero tolerance policies. Although this shift towards get-tough policies encompassed increased preventative security measures such as police guards, metal detectors, and locker searches, this Comment only focuses upon zero tolerance policies as the most pervasive cause of injustice for students. This Comment will now explore the various legal avenues by which opponents of the zero tolerance approach have challenged such policies, beginning with an analysis of the federal Gun-Free Schools Act of 1994.

2. The Federal Gun-Free Schools Act of 1994 and its aftermath

The zero tolerance approach to school discipline was given the federal seal of approval when Congress passed the Gun-Free Schools Act of 1994. This Act conditions federal funding for public schools on each state's adoption of legislation requiring at least a one-year expulsion for any student who brings a firearm to school. Yet, the same clause in the Act also provides a discretionary exception to this seemingly mandatory policy: "State law shall allow the chief administering officer of such local educational agency to modify such expulsion requirement for a student on a case-by-case basis." The Act also notes that the term "weapon" means only a firearm, defined as a weapon that will eject a projectile such as a bullet or pellet by an explosive action, or a weapon that is designed to do so or can be readily converted to do so. Additionally, the Act explicitly states that it does not prevent states from providing alternative educational services for students expelled in conjunction with the Act. Lastly, it requires local educational bodies to maintain a policy of referring students who bring a firearm or weapon to school to the criminal justice or juvenile delinquency system.

Following the enactment of the Act, almost all states complied with the federal statute by enacting zero tolerance policies by 1995 and the remaining states complied shortly thereafter. Since then, the percentage of schools with such policies has never fallen below seventy-five percent, and in 1998, nine out of ten public schools reported zero tolerance policies for firearms and weapons. In fact, by 1998 the percentage of schools with zero tolerance polices for specified infractions was as follows: ninety-four percent for firearms, ninety-one percent for other weapons, eighty-eight percent for drugs, eighty-seven percent for alcohol, and seventy-nine percent for violence and tobacco. In contrast to the listed offenses, the original language of the Gun-Free Schools Act of 1994 only encouraged zero tolerance policies for possessing a firearm or other explosive device.

Under the federal Act, states must maintain current zero tolerance policies regarding firearms or weapons such as bombs or other explosives, but states could legally abandon zero tolerance policies regarding other misbehavior including drugs, alcohol, tobacco, or other misconduct unspecified by the Act. A guidance document issued by the Department of Education notes that the federal Act establishes the minimum punishment states must impose for firearm possession, not the maximum; thus, state legislators, state educational agencies, and local educational agencies may broaden federal definitions of offenses and punishments. However, under the federal Act, state law must allow local and state educational agencies and officials to modify the one-year expulsion requirement when evaluating each individual case. Therefore, school officials are not required to expel students under federal law. In conclusion, challenging zero tolerance policies by challenging the Gun-Free Schools Act of 1994 implicates state interpretations of the Act, rather than the Act itself, although, as noted, states can legally interpret the Act in an expansive manner. Therefore, challenging the Act at the federal or state level will likely yield little success.

D. Procedural and Substantive Due Process Challenges to Disciplinary Decisions

Opponents of zero tolerance policies can also challenge zero tolerance policies on due process grounds under the Fifth and Fourteenth Amendments to the United States Constitution, which provide that neither the federal government, nor states, can deprive any person of life, liberty, or property without due process of law. In *Goss v. Lopez*, the Supreme Court held that when the government deprives an individual of a property interest, such as depriving a student of their right to public education due to a suspension or an expulsion, minimum procedural due process requirements apply. Under *Goss*, minimum due process includes notice and the opportunity to be heard prior to suspensions, although, the opportunity to be heard need only be an informal conversation between the student and the vice-principal. *Goss* only addressed suspensions for ten days or less, but the Court noted that longer suspensions or expulsions might entail more formal procedures.

Procedural due process challenges to expulsions and suspensions under zero tolerance policies may be successful when a school fails to provide minimum procedures discussed above, a more likely occurrence in states that have no due process requirements. For example, Arizona, Colorado, Georgia and Iowa have zero tolerance policies requiring one-year expulsions under the Gun-Free Schools Act of 1994; however, these states have no requirements regarding procedural due process. Therefore, schools that fails to provide notice and an opportunity to be heard directly violate the minimum procedural due process requirements established in Goss and can be challenged on such grounds. Yet, most schools provide notice and some kind of hearing to meet minimum due process requirements. Therefore, procedural due process challenges generally will be futile because schools provide the basic due process requirements and summarily discharge students.

Substantive due process challenges to zero tolerance policies generally contest the mandatory nature of the policies as excessive and lacking a rational connection to legitimate educational goals. However, most cases have held that zero tolerance polices mandating specific punishments for certain behaviors do not violate substantive due process. To successfully challenge a zero tolerance policy or disciplinary decision on substantive due process grounds, one must show an "extraordinary departure from established norms" that is "wholly arbitrary." Thus, if the government provides some reasonable justification for its policy or decision, it will likely withstand judicial scrutiny. Moreover, courts generally defer to local school systems concerning disciplinary decisions; thus, substantive due process challenges have had little success.

In conclusion, both procedural and substantive due process challenges are likely to be successful only in cases of blatant omissions of minimum procedures or extreme policies that present no rational connection. Schools generally provide basic procedures and rational policies that courts are reluctant to overturn, effectively blocking due process challenges to zero tolerance policies in all but the most egregious cases. Therefore, due process challenges will not prove useful in undermining zero tolerance policies.

III. Faculty, Staff and Procedural Due Process

BOARD OF REGENTS v. ROTH
408 U.S. 564 (1972)

MR. JUSTICE STEWART delivered the opinion of the Court.

In 1968 the respondent, David Roth, was hired for his first teaching job as assistant professor of political science at Wisconsin State University-Oshkosh. He was hired for a fixed term of one academic year. The notice of his faculty appointment specified that his employment would begin on September 1, 1968, and would end on June 30, 1969.[1] The respondent completed that term. But he was informed that he would not be rehired for the next academic year.

The notice of his appointment provided that: "David F. Roth is hereby appointed to the faculty of the Wisconsin State University Position number 0262. (Location:) Oshkosh as (Rank:) Assistant Professor of (Department:) Political Science this (Date:) first day of (Month:) September (Year:) 1968." The notice went on to specify that the respondent's "appointment basis" was for the "academic year." And it provided that "regulations governing tenure are in accord with Chapter 37.31, Wisconsin Statutes. The employment of any staff member for an academic year shall not be for a term beyond June 30th of the fiscal year in which the appointment is made."

The respondent had no tenure rights to continued employment. Under Wisconsin statutory law a state university teacher can acquire tenure as a "permanent" employee only after four years of year-to-year employment. Having acquired tenure, a teacher is entitled to continued employment "during efficiency and good behavior." A relatively new teacher without tenure, however, is under Wisconsin law entitled to nothing beyond his one-year appointment.[2] There are no statutory or

---

[1] The respondent had no contract of employment. Rather, his formal notice of appointment was the equivalent of an employment contract.

[2] Wis. Stat. § 37.31 (1) (1967), in force at the time, provided in pertinent part that:

administrative standards defining eligibility for re-employment. State law thus clearly leaves the decision whether to rehire a nontenured teacher for another year to the unfettered discretion of university officials.

The procedural protection afforded a Wisconsin State University teacher before he is separated from the University corresponds to his job security. As a matter of statutory law, a tenured teacher cannot be "discharged except for cause upon written charges" and pursuant to certain procedures.[3] A nontenured teacher, similarly, is protected to some extent during his one-year term. Rules promulgated by the Board of Regents provide that a nontenured teacher "dismissed" before the end of the year may have some opportunity for review of the "dismissal." But the Rules provide no real protection for a nontenured teacher who simply is not re-employed for the next year. He must be informed by February 1 "concerning retention or nonretention for the ensuing year." But "no reason for non-retention need be given. No review or appeal is provided in such case."

In conformance with these Rules, the President of Wisconsin State University-Oshkosh informed the respondent before February 1, 1969, that he would not be rehired for the 1969-1970 academic year. He gave the respondent no reason for the decision and no opportunity to challenge it at any sort of hearing.

The respondent then brought this action in Federal District Court alleging that the decision not to rehire him for the next year infringed his Fourteenth Amendment rights. He attacked the decision both in substance and procedure. First, he alleged that the true reason for the decision was to punish him for certain statements critical of the University administration, and that it therefore violated his right to freedom of speech. Second, he alleged that the failure of University officials to give him notice of any reason for nonretention and an opportunity for a hearing violated his right to procedural due process of law.

The District Court granted summary judgment for the respondent on the procedural issue, ordering the University officials to provide him with reasons and a hearing. The Court of Appeals, with one judge dissenting, affirmed this partial summary judgment. We granted certiorari. The only question presented to us at this stage in the case is whether the respondent had a constitutional right to a statement of reasons and a hearing on the University's decision not to rehire him for another year.

I

The requirements of procedural due process apply only to the deprivation of interests encompassed by the Fourteenth Amendment's protection of liberty and property. When protected interests are

---

"All teachers in any state university shall initially be employed on probation. The employment shall be permanent, during efficiency and good behavior after 4 years of continuous service in the state university system as a teacher."

[3] Wis. Stat. § 37.31 (1) further provided that:

> No teacher who has become permanently employed as herein provided shall be discharged except for cause upon written charges. Within 30 days of receiving the written charges, such teacher may appeal the discharge by a written notice to the president of the board of regents of state colleges. The board shall cause the charges to be investigated, hear the case and provide such teacher with a written statement as to their decision.

implicated, the right to some kind of prior hearing is paramount.[7] But the range of interests protected by procedural due process is not infinite.

The District Court decided that procedural due process guarantees apply in this case by assessing and balancing the weights of the particular interests involved. It concluded that the respondent's interest in re-employment at Wisconsin State University-Oshkosh outweighed the University's interest in denying him re-employment summarily. Undeniably, the respondent's re-employment prospects were of major concern to him—concern that we surely cannot say was insignificant. And a weighing process has long been a part of any determination of the form of hearing required in particular situations by procedural due process. But, to determine whether due process requirements apply in the first place, we must look not to the "weight" but to the nature of the interest at stake. We must look to see if the interest is within the Fourteenth Amendment's protection of liberty and property.

[T]he Court has fully and finally rejected the wooden distinction between "rights" and "privileges" that once seemed to govern the applicability of procedural due process rights. The Court has also made clear that the property interests protected by procedural due process extend well beyond actual ownership of real estate, chattels, or money. By the same token, the Court has required due process protection for deprivations of liberty beyond the sort of formal constraints imposed by the criminal process.

Yet, while the Court has eschewed rigid or formalistic limitations on the protection of procedural due process, it has at the same time observed certain boundaries. For the words "liberty" and "property" in the Due Process Clause of the Fourteenth Amendment must be given some meaning.

II

"While this Court has not attempted to define with exactness the liberty . . . guaranteed [by the Fourteenth Amendment], the term has received much consideration and some of the included things have been definitely stated. Without doubt, it denotes not merely freedom from bodily restraint but also the right of the individual to contract, to engage in any of the common occupations of life, to acquire useful knowledge, to marry, establish a home and bring up children, to worship God according to the dictates of his own conscience, and generally to enjoy those privileges long recognized . . . as essential to the orderly pursuit of happiness by free men." *Meyer v. Nebraska*,

---

[7] Before a person is deprived of a protected interest, he must be afforded opportunity for some kind of a hearing, "except for extraordinary situations where some valid governmental interest is at stake that justifies postponing the hearing until after the event." *Boddie v. Connecticut*, 401 U.S. 371, 379. "While 'many controversies have raged about . . . the Due Process Clause,' . . . it is fundamental that except in emergency situations (and this is not one) due process requires that when a State seeks to terminate [a protected] interest . . . , it must afford 'notice and opportunity for hearing appropriate to the nature of the case' before the termination becomes effective." *Bell v. Burson*, 402 U.S. 535, 542. For the rare and extraordinary situations in which we have held that deprivation of a protected interest need not be preceded by opportunity for some kind of hearing.

262 U.S. 390, 399. ...There might be cases in which a State refused to reemploy a person under such circumstances that interests in liberty would be implicated. But this is not such a case.

The State, in declining to rehire the respondent, did not make any charge against him that might seriously damage his standing and associations in his community. It did not base the nonrenewal of his contract on a charge, for example, that he had been guilty of dishonesty, or immorality. Had it done so, this would be a different case. ... In such a case, due process would accord an opportunity to refute the charge before University officials. In the present case, however, there is no suggestion whatever that the respondent's "good name, reputation, honor, or integrity" is at stake.

Similarly, there is no suggestion that the State, in declining to re-employ the respondent, imposed on him a stigma or other disability that foreclosed his freedom to take advantage of other employment opportunities. The State, for example, did not invoke any regulations to bar the respondent from all other public employment in state universities. Had it done so, this, again, would be a different case. ... The Court has held, for example, that a State, in regulating eligibility for a type of professional employment, cannot foreclose a range of opportunities "in a manner . . . that contravene[s] . . . Due Process," *Schware v. Board of Bar Examiners*, 353 U.S. 232, 238, and, specifically, in a manner that denies the right to a full prior hearing.

To be sure, the respondent has alleged that the nonrenewal of his contract was based on his exercise of his right to freedom of speech. But this allegation is not now before us. The District Court stayed proceedings on this issue, and the respondent has yet to prove that the decision not to rehire him was, in fact, based on his free speech activities.[14]

Hence, on the record before us, all that clearly appears is that the respondent was not rehired for one year at one university. It stretches the concept too far to suggest that a person is deprived of "liberty" when he simply is not rehired in one job but remains as free as before to seek another.

To have a property interest in a benefit, a person clearly must have more than an abstract need or desire for it. He must have more than a unilateral expectation of it. He must, instead, have a legitimate claim of entitlement to it. It is a purpose of the ancient institution of property to protect those claims upon which people rely in their daily lives, reliance that must not be arbitrarily undermined. It is a purpose of the constitutional right to a hearing to provide an opportunity for a person to vindicate those claims.

.....

Thus, the terms of the respondent's appointment secured absolutely no interest in re-employment for the next year. They supported absolutely no possible claim of entitlement to re-employment. Nor, significantly, was there any state statute or University rule or policy that secured his interest

[14] When a State would directly impinge upon interests in free speech or free press, this Court has on occasion held that opportunity for a fair adversary hearing must precede the action, whether or not the speech or press interest is clearly protected under substantive First Amendment standards. In the respondent's case, however, the State has not directly impinged upon interests in free speech or free press in any way comparable to a seizure of books or an injunction against meetings. Whatever may be a teacher's rights of free speech, the interest in holding a teaching job at a state university, simpliciter, is not itself a free speech interest.

in re-employment or that created any legitimate claim to it.[16] In these circumstances, the respondent surely had an abstract concern in being rehired, but he did not have a property interest sufficient to require the University authorities to give him a hearing when they declined to renew his contract of employment.

We must conclude that the summary judgment for the respondent should not have been granted, since the respondent has not shown that he was deprived of liberty or property protected by the Fourteenth Amendment. The judgment of the Court of Appeals, accordingly, is reversed and the case is remanded for further proceedings consistent with this opinion.

CLEVELAND BOARD OF EDUCATION v. LOUDERMILL
470 U.S. 532 (1985)

OPINION: JUSTICE WHITE delivered the opinion of the Court.

In these cases we consider what pretermination process must be accorded a public employee who can be discharged only for cause.

I

In 1979 the Cleveland Board of Education, petitioner in No. 83-1362, hired respondent James Loudermill as a security guard. On his job application, Loudermill stated that he had never been convicted of a felony. Eleven months later, as part of a routine examination of his employment records, the Board discovered that in fact Loudermill had been convicted of grand larceny in 1968. By letter dated November 3, 1980, the Board's Business Manager informed Loudermill that he had been dismissed because of his dishonesty in filling out the employment application. Loudermill was not afforded an opportunity to respond to the charge of dishonesty or to challenge his dismissal. On November 13, the Board adopted a resolution officially approving the discharge.

Under Ohio law, Loudermill was a "classified civil servant." Ohio Rev. Code Ann. § 124.11 (1984). Such employees can be terminated only for cause, and may obtain administrative review if discharged. § 124.34. Pursuant to this provision, Loudermill filed an appeal with the Cleveland Civil Service Commission on November 12. The Commission appointed a referee, who held a hearing on January 29, 1981. Loudermill argued that he had thought that his 1968 larceny conviction was for a misdemeanor rather than a felony. The referee recommended reinstatement. On July 20, 1981, the full Commission heard argument and orally announced that it would uphold

---

[16] To be sure, the respondent does suggest that most teachers hired on a year-to-year basis by Wisconsin State University-Oshkosh are, in fact, rehired. But the District Court has not found that there is anything approaching a "common law" of re-employment, *see Perry v. Sindermann*, post, at 602, so strong as to require University officials to give the respondent a statement of reasons and a hearing on their decision not to rehire him.

the dismissal. Proposed findings of fact and conclusions of law followed on August 10, and Loudermill's attorneys were advised of the result by mail on August 21.

Although the Commission's decision was subject to judicial review in the state courts, Loudermill instead brought the present suit in the Federal District Court for the Northern District of Ohio. The complaint alleged that § 124.34 was unconstitutional on its face because it did not provide the employee an opportunity to respond to the charges against him prior to removal. As a result, discharged employees were deprived of liberty and property without due process. The complaint also alleged that the provision was unconstitutional as applied because discharged employees were not given sufficiently prompt postremoval hearings.

Before a responsive pleading was filed, the District Court dismissed for failure to state a claim on which relief could be granted. *See* Fed. Rule Civ. Proc. 12(b)(6). It held that because the very statute that created the property right in continued employment also specified the procedures for discharge, and because those procedures were followed, Loudermill was, by definition, afforded all the process due. The post-termination hearing also adequately protected Loudermill's liberty interests. Finally, the District Court concluded that, in light of the Commission's crowded docket, the delay in processing Loudermill's administrative appeal was constitutionally acceptable. App. to Pet. for Cert. in No. 83-1362, pp. A36-A42.

****

II

Property interests are not created by the Constitution, "they are created and their dimensions are defined by existing rules or understandings that stem from an independent source such as state law . . . ." *Board of Regents v. Roth, supra*, at 577. *See also Paul v. Davis*, 424 U.S. 693, 709 (1976). The Ohio statute plainly creates such an interest. Respondents were "classified civil service employees," Ohio Rev. Code Ann. § 124.11 (1984), entitled to retain their positions "during good behavior and efficient service," who could not be dismissed "except . . . for . . . misfeasance, malfeasance, or nonfeasance in office," § 124.34.[4] The statute plainly supports the conclusion, reached by both lower courts, that respondents possessed property rights in continued employment. Indeed, this question does not seem to have been disputed below.[5]

The Parma Board argues, however, that the property right is defined by, and conditioned on, the legislature's choice of procedures for its deprivation. Brief for Petitioner in No. 83-1363, pp. 26-

---

[4] The relevant portion of § 124.34 provides that no classified civil servant may be removed except "for incompetency, inefficiency, dishonesty, drunkenness, immoral conduct, insubordination, discourteous treatment of the public, neglect of duty, violation of such sections or the rules of the director of administrative services or the commission, or any other failure of good behavior, or any other acts of misfeasance, malfeasance, or nonfeasance in office."

[5] The Cleveland Board of Education now asserts that Loudermill had no property right under state law because he obtained his employment by lying on the application. It argues that had Loudermill answered truthfully he would not have been hired. He therefore lacked a "legitimate claim of entitlement" to the position. Brief for Petitioner in No. 83-1362, pp. 14-15.

27. The Board stresses that in addition to specifying the grounds for termination, the statute sets out procedures by which termination may take place.[6] The procedures were adhered to in these cases. According to petitioner, "[to] require additional procedures would in effect expand the scope of the property interest itself." *Id.*, at 27. *See also* Brief for State of Ohio et al. as Amici Curiae 5-10.

.....

In short, once it is determined that the Due Process Clause applies, "the question remains what process is due." *Morrissey v. Brewer*, 408 U.S. 471, 481 (1972). The answer to that question is not to be found in the Ohio statute.

III

An essential principle of due process is that a deprivation of life, liberty, or property "be preceded by notice and opportunity for hearing appropriate to the nature of the case." *Mullane v. Central Hanover Bank & Trust Co.*, 339 U.S. 306, 313 (1950). We have described "the root requirement" of the Due Process Clause as being "that an individual be given an opportunity for a hearing before he is deprived of any significant property interest."[7] *Boddie v. Connecticut*, 401 U.S. 371, 379 (1971) (emphasis in original); *see Bell v. Burson*, 402 U.S. 535, 542 (1971). This principle requires "some kind of a hearing" prior to the discharge of an employee who has a constitutionally protected property interest in his employment. *Board of Regents v. Roth*, 408 U.S., at 569-570; *Perry v. Sindermann*, 408 U.S. 593, 599 (1972).

The need for some form of pretermination hearing, recognized in these cases, is evident from a balancing of the competing interests at stake. These are the private interest in retaining employment, the governmental interest in the expeditious removal of unsatisfactory employees and the avoidance of administrative burdens, and the risk of an erroneous termination. *See Mathews v. Eldridge*, 424 U.S. 319, 335 (1976).

First, the significance of the private interest in retaining employment cannot be gainsaid. We have frequently recognized the severity of depriving a person of the means of livelihood. *See Fusari v. Steinberg*, 419 U.S. 379, 389 (1975); *Bell v. Burson, supra*, at 539; *Goldberg v. Kelly*, 397 U.S.

---

[6] After providing for dismissal only for cause, see n. 4, *supra*, § 124.34 states that the dismissed employee is to be provided with a copy of the order of removal giving the reasons therefor. Within 10 days of the filing of the order with the Director of Administrative Services, the employee may file a written appeal with the State Personnel Board of Review or the Commission. "In the event such an appeal is filed, the board or commission shall forthwith notify the appointing authority and shall hear, or appoint a trial board to hear, such appeal within thirty days from and after its filing with the board or commission, and it may affirm, disaffirm, or modify the judgment of the appointing authority." Either side may obtain review of the Commission's decision in the State Court of Common Pleas.

[7] There are, of course, some situations in which a postdeprivation hearing will satisfy due process requirements. *See Ewing v. Mytinger & Casselberry, Inc.*, 339 U.S. 594 (1950); *North American Cold Storage Co. v. Chicago*, 211 U.S. 306 (1908).

254, 264 (1970); *Sniadach v. Family Finance Corp.*, 395 U.S. 337, 340 (1969). While a fired worker may find employment elsewhere, doing so will take some time and is likely to be burdened by the questionable circumstances under which he left his previous job. *See Lefkowitz v. Turley*, 414 U.S. 70, 83-84 (1973).

Second, some opportunity for the employee to present his side of the case is recurringly of obvious value in reaching an accurate decision. Dismissals for cause will often involve factual disputes. *Cf. Califano v. Yamasaki*, 442 U.S. 682, 686 (1979). Even where the facts are clear, the appropriateness or necessity of the discharge may not be; in such cases, the only meaningful opportunity to invoke the discretion of the decision maker is likely to be before the termination takes effect. *See Goss v. Lopez*, 419 U.S., at 583-584; *Gagnon v. Scarpelli*, 411 U.S. 778, 784-786 (1973).

The governmental interest in immediate termination does not outweight these interests. As we shall explain, affording the employee an opportunity to respond prior to termination would impose neither a significant administrative burden nor intolerable delays. Furthermore, the employer shares the employee's interest in avoiding disruption and erroneous decisions; and until the matter is settled, the employer would continue to receive the benefit of the employee's labors. It is preferable to keep a qualified employee on than to train a new one. A governmental employer also has an interest in keeping citizens usefully employed rather than taking the possibly erroneous and counterproductive step of forcing its employees onto the welfare rolls. Finally, in those situations where the employer perceives a significant hazard in keeping the employee on the job,[10] it can avoid the problem by suspending with pay.

IV

The foregoing considerations indicate that the pretermination "hearing," though necessary, need not be elaborate. We have pointed out that "[the] formality and procedural requisites for the hearing can vary, depending upon the importance of the interests involved and the nature of the subsequent proceedings." *Boddie v. Connecticut*, 401 U.S. at 378. *See Cafeteria Workers v. McElroy*, 367 U.S. 886, 894-N95 (1961). In general, "something less" than a full evidentiary hearing is sufficient prior to adverse administrative action. *Mathews v. Eldridge*, 424 U.S., at 343. Under state law, respondents were later entitled to a full administrative hearing and judicial review. The only question is what steps were required before the termination took effect.

.....

The essential requirements of due process and all that respondents seek or the Court of Appeals required, are notice and an opportunity to respond. The opportunity to present reasons, either in person or in writing, why proposed action should not be taken is a fundamental due process

---

[10] In the cases before us, no such danger seems to have existed. The examination Donnelly failed was related to driving school buses, not repairing them. *Id.*, at 39-40. As the Court of Appeals stated, "[no] emergency was even conceivable with respect to Donnelly." 721 F.2d, at 562. As for Loudermill, petitioner states that "to find that we have a person who is an ex-felon as our security guard is very distressful to us." Tr. of Oral Arg. 19. But the termination was based on the presumed misrepresentation on the employment form, not on the felony conviction. In fact, Ohio law provides that an employee "shall not be disciplined for acts," including criminal convictions, occurring more than two years previously. *See* Ohio Admin. Code § 124-3-04 (1979). Petitioner concedes that Loudermill's job performance was fully satisfactory.

requirement. *See* Friendly, "Some Kind of Hearing," 123 U. Pa. L. Rev. 1267, 1281 (1975). The tenured public employee is entitled to oral or written notice of the charges against him, an explanation of the employer's evidence, and an opportunity to present his side of the story. *See Arnett v. Kennedy*, 416 U.S., at 170-71 (opinion of POWELL, J.); *Id.* at 195-96 (opinion of WHITE, J.); *see also Goss v. Lopez*, 419 U.S., at 581. To require more than this prior to termination would intrude to an unwarranted extent on the government's interest in quickly removing an unsatisfactory employee.

V

Our holding rests in part on the provisions in Ohio law for a full post-termination hearing. In his cross-petition Loudermill asserts, as a separate constitutional violation, that his administrative proceedings took too long. The Court of Appeals held otherwise, and we agree. The Due Process Clause requires provision of a hearing "at a meaningful time." E. g., *Armstrong v. Manzo*, 380 U.S. 545, 552 (1965). At some point, a delay in the post-termination hearing would become a constitutional violation. *See Barry v. Barchi*, 443 U.S., at 66. In the present case, however, the complaint merely recites the course of proceedings and concludes that the denial of a "speedy resolution" violated due process. App. 10. This reveals nothing about the delay except that it stemmed in part from the thoroughness of the procedures. A 9-month adjudication is not, of course, unconstitutionally lengthy per se. Yet Loudermill offers no indication that his wait was unreasonably prolonged other than the fact that it took nine months. The chronology of the proceedings set out in the complaint, coupled with the assertion that nine months is too long to wait, does not state a claim of a constitutional deprivation.

VI

We conclude that all the process that is due is provided by a pretermination opportunity to respond, coupled with post-termination administrative procedures as provided by the Ohio statute. Because respondents allege in their complaints that they had no chance to respond, the District Court erred in dismissing for failure to state a claim.

SEGAL v. CITY OF NEW YORK

459 F.3d 207 (2d Cir. 2006)

JUDGES: Before: WALKER, Chief Judge, NEWMAN and SOTOMAYOR, Circuit Judges.

JOHN M. WALKER, JR., Chief Judge:

Not every wrong committed at the hands of the government is cognizable as a constitutional violation. In this case, we harbor little doubt that the defendants-appellees committed certain errors during the course of an investigation that ultimately led to the plaintiff-appellant's termination.

Whether this constitutes a deprivation of liberty without due process of law, and is therefore cognizable in an action brought under 42 U.S.C. § 1983, is a separate question.

The undisputed facts establish that the plaintiff-appellant, an at-will government employee, had available to her an adequate post-termination hearing that accorded with the requirements of due process. Because, in our view, the availability of this post-termination name-clearing hearing is sufficient to defeat her "stigma-plus" claims,[1] the defendants are entitled to judgment as a matter of law. We therefore affirm the judgment of the district court, which rested on such a holding.

In September 2002, plaintiff-appellant Sarrit Segal was appointed a probationary teacher for the New York City Department of Education ("DOE" or "Department") and was assigned to teach kindergarten at P.S. 396 in the Bronx. By all accounts, Ms. Segal appears to have been a good teacher. On her first performance evaluation she received an above-scale rating of "satisfactory plus" and a note from the principal that indicated, "It is a pleasure to have you as a member of our school community." During the following school year, however, an incident occurred in Segal's classroom that prompted an investigation and in turn resulted in her termination.

On March 5, 2004, Assistant Principal Joseph Ponzo reported to the DOE's Office of Special Investigations that he had received information that Segal had failed to assist a student (hereinafter "Student A") when that student was attacked by other children in Segal's kindergarten classroom. Although Segal was not immediately removed from her classroom duties, the Office of Special Investigations assigned Ness Matos (a DOE confidential investigator) to investigate the incident.

According to Matos's May 6, 2004, report, Segal called the school guidance counselor, Obdulia Karamanos, to report a "riot" in her classroom after she was unable to separate a group of children who were attacking Student A. When Karamanos arrived, she found Segal standing near the children, who were in a circle attacking Student A as that child lay on the floor. Karamanos managed to separate the children and remove Student A from the classroom; she expressed shock because, from her perspective, Segal appeared to have stood by and watched the incident without intervening. In completing his report, Matos also spoke with several students, all of whom were implicated in one way or another in the attack on Student A. The children's ages ranged from five to six. Several of the children stated that Student A had hit them, and that Segal directed them to strike back. Segal denied these allegations; she stated that she tried to stop the children from attacking Student A, and, when that proved impossible, she called for outside help, eventually reaching Karamanos after her calls to the principal and the assistant principal went unanswered. Based on these interviews, Matos chose to believe the story of some of the children; he concluded that "Ms. Segal's claim that she did not instruct the students to hit Student A, and that she did try to stop the hitting[,] is not credible and not supported by witness statements." He recommended that the Department terminate Segal's employment and place her name on the Department's Ineligible/Inquiry List, which would essentially render her ineligible for future employment with the Department.

---

[1] 'Stigma plus' refers to a claim brought for injury to one's reputation (the stigma) coupled with the deprivation of some 'tangible interest' [e.g., the loss of government employment] or property right (the plus), without adequate process." *DiBlasio v. Novello*, 344 F.3d 292, 302 (2d Cir. 2003).

Segal argues that due process requires a pre-termination name-clearing hearing, based in part on the severity of the accusations leveled against her, and, even if a post-termination hearing will suffice, both the Department's [procedures] are inadequate for name-clearing purposes.

Segal has conceded, as she must, that she has no property interest in her continued employment at the Department. As a probationary employee, she did not have "a legitimate claim of entitlement" to her position as kindergarten teacher. *Bd. of Regents of State Colls. v. Roth*, 408 U.S. 564, 577, 92 S. Ct. 2701, 33 L. Ed. 2d 548 (1972). Instead, Segal asserts that her liberty was deprived without due process of law.

We have recognized that a probationary employee can "invoke the protections of the Due Process Clause" where that employee has suffered a loss of reputation "coupled with the deprivation of a more tangible interest, such as government employment." *Patterson v. City of Utica*, 370 F.3d 322, 330 (2d Cir. 2004). Such an action is referred to as a stigma-plus claim; it involves an "injury to one's reputation (the stigma) coupled with the deprivation of some 'tangible interest' or property right (the plus), without adequate process." *DiBlasio v. Novello*, 344 F.3d 292, 302 (2d Cir. 2003).

In an action based on a termination from government employment, a plaintiff must satisfy three elements in order to demonstrate a deprivation of the stigma component of a stigma-plus claim. *See Patterson*, 370 F.3d at 330. First, the plaintiff "must . . . show that the government made stigmatizing statements about [her] - statements that call into question [the] plaintiff's 'good name, reputation, honor, or integrity.'" *Id.* (quoting *Quinn v. Syracuse Model Neighborhood Corp.*, 613 F.2d 438, 446 (2d Cir. 1980)). We have also said that statements that "denigrate the employee's competence as a professional and impugn the employee's professional reputation in such a fashion as to effectively put a significant roadblock in that employee's continued ability to practice his or her profession" will satisfy the stigma requirement. *Donato v. Plainview-Old Bethpage Cent. Sch. Dist.*, 96 F.3d 623, 630-31 (2d Cir. 1996).[5]

Second, a plaintiff must prove these stigmatizing statements were made public. Third, the plaintiff must show that the stigmatizing statements were made concurrently with, or in close temporal relationship to, the plaintiff's dismissal from government employment.

We assume, for purposes of this appeal, that Segal has brought forth evidence which demonstrates a deprivation of her liberty interest. Segal was terminated; she also presented facts in support of her claim that she was stigmatized during the course of her termination. The Matos report and Superintendent DiBartolomeo's letter all but accuse Segal of having inflicted corporal punishment upon a student under her care and supervision. Such statements would be highly stigmatizing and damaging to a school teacher. She also has presented evidence that suggests that these statements

---

[5] "A plaintiff generally is required only to raise the falsity of these stigmatizing statements as an issue, not prove they are false." *Patterson*, 370 F.3d at 330; *see also Brandt v. Bd. of Coop. Educ. Servs.*, 820 F.2d 41, 43-44 (2d Cir. 1987) ("If Brandt had to prove the falsity of the charges before he could obtain a hearing, there would be no need for the hearing." (emphasis removed)).

were placed in her personnel file prior to her termination, where they remain. We have previously held that the placement of statements in an employee's personnel file may satisfy the contemporaneous public disclosure elements of a stigma-plus claim.

Because stigma plus is a species within the phylum of procedural due process claims, however, it is not enough that the plaintiff has demonstrated the deprivation of her liberty interest; in order to bring a successful stigma-plus claim, the plaintiff also must demonstrate that her liberty was deprived without due process of law. Stated differently, the availability of adequate process defeats a stigma-plus claim. ...Like any procedural due process claim, a stigma-plus claim enforces a limited but important right: the right to be heard "at a meaningful time and in a meaningful manner." *Goldberg v. Kelly*, 397 U.S. 254, 267, 90 S. Ct. 1011, 25 L. Ed. 2d 287 (1970).[6] The limited nature of this right is especially apparent where the plaintiff, like Segal, is an at-will government employee. An at-will government employee may be terminated for cause or for no cause whatsoever. ...Of course, this all raises the familiar question in any procedural due process case: What process is adequate? What process is due?

****

We now hold that, in this case involving an at-will government employee, the availability of an adequate, reasonably prompt, post-termination name-clearing hearing is sufficient to defeat a stigma-plus claim and that the procedures available ...were adequate to protect Segal's reputational and professional interests. Due process does not require a pre-termination name-clearing hearing on the facts in this case. Our decision results from applying the familiar balancing test articulated in *Mathews v. Eldridge*, 424 U.S. 319, 335, 96 S. Ct. 893, 47 L. Ed. 2d 18 (1976).

In [*Matthews*] the Supreme Court set forth a three-part test for evaluating whether the process afforded by the government is constitutionally adequate: (1) "the [nature of the] private interest that will be affected by the [governmental] action"; (2) "the Government's interest, including the function involved and the fiscal and administrative burdens that the additional or substitute procedural requirement would entail"; and (3) "the risk of an erroneous deprivation of such interest through the procedures used, and the probable value, if any, of additional or substitute procedural safeguards." *Id.* at 335. "A court must balance these factors to determine what type of procedures would assure fairness in a particular case." *Patterson*, 370 F.3d at 336.

The private interests presented by Segal, an at-will employee, are her reputational interest, and how that interest can effect [her] standing in the community and [her] future job prospects. In contrast, a tenured government employee would have interests in both her reputation and her right to continued employment.

The government interest at stake in a stigma-plus claim is its ability to execute and explain its personnel decisions quickly. This interest is heightened in the case of an at-will employee. The government has wide latitude when it comes to retaining or dismissing such employees.

[6] Where an at-will employee disagrees with the outcome reached at an otherwise adequate name-clearing hearing, she may have non-constitutional avenues in which to seek redress. For example, state law may provide her an opportunity to petition a court to review the name-clearing panel's adverse determination.

Traditionally, the government has used this latitude to establish a probationary, at-will period before affording such employees the rights and privileges associated with tenured employment, including the right to a pre-termination hearing, *see, e.g., Roth*, 408 U.S. at 577.

As for the third factor, we have said that [t]he risk inherent in a stigma-plus claim is the risk that the false charges against the plaintiff will go unrefuted and that [her] name will remain stigmatized. The risk will vary depending on the effectiveness of the procedures available and the promptness by which they are afforded.

Chancellor's Regulation C-31 sets out the procedures under which a non-tenured Department employee may be terminated. This regulation provides that the District Superintendent must notify the Department's Office of Appeals and Reviews of the need to terminate a non-tenured employee. The Office of Appeals and Reviews will then convene a "Technical Assistance Conference," without the employee's participation, at which the conferees review the relevant facts provided by the Superintendent to determine whether it is advisable to fire the employee. The conferees submit their recommendation to the Chancellor. If the Chancellor accepts a recommendation to terminate the employee, he may issue a notice of discontinuance, at which point the employee is formally terminated by the Department, or he may simply indicate his intent to terminate the employee. Either way, the Chancellor must provide the employee with the specific reasons for his decision. The employee has 15 school days from the date of service in which to appeal the Chancellor's decision either terminating her employment or expressing an intent to do so. During the pendency of the review, an employee who has not been terminated is suspended without pay. Thus, the C-31 regulation provides for pre- or post-termination review, depending on whether the Chancellor determines that, in a given case, immediate dismissal is warranted.

The C-31 regulation provides for extensive procedures to review the Chancellor's initial decision: (1) the right to a hearing, if the employee requests one; (2) notice, at least three weeks before the hearing, of the time, date, and place of the hearing; (3) written notice of the employee's rights at the hearing; and the rights (4) to be represented by an advocate selected by the employee's union, (5) to present all relevant evidence, (6) to call witnesses on the employee's behalf, (7) to cross-examine witnesses, and (8) to make an oral presentation. The hearing must be held within one year of the employee's request for a hearing. At the hearing, the Department must present evidence to support its decision but is not obligated to call witnesses. The Chancellor is authorized to uphold his previous decision to terminate, to execute his previous intention to terminate, or to reinstate the employee. The employee is notified in writing of the Chancellor's decision. ...In our view, the procedures available at the hearing were sufficient to safeguard Segal's reputational and professional interests.

Jennifer M. Brun: Determining the Appropriate Level of Judicial Deference to Public School Board Determinations of Cause in Wrongful Termination Cases, 38 Idaho L. Rev. 781 (2002)*

[I]t may be helpful to provide a general oversight of levels of review a court may use in making determinations of just cause in wrongful termination cases. The levels of review can be broken down into four general categories.

First, a reviewing court may use the arbitrary and capricious standard. At this level, courts will not usually interfere with the exercise of the school boards' discretion unless the school board abused its power by acting arbitrarily or capriciously. Courts generally use the arbitrary and capricious standard where there is no hearing or formal findings on record. Most school boards are required by statute to hold a hearing and to provide the reasoning used to make determinations of just cause. Therefore, this standard would seem inappropriate if used in Idaho because Idaho law mandates that school boards not only hold a hearing to determine just cause for termination but also that school boards provide to the employee their reasoning for making such a determination.

The second level of review a court may use is the substantial evidence standard. At this level, in the absence of fraud, a reviewing court is bound by the findings of fact previously made if those findings are supported by substantial evidence. The reviewing court does not substitute its conclusion for that of the school board but reviews the record only to determine whether substantial evidence supports the board's decision and whether the board exercised its discretion reasonably.

The third level of review, a branch of the substantial evidence standard, is the whole record review. At this level, if the specific evidence cited in the board's reasoning for making its determination of just cause is inadequate to support the ultimate conclusion, a reviewing court should review the entire record of proceedings to determine whether there is substantial evidence from which the ultimate conclusion could be reasonably inferred; this should provide a reviewing court with the same amount of information that the school board had at the time it made its decision.

The fourth level of review is de novo. At this level, the reviewing court does not hear new evidence but makes an independent decision regarding the facts and law based on the record developed before the school board.

.....

[T]he current trend in other states is to afford considerable deference to a school board's determination of cause, subject to any decision of the school board deemed arbitrary, rather than one arrived at reasonably. Some courts would even rephrase the issue to define the burden placed on school boards as entailing a finding that the school board's decisions were made reasonably, in good faith, and based upon substantial evidence. This is a combination of both the arbitrary and capricious standard and the substantial evidence standards of review.

In California, the question placed before the jury usually involves whether "the factual basis on which the employer concluded a dischargeable act had been committed [was] reached honestly, after an appropriate investigation and for reasons that are not arbitrary or pretextual."

.....

In [the State of Ohio] in *Dworken v. Cleveland Board of Education*, the Ohio Supreme Court found, "in the absence of fraud, abuse of discretion, arbitrariness or unreasonableness . . . this court will not interfere with that authority nor substitute its judgment for that of defendant board upon matters delegated to it to decide in conducting the affairs of its schools." The rule spelled out in *Dworken* is widely adopted in modern codes of administrative law. Essentially the rule set forth in *Dworken* replicates an abuse of discretion standard which covers a variety of possible errors by the school board such as unfairness, errors of judgment, findings that lack any basis in fact, and inconsistent use of procedures or policies.

.....

In [the State of Oregon] in *Simpson v. Western Graphics Corp.*, the Oregon Supreme Court reviewed a decision by the trial court that found the plaintiff's discharge was for just cause and therefore, a breach of contract did not occur. Although this case can be distinguished from the specific topic at issue, it is similar in that the two parties mutually agreed, through written contract, that discharge could only occur for "just cause." The supreme court affirmed the trial court's conclusions of law in regard to the level of deference afforded to the employer in determining "just cause":

> To constitute "just cause," the employer (or agent of the employer) must make a good faith determination of a sufficient cause for discharge based on facts reasonably believed to be true and not for any arbitrary, capricious, or illegal reason. It is not necessary that the alleged reason for discharge . . . actually in fact occurred, but only that the evidence of threats existed which the employer reasonably believed in good faith after an investigation.

.....

Nevada has also followed the standard used in *Simpson* and that set forth in *Baldwin*. In a wrongful termination case challenging a discharge by a former employee, the Nevada Supreme Court found that "just cause" is one that is not for any arbitrary, capricious, or illegal reason, and which, based on the supported facts before the employer, can be reasonably believed (by the employer) to be true. At the trial level, both parties agreed to the applicable standard and stipulated that the plaintiff had the burden of proving by a preponderance of the evidence "whether Southwest [the defendant] 'reasonably believed' that Vargas [the plaintiff] had sexually harassed other employees." On appeal, the plaintiff seemed to step back from his agreement on the applicable standard and instead tended to "advocate a rule that would allow for de novo factual review of the issue of good cause by a jury." Therefore, the court reviewed the instructions given to the jury regarding the applicable standard and also discussed the rationale behind the use of "just cause" language in employment contracts. The Nevada Supreme Court relied on Simpson in its conclusion that when an employment contract included "just cause" language, "the employer agreed to the substantive standard embodied in the term 'just cause,' but did not agree to a secondary level of fact-finding authority." The court provided a descriptive explanation:

Allowing a jury to trump the factual findings of an employer that an employee has engaged in misconduct rising to the level of "good cause" for discharge, made in good faith and in pursuit of legitimate business objectives, is a highly undesirable prospect. In effect, such a system would create the equivalent of a preeminent fact-finding board unconnected to the challenged employer that would have the ultimate right to determine anew whether the employer's decision to terminate an employee was based upon an accurate finding of misconduct, and whether any such misconduct was qualitatively and quantitatively sufficient to constitute good cause for discharge. This ex officio "fact-finding board," unattuned to the practical aspects of employee suitability over which it would exercise consummate power, and unexposed to the entrepreneurial risks that form a significant basis of every state's economy, would be empowered to impose substantial monetary consequences on employers whose employee termination decisions are found wanting.

However, the court then recognized the opposing side of the issue allowing complete review of the employer's decision. "On the other hand, in the absence of an unequivocal at-will termination, an employer's discretion to declare the presence of good cause for termination cannot be immune to challenge; otherwise, an employee's contractual entitlements to continuing employment would be without substance or effect."

After reviewing both sides of the issue, the Nevada Supreme Court adopted the "qualified Simpson approach" and concretely stated, "the employer is the ultimate finder of facts constituting good cause for termination." The process of weighing the interests and needs of both sides did not result in a finding of full judicial review of these decisions nor absolute judicial deference, but instead came to a result that balanced the two.

D. Distinguishing between Subjectivity and Objectivity

The Supreme Court of New Mexico similarly balanced the needs of both sides.... However, in addressing its own concerns with the *Baldwin* standard, the court made a relevant distinction between a subjective and objective standard. The court recognized that the trial court correctly denied the defendant's request for a jury instruction "because it erroneously suggested the jury could find good cause from the employer's subjective good faith belief as opposed to an objective standard of reasonable belief." In reaching its final decision, the court made it clear an objective standard of reasonable belief must be used in these instances.

Also the North Dakota Supreme Court focused on subjective/objectiveness and determined that the former employer's decision to terminate the employee for cause should be assessed by a trier of fact under an objective good-faith standard or reasonableness standard. In adopting the objective good-faith standard, the court stated:

[An employer is justified in terminating an employee for good cause for] fair and honest reasons, regulated by good faith on the part of the employer, that are not trivial, arbitrary or capricious, unrelated to business needs or goals, or pretextual. A reasoned conclusion, in short, supported by substantial evidence gathered through an adequate investigation that includes notice of the claimed misconduct and a chance for the employee to respond.

The North Dakota Supreme Court clearly emphasized that an objective good-faith standard must be applied to reach a fair and accurate result.

.....

In South Dakota cases in which the employee has asked for judicial review, the courts have afforded great deference to the school board decision. In affording this great deference, the South Dakota Supreme Court applies a two-step inquiry: first, the court determines whether the board complied with all of the procedural requirements and second, whether the board's decision was "arbitrary, capricious, or an abuse of discretion." The second prong can be further described as applying the "substantial evidence" and "clearly erroneous" standards. The former standard determines whether there is substantial evidence to support the school board's determination. With either standard, the court still does not perform a review de novo of the school board's determination.

Under the substantial evidence rule, courts do not substitute their independent appraisal of the evidence, but look to see if there is "such relevant evidence as a reasonable mind might accept as adequate to support a conclusion." While this rule limits review, it does not avoid it, and courts will reverse findings that, in their judgment, lack reasonable probative support.

.....

Washington clarifies what exactly can be reviewed by the superior court when an employee challenges a school board finding to terminate. Washington uses concepts of administrative law to determine what level of deference should be afforded to school board determinations of cause. Washington is different than Idaho in that it considers a school board hearing an "administrative hearing" held by an "administrative agency." Therefore, an action to terminate an employee for cause is exercising a judicial function and can be reviewable de novo by the courts.

The Washington Supreme Court extended its analysis to specify that the hearing to the superior court afforded by statute to employees challenging a determination of cause is not only reviewable de novo, but can include an independent evidentiary and fact-finding trial. The Washington Appellate Court recognized that by allowing a de novo hearing, which entails a full review of evidence and facts, the superior court is substituting its opinion for that of the school board—it is re-deciding the case.

As previously stated in its analysis of these cases, the Washington Supreme Court closely followed those rules identified in administrative law. It based the level of deference afforded to school board determinations on whether or not the action was essentially administrative or judicial in nature. If the decision resembled a more administrative function, a review could determine whether or not the action was arbitrary, capricious, or contrary to law; if the action was considered judicial, it could be reviewed de novo. The school board's determination of "cause" is considered a "quasi-judicial" function for these purposes. Therefore, the court determined that the decision justified de novo review.

.....

The United States Congress has not provided any specific statutory constraints on the federal court's ability to review local school board decision-making power. However, a number of Supreme Court decisions set forth a "standard for federal court review of local school board decision-making that provides for significant judicial deference to school board decision-making." Granted, these cases address the issue of school board decisions in student discipline cases, however, the holdings do provide some insight on the Supreme Court's viewpoint on the reliability and expertise of school board members in making decisions. In cases revolving around the issue of a court's review of a school board decision based on student discipline, the Supreme Court clearly believes it should avoid interfering with the processes and procedures of school boards.

Notes and Comments

1. Are there any significant differences between the treatment of students under procedural due process from that of school officials? How would you articulate any distinctions?

2. Under what circumstances might school officials properly fire an employee without a pre-deprivation hearing? Can you foresee the need for a school district to implement a uniform policy in this regard?

Chapter Five
The Right to Privacy and Freedom from Unreasonable Searches and Seizures

> I am reluctant to believe that there is any disagreement between the majority and myself on the proposition that school officials should be accorded the widest authority in maintaining discipline and good order in their institutions. To translate that proposition into a workable constitutional rule, I would, in cases like this, cast upon those complaining the burden of showing that a particular school measure was motivated by other than legitimate school concerns.
> Justice Harlan, dissenting, in Tinker v. Des Moines Independent Community School District, 393 U.S. 503, 526 (1969).

> Although "'special needs' inhere in the public school context," those needs are not so expansive or malleable as to render reasonable any program of student drug testing a school district elects to install. The particular testing program upheld today is not reasonable, it is capricious, even perverse: ... testing a student population least likely to be at risk from illicit drugs and their damaging effects.
> Justice Ginsberg, dissenting, in *Board of Education v. Earls*, 536 U.S. 822, 843 (2002).

The Fourth Amendment to the United States Constitution protects "the right of the people to be secure in their persons, houses, papers, and effects, against unreasonable searches and seizures." These protections were designed to limit the power of government officials primarily in the context of criminal law. Its application to other aspects of government conduct has been uneven and inconsistent. As a result, the notion of what constitutes an "unreasonable" search and seizure is difficult to generalize. The Fourth Amendment has become more categorical, making the facts of each case in the relevant context essential to a correct application of the law.

The study of the application of the Fourth Amendment in public education appears to be caught between the two philosophies expressed above from the *Tinker* and *Earls* decisions. The views act as opposite and irresistible forces in the constitutional rights debate. Justice Harlan speaks for the viewpoint that encourages deference to the policies of educators in the absence of evidence of bad faith. This approach has deep roots in education law and routinely has an influence on the courts and other institutions (see Chapter One for a detailed discussion of the institutional interests in public education).

Under this view, the resolution of doubts about the constitutionality of a campus policy would favor most often the educator. On the other end of the pendulum, Justice Ginsberg's position represents a construction of the Bill of Rights that resolves disputes regarding the constitutionality of campus rules in favor of constitutional rights. This approach rests on the assumption that the Bill of Rights was designed to act as a limit on all government officials—including educators. Therefore, in the absence of evidence of a "special need," Fourth Amendment rights should be vindicated.

The prevailing doctrine currently favors Justice Harlan and the deference philosophy. Try to determine the limits, if any, on such an interpretation of the Fourth Amendment. Should abuses of the Fourth Amendment be strictly construed or should educators be given the benefit of the doubt? What about the rights of faculty and staff? Should the guarantees of the Fourth Amendment apply in the same manner to students and staff alike? Also, notice the effect of state constitutional law on the question of unreasonable searches and seizures. Should state courts interpret privacy rights in a manner that strengthen individual rights and ignores more the lenient federal constitutional law? Finally. what, if anything, do the federal privacy laws (FERPA and HIPAA) add to privacy protection for educators and students?

I. The Fourth Amendment and Students

A. "Pat-downs," Book Bags, and Strip Searches

NEW JERSEY v. T. L. O.
469 U.S. 325 (1985)

JUSTICE WHITE delivered the opinion of the Court.

We granted certiorari in this case to examine the appropriateness of the exclusionary rule as a remedy for searches carried out in violation of the Fourth Amendment by public school authorities. Our consideration of the proper application of the Fourth Amendment to the public schools, however, has led us to conclude that the search that gave rise to the case now before us did not violate the Fourth Amendment. Accordingly, we here address only the questions of the proper standard for assessing the legality of searches conducted by public school officials and the application of that standard to the facts of this case.

On March 7, 1980, a teacher at Piscataway High School in Middlesex County, N. J., discovered two girls smoking in a lavatory. One of the two girls was the respondent T.L.O., who at that time was a 14-year-old high school freshman. Because smoking in the lavatory was a violation of a school rule, the teacher took the two girls to the Principal's office, where they met with Assistant Vice Principal Theodore Choplick. In response to questioning by Mr. Choplick, T.L.O.'s companion admitted that she had violated the rule. T.L.O., however, denied that she had been smoking in the lavatory and claimed that she did not smoke at all.

Mr. Choplick asked T.L.O. to come into his private office and demanded to see her purse. Opening the purse, he found a pack of cigarettes, which he removed from the purse and held before T.L.O. as he accused her of having lied to him. As he reached into the purse for the cigarettes, Mr. Choplick also noticed a package of cigarette rolling papers. In his experience, possession of rolling papers by high school students was closely associated with the use of marihuana. Suspecting that a closer examination of the purse might yield further evidence of drug use, Mr. Choplick proceeded to search the purse thoroughly. The search revealed a small amount of marihuana, a pipe, a number of empty plastic bags, a substantial quantity of money in one-dollar bills, an index card that appeared to be a list of students who owed T.L.O. money, and two letters that implicated T.L.O. in marihuana dealing.

Mr. Choplick notified T.L.O.'s mother and the police, and turned the evidence of drug dealing over to the police. At the request of the police, T.L.O.'s mother took her daughter to police headquarters, where T.L.O. confessed that she had been selling marihuana at the high school. On the basis of the confession and the evidence seized by Mr. Choplick, the State brought delinquency charges against T.L.O. in the Juvenile and Domestic Relations Court of Middlesex County.[1] Contending that Mr. Choplick's search of her purse violated the Fourth Amendment, T.L.O. moved to suppress the evidence found in her purse as well as her confession, which, she argued, was tainted by the allegedly unlawful search. The Juvenile Court denied the motion to suppress.

In determining whether the search at issue in this case violated the Fourth Amendment, we are faced initially with the question whether that Amendment's prohibition on unreasonable searches and seizures applies to searches conducted by public school officials. We hold that it does.

.....

We have held school officials subject to the commands of the First Amendment, *see Tinker v. Des Moines Independent Community School District*, 393 U.S. 503 (1969), and the Due Process Clause of the Fourteenth Amendment, *see Goss v. Lopez*, 419 U.S. 565 (1975). If school authorities are state actors for purposes of the constitutional guarantees of freedom of expression and due process, it is difficult to understand why they should be deemed to be exercising parental rather than public authority when conducting searches of their students. More generally, the Court has recognized that "the concept of parental delegation" as a source of school authority is not entirely "consonant with compulsory education laws." *Ingraham v. Wright*, 430 U.S. 651, 662 (1977). Today's public school officials do not merely exercise authority voluntarily conferred on them by individual parents; rather, they act in furtherance of publicly mandated educational and disciplinary policies. In carrying out searches and other disciplinary functions pursuant to such policies, school officials act as representatives of the State, not merely as surrogates for the parents, and they cannot claim the parents' immunity from the strictures of the Fourth Amendment.

To hold that the Fourth Amendment applies to searches conducted by school authorities is only to begin the inquiry into the standards governing such searches. .... A search of a child's person or of a closed purse or other bag carried on her person,[5] no less than a similar search carried out on an adult, is undoubtedly a severe violation of subjective expectations of privacy.

---

[1] T.L.O. also received a 3-day suspension from school for smoking cigarettes in a nonsmoking area and a 7-day suspension for possession of marihuana. On T.L.O.'s motion, the Superior Court of New Jersey, Chancery Division, set aside the 7-day suspension on the ground that it was based on evidence seized in violation of the Fourth Amendment. *(T.L.O.) v. Piscataway Bd. of Ed.*, No. C.2865-79 (Super. Ct. N. J., Ch. Div., Mar. 31, 1980). The Board of Education apparently did not appeal the decision of the Chancery Division.

[5] We do not address the question, not presented by this case, whether a schoolchild has a legitimate expectation of privacy in lockers, desks, or other school property provided for the storage of school supplies. Nor do we express any opinion on

To receive the protection of the Fourth Amendment, an expectation of privacy must be one that society is "prepared to recognize as legitimate." The State of New Jersey has argued that because of the pervasive supervision to which children in the schools are necessarily subject, a child has virtually no legitimate expectation of privacy in articles of personal property "unnecessarily" carried into a school. This argument has two factual premises: (1) the fundamental incompatibility of expectations of privacy with the maintenance of a sound educational environment; and (2) the minimal interest of the child in bringing any items of personal property into the school. Both premises are severely flawed.

.....

Against the child's interest in privacy must be set the substantial interest of teachers and administrators in maintaining discipline in the classroom and on school grounds. Maintaining order in the classroom has never been easy, but in recent years, school disorder has often taken particularly ugly forms: drug use and violent crime in the schools have become major social problems. Even in schools that have been spared the most severe disciplinary problems, the preservation of order and a proper educational environment requires close supervision of schoolchildren, as well as the enforcement of rules against conduct that would be perfectly permissible if undertaken by an adult. "Events calling for discipline are frequent occurrences and sometimes require immediate, effective action." *Goss v. Lopez*, 419 U.S., at 580. Accordingly, we have recognized that maintaining security and order in the schools requires a certain degree of flexibility in school disciplinary procedures, and we have respected the value of preserving the informality of the student-teacher relationship.

.....

The school setting also requires some modification of the level of suspicion of illicit activity needed to justify a search. Ordinarily, a search—even one that may permissibly be carried out without a warrant—must be based upon "probable cause" to believe that a violation of the law has occurred. However, "probable cause" is not an irreducible requirement of a valid search. ... We join the majority of courts that have examined this issue in concluding that the accommodation of the privacy interests of schoolchildren with the substantial need of teachers and administrators for freedom to maintain order in the schools does not require strict adherence to the requirement that searches be based on probable cause to believe that the subject of the search has violated or is violating the law. Rather, the legality of a search of a student should depend simply on the reasonableness, under all the circumstances, of the search. Determining the reasonableness of any search involves a twofold inquiry: first, one must consider whether the . . . action was justified at its inception; second, one must determine whether the search as actually conducted "was reasonably related in scope to the circumstances which justified the interference in the first place,"

---

the standards (if any) governing searches of such areas by school officials or by other public authorities acting at the request of school officials.

Under ordinary circumstances, a search of a student by a teacher or other school official[7] will be "justified at its inception" when there are reasonable grounds for suspecting that the search will turn up evidence that the student has violated or is violating either the law or the rules of the school. Such a search will be permissible in its scope when the measures adopted are reasonably related to the objectives of the search and not excessively intrusive in light of the age and sex of the student and the nature of the infraction.

This standard will, we trust, neither unduly burden the efforts of school authorities to maintain order in their schools nor authorize unrestrained intrusions upon the privacy of schoolchildren. By focusing attention on the question of reasonableness, the standard will spare teachers and school administrators the necessity of schooling themselves in the niceties of probable cause and permit them to regulate their conduct according to the dictates of reason and common sense. At the same time, the reasonableness standard should ensure that the interests of students will be invaded no more than is necessary to achieve the legitimate end of preserving order in the schools.

.....

A teacher had reported that T.L.O. was smoking in the lavatory. Certainly this report gave Mr. Choplick reason to suspect that T.L.O. was carrying cigarettes with her; and if she did have cigarettes, her purse was the obvious place in which to find them. Mr. Choplick's suspicion that there were cigarettes in the purse was not an "inchoate and unparticularized suspicion or 'hunch,'" rather, it was the sort of "common-sense [conclusion] about human behavior" upon which "practical people"—including government officials—are entitled to rely. Of course, even if the teacher's report were true, T.L.O. might not have had a pack of cigarettes with her; she might have borrowed a cigarette from someone else or have been sharing a cigarette with another student. But the requirement of reasonable suspicion is not a requirement of absolute certainty: "sufficient probability, not certainty, is the touchstone of reasonableness under the Fourth Amendment. . . ." Because the hypothesis that T.L.O. was carrying cigarettes in her purse was not itself not unreasonable, it is irrelevant that other hypotheses were also consistent with the teacher's accusation. Accordingly, it cannot be said that Mr. Choplick acted unreasonably when he examined T.L.O.'s purse to see if it contained cigarettes.

.....

The suspicion upon which the search for marihuana was founded was provided when Mr. Choplick observed a package of rolling papers in the purse as he removed the pack of cigarettes. Although T.L.O. does not dispute the reasonableness of Mr. Choplick's belief that the rolling papers indicated the presence of marihuana, she does contend that the scope of the search Mr. Choplick conducted

---

[7] We here consider only searches carried out by school authorities acting alone and on their own authority. This case does not present the question of the appropriate standard for assessing the legality of searches conducted by school officials in conjunction with or at the behest of law enforcement agencies, and we express no opinion on that question. *Cf. Picha v. Wielgos*, 410 F.Supp. 1214, 1219-21 (ND Ill. 1976) (holding probable-cause standard applicable to searches involving the police).

exceeded permissible bounds when he seized and read certain letters that implicated T.L.O. in drug dealing. This argument, too, is unpersuasive. The discovery of the rolling papers concededly gave rise to a reasonable suspicion that T.L.O. was carrying marihuana as well as cigarettes in her purse. This suspicion justified further exploration of T.L.O.'s purse, which turned up more evidence of drug-related activities: a pipe, a number of plastic bags of the type commonly used to store marihuana, a small quantity of marihuana, and a fairly substantial amount of money. Under these circumstances, it was not unreasonable to extend the search to a separate zippered compartment of the purse; and when a search of that compartment revealed an index card containing a list of "people who owe me money" as well as two letters, the inference that T.L.O. was involved in marihuana trafficking was substantial enough to justify Mr. Choplick in examining the letters to determine whether they contained any further evidence. In short, we cannot conclude that the search for marihuana was unreasonable in any respect.

DISSENT: JUSTICE BRENNAN, with whom JUSTICE MARSHALL joins, concurring in part and dissenting in part.

I fully agree with Part II of the Court's opinion. Teachers, like all other government officials, must conform their conduct to the Fourth Amendment's protections of personal privacy and personal security. .... I do not, however, otherwise join the Court's opinion.

On my view of the case, we need not decide whether the initial search conducted by Mr. Choplick—the search for evidence of the smoking violation that was completed when Mr. Choplick found the pack of cigarettes—was valid. For Mr. Choplick at that point did not have probable cause to continue to rummage through T.L.O.'s purse. Mr. Choplick's suspicion of marihuana possession at this time was based solely on the presence of the package of cigarette papers.

SAFFORD UNIFIED SCHOOL DISTRICT v. REDDING
557 U.S. 364 (2010)

SOUTER, J.

The issue here is whether a 13–year–old student's Fourth Amendment right was violated when she was subjected to a search of her bra and underpants by school officials acting on reasonable suspicion that she had brought forbidden prescription and over-the-counter drugs to school. Because there were no reasons to suspect the drugs presented a danger or were concealed in her underwear, we hold that the search did violate the Constitution, but because there is reason to question the clarity with which the right was established, the official who ordered the unconstitutional search is entitled to qualified immunity from liability.

The events immediately prior to the search in question began in 13–year–old Savana Redding's math class at Safford Middle School one October day in 2003. The assistant principal of the school, Kerry Wilson, came into the room and asked Savana to go to his office. There, he showed her a day planner, unzipped and open flat on his desk, in which there were several knives, lighters, a permanent marker, and a cigarette. Wilson asked Savana whether the planner was hers; she said it was, but that a few days before she had lent it to her friend, Marissa Glines. Savana stated that none of the items in the planner belonged to her.

Wilson then showed Savana four white prescription-strength ibuprofen 400–mg pills, and one over-the-counter blue naproxen 200–mg pill, all used for pain and inflammation but banned under school rules without advance permission. He asked Savana if she knew anything about the pills. Savana answered that she did not. Wilson then told Savana that he had received a report that she was giving these pills to fellow students; Savana denied it and agreed to let Wilson search her belongings. Helen Romero, an administrative assistant, came into the office, and together with Wilson they searched Savana's backpack, finding nothing.

At that point, Wilson instructed Romero to take Savana to the school nurse's office to search her clothes for pills. Romero and the nurse, Peggy Schwallier, asked Savana to remove her jacket, socks, and shoes, leaving her in stretch pants and a T-shirt (both without pockets), which she was then asked to remove. Finally, Savana was told to pull her bra out and to the side and shake it, and to pull out the elastic on her underpants, thus exposing her breasts and pelvic area to some degree. No pills were found.

Savana's mother filed suit against Safford Unified School District # 1, Wilson, Romero, and Schwallier for conducting a strip search in violation of Savana's Fourth Amendment rights. The individuals (hereinafter petitioners) moved for summary judgment, raising a defense of qualified immunity. The District Court for the District of Arizona granted the motion on the ground that there was no Fourth Amendment violation, and a panel of the Ninth Circuit affirmed. 504 F.3d 828 (2007).

A closely divided Circuit sitting en banc, however, reversed.

…………....

We granted certiorari, and now affirm in part, reverse in part, and remand.

II

……….

In *T.L.O.,* we recognized that the school setting "requires some modification of the level of suspicion of illicit activity needed to justify a search," 469 U.S., at 340, 105 S.Ct. 733, and held that for searches by school officials "a careful balancing of governmental and private interests suggests that the public interest is best served by a Fourth Amendment standard of reasonableness that stops short of probable cause," *id.,* at 341, 105 S.Ct. 733. We have thus applied a standard of reasonable suspicion to determine the legality of a school administrator's search of a student, *id.,* at 342, 345, 105 S.Ct. 733, and have held that a school search "will be permissible in its scope when the measures adopted are reasonably related to the objectives of the search and not excessively intrusive in light of the age and sex of the student and the nature of the infraction," *id.,* at 342, 105 S.Ct. 733.

A number of our cases on probable cause have an implicit bearing on the reliable knowledge element of reasonable suspicion, as we have attempted to flesh out the knowledge component by looking to the degree to which known facts imply prohibited conduct, the specificity of the information received, and the reliability of its source. ...Perhaps the best that can be said generally about the required knowledge component of probable cause for a law enforcement officer's evidence search is that it raise a "fair probability," or a "substantial chance," of discovering evidence of criminal activity. The lesser standard for school searches could as readily be described as a moderate chance of finding evidence of wrongdoing.

III

A

In this case, the school's policies strictly prohibit the nonmedical use, possession, or sale of any drug on school grounds, including " '[a]ny prescription or over-the-counter drug, except those for which permission to use in school has been granted pursuant to Board policy.' "[28] A week before Savana was searched, another student, Jordan Romero (no relation of the school's administrative assistant), told the principal and Assistant Principal Wilson that "certain students were bringing drugs and weapons on campus," and that he had been sick after taking some pills that "he got from a classmate." On the morning of October 8, the same boy handed Wilson a white pill that he said Marissa Glines had given him. He told Wilson that students were planning to take the pills at lunch.

Wilson learned from Peggy Schwallier, the school nurse, that the pill was Ibuprofen 400 mg, available only by prescription. Wilson then called Marissa out of class. Outside the classroom, Marissa's teacher handed Wilson the day planner, found within Marissa's reach, containing various contraband items. Wilson escorted Marissa back to his office.

In the presence of Helen Romero, Wilson requested Marissa to turn out her pockets and open her wallet. Marissa produced a blue pill, several white ones, and a razor blade. Wilson asked where the blue pill came from, and Marissa answered, " 'I guess it slipped in when *she* gave me the IBU 400s.' " *Id.,* at 13a. When Wilson asked whom she meant, Marissa replied, " 'Savana Redding.' " *Ibid.* Wilson then enquired about the day planner and its contents; Marissa denied knowing anything about them. Wilson did not ask Marissa any followup questions to determine whether

---

[28] When the object of a school search is the enforcement of a school rule, a valid search assumes, of course, the rule's legitimacy. But the legitimacy of the rule usually goes without saying as it does here. The Court said plainly in *New Jersey v. T.L.O.,* 469 U.S. 325, 342, n. 9, 105 S.Ct. 733, 83 L.Ed.2d 720 (1985), that standards of conduct for schools are for school administrators to determine without second-guessing by courts lacking the experience to appreciate what may be needed. Except in patently arbitrary instances, Fourth Amendment analysis takes the rule as a given, as it obviously should do in this case. There is no need here either to explain the imperative of keeping drugs out of schools, or to explain the reasons for the school's rule banning all drugs, no matter how benign, without advance permission. Teachers are not pharmacologists trained to identify pills and powders, and an effective drug ban has to be enforceable fast. The plenary ban makes sense, and there is no basis to claim that the search was unreasonable owing to some defect or shortcoming of the rule it was aimed at enforcing.

there was any likelihood that Savana presently had pills: neither asking when Marissa received the pills from Savana nor where Savana might be hiding them.

....

Wilson had other reports of their friendship from staff members, who had identified Savana and Marissa as part of an unusually rowdy group at the school's opening dance in August, during which alcohol and cigarettes were found in the girls' bathroom. Wilson had reason to connect the girls with this contraband, for Wilson knew that Jordan Romero had told the principal that before the dance, he had been at a party at Savana's house where alcohol was served. Marissa's statement that the pills came from Savana was thus sufficiently plausible to warrant suspicion that Savana was involved in pill distribution.

This suspicion of Wilson's was enough to justify a search of Savana's backpack and outer clothing.[29] If a student is reasonably suspected of giving out contraband pills, she is reasonably suspected of carrying them on her person and in the carryall that has become an item of student uniform in most places today. If Wilson's reasonable suspicion of pill distribution were not understood to support searches of outer clothes and backpack, it would not justify any search worth making. And the look into Savana's bag, in her presence and in the relative privacy of Wilson's office, was not excessively intrusive, any more than Romero's subsequent search of her outer clothing.

B

Here it is that the parties part company, with Savana's claim that extending the search at Wilson's behest to the point of making her pull out her underwear was constitutionally unreasonable. The exact label for this final step in the intrusion is not important, though strip search is a fair way to speak of it. .... The very fact of Savana's pulling her underwear away from her body in the presence of the two officials who were able to see her necessarily exposed her breasts and pelvic area to some degree, and both subjective and reasonable societal expectations of personal privacy support the treatment of such a search as categorically distinct, requiring distinct elements of justification on the part of school authorities for going beyond a search of outer clothing and belongings.

Savana's subjective expectation of privacy against such a search is inherent in her account of it as embarrassing, frightening, and humiliating.

....

The indignity of the search does not, of course, outlaw it, but it does implicate the rule of reasonableness as stated in *T.L.O.,* that "the search as actually conducted [be] reasonably related in

---

[29] There is no question here that justification for the school officials' search was required in accordance with the *T.L.O.* standard of reasonable suspicion, for it is common ground that Savana had a reasonable expectation of privacy covering the personal things she chose to carry in her backpack, cf. 469 U.S., at 339, and that Wilson's decision to look through it was a "search" within the meaning of the Fourth Amendment.

scope to the circumstances which justified the interference in the first place." 469 U.S., at 341, 105 S.Ct. 733 (internal quotation marks omitted). The scope will be permissible, that is, when it is "not excessively intrusive in light of the age and sex of the student and the nature of the infraction." *Id.,* at 342, 105 S.Ct. 733.

Here, the content of the suspicion failed to match the degree of intrusion. Wilson knew beforehand that the pills were prescription-strength ibuprofen and over-the-counter naproxen, common pain relievers equivalent to two Advil, or one Aleve. He must have been aware of the nature and limited threat of the specific drugs he was searching for, and while just about anything can be taken in quantities that will do real harm, Wilson had no reason to suspect that large amounts of the drugs were being passed around, or that individual students were receiving great numbers of pills.

Nor could Wilson have suspected that Savana was hiding common painkillers in her underwear. Petitioners suggest, as a truth universally acknowledged, that "students ... hid[e] contraband in or under their clothing," Reply Brief for Petitioners 8, and cite a smattering of cases of students with contraband in their underwear, *id.,* at 8–9. But when the categorically extreme intrusiveness of a search down to the body of an adolescent requires some justification in suspected facts, general background possibilities fall short; a reasonable search that extensive calls for suspicion that it will pay off. But nondangerous school contraband does not raise the specter of stashes in intimate places, and there is no evidence in the record of any general practice among Safford Middle School students of hiding that sort of thing in underwear; neither Jordan nor Marissa suggested to Wilson that Savana was doing that, and the preceding search of Marissa that Wilson ordered yielded nothing. …

In sum, what was missing from the suspected facts that pointed to Savana was any indication of danger to the students from the power of the drugs or their quantity, and any reason to suppose that Savana was carrying pills in her underwear. We think that the combination of these deficiencies was fatal to finding the search reasonable.

In so holding, we mean to cast no ill reflection on the assistant principal, for the record raises no doubt that his motive throughout was to eliminate drugs from his school and protect students from what Jordan Romero had gone through. … We do mean, though, to make it clear that the *T.L.O.* concern to limit a school search to reasonable scope requires the support of reasonable suspicion of danger or of resort to underwear for hiding evidence of wrongdoing before a search can reasonably make the quantum leap from outer clothes and backpacks to exposure of intimate parts. The meaning of such a search, and the degradation its subject may reasonably feel, place a search that intrusive in a category of its own demanding its own specific suspicions.

JUSTICE STEVENS, with whom JUSTICE GINSBURG joins, concurring in part and dissenting in part.

In *New Jersey v. T.L.O.,* 469 U.S. 325, 105 S.Ct. 733, 83 L.Ed.2d 720 (1985), the Court established a two-step inquiry for determining the reasonableness of a school official's decision to search a student. … Nothing the Court decides today alters this basic framework. It simply applies *T.L.O.* to declare unconstitutional a strip search of a 13–year–old honors student that was based on a groundless suspicion that she might be hiding medicine in her underwear. This is, in essence, a case in which clearly established law meets clearly outrageous conduct. …Therefore, I disagree with its decision to extend qualified immunity to the school official who authorized this unconstitutional search.

JUSTICE THOMAS, concurring in the judgment in part and dissenting in part.

I agree with the Court that the judgment against the school officials with respect to qualified immunity should be reversed. See *ante,* at 2643 – 2644. Unlike the majority, however, I would hold that the search of Savana Redding did not violate the Fourth Amendment. The majority imposes a vague and amorphous standard on school administrators. It also grants judges sweeping authority to second-guess the measures that these officials take to maintain discipline in their schools and ensure the health and safety of the students in their charge.

…………

Redding would not have been the first person to conceal pills in her undergarments. … Nor will she be the last after today's decision, which announces the safest place to secrete contraband in school. … Judges are not qualified to second-guess the best manner for maintaining quiet and order in the school environment. Such institutional judgments, like those concerning the selection of the best methods for restraining students from assaulting one another, abusing drugs and alcohol, and committing other crimes, involve a host of policy choices that must be made by locally elected representatives, rather than by federal judges interpreting the basic charter of Government for the entire country.

IN THE MATTER OF T.A.S.
713 S.E.2d 211 (N.C. Ct. App. 2011)

OPINION BY: BEASLEY, Judge

T.A.S. appeals the trial court's order denying her motion to suppress evidence obtained during a school-wide student search at the Brunswick County Academy (Academy) that extended from the students' personal effects and jackets to their pockets, shoes, and socks and finally beneath the girls' outer clothing. Following the trial court's ruling, T.A.S. admitted to the offenses while "preserving her right to appeal the denial of her motion to suppress." Where the blanket search of the entire school lacked any individualized suspicion as to which students were responsible for the alleged infraction or any particularized reason to believe the contraband sought presented an imminent threat to school safety, the search of T.A.S.'s bra was constitutionally unreasonable and we reverse the trial court's order denying her suppression motion.

I. Background
Charged with possession of a Schedule III substance and drug paraphernalia, T.A.S. filed a motion to suppress, which was heard on 20 February 2009. Sandra Robinson, the Academy's principal and the State's only witness, testified that the Academy is an alternative school in the Brunswick County

School System. Many of its students are assigned there because of disciplinary infractions at traditional schools, including behavioral problems and substance abuse or weapons violations on campus. While T.A.S. was a student at the Academy in November 2008, the record does not indicate the basis for her attendance.

To enter the Academy, students must pass through a metal detector, at which time their book bags, purses, and coats are also searched. More thorough searches of their persons are frequently conducted, sometimes in response to information from other students but regularly without any "leads." On 5 November 2008, one of these more extensive searches was ordered after Ms. Robinson was informed by other students that pills of a type that "would cause kids to be unsafe" were currently coming into the school but had no further clues as to their nature or which students were responsible. The only details learned by administrators were that some of these students were hiding the pills in places not normally searched when they came through the metal detectors, like shoe tongues, socks, bras, and underwear.

After passing through the metal detectors that morning, all students were required to wait in the lunchroom to be brought one-by-one to a classroom to be searched, where they emptied their book bags, had their jackets thoroughly searched, removed their shoes, and emptied their pockets. A staff member whose sex is not specified in the record conducted the searches and patted down the students' socks. The girls were required to perform a "bra lift," where they "pull their shirts out," "shake them," and "go underneath themselves with their thumb in the middle of their bra [to] pull it out." Other administrators and a resource officer, whose sexes are likewise unspecified, were also in the room, and a male law enforcement officer was present throughout-apparently regardless of the sex of the student being searched-solely to observe. During T.A.S.'s search, a white powder identified as Percocet and drug paraphernalia were found.

The trial court found "[t]here was no specific information regarding a particular student" and that a general search was nevertheless conducted "without any reasonable suspicion as to a particular student." Nevertheless, it concluded that the search was reasonable under the circumstances based on companion findings that many Academy students are there because "of school policy violations regarding drugs and weapons"; pills, often prescribed to someone else, are found at the Academy two to three times every nine weeks; there is a "no penalty disclosure" policy in place during these searches; "[g]eneralized searches for weapons have been upheld because of special circumstances that permitted requiring male students to take off shoes, socks and empty pockets because of reports of weapons at school"; and "[n]o private parts were exposed" during the instant search. The trial court thus denied T.A.S.'s motion. We conclude, however, that at the point the Academy required T.A.S. to pull out her bra in searching her person for evidence of pills of an unknown nature and quantity, "the content of the suspicion failed to match the degree of intrusion," *Safford Unified Sch. Dist. # 1 v. Redding,* —U.S. —, —, 129 S.Ct. 2633, 2636, 174 L.Ed.2d 354, 359 (2009), and the search was accordingly unreasonable.

……

Where searching T.L.O.'s purse was clearly less intrusive than searching a student's person, the Court likewise had no occasion to address the applicability of the "twofold inquiry" or the requisite level of suspicion to a search involving, e.g., a pat-down, "bra-lift," or removal of outer clothing.

Recently, however, some lingering questions were resolved where the Court applied the *T.L.O.* framework to new facts in *Redding*—the strip search-and also sought to clarify the law. *See Redding,* — U.S. at ——, 129 S.Ct. at 2643, 174 L.Ed.2d at 366 (noting the lower courts' "divergent conclusions" in applying *T.L.O.* to such searches). *Redding* evaluated the constitutionality of a student strip search under the same reasonableness test that was applied to T.L.O.'s purse despite the distinct nature of the two searches. But similar to *T.L.O.*, there was an individualized suspicion that thirteen-year-old Savana Redding was violating a school rule.

.....

The Court ... held that his search of Savana's backpack and a female administrator's search of her outer clothing-including her jacket, socks, and shoes—were justified. *Id.* at ——, 129 S.Ct. at 2649, 174 L.Ed.2d at 363. However, when the nurse subsequently required Savana to remove her clothes down to her underwear and directed her to "pull her bra out and to the side and shake it," *id.* at ——, 129 S.Ct. at 2638, 174 L.Ed.2d at 360, "the content of the suspicion failed to match the degree of intrusion," *id.* at ——, 129 S.Ct. at 2642, 174 L.Ed.2d at 364, which subjected her private parts to some degree of exposure. Thus, while the search of Savana's outer clothing and backpack was justified at its inception and not excessively intrusive—satisfying the two-pronged *T.L.O.* inquiry—the known "nature and limited threat" of the pain relievers sought, the absence of reasonable grounds "to suspect that large amounts of the drugs were being passed around," and the lack of any indication "that Savana was hiding common painkillers in her underwear" rendered the strip search unreasonable. *Id.* at ——, 129 S.Ct. at 2642–43, 174 L.Ed.2d at 365. In reaching this conclusion, the Court explained that "the categorically extreme intrusiveness of a search down to the body of an adolescent requires some justification in suspected facts," and "a reasonable search that extensive calls for suspicion that pays off." *Id.* Simply put, "general background possibilities fall short," as evidenced in *Redding:*

> [W]hat was missing from the suspected facts that pointed to Savana was any indication of danger to the students from the power of the drugs or their quantity, and any reason to suppose that Savana was carrying pills in her underwear. We think that the combination of these deficiencies was fatal to finding the search reasonable.

Id. The Court then announced a new standard, within the *T.L.O.* framework, for strip searches which, to be reasonable in scope, "require the support of reasonable suspicion of danger or of resort to underwear for hiding evidence of wrongdoing before a search can reasonably make the quantum leap from outer clothes and backpacks to exposure of intimate parts." *Id.*

......

B. The Suspicionless Search of T.A.S.

While certain aspects of the search here may have been reasonable based on the general suspicion that pills were coming into the school—possibly by concealment in some students' undergarments—the search of T.A.S.'s bra, without individualized grounds for suspecting that she had the pills on her person, was excessively intrusive. Once the search extended to such intimate places, the generalized suspicion upon which the trial court relied was no longer sufficient to justify the heightened intrusion. Thus, in light of *T.L.O.* and *Redding,* the search was not reasonable under the circumstances.

As in *Redding,* Academy administrators "ma[d]e the quantum leap from outer clothes and backpacks," *Redding,* — U.S. at ——, 129 S.Ct. at 2643, 174 L.Ed.2d at 365, by requiring each female student to do a "bra lift" by pulling out her shirt, shaking it, and going underneath her shirt to pull her bra away from her body. ...

As in *Redding* ...Academy officials failed to ask additional questions to determine the exigency of the situation. Rather than conduct intrusive bra-lifts, the school should have followed up with the student informants to ascertain the identity of the violators or inquired further to determine the nature of the substances. Moreover, while not expedient but to ensure Fourth Amendment protections along with the dignity and sanctity of T.A.S. and the other girls, T.A.S.'s parents could have been called before the bra-lift was conducted. These failures clearly weaken the argument that the search of T.A.S. was constitutional, as they indicate that *Redding*' s additional factors appended to the "reasonableness-in-scope" prong of the *T.L.O.* standard when a search extends beneath the outer clothing—namely, "reasonable suspicion of danger or of resort to underwear"—were not met here. Still, it is the lack of any reason to suspect T.A.S. that is the fatal element here. The trial court, however, relied on "cases where special circumstances" eliminated the need for individualized suspicion and suspicionless searches were upheld, but, of the examples listed in its order, the only one relevant to the context here "involved random drug testing of student athletes."

.....

T.A.S. thus clearly had a legitimate expectation of privacy beneath her outer clothing and had no reason to believe that her body would be subjected to exposure, especially when school officials had no basis for suspecting her. For, notwithstanding the fact that she attends an alternative school and is subjected to other, lesser intrusions upon entry each day, "when the *categorically extreme intrusiveness* of a search down to the body of an adolescent requires some justification in suspected facts, general background possibilities fall short; *a reasonable search that extensive calls for suspicion that it will pay off.*" *Redding,* — U.S. at ——, 129 S.Ct. at 2642, 174 L.Ed.2d at 365 (emphasis added). While attending an alternative school may compel the students to expect to be subjected to the inconvenience of passing through a metal detector or the moderate intrusiveness of having their backpacks searched each day, such does not demand an expectation that their underwear will be searched. *Redding*'s indication that strip searches are sui generis, intruding on a privacy interest distinct from all other types of searches, suggests that the suspicionless search rationale of *Vernonia* and the cases upon which it relies will not support a search of this kind, as "the content of the suspicion [will undoubtedly] fail[ ] to match the degree of intrusion." *Id.* at ——, 129 S.Ct. at 2642, 174 L.Ed.2d at 364.

.....

Finally, while deterring drug use by students is clearly an important governmental interest, and possibly even more weighty at the Academy where many students have been in violation of the school district's substance abuse policy, the government's interest is 'diluted' when a school searches a group of students 'without reason to suspect that any particular student was responsible for the alleged' infraction. Indeed, without any individualized suspicion, the intrusiveness of the search of each individual is that much less likely to be successful. Here, despite the complete lack of any reasonable belief than any single student possessed any pills, the Academy searched all 134 of its students. Further, the school required all of the girls to perform the "bra lift" even if nothing revealed during the less intrusive part of the search suggested that the student was hiding contraband in her underwear. A search of the entire student body based on vague tips from unidentified students—where no follow-up investigation was made to determine who the actual perpetrators may be, how many students were estimated to be bringing pills into the school, or the nature and level of danger of the pills—was not an appropriate method of discovering the wrongdoers. *See Redding,* —— U.S. at ——, 129 S.Ct. at 2635, 174 L.Ed.2d at 362 (holding the required knowledge under the reasonable suspicion standard is that a school administrator's search of each student must forecast "a moderate chance of finding evidence of wrongdoing").

.....

[T]he fact remains that there was no reason to suspect any of the students searched in the first place. Thus, proceeding to inspect T.A.S.'s bra was unreasonably excessive in scope, given that no additional facts, either known to the Academy prior to the less intrusive search of her belongings and outer clothing or discovered in the course thereof, could have caused officials to suspect *her in particular* or to believe that there were reasonable grounds for resorting to *her* underwear.

In light of the foregoing, when any group search is conducted in the absence of individualized suspicion, even if the circumstances otherwise permit less invasive searches—ranging from personal effects and jackets, to pat-downs of the outer clothing, and even to searches of pockets, shoes, and socks—such a search that subjects the students' undergarments or unclothed bodies to exposure is unconstitutional if school officials do not have reasonable grounds to believe the particular student possesses the item sought, unless the item is reasonably believed to be imminently dangerous. Reversed.

Steelman, Judge dissenting.

Where TAS had a diminished privacy interest due to her attendance at an alternative school, the nature of the intrusion occasioned by the search in question was minimal, the governmental concern involved was important and immediate, and the search in question was an effective means of addressing that concern, the trial court did not err in denying TAs' motion to suppress. I must respectfully dissent.

Additional facts should be noted. Students were sent to Brunswick County Academy ("the Academy") for violating the Brunswick County Code of Conduct, by engaging in violent behaviors and/or substance abuse. Pills, typically prescription medications, were discovered at the Academy two to three times within every nine week period. The Academy had a "no penalty disclosure" policy. If students voluntarily turned over items that were not allowed at the Academy, such as pills or weapons, then the student was not punished and law enforcement was not contacted. The

Academy notified the student's parents, and the parents were required to pick up the contraband. Finally, the Academy's principal stated that during the search in question the girls' shirts remained down at all times, and no body parts were seen by the persons conducting the search.

.....

The rationale of *Safford* is not applicable to the instant case. ...[It] is distinguishable from *Safford* based on the specific tip in the instant case that pills were coming into the school in the female students' bras, and the less intrusive nature of the search in the instant case.

T.S. v. STATE
863 N.E.2d 362 (Ind. Ct. App. 2007)

T.S., a minor, appeals from a proceeding in which he was adjudicated a juvenile delinquent based on the juvenile court's finding that T.S. committed an act that if committed by an adult would be the crime of possession of marijuana, a Class A misdemeanor. On appeal, T.S. raises the sole issue of whether the trial court erred in denying T.S.'s motion to suppress evidence he claims was obtained in violation of Article I, Section 11 of the Indiana Constitution, and the Fourth, Fifth, and Fourteenth Amendments to the United States Constitution. Concluding that the procedure through which the evidence against T.S. was obtained did not violate T.S.'s federal or state constitutional rights, we affirm.

On October 13, 2005, Sergeant Mark Driskell, of the Indiana Public Schools Police ("IPSP"), received a phone call in the Broad Ripple High School ("BRHS") IPSP office. Sergeant Driskell testified that "[t]here was a female who [sic] I did not identify. . . . [S]he indicated that there was a student at Broad Ripple high school by the name of [T.S.] and that he had marijuana in right front pant pocket." Sergeant Driskell testified that he had "no idea" who the anonymous caller was. The tipster did not state how she knew T.S had marijuana in his possession.

After receiving this call, Sergeant Driskell went to T.S.'s gym class, and told him to accompany him to the locker room. Sergeant Driskell testified that this call was the only basis on which he removed T.S. from class. After reaching the locker room, Sergeant Driskell told T.S. to change out of his gym uniform into his street clothes. After T.S. had finished dressing, Sergeant Driskell asked T.S. if "he had anything on him that he shouldn't have." *Id.* at 38. At this point, T.S. pulled a small plastic baggie containing marijuana out of his front pocket and handed it to Sergeant Driskell. Sergeant Driskell then reached into T.S.'s pocket and pulled out another small baggie of marijuana. T.S. gave a slightly different description of the events. T.S. testified that when they reached the locker room, Sergeant Driskell told T.S. about the anonymous tip, put his hand on T.S.'s chest, and said that he knew T.S. had some marijuana because his heart was beating quickly. T.S. testified he then told Sergeant Driskell that he did have marijuana, walked over to his locker, and opened it. T.S. testified that when he opened his locker, Sergeant Driskell grabbed T.S.'s pants out, went through the pockets, and pulled out the two baggies of marijuana. When asked about T.S.'s version of events, Sergeant Driskell testified that he did not recall placing his hand on T.S.'s chest and that T.S. had handed him the first baggie of marijuana.

.....

The seminal case regarding searches and seizures that occur in schools is *New Jersey v. T.L.O.*, 469 U.S. 325 (1985). In *T.L.O.*, the United States Supreme Court held that the Fourth Amendment does apply to school searches and seizures, but that:

> The accommodation of the privacy interests of schoolchildren with the substantial need of teachers and administrators for freedom to maintain order in the schools does not require strict adherence to the requirement that searches be based on probable cause to believe that the subject of the search has violated or is violating the law. Rather, the legality of a search of a student should depend simply on the reasonableness, under all the circumstances, of the search.

The Court developed a two prong test for determining the reasonableness of a search: (1) whether the action was justified at its inception; and (2) whether the search "was reasonably related in scope to the circumstances which justified the interference in the first place." *Id.* (quoting *Terry v. Ohio*, 392 U.S. 1, 20 (1968)). The first prong will be satisfied if "there are reasonable grounds for suspecting that the search will turn up evidence that the student has violated or is violating either the law or the rules of the school." *Id.* The second prong will be satisfied if "the measures adopted are reasonably related to the objectives of the search and not excessively intrusive in light of the age and sex of the student and the nature of the infraction." *Id.* In *T.L.O.*, the Court explicitly left open the question of whether the exclusionary rule applied to school searches. *Id.* at 333 n.3. However, the decisions of Indiana courts subsequent to *T.L.O.* indicate that the exclusionary rule is the remedy for Fourth Amendment violations occurring in schools. *See Myers*, 839 N.E.2d at 1161 (holding that trial court properly denied defendant's motion to suppress because search conducted by school officials was reasonable); *D.I.R. v. State*, 683 N.E.2d 251, 253 (Ind. Ct. App. 1997) (reversing defendant's delinquency adjudication because evidence was discovered during unreasonable search in a school).

T.L.O. left open many questions with which courts still struggle. The case before us raises three questions undecided by *T.L.O.*: (1) the level of cause required for an IPSP officer who initiates an encounter with a student without the involvement of other school officials; (2) whether the encounter between Sergeant Driskell and T.S. constituted a seizure; and (3) the standard for determining the constitutionality of a seizure occurring in a school.

T.L.O. left open the question of what standard applies to searches conducted by police officers on school property, or by police officers employed by the school system. However, our supreme court has noted that other jurisdictions divide school searches into three categories and use the following set of standards:

> (1) where school officials initiate the search or police involvement is minimal, the reasonableness standard is applied; (2) where the search is conducted by the school resource officer on his or her own initiative to further educationally related goals, the reasonableness standard is applied; and (3) where "outside" police officers

> initiate the search of a student for investigative purposes, the probable cause and warrant requirements are applied.
> *Myers v. State*, 839 N.E.2d at 1160.

Our supreme court then stated:

> We find this approach and analysis persuasive. Thus, where a search is initiated and conducted by school officials alone, or where school officials initiate a search and police involvement is minimal, the reasonableness standard is applicable. And the ordinary warrant requirement will apply where "outside" police officers initiate, or are predominantly involved in, a school search of a student or student property for police investigative purposes.

We note that our supreme court did not explicitly adopt the three categories used by other jurisdictions, and merely found them "persuasive." The language it used in announcing its test adopts the approach taken for the first and third categories, but omits the second category of a school resource officer acting on his or her own initiative. However, this omission can be explained because the facts of *Myers* made possible only a conclusion that the search fell under either the first or third categories. We thus conclude that the Myers court adopted the three-part test, and that the later statement omitting the second category is merely a restatement of the two categories relevant to the facts of Myers. Therefore, we must decide whether Sergeant Driskell was an "outside" police officer or a school resource officer acting to further educationally related goals.

.....

At the time of the incident, Sergeant Driskell was employed by the IPSP and was working in BRHS. He received the anonymous call in BRHS's IPSP office. We have previously held that employees of the IPSP who act in their capacity as security officers are considered school officials and that their conduct is therefore governed by *T.L.O.*

.....

Other courts have held that searches conducted by school police officers were governed by the reasonableness standard based on the rationale that by ferreting out drugs, the officers were working in the furtherance of educational goals. .... Other courts have not based their holding solely on the officer's status as a school police officer, but have examined the involvement of other school administrators in the officer's action......... Finally, courts have found relevant the officer's purpose in conducting the search.

.....

We conclude that Sergeant Driskell acted as school resource officer acting to further educationally related goals. Although Sergeant's Driskell's encounter with T.S. ultimately resulted in Sergeant Driskell taking T.S. to the police station, Sergeant Driskell testified that, at the time he initiated the encounter, he intended to take T.S. to the Dean's office. Therefore, although Sergeant Driskell did not act in conjunction with other school officials prior to the initial contact with T.S., when he initiated contact, he had the intent to involve the school's dean. Such intent indicates that Sergeant

Driskell was concerned with a possible violation of school rules, and not solely a criminal violation. We also agree with the rationale of the North Carolina and Pennsylvania courts that the presence of drugs on school property presents a serious threat to a learning environment. Therefore, Sergeant Driskell acted not only to ferret out criminal activity, but also to preserve an environment conducive to education.

.....

After considering the reduced expectation of privacy that students enjoy in public schools, we hold that Sergeant Driskell acted reasonably in investigating the tip. Removing T.S. from class, although certainly an intrusion on his privacy, was not an invasive intrusion. Indeed, school officials routinely remove students from class for a variety of reasons. Although, as T.S. points out, it may cause more embarrassment for a student to be removed by a police officer, the officers to which this holding applies are also people whom students routinely see in the hallways, and are in the schools not only to enforce laws, but also to maintain a safe environment conducive to learning. As discussed above, the presence of drugs in schools is a serious problem that jeopardizes the learning environment. We think it reasonable that an officer charged with maintaining this environment investigate a tip indicating that a student has drugs on school property by removing the student from class for questioning with the intent of taking the student to the dean's office. Therefore, the seizure of T.S. did not violate his Fourth Amendment rights......... we [also] conclude that given the totality of the circumstances, most importantly the school setting and Sergeant Driskell's role within the school, Sergeant Driskell's seizure of T.S. was reasonable under the Indiana constitution.

Notes and Comments

1. *T.L.O.* and the "Moderate Chance of Finding Wrongdoing."

The Safford Court sets the modern standard for deferring to school officials on matters of student searches. "The lesser standard for school searches could as readily be described as a moderate chance of finding evidence of wrongdoing." *Safford Unified Sch. Dist. No. 1 v. Redding*, 557 U.S. 364, 371, (2009). Do the following lower court cases suggest a standard of what is a "moderate chance of finding wrongdoing?"

-- In California, the Court of Appeal, Second District ruled that a school administrator's search of a student was reasonable because it was based on an individualized suspicion of wrongdoing. The administrator discovered a knife after a teacher reported that the student might be under the influence of drugs in violation of school policy. The court held that the teacher's report provided the reasonable suspicion necessary for a search. *In re M.C.*, No. 2D JUV. B282779, 2018 WL 1079741 (Cal. Ct. App. Feb. 28, 2018).

-- In Louisiana, the Court of Appeal of Louisiana upheld a search of a student by an educator. The teacher observed what he believed to be a hand-to-hand transaction between two students, one of whom was known to have issues with marijuana. The teacher asked the student to remove what he placed into his pocket and discovered marijuana. *State in Interest of K.L.*, 2016-1151 (La. App. 4 Cir. 4/10/17), 217 So. 3d 628.

-- In Missouri, the Missouri court of Appeals ruled that the pat-down search of a student, pursuant to school policy authorizing searches of all students who arrive at school more than 30 minutes late, was unreasonable and thus unconstitutional under the Fourth Amendment. *State v. Charles Williams*, 521 S.W.3d 689 (Mo. Ct. App. 2017).

-- In Maryland, the court of appeals ruled against school officials who searched a student after he was found in possession of a validly prescribed medication. The court ruled that even though the student violated school rules by failing to give the medicine to the school nurse, such a violation did not support an inference or suspicion that the student possessed additional medication or contraband. *In re Kavon P.*, No. 2499 SEPT. TERM 2014, 2016 WL 3031711 (Md. Ct. Spec. App. May 27, 2016).

2. *T.L.O.* and Searches by School Resource Officers

to act under *T.L.O.* in searching students was well established. A federal court surveying this phenomenon in a case decided contemporaneously with *T.S.* concluded,

> [T]he weight of authority holds... that a search of a student on school grounds by a school resource officer at the request of school officials should be deemed a search by a school employee for Fourth Amendment purposes and thus is subject to the reasonableness standard, not the probable cause standard.
> *Wilson v. Cahokia Sch. Dist. # 187*, 470 F. Supp. 2d 897 (S.D. Ill. 2007).

After *T.L.O.*, the **lower** courts began to ignore the distinction between the campus enforcement of criminal law and discipline under school codes of conduct and instead shifted the focus to whether "school officials" were furthering legitimate educational interests when regulating student activity. The SRO is now seen as having been brought into the safe school environment, not as an outsider, but as a core part of the educational family. A police officer on assignment to the school as a resource officer is a *school official* when furthering legitimate educational interests. Therefore, a search of a student on school grounds by an SRO, either at the request of educators or on the officer's own initiative, is deemed a search by a school official for purposes of *T.L.O.* In the seminal case to extend *T.L.O.* to police officers, the court reasoned that,

> Were we to conclude otherwise, our decision might serve to encourage teachers and school officials, who generally are untrained in proper pat down procedures or in neutralizing dangerous weapons, to conduct a search of a student suspected of carrying a dangerous weapon on school grounds without the assistance of a school liaison officer or other law enforcement official. *State of Wisconsin v. Angelia* D.B., (211 Wis. 2d 140, 155; 564 N.W.2d 682, 688 (1997))

See, D.L. v. State, 877 N.E.2d 500 (2007); *In re William V.*, 111 Cal. App. 4th 1464, 4 Cal. Rptr. 3d 695, 699-700 (Cal. Ct. App. 2003); *Russell v. State*, 74 S.W.3d 887, 892-93 (Tex. App. 2002); *New York v. Jameel Butler*, 725 N.Y.S.2d 534 (2001). *In re Josue T.*, 1999 NMCA 115, 128 N.M. 56, 989 P.2d 431, 436-37 (N.M. Ct. App. 1999), In re K.J., 18 Cal. App. 5th 1123, 227 Cal. Rptr. 3d 380 (Ct. App. 2018), review denied (Apr. 11, 2018).

3. Cell Phone Searches and Student Privacy

There are numerous cases in which the courts have considered the application of the rules of the *TLO* decision to cell phones. In the first spate of court decisions, all courts upheld school enforcement of policies that prohibited phones and other communicative devices on campus. *Price v. New York City Bd. of Educ.*, 51 A.D.3d 277 (N.Y. App. Div. 1st Dep't 2008); *Laney v. Farley*, 501 F.3d 577 (6th Cir. 2007); *Requa v. Kent Sch. Dist. No. 415*, 492 F. Supp. 2d 1272 (W.D. Wash. 2007).

As to the searches of student phones, the early cases apply the more forgiving standard of the *TLO* decision. In *Miller v. Skumanick*, 605 F. Supp. 2d 634 (M.D. Pa. 2009), officials confiscated several students' cell phones, examined them and discovered that the students were engaged in "sexting". In addition to school discipline, the phones were turned over to the District Attorney who began a criminal investigation. The searches were not challenged by the parents, but the parents sued to stop the district attorney from initiating criminal charges for two nude photographs. In *Klump v. Nazareth Area Sch. Dist.*, 425 F. Supp. 2d 622 (E.D. Pa. 2006), the trial court agreed that the seizure of a student's cell phone and search of the phone number directory and call log was valid. But the court ruled that school officials crossed the line when they pretended to be the student while sending an instant message to the student's brother and calling nine other students listed in phone number directory to determine whether they, too, were violating the school's cell phone policy. One exception is the United States District Court decision in *Gallimore v. Henrico Cty. Sch. Bd.*, 38 F. Supp. 3d 721, 725 (E.D. Va. 2014), where the court held that the search a student's cell phone was not "reasonably related to the objective of the search—finding evidence of drug use on the school bus earlier that day."

More recently, the courts have abandoned any effort to add rigor to the reasonable suspicion calculus, creating a presumption in favor of student cell phone searches. In Georgia, the United States District Court ruled that the search of a student's cell phone without a warrant during an investigation of alleged threats made against the student did not violate the Fourth Amendment. "Though technology has changed since T.L.O. was handed down, a school official's search of a student's cell phone on school property and during the school day still fits within the framework announced in T.L.O." *Jackson v. McCurry*, 303 F. Supp. 3d 1367, 1378 (M.D. Ga. 2017), aff'd, 762 F. App'x 919 (11th Cir. 2019). In California, the California Court of Appeal ruled that school officials may search the cell phone of a student when they have a reasonable belief that school rules have been violated. The court affirmed the trial court ruling that the student's cell phone was lawfully seized and searched when video recordings of female students in the locker room were posted on the Internet. *In re Adrian O.*, No. C084538, 2019 WL 1292401 (Cal. Ct. App. Mar. 21, 2019). In Washington State, the United States District Court held that school officials did not violate the Fourth Amendment rights of a student by confiscating his cell phone while conducting a disciplinary investigation regarding the student's forging of a permission slip. The court reasoned that the confiscation was consistent with a reasonable school policy to take cell phones to prevent a student from contacting anyone while an investigation was ongoing. *Rorvik v. Snohomish Sch. Dist.*, No. C17-0946-JCC, 2018 WL 3917932 (W.D. Wash. Aug. 16, 2018), appeal dismissed, No. 18-35760, 2018 WL 7575588 (9th Cir. Dec. 19, 2018). In California, the California Court of Appeal ruled that school administrators had authority to seize and searched a student cell phone based on the student's suspected involvement in an incident in which a firearm was discovered on campus. The phone contained digital images of the student holding the firearm. *In re Rafael C.*, 200 Cal. Rptr. 3d 305 (Ct. App.), as modified on denial of reh'g (Apr. 21, 2016), review granted and opinion superseded sub nom. *In re R.C.*, 372 P.3d 903 (Cal. 2016).

4. Strip Searches and Student Privacy after *Safford.*

Before *Safford*, the law on strip searches had been carefully assembled by the lower courts in the absence of guidance by the U.S. Supreme Court. State and federal courts resolving these disputes focused a great deal on the level of suspicion possessed by the government official conducting the search, the severity of the illegality that prompted the search and the climate (degree of exigency or danger) in which the search is conducted. The controlling rule was derived from decisions in settings other then the educational environment. The Eleventh Circuit, in *Justice v. Peachtree City*, 961 F.2d 188, 192-193 (11th Cir. Ga. 1992), in which the court upheld a strip search of juveniles by police officers who arrested them for loitering and truancy, provides an excellent narrative on this body of law:

> [C]hildren are especially susceptible to possible traumas from strip searches. . . . ... Thus, the strip search of a juvenile based on less than probable cause "instinctively gives us the most pause." Bell, 441 U.S. at 558.
>
> Finally, the nature of the infraction here—a small theft—is insufficient as a matter of law to permit a strip search. *T.L.O.* directs us to consider the nature of the infraction because, although keeping order in the school is important, it is not determinative. Students' privacy rights must be weighed in the balance. Strip searching a student is permissible only in extraordinary cases, and only to prevent imminent harm.

Therefore, prior to ruling in *Safford*, the emerging standard on strip searches in educational settings favored the educator when the search was based upon factors that would satisfy probable cause or which would create an exigency on campus. Strip searches based upon reasonable suspicion or no suspicion would be upheld if the circumstances involved dangerous contraband (guns and drugs) or nondangerous items of substantial value, or low value items stolen in a manner that creates a risk of a substantial disruption and danger on campus. See, *Oliver by Hines v. McClung*, 919 F. Supp. 1206, 1216-19 (N.D. Ind. 1995) (strip search of seventh graders for $4.50 unconstitutionally unreasonable); *State ex rel. Galford v. Mark Anthony B.*, 189 W. Va. 538, 433 S.E.2d 41, 49 (W. Va. 1993) (strip search for $100 unconstitutionally unreasonable in scope because no threat of danger).

After *Safford*, the lower courts find that much of the prior approach. After *Safford*, a strip search of a student will be upheld if (1) there is any indication of danger to the students because of the nature of the item sought OR (2) there is reasonable suspicion that the student is concealing the item sought in his or her underwear.

Do the outcomes of the following two cases provide a persuasive rationale for applying Safford in public schools? In Texas, the United States Court of Appeals for the Fifth Circuit ruled that an assistant principal, who ordered a strip-search of twenty-two female students to find missing $50 in cash, violated the girls' constitutional rights unless educators reasonably suspected that the missing $50 cash (1) would be found on that particular girl's person and either (2) would be found specifically in that girl's underwear or (3) would pose a dangerous threat to students. The court ruled that the school district could also be liable for permitting its employees to conduct invasive searches without providing training as to how to do so. *Littell v. Hous. Indep. Sch. Dist.*, 894 F.3d 616 (5th Cir. Jun. 27, 2018). In Georgia, the United States Court of Appeals for the Eleventh Circuit ruled that an assistant principal's strip search of a student for the presence of illegal drugs was valid at its inception; but that forcing the student to strip until he was fully naked in front of his peers was unconstitutionally excessive in scope. The court held that the law was clearly established so that the educator was not entitled to qualified immunity. *D.H. v. Clayton Cnty. Sch. Dist.*, 830 F.3d 1306 (11th Cir. 2016).

5. Test your "Strip Search IQ" on the following scenarios in light of *Safford*. Are the strip searches lawful under the Safford test?

-- A teacher discovered that during the school day her desk had been disturbed, resulting in the removal of an iPod. The students refused to tell the teacher who had taken it. The assistant principal instructed the students to open their book bags, pull out their pockets, and untuck their shirts, but the iPod was not found. A school resource officer was told to search five students in a storage closet, where they were required to remove their clothing. One of the students, who did not have the iPod filed a lawsuit over the incident.

-- Two students reported to their instructor, that cash, a credit card, and two gift cards were missing from their purses. The teacher stopped his instruction, directed the students to sit down, and searched each student's books, shoes, socks, and pockets. Then several school officials collaborated to take the students into the restroom one at a time for a strip search. Female students were told to unhook and shake their bras underneath their tops and take their pants halfway down their thighs. Several students challenged these searches in the restroom.

-- School administrators collaborated with members of the staff to combat vandalism of the bathrooms. The school custodian would occasionally climb up above the panels in the bathroom ceiling and look down into the stalls of both the boys' and girls' restrooms. One day, a student was observed by the custodian entering a stall and marking on the inside door. The custodian followed into the hallway, searched him, and led him away to school administrators. The student was arrested and charged with a felony. The student filed suit to challenge the search.

-- High school administrators asked a female SRO to assist in randomly searching female students as they arrived on school buses. The searches were in response to reports by teachers that girls were starting to bring in cigarettes and marijuana cigarettes in their bras and their socks and possibly their underwear. The SRO asked the students to untuck their shirts, lift their bras away from their chest, and shake the bra so that anything tucked in it would fall out. One student filed a lawsuit after submitting to such a search.

-- During the semester, administrators received reports on a student who was suspected of bringing cocaine and marijuana to school. Both the police and a student supplied information that the student was selling the drugs on campus. Later, the student was found in possession of a live bullet while on campus. The next day, a teacher discovered the student outside the building in violation of school rules. When she reported the infraction, she shared her belief that the student was crouching drugs. Administrators also observed an unusual bulge in the student's crotch area. They escorted the student to the boys' locker room where the student removed his street clothes and put on a gym uniform during which the administers inspected his naked body and physically inspected his clothes. They found no evidence of drugs or any other contraband.

B. Drug Testing

VERNONIA SCHOOL DISTRICT 47J v. ACTON
515 U.S. 646 (1995)

JUSTICE SCALIA delivered the opinion of the Court.

The Student Athlete Drug Policy adopted by School District 47J in the town of Vernonia, Oregon, authorizes random urinalysis drug testing of students who participate in the District's school athletics programs. We granted certiorari to decide whether this violates the Fourth and Fourteenth Amendments to the United States Constitution.

Petitioner Vernonia School District 47J (District) operates one high school and three grade schools in the logging community of Vernonia, Oregon. As elsewhere in small-town America, school sports play a prominent role in the town's life, and student athletes are admired in their schools and in the community.

Drugs had not been a major problem in Vernonia schools. In the mid-to-late 1980's, however, teachers and administrators observed a sharp increase in drug use. ..... Students became increasingly rude during class; outbursts of profane language became common.

Not only were student athletes included among the drug users but, as the District Court found, athletes were the leaders of the drug culture...... Initially, the District responded to the drug problem by offering special classes, speakers, and presentations designed to deter drug use. It even brought in a specially trained dog to detect drugs, but the drug problem persisted.

At that point, District officials began considering a drug-testing program. They held a parent "input night" to discuss the proposed Student Athlete Drug Policy (Policy), and the parents in attendance gave their unanimous approval. The school board approved the Policy for implementation in the fall of 1989. Its expressed purpose is to prevent student athletes from using drugs, to protect their health and safety, and to provide drug users with assistance programs.

The Policy applies to all students participating in interscholastic athletics. Students wishing to play sports must sign a form consenting to the testing and must obtain the written consent of their parents. Athletes are tested at the beginning of the season for their sport. In addition, once each week of the season the names of the athletes are placed in a "pool" from which a student, with the supervision of two adults, blindly draws the names of 10% of the athletes for random testing. Those selected are notified and tested that same day, if possible.

The samples are sent to an independent laboratory, which routinely tests them for amphetamines, cocaine, and marijuana. Other drugs, such as LSD, may be screened at the request of the District, but the identity of a particular student does not determine which drugs will be tested. The laboratory's procedures are 99.94% accurate. .... Only the superintendent, principals, vice-principals, and athletic directors have access to test results, and the results are not kept for more than one year.

If a sample tests positive, a second test is administered as soon as possible to confirm the result. If the second test is negative, no further action is taken. If the second test is positive, the athlete's parents are notified, and the school principal convenes a meeting with the student and his parents, at which the student is given the option of (1) participating for six weeks in an assistance program that includes weekly urinalysis, or (2) suffering suspension from athletics for the remainder of the current season and the next athletic season. The student is then retested prior to the start of the next athletic season for which he or she is eligible. The Policy states that a second offense results in automatic imposition of option (2); a third offense in suspension for the remainder of the current season and the next two athletic seasons.

In the fall of 1991, respondent James Acton, then a seventh grader, signed up to play football at one of the District's grade schools. He was denied participation, however, because he and his parents refused to sign the testing consent forms. The Actons filed suit, seeking declaratory and injunctive relief from enforcement of the Policy on the grounds that it violated the Fourth and Fourteenth Amendments to the United States Constitution and Article I, § 9, of the Oregon Constitution.

The Fourth Amendment to the United States Constitution provides that the Federal Government shall not violate "the right of the people to be secure in their persons, houses, papers, and effects, against unreasonable searches and seizures" . . . ."..As the text of the Fourth Amendment indicates, the ultimate measure of the constitutionality of a governmental search is "reasonableness."

We have found such "special needs" to exist in the public school context. There, the warrant requirement "would unduly interfere with the maintenance of the swift and informal disciplinary procedures [that are] needed," and "strict adherence to the requirement that searches be based on probable cause" would undercut "the substantial need of teachers and administrators for freedom to maintain order in the schools." *T.L.O.*, 469 U.S. at 340, 341. The school search we approved in *T.L.O.*, while not based on probable cause, was based on individualized suspicion of wrongdoing. As we explicitly acknowledged, however, "'the Fourth Amendment imposes no irreducible requirement of such suspicion'"

Fourth Amendment rights, no less than First and Fourteenth Amendment rights, are different in public schools than elsewhere; the "reasonableness" inquiry cannot disregard the schools' custodial and tutelary responsibility for children. For their own good and that of their classmates, public school children are routinely required to submit to various physical examinations, and to be vaccinated against various diseases. According to the American Academy of Pediatrics, most public schools "provide vision and hearing screening and dental and dermatological checks. . . . Others also mandate scoliosis screening at appropriate grade levels." Committee on School Health, American Academy of Pediatrics, School Health: A Guide for Health Professionals 2 (1987). In the 1991-1992 school year, all 50 States required public school students to be vaccinated against diphtheria, measles, rubella, and polio. U.S. Dept. of Health & Human Services, Public Health Service, Centers for Disease Control, State Immunization Requirements 1991-1992, p. 1. Particularly with regard to medical examinations and procedures, therefore, "students within the school environment have a lesser expectation of privacy than members of the population generally."

Legitimate privacy expectations are even less with regard to student athletes. School sports are not for the bashful. They require "suiting up" before each practice or event, and showering and changing afterwards. Public school locker rooms, the usual sites for these activities, are not notable for the privacy they afford. ......

There is an additional respect in which school athletes have a reduced expectation of privacy. By choosing to "go out for the team," they voluntarily subject themselves to a degree of regulation even higher than that imposed on students generally. In Vernonia's public schools, they must submit to a preseason physical exam (James testified that his included the giving of a urine sample), they must acquire adequate insurance coverage or sign an insurance waiver, maintain a minimum grade point average, and comply with any "rules of conduct, dress, training hours and related matters as may be established for each sport by the head coach and athletic director with the principal's approval."

Having considered the scope of the legitimate expectation of privacy at issue here, we turn next to the character of the intrusion that is complained of. ...... Under [the policy], the privacy interests compromised by the process of obtaining the urine sample are in our view negligible.

The other privacy-invasive aspect of urinalysis is, of course, the information it discloses concerning the state of the subject's body, and the materials he has ingested. In this regard it is significant that the tests at issue here look only for drugs, and not for whether the student is, for example, epileptic, pregnant, or diabetic...... Moreover, the results of the tests are disclosed only to a limited class of school personnel who have a need to know; and they are not turned over to law enforcement authorities or used for any internal disciplinary function.

That the nature of the concern is important—indeed, perhaps compelling—can hardly be doubted. .... As to the efficacy of this means for addressing the problem: It seems to us self-evident that a drug problem largely fueled by the "role model" effect of athletes' drug use, and of particular danger to athletes, is effectively addressed by making sure that athletes do not use drugs.

Taking into account all the factors we have considered above—the decreased expectation of privacy, the relative unobtrusiveness of the search, and the severity of the need met by the search—we conclude Vernonia's Policy is reasonable and hence constitutional.

.... We caution against the assumption that suspicionless drug testing will readily pass constitutional muster in other contexts. The most significant element in this case is the first we discussed: that the Policy was undertaken in furtherance of the government's responsibilities, under a public school system, as guardian and tutor of children entrusted to its care. We may note that the primary guardians of Vernonia's schoolchildren appear to agree. The record shows no objection to this districtwide program by any parents other than the couple before us here—even though, as we have described, a public meeting was held to obtain parents' views. We find insufficient basis to contradict the judgment of Vernonia's parents, its school board, and the District Court, as to what was reasonably in the interest of these children under the circumstances.

CONCUR: JUSTICE GINSBURG, concurring.

The Court constantly observes that the School District's drug-testing policy applies only to students who voluntarily participate in interscholastic athletics. Correspondingly, the most severe sanction allowed under the District's policy is suspension from extracurricular athletic programs. I comprehend the Court's opinion as reserving the question whether the District, on no more than the showing made here, constitutionally could impose routine drug testing not only on those seeking to engage with others in team sports, but on all students required to attend school.

DISSENT: JUSTICE O'CONNOR, with whom JUSTICE STEVENS and JUSTICE SOUTER join, dissenting.

On this record, then, it seems to me that the far more reasonable choice would have been to focus on the class of students found to have violated published school rules against severe disruption in class and around campus—disruption that had a strong nexus to drug use, as the District established at trial. Such a choice would share two of the virtues of a suspicion-based regime: testing dramatically fewer students, tens as against hundreds, and giving students control, through their behavior, over the likelihood that they would be tested.

I cannot avoid the conclusion that the District's suspicionless policy of testing all student athletes sweeps too broadly, and too imprecisely, to be reasonable under the Fourth Amendment.

BOARD OF EDUCATION v. EARLS
536 U.S. 822 (2002)

JUSTICE THOMAS delivered the opinion of the Court.

The Student Activities Drug Testing Policy implemented by the Board of Education of Independent School District No. 92 of Pottawatomie County (School District) requires all students who participate in competitive extracurricular activities to submit to drug testing. Because this Policy reasonably serves the School District's important interest in detecting and preventing drug use among its students, we hold that it is constitutional.

The city of Tecumseh, Oklahoma, is a rural community located approximately 40 miles southeast of Oklahoma City. The School District administers all Tecumseh public schools. In the fall of 1998, the School District adopted the Student Activities Drug Testing Policy (Policy), which requires all middle and high school students to consent to drug testing in order to participate in any extracurricular activity. In practice, the Policy has been applied only to competitive extracurricular activities sanctioned by the Oklahoma Secondary Schools Activities Association, such as the Academic Team, Future Farmers of America, Future Homemakers of America, band, choir, pom pon, cheerleading, and athletics. Under the Policy, students are required to take a drug test before participating in an extracurricular activity, must submit to random drug testing while participating in that activity, and must agree to be tested at any time upon reasonable suspicion. The urinalysis tests are designed to detect only the use of illegal drugs, including amphetamines, marijuana, cocaine, opiates, and barbituates, not medical conditions or the presence of authorized prescription medications.

At the time of their suit, both respondents attended Tecumseh High School. Respondent Lindsay Earls was a member of the show choir, the marching band, the Academic Team, and the National Honor Society. Respondent Daniel James sought to participate in the Academic Team. Together with their parents, Earls and James brought a 42 U.S.C. § 1983 action against the School District, challenging the Policy both on its face and as applied to their participation in extracurricular activities. ...... They also argued that the School District failed to identify a special need for testing students who participate in extracurricular activities, and that the "Drug Testing Policy neither addresses a proven problem nor promises to bring any benefit to students or the school." ....

Significantly, this Court has previously held that "special needs" inhere in the public school context. While schoolchildren do not shed their constitutional rights when they enter the schoolhouse, "Fourth Amendment rights . . . are different in public schools than elsewhere; the 'reasonableness' inquiry cannot disregard the schools' custodial and tutelary responsibility for children." *Vernonia, supra,* 515 U.S. at 656. In particular, a finding of individualized suspicion may not be necessary when a school conducts drug testing. In *Vernonia,* this Court held that the suspicionless drug testing of athletes was constitutional. The Court, however, did not simply authorize all school drug testing, but rather conducted a fact-specific balancing of the intrusion on the children's Fourth Amendment rights against the promotion of legitimate governmental interests. Applying the principles of *Vernonia* to the somewhat different facts of this case, we conclude that Tecumseh's Policy is also constitutional.

We first consider the nature of the privacy interest allegedly compromised by the drug testing..... A student's privacy interest is limited in a public school environment where the State is responsible for maintaining discipline, health, and safety. Schoolchildren are routinely required to submit to physical examinations and vaccinations against disease. Securing order in the school environment sometimes requires that students be subjected to greater controls than those appropriate for adults. ...... [S]tudents who participate in competitive extracurricular activities voluntarily subject themselves to many of the same intrusions on their privacy as do athletes. Some of these clubs and activities require occasional off-campus travel and communal undress. All of them have their own rules and requirements for participating students that do not apply to the student body as a whole. ..... We therefore conclude that the students affected by this Policy have a limited expectation of privacy.

Next, we consider the character of the intrusion imposed by the Policy. Urination is "an excretory function traditionally shielded by great privacy." But the "degree of intrusion" on one's privacy caused by collecting a urine sample "depends upon the manner in which production of the urine sample is monitored." This procedure is virtually identical to that reviewed in *Vernonia*, except that it additionally protects privacy by allowing male students to produce their samples behind a closed stall.

.....

In addition, the Policy clearly requires that the test results be kept in confidential files separate from a student's other educational records and released to school personnel only on a "need to know" basis. ....Moreover, the test results are not turned over to any law enforcement authority. Nor do the test results here lead to the imposition of discipline or have any academic consequences. Rather, the only consequence of a failed drug test is to limit the student's privilege of participating in extracurricular activities... [W]e conclude that the invasion of students' privacy is not significant.

Finally, this Court must consider the nature and immediacy of the government's concerns and the efficacy of the Policy in meeting them. The health and safety risks identified in *Vernonia* apply with equal force to Tecumseh's children. Indeed, the nationwide drug epidemic makes the war against drugs a pressing concern in every school. Additionally, the School District in this case has presented specific evidence of drug use at Tecumseh schools. Teachers testified that they had seen students who appeared to be under the influence of drugs and that they had heard students speaking openly about using drugs. A drug dog found marijuana cigarettes near the school parking lot. Police officers once found drugs or drug paraphernalia in a car driven by a Future Farmers of America member. And the school board president reported that people in the community were calling the board to discuss the "drug situation." We decline to second-guess the finding of the District Court that "viewing the evidence as a whole, it cannot be reasonably disputed that the [School District] was faced with a 'drug problem' when it adopted the Policy." Likewise, the need to prevent and deter the substantial harm of childhood drug use provides the necessary immediacy for a school testing policy. Indeed, it would make little sense to require a school district to wait for a substantial portion of its students to begin using drugs before it was allowed to institute a drug testing program designed to deter drug use....... Given the nationwide epidemic of drug use, and the evidence of increased drug use in Tecumseh schools, it was entirely reasonable for the School District to enact this particular drug testing policy. ...... As we cannot articulate a threshold level of drug use that would suffice to justify a drug testing program for schoolchildren, we refuse to fashion what would in effect be a constitutional quantum of drug use necessary to show a "drug problem."

Finally, we find that testing students who participate in extracurricular activities is a reasonably effective means of addressing the School District's legitimate concerns in preventing, deterring, and detecting drug use. While in *Vernonia* there might have been a closer fit between the testing of athletes and the trial court's finding that the drug problem was "fueled by the 'role model' effect of athletes' drug use," such a finding was not essential to the holding. *Vernonia* did not require the school to test the group of students most likely to use drugs, but rather considered the constitutionality of the program in the context of the public school's custodial responsibilities. Evaluating the Policy in this context, we conclude that the drug testing of Tecumseh students who participate in extracurricular activities effectively serves the School District's interest in protecting the safety and health of its students.

[W]e express no opinion as to its wisdom. Rather, we hold only that Tecumseh's Policy is a reasonable means of furthering the School District's important interest in preventing and deterring drug use among its schoolchildren. Accordingly, we reverse the judgment of the Court of Appeals.

CONCUR: JUSTICE BREYER, concurring.

In my view, this program does not violate the Fourth Amendment's prohibition of "unreasonable searches and seizures." I reach this conclusion primarily for the reasons given by the Court, but I would emphasize several underlying considerations, which I understand to be consistent with the Court's opinion.

First, not everyone would agree with this Court's characterization of the privacy-related significance of urine sampling as "negligible." When trying to resolve this kind of close question involving the interpretation of constitutional values, I believe it important that the school board provided an opportunity for the airing of these differences at public meetings designed to give the entire community "the opportunity to be able to participate" in developing the drug policy. The board used this democratic, participatory process to uncover and to resolve differences, giving weight to the fact that the process, in this instance, revealed little, if any, objection to the proposed testing program.

Second, the testing program avoids subjecting the entire school to testing. And it preserves an option for a conscientious objector. He can refuse testing while paying a price (nonparticipation) that is serious, but less severe than expulsion from the school.

Third, a contrary reading of the Constitution, as requiring "individualized suspicion" in this public school context, could well lead schools to push the boundaries of "individualized suspicion" to its outer limits, using subjective criteria that may "unfairly target members of unpopular groups," or leave those whose behavior is slightly abnormal stigmatized in the minds of others.

DISSENT: JUSTICE O'CONNOR, with whom JUSTICE SOUTER joins, dissenting.

I dissented in Vernonia and continue to believe that case was wrongly decided. Because Vernonia is now this Court's precedent, and because I agree that petitioners' program fails even under the balancing approach adopted in that case, I join JUSTICE GINSBURG's dissent.

JUSTICE GINSBURG, JUSTICE STEVENS, JUSTICE O'CONNOR, and JUSTICE SOUTER join, dissenting.

The particular testing program upheld today is not reasonable, it is capricious, even perverse: Petitioners' policy targets for testing a student population least likely to be at risk from illicit drugs and their damaging effects. I therefore dissent.

Not only did the Vernonia and Tecumseh districts confront drug problems of distinctly different magnitudes, they also chose different solutions: Vernonia limited its policy to athletes; Tecumseh indiscriminately subjected to testing all participants in competitive extracurricular activities. Urging that "the safety interest furthered by drug testing is undoubtedly substantial for all children, athletes and nonathletes alike," the Court cuts out an element essential to the *Vernonia* judgment.

The Vernonia district, in sum, had two good reasons for testing athletes: Sports team members faced special health risks and they "were the leaders of the drug culture." No similar reason, and no other tenable justification, explains Tecumseh's decision to target for testing all participants in every competitive extracurricular activity.

Nationwide, students who participate in extracurricular activities are significantly less likely to develop substance abuse problems than are their less-involved peers. ..... Tecumseh's policy thus falls short doubly if deterrence is its aim: It invades the privacy of students who need deterrence least, and risks steering students at greatest risk for substance abuse away from extracurricular involvement that potentially may palliate drug problems. .... A program so sweeping is not sheltered by *Vernonia*; its unreasonable reach renders it impermissible under the Fourth Amendment.

C. Suspicionless Student Searches

JANE DOE v. LITTLE ROCK SCHOOL DISTRICT

380 F.3d 349 (8th Cir. 2004)

MORRIS SHEPPARD ARNOLD, Circuit Judge.

This case requires us to decide whether the practice of the Little Rock School District (LRSD) that subjects secondary public school students to random, suspicionless searches of their persons and belongings by school officials is unconstitutional. We conclude that such searches violate the students' fourth amendment rights because they unreasonably invade their legitimate expectations of privacy.

Jane Doe is a secondary school student in the LRSD. One day during the school year, all of the students in Ms. Doe's classroom were ordered to leave the room after removing everything from their pockets and placing all of their belongings, including their backpacks and purses, on the desks in front of them. While the students were in the hall outside their classroom, school personnel searched the items that the students had left behind, including Ms. Doe's purse, and they discovered marijuana in a container in her purse. The parties have stipulated that LRSD has a practice of regularly conducting searches of randomly selected classrooms in this manner.

In her amended complaint, Ms. Doe, individually and on behalf of a class of "all secondary public school students who have started seventh grade in the [LRSD] as of the 1999-2000 school year," claimed that this method of conducting searches is unconstitutional, and sought declaratory and injunctive relief pursuant to 42 U.S.C. § 1983. After certifying the case as a class action, the district court entered judgment for the LRSD and dismissed the complaint with prejudice. We reverse.

.....

II.

We [apply TLO] and ask first whether secondary public school students in the LRSD retain any legitimate expectations of privacy. The district court, quoting *Earls*, 536 U.S. at 830, noted that a " 'student's privacy interest is limited in a public school environment where the State is responsible for maintaining discipline, health, and safety.' " Students in public schools do indeed have lesser expectations of privacy than people generally have in public situations, due in large part to the government's responsibilities "as guardian and tutor of children entrusted to its care." *Vernonia*, 515 U.S. at 665 (footnote omitted). Public school students' privacy interests, however, are not nonexistent. We think it is clear that schoolchildren are entitled to expect some degree of privacy in the personal items that they bring to school.

As a general matter, "the Fourth Amendment provides protection to the owner of every container that conceals its contents from plain view," *United States v. Ross*, 456 U.S. 798, 822-23, 72 L. Ed. 2d 572, 102 S. Ct. 2157 (1982), and public school students thus retain a protection against "unreasonable" searches of their backpacks and purses by school officials. Schoolchildren have a legitimate need to bring items of personal property into their schools, which are their "homes away from home" where they are required by compulsory attendance laws to spend a substantial portion of their waking hours. They "at a minimum must bring to school not only the supplies needed for their studies, but also keys, money, and the necessaries of personal hygiene and grooming," and they may also carry with them "such nondisruptive yet highly personal items as photographs, letters, and diaries." *T.L.O.*, 469 U.S. at 339. Unlike prisoners, who "retain no legitimate expectations of privacy in their cells" after having been convicted and incarcerated, *see id.* at 338, public school students have traditionally been treated as presumptively responsible persons entitled to some modicum of privacy in their personal belongings, at least to the extent that recognition of such privacy interests does not unduly burden the maintenance of security and order in schools.

The Supreme Court has observed that there is a tension between the types of privacy "interests protected by the Fourth Amendment and the interest of the States in providing a safe environment conducive to education in the public schools," *id.* at 332 n.2, and has concluded that the fourth amendment allows school officials some flexibility in resolving this tension. But it has characterized as "severely flawed" a state's argument that "because of the pervasive supervision to which children in the schools are necessarily subject, a child has virtually no legitimate expectation of privacy in articles of personal property 'unnecessarily' carried into a school." *Id.* at 338. While the Court has acknowledged that students' privacy rights are limited due to the "difficulty of maintaining discipline in the public schools," and that "drug use and violent crime in the schools have become major social problems," it has stated that "the situation is not so dire that students in the schools may claim no legitimate expectations of privacy." *Id.* at 338-39.

...

As the district court noted, a passage that was added to the LRSD's current Secondary Student Rights and Responsibilities Handbook, which is distributed to students at the beginning of the school year, provides that "book bags, backpacks, purses and similar containers are permitted on school property as a convenience for students," and that "if brought onto school property, such containers and their contents are at all times subject to random and periodic inspections by school officials." But we do not think that this handbook passage has effected a waiver by LRSD students of any expectations of privacy that they would otherwise have. The students are required by state law to attend school, and have not entered into a contract that incorporates the handbook or voluntarily assented to be bound by its terms. The lack of mutual consent to the student handbook makes it fundamentally different from an employee handbook, which may create an enforceable contract between an employer and employee under traditional contract principles. The LRSD may not deprive its students of privacy expectations protected by the fourth amendment simply by announcing that the expectations will no longer be honored.

III.

Given that public school students retain some legitimate expectation of privacy in their persons and belongings, we are bound to inquire into the character of the intrusion that the LRSD's search practice imposes. We respectfully disagree with the district court's determination that the search practices of the LRSD are "minimally intrusive."

Unlike the suspicionless searches of participants in school sports and other competitive extracurricular activities that the Supreme Court approved in *Vernonia* and *Earls*, in which "the privacy interests compromised by the process" of the searches were deemed "negligible," *Vernonia*, 515 U.S. at 658, *see Earls*, 536 U.S. at 832-33, the type of search at issue here invades students' privacy interests in a major way. "A search of a child's person or of a closed purse or other bag carried on her person, no less than a similar search carried out on an adult, is undoubtedly a severe violation of subjective expectations of privacy." *T.L.O.*, 469 U.S. at 337-38 (footnote omitted). Students often carry items of a personal or private nature in their pockets and bags, and many students (whether or not they are carrying contraband) must surely feel uncomfortable or embarrassed when officials decide to rifle through their personal belongings.

Whatever privacy interests the LRSD students have in the personal belongings that they bring to school are wholly obliterated by the search practice at issue here, because all such belongings are subject to being searched at any time without notice, individualized suspicion, or any apparent limit to the extensiveness of the search. Full-scale searches that involve people rummaging through personal belongings concealed within a container are manifestly more intrusive than searches effected by using metal detectors or dogs. Indeed, dogs and magnetometers are often employed in conducting constitutionally reasonable large-scale "administrative" searches precisely because they are minimally intrusive, and provide an effective means for adducing the requisite degree of individualized suspicion to conduct further, more intrusive searches. The type of search that the LRSD has decided to employ, in contrast, is highly intrusive, and we are not aware of any cases indicating that such searches in schools pass constitutional muster absent individualized suspicion, consent or waiver of privacy interests by those searched, or extenuating circumstances that pose a grave security threat.

Another relevant consideration is the purpose for which the fruits of the searches at issue are used. In *Vernonia* and *Earls*, which involved drug testing of voluntary participants in competitive extracurricular activities, the results of the searches at issue were never disclosed to law enforcement authorities, and the most serious form of discipline that could possibly result from failing the tests was exclusion from the relevant extracurricular activities. *See Earls*, 536 U.S. at 833; *Vernonia*, 515 U.S. at 651. The Court in *Earls*, 536 U.S. at 834, found that "the limited uses to which the test results are put" contributed significantly to a conclusion that the invasion of the students' privacy was insignificant. In sharp contrast to these cases, the fruits of the searches at issue here are apparently regularly turned over to law enforcement officials and are used in criminal proceedings against students whose contraband is discovered. In fact, Ms. Doe was convicted of a misdemeanor as a result of the search of her purse. Because the LRSD's searches can lead directly to the imposition of punitive criminal sanctions, the character of the intrusions is qualitatively more severe than that in *Vernonia* and *Earls*. Rather than acting *in loco parentis*, with the goal of promoting the students' welfare, the government officials conducting the searches are in large part playing a law enforcement role with the goal of ferreting out crime and collecting evidence to be used in prosecuting students.

IV.

We consider finally the nature and immediacy of the governmental concerns that gave rise to the searches at issue here. A sliding scale is used in evaluating the reasonableness of a search, that is, the government is entitled to inflict more serious intrusions upon legitimate expectations of privacy as the governmental interest served by the intrusions becomes more compelling. A governmental interest need not meet some "fixed, minimum quantum of governmental concern," but merely has to be "*important enough* to justify the particular search at hand," considering the degree of its intrusiveness. *Vernonia*, 515 U.S. at 661. The district court determined that the LRSD's search practice is "directed towards an immediate, legitimate need." It failed, however, to point to any evidence indicating that the LRSD has experienced any significant and immediate difficulties sufficient to give rise to a special need for such an unprecedented practice.

We conclude that the LRSD has in fact failed to demonstrate the existence of a need sufficient to justify the substantial intrusions upon the students' privacy interests that the search practice entails. While the LRSD has expressed some generalized concerns about the existence of weapons and drugs in its schools, it conceded at oral argument that there is nothing in the record regarding the magnitude of any problems with weapons or drugs that it has actually experienced. All schools surely have an interest in minimizing the harm that the existence of weapons and controlled substances might visit upon a student population, but public schools have never been entitled to conduct random, full-scale searches of students' personal belongings because of a mere apprehension.

.....

V.

While the line separating reasonable and unreasonable school searches is sometimes indistinct, we think it plain enough that the LRSD's search practice crosses it. In light of the government's legitimate interest in maintaining discipline and safety in the public schools, the privacy that students in those schools are reasonably entitled to expect is limited. The LRSD's search practice, however, effectively reduces these expectations to nothing, and the record contains no evidence of unique circumstances that would justify significant intrusions. The mere assertion that there are substantial problems associated with drugs and weapons in its schools does not give the LRSD *carte blanche* to inflict highly intrusive, random searches upon its general student body. We therefore reverse the judgment of the district court, and we remand for entry of a judgment not inconsistent with this opinion.

DISSENT

BEAM, Circuit Judge, concurring and dissenting.

In my view, Vernonia and Earls appreciate the limited expectation of privacy, but allow a school to search if the search is not too intrusive, if the school's concerns are immediate, and if the means employed to serve the school's concerns serve that immediate concern. Obviously, this test

notion of reasonableness in the context of government action. Thus, a useful benchmark is prior cases that have applied this test.

It seems to me that the "nature of the intrusion" in this case was noticeably less intrusive than the extraction and testing of body fluids discussed in Earls and Vernonia and tends to support an affirmance of the district court. But it is the immediacy of the school's concerns that I believe is misstated here. I agree with Judge Bowman's opinion in Miller v. Wilkes, 172 F.3d 574 (8th Cir. 1999) (now vacated because of Miller's exodus from the subject school system). Judge Bowman, acknowledging Vernonia, states, "Drug and alcohol abuse in public schools is a serious social problem today in every part of the country. (Indeed, to the extent any party thinks it necessary to do so, we take judicial notice of that fact. See Fed. R. Evid. 201 (generally known fact).)" The same is true, I submit, with the dangers of weapons that may pose threats of bodily harm to members of the student body. And, in this case, the stipulated facts address that specific problem. ...And I believe the random searches serve that concern by deterring possession.

Finally, although a close question on the stipulated facts and the evidence the district court was entitled to consider through judicial notice, I agree with the court's analysis of Doe's individual claim. The distinguishing feature to me is the police involvement in the fruits of Doe's search. ...By turning the fruits of its search over to police, the school reduced the extent to which it was acting under its "'custodial and tutelary responsibility'" Earls, 536 U.S. at 830 (quoting Vernonia, 515 U.S. at 656), and instead, brought it much closer to acting in the investigatory role for which the probable-cause standard is intended. Id. at 828. In other words, its "special needs," Vernonia, 515 U.S. at 653, became ordinary. ...Ironically, calling upon the police after random searches probably heightens the extent to which the searches serve a school's immediate concern with deterrence and thereby may make other students safer. But it also brings into the picture notions of detection and criminal punishment--not-so-peculiar facets of police work--that make the student's shepherd much more like the criminal's.

On balance, I conclude that the school district's search was unreasonable as to Doe. Thus, the declaratory judgment and injunction should issue on Doe's behalf. If, however, LRSD conducts its searches without individualized suspicion and refrains from sharing the fruits thereof with the police, I believe its actions are fully constitutional. The class has shown no more than that here. In sum, I concur in the court's reversal regarding Doe's individual claim but would affirm the district court on the class claim.

Bernard James and Joanne E. K. Larson: The Doctrine of Deference: Shifting Constitutional Presumptions and The Supreme Court's Restatement of Student Rights After *Board of Education v. Earls*, 56 S.C. Law Review 1 (2004)*

The Court in *Earls* set forth what is nearly a complete equation for a deferential model on the authority of educators, largely culling the key components from the *Tinker–Vernonia* line of cases. The model is a testament to the changes in both the outcome of student-rights disputes in public schools as well as a primer on the philosophical shift of the Court over this same time period. Most importantly, its elements provide a glimpse into the future of both law and educational policymaking suggesting that the judicial role will hereafter be narrowly confined to a predictable set of inquiries.

In application to future conflicts over student rights, the model promises to provide a nomenclature for policy formulation and a barometer for resolving disputes over the reasonableness of the actions of educators. Four factors provide the basic framework:

- *The Education Mission Factor*: this factor acts as a limit on the presumption of validity, covering campus policies that are "undertaken in furtherance of the government's responsibilities, under a public school system, as guardian and tutor of children entrusted to its care."

- *The Custodial Factor*: this factor is based on the historical view that educators have a natural zone of authority, if not a legal duty as to "(1) children, who (2) have been committed to the temporary custody of the State as schoolmaster."

- *The Due Process Factor*: this element serves to validate the reasonableness of a policy. It is based on an emerging view that there should be a link between the educator's

---

interest in implementing a policy and the effects created by the disciplinary process when the law is enforced.

- *The Accountability Factor*: this requires that the challenged policy actually represent the views of the affected community, giving rise to an expectation that educators will reach out for parental input by providing a democratic, participatory process to "uncover and to resolve differences," particularly over controversial policies.

As a constitutional restatement the model comes remarkably close to codifying Justice Harlan's dissent in *Tinker* in a manner that, at least at first glance, produces for educators an almost total exemption from ordinary Fourth Amendment analysis. In place of the traditional objective, fact-based balancing of interests comes a set of context-dependent presumptions accompanied by a framework designed to standardize the judicial search for arbitrary, abusive, and bad-faith policymaking by educators. [D]ebates over education policies, like suspicionless drug testing, metal detectors, or drug sniffer dogs, remain just as controversial for educators, but less so for the courts due to the shift in presumptions about the authority of educators in the absence of a finding of bad faith.

Interestingly, the elements that emerge from the restatement are neither novel nor particularly surprising. Each factor, standing alone, is well-established in narrower education law contexts. What is significant is the synergistic effect the Court derives by combining the elements in a manner that shifts presumptions in favor of educators and burdens toward opponents of school-safety reforms.

For example, the custodial and the education-mission factors are traditional notions in education law such that their exclusion from any restatement would be peculiar. Judicial references to both appear frequently, often as dispositive factors in court decisions involving the authority of educators. As a result, the Court in both the *Vernonia* and *Earls* decisions does little more than formalize judicial notice already taken of the fact that educators operate from a position of strength when they act in good faith to further legitimate educational interests.

In *Vernonia*, the majority, without benefit of any citation, appeared to herald this formalization: "The most significant element in this case is the first we discussed: that the Policy was undertaken in furtherance of the government's responsibilities, under a public school system, as guardian and tutor of children entrusted to its care." *Vernonia*, 515 U.S. at 664.

Later in *Earls*, the justices, citing back to *Vernonia*, completed the formalization of these elements:

> Respondents argue that because children participating in nonathletic extracurricular activities are not subject to regular physicals and communal undress, they have a stronger expectation of privacy than the athletes tested in *Vernonia*. This distinction, however, was not essential to our decision in *Vernonia*, which depended primarily upon the school's custodial responsibility and authority. *Earls*, 536 U.S. at 831 (citations omitted).

Examined separately, the education mission is frequently viewed as a compelling interest by judges, effectively allowing schools to overcome assertions of student rights with a showing of the deleterious effects, overt or subtle, caused by the exercise of those rights. When applying the precedent in regard to the education mission, courts typically recite the mantra of "[t]he broad authority to control the conduct of students granted to school official permits a good deal of latitude in determining which policies will best serve educational and disciplinary goals." *Sypniewski v. Warren Hills Reg'l Bd. of Educ.*, 307 F.3d 243, 259 (3d Cir. 2002), *cert denied*, 538 U.S. 1033 (2003).

.....

Similarly, the notion of the custodial interest of educators, when examined apart from the education mission, supports a more deferential restatement of the law. Judicial discussions about the custodial interest are occasionally tied to the education mission, but are more routinely found in a separate body of case law organized around the notion of in loco parentis. Its prominence in *Earls* serves to essentially codify a type of utilitarianism about the interest of educators to provide a safe, effective learning environment for students, which outweighs the rights of the few or of the individual student.

.....

[R]equirements of due process in a public school setting emerge from the seminal school discipline case of *Goss v. Lopez*. *Lopez* has been thought of as mainly a procedural case, but, in fact, its influence in school discipline has been quite substantive, creating an incentive for educators to ruminate the decisions regarding punishment for code violations. This link, of both process and substance, between the type of punishment and its severity has led to a judicial expectation of proportionality in school discipline that works its way into the *Earls* formula.

.....

[T]he references in *Earls* to some form of accountability should not be left to speculation nor attributed to a form of judicial altruism. It is woven throughout both the *Earls* and *Vernonia* rationale, making discussion of its future impact on education-law development a serious matter, especially in light of the Court's decision to defer to local decisionmakers. Whatever else the Court intended, an unmistakable preference emerges to restrain judicial intervention in student discipline disputes when the policy in question is forged through community dialogue and participation.

Justice Thomas's majority opinion in *Earls* chronicles the participatory efforts of the Oklahoma educators. After summarizing the process, which included the observations and beliefs of teachers, administrators, law enforcement officials, the school board, and members of the community, the *Earls* majority concluded that deference was appropriate: "We decline to second-guess the finding of the District Court that [v]iewing the evidence as a whole, it cannot be reasonably disputed that the [School District] was faced with a 'drug problem' when it adopted the Policy." *Earls*, 536 U.S. at 835.

Justice Breyer, in his concurrence in *Earls*, gives weight to such a factor:

> When trying to resolve this kind of close question involving the interpretation of constitutional values, I believe it important that the school board provided an opportunity for the airing of these differences at public meetings designed to give the entire community "the opportunity to be able to participate" in developing the drug policy.... The board used this democratic, participatory process to uncover and to resolve differences, giving weight to the fact that the process, in this instance, revealed little, if any, objection to the proposed testing program. *Earls* at 842. (Breyer, J., concurring).

Notes and Comments

1. What appears to bother the dissenters the most about the deference approach to Fourth Amendment rights? Is there a compromise solution somewhere in the middle of the dispute? How would you summarize the status of student privacy rights to a school official based on *TLO*, *Acton* and *Earls*?

2. *TLO*, *Acton* and *Earls* and Substantive Due Process
As discussed *infra*, in Chapter Thirteen, the Due Process Clause of the Fourteenth Amendment provides the right to be free from, and to obtain judicial relief for, unjustified intrusions on personal security. The seminal case on these constitutional torts is *Rochin v. California*, 342 U.S. 165 (1952). In *Rochin*, the Court overturned the conviction of a defendant whose stomach was pumped against his will to produce the only evidence (morphine capsules) used against him. Justice Frankfurter wrote for the Court that,

> [W]e are compelled to conclude that the proceedings by which this conviction was obtained do more than offend some fastidious squeamishness or private sentimentalism about combating crime too energetically. This is conduct that shocks the conscience. Illegally breaking into the privacy of the petitioner, the struggle to open his mouth and remove what was there, the forcible extraction of his stomach's content...... They are methods too close to the rack and the screw to permit of constitutional differentiation........ It would be a stultification of the responsibility, which the course of constitutional history has cast upon this Court to hold that in order to convict a man the police cannot extract by force what is in his mind but can extract what is in his stomach.

Can one make a creditable argument that mandatory student drug testing violates substantive due process? Does the spirit of the "shock the conscience" standard suggest that the Fourteenth Amendment should protect students in such instances even though the Fourth Amendment does not? One commentator notes;

> Students' interest in personal security, whether it is implicated by school officials' using physical force to control or punish them, lies doctrinally near the chasm between the Fourth and Fourteenth Amendments. Nevertheless, a student's interest in bodily integrity, under the Court's modern jurisprudence, should fall within the protections of the Fourth Amendment….. The difference between the Fourth and Fourteenth Amendment is doctrinally significant because the Supreme Court has created multiple standards for personal security claims depending on the context of the incident challenged. Although the Court has articulated numerous standards to establish a violation of substantive due process, its most recent exegesis of personal security litigation in *County of Sacramento v. Lewis* suggests that students' personal security claims will virtually always fail if they are litigated under substantive due process, and not fail so consistently if litigated under the Fourth Amendment.

Kathryn R. Urbonya: Public School Officials' Use of Physical Force as a Fourth Amendment Seizure: Protecting Students from the Constitutional Chasm Between the Fourth and Fourteenth Amendments, 69 Geo. Wash. L. Rev. 1, 40, 54 (2000).

3. *Acton* and *Earls* and the Curricular, Extra-curricular Distinction

One issue that the Court does not raise in the *Acton* and *Earls* decisions is the nature of the activity. Both cases involve extra-curricular activities. The outcomes in the cases are easier to justify with reference to the traditional right/privilege distinction. According to this rule, participation in extra-curricular activities is not a right, but a privilege. Therefore, unlike curricular activities, educators may place conditions and impose punishments appropriate to the activity and the legitimate interest of educators. See, *In re U.S. ex. rel. Missouri State High School Activities Association*, 682 F.2d 147, 153 (8th Cir. 1982), *cert. denied*, 449 U.S. 1124, 101 S. Ct. 939, 67 L. Ed. 2d 109 (1981) ("a student's interest in participating in a single year of interscholastic athletics amounts to a mere expectation rather than a constitutionally protected claim of entitlement."). See also Part II, Chapter Four, and notes after *Langley v. Monroe County School District.*

One reason that the Court may have ignored the curricular, extra-curricular element in *Acton* and *Earls* is the doctrine of unconstitutional conditions. Under this doctrine, the government may not condition the receipt of its benefits upon the non-assertion of constitutional rights even if receipt of such benefits is in all other respects a "mere privilege" and theoretically allows individuals to challenge government action, which indirectly inhibits or penalizes the exercise of constitutional rights. *See Perry v. Sinderman*, 408 U.S. 593 (1972) (holding that although a person has no right to a valuable governmental benefit, that benefit may not be denied to a person on a basis that infringes his constitutionally protected interests, especially his interest in freedom of speech); *Legal Serv. Corp. v. Velasquez*, 531 U.S. 533 (2001) (declaring unconstitutional a federal statute restricting the ability of legal services providers who receive federal funds to engage in activity protected by the First Amendment); *Rust v. Sullivan*, 500 U.S. 173 (1991) (rejecting a challenge to federal regulations prohibiting federally funded health care clinics from providing information regarding the use of abortion as a family planning alternative).

The Justices in *Acton* and *Earls* appear to lay the matter of the curricular, extra-curricular distinction to rest in cases arising out of the Fourth Amendment by giving educators generalized power to implement policies that are designed to protect students and the educational environment. Does this mean that educators have the power to implement a mandatory drug testing policy for the entire student body? For example, in *Linke v. Northwest Schools*, 763 N.E.2d 972 (2002), the Indiana courts applied the state constitution to uphold an expanded random drug testing policy. The policy applied to athletes and students participating in other extra-curricular activities and students driving to school. In *Ziegler v. Martin Cty. Sch. Dist.*, 831 F.3d 1309 (11th Cir. 2016), the Eleventh Circuit upheld a school policy of applying school rules to the school-sponsored prom, including the zero tolerance policy that specifically applied to off-campus activities. The court upheld the decision of school officials to give breathalyzer tests to students who rode a party bus to the prom. The court reasoned that the students did not have an expectation of privacy on the party bus and that educators had a reasonable basis for believing students had violated school's rules after finding an empty champagne bottle and plastic cups on the bus. The court did find that school officials unreasonably detained all of the students while each of them were administered breath test for blood alcohol concentration, rather than allowing those who tested alcohol free to enter prom.

4. *Vernonia, Earls* and Suspicionless Searches for Weapons and Drugs

State courts and federal lower courts apply the rule of the *Vernonia* and *Earls* cases to permit educators to conduct suspicionless searches of the entire student body. These searches are much less intrusive than the urine-based drug tests. As such, the authority for the searches is arguably justified by logic; the "greater power" to drug test students implies the "lesser power" of requiring all students to submit to searches for contraband. *See In Re F. B. v. Pennsylvania*, 555 Pa. 661, 726 A.2d 361 (1999) (knife seized during a search for weapons conducted as a precondition to entry for all students.); *Brousseau v Westerly et al.,* 11 F. Supp. 2d 177 (D. Rhode Island, 6/11/98) (all students searched in cafeteria when a knife was discovered missing in the cafeteria.); *Beth Smith v. James McGlothlin*, 119 F.3d 786 (U.S. Ct. of Appeals, 9th Cir.) (1997) (Principal searched a group of students after seeing a cloud of smoke and what he believed to be the discarding of cigarettes.); *DesRoches v. Caprio,* 156 F.3d 571, (4th Cir. Va. 1998) (search of all students' backpacks when a fellow student reported their shoes missing after school-sponsored trip.); *In the Interest of L.E.*, 589 S.W.3d 593 (Mo. Ct. App. 2019), transfer denied (Nov. 19, 2019) (upholding the search of a student's backpack during a routine search where all students are required to walk through a metal detector and have their bags hand-searched by either a school safety officer or a teacher.); *Woods as Next Friend of T.W. v. Rio Rancho Pub. Sch.*, No. 17-CV-492-WJ-JHR, 2019 WL 251734 (D.N.M. Jan. 17, 2019) (upholding the search of an entire class after a student reported that someone stole $210.); *In re R.H.*, No. B267146, 2016 WL 3179388 (Cal. Ct. App. May 27, 2016) (upholding school policy of randomly selecting one classroom to search each day for weapons and drugs. A student was found with a knife in his folder.)

5. *TLO, Acton* and *Earls* and State Constitutional Law

State courts have addressed the question of the constitutionality of random drug testing polices under the rights of privacy guaranteed under state constitutions. As a matter of autonomy, a State may provide individual rights at a level that exceeds federal constitutional law standards. In Washington State, the Washington Court of Appeals ruled that the search of a non-student's backpack, due to the smell of marijuana was unreasonable. The court reasoned that the "school search exception," which under the Washington Constitution allows school authorities to conduct a search of a student without probable cause only applies to non-students if the nonstudent presents a credible threat of physical harm and when the scope of the search conducted is directly related to that threat. *State v. A.S.*, 430 P.3d 703 (Wash. Ct. App. 2018), review denied, 193 Wash. 2d 1004, 438 P.3d 125 (2019). In Oregon, the court upheld a drug testing policy for student athletes, holding that it did not violate rights under Or. Const. (art. I, § 9A.). *Weber v. Oakridge Sch. Dist.* 76, 184 Ore. App. 415; 56 P.3d 504 (2002).

> Under the Oregon Constitution, the determinative question is whether any search required by an administrative policy is reasonable in relation to its purpose. To be reasonable, the search need not be the least restrictive means to accomplish an end.......Because the urinalysis component of the district's policy was authorized by a politically accountable body, involves no discretion by the person or persons directing it, and has not been shown to be unreasonable in relation to the purposes of the policy, we conclude that [the policy is valid].

In *Theodore v. Del. Valley Sch. Dist.*, 575 Pa. 321, 836 A.2d 76, (2003), the Supreme Court of Pennsylvania invalidated a drug testing program that it admitted would have passed muster under the Fourth Amendment. The case appears below. What problems does a State create when it overrules a U.S. constitutional law using its state constitution? Is it clear why this particular drug testing policy fails? Is it possible that public school officials could still prevail under the more rigorous standard when the case is remanded for further proceedings? Finally, read closely the decision below of the Colorado Supreme Court in *University of Colorado v. Derdeyn*, 863 P.2d 929 (1993). The U. S. Supreme Court denied a writ of certiorari to review the case (511 U.S. 1070 (1994)). Does the ruling create a different standard of privacy for college students?

THEODORE v. DELAWARE VALLEY SCHOOL DISTRICT
836 A.2d 76 (Pa. 2003)

OPINION OF THE COURT: MR. JUSTICE CASTILLE

In 1998, the Delaware Valley School District (the "School District" or "District") adopted a policy which authorizes random, suspicionless drug and alcohol testing of students who hold school parking permits or participate in voluntary extracurricular activities. Appellees Louis and Mary Ellen Theodore, whose two daughters were subject to the policy, filed a complaint seeking to enjoin the testing policy on grounds that, inter alia, it violated their daughters' right to privacy under Article I, Section 8 of the Pennsylvania Constitution. The primary question in this appeal is whether, for purposes of the preliminary objections subsequently filed by the School District, the policy must be deemed constitutional as a matter of law. Because we reject the District's argument that the policy is constitutional as a matter of law, we affirm the decision of the Commonwealth Court which reinstated the complaint and permitted the case to go forward.

The District…adopted Policy 227…which required all middle and high school students seeking to participate in extracurricular activities or requesting permission to drive to school or park at school to sign, or have a parent sign, a "contract" consenting to testing for alcohol and controlled substances. The policy defines extracurricular activities as all athletics, clubs, and other activities in which students participate on a voluntary basis, and for which academic credit is not awarded. The policy includes the following statement of purpose:

> As representatives of the school district and leaders in their schools, students involved in extracurricular programs and students who drive to school are expected to exemplify high standards by the public and are held in high esteem by other students. Participants in extracurricular programs and those who drive to school are expected to accept the responsibilities accompanying these opportunities.
>
> Deterring drug use by school students is important. School years are the time when the physical, psychological, and addictive effects of drugs are most severe. The effects of a drug-infested school are visited not just upon the users, but upon the entire student body and faculty, because the educational process is disrupted.
>
> With regard to school athletes and student drivers, the risk of immediate physical harm to the drug and alcohol user or those with whom he/she is playing a sport or sharing the highway is particularly high. Apart from psychological effects, which include impairment of judgment, slowing of reaction time, and a lessening of the perception of pain, alcohol and the particular drugs screened by this policy pose substantial physical risks to athletes and drivers. Extracurricular participants, whether athletes or not, are student leaders and, as such, serve as role models for their peers and for young children as well. The use of drugs and alcohol by these role models exacerbates the problem of illegal substances in our schools.

Jennifer Lynn Theodore and Kimberly Ann Theodore were subject to mandatory urinalysis testing under Policy 227 because Jennifer participated in the National Honor Society, Science Olympiad, and Scholastic Bowl, while Kimberly participated in tennis, swimming, and track, and had a parking permit. Both girls were required to provide urine samples. Both tests returned negative for any banned substance. In January, 1999, the students' parents filed suit seeking to enjoin the School District from continuing to test students.

…..

The District contends that Policy 227 is virtually identical to the policy at issue in Earls. The District argues that Article I, Section 8 should not be construed as imposing greater limitations upon the authority of public schools to conduct student drug tests beyond those imposed by the Fourth Amendment, as all public schools possess an inherent "special need" to drug test the pupils under their care.

Appellees respond that Article I, Section 8 provides students with greater protection than the Fourth Amendment in this instance, consistently with the viewpoint articulated in the Earls dissent.

.....

We have little doubt that, if this case presented a Fourth Amendment challenge, the intervening decision in Earls would require us to reverse the Commonwealth Court.

The Article I, Section 8 question, however, is more difficult. "The cases decided under Article I, [Section] 8, have recognized a 'strong notion of privacy, which is greater than that of the Fourth Amendment.'" *Commonwealth v. Glass*, 562 Pa. 187, 754 A.2d 655, 662 (Pa. 2000) (quoting *Commonwealth v. Walston*, 555 Pa. 223, 724 A.2d 289, 292 (Pa. 1998)). Thus, as we held in *In the Interest of F.B.*, "the unique policy concerns safeguarding the individual right to privacy in Pennsylvania bring a greater degree of scrutiny to all searches where the protection of Article I, Section 8 is invoked." 726 A.2d at 365. Moreover, we also specifically held that Article I, Section 8 "mandates greater scrutiny in the school environment." *Id.*

The *In the Interest of F.B.* Court concluded that the appropriate state constitutional test in the school environment involves balancing four factors: (1) the students' privacy interests, (2) the nature of the intrusion created by the search, (3) notice, and (4) "the overall purpose to be achieved by the search and the immediate reasons prompting the decision to conduct the actual search." 726 A.2d at 365. The Court looked for guidance to *Vernonia*, and noted that the test it ultimately fashioned bore a "great similarity" to the *Vernonia* test, *id.* at 365—albeit the notice prong lacks a counterpart in *Vernonia*. We recognize that the fourth prong of the *In the Interest of F.B.* test is stated somewhat differently than its *Vernonia* counterpart. Vernonia expressed this concern in terms of the "nature and immediacy" of the governmental interest and the "efficacy" of its chosen means in advancing that interest, *see* 515 U.S. at 660, 115 S. Ct. at 2394, while *In the Interest of F.B.* spoke in terms of the government's "overall purpose" and "immediate reasons" for conducting the search. 726 A.2d at 365. But, the analytical point is the same: the reasonableness of a search will depend in part upon a measure of the reason and purpose for the search and the government's chosen means of effecting it. This consideration is appropriate, for if the method is not efficacious, then the government's need to conduct the intrusion is correspondingly diminished.

In the Interest of F.B. involved a suspicionless search of the entire student body for weapons, but there is no reason why the school search test formulated there should not also apply to searches which target a defined subset of the student population for after-the-fact evidence of drug or alcohol use. In addition, the fact that the U.S. Supreme Court relaxed its scrutiny in this area since we last visited the question, see Earls, is no reason for this Court to reconsider the *Vernonia*-based test we formulated in *In the Interest of F.B.*

In In the Interest of F.B., this Court adopted an approach based upon *Vernonia*; we did not adopt the very different, hands-off approach later articulated in *Earls*. *See Earls*, 536 U.S. at 845, 122 S. Ct. at 2573 (Ginsburg, J., dissenting) ("Had the Vernonia Court agreed that public school attendance, in and of itself, permitted the State to test each student's blood or urine for drugs, the opinion in *Vernonia* could have saved many words."). Accordingly, the test articulated in *In the Interest of F.B.* controls our query under Article I, Section 8.

In the Interest of F.B. considered a search of all students entering a public high school for weapons. All students were required to pass through a stationary metal detector with the potential for a follow-up scan of their bodies with a hand-held metal detector. In addition, the students' book bags, purses and coats were physically inspected, and each student was required to empty his or her pockets for examination. Looking to the students' privacy interest, we found that "the search of a person always involves a greater degree of intrusion upon one's privacy interest than the search of a thing." *Id.* (citing *Commonwealth v. Martin*, 534 Pa. 136, 626 A.2d 556 (Pa. 1993)). Turning to the nature of the intrusion, we found the intrusion to be minimal given that the search was non-invasive; indeed, it was no different from the intrusion experienced by air travelers and those seeking to enter government buildings, where metal detectors, hand-held scanners and x-ray machines are routinely employed. The third factor, notice, weighed in favor of upholding the search, because the school's policy manual contained information regarding point-of-entry weapons searches and notices were routinely mailed to students' homes and were posted prominently in the school building. As to the fourth factor, this Court noted that the need to ban weapons entirely from the school environment is "obvious" and there was no "logical argument" in opposition to such a policy.

Also instructive in this area is this Court's earlier plurality decision in *Commonwealth v. Cass*, 551 Pa. 25, 709 A.2d 350 (Pa. 1998). There, we approved of a general and suspicionless search of all student lockers for evidence of drug use. Key factors present in Cass included that: there was evidence of a specific and increasing drug problem in the school to which officials were responding; it was reasonable for those officials to believe that evidence of drug use could be found in some student lockers; the general "search" consisted of a trained canine sniffing the lockers; a canine search of the outside of a school-owned locker is not intrusive; all lockers were subject to the canine sniff, not just a select few; students were forewarned of the possibility of locker searches; the students had only a limited expectation of privacy in the school-owned lockers; and searches of the interior of the lockers occurred only if there was particularized suspicion, i.e., the canine alerted to drugs at the locker. 709 A.2d at 361-62.

With the teaching of *Cass, In the Interest of F.B.*, and *Vernonia* in mind, we have no doubt that Policy 227 cannot survive an Article I, Section 8 challenge on its face, so as to presently entitle the District to a demurrer. First, since the students' privacy rights here—rights which were rather summarily dismissed by Earls—have greater meaning under Article I, Section 8, the testing authorized by the District cannot be viewed as a trivial incursion on privacy. While students' privacy expectations are lessened by virtue of their presence at school, students may reasonably anticipate that the privacy associated with their excretory functions will be diminished at school only modestly via the need to use public restrooms. Thus, it is significant that the District here has elected not merely to conduct searches of student lockers, clothing, or personal belongings, as in *Cass* and *In the Interest of F.B.,* but seeks bodily fluids as well as an ensuing chemical analysis of the sample obtained.

. . . . .

Turning to the third factor, although the timing of the tests were deliberately made unknowable to the students, the District provided general notice by providing copies of the policy and requiring signatures of parents and students on a contract prior to the students' involvement in any extracurricular activity or obtaining a parking permit.

We are left then with a final consideration of the reasons the District enacted the policy and the efficacy and reasonableness of the policy in furthering the purpose identified. Any analysis of efficacy obviously must include an inquiry into the reasonableness of selecting only the targeted students for testing.

In forwarding its preliminary objection here, the District did not suggest that there is a specialized need to test for drugs and alcohol because of an existing drug or alcohol problem in the District, much less a problem that is particular to the targeted students. As to other extracurricular participants, however, the only explanation given is that those participants, like athletes and drivers, are "student leaders and, as such, serve as role models for their peers." These students, it appears, have been selected for testing for symbolic purposes—i.e., their privacy rights are deemed forfeit so as to set an example for other students.

The compelling need to combat and deter drug use among students is obvious, and the District's desire to take action in that regard is certainly understandable, particularly in light of the school's duty to maintain a safe, appropriate environment for learning. The tragic fact that there is a continuing drug problem among certain youth in America certainly justifies some responsive measures in public schools. However, we agree with the *Commonwealth* Court plurality and concurrence below that the means chosen by this District to effectuate that general policy are unreasonable given the heightened protection of privacy under the Pennsylvania Constitution.

This case has been presented procedurally to this Court on preliminary objections. The District at this stage of the matter has offered no reason to believe that a drug problem actually exists in its schools, much less that the means chosen to address any latent drug problem would actually tend to address that problem, rather than simply coerce those students who would have the most to lose if they violated or challenged the policy. This case thus stands in stark contrast to *Vernonia.* Policy 227 was not adopted by a school district at its "wit's end" as a last-ditch effort to address a pervasive and disruptive "drug culture" which other, lesser measures had failed to eradicate. To the contrary, the most that the District proffered was "publicity" in the form of a local newspaper article reporting on a single, $3 drug sale that took place at the Delaware Valley High School in the past year—an article that does not address whether the students involved were athletes, drivers, or participants in extracurricular activities.

. . . . .

Were the suspicionless drug and alcohol testing in this case confined to student- athletes and students with driving/parking privileges, the question obviously would be closer. Policy 227, however, captures students involved in all extracurricular activities. Students in the band, chess club, drama club, or academic clubs simply do not pose the same sort of danger to themselves or others.

. . . . .

In short, Policy 227 cannot be deemed constitutional on its face because it authorizes a direct invasion of student privacy, with no suspicion at all that the students targeted are involved with alcohol or drugs, or even that they are more likely to be involved than the students who are exempted from the policy. The policy stands in stark contrast to the policy approved in *Vernonia*, where a drug culture led by the targeted student- athletes, who already had a lesser expectation of privacy, was proven to exist in the school.

.....

On the current state of this record, the suspicionless search policy at issue has not been supported by sufficient proof that there is an actual drug problem in the Delaware Valley School District; by individualized proof that the targeted students are at all likely to be part of whatever drug problem may (or may not) exist; or by reasonable proof that the policy actually addresses whatever drug problem may exist. Because the policy is not so supported, we hold that the *Commonwealth* Court correctly reinstated the complaint filed on behalf of the affected students.

Notes and Comments

1. Lower Courts, Educators' Authority, and Suspicionless Searches
After *Acton* and *Earls*, litigation over suspicionless search policies has not resulted in a rubber stamp in favor of public educators. The validity of a student search still depends on the reasonableness, under all the circumstances, of the search. And there is a presumption of validity for a suspicionless search policy that is implemented in good faith for the purpose of safety and security. However, lower courts still struggle with these cases.

Lower courts have developed a rigorous rule of thumb to invalidate search policies by educators that appear to be tacit law enforcement operations or criminal investigations rather than centered on school discipline and order. See *Doe v. Little Rock Sch. Dist.*, 380 F.3d 349 (8th Cir. Ark. 2004) (targeted searches for evidence of illegal activity require individualized suspicion). See also, *In re T.A.S.*, 713 S.E.2d 211 (N.C. Ct. App. 2011). Beyond this, there is much mishandling of suspicionless search cases by judges who do not understand the modern authority of educators as redefined by the U.S. Supreme Court.

The error in these decisions is easy to identify and explain. Policymakers need to understand this and avoid implementing policies that confuse the presumption of good faith and fair focus. When lower courts struggle, it is usually with respect to one or both of the following two elements:

(a) Ignoring the "Special Needs" Inherent in Public Schools.

A few lower courts have raised the hurdle of validity for suspicionless student search policies by requiring an empirical and specific "special need" or at least a crisis of undeniable proportion. In these decisions, individualized suspicion is seen as the standard unless educators can articulate a dire need to search the group. *Acton* and *Earls* are tolerated by these courts as decisions limited to the narrow area of extra-curricular policies. The error is a common one. It is attributable to the failure of these judges to understand the unique evolution of the "special needs" doctrine after its introduction into public education law in TLO. This error is combined with a narrow characterization of *Acton* and *Earls* to effectively remove an essential tool from school safety teams.

The possibility of this error was anticipated by the Court in *Acton* and *Earls*. In each case, the Supreme Court speaks beyond the extra-curricular facts before it. Ruling more broadly, the justices give judicial notice of a new branch of "special needs" unique to public education law where "special needs" automatically exist because the duty to protect exists. In Acton, the Court quotes TLO to announce that, ""special needs" inhere in the public school context." Acton, (515 U.S. at 653); *TLO* (469 U.S. at 339-340). Later the justices hold that, "Fourth Amendment rights . . . are different in public schools than elsewhere; the 'reasonableness' inquiry cannot disregard the schools' custodial and tutelary responsibility for children." *Acton*, 515 U.S. at 656). In *Earls*, the Court is explicit:

> We reject the Court of Appeals' novel test that "any district seeking to impose a random suspicionless drug testing policy as a condition to participation in a school activity must demonstrate that there is some identifiable drug abuse problem among a sufficient number of those subject to the testing, such that testing that group of students will actually redress its drug problem." *Earls* (536 U.S. at 836).

In other words, when, a group search is conducted in good faith for the purpose of safety and security individualized suspicion is not required. Undesirable incidents that are foreseeable, but not chronic, as well as those that are routine and disruptive, justify suspicionless searches. The need to prevent and deter the activity from taking root on campus provides the justification for the search at its inception. The critical mass of lower court decisions apply this standard because to do otherwise makes for poor logic as well as unnecessary student victimization by requiring educators to wait until a problem is deeply rooted before intervention is permitted.

(b) Second-Guessing the Subjective Intent of School Officials.

More than a few lower courts cannot resist second-guessing school officials judgment, missing the unique evolution of the "special needs" doctrine in public education law after *TLO* in three distinct ways. First, these judges ignore the special deference that should be given to local educators' and communities' decisions about what policies best serve their responsibilities as educators and protectors of campus safety. This deference has been applied by the Court as far back as *Epperson v. Arkansas*, 393 U.S. 97, 104 (1968), when the justices, while resolving a conflict over the teaching of evolution, noted: "[j]udicial interposition in the operation of the public school system of the Nation raises problems requiring care and restraint...By and large, public education in our Nation is committed to the control of state and local authorities." Since, Epperson, the Court have confirmed a position of deference to school policies in the absence of proof of bad-faith in light of clearly established law. See *Bethel School Dist. No. 403 v. Fraser*, (478 U.S. 675, 685 (1986)). *Hazelwood School District v. Kuhlmeier*, (484 U.S. 260, 266 (1988)). *Grutter v. Bollinger*, (539 U.S. 306, 328 (2003)). The Fourth Amendment is now a part of this relaxed standard of judicial review. In Acton, the Court applies it with little fanfare, upholding the drug testing policy because the "relevant question is whether the search is one that a reasonable guardian and tutor might undertake." *Acton*, (515 U.S. at 665). Many lower court judges, less familiar with education law, bring a more rigorous level of judicial review to the analysis.

Second, lower courts refuse to credit the subjective intentions of educators, missing the shift in application of the Fourth Amendment in the "special needs" context. Outside of this context, Fourth Amendment reasonableness is an objective inquiry in which courts ask whether the circumstances, viewed objectively, justify conduct of the government official. See, *Scott v. United States*, 436 U.S. 128, 138 (1978)). Valid policies are deemed reasonable without regard for the subjective intent motivating the government official. See, *Whren v. United States*, 517 U.S. 806, 814 (1996)). In other words, outside of the "special needs" context, the Fourth Amendment regulates conduct rather than intention. See, Bond v. United States, 529 U.S. 334, 338, n. 2 (2000)). However, the "special needs" cases are dispositive exceptions to this rule. Therefore, in suspicionless search cases the actual intent of educators matter to the outcome, for example, the intent to deter drug use in public schools. See, Acton (515 U.S. at 653). In the absence of an abuse of discretion, judicial second-guessing is not appropriate. In pubic education law, the standard for an abuse of discretion is a high one:

> An abuse of discretion is not merely an error of judgment, but if in reaching a conclusion, the law is overridden or misapplied, or the judgment exercised is manifestly unreasonable, or the result of partiality, prejudice, bias or ill will, as shown by the evidence of record, discretion is abused."

Parents United for Better Schools v. Board of Education, 148 F.3d 260 (3rd Cir. 1998).

(c) Applying a "Least Intrusive" Search Requirement.

The third way courts err is merely an object lesson of the preceding two. Courts err in invalidating suspicionless search policies by pointing to a host of alternative ways in which educators might have acted without intruding on student's Fourth Amendment rights. The U.S. Supreme Court has repeatedly refused to declare that only "the 'least intrusive' search practicable can be reasonable under the Fourth Amendment." *Acton*, (515 U.S. at 663). See also *Earls*, (536 U.S. at 837). This is especially discouraged in the "special needs" context because, "judges engaged in post hoc evaluations of government conduct can almost always imagine some alternative means by which the objectives of the government might have been accomplished," *Skinner v. Railway Labor Executives' Ass'n*, (489 U.S. 602, 629 (1989)). Therefore, even when there are ways that school officials could have performed a search in a more selective or less intrusive manner, it does not mean that the school policy is invalid. When a suspicionless search is motivated by a legitimate school safety purpose, and not excessive in scope, the search carries a presumption of validity. Lower courts err by holding to the contrary.

2. Test your "Suspicionless Search IQ" on the following scenarios:

A. The local public high school conducts frequent "point of entry searches" to prevent weapons and drugs. The search policy is in the manual of the School District and notices are posted throughout the school and mailed home. All students are required to stand in line before a table and empty their pockets while their backpacks and coats are searched. The students are each scanned by a hand-held metal detector before being permitted to enter the school. The actual searches are conducted by SROs. Will students win a lawsuit brought against the school for an illegal suspicionless search?

B. A student at a public high school, was observed by an SRO returning to campus in the middle of the school day. The student had been absent from his period 1 and 2 classes, present for his period 3 class, and then absent from his period 4 class. The high school searches students who leave campus and then return during the school day. The policy is in the behavior code section of the student handbook. The purpose of the rule is to keep students from bringing contraband onto campus. The assistant principal called the student to his office and asked him to empty his pockets, finding a plastic bag containing 44 pills of Ecstasy. Should the court grant the student's motion to suppress evidence obtained as a result of the search?

C. Tiffy and other students at her Middle School ate pizza for lunch in the school cafeteria. One of the cafeteria workers was unable to find a knife that was used to cut the pizza. The missing knife was approximately 13 1/2 inches long and had a nine inch serrated metal blade. When educators could not locate it, they asked any student who knew of its whereabouts to come forward. In the absence of any response, the SRO was asked to conduct a pat-down search of the students present in the cafeteria. The male SRO patted down the male students while the female assistant principal patted down the female students. The knife was not found. Will Tiffy win a lawsuit brought against the school for an illegal suspicionless search?

D. Mortimer's high school has a practice of regularly conducting searches of randomly selected classrooms. One day Mortimer, along with his classmate, were ordered to leave the classroom after removing everything from their pockets and placing all of their belongings, including their backpacks and purses, on the desks in front of them. While the students were in the hall outside their classroom, the SRO and other school officials searched the items that the students had left behind, including Mortimer's bookbag, and they discovered marijuana in a container in his bag. The parties have stipulated that the school has a practice of regularly conducting searches of randomly selected classrooms in this manner. Should the court grant the student's motion to suppress evidence obtained as a result of the search?

E. A public school has a policy that, "a drug detection dog may be used to sniff backpacks, book bags, gym bags, purses or other similar items, when such items are not in the physical possession of a student or person." One day, educators asked the SRO to bring a canine unit to assist with drug detection in a classroom. The SRO waited while the students were taken to the opposite end of the third-floor hallway. The SRO walked the dog down the aisles between the desks. The canine alerted to a backpack. The SRO examined the bag and found a plastic bag containing marijuana. Should the court grant the student's motion to suppress evidence obtained as a result of the search?

E. Student Privacy at Institutions of Higher Education

As the litigation of drug testing in high school athletic programs was settling down, litigation challenging the constitutionality of these testing schemes in higher education became a major issue. There is considerable confusion regarding drug testing of students in higher education. Much of the confusion stems from the legal decisions involving college athletes who are increasingly drug tested as a condition for eligibility in NCAA regulated sports.

The NCAA is deemed a private entity. *In National Collegiate Athletic Ass'n v. Tarkanian*, 488 U.S. 179 (1988), the Court held that the NCAA is not a government actor for purposes of the individual rights guaranteed by the Constitution. The Court concluded that Coach Tarkanian's employer (the University Nevada Las Vegas), a state institution was the proper defendant in the case.

> [A]lthough, Nevada had some impact on the NCAA's policy determinations…the NCAA's several hundred other public and private member institutions each similarly affected those policies. Those institutions, the vast majority of which were located in States other than Nevada, did not act under color of Nevada law. It necessarily follows that the source of the legislation adopted by the NCAA is not Nevada but the collective membership, speaking through an organization that is independent of any particular State. 488 U.S. at 193.

Thus, the NCAA is beyond the reach of the Fourth amendment rules. [Note: courts have uniformly held K-12 athletic associations to be state actors. *See Brentwood Academy v. Tennessee Secondary Sch. Ath. Ass'n*, 531 U.S. 288 (2001)]. In addition, the NCAA does not receive federal funding of any kind and is thus beyond the reach of statutory privacy protections. Therefore, the NCAA can regulate with a sort of impunity leaving state institutions to fight it out with their institutions over the legal issues.

Athletes are clearly stuck in the middle with their interests. They must submit to testing by the NCAA if they wish to continue competing at the highest level of skill and exposure. Their institutions, likewise, must continue testing their athletes to participate in NCAA sanctioned events.

Adding to this confusion is the decision in *Hill v. Nat'l Collegiate Athletic Ass'n*, 865 P.2d 633 (Cal. 1994) that held that the NCAA's testing policies do not violate the right to privacy. In *Hill*, the California Supreme Court applied the state constitution and its right to privacy (which applies to both public and private actors). The court upheld the NCAA testing program.

[T]he NCAA's decision to enforce a ban on the use of drugs by means of a drug testing program is reasonably calculated to further its legitimate interest in maintaining the integrity of intercollegiate athletic competition…. The NCAA also has an interest in protecting the health and safety of student athletes who are involved in NCAA-regulated competition…. If athletic drug use became widespread because of a growing perception that drug users thereby obtained a "competitive edge," the integrity and reputation of NCAA athletic competition could be seriously threatened. The

NCAA is not required by state constitutional privacy principles to stay its hand until a "minor" problem becomes a "major" one." 865 P.2d at 660-62.

The Supreme Court of the Colorado addresses the issue in the leading case on the question.

University of Colorado v. Derdeyn
863 P.2d 929 (Colo. 1993)

Opinion By: Lohr

We granted certiorari in order to determine whether random, suspicionless urinalysis-drug-testing of intercollegiate student athletes by the University of Colorado, Boulder (CU), violates the Fourth Amendment to the United States Constitution or Article II, Section 7, of the Colorado Constitution. Following a bench trial conducted in August of 1989 in which a class of current and prospective CU athletes challenged the constitutionality of CU's drug-testing program, the Boulder County District Court permanently enjoined CU from continuing its program. The trial court found that CU had not obtained voluntary consent from its athletes for such testing, and it declared such testing unconstitutional under both the federal and state constitutions. The Colorado Court of Appeals generally affirmed. We agree with the court of appeals, that in the absence of voluntary consents, CU's random, suspicionless urinalysis-drug-testing of student athletes violates the Fourth Amendment to the United States Constitution and Article II, Section 7, of the Colorado Constitution. We further agree that the record supports the finding of the trial court that CU failed to show that consents to such testing given by CU's athletes are voluntary for the purposes of those same constitutional provisions. Accordingly, we affirm the judgment of the court of appeals.

……

CU began a drug-testing program in the fall of 1984 for its intercollegiate student athletes. CU has since amended its program in various ways, but throughout the existence of the program participation was mandatory in the sense that if an athlete did not sign a form consenting to random urinalysis pursuant to the program, the student was prohibited from participating in intercollegiate athletics at CU.[3]

CU's drug-testing program originally required a urine test for certain proscribed drugs at each intercollegiate athlete's annual physical and also required random urine tests thereafter. Counseling was mandated following a first positive result.[4] The penalty for a second positive included a seven-

---

[3] In written descriptions, CU itself has always characterized its drug-testing program as "a mandatory program of drug education, testing, and counseling/rehabilitation."

[4] The proscribed drugs as specified by CU in its 1984 form entitled "UNIVERSITY OF COLORADO INTERCOLLEGIATE ATHLETICS DRUG EDUCATION PROGRAM" (the 1984 Form) were amphetamines, barbiturates, cocaine, methaqualudes, opiates, morphine, codeine, PCP (angel dust) and analogues, and tetrahydrocannabinol (THC or marijuana).

day suspension from participation in intercollegiate athletics, and the penalty for a third positive included a minimum one-year suspension. No specific monitoring procedures were prescribed for the collection of the urine samples, and two students testified that during this phase of the program they were not monitored during the act of urination. According to CU's 1984 Form describing the program, all test results were sent to the "Team Physician." The intercollegiate student athletes also were required to give their consent to releasing test results to the Head Athletic Trainer at [CU]; my parent(s) or legal guardian(s) or spouse; the head coach of any intercollegiate sport in which I am a team member; the Athletic Director of [CU]; and the Drug Counseling Program at the Wardenburg Student Health Center.

The 1984 Form gave no general or specific assurances of confidentiality.

Sometime thereafter, CU amended its program for the first time. The penalty for a first positive was changed to include suspension for "the current competitive season," and the penalty for a second positive was changed to include permanent suspension from "any activity sponsored by the University of Colorado Athletic Department." Following a first positive, the athlete was also required success fully to complete a substance abuse rehabilitation program as a condition for further participation in intercollegiate athletics. The first amended program also provided that the "collection of the specimen will be observed [sic], and the athlete may be asked to disrobe in order to protect the integrity of the testing procedure."[8] Test results were still sent to the "Team Physician," but following a first positive, the first amended program stated:

> The Team Physician will inform the Head Athletic Trainer. The Head Athletic Trainer will advise the Athletic Director. The Athletic Director will notify the athlete's Head Coach(es). Additionally, the athlete will be required to . . . participate in a conference telephone call between the athlete, his/her parent(s) or legal guardian(s) of the positive test results.

CU still gave no general or specific assurances of confidentiality of test results.

---

[8] One male student athlete testified that during this phase of the program the trainer would hand you a bottle, a screw cap bottle and you and the trainer would adjourn to a restroom where the trainer would physically observe you filling up the bottle with your urine.......

I mean that the trainer would actually watch you urinate, you weren't allowed to turn your back, talking about full frontal exposure of your body.

A female student athlete testified:

Some female trainer had to be in the restroom watching you, in the actual stall watching you while you went to the bathroom.

Another female student athlete testified:

That is what we called it, after a while, "the pee team". You kind of got flippant about it after a while because it was so embarrassing and everybody had to do it so we made jokes about it so that, you know, it wouldn't be as bad. Then, you would go into the bathroom with one of the trainers because at that time the training room was in the track office so you got one of the trainers and you went to the bathroom and she gave you a coke cup and you peed in the cup with the door open so she could watch and then you take your urine sample and you pour it in the bottle and screw the bottle up and she writes your number or whatever on it and then takes it away.

CU's second amended program changed the penalty for a first positive from suspension for "the current competitive season," to suspension for "a twelve month period." In all other relevant respects the program remained unaltered.

CU's third amended program, which became effective August 14, 1988, contained numerous changes. First, it added alcohol, "over-the-counter drugs," and "performance-enhancing substances such as anabolic steroids" to the list of drugs for which students could be tested. Second, the term "athlete" was defined to include "all student participants in recognized intercollegiate sports, including but not limited to student athletes, cheerleaders, student trainers and student managers." Third, random "rapid eye examination (REE)" testing was substituted for random urinalysis, and a urinalysis was performed only after a "finding of reasonable suspicion that an athlete has used drugs," and at the athlete's annual physical examination. Failure to perform adequately on an REE was considered "prima facie reasonable suspicion of drug use [except with regard to steroids]," and the student was required to provide a urine specimen for testing purposes if the student did not perform adequately on the REE. In addition, if a student exhibited "physical or behavioral characteristics indicating drug use including, but not limited to: tardiness, absenteeism, poor heath [sic] habits, emotional swings, unexplained performance changes, and/or excessive aggressiveness," this was also considered reasonable suspicion of drug use, and the student was required to take a urine test. Fourth, urine samples were to be collected "within the Athletic Department facilities," and athletes were "directed to provide a urine specimen in a private and enclosed area" while a monitor remained outside. The monitor would then receive "the sample from the athlete and check [] the sample for appropriate color, temperature, specific gravity and other properties to determine that no substitution or tampering has occurred." Fifth, the athletes were required to give their consent to releasing test results to the Head Athletic Trainer at [CU]; my parent(s) or legal guardian(s), if I am under the age of 21; the head coach of any intercollegiate sport in which I am a team member; the Athletic Director of [CU]; my work supervisor (if applicable) and the Drug Counseling Program at the Wardenburg Student Health Center.

Finally, although CU still gave no general assurances of confidentiality, it did specify in its third amended program that communications between an athlete and physicians at Wardenburg Student Health Center would be confidential.

……

The Fourth Amendment to the United States Constitution protects individuals from unreasonable searches conducted by the government, even when the government acts as the administrator of an athletic program in a state school or university. *See Schaill ex rel. Kross v. Tippecanoe County Sch. Corp.*, 864 F.2d 1309 (7th Cir. 1989); *Brooks v. East Chambers Consol. Indep. Sch. Dist.*, 730 F. Supp. 759 (S.D. Tex. 1989); *cf. New Jersey v. T.L.O.*, 469 U.S. 325, 333-37 (1985). Furthermore, expectations of privacy that society has long recognized as reasonable . . . these intrusions must be deemed searches under the Fourth Amendment. *Skinner*, 489 U.S. at 617. It follows that CU's urinalysis-drug-testing program must meet the reasonableness requirement of the Fourth Amendment.

It is clear that CU's drug-testing program is not designed to serve the ordinary needs of law enforcement. We must therefore balance individual student athletes' privacy expectations against

CU's governmental interests to determine whether CU's random, warrantless, suspicionless urinalysis-drug-testing program is unreasonable under the Fourth Amendment.

.....

A

CU argues that its drug-testing program is reasonable under the Fourth Amendment because of the student athletes' diminished expectations of privacy and the compelling governmental interests served by the program. We therefore consider in turn (1) the degree to which CU's drug-testing program intrudes on the reasonable expectations of privacy of student athletes and (2) the magnitude of the governmental interests served by the program. We then balance these factors in order to determine whether CU's drug-testing program is reasonable under the Fourth Amendment.

Although nonvoluntary, random, suspicionless urinalysis-drug-testing by the government always intrudes on an individual's Fourth Amendment privacy interests, the magnitude of that intrusion can vary from context to context. .... Specifically, CU asserts that (a) collection of the urine sample in a closed stall with aural monitoring minimizes any intrusion. CU also asserts that student athletes' expectations of privacy with regard to urinalysis are diminished because (b) they routinely give urine samples as part of annual, general medical examinations; because (c) they submit to extensive regulation of their on- and off-campus behavior, including maintenance of required levels of academic performance, monitoring of course selection, training rules, mandatory practice sessions, diet restrictions, attendance at study halls, curfews, and prohibitions on alcohol and drug use; because (d) they must submit to the NCAA's random urinalysis-drug-testing program as a condition of participating in NCAA competition; because (e) the consequences of refusing to provide a urine sample are not severe; and because (f) positive test results are confidential and are not used for the purposes of criminal law enforcement.

.....

We are unaware of any case that holds that the determination of the magnitude of the intrusion of a drug-testing program on the privacy interests of individuals is a factual issue for the trial court to which appellate courts must defer. On the other hand, such a determination, while not a pure question of fact, is certainly one that is dependent upon many facts that can vary from case to case, and therefore a trial court is especially well positioned to assess the magnitude of an intrusion of a drug-testing program on the reasonable privacy expectations of an individual. We therefore owe respectful attention to the trial court's findings and conclusions in this case, and its findings and conclusions in no way support CU's assertion that its drug-testing program does not significantly intrude on the privacy interests of intercollegiate student athletes.

Second, it cannot be said that university students, simply because they are university students, are entitled to less protection than other persons under the Fourth Amendment. *See Morale v. Grigel*, 422 F. Supp. 988, 997, 998 (D.N.H. 1976) (stating that a " college cannot, in this day and age, protect students under the aegis of in loco parentis authority from the rigors of society's rules and laws, just as it cannot, under the same aegis, deprive students of their constitutional rights," and holding that a warrantless search of a student's dormitory room for stolen goods violated the Fourth Amendment even though the purpose of the search was not to obtain criminal evidence); *Collier v. Miller*, 414 F. Supp. 1357, 1359, 1367, 1367 n.11 (S.D. Tex. 1976) (holding unconstitutional a random search, without probable cause, of a Houston University student's purse for alcoholic beverages, bottles, or weapons, as she entered a university pavilion for a rock concert, and explaining that "the defendants do not argue in their brief that a different Fourth Amendment standard should apply to schools, nor would this Court find such an argument meritorious."); *Smyth v. Lubbers*, 398 F. Supp. 777, 786 (W.D. Mich. 1975) (holding that adult college students have the same interest in the privacy of their rooms as any adult has in the privacy of his home); ...We therefore find of only marginal relevance holdings by other courts that high school student athletes have a diminished expectation of privacy under the Fourth Amendment.

.....

Continuation of such scholarships at CU is dependent upon continued participation in the intercollegiate athletic program, which in turn requires consent to the drug-testing program. Furthermore, many intercollegiate athletes pursue professional careers as high school or college coaches, or as administrators in athletic or recreational programs. Thus, for example, one student athlete who graduated from CU by the time of the trial testified that she worked as a track coach at CU. Another testified that she just recently obtained employment coaching girls' volleyball and basketball at a local high school. While having participated in intercollegiate athletics may not be a formal requirement for such jobs, it is commonplace that applicants with experience at the intercollegiate athletic level will not be disadvantaged in seeking such jobs in comparison with those who lack such experience. Also, we recognize that for many student athletes, participation in intercollegiate athletics is an activity highly valued for its own sake. We therefore believe that the consequences of not being able to participate in intercollegiate athletics must be accorded significant weight.

.....

We have not been persuaded that CU's athletes have a greatly diminished expectation of privacy, nor are we persuaded that CU's program is not significantly intrusive. In addition, we question whether some of the interests asserted by CU are even significant for Fourth Amendment purposes. For example, although the integrity of its athletic program is, like all the other interests asserted by CU, a valid and commendable one, it does not seem to be very significant for Fourth Amendment purposes........... Similarly, although the promotion of fair competition builds character in athletes and enhances the entertainment value of athletic events, CU does not explain why the promotion of fair competition is itself an important governmental interest, just as it does not explain why preventing the disqualification of its athletes at sporting events is an important governmental interest.

We therefore hold, based on a balancing of the privacy interests of the student athletes and the governmental interests of CU, that CU's drug-testing program is unconstitutional under the Fourth Amendment. More specifically, we hold that random, suspicionless urinalysis-drug-testing by CU of student athletes is unconstitutional under the Fourth Amendment if that testing is conducted according to the procedures utilized in any of CU's drug-testing programs to the date of trial, or if that testing is conducted in a manner substantially similar to any of the procedures utilized in any of CU's drug-testing programs to the date of trial. Furthermore, because the Colorado Constitution provides at least as much protection from unreasonable searches and seizures as does the Fourth Amendment, CU's drug-testing program is also unconstitutional under Article II, Section 7, of the Colorado Constitution.

II. Faculty, Staff and the Fourth Amendment

HEARN v. BOARD OF PUBLIC EDUCATION

191 F.3d 1329 (11th Cir. 1999)

HILL, Senior Circuit Judge:

I.

Sherry Hearn was a teacher in Savannah for many years. She was employed under a contract which required that she abide by the policies of the Board of Education of Chatham County (Board).

In 1992, the county enacted its "Safe School Plan" which called for "zero-tolerance" of drugs, alcohol and weapons. ….In April of 1996, campus and Chatham County, Georgia police conducted a "drug lockdown" and random drug search at Hearn's high school in Savannah. Hearn's car was in the school's rear parking lot, unlocked and with its passenger side window down.

The Chatham County deputy's drug-sniffing dog alerted at Hearn's vehicle. The deputy let the dog enter the car through the passenger window. The dog alerted on the vehicle's closed ashtray. A campus officer opened it and found a partially burned, hand-rolled cigarette. He testified that he field-tested it for marijuana, and it tested positive. The officers noticed the faculty parking permit on the dash and took it with them.

The officers went to the school's principal, Linda Herman, and informed her of these events. She summoned Hearn, who denied knowledge or possession of any marijuana. One of the County's officers "Mirandized" Hearn, telling her that she probably would be charged with criminal possession of marijuana.

Herman informed Hearn that, under [District policy], she must take a urinalysis drug test within two hours. Hearn refused. Herman gave Hearn a warning letter which directed her to take the drug test. The letter stated:

> In the course of a drug search, a substance [found to have tested positive for cannabinoid] was found in your personal vehicle.… Based on this finding, in compliance with BOE Policy 766—Drug Free Workplace, you are hereby directed

> to submit to a drug test for reasonable suspicion within [the two-hour limit]. Your failure to comply may result in disciplinary action.

Hearn, however, continued to refuse to take the drug test.

Later, the Superintendent of Schools for Chatham County suspended her. He recommended that she be terminated for "insubordination" and "other good and sufficient cause" as the result of her failure to consent to take the drug test within the prescribed two hour period……The Board provided Hearn with a hearing. She appeared with counsel and testified. At the end of the hearing, the Board made no findings of fact, but voted to accept the superintendent's recommendation and terminated Hearn. Hearn appealed to the State Board of Education, which issued a written opinion upholding the Board.

II.

Hearn's termination was for insubordination—her refusal to take the drug test within the prescribed two hour period. She argues that she cannot be terminated for her refusal because she was under no obligation to take the drug test. She was not obliged to take the test because there was no "reasonable suspicion" as required by the Board's policy prior to directing an employee to take the test. There was no reasonable suspicion because the search of her car was illegal under both the Board's own policy which requires an employee's consent or a search warrant in order to search an employee's personal property at school, and under the Fourth Amendment. We find no merit in either of these contentions.

……..

Reasonable suspicion arose in the context of a drug sweep of a parking lot by local law enforcement officers whose dog alerted at Hearn's car—a law enforcement event. Neither the Board's policy nor Hearn's contract of employment trumps the legal authority of law enforcement officers to perform such a sweep or the subsequent search. The officers' authority is limited only by the Constitution.

Hearn implicitly recognizes this distinction. …Her argument is that since a campus police officer actually found the marijuana, the Board's policy governed his search and it should not have been conducted without her consent. Because the search was without her consent, no reasonable suspicion could arise from it and she was not required to consent to the drug test.

We find no basis in the law or in the real world to distinguish two legally distinct events in the one sweep and search. Merely because a campus police officer was present during the sweep and happened to be the one to find the marijuana does not change the fact that this was a law enforcement event, not bound by any school policy or employment contract. Even if, as Hearn argues, the Board's policy gave employee's a heightened expectation of privacy with regard to their personal property at school, that expectation does not bind local law enforcement. They are not parties to the contract. Whatever expectation of privacy Hearn had in her vehicle during a law enforcement event must be located in constitutional law, not local school board policies.

Second, the Constitution does not provide Hearn with any expectation of privacy in the odors emanating from her car. A dog sniff of a person's property located in a public place is not a search within the meaning of the Fourth Amendment. *United States v. Place*, 462 U.S. 696 (1983); *Merrett v. Moore*, 58 F.3d 1547 (11th Cir.1995); *United States v. Seals*, 987 F.2d 1102 (5th Cir.1993); *United States v. Morales-Zamora*, 914 F.2d 200 (10th Cir.1990); *United States v. Rodriguez-Morales*, 929 F.2d 780 (1st Cir. 1991).... Furthermore, the alerting of a drug-sniffing dog to a person's property supplies not only reasonable suspicion, but probable cause to search that property.

Thus, there was a reasonable suspicion generated by these circumstances regarding Hearn's possible drug use. At this point, the Board's policy was triggered. Hearn's refusal to give her consent to Board's request for a drug test gave rise to the possibility of her termination under that policy. Her subsequent termination, therefore, did not violate neither her contract of employment nor the Board's policy, and she is not due to be reinstated for these reasons.

......

III.

Hearn's contract with the Board does not vitiate the authority of the law enforcement officers to search her car under the circumstances of this case. Nor were any of Hearn's constitutional rights violated. Accordingly, the judgment of the district court is AFFIRMED.

FERGUSON, District Judge, dissenting:

I respectfully dissent.

It is important to note at the outset that this highly publicized case does not arise from a criminal proceeding. For that reason, in my opinion, the majority's scholarly discussion of probable cause is not dispositive on the questions presented. Central to one of the causes of action is whether reasonable suspicion as a basis for the termination of a teacher's employment was obtained in violation of an employment agreement.

There was no police detention or arrest; no law enforcement report of a crime; no probable cause affidavit filed; and no magistrate determination of probable cause. What is shown by undisputed facts is that a school security officer, assisted by a city police canine officer who had been invited to assist the school in enforcement of its anti-drug policy, conducted a sweep search within the walls of a high school campus. During a walk through the student parking lot the dog alerted to the presence of a controlled substance outside the plaintiff's vehicle. ... Purportedly the cigarette remnant field tested positive for marijuana. All of these events occurred before noon in the student lot where the vehicle was parked, unlocked and with the windows down. The substance was turned over to police and consumed during a police laboratory analysis. It was argued by counsel for Mrs. Hearns, and not disputed, that she was with her class at all times during the morning hours.

We may only speculate as to why no criminal action was taken. … Notwithstanding the reason it is clear that after the substance was seized by the school board, law enforcement officials totally distanced themselves from any further involvement in the case.

This is a simple civil case based on administrative action where the plaintiff alleges among other things, that the defendant, her employer, breached an employment agreement which had been hammered out to control the conduct of the parties in exactly the situation presented here. The contract provides that faculty and administrators are insulated from searches of their desks, personal items or vehicles by school personnel except with the prior consent of the employee, which consent shall not be withheld where there is reasonable suspicion to believe that the employee has violated a policy, regulation or criminal law.

……

Abandoning its earlier position, the Board does not argue here that the contract permits it to search without consent where the Administration has a suspicion that an employee has violated its drug policy. … The new theories advanced by the Board, in defense to this federal lawsuit, are that the finding of reasonable suspicion is untainted because the dog's alert outside the vehicle, without the search, was sufficient to justify the administrative action, or no warrant was needed for an intrusive search because a local law enforcement officer was present. Neither theory was advanced by the Board during administrative proceedings and cannot be reconciled with the facts. Mrs. Hearn's injury resulted from an administrative action, which was governed by Board policy, unrelated to anything that could have been done in a criminal action. The local police officer did no more than bring a drug detection dog to the campus. He was then directed by the school board officer.

……

[T]here are relevant factors beyond principles of contract law which have chilling ramifications. The plaintiff had been very critical of the School Board's policy of campus lock down searches for drugs which she likened to police state tactics. Because of her classroom criticism of the practice as unconstitutional, she was not in favor with the employer. Expectations of privacy guaranteed by the policy were ignored and the penalty imposed was the professional equivalent of the death penalty. The twenty-seven (27) year stellar career of a 1994 "Teacher of the Year" is shattered with only three (3) years remaining to retirement with benefits.

Unquestionably the plaintiff's termination from employment as a teacher for not submitting to a drug test was an "intra school event". On the collateral point, whether the search for and seizure of contraband from the interior of the plaintiff's vehicle by a school board officer was a "law enforcement event", presents at least an issue of fact.

In my view this fact-driven case should go to a jury.

Friedenberg v. School Board of Palm Beach County
911 F.3d 1084 (11th Cir. 2018)

Marcus, Circuit Judge:

A suspicionless search by the government is presumptively unconstitutional. So goes the basic hornbook law of the Fourth Amendment. The details are a bit more complex. Suspicionless searches are permissible in a narrow band of cases where they serve sufficiently powerful and unique public needs. The force of these needs depends heavily on the context in which the search takes place.

At issue today is a matter of first impression—whether a county school board may require all applicants for substitute teacher positions to submit to and pass a drug test as a condition of employment. That is, to put it more directly, whether the Palm Beach County School Board (the "School Board") may, without any suspicion of wrongdoing, collect and search—by testing—the urine of all prospective substitute teachers. We think that the School Board has a sufficiently compelling interest in screening its prospective teachers to justify this invasion of the privacy rights of job applicants, and thus conclude that the School Board has not violated the constitutional mandate barring unreasonable searches and seizures. As we see it, ensuring the safety of millions of schoolchildren in the mandatory supervision and care of the state, and ensuring and impressing a drug-free environment in our classrooms, are compelling concerns. Because we recognize today a special need to conduct such testing, and because the balance of interests weighs heavily in its favor, we hold that the suspicionless testing of substitute teacher applicants in Palm Beach County is permissible and affirm the district court's denial of a preliminary injunction.

……

Joan Friedenberg applied for several advertised positions—tutor, substitute teacher, and early childhood aide—in the Palm Beach County School District. Among other things, the online application required Friedenberg to agree to be tested for drugs. In February 2017, Friedenberg received a conditional offer to become a substitute teacher. She was told, however, that she would need to be fingerprinted—for a full background check—and would need to pass a drug test before she could be officially hired. Friedenberg was fingerprinted but refused to submit to drug testing.

Since our constitutional analysis depends in substantial measure on the specific facts and the unique circumstances found in our public schools, we are obliged to examine closely the testing protocol adopted by the School District, the efficacy of the testing regime, and the duties and responsibilities of substitute public school teachers. The drug testing was required under the School District's "Drug and Alcohol-Free Workplace" policy, which provides for drug testing to be performed in conformity with Florida's Administrative Code. See Fla. Admin Code. R. 59A-24.005(3). The policy required, among other things, pre-employment drug testing of all job applicants. The relevant provision read this way:

Pre-employment screening will be required of all applicants before employment with the District. Any applicant who tests positive in the pre-employment screening for a drug as defined in this Policy will not be hired and is not eligible to re-apply for employment with the District for one year following the confirmed positive test.

......

Select information from the drug testing is reported to the School Board. Among other things, positive test results, including the substance or substances for which the specimen tested positive, are reported. The reports also indicate whether an individual refused testing or left the testing site. Five individuals within the School Board's Department of Risk and Benefits Management receive this information. The results are held in a "confidential electronic medical folder" and are not reported to any law enforcement official. The hiring school site or department is informed only that the applicant did not pass a medical examination. Moreover, self-disclosed information about medications is seen only by the collection staff and a review officer—a position the District outsources.

......

The typical workday of a substitute teacher in the School District includes five to six hours of classroom time, generally alone with students. Before the school day, substitute teachers check in and are seen by others, such as a school principal, in the school office; they also check out at the office at the end of the day. During the day, substitutes may be monitored by supervisors or by other teachers through classroom visits or perhaps when taking students to lunch, recess, or other locations. Substitute teachers also have a variety of safety-related responsibilities which include monitoring students for safety purposes, such as preventing or stopping fights; reporting and addressing hazards or other unsafe circumstances; detecting and promptly responding to student health issues; detecting and reporting student drug use or possession; and reporting suspected child abuse. As the Chief of the County's school district police explained, school personnel, including substitute teachers, are "on the frontlines of securing the campus and are often the first responders to any given incident."

According to the School District's Substitute Teacher Handbook, a substitute teacher's specific responsibilities include addressing student behavior and emergencies. Thus, for example, any complaint about student illness "should receive immediate attention." Student accidents must be reported immediately as well. And control of the classroom is characterized as "a primary concern." The Handbook further provides: "It is [the substitute teacher's] responsibility to discuss any limitation or restriction with the substitute contact before [the substitute teacher] begin[s] the assignment so that [the substitute teacher] will be prepared to provide safety and accountability for students in any situation and at all times." And the Handbook says that substitutes are "as legally responsible *1090 for students, equipment, and materials as is the regular teacher."

......

The Fourth Amendment protects the "right of the people to be secure in their persons ... against unreasonable searches and seizures." U.S. Const. amend. IV. Undeniably the school district's urinalysis drug tests are searches that implicate the Fourth Amendment. See, e.g., Nat'l Treasury

Emps. Union v. Von Raab, 489 U.S. 656, 665, 109 S.Ct. 1384, 103 L.Ed.2d 685 (1989). We consider whether the search is a reasonable one.

"The default rule in this context ... is that 'to be reasonable under the Fourth Amendment, a search ordinarily must be based on individualized suspicion of wrongdoing.' " AFSCME v. Scott, 717 F.3d 851, 866 (11th Cir. 2013) (quoting Chandler v. Miller, 520 U.S. 305, 313, 117 S.Ct. 1295, 137 L.Ed.2d 513 (1997)). However, "neither a warrant nor probable cause, nor, indeed, any measure of individualized suspicion, is an indispensable component of reasonableness in every circumstance." Von Raab, 489 U.S. at 665, 109 S.Ct. 1384. The Supreme Court has developed a narrow exception to the Fourth Amendment expectation of individualized suspicion where a search "serves special governmental needs." Id.; Griffin v. Wisconsin, 483 U.S. 868, 873, 107 S.Ct. 3164, 97 L.Ed.2d 709 (1987) (search made without individualized suspicion of wrongdoing can be reasonable "when special needs, beyond the normal need for law enforcement, make the warrant and probable-cause requirement impracticable" (quotation omitted)). The special need must raise a "concern[ ] other than crime detection," and in order to satisfy the Fourth Amendment, the special need must be "substantial — important enough to override the individual's acknowledged privacy interest, sufficiently vital to suppress the Fourth Amendment's normal requirement of individualized suspicion." Chandler v. Miller, 520 U.S. 305, 314, 318, 117 S.Ct. 1295, 137 L.Ed.2d 513 (1997).

When a special need is claimed, we are obliged to "undertake a context-specific inquiry, examining closely the competing private and public interests advanced by the parties." Id. at 314, 117 S.Ct. 1295. And "[i]n limited circumstances, where the privacy interests implicated by the search are minimal, and where an important governmental interest furthered by the intrusion would be placed in jeopardy by a requirement of individualized suspicion, a search may be reasonable despite the absence of such suspicion." Skinner v. Ry. Labor Execs. Ass'n, 489 U.S. 602, 624, 109 S.Ct. 1402, 103 L.Ed.2d 639 (1989). As we wrote in AFSCME v. Scott, 717 F.3d 851 (11th Cir. 2013), a " 'compelling state interest,' in the Fourth Amendment context, [does not describe] a fixed, minimum quantum of governmental concern." Id. at 717 F.3d at 867 (quotations omitted). Resolving a case like this one requires identifying what interest the government has, then measuring the weight of that interest and, eventually, balancing it against other factors.

Our consideration of the merits then is twofold. Once a plaintiff has shown that the government conducted a search without individualized suspicion—which the School Board concedes—the burden shifts to the government to establish that it has a "special need" sufficient to warrant departure from the Fourth Amendment's baseline requirement of individualized suspicion. See Id. at 880. If a special need is presented, we "undertake a context-specific inquiry, examining closely the competing private and public interests advanced by the parties to determine the reasonableness of the search." Lebron v. Sec'y, Fla. Dep't of Children & Families, 710 F.3d 1202, 1207 (11th Cir. 2013) (quotation omitted). At this balancing stage, "the ultimate burden of persuasion remains squarely on the plaintiff." AFSCME, 717 F.3d at 880. On this record, and in the unique context of public schools, we are satisfied that the School Board's testing regime as applied to substitute teacher applicants is a reasonable one, and the district court committed no abuse of discretion in denying a preliminary injunction.

III.

Neither the Supreme Court nor this Court has ever faced the question whether there is a sufficiently compelling need to justify the invasion of privacy entailed in suspicionless drug testing of public school teachers. But we are not writing on a blank slate. The Supreme Court has considered the constitutionality of suspicionless drug-testing regimes five times in the past thirty years. It has found special needs compelling enough to permit suspicionless drug testing of public school students participating in extracurricular activities and also of government employees whose work implicates public safety.

……

For our purposes, the relevant precedent begins with the Supreme Court's declaration that, for Fourth Amendment purposes, public schools are unique. In New Jersey v. T.L.O., 469 U.S. 325, 105 S.Ct. 733, 83 L.Ed.2d 720 (1985), the Court set out as a foundational principle that "[a]lthough the underlying command of the Fourth Amendment is always that searches and seizures be reasonable, what is reasonable depends on the context within which a search takes place." Id. at 337, 105 S.Ct. 733. In that case, a student had been caught smoking in a school lavatory and a school administrator had searched her purse. Id. at 328, 105 S.Ct. 733. It will come as no surprise that the administrator, an Assistant Vice Principal, had not sought or obtained a warrant before performing this search. See id. The Assistant Vice Principal was a state actor and the Fourth Amendment was applicable to this warrantless search, see id. at 336, 105 S.Ct. 733, but the Court held that the search was constitutional, Id. at 332–33, 105 S.Ct. 733.

The Court weighed the student's privacy interests against "the school's equally legitimate need to maintain an environment in which learning can take place." Id. at 340, 105 S.Ct. 733. Students had "perfectly legitimate reasons" to bring personal property to school, and to expect some level of privacy against searches of that property. See Id. at 338–39, 105 S.Ct. 733. Notwithstanding "the difficulty of maintaining discipline in the public schools," "the situation [was] not so dire" that schools would be treated, for Fourth Amendment purposes, like prisons, and students treated like prisoners who had no "legitimate expectations of privacy." Id. at 338, 105 S.Ct. 733 (noting that a prisoner's interest in privacy was negligible when compared to the government interest in preserving order in prisons) (quoting Ingraham v. Wright, 430 U.S. 651, 669, 97 S.Ct. 1401, 51 L.Ed.2d 711 (1977)). School officials, nonetheless, had a "substantial interest ... in maintaining discipline in the classroom and on school grounds." Id. at 339, 105 S.Ct. 733. To do this required "close supervision" and "the enforcement of rules against conduct that would be perfectly permissible if undertaken by an adult."

Balancing these competing values, the Court determined that the need for school administrators to preserve order tipped the scales against the student's interest in privacy. See id. at 340–43, 105 S.Ct. 733. Students would not be stripped of their privacy interests under the Fourth Amendment, but their rights would be less robust than a typical adult's right to be free from a search by a typical government agent. At the core of the Court's holding was "the need to maintain an environment in which learning [could] take place." Id. at 340, 105 S.Ct. 733. The school setting itself "require[d] some easing of the restrictions to which searches by public authorities are ordinarily subject." Id.

Going forward, the Court has taken to describing contexts, like schools, where the warrant requirement has been relaxed, as presenting "special needs." This terminology was coined by Justice Blackmun, concurring in the judgment in T.L.O., who described the school setting as among "those exceptional circumstances in which special needs, beyond the normal need for law enforcement, make the warrant and probable-cause requirement impracticable...." Id. at 351, 105 S.Ct. 733 (Blackmun, J., concurring in the judgment). Justice Blackmun's terminology was adopted by a majority of the Court in O'Connor v. Ortega, 480 U.S. 709, 107 S.Ct. 1492, 94 L.Ed.2d 714 (1987), which held that "special needs" were also present in government workplaces. Id. at 725, 107 S.Ct. 1492 (plurality opinion); id. at 732, 107 S.Ct. 1492 (Scalia, J., concurring in the judgment). There, a plurality held that public employers could conduct searches of employees' offices, desks, filing cabinets, and the like, without warrants. See id. at 725–26, 107 S.Ct. 1492 (plurality opinion). If a public employer intruded on an employee's protected privacy interest through a "legitimate work-related" search or an "investigation[ ] of work related misconduct," the employer's search "[would] be judged by the standard of reasonableness." Id. at 725, 107 S.Ct. 1492. Later that same Term, the Court found that "special needs, beyond the normal need for law enforcement" also justified reasonable, warrantless searches of a probationer's home by probation officers. See Griffin, 483 U.S. at 875–76, 107 S.Ct. 3164.

The "special needs" that justified warrantless searches in schools returned in two drug-testing cases that are highly instructive for our analysis today. In the first of these, Vernonia School District 47J v. Acton, 515 U.S. 646, 115 S.Ct. 2386, 132 L.Ed.2d 564 (1995), the Supreme Court considered suspicionless drug testing of student athletes in an Oregon public school district. The district, after observing an increase in drug use and drug-related problems among the student body, had required all students participating in school athletics to take drug tests. Id. at 649–50, 115 S.Ct. 2386. The Court upheld this testing regime as constitutional. Id. at 666, 115 S.Ct. 2386. Citing T.L.O., the Court emphasized that it had previously "found ... 'special needs' to exist in the public school context." Id. at 653, 115 S.Ct. 2386 (citing T.L.O., 469 U.S. at 340–41, 105 S.Ct. 733). These special needs were critical for the Court, which observed in no uncertain terms that "Fourth Amendment rights ... are different in public schools than elsewhere." Id. at 656, 115 S.Ct. 2386. In the end, the Court concluded that the school context was determinative. Id. at 665, 115 S.Ct. 2386 ("We caution against the assumption that suspicionless drug testing will readily pass constitutional muster in other contexts. The most significant element ... [is] that the Policy was undertaken in furtherance of the government's responsibilities, under a public school system, as guardian and tutor of children entrusted to its care.").

Vernonia's reasoning differed from T.L.O.'s, though, in that Vernonia also focused on the status of students, who it identified as "(1) children, who (2) have been committed to the temporary custody of the State as schoolmaster." Id. at 654, 115 S.Ct. 2386. Children "lack some of the most fundamental rights of self-determination" and "are subject ... to the control of their parents or guardians." Id. School teachers and administrators "stand in loco parentis over the children entrusted to them." Id. at 654, 115 S.Ct. 2386. They exercise a "degree of supervision and control that could not be exercised over free adults." Id. at 655, 115 S.Ct. 2386.

While "reasonableness" remained the touchstone for measuring the lawfulness of a Fourth Amendment search, the school setting and the status of students informed what would be reasonable: "the 'reasonableness' inquiry cannot disregard the schools' custodial and tutelary responsibility for children." Id. at 656, 115 S.Ct. 2386. In schools, students "have a lesser expectation of privacy than members of the population generally," and student athletes could expect even less privacy than typical students. Id. at 657, 115 S.Ct. 2386 (quoting T.L.O., 469 U.S. at 348, 105 S.Ct. 733 (Powell, J., concurring)). The Court considered the government's interest in deterring drug use by schoolchildren and the efficacy of this testing regime in furthering that interest. See id. at 661–64, 115 S.Ct. 2386. Ultimately, "the relevant question is whether the search is one that a reasonable guardian or tutor might undertake." Id. 665, 115 S.Ct. 2386.

Seven years later, in Board of Education v. Earls, 536 U.S. 822, 122 S.Ct. 2559, 153 L.Ed.2d 735 (2002), the Supreme Court once again upheld suspicionless drug testing of public school students. This time, the policy in question provided for suspicionless drug testing of all students participating in any competitive extracurricular activities—not just athletics but "the Academic Team, Future Farmers of America, Future Homemakers of America, band, choir, pom–pom, [and] cheerleading." Id. at 826, 122 S.Ct. 2559. These students were "required to take a drug test before participating in an extracurricular activity, [and had to] submit to random drug testing while participating in that activity." Id. Once again, the Court emphasized the unique setting of our public schools for Fourth Amendment purposes. Id. at 830, 122 S.Ct. 2559. Looking to Vernonia and T.L.O., the Court reiterated that "Fourth Amendment rights are different in public schools." Id. at 829–30, 122 S.Ct. 2559 (quoting Vernonia, 515 U.S. at 656, 115 S.Ct. 2386) (alteration adopted). Indeed, again in Earls, "the context of the public school environment serve[d] as the backdrop for the analysis of the privacy interest at stake and the reasonableness of the drug testing policy in general." Id. at 830, 122 S.Ct. 2559. And still again the Supreme Court concluded that our public schools had a sufficiently compelling interest in the prevention and deterrence of student drug use to create a "special need" for Fourth Amendment purposes. Id. at 838, 122 S.Ct. 2559.

The Court elaborated on the unique nature of the school setting. Students have reduced privacy interests "in a public school environment where the State is responsible for maintaining discipline, health, and safety." Id. at 830, 122 S.Ct. 2559. Schools have a responsibility to maintain control, drawn from the need to educate and to create an environment conducive to learning. Id. at 831, 122 S.Ct. 2559 (quoting New Jersey v. T.L.O., 469 U.S. 325, 350, 105 S.Ct. 733, 83 L.Ed.2d 720 (1985) (Powell, J., concurring)). Just as in previous cases, the Court considered "the nature of the privacy interest," id. at 830, 122 S.Ct. 2559, and "the character of the intrusion," id. at 832, 122 S.Ct. 2559, as balanced against "the nature and immediacy of the government's concerns and the efficacy of the Policy in meeting them," id. at 834, 122 S.Ct. 2559. And just like in T.L.O. and Vernonia, the warrantless searches passed constitutional muster. Id. at 838, 122 S.Ct. 2559.

……

In two cases that arose outside the school context, the Court identified still other versions of "special needs," and made it abundantly clear that adult government employees in some safety-sensitive positions could be required to pass suspicionless drug tests as a condition of their employment.

The first of these cases was Skinner v. Railway Labor Executives Ass'n, 489 U.S. 602, 109 S.Ct. 1402, 103 L.Ed.2d 639 (1989). There, the Supreme Court concluded that the government had a sufficiently compelling reason to test railroad employees who had been involved in railroad accidents,2 because "[t]he Government's interest in regulating the conduct of railroad employees to ensure safety ... present[ed] special needs beyond normal law enforcement that may justify departures from the usual warrant and probable-cause requirements." Id. at 620, 109 S.Ct. 1402. Evidence had established that "on-the-job intoxication was a significant problem in the railroad industry," and that in about a decade, there had been twenty-one significant accidents causing deaths and injuries that had involved alcohol or drug use. Id. at 607, 109 S.Ct. 1402. The delay imposed by a warrant requirement would frustrate detection of misconduct because alcohol and certain other drugs would leave the bloodstream before they could be detected. See id. at 623, 109 S.Ct. 1402. Skinner established the basic proposition that the government had an important interest in safety because the protection of life and property depended on railroad employees working effectively. Id. at 620, 109 S.Ct. 1402.

......

On the same day Skinner was handed down, the Supreme Court also upheld the suspicionless urine testing of two distinct groups of safety-sensitive Customs Service employees: those applying for positions directly involved in drug interdiction and those applying for positions that would require carrying a firearm. Von Raab, 489 U.S. at 664, 109 S.Ct. 1384. Testing was performed after qualification for the position but before beginning in either role. Id. at 661, 109 S.Ct. 1384. The testing regime, the government urged, was about both prevention and deterrence. It was meant "to deter drug use among those eligible for promotion to sensitive positions ... and to prevent the promotion of drug users to those positions." Id. at 666, 109 S.Ct. 1384. These dual needs "present[ed] a special need that may justify departure from the ordinary warrant and probable-cause requirements" of the Fourth Amendment.

Von Raab relied heavily on the unique functions performed by these Customs employees. Id. at 668, 109 S.Ct. 1384. Customs employees did not all face the moment-to-moment life-and-death situations that railroad employees did, but, the Customs Service was, as the Court put it, "our Nation's first line of defense against one of the greatest problems affecting the health and welfare of our population"—drug smuggling. Id. The Supreme Court suggested that employees involved in drug interdiction could be tested because drug users would be "unsympathetic to their mission of interdicting narcotics," or might even actively participate in a drug trafficking scheme. Id. at 670, 109 S.Ct. 1384. These employees also were at risk of physical violence by traffickers, temptation from access to seized drugs, and susceptible to being targeted for bribery. Id. at 669, 109 S.Ct. 1384. The government thus had a "compelling interest" in ensuring that those employees were "physically fit, and [had] unimpeachable integrity and judgment." Id. at 670, 109 S.Ct. 1384. Moreover, employees whose jobs required them to carry firearms "discharge[d] duties fraught with such risks of injury to others that even a momentary lapse of attention c[ould] have disastrous consequences." Id. (quoting Skinner, 489 U.S. at 628, 109 S.Ct. 1402).

The Court concluded that, when balancing the interests involved, "the Government's need to conduct the suspicionless searches ... outweigh[ed] the privacy interests of employees engaged directly in drug interdiction, and of those who otherwise are required to carry firearms." Id. at 668, 109 S.Ct. 1384. Like the employees in Skinner, Customs Service employees entering these specialized roles had diminished expectations of privacy because they could reasonably expect they would be subjected to additional precautions and inquiries. Id. at 672, 109 S.Ct. 1384. While collecting urine could be a "substantial" invasion of privacy in other settings, the workplace can "render entirely reasonable certain work-related intrusions ... that might be viewed as unreasonable in other contexts." Id. at 671, 109 S.Ct. 1384. The "compelling interests in safety and in the integrity of our borders" outweighed the privacy interests implicated, and so the testing was found to be reasonable. Id. at 672, 677, 109 S.Ct. 1384.

......

C.

In short, Supreme Court precedent boils down to this: searches must be reasonable; to determine whether a warrantless search is reasonable, we consider whether the government has demonstrated a "special need" to circumvent the warrant requirement, and, if so, we weigh this against the public and private interests at stake. See Lebron, 710 F.3d at 1206–07. This calculus is highly dependent on the context of the search and the status or role of the person being searched, and it plays out uniquely in schools, where teachers and administrators have a "legitimate need to maintain an environment in which learning can take place." T.L.O., 469 U.S. at 340, 105 S.Ct. 733; see id. at 340–43, 105 S.Ct. 733; see also Earls, 536 U.S. at 831, 122 S.Ct. 2559 ("Securing order in the school environment sometimes requires that students be subjected to greater controls than those appropriate for adults."). In many circumstances, students in schools can be required to take drug tests because of the unique context of the school and because teachers and administrators are responsible for their wellbeing. See Earls, 536 U.S. at 838, 122 S.Ct. 2559. Still another line of cases tells us that where drug use or intoxication would present a significant risk to public safety, adult employees in safety-sensitive positions may be tested. Chandler, 520 U.S. at 323, 117 S.Ct. 1295. The testing regime instituted by the School Board of Palm Beach County implicates the entirety of the Court's precedent and requires that we synthesize the cases addressing searches in schools with those addressing safety-sensitive positions.

IV.

To determine whether the government has demonstrated a "special need" justifying a departure from probable cause and warrant requirements, we first evaluate the danger against which the testing regime is intended to guard; that is, the danger posed by drug-addicted teachers in the classroom. We conclude that a special need is evident. The danger posed by intoxicated teachers is significant and it is "readily apparent" that the School Board "has a compelling interest in ensuring" that teachers—including substitutes—are not habitual drug users. Von Raab, 489 U.S. at 670, 109 S.Ct. 1384; cf. id. ("It is readily apparent that the Government has a compelling interest in ensuring that front-line interdiction personnel are physically fit, and have unimpeachable integrity and judgment.").

......

In order to evaluate the danger posed by substitute teacher drug use, we begin with the long-accepted notion that danger is measured by how likely it is that harm will occur and how serious that harm will be if it does occur. Here, the first variable, the probability of harm, is itself a function of the likelihood that a teacher will be intoxicated and the likelihood that a dangerous situation will arise. In most instances, one or the other would not, alone, cause the type of harm we see as relevant here. Our calculation does not end with this figure, though. As Judge Learned Hand famously put it, negligence is determined not just by the probability of harm but also by "the gravity of the resulting injury." United States v. Carroll Towing Co., 159 F.2d 169, 173 (2d Cir. 1947). The danger, then, against which the testing regime is intended to guard may be measured by (a) the likelihood that a teacher will be intoxicated; (b) the likelihood that a dangerous and urgent situation will arise in school to which that teacher cannot effectively respond; and (c) the gravity of harm that would occur if that teacher fails to respond effectively. While the first of these probabilities may not be particularly high, a serious danger is nonetheless present because the second and third are quite high indeed.

To state the obvious, our schools have a singular custodial and tutelary responsibility for our nation's most precious resource—our children. Parents are compelled, under force of law, to place their children in the care of the schools. Our teachers—substitute or otherwise—are directly given the responsibility to ensure the safety and protection of our children. Each family sending a child into the care and custody of the schools is counting on these teachers not only to educate them, but to keep them safe. It is to them that we look to safeguard the classroom and protect our students. Like teachers, substitute teachers are on the front lines. After all, students are at school all day long. Teachers have close interaction with students as young as five and as old as eighteen for the better part of every school day for many years of their lives.

While we cannot predict when or where a substitute teacher will face a situation in which a child's health or safety is at stake, we know with confidence that these situations will occur. …More generally, an obvious and basic step necessary to ensure student safety is ensuring that the guardian in closest daily contact with students is able to respond, and to do so promptly and without any cognitive or physical impairment.

If schools are going to be able to handle emergencies that threaten children's safety, teachers will need to be able to identify and respond to emergencies quickly, decisively, and with sound judgment. To take one example among the many dangers that will arise, we know for sure that kids get sick. A child's illness may be benign or can be anything but benign. A child's fever may quickly develop and spike—it could be nonexistent in the morning and yet require medical attention before the end of the school day. A student may develop a life-or-death allergic reaction even more rapidly…There may be no time to waste in seeking help. Nor is there time to waste when a child falls into diabetic shock or suffers a seizure, fainting spell, or asthma attack.

Teachers must also expeditiously recognize and respond to violent situations. The hard fact of life is that during school hours, bad things can happen to kids, and those front-line responders most directly supervising students—our teachers and substitute teachers—must be able to respond properly. It is not remote, idle, or fanciful to posit with some confidence that students, particularly teenagers, will engage in conflict at school. When students get into fights, a teacher will likely be in the best position to stop it, to diffuse it before it turns serious, or to seek help if the situation intensifies. Sadly, we need only look to recent events to know that teachers may, at a moment's notice, become those most readily able to protect our students from deadly and immediate harm from outside the school as well. School shootings are a real and palpable possibility. They are not so remote as to be only a hypothetical: in the first half of this year alone, school shooting incidents resulted in nearly three dozen deaths and numerous injuries.

As acute situations arise, and we know they will, the danger posed by leaving children, especially young children, in the care of an intoxicated teacher is profound. A teacher under the influence of drugs is significantly less likely to respond promptly, efficiently, and with sound judgment than a sober and clearheaded teacher. As we have said, it is not particularly likely that intoxicated teachers will regularly find themselves in front of a classroom. In some instances, if a teacher arrived at work high or drunk, a coworker might notice that something was wrong and would intervene—but we will not require the School Board to count on this, just at the Supreme Court did not rely on railroad workers to report one another. Since the School Board considers this a danger to be guarded against, we will consider their proposed solution, rather than waving away the problem.

The probability of harm is significant because it is a function not only of the relatively small chance of an intoxicated teacher in the classroom but also of the much larger chance that an emergency will occur. If a teacher who is responsible for the wellbeing and safety of a classroom of students is intoxicated on the job, there is a very realistic probability that a serious situation requiring a swift and effective adult response would emerge. Thus, we consider the gravity of the harm that could befall a child—not to mention that child's family—if the theoretically responsible adult fails to respond properly…We know with a high degree of confidence that serious problems will arise, that substitute teachers just like permanent teachers are the first and primary line of protection for minor students in the care of the public schools, and that an intoxicated guardian may well be unable to respond properly and promptly.

The danger that would be posed by drug-using individuals overseeing our classrooms is, we think, concrete and substantial. The government, therefore, has a significant safety-based interest in regulating the conduct of teachers to ensure safety in the public schools…We don't know that disastrous consequences would necessarily occur if a drug-using teacher were supervising a classroom, but the government has a powerful interest in not taking that chance.

……

Reasoning along similar lines, the Sixth Circuit has addressed and upheld the suspicionless drug-testing of public school teachers. Knox Cty. Educ. Ass'n v. Knox Cty. Bd. of Educ., 158 F.3d 361 (6th Cir. 1998). That court spoke in no uncertain terms about the special needs presented in our schools. It too emphasized the compelling nature of the government interests involved, observing that it could "imagine few governmental interests more important to a community than that of insuring the safety and security of its children while they are entrusted to the care of teachers and administrators." Id. at 374–75. The Sixth Circuit looked at the unique responsibilities placed on our teachers as well—to protect the students they serve, to respond with alacrity to the variety of problems as they arise, and to ensure an environment conducive to learning. Id. Additionally, the

Sixth Circuit noted that teachers acted as role models, and their actions readily affect the "perceptions, and thoughts and values" of students. Id. at 375 ("[T]eachers occupy a singularly critical and unique role in our society in that ... they occupy a position of immense direct influence on a child, with the potential for both good and bad.")

……

We recognize that there is a difference between a substitute teacher and a full-time classroom teacher. And, we note, the sufficiently compelling special need we recognize today is limited to the question before us: drug testing of provisionally hired substitute teachers. Substitute teachers, compared to full-time classroom teachers, may receive more regular supervision, which increases the potential that some school official may recognize when something is wrong with the substitute teacher. But at the end of the day, there is no real distinction between the responsibilities assumed by substitute teachers and full-time classroom teachers except for the amount of time they spend in the classroom. Substitute teachers, just like regular teachers, are the first responders in the classroom, and serve as the primary (and frequently only) caretakers for young children under the government's guardianship during the time they are at work. Their basic obligations are the same: to safeguard and teach those in their care.

Today we are asked to consider only the testing of substitute teachers, but we do not think that by recognizing a special need in this unique setting we have opened the floodgates to indiscriminate suspicionless searches. We have always required, as we do today, an exceptional showing of a special need to allow a suspicionless search, and not all government jobs present the same needs. We have repeatedly observed that the "special needs" calculus requires a careful, case-by-case examination of whether the duties and responsibilities surrounding the job are compelling enough to justify the invasion of privacy. In every case, the court must weigh privacy interests against the government's need…Front-line responders in this unique setting likely will be called on to solve the problem, navigate around a dangerous and unfolding event, break up a fight before it escalates, seek out emergency medical treatment, or provide direction and as much protection as possible if an unthinkable emergency occurs. Thus, we conclude that there is a powerful special need in this unique setting justifying the imposition of a suspicionless drug testing regime for substitute teacher applicants.

V.

Once a special need has been established, controlling precedent requires that we weigh the competing private and government interests implicated by the search. We must evaluate the reasonableness of the search by "balanc[ing] the individual's privacy expectations against the Government's interests to determine whether it is impractical to require a warrant or some level of individualized suspicion in the particular context." Von Raab, 489 U.S. at 665–66, 109 S.Ct. 1384. At the balancing stage, once the government has carried its burden of establishing the special need, the burden returns to the plaintiff to persuade the court that the balance weighs in its favor. See AFSCME, 717 F.3d at 880. The Supreme Court has laid out four factors to be used in conducting this balancing: the strength of the individuals' expectation of privacy, measured in light of their chosen profession or special status; the nature and extent of the testing regime's intrusion on privacy; the nature of the government's special need; and the testing regime's efficacy at achieving the government's aims. A showing of an existing problem "would shore up an assertion of special need for a suspicionless general search program." Chandler, 520 U.S. at 319, 117 S.Ct. 1295; see also Earls, 536 U.S. at 835, 122 S.Ct. 2559. But the government need not present empirical data concerning the extent of a drug problem peculiar to the group it seeks to test. See Earls, 536 U.S. at 835, 122 S.Ct. 2559; Von Raab, 489 U.S. at 660–61, 109 S.Ct. 1384.

In making this calculus we are satisfied that the intrusion on privacy has been reasonably minimized by the School District and that the reasons offered for the search are compelling. Again, it comes down to the fact that schools are different. Reasonable expectations of privacy depend on circumstance, and the government is justified in demanding more from those to whom our country's children are entrusted.

……

VI.

The long and the short of it is that we are satisfied that the testing regime adopted by the Palm Beach County School Board serves a preventive and deterrent function. When we balance all the interests as we are required to do, the School Board clearly has carried the day. Friedenberg has a diminished privacy interest owing to the unique Fourth Amendment context of the public schools. Plainly, the School Board has made only a minimal intrusion on that privacy interest. It has done so in the service of a serious and compelling need. And the testing regime appears to us be reasonably effective and altogether reasonable. Friedenberg has not established a substantial likelihood of success on the merits. On this preliminary record, and on these facts, we can discern no abuse of discretion in the district court's denial of a preliminary injunction.

Ralph D. Mawdsley: School Board Control Over Education and a Teacher's Right to Privacy, 23 St. Louis U. Pub. L. Rev. 609 (2004)*

Physical privacy for teachers, as for other employees, means intrusion into their persons and property, particularly as related to searches of a person's property and searches in the form of requiring urine samples for drug testing purposes. Searches are intrusions on a person's privacy, and the Fourth Amendment ensures that a person's expectation of privacy will not be intruded upon by government officers unless probable cause exists.

However, not all public places are the same in terms of an expectation of privacy, as the Supreme Court indicated in three student search cases involving drugs, *New Jersey v. T.L.O.*, *Vernonia School District 47J v. Acton*, and *Board of Education of Independent School District No. 92 of Pottawatomie County v. Earls*. The Court held in all three cases that probable cause did not apply to searches of students by school officials and that officials needed only reasonable suspicion to conduct a search. As the Supreme Court has yet to decide a school employee search and seizure case, the question becomes the extent to which diminished expectation of privacy for students, in large part because of the confined and custodial nature of schools, should also apply to teachers.

In *T.L.O.*, where the Court upheld an individualized suspicion search of a girl's purse that produced evidence of drug dealing, the Court, for the first time, articulated that student searches required only reasonable suspicion but had to be reasonable both as to inception of the search and the scope of the search. Thus, in *T.L.O.*, a charge by the teacher that T.L.O. was smoking in the restroom, along with the girl's denial that she had been smoking, provided reasonable suspicion to open the purse and to look for cigarettes and, upon seeing and removing a pack of cigarettes, to continue the search when drug-related items were seen.

The *T.L.O.* Court found the probable cause standard of the Fourth Amendment "unsuited to the school environment" because a requirement that school officials secure a search warrant before conducting student searches "would unduly interfere with the maintenance of the swift and informal disciplinary procedures needed in the schools." In finding that reasonable suspicion, despite diminishing the privacy rights of students, was an appropriate standard because of "the substantial need of teachers and administrators for freedom to maintain order in the schools," could the Court apply that holding to teachers as well?

In *Earls*, the Court, reinforcing its decision in *Vernonia* by upholding mandatory universal and random drug testing for students participating in extracurricular activities, observed that individualized suspicion for a search was not required because of "the schools' custodial and tutelary responsibility for children." The *Earls* Court opined that "while school children do not shed their constitutional rights when they enter the schoolhouse" under *Tinker v. Des Moines Independent Community School District*, the Court in *Vernonia* added that "Fourth Amendment rights ... are different in public schools than elsewhere." Clearly, the context for diminished privacy in *T.L.O.*, *Vernonia*, and *Earls* involves students, but one can argue that setting a lower reasonable suspicion standard for students and requiring a higher probable cause standard for teacher searches in the same school environment would be inconsistent and anomalous. Because teacher constitutional rights in schools owe their origin to the same *Tinker* Court decision as for students, teacher rights, arguably, should be subject to the same ebb and flow of Supreme Court interpretation as for student rights.

In the absence of a Supreme Court decision addressing school employee search and seizure, the closest case is *O'Connor v. Ortega* where the Court, relying heavily on *T.L.O.*, set forth guidelines for search and seizure of public employee property. In *O'Connor*, public hospital supervisors conducted a search of the office of a doctor in charge of residents, purportedly looking for evidence of alleged sexual harassment and suspected coercion of past residents to donate money for the doctor's new computer. The search, which involved mainly looking through the doctor's personal possessions, revealed no evidence of either allegation. When completed, the doctor's personal possessions and hospital property were boxed together, and despite the supervisors' claim that they entered the office in part to take inventory, no inventory in fact was taken.

In applying *T.L.O.*, the Court in *O'Connor* opined that the employer must "balance the invasion of the employee's legitimate expectations of privacy against the government's need for supervision, control, and the efficient operation of the workplace." The Court defined workplace broadly so as to include all of those areas over which the employer exerts control, which for teachers could include areas such as hallways, break rooms, desks, file cabinets, and classrooms.

An employee's expectation of privacy is determined by the circumstances of the workplace, which the *O'Connor* Court indicated is influenced by the amount of access employees have to an area. In *O'Connor*, the Court suggested that the employee had a greater expectation of privacy where he did not share his locked office with other employees, a marked difference, one could argue, from a teacher's classroom where school administrators, other teachers, substitute teachers, janitors, and students have ready access to the room. The *O'Connor* Court also observed that the hospital had no policy regarding personal items at the workplace, although the Court cautioned that absence of such a policy did not create an expectation of privacy where one would not otherwise exist. In other words, personal items, such as pictures and letters on a teacher's desk, are still part of the workplace and might be the subject of a search.

Applying the *T.L.O.* requirement of reasonableness for a search as to inception and scope, the *O'Connor* Court found reasonable grounds for searching an employee's office to include finding a record, report, or file, conducting an inventory of items in the office, and investigating alleged misconduct. The scope of a search in the workplace was more problematic for the Court, and it cautioned that a workplace did not necessarily apply to a piece of closed personal luggage, a handbag, or a briefcase that happens to be within the employee's workspace. Whether an employer could search personal items would depend on whether the particular items for which the search has been conducted might reasonably be located in the places being searched.

Ultimately, the search in *O'Connor* failed the test under *T.L.O.* because it was "at best, a general and unbounded pursuit of anything that might tend to indicate any sort of malfeasance—a search that is almost by definition, unreasonable." Seventeen years after filing his lawsuit for unlawful search and seizure (and eleven years after the Supreme Court decision), the doctor who had been discharged recovered $ 376,000 in compensatory damages and $ 60,000 in punitive damages against the two supervisors.

Cases applying the search principles of *T.L.O.* and *O'Connor* to school employees are rare. However, a recent Ohio appeals court decision examined employees' expectation of privacy where a building principal, suspecting third shift janitors of taking unauthorized breaks, installed a hidden video camera in a break room. The videotape revealed that janitors were taking unauthorized breaks and, upon being disciplined, they challenged the videotaping as an unlawful search. In upholding the principal's action, the court observed that the janitors could have no reasonable expectation of privacy in a break room that was accessible to all employees and contained a washing machine, clothes dryer, cleaning supplies, lockers, a refrigerator, and a microwave oven. The inception of the search was justified by the principal's reasonable suspicion about the unauthorized breaks, and the scope of the search was acceptable because it was less intrusive than it could have been as the principal had turned off the sound and recorded only the visual images.

Both T.*L.O.* and *O'Connor* suggest that teachers would have a reduced expectation of privacy regarding most places in schools, at least as to classrooms where teachers work and file cabinets where teachers store items. In such places, school officials would need only reasonable suspicion that the search would turn up evidence of work-related misconduct or work-related items such as records or files. The scope of a search would meet Fourth Amendment requirements as long as the measures adopted for the search are reasonably related to the search's objectives and are not excessively intrusive "in light of ... the nature of the [misconduct]." Relying on *T.L.O.*, the *O'Connor* Court held that:

> Public employer intrusions on the constitutionally protected privacy interests of government employees for non-investigatory, work-related purposes, as well as for investigations of work-related misconduct, should be judged by the standard of reasonableness.

The Court is silent as to the appropriate standard for searches of personal places such as teacher purses or brief cases. However, it is arguable that the reasonable suspicion, inception, and scope tests from *T.L.O.* would apply in much the same way as for students.

Suspicionless searches of teachers would be difficult to justify using the student cases of *Vernonia* and *Earls*. In those cases, the Supreme Court supported drug testing for students in extracurricular activities because participation was voluntary and because the extracurricular groups had rules not applicable to non-participating students. If students chose not to participate, or decided to cease participation, suspicionless searches would no longer apply and searches of those students could only be conducted under *T.L.O.'s* individualized suspicion standard. If suspicionless searches are to be used for teachers, they obviously need a different legal rationale than the one used for students.

Although a number of courts have upheld the use of random drug tests for janitors and school bus workers, the Sixth Circuit's opinion in *Knox County Education Association v. Knox County Board of Education* is the highest court decision to date upholding random drug testing for teachers. The court in *Knox County* likened teachers to other "safety sensitive" positions, such as customs employees and railway employees, positions for which the Supreme Court has upheld random drug testing. The Sixth Circuit found that a school board has a very strong interest in having teachers (and administrators) sober and not under the influence of drugs, because they must act immediately to protect students when a dangerous event occurs and because they are in "a unique position to observe children and learn if they are involved in activities which can lead to harm or injury to themselves or others." The court determined that the teachers' expectation of privacy was diminished because the taking of a drug sample was not intrusive and because the teaching profession is highly regulated. The teachers' concerns regarding the intrusiveness of the drug test was satisfied because providing the drug sample could be done in private without monitoring, except in cases where there is reason to believe a teacher will adulterate the sample. The court also observed that "when people enter the education profession they do so with the understanding that the profession is heavily regulated as to the conduct of people in the field, as well as to the responsibilities that they undertake toward their students and colleagues ...." As a result, "teachers should not be surprised if their own use of drugs is subject to regulation and testing ...."

Absent state statutes, collective bargaining agreements, or school board policies regulating teacher searches, the expectation of privacy that teachers have in their person or property follows the standard already set forth regarding students. Although only one federal appeals court has thus far ruled, suspicionless searches (drug testing) do not appear to be excessively intrusive on the privacy of teachers and are constitutionally permissible, although the justification for such testing differs from the one given for the testing of students.

III. The Family Educational Rights and Privacy Act (FERPA)

> "No funds shall be made available...to any educational agency or institution which has a policy or practice of permitting the release of education records... of students without the written consent of their parents to any individual, agency, or organization." 20 U.S.C.A. §§ 1232g(b)(1).

The Family Educational Rights and Privacy Act (FERPA) creates an intriguing form of educational records privacy. Also known as the Buckley Amendment (for one of its sponsors), FERPA has as its primary aim the protection of the privacy interests of students through standards for record-keeping designed to discourage unwarranted and abusive disclosure.

FERPA was enacted to further the twin goals of providing parents access to education records and limiting nonconsensual disclosure. Its sponsors announced that

> [t]he purpose of the Act is twofold—to assure parents of students, and students themselves if they are over the age of 18 or attending an institution of post secondary education, access to their education records and to protect such individuals rights to privacy by limiting the transferability of their records without their consent.". Joint Statement in Explanation of Buckley/Pell Amendment, Congressional Record, December 13, 1974; pp. 39862.

Under FERPA, the Department of Education has promulgated rules that govern privacy rights with respect to education records. Failure to comply with FERPA could result in the loss of federal education funding. Therefore, reach of FERPA is broad, covering practically every public primary and secondary school as well as public and private universities and colleges. As the material below illustrates, a curtain of uncertainty often exists over enforcement of the provisions of FERPA. In addition, the courts have taken a narrow view of the scope of education record privacy under FERPA. As a result, student claims under FERPA can be difficult to assert and compliance with its disclosure provisions confusing difficult to describe.

A. Remedies under FERPA

GONZAGA UNIVERSITY v. DOE
536 U.S. 273 (2002)

Chief Justice Rehnquist delivered the opinion of the Court.

The question presented is whether a student may sue a private university for damages to enforce provisions of the Family Educational Rights and Privacy Act of 1974 (FERPA or Act), 88 Stat. 571, 20 U.S.C. § 1232g which prohibit the federal funding of educational institutions that have a policy or practice of releasing education records to unauthorized persons. We hold such an action foreclosed because the relevant provisions of FERPA create no personal rights to enforce under 42 U.S.C. § 1983.

Respondent John Doe is a former undergraduate in the School of Education at Gonzaga University, a private university in Spokane, Washington. He planned to graduate and teach at a Washington public elementary school. Washington at the time required all of its new teachers to obtain an affidavit of good moral character from a dean of their graduating college or university. In October 1993, Roberta League, Gonzaga's "teacher certification specialist," overheard one student tell another that respondent engaged in acts of sexual misconduct against Jane Doe, a female undergraduate. League launched an investigation and contacted the state agency responsible for teacher certification, identifying respondent by name and discussing the allegations against him. Respondent did not learn of the investigation, or that information about him had been disclosed, until March 1994, when he was told by League and others that he would not receive the affidavit required for certification as a Washington schoolteacher.

Respondent then sued Gonzaga and League (petitioners) in state court. He alleged violations of Washington tort and contract law, as well as a pendent violation of §1983 for the release of personal information to an "unauthorized person" in violation of FERPA. A jury found for respondent on all counts, awarding him $1,155,000, including $150,000 in compensatory damages and $300,000 in punitive damages on the FERPA claim.... The Washington Court of Appeals reversed in relevant part, concluding that FERPA does not create individual rights. .... The Washington Supreme Court reversed that decision, and ordered the FERPA damages reinstated.

Like the Washington Supreme Court and the state court of appeals below, other state and federal courts have divided on the question of FERPA's enforceability under § 1983. The fact that all of these courts have relied on the same set of opinions from this Court suggests that our opinions in this area may not be models of clarity. We therefore granted certiorari, 534 U.S. 1103 (2002), to resolve the conflict among the lower courts and in the process resolve any ambiguity in our own opinions.

Congress enacted FERPA under its spending power to condition the receipt of federal funds on certain requirements relating to the access and disclosure of student educational records. The Act directs the Secretary of Education to withhold federal funds from any public or private "educational agency or institution" that fails to comply with these conditions.

The Act directs the Secretary of Education to enforce this and other of the Act's spending conditions. § 1232g(f). The Secretary is required to establish an office and review board within the Department of Education for "investigating, processing, reviewing, and adjudicating violations of [the Act]." § 1232g(g). Funds may be terminated only if the Secretary determines that a recipient institution "is failing to comply substantially with any requirement of [the Act]" and that such compliance "cannot be secured by voluntary means." §§ 1234c(a), 1232g(f).

Respondent contends that this statutory regime confers upon any student enrolled at a covered school or institution a federal right, enforceable in suits for damages under § 1983, not to have "education records" disclosed to unauthorized persons without the student's express written consent. But we have never before held, and decline to do so here, that spending legislation drafted in terms resembling those of FERPA can confer enforceable rights.

****

Our more recent decisions... have rejected attempts to infer enforceable rights from Spending Clause statutes. In *Suter v. Artist M.*, 503 U.S. 347 (1992), the Adoption Assistance and Child Welfare Act of 1980 required States receiving funds for adoption assistance to have a "plan" to make "reasonable efforts" to keep children out of foster homes. A class of parents and children sought to enforce this requirement against state officials under § 1983, claiming that no such efforts had been made. We read the Act... and found no basis for the suit, saying:

> Careful examination of the language . . . does not unambiguously confer an enforceable right upon the Act's beneficiaries. The term 'reasonable efforts' in this context is at least as plausibly read to impose only a rather generalized duty on the State, to be enforced not by private individuals, but by the Secretary in the manner [of reducing or eliminating payments]. *Id.*, at 363.

Since the Act conferred no specific, individually enforceable rights, there was no basis for private enforcement, even by a class of the statute's principal beneficiaries. *Id.* at 357.

Similarly, in *Blessing v. Freestone*, 520 U.S. 329 (1997), Title IV—D of the Social Security Act required States receiving federal child-welfare funds to "substantially comply" with requirements designed to ensure timely payment of child support. Five Arizona mothers invoked §1983 against state officials on grounds that state child-welfare agencies consistently failed to meet these requirements. We found no basis for the suit, saying,

> Far from creating an individual entitlement to services, the standard is simply a yardstick for the Secretary to measure the system wide performance of a State's Title IV—D program. Thus, the Secretary must look to the aggregate services provided by the State, not to whether the needs of any particular person have been satisfied. *Id.* at 343 (emphases in original).

Because the provision focused on "the aggregate services provided by the State," rather than "the needs of any particular person," it conferred no individual rights and thus could not be enforced by §1983. We emphasized: "[T]o seek redress through §1983 … a plaintiff must assert the violation of a federal right, not merely a violation of federal law." *Id.* at 340 (emphases in original).

Section 1983 provides a remedy only for the deprivation of "rights, privileges, or immunities secured by the Constitution and laws" of the United States. Accordingly, it is rights, not the broader or vaguer "benefits" or "interests," that may be enforced under the authority of that section. [O]ur implied right of action cases should guide the determination of whether a statute confers rights enforceable under § 1983.

.....

With this principle in mind, there is no question that FERPA's nondisclosure provisions fail to confer enforceable rights. To begin with, the provisions entirely lack the sort of "rights-creating" language critical to showing the requisite congressional intent to create new rights. Unlike the individually focused terminology of Titles VI and IX ("no person shall be subjected to discrimination"), FERPA's provisions speak only to the Secretary of Education, directing that "[n]o funds shall be made available" to any "educational agency or institution" which has a prohibited "policy or practice." 20 U.S.C. § 1232g(b)(1). This focus is two steps removed from the interests of individual students and parents and clearly does not confer the sort of "individual entitlement" that is enforceable under § 1983.

FERPA's nondisclosure provisions further speak only in terms of institutional policy and practice, not individual instances of disclosure. .... Recipient institutions can further avoid termination of funding so long as they "comply substantially" with the Act's requirements. § 1234c(a). … For reasons expressed repeatedly in our prior cases, however, such provisions cannot make out the requisite congressional intent to confer individual rights enforceable by § 1983.7

Our conclusion that FERPA's nondisclosure provisions fail to confer enforceable rights is buttressed by the mechanism that Congress chose to provide for enforcing those provisions. Congress expressly authorized the Secretary of Education to "deal with violations" of the Act, § 1232g(f) (emphasis added), and required the Secretary to "establish or designate [a] review board" for investigating and adjudicating such violations, § 1232g(g). Pursuant to these provisions, the Secretary created the Family Policy Compliance Office (FPCO) "to act as the Review Board required under the Act and to enforce the Act with respect to all applicable programs." 34 CFR §§ 99.60(a) and (b) (2001). The FPCO permits students and parents who suspect a violation of the Act to file individual written complaints. § 99.63. If a complaint is timely and contains required information, the FPCO will initiate an investigation, §§ 99.64(a)—(b), notify the educational institution of the charge, § 99.65(a), and request a written response, § 99.65. If a violation is found, the FPCO distributes a notice of factual findings and a "statement of the specific steps that the agency or institution must take to comply" with FERPA. §§ 99.66(b) and (c)(1). These administrative procedures squarely distinguish this case from Wright and Wilder, where an aggrieved individual lacked any federal review mechanism, and further counsel against our finding a congressional intent to create individually enforceable private rights.

Congress finally provided that "[e]xcept for the conduct of hearings, none of the functions of the Secretary under this section shall be carried out in any of the regional offices" of the Department of Education. 20 U.S.C. § 1232g(g). This centralized review provision was added just four months after FERPA's enactment due to "concern that regionalizing the enforcement of [FERPA] may lead to multiple interpretations of it, and possibly work a hardship on parents, students, and institutions." 120 Cong. Rec. 39863 (1974) (joint statement). It is implausible to presume that the same Congress nonetheless intended private suits to be brought before thousands of federal- and state-court judges, which could only result in the sort of "multiple interpretations" the Act explicitly sought to avoid.

In sum, if Congress wishes to create new rights enforceable under § 1983, it must do so in clear and unambiguous terms–no less and no more than what is required for Congress to create new rights enforceable under an implied private right of action. FERPA's nondisclosure provisions contain no rights-creating language, they have an aggregate, not individual, focus, and they serve primarily to direct the Secretary of Education's distribution of public funds to educational institutions. They therefore create no rights enforceable under § 1983. Accordingly, the judgment of the Supreme Court of Washington is reversed, and the case is remanded for further proceedings not inconsistent with this opinion.

JUSTICE BREYER, with whom JUSTICE SOUTER joins, concurring in the judgment.

I would not, in effect, pre-determine an outcome through the use of a presumption—such as the majority's presumption that a right is conferred only if set forth "unambiguously" in the statute's "text and structure.".

At the same time, I do not believe that Congress intended private judicial enforcement of this statute's "school record privacy" provisions. The Court mentions most of the considerations I find persuasive... I would add one further reason. Much of the statute's key language is broad and nonspecific. The statute, for example, defines its key term, "education records," as (with certain enumerated exceptions) "those records, files, documents, and other materials which (i) contain information directly related to a student; and (ii) are maintained by an educational . . . institution." 20 U.S.C. § 1232g(a)(4)(A). This kind of language leaves schools uncertain as to just when they can, or cannot, reveal various kinds of information. It has led, or could lead, to legal claims that would limit, or forbid, such practices as peer grading, *see Owasso Independent School Dist. No. I-011 v. Falvo*, 534 U.S. 426 (2002), teacher evaluations, *see Moore v. Hyche*, 761 F. Supp. 112 (ND Ala. 1991), school "honor society" recommendations, *see Price v. Young*, 580 F. Supp. 1 (ED Ark. 1983), or even roll call responses and "bad conduct" marks written down in class, *see Tr. of Oral Arg. in Falvo, supra*, O.T. 2001, No. 00-1073, pp. 37-38. And it is open to interpretations that invariably favor confidentiality almost irrespective of conflicting educational needs or the importance, or common sense, of limited disclosures in certain circumstances, say, where individuals are being considered for work with young children or other positions of trust.

Under these circumstances, Congress may well have wanted to make the agency remedy that it provided exclusive—both to achieve the expertise, uniformity, wide-spread consultation, and resulting administrative guidance that can accompany agency decision making and to avoid the comparative risk of inconsistent interpretations and misincentives that can arise out of an occasional inappropriate application of the statute in a private action for damages.

Notes and Comments

1. Role of the Courts and Litigation after *Gonzaga*
What is the role of the courts after Gonzaga? What, if any, controversies surrounding FERPA can be litigated? Is the U.S. Department of Education the sole arbiter of disputes involving FERPA? For a thoughtful analysis of when suits can be brought see David Sloss: Constitutional Remedies for Statutory Violations, 89 Iowa L. Rev. 355 (2004).

2. State Data Accumulation and Privacy: *Whalen v. Roe*
In privacy rights discussions it is important to distinguish between data gathering and data disclosure. While a citizen's right to privacy can be violated by intrusive means of gathering information, the right to privacy does not generally prohibit government from gathering and compiling data. Assuming the means used to gather the data are valid, governments are expected to make frequent assessments of the general welfare as a means to exercise of the police power. In *Whalen v. Roe*, 429 U.S. 589 (1977) the Supreme Court addresses this issue directly in a lawsuit challenging a state law that required that records be kept of all persons receiving prescriptions for controlled substances with a potential for abuse, The Court held that the law adequately protected privacy when it limited access to the lists and built in protection from disclosures. State agencies may gather information on citizens. States have "broad latitude" in uses to which data is put. However, the data must be adequately protected from unauthorized disclosure.

B. Defining the "Education Record" under FERPA

OWASSO INDEPENDENT SCHOOL DISTRICT NO. I-011 v. FALVO
534 U.S. 426 (2002)

JUSTICE KENNEDY delivered the opinion of the Court.

I

Three of respondent Kristja J. Falvo's children are enrolled in Owasso Independent School District No. I-011, in a suburb of Tulsa, Oklahoma. The children's teachers, like many teachers in this country, use peer grading. In a typical case, the students exchange papers with each other and score them according to the teacher's instructions, then return the work to the student who prepared it. The teacher may ask the students to report their own scores. In this case it appears the student could either call out the score or walk to the teacher's desk and reveal it in confidence, though by that stage, of course, the score was known at least to the one other student who did the grading. Both the grading and the system of calling out the scores are in contention here.

Respondent claimed the peer grading embarrassed her children. She asked the school district to adopt a uniform policy banning peer grading and requiring teachers either to grade assignments themselves or at least to forbid students from grading papers other than their own. The school district declined to do so, and respondent brought a class action against the school district.

.....Respondent alleged the school district's grading policy violated FERPA and other laws not relevant here. The United States District Court for the Northern District of Oklahoma granted summary judgment in favor of the school district's position. ... The Court of Appeals for the Tenth Circuit reversed. .....We granted certiorari to decide whether peer grading violates FERPA. Finding no violation of the Act, we reverse.

II

At the outset, we note it is an open question whether FERPA provides private parties, like respondent, with a cause of action enforceable under § 1983. We have granted certiorari on this issue in another case. *See Gonzaga Univ. v. Doe*, 534 U.S. 1103, 122 S. Ct. 865, 151 L. Ed. 2d 738 (2002)..... In these circumstances we assume, but without so deciding or expressing an opinion on the question, that private parties may sue an educational agency under § 1983 to enforce the provisions of FERPA here at issue. ...With these preliminary observations concluded, we turn to the merits.

The parties appear to agree that if an assignment becomes an education record the moment a peer grades it, then the grading, or at least the practice of asking students to call out their grades in class, would be an impermissible release of the records under § 1232g(b)(1). Without deciding the point, we assume for the purposes of our analysis that they are correct. The parties disagree, however, whether peer-graded assignments constitute education records at all. The papers do contain information directly related to a student, but they are records under the Act only when and if they "are maintained by an educational agency or institution or by a person acting for such agency or institution." § 1232g(a)(4)(A).

.....

Respondent, adopting the reasoning of the Court of Appeals, contends student-graded assignments fall within the definition of education records. That definition contains an exception for "records of instructional, supervisory, and administrative personnel . . . which are in the sole possession of the maker thereof and which are not accessible or revealed to any other person except a substitute." § 1232g(a)(4)(B)(i). The Court of Appeals reasoned that if grade books are not education records, then it would have been unnecessary for Congress to enact the exception. Grade books and the grades within, the court concluded, are "maintained" by a teacher and so are covered by FERPA. The court recognized that teachers do not maintain the grades on individual student assignments until they have recorded the result in the grade books. It reasoned, however, that if Congress forbids teachers to disclose students' grades once written in a grade book, it makes no sense to permit the disclosure immediately beforehand. The court thus held that student graders maintain the grades until they are reported to the teacher.

The Court of Appeals' logic does not withstand scrutiny. Its interpretation, furthermore, would effect a drastic alteration of the existing allocation of responsibilities between States and the National Government in the operation of the Nation's schools. We would hesitate before interpreting the statute to effect such a substantial change in the balance of federalism unless that is the manifest purpose of the legislation. This principle guides our decision.

First, the student papers are not, at that stage, "maintained" within the meaning of § 1232g(a)(4)(A). The ordinary meaning of the word "maintain" is "to keep in existence or continuance; preserve; retain." Random House Dictionary of the English Language 1160 (2d ed. 1987). Even assuming the teacher's grade book is an education record—a point the parties contest and one we do not decide here—the score on a student-graded assignment is not "contained therein," § 1232g(b)(1), until the teacher records it. The teacher does not maintain the grade while students correct their peers' assignments or call out their own marks. Nor do the student graders maintain the grades within the meaning of § 1232g(a)(4)(A). The word "maintain" suggests FERPA records will be kept in a filing cabinet in a records room at the school or on a permanent secure database, perhaps even after the student is no longer enrolled. The student graders only handle assignments for a few moments as the teacher calls out the answers. It is fanciful to say they maintain the papers in the same way the registrar maintains a student's folder in a permanent file.

[Second], Court of Appeals was further mistaken in concluding that each student grader is "a person acting for" an educational institution for purposes of § 1232g(a)(4)(A). 233 F.3d at 1216. The phrase "acting for" connotes agents of the school, such as teachers, administrators, and other school employees. Just as it does not accord with our usual understanding to say students are "acting for" an educational institution when they follow their teacher's direction to take a quiz, it is equally awkward to say students are "acting for" an educational institution when they follow their teacher's direction to score it. Correcting a classmate's work can be as much a part of the assignment as taking the test itself. It is a way to teach material again in a new context, and it helps show students how to assist and respect fellow pupils. By explaining the answers to the class as the students correct the papers, the teacher not only reinforces the lesson but also discovers whether the students have understood the material and are ready to move on. We do not think FERPA prohibits these educational techniques. We also must not lose sight of the fact that the phrase "by a person acting for [an educational] institution" modifies "maintain." Even if one were to agree students are acting for the teacher when they correct the assignment, that is different from saying they are acting for the educational institution in maintaining it.

Under the Court of Appeals' broad interpretation of education records, every teacher would have an obligation to keep a separate record of access for each student's assignments. Indeed, by that court's logic, even students who grade their own papers would bear the burden of maintaining records of access until they turned in the assignments. We doubt Congress would have imposed such a weighty administrative burden on every teacher, and certainly it would not have extended the mandate to students.

Also FERPA requires "a record" of access for each pupil. This single record must be kept "with the education records." This suggests Congress contemplated that education records would be kept in one place with a single record of access. By describing a "school official" and "his assistants" as the personnel responsible for the custody of the records, FERPA implies that education records are institutional records kept by a single central custodian, such as a registrar, not individual assignments handled by many student graders in their separate classrooms.

FERPA also requires recipients of federal funds to provide parents with a hearing at which they may contest the accuracy of their child's education records. § 1232g(a)(2). The hearings must be conducted "in accordance with regulations of the Secretary," *ibid.*, which in turn require adjudication by a disinterested official and the opportunity for parents to be represented by an attorney. 34 CFR § 99.22 (2001). It is doubtful Congress would have provided parents with this elaborate procedural machinery to challenge the accuracy of the grade on every spelling test and art project the child completes.

Respondent's construction of the term "education records" to cover student homework or classroom work would impose substantial burdens on teachers across the country. It would force all instructors to take time, which otherwise could be spent teaching and in preparation, to correct an assortment of daily student assignments. Respondent's view would make it much more difficult for teachers to give students immediate guidance. The interpretation respondent urges would force teachers to abandon other customary practices, such as group grading of team assignments. Indeed, the logical consequences of respondent's view are all but unbounded. At argument, counsel for respondent seemed to agree that if a teacher in any of the thousands of covered classrooms in the Nation puts a happy face, a gold star, or a disapproving remark on a classroom assignment, federal law does not allow other students to see it.

We doubt Congress meant to intervene in this drastic fashion with traditional state functions. Under the Court of Appeals' interpretation of FERPA, the federal power would exercise minute control over specific teaching methods and instructional dynamics in classrooms throughout the country. The Congress is not likely to have mandated this result, and we do not interpret the statute to require it.

For these reasons, even assuming a teacher's grade book is an education record, the Court of Appeals erred, for in all events the grades on students' papers would not be covered under FERPA at least until the teacher has collected them and recorded them in his or her grade book. We limit our holding to this narrow point, and do not decide the broader question whether the grades on individual student assignments, once they are turned in to teachers, are protected by the Act.

The judgment of the Court of Appeals is reversed, and the case is remanded for further proceedings consistent with this opinion.

JUSTICE SCALIA, concurring in the judgment.

I agree with the Court that peer-graded student papers do not constitute "education records" while they remain in the possession of the peer grader because, as the Court explains, a student who grades another's work is not "a person acting for" the school in the ordinary meaning of that phrase. Ante, at 6-7. I cannot agree, however, with the other ground repeatedly suggested by the Court: that education records include only documents kept in some central repository at the school. Ante, at 6 ("The word 'maintain' suggests FERPA records will be kept in a filing cabinet in a records room at the school or on a permanent secure database . . . . It is fanciful to say [student graders] maintain the papers in the same way the registrar maintains a student's folder in a permanent file"), ("FERPA implies that education records are institutional records kept by a single central custodian, such as a registrar . . .").

As the Court acknowledges, Ante, at 2, 5, Congress expressly excluded from the coverage of FERPA "records of instructional . . . personnel . . . which are in the sole possession of the maker thereof and which are not accessible or revealed to any other person except a substitute," 20 U.S.C. § 1232g(a)(4)(B)(i). Respondent argues that this exception, which presumably encompasses many documents a teacher might create and keep in the classroom, including a grade book, would be rendered superfluous if education records included only "institutional records kept by a single central custodian, such as a registrar." We do not, of course, read statutes in such fashion as to render entire provisions inoperative. *United States v. Nordic Village, Inc.*, 503 U.S. 30, 35-36 (1992).

The Court does not explain why respondent's argument is not correct, and yet continues to rely upon the "central custodian" principle that seemingly renders the exception for "records of instructional . . . personnel" superfluous. Worse still, while thus relying upon a theory that plainly excludes teachers' grade books, the Court protests that it is not deciding whether grade books are education records, Ante, at 6. In my view, the Court's endorsement of a "central custodian" theory of records is unnecessary for the decision of this case, seemingly contrary to § 1232g(a)(4)(B)(i), and (when combined with the Court's disclaimer of any view upon the status of teachers' grade books) incurably confusing. For these reasons, I concur only in the judgment of the Court.

BRV, INC. v. SUPERIOR COURT

49 Cal. Rptr. 3d 519 (Ct. App. 2006)

NICHOLSON, Acting P. J.

We must determine whether the California Public Records Act (Gov. Code, § 6250 et seq.; Public Records Act or the Act) requires the report to be released or allows it to remain confidential. Under the circumstances presented here, we conclude the Public Records Act requires disclosure, subject to conditions.

Real party in interest Dunsmuir Joint Union High School District (the District) operates Dunsmuir High School. The school serves about 135 students in grades nine through 12. In March 2004, the District received approximately 13 letters complaining about the behavior of real party in interest Robert Morris, superintendent of the District and principal of Dunsmuir High School. The letters alleged Morris verbally abused students in disciplinary settings and sexually harassed female students.

On April 22, 2004, the District's board of trustees (the Board) met in closed session, where it listened to parents voice their complaints about Morris.... On May 4, 2004, the Board convened a special meeting. Following the closed session, the Board in open session voted unanimously to retain Diane Davis, a private investigator, to investigate the complaints against Morris.... The Board directed Davis to interview complaining witnesses by telephone and to prepare written summaries of those interviews. It also asked Davis to provide her conclusions regarding the truth of the complaints and whether the evidence provided by the complainants supported the allegations.

On May 11, 2004, the Board met in closed session with Morris for over two hours. At the conclusion of the closed session, it was announced that Morris had requested, and the Board had agreed, that Morris's employment contract would not be renewed after its scheduled expiration in June 2006.

Meanwhile, Davis conducted numerous interviews. The District informed the trial court Davis interviewed 27 people. She interviewed parents, current students, former students, and District employees. She prepared 25 summaries documenting these interviews. Davis prepared nine additional memoranda recording various investigative steps she took. Also, Davis prepared a lengthy letter detailing her findings and opinions following her investigation. She dated the report June 24, 2004, and submitted the letter, the interview summaries, the additional memoranda, and her interview notes as her report to the District.

Under cover of letters dated July 19, 2004, the Board transmitted to a limited number of complainants a copy of Davis's interview summary of that complainant, and solicited the complainant's review and comment. Petitioner BRV, Inc. (BRV), publisher of the Redding Record Searchlight newspaper, obtained copies of eight such letters, nine interview summaries, and the responses of each complainant to those summaries. They are included in the record. The word "Confidential" appears at the top of each interview summary.

On July 23, 2004, Morris resigned from his positions effective December 31, 2004, conditioned on the Board accepting a written agreement between him and the District, also dated July 23, 2004. .... The District agreed not to release any documents in Morris's personnel file except with Morris's consent or as required by law. The District also agreed to "seal and place in a sealed envelope in [Morris's] personnel file any and all documents relating to the investigation conducted by Diane Davis on behalf of the District and no information on such investigation shall be released to any third party except as required by law or in accordance with any court order or subpoena."

Between July and August 2004, some 40 tort claims were filed with the District regarding Morris's conduct and Davis's investigation.... On July 29, 2004, BRV filed a request with the District under the Public Records Act to obtain copies of Davis's report, any documentation relating to the District's retention of Davis, and any letter of resignation submitted by Morris.... On August 9, 2004, the District provided BRV with everything it had requested except Davis's report. The District stated Davis's report was exempt from disclosure under the Public Records Act...... [T]he trial court determined almost all of Davis's report, including the interview summaries she prepared, were not required to be disclosed under the Public Records Act's personnel records exception, section 6254, subdivision (c). It ordered only those portions of the report regarding complaints of Morris yelling at students be disclosed. All other portions would remain confidential, even though they tended to exonerate Morris. The court found this to be an odd result, but felt constrained by case law not to disclose complaints that were determined not to be credible or to concern serious matters.

BRV sought writ relief from this court, claiming the trial court erred. We issued an alternative writ, and now address the merits.

DISCUSSION

****

II

Statutory Background

All public records are subject to disclosure unless the Public Records Act expressly provides otherwise. (*Williams v. Superior Court* (1993) 5 Cal.4th 337, 346). The trial court found two exemptions relevant here. The first, subdivision (c) of section 6254, exempts from disclosure "[p]ersonnel, medical, or similar files, the disclosure of which would constitute an unwarranted invasion of personal privacy." The second is the Act's so-called "catchall exception," section 6255. This provision allows an agency to withhold public records where no express exemption may apply if the agency can demonstrate "that on the facts of the particular case the public interest served by not disclosing the record clearly outweighs the public interest served by disclosure of the record." (§ 6255, subd. (a).)

CA(3)(3) We directed the parties to address in supplemental briefing a third exemption that may apply, one originally raised by the District at trial. Under Education Code section 49076, a school district may not grant any person access to "pupil records" without written parental consent or judicial order except under circumstances not relevant here. (Ed. Code, § 49076.) This statute prevails over the Public Records Act. (Ed. Code, § 49060; Gov. Code, § 6254, subd. (k).) We thus turn our attention first to this provision, determining whether Davis's report constitutes "pupil records" within the meaning of Education Code section 49076.

III

Pupil Records

Education Code section 49076 is part of a statutory response to Congress's adoption of the Family Educational Rights and Privacy Act of 1974 (FERPA), 20 U.S.C. § 1232g. "Congress enacted FERPA 'to assure parents of students … access to their educational records and to protect such individuals' rights to privacy by limiting the transferability of their records without their consent.' [Citation.] Under its terms, educational institutions, with a few exceptions not material here, must obtain written parental consent prior to releasing students' records or information derived there from. The statute takes a carrot-and-stick approach: the carrot is federal funding; the stick is the termination of such funding to any educational institution 'which has a policy or practice of permitting the release of educational records (or personally identifiable information contained therein ...) of students without the written consent of their parents.' (20 U.S.C. § 1232g(b)(1).)" (*Frazier v. Fairhaven School Committee* (1st Cir. 2002) 276 F.3d 52, 67–68.) The California Legislature adopted a statutory scheme to eliminate potential conflicts between FERPA and state law, including the Public Records Act. (Ed. Code, § 49060.)

California law defines "pupil records" as "any item of information directly related to an identifiable pupil, other than directory information, which is maintained by a school district ...." (Ed. Code, § 49061, subd. (b).). FERPA defines " 'education records' " in nearly identical terms. (20 U.S.C. § 1232g(a)(4)(A).)

Implementing regulations promulgated by the State Department of Education further explain the term: "'Pupil Record' means information relative to an individual pupil gathered within or without the school system and maintained within the school system, regardless of the physical form in which it is maintained. Essential in this definition is the idea that any information which is maintained for the purpose of second party review is considered a pupil record." (Cal. Code Regs., tit. 5, § 430, subd. (d).)

Judicial authority interpreting the term is scant. Federal courts interpreting FERPA, for example, have held the following records not to be education records: students' individual assignments handled by student graders in their separate classrooms (*Owasso Independent School Dist. No. I-011 v. Falvo* (2002) 534 U.S. 426, 432–36 [151 L. Ed. 2d 896, 904–06, 122 S. Ct. 934] (*Falvo*)); transcripts of students' depositions in a sexual harassment case against a school coach that were not maintained by the school (*Jennings v. University of N.C. at Chapel Hill* (M.D.N.C. 2004) 340 F. Supp. 2d 679, 683–84); and a voluntary student survey participated in anonymously (*C.N. v. Ridgewood Bd. of Educ.* (D.N.J. 2001) 146 F. Supp. 2d 528, 538, affd, in part, rev'd, in part (3d Cir. 2001) 281 F.3d 219).

Records found by federal courts to be education records under FERPA include student disciplinary records (*U.S. v. Miami University* (S.D. Ohio 2000) 91 F. Supp. 2d 1132, 1149), and district records relating to a student's juvenile court proceedings and kept in the school district's attorney's files (*Belanger v. Nashua, New Hampshire, School Dist.* (D.N.H. 1994) 856 F. Supp. 40, 50 (*Belanger*)).

The *Belanger* court noted Congress intended the definition of "education record" to be broad. The current definition, enacted in 1974, "'define[s] "education records" in order to make clear what documents and other material parents and students will have access to ... [The] intent to be that, except as provided in the definition, parents and students should have access to everything in institutional records maintained for each student in the normal course of business and used by the institution in making decisions that affect the life of the student. 120 Cong. Rec. at 39858–39859 (emphasis added)." (*Belanger, supra,* 856 F. Supp. at p. 49.)

Nonetheless, in holding students' assignments were not education records, the Supreme Court clarified that not every record in a school concerning a student is an education record. The court relied in part on a provision of FERPA that requires agencies to keep a separate record listing those who request access to a student's education records. (20 U.S.C. § 1232g(b)(4)(A).) "FERPA requires 'a record' of access for each pupil. This single record must be kept 'with the education records.' This suggests Congress contemplated that education records would be kept in one place with a single record of access. By describing a 'school official' and 'his assistants' as the personnel responsible for the custody of the records, FERPA implies that education records are institutional records kept by a single central custodian, such as a registrar, not individual assignments handled by many student graders in their separate classrooms." (*Falvo, supra*, 534 U.S. at pp. 434–35, italics added.)

The Tenth Circuit Court of Appeals also limited the scope of "education records" in an unreported decision that court's local rule allows us to cite for persuasive value. In *Jensen v. Reeves* (10th Cir. 2001) 3 Fed.Appx. 905 (Jensen), a school official sent reports to the parents of victims and witnesses of a particular student's verbal and physical harassment. In one instance, the report explained the investigation conducted in response to a complaint, the facts discerned, and the discipline taken against the offending student. In another instance, the reports summarized the incident, explained the addressee's child had been involved and had been interviewed, and stated the alleged perpetrator had been warned. (*Id.* at p. 910.)

The Court of Appeals determined the school did not violate FERPA by releasing the investigation reports. The reports were not "education records." "[T]he contemporaneous disclosure to the parents of a victimized child of the results of any investigation and resulting disciplinary actions taken against an alleged child perpetrator does not constitute a release of an 'education record' within the meaning of 20 U.S.C. § 1232g(a)(4)(A). Reading such disclosures to fall within the ambit of § 1232g would place educators in an untenable position: they could not adequately convey to the parents of affected students that adequate steps were being undertaken to assure the safety of the student. Nor do we think that such a targeted, discrete, contemporaneous disclosure fits within the bounds of the plain language of § 1232g(a)(4)(A)." (*Jensen, supra*, 3 Fed. Appx. at p. 910.)

Even less authority exists interpreting the California statute. *Poway Unified School Dist. v. Superior Court* (1998) 62 Cal.App.4th 1496 [73 Cal. Rptr. 2d 777] (*Poway Unified*), is the only reported California case found by the parties and us addressing the issue. There, a newspaper sought access to tort claims filed against a school district arising from hazing incidents at a high school. One claim was filed by a student who pled guilty in juvenile court to sodomizing another student with a broomstick. The claim included a description of prurient details about the attack. (*Id.* at pp. 1499–1500.)

Although the Court of Appeal acknowledged Education Code section 49061 defined "pupil records" broadly (*Poway Unified, supra*, 62 Cal. App. 4th at pp. 1506–07), it determined neither the statute nor FERPA prevented releasing the tort claims to the media. "It defies logic and common sense to suggest that a Claims Act claim, even if presented on behalf of a student, is an 'education record' or 'pupil record' within the purview of these exemptions. Just because a litigant has chosen to sue a school does not transmogrify the Claims Act claim into such a record. We therefore conclude the release of such a claim implicates neither FERPA nor its California counterpart." (*Id.* at p. 1507.)

Certainly the language of the statute, though broadly written, does not encompass every document that relates to a student in any way and is kept by the school in any fashion. A pupil record is one that "directly relates" to a student and is "maintained" by the school. We agree with the Supreme Court that the statute was directed at institutional records maintained in the normal course of business by a single, central custodian of the school. Typical of such records would be registration forms, class schedules, grade transcripts, discipline reports, and the like.

The Davis report, however, does not fall within that group. True, it identifies students by name and details actions taken by them and against them, some of which violated school policy and subjected them to discipline. However, the report was not directly related to the private educational interests of the students. Its purpose was to investigate complaints of malfeasance allegedly committed by the highest administrator in the District.

The report was not something regularly done in the normal course of business, as illustrated by the fact it required a Board resolution to initiate. It also was not the type of report regularly maintained in a central location along with education records such as those described above in separate files for each student.

For all of the above reasons, we conclude the Davis report and its accompanying summaries were not pupil records within the meaning of Education Code sections 49061 and 49076.

[The court held that state law did not prevent disclosure of the records.]

Notes and Comments

1. The "Education Record" under FERPA

The focus of FERPA is on the "education record." The "education record" is defined as "those records, files, documents, and other materials that contain information directly related to a student; and are maintained by an education agency or institution or by a person acting for such an agency." 20 U.S.C. § 1232g(a)(4)(A). Generally, most written information schools maintain on students (in any form, including computerized databases) will be considered an education record. Nevertheless, written information that pertains directly to a student that is not maintained by the school or by an agent of the school is not an education record. If the information is not an education record, FERPA does not apply.

FERPA, is a "hard copy law". FERPA does not apply to oral communication between educators and others concerning information the knowledge of which does not rely on the education record.

The U.S. Department of Education and Federal courts interpreting FERPA, have held the following records not to be education records:

- Students' individual assignments handled by student graders in their separate classrooms (*Owasso Independent School Dist. No. I-011 v. Falvo*, 534 U.S. 426 (2002);

- Transcripts of students' depositions in a sexual harassment case against a school coach that were not maintained by the school (*Jennings v. University of N.C. at Chapel Hill* 340 F. Supp. 2d 679 (M.D.N.C. 2004));

- A voluntary student survey participated in anonymously (*C.N. v. Ridgewood Bd. of Educ.* 146 F. Supp. 2d 528, (D.N.J. 2001), *aff'd.* in part, *rev'd.* in part 281 F.3d 219 (3d Cir. 2001)).

- Records of instructional, supervisory, and administrative personnel . . . which are in the sole possession of the maker thereof and which are not accessible or revealed to any other person except a substitute." § 1232g(a)(4)(B)(i); and

- School law enforcement unit records. These are records kept by "[a] law enforcement unit of the education agency or institution that is created by that law enforcement unit for the purpose of law enforcement." 20 U.S.C. § 1232g(a)(4)(B)(ii).

In what category would you place video recordings from cameras in school buses, building hallways and classrooms? Would it matter if the tape was recorded over every 24-48 hours? What if the records were saved to a storage device and kept?

2. Records Management Policies under FERPA

FERPA attempts to eliminate the abuse of student records by creating a minimum standard for educational record management. School Districts are required to have a written policy that discloses its record keeping practices, 20 U.S.C. § 1232g(e) and 34 C.F.R. § 99.7(a).

This policy must be disclosed periodically to students and parents. FERPA thus forces educators to announce valid guidelines and then to live by them. The minimum standard requires that students be given access to the contents in their educational record file. The access must be meaningful: schools must make location and access an easy matter by spelling out where records are kept, 34 C.F.R. § 99.6(a)(2)(iv). Students are permitted to challenge the veracity of the contents of information contained in the file, 20 U.S.C. § 1232g(a)(2) and 34 C.F.R. § 99.6(a)(7). A log chronicling the use of the educational record file and its contents must be kept, in effect, forcing the educators to "log in" and "log out" of a student's file, 34 C.F.R. § 99.6(a)(5) and s 99.32.

3. Video and Audio Surveillance, FERPA, and Privacy

Despite the sophistication of video surveillance technology (VST), the law that applies is familiar and well known to both educators and law enforcement. Federal law claims will arise out of the Fourth Amendment and statutes on data privacy. State claims may also arise out of similar state provisions. The Fourth Amendment comes into play only in those situations where the individuals who fall under the lens of the camera have a reasonable expectation of privacy and requires that educators have at least individualized suspicion. See *New Jersey v. T.L.O.*, 469 U.S. 325 (1985). In all other cases the validity of VST is straightforward and uncomplicated. If all methods of video surveillance were regulated by the Fourth Amendment, T.L.O. would be read to prohibit educators' use of the technology, unless they first developed individualized suspicion. That would effectively eliminate VST as a deterrent and seriously limit its usefulness as an school safety device, except in those rare instances when individualized suspicion is developed in other ways and cameras are needed to provide corroboration or help capture a person who continues to disrupt the school environment. Therefore, in public places the validity of the use of VSE is a moot issue. School officials may observe and record what they lawfully can see with the naked eye. In Ohio, the United States District Court held that classroom video of a student without prior parental consent does not implicate the right to privacy under the Fourth Amendment. The court reasoned that a student's reasonable expectation of privacy is limited. While video surveillance in a school locker-room invades a student's reasonable expectation of privacy, video surveillance in other common areas does not implicate privacy rights. The court said that, "[a]lthough [courts have] recognized that video surveillance in a school locker-room invades a student's reasonable expectation of privacy, this holding cannot be understood to mean that the Fourth Amendment covers all instances in which a student is videotaped at school in any location (i.e., classroom, hallway), in any manner, and for any duration, without parental consent." *Gregory v. W. Clermont Local Sch. Dist. Bd. of Educ.*, 414 F. Supp. 3d 1064, 1079 (S.D. Ohio 2019). See *State v. McLellan*, 144 N.H. 602, 604-05, 744 A.2d 611 (N.H. 1999) (no reasonable expectation of privacy by janitor in public school classroom because classroom was open to students and school staff); *Goodwin v. Moyer*, 2006 U.S. Dist. LEXIS 18492 (M.D. Pa. 2006) (no reasonable expectation of privacy for public school's bus driver subjected to video monitoring on school bus); *Thompson v. Johnson County Community College*, 930 F.Supp. 501, 507 (D. Kan. 1996) (no reasonable expectation of privacy in locker area used by security personnel of community college because area video taped was not reserved for the exclusive use of security personnel); *Brannen v. Kings Local School Dist.*, 144 Ohio App.3d 620 (12th Dist. 2001) (no reasonable expectation of privacy in public school's break room used by third shift custodians because teachers and principal also had "unfettered access" to break room); *Plock v. Bd. of Educ.*, 545 F. Supp. 2d 755 (N.D. IL 2007) (school teachers do not have an expectation of privacy in their classrooms). When educators cross the constitutional line, it is usually beyond quibble. The surveillance is overzealous and captures students in settings and at times when the expectation of privacy is beyond any intrusion, i.e. the private areas of school bathrooms, lockers, off-campus dwellings and automobiles. See, *Brannum v. Overton Cty. Sch. Bd.*, 516 F.3d 489, 494, 497 (6th Cir. 2008) (student locker room); *Doe v. Dearborn Pub. Schs*, 2008 U.S. Dist. LEXIS 25514 (E.D. Mich. 2008) (faculty locker room).

The same rules apply to disputes over audio surveillance. Collecting audio data is prohibited under Title I of the Electronic Communications Privacy Act of 1986. See U.S.C. §§ 2510-2521. State statutes similarly provide a right of action in court for persons whose conversations have been recorded. However, all of these laws, federal and state, protect only protect communications in circumstances where the speaker has a reasonable, as well as a subjective, expectation of privacy. See *Kee v. City of Rowlett*, 247 F.3d 206 (5th Cir. 2001), and *United States v. Longoria*, 177 F.3d 1179 (10th Cir. 1999). State legislators are beginning to provide a context for the use of VSE. The laws of 13 states expressly prohibit the installation or use of cameras in private places. In Alabama, Arkansas, California, Delaware, Georgia, Hawaii, Kansas, Maine, Michigan, Minnesota, New Hampshire, South Dakota and Utah, installation of VST without permission is against the law.

C. Disclosure of Private Information under FERPA

Connecticut Office v. Hartford Board of Education
464 F.3d 229 (2d Cir. 2006)

SOTOMAYOR, Circuit Judge:

This appeal raises the question of whether the Protection and Advocacy for Individuals with Mental Illness Act ("PAIMI"), the Developmental Disabilities Assistance and Bill of Rights Act of 2000 ("DD Act"), and the Protection and Advocacy of Individual Rights Act ("PAIR"), (collectively, the "P&A Acts") authorize plaintiffs-appellees the State of Connecticut Office of Protection and Advocacy ("OPA") (1) to observe and interview students at the Hartford Transitional Learning Academy (the "Academy"), a therapeutic school for students who are seriously emotionally disturbed, in order to investigate complaints of abuse and neglect at the school, and (2) to obtain a directory of students with contact information for their parents or guardians. For the reasons that follow, we hold that the P&A Acts authorize OPA to access the Academy during school hours and to obtain a directory of students and contact information for their parents or guardians.

[Defendants] on appeal that, even if the P&A Acts authorize OPA to access the Academy and its students and to obtain a list of students and contact information for their parents or guardians, the Family Educational Rights and Privacy Act ("FERPA"), and the Individuals with Disabilities Education Act ("IDEA"), nonetheless bar their compliance with OPA's requests. Following oral argument and the submission of a joint amicus brief by the United States Departments of Education and Health and Human Services, however, defendants abandoned their arguments based on FERPA and the IDEA, and we therefore do not address them. We affirm the injunction.

I. Factual Background

The Academy is a public school in Hartford, Connecticut, that is under defendants' authority. The Academy provides a "therapeutic educational program" for children who are seriously emotionally disturbed and who present challenging behavioral problems. All students enrolled at the Academy have been identified as requiring special education or related services under the IDEA. The parents or guardians of students enrolled there are required to sign a document acknowledging the school's use of physical restraints and seclusion.

OPA alleges that it received complaints from parents of students at the Academy about the inappropriate use of physical restraints and seclusion at the school. Parents also complained that students had been injured during the restraint process. As a result of these complaints, as well as allegations that students had been placed at the Academy without proper behavioral assessments or adequate individualized educational plans as required by the IDEA, OPA determined that it had probable cause to suspect that Academy students had been, or were at risk of being, subject to abuse and neglect. In conjunction with the State of Connecticut Office of the Child Advocate ("OCA"), OPA opened an investigation into possible abuse and neglect at the Academy. OCA is a state-created agency charged with monitoring services provided to children by the State of Connecticut or by organizations, such as school districts, that receive state funds, and with reviewing complaints about those services.

****

On appeal, defendants assert that the district court erred in concluding that the Academy is a "facility" to which OPA is entitled to have reasonable access under PAIMI because the implementing regulations limit the term "facility" to residential facilities, which the Academy is not. ......Initially, defendants also asserted that FERPA and the IDEA prohibited them from allowing OPA to access the Academy, its students or the students' contact information. Specifically, they argued that, regardless of any authority OPA might have under the P&A Acts, FERPA and the IDEA prohibit them from allowing OPA to be present at the Academy during school hours or to interview Academy students without the consent of their parents or guardians.[3] Similarly, without such permission, defendants asserted, the release of the names of students and contact information for their parents or guardians is prohibited by FERPA. For the reasons we will explain, defendants have since abandoned these arguments.

Following oral argument, we invited the United States Departments of Education ("DOE") and Health and Human Services ("HHS") to file amicus briefs in this case providing their interpretations of the relevant statutory provisions. DOE and HHS accepted our invitation and filed a joint brief with the Court, which, in significant part, rejects defendants' arguments. With respect to defendants' FERPA defense, the agencies explain that FERPA's non-disclosure requirements are limited to tangible records and information derived from records and that FERPA does not prohibit an OPA representative from observing a classroom or speaking with students. They note that DOE has previously adopted this interpretation in informal guidance. DOE and HHS also explain that, to the extent FERPA prohibits defendants from releasing the names and contact information for students who OPA has probable cause to believe were subject to abuse or neglect, the P&A Acts should be construed "as a limited override of FERPA's non-disclosure requirements" in the circumstances presented by this case.

In response to the agencies' submission, defendants notified this Court that, although they do not agree with the view articulated in the joint amicus brief, they will defer to the agencies' interpretation of FERPA.

---

[3] The IDEA requires schools that receive federal funds for special education, such as the Academy, to abide by the terms of FERPA. *See* 20 U.S.C. § 1417(c). It does not impose any further non-disclosure requirements. We therefore discuss defendants' non-disclosure argument only with reference to FERPA.

Jensen v. Reeves
3 F. App'x 905 (10th Cir. 2001)

ORDER AND JUDGMENT

After C.J. was suspended from Sharon Elementary School for engaging in several alleged incidents of misconduct, his parents, Carl and Judy Jensen, filed this civil rights action… The Plaintiffs' civil rights complaint alleged the following seven general causes of action: …. (6) the Defendants violated their privacy rights under the United States Constitution, the Family Educational Rights and Privacy Act ("FERPA").

****

In their first amended complaint, the Plaintiffs asserted that Reeves violated their right to privacy, which right arose under the Fourth Amendment, the Fourteenth Amendment, and FERPA. The district court concluded that the Plaintiffs' privacy claims based on the Fourth and Fourteenth Amendments failed to state a claim because Reeves' investigation of the complaints against C.J. was reasonable and Reeves' suspension decision was made in conformity with *Lopez*. The district court concluded that the Plaintiffs' privacy claims based on FERPA failed to state a claim because: (1) Reeves' alleged disclosure to the parents of children involved as victims or witnesses did not constitute a prohibited disclosure of an educational record under 20 U.S.C. § 1232g; (2) FERPA only regulates the release of records pursuant to a policy or practice and there was nothing in the complaint to indicate Reeves' disclosures were pursuant to such a policy or practice; and (3) FERPA does not create a private cause of action enforceable under § 1983.

…..Accordingly, with the exception of the brief comments set out below with regard to the Plaintiffs' FERPA claims, this court affirms the district court's 12(b)(6) dismissal of the Plaintiffs' federal claims for substantially those reasons set forth in the district court's order of dismissal filed March 29, 1999.

……

The Plaintiffs' complaint identifies two disclosures that purportedly implicate FERPA's privacy provisions. The first disclosure occurred on October 31, 1997, in a memorandum sent by Reeves to the parents of a female student named L.P. According to the amended complaint, "the memorandum outlined what had been done in response to a harassment complaint that had been filed against C.J. The memorandum indicated that matters had been investigated in accordance with district policy and C.J. would lose his lunch privileges during the first week of November and be required to stay in the principal's office." Like the district court, we conclude that the contemporaneous disclosure to the parents of a victimized child of the results of any investigation and resulting disciplinary actions taken against an alleged child perpetrator does not constitute a release of an "education record" within the meaning of 20 U.S.C. § 1232g(a)(4)(A). Reading such disclosures to fall within the ambit of § 1232g would place educators in an untenable position: they could not adequately convey to the parents of affected students that adequate steps were being undertaken to assure the safety of the student. Nor do we think that such a targeted, discrete, contemporaneous disclosure fits within the bounds of the plain language of § 1232g(a)(4)(A). Finally, we note that this particular disclosure is completely unlike the broad, routinized disclosures of student grades at issue in *Falvo. See* 233 F.3d at 1203.

The second disclosure set out in the Plaintiffs' amended complaint related to a separate playground incident that allegedly occurred on March 2, 1999. The amended complaint alleges that on March 4th, Reeves sent a series of memoranda to "the parents of students who had claimed they had been hit or touched by C.J. as well as other students who had reported were [sic] witnesses to the conduct of C.J." In both their appellate brief and at oral argument, the Plaintiffs emphasized that this second disclosure went not only to the parents of the children allegedly assaulted by C.J., but also to the parents of children who simply witnessed the incident. This court need not decide how a broader, yet still contemporaneous, disclosure to the parents of children witnesses, in addition to the parents of alleged victims, would affect the calculus set out above because the memoranda identified in the amended complaint simply do not disclose anything that could qualify as an education record under § 1232g(a)(4)(A). Instead, the memoranda all reflect the following information:

> (1) an incident allegedly occurred on the playground involving C.J. and a number of other children; (2) C.J. was allegedly verbally and/or physically abusive to several children during the incident; (3) each addressee's child had been questioned about the incident and each reported C.J. had been abusive in some manner; (4) C.J. was informed that *if he had been* abusive, he must stop such behavior immediately; and (5) C.J. was warned that there were consequences for abusive behavior.

As should be apparent, the memoranda identified in the complaint disclosed no more than the fact that the addressee's child had been involved in an alleged incident involving C.J., either as a victim or witness, and that the addressee's child had been questioned about the incident. The memoranda do not disclose whether C.J. was ultimately found to be at fault, whether he was punished, or, if so, what that punishment was. The Plaintiffs have not identified, and this court has not found, a single case holding that the extremely limited type of information conveyed here constitutes an education record under § 1232g. Accordingly, this court concludes that the district court did not err in dismissing the Plaintiffs' FERPA claim pursuant to Fed. R. Civ. P. 12(b)(6).

FERPA Regulations: A Response to Campus Shootings, 9/11-Terrorism, and New Technology

From time-to time, the US Department of Education adopts new regulations governing disclosures under FERPA. The rules ordinarily represent a compilation of the private letters of guidance that the Office of FERPA Compliance had issued since its last regulatory enactment. The rules below also implement changes in FERPA necessary after four events:

> - The Supreme Court decision in *Gonzaga University v. Doe*, 536 U.S. 273 (2002), that states that the USDOE may not take any enforcement action involving FERPA

disclosures without first finding that the violation constituted a policy or practice of the agency or institution;

- Increased demand for education record disclosures following the shootings at Columbine High School in Littleton, Colo., in the spring of 1999, and Virginia Tech University in April 2007 and state laws requiring record disclosures;

-The enactment of the USA Patriot Act (Pub. L. 107-56), passed on October 26, 2001, which included a terrorism exception to disclosures form the education record; and

-The passage of the Campus Sex Crimes Prevention Act, section 1601(d) of the Victims of Trafficking and Violence Protection Act of 2000 (Pub. L. 106-386), enacted October 28, 2000.

The new rules make the following changes in the FERPA regulations:

• Amends CFR § 99.5 to clarify the conditions under which an educational agency or institution may disclose personally identifiable information from an eligible student's education records to a parent without the prior written consent of the eligible student;

• Amends CFR § 99.31(a)(1) to authorize the disclosure of education records without consent to contractors, consultants, volunteers, and other outside parties to whom an educational agency or institution has outsourced institutional services or functions;

• Amends CFR § 99.31(a)(1) to ensure that teachers and other school officials only gain access to education records in which they have legitimate educational interests;

• Amends CFR § 99.31(a)(2) to permit educational agencies and institutions to disclose education records, without consent, to another institution even after the student has enrolled or transferred so long as the disclosure is for purposes related to the student's enrollment or transfer;

• Amends CFR § 99.31(a)(6) to require that an educational agency or institution may disclose personally identifiable information under this section only if it enters into a written agreement with the organization specifying the purposes of the study and the use and destruction of the data;

• Amends CFR § 99.31 to include a new subsection to provide standards for the release of information from education records that has been de-identified;

• Amends CFR § 99.35 to permit State and local educational authorities and Federal officials listed in § 99.31(a)(3) to make further disclosures of personally identifiable information from education records on behalf of the educational agency or institution; and

• Amends CFR § 99.36 to remove the language requiring strict construction of this exception and add a provision stating that if an educational agency or institution determines that there is an articulable and significant threat to the health or safety of a student or other individual, it may disclose the information to any person, including parents, whose knowledge of the information is necessary to protect the health or safety of the student or other individuals.

Notes and Comments

1. FERPA Disclosures and Exceptions to Prior Parental Consent

The essential starting point for FERPA disclosures is always notice to, and consent from, the parent or guardian prior to the sharing of the contents of the education record. However, the federal law has refined a list of the circumstances when disclosure is permitted without prior written consent. It includes disclosures that are made:

• To comply with a judicial order or lawfully issued subpoena. 34 CFR 99.31(a)(9)

• In connection with a health or safety emergency. 34 CFR 99.31(a)(10);

• To provide "directory information" (student name, address, date of birth, dates of attendance, etc.). 34 CFR 99.37;

• To State and local officials in compliance with a State statute that requires or authorizes information sharing. 34 CFR 99.31(a)(5) and 34 CFR 99.38;

• To provide information from the school's law enforcement unit records file that is usually maintained by the SRO. 34 CFR 99.3 and 99.8.

• To other school officials, including teachers, within the school or school district. 34 CFR 99.31(a)(1);

• To officials of another school, school system, or postsecondary institution where the student seeks or intends to enroll. 34 CFR 99.34;

• To teachers and school officials in other schools when the information concerns disciplinary action taken against the student for conduct. 34 CFR 99.36.

For more, see Medaris, M.L., Campbell, E., & James, B. (1997, June): Sharing information: A Guide to the Family Educational Rights and Privacy Act and Participation in Juvenile Justice

Programs. Washington, D.C.: U.S. Department of Justice, Office of Juvenile Justice and Delinquency Prevention and U.S. Department of Education, Family Policy Compliance Office.

2. Student Record Disclosures and "Directory Information"
"Directory Information" from the education record may be disclosed without prior parental consent after a school gives notice of its intention to do so. A critical distinction exists between "directory information" and all other information present in the file. School districts are permitted to choose how much benign or "directory information" from the education record it will disclose.

The items of directory information are made up of information not generally considered by the Department of Education to be harmful or an invasion of privacy if disclosed. In most instances disclosure is helpful to both the institution and the student. Even so, school districts must establish a policy and give notice as to the type of directory information it intends to disclose. Parents who wish to retain the right to consent to disclosures of directory information must so advise the school. Directory information includes, but is not limited to the following:

- student name
- address and telephone
- date, place of birth
- major field of study
- official activities
- dates of attendance
- height and weight for sports
- degrees and awards received
- most recent previous education institution

See 20 U.S.C. § 1232g(a)(5)(B) and 34 C.F.R. § 99.3, 99.6(a)(6) and § 99.37.

3. FERPA Disclosures and State Juvenile Record Sharing Laws
In many States, the disclosure of juvenile record information is seen as essential to the legislative reform designed to enhance supervision and intervention of juveniles. This recurring theme has important implications for educators who are always included on these interagency teams. What are the FERPA implications for educators who are required to provide information from education records for other state and local agencies? May an educator opt out of such programs? Does FERPA provide an excuse for refusing to participate in interagency collaboration?

The basis for the great interest in interagency collaboration is the belief that state and local agencies make better decisions when the quality of the information regarding juveniles is available in a timely fashion. The laws of the reform states have some, if not all of the following components:

* Provisions clearly authorizing or requiring collaboration among state and local juvenile justice agencies;

* Statutes requiring record sharing among agencies who provide supervision and intervention services as to known juvenile offenders under court supervision;

* Laws mandating the inclusion of schools (public and private) in the interagency team as to both known offenders and juveniles considered at-risk; and

* Policies that authorize or require school-based collaboration between schools (public and private) and law enforcement, for the purpose of maintaining safe campuses.

* Programs that broaden interagency collaboration into proactive efforts that compile risk factors of juveniles who are (or may be) at-risk for delinquent behavior.

California law expresses the authorization in this manner:

Wel. and Inst. Code § 827.1. Computerized data base system; authorized access; security procedures

> (a) Notwithstanding any other provision of law, a city, county, or city and county may establish a computerized data base system within that city, county, or city and county that permits the probation department, law enforcement agencies, and school districts to access probation department, law enforcement, school district, and juvenile court information and records which are nonprivileged and where release is authorized under state or federal law or regulation, regarding minors under the jurisdiction of the juvenile court.

Florida law provides a mandatory structure for interagency information sharing.

> Juv. Code § 985.046. Statewide information-sharing system; interagency workgroup
>
> (1) The Department of Education, the Department of Juvenile Justice, and the Department of Law Enforcement shall create an information-sharing workgroup for the purpose of developing and implementing a workable statewide system of sharing information among school districts, state and local law enforcement agencies, providers, the Department of Juvenile Justice, and the Department of Education. The system shall build on processes previously authorized in statute and on any revisions to federal statutes on confidentiality. The information to be shared shall focus on youth who are involved in the juvenile justice system, youth who have been tried as adults and found guilty of felonies, and students who have been serious discipline problems in schools. The participating agencies shall implement improvements that maximize the sharing of information within applicable state and federal statutes and rules and that utilize statewide databases and data delivery systems to streamline access to the information needed to provide joint services to disruptive, violent, and delinquent youth.
>
> (2) The interagency workgroup shall be coordinated through the Department of Education and shall include representatives from the state agencies specified in subsection (1), school superintendents, school district information system

> directors, principals, teachers, juvenile court judges, police chiefs, county sheriffs, clerks of the circuit court, the Department of Children and Family Services, providers of juvenile services including a provider from a juvenile substance abuse program, and circuit juvenile justice managers.

Connecticut law requires notice to educators as part of an "early warning" that allows school officials to determine how, if at all, to respond to the delinquency of a juvenile who is also a student. Educators receive information from law enforcement records and are given discretion in sharing it.

Ed. Code § 10-233h. Arrested students. Reports by police, disclosure, confidentiality. Police testimony at expulsion hearings.

> If any person who is at least seven years of age but less than twenty-one years of age and an enrolled student is arrested for a violation of section 53-206c, a class A misdemeanor or a felony, the municipal police department or Division of State Police within the Department of Public Safety that made such arrest shall, not later than the end of the weekday following such arrest, orally notify the superintendent of schools of the school district in which such person resides of the identity of such person and the offense or offenses for which he was arrested and shall, within seventy-two hours of such arrest, provide written notification of such arrest, containing a brief description of the incident, to such superintendent. The superintendent shall maintain such written report in a secure location and the information in such report shall be maintained as confidential in accordance with section 46b-124. The superintendent may disclose such information only to the principal of the school in which such person is a student or to the principal or supervisory agent of any other school in which the superintendent knows such person is a student. The principal or supervisory agent may disclose such information only to special services staff or a consultant, such as a psychiatrist, psychologist or social worker, for the purposes of assessing the risk of danger posed by such person to himself, other students, school employees or school property and effectuating an appropriate modification of such person's educational plan or placement, and for disciplinary purposes. If the arrest occurred during the school year, such assessment shall be completed not later than the end of the next school day…

Iowa law broadens the role of educators on the interagency team with the following provisions:

Ed Code 280.25 Information sharing—interagency agreements.

> 1. The board of directors of each public school and the authorities in charge of each accredited nonpublic school shall adopt a policy and the superintendent of each public school shall adopt rules which provide that the school district or school may share information contained within a student's permanent record pursuant to an interagency agreement with state and local agencies that are part of the juvenile

> justice system. These agencies include, but are not limited to, juvenile court services, the department of human services, and local law enforcement authorities. The disclosure of information shall be directly related to the juvenile justice system's ability to effectively serve, prior to adjudication, the student whose records are being released.

IV. The Health Insurance Portability and Accountability Act (HIPAA)

> [I]nformation that is created or received by a healthcare provider ... that relates to the physical or mental health of an individual, as well as the provision of healthcare to an individual or payment for the provision of healthcare to an individual, and that identifies the individual or could be used to identify the individual [is private]. 42 U.S.C. § 1320d(6); 45 C.F.R. § 160.103.

The Health Insurance Portability and Accountability Act (HIPAA), (Pub. L. No. 104-191, 110 Stat. 1936; codified primarily in sections of 42 U.S.C. and 29 U.S.C), was enacted to improve the portability of patients' health records while maintaining the privacy and security of the information. HIPAA requires health plans and hospitals to ensure the confidentiality and security of patient information. Its records privacy provisions set national standards for the protection of health information, particularly health care transactions that are performed electronically. HIPAA imposes standardization in the way health care records, including provider billings, are prepared and transmitted. Medical providers, insurance companies, claims clearinghouses, employers that self-insure workers' health benefits are the primary entities covered under HIPAA. The changes will also impact nearly all Medicaid providers, including those providing general health care, pharmacy, mental health, dental, nursing home care, vision and hearing for Medicaid patients. All covered entities are required to implement privacy systems and to require that persons and business with whom they interact will implement privacy systems to compliment the goals of HIPAA. The HIPAA Privacy Rule also requires covered entities to protect individuals' health records and other identifiable health information by requiring appropriate safeguards to protect privacy, and setting limits and conditions on the uses and disclosures that may be made of such information without patient authorization. The rule also gives patients rights over their health information, including rights to examine and obtain a copy of their health records, and to request corrections. Failure to timely implement these standards may, under certain circumstances, trigger the imposition of civil or criminal penalties. *See* 42 U.S.C. § 1320d(6).

Educators fall under the definition of entities covered by the provisions of HIPAA when they engage in electronic disclosures of student health care information. Records of these services and records relating to special medical conditions of students cannot be disclosed except as provided by the Privacy Rule found in 45 C.F.R. § 160.103.

The materials below provide an overview of how the Privacy Rule operates in a school setting. HIPAA works together with the provisions of a variety of statutes that speak to student records making compliance with its mandates a matter of some complexity.

Protection & Advocacy v. Freudenthal
412 F. Supp. 2d 1211 (D. Wyo. 2006)

Honorable Alan B. Johnson, United States District Court Judge.

This Court has been asked to decide whether the confidentiality provisions of two federal statutes, the Health Insurance Portability and Accountability Act (HIPAA), 42 U.S.C. § 1320d to d-8, and the federal Medicaid Act, 42 U.S.C. § 1396a(a)(7), prohibit the Plaintiff from accessing records at the Wyoming State Hospital and the Wyoming State Training School [to investigate incidents of abuse and neglect of individuals with developmental disabilities] in accordance with the access authority set forth in the Protection and Advocacy for Individuals with Mental Illness Act, (hereinafter the "PAIMI Act"), 42 U.S.C. § 10801 et seq., the Developmental Disabilities Assistance and Bill of Rights Act (hereinafter, "DD Act"), 42 U.S.C. § 15001 et seq., and the Protection and Advocacy for Individual Rights Act (hereinafter, the "PAIR Act"), 29 U.S.C § 794e, (collectively referred to as the "P&A" acts).

In its Amended Complaint, Plaintiff asserts that Defendants have denied access to records at the Wyoming State Hospital and Wyoming State Training School in violation of the P&A acts. Defendants raise the issue of the extent to which HIPAA and the Medicaid Act affect the disclosure requirements in the P&A acts.

The Court holds that neither HIPAA nor the Medicaid Act bars the Plaintiff from accessing records at the Wyoming State Hospital and the Wyoming State Training School as long as the disclosure is required by a P&A act and P&A complies with all requirements set forth in the P&A act.

FINDINGS OF FACT

.....

The Wyoming State Hospital (hereinafter, "State Hospital") is a state institution which was established in 1886. It is the only publicly funded, psychiatric inpatient facility in the State. The State Hospital is an agency within the Wyoming Department of Health, and is a "covered entity," as that term is defined in the Health Insurance Portability and Accountability Act (hereinafter, "HIPAA"), 42 U.S.C. § 1320d.

The Wyoming State Training School (hereinafter, "State Training School") is a state institution which was opened in 1912, originally as an inpatient facility for persons with developmental disabilities. The State Training School continues to serve individuals with developmental disabilities. It also provides support and services to individuals who are dually diagnosed with developmental disabilities and mental illness. The State Training School also provides inpatient services for persons with traumatic brain injuries. The State Training School is an agency within the Wyoming Department of Health and is a "covered entity," as that term is defined in HIPAA.

The Wyoming Medicaid program pays for services to some of the patients of the State Training School.

II. ISSUES

The parties agree that the P&A acts authorize P&A to obtain patient and other records from the State Hospital and State Training School in certain circumstances. However, Defendants question the extent to which HIPAA and the Medicaid Act affect those rights of access. Thus, the parties have asked the Court to rule on the interplay between the P&A acts, which confer a right to access patient records under certain circumstances, and HIPPA and the Medicaid Act, which safeguard protected health information. The parties, through negotiations, have established a mutually acceptable access agreement (Appendix A), but it cannot be implemented if HIPAA or the Medicaid Act bar disclosure of the records to P&A.

CONCLUSIONS OF LAW

The issue of P&A's access to records requires the Court to consider other federal statutes which impose confidentiality requirements to protect individual records. The requirements regarding access and confidentiality rights relevant to this case are set forth in the PAIMI, DD and PAIR acts; in HIPAA, 42 U.S.C. § 1320d to d-8; and in the federal Medicaid confidential data standards, as established by § 1902(a)(7) of the Social Security Act (hereinafter, "Medicaid"), 42 U.S.C. § 1396a(a)(7).

****

B. The Health Insurance Portability and Accountability Act (HIPAA) and the Medicaid Act

Congress enacted HIPAA, 42 U.S.C. § 1320d to d-8 , in part, to address concerns about the confidentiality of individually identifiable health information, particularly in an era of electronic communication. Effective as of April 14, 2003, the U.S. Department of Health and Human Services, (hereinafter "DHHS"), promulgated a Privacy Rule protecting all individually identifiable health information held or transmitted by a covered entity or its business associate in any form or media. The Privacy Rule calls this information "protected health information." 45 C.F.R. § 160.103. HIPAA defines terms and imposes requirements for exchanging health information and provides civil and criminal penalties for violations. 42 U.S.C. § 1320d-5 to d-6.

The parties agree that both the State Hospital and State Training School, agencies within the Wyoming Department of Health, are covered entities under HIPAA and the Privacy Rule, as defined in the regulations at 45 C.F.R. § 160.103.

The drafters of the Privacy Rule clearly anticipated its potential conflict with other federal laws and addressed the issue in the preamble to the rule. The Court will consider the drafters' comments at length, as an agency's interpretation of its own regulations is entitled to substantial deference. "The agency's construction of its own regulation is controlling 'unless it is plainly erroneous or inconsistent with the regulation.'" *Wyoming Outdoor Council v U.S. Forest Service, supra*, at 165 F.3d 44, citing United States v. *Larionoff*, 431 U.S. 864, 872 (1977) (quoting *Bowles v. Seminole Rock Co.*, 325 U.S. 410, 414 (1945).)

The preamble to the Privacy Rule states, under the heading of "Relationship to Other Federal Laws:" "Covered entities subject to these rules are also subject to other federal statutes and regulations." Further, the preamble advised that "covered entities will need to determine how the privacy regulation will affect their ability to comply with other federal laws." 65 Fed. Reg. 82481 (December 28, 2000).

The Privacy Rule was intended to develop a procedure for handling protected health information and not to create or change substantive law, as indicated in the following statement in the preamble to the rule:

> Many apparent conflicts will not be true conflicts. For example, if a conflict appears to exist because a previous statute or regulation requires a specific use or disclosure of protected health information that the rules below appear to prohibit, the use or disclosure pursuant to that statute or regulation would not be a violation of the privacy regulation because § 164.512(a) permits covered entities to use or disclose protected health information as required by law.

65 Fed. Reg. 82481-82482 (December 28, 2000).

The drafters did not intend the Privacy Rule to interfere with the operation of P&A acts where access to records is required, as illustrated in the following comment and response in the preamble:

> Comment: One commenter urged HHS [Health and Human Services] to ensure that the regulation would not impede access to individually identifiable health information to entities that are part of the Protection and Advocacy System to investigate abuse and neglect as authorized by the Developmental Disabilities Bill of Rights Act.

> Response: The Developmental Disabilities Assistance and Bill of Rights Act of 2000 ("DD Act") mandates specific disclosures of individually identifiable health information to Protection and Advocacy systems designated by the chief elected official of the states and territories. Therefore covered entities may make these disclosures under § 164.512(a) without first obtaining an individual's authorization, except in those circumstances in which the DD Act requires the individual's authorization. Therefore, the rules below will not impede the functioning of the existing Protection and Advocacy System.

65 Fed. Reg. 82594 (December 28, 2000).

The Privacy Rule provision governing disclosures "required by law" is 45 C.F.R. § 164.512(a)(1), which states as follows:

> A covered entity may use or disclose protected health information to the extent that such use or disclosure is required by law and the use or disclosure complies with and is limited to the relevant requirements of law.

DHHS has designated its Office of Civil Rights, (hereinafter "OCR"), as the agency to enforce the Privacy Rule. OCR operates a web site on which it provides information and answers to questions about the Privacy Rule. The web site reports the OCR was asked the following question:

> May a covered entity disclose protected health information to a Protection and Advocacy system where the disclosure is required by law?

The Office of Civil Rights responded, in the affirmative, stating, in part:

> Yes. The Privacy Rule permits a covered entity to disclose protected health information (PHI) without the authorization of the individual to a state-designated Protection and Advocacy (P&A) system to the extent that such disclosure is required by law and the disclosure complies with the requirements of that law. http://answers.hhs.gov.

In the case at hand, the Court has quoted extensively from the preamble to the Privacy Rule because there is apparently only one case in which a court has considered the interplay between HIPAA and the P&A acts. The case is *Ohio Legal Rights Service v. Buckeye Ranch, Inc*., 365 F. Supp. 2d 877 (S.D. Ohio 2005). Although the court based its decision on Ohio state law, the opinion is helpful for its interpretation of the HIPAA regulation on disclosures required by law. 45 C.F.R. § 164.512(a).

The case involved two parallel investigations by Ohio Legal Rights Service (hereinafter, "OLRS"), a designated protection and advocacy system. In relevant part, OLRS was investigating the possible abuse of a 13-year old whose wrist was apparently fractured during a restraint at Buckeye Ranch, a residential facility for children with mental illness. The Buckeye Ranch refused P&A access to the records arguing that HIPAA prohibited it from disclosing the records and that Buckeye Ranch would face civil and criminal penalties if it released individually identifiable health information. This is the same concern the State Hospital and State Training School have raised in this case.

The court found that the HIPAA Privacy Rule did not bar disclosure of records to P&A, but that Buckeye Ranch acted appropriately in refusing to produce the records because P&A had not asserted probable cause as required under the PAIMI Act:

> The Court is certainly aware of OLRS's important mission of defending mentally ill individuals from abuse and neglect. Nonetheless, OLRS's requests for the seclusion and restraint logs were not based on a finding of probable cause... Buckeye Ranch cannot be faulted for refusing to produce the logs when it did not know OLRS had probable cause to believe that incidents of abuse and neglect had occurred. *Id.*

In addressing the Privacy Rule's "required by law" provision at 45 C.F.R. § 164.512(a)(1), the court stated:

> Subparagraph (1) is an exception that stands on its own, allowing a covered entity to make a disclosure otherwise prohibited by HIPAA if that disclosure is required by another law. In disclosing the information, the covered entity must simply comply with the requirements of the other law—HIPAA imposes no further conditions. Ohio Legal Rights Service v. Buckeye Ranch, Inc., supra, at 365 F. Supp. 2d 886.

The court supported its interpretation of the Privacy Rule provision by quoting from the commentary to the HIPAA rule, stating in part:

> A reading of the final commentary accompanying the HIPAA regulations confirms that the Court's interpretation is correct. The commentary notes that the phrase 'required by law' is intended to be read broadly to include the full array of binding legal authority, such as constitutions, statutes, rules, regulations....It encompasses federal, state or local actions with legally binding effect.... 65 Fed. Reg. 82462, 82668.'
> *Ohio Legal Rights Service*, *Id.* at 365 F. Supp. 2d 886 .

In the case at hand, the Court, in interpreting 45 C.F.R. § 164.512(a)(1), adopts the reasoning of DHHS and of the court in *Ohio Legal Rights Service v. Buckeye Ranch, Inc., supra.* Accordingly, the Court specifically finds as a matter of law that the HIPAA Privacy Rule does not bar the State Hospital and State Training School from disclosing "protected health information" without the authorization of the individual to P&A if such disclosure is required by a P&A act, and that P&A complies with the requirements set forth in the act.

Medicaid is a program that pays for medical assistance for certain individuals and families with low incomes and resources. The program became law in 1965 and is jointly funded by the federal and state governments to assist states in providing assistance for long-term medical care to people who meet certain eligibility criteria. Medicaid is the largest source of funding for medical and health-related services for people with limited income.

The federal Medicaid confidential data standard, as established by § 1902(a)(7) of the Social Security Act (Medicaid), contains requirements for disclosure of records. 42 U.S.C. § 1396a(a)(7). Records may be released pursuant to 42 C.F.R. § 431.302 for purposes which are directly related to State plan administration, including:

(a) Establishing eligibility;

(b) Determining the amount of medical assistance;

(c) Providing services for recipients; and

(d) Conducting or assisting an investigation, prosecution, or civil or criminal proceeding related to the plan.

The Wyoming State Medicaid program pays for services to some patients at the State Training School. The Wyoming State Medicaid program considers a request from P&A for records as falling within subsection (d) of § 431.302 because it regards P&A as investigating whether or not the facility provided adequate services or adequate safeguards for its clients.

The Court adopts the Wyoming State Medicaid interpretation of 42 C.F.R. § 431.302(d). Accordingly, the Court specifically finds as a matter of law that the State Hospital and the State Training School do not violate the confidentiality provisions of the Medicaid act and regulations by disclosing records to P&A so long as the disclosure is authorized by a P&A act, and the requirements for disclosures are met.

II. DISCLOSURE OF RECORDS

The parties have reached agreement on a protocol to govern P&A's access to records of the State Hospital and State Training School. The DD Act at 42 U.S.C. § 15043(a)(2)(B) grants P&A "authority to investigate incidents of abuse and neglect of individuals with developmental disabilities if the incidents are reported to the system or if there is probable cause to believe the incidents occurred." The PAIMI Act at 42 U.S.C. § 10805(a)(1)(A) grants P&A "authority to investigate incidents of abuse and neglect of individuals with mental illness if the incidents are reported to the system or if there is probable cause to believe the incidents occurred."

In its investigation of alleged abuse and neglect, P&A is entitled to access a broad range of records. The DD Act and its implementing regulations authorize access at 42 U.S.C. § 15043(c) and 45 C.F.R. § 1386.22; these provisions apply as well to requests under the PAIR Act. 29 U.S.C. § 794e(f)(1)-(2). The PAIMI Act and its implementing regulations authorize access to records at 42 U.S.C. § 10805(a)(l)(A) and 42 C.F.R. § 51.41.

The DD and PAIMI acts delineate the circumstances under which P&A is authorized to obtain individual patient records. 42 U.S.C. § 15043(a)(2)(1)(i) and 42 U.S.C. § 10805(a)(4)(A).

As the statutes provide, P&A sometimes requests records on the basis of probable cause to believe that a person with a disability has been subjected to abuse or neglect. The law is well established that in requesting records, P&A makes the decision as to whether probable cause exists. As the court stated in a 2003 case in Connecticut:

> ...it is now a settled principle that the P&A is the 'final arbiter of probable cause for triggering its authority to access all records for an individual that may have been subject to abuse or neglect.' *Arizona Center for Disability Law v. Allen*, 197 F.R.D. 689, 693 (D. Ariz. 2000). Such a position has been overwhelmingly agreed with by other courts.

Office of Protection and Advocacy for Persons with Disabilities v. Armstrong, 266 F. Supp. 2d 303, 318 (D. Conn. 2003).

P&A is entitled to access an individual's records upon a finding of probable cause so long as the other requirements set forth at 42 U.S.C.§ 15043(a)(2)(I)(ii) and (iii); 42 U.S.C.§ 15043 (a)(2)(J)(ii)(I) and (II); or 42 U.S.C. § 10805(a)(4)(B) or (C) are met.

Where a release of records is specifically allowed under the PAIMI or DD acts, HIPAA does not bar disclosure since such records are produced based on the "as required by law" exception to HIPAA. If there is no probable cause, HIPAA would prohibit facilities from disclosing incident reports that contain protected health information without the authorization of the individual.

The primary purpose of HIPAA's Privacy Rule is to safeguard the privacy of medical protected health information. However, these incident reports contain information which can be helpful to P&A in monitoring compliance with patients' rights and in determining whether there is probable cause to believe that abuse or neglect has occurred. The analysis of the release of the incident reports must take into account these different interests. The Court finds that the purpose of all statutes can be met by providing the incident reports to P&A with names and identifying information redacted.

If P&A, after its review of the reports, determines there is probable cause to believe that a patient has been subject to abuse or neglect or that the health or safety of the individual is in serious or immediate jeopardy, it can make an appropriate request for more information. The State Hospital can then provide an unredacted report pursuant to 42 C.F.R. § 51.41(c)(2)(i):

> (2) Reports prepared by an agency charged with investigating abuse, neglect, or injury occurring at a facility rendering care or treatment, or by or for a facility itself, that describe any of the following:
>
> (i) Abuse, neglect or injury occurring at the facility.

The State Training School can then provide an unredacted report pursuant to 45 C.F.R.§ 1386.22(b):

> (2) Reports prepared by an agency charged with investigating incidents of abuse or neglect, injury or death occurring in the facility or while the individual with a developmental disability is under the care of a member of the staff of a facility, or by such a facility that describe any or all of the following:
>
> (i) Abuse, neglect, injury or death;

P&A can then proceed with the requirements set forth in 42 U.S.C. § 10805(a)(4) and 42 U.S.C. § 15043(a)(2)(I) or (J).

The Court specifically finds that this protocol for disclosing incident reports does not violate the HIPAA Privacy Rule or the Medicaid regulations on confidentiality.

The DD Act at 42 U.S.C. § 15043(a)(2)(J) requires P&A to have access to records no later than three business days after it makes a written request, but that P&A shall have immediate access, no later than twenty-four hours after it makes a request without consent from another party, if P&A determines there is probable cause to believe the "health or safety of the individual is in serious or immediate jeopardy" or in any case of death of a person with a developmental disability.

Neither the PAIMI Act nor its regulations establishes specific deadlines for production of records. The PAIMI regulations at 42 C.F.R. § 51.41(a) merely say, "Access to records shall be extended promptly to all authorized agents of a P&A system."

The Court finds that the parties may use the deadlines in the DD Act as a guideline for requests under the PAIMI Act, but, this approach should reflect a good faith analysis of the nature and extent of the request. A narrow request for a small number of records should not require the full three days allowed under DD Act, while a very broad and time intensive request should be allowed some leeway.

The Court finds that the access agreement complies with the current and controlling law and will be the authoritative and enforceable document regarding P&A's access to information and records at the State Hospital and State Training School until or unless the laws and controlling legal precedents change. If the relevant laws are amended, additional relevant laws are passed, or controlling case law deems any provision illegal, the parties will revise the access agreement accordingly.

ORDER

WHEREFORE, THE COURT ORDERS:

1. The HIPAA Privacy Rule does not bar the State Hospital or State Training School from disclosing "protected health information" without the authorization of the individual to P&A so long as the disclosure is required by a P&A act and P&A meets all requirements under the act.

2. The Medicaid confidentiality provision does not bar the State Hospital or State Training School from disclosing records to P&A so long as the disclosure is authorized by a P&A act and P&A meets all requirements under the act.

3. The process set forth in this Order and the Access Agreement shall govern the release of records to P&A subject to changes in applicable laws.

4. As the parties have resolved the main substantive issue in this case and have informed this Court that they no longer wish to pursue residual issues in this case, the Plaintiff's case for retaliation is dismissed with prejudice and the Defendant's claim for copying costs is dismissed with prejudice.

5. The above-captioned case is dismissed with prejudice and each party shall bear its own costs and fees.

Susan P. Stuart: Lex-Praxis of Education Informational Privacy for Public School Children. 84 Neb. L. Rev. 1158 (2006)*

Public schools are information-collection machines. Public schools are also the government. Consequently, there is a confluence of concerns about what the government can and should do about protecting the privacy of schoolchildren in that information. Local educational agencies must concern themselves with the legalities of the collection, maintenance, and disclosure of student information, generated both by the agency itself and by the student. Unfortunately, the federal statutes and regulations designed to protect the privacy of that information have run amok.

****

D. Student Medical Information

One point of similarity between special education students and general education students is the concern about medical information regardless of disability. Educational agencies must be familiar with four principle areas of privacy protection with regard to students' medical information: (i) the general constitutional protections; (ii) Health Insurance Portability and Accountability Act of 1996 ("HIPAA"); 111 (iii) the privilege of school nursing files; and (iv) substance abuse documentation.

1. Medical Records, Generally

The medical files of any child with a serious medical condition—whether disabling or not - may be at the fingertips of school personnel. Even if not for use under IDEA, such records are maintained for health and safety purposes. Similar concerns surround those records generated by and kept by school psychologists or other therapists employed by the school, providing services to both IDEA-protected children and others. The privacy concern is disclosure of and access to that medical information.

2. HIPAA

In Spring 2001, health data privacy protections were mandated by HIPAA. The impetus for these privacy protections arose from the personal nature of health information and the proliferation of electronic databases to collect and store that information. This type of "protected health information" includes intimate details of both physical and mental health - information traditionally protected by the doctor-patient privilege - and could be the source of stigmatization and discrimination if disclosed.

HIPAA regulates electronic communications between health-care providers and health insurers to protect individually identifiable health information. For determining whether they must conform to HIPAA, schools must be either a "health care provider" or any person who, "in the normal course

---

of business, furnishes, bills, or is paid for 'health care'" and who transmits health information electronically. A protected HIPAA transaction is an exchange of information to carry out financial and administrative activities concerning health care. The protected product, "individually identifiable health information," is

> [HIPAA protects] information that is created or received by a healthcare provider ... that relates to the physical or mental health of an individual, as well as the provision of healthcare to an individual or payment for the provision of healthcare to an individual, and that identifies the individual or could be used to identify the individual. See 42 U.S.C. 1320d(6); 45 C.F.R. 160.103.

Based on the circuitous language of HIPAA, a local educational agency would benefit from some expert advice on determining its status under the statute.

What is equally important to note, however, is that "education records" covered by FERPA originally had been excluded from the HIPAA privacy rule's classification for "protected health information." However, the definition of "protected health information" was removed from the HIPAA privacy rule. Apparently, the DOE assumes that FERPA-related records are excluded from HIPAA's protection because the exclusion still exists in regulations for the Social Security Act. Thus, the protection of and access to FERPA-related health records under HIPAA remain a mystery.

Regardless, HIPAA's protected health information would still likely include any documentation, such as personal notes or information, held solely by an individual school psychologist or physical therapist. Those records are typically considered outside the scope of FERPA-protected education records and would therefore not be affected one way or the other by HIPAA coverage of FERPA records. Except for a few limited circumstances, the patient must consent to the disclosure and use of this personal health information under HIPAA. One of those limited circumstances is when parents of an unemancipated minor may be entitled to disclosure of or access to the records as the child's personal representatives unless prohibited by state law.

There are also two particular functions with which public schools must be concerned under HIPAA: student health clinics and school nurses. HIPAA regulates either function if it transmits information electronically. Student health clinics would most clearly come within the protections of HIPAA because of the type of information they obtain and because the information is not likely to fall within the FERPA exceptions. The situation is a bit more complicated with regard to a school nurse. If the nurse transmits electronic health information in a HIPAA transaction, she is covered. If she does not transmit electronically, then it depends upon whether her employer - the local school - ever transmits electronic health information. If so, the nurse is also within HIPAA. However, if the employer does transmit electronically but takes action to exclude the nursing program from HIPAA coverage as a "hybrid" entity, the school nurse is not covered. The whole rigamarole is pretty convoluted, but the gist of HIPAA is that schools may have to comply with HIPAA's use and disclosure requirements, notice and access requirements, and administrative procedural requirements.

The HIPAA privacy rule is a short list of permitted and required disclosures of protected health information; all other disclosures are prohibited. Required disclosures are made to the affected individual under a right of access and to the Department of Health and Human Services to check HIPAA compliance. Permitted disclosures are made to the individual; to carry out health care treatment and its payment in accordance with patient authorization or advance notice to the patient as agreed; and for certain health and safety issues. An educational agency that is required to follow HIPAA and its privacy rules must be prepared to implement procedures for statutorily mandated patient access to and power to amend her health records; procedures to maintain the privacy of health records and to notify patients of such procedures; and procedures for confidential communications and accounting for actual disclosures. Among those duties, the educational agency must designate a privacy officer responsible for implementing the various privacy, administrative, technical, and physical standards and safeguards necessary to comply with HIPAA and its regulations. Because of the intricacies involved in HIPAA compliance, an educational agency should make certain this officer is adequately trained and that all notices and procedures follow a national standard rather than a local standard. Although the appropriate notices of individual rights under HIPAA could be disseminated with other notices, the formulation and implementation of these complex matters is not lightly left to the local educational agencies themselves.

3. School Nurses

HIPAA does not cover all the privacy issues inherent in school nursing duties. For nurses to comply with appropriate nursing standards, they have to keep "process documentation." And although that documentation need not necessarily become part of a state-required school health record—for immunizations, for instance—nor otherwise entered in the student's cumulative record, there is the potential that such systematic documentation could be considered an educational record under FERPA, subject to the same problematic disclosure standards and parental access.

School nurses often keep systematic process documentation through daily logs of student visits in order to provide a plan of appropriate nursing care to the students. Not all of this information is transferred to the school health record forms, and some of the information remaining in these logs is confidential. The logs must be maintained for the nursing process but are separate from the formally maintained records. However, these logs might be accessible under FERPA because they probably are not the "personal notes" that might otherwise be exempt from disclosure as education records. Thus, a school nurse runs into a real conflict if approached for health advice, particularly from a mature minor, if she documents that meeting in accordance with nursing standards. Parents may be able to access that documentation under FERPA.

4. Drug and Alcohol Abuse Records

Any student who is a patient in a federally assisted drug or alcohol abuse program has a nearly absolute right of confidentiality in those records under the Public Health Services Act. The confidentiality of the information resides in the patient, and disclosure usually requires written consent. If state law confers the legal capacity upon minors to obtain substance abuse treatment, then only the minor patient may consent to disclosure; however, if state law requires the consent of a parent or guardian for such treatment, then both the minor and parent must sign the consent unless the minor "lacks the capacity for rational choice." Disclosure without such consent is limited to medical emergencies, certain research projects, audit and evaluation procedures, and certain court orders. The disclosure of these records is even circumscribed in criminal proceedings in the absence of "good cause" for the information in investigating or charging a patient.

A school may be affected by the Public Health Services Act if it is an "entity ... who holds itself out as providing, and provides, alcohol or drug abuse diagnosis, treatment or referral for treatment" that receives federal assistance. Such "treatment" certainly includes substance abuse education and prevention and likely includes any counseling undertaken at an educational agency. Federal assistance need not be directly related to the provision of drug or alcohol treatment to require a governmental agency to comply with the statute's confidentiality provisions. Because these written records must be locked up and secure, they should be separated from the usual education records. Depending upon state law treatment of minors, parental access to the records may be limited so segregating those records is a wise idea.

This statute also raises a dilemma for the increasingly common drug-testing programs in schools—programs designed to control drug use by agencies that receive federal funds. The statute's restrictions on disclosure do not apply to law enforcement personnel for crimes on the premises. However, if, for example, a student tests positive for Tetrahydrocannabinol (commonly called THC) during a school-implemented drug test after having smoked marijuana two weeks before, the student has not really committed a "crime on the premises" under the statute. Furthermore, because the statute's confidentiality provision is not confined to written records, a school that takes disciplinary action as a result of a drug test - such as prohibiting the student from taking part in extracurricular activities - might be "publicizing" this information in violation of the statute.

....

F. Government Accountability and Education Statistics

The No Child Left Behind Act of 2001 ("NCLB"), a comprehensive school reauthorization of the Elementary and Secondary Education Act of 1965, was intended to reform public education and affects educational privacy issues only tangentially. As mentioned above, NCLB specifically amended PPRA. Other than that, however, only its provisions addressing government accountability and transparency have any other effect on schoolchildren's individually identifiable personal information. As NCLB insists on testing and assessment as the means and methods for school improvement and accountability in reading and mathematics, schools must necessarily allow public access to those records. However, individual assessment statistics become part of the student's education records and are otherwise protected by the provisions of FERPA. Also exempted from NCLB's public access is personally identifiable information about students, their academic achievement, and their parents.

Similar protections are included in the Education Sciences Reform Act of 2002. That Act created an Institute of Education Sciences within the DOE to "provide national leadership" in the progress and condition of education in the United States. Within the Institute are the National Center for Education Research, the National Center for Education Statistics ("NCES"), 171 and the National Center for Education Evaluation and Regional Assistance, all of which feed on statistical and other research data to justify their missions. The Institute is specifically bound by the confidentiality provisions of FERPA, PPRA, and the Privacy Act of 1974 with regard to individually identifiable information, but the remaining data is widely available to the public, especially via the Internet.

The USA Patriot Act, however, carved out an exception to the confidentiality protection otherwise required of the NCES. The United States Department of Justice now has the power to collect individually identifiable information possessed by the NCES by applying in writing and averring that the information is relevant to a terrorism investigation under circumstances similar to the seizure of educational records otherwise protected under FERPA.

....

I. School Lunch Programs

One last privacy program that deserves mention is the National School Lunch Program. Similar to other federal privacy regimes, like HIPAA, the school lunch program confidentiality directives are fairly inflexible regarding whether or not to divulge confidential information. Local educational agencies are best served by following the advice of legal counsel and the directives of the United States Department of Agriculture ("USDA") in putting together a local privacy policy. Student eligibility for free and reduced-price breakfasts and lunches requires the compilation of sensitive student and household information, including all sources of income (welfare, unemployment compensation, and the like), SSNs of the applicant-adult, and food stamp information. The types of information that can be disclosed—all eligibility information versus eligibility status only—and the types of consent required depend upon the governmental agency administering the related program. Such programs include education programs, Medicaid, State Children's Health Insurance Programs ("SCHIP"s), and federal, state, and local enforcement laws.

Any violation of these confidentiality regulations is subject to criminal sanctions. Security measures require that only persons with a direct connection to the lunch program may have access to this information. All other disclosures may be made only upon requiring written parental consent with clear identification of the information that will be shared and with whom and providing the option to pick and choose the programs with which the educational agencies may share information. Because the disclosure, access, collection, maintenance, and use protocols for this information are so narrow and are limited to aid recipients, a local policy should be formulated and published, but the individual situational notices could be limited to those who apply for assistance.

Notes and Comments

1. HIPAA and State Laws

The HIPAA Privacy Rule has a rather complex preemption provision. HIPAA preempts state law when it conflicts with or is less restrictive than the Privacy Rule. *See* 45 C.F.R. § 160.202 and 45 C.F.R. § 160.203(b). State law is exempt from the Privacy Rule when it:

> (1) relates to the privacy of individually identifiable health information and provides greater privacy protections or privacy rights with respect to such information;
>
> (2) provides for the reporting of disease or injury, child abuse, birth, or death, or for public health surveillance, investigation, or intervention; or
>
> (3) requires certain health plan reporting, such as for management or financial audits.

State laws may be saved from preemption by specific request of a state. The U.S. Department of Health and Human may, after review of a "contrary" state law, allow an exemption of the statute if it:

> (1) is necessary to prevent fraud and abuse related to the provision of or payment for health care;
>
> (2) is necessary to ensure appropriate State regulation of insurance and health plans to the extent expressly authorized by statute or regulation;
>
> (3) is necessary for State reporting on health care delivery or costs,;
>
> (4) is necessary for purposes of serving a compelling public health, safety, or welfare need, and, if a Privacy Rule provision is at issue, if the Secretary determines that the intrusion into privacy is warranted when balanced against the need to be served; or
>
> (5) has as its principal purpose the regulation of the manufacture, registration, distribution, dispensing, or other control of any controlled substances (as defined in 21 U.S.C. 802), or that is deemed a controlled substance by State law.

As a result, HIPAA provisions are not designed to affect or modify legitimate information exchanges that are authorized or required under federal, state and local law. Most, if not all, of its privacy regulations may yield to the information needs of juvenile justice agencies that collaborate with educators in providing services to children. HIPAA recognizes that these agencies and public officials will need protected health information to deal effectively with public safety threats, emergencies, and crime. The entity covered under HIPAA, that would otherwise need prior authorization, would simply share the information as required under state law. A state or local agency receiving the information is not a covered entity under HIPAA.

The Privacy rule permits covered entities to disclose needed information to public agencies and officials in a variety of ways (45 CFR 164.512):

> 1. Directly to public health authorities for the purpose of preventing or controlling disease, injury, or disability (including the reporting of disease, injury, vital events such as birth or death, and the conduct of public health surveillance, public health investigations, and public health interventions).

2. Directly to agencies authorized to receive reports of victims of abuse, neglect, or domestic violence (including a social service or protective services agency, authorized by law to receive reports of such abuse, neglect, or domestic violence).

1. Directly to the FDA and related agencies for the purpose of monitoring the quality, safety or effectiveness of such FDA-regulated products or activities.

2. Directly to agencies authorized by law to notify persons who may have been exposed to a communicable disease or who may otherwise be at risk of contracting or spreading a disease or condition.

3. Directly to agencies authorized to conduct audits, inspections, investigations, (criminal, administrative, or civil) related to determining compliance with health care laws and regulations.

4. As directed by any judicial or administrative proceeding as a result of a court order, or subpoena, discovery request, or other lawful process.

......

7. Directly to a law enforcement official as required by law (including investigation demands and informal administrative requests, formal requests through warrants and other process, mandatory reporting of certain types of wounds and injuries, or information that may serve to identify or locate a suspect, fugitive, material witness, or missing person). However, HIPAA specifically prohibits disclosure of DNA information for the purpose of suspect identification, absent some other legal requirements such as a warrant.

2. HIPAA and other Federal Laws

The HIPAA Privacy Rule coexists with other federal laws, such as the Federal Privacy Act of 1974, The Federal Educational Rights and Privacy Act and other federal statutes that govern specific areas of records privacy other than patient health data.

The U.S. Department of Health and Human Services has issued regulations and other clarifying statements designed to prevent confusion over FERPA and HIPAA privacy rights.

- Student health records covered under FERPA are excluded from the HIPAA privacy rule in both primary and secondary schools as well as postsecondary institutions that provide health or medical services to students.

- A school district will be considered a covered entity under HIPAA if it has a self-insured health plan; operates as a health-care clearinghouse (for example, providing billing services for other districts); or acts as a health-care provider and transmits health information electronically (for example, billing Medicaid electronically to get reimbursement for services provided to students).

- HIPAA covers protected health information. But "protected health information" (PHI), excludes student health information in a student's educational records. This information is covered by FERPA. School Nurses do not have to comply with HIPAA, even though a school nurse might be a covered entity—because he transmits health information electronically to obtain Medicaid reimbursement for IDEA related services.

- An educational record under FERPA does not include school staff records kept only by the person who created them. It also excludes records created by a district's school resource officers, records that relate to a student's employment in a district, and records for students who are 18 years or older. These records are also exempt from HIPAA, unless they contain "protected health information."

- Both FERPA and HIPAA exempt disclosures to police for legitimate law enforcement purposes.

- The records of school counselors made while providing therapeutic counseling may be covered under FERPA or HIPAA depending on the contents of the records and how they are kept. A counselor's personal notes are exempt from FERPA. They are not exempt from HIPAA if they contain "protected health information" (PHI) which is identifiable to a student. A counselor's notes that are kept by the school with the other records of the student are covered by FERPA and exempt from HIPAA.

For a useful guide on HIPAA, *see*; Joint Guidance on the Application of the *Family Educational Rights and Privacy Act* (*FERPA*) and the *Health Insurance Portability and Accountability Act of 1996* (*HIPAA*) to Student Health Records, (www.ed.gov/policy/gen/guid/fpco/doc/ferpa-hippa-guidance.pdf).

3. HIPAA and Authorizations for the Release of Student Health Records

Students and parents may authorize disclosures that are otherwise subject to the privacy provisions of HIPAA. A valid authorization must be written in plain language and should include all of the items listed below. The school must provide the student or parent with a signed copy of the authorization. Below are the elements that should be included in proper release and authorization:

1. A specific and meaningful description of the information.

2. The name or other specific identification of the person(s) (or class of persons) authorized to make the requested use or disclosure.

3. The name or other specific identification of the person(s) (or class of persons) to whom the covered entity may make the requested use or disclosure.

4. An expiration date or event that relates to the individual or the use or disclosure purpose.

5. A statement of the individual is right to revoke the authorization in writing (and procedures for doing so and exceptions to this right).

6. A statement that any personal health information used or disclosed based on the authorization may be subject to re-disclosure by the recipient and may no longer be protected by HIPAA'.

7. A statement of the ability or inability to condition treatment, payment, enrollment or eligibility for benefits on the authorization (and the implications of that).

8. The individual's dated signature.

9. If an individual's personal representative signs the authorization, a description of that representative's authority to act on the individual's behalf.

Chapter Six
Safe Schools, Criminal Procedure and Law Enforcement on Campus

> [I]n recent years, school disorder has often taken particularly ugly forms: drug use and violent crime in the schools have become major social problems. Even in schools that have been spared the most severe disciplinary problems, the preservation of order and a proper educational environment requires close supervision of schoolchildren. Accordingly, we have recognized that maintaining security and order in the schools requires a certain degree of flexibility in school disciplinary procedures, and we have respected the value of preserving the informality of the student-teacher relationship. *New Jersey v. T.L.O.*, 469 U.S. 325 (1985).

> Questioning of a student by a principal, whose duties include the obligations to maintain order, protect the health and safety of pupils and maintain conditions conducive to learning, cannot be equated with custodial interrogation by law enforcement officers. *In re Corey L.*, 203 Cal. App. 3d 1020, 1024 (Cal. App. 1st Dist. 1988).

There is renewed interest in criminal procedure in the context of pubic education. The movement is of relatively recent vintage and is not without some reluctance and confusion on the part of school officials. While it is fair to say that educators initially found themselves in reactive mode in responding to increasing incidents of crime on campus, chronic bullying and random, but deadly crisis events has prompted an interest in implementing safe schools methods that resemble traditional law enforcement. School district police units are now common at the K-12 level and on college campuses. Juvenile justice courts routinely adjudicate students delinquent for campus misconduct.

The cases and materials below examine the following questions: Should the procedural rules that protect the rights of individuals apply with greater rigor on school campuses? Should students receive at least as much protection from illegal searches, seizures and unfair interrogation techniques as citizens in the neighborhood? How much should educators be able to utilize traditional law enforcement officers on campus before ordinary robust criminal procedures apply? Should the standard be the same in both K-12 and higher education settings?

Note the competing voices in this important area of education reform. Should federal law control in the matter of safe school policies? Should states be free to construct their own solutions to uniquely local problems? There is a visceral link to issues of liability when discussions safe schools. Part V of the course will provide more on the duty of educators to provide a safe learning environment. However, it is worth keeping the following question in mind as you read this section: Why does it appear to be so difficult for educators to maintain a safe campus?

I. Educators as Guarantors of Student Safety

A. The Problem of Unsafe Schools

Bryan Vossekuil et al., U.S. Secret Service & Dep't of Educ., The Final Report and Findings of the Safe School Initiative (2002)

Littleton, Colorado; Springfield, Oregon; West Paducah, Kentucky; Jonesboro, Arkansas. These communities have become familiar to many Americans as the locations where school shootings have occurred in recent years. School shootings are a rare, but significant, component of school violence in America. It is clear that other kinds of problems are far more common than the targeted attacks that have taken place in schools across this country. However, each school-based attack has had a tremendous and lasting effect on the school in which it occurred, the surrounding community, and the nation as a whole.

....

Public policymakers, school administrators, police officials and parents continue to search for explanations for the targeted violence that occurred at Columbine High School and other schools across the country, and seek assurance that similar incidents will not be repeated at educational institutions in their communities. While the quest for solutions to the problem of targeted school violence is of critical importance, reports from the Department of Education, the Justice Department and other sources indicate that few children are likely to fall prey to life-threatening violence in school settings.

To put the problem of targeted school-based attacks in context, from 1993 to 1997 the odds that a child in grades 9-12 would be threatened or injured with a weapon in school were 7 to 8 percent, or 1 in 13 or 14; the odds of getting into a physical fight at school were 15 percent, or 1 in 7.7 In contrast, the odds that a child would die in school–by homicide or suicide–are, fortunately, no greater than 1 in 1 million. In 1998, students in grades 9-12 were the victims of 1.6 million thefts and 1.2 million nonfatal violent crimes, while in this same period 60 school-associated violent deaths were reported for this student population. ...Nevertheless, the impact of targeted school-based attacks cannot be measured in statistics alone. While it is clear that other kinds of problems in American schools are far more common than the targeted violence that has taken place in schools in this country, the high-profile shootings that have occurred in schools over the past decade have resulted in increased fear among students, parents and educators. School shootings are a rare, but significant, component of the problem of school violence. Each school-based attack has had a tremendous and lasting effect on the school in which it occurred, the surrounding community and the nation as a whole. In the wake of these attacks, fear of future targeted school violence has become a driving force behind the efforts of school officials, law enforcement professionals and parents to identify steps that can be taken to prevent incidents of violence in their schools.

[T]here are productive actions that educators, law enforcement officials and others can pursue in response to the problem of targeted school violence. Specifically, Initiative findings suggest that these officials may wish to consider focusing their efforts to formulate strategies for preventing these attacks in two principal areas:

- developing the capacity to pick up on and evaluate available or knowable information that might indicate that there is a risk of a targeted school attack; and,

- employing the results of these risk evaluations or "threat assessments" in developing strategies to prevent potential school attacks from occurring.

Support for these suggestions is found in 10 key findings of the Safe School Initiative study. These findings are as follows:

- Incidents of targeted violence at school rarely were sudden, impulsive acts.

- Prior to most incidents, other people knew about the attacker's idea and/or plan to attack.

- Most attackers did not threaten their targets directly prior to advancing the attack.

- There is no accurate or useful "profile" of students who engaged in targeted school violence.

- Most attackers engaged in some behavior prior to the incident that caused others concern or indicated a need for help.

- Most attackers had difficulty coping with significant losses or personal failures. Moreover, many had considered or attempted suicide.

- Many attackers felt bullied, persecuted or injured by others prior to the attack.

- Most attackers had access to and had used weapons prior to the attack.

- In many cases, other students were involved in some capacity.

- Despite prompt law enforcement responses, most shooting incidents were stopped by means other than law enforcement intervention.

Daniel B. Weddle: Bullying in Schools: The Disconnect Between Empirical Research and Constitutional, Statutory, and Tort Duties to Supervise, 77 Temp. L. Rev. 641 (2004)[*]

At Ohlone Elementary School in Watsonville, California, a boy attacked a younger student in a school restroom, choking him, kicking him repeatedly in the groin, and throwing him to ground so hard that the fall broke the younger boy's leg. The younger boy crawled to the door, pleading for help. According to the victim's mother, the older boy and his brother had attacked the younger boy

---

at school just over one month before; although she had reported the earlier attack to the principal, no disciplinary action ever occurred.

In Boiling Springs, Pennsylvania, Ian Dum was tormented daily from the time he was in fourth grade, when he first began to suffer symptoms of Tourette's syndrome, until well into high school. His classmates taunted him, tied his shoes together, and once followed him around the halls whispering his name and then telling him he was hallucinating. Because they knew he suffered from a severe germ phobia, they poked him in order to aggravate his phobia. Ian eventually left school in his sophomore year, sank into a suicidal depression, and was hospitalized for psychiatric treatment. In his final two years of school, administrators allegedly told him he was overreacting when he reported the bullying.

Nearly two decades of educational research has repeatedly demonstrated that one of the most damaging and pervasive problems in our schools today is bullying. That research has shown that bullying leaves its victims with serious and often life-long emotional problems. It has revealed that bullies are substantially more likely than their peers to commit felonies later in their lives. It has even demonstrated that witnesses to the bullying are often affected in serious, lasting ways. Most importantly, it has proven that school officials can dramatically reduce the prevalence of bullying if they implement proven bullying prevention strategies. Nevertheless, in most schools today, bullying goes on unabated and virtually unchallenged by school officials.

The educational community knows that these children are being tormented; it knows that they are being damaged in ways that will haunt them—and in some cases, entire communities—for years to come. It also knows how to reduce dramatically the prevalence of the torment; and it knows that school officials must lead the way in doing so. Current legal theories, however, whether found in federal or state law, whether based in statutory or common law, are simply not aligned with what empirical research has shown to be true. Therefore, the law provides those who could stop the torment no real incentive to inform themselves and to act, and it provides victims of the torment no remedy against the school officials who could have protected them.

****

A. A Working Definition of Bullying

Perhaps, then, it would be best to begin by defining "bullying." Bullying is not the garden-variety trouble all children have with others from time to time. It is not mere teasing or even being pushed around a little by another child. It is not occasional insults or exclusion by the popular students. All of those encounters are suffered by all children on one level or another, and they may be ultimately harmless or at least limited in their impact. Of course, they may also be the sparks that signal a forest fire of ongoing torment that is either coming or has already arrived for some child. By themselves, however, they are not what educational research has identified as truly damaging.

Bullying, as it is usually defined in the educational research, is a persistent pattern of intimidation and harassment directed at a particular student in order to humiliate, frighten, or isolate the child. The victim usually has no effective way to resist or end the torment, either because of an imbalance of power or because the bully can so effectively lie his way out of trouble when necessary and return to retaliate. Bullying is a sustained, cruel, and inescapable torment that sometimes continues for years. It is, in fact, a form of child abuse perpetrated by the child's peers. Given bullying's effects on victims, one researcher places bullying "in the same league as harassment, discrimination, racism, violence, assault, stalking, physical abuse, sexual abuse, molestation, and rape." It isn't Opie's nemesis.

Nor is bullying limited to boys bullying boys. Both boys and girls engage in bullying - boys most often in physical intimidation and girls most often in psychological intimidation. Girls' bullying tends to be less visible, consisting of "social alienation, intimidation, malicious gossip, note writing, and peer manipulation." Although girls' bullying typically lacks the physical threat usually associated with boys' bullying, its effects are just as debilitating because it tends to force its victims into social isolation and despair. Bystanders are as reluctant to challenge the female bully who can effectively destroy their peer relationships as boys are to challenge the male bully who can beat them physically....

B. The Effects of Bullying

The effects of bullying, as defined above, are well documented and disturbing. They are long lasting and debilitating, not only for the victims, as one might expect, but also for the bullies themselves, as well as bystanders.

The effects on victims are, the most disturbing. Not only do victims suffer the immediate pain and humiliation of being the subject of a bully's torment, they suffer emotional and psychological effects that can remain with them well into their adult lives, as well as physical ailments and academic problems. One study showed that nearly fifteen percent of the middle and high school children surveyed believed that "bullying had severely impacted their physical, social, and academic well-being." .....

These children often begin to believe that the bullies' derogatory remarks are deserved and that they themselves are weak and inferior because they cannot effectively stop the aggression. These reactions are not limited to children who might have been predicted to become victims because of their timidity or other behaviors one might imagine would invite the aggression of bullies. Rather, even those who are "physically and psychologically robust" may suffer severe reactions to being victims of bullying as they recognize their vulnerability. Despite their earlier psychological and emotional health, their coping skills often deteriorate and are reflected in nervousness, an inability to concentrate, and problems with "flashbacks" of being bullied. They suffer physical problems that include "more frequent stomachaches, headaches, and problems with bed-wetting than their non-bullied peers."

In addition, they become increasingly isolated, both socially and psychologically, as the bullying persists. Because victims of bullying often regard themselves as being "at the bottom of the social heap," they are often ashamed to admit what is happening to them and fail to seek help or to alert adults to the source of their problems. Their peers, on the other hand, steer clear of them to avoid the bully's attention. Victims begin to avoid school to escape the torment that accompanies it. Left alone to find ways to cope with the bullying and to defend themselves against it, they begin to accept the bullying as inevitable and deserved. The pattern of victimization does not confine itself to a single school year for a child; many students who are victims early in their schooling are still being victimized years later. Ultimately, victims begin to view the world as a "horrible and unsafe place," where they will not live—and perhaps do not deserve to live—happily.

.....

These dark thoughts sometimes turn outward and move from suicide to violence against the teachers and peers who make up the victims' worlds. Several school shootings in the United States, including the violence at Columbine High School in Colorado, have been tied to the shooters' having been bullied. Where bullying flourishes and protection seems lacking from school officials, it should be no surprise that some victims and even bystanders begin to look for protection where they can find it—in weapons, fighting, tough [images, and retaliation.

....

C. The Prevalence of Bullying in Schools

Bullying has increased in frequency and seriousness in schools in recent years and now constitutes a significant problem. Most studies suggest that as many as fifteen percent of all students are either victims or perpetrators, and one survey suggested that the figure may be as high as twenty percent. Bullying seems to be most prevalent in the junior high and middle school years, but it is also present in both elementary and high schools.

.....

Nevertheless, teachers and other school personnel seldom address bullying directly with students, and many believe that bullying is nothing more than a normal part of growing up that should be ignored unless it "crosses the line into assault or theft." Several studies have shown, however, that when teachers' perceptions are compared with those of students, the teachers' assumptions about bullying underestimate the prevalence and severity of the problem. Among children, the most common and pressing fear has long been the fear of being bullied.

This relative ignorance on the part of adults creates a perfect environment for bullying because bullying "is a problem which flourishes best on a bed of secrecy, hidden from those who could help." It occurs behind the backs of adults who might intervene and depends upon the immaturity or fear that prevents victims and bystanders from finding help for the victims. Although exposing the problem and addressing it directly most often tends to discourage further bullying, student victims themselves tend not to trust adults enough to ask for help because they perceive little chance of real help and fear that adult intervention will inspire more bullying. In addition, victims are often unwilling to tell adults of their plight because doing so seems like a humiliating admission of their own weakness, as well as an admission of their unpopularity. Adults often do not realize the intensity or duration of bullying against a particular child, and therefore fail to respond adequately to the child's plight, even when an incident does finally bring the problem to the adults' attention.

Unfortunately, children do not typically know how to intervene in a bullying situation and need the adults in their lives to model and encourage intervention. Adults, on the other hand, often fear that intervening will exacerbate the problem, resulting in better-hidden retribution against the victim.

....

D. The School as the Solution

....

Where schools, in good faith, put in place such positive, directed, and sustained efforts to change school climate, bullying drops dramatically. Fewer children are victimized, fewer bullies develop life-long antisocial perspectives, and the school as a whole becomes a safer environment for everyone involved.

Unfortunately, too few schools have taken such serious steps because, apparently, too few school officials truly believe what the research reveals about the effects of bullying, its prevalence, and its prevention. Courts and legislatures suffer from the same lack of understanding and do too little to force schools to change. Educators know what to do; they know it can be done; they know it is not prohibitively expensive; they know it will have positive collateral effects on the entire educational process; and they know it will save children from injuries that may well last their entire lives.

Nevertheless, courts and legislators stop short of requiring schools across the country to make the necessary changes. State and federal laws fail to create the incentives that will force reluctant school officials to move aggressively against a culture of bullying in their schools. Causes of action under federal statutory and constitutional law seldom succeed, nor do actions based in state statutory and common law. Where states have enacted legislation to require schools to implement vigorous anti-bullying policies, the statutes fail to require the kinds of processes that make those policies effective.

B. Statutory Reform for Safe Schools

TITLE 20. EDUCATION
CHAPTER 70 21ST CENTURY SCHOOLS
SAFE AND DRUG-FREE SCHOOLS AND COMMUNITIES
20 U.S.C. § 7101

....

§ 7101. Short title

This part may be cited as the "Safe and Drug-Free Schools and Communities Act".

§ 7102. Purpose

The purpose of this part is to support programs that prevent violence in and around schools; that prevent the illegal use of alcohol, tobacco, and drugs; that involve parents and communities; and that are coordinated with related Federal, State, school, and community efforts and resources to foster a safe and drug-free learning environment that supports student academic achievement, through the provision of Federal assistance to—

(1) States for grants to local educational agencies and consortia of such agencies to establish, operate, and improve local programs of school drug and violence prevention and early intervention;

(2) States for grants to, and contracts with, community-based organizations and public and private entities for programs of drug and violence prevention and early intervention, including community-wide drug and violence prevention planning and organizing activities;

(3) States for development, training, technical assistance, and coordination activities; and

(4) public and private entities to provide technical assistance; conduct training, demonstrations, and evaluation; and to provide supplementary services and community-wide drug and violence prevention planning and organizing activities for the prevention of drug use and violence among students and youth.

§ 7113. State application

(a) ... [A] State shall submit to the Secretary, at such time as the Secretary may require, an application that—

(1) contains a comprehensive plan for the use of funds by the State educational agency and the chief executive officer of the State to provide safe, orderly, and drug-free schools and communities through programs and activities that complement and support activities of local educational agencies...;

(2) describes how activities funded under this subpart will foster a safe and drug-free learning environment that supports academic achievement;

(3) provides an assurance that the application was developed in consultation and coordination with appropriate State officials and others, including the chief executive officer, the chief State school officer, the head of the State alcohol and drug abuse agency, the heads of the State health and mental health agencies, the head of the State criminal justice planning agency, the head of the State child welfare agency, the head of the State board of education, or their designees, and representatives of parents, students, and community-based organizations;

(4) describes how the State educational agency will coordinate such agency's activities under this subpart with the chief executive officer's drug and violence prevention programs under this subpart and with the prevention efforts of other State agencies and other programs, as appropriate....

DISTRICT OF COLUMBIA
Code § 5-132.04 (2008)
TITLE 5. POLICE, FIREFIGHTERS, AND CHIEF MEDICAL EXAMINER
CHAPTER 1. METROPOLITAN POLICE
SUBCHAPTER XVI-A. SCHOOL SAFETY DIVISION

§ 5-132.02. Establishment of the Metropolitan Police Department School Safety Division; functions of the School Safety Division

(a) There is established within the Metropolitan Police Department a School Safety Division that shall provide security for the District of Columbia Public Schools.

(b) The School Safety Division shall be headed by a Director, appointed by, and reporting to, the Chief of Police with rank equal to an Assistant Chief.

(c) The School Safety Division shall:

(1) Hire all school security personnel for DCPS;

(2) Deploy school security personnel to DCPS;

(3) Provide oversight over school security personnel and be responsible for administering all disciplinary actions related to school security personnel, including termination;

(4) Execute, approve, monitor, and provide oversight over any contract for school security personnel; and

(5) Create and implement security and emergency operations plans for DCPS in concert with the Superintendent.

FLORIDA STATUTES. TITLE 48. K-20 EDUCATION CODE
CHAPTER 1006. SUPPORT FOR LEARNING
PART I. PUBLIC K-12 EDUCATION SUPPORT FOR LEARNING AND STUDENT SERVICES
SUBPART C. STUDENT DISCIPLINE AND SCHOOL SAFETY

§ 1006.12. School Resource Officers and School Safety Officers

(1) District school boards may establish school resource officer programs, through a cooperative agreement with law enforcement agencies or in accordance with subsection (2).

(a) School resource officers shall be certified law enforcement officers, as defined in s. 943.10(1), who are employed by a law enforcement agency as defined in s. 943.10(4). The powers and duties of a law enforcement officer shall continue throughout the employee's tenure as a school resource officer.

(b) School resource officers shall abide by district school board policies and shall consult with and coordinate activities through the school principal, but shall be responsible to the law enforcement agency in all matters relating to employment, subject to agreements between a district school board and a law enforcement agency. Activities conducted by the school resource officer which are part of the regular instructional program of the school shall be under the direction of the school principal.

(2) (a) School safety officers shall be law enforcement officers, as defined in § 943.10(1), certified under the provisions of chapter 943 and employed by either a law enforcement agency or by the district school board. If the officer is employed by the district school board, the district school board is the employing agency for purposes of chapter 943, and must comply with the provisions of that chapter.

(b) A district school board may commission one or more school safety officers for the protection and safety of school personnel, property, and students within the school district. The district school superintendent may recommend and the district school board may appoint one or more school safety officers.

(c) A school safety officer has and shall exercise the power to make arrests for violations of law on district school board property and to arrest persons, whether on or off such property, who violate any law on such property under the same conditions that deputy sheriffs are authorized to make arrests. A school safety officer has the authority to carry weapons when performing his or her official duties.

(d) A district school board may enter into mutual aid agreements with one or more law enforcement agencies as provided in chapter 23. A school safety officer's salary may be paid jointly by the district school board and the law enforcement agency, as mutually agreed to.

PENNSYLVANIA STATUTES
TITLE 24. EDUCATION
CHAPTER 1. PUBLIC SCHOOL CODE OF 1949
ARTICLE XIII-A. SAFE SCHOOLS

§ 13-1302-A. Office for Safe Schools

(a) There is hereby established in the Department of Education an Office for Safe Schools.

(b) The office shall have the following powers and duties:

(1) To coordinate antiviolence efforts between school, professional, parental, governmental, law enforcement and community organizations and associations.

(2) To collect, develop and disseminate information, policies, strategies and other information to assist in the development of programs to impact school violence.

(3) To provide direct training to school employees, parents, law enforcement officials and communities on effective measures to combat school violence.

(4) To advise school entities and nonpublic schools on the development of policies to be used regarding possession of weapons by any person, acts of violence and protocols for coordination with and reporting to law enforcement officials and the Department of Education.

(5) To develop forms to be used by school entities for reporting incidents involving acts of violence and possession of weapons on school property.

(c) In addition to the powers and duties set forth under subsection (a), the office is authorized to make targeted grants to schools to fund programs which address school violence, including, but not limited to, the following programs:

(1) Conflict resolution or dispute management.

(2) Peer helpers programs.

(3) Risk assessment, safety-related or violence prevention curricula.

(4) Classroom management.

(5) Student codes of conduct.

(6) Training to undertake a districtwide assessment of risk factors that increase the likelihood of problem behaviors among students.

(7) Development and implementation of research-based violence prevention programs that address risk factors to reduce incidents of problem behaviors among students.

(8) Comprehensive, districtwide school safety and violence prevention plans.

(9) Security planning, purchase of security-related technology which may include metal detectors, protective lighting, surveillance equipment, special emergency communications equipment, electronic locksets, deadbolts and theft control devices and training in the use of security-related technology. Security planning and purchase of security-related technology shall be based on safety needs identified by the school entity's board of directors.

(10) Institution of student, staff and visitor identification systems.

(11) Establishment or enhancement of school security personnel, including school resource officers.

(12) Provision of specialized staff and student training programs, including training for Student Assistance Program team members in elementary, middle and high schools in the referral of students at risk of violent behavior to appropriate community-based services, including mental health services.

(13) Alternative education programs provided for in Article XIX-C.

(14) Counseling services for students enrolled in alternative education programs.

(d) Grant applications shall contain information as the office may require. The office shall conduct a thorough annual evaluation of each program for which a grant under this section is made.

C. Judicial Expansion of Educators' Authority to Maintain Safe Schools

NEW JERSEY v. T. L. O.
469 U.S. 325 (1985)

[This case appears in Chapter Five on page 282]

IN RE F.B.

658 A.2d 1378 (Pa. Super. Ct. 1995)

OPINION BY JOHNSON, J.:

In this appeal, we are asked to determine whether the search of a student by school officials as part of a school-wide search of students for weapons was reasonable under the circumstances where the officials had no individualized suspicion that the student was armed. Finding that no individualized suspicion was required under the circumstances, we conclude that the search was reasonable. Accordingly, we affirm the trial court order which directed that F.B. (the juvenile) remain on probation after he was adjudicated delinquent.

Students at University High School in the City of Philadelphia are prohibited from bringing weapons or drugs onto school property. If students are found in possession of these items, they are arrested. Letters are sent home throughout the year informing parents and students of this policy.

To enforce this policy, the Philadelphia school district employs police officers to conduct in-house metal-detector scans and bag searches of the students at University High School. Signs are posted on the front door and throughout the school notifying the students of these searches. Upon entering the building, the students are led into the gymnasium where they form lines and, one by one, step up to a table. Once at the table, each student empties his pockets and surrenders his jacket and any bags he may be carrying. While an officer searches the student's belongings, the student is told to step to the end of the table where he is scanned by a metal detector. If no drugs or weapons are found, the student is permitted to retrieve his belongings. Every student is searched in this manner until the gymnasium becomes too crowded, at which time school administrators randomly select students to be searched.

The trial court found that when the juvenile, a University High School student, stepped up to the table and emptied his pockets, he discarded a Swiss-type folding knife. The juvenile then was escorted to a holding room where he was placed under arrest for possessing a weapon on school property. The trial court … adjudicated him delinquent. This appeal followed.

On appeal, the juvenile contends that the trial court erred in denying his suppression motion because the police searched him without reasonable suspicion or probable cause to believe that he had violated any school regulation. Thus, he argues that the search violated his rights against unreasonable searches and seizures under both the United States and Pennsylvania Constitutions.

I. UNITED STATES CONSTITUTION

The United States Supreme Court, in *New Jersey v. T.L.O.*, 469 U.S. 325 (1985), held that the Fourth Amendment's prohibition of unreasonable searches and seizures applies to searches conducted by public school officials. … First, it must be determined whether the action was justified at its inception. Second, it must be determined whether the search, as conducted, was reasonably related in scope to the circumstances that justified the interference in the first place.

The juvenile contends that the search was unreasonable in light of the *T.L.O.* factors. Specifically, he argues that the search was not justified at its inception because there were no reasonable grounds to believe that he was carrying contraband. The juvenile asserts that the *T.L.O.* requirements cannot be evaded merely by searching the entire student population. Rather, he maintains that "individualized suspicion" must be required when school authorities subject students to such highly intrusive searches. Whether school officials need individualized suspicion to search students is an issue of first impression in this Commonwealth.

The *T.L.O.* Court determined that, ordinarily, a student search is justified at its inception where "there are reasonable grounds for suspecting that the search will turn up evidence that the student has violated or is violating either the law or the rules of the school." *T.L.O., supra*, at 342. However, the Supreme Court in *T.L.O.* did not decide whether individualized suspicion is an essential element of the reasonableness standard that it adopted for searches by school authorities. *Id.* at 342 n.8. In fact, the Supreme Court pointed out that it previously had concluded that the Fourth Amendment imposes no irreducible requirement of individualized suspicion. Id. In addition, the Court noted that exceptions to the requirement of individualized suspicion are appropriate

> where the privacy interests implicated by a search are minimal and where "other safeguards" are available "to assure that the individual's reasonable expectation of privacy is not 'subject to the discretion of the official in the field.'" *Delaware v. Prouse*, 440 U.S. 648, 654-655 (1979).

For example, the United States Supreme Court, as well as courts across the country, have permitted administrative searches where law enforcement authorities have no individualized suspicion when the searches are conducted as part of a general regulatory scheme to ensure the public safety, rather than as part of a criminal investigation to secure evidence of crime. Such searches are reasonable when the intrusion involved in the search is no greater than necessary to satisfy the governmental interest justifying the search, i.e., courts balance the degree of intrusion against the need for the search. Thus, courts have approved airport searches, *Commonwealth v. Vecchione*, 327 Pa. Super. 548, 476 A.2d 403 (1984); courthouse security measures, *McMorris v. Alioto*, 567 F.2d 897 (9th Cir. 1978); *Downing v. Kunzig*, 454 F.2d 1230 (6th Cir. 1972); *Legal Aid Soc. of Orange County v. Crosson*, 784 F. Supp. 1127 (S.D.N.Y. 1992); license and registration vehicle stops, *Commonwealth v. Blouse*, 531 Pa. 167, 611 A.2d 1177 (1992); and border-patrol checkpoints, *United States v. Martinez-Fuerte*, 428 U.S. 543 (1976).

Nevertheless, the juvenile alleges that the search in the present case does not fall within the exceptions set forth in *T.L.O.* First, the juvenile claims that his privacy interest is not minimal because this was a search of his person. However, we must balance the school's compelling interest in promoting an environment which is safe and conducive to learning against the schoolchild's privacy interest. As a New York court recognized, "if schools cannot operate in a violence-free atmosphere, then education will suffer, a result which ultimately threatens the well-being of everyone." *People v. Dukes*, 151 Misc. 2d 295, 300, 580 N.Y.S.2d 850, 853 (1992). We find that the school's interest in ensuring security for its students far outweighs the juvenile's privacy interest. In addition, the trial court found, and we agree, that, in light of the school's efforts to make students and parents aware of their search policy, "the [juvenile]'s expectation of privacy was greatly reduced by the notice he received prior to the search." Therefore, under these circumstances, we believe that the juvenile's privacy interest is minimal.

Next, the juvenile asserts that there were no safeguards assuring that his expectation of privacy was not subjected to the discretion of the official in the field. *See T.L.O., supra.* Namely, he charges that there were no written guidelines governing the search. Although we believe written guidelines would be prudent, we find that there were "other safeguards" present in this case. Specifically, the officers who conducted the student searches followed a uniform procedure as they searched each student, i.e., after each student's personal belongings were searched, the student was scanned by a metal detector. This uniformity served to safeguard the students from the discretion of those conducting the search.

Nevertheless, the juvenile suggests that school administrators had complete discretion to choose which students to search randomly after the gymnasium became crowded. However, we need not determine whether the random selection process subjected students to the discretion of school administrators because the juvenile does not allege that he was among those randomly chosen. Thus, this question is not properly before our Court, and we will not consider it. Because the juvenile's privacy interest was minimal and his expectation of privacy was not subjected to the discretion of the official in the field, no individualized suspicion was required to search the juvenile. *See T.L.O., supra.*

Here, the trial court applied the reasonableness factors set forth in *T.L.O.* and found that the search was justified at its inception because of the high rate of violence in the Philadelphia public schools. Further, the court found that it was reasonable to search all students prior to entering the school because there is no way to know which students are carrying weapons. Therefore, the trial court concluded, and we agree, that the search of the juvenile satisfied the *T.L.O.* test for reasonableness.

Insofar as school authorities in the present case were also searching for drugs, we do not determine whether the need to promote safety in the school also served to justify this aspect of the search. That question is not properly before us because only a weapon was discovered in the juvenile's possession.

Accordingly, having determined that no individualized suspicion was required in this case, we conclude that this search did not violate the juvenile's Fourth Amendment rights because it satisfied the *T.L.O.* test for reasonableness..... [W]e likewise decline to address a state constitutional analysis.

T.S. v. STATE

863 N.E.2d 362 (Ind. Ct. App. 2007)

[This case appears in Chapter Five on page 296]

Notes and Comments

1. The Juvenile Justice System and the Safe Schools Movement

The juvenile justice system emerged as part of the criminal justice reform movement of the late 19th century. The creation of the first juvenile court in Chicago, Illinois in 1899 and it expansion into all 50 states soon thereafter was based on the belief that punishment for juveniles who committed crimes should be a more thoughtful, less punitive procedure.

This more forgiving system was severed from the adult criminal justice system largely on the belief that juvenile delinquents were a product of many factors: a bad peer influences, a bad family and poor community resources for intervention. This diversion from the usual criminal courts was thought to be the best way to redeem juveniles from the certain lost life if they were to be placed in the more punitive adult system. Juvenile court judges began issuing a finding of delinquency, instead of a conviction. In less severe cases of misconduct, courts created an even more novel nomenclature by ruling that the wayward child was merely a "child-in-need-of-supervision," or guilty of committing a "status offense." Punishment often combined court ordered supervision, treatment, and counseling.

The alternate system for juveniles was not, however, completely divorced from constitutional individual rights. The Supreme Court, while acknowledging the juvenile justice system, made clear the application of essential rights in a variety of contexts. *See In re Winship*, 397 U.S. 358 (1970) (right to proof beyond reasonable doubt); *Breed v. Jones*, 421 U.S. 519 (1975) (protection from double jeopardy); *Planned Parenthood of Missouri v. Danforth*, 428 U.S. 52 (1976) (right to abortion without parental consent); *Tinker v. Des Moines Indep. Cmty. Sch. Dist.*, 393 U.S. 503 (1969) (right to freedom of speech and expression); *Goss v. Lopez*, 419 U.S. 565 (1975) (right to due process before being suspended from school); *In re Scott K.*, 595 P.2d 105 (Cal. 1979) (right to be free from unreasonable search and seizure).

In general, the recent wave of juvenile justice reform is comprehensive, affecting most every aspect of the interest of a State in the welfare of juveniles. The reform seeks to enhance the impact of the system on the lives of juveniles through either punitive intervention or a rehabilitative prevention emphasis, occasionally utilizing both. The reform strategy rests on two elements:

> (1) preventing youth from becoming delinquent by focusing prevention programs on at-risk youth; and
>
> (2) improving the juvenile justice system response to delinquent treatment alternatives that include immediate intervention, intermediate sanctions, and

> community-based corrections sanctions, incorporating restitution and community service when appropriate. (Wilson and Howell, 1994).

In most of the states, the reform efforts move in both directions. At the punitive end, the law prompts an early determination as to whether an offender is amenable to rehabilitation within the traditional juvenile treatment period. Juvenile courts transfer jurisdiction, through certification or waiver, to the adult criminal court for certain serious, violent or recidivist offenders who are deemed to be beyond the scope of the twin concerns of the system: parens patriae and rehabilitation and treatment of the juvenile. A California study of certification concludes that

> [a] new conceptual framework is emerging that seems to assume contemporary children not only act but reason like adults. Commit a heinous crime, and you are an adult for the purpose of prosecution. (Dowie, 1993).

At the rehabilitative end of the reform scale, the state laws seek to prevent juvenile delinquency by enhancing supervision and improving delivery of needed prevention programs. These prevention efforts reach out to the serious and habitual juvenile offenders (who remain in the system and are not certified as adults) as well as to the juveniles who are identified as being at risk of delinquency.

For example, California law authorizes both early intervention programs (Cal. Wel. & Inst. Code § 601.5 (1999)) as well as serious offender comprehensive action teams (Cal. Wel. & Inst. Code § 503 (1999). The Interagency Children's Services Act, (Cal. Wel. & Inst. Code § 18986 (1999)), seeks to create a general, coordinated children's services system to "Ensur[e] collaboration and countywide planning for the provision of children's services". (Cal. Wel. & Inst. Code @ 18986.14 (1999)). The most recent program, The Community Law Enforcement and Recovery (CLEAR) Demonstration Project, is designed to "provide a flexible and coordinated response to crime perpetrated by criminal street gangs" and "to coordinate prevention and intervention strategies with community-based organizations." (Cal. Pen. Code @ 14000 (1999)). All four cooperative models are based on the theme of creating a team climate among local agencies with a common interest in effective intervention in the life of a juvenile.

Public Schools quickly became an essential member of the juvenile justice team. Court ordered diversion programs had much in common with the compulsory attendance laws. Moreover, the placement of juvenile delinquent in school provided both a natural place of supervision and hub for rehabilitation. State officials began to assemble legislation around an interagency-focused system of juvenile services and much of the system that is in place today took shape. State officials began to assemble legislation around an interagency-focused system of juvenile services and much of the system that is in place today took shape. The vision for the interagency component of state juvenile justice reform is a variation on the national theme of cooperation and focused delivery of services to juveniles in need. A majority of the states now either has implemented some version of this model or is now, considering which aspect of the concept best suits their sense of the needs of the known juvenile offenders and the children at risk of becoming delinquent within their jurisdiction.

No one could foresee the spate of targeted violence in schools. From 1974-2000, thirty-seven shootings occurred on public school campuses. In response to these vents, most state and local agencies began circling the wagon around school campuses with a concerted effort to keep schools safe. Metal detectors, police and crisis planning have now become second nature at most public schools. One unintended consequence of the safe schools movement is legal uncertainty about the rights of juvenile in the midst of educators and police.

2. Safe Schools and Juvenile Justice Scholarship

For more on the history of the juvenile justice system, see Anthony M. Platt, *The Child Savers: The Invention of Delinquency* (2d ed., University of Chicago Press 1977); Christopher P. Manfredi, *The Supreme Court and Juvenile Justice* 32 (Univ. Press of Kan. (1997); Cynthia Conward, *The Juvenile Justice System: Not Necessarily in the Best Interests of the Children*, 33 New Eng. L. Rev. 39, 42-43 (1998); and Barry C. Feld, *The Transformation of the Juvenile Court-Part II: Race and the Crackdown on Youth Crime*, 84 Minn. L. Rev. 327 (1999). For more on the safe schools movement, see, Vossekuil, B., Fein, R., Reddy, M., Borum, R., & Modzeleski, W., *The Final Report and Findings of the Safe School Initiative: Implications for the Prevention of School Attacks in the United States*, U.S. Department of Education, Office of Elementary and Secondary Education, Safe and Drug-Free Schools Program and U.S. Secret Service, National Threat Assessment Center, Washington, D.C., 2002.; Ronald Stephens, *School Crime and Violence: Victims' Rights*, National School Safety Center (1992).

II. The Fifth Amendment and Student Interrogations

The rules of interrogation are called "*Miranda* warnings" in reference to the seminal case of *Miranda v. Arizona*, (384 U.S. 436 (1966)), where the "right to remain silent..." warnings were first required. The *Miranda* warnings are considered a part of the jurisprudence of the Fifth Amendment; "No person... shall be compelled in any criminal case to be a witness against himself." The rules apply to both juveniles and adults alike; a *Miranda* warning is required whenever a police officer conducts a custodial interrogation of a person, including a student on campus. When there is uncertainty over whether or not a person is "in custody", courts typically use a reasonableness test measured from the point of view of the person being interrogated. Thus, *Miranda* warnings must be given when a person reasonably believes his freedom to leave has been curtailed. It is irrelevant whether the police have probable cause to arrest the person, or whether the police officer subjectively believes that the person is not in custody.

Schools are more violent and misbehavior is more proactively targeted. Schools now have dedicated police officers (known as "school resource officers" or SROs) on campus to help combat and prevent criminal activity. As a result of these changes, students are being questioned and, on occasion, arrested at school during school hours in connection with both on-campus and off-campus crimes. Therefore, there is a great interest in providing clear direction as to whom, when and how educators and police are to question a student at school during hours without violating the constitutional right of students.

This section explores the difficult questions that arise when students may be questioned at school for criminal behavior. Unlike the clarity provided by *New Jersey v. T.L.O.*, (*see* Chapter Eight on the Fourth Amendment), the area of student interrogations has not led to any single line of analysis.

The U.S. Supreme Court has yet to consider the issue and, thus, there is some uncertainty about whether a teacher or principal may, or may not, question a student at school during school hours without offending the Fifth Amendment right against self-incrimination. As a result, federal and state courts wrestle with the issue of where the line should be drawn between student rights and the authority of school officials.

J.D.B. v. North Carolina

564 U.S. 261 (2011)

SOTOMAYOR, J.

This case presents the question whether the age of a child subjected to police questioning is relevant to the custody analysis of *Miranda v. Arizona,* 384 U.S. 436, 86 S.Ct. 1602, 16 L.Ed.2d 694 (1966). It is beyond dispute that children will often feel bound to submit to police questioning when an adult in the same circumstances would feel free to leave. Seeing no reason for police officers or courts to blind themselves to that commonsense reality, we hold that a child's age properly informs the *Miranda* custody analysis.

I

A

Petitioner J.D.B. was a 13–year–old, seventh-grade student attending class at Smith Middle School in Chapel Hill, North Carolina when he was removed from his classroom by a uniformed police officer, escorted to a closed-door conference room, and questioned by police for at least half an hour.

This was the second time that police questioned J.D.B. in the span of a week. Five days earlier, two home break-ins occurred, and various items were stolen. Police stopped and questioned J.D.B. after he was seen behind a residence in the neighborhood where the crimes occurred. That same day, police also spoke to J.D.B.'s grandmother—his legal guardian—as well as his aunt.

Police later learned that a digital camera matching the description of one of the stolen items had been found at J.D.B.'s middle school and seen in J.D.B.'s possession. Investigator DiCostanzo, the juvenile investigator with the local police force who had been assigned to the case, went to the school to question J.D.B. Upon arrival, DiCostanzo informed the uniformed police officer on detail to the school (a so-called school resource officer), the assistant principal, and an administrative intern that he was there to question J.D.B. about the break-ins. Although DiCostanzo asked the school administrators to verify J.D.B.'s date of birth, address, and parent contact information from school records, neither the police officers nor the school administrators contacted J.D.B.'s grandmother.

The uniformed officer interrupted J.D.B.'s afternoon social studies class, removed J.D.B. from the classroom, and escorted him to a school conference room.[30] There, J.D.B. was met by DiCostanzo, the assistant principal, and the administrative intern. The door to the conference room was closed. With the two police officers and the two administrators present, J.D.B. was questioned for the next 30 to 45 minutes. Prior to the commencement of questioning, J.D.B. was given neither *Miranda* warnings nor the opportunity to speak to his grandmother. Nor was he informed that he was free to leave the room.

Questioning began with small talk—discussion of sports and J.D.B.'s family life. DiCostanzo asked, and J.D.B. agreed, to discuss the events of the prior weekend. Denying any wrongdoing, J.D.B. explained that he had been in the neighborhood where the crimes occurred because he was seeking work mowing lawns. DiCostanzo pressed J.D.B. for additional detail about his efforts to obtain work; asked J.D.B. to explain a prior incident, when one of the victims returned home to find J.D.B. behind her house; and confronted J.D.B. with the stolen camera. The assistant principal urged J.D.B. to "do the right thing," warning J.D.B. that "the truth always comes out in the end." App. 99a, 112a.

Eventually, J.D.B. asked whether he would "still be in trouble" if he returned the "stuff." *Ibid.* In response, DiCostanzo explained that return of the stolen items would be helpful, but "this thing is going to court" regardless. *Id.,* at 112a; *ibid.* ("[W]hat's done is done[;] now you need to help yourself by making it right"); see also *id.,* at 99a. DiCostanzo then warned that he may need to seek a secure custody order if he believed that J.D.B. would continue to break into other homes. When J.D.B. asked what a secure custody order was, DiCostanzo explained that "it's where you get sent to juvenile detention before court." *Id.,* at 112a.

After learning of the prospect of juvenile detention, J.D.B. confessed that he and a friend were responsible for the break-ins. DiCostanzo only then informed J.D.B. that he could refuse to answer the investigator's questions and that he was free to leave.[31] Asked whether he understood, J.D.B. nodded and provided further detail, including information about the location of the stolen items. Eventually J.D.B. wrote a statement, at DiCostanzo's request. When the bell rang indicating the end of the school day, J.D.B. was allowed to leave to catch the bus home.

---

[30] Although the State suggests that the "record is unclear as to who brought J.D.B. to the conference room, and the trial court made no factual findings on this specific point," Brief for Respondent 3, n. 1, the State agreed at the certiorari stage that "the SRO [school resource officer] escorted petitioner" to the room, Brief in Opposition 3.

[31] The North Carolina Supreme Court noted that the trial court's factual findings were "uncontested and therefore ... binding" on it. *In re J.D.B.,* 363 N.C. 664, 668, 686 S.E.2d 135, 137 (2009). The court described the sequence of events set forth in the text. See *id.,* at 670–671, 686 S.E.2d, at 139. ("Immediately following J.D.B.'s initial confession, Investigator DiCostanzo informed J.D.B. that he did not have to speak with him and that he was free to leave" (internal quotation marks and alterations omitted)). Though less than perfectly explicit, the trial court's order indicates a finding that J.D.B. initially confessed prior to DiCostanzo's warnings. See App. 99a.
Nonetheless, both parties' submissions to this Court suggest that the warnings came after DiCostanzo raised the possibility of a secure custody order but before J.D.B. confessed for the first time. See Brief for Petitioner 5; Brief for Respondent 5. Because we remand for a determination whether J.D.B. was in custody under the proper analysis, the state courts remain free to revisit whether the trial court made a conclusive finding of fact in this respect.

B

Two juvenile petitions were filed against J.D.B., each alleging one count of breaking and entering and one count of larceny. J.D.B.'s public defender moved to suppress his statements and the evidence derived therefrom, arguing that suppression was necessary because J.D.B. had been "interrogated by police in a custodial setting without being afforded *Miranda* warning[s]," App. 89a, and because his statements were involuntary under the totality of the circumstances test, *id.*, at 142a; see *Schneckloth v. Bustamonte,* 412 U.S. 218, 226, 93 S.Ct. 2041, 36 L.Ed.2d 854 (1973) (due process precludes admission of a confession where "a defendant's will was overborne" by the circumstances of the interrogation). After a suppression hearing at which DiCostanzo and J.D.B. testified, the trial court denied the motion, deciding that J.D.B. was not in custody at the time of the schoolhouse interrogation and that his statements were voluntary. As a result, J.D.B. entered a transcript of admission to all four counts, renewing his objection to the denial of his motion to suppress, and the court adjudicated J.D.B. delinquent.

A divided panel of the North Carolina Court of Appeals affirmed. *In re J.D.B.,* 196 N.C.App. 234, 674 S.E.2d 795 (2009). The North Carolina Supreme Court held, over two dissents, that J.D.B. was not in custody when he confessed, "declin[ing] to extend the test for custody to include consideration of the age ... of an individual subjected to questioning by police." *In re J.D.B.,* 363 N.C. 664, 672, 686 S.E.2d 135, 140 (2009).[32] We granted certiorari to determine whether the *Miranda* custody analysis includes consideration of a juvenile suspect's age. 562 U.S. ——, 131 S.Ct. 502, 178 L.Ed.2d 368 (2010).

II

A

Any police interview of an individual suspected of a crime has "coercive aspects to it." *Oregon v. Mathiason,* 429 U.S. 492, 495, 97 S.Ct. 711, 50 L.Ed.2d 714 (1977) *(per curiam).* Only those interrogations that occur while a suspect is in police custody, however, "heighte[n] the risk" that statements obtained are not the product of the suspect's free choice. *Dickerson v. United States,* 530 U.S. 428, 435, 120 S.Ct. 2326, 147 L.Ed.2d 405 (2000).

By its very nature, custodial police interrogation entails "inherently compelling pressures." *Miranda,* 384 U.S., at 467, 86 S.Ct. 1602. Even for an adult, the physical and psychological isolation of custodial interrogation can "undermine the individual's will to resist and ... compel him to speak where he would not otherwise do so freely." *Ibid.* Indeed, the pressure of custodial interrogation is so immense that it "can induce a frighteningly high percentage of people to confess to crimes they never committed." *Corley v. United States,* 556 U.S. 303, ——, 129 S.Ct. 1558,

---

[32] J.D.B.'s challenge in the North Carolina Supreme Court focused on the lower courts' conclusion that he was not in custody for purposes of *Miranda v. Arizona,* 384 U.S. 436, 86 S.Ct. 1602, 16 L.Ed.2d 694 (1966). The North Carolina Supreme Court did not address the trial court's holding that the statements were voluntary, and that question is not before us.

1570, 173 L.Ed.2d 443 (2009) (citing Drizin & Leo, The Problem of False Confessions in the Post–DNA World, 82 N.C. L. Rev. 891, 906–907 (2004)); see also *Miranda,* 384 U.S., at 455, n. 23, 86 S.Ct. 1602. That risk is all the more troubling—and recent studies suggest, all the more acute—when the subject of custodial interrogation is a juvenile. See Brief for Center on Wrongful Convictions of Youth et al. as *Amici Curiae* 21–22 (collecting empirical studies that "illustrate the heightened risk of false confessions from youth").

Recognizing that the inherently coercive nature of custodial interrogation "blurs the line between voluntary and involuntary statements," *Dickerson,* 530 U.S., at 435, 120 S.Ct. 2326, this Court in *Miranda* adopted a set of prophylactic measures designed to safeguard the constitutional guarantee against self-incrimination. Prior to questioning, a suspect "must be warned that he has a right to remain silent, that any statement he does make may be used as evidence against him, and that he has a right to the presence of an attorney, either retained or appointed." 384 U.S., at 444, 86 S.Ct. 1602; see also *Florida v. Powell,* 559 U.S. ——, ——, 130 S.Ct. 1195, 1198, 175 L.Ed.2d 1009 (2010) ("The four warnings *Miranda* requires are invariable, but this Court has not dictated the words in which the essential information must be conveyed"). And, if a suspect makes a statement during custodial interrogation, the burden is on the Government to show, as a "prerequisit[e]" to the statement's admissibility as evidence in the Government's case in chief, that the defendant "voluntarily, knowingly and intelligently" waived his rights.[33] *Miranda,* 384 U.S., at 444, 475–476, 86 S.Ct. 1602; *Dickerson,* 530 U.S., at 443–444, 120 S.Ct. 2326.

Because these measures protect the individual against the coercive nature of custodial interrogation, they are required " 'only where there has been such a restriction on a person's freedom as to render him "in custody." ' " *Stansbury v. California,* 511 U.S. 318, 322, 114 S.Ct. 1526, 128 L.Ed.2d 293 (1994) *(per curiam)* (quoting *Oregon v. Mathiason,* 429 U.S. 492, 495, 97 S.Ct. 711, 50 L.Ed.2d 714 (1977) *(per curiam)*). As we have repeatedly emphasized, whether a suspect is "in custody" is an objective inquiry.

"Two discrete inquiries are essential to the determination: first, what were the circumstances surrounding the interrogation; and second, given those circumstances, would a reasonable person have felt he or she was at liberty to terminate the interrogation and leave. Once the scene is set and the players' lines and actions are reconstructed, the court must apply an objective test to resolve the ultimate inquiry: was there a formal arrest or restraint on freedom of movement of the degree associated with formal arrest." *Thompson v. Keohane,* 516 U.S. 99, 112, 116 S.Ct. 457, 133 L.Ed.2d 383 (1995) (internal quotation marks, alteration, and footnote omitted). See also *Yarborough v. Alvarado,* 541 U.S. 652, 662–663, 124 S.Ct. 2140, 158 L.Ed.2d 938 (2004); *Stansbury,* 511 U.S., at 323, 114 S.Ct. 1526; *Berkemer v. McCarty,* 468 U.S. 420, 442, and n. 35, 104 S.Ct. 3138, 82 L.Ed.2d 317 (1984).

Rather than demarcate a limited set of relevant circumstances, we have required police officers and courts to "examine all of the circumstances surrounding the interrogation," *Stansbury,* 511 U.S., at

---

[33] *Amici* on behalf of J.D.B. question whether children of all ages can comprehend *Miranda* warnings and suggest that additional procedural safeguards may be necessary to protect their *Miranda* rights. Brief for Juvenile Law Center et al. as *Amici Curiae* 13–14, n. 7. Whatever the merit of that contention, it has no relevance here, where no *Miranda* warnings were administered at all.

322, 114 S.Ct. 1526, including any circumstance that "would have affected how a reasonable person" in the suspect's position "would perceive his or her freedom to leave," *id.*, at 325, 114 S.Ct. 1526. On the other hand, the "subjective views harbored by either the interrogating officers or the person being questioned" are irrelevant. *Id.*, at 323, 114 S.Ct. 1526. The test, in other words, involves no consideration of the "actual mindset" of the particular suspect subjected to police questioning. *Alvarado,* 541 U.S., at 667, 124 S.Ct. 2140; see also *California v. Beheler,* 463 U.S. 1121, 1125, n. 3, 103 S.Ct. 3517, 77 L.Ed.2d 1275 (1983) *(per curiam).*

The benefit of the objective custody analysis is that it is "designed to give clear guidance to the police." *Alvarado,* 541 U.S., at 668, 124 S.Ct. 2140. But see *Berkemer,* 468 U.S., at 441, 104 S.Ct. 3138 (recognizing the "occasiona[l] ... difficulty" that police and courts nonetheless have in "deciding exactly when a suspect has been taken into custody"). Police must make in-the-moment judgments as to when to administer *Miranda* warnings. By limiting analysis to the objective circumstances of the interrogation, and asking how a reasonable person in the suspect's position would understand his freedom to terminate questioning and leave, the objective test avoids burdening police with the task of anticipating the idiosyncrasies of every individual suspect and divining how those particular traits affect each person's subjective state of mind. See *id.*, at 430–431, 104 S.Ct. 3138 (officers are not required to "make guesses" as to circumstances "unknowable" to them at the time); *Alvarado,* 541 U.S., at 668, 124 S.Ct. 2140 (officers are under no duty "to consider ... contingent psychological factors when deciding when suspects should be advised of their *Miranda* rights").

B

The State and its *amici* contend that a child's age has no place in the custody analysis, no matter how young the child subjected to police questioning. We cannot agree. In some circumstances, a child's age "would have affected how a reasonable person" in the suspect's position "would perceive his or her freedom to leave." *Stansbury,* 511 U.S., at 325, 114 S.Ct. 1526. That is, a reasonable child subjected to police questioning will sometimes feel pressured to submit when a reasonable adult would feel free to go. We think it clear that courts can account for that reality without doing any damage to the objective nature of the custody analysis.

A child's age is far "more than a chronological fact." *Eddings v. Oklahoma,* 455 U.S. 104, 115, 102 S.Ct. 869, 71 L.Ed.2d 1 (1982); accord, *Gall v. United States,* 552 U.S. 38, 58, 128 S.Ct. 586, 169 L.Ed.2d 445 (2007); *Roper v. Simmons,* 543 U.S. 551, 569, 125 S.Ct. 1183, 161 L.Ed.2d 1 (2005); *Johnson v. Texas,* 509 U.S. 350, 367, 113 S.Ct. 2658, 125 L.Ed.2d 290 (1993). It is a fact that "generates commonsense conclusions about behavior and perception." *Alvarado,* 541 U.S., at 674, 124 S.Ct. 2140 (BREYER, J., dissenting). Such conclusions apply broadly to children as a class. And, they are self-evident to anyone who was a child once himself, including any police officer or judge.

Time and again, this Court has drawn these commonsense conclusions for itself. We have observed that children "generally are less mature and responsible than adults," *Eddings,* 455 U.S., at 115–116, 102 S.Ct. 869; that they "often lack the experience, perspective, and judgment to recognize and avoid choices that could be detrimental to them," *Bellotti v. Baird,* 443 U.S. 622, 635, 99 S.Ct. 3035, 61 L.Ed.2d 797 (1979) (plurality opinion); that they "are more vulnerable or susceptible to ... outside pressures" than adults, *Roper,* 543 U.S., at 569, 125 S.Ct. 1183; and so on. See *Graham v. Florida,* 560 U.S. ——, ——, 130 S.Ct. 2011, 2026, 176 L.Ed.2d 825 (2010) (finding no reason to "reconsider" these observations about the common "nature of juveniles"). Addressing the specific context of police interrogation, we have observed that events that "would leave a man cold and unimpressed can overawe and overwhelm a lad in his early teens." *Haley v. Ohio,* 332 U.S. 596, 599, 68 S.Ct. 302, 92 L.Ed. 224 (1948) (plurality opinion); see also *Gallegos v. Colorado,* 370 U.S. 49, 54, 82 S.Ct. 1209, 8 L.Ed.2d 325 (1962) ("[N]o matter how sophisticated," a juvenile subject of police interrogation "cannot be compared" to an adult subject). Describing no one child in particular, these observations restate what "any parent knows"—indeed, what any person knows—about children generally. *Roper,* 543 U.S., at 569, 125 S.Ct. 1183.[34]

……

In other words, a child's age differs from other personal characteristics that, even when known to police, have no objectively discernible relationship to a reasonable person's understanding of his freedom of action. *Alvarado,* holds, for instance, that a suspect's prior interrogation history with law enforcement has no role to play in the custody analysis because such experience could just as easily lead a reasonable person to feel free to walk away as to feel compelled to stay in place. 541 U.S., at 668, 124 S.Ct. 2140. Because the effect in any given case would be "contingent [on the] psycholog[y]" of the individual suspect, the Court explained, such experience cannot be considered without compromising the objective nature of the custody analysis. *Ibid.* A child's age, however, is different. Precisely because childhood yields objective conclusions like those we have drawn ourselves—among others, that children are "most susceptible to influence," *Eddings,* 455 U.S., at 115, 102 S.Ct. 869, and "outside pressures," *Roper,* 543 U.S., at 569, 125 S.Ct. 1183—considering age in the custody analysis in no way involves a determination of how youth "subjectively affect[s] the mindset" of any particular child, Brief for Respondent 14.[35]

……

Reviewing the question *de novo* today, we hold that so long as the child's age was known to the officer at the time of police questioning, or would have been objectively apparent to a reasonable officer, its inclusion in the custody analysis is consistent with the objective nature of that test.[36]

---

[34] Although citation to social science and cognitive science authorities is unnecessary to establish these commonsense propositions, the literature confirms what experience bears out. See, *e.g., Graham v. Florida,* 560 U.S. ——, ——, 130 S.Ct. 2011, 2026, 176 L.Ed.2d 825 (2010) ("[D]evelopments in psychology and brain science continue to show fundamental differences between juvenile and adult minds").

[35] Thus, contrary to the dissent's protestations, today's holding neither invites consideration of whether a particular suspect is "unusually meek or compliant," *post,* at 2413 (opinion of ALITO, J.), nor "expan[ds]" the *Miranda* custody analysis, *post,* at 2412 – 2413, into a test that requires officers to anticipate and account for a suspect's every personal characteristic, see *post,* at 2414 – 2415.

[36] This approach does not undermine the basic principle that an interrogating officer's unarticulated, internal thoughts are never—in and of themselves—objective circumstances of an interrogation. See *supra,* at 2402; *Stansbury v. California,* 511 U.S. 318, 323, 114 S.Ct. 1526, 128 L.Ed.2d 293 (1994) *(per curiam).* Unlike a child's youth, an officer's purely

This is not to say that a child's age will be a determinative, or even a significant, factor in every case. Cf. *ibid.* (O'Connor, J., concurring) (explaining that a state-court decision omitting any mention of the defendant's age was not unreasonable under AEDPA's deferential standard of review where the defendant "was almost 18 years old at the time of his interview"); *post,* at 2417 (suggesting that "teenagers nearing the age of majority" are likely to react to an interrogation as would a "typical 18–year–old in similar circumstances"). It is, however, a reality that courts cannot simply ignore.

III

……

Relying on our statements that the objective custody test is "designed to give clear guidance to the police," *Alvarado,* 541 U.S., at 668, 124 S.Ct. 2140, the State next argues that a child's age must be excluded from the analysis in order to preserve clarity. Similarly, the dissent insists that the clarity of the custody analysis will be destroyed unless a "one-size-fits-all reasonable-person test" applies. *Post,* at 2415. In reality, however, ignoring a juvenile defendant's age will often make the inquiry more artificial, see *supra,* at 2404 – 2405, and thus only add confusion. And in any event, a child's age, when known or apparent, is hardly an obscure factor to assess. Though the State and the dissent worry about gradations among children of different ages, that concern cannot justify ignoring a child's age altogether. Just as police officers are competent to account for other objective circumstances that are a matter of degree such as the length of questioning or the number of officers present, so too are they competent to evaluate the effect of relative age. Indeed, they are competent to do so even though an interrogation room lacks the "reflective atmosphere of a [jury] deliberation room," *post,* at 2416. The same is true of judges, including those whose childhoods have long since passed, see *post,* at 2416. In short, officers and judges need no imaginative powers, knowledge of developmental psychology, training in cognitive science, or expertise in social and cultural anthropology to account for a child's age. They simply need the common sense to know that a 7–year–old is not a 13–year–old and neither is an adult.

……

The question remains whether J.D.B. was in custody when police interrogated him. We remand for the state courts to address that question, this time taking account of all of the relevant circumstances of the interrogation, including J.D.B.'s age at the time. The judgment of the North Carolina Supreme Court is reversed, and the case is remanded for proceedings not inconsistent with this opinion.

---

internal thoughts have no conceivable effect on how a reasonable person in the suspect's position would understand his freedom of action. See *id.,* at 323–325, 114 S.Ct. 1526; *Berkemer v. McCarty,* 468 U.S. 420, 442, 104 S.Ct. 3138, 82 L.Ed.2d 317 (1984). Rather than "overtur[n]" that settled principle, *post,* at 2415, the limitation that a child's age may inform the custody analysis only when known or knowable simply reflects our unwillingness to require officers to "make guesses" as to circumstances "unknowable" to them in deciding when to give *Miranda* warnings, *Berkemer,* 468 U.S., at 430–431, 104 S.Ct. 3138.

DISSENT: ALITO, J. with whom THE CHIEF JUSTICE, SCALIA, J. and THOMAS, J. join, dissenting.

Today's decision shifts the *Miranda* custody determination from a one-size-fits-all reasonable-person test into an inquiry that must account for at least one individualized characteristic—age—that is thought to correlate with susceptibility to coercive pressures. Age, however, is in no way the only personal characteristic that may correlate with pliability, and in future cases the Court will be forced to choose between two unpalatable alternatives. It may choose to limit today's decision by arbitrarily distinguishing a suspect's age from other personal characteristics—such as intelligence, education, occupation, or prior experience with law enforcement—that may also correlate with susceptibility to coercive pressures. Or, if the Court is unwilling to draw these arbitrary lines, it will be forced to effect a fundamental transformation of the *Miranda* custody test—from a clear, easily applied prophylactic rule into a highly fact-intensive standard resembling the voluntariness test that the *Miranda* Court found to be unsatisfactory.

For at least three reasons, there is no need to go down this road. First, many minors subjected to police interrogation are near the age of majority, and for these suspects the one-size-fits-all *Miranda* custody rule may not be a bad fit. Second, many of the difficulties in applying the *Miranda* custody rule to minors arise because of the unique circumstances present when the police conduct interrogations at school. The *Miranda* custody rule has always taken into account the setting in which questioning occurs, and accounting for the school setting in such cases will address many of these problems. Third, in cases like the one now before us, where the suspect is especially young, courts applying the constitutional voluntariness standard can take special care to ensure that incriminating statements were not obtained through coercion.

Safeguarding the constitutional rights of minors does not require the extreme makeover of *Miranda* that today's decision may portend.

B.A. v. State

100 N.E.3d 225 (Indiana Sup. Ct. 2018)

Rush, Chief Justice.

The vital mission of educating our youth requires schools to daily provide safety, security, and student discipline. In recent decades, schools have turned to resource officers for help. These officers protect students and staff, offer mentorship—and, yes, help with discipline and criminal investigations. As their presence has grown, so too have questions of students' constitutional rights. Today we address for the first time one of those questions: when are students entitled to Miranda warnings at school?

Here, in response to a bomb threat on a bathroom wall, thirteen-year-old B.A. was escorted from his bus and questioned in a vice-principal's office. Officers hovered over B.A. and encouraged him to confess, but no one gave him Miranda warnings. We hold that B.A. was in police custody and under police interrogation, so he should have been Mirandized. We therefore reverse his delinquency adjudications.

……

Scribbled in pink marker in a Decatur Middle School boys' bathroom came the threat: "I will Got A bomb in the school Monday 8th 2016 not A Joke." School Resource Officer Tutsie "immediately went into investigative mode" and soon narrowed the suspects to two students—including thirteen-year-old B.A. The next Monday, February 8, 2016, school resource officers and administrators walked through the school and found it safe. Then, when B.A.'s bus arrived, Vice–Principal Remaly and School Resource Officer Lyday removed B.A. from his bus and escorted him to Remaly's office. B.A. sat in front of Remaly's desk while Officer Lyday stood a few feet away. Early in B.A.'s interview, Officer Tutsie came in and took Officer Lyday's spot while Officer Lyday moved to sit at a conference table behind B.A. Around that same time, a third school resource officer—Officer Wheeler—came in and sat at the conference table. All three officers wore police uniforms.

Vice–Principal Remaly led the interview, asking if B.A. knew why he was there. B.A. maintained that he did not. To see if B.A.'s handwriting matched the bomb threat, Officer Tutsie handed B.A. written sentences and told B.A. how to copy them. After B.A. copied the sentences, Remaly decided that the handwriting sample matched the threat and asked B.A. why he did it. Then Officer Lyday interrupted to say, "Come on, man, just—just tell the truth." B.A. started crying, lowered his head, and said "I don't know. I'm sorry." Remaly then ended the interview—which had lasted fifteen minutes—and called B.A.'s mother. When she arrived and asked B.A. what happened, he told her, "I'm sorry mom, it was a joke" and admitted that it was a dumb thing to do.

With these admissions, Remaly suspended B.A. from school, pending expulsion. He then turned B.A. over to the school resource officers, who arrested him and took him to the Marion County Juvenile Detention Center. The State alleged that B.A. was delinquent for committing false reporting, a Level 6 felony if committed by an adult, and institutional criminal mischief, a Class A misdemeanor if committed by an adult. [T]he juvenile court denied the motion [to suppress the evidence from his interview] and found B.A. delinquent on both counts.

……

The parties agree that Miranda warnings protect students at school but disagree whether B.A. was entitled to the warnings. The critical inquiry is whether he was under custodial interrogation. B.A. argues that he was in custody under the totality of the circumstances and that he was interrogated because police officers participated in his interview. The State responds that the officers' presence was noncoercive and that they did not directly question B.A.

We start by exploring how Miranda ties into modern schools' efforts to stay safe and crime-free. We then explain the tests for police custody and police interrogation in a school setting and apply them to the undisputed facts here. We conclude that because B.A. was under custodial interrogation yet not Mirandized, his incriminating statements should have been suppressed. The juvenile court therefore abused its discretion.

I. Miranda warnings protect students under custodial interrogation.

Our schools face the monumental task of shielding students from an array of dangers in order to provide safe learning environments. Partnering with school resource officers is a key part of that effort; sworn law enforcement officers protect nearly half of the country's public schools. These officers wear many hats. They ensure school safety and mentor and educate students, but they also investigate crimes and make arrests.3 See Ind. Code §§ 20–26–18.2–1, -3, -16–6(b) (2017). This means that school discipline sometimes falls under the watchful eye of the police.

For students, the stakes of the disciplinary process are high. Students can be suspended and expelled, as B.A. was here. But those educational consequences are just the tip of the iceberg since school police officers' involvement can also lead to criminal charges. ...Ultimately, as the law-enforcement presence grows in today's schools, so does the discussion of students' rights. Indeed, the right, while sometimes 'a shelter to the guilty,' is often 'a protection to the innocent. Because of that important role, as explained below, the right against self-incrimination is protected by Miranda warnings.

......

Children are particularly vulnerable to that coercion, making Miranda warnings especially important when police place a student under custodial interrogation at school. J.D.B. v. North Carolina, 564 U.S. 261, 269, 276, 131 S.Ct. 2394, 180 L.Ed.2d 310 (2011). In other words, students surely enjoy Miranda rights just as teachers, parents, janitors, cafeteria staff, or other adults at a school do. See J.D.B., 564 U.S. at 276, 131 S.Ct. 2394. "It would indeed be surprising if the privilege against self-incrimination were available to hardened criminals but not to children."

In J.D.B. the Supreme Court of the United States considered custodial interrogation in schools. There, a police officer pulled a thirteen-year-old seventh grader out of class, took him to a conference room, and questioned him for at least half an hour. The Court held that a juvenile suspect's age is relevant to Miranda's custody analysis, as long as it's known by the interviewing officer or would be objectively apparent to a reasonable officer. Though the Court did not decide whether J.D.B. was under custodial interrogation, the implication is unmistakable: Miranda warnings protect students when they are placed under custodial interrogation at school.

Courts have understandably grappled with the custodial interrogation test in schools. For example, the Colorado Supreme Court applied J.D.B. and held that a seventh-grader was not entitled to Miranda warnings at school because he was not in custody. People v. N.A.S., 329 P.3d 285, 290 (Colo. 2014). The Supreme Court of Kentucky similarly applied J.D.B., finding that a student was entitled to Miranda warnings because he was under custodial interrogation, even in a school-discipline matter. N.C., 396 S.W.3d at 862–63. And the Supreme Court of Pennsylvania held that Miranda warnings were required when school police officers questioned a student at school. In re R.H., 568 Pa. 1, 791 A.2d 331, 334 (2002). So, cases before and after J.D.B. reveal the challenge of determining custodial interrogation (and thus whether Miranda warnings are required) in schools.

These cases also show that there is no "educational purpose" exception to Miranda. Instead, "confessions of juveniles require special caution." In re Gault, 387 U.S. 1, 45, 87 S.Ct. 1428, 18 L.Ed.2d 527 (1967). Rather than using special caution, that exception would swallow the Miranda rule, leaving less protection for students than for other suspects.

Also in keeping with special protections for juveniles, our legislature has crafted Indiana's juvenile waiver statute. See I.C. § 31–32–5–1. When Miranda applies to minor students, this statute does too. It allows an unemancipated juvenile to waive Miranda rights only through counsel or a custodial parent, guardian, custodian, or guardian ad litem. Id. If the statute is not followed, the State cannot use any statements as evidence. D.M. v. State, 949 N.E.2d 327, 333–34 (Ind. 2011).

This background leads to two points worth emphasizing. First, Miranda's key exception—for public safety—will of course apply in schools in cases of imminent danger. See New York v. Quarles, 467 U.S. 649, 655, 104 S.Ct. 2626, 81 L.Ed.2d 550 (1984); Bailey v. State, 763 N.E.2d 998, 1001–02 (Ind. 2002). So when police face the pressing need to secure the safety of students at school in light of present-day threats, Miranda warnings may be bypassed. See Quarles, 467 U.S. at 657–59, 104 S.Ct. 2626. Here though, as the parties agree, B.A.'s school was in no danger at the time of his interview.

And second, none of this is to say that schools and their resource officers must avoid placing students under custodial interrogation. Students sometimes commit crimes that school resource officers will have to investigate, often by interviewing suspects. This proper role of resource officers may place students in custody. When it does, officers must give Miranda warnings and follow Indiana's juvenile waiver statute before asking questions. See S.G. v. State, 956 N.E.2d 668, 675 (Ind. Ct. App. 2011), trans. denied; I.C. § 31–32–5–1.

In sum, Miranda warnings and Indiana's juvenile waiver statute apply when minor students are placed under custodial interrogation. We now turn to the more complex discussion: the custodial interrogation test in schools.

C. The custodial interrogation test in schools.

The initial step in the custody analysis asks whether a reasonable person in the suspect's situation would feel free to leave. Of course, no student feels free to just walk out of the principal's office, so this step points toward custody. See Schall v. Martin, 467 U.S. 253, 265, 104 S.Ct. 2403, 81 L.Ed.2d 207 (1984) ("[J]uveniles, unlike adults, are always in some form of custody."). But that does not end the analysis. For there to be custody, the suspect's situation must also present the same inherently coercive pressures as the type of station house questioning at issue in Miranda. In schools, the extent of those pressures shifts along a spectrum based on how much coercive power of law enforcement is brought to bear against the student.

On one end of the spectrum lies traditional school discipline. This discipline—handed down by school officials alone—does not place students in custody because police officers aren't involved. So, as in today's companion opinion D.Z. v. State, when school officials are not agents of the police, a clear rule applies: they can question students without providing Miranda warnings. And even if a police officer is present, a single officer's unintimidating presence is unlikely to create custody.

On the other end of the spectrum lie armed and uniformed police officers who pull students from class in handcuffs before questioning them. And "even when a private party such as a school initiates an investigation," an officer's "pervasive presence" will probably create custody. These fairly well-defined ends of the custody spectrum provide the clearest guidance.

Many cases, though, will fall in the spectrum's messy middle, posing difficulty deciding exactly when a suspect has been taken into custody. In schools, under Miranda's totality-of-the-circumstances test, myriad factors may be relevant:

- The number of officers present and how they are involved.
- Whether the setting is a traditional school-discipline environment or is police dominated.
- What the student is told about the interview.
- The length of the interview.
- The student's age.
- Whether the student is arrested after the interview.
- The relationship between the parties, including whether police officers act as teachers, counselors, or law enforcement agents. Some schools embrace all three roles for their resource officers, while in other schools one role dominates.

This list is not exhaustive given Miranda's totality-of-the-circumstances test, but it offers some factors that may be relevant in the school setting. Of course, a bright-line rule for custody would be easier for schools, police, and courts to apply in these close cases. But despite its challenges, we cannot replace Miranda's custody spectrum with a simple, clear line. Such a line could not account for each case's nuances, as Miranda's totality-of-the-circumstances test requires.

......

Police custody alone does not trigger Miranda; there must be police interrogation as well. Interrogation under Miranda refers not only to express questioning, but also to any words or actions on the part of the police that the police should know are reasonably likely to elicit an incriminating response from the suspect.

......

When B.A. arrived at school that Monday morning, a uniformed Officer Tutsie escorted him from his bus straight to Vice–Principal Remaly's office. As Remaly talked with B.A., at least one officer—and often three—stayed at all times between B.A. and the door. There's no indication that any of these officers had built a relationship with B.A., or that B.A. had any disciplinary history with them. In fact, only one officer, Officer Wheeler, typically worked at the middle school. The officers were aware, though, that B.A. was a young middle-schooler. So they knew that a reasonable person in B.A.'s shoes would be "more vulnerable or susceptible to ... outside pressures" than would adults or older teenagers.

Despite B.A.'s youth and the severity of the situation, no one called his mom until after his interview. This left him in an unfamiliar, police-overshadowed situation without parental or other support. No one told B.A. that he was free to call his mother, leave the room, take a break, or go to class. See C.H., 763 N.W.2d at 715 (finding it "crucial" whether juveniles are told they are free to leave). Instead, after the interview and, finally, a brief meeting with B.A.'s mother, officers arrested B.A. to take him "downtown" to the juvenile detention center. [T]he consistent police presence would place considerable coercive pressure on a reasonable student in B.A.'s situation. So this case lies solidly on the "custody" end of the student-confinement spectrum.

……

Officer Tutsie himself prepared a handwriting test, handed it to B.A., and explained to B.A. how to copy the sentences. As he testified, this test "was investigation material that only a police officer can probably have experience to do." And its aim was obtaining a sample to compare to the pink-marker bomb threat. Then, Officer Lyday told B.A., "Come on, man, just—just tell the truth." In context, B.A. surely saw this for what it was: an order to fess up. This tag-team probe, though limited, was interrogation because the officers should have known that it was "reasonably likely to elicit an incriminating response," And it worked, finally prompting B.A.'s tearful confession and trip to juvenile detention…We accordingly reverse his delinquency adjudications and remand this case to the juvenile court.

D.Z. v. State

100 N.E.3d 246 (Indiana Sup. Ct. 2018)

Rush, Chief Justice.

As today's companion opinion B.A. holds, Miranda warnings protect students—no less than adults at a school—when police place them under custodial interrogation. Custodial interrogation, though, requires police involvement. So when school officials alone meet with students, a clear rule governs: Miranda warnings are not required.

Here, only an assistant principal interviewed D.Z., so Miranda warnings were not required. We also find no reversible evidentiary error and that sufficient evidence supports D.Z.'s criminal-mischief adjudication, so we affirm the juvenile court.

……

In early March 2017, sexual graffiti on boys-bathroom walls at Brownsburg High School prompted a school investigation. Assistant Principal Demetrius Dowler soon enlisted school resource officer Nathan Flynn's help finding a suspect. From surveillance video, they pinpointed seventeen-year-old D.Z. Assistant Principal Dowler called D.Z. into his office for a closed-door discussion. With only the two of them in the room, Dowler detailed his investigation and said that he knew D.Z. was the culprit. D.Z. remorsefully responded that he didn't know why he did it, that he knew it was wrong, and that he didn't have anything against the girls named in the graffiti.

Assistant Principal Dowler suspended D.Z. for five days and told Officer Flynn of D.Z.'s confession. Flynn then went into Dowler's office to talk to D.Z., who again confessed. At the end of that conversation, Flynn told D.Z. that he was being charged with a crime. The next month, the State filed a delinquency petition alleging that D.Z. committed criminal mischief and harassment. At the factfinding hearing, the parties agreed that D.Z.'s incriminating statements to Officer Flynn should be suppressed since D.Z. was never Mirandized. But they disagreed about the earlier statements to Assistant Principal Dowler. The juvenile court admitted them over D.Z.'s objection. At the end of the hearing, the court found that the State failed to prove harassment, but that D.Z. had committed criminal mischief, a Class B misdemeanor if committed by an adult.

……

In today's companion opinion B.A. v. State, we explore[d] how Miranda and its custodial interrogation test apply in today's schools. As we explain there, when police officers are present at and involved in a suspect's interview, the custody and interrogation analyses are fact-specific and can result in close calls.

But when police officers aren't present, a clear rule applies: students are neither in custody nor under interrogation, unless school officials are acting as agents of the police. Ritchie v. State, 875 N.E.2d 706, 717 (Ind. 2007) ("[C]ivilians conducting their own investigation need not give Miranda warnings."). Here, unlike in B.A., the clear rule governs; Officer Flynn was not in the room when Assistant Principal Dowler talked with D.Z. So D.Z. was entitled to Miranda warnings only if Dowler was an agent of the police. See Sears v. State, 668 N.E.2d 662, 668 (Ind. 1996) ("The police ... cannot avoid their duty under Miranda by attempting to have someone act as their agent in order to bypass the Miranda requirements."), overruled on other grounds by Scisney v. State, 701 N.E.2d 847, 848–49 (Ind. 1998).

There must be some evidence of an agency relationship before we can find one. [N]o evidence suggests that police directed or encouraged Assistant Principal Dowler to act on their behalf. Quite the reverse; Dowler asked Officer Flynn—the only officer mentioned in the record—to help with his ongoing school investigation. And while Dowler did share D.Z.'s confession with Officer Flynn, the focus was not on criminal charges but on finding out who was doing the graffiti. Nor does Officer Flynn's interview with D.Z. show an agency relationship simply because it came on the heels of Dowler's interview. Yes, Officer Flynn knew during his investigation that criminal charges were possible. And he did tell D.Z. at the end of his interview that criminal charges were coming. But that is not enough to show that Dowler's interview was pretextual priming for Officer Flynn's interrogation.

Assistant Principal Dowler thus was not acting as an agent of the police. But even if he had been, Miranda warnings wouldn't be required here. Miranda's premise is that "the interaction of custody and official interrogation" creates the danger of coercion. Illinois v. Perkins, 496 U.S. 292, 297, 110 S.Ct. 2394, 110 L.Ed.2d 243 (1990). Since that coercion "is determined from the perspective of the suspect," an agency relationship implicates Miranda only if the suspect is aware enough of the underlying police involvement to create a "coercive atmosphere." Id. at 296, 110 S.Ct. 2394; Ritchie, 875 N.E.2d at 717 (recognizing that the "essential ingredients" of a coercive atmosphere are absent when the suspect "speaks freely to someone whom he believes is not an officer"). Here no evidence shows that D.Z. even knew that Assistant Principal Dowler had talked to Officer Flynn. For these reasons, the juvenile court correctly denied D.Z.'s motion to suppress his incriminating statements to Assistant Principal Dowler.

Meg Penrose: Miranda, Please Report to the Principal's Office, 33 Fordham Urb. L.J. 775 (2006)*

In many, if not most cases, courts have been reluctant to view school officials—even those individuals employed at schools as [School Resource Officer] SROs—as state actors falling within the ambit of *Miranda*. Rather than considering the inherently coercive and custodial nature of the school setting, courts frequently focus only on whether a reasonable student would feel he or she was free to exit the interview. It is naive to assume that an individual pulled involuntarily out of class would feel capable of exercising the right simply to return from where he or she was removed. This dogmatic application, while consistent with the literal *Miranda* "custody" requirement, turns a blind eye to the reality that most students do not recognize, much less exert, an ability to rebuff the school official's inquisitorial advances. Thus, courts continue to take a constrained view of *Miranda's* applicability in schools by assessing, under the totality of the circumstances, whether a particular juvenile believed he or she was "in custody" while being questioned by school officials.

****

Beyond the obvious factors of police/school entanglement, courts scrutinize school interviews and assess custody by considering: (1) the age of juvenile; (2) whether the law enforcement figure is in uniform, armed, and participating in the interview; and (3) whether the juvenile was informed that he or she had the right to leave the interview because she was not under arrest. Curiously, however, courts do not seem concerned about the broad latitude given to school officials to question students on non-school offenses such as burglaries, sexual assaults, or other off-campus behavior. Courts should vigilantly assess whether school officials are working in concert with law enforcement and thereby abandoning their in loco parentis role. Likewise, courts should evaluate whether the school official is tending to or inquiring about matters related to the safety, order, and discipline of the campus, not merely the business of students and their off-campus lives. Abandoning the narrow

---

focus of custody and opting for a more scrutinizing assessment of why a particular juvenile is being interviewed on campus by school officials should preclude school officials and SROs from immunizing their pseudo-law enforcement activities under the guise of *T.L.O.* and its progeny.

Where the behavior is school-related and deals strictly with disciplinary issues, the Fifth Amendment poses no obstacle to school officials furthering the safety and order of their charges. Unfortunately, the current state of affairs often involves school officials with non-school-related offenses and asks them to "assist" in interviewing potential criminal suspects. Where the purpose of the interview, even remotely, is to elicit evidence intended for use in criminal proceedings, the dynamic of the exchange transforms immediately into a setting where the Fifth Amendment and its full protections should be afforded and honored. It is this latter scenario where a silver platter doctrine equivalent should be applied to prevent school officials from unjustly stripping juveniles of their constitutionally guaranteed rights. Schools should limit themselves and their investigations to school-related disciplinary issues. Nothing in *T.L.O.*, *Acton*, or *Earls* hinted that they enjoy any greater powers.

The majority of cases assessing *Miranda's* viability on school campuses bypass the important question of whether school officials are working in concert with police officers to effectuate criminal prosecutions of juveniles. The assumption is that school officials are not working, either tacitly or patently, as agents of the police. However, unlike the scenarios presented in *T.L.O.* and *Acton*, many modern cases illustrate that school officials do work in tandem with police to ensure that juveniles not only receive school penalties for misbehavior, but also face criminal prosecution for violating state criminal codes. While juveniles should not escape criminal prosecution for criminal behavior, the mandates of criminal procedure should fully extend to juveniles who are interrogated by the same individuals likely to participate in their subsequent criminal prosecution. For better or worse, school officials are increasingly becoming active participants in the criminal process.

In recent years, schools have been legislatively required or have voluntarily consented to participate in programs requiring the reporting of any behavior that, while possibly violating a school rule, qualifies as a criminal offense. Schools now routinely collaborate with police officers when a student is found to have drugs, drug paraphernalia, or weapons which clearly violate both school regulations and criminal law. Schools also assist the police in investigating allegations relating to assaults (fighting) and sexual assaults (incest or rape), the majority of which occur off-campus. It is in these latter instances, particularly, that school involvement cannot encompass anything other than pseudo-police behavior. Non-school events that have predominantly, if not exclusively, non-school effects should disqualify school officials from working in concert with police officers without invoking traditional criminal procedure protections.

Frequently, local school districts employ police officers with dual assignments as both teacher and law enforcement officer. Courts should not readily dismiss the police qualities these individuals possess and express while working on school campuses. Rather, courts should accept that these individuals possess the full arsenal of police powers: search, seizure, arrest, and, most notably, interrogation. It is time that our jurisprudence reflect the growing reality that school officials, not just school resource officers, are taking on a greater and more active role in their communities' efforts to eradicate juvenile crime.

While the era of *T.L.O.* proved vital in making schools safe for learning purposes by empowering school officials with the ability to perform searches under the less stringent reasonable suspicion standard, the modern decisions of *Acton* and *Earls* reflect a concern that juvenile crime can best be quelled with the proactive assistance of school officials. Yet, both *Acton* and *Earls* are remarkable in that each decision ratified the suspicionless urine searches at issue because the results were not turned over to law enforcement. Instead, students testing positive for drug use in each instance were required to submit to non-criminal sanctions—a fact that should not go unnoticed. As school officials and SROs take more initiative in eradicating crime on campuses, courts should recognize the limited reach of *T.L.O.*, *Acton*, and *Earls*.

School safety can remain a paramount concern without resulting in simultaneous criminal prosecutions. If school safety is the true concern, something that is debatable at this point, then police involvement is not relevant because the sanctions should be limited to those required to keep students and school officials safe. But as school officials and SROs continue to take a more active role in working with police officers to provide police with information gleaned from schoolhouse interviews, courts should evaluate whether the "prosecution of the [student] being questioned is among the purposes, definite or contingent, for which the information is elicited."

State v. Pablo

100 N.E.3d 1068 (Ohio 2017)

Plaintiff-appellant, State of Ohio, appeals a decision of the Franklin County Court of Common Pleas issued on December 21, 2016 which suppressed statements the defendant-appellee, David Pablo, made to the police in an interrogation on September 24, 2014. Because Pablo was not afforded the presence of a parent or responsible adult in determining whether to waive his Miranda rights, because he had no prior experience with the police, because English was not his first or primary language, because evidence suggested his level of intelligence was not high, and because he indicated that he signed the rights waiver form because he thought he had to, we agree with the trial court. Under the totality of the circumstances, Pablo's Miranda waiver was not valid and Pablo's statement to the police was correctly suppressed.

Pablo was charged as a juvenile with three counts of rape, two counts of kidnapping, one count of gross sexual imposition, and one count of felonious assault in connection with two incidents involving two different women on September 9 and 22, 2014. ... Pablo filed a motion to suppress statements made to the police during an interrogation...At the hearing, the State presented a Miranda rights form, signed by Pablo, and a video recording of the interrogation. In addition, three witnesses testified, one of the detectives who interviewed Pablo, Pablo himself, and Pablo's mother.

The detective testified ... that after he became suspicious (for reasons which are not disclosed in the record) that Pablo was involved in the incidents with the two women, he traveled to Pablo's school. The detective said that Pablo had been brought to an administrator's office at the school and that after telling Pablo the police needed to talk to him, he had a patrol officer transport Pablo to the Franklin County Sheriff's Office. The detective testified that a "translator" from the school called Pablo's parents but the detective admitted he was not in the room when the call took place; he testified that, to the extent he could overhear, he did not understand what he heard. Video revealed that at the Franklin County Sheriff's Office, two detectives interviewed Pablo for approximately 26 minutes in an interrogation room. In addition to having Pablo sign the Miranda rights form, one of the detectives read Pablo the rights portion of the form verbatim, pausing after each right to ask Pablo if he understood. In each pause, Pablo nodded to some visible degree. After the reading, Pablo signed the form.

……

Pablo testified that he had just turned 16 and was in ninth grade (having been held back). He testified that he was a "D" student and that while he understands and speaks English fully (having lived in the United States his whole life), his first and primary language is Spanish. He recounted that the principal took him out of class and to the office where a detective and two officers were waiting. The detective told him to put his hands behind his back and he was then taken to the police station. He had never been interrogated or even visited a police station before. Id. No one offered him a phone call, or to let someone know where he was, or to notify his parents. Although he admitted that he understood that the police were telling him he had the right to talk to a lawyer, he signed the form because he thought he had to sign. He did not read it. He confirmed that the detectives made neither threats nor promises and admitted that he never asked permission to telephone his parents.

Pablo's mother testified by means of an interpreter. She testified that Pablo did not come home from school in a timely fashion and that she had been worried. She only found out that he had been arrested around midnight when her sister saw it on the news and contacted her. Id. She testified that the school had contacted her before at home and knew her number. Despite the fact that she was home that day, no one from the school or the police contacted her.

……

Due process protects juveniles with the result that they are afforded the right to Miranda warnings. In re Gault, 387 U.S. 1, 55, 87 S.Ct. 1428, 18 L.Ed.2d 527 (1967). With respect to whether a juvenile has validly waived his Miranda rights, the Supreme Court of Ohio has said:

> If custodial interrogation continues in the absence of an attorney after a police officer advises a suspect of his rights, the government bears "a heavy burden" to demonstrate by a preponderance of the evidence that the suspect "knowingly and intelligently waived his privilege against self-incrimination and his right to retained or appointed counsel" before speaking to the police. A court may not presume a valid waiver either from the suspect's silence after warnings are given or from the fact that the suspect eventually confessed. Rather, the record must show 'that an accused was offered counsel but intelligently and understandingly rejected the offer. Anything less is not waiver.' If the state does not satisfy its burden, "no evidence obtained as a result of interrogation can be used."

> To determine whether a suspect knowingly, intelligently, and voluntarily waived his Miranda rights, courts examine the totality of the circumstances. When the suspect is a juvenile, the totality of the circumstances includes "the juvenile's age, experience, education, background, and intelligence" as well as his "capacity to understand the warnings given him, the nature of his Fifth Amendment rights, and the consequences of waiving those rights."
> State v. Barker, 149 Ohio St.3d 1, 2016-Ohio-2708, 73 N.E.3d 365, ¶ 23–24.

Whether a juvenile has voluntarily confessed (following a valid waiver of rights under Miranda), the Supreme Court has explained:

> In deciding whether a juvenile's confession is involuntarily induced, [a trial] court should consider the totality of the circumstances, including the age, mentality and prior criminal experience of the accused; the length, intensity, and frequency of interrogation; and the existence of physical deprivation or inducement.
> In re Watson, 47 Ohio St.3d 86, 548 N.E.2d 210 (1989).

Some jurisdictions have recognized an "independent advice/interested adult" principle which holds that a juvenile can only validly waive his rights to an attorney and to remain silent if both the child and a parent (or other "interested adult") are advised of those rights and are given the opportunity to confer regarding the advisability of waiving, free from coercion, force, or inducement. Id. at 89, 548 N.E.2d 210. The Supreme Court has expressly declined to adopt the "independent advice/interested adult" view as a per se rule in juvenile interrogations. Id. at 89–90, 548 N.E.2d 210. But the Court has not forbidden it as a consideration under the "totality of the circumstances." Id. at paragraph one of the syllabus. And the Supreme Court has explained that, "[a] juvenile's access to advice from a parent, guardian or custodian also plays a role in assuring that the juvenile's waiver is knowing, intelligent, and voluntary." Barker at ¶ 24.

……

Consistent with the record, the trial court noted in its decision that Pablo had just turned 16 at the time of the interrogation, was a poor student repeating ninth grade, and had no previous contact with the police. The record is clear that the trial court considered " 'the juvenile's age, experience, education, background, and intelligence' as well as his 'capacity to understand the warnings given him, the nature of his Fifth Amendment rights, and the consequences of waiving those rights.' " Barker at ¶ 24. These considerations are also relevant and significant to determining voluntariness such as, "the age, mentality and prior criminal experience of the accused." In re Watson at paragraph one of the syllabus. In admitting the videotaped confession and hearing testimony about its circumstances and character, the trial court also would have considered (though it did not explicitly mention) other voluntariness factors including, "the length," (short, 26 minutes), "intensity," (low key) "frequency of interrogation" (one session), and "the existence of physical deprivation or inducement" (essentially none).

……

The trial court also considered what the school and police did (essentially nothing) to ensure that Pablo's parents were aware of the situation and could assist Pablo in understanding his rights. This is important because, "[a] juvenile's access to advice from a parent, guardian or custodian also plays a role in assuring that the juvenile's waiver is knowing, intelligent, and voluntary." Barker at ¶ 24. And parental involvement may have been of enhanced importance here, as the trial court noted. Pablo did not achieve high grades in school. He had no prior experience with the police. And Pablo's first and primary language is Spanish, not English. There is further evidence of this from the detective's testimony that an interpreter had to call Pablo's home from his school.

We find the trial court acted within the valid exercise of its factfinding discretion to conclude that the evidence did not support a finding that Pablo's waiver of his Miranda rights, unaccompanied by a parent or interested adult to assist him, was knowing and voluntary. Under the law, someone in their early to mid-teens " 'cannot be compared with an adult in full possession of his senses and knowledgeable of the consequences of his admissions.' " Barker at ¶ 39. Accordingly, we agree that, under all of the factual circumstances cited by the trial court and as contained in the record, Pablo's waiver of his Miranda rights was not knowing and voluntary and as such does not stand.

State v. Daniell
346 Ga. App. 792 (2018)

The State appeals the grant of a motion to suppress a statement given by a high school student during the school's attempt to determine why another student was found unconscious in the school restroom. We reverse.

On March 8, 2016, the victim, a ninth grade student at Villa Rica High School, was found unconscious in the school restroom. He revived but could not recall what had happened. The assistant principal reviewed hallway surveillance video and observed the victim enter the restroom with the defendant, Hunter Daniell, and another student, Shane Black. Shortly thereafter, a fourth student entered the restroom as well. Because Daniell and Black exited the restroom without the victim, they were called to the administrative offices, with Daniell being interviewed in the principal's office and Black being interviewed in the assistant principal's office. At first, Daniell told the principal that he had no idea what happened, but later changed his story and stated he thought the fourth student who entered the restroom may have hit the victim. But the principal and assistant principal had observed Daniell and Black texting each other and suspected they were trying to coordinate their stories.

Officer Michelle Moore, a corporal with the Villa Rica Police Department who served as the high school's resource officer, was summoned to the principal's office. The assistant principal told her he had seen the two texting about saying the fourth student had struck the victim. At first, Officer Moore didn't know whether the victim had just had a medical problem or if the fourth student had attacked him, and she didn't consider Daniell as a suspect; she just wanted to find out if Daniell knew what happened. She suspected Daniell and Black knew more than what they were telling, and because the two had been texting each other, she seized their cell phones as evidence and informed them she would be requesting a search warrant. Daniell's mother arrived soon afterward and told her son to not cover up for anybody and to tell what he knew about the incident. Daniell then stated that he choked the victim until he was unconscious and then dropped him to the floor.

No one expected that admission. Officer Moore decided she needed to tell the victim's mother, who had taken her son to the emergency room. She asked Daniell if he was willing to write a statement while she made the call, and Daniell did so. When she called the victim's mother, Officer Moore did not know whether the matter would be handled administratively through the school or through a criminal prosecution. At that point, Daniell was not under arrest; he was not restrained; he was free to leave, and there was even a nearby exit door leading to the parking lot; and he was unsupervised while Officer Moore stepped out of the room and went to the reception area to make the call. But when the victim's mother indicated she wanted Daniell prosecuted, Officer Moore returned and placed him under arrest for aggravated assault.

The trial court found that after Officer Moore seized Daniell's cell phone, the situation became a custodial interrogation requiring the Miranda warnings. Because Officer Moore had not informed Daniell of his rights before his subsequent oral and written admissions, the trial court suppressed those statements. On appeal, the State contends the trial court erred in finding there was a custodial interrogation that implicated the Miranda warnings.

Law enforcement officers are required to give Miranda warnings prior to questioning only where the subject is in police custody, having either been formally arrested or restrained to an extent associated with such an arrest. Where one has not been arrested, he will be considered to be in custody only under circumstances where a reasonable person in the same situation would perceive that he was deprived of his freedom of action in a meaningful way. Jacobs v. State, 338 Ga. App. 743, 745 (1), 791 S.E.2d 844 (2016). (Citation and punctuation omitted.)

A trial court must consider the totality of the circumstances to determine whether a reasonable person would believe he is not at liberty to leave. Factors indicating a defendant is not in custody include that the defendant voluntarily accompanied an officer to another location, that the officer told the defendant he was not under arrest or otherwise in custody, that the defendant was allowed to speak to others, and that the defendant was not handcuffed or otherwise restrained.

Jacobs, supra. (Citation omitted.)

In the instant case, Daniell was in the school principal's office; he had been called there by the school principal, not Officer Moore. When Officer Moore arrived, she did not think of Daniell as a suspect and did not treat him like one. She was simply trying to find out what had caused a student to end up unconscious on the restroom floor. Daniell was allowed to speak to his mother, and actually it was his mother who elicited Daniell's statement. Daniell was not restrained while he was in the principal's office. Even after Daniell admitted choking the victim, Officer Moore never restrained him or told him he was not free to leave, and she left him entirely unsupervised, with a clearly marked exit door near the office, while she left the room to contact the victim's mother. Being called to the principal's office did not constitute an arrest, and being questioned by his own mother did not constitute a police interrogation. No doubt, under the circumstances, Daniell had reason to feel he was in some trouble, but this situation did not transform into a custodial interrogation, even after Officer Moore took away his cell phone. Considering the totality of the circumstances in this case, we conclude that a reasonable person would not perceive he was deprived of his freedom of action in a meaningful way.

Even if Daniell were considered to have been in custody, the fact that his own mother elicited the statement militates against suppression of the statement. "Numerous cases hold that Miranda is not implicated when a suspect in custody is questioned or encouraged to confess by a father, mother, wife, or girl friend." Cook v. State, 270 Ga. 820, 826 (2), 514 S.E.2d 657 (1999). Accordingly, the trial court should not have suppressed Daniell's statement.

Pamela M. Henry-Mays, Farewell *Michael C.*, Hello *Gault*: Considering the Miranda Rights of Learning Disabled Children, 34 N. Ky. L. Rev. 343 (2007)*

Not all juveniles are created equal. Juveniles, who run afoul of the law, have a range of mental capacities. For some juveniles, a lack of worldly experience is compounded by a mental deficiency that renders their intelligence, moral aptitude, and resistance to suggestion far below that of their peers. Many of these children receive special education services from local school systems. Unfortunately, children qualifying for such services constitute a majority of those currently in the juvenile justice system.

A concerned Ohio court offered an interesting solution to the dilemmas posed by special education children during custodial interrogation. According to the court, the best protection for the rights of such children was the presence of a special education teacher or counselor. Because of familiarity with the child's propensities and capabilities, the special education teacher or counselor would have the insight necessary to protect the child. The court's employment of a per se interested adult standard is an excellent solution. However, special education teachers and counselors are not the best choices. Indeed, the conflicts implicit in their presence may prove to do more harm than good for that child and others.

.....

[T]he states have taken a variety of approaches when faced with a child possessing intellectual limitations that affect their ability to knowingly, intelligently, and voluntarily waive their rights. The most troubling circumstance for the courts is not when a child is clearly designated as mentally retarded. Rather, it is the child enrolled in a special education program that provides difficulty. Such children possess disabilities that most often focus on their ability or inability, rather, to process information.

......

In order for a child to waive their *Miranda* rights effectively, three elements are necessary. First, the child must have an understanding of what the words and phrases contained in the warnings mean. Then, effective waiver requires both the ability to reason about the consequences of the decision to waive or invoke those rights and an accurate understanding of the function of the *Miranda* rights. While special education children may understand each individual word of the *Miranda* rights being read to them, they have little understanding of what those rights mean as a whole. Research has shown that the ability to understand what the rights mean correlates with experience with the juvenile justice system, I.Q., and age.

Moreover, juveniles have great difficulty foreseeing what waiver of their *Miranda* rights may mean to them in the future. When asked about their reasons for waiving their rights, most juveniles were more concerned with their immediate detention or release. Long-range consequences were simply too far away for them to identify or comprehend. For example, in a laboratory study, 72 participants were accused of stealing 100 dollars. Fifty-eight percent waived their rights. The innocent were more likely than the guilty to waive their rights for strategic self-presentation reasons. They believed that others would be able to judge correctly their innocence or guilt based on their denials.

This inability to foresee the effects of waiver of rights translates into high rates of false confessions among juveniles. In another study, persons age twelve to twenty-six were told not to strike a key on a keyboard during a typing test. Each was confronted with proof that they had done so, though none actually had. Among those who were ages twelve to thirteen the false confession rate was 78 percent, and among those who were fifteen to sixteen, the false confession rate was 72 percent.

Especially troublesome in the interrogation of juveniles, is the wide spread practice of training of law enforcement officers in the Reid technique of interrogation. The Reid technique attempts to cause suspects to engage in self-incrimination by creating increased anxiety and despair and minimizing the consequences of confession. The urge to confess to real or imagined transgressions originates in the fear of loosing the love of family and others, and the fear of retaliation. Juvenile suspects are particularly vulnerable to false confessions under interrogation by authority figures. The presence of parents or other friends does little to mitigate this effect and may even worsen it. Most often parents do not believe that children should be allowed to remain silent and recommend that their children speak. Parents may even coerce their children to make statements out of embarrassment or anger.

Additionally, juveniles have little understanding of the purpose of *Miranda* rights. They do not understand that these rights trump the ability of the police to continue the interrogation, as they will. Many normal juveniles do not view *Miranda* rights as entitlements but rather as rules that can be changed by adults. Juveniles also have different interpretations of what the words of *Miranda* mean. "Anything you say may be used against you" in the mind of a child may become "you had better talk to the police." If normal children hold such misconceptions, how might a special education child perceive *Miranda* warnings? One special education teacher, who works with EBD children, believed that his students "would not even hear them as rights, but as a challenge."

[T]he use of special education teachers to protect those rights is not practical…..To state the obvious, school personnel and teachers in particular, are not law enforcement personnel. However, in many ways they are similar since part of what teachers do every day is protect the individual from abuse by the group, and the group from abuse by the individual. School personnel, just like law enforcement, exercise authority, and control over the school community.

While special education students do need extra protection during custodial interrogations, protection should not come in the form of pro se representation by special education teachers. Teachers, like parole officers, have conflicting loyalties when it comes to their students. On the one hand, most teachers would help a child in any way that they could. On the other, helping one child may not be in another child's best interest. Asking teachers to choose the good of one child over another would violate the spirit of the relationship between the children and the teacher and the teacher and the parents. Additionally, when asked, special education teachers have expressed great uneasiness with being involved in criminal matters and would rather parents were involved. Most respondents saw no role for themselves in the interrogation of a juvenile by the police even when that student was one on their own caseload. Moreover, they expressed fear that such a requirement would open them up to increased liability and lawsuits.

The path toward a solution that provides the extra protections needed by juveniles with learning disabilities, and juveniles, in general, begins in federal law. Congress [recently] passed section 18 U.S.C.A. § 5033 205 of the Federal Juvenile Delinquency Act. Under 18 U.S.C.A. § 5033, when a juvenile is taken into custody for delinquent behavior, the arresting officer must inform the juvenile of his rights in language that is comprehensive to the juvenile. Moreover, the section requires that the arresting officer not only inform the Attorney General of the arrest, but also inform the child's parents, guardians, or custodians of both the nature of the offense, and the rights of the juvenile. The juvenile must also appear before a magistrate forthwith.

Section 5033 embodies many of the elements of the per se approach to juvenile interrogation, while maintaining a degree of the flexibility found in totality of the circumstances approach. The law contains a systematic process for law enforcement personnel to follow. .... Another element in finding the path to a solution which provides extra protection for students with learning disabilities does lie in the schools. Somewhere, in between the Pythagorean Theorem and mitosis, schools can teach all students what rights Miranda protects and the importance of preserving those rights. Courts have repeatedly ruled both for adults and for juveniles that an invocation of silence or the request for counsel ends custodial interrogation and that the right to counsel exists for all. What a small piece of information to teach our children. By combining education with state laws patterned after 18 U.S.C.A. § 5033, the courts can begin to find a middle ground between protecting the child and protecting society.

Notes and Comments

1. The School Resource Officer and Student Interrogations

J.D.B. formalizes the factor of age when juveniles are being questioned on campus by police. Significantly, *J.D.B.* does not represent a radical departure from the rules that previously applied in the public school setting. Essentially, the U.S. Supreme Court in *J.D.B.* endorses, without citations, the course previously plotted by the many state court decisions that ruled that special caution is required when young, impressionable children encounter school resource officers while on campus. These state court cases, now codified by *J.D.B.*, create a list of sorts to regulate the interrogation setting on campus.

(a). *Miranda* does not apply to school officials. See, *In re D.E.M.*, 727 A.2d 570 (Pa. 1999), *State v. C.G.*, 2000 Wash. App. LEXIS 1304 (Wash. Ct. App. 2000).

(b). *Miranda* does apply to police of all kinds, including the school resource officer. See, *In re K.D.L.*, 700 S.E.2d 766 (N.C. Ct. App. 2010), *In re C.E.*, 2011 WL 2581921 (Cal. Ct. App. 2011), *Kalmakoff v. State*, 2011 WL 3241860 (Alaska 2011), *In re Welfare of G.S.P.*, 610 N.W.2d 651 (Minn. Ct. App. 2000). In re I.J., 906 A.2d 249, 263-64 (D.C. App. 2006), In re D.A.R., 73 S.W.3d 505, 512 (Tex. App. 2002).

(c). If police question a student, then police must insure that the student understands that he is not under arrest, can leave if he wants to, and does not have to answer questions from the police. See, *In re Loredo*, 865 P.2d 1312 (Or. Ct. App. 1993), *In re Killitz*, 651 P.2d 1382 (Or. Ct. App. 1982), *In re Welfare of G.S.P.*, 610 N.W.2d 651 (Minn. Ct. App. 2000), *Kalmakoff v. State*, 2011 WL 3241860 (Alaska 2011).

(d). Particular care should be given to police questioning of students of tender years and fragile sensibilities. See, *In re John Doe*, 130 Idaho 811; 948 P.2d 166 (1997), *In re Welfare of G.S.P.*, 610 N.W.2d 651 (Minn. App. 2000), *State v. D.R.*, 84 Wn. App. 832, 930 P.2d 350, 353 (Wash. App. 1997).

This rule is compatible with the legal reform in school safety regarding police. Fourth Amendment law recognizes the SRO when acting as a resource to the educator's desire to maintain a safe campus, but treats police as an outsider for all other collaboration. The courts have divided the student search rules into three scenarios:

(1) Where school officials initiate the search or police involvement is minimal, the reasonableness standard is applied;

(2) Where the search is conducted by the school resource officer on his or her own initiative to further educationally related goals, the reasonableness standard is applied; and

(3) Where "outside" police officers initiate the search of a student for investigative purposes, the probable cause and warrant requirements are applied.

J.D.B. effectively treats all police as outsiders when (1) the event that causes the questioning does not involve school safety, and (2) when the event involves school safety but a competent educator is available to perform the necessary *tasks in-loco parentis*.

2. State Statutory Reform on Student Interrogations

State statutes now provide guidelines on student interrogations. Where a state has given students some form of protection from interrogation, whether by state statute or school district policy, that protection must be honored. Do you believe that these provisions are sufficient to protect students from self-incrimination?

> Arkansas Code 6-18-221
> "Any school district [collaborating with Police] shall include in its attendance policy a notice to parents and students that … unsupervised students found off school premises during school hours shall be subject to questioning by a law enforcement officer under the program."

> Arkansas Code 6-18-513
> "The principal…shall make a reasonable, good faith effort to notify the student's parent…that the student has been reported to, interviewed by, or taken into custody by law enforcement personnel."

> Colorado Code 22-33-106.3
> "A public school employee shall not use a student's statement concerning an act alleged to have been committed by the student that results in mandatory expulsion pursuant to section 22-33-106(1)(d), in the expulsion hearing, unless the statement is signed by the student and a parent, guardian, or legal or physical custodian is present when the student signs the statement."

> New Mexico Code 32A-2-14(c)
> "A child subject to the provisions of the Delinquency Act is entitled to the same basic rights as an adult. Notwithstanding any other provision to the contrary, no confessions, statements or admissions may be introduced against a child under the age of thirteen years on the allegations of the petition. There is a rebuttable presumption that any confessions, statements or admissions made by a child thirteen or fourteen years old to a person in a position of authority are inadmissible."

> Oklahoma Code 10, § 1109(a):
> "No information gained by questioning a child nor any evidence subsequently obtained as a result of such information shall be admissible …unless the questioning … by any law enforcement officer or investigative agency, or employee of the court, or the Department of Human Services is done in the presence of the parents."

> Rhode Island Code 16-21.5-2
> "Before making an elementary school pupil available to a law enforcement officer for the purpose of being questioned, the principal of the elementary school shall take immediate steps to obtain the oral consent of the parent or guardian of the pupil to permit the questioning."

> Rhode Island Code 16-21.5-3
> "Before making a high school pupil under eighteen (18) years of age available to a law enforcement officer for the purpose of questioning, the principal of the school shall inform the pupil that the pupil has the right to request that his or her

> parent or guardian or an adult family member, or person on the list of emergency contacts for the pupil be present during the questioning."

3. *Miranda*, Student Interrogations and Exigent Circumstances

The warnings required under *Miranda* are not absolute. One traditional *Miranda* exception, the public safety exception, (*see N.Y. v. Quarles*, 467 U.S. 649 (1984)); broadens the latitude of questioning. (*see also Commonwealth v. Dillion*, 863 N.E.2d 1287 (Mass. 2007)). This exception, when applied to campus settings in an era of school shootings provides a much-needed tool for teachers and administrators to avert violence. In *Dillion*, a police officer questioned a student after he was observed on campus showing to other students a clear plastic bag containing over fifty bullets. The trial court ruled that the student's *Miranda* rights were violated because the public safety exception was not applicable. The appellate court reversed.

> [The police officer] was faced with an emergency situation that required protecting approximately 890 children at the middle school and residents of the neighborhood. In these circumstances, where the juvenile possessed a clear plastic bag containing over fifty bullets and was observed showing the bag to other students, Partello reasonably concluded that there was an immediate need to question the juvenile about the presence of a firearm because the obligation of protecting other students and community members outweighed the administration of *Miranda* warnings to the juvenile in the presence of an interested adult. The juvenile's possession of over fifty bullets alone was enough to support the inference that a gun was in close proximity and to invoke the public safety exception to the requisite *Miranda* warnings. 863 N.E.2d, at 1290.

4. Interrogations and the Role of Educators after *J.D.B.*

After *J.D.B.*, it is clear that school officials must be considered protective guardians when it comes to on-campus interrogations by police officers. This duty, while contrary to the usual collaborative relationship with police, is required to discourage abuse by the coercive appearance of both public officials in the eyes of the student in question. Courts are wary that students who are younger and who also have no prior experience with questioning by police or school officials may reasonably believe that they are either in police custody or believe that they are in trouble with the school and thus be more likely to make incriminating statements. The Idaho Court of Appeals underscores this in *In re John Doe*, 130 Idaho 811; 948 P.2d 166 (1997), where a ten-year-old boy was told by educators to leave his fifth-grade classroom and go to the faculty lounge to be interrogated by an SRO without receiving *Miranda* warning of any kind.

> "We think it unlikely that the environment of a principal's office or a faculty room is considered by most children to be a familiar or comfortable setting, for students normally report to these locations for disciplinary reasons, as Doe had in the past. It is also unlikely that any ten-year-old would feel free to simply leave the administrative area of the school after having been summoned there by school authorities for a police interview. We are persuaded that under these circumstances a child ten years of age would have reasonably believed that his appearance at the

> designated room and his submission to the questioning was compulsory and that he was subject to restraint which, from such a child's perspective, was the effective equivalent of arrest." 948 P.2d at 172-74.

Otherwise, the role of educators does not change after *J.D.B.*. Before, *J.D.B.*., the attention of the Court focused solely on student rights arising out of the First and the Fourth Amendments. The rules from these cases are more favorable toward school officials than students. Recently, in *Morse v. Frederick*, 551 U.S. 393 (2007), the Court set forth the controlling principle.

> "[T]he constitutional rights of students in public school are not automatically coextensive with the rights of adults in other settings…Drawing on the principles applied in our student speech cases, we have held in the Fourth Amendment context that "while children assuredly do not 'shed their constitutional rights . . . at the schoolhouse gate,' . . . the nature of those rights is what is appropriate for children in school." *Vernonia Sch. Dist. 47J v. Acton*, 515 U.S. 646, 655-56, (1995). In particular, "the school setting requires some easing of the restrictions to which searches by public authorities are ordinarily subject." *New Jersey v. T.L.O.*, 469 U.S. 325, 340 (1985). ("Fourth Amendment rights, no less than First and Fourteenth Amendment rights, are different in public schools than elsewhere . . ."); *Bd. of Educ. v. Earls*, 536 U.S. 822, 829-30 (2002) ("'special needs' inhere in the public school context"; "while schoolchildren do not shed their constitutional rights when they enter the schoolhouse, Fourth Amendment rights . . . are different in public schools than elsewhere; the 'reasonableness' inquiry cannot disregard the schools' custodial and tutelary responsibility for children."

Morse v. Frederick, 551 U.S. 393, 396 - 406 (2007).

After J.D.B., as a matter of constitutional law, educators should make sure that students fully understand what it is they are being asked to do. When incidents are school-related, the best practice is for educators to conduct the questioning; no warnings of any kind are required. Any confusion over the role of age in a police interrogation will be resolved in favor of the student, especially as the age of the juvenile decreases. However, the Supreme Court does not change the nature of the authority of the educator to question students as a means of keeping the campus safe for learning. In this context, *J.D.B.* is not a school safety case at all, but instead is specifically about limitations on outside government officials who come onto campus.

5. When does the educator become an agent of law enforcement?

One obstacle to better collaboration school officials and law enforcement is a misunderstanding of how the rules of agency apply. On one side of the line is a school official standing *in loco parentis* and acting independently of the police when resolving a school disciplinary incident that may or may not involve criminal activity. The other side of the line is a school official whose actions are coerced, dominated, or directed by police for law enforcement purposes, not for school disciplinary purposes. The principle questions are straightforward. When does the educator become an agent of law enforcement? Does the implementation of a school resource officer program create a great risk that the tasks performed by educators will be measured by the rules that apply to police?

The courts have uniformly held that a school principal or other school official who questions a student about a possible violation of law or school regulation does not, absent other circumstances, act as a law enforcement officer or agent of the police. See, *In re Navajo County Juvenile Action*, No. JV91000058, 183 Ariz. 204, 901 P.2d 1247, 1249 (Ariz.Ct.App.1995); *In re Corey L.*, 203 Cal.App.3d 1020, 250 Cal. Rptr. 359, 361 (Cal.Ct.App.1988); *S.A. v. State*, 654 N.E.2d 791, 797 (Ind.Ct.App.1995); *Commonwealth v. Snyder*, 413 Mass. 521, 597 N.E.2d 1363, 1369 (Mass.1992); *State v. Tinkham*, 143 N.H. 73, 719 A.2d 580, 583–84 (N.H.1998); *State v. Biancamano*, 284 N.J.Super. 654, 666 A.2d 199, 203 (N.J.Super.Ct.App.Div.1995); *In re Harold S.*, 731 A.2d 265, 268 (R.I.1999); *In re V.P.*, 55 S.W.3d 25, 33 (Tex.App.2001). *J.D. v. Commonwealth*, 42 Va.App. 329, 335, 591 S.E.2d 721 (2004).

The rule has been extended to prevent non-sworn school security officers from being agents of law enforcement despite the fact that their duties specifically include investigating and preventing disruptions that may be violations of the law. See, *In the Matter of L.A.,* 270 Kan. 879, 21 P.3d 952 (2001). See, *State v. Wolfer*, 39 Wash. App. 287, 693 P.2d 154 (1984). However, conduct by school resource officers and other sworn school police are "law enforcement officers" for Fourth and Fifth Amendment purposes. This is so even when the SRO is considered an employee of the school district. See, *In re R.H.*, 568 Pa. 1, 791 A.2d 331 (2002). And where police have a "silent understanding" with school officials designed to delegate investigations over to educators where constitutional restraints would make certain evidence inaccessible to police, the courts will find the educators to be police agents. See, *State v. Heirtzler*, 147 N.H. 344, 789 A.2d 634 (2001).

Can the following two cases be reconciled with the rule? (1) In Missouri, the United States District Court refused to dismiss claims brought against educators and police for detaining a student without probable cause or exigent circumstances. The court ruled that the in-school police interview about a non-school incident was a seizure under the Fourth Amendment and that educators were acting as agents of the police. The court found that the interrogation violated school policy that required the presence of an administrator and parental notice. *L.G. v. Columbia Pub. Sch.*, Case No. 2:19-cv-04191-NKL (W.D. Mo. May. 12, 2020). (2) In Connecticut, the United States District Court held that an educator does not become an agent of police when he telephones local police, informs them about a threatening e-mail, and thereafter responds to police inquiries by giving them information about suspected students. The police investigation resulted in removing a suspected student from a school bus, arresting and detaining him for about an hour, and then releasing him, without further charge or action against him. *Ortolaza ex rel E. v. Capitol Region Educ. Council*, 388 F. Supp. 3d 109 (D. Conn. 2019).

III. Campus Policing and Excessive Force

New Jersey v. T.L.O., 469 U.S. 325, 341 (1985) establishes that when students raise Fourth Amendment claims to challenge school search and seizure policies, courts do not apply the probable cause standard to school officials. ("[T]he substantial need of teachers and administrators for freedom to maintain order in the schools does not require strict adherence to the requirement that searches be based on probable cause."). Instead, courts use a standard that balances the legitimate competing interests of *in loco parentis* authority, the rights of parents, and the right of students to be free from unreasonable seizures and searches. On campus, "the legality of a search of a student . . . depend simply on the reasonableness, under all the circumstances, of the search." *T.L.O.,* 469 U.S. at 341. Two elements combine to control the reasonableness assessment by the courts. First, courts must determine whether the conduct of a school official is "justified at its inception." *T.L.O.*, 469 U.S. at 341-42. Second, courts must determine whether the conduct is "reasonably related in scope to the circumstances which justified the interference in the first place." *ibid.* In the application of these standards, the U.S. Supreme Court intends to defer to the judgment of educators when seizures and searches "are reasonably related to the objectives of the [seizure and] search and not excessively intrusive in light of the age and sex of the student and the nature of the infraction." *T.L.O.,* 469 U.S. at 342; see also *Safford Unified Sch. Dist. No. 1 v. Redding*, 557 U.S. at 370.

There is enormous confusion over the issue of how these rules apply to the police who are deployed on public school campuses. Under what circumstances do the seizures and searches conducted by police officers fall on the unconstitutional side of the line? The answer is tricky. Courts currently view school resource officers as "school officials" when acting in concert with educators to promote campus safety through some type of collaborative agreement. "[T]he weight of authority holds… that a search of a student on school grounds by a school resource officer at the request of school officials should be deemed a search by a school employee for Fourth Amendment purposes and thus is subject to the reasonableness standard, not the probable cause standard." *Wilson v. Cahokia Sch. Dist. # 187*, 470 F. Supp. 2d 897, 2007 U.S. Dist. LEXIS 3974 (S.D. Ill. 2007). See also, *D.L. v. State*, 877 N.E.2d 500 (2007*); In re William V.*, 111 Cal. App. 4th 1464, 4 Cal. Rptr. 3d 695, 699-700 (Cal. Ct. App. 2003); *Russell v. State*, 74 S.W.3d 887, 892-93 (Tex. App. 2002); *In the Matter of D.D.*, 554 S.E.2d 346 (2001); *New York v. Jameel Butler*,725 N.Y.S.2d 534 (2001); *Shade v. City of Farmington*, 309 F.3d 1054 (8th Cir. Minn. 2002); *People v. Dilworth*, 169 Ill. 2d 195, 661 N.E.2d 310, 317, 214 Ill. Dec. 456 (Ill. 1996); *In re Josue T.*, 1999 NMCA 115, 128 N.M. 56, 989 P.2d 431, 436-37 (N.M. Ct. App. 1999); *In re Angelia D.B.*, 211 Wis. 2d 140, 564 N.W.2d 682, 687 (Wis. 1997); *Cason v. Cook*, 810 F.2d 188, 191-92 (8th Cir. 1987).

As to seizures, the law is in a state of flux. Educators, by virtue of their *in loco parentis* authority have Eighth Amendment immunity in the use of physicality against students. And as summarized above, the case of *T.L.O.* controls student challenges to the use of force by traditional educators.

Even so, the rules are unsettled as to the use of force by school police. The Eighth Circuit in the case of *K.W.P. v. Kansas City Public Schools*, 931 F.3d 813, 822 (8th Cir. 2019) summarizes the debate among the courts wherein some judges hold that school police are not a "school official" for purposes of resolving an excessive-force claim under the Fourth Amendment.

> Our sister circuits are divided on whether to apply *T.L.O.*'s reasonableness standard or the objective reasonableness standard set forth in *Graham v. Connor*, 490 U.S. 386, 109 S.Ct. 1865, 104 L.Ed.2d 443 (1989), to law enforcement seizures of students. Compare Gray, 458 F.3d at 1304 ("apply[ing] the reasonableness standard articulated in ... T.L.O. ... to school seizures by law enforcement officers"), with E.W. by & through T.W. v. Dolgos, 884 F.3d 172, 179 (4th Cir. 2018) (applying Graham standard to school resource officer's seizure of student); Hawker v. Sandy City Corp., 591 F. App'x 669, 674 (10th Cir. 2014)

(applying Graham standard to school resource officer's seizure of student). Some courts have opted to apply both the Graham and T.L.O. standards in analyzing a claim of unreasonable seizure and excessive force. See, e.g., C.B. v. City of Sonora, 769 F.3d 1005, 1030 (9th Cir. 2014) (en banc); Hoskins v. Cumberland Cty. Bd. of Educ., No. 2:13-cv-15, 2014 WL 7238621, at *11 (M.D. Tenn. Dec. 17, 2014).

The cases below reflect a good faith attempt to resolve the dispute over the rules that apply to school police officers. The case of *Graham v. Connor*, 490 U.S. 386, 399 (1989), is recognizable to school police officers as the same law that applies off campus in non-school settings "when a law enforcement officer is accused of using excessive force in the course of an arrest, investigatory stop, or other "seizure" of a free citizen." *Graham v. Connor*, 490 U.S. 386, 399 (1989). The U.S. Supreme Court in *Graham* says that, "a law-enforcement officer's right to make an arrest necessarily carries with it the right to use some degree of physical coercion to effect it…[n]ot every push or shove, even if it may later seem unnecessary… violates the Fourth Amendment." *Graham v. Connor*, 490 U.S. at 396. After this, the focus of *Graham* combines the so-called "reasonable officer on the scene" test (determining if an officer's actions were objectively reasonable using the totality of the circumstances) with one or more of these three factors: (1) The severity of the crime; (2) Whether the person poses an immediate threat to the safety of the officers or others; (3) Whether the person is actively resisting arrest or attempting to evade arrest by flight. In the school environment, the courts add a fourth element: the age of the student.

Taken together, the *T.L.O.* and the *Graham* cases suggest the following rules for resolving disputes involving school-based police:

(1) As the age of the student decreases the amount of force used should be reduced accordingly;

(2) When the offense involves only a school code of conduct violation or a petty misdemeanor the amount of force should be reduced accordingly;

(3) Increased use of force is justified only when the conduct of the student escalates a tense situation. The physicality of school police is permitted to protect the safety of others as well as the safety of the official and to deescalate the situation.

E.W. v. Dolgos

884 F.3d 172 (4th Cir. 2018)

GREGORY, Chief Judge:

This matter involves a school resource officer's decision to handcuff a calm, compliant elementary school student for fighting with another student three days prior…[T]he district court concluded that the officer's conduct did not amount to a constitutional violation...For the reasons that follow, we affirm the district court's judgment.

I.

......

On Tuesday, January 6, 2015, ten-year-old E.W. rode a school bus to East Salisbury Elementary School in Salisbury, Maryland. E.W. sat in an aisle seat on one side of the bus while another student, A.W., sat diagonally across from her in an aisle seat one row behind E.W. on the opposite side of the bus. The two schoolgirls both had their feet in the aisle: E.W. was facing sideways with her feet in the aisle, and A.W. was facing forward with her left leg in the aisle, extended in the direction of E.W.

Video footage from the school bus's surveillance camera shows A.W. swaying her left knee from side to side in the aisle. Several seconds later A.W. raised her left leg in the air and made a sudden, stomping motion in the direction of E.W.'s leg. ...The two girls appear to trade kicks before E.W. put her leg down and A.W. slid lower into her seat...E.W. then stood over A.W. and began hitting her, swinging her arms downward because of their height difference. Although the seat in front of A.W. obscured the camera's view of the scuffle, the way A.W. was sitting suggests that E.W.'s swings likely landed on A.W.'s left arm, shoulder, and possibly her head. After four seconds, E.W. returned to her seat. Shortly thereafter, E.W. looked at A.W., stood up, and again moved in A.W.'s direction. A.W. raised her leg in the air, and E.W. kicked at A.W.'s shoe several times while A.W. kicked back. During the exchange of kicks, A.W. appeared to laugh and say something to E.W. This exchange drew the attention of the bus driver, who called both E.W. and A.W. to the front of the bus and eventually suspended both girls from the bus for three days.

On Friday, January 9, 2015, the school contacted Appellee Rosemary Dolgos, a deputy sheriff and school resource officer ("SRO") in Wicomico County, about the scuffle. When she arrived at the school, Dolgos watched the surveillance video described above. Dolgos spoke to A.W. first, asking her if she was injured. A.W. pulled up her left pant leg, and Dolgos observed "two small, bluish bruise[s]" above the left knee and one on the side of A.W.'s leg. Notably, no other injuries, including upper body injuries, were reported.

E.W. was then removed from class and placed in a closed office with Dolgos and two school administrators. Dolgos told E.W. that she was there to discuss what took place on the bus. But, in Dolgos's estimation, "E.W. [did not] seem to care." E.W. explained, "A.W. stepped on my shoe so I kicked her and started to hit her." Dolgos attempted to emphasize to E.W. the seriousness of the situation and the possible repercussions, telling her that adults could be jailed for such behavior. Still, in Dolgos's opinion, "E.W. continued to act as if the situation simply was not a 'big deal.' " Dolgos then decided to take E.W. into custody.

Dolgos placed E.W. in handcuffs from behind and reseated her. Dolgos inserted two fingers between the handcuffs and E.W.'s wrists to ensure that they were not too tight. In her affidavit, Dolgos stated that she was concerned about the physical safety of herself and the school administrators because of both the incident she observed in the surveillance video and E.W.'s apathy. Dolgos expressed concern in the affidavit that E.W. might act violently against her or someone else if she attempted to walk E.W. from the school to her patrol car. Dolgos also admitted, however, that she had no idea whether E.W. had "any past or current behavioral issues or past involvements with law enforcement." According to Dolgos, E.W. stood 4'4" and weighed about 95 pounds, while Dolgos stands 5'4" and weighs 155 pounds.

Immediately after being handcuffed, E.W. began to cry. She explained that she did not want to go to jail and that she would not hit A.W. again. Dolgos kept her handcuffed for about two minutes as she cried and apologized. Dolgos averred that E.W. never complained that the handcuffs were too tight or displayed bruises to her. Rather, "[i]n response" to E.W.'s show of remorse, Dolgos decided not to arrest E.W. and removed the handcuffs. J.A. 24–25. "Based on [E.W.'s] remorse," Dolgos further decided to release E.W. to her parents. The school contacted E.W.'s mother, T.W., and Dolgos informed T.W. that she would refer the matter to the Wicomico County Department of Juvenile Services. T.W. responded by asking, "[f]or a kid fight?" and "[s]o you're going to put my 10 year old daughter in the system when she's 10?" Frustrated and upset by the treatment of her daughter, T.W. retrieved E.W. from the school.

On December 29, 2015, E.W., by and through T.W., filed this suit against Dolgos,1 alleging (1) a violation of the Fourth Amendment under 42 U.S.C. § 1983 for unreasonable seizure and excessive force; (2) a violation of Article 26 of the Maryland Declaration of Rights; (3) battery; and (4) assault. Dolgos filed a motion to dismiss or, in the alternative, for summary judgment, which the district court construed as one for summary judgment and then granted. In a short paragraph, without citing any case law, the district court concluded that Dolgos's actions did not amount to excessive force because E.W. was handcuffed for only two minutes and then released to her mother. The court further concluded that Dolgos was "at least" entitled to qualified immunity as to the § 1983 claim. And as to the state law claims, the court found that E.W. failed to prove that Dolgos acted with malice or gross negligence. E.W. timely appealed.

II.

……

A.

We begin by considering whether Dolgos used excessive force in violation of the Fourth Amendment when she handcuffed E.W. "The Fourth Amendment prohibition on unreasonable seizures bars police officers from using excessive force to seize a free citizen." Jones v. Buchanan, 325 F.3d 520, 527 (4th Cir. 2003) (citing Graham v. Connor, 490 U.S. 386, 395, 109 S.Ct. 1865, 104 L.Ed.2d 443 (1989)). We analyze whether an officer has used excessive force under an objective reasonableness standard. Purnell, 652 F.3d at 531. Determining the reasonableness of an officer's actions "requires a careful balancing of the nature and quality of the intrusion on the individual's Fourth Amendment interests against the countervailing governmental interests at stake." Ray, 781 F.3d at 101 (quoting Graham, 490 U.S. at 396, 109 S.Ct. 1865). We examine the officer's actions "in light of the facts and circumstances confronting [her], without regard to [her] underlying intent or motivation." Graham, 490 U.S. at 397, 109 S.Ct. 1865; accord Pegg v.

Herrnberger, 845 F.3d 112, 120 (4th Cir. 2017) ("Subjective factors involving the officer's motives, intent, or propensities are not relevant." (quoting Rowland v. Perry, 41 F.3d 167, 173 (4th Cir. 1994))).

For this inquiry, Graham encourages us to evaluate three factors: "the severity of the crime at issue, whether the suspect poses an immediate threat to the safety of the officers or others, and whether he is actively resisting arrest or attempting to evade arrest by flight." 490 U.S. at 396, 109 S.Ct. 1865. But these factors are not "exclusive," and we may identify other "objective circumstances potentially relevant to a determination of excessive force." Kingsley v. Hendrickson, —— U.S. ——, 135 S.Ct. 2466, 2473, 192 L.Ed.2d 416 (2015). Here, we believe it prudent to consider also the suspect's age and the school context. The ultimate "question [is] whether the totality of the circumstances justified a particular sort of ... seizure." Jones, 325 F.3d at 527–28 (alternation in original) (quoting Tennessee v. Garner, 471 U.S. 1, 8–9, 105 S.Ct. 1694, 85 L.Ed.2d 1 (1985)); see Ray, 781 F.3d at 101 ("To properly consider the reasonableness of the force employed we must 'view it in full context, with an eye toward the proportionality of the force in light of all the circumstances.' " (quoting Waterman v. Batton, 393 F.3d 471, 481 (4th Cir. 2005))).

Here, the parties dispute whether handcuffing E.W. was justified under the circumstances. E.W. asserts that such physical restraint was unnecessary because Dolgos did not have a reasonable safety concern. Dolgos argues in response that because she had probable cause to arrest E.W. for assaulting A.W., as seen on video and as E.W. concedes, see Md. Code Ann, Crim. Law § 3–203(a) (West 2015) (defining second-degree assault), she was justified in using handcuffs to effectuate the arrest.

In Brown v. Gilmore, we stated that "a standard procedure such as handcuffing would rarely constitute excessive force where the officers were justified ... in effecting the underlying arrest." 278 F.3d 362, 369 (4th Cir. 2002). There, the plaintiff brought an excessive force claim based on allegations that a police officer had handcuffed her, causing her wrists to swell, dragged her to the police cruiser, and then pulled her into the vehicle. Id. at 365–66, 369. We found that the circumstances justified the "minimal level of force applied" because, as the officer approached a crowded scene on the street, he attempted to arrest the plaintiff for failure to follow another officer's orders to move her car. Id. at 369. We stated that it was not "unreasonable for the officers to believe that a suspect who had already disobeyed one direct order would balk at being arrested. Handcuffing [the plaintiff] and escorting her to a police vehicle was thus reasonable under the circumstances." Id.

But this Court has never held that using handcuffs is per se reasonable. Rather, the Fourth Amendment requires us to assess the reasonableness of using handcuffs based on the circumstances. See United States v. Drayton, 536 U.S. 194, 201, 122 S.Ct. 2105, 153 L.Ed.2d 242 (2002) ("[F]or the most part per se rules are inappropriate in the Fourth Amendment context."); Garner, 471 U.S. at 7–8, 105 S.Ct. 1694 (holding that probable cause to arrest does not automatically justify manner in which search or seizure is conducted). A lawful arrest does not categorically legitimize binding a person's wrists in chains. See Soares v. State of Conn., 8 F.3d 917, 921 (2d Cir. 1993) ("[W]e reject defendants' invitation to adopt a per se rule that the use of handcuffs in effecting an arrest is always reasonable."). And the troubling facts of the present case highlight why such a per se rule would be ill-advised.

The circumstances in this case are markedly different from those in Brown. We are not considering the typical arrest of an adult (or even a teenager) or the arrest of an uncooperative person engaged in or believed to be engaged in criminal activity. Rather, we have a calm, compliant ten-year-old being handcuffed on school grounds because she hit another student during a fight several days prior. These considerations, evaluated under the Graham framework, demonstrate that Dolgos's decision to handcuff E.W. was unreasonable.

The first factor considers the severity of the underlying offense. Graham, 490 U.S. at 396, 109 S.Ct. 1865. At the time Dolgos handcuffed E.W., Dolgos knew that E.W. had at most committed misdemeanor assault in the second degree by hitting another little girl for stepping on her foot. See Md. Code Ann. Crim. Law § 3–203(a). But because assault is an offense that can be considered violent if committed by any person, even a child, we find that this factor weighs against E.W. This finding is tempered, though, by the fact that the offense is a misdemeanor.

The second factor identified in Graham, whether the suspect poses an immediate threat to the safety of the officer or others, weighs strongly in E.W.'s favor. See 490 U.S. at 396, 109 S.Ct. 1865. In assessing the threat an individual poses, it is often useful to consider the suspect's conduct at the time of the arrest and "the size and stature of the parties involved." See Solomon v. Auburn Hills Police Dep't, 389 F.3d 167, 174 (6th Cir. 2004); see also C.B. v. City of Sonora, 769 F.3d 1005, 1030 (9th Cir. 2014) (en banc). In Solomon, the Sixth Circuit concluded that a suspect did not pose a safety threat because she had no weapons, she made no threats, and she was several inches shorter and weighed one hundred pounds less than the arresting officers. 389 F.3d at 174. Similarly, in Sonora, the Ninth Circuit held that "a calm, compliant, but nonresponsive 11-year-old child," who weighed about eighty pounds and stood around 4'8" tall, did not pose a safety threat, particularly given the child was "surrounded by four or five adults at all times." 769 F.3d at 1030.

Here, Dolgos could not have reasonably believed that E.W. presented any immediate risk of harm to anyone. Like the adult suspect in Solomon, E.W. had no weapons and made no threats, see 389 F.3d at 174, and like the eleven-year-old in Sonora, she was calm and compliant as Dolgos spoke to her, see 769 F.3d at 1030. In fact, Dolgos recognized that E.W. appeared calm. See J.A. 23–24. Also similar to the suspects in Solomon and Sonora, E.W., at 4'4" and ninety-five pounds, was quite small relative to Dolgos, the arresting officer, who was a foot taller and sixty pounds heavier. See Sonora, 769 F.3d at 1030; Solomon, 389 F.3d at 174. Not to mention, E.W. was in a closed office and surrounded by two school administrators and a deputy sheriff. Given these facts, E.W. posed little threat even if she were to become aggressive.

The significant time that had elapsed—without incident—since the fight on the bus further negates any notion that E.W. posed an immediate threat. While the scuffle took place on Tuesday, January 6, East Salisbury Elementary School waited three days to even contact Dolgos. In the interim, E.W. was allowed to and did in fact attend school without incident, indicating that she did not pose a risk to the children around her, much less to the adults. See Williams v. Nice, 58 F.Supp.3d 833, 838 (N.D. Ohio 2014) (finding reduced need to use force because student was no longer disruptive when officer arrived). When Dolgos interacted with E.W. on Friday, January 9, E.W. was not hostile or even disobedient. Rather, E.W. remained seated and submissive during the entire interview, even as Dolgos placed the handcuffs on her.

Moreover, Dolgos had no reason to think that the scuffle between E.W. and A.W. was anything but an isolated incident. E.W. had no prior behavioral issues or involvement with law enforcement, nor did Dolgos have any indication that she did. The use of force is an intrusion on Fourth Amendment rights, and an officer must have a reason for using or escalating force. See Graham, 490 U.S. at 396, 109 S.Ct. 1865 (intrusions on Fourth Amendment rights must be reasonably necessary given countervailing governmental interests). Even as to the altercation on the school bus, E.W., while unjustified in retaliating, did not become violent without physical provocation by A.W. Indeed, even a child with a history of attacking school officials should not be handcuffed if, at the time of handcuffing, she did not present a danger. See S.R. v. Kenton Cty. Sheriff's Office, No. 15-143, 2017 WL 4545231, at *5–6, *9 (E.D. Ky. Oct. 11, 2017) (hereinafter " Kenton II"). All of these circumstances, taken together, show that E.W. posed no immediate threat to the safety of the officer or others to justify the use of handcuffs.

The third factor discussed in Graham, whether the suspect is actively resisting arrest or attempting to evade arrest by flight, also strongly favors E.W. See 490 U.S. at 396, 109 S.Ct. 1865. Dolgos does not even suggest that E.W. attempted to resist or flee from the office at any point. See, e.g., Sonora, 769 F.3d at 1030 (handcuffing student was unreasonable in part because no evidence suggested that nonresponsive eleven-year-old was likely to run away); Solomon, 389 F.3d at 173–74 (unreasonable use of force in part because arrestee did not attempt to flee or otherwise resist arrest). Cf. Brown, 278 F.3d at 369–70 (finding that officer was justified in handcuffing plaintiff who was actively and violently resisting arrest).

The suspect's age again favors E.W. Circuit and district courts around the country have recognized that youth is an important consideration when deciding to use handcuffs during an arrest.[4] The Ninth Circuit, applying the Graham factors, held that officers who handcuffed an eleven-year-old child used excessive force. Tekle v. United States, 511 F.3d 839, 846 (9th Cir. 2007) ("He was cooperative and unarmed and, most importantly, he was eleven years old."); see also Ikerd v. Blair, 101 F.3d 430, 435 (5th Cir. 1996) (holding that officer used excessive force against ten-year-old girl under Graham analysis). In addition, the Eleventh Circuit has held that "handcuffing was excessively intrusive given [the arrestee's] young age." Gray ex rel. Alexander v. Bostic, 458 F.3d 1295, 1300–01, 1306 (11th Cir. 2006) (denying qualified immunity to SRO who handcuffed nine-year-old student for five minutes). Several district courts have similarly held that young age is a "uniquely" or "highly relevant" consideration under Graham. See Kenton II, 2017 WL 4545231, at *9 (holding that handcuffing eight-year-old child violated constitution); Hoskins v. Cumberland Cty. Bd. of Educ., No. 13-15, 2014 WL 7238621, at *7, 11 (M.D. Tenn. Dec. 17, 2014) (noting that eight-year-old student "was a startlingly young child to be handcuffed"); see also James v. Frederick Cty. Pub. Sch., 441 F.Supp.2d 755, 757, 759 (D. Md. 2006) (concluding that handcuffing eight-year-old child suggested excessive force). Here, E.W. was only ten years old at the time of the arrest. She therefore falls squarely within the tender age range for which the use of handcuffs is excessive absent exceptional circumstances.

[4] This consideration makes particular sense given the risk of lasting trauma among children exposed to the criminal justice system at young age. E.g., Sonora, 769 F.3d at 1012 ("Following [handcuffing]

incident, C.B. experienced a host of psychological and emotional problems, including difficulty sleeping, low self-esteem, anger, irritability, and depression.").

……

The location of the arrest also weighs in E.W.'s favor because all relevant activity took place in the school context. Courts have found that officers should exercise more restraint when dealing with student misbehavior in the school context. See Hoskins, 2014 WL 7238621, at *7 (holding that school setting, along with suspect's young age, is "uniquely relevant" consideration under Graham analysis); see, e.g., Sonora, 769 F.3d at 1030 (noting significance of school setting); Kenton I, at *4–5 (same). Society expects that children will make mistakes in school—and, yes, even occasionally fight. That teachers handle student misbehavior and unruliness "on a routine basis without the use of any force" suggests that force is generally unnecessary in the school context. See Nice, 58 F.Supp.3d at 838. Furthermore, as with age, the school context presents unique considerations not present when officers patrol the streets. The use of handcuffs, for instance, may undermine students' perception of the school and their willingness to attend, thereby disrupting their education far beyond the time they actually spend in handcuffs. And being handcuffed is often a source of stigma, which can lead to alienation and further disrupt long-term outcomes. In other words, the use of handcuffs and force is not reasonably expected in the school context because it is counterproductive to the mission of schools and school personnel. For these reasons, the school setting—especially an elementary school—weighs against the reasonableness of using handcuffs.

Viewing the facts in the light most favorable to E.W., the totality of the circumstances weighs against Dolgos and demonstrates that her actions were not " 'objectively reasonable' in light of the facts and circumstances confronting" her. Graham, 490 U.S. at 397, 109 S.Ct. 1865. Our reasonableness analysis incorporates "the fact that police officers are often forced to make split-second judgments—in circumstances that are tense, uncertain, and rapidly evolving—about the amount of force that is necessary in a particular situation." Id. But the circumstances here were by no means tense, uncertain, or rapidly evolving such that Dolgos was required to make any split-second decisions. Dolgos observed a ten-year-old girl sit calmly and compliantly in a closed office surrounded by three adults and answer questions about an incident with another little girl that had occurred several days prior. Although Dolgos stated she "believed there was a possibility that [E.W.] could physically act out against me or anyone else nearby as we left the school to go to my patrol car," J.A. 24, and although E.W. argues that Dolgos handcuffed her at the outset merely because E.W. "didn't seem to care" about the incident with A.W., J.A. 23, Dolgos's subjective motives are not relevant to our reasonableness inquiry. We consider neither whether Dolgos had a subjective safety concern nor whether she intended to teach E.W. to appreciate the consequences of her actions.[10] Rather, we consider whether a reasonable officer would have determined that E.W. should be handcuffed as a means of effectuating her arrest.

[10] Contrary to the concurrence's conclusion, we are not allowed to consider that Dolgos handcuffed E.W. for safety reasons related to the transport. Post at 190–91; see Pegg, 845 F.3d at 120 ("Subjective factors involving the officer's motives, intent, or propensities are not relevant.").

……

Dolgos took a situation where there was no need for any physical force and used unreasonable force disproportionate to the circumstances presented. We therefore find that Dolgos's actions amount to excessive force. As such, E.W. has demonstrated a violation of her constitutional rights under the Fourth Amendment.

B.

Because we conclude that Dolgos's conduct was unreasonable and violated E.W.'s Fourth Amendment rights, we must next examine whether Dolgos violated a clearly established right. A right is "clearly established" if "the contours of the right [are] sufficiently clear that a reasonable officer would understand that what he is doing violates that right." Hill v. Crum, 727 F.3d 312, 321 (4th Cir. 2013) (quoting Wilson v. Layne, 526 U.S. 603, 615, 119 S.Ct. 1692, 143 L.Ed.2d 818 (1999))...At the time Dolgos seized E.W., the law was clear that, as a general matter, an officer must carefully measure the force used to respond to the particulars of a case, including the wrongdoing at issue, the safety threat posed by the suspect, and any attempt to evade arrest or flee. Here, Dolgos handcuffed a calm, compliant ten-year-old who was surrounded by multiple adults in a closed room for hitting another child three days earlier. While E.W.'s right not to be unreasonably handcuffed is clearly implicated by "more general applications of the core constitutional principle invoked," Owens, 372 F.3d at 279 (quoting Amaechi v. West, 237 F.3d 356, 362–63 (4th Cir. 2001)), namely, the right to be free from the use of excessive and unreasonable police force, we cannot say that her seizure amounts to an "obvious case" such that Graham put Dolgos on sufficient notice that her conduct was unlawful.

......

Although precedent supports the conclusion that Dolgos acted unreasonably and violated E.W.'s Fourth Amendment rights, it did not put Dolgos on sufficient notice that her conduct was unlawful. Indeed, this Court previously stated that the use of handcuffs would "rarely" be considered excessive force when the officer has probable cause for the underlying arrest. See Brown, 278 F.3d at 369. And the parties do not point us to any controlling authority sufficiently similar to the situation Dolgos confronted. In fact, E.W. chiefly relies on Graham to define the clearly established law. Without more, we cannot conclude that it would have necessarily been clear to a reasonable officer that handcuffing E.W. would give rise to a Fourth Amendment violation. We emphasize, however, that our excessive force holding is clearly established for any future qualified immunity cases involving similar circumstances.

Accordingly, we conclude that E.W.'s right not to be handcuffed under the circumstances of this case was not clearly established at the time of her seizure. As such, Dolgos is entitled to qualified immunity, and we affirm the district court as to the § 1983 claim.

K.W.P. v. Kansas City Public Schools
931 F.3d 813 (8th Cir. 2019)

SMITH, Chief Judge.

K.W.P., an elementary student, sued Kansas City Public Schools (KCPS), Officer Brandon Craddock, and Principal Anne Wallace for violations of K.W.P.'s rights under the Fourth and Fourteenth Amendments pursuant to 42 U.S.C. § 1983. K.W.P. alleged that Officer Craddock unreasonably seized him and used excessive force by handcuffing him and failing to remove the handcuffs. He alleged that Principal Wallace approved Officer Craddock's seizure by failing to instruct Officer Craddock to remove the handcuffs despite K.W.P. posing no imminent threat to anyone and complying with instructions. K.W.P. sued KCPS for municipal liability and failure to train and supervise Officer Craddock on the use of handcuffs on elementary-age children. Officer Craddock and Principal Wallace moved for summary judgment based on qualified immunity on the claim of unreasonable seizure and excessive force, and KCPS moved for summary judgment on the municipal liability claim. The district court determined that disputed material facts precluded dismissal of K.W.P.'s claims against Officer Craddock and Principal Wallace. The court also denied summary judgment to KCPS. KCPS, Officer Craddock, and Principal Wallace appeal the denial of summary judgment.

Construing the facts in the light most favorable to K.W.P., we conclude that neither Officer Craddock nor Principal Wallace violated K.W.P.'s constitutional rights; thus, they are entitled to qualified immunity on K.W.P.'s claim of unreasonable seizure and excessive force. As a result, we necessarily hold that K.W.P.'s municipal liability claim also fails. Therefore, we reverse the district court's denial of summary judgment to Officer Craddock, Principal Wallace, and KCPS and remand for entry of summary judgment in their favor on K.W.P.'s claims.

I. Background

a. Underlying Facts

"We recite the facts in the light most favorable to [K.W.P.], as the nonmoving part[y]." O'Brien v. Dep't of Agric., 532 F.3d 805, 808 (8th Cir. 2008).

K.W.P., a seven-year-old boy in the second grade, attended George Melcher Elementary School within the KCPS system. On April 30, 2014, while in Ms. Beverly Cole's class, a classmate teased K.W.P. incessantly, distracting him from his school work. The classmate's actions antagonized him to the point of frustration. In response, K.W.P. yelled at the classmate and desired to physically confront him, stating that he "didn't get to push [the student], but [he] wanted to." As tensions escalated, a second adult school employee entered the classroom. According to K.W.P., she was "yelling" at him to "sit down" and telling him "you better sit down, you are about to get in trouble, the security guard [is] coming." According to K.W.P., that woman made him "even madder." K.W.P. did not pay any attention to what she was saying. K.W.P. admitted that he was "hollering" at the other student things such as "leave me alone, I'm not paying attention to you."

At this point, Officer Craddock, who was in the school at the time, was asked by a staff member to step inside Ms. Cole's classroom to assist with an "out of control" student. Officer Craddock is employed by KCPS as a patrol officer. Officer Craddock did not know K.W.P. or have any previous dealings with him. K.W.P. testified that by the time he noticed Officer Craddock, he was "sitting in [his] seat." K.W.P. believed he had "stopped" "hollering" when he noticed Officer Craddock. Id. K.W.P. clarified: I remember, [Officer Craddock]—like at first I was yelling, because I didn't know he was there, I said [omitted], I just heard somebody shout ... "if you don't get up in three seconds, I'm going to come and get you." And then—like it was a very deep voice. And then as soon as I heard that, like I just had turned around and then I looked back at [omitted] and then I just started to be still.

And then that's when he was counting down to three. And as soon as he said 1, I had pushed like, pushed out my chair like that and then got up and walked towards him.

Officer Craddock asked K.W.P. to accompany him into the hallway. After the second request, K.W.P. complied and went into the hallway. K.W.P. admitted that he did not want to go with Officer Craddock. K.W.P. testified that he responded to Officer Craddock's request to accompany him by "push[ing] [his] chair out in a negative way" because he was "angry," "emotional," and "didn't want to go with [Officer Craddock]."

Once in the hallway, Officer Craddock told K.W.P. that he was not in trouble. Officer Craddock wanted K.W.P. to follow him and would not allow K.W.P. back into the classroom. K.W.P. admitted that he "didn't want to go with the officer" and that he was "attempting to not go with the police officer." He also admitted he was "trying to get away" and "wanted to stand up for [himself]." Officer Craddock bent down to K.W.P.'s level and said, "Son, I need you to calm down." K.W.P. told Officer Craddock that he "didn't want to go with [him]." K.W.P. admitted that he was "resisting going with him" and "didn't want to cooperate with the officer." According to K.W.P. he "tried to calm down, ... but [he] couldn't."

K.W.P. recalled Officer Craddock telling him "several times to stop walking away." Officer Craddock put his hand on K.W.P.'s back to guide him in the direction that Officer Craddock was walking. Eventually, Officer Craddock "grabbed [K.W.P.'s] [left] wrist." During this time, K.W.P. admitted he was "crying real loud" and "screaming." K.W.P. recalled "jerking [his] body away" because he has "a problem with people just grabbing [his] wrists and like trying to make [him] go somewhere." K.W.P. admitted that during the encounter, Officer Craddock told him that he "wasn't in trouble." Yet, K.W.P. testified that when Officer Craddock tried to grab his left wrist, K.W.P. "tr[ied] even more to get away from him." K.W.P. agreed that he "could have got[ten] hurt" when he was "trying to go in the opposite direction and [Officer Craddock] [was] trying to pull [K.W.P.] towards the front office." K.W.P. admitted that he was "aggressively trying to pull away." When Officer Craddock reached out his arm to block K.W.P. from getting away, K.W.P. tried to push past him. K.W.P. continued to forcefully pull away from Officer Craddock's grasp. K.W.P. began crying. Officer Craddock told K.W.P., "Son, if you don't calm down, I'm going to have to put the cuffs on." K.W.P. saw a handrail on the side of the hallway and grabbed it.

Officer Craddock handcuffed K.W.P. with his hands behind him. K.W.P. admitted getting "more upset after [Officer Craddock] put the handcuffs on" him and that he was "still trying to get away."

Officer Craddock double-locked the handcuffs so they would not tighten on K.W.P.'s wrists. K.W.P. finally "got tired and stopped trying to resist what was happening to him." According to K.W.P., once in the front office, he obeyed Officer Craddock's directions, sat in a chair, and did not attempt to leave.

Principal Wallace first saw K.W.P. while he was seated in the front office and in handcuffs. Principal Wallace did not advise Officer Craddock to remove the handcuffs. Principal Wallace had a prior history with K.W.P., having restrained him a couple of months prior.[3] Principal Wallace left to go to an adjoining office to complete unrelated paperwork. Officer Craddock also left the front office. When K.W.P.'s father arrived, only the secretary was present in the front office. K.W.P.'s father then left the office to retrieve Officer Craddock. K.W.P.'s father asked Officer Craddock why he had handcuffed K.W.P. Officer Craddock responded that he did it for "safety." Defs.' Suggestions in Supp. of Mot. for Summ. J., Ex. 8, Wiley Dep., at 3, K.W.P. v. Kan. City Pub. Schs. (W.D. Mo. Aug. 30, 2017), ECF No. Doc. 70-8. According to K.W.P.'s father, Officer Craddock told him that "he made a split decision of what he thought was right and [took K.W.P.] ... out of the classroom ... and [took] him out into the hallway and tr[ied] to calm him down or resolve ... what he thought was the problem in the situation." Id. When Officer Craddock and K.W.P.'s father returned to the front office, Officer Craddock removed the handcuffs from K.W.P.

> [3] In February 2014, Principal Wallace witnessed K.W.P. punch a student while in line after a fire drill. Principal Wallace advised K.W.P. to keep his hands to himself; in response, K.W.P. responded, "Quit talking to me." Principal Wallace advised K.W.P. that his response was unacceptable and that she was going to call his mother. K.W.P. "got mad, and he tried to leave the school playground, which [Principal Wallace] would not allow him to do." Principal Wallace grabbed K.W.P. by the wrist "to guide him into the office so that [she] could call [his] [m]om." K.W.P. was "screaming the whole way and pulling and resisting, trying to pull away from [Principal Wallace]." K.W.P. confirmed that he was, in fact, "trying to get away from [Principal Wallace]." Once in the office, Principal Wallace called K.W.P.'s mother and told her that K.W.P. "was trying to leave out of her office." Principal Wallace also advised K.W.P.'s mother that she "restrained [K.W.P.] because she didn't want him to run out into the street."

K.W.P. was handcuffed for a total of 20 minutes. For 15 of those 20 minutes, K.W.P. was seated in the front office. The handcuffs made K.W.P.'s wrists tender and red. He also alleged that he suffered mental and emotional distress.

......

II. Discussion

On appeal, the defendants argue that, construing the facts in the light most favorable to K.W.P., (1) Officer Craddock did not violate K.W.P.'s constitutional rights in handcuffing K.W.P., and (2) Officer Craddock and Principal Wallace did not violate his rights by keeping him in handcuffs once seated in the front office. They assert that Officer Craddock's and Principal Wallace's actions were reasonable based on "(1) the severity of K.W.P.'s conduct, (2) the fact that he was a safety threat, (3) he was aggressively resisting, and (4) he had a history of being a flight risk and engaging in unsafe behavior." They also argue that neither Officer Craddock nor Principal Wallace violated a clearly established constitutional right. Thus, they assert, Officer Craddock and Principal Wallace are entitled to qualified immunity on K.W.P.'s claim of unreasonable seizure and excessive force. Finally, they argue that KCPS was entitled to summary judgment on K.W.P.'s municipal liability claim because (1) "no employee of KCPS violated K.W.P.'s constitutional rights," and (2) "no evidence [exists] that ... KCPS's training practices were inadequate, ... that it was deliberately indifferent to the rights of others such that its failure to train reflects a deliberate or conscious choice by KCPS, or ... [that] KCPS's alleged deficiency 'actually caused' K.W.P.'s injury." Id. at 21–22 (quoting City of Canton v. Harris, 489 U.S. 378, 391, 109 S.Ct. 1197, 103 L.Ed.2d 412 (1989)).

A. Qualified Immunity

We will first address Officer Craddock's and Principal Wallace's arguments that they are entitled to qualified immunity on K.W.P.'s claim of unreasonable seizure and excessive force.

Courts apply a two-part test in determining whether a government official is entitled to qualified immunity:

First, "whether the facts alleged, construed in the light most favorable to [the plaintiff], establish a violation of a constitutional or statutory right," and second, "whether that right was clearly established at the time of the alleged violation, such that a reasonable official would have known that her actions were unlawful."

……

1. Constitutional Violation

K.W.P. has brought a claim of unreasonable seizure and excessive force against Officer Craddock and Principal Wallace. K.W.P.'s allegations that Officer Craddock unreasonably seized him and used excessive force in handcuffing him with Principal Wallace's approval are intertwined. See Gray ex rel. Alexander v. Bostic, 458 F.3d 1295, 1304 (11th Cir. 2006) (stating that the "excessive force claim is not an independent claim, but rather is subsumed in [the] illegal seizure claim").

The Supreme Court has previously held that "the legality of a search of a student ... depend[s] simply on the reasonableness, under all the circumstances, of the search." New Jersey v. T.L.O., 469 U.S. 325, 341, 105 S.Ct. 733, 83 L.Ed.2d 720 (1985) (involving school official's search of a student). A two-fold inquiry applies in determining whether such search is reasonable: "first, one must consider 'whether the ... action was justified at its inception'; second, one must determine whether the search as actually conducted 'was reasonably related in scope to the circumstances which justified the interference in the first place.' " Id. (ellipsis in original) (quoting Terry v. Ohio, 392 U.S. 1, 20, 88 S.Ct. 1868, 20 L.Ed.2d 889 (1968)). This standard balances "the privacy interests of schoolchildren with the substantial need of teachers and administrators for freedom to maintain order in the schools." Id. It "neither unduly burden[s] the efforts of school authorities to maintain order in their schools nor authorize[s] unrestrained intrusions upon the privacy of schoolchildren." Id. at 342–43, 105 S.Ct. 733. Instead, "[b]y focusing attention on the question of reasonableness, the standard ... spare[s] teachers and school administrators the necessity of schooling themselves in the niceties of probable cause and permit[s] them to regulate their conduct according to the dictates of reason and common sense." Id. at 343, 105 S.Ct. 733. But it also "ensure[s] that the interests of students will be invaded no more than is necessary to achieve the legitimate end of preserving order in the schools."

We have held that T.L.O.'s reasonableness standard governs law enforcement searches that school officials initiate. Shade v. City of Farmington, 309 F.3d 1054, 1061 (8th Cir. 2002) ("Because school officials initiated the investigation and search of Shade in furtherance of the school's interest in maintaining a safe learning environment, and because they asked officers to assist them in furtherance of that interest, we hold that T.L.O.'s two-part inquiry governs the lawfulness of the search conducted by Officer Dau."). We have not previously determined whether T.L.O.'s reasonableness standard governs law enforcement seizures of students. Cf. Burlison v. Springfield Pub. Sch., 708 F.3d 1034, 1039–40 (8th Cir. 2013) (applying T.L.O. to the search and seizure of a student's backpack).

Our sister circuits are divided on whether to apply T.L.O.'s reasonableness standard or the objective reasonableness standard set forth in Graham v. Connor, 490 U.S. 386, 109 S.Ct. 1865, 104 L.Ed.2d 443 (1989), to law enforcement seizures of students.[4] Compare Gray, 458 F.3d at 1304 ("apply[ing] the reasonableness standard articulated in ... T.L.O. ... to school seizures by law enforcement officers"), with E.W. by & through T.W. v. Dolgos, 884 F.3d 172, 179 (4th Cir. 2018) (applying Graham standard to school resource officer's seizure of student); Hawker v. Sandy City Corp., 591 F. App'x 669, 674 (10th Cir. 2014) (applying Graham standard to school resource officer's seizure of student). Some courts have opted to apply both the Graham and T.L.O. standards in analyzing a claim of unreasonable seizure and excessive force. See, e.g., C.B. v. City of Sonora, 769 F.3d 1005, 1030 (9th Cir. 2014) (en banc); Hoskins v. Cumberland Cty. Bd. of Educ., No. 2:13-cv-15, 2014 WL 7238621, at *11 (M.D. Tenn. Dec. 17, 2014).

[4] In Graham, the Supreme Court determined that "[t]he Fourth Amendment's objective reasonableness standard governs a claim that an officer used excessive force 'in the course of making an arrest, investigatory stop, or other 'seizure.' " Brossart v. Janke, 859 F.3d 616, 624 (8th Cir. 2017) (quoting Graham, 490 U.S. at 388, 109 S.Ct. 1865). "[T]he question is whether the officers' actions are 'objectively reasonable' in light of the facts and circumstances confronting them, without regard to their underlying intent or motivation." Graham, 490 U.S. at 397, 109 S.Ct. 1865. When applying the objective reasonableness standard, we must pay "careful attention to the facts and circumstances of each particular case, including the severity of the crime at issue, whether the suspect poses an immediate threat to the safety of the officers or others, and whether he is actively resisting arrest or attempting to evade arrest by flight." Id. at 396, 109 S.Ct. 1865. We judge "[t]he 'reasonableness' of a particular use of force ... from the perspective of a reasonable officer on the scene, rather than with the 20/20 vision of hindsight." Id. The objective reasonableness standard "embod[ies] allowance for the fact that police officers are often forced to make split-second judgments—in circumstances that are tense, uncertain, and rapidly evolving—about the amount of force that is necessary in a particular situation." Id. at 396–97, 109 S.Ct. 1865.

Applying the T.L.O. standard, the Eleventh Circuit has held "that a law enforcement officer, acting as a school resource officer, who handcuffs a compliant nine-year-old child for purely punitive purposes has unreasonably seized the child in violation of the Fourth Amendment." Gray ex rel. Alexander v. Bostic, 720 F.3d 887, 892 (11th Cir. 2013) (emphases added). In that case, a nine-year-old child threatened to "do something" physically to her physical education coach after the coach told her to "[c]ome to the wall" in gym class for not complying with his instructions. Gray,

458 F.3d at 1300 (alteration in original). A school resource officer witnessed the exchange and intervened. Id. at 1301. He escorted the child out of the gym and into a lobby area. Id. The officer then handcuffed the child, stating, " '[T]his is how it feels when you break the law,' and '[T]his is how it feels to be in jail.' " Id. (alterations in original). The child began crying. Id. The handcuffs remained on the child for five minutes. Id. The reason the officer detained and handcuffed the student was " 'to impress upon her the serious nature of committing crimes that can lead to arrest, detention or incarceration' and 'to help persuade her to rid herself of her disrespectful attitude.' " Id. The child brought claims against the officer for excessive force and unreasonable seizure. Id. at 1302. The district court denied the officer's motion for qualified immunity, and the officer appealed. Id. at 1303.

The court, applying T.L.O.'s first prong, concluded that the officer "stopping [the child] to question her about her conduct was reasonable" because he had "witnessed [the child] threaten to do something physically to her teacher." Id. at 1305. But, under T.L.O.'s second prong, the court determined that "the handcuffing was excessively intrusive given [the child's] young age and the fact that it was not done to protect anyone's safety." Id. at 1306 (emphasis added). The facts taken in the light most favorable to the student showed that when the officer handcuffed the child, "there was no indication of a potential threat to anyone's safety. The incident was over, and [the child], after making the comment, had promptly complied with her teachers' instructions." Id. (emphasis added). The court found "no evidence that [the child] was gesturing or engaging in any further disruptive behavior." Id. (emphasis added). Instead, the child "had cooperated with her teachers and did not pose a threat to anyone's safety." Id. (emphasis added). In emphasizing that the child posed no safety threat, the court cited the officer's admission "that he handcuffed [the child] to persuade her to get rid of her disrespectful attitude and to impress upon her the serious nature of committing crimes. In effect, [the officer's] handcuffing of [the child] was his attempt to punish [her] in order to change her behavior in the future." Id. As a result, the court held that the officer's handcuffing of the child constituted a violation of her Fourth Amendment rights. Id.

The Fourth Circuit reached a similar conclusion in E.W. by applying the Graham standard.

……

The Ninth Circuit likewise determined—utilizing both the T.L.O. and Graham standards—that officers' "use of handcuffs on a calm, compliant, but nonresponsive 11-year-old child was unreasonable." C.B., 769 F.3d at 1030. There, a sixth-grade student with ADHD experienced a period of unresponsiveness and refused to leave the playground. Id. at 1010. A coach called the police out of concern for the student's safety. Id. at 1011. A police chief arrived, and the coach whispered to him that the student was a "runner" not on his medicine, despite the fact the student had never previously attempted to run from her. Id. The coach advised the police chief she no longer wanted the student on school grounds. Id. The student "remained completely quiet and unresponsive throughout the time [the police chief] was with him." Id. Another officer arrived, learned that the student was a "runner," and tried to engage in conversation with the student. Id. The student "remained unresponsive." Id. The police chief instructed the officer to handcuff the student. Id. The student immediately complied with the officer's directive to put his hands behind his back, and the officer handcuffed the student. Id. The student began to cry upon being handcuffed. Id. The officers and coach then escorted the student from the playground and "directed [the student]—still in handcuffs—into the back seat" of the police car. Id. at 1012. "During this entire time, no one spoke to [the student] or explained to him why he had been handcuffed, that he was not under arrest, or where the police were taking him." Id. The student "remained handcuffed during the approximately thirty-minute ride to his uncle's place of business." Id. The student filed suit for, among other things, unlawful seizure and excessive force. Id. The case proceeded to trial, and the jury returned a verdict in favor of the student. Id. at 1015.

On appeal, the officers argued that the district court had erred in denying them judgment as a matter of law based on qualified immunity. Id. at 1022. The court first determined that "applying T.L.O.'s reasonableness standard d[id] not aid [the officers]" in defeating the student's unlawful seizure claim. Id. at 1024. While the officers were called to investigate a report of an "out of control" student, upon their arrival to the school, the officers "found ... a quiet but nonresponsive child." Id. The officers never "consider[ed] any less intrusive solutions, such as ordering [the student] to return inside the school building, or asking a guardian to pick up the child." Id. The court concluded that the circumstances demonstrated that "the officers' decision to seize [the student] and remove him from school grounds was not reasonable." Id. As a result, it held that "taking the evidence in the light most favorable to [the student], a reasonable jury could conclude that [the officers] violated [his] Fourth Amendment rights when they seized him and took him into custody." Id. at 1026.

The Ninth Circuit then separately analyzed the student's excessive force claim that the officers violated his Fourth Amendment rights by removing him from school and handcuffing him for 25 to 30 minutes. Id. at 1029. The court observed that "whether T.L.O. or Graham governed [the officers'] actions at any given moment [was] of little consequence" because the officers' "use of handcuffs on a calm, compliant, but nonresponsive 11-year-old child was unreasonable under either standard." Id. at 1030. While the officers were told the student might be a "runner," the student "never did anything that suggested he might run away or that he otherwise posed a safety threat." Id. As a result, the court held "that the decision to use handcuffs on [the student] was unreasonable, notwithstanding [the coach's] unexplained statement that [the student] was a 'runner,' " and that the "decision to leave [the student] in handcuffs for the duration of the half-hour commute to his uncle's business—a commute that took place in a vehicle equipped with safety locks that made escape impossible—was clearly unreasonable." Id.; see also Hoskins, 2014 WL 7238621, at *6 (analyzing unreasonable seizure claim under T.L.O. and Graham standards and holding that an officer's handcuffing of an eight-year-old second grader with special needs, who had threatened and swung his fist at his teacher, constituted an unlawful seizure).

In contrast to Gray, E.W., and C.B., where the courts found violations of the students' constitutional rights, the Tenth Circuit applied Graham in holding that a school resource officer's use of force was reasonable against a nine-year-old boy when the officer arrested and performed a twist-lock on the student, who was suspected of stealing an iPad at school. Hawker, 591 F. App'x at 671. In that case, upon the officer's arrival to the school, she saw the student "sitting on the floor in the hallway against a wall." Id. The principal informed the officer that she wanted to file theft charges against the student. Id. The officer then advised the student, "We can do this the easy way by you talking to me, or we can do this the difficult way or hard way by you not talking to me." Id. (citation omitted). The student looked at the officer, but he said nothing. Id. The officer then " 'grabbed' his arm and 'yanked' him up off the floor." Id. (citation omitted). The student responded by grabbing the officer's arm. Id. In response, the officer "put [the student] in a twist-lock, pushed him against the wall, and handcuffed him. [The student] kicked at [the officer] and cried 'You're hurting me.' " Id. (citation omitted). The officer then took the student to the principal's office and issued him a theft citation. Id. Subsequently, the student's parents brought suit against the officer for excessive force. Id. The sole issue on appeal was "whether [the officer's] use of a twist-lock to effectuate the arrest constitute[d] excessive force." Id. at 672.

Applying Graham, the Tenth Circuit determined that the use of the twist-lock was objectively reasonable based on the facts. The court concluded that the first Graham factor—the severity of the crime—weighed in favor of the student because the crime was misdemeanor theft offense and "relatively minor." Id. at 674. But it found that the second and third factors—immediate threat to safety and resisting arrest—weighed against the student because the officer "could objectively and reasonably view [the student's] grabbing her arm as resisting arrest and escalating a tense situation. For safety, it was objectively reasonable for [the officer] to deescalate the situation and command [the student's] compliance by using a twist-lock." Id. at 675. The court acknowledged the student's age (nine years old) and weight (67 pounds) as "factors in the totality-of-the circumstances reasonableness calculation," but it concluded that such "factors alone do not render force used against him unreasonable per se." Id. According to the court, "An arrestee's age and small demeanor do not necessarily undermine an officer's concern for safety and need to control the situation." Id. The key, according to the court, is if force was used "on an individual posing no immediate threat." Id. The court determined that a reasonable officer could have viewed the student's grabbing of the officer's arm "an act of violent resistance" and that officer's "actions in this case simply d[id] not rise to the level of a constitutional violation." Id. Therefore, the court held that the officer was entitled to qualified immunity. Id.

In the present case, K.W.P. avers that we need not resolve whether the Graham or T.L.O. standard applies because "the result in this case would be the same under either standard." We agree but reach a different conclusion as to the result. We hold that, applying either the Graham or T.L.O. standard, and construing the facts in the light most favorable to K.W.P., neither Officer Craddock nor Principal Wallace violated K.W.P.'s right to be free from unreasonable seizure and excessive force.

First, as to the initial handcuffing, unlike the calm, compliant children in Gray, E.W., and C.B. who did not engage in further disruptive behavior and posed no risks to anyone's safety, K.W.P.'s own admissions indicate that he attempted to flee from Officer Craddock upon his removal from the classroom and that his escape efforts posed a safety risk to himself. K.W.P. does not challenge as unlawful Officer Craddock's initial removal of him from the classroom for being disruptive. Once removed from the classroom, K.W.P. resisted Officer Craddock's directive for K.W.P. to accompany Officer Craddock to the office. K.W.P. admitted, among other things, that he "didn't want to go with the officer," was "attempting to not go with the police officer," was "trying to get away," "wanted to stand up for [himself], told Officer Craddock that he "didn't want to go with [him]," was "resisting going with [Officer Craddock]," "didn't want to cooperate with the officer," "tried to calm down ... but [he] couldn't," was "crying real loud" and "screaming" when Officer Craddock grabbed his left wrist, was "jerking [his] body away," "tr[ied] even more to get away from" Officer Craddock when he grabbed K.W.P.'s wrist, tried to push past Officer Craddock, continued to aggressively pull away from Officer Craddock's grasp, and grabbed a handrail. K.W.P. further admitted that his actions could have resulted in him getting hurt. In applying the objective reasonableness standard to the undisputed facts, a reasonable officer could have concluded that K.W.P.'s admitted conduct constituted "an act of violent resistance." Hawker, 591 F. App'x at 675.

Second, K.W.P. challenges as unlawful the 15 minutes that he was seated in the front office and handcuffed. Once again, applying either the Graham or T.L.O. standard, neither Officer Craddock nor Principal Wallace violated K.W.P.'s right to be free from unreasonable seizure and excessive force in the extended handcuffing. Construing the facts in the light most favorable to K.W.P., K.W.P. had stopped resisting by the time that he reached the front office, sat in a chair pursuant to Officer Craddock's commands, and did not attempt to leave. Nevertheless, the case remains distinguishable from other cases in which courts have found extended handcuffing violative of the Fourth Amendment. Here, K.W.P. remained handcuffed in the front office for only 15 minutes; by comparison, the student in C.B. remained handcuffed for 25 to 30 minutes, 769 F.3d at 1029, and the student in Hoskins remained handcuffed for 45 minutes. Our conclusion that no constitutional violation occurred also rests on K.W.P.'s behavior justifying the initial handcuffing. Unlike the students in Gray, E.W., and C.B. who were complaint with the school resource officer from the outset of their encounter, K.W.P. had actively resisted Officer Craddock just prior to arriving to the front office. A reasonable officer could conclude that, based on K.W.P.'s recent resistance, keeping him in handcuffs for 15 minutes until a parent arrived was a reasonable course of action and was necessary to prevent K.W.P. from trying to leave and posing harm to himself. Cf. Hoskins, 2014 WL 7238621, at *11 ("[T]he scope of the seizure—that is, the handcuffing of the child for forty-five minutes, even after his parents arrived at the school and were present in the room with him—was unreasonable." (emphasis added)).

Furthermore, Principal Wallace's failure to intervene and have Officer Craddock remove the handcuffs was reasonable in light of her previous experience with K.W.P. The undisputed facts show that just two months prior to the incident at issue, K.W.P. tried to leave the playground after getting mad at Principal Wallace for instructing him not to hit others. When Principal Wallace grabbed K.W.P.'s wrist to take him to the office to call his mother, K.W.P. actively resisted by trying to pull away from Principal Wallace.

Accordingly, we hold that, applying either the Graham or T.L.O. standard and viewing the facts in the light most favorable to K.W.P., neither Officer Craddock nor Principal Wallace violated K.W.P.'s right to be free from unreasonable seizure and excessive force and are therefore entitled to qualified immunity on this claim.

……

III. Conclusion

Accordingly, we reverse the district court's denial of summary judgment to Officer Craddock, Principal Wallace, and KCPS and remand for entry of summary judgment in their favor on K.W.P.'s claims.

Carter v. Pointe Coupee Parish School Board
268 So. 3d 1064 (La. App. 2018)

CHUTZ, J.

Defendants-appellants, Stephen Lewis and the City of New Roads (the City), appeal the trial court's judgment, awarding damages to twenty-two minor plaintiffs-appellees for the injuries sustained at Rosenwald Elementary School in Point Coupee Parish. Finding the claims of seven of the minor plaintiffs prescribed before they were filed, we reverse in part. Additionally, we amend the judgment to award to the minors' representatives the damages sustained by nine minors and, as amended, affirm the trial court's judgment against Lewis and the City.

FACTUAL AND PROCEDURAL BACKGROUND

Lewis was a police officer employed by the City and used by the Point Coupee Parish School Board (PCPSB) at Rosenwald Elementary School as a resource officer on March 6, 2012, pursuant to a contract between PCPSB and the City. According to the testimony adduced at trial and the defendants' stipulation, an incident occurred on campus on March 6, 2012, where at least twenty-two elementary school children were identified as bullies by Lewis, the teacher in the classroom, and/or fellow classmates. Lewis removed the identified children into the hallway and directed them to wait in a line until all the children were gathered. He then ordered them outside and directed the children identified as bullies to kneel in gravel for between ten and forty minutes, with the majority of the students recalling they knelt for between ten and twenty minutes. Some children stated that Lewis yelled at them; others said that when they refused to kneel or squirmed due to the pain, he threatened to keep them kneeling for a longer period of time. All of the children involved in the incident who testified recalled that Lewis was dressed as a police officer and most recalled that he had his gun and handcuffs. Several of those who had been minors involved in the incident stated that during the incident, Lewis made physical contact with them, indicating that as he or she attempted to rise from the kneeling position, Lewis pushed him/her back to the ground, touching his or her shoulders in the process. Some of the children stated that Lewis ordered them to put mud on their faces or to go into a muddy ditch, but ultimately stated he did not follow through on the threats. Eventually, Lewis allowed the children to stand up, and they left as a group.

On March 6, 2013, the mothers of fifteen of the children instituted this lawsuit, naming PCPSB, its insurer, and Lewis as defendants. By amended petition, filed on August 14, 2013, the City was added as a named defendant. The City and Lewis answered the petition and the amending petition. The matter proceeded to a trial on the merits commencing on January 16, 2018. On March 5, 2018, the trial court signed a judgment, awarding $5,000 for the damages sustained on March 6, 2012 by each of those who had been identified as a bully and subjected to Lewis's actions. The City and Lewis appeal.

DAMAGES

On appeal, without challenging the quantum of each award, the City and Lewis assert that because the record is devoid of any medical evidence supporting physical, emotional, and psychological injuries, the trial court erred in awarding any damages to the minors. Thus, they ask that this court reverse the awards of $5,000 as damages sustained by each minor.

……

The testimonial evidence admitted at trial established that Lewis's conduct was clearly directed at the children who were singled out of their classrooms for special treatment as a result of having been identified either by Lewis, a teacher, or other students as a bully. Lewis not only threatened them, he also used his supervisory power to order the children to kneel in gravel. Several minors (and those who had been minors on March 6, 2012) as well as their parents testified that the child experienced fear for his or her personal well-being or felt "bad" or otherwise burdened for having been singled out as a bully. Indeed, many of those who testified indicated that they were afraid Lewis would hurt them with his gun or cause them some other type of physical harm. The testimony established that most of the children developed distrust in law enforcement after the incident. A reasonable factual basis exists to support the trial court's implicit finding that Lewis's actions were an affront to the personal integrity and privacy, as well as mental tranquility, of each child and sufficiently caused their damages. Therefore, the trial court's awards are not manifestly erroneous.

THE CITY'S LIABILITY FOR LEWIS'S ACTIONS

The City and Lewis contend that the trial court erred in finding the City liable to the minors for Lewis's conduct. They urge that under the facts of this case, PCPSB was solely responsible for Lewis's actions on March 6, 2012, and as such, the City owed no duty to the children. As such, the City suggests that it cannot be liable to plaintiffs. We disagree.

……

The evidence in this case established that on March 6, 2012, the City had a contractual relationship with PCPSB whereby the City sent police officers over to PCPSB schools to function as resource officers. And in its answer to the lawsuit, the City admitted that Lewis did not "maintain an employment relationship with [PCPSB]" at the time of the incident. Thus, as the Rosenwald Elementary School Resource Officer, Lewis was PCPSB's "borrowed employee" from the City, the City was Lewis's "general employer," and PCPSB was Lewis's "special employer." Both the general employer and the special employer may be solidarily liable for the torts of the borrowed employee.

The general employer has a heavy burden of overcoming the presumption that it retained control (and thus remained liable for his employee's tort) and of proving that "the relationship of master and servant which previously existed between the general employer and employee has been suspended, that a new such relationship has been created between the borrowing employer and that employee, and that such new relationship was in existence at the time the accident occurred." LeJeune, 365 So.2d at 480 (quoting Vincent v. Ryder Enterprises, Inc., 352 So.2d 1061, 1067 (1977)). That an employee may have been a borrowed employee of the special employer for some purposes, such as working under the direction of the special employer at the time of the incident, does not relieve the general employer of its liability for its employee's negligent acts done in the pursuance of duties designated for the employee by his general employer, with whom the employee continued in a paying working relationship and who had the sole right to discharge him. This is especially so where the employee was loaned out to another in a continuing arrangement between the employers for their mutual benefit. See LeJeune, 365 So.2d at 481.

In the imposition of vicarious liability for the general employer whose employee was working under the direction of the special employer at the time of the incident, specific conduct may be considered within the scope of employment even though it is done in part to serve the purposes of the special employer. The fact that the predominant motive of the employee is to benefit the special employer does not prevent the act from being within the scope of employment. See Ermert, 559 So.2d at 476-77. If the purpose of serving the general employer's business actuates the employee to any appreciable extent, the general employer is subject to liability if the act is otherwise within the service. Id., 559 So.2d at 477.

The two-master rule is the more sensible rule in cases where the general employer is at least sometimes engaged in the business of lending out people and equipment. In such situations, the general employer's business is being furthered even if it does not control the details of the actual work. Moreover, the special employer benefits: it is its work that is being done as well. In such situations, the relevant enterprise benefitted by the work consists of the combination of the general and special employers. The two-master rule represents a triumph of function over (legal) fiction. See Thomas C. Galligan, Jr., A Primer on the Patterns of Louisiana Workplace Torts, 55 Louisiana Law Review 91 (1994). See also Morgan v. ABC Mfr., 97-0956 (La. 5/1/98), 710 So.2d 1077, 1083 (holding that where a general employer is in the business of hiring its employees out under the supervision of others, the general employer remains liable for the "borrowed" employees' torts under La. C.C. art. 2320).

……

With these precepts in mind, we find no manifest error in the trial court's conclusion that Lewis was in the course and scope of his employment at the time of the March 6, 2012 incident. Thus, the trial court correctly concluded that the City was vicariously liable under Article 2320 to the plaintiffs for Lewis's actions on March 6, 2012. See Ermert, 559 So.2d at 476-77. The evidence established that while acting in his capacity as a resource officer and, more particularly on March 6, 2012, when he removed the minor children from their classrooms and forced them to kneel on gravel in an effort to punish those identified as bullies in the elementary school, Lewis was dressed as police officer of the City. He carried a gun and handcuffs, and a police vehicle, identified as a marked unit of the City, was parked in front of the school while he was on duty as a resource officer.

Although the City of New Roads Mayor Anthony R. Daisy testified that while he was administering his duties as a resource officer, Lewis was under the supervision and direction of the Rosenwald Elementary School principal and assistant principal and that the PCPSB paid his salary during those times, the mayor admitted that when police officers are off duty, they are not permitted to either wear a City police uniform or carry their guns or handcuffs. Mayor Daisy also conceded that the City hired Lewis, trained him, and retained the right to fire the police officer. We find the trial court could reasonably infer from the testimonial evidence that the resource officer was at the elementary school at the request of the PCPSB to maintain safety and order on campus, functions that are regular duties of police departments. Accordingly, there is no error in the trial court's conclusion that the City was liable to the plaintiffs for the damages caused by Lewis on March 6, 2012.

Notes and Comments

1. Excessive Force IQ Test
In which scenario below should liability be found?

- A case involving a school police officer's conduct of placing a student in a choke hold and carrying her to the administrative office while the student was "squirming, wiggling, twisting, and turning to get away." The student had punched another student in the face and was combative toward the officer who was trying to break up the fight and deescalate the situation. *Hines v. Jefferson*, 338 F. Supp. 3d 1288 (N.D. Ga. 2018), aff'd, 795 F. App'x 707 (11th Cir. 2019).

- A case involving a school police officer handcuffed who a special needs student who refused to do his classwork, took off his shoes and threw them at a staff members and administrators, ran and hid in the school, ate food off the cafeteria floor, and locked himself in a bathroom. The student's conduct was outside the scope of his Behavioral Improvement Program. *J.V. & M.Q. v. Winston Brooks*, 2020 WL 2126792 (N.M. Ct. App. 2020))

- A case involving a school police officer who decided to arrest a 16 year-old special needs student for disrupting the classroom with persistent and loud speech, by grabbing the student and the desk in which she was sitting, flipped them backward, and pulling her out of the desk. *Murphy v. Fields*, 2019 WL 7195889 (D.S.C. 2019), *report and recommendation adopted*, 2019 WL 5417735 (D.S.C. 2019), *appeal dismissed sub nom.*, 2020 WL 2551049 (4th Cir. 2020).

- A case involving a school police officer who discharged pepper spray to break up an altercation between the athletes at a high school soccer game after verbal commands and physically separating the athletes was no longer effective. *Hernandez v. Blackburn*, 2019 WL 2455272 (Tex. App. 2019).

- A case involving a school police officer who deployed a taser that struck a special needs student who left campus without authorization and ran away from pursuing school officials. The student, after being tased, failed to submit and eluded the officer as well as the educators. *Lucero Y Ruiz De Gutierrez v. Albuquerque Pub. Sch.*, 2019 WL 203171 (D.N.M. 2019).

Part III
Equality, Discrimination, and Special Education

Chapter Seven
Equal Protection of the Laws

Today [education] is a principal instrument in awakening the child to cultural values, in preparing him for later professional training, and in helping him to adjust normally to his environment. In these days, it is doubtful that any child may reasonably be expected to succeed in life if he is denied the opportunity of an education. Such an opportunity, where the state has undertaken to provide it, is a right which must be made available to all on equal terms. *Brown v. Board of Education*, 347 U.S. 483 (1953)

I. Racial Discrimination

BROWN v. BOARD OF EDUCATION
347 U.S. 483 (1953)

[This case appears in Chapter One on page 46]

FREEMAN v. PITTS
503 U.S. 467 (1992)

OPINION: JUSTICE KENNEDY delivered the opinion of the Court.

DeKalb County, Georgia, is a major suburban area of Atlanta. This case involves a court-ordered desegregation decree for the DeKalb County School System (DCSS). DCSS now serves some 73,000 students in kindergarten through high school and is the 32d largest elementary and secondary school system in the Nation.

DCSS has been subject to the supervision and jurisdiction of the United States District Court for the Northern District of Georgia since 1969, when it was ordered to dismantle its dual school system. In 1986, petitioners filed a motion for final dismissal. The District Court ruled that DCSS had not achieved unitary status in all respects but had done so in student attendance and three other categories. In its order the District Court relinquished remedial control as to those aspects of the system in which unitary status had been achieved, and retained supervisory authority only for those aspects of the school system in which the district was not in full compliance. The Court of Appeals for the Eleventh Circuit reversed, 887 F.2d 1438 (1989), holding that a district court should retain full remedial authority over a school system until it achieves unitary status in six categories at the same time for several years. We now reverse the judgment of the Court of Appeals and remand, holding that a district court is permitted to withdraw judicial supervision with respect to discrete categories in which the school district has achieved compliance with a court-ordered desegregation plan. A district court need not retain active control over every aspect of school administration until a school district has demonstrated unitary status in all facets of its system.

I

A

For decades before our decision in *Brown v. Board of Education*, 347 U.S. 483 (1954) (*Brown I*), and our mandate in *Brown v. Board of Education*, 349 U.S. 294, 301 (1955) (*Brown II*), which ordered school districts to desegregate with "all deliberate speed," DCSS was segregated by law. DCSS' initial response to the mandate of *Brown II* was an all too familiar one. Interpreting "all deliberate speed" as giving latitude to delay steps to desegregate, DCSS took no positive action toward desegregation until the 1966-1967 school year, when it did nothing more than adopt a freedom of choice transfer plan. Some black students chose to attend former de jure white schools, but the plan had no significant effect on the former de jure black schools.

In 1968, we decided *Green v. School Bd. of New Kent County*, 391 U.S. 430, 20 L. Ed. 2d 716, 88 S. Ct. 1689. We held that adoption of a freedom of choice plan does not, by itself, satisfy a school district's mandatory responsibility to eliminate all vestiges of a dual system. *Green* was a turning point in our law in a further respect. Concerned by more than a decade of inaction, we stated that "'the time for mere "deliberate speed" has run out.'" *Id.*, at 438, quoting *Griffin v. Prince Edward County School Bd.*, 377 U.S. 218, 234 (1964). We said that the obligation of school districts once segregated by law was to come forward with a plan that "promises realistically to work, and promises realistically to work now." The case before us requires an understanding and assessment of how DCSS responded to the directives set forth in *Green*.

Within two months of our ruling in *Green*, respondents, who are black schoolchildren and their parents, instituted this class action in the United States District Court for the Northern District of Georgia. After the suit was filed, DCSS voluntarily began working with the Department of Health, Education, and Welfare to devise a comprehensive and final plan of desegregation. The District Court, in June 1969, entered a consent order approving the proposed plan, which was to be implemented in the 1969-1970 school year. The order abolished the freedom of choice plan and adopted a neighborhood school attendance plan that had been proposed by DCSS and accepted by the Department of Health, Education, and Welfare subject to a minor modification. Under the plan all of the former de jure black schools were closed, and their students were reassigned among the remaining neighborhood schools. The District Court retained jurisdiction.

Between 1969 and 1986, respondents sought only infrequent and limited judicial intervention into the affairs of DCSS. They did not request significant changes in student attendance zones or student assignment policies. In 1976, DCSS was ordered to expand its Majority-to-Minority (M-to-M) student transfer program, allowing students in a school where they are in the majority race to transfer to a school where they are in the minority; to establish a biracial committee to oversee the transfer program and future boundary line changes; and to reassign teachers so that the ratio of black to white teachers in each school would be, in substance, similar to the racial balance in the school population system wide. From 1977 to 1979, the District Court approved a boundary line change for one elementary school attendance zone and rejected DCSS proposals to restrict the M-to-M transfer program. In 1983, DCSS was ordered to make further adjustments to the M-to-M transfer program.

In 1986, petitioners filed a motion for final dismissal of the litigation. They sought a declaration that DCSS had satisfied its duty to eliminate the dual education system, that is to say a declaration that the school system had achieved unitary status. *Green*, *supra*, at 441. The District Court approached the question whether DCSS had achieved unitary status by asking whether DCSS was unitary with respect to each of the factors identified in Green. The court considered an additional factor that is not named in Green: the quality of education being offered to the white and black student populations.

The District Court found DCSS to be "an innovative school system that has travelled the often long road to unitary status almost to its end," noting that "the court has continually been impressed by the successes of the DCSS and its dedication to providing a quality education for all students within that system." App. to Pet. for Cert. 71a. It found that DCSS is a unitary system with regard to student assignments, transportation, physical facilities, and extracurricular activities, and ruled that it would order no further relief in those areas. The District Court stopped short of dismissing the case, however, because it found that DCSS was not unitary in every respect. The court said that vestiges of the dual system remain in the areas of teacher and principal assignments, resource allocation, and quality of education. DCSS was ordered to take measures to address the remaining problems.

B

Proper resolution of any desegregation case turns on a careful assessment of its facts. *Green*, *supra*, at 439. Here, as in most cases where the issue is the degree of compliance with a school desegregation decree, a critical beginning point is the degree of racial imbalance in the school district, that is to say a comparison of the proportion of majority to minority students in individual schools with the proportions of the races in the district as a whole. This inquiry is fundamental, for under the former de jure regimes racial exclusion was both the means and the end of a policy motivated by disparagement of, or hostility towards, the disfavored race. In accord with this principle, the District Court began its analysis with an assessment of the current racial mix in the schools throughout DCSS and the explanation for the racial imbalance it found. Respondents did not contend on appeal that the findings of fact were clearly erroneous, and the Court of Appeals did not find them to be erroneous. The Court of Appeals did disagree with the conclusion reached by the District Court respecting the need for further supervision of racial balance in student assignments.

In the extensive record that comprises this case, one fact predominates: Remarkable changes in the racial composition of the county presented DCSS and the District Court with a student population in 1986 far different from the one they set out to integrate in 1969. Between 1950 and 1985, DeKalb County grew from 70,000 to 450,000 in total population, but most of the gross increase in student enrollment had occurred by 1969, the relevant starting date for our purposes. Although the public school population experienced only modest changes between 1969 and 1986 (remaining in the low

70,000's), a striking change occurred in the racial proportions of the student population. The school system that the District Court ordered desegregated in 1969 had 5.6% black students; by 1986 the percentage of black students was 47%.

To compound the difficulty of working with these radical demographic changes, the northern and southern parts of the county experienced much different growth patterns. The District Court found that "as the result of these demographic shifts, the population of the northern half of DeKalb County is now predominantly white and the southern half of DeKalb County is predominantly black." App. to Pet. for Cert. 38a. In 1970, there were 7,615 nonwhites living in the northern part of DeKalb County and 11,508 nonwhites in the southern part of the county. By 1980, there were 15,365 nonwhites living in the northern part of the county, and 87,583 nonwhites in the southern part. Most of the growth in the nonwhite population in the southern portion of the county was due to the migration of black persons from the city of Atlanta. Between 1975 and 1980 alone, approximately 64,000 black citizens moved into southern DeKalb County, most of them coming from Atlanta. During the same period, approximately 37,000 white citizens moved out of southern DeKalb County to the surrounding counties.

The District Court made findings with respect to the number of nonwhite citizens in the northern and southern parts of the county for the years 1970 and 1980 without making parallel findings with respect to white citizens. Yet a clear picture does emerge. During the relevant period, the black population in the southern portion of the county experienced tremendous growth while the white population did not, and the white population in the northern part of the county experienced tremendous growth while the black population did not.

The demographic changes that occurred during the course of the desegregation order are an essential foundation for the District Court's analysis of the current racial mix of DCSS. As the District Court observed, the demographic shifts have had "an immense effect on the racial compositions of the DeKalb County schools." *Ibid.* From 1976 to 1986, enrollment in elementary schools declined overall by 15%, while black enrollment in elementary schools increased by 86%. During the same period, overall high school enrollment declined by 16%, while black enrollment in high schools increased by 119%. These effects were even more pronounced in the southern portion of DeKalb County.

Concerned with racial imbalance in the various schools of the district, respondents presented evidence that during the 1986-1987 school year DCSS had the following features: (1) 47% of the students attending DCSS were black; (2) 50% of the black students attended schools that were over 90% black; (3) 62% of all black students attended schools that had more than 20% more blacks than the system-wide average; (4) 27% of white students attended schools that were more than 90% white; (5) 59% of the white students attended schools that had more than 20% more whites than the system-wide average; (6) of the 22 DCSS high schools, five had student populations that were more than 90% black, while five other schools had student populations that were more than 80% white; and (7) of the 74 elementary schools in DCSS, 18 are over 90% black, while 10 are over 90% white. *Id.*, at 31a. (Respondents' evidence on these points treated all nonblack students as white. The District Court noted that there was no evidence that nonblack minority students constituted even 1% of DCSS student population.)

Respondents argued in the District Court that this racial imbalance in student assignment was a vestige of the dual system, rather than a product of independent demographic forces. In addition to the statistical evidence that the ratio of black students to white students in individual schools varied to a significant degree from the system wide average, respondents contended that DCSS had not used all available desegregative tools in order to achieve racial balancing. Respondents pointed to the following alleged shortcomings in DCSS' desegregative efforts: (1) DCSS did not break the county into subdistricts and racially balance each subdistrict; (2) DCSS failed to expend sufficient funds for minority learning opportunities; (3) DCSS did not establish community advisory organizations; (4) DCSS did not make full use of the freedom of choice plan; (5) DCSS did not cluster schools, that is, it did not create schools for separate grade levels which could be used to establish a feeder pattern; (6) DCSS did not institute its magnet school program as early as it might have; and (7) DCSS did not use busing to facilitate urban to suburban exchanges.

According to the District Court, respondents conceded that the 1969 order assigning all students to their neighborhood schools "effectively desegregated the DCSS for a period of time" with respect to student assignment. *Id.* at 35a. The District Court noted, however, that despite this concession respondents contended there was an improper imbalance in two schools even in 1969. Respondents made much of the fact that despite the small percentage of blacks in the county in 1969, there were then two schools that contained a majority of black students: Terry Mill Elementary School was 76% black, and Stoneview Elementary School was 51% black.

The District Court found the racial imbalance in these schools was not a vestige of the prior de jure system. It observed that both the Terry Mill and Stoneview schools were de jure white schools before the freedom of choice plan was put in place. It cited expert witness testimony that Terry Mill had become a majority black school as a result of demographic shifts unrelated to the actions of petitioners or their predecessors. In 1966, the overwhelming majority of students at Terry Mill were white. By 1967, due to migration of black citizens from Atlanta into DeKalb County—and into the neighborhood surrounding the Terry Mill School in particular—23% of the students at Terry Mill were black. By 1968, black students constituted 50% of the school population at Terry Mill. By 1969, when the plan was put into effect, the percentage of black students had grown to 76. In accordance with the evidence of demographic shifts, and in the absence of any evidence to suggest that the former dual system contributed in any way to the rapid racial transformation of the Terry Mill student population, the District Court found that the pre-1969 unconstitutional acts of petitioners were not responsible for the high percentage of black students at the Terry Mill school in 1969. Its findings in this respect are illustrative of the problems DCSS and the District Court faced in integrating the whole district.

Although the District Court found that DCSS was desegregated for at least a short period under the court-ordered plan of 1969, it did not base its finding that DCSS had achieved unitary status with respect to student assignment on that circumstance alone. Recognizing that "the achievement of unitary status in the area of student assignment cannot be hedged on the attainment of such status for a brief moment," *Id.* at 37a, the District Court examined the interaction between DCSS policy and demographic shifts in DeKalb County.

The District Court noted that DCSS had taken specific steps to combat the effects of demographics on the racial mix of the schools. Under the 1969 order, a biracial committee had reviewed all proposed changes in the boundary lines of school attendance zones. Since the original desegregation order, there had been about 170 such changes. It was found that only three had a partial segregative effect. An expert testified, and the District Court found, that even those changes had no significant effect on the racial mix of the school population, given the tremendous demographic shifts that were taking place at the same time.

The District Court also noted that DCSS, on its own initiative, started an M-to-M program in the 1972 school year. The program was a marked success. Participation increased with each passing year, so that in the 1986-1987 school year, 4,500 of the 72,000 students enrolled in DCSS participated. An expert testified that the impact of an M-to-M program goes beyond the number of students transferred because students at the receiving school also obtain integrated learning experiences. The District Court found that about 19% of the students attending DCSS had an integrated learning experience as a result of the M-to-M program. *Id.* at 40a.

In addition, in the 1980's, DCSS instituted a magnet school program in schools located in the middle of the county. The magnet school programs included a performing arts program, two science programs, and a foreign language program. There was testimony in the District Court that DCSS also had plans to operate additional magnet programs in occupational education and gifted and talented education, as well as a preschool program and an open campus. By locating these programs in the middle of the county, DCSS sought to attract black students from the southern part of the county and white students from the northern part.

Further, the District Court found that DCSS operates a number of experience programs integrated by race, including a writing center for fifth and seventh graders, a driving range, summer school programs, and a dialectical speech program. DCSS employs measures to control the racial mix in each of these special areas.

In determining whether DCSS has achieved unitary status with respect to student assignment, the District Court saw its task as one of deciding if petitioners "have accomplished maximum practical desegregation of the DCSS or if the DCSS must still do more to fulfill their affirmative constitutional duty." *Id.* at 41a. Petitioners and respondents presented conflicting expert testimony about the potential effects that desegregative techniques not deployed might have had upon the racial mix of the schools. The District Court found that petitioners' experts were more reliable, citing their greater familiarity with DCSS, their experience, and their standing within the expert community.

The District Court made these findings:

"[The actions of DCSS] achieved maximum practical desegregation from 1969 to 1986. The rapid population shifts in DeKalb County were not caused by any action on the part of the DCSS. These demographic shifts were inevitable as the result of suburbanization, that is, work opportunities arising in DeKalb County as well as the City of Atlanta, which attracted blacks to DeKalb; the decline in the number of children born to white families during this period while the number of children born to black families did not decrease; blockbusting of formerly white neighborhoods leading to selling and buying of real estate in the DeKalb area on a highly dynamic basis; and the completion of Interstate 20, which made access from DeKalb County into the City of Atlanta much easier. . . . There is no evidence that the school system's previous unconstitutional conduct may have contributed to this segregation. This court is convinced that any further actions taken by defendants, while the actions might have made marginal adjustments in the population trends, would not have offset the factors that were described above and the same racial segregation would have occurred at approximately the same speed." *Id.* at 44a-45a.

The District Court added:

"Absent massive bussing, which is not considered as a viable option by either the parties or this court, the magnet school program and the M-to-M program, which the defendants voluntarily implemented and to which the defendants obviously are dedicated, are the most effective ways to deal with the effects on student attendance of the residential segregation existing in DeKalb County at this time." *Id.* at 46a.

In accordance with its fact finding, the District Court held that it would order no further relief in the areas of student assignment, transportation, physical facilities, and extracurricular activities. The District Court, however, did order DCSS to establish a system to balance teacher and principal assignments and to equalize per-pupil expenditures throughout DCSS. Having found that blacks were represented on the school board and throughout DCSS administration, the District Court abolished the biracial committee as no longer necessary.

Both parties appealed to the United States Court of Appeals for the Eleventh Circuit. The Court of Appeals affirmed the District Court's ultimate conclusion that DCSS has not yet achieved unitary status, but reversed the District Court's ruling that DCSS has no further duties in the area of student assignment. ....The Court of Appeals held that petitioners bore the responsibility for the racial imbalance, and in order to correct that imbalance would have to take actions that "may be administratively awkward, inconvenient, and even bizarre in some situations," *Swann v. Charlotte-Mecklenburg Bd. of Education*, 402 U.S. 1, 28 (1971), such as pairing and clustering of schools, drastic gerrymandering of school zones, grade reorganization, and busing. We granted certiorari, 498 U.S. 1081 (1991).

II

Two principal questions are presented. The first is whether a district court may relinquish its supervision and control over those aspects of a school system in which there has been compliance with a desegregation decree if other aspects of the system remain in noncompliance. As we answer this question in the affirmative, the second question is whether the Court of Appeals erred in reversing the District Court's order providing for incremental withdrawal of supervision in all the circumstances of this case.

A

The duty and responsibility of a school district once segregated by law is to take all steps necessary to eliminate the vestiges of the unconstitutional de jure system. This is required in order to ensure that the principal wrong of the de jure system, the injuries and stigma inflicted upon the race disfavored by the violation, is no longer present. This was the rationale and the objective of *Brown I* and *Brown II.*

.....

The concept of unitariness has been a helpful one in defining the scope of the district courts' authority, for it conveys the central idea that a school district that was once a dual system must be examined in all of its facets, both when a remedy is ordered and in the later phases of desegregation when the question is whether the district courts' remedial control ought to be modified, lessened, or withdrawn.

.....

That the term "unitary" does not have fixed meaning or content is not inconsistent with the principles that control the exercise of equitable power. The essence of a court's equity power lies in its inherent capacity to adjust remedies in a feasible and practical way to eliminate the conditions or redress the injuries caused by unlawful action. Equitable remedies must be flexible if these underlying principles are to be enforced with fairness and precision. In this respect, as we observed in *Swann*, "a school desegregation case does not differ fundamentally from other cases involving the framing of equitable remedies to repair the denial of a constitutional right. The task is to correct, by a balancing of the individual and collective interests, the condition that offends the Constitution." *Swann*, 402 U.S. at 15-16. The requirement of a unitary school system must be implemented according to this prescription.

Today, we make explicit the rationale that was central in *Spangler*. A federal court in a school desegregation case has the discretion to order an incremental or partial withdrawal of its supervision and control. This discretion derives both from the constitutional authority which justified its intervention in the first instance and its ultimate objectives in formulating the decree. The authority of the court is invoked at the outset to remedy particular constitutional violations. In construing the remedial authority of the district courts, we have been guided by the principles that "judicial powers may be exercised only on the basis of a constitutional violation," and that "the nature of the violation determines the scope of the remedy." *Swann*, *supra*, at 16. A remedy is justifiable only insofar as it advances the ultimate objective of alleviating the initial constitutional violation.

We have said that the court's end purpose must be to remedy the violation and, in addition, to restore state and local authorities to the control of a school system that is operating in compliance with the Constitution. .....Partial relinquishment of judicial control, where justified by the facts of the case, can be an important and significant step in fulfilling the district court's duty to return the operations and control of schools to local authorities. .... Just as a court has the obligation at the outset of a desegregation decree to structure a plan so that all available resources of the court are directed to comprehensive supervision of its decree, so too must a court provide an orderly means for withdrawing from control when it is shown that the school district has attained the requisite degree of compliance. A transition phase in which control is relinquished in a gradual way is an appropriate means to this end.

As we have long observed, "local autonomy of school districts is a vital national tradition." *Dayton Bd. of Education v. Brinkman*, 433 U.S. 406, 410 (1977) (*Dayton I*). Returning schools to the control of local authorities at the earliest practicable date is essential to restore their true accountability in our governmental system.

We hold that in the course of supervising desegregation plans, federal courts have the authority to relinquish supervision and control of school districts in incremental stages, before full compliance has been achieved in every area of school operations. While retaining jurisdiction over the case, the court may determine that it will not order further remedies in areas where the school district is in compliance with the decree. That is to say, upon a finding that a school system subject to a court-supervised desegregation plan is in compliance in some but not all areas, the court in appropriate cases may return control to the school system in those areas where compliance has been achieved, limiting further judicial supervision to operations that are not yet in full compliance with the court decree. In particular, the district court may determine that it will not order further remedies in the area of student assignments where racial imbalance is not traceable, in a proximate way, to constitutional violations.

A court's discretion to order the incremental withdrawal of its supervision in a school desegregation case must be exercised in a manner consistent with the purposes and objectives of its equitable power. Among the factors which must inform the sound discretion of the court in ordering partial withdrawal are the following: whether there has been full and satisfactory compliance with the decree in those aspects of the system where supervision is to be withdrawn; whether retention of judicial control is necessary or practicable to achieve compliance with the decree in other facets of the school system; and whether the school district has demonstrated, to the public and to the parents and students of the once disfavored race, its good-faith commitment to the whole of the court's decree and to those provisions of the law and the Constitution that were the predicate for judicial intervention in the first instance.

In considering these factors, a court should give particular attention to the school system's record of compliance. A school system is better positioned to demonstrate its good-faith commitment to a constitutional course of action when its policies form a consistent pattern of lawful conduct directed to eliminating earlier violations. And, with the passage of time, the degree to which racial imbalances continue to represent vestiges of a constitutional violation may diminish, and the practicability and efficacy of various remedies can be evaluated with more precision.

These are the premises that guided our formulation in Dowell of the duties of a district court during the final phases of a desegregation case: "The District Court should address itself to whether the Board had complied in good faith with the desegregation decree since it was entered, and whether the vestiges of past discrimination had been eliminated to the extent practicable." 498 U.S. at 249-50.

B

****

The findings of the District Court that the population changes which occurred in DeKalb County were not caused by the policies of the school district, but rather by independent factors, are consistent with the mobility that is a distinct characteristic of our society.

The effect of changing residential patterns on the racial composition of schools, though not always fortunate, is somewhat predictable. Studies show a high correlation between residential segregation and school segregation.

Where resegregation is a product not of state action but of private choices, it does not have constitutional implications. It is beyond the authority and beyond the practical ability of the federal courts to try to counteract these kinds of continuous and massive demographic shifts. To attempt such results would require ongoing and never-ending supervision by the courts of school districts simply because they were once de jure segregated. Residential housing choices, and their attendant effects on the racial composition of schools, present an ever-changing pattern, one difficult to address through judicial remedies.

As the de jure violation becomes more remote in time and these demographic changes intervene, it becomes less likely that a current racial imbalance in a school district is a vestige of the prior de jure system. The causal link between current conditions and the prior violation is even more attenuated if the school district has demonstrated its good faith. In light of its finding that the demographic changes in DeKalb County are unrelated to the prior violation, the District Court was correct to entertain the suggestion that DCSS had no duty to achieve system-wide racial balance in the student population.

The requirement that the school district show its good-faith commitment to the entirety of a desegregation plan so that parents, students, and the public have assurance against further injuries or stigma also should be a subject for more specific findings.

When a school district has not demonstrated good faith under a comprehensive plan to remedy ongoing violations, we have without hesitation approved comprehensive and continued district court supervision.

****

In contrast to the circumstances in *Penick* and *Brinkman*, the District Court in this case stated that throughout the period of judicial supervision it has been impressed by the successes DCSS has achieved and its dedication to providing a quality education for all students, and that DCSS "has travelled the often long road to unitary status almost to its end." With respect to those areas where compliance had not been achieved, the District Court did not find that DCSS had acted in bad faith or engaged in further acts of discrimination since the desegregation plan went into effect. This, though, may not be the equivalent of a finding that the school district has an affirmative commitment to comply in good faith with the entirety of a desegregation plan, and further proceedings are appropriate for this purpose as well.

The judgment is reversed, and the case is remanded to the Court of Appeals. It should determine what issues are open for its further consideration in light of the previous briefs and arguments of the parties and in light of the principles set forth in this opinion. Thereupon it should order further proceedings as necessary or order an appropriate remand to the District Court.

CONCUR: JUSTICE SCALIA, concurring.

The District Court in the present case found that the imbalances in student assignment were attributable to private demographic shifts rather than governmental action. Without disturbing this finding, and without finding that revision of student assignments was necessary to remedy some other unlawful government action, the Court of Appeals ordered DeKalb County to institute massive busing and other programs to achieve integration. The Court convincingly demonstrates that this cannot be reconciled with our cases, and I join its opinion.

.....

Identifying and undoing the effects of some violations of the law is easy. Where, for example, a tax is found to have been unconstitutionally imposed, calculating the funds derived from that tax (which must be refunded), and distinguishing them from the funds derived from other taxes (which may be retained), is a simple matter. That is not so with respect to the effects of unconstitutionally operating a legally segregated school system; they are uncommonly difficult to identify and to separate from the effects of other causes. But one would not know that from our instructions to the lower courts on this subject, which tend to be at a level of generality that assumes facile reduction to specifics. "'[Desegregation] decrees,'" we have said, "'exceed appropriate limits if they are aimed at eliminating a condition that does not violate the Constitution or does not flow from such a violation,'" *Board of Education of Oklahoma City Public Schools v. Dowell*, 498 U.S. 237, 247 (1991); *Milliken v. Bradley*, 433 U.S. 267, 282 (1977).

At some time, we must acknowledge that it has become absurd to assume, without any further proof, that violation of the Constitution dating from the days when Lyndon Johnson was President, or earlier, continue to have an appreciable effect upon current operation of schools. We are close to that time. While we must continue to prohibit, without qualification, all racial discrimination in the operation of public schools, and to afford remedies that eliminate not only the discrimination but its identified consequences, we should consider laying aside the extraordinary, and increasingly counter-factual, presumption of *Green*. We must soon revert to the ordinary principles of our law, of our democratic heritage, and of our educational tradition: that plaintiffs alleging equal protection violations must prove intent and causation and not merely the existence of racial disparity, that public schooling, even in the South, should be controlled by locally elected authorities acting in conjunction with parents; and that it is "desirable" to permit pupils to attend "schools nearest their homes."

VILLANUEVA v. CARERE
85 F.3d 481 (10th Cir. 1996)

HENRY, Circuit Judge.

Plaintiffs-appellants, a class of Hispanic parents and their children (the Parents), brought this action to enjoin the closing of two Pueblo, Colorado public schools and the opening of a charter school pursuant to the Colorado Charter Schools Act, Colo. Rev. Stat. §§ 22-30.5-101 to -114 (the Act). The Parents alleged that the decisions of defendant-appellee the Board of Education for Pueblo School District No. 60 (the Board) to close the schools at which their children were enrolled and, three months before, to approve the opening of a charter school had deprived them of their Fourteenth Amendment right to equal protection of the laws and of those rights guaranteed by Title VI of the Civil Rights Act of 1964, 42 U.S.C. §§ 2000d to 2000d-4a. In addition to raising various other claims, which they have not pursued on appeal, the Parents also challenged the constitutionality of the Charter Schools Act under the Equal Protection Clause. The State of Colorado and the Colorado State Board of Education intervened to defend the Act.

I. BACKGROUND

Pueblo School District 60 (the District), comprised of some thirty-three elementary, middle, and high schools, an alternative school, and a day care facility, enrolls approximately 18,000 students of whom almost exactly 50% are Hispanic and about 64% are minorities. In recent years, the District has experimented with innovative approaches to education, forging an educational and administrative alliance with the University of Southern Colorado to improve educational quality and allocate resources more efficiently. As required by Colorado law, District 60 operates under a "schools of choice" system, in which parents may send their children to any school in the District, *see* Colo. Rev. Stat. §§ 22-36-101 to -106, although free transportation generally is not provided to those who choose to attend schools outside their neighborhood.

The Colorado Charter Schools Act authorizes local school boards to contract with interested parties to establish charter schools—public schools that are managed by their sponsors and financed primarily with the local school district's funds. *See* Colo. Rev. Stat. §§ 22-30.5-101 to -112. In late 1993, the University of Southern Colorado submitted to the Board an application to establish in District 60 a charter school known as Pueblo School for Arts and Sciences (PSAS), which proposed to use nontraditional pedagogic methods to address especially the needs of "at-risk" and minority students.[1] The proposal asserted the sponsors' commitment to admit a student body reflecting the make-up of "the educational community of Pueblo in terms of gender, ethnicity, and economic status," to use "targeted recruitment" "only to maintain a balanced and diverse student body," and to admit students on a first-come, first-served basis, without regard to test scores. The sponsors emphasized the importance of a strong "community/school partnership," by requiring parents annually to perform eighteen hours of service to the school. In December 1993, the Board voted pursuant to its authority under the Act to approve the application of PSAS.

---

[1] The Act defines an "at-risk pupil" as "a pupil who, because of physical, emotional, socioeconomic, or cultural factors, is less likely to succeed in a conventional educational environment." Colo. Rev. Stat. § 22-30.5-103(1)(a).

The administrators of PSAS sought to ensure geographic and ethnic diversity by dividing District 60 into eight regions for purposes of soliciting enrollment applications; students were admitted on a first-come, first-served basis within each region. Application forms notified parents of the community service requirement, a mandatory pre-admission parental interview, and the requirement that parents provide transportation for their children, and informed parents that admission was to be based upon commitment to the school and not upon previous student performance. The forms also requested information about parents' place of employment.

In practice, no parental interviews were held until after admission. Community groups publicized the charter school among the Hispanic community in Pueblo. In its first year, 1994-95, the projected enrollment at PSAS included 52% Hispanic students and 62% minority students.

In February 1994, three months after the vote to approve PSAS, the Board voted to close Hyde Park Elementary School and Spann Elementary School. Approximately 75% of students in each school were Hispanic. The issue of school closures had been before the Board for three years.

Both schools hosted programs for "at-risk" students, including federally funded breakfast and lunch programs and school-wide Chapter I programs that contributed to maintaining pupil-teacher ratios below the District average. In addition, Hyde Park was one of eighteen schools chosen nationwide to host a Parent Resource and Involvement Strength Education (P.R.A.I.S.E.) program, which successfully encouraged broad parental involvement at the school.

In deciding which schools to close, the Board considered primarily four factors: (1) the present and projected enrollment at the schools to be closed and (2) at nearby schools; (3) the percentage of space utilized; and (4) the total cost per student. The Board did not directly consider the impact of school closures on the surrounding communities or the quality of educational programs at the schools chosen for closure.

Of the students formerly attending Hyde Park and Spann, most were to be transferred to other schools consisting predominantly (over 70%) of minority students. In turn, to make room for the incoming students, one of the "receiving schools" was to transfer about forty-four students to another predominantly minority school. While many of the former Hyde Park and Spann students were to be bussed, some would be able to walk to school; some of the latter would now, unlike in the past, have to cross busy intersections. In deciding where to transfer these students, the District considered factors including the proximity and capacity of receiving schools and the desire to have former Hyde Park and Spann teachers follow the students. The District planned to transfer the P.R.A.I.S.E. program to one of these receiving schools and also to have Chapter I funding follow qualifying Hyde Park and Spann students to the receiving schools.

II. DISCUSSION

A. Discriminatory Intent

Proof of racially discriminatory intent or purpose is required to demonstrate a race-based violation of the Equal Protection Clause. *Washington v. Davis*, 426 U.S. 229, 239 (1976). The discriminatory purpose need not be the only purpose, but it must be "a motivating factor in the decision." *Arlington Heights v. Metropolitan Hous. Dev. Corp.*, 429 U.S. 252, 265-66 (1977).

As the parties properly acknowledge, we may reverse the trial court's finding of no discriminatory intent only if it is clearly erroneous. *See, e.g., Dowell v. Board of Educ. of Okla. City Pub. Schs.*, 8 F.3d 1501, 1518 (10th Cir. 1993). Not only is this standard of review well-established, but its rationale is exemplified by a case such as this one. The district court heard extensive testimony before making its factual determinations, which included findings that the defendant Board members did not intend to discriminate against Hispanic students, and that they were sincere in their stated purpose of striving to improve the quality of education in the District. Findings such as these, based on the trial court's determination of the credibility of witnesses, demand of the appellate court a heightened degree of deference.

Although the Parents presented no direct evidence of discriminatory intent, the district court's inquiry could not stop there. "Determining whether invidious discriminatory purpose was a motivating factor demands a sensitive inquiry into such circumstantial and direct evidence of intent as may be available." *Arlington Heights*, 429 U.S. at 266. The Parents' claim that discriminatory intent was a motivating factor in the school closings decision rests principally on four allegations: that the closures resulted in overcrowded classrooms in the selected receiving schools; that the Board failed to consider the high quality of the educational programs offered at Hyde Park and Spann or the impact of school closings on the affected communities; that the Board did not make adequate arrangements to ensure that the P.R.A.I.S.E. program and high levels of parental involvement would be maintained after the closures; and that the Board improperly took into consideration the ethnic mix of the closed and receiving schools.

However, the evidence concerning these allegations, when viewed in concert with "the totality of the relevant facts," *see Davis*, 426 U.S. at 242, is insufficient to lead us to conclude that the district court's finding of a lack of discriminatory intent was clearly erroneous. Indeed, several of the Board members and the Superintendent are themselves Hispanic, and have notable records of commitment to the Hispanic and minority communities of Pueblo, including long years of service to the plurality-Hispanic District 60. The Parents' separate claim of discriminatory intent in the implementation of admissions procedures for PSAS similarly rests on circumstantial evidence which, in the face of the clear purpose of the charter school and its admissions procedure—to serve at-risk students and to admit a broad cross-section of the community—is inadequate to lead us to a different conclusion than that of the district court. Because the district court correctly found that the Board did not intentionally discriminate against Hispanic parents, we hold that it properly found for the Appellees with respect to the Parents' equal protection claims.

B. Discriminatory Impact

The Parents also argue that the school closures and the implementation of the PSAS admissions procedure violated their right under Title VI of the Civil Rights Act of 1964, 42 U.S.C. §§ 2000d to 2000d-4a, to be free from discrimination "under any program or activity receiving Federal financial assistance," *Id.* § 2000d. Although Title VI itself proscribes only intentional discrimination, certain regulations promulgated pursuant to Title VI prohibit actions that have a disparate impact on groups protected by the act, even in the absence of discriminatory intent. *Guardians Ass'n. v. Civil Serv. Comm'n.*, 463 U.S. 582, 584 (1983).

The district court found that the Parents had failed to demonstrate that the school closures would have a discriminatory impact on Hispanic students. In rejecting the Parents' broadly pleaded disparate impact claim, the district court made factual findings supporting its conclusion that there had been no demonstrated adverse impact on Hyde Park and Spann students as a group, regardless of ethnicity. Because it is these findings which the Parents challenge on appeal, our review is for clear error. *See Ortega v. Safeway Stores, Inc.*, 943 F.2d 1230, 1244 n.29 (Colo. 1991)

Upon a careful examination of the record, we cannot say that the district court's findings were clearly erroneous. The schools to which the student appellants were transferred had facilities comparable to those of the closed schools and, although the testimony indicates some confusion about this, we conclude that the court did not err in determining that the receiving schools would not be over-crowded. Moreover, Chapter I funding and the P.R.A.I.S.E. program were to follow qualified students to the receiving schools. Significantly, that the transfers resulted in high percentages of at-risk and minority students at receiving schools has little relevance to the issue of disparate impact because Hyde Park and Spann, the very schools that the appellants have fought to resurrect, themselves enrolled high percentages of such students.

We briefly respond to the Parents' argument, not directly addressed in the district court's order, that Hispanic students were disparately impacted by the opening of PSAS. Clearly this cannot be the case, as the uncontroverted evidence shows that the 1994-95 projected enrollment at PSAS was about 50% Hispanic, compared with approximately the same proportion of Hispanic students in the district-wide population.

Because the district court's findings that neither the school closings nor the opening of PSAS resulted in a negative disparate impact on the Hispanic population is not clearly erroneous, we hold that the court correctly found for the Appellees with respect to the Parents' Title VI claims.

C. The Colorado Charter Schools Act

We conduct plenary review of the district court's determination that the Parents have failed to establish that the Charter Schools Act passed by the Colorado legislature violates the Equal Protection Clause of the Fourteenth Amendment. We begin our review with the venerable presumption that the acts of a state legislature are constitutional. *See Parham v. Hughes*, 441 U.S. 347 (1979) (employing the presumption of validity against a challenge under the Equal Protection

Clause). Moreover, courts pay particular deference to the states in decisions involving "the most persistent and difficult questions of educational policy" because our "lack of specialized knowledge and experience counsels against premature interference with the informed judgments made at the state and local levels." *San Antonio Indep. Sch. Dist. v. Rodriguez,* 411 U.S. 1, 42 (1973). "The very complexity of the problems of financing and managing a statewide public school system suggests that 'there will be more than one constitutionally permissible method of solving them,' and that, within the limits of rationality, 'the legislature's efforts to tackle the problems' should be entitled to respect." *Id.* (quoting *Jefferson v. Hackney*, 406 U.S. 535, 546-47 (1972)).

The Parents challenge the provision of the Act that reserves thirteen charters for "applications which are designed to increase the educational opportunities of at-risk pupils," Colo. Rev. Stat. § 22-30.5-109(2)(a), because they allege that it creates a suspect classification. The Act defines "at-risk pupils" as those "who, because of physical, emotional, socioeconomic, or cultural factors, [are] less likely to succeed in a conventional educational environment." *Id.* § 22-30.5-103(1)(a). The Parents argue that the word "cultural" in this definition "is a code-word for ethnic minority," and that the Act therefore separates and classifies students according to race and ethnicity. Such criteria are traditionally suspect and would thus trigger strict scrutiny, which is almost always fatal to a classification. *See Fullilove v. Klutznick*, 448 U.S. 448, 519 (1980) (Marshall, J., concurring).

We share the Parents' concern with the practice of drawing classifications based on "culture," which might in some circumstances be used as a proxy for ethnicity, race, national origin or some other suspect classification. However, we believe that, reading the Act in its entirety, it simply does not create any classification of students, and therefore it cannot create a suspect classification. The Act expressly requires of charter schools that "enrollment must be open to any child who resides within the school district" and that "enrollment decisions shall be made in a nondiscriminatory manner." Colo. Rev. Stat. § 22-30.5-104(3). Moreover, under the Colorado Public Schools of Choice Act, *Id.* §§ 22-36-101 to -106, enrollment in any public school generally is open to any child in Colorado, *Id.* § 22-36-101. Hence, charter schools designed to increase the educational opportunities of at-risk pupils must admit on an equal basis applicants who are not so classified, and, conversely, at-risk students are not required to attend such schools but may attend any public school they and their parents choose. Therefore, even though we might agree in other contexts that treating students differently on the basis of "culture" could trigger strict scrutiny, the carefully crafted provisions of the Act mandating open enrollment and expressly proscribing discrimination convince us that no suspect classification has been created.[3] Because the Act creates no suspect classification, and because no fundamental right is alleged to be affected, the correct standard is whether the challenged state action rationally furthers a legitimate state purpose.

One of the stated purposes of the Act is to allow communities to "create new, innovative, and more flexible ways of educating all children within the public school system." Colo. Rev. Stat. § 22-30.5-102(3). Colorado has a legitimate interest in encouraging innovation in education. *See*

---

[3] We note the district court's concern with the "modified first come/first served," Aplts' App. at 283, admissions procedure that was implemented at PSAS, which seems to favor children of parents with the resources and the acumen to apply early. *See id.* at 283-85. Though we do not believe this rises to an actionable level, we also note that the federal Charter Schools Act requires schools receiving funds under the Act to admit students on the basis of a lottery, see 20 U.S.C. § 8066(1)(H), indicating that Congress apparently shared the district court's concern.

Rodriguez, 411 U.S. at 50 ("No area of social concern stands to profit more from a multiplicity of viewpoints and from a diversity of approaches than does public education."). We hold that the Charter Schools Act is rationally related to that interest.

III. CONCLUSION

We cannot fail to observe the acrimony in this long-standing community battle. Perhaps it comes from the fact that although education is not a "fundamental right" in the United States, good parents nonetheless have fundamental aspirations about the education of their children. Hence it is not surprising that these convictions should produce conflicts that run equally deep. Yet all disagreements cannot be resolved by the federal courts, especially when they relate to local educational policies upon which both warring factions hold deep and sincere beliefs. This question is political, not legal.

Notes and Comments

1. School Desegregation Terminology: De facto v. De jure Discrimination
De jure segregation ("by law") is that which is tied to intentional acts of government. De facto segregation ("by the facts") is not attributable to government because it exists outside of-and often in spite of-the law. The distinction is critical in school desegregation cases. It has been recognized in other areas of discrimination law as well. For example, the Court has cautioned state and local governments that they should ignore private biases in policymaking or else risk converting the effects of the private bias into a de jure conflict. *See Palmore v. Sidoti*, 466 U.S. 429 (1984) (Child custody dispute in which the judge disqualifies the mother who remarried into an interracial marriage because of the potential for racial conflict within the community). The justices revisit the distinction as well in the affirmative action cases below. Especially note the discussion of de jure and de facto effects in *Parents Involved v. Seattle School District No. 1.*

2. The Desegregation Cases from *Brown* to *Freeman*: "All Deliberate Speed"
The period of litigation after *Brown* focused primarily on two concerns. First, the Court struggled to articulate the role of the federal courts in monitoring local school districts for compliance with its antidiscrimination mandate. Second, and perhaps most importantly, several decisions hashed out the question of when and how a local school district would be found to be segregated.

In 1971, the Supreme Court announced its decision in the case *Swann v. Charlotte-Mecklenburg Board of Education*, 402 U.S. 1 (1971). The Court in *Swann* reaffirmed the traditional equity power of the federal judiciary to remedy violations of the Constitution. Chief Justice Burger then proceeded to limit its application in public school desegregation cases. "If school authorities fail in their affirmative obligations," reasoned Chief Justice Burger, "judicial authority may be invoked." The ruling in *Swann* settled norms for the officials of state public school systems who thereafter could anticipate robust federal involvement in dismantling segregated schools. After *Swann*, the primary obligation to provide a remedy for unlawful segregation in schools rested with federal courts. The judges-primarily district court judges-were supposed to fashion decrees relying on the traditional equity power of the federal judiciary. Traditionally, equity has been characterized by a practical flexibility in shaping its remedies and by a facility for adjusting and reconciling public and private needs." 349 U.S. at 300.

The next major decision occurred in 1974 in *Milliken v. Bradley*. 418 U.S. 717 (1974). The Court was faced with reviewing an order of the District Court (affirmed by the Court of Appeals) that imposed an inter-district desegregation remedy on the entire State of Michigan because of the policies of the Michigan State Board of Education. All of the Justices agreed with the findings of the lower courts that several acts by the State Board contributed to the pattern of segregation that existed in the City of Detroit public schools. These actions helped to create a scheme of metropolitan schools that were segregated with blacks at the core and whites at the periphery. Of the 86 school districts in the Detroit metropolitan area, the racial composition was 81% white and 19% black. Within the City of Detroit, the school ratio was 64% black and 34% white with most schools either all-white or all-black. *See Milliken v. Bradley*, 418 U.S. 717, 765 (1974) (White, J., dissenting). The lower courts approved of a remedy that would effectively combine fifty-three school districts with the City of Detroit district to "achieve the greatest degree of actual desegregation." *Milliken v. Bradley*, 418 U.S. 717, 734 (1974) However, a majority of justices, led by Chief Justice Burger, ruled that the order was too broad and that the remedy should be confined to the area where the segregation actually occurred-the Detroit City school system. The Court reasoned:

> [O]ur assumption, ... that state agencies did participate in the maintenance of the Detroit system, should make it clear that it is not on this point that we part company. The difference between [the majority and the dissenters] arises instead from established doctrine laid down by our cases. [These cases] addressed the issue of constitutional wrong in terms of an established geographic and administrative school system.... *Id.* at 746.

Milliken narrowed the scope of judicial power to correct segregated schools version of agency theory to insulate local subdivisions from accountability for discrimination caused by the policies of the Michigan State Board of Education. Justice Burger wrote:

> No single tradition in public education is more deeply rooted than local control over the operation of schools; local autonomy has long been thought essential both to the maintenance of community concern and support for public schools and to the quality of the educational process.... [A] review of the scope and character of these local powers indicates the extent to which the interdistrict remedy approved by the two courts could disrupt and alter the structure of public education in Michigan. *Milliken*, 418 U.S. at 742-43.

Justice White, one of the four dissenters in *Milliken*, noted:

> The core of my disagreement is that deliberate acts of segregation and their consequences will go unremedied, not because a remedy would be infeasible or unreasonable in terms of the usual criteria governing school desegregation cases, but because an effective remedy would cause what the Court considers to be undue administrative inconvenience to the State. The result is that the State of Michigan, the entity at which the Fourteenth Amendment is directed, has successfully insulated itself from its duty to provide effective desegregation remedies by vesting sufficient power over its public schools in its local school districts. If this is the case in Michigan, it will be the case in most States. *Id.* at 763 (White, J., dissenting).

After *Milliken*, the Supreme Court began a pattern of issuing rulings that effectively narrowed the equity powers of federal district court judges as to both the breadth of desegregation orders as well as the scope of discretion by which these judges would evaluate compliance with the orders.

The decision in 1976 in *Pasadena City Board of Education v. Spangler* 427 U.S. 424 (1976) encouraged an extension of the *Milliken* non-responsibility rationale through application of the de facto/de jure dichotomy. In *Spangler*, the Court reversed the ruling of the district and circuit courts that continued the supervision of the district court on pupil assignments in the Pasadena School District. The district court based its decision, in part, on "a 3-year pattern of opposition by a number of the members of the Board of Education to both the spirit and letter" of the desegregation plan. *Id.* at 442 (Marshall, J., dissenting). This finding served as a counterpoint to the fact that the school district had achieved the pupil assignment goals set in the plan during the first year. Thereafter, the pupil assignment goal, that there be no school in the district with a majority of any minority students, was not met. Goals set in other areas, including hiring and promoting teachers and administrators, were also not met.

The *Spangler* Court, however, decided that the initial year of compliance with the goal justified restriction on the equity powers of the court. The key to the Court's logic was the fact that the shift away from the pupil attendance goals "resulted from people randomly moving into, out of, and around the PUSD [Pasadena Unified School District] area." *Spangler*, 427 U.S. at 435-36. The Court ruled that one year of compliance was enough to take the issue of pupil assignments out of the remedial authority of the courts. "For having once implemented a racially neutral attendance pattern in order to remedy the perceived constitutional violations on the part of the defendants, the District Court had fully performed its function...." *Id.* at 436-37.

After *Swann*, *Milliken*, and *Spangler*, federal district courts were hard pressed to fashion effective desegregation plans. Demographic changes, combined with the reorganization of state educational systems into literally hundreds of local and independent school districts, left judges tinkering with remedies in school districts that were mostly minority and primarily poor. Some observer of these events concluded that the Supreme Court had simply changed its jurisprudence to fit its conclusion that busing, the most common remedy at the time, was not desirable as a solution to educational equality problems arising from racial classifications. *See* Robert A. Sedler, Metropolitan Desegregation in the Wake of Milliken: The View Largely From Within, 1975 Wash. U. L.Q. 535; Leonard P. Strickman, School Desegregation at the Crossroads, 70 Nw. U. L. Rev. 725 (1975).

Sheryll D. Cashin: American Public Schools Fifty Years After *Brown*: A Separate and Unequal Reality, 47 How. L.J. 341 (2004)[*]

Public schools became more segregated in the 1990s. More so than our neighborhoods, our schools are bastions of race and class privilege on the one hand, and race and class disadvantage on the other. Black and Latino schoolchildren are bearing the heaviest costs of this separation. They tend to be relegated to high-poverty; overwhelmingly minority schools that are characterized by poorer test scores, less experienced teachers, and fewer resources than the type of public schools most white children attend. This Essay argues that public schooling has become the "great equalizer" in America because it tends to place white children in predominantly white middle class schools and black and Latino children in predominantly minority, heavily poor schools.

We have come full circle since the momentous decision of *Brown v. Board of Education*. Issued on May 17, 1954, it has entered the psyche and lexicon of average Americans everywhere. *Brown* is the one Supreme Court decision that most school children can easily identify. The other might be *Roe v. Wade*, or, more ignominiously, *Dred Scott v. Sandford.* As I write this Essay, a national commission created by the Bush Administration is planning a series of events to celebrate the decision's semi-centennial anniversary. Everyone, with the exception of certain radical political factions or fringe elements of American society, now venerates, or at least pretends to venerate, the opinion which repudiated the principle of "separate but equal." In four short pages, the Supreme Court unanimously overturned a nearly sixty-year old standard, announced in *Plessy v. Ferguson*, that "separate but equal" would do for black people under the United States Constitution's Equal Protection Clause. *Plessy's* insidious edict ultimately legitimated Jim Crow segregation in all manners of human discourse, from the "Whites-only" train coaches at issue in *Plessy*, to other public accommodations, including housing, voting, and of course, public education.

The *Brown* Court stopped short of saying that separate but equal was illegitimate in all spheres. It would take another decade-plus of civil rights struggle and federal legislation to embed that idea into our national way of being on "the Negro problem." *Brown* did, however, ignite a spark that enabled civil rights revolutionaries to envision and fight for a different America. The nine justices, or maybe Chief Justice Warren, the opinion's author, seemed most concerned with the effect of state-mandated segregation on the psyches of "Negro" children. It did not matter that their schools' physical facilities and other "tangible" factors such as school transportation or teacher qualifications might, at least in theory, be made equal. "To separate them from others of similar age and qualifications solely because of their race generates a feeling of inferiority as to their status in the community that may affect their hearts and minds in a way unlikely ever to be undone." So in public education, according to the *Brown* Court, "separate educational facilities are inherently

---

unequal" because of the feelings of inferiority they engender. The Court seemed swayed by the social science research of Dr. Kenneth Clark and others in demonstrating that such feelings of inferiority were in fact being cultivated in black children.

Implicitly, the Court was saying that state-sanctioned separation, even into ostensibly equal facilities, is what sends a message of inferiority to black children. This seems to be a point of general agreement in American society and the reason the decision is afforded near-sacred status in the annals of Supreme Court jurisprudence. It is now accepted common wisdom that state-sanctioned racial apartheid of school children or adults is both morally repugnant and inconsistent with the equality principles embodied in our Constitution's Equal Protection Clause. *Brown* is a decision which should make us proud of ourselves because it represents an idea that is fundamental to our democratic values. It recaptured or re-imagined the idea that there should be at least one institution in American society that provides a common experience of citizenship and equal opportunity, regardless of the lottery of birth. And yet, the idea and vision animating Brown could not be farther from the reality that is American public education today. Indeed, we are not even living up to the repugnant principle announced in *Plessy v. Ferguson*. Our schools are separate, but hardly equal.

Any sincere fifty-year celebration of *Brown v. Board of Education* could not occur without a deep ambivalence and a mourning of our collective failure to live up to the promise and vision that animated the decision.

With the loss of racial integration in schools, we are also creating economic homogeneity, which in turn is creating separate educational tracks that vary greatly in quality. The overlay of race and class for our children can be seen in the following national statistics for elementary school children in the 1999-2000 school year. Nationally, white elementary school students are in schools that are 30% poor. Asians children are in schools that are 43% poor. By contrast, black and Latino elementary children are in schools where two-thirds of their classmates are poor (65% for blacks, 66% for Latinos). Older students have similar experiences. Overall, the average black or Latino student attends classes where almost half of their peers receive free or reduced-price lunch. The average white student, on the other hand, attends schools where less than one in five of their peers are classified as poor.

The urban-suburban divide explains much of this class dichotomy. Primarily, black and Latino students attend urban schools. The middle classes of all races have been moving to suburbs, leaving behind large numbers of minority poor students, especially in the school districts of America's largest cities, and in older, distressed suburbs. The numbers in the nation's largest urban school districts are staggering. As of 2000, between 85-90% of the students in New York, Los Angeles, Chicago, Miami-Dade, and Houston—the five largest school central city districts—were minorities. Additionally, 96% of the students were minorities in Detroit, New Orleans and Santa Ana, as were 95% in Washington, DC, 92% in Dallas, and 88% in Baltimore. Overall, the twenty-seven largest school districts, which serve almost one-quarter of black and Latino public school students, have lost the vast majority of their white enrollment. Not surprisingly, a large percentage of the students remaining in urban school systems were poor. For example, in the five largest urban school systems, typically more than 70% of the students are eligible to receive free or reduced price lunch.

In sum, the average experience for white public school students is a middle-class experience while the average experience for black and Latino students is one of high or concentrated poverty. How we will live up to the equality premise, if not the integrationist premise of *Brown*, given our separated living patterns, is America's unique conundrum.

GRUTTER v. BOLLINGER
539 U.S. 306 (2003)

Justice O'Connor delivered the opinion of the Court.

This case requires us to decide whether the use of race as a factor in student admissions by the University of Michigan Law School (Law School) is unlawful.

I

A

The Law School ranks among the Nation's top law schools. It receives more than 3,500 applications each year for a class of around 350 students. Seeking to "admit a group of students who individually and collectively are among the most capable," the Law School looks for individuals with "substantial promise for success in law school" and "a strong likelihood of succeeding in the practice of law and contributing in diverse ways to the well-being of others." More broadly, the Law School seeks "a mix of students with varying backgrounds and experiences who will respect and learn from each other." In 1992, the dean of the Law School charged a faculty committee with crafting a written admissions policy to implement these goals. In particular, the Law School sought to ensure that its efforts to achieve student body diversity complied with this Court's most recent ruling on the use of race in university admissions. Upon the unanimous adoption of the committee's report by the Law School faculty, it became the Law School's official admissions policy.

The hallmark of that policy is its focus on academic ability coupled with a flexible assessment of applicants' talents, experiences, and potential "to contribute to the learning of those around them." The policy requires admissions officials to evaluate each applicant based on all the information available in the file, including a personal statement, letters of recommendation, and an essay describing the ways in which the applicant will contribute to the life and diversity of the Law School. In reviewing an applicant's file, admissions officials must consider the applicant's undergraduate grade point average (GPA) and Law School Admissions Test (LSAT) score because they are important (if imperfect) predictors of academic success in law school. The policy stresses that "no applicant should be admitted unless we expect that applicant to do well enough to graduate with no serious academic problems."

The policy makes clear, however, that even the highest possible score does not guarantee admission to the Law School. Nor does a low score automatically disqualify an applicant. Rather, the policy requires admissions officials to look beyond grades and test scores to other criteria that are important to the Law School's educational objectives. So-called "'soft' variables" such as "the enthusiasm of recommenders, the quality of the undergraduate institution, the quality of the applicant's essay, and the areas and difficulty of undergraduate course selection" are all brought to bear in assessing an "applicant's likely contributions to the intellectual and social life of the institution."

The policy does, however, reaffirm the Law School's longstanding commitment to "one particular type of diversity," that is, "racial and ethnic diversity with special reference to the inclusion of students from groups which have been historically discriminated against, like African-Americans, Hispanics and Native Americans, who without this commitment might not be represented in our student body in meaningful numbers." By enrolling a "'critical mass' of [underrepresented] minority students," the Law School seeks to "ensure their ability to make unique contributions to the character of the Law School."

The policy does not define diversity "solely in terms of racial and ethnic status." Nor is the policy "insensitive to the competition among all students for admission to the Law School." Rather, the policy seeks to guide admissions officers in "producing classes both diverse and academically outstanding, classes made up of students who promise to continue the tradition of outstanding contribution by Michigan Graduates to the legal profession."

Petitioner Barbara Grutter is a white Michigan resident who applied to the Law School in 1996 with a 3.8 grade point average and 161 LSAT score. The Law School initially placed petitioner on a waiting list, but subsequently rejected her application. In December 1997, petitioner filed suit in the United States District Court for the Eastern District of Michigan.

[T]he District Court concluded that the Law School's use of race as a factor in admissions decisions was unlawful. Applying strict scrutiny, the District Court determined that the Law School's asserted interest in assembling a diverse student body was not compelling because "the attainment of a racially diverse class . . . was not recognized as such by *Bakke* and is not a remedy for past discrimination." The District Court went on to hold that even if diversity were compelling, the Law School had not narrowly tailored its use of race to further that interest. The District Court granted petitioner's request for declaratory relief and enjoined the Law School from using race as a factor in its admissions decisions.... Sitting en banc, the Court of Appeals reversed the District Court's judgment and vacated the injunction.

II

A

Since this Court's splintered decision in *Bakke*, Justice Powell's opinion announcing the judgment of the Court has served as the touchstone for constitutional analysis of race-conscious admissions policies. Public and private universities across the Nation have modeled their own admissions programs on Justice Powell's views on permissible race-conscious policies.

****

Justice Powell approved the university's use of race to further only one interest: "the attainment of a diverse student body." With the important proviso that "constitutional limitations protecting individual rights may not be disregarded," Justice Powell grounded his analysis in the academic freedom that "long has been viewed as a special concern of the First Amendment." *Id.* at 312. Justice Powell emphasized that nothing less than the "'nation's future depends upon leaders trained through wide exposure' to the ideas and mores of students as diverse as this Nation of many peoples." *Id.* at 313. In seeking the "right to select those students who will contribute the most to the 'robust exchange of ideas,'" a university seeks "to achieve a goal that is of paramount importance in the fulfillment of its mission." 438 U.S. at 313. Both "tradition and experience lend support to the view that the contribution of diversity is substantial." *Ibid.*

Justice Powell was, however, careful to emphasize that in his view race "is only one element in a range of factors a university properly may consider in attaining the goal of a heterogeneous student body." *Id.* at 314... For Justice Powell, "it is not an interest in simple ethnic diversity, in which a specified percentage of the student body is in effect guaranteed to be members of selected ethnic groups," that can justify the use of race. *Id.* at 315. Rather, "the diversity that furthers a compelling state interest encompasses a far broader array of qualifications and characteristics of which racial or ethnic origin is but a single though important element." *Ibid.*

****

Strict scrutiny is not "strict in theory, but fatal in fact." Although all governmental uses of race are subject to strict scrutiny, not all are invalidated by it. As we have explained, whenever the government treats any person unequally because of his or her race, that person has suffered an injury that falls squarely within the language and spirit of the Constitution's guarantee of equal protection. But that observation says nothing about the ultimate validity of any particular law; that determination is the job of the court applying strict scrutiny. When race-based action is necessary to further a compelling governmental interest, such action does not violate the constitutional guarantee of equal protection so long as the narrow-tailoring requirement is also satisfied.

****

Today, we hold that the Law School has a compelling interest in attaining a diverse student body.... The Law School's educational judgment that such diversity is essential to its educational mission is one to which we defer. The Law School's assessment that diversity will, in fact, yield educational benefits is substantiated by respondents and their amici. Our scrutiny of the interest asserted by the

Law School is no less strict for taking into account complex educational judgments in an area that lies primarily within the expertise of the university. Our holding today is in keeping with our tradition of giving a degree of deference to a university's academic decisions, within constitutionally prescribed limits. As part of its goal of "assembling a class that is both exceptionally academically qualified and broadly diverse, "the Law School seeks to "enroll a 'critical mass' of minority students." ... These benefits are substantial. As the District Court emphasized, the Law School's admissions policy promotes "cross-racial understanding," helps to break down racial stereotypes, and "enables [students] to better understand persons of different races." ... In addition to the expert studies and reports entered into evidence at trial, numerous studies show that student body diversity promotes learning outcomes, and "better prepares students for an increasingly diverse workforce and society, and better prepares them as professionals."

****

B

Even in the limited circumstance when drawing racial distinctions is permissible to further a compelling state interest, government is still constrained in how it may pursue that end: [T]he means chosen to accomplish the [government's] asserted purpose must be specifically and narrowly framed to accomplish that purpose. ... Since Bakke, we have had no occasion to define the contours of the narrow-tailoring inquiry with respect to race-conscious university admissions programs....

To be narrowly tailored, a race-conscious admissions program cannot use a quota system—it cannot "insulate each category of applicants with certain desired qualifications from competition with all other applicants." *Bakke*, *supra*, at 315, (opinion of Powell, J.). Instead, a university may consider race or ethnicity only as a "'plus' in a particular applicant's file," without "insulating the individual from comparison with all other candidates for the available seats." *Id.* at 317. In other words, an admissions program must be "flexible enough to consider all pertinent elements of diversity in light of the particular qualifications of each applicant, and to place them on the same footing for consideration, although not necessarily according them the same weight." *Ibid.*

We are satisfied that the Law School's admissions program, like the Harvard plan described by Justice Powell, does not operate as a quota. Properly understood, a "quota" is a program in which a certain fixed number or proportion of opportunities are "reserved exclusively for certain minority groups." *Richmond v. J. A. Croson Co.*, *supra*, at 496. Quotas "'impose a fixed number or percentage which must be attained, or which cannot be exceeded,'" *Local 28 of Sheet Metal Workers' Int'l Ass'n v. EEOC*, 478 U.S. 421, 495 (1986) and "insulate the individual from comparison with all other candidates for the available seats." *Bakke*, *supra*, at 317. (opinion of Powell, J.). In contrast, "a permissible goal . . . requires only a good-faith effort . . . to come within a range demarcated by the goal itself," *Sheet Metal Workers v. EEOC*, *supra*, at 495 and permits consideration of race as a "plus" factor in any given case while still ensuring that each candidate "competes with all other qualified applicants," *Johnson v. Transportation Agency, Santa Clara Cty.*, 480 U.S. 616, 638 (1987).

****

The Law School's current admissions program considers race as one factor among many, in an effort to assemble a student body that is diverse in ways broader than race. Because a lottery would make that kind of nuanced judgment impossible, it would effectively sacrifice all other educational values, not to mention every other kind of diversity. .... We are satisfied that the Law School adequately considered race-neutral alternatives currently capable of producing a critical mass without forcing the Law School to abandon the academic selectivity that is the cornerstone of its educational mission.

****

We take the Law School at its word that it would "like nothing better than to find a race-neutral admissions formula" and will terminate its race-conscious admissions program as soon as practicable. It has been 25 years since Justice Powell first approved the use of race to further an interest in student body diversity in the context of public higher education. Since that time, the number of minority applicants with high grades and test scores has indeed increased. We expect that 25 years from now, the use of racial preferences will no longer be necessary to further the interest approved today.

IV

The judgment of the Court of Appeals for the Sixth Circuit, accordingly, is affirmed.

Chief Justice Rehnquist, with whom Justice Scalia, Justice Kennedy, and Justice Thomas join, dissenting.

I agree with the Court that, "in the limited circumstance when drawing racial distinctions is permissible," the government must ensure that its means are narrowly tailored to achieve a compelling state interest. I do not believe, however, that the University of Michigan Law School's (Law School) means are narrowly tailored to the interest it asserts.

Although the Court recites the language of our strict scrutiny analysis, its application of that review is unprecedented in its deference.

.....

I do not believe that the Constitution gives the Law School such free rein in the use of race. The Law School has offered no explanation for its actual admissions practices and, unexplained, we are bound to conclude that the Law School has managed its admissions program, not to achieve a "critical mass," but to extend offers of admission to members of selected minority groups in proportion to their statistical representation in the applicant pool. But this is precisely the type of racial balancing that the Court itself calls "patently unconstitutional."

Finally, I believe that the Law School's program fails strict scrutiny because it is devoid of any reasonably precise time limit on the Law School's use of race in admissions. ... The Court suggests a possible 25-year limitation on the Law School's current program. Respondents, on the other hand, remain more ambiguous. Thus, an important component of strict scrutiny—that a program be limited in time—is casually subverted.

Justice Kennedy, dissenting.

The Court, in a review that is nothing short of perfunctory, accepts the University of Michigan Law School's assurances that its admissions process meets with constitutional requirements.

The Court's refusal to apply meaningful strict scrutiny will lead to serious consequences. By deferring to the law schools' choice of minority admissions programs, the courts will lose the talents and resources of the faculties and administrators in devising new and fairer ways to ensure individual consideration. … If universities are given the latitude to administer programs that are tantamount to quotas, they will have few incentives to make the existing minority admissions schemes transparent and protective of individual review. The unhappy consequence will be to perpetuate the hostilities that proper consideration of race is designed to avoid.

Justice Scalia, with whom Justice Thomas joins, concurring in part and dissenting in part.

I join the opinion of The Chief Justice. …I also join Parts I through VII of Justice Thomas's opinion. I find particularly unanswerable his central point: that the allegedly "compelling state interest" at issue here is not the incremental "educational benefit" that emanates from the fabled "critical mass" of minority students, but rather Michigan's interest in maintaining a "prestige" law school whose normal admissions standards disproportionately exclude blacks and other minorities. If that is a compelling state interest, everything is.

Justice Thomas, with whom Justice Scalia joins as to Parts I-VII, concurring in part and dissenting in part.

A close reading of the Court's opinion reveals that all of its legal work is done through one conclusory statement: The Law School has a "compelling interest in securing the educational benefits of a diverse student body." *Ante*, at 156. No serious effort is made to explain how these benefits fit with the state interests the Court has recognized (or rejected) as compelling, or to place any theoretical constraints on an enterprising court's desire to discover still more justifications for racial discrimination.

Under the proper standard, there is no pressing public necessity in maintaining a public law school at all and, it follows, certainly not an elite law school. Likewise, marginal improvements in legal education do not qualify as a compelling state interest.

…..

The Court bases its unprecedented deference to the Law School—a deference antithetical to strict scrutiny—on an idea of "educational autonomy" grounded in the First Amendment. Ante, at 156.

In my view, there is no basis for a right of public universities to do what would otherwise violate the Equal Protection Clause.

PARENTS INVOLVED IN COMMUNITY SCHOOLS v. SEATTLE SCHOOL DISTRICT NO. 1
551 U.S. 701 (2007)

Chief Justice Roberts announced the judgment of the Court, and delivered the opinion of the Court with respect to Parts I, II, III-A, and III-C, and an opinion with respect to Parts III-B and IV, in which Justices Scalia, Thomas, and Alito join.

The school districts in these cases voluntarily adopted student assignment plans that rely upon race to determine which public schools certain children may attend. The Seattle school district classifies children as white or nonwhite; the Jefferson County school district as black or "other." In Seattle, this racial classification is used to allocate slots in oversubscribed high schools. In Jefferson County, it is used to make certain elementary school assignments and to rule on transfer requests. In each case, the school district relies upon an individual student's race in assigning that student to a particular school, so that the racial balance at the school falls within a predetermined range based on the racial composition of the school district as a whole. Parents of students denied assignment to particular schools under these plans solely because of their race brought suit, contending that allocating children to different public schools on the basis of race violated the Fourteenth Amendment guarantee of equal protection. The Courts of Appeals below upheld the plans. We granted certiorari, and now reverse.

I

Both cases present the same underlying legal question—whether a public school that had not operated legally segregated schools or has been found to be unitary may choose to classify students by race and rely upon that classification in making school assignments.

Seattle School District No. 1 operates 10 regular public high schools. In 1998, it adopted the plan at issue in this case for assigning students to these schools. The plan allows incoming ninth graders to choose from among any of the district's high schools, ranking however many schools they wish in order of preference.

Some schools are more popular than others. If too many students list the same school as their first choice, the district employs a series of "tiebreakers" to determine who will fill the open slots at the oversubscribed school. The first tiebreaker selects for admission students who have a sibling currently enrolled in the chosen school. The next tiebreaker depends upon the racial composition of the particular school and the race of the individual student. In the district's public schools approximately 41 percent of enrolled students are white; the remaining 59 percent, comprising all other racial groups, are classified by Seattle for assignment purposes as nonwhite. If an oversubscribed school is not within 10 percentage points of the district's overall white/nonwhite racial balance, it is what the district calls "integration positive," and the district employs a tiebreaker that selects for assignment students whose race "will serve to bring the school into balance."

Seattle...employs the racial tiebreaker in an attempt to address the effects of racially identifiable housing patterns on school assignments. Most white students live in the northern part of Seattle, most students of other racial backgrounds in the southern part.

****

Jefferson County Public Schools operates the public school system in metropolitan Louisville, Kentucky. ..... Approximately 34 percent of the district's 97,000 students are black; most of the remaining 66 percent are white. The plan requires all nonmagnet schools to maintain a minimum black enrollment of 15 percent, and a maximum black enrollment of 50 percent. If a school has reached the "extremes of the racial guidelines," a student whose race would contribute to the school's racial imbalance will not be assigned there. Transfers may be requested for any number of reasons, and may be denied because of lack of available space or on the basis of the racial guidelines.

****

III

A

[O]ur prior cases, in evaluating the use of racial classifications in the school context, have recognized two interests that qualify as compelling. The first is the compelling interest of remedying the effects of past intentional discrimination. *See Freeman v. Pitts*, 503 U.S. 467, 494 (1992). Yet the Seattle public schools have not shown that they were ever segregated by law, and were not subject to court-ordered desegregation decrees. The Jefferson County public schools were previously segregated by law and were subject to a desegregation decree entered in 1975. In 2000, the District Court that entered that decree dissolved it, finding that Jefferson County had "eliminated the vestiges associated with the former policy of segregation and its pernicious effects," and thus had achieved "unitary" status. Jefferson County accordingly does not rely upon an interest in remedying the effects of past intentional discrimination in defending its present use of race in assigning students.

The second government interest we have recognized as compelling for purposes of strict scrutiny is the interest in diversity in higher education upheld in *Grutter*, 539 U.S., at 328. The specific interest found compelling in *Grutter* was student body diversity "in the context of higher education." *Ibid.* The diversity interest was not focused on race alone but encompassed "all factors that may contribute to student body diversity." *Id.* at 337. We described the various types of diversity that the law school sought:

> "[The law school's] policy makes clear there are many possible bases for diversity admissions, and provides examples of admittees who have lived or traveled widely abroad, are fluent in several languages, have overcome personal adversity and family hardship, have exceptional records of extensive community service, and have had successful careers in other fields." *Id.* at 338.

In the present cases, by contrast, race is not considered as part of a broader effort to achieve "exposure to widely diverse people, cultures, ideas, and viewpoints," *ibid.*; race, for some students, is determinative standing alone. The districts argue that other factors, such as student preferences, affect assignment decisions under their plans, but under each plan when race comes into play, it is decisive by itself. It is not simply one factor weighed with others in reaching a decision, as in *Grutter*; it is the factor. Like the University of Michigan undergraduate plan struck down in *Gratz*, 539 U.S., at 275, the plans here "do not provide for a meaningful individualized review of applicants" but instead rely on racial classifications in a "nonindividualized, mechanical" way. *Id.*, at 276, 280 (O'Connor, J., concurring).

Even when it comes to race, the plans here employ only a limited notion of diversity, viewing race exclusively in white/nonwhite terms in Seattle and black/"other" terms in Jefferson County.... It is hard to understand how a plan that could allow these results can be viewed as being concerned with achieving enrollment that is "'broadly diverse,'" *Grutter*, *supra*, at 329...... The present cases are not governed by *Grutter*.

B

Perhaps recognizing that reliance on *Grutter* cannot sustain their plans, both school districts assert additional interests, distinct from the interest upheld in *Grutter*, to justify their race-based assignments. In briefing and argument before this Court, Seattle contends that its use of race helps to reduce racial concentration in schools and to ensure that racially concentrated housing patterns do not prevent nonwhite students from having access to the most desirable schools. Jefferson County has articulated a similar goal, phrasing its interest in terms of educating its students "in a racially integrated environment." Each school district argues that educational and broader socialization benefits flow from a racially diverse learning environment, and each contends that because the diversity they seek is racial diversity—not the broader diversity at issue in *Grutter*—it makes sense to promote that interest directly by relying on race alone.

The plans are tied to each district's specific racial demographics, rather than to any pedagogic concept of the level of diversity needed to obtain the asserted educational benefits. .....The districts offer no evidence that the level of racial diversity necessary to achieve the asserted educational benefits happens to coincide with the racial demographics of the respective school districts—or rather the white/nonwhite or black/"other" balance of the districts, since that is the only diversity addressed by the plans.

This working backward to achieve a particular type of racial balance, rather than working forward from some demonstration of the level of diversity that provides the purported benefits, is a fatal flaw under our existing precedent. .....Accepting racial balancing as a compelling state interest would justify the imposition of racial proportionality throughout American society, contrary to our repeated recognition that] "[a]t the heart of the Constitution's guarantee of equal protection lies the simple command that the Government must treat citizens as individuals, not as simply components of a racial, religious, sexual or national class." *Miller v. Johnson*, 515 U.S. 900, 911 (1995) (quoting *Metro Broadcasting*, 497 U.S., at 602 (O'Connor, J., dissenting).

C

While we do not suggest that greater use of race would be preferable, the minimal impact of the districts' racial classifications on school enrollment casts doubt on the necessity of using racial classifications. In *Grutter*, the consideration of race was viewed as indispensable in more than tripling minority representation at the law school—from 4 to 14.5 percent.

The districts have also failed to show that they considered methods other than explicit racial classifications to achieve their stated goals. Narrow tailoring requires "serious, good faith consideration of workable race-neutral alternatives," *Grutter*, *supra*, at 339, and yet in Seattle several alternative assignment plans—many of which would not have used express racial classifications—were rejected with little or no consideration. Jefferson County has failed to present any evidence that it considered alternatives, even though the district already claims that its goals are achieved primarily through means other than the racial classifications.

IV

.....

Before *Brown*, schoolchildren were told where they could and could not go to school based on the color of their skin. The school districts in these cases have not carried the heavy burden of demonstrating that we should allow this once again—even for very different reasons. For schools that never segregated on the basis of race, such as Seattle, or that have removed the vestiges of past segregation, such as Jefferson County, the way "to achieve a system of determining admission to the public schools on a nonracial basis," *Brown II*, 349 U.S., at 300-301, is to stop assigning students on a racial basis. The way to stop discrimination on the basis of race is to stop discriminating on the basis of race.

The judgments of the Courts of Appeals for the Sixth and Ninth Circuits are reversed, and the cases are remanded for further proceedings.

Justice Kennedy, concurring in part and concurring in the judgment.

Diversity, depending on its meaning and definition, is a compelling educational goal a school district may pursue.

.....

This is by way of preface to my respectful submission that parts of the opinion by The Chief Justice imply an all-too-unyielding insistence that race cannot be a factor in instances when, in my view, it may be taken into account. The plurality opinion is too dismissive of the legitimate interest government has in ensuring all people have equal opportunity regardless of their race. ... The plurality opinion is at least open to the interpretation that the Constitution requires school districts to ignore the problem of de facto resegregation in schooling. I cannot endorse that conclusion. To the extent the plurality opinion suggests the Constitution mandates that state and local school authorities must accept the status quo of racial isolation in schools, it is, in my view, profoundly mistaken.

In the administration of public schools by the state and local authorities it is permissible to consider the racial makeup of schools and to adopt general policies to encourage a diverse student body, one aspect of which is its racial composition. If school authorities are concerned that the student-body compositions of certain schools interfere with the objective of offering an equal educational opportunity to all of their students, they are free to devise race-conscious measures to address the problem in a general way and without treating each student in different fashion solely on the basis of a systematic, individual typing by race.

School boards may pursue the goal of bringing together students of diverse backgrounds and races through other means, including strategic site selection of new schools; drawing attendance zones with general recognition of the demographics of neighborhoods; allocating resources for special programs; recruiting students and faculty in a targeted fashion; and tracking enrollments, performance, and other statistics by race. These mechanisms are race conscious but do not lead to different treatment based on a classification that tells each student he or she is to be defined by race, so it is unlikely any of them would demand strict scrutiny to be found permissible. *See Bush v. Vera*, 517 U.S. 952, 958, (1996) (plurality opinion) ("Strict scrutiny does not apply merely because redistricting is performed with consciousness of race. . . . Electoral district lines are 'facially race neutral' so a more searching inquiry is necessary before strict scrutiny can be found applicable in redistricting cases than in cases of 'classifications based explicitly on race'"(quoting *Adarand*, 515 U.S., at 213)). Executive and legislative branches, which for generations now have considered these types of policies and procedures, should be permitted to employ them with candor and with confidence that a constitutional violation does not occur whenever a decision maker considers the impact a given approach might have on students of different races. Assigning to each student a personal designation according to a crude system of individual racial classifications is quite a different matter; and the legal analysis changes accordingly.

Each respondent has asserted that its assignment of individual students by race is permissible because there is no other way to avoid racial isolation in the school districts. Yet, as explained, each has failed to provide the support necessary for that proposition. *Cf. Croson*, 488 U.S., at 501, 109 S. Ct. 706, 102 L. Ed. 2d 854 ("The history of racial classifications in this country suggests that blind judicial deference to legislative or executive pronouncements of necessity has no place in equal protection analysis"). And individual racial classifications employed in this manner may be considered legitimate only if they are a last resort to achieve a compelling interest. *See Id.* at 519, 109 S. Ct. 706, 102 L. Ed. 2d 854 (Kennedy, J., concurring in part and concurring in judgment).

In the cases before us it is noteworthy that the number of students whose assignment depends on express racial classifications is limited. [I]n the context of these plans, the small number of assignments affected suggests that the schools could have achieved their stated ends through different means. These include the facially race-neutral means set forth above or, if necessary, a more nuanced, individual evaluation of school needs and student characteristics that might include race as a component. The latter approach would be informed by *Grutter*, though of course the criteria relevant to student placement would differ based on the age of the students, the needs of the parents, and the role of the schools.

.....

The decision today should not prevent school districts from continuing the important work of bringing together students of different racial, ethnic, and economic backgrounds. Due to a variety of factors—some influenced by government, some not—neighborhoods in our communities do not reflect the diversity of our Nation as a whole. Those entrusted with directing our public schools can bring to bear the creativity of experts, parents, administrators, and other concerned citizens to find a way to achieve the compelling interests they face without resorting to widespread governmental allocation of benefits and burdens on the basis of racial classifications.

With this explanation I concur in the judgment of the Court.

Notes and Comments

1. Affirmative Action K-12 after Grutter, Gratz and Seattle School District No. 1
In what manner does affirmative action survive after these cases? Is the Michigan Law School policy easily adaptable for other institutions of higher education? Is diversity a compelling interest in primary and secondary schools?

Give special attention to the concurring opinion by Justice Kennedy in Seattle School District No. 1. His vote controls the outcome of the plurality decision and sheds light on how K-12 schools might respond to the ruling. Do you agree with Justice Kennedy's suggestions on how diversity might properly be brought into education policymaking? Would the Court still apply strict scrutiny to such plans?

2. Affirmative Action and State Constitutions
States, through their constitutions, may provide a greater level of protection for individual rights. *See Michigan v. Long*, 463 U.S. 1032 (1983) (Right to be free form unreasonable search and seizure subject to upgrade under state law with a plain statement).

After *Grutter*, several states have asked voters to amend their constitution to end affirmative action by preventing preferential treatment based on race, sex, color ethnicity or national origin in the areas of public employment, education and contracting. Voters have approved affirmative action bans in California, Michigan, Nebraska and Washington State. In Colorado, voters rejected such a proposal. The movement against affirmative action is led and funded primarily by the California-based American Civil Rights Institute, run by Ward Connerly, a former University of California regent.

The impact of these bans on student admissions is not yet clear. In Michigan, two years after the ban took effect, student enrollments varied. At Wayne State University minority medical student enrollment dropped from 43 to 14 between 2006 and 2008, but law school enrollment increased from 20 in 2006 to 24 in 2008. The University of Michigan also maintained its diversity. In 2008, the freshman class at the University of Michigan showed a 12% increase in the number of African Americans out of 5,992 students. The percentage of non-minority students in the 2008 freshman class held steady at 65.6 %.

After *Grutter*, several alternatives exist to race-based student preferences. Colleges and universities may target minority students in their recruitment efforts by concentrating on geographic areas, schools and counselors at high schools that have large minority populations. In addition, state legislators can modify the admissions process to increase the pool of qualified minority students. Under Texas law, in-state students are guaranteed admission to any state university ranked in the top 10 percent of their graduating high school class. (*See* Tex. Educ. Code § 51.803). California has a similar plan that targets the top four percent. Florida's guaranteed admissions plan applies to the top twenty percent. Schools can also target minority students through scholarship programs designed to target high schools in economically disadvantaged areas.

II. Alienage Discrimination

PLYLER v. DOE
457 U.S. 202 (1982)

[This case is reported in Chapter Three on page 164]

Stuart Biegel: The Wisdom of *Plyler v. Doe*,
17 Chicano-Latino L. Rev. 46 (1995)*

The *Plyler* Court determined that a Texas law prohibiting undocumented children from attending public schools infringed upon the important interests of a burdened class. In doing so, the Court based its reasoning on the emerging heightened scrutiny jurisprudence in federal Equal Protection Clause cases.

Although the Court was unwilling to extend the rationale of *Plyler* to a different set of facts in 1988 [*Kadramas v. Dickinson Public Schools*, 487 U.S. 459 (1988)], prospective plaintiffs in a school choice context may find the federal courts much more receptive today. The gulf between the "haves" and the "have-nots" in America continues to widen, and federal judges may very well decide that it is time to step in and help reverse this dangerous trend.

. . . .

A Fourteenth Amendment case can be built by employing *Plyler v. Doe* and other recent cases where the Court covertly applied heightened scrutiny. Read together with these cases, *Plyler* stands for the proposition that the federal courts will apply an intermediate level of review under the Equal Protection Clause to protect burdened classes that have been denied important interests. The "fundamental rights" approach set forth by the Court identifies a disadvantaged class of children and documents the extent to which they have been deprived of an education. The extent and nature of the deprivation of equal education opportunity appears to determine whether heightened scrutiny applies.

A. The Implicated Class: Children of Poverty

The Fourteenth Amendment heightened scrutiny framework requires the identification of a disadvantaged class. To qualify as a group that has been burdened in this manner, plaintiffs must be "a discrete class of children not accountable for their disabling status."

Poor families challenging tuition requirements, additional fees for educational services in a publicly funded choice program, or both, would be likely to qualify as a disadvantaged class for equal protection purposes. The existence of a growing underclass of students who are not accountable for their low socioeconomic status has been documented in great detail by the Panel on High-Risk Youth of the Commission on Behavioral and Social Sciences and Education. Such young people would certainly not have the resources available to fund any part of their education in either a public school or a private school choice context. These students would argue that by virtue of their disabling status they are denied equal access to quality education in a deregulated school setting.

B. Documenting the Deprivation of an Important Interest

Under the Equal Protection Clause, heightened scrutiny is triggered only if both a burdened class and an important interest have been identified. The *Plyler* Court recognized unequivocally that education is an important interest. Yet such recognition is merely the beginning of the analysis.

Both the extent of the deprivation generally and the denial of equal educational opportunity specifically must be explored.

1. The Extent of the Deprivation

Federal courts often ask whether the injury sustained by plaintiff in a Fourteenth Amendment education case is absolute or relative. …An absolute deprivation of education is likely to result in a victory for the plaintiffs in a school choice lawsuit. It is unclear, however, whether tuition or other fee requirements are an absolute or a relative deprivation. Parents of disenfranchised children will argue that a deregulated choice system absolutely deprives them of education at the best schools when they are unable to attend because they cannot afford the balance of the tuition or come up with the additional fees. Defendants will contend, however, that the deprivation is only relative since the children can always attend some school.

2. The Denial of Equal Educational Opportunity

Under *Plyler*, a two-part analysis is employed to ascertain the nature of the denial of equal opportunity. First, did the policy or practice constitute an unreasonable obstacle to advancement on the basis of individual merit? Second, what are the consequences of the deprivation for both the individual and society? ... A denial of equal educational opportunity occurs when "barriers present unreasonable obstacles to advancement on the basis of individual merit."

The Supreme Court warned in *Plyler* that "we cannot ignore the significant social costs borne by our Nation when select groups are denied the means to absorb the values and skills upon which our social order rests." Such costs include the adverse effects on the economy of a poorly trained work force, and the breakdown of social order when angry, frustrated, and unsuccessful students leave school and turn increasingly to violence and crime. All Americans are adversely affected when publicly funded schools fail to address the needs of today's young people. Therefore, the deprivation results in an enormous cost to society.

Once a burdened class and an important interest in education have been identified, plaintiffs employing the Fourteenth Amendment must address the nature of the denial of equal educational opportunity by employing the *Plyler* two-part analysis. First, did the policy or practice constitute an unreasonable obstacle to advancement on the basis of individual merit? Second, what are the consequences of the deprivation for both the individual and society?

Under *Plyler*, a denial of equal educational opportunity has occurred when "barriers present [] unreasonable obstacles to advancement on the basis of individual merit." Plaintiffs challenging academic requirements of secondary schools in a choice program would argue that admissions decisions based on prior academic performance create unreasonable obstacles to achieving an education. Defendants would counter, however, that decisions based on performance in school are completely consistent with the apparent "right of advancement based on individual merit" set forth by Justice Brennan. Indeed, what better indicators of individual merit are there in a school setting?

Whether these "obstacles" are deemed unreasonable is likely to depend on the existence of viable alternatives. Plaintiff may suggest that not all applicants to secondary schools should have to demonstrate ability or achievement. If the new choice system is to be fair and equitable, care must be taken to ensure that it does not become completely stratified. Students who are not doing as well as others must be accommodated. Either a certain number of places should be reserved at every school for students who have not been successful, or admissions decisions should not be based on merit at all.

Plyler is much more than simply a unique confluence of theories that was cobbled together to fit the facts of the Texas litigation. Indeed, *Plyler* ... can serve as the framework for a variety of lawsuits that might be filed by economically disadvantaged plaintiffs in an education setting. The recent proliferation of school choice programs for both public and private school students presents only one possible avenue of litigation in this regard.

Plyler v. Doe sets forth a viable, principled approach for resolving constitutional disputes by balancing the interests of the plaintiffs against the interests of the public entities. After examining the *Plyler* decision in light of other major cases that have employed a similar approach, members of the federal judiciary must think twice before deciding that *Plyler* is no longer a controlling precedent.

MARTINEZ v. BYNUM
461 U.S. 321 (1983)

JUSTICE POWELL delivered the opinion of the Court.

This case involves a facial challenge to the constitutionality of the Texas residency requirement governing minors who wish to attend public free schools while living apart from their parents or guardians.

I

Roberto Morales was born in 1969 in McAllen, Texas, and is thus a United States citizen by birth. His parents are Mexican citizens who reside in Reynosa, Mexico. He left Reynosa in 1977 and returned to McAllen to live with his sister, petitioner Oralia Martinez, for the primary purpose of attending school in the McAllen Independent School District. Although Martinez is now his custodian, she is not—and does not desire to become—his guardian. As a result, Morales is not entitled to tuition-free admission to the McAllen schools. ...Respondent McAllen Independent School District therefore denied Morales' application for admission in the fall of 1977.

****

After a hearing on the merits, the District Court granted judgment for the defendants. The court concluded that § 21.031(d) was justified by the State's "legitimate interest in protecting and preserving the quality of its educational system and the right of its own bona fide residents to attend state schools on a preferred tuition basis." In an appeal by two plaintiffs, the United States Court of Appeals for the Fifth Circuit affirmed. In view of the importance of the issue, we granted certiorari. We now affirm.

II

This Court frequently has considered constitutional challenges to residence requirements. On several occasions the Court has invalidated requirements that condition receipt of a benefit on a minimum period of residence within a jurisdiction, but it always has been careful to distinguish such durational residence requirements from bona fide residence requirements. ... This was not an empty distinction. JUSTICE MARSHALL, writing for the Court, again emphasized that "States have the power to require that voters be bona fide residents of the relevant political subdivision." *Id.* at 343. …

We specifically have approved bona fide residence requirements in the field of public education. The Connecticut statute before us in *Vlandis v. Kline*, 412 U.S. 441 (1973), for example, was unconstitutional because it created an irrebuttable presumption of nonresidency for state university students whose legal addresses were outside of the State before they applied for admission. The statute violated the Due Process Clause because it in effect classified some bona fide state residents as nonresidents for tuition purposes. But we "fully [recognized] that a State has a legitimate interest in protecting and preserving . . . the right of its own bona fide residents to attend [its colleges and universities] on a preferential tuition basis." *Id.*, at 452-453. This "legitimate interest" permits a "State [to] establish such reasonable criteria for in-state status as to make virtually certain that students who are not, in fact, bona fide residents of the State, but who have come there solely for educational purposes, cannot take advantage of the in-state rates." *Id.* at 453-454. …

A bona fide residence requirement, appropriately defined and uniformly applied, furthers the substantial state interest in assuring that services provided for its residents are enjoyed only by residents. Such a requirement with respect to attendance in public free schools does not violate the Equal Protection Clause of the Fourteenth Amendment. It does not burden or penalize the constitutional right of interstate travel, for any person is free to move to a State and to establish residence there. A bona fide residence requirement simply requires that the person does establish residence before demanding the services that are restricted to residents.

****

III

The central question we must decide here is whether § 21.031(d) is a bona fide residence requirement. Although the meaning may vary according to context, residence" generally requires both physical presence and an intention to remain. As the Supreme Court of Maine explained over a century ago:

"When . . . a person voluntarily takes up his abode in a given place, with intention to remain permanently, or for an indefinite period of time; or, to speak more accurately, when a person takes up his abode in a given place, without any present intention to remove there from, such place of abode becomes his residence. . . ." *Inhabitants of Warren v. Inhabitants of Thomaston*, 43 Me. 406, 418 (1857).

This classic two-part definition of residence has been recognized as a minimum standard in a wide range of contexts time and time again.

****

Section 21.031 is far more generous than this traditional standard. It compels a school district to permit a child such as Morales to attend school without paying tuition if he has a bona fide intention to remain in the school district indefinitely, for he then would have a reason for being there other than his desire to attend school: his intention to make his home in the district. Thus § 21.031 grants the benefits of residency to all who satisfy the traditional requirements. The statute goes further and extends these benefits to many children even if they (or their families) do not intend to remain in the district indefinitely. As long as the child is not living in the district for the sole purpose of attending school, he satisfies the statutory test. … Since there is no indication that this extension of the traditional definition has any impermissible basis, we certainly cannot say that § 21.031(d) violates the Constitution. ….

CONCUR: JUSTICE BRENNAN, concurring.

I join the Court's opinion. I write separately, however, to stress that this case involves only a facial challenge to the constitutionality of the Texas statute. In upholding the statute, the Court does not pass on its validity as applied to children in a range of specific factual contexts. In particular, the Court does not decide whether the statute is constitutional as applied to Roberto Morales, a United States citizen whose parents are nonresident aliens. If this question were before the Court, I believe that a different set of considerations would be implicated which might affect significantly an analysis of the statute's constitutionality.

Notes and Comments

1. How would you summarize the obligations of public school officials toward aliens? Would your answer distinguish between resident aliens (legal) and illegal aliens?

2. Is *Plyler* still good law? Does it survive the decision of the U.S. Supreme Court in *Martinez v. Bynum*? What should one make of the concurring opinion of Justice Brennan in *Martinez*?

AMBACH v. NORWICK
441 U.S. 68 (1979)

MR. JUSTICE POWELL delivered the opinion of the Court.

This case presents the question whether a State, consistently with the Equal Protection Clause of the Fourteenth Amendment, may refuse to employ as elementary and secondary school teachers aliens who are eligible for United States citizenship but who refuse to seek naturalization.

I

New York Education Law § 3001 (3) forbids certification as a public school teacher of any person who is not a citizen of the United States, unless that person has manifested an intention to apply for citizenship. The Commissioner of Education is authorized to create exemptions from this prohibition, and has done so with respect to aliens who are not yet eligible for citizenship. Unless a teacher obtains certification, he may not work in a public elementary or secondary school in New York.

Appellee Norwick was born in Scotland and is a subject of Great Britain. She has resided in this country since 1965 and is married to a United States citizen. Appellee Dachinger is a Finnish subject who came to this country in 1966 and also is married to a United States citizen. Both Norwick and Dachinger currently meet all of the educational requirements New York has set for certification as a public school teacher, but they consistently have refused to seek citizenship in spite of their eligibility to do so. Norwick applied in 1973 for a teaching certificate covering nursery school through sixth grade, and Dachinger sought a certificate covering the same grades in 1975. Both applications were denied because of appellees' failure to meet the requirements of § 3001 (3). Norwick then filed this suit seeking to enjoin the enforcement of § 3001 (3), and Dachinger obtained leave to intervene as a plaintiff.

II

A

The decisions of this Court regarding the permissibility of statutory classifications involving aliens have not formed an unwavering line over the years. State regulation of the employment of aliens long has been subject to constitutional constraints.

.....

[S]ome state functions are so bound up with the operation of the State as a governmental entity as to permit the exclusion from those functions of all persons who have not become part of the process of self-government. In *Sugarman*, [*Sugarman v. Dougall*, 413 U.S. 634 (1973)] we recognized that a State could, "in an appropriately defined class of positions, require citizenship as a qualification for office." We went on to observe:

> Such power inheres in the State by virtue of its obligation, already noted above, 'to preserve the basic conception of a political community.' . . . And this power and responsibility of the State applies, not only to the qualifications of voters, but also to persons holding state elective or important nonelective executive, legislative, and judicial positions, for officers who participate directly in the formulation, execution, or review of broad public policy perform functions that go to the heart of representative government. 413 U.S., at 647 (citation omitted).

The exclusion of aliens from such governmental positions would not invite as demanding scrutiny from this Court. The rule for governmental functions, which is an exception to the general standard applicable to classifications based on alienage, rests on important principles inherent in the Constitution. The distinction between citizens and aliens, though ordinarily irrelevant to private activity, is fundamental to the definition and government of a State.

.....

B

In determining whether, for purposes of equal protection analysis, teaching in public schools constitutes a governmental function, we look to the role of public education and to the degree of responsibility and discretion teachers possess in fulfilling that role. Each of these considerations supports the conclusion that public school teachers may be regarded as performing a task "that [goes] to the heart of representative government." *Sugarman v. Dougall, supra*, at 647.

. . . .

Within the public school system, teachers play a critical part in developing students' attitude toward government and understanding of the role of citizens in our society. Alone among employees of the system, teachers are in direct, day-to-day contact with students both in the classrooms and in the other varied activities of a modern school. In shaping the students' experience to achieve educational goals, teachers by necessity have wide discretion over the way the course material is communicated to students. They are responsible for presenting and explaining the subject matter in a way that is both comprehensible and inspiring. No amount of standardization of teaching materials or lesson plans can eliminate the personal qualities a teacher brings to bear in achieving these goals. Further, a teacher serves as a role model for his students, exerting a subtle but important influence over their perceptions and values. Thus, through both the presentation of course materials and the example he sets, a teacher has an opportunity to influence the attitudes of students toward government, the political process, and a citizen's social responsibilities. This influence is crucial to the continued good health of a democracy.

III

The people of New York, acting through their elected representatives, have made a judgment that citizenship should be a qualification for teaching the young of the State in the public schools, and § 3001 (3) furthers that judgment.

III. Gender Discrimination

U. S. v. VIRGINIA
518 U.S. 515 (1996)

JUSTICE GINSBURG delivered the opinion of the Court.

Virginia's public institutions of higher learning include an incomparable military college, Virginia Military Institute (VMI). The United States maintains that the Constitution's equal protection guarantee precludes Virginia from reserving exclusively to men the unique educational opportunities VMI affords. We agree.

I

Founded in 1839, VMI is today the sole single-sex school among Virginia's 15 public institutions of higher learning. VMI's distinctive mission is to produce "citizen-soldiers," men prepared for leadership in civilian life and in military service. VMI pursues this mission through pervasive training of a kind not available anywhere else in Virginia. Assigning prime place to character development, VMI uses an "adversative method" modeled on English public schools and once characteristic of military instruction. VMI constantly endeavors to instill physical and mental discipline in its cadets and impart to them a strong moral code. The school's graduates leave VMI with heightened comprehension of their capacity to deal with duress and stress, and a large sense of accomplishment for completing the hazardous course.

VMI has notably succeeded in its mission to produce leaders; among its alumni are military generals, Members of Congress, and business executives. The school's alumni overwhelmingly perceive that their VMI training helped them to realize their personal goals. VMI's endowment reflects the loyalty of its graduates; VMI has the largest per-student endowment of all undergraduate institutions in the Nation.

Neither the goal of producing citizen-soldiers nor VMI's implementing methodology is inherently unsuitable to women. And the school's impressive record in producing leaders has made admission desirable to some women. Nevertheless, Virginia has elected to preserve exclusively for men the advantages and opportunities a VMI education affords.

II

A

From its establishment in 1839 as one of the Nation's first state military colleges, *see* 1839 Va. Acts, ch. 20, VMI has remained financially supported by Virginia and "subject to the control of the [Virginia] General Assembly," Va. Code Ann. § 23-92 (1993). …VMI today enrolls about 1,300 men as cadets.[2] Its academic offerings in the liberal arts, sciences, and engineering are also available at other public colleges and universities in Virginia. But VMI's mission is special. It is the mission of the school "'to produce educated and honorable men, prepared for the varied work of civil life, imbued with love of learning, confident in the functions and attitudes of leadership, possessing a high sense of public service, advocates of the American democracy and free enterprise system, and ready as citizen-soldiers to defend their country in time of national peril.'" 766 F. Supp. 1407, 1425 (WD Va. 1991) (quoting Mission Study Committee of the VMI Board of Visitors, Report, May 16, 1986).

In contrast to the federal service academies, institutions maintained "to prepare cadets for career service in the armed forces," VMI's program "is directed at preparation for both military and civilian life"; "only about 15% of VMI cadets enter career military service." 766 F. Supp. at 1432.

VMI produces its "citizen-soldiers" through "an adversative, or doubting, model of education" which features "physical rigor, mental stress, absolute equality of treatment, absence of privacy, minute regulation of behavior, and indoctrination in desirable values." As one Commandant of Cadets described it, the adversative method "dissects the young student," and makes him aware of

---

[2] Historically, most of Virginia's public colleges and universities were single-sex; by the mid-1970's, however, all except VMI had become coeducational.

his "limits and capabilities," so that he knows "how far he can go with his anger. . . how much he can take under stress, . . . exactly what he can do when he is physically exhausted." ...

VMI cadets live in spartan barracks where surveillance is constant and privacy nonexistent; they wear uniforms, eat together in the mess hall, and regularly participate in drills. *Id.* at 1424, 1432. Entering students are incessantly exposed to the rat line, "an extreme form of the adversative model," comparable in intensity to Marine Corps boot camp. *Id.* at 1422. Tormenting and punishing, the rat line bonds new cadets to their fellow sufferers and, when they have completed the 7-month experience, to their former tormentors..

VMI's "adversative model" is further characterized by a hierarchical "class system" of privileges and responsibilities, a "dyke system" for assigning a senior class mentor to each entering class "rat," and a stringently enforced "honor code," which prescribes that a cadet "'does not lie, cheat, steal nor tolerate those who do.'" *Id.* at 1422-23.

III

The cross-petitions in this case present two ultimate issues. First, does Virginia's exclusion of women from the educational opportunities provided by VMI—extraordinary opportunities for military training and civilian leadership development—deny to women "capable of all of the individual activities required of VMI cadets," ...the equal protection of the laws guaranteed by the Fourteenth Amendment? Second, if VMI's "unique" situation as Virginia's sole single-sex public institution of higher education—offends the Constitution's equal protection principle, what is the remedial requirement?

IV

...Parties who seek to defend gender-based government action must demonstrate an "exceedingly persuasive justification" for that action....As a plurality of this Court acknowledged a generation ago, "our Nation has had a long and unfortunate history of sex discrimination." *Frontiero v. Richardson*, 411U.S. 677, 684 (1973). Through a century plus three decades and more of that history, women did not count among voters composing "We the People"; not until 1920 did women gain a constitutional right to the franchise. *Id.* at 685. And for a half century thereafter, it remained the prevailing doctrine that government, both federal and state, could withhold from women opportunities accorded men so long as any "basis in reason" could be conceived for the discrimination.

.....

...To summarize the Court's current directions for cases of official classification based on gender: Focusing on the differential treatment or denial of opportunity for which relief is sought, the reviewing court must determine whether the proffered justification is "exceedingly persuasive." The burden of justification is demanding and it rests entirely on the State. The State must show "at least that the [challenged] classification serves 'important governmental objectives and that the discriminatory means employed' are 'substantially related to the achievement of those objectives.'" The justification must be genuine, not hypothesized or invented post hoc in response to litigation. And it must not rely on overbroad generalizations about the different talents, capacities, or preferences of males and females.

The heightened review standard our precedent establishes does not make sex a proscribed classification. Supposed "inherent differences" are no longer accepted as a ground for race or national origin classifications. *See Loving v. Virginia*, 388 U.S. 1 (1967). Physical differences between men and women, however, are enduring: "The two sexes are not fungible; a community made up exclusively of one [sex] is different from a community composed of both." *Ballard v. United States*, 329 U.S. 187, 193 (1946).

"Inherent differences" between men and women, we have come to appreciate, remain cause for celebration, but not for denigration of the members of either sex or for artificial constraints on an individual's opportunity. Sex classifications may be used to compensate women "for particular economic disabilities [they have] suffered," *Califano v. Webster*, 430 U.S. 313, 320 (1977) (per curiam), to "promote equal employment opportunity," *See California Federal Sav. & Loan Assn. v. Guerra*, 479 U.S. 272, 289 (1987), to advance full development of the talent and capacities of our Nation's people. But such classifications may not be used, as they once were, see *Goesaert*, 335 U.S., at 467, to create or perpetuate the legal, social, and economic inferiority of women.

Measuring the record in this case against the review standard just described, we conclude that Virginia has shown no "exceedingly persuasive justification" for excluding all women from the citizen-soldier training afforded by VMI. We therefore affirm the Fourth Circuit's initial judgment, which held that Virginia had violated the Fourteenth Amendment's Equal Protection Clause. Because the remedy proffered by Virginia—the Mary Baldwin VWIL program—does not cure the constitutional violation, i.e., it does not provide equal opportunity, we reverse the Fourth Circuit's final judgment in this case.

.....

Virginia describes the current absence of public single-sex higher education for women as "an historical anomaly." But the historical record indicates action more deliberate than anomalous: First, protection of women against higher education; next, schools for women far from equal in resources and stature to schools for men; finally, conversion of the separate schools to coeducation. The state legislature, prior to the advent of this controversy, had repealed "all Virginia statutes requiring individual institutions to admit only men or women." 766 F. Supp. at 1419. And in 1990, an official commission, "legislatively established to chart the future goals of higher education in Virginia," reaffirmed the policy "of affording broad access" while maintaining "autonomy and diversity." 976 F.2d at 898-99 (quoting Report of the Virginia Commission on the University of the 21st Century). Significantly, the Commission reported:

> Because colleges and universities provide opportunities for students to develop values and learn from role models, it is extremely important that they deal with faculty, staff, and students without regard to sex, race, or ethnic origin. *Id.* at 899 (emphasis supplied by Court of Appeals deleted). This statement, the Court of Appeals observed, "is the only explicit one that we have found in the record in

> which the Commonwealth has expressed itself with respect to gender distinctions. *Ibid.*

.....

In sum, we find no persuasive evidence in this record that VMI's male-only admission policy "is in furtherance of a state policy of 'diversity.'" *See* 976 F.2d at 899. No such policy, the Fourth Circuit observed, can be discerned from the movement of all other public colleges and universities in Virginia away from single-sex education. *See ibid.* That court also questioned "how one institution with autonomy, but with no authority over any other state institution, can give effect to a state policy of diversity among institutions." *Ibid.* A purpose genuinely to advance an array of educational options, as the Court of Appeals recognized, is not served by VMI's historic and constant plan—a plan to "afford a unique educational benefit only to males." *Ibid.* However "liberally" this plan serves the State's sons, it makes no provision whatever for her daughters. That is not equal protection.

B

.....

It may be assumed, for purposes of this decision, that most women would not choose VMI's adversative method. As Fourth Circuit Judge Motz observed, however, in her dissent from the Court of Appeals' denial of rehearing en banc, it is also probable that "many men would not want to be educated in such an environment." 52 F.3d at 93. (On that point, even our dissenting colleague might agree.) Education, to be sure, is not a "one size fits all" business. The issue, however, is not whether "women—or men—should be forced to attend VMI"; rather, the question is whether the State can constitutionally deny to women who have the will and capacity, the training and attendant no opportunities that VMI uniquely affords.

.....

Medical faculties similarly resisted men and women as partners in the study of medicine. ... More recently, women seeking careers in policing encountered resistance based on fears that their presence would "undermine male solidarity," ... deprive male partners of adequate assistance, ... and lead to sexual misconduct. Field studies did not confirm these fears.

Women's successful entry into the federal military academies, and their participation in the Nation's military forces, indicate that Virginia's fears for the future of VMI may not be solidly grounded. The State's justification for excluding all women from "citizen-soldier" training for which some are qualified, in any event, cannot rank as "exceedingly

persuasive," as we have explained and applied that standard.

Virginia and VMI trained their argument on "means" rather than "end," and thus misperceived our precedent. Single-sex education at VMI serves an "important governmental objective," they maintained, and exclusion of women is not only "substantially related," it is essential to that objective. By this notably circular argument, the "straightforward" test Mississippi Univ. for Women described, *see* 458 U.S., at 724-725, was bent and bowed.

The State's misunderstanding and, in turn, the District Court's, is apparent from VMI's mission: to produce "citizen-soldiers," individuals "'imbued with love of learning, confident in the functions and attitudes of leadership, possessing a high sense of public service, advocates of the American democracy and free enterprise system, and ready . . . to defend their country in time of national peril.'" 766 F. Supp., at 1425 (quoting Mission Study Committee of the VMI Board of Visitors, Report, May 16, 1986).

Surely that goal is great enough to accommodate women, who today count as citizens in our American democracy equal in stature to men. Just as surely, the State's great goal is not substantially advanced by women's categorical exclusion, in total disregard of their individual merit, from the State's premier "citizen-soldier" corps. Virginia, in sum, "has fallen far short of establishing the 'exceedingly persuasive justification,'" Mississippi Univ. for Women, 458 U.S., at 731, that must be the solid base for any gender-defined classification.

****

VI

In the second phase of the litigation, Virginia presented its remedial plan—maintain VMI as a male-only college and create VWIL as a separate program for women. ... The constitutional violation in this case is the categorical exclusion of women from an extraordinary educational opportunity afforded men. A proper remedy for an unconstitutional exclusion, we have explained, aims to "eliminate [so far as possible] the discriminatory effects of the past" and to "bar like discrimination in the future." *Louisiana v. United States*, 380 U.S. 145, 154 (1965).

Virginia chose not to eliminate, but to leave untouched, VMI's exclusionary policy. For women only, however, Virginia proposed a separate program, different in kind from VMI and unequal in tangible and intangible facilities. ... VWIL affords women no opportunity to experience the rigorous military training for which VMI is famed. ...Instead, the VWIL program "deemphasizes" military education ... and uses a "cooperative method" of education "which reinforces self-esteem,"

VWIL students participate in ROTC and a "largely ceremonial Virginia Corps of Cadets, see 44 F.3d at 1234, but Virginia deliberately did not make VWIL a military institute. The VWIL House is not a military-style residence and VWIL students need not live together throughout the 4-year program, eat meals together, or wear uniforms during the school day. *See* 852 F. Supp. at 477, 495. VWIL students thus do not experience the "barracks" life "crucial to the VMI experience," the spartan living arrangements designed to foster an "egalitarian ethic." *See* 766 F. Supp. at 1423-24. "The most important aspects of the VMI educational experience occur in the barracks," the District Court found, *Id.*, at 1423, yet Virginia deemed that core experience nonessential, indeed inappropriate, for training its female citizen-soldiers.

****

...In contrast to the generalizations about women on which Virginia rests, we note again these dispositive realties: VMI's "implementing methodology" is not "inherently unsuitable to women," 976 F.2d at 899; "some women . . . do well under [the] adversative model," 766 F. Supp. at 1434 (internal quotation marks omitted); "some women, at least, would want to attend [VMI] if they had the opportunity," *Id.*, at 1414; "some women are capable of all of the individual activities required of VMI cadets," *Id.*, at 1412,and "can meet the physical standards [VMI] now imposes on men," 976 F.2d at 896. It is on behalf of these women that the United States has instituted this suit, and it is for them that a remedy must be crafted,[19] a remedy that will end their exclusion from a state-supplied educational opportunity for which they are fit, a decree that will "bar like discrimination in the future." *Louisiana*, 380 U.S., at 154.

B

In myriad respects other than military training, VWIL does not qualify as VMI's equal. VWIL's student body, faculty, course offerings, and facilities hardly match VMI's. Nor can the VWIL graduate anticipate the benefits associated with VMI's 157-year history, the school's prestige, and its influential alumni network.

****

Virginia, in sum, while maintaining VMI for men only, has failed to provide any "comparable single-gender women's institution." *Id.* at 1241. Instead, the Commonwealth has created a VWIL program fairly appraised as a "pale shadow" of VMI in terms of the range of curricular choices and faculty stature, funding, prestige, alumni support and influence.

.....

VII

VMI, too, offers an educational opportunity no other Virginia institution provides, and the school's "prestige"—associated with its success in developing "citizen-soldiers"—is unequaled. Virginia has closed this facility to its daughters and, instead, has devised for them a "parallel program," with a faculty less impressively credentialed and less well paid, more limited course offerings, fewer opportunities for military training and for scientific specialization. ... There is no reason to believe that the admission of women capable of all the activities required of VMI cadets would destroy the Institute rather than enhance its capacity to serve the "more perfect Union."

---

[19] Admitting women to VMI would undoubtedly require alterations necessary to afford members of each sex privacy from the other sex in living arrangements, and to adjust aspects of the physical training programs. .... Experience shows such adjustments are manageable.

For the reasons stated, the initial judgment of the Court of Appeals, is affirmed, the final judgment of the Court of Appeals is reversed, and the case is remanded for further proceedings consistent with this opinion.

It is so ordered.

Justice Thomas took no part in the consideration or decision of this case.

CONCUR: CHIEF JUSTICE REHNQUIST, concurring in judgment.

The Court holds first that Virginia violates the Equal Protection Clause by maintaining the Virginia Military Institute's (VMI's) all-male admissions policy, and second that establishing the Virginia Women's Institute for Leadership (VWIL) program does not remedy that violation. While I agree with these conclusions, I disagree with the Court's analysis and so I write separately.

.....

While terms like "important governmental objective" and "substantially related" are hardly models of precision, they have more content and specificity than does the phrase "exceedingly persuasive justification." That phrase is best confined, as it was first used, as an observation on the difficulty of meeting the applicable test, not as a formulation of the test itself... To avoid introducing potential confusion, I would have adhered more closely to our traditional, "firmly established," *Hogan, supra*, at 723; *Heckler, supra*, at 744, standard that a gender-based classification "must bear a close and substantial relationship to important governmental objectives." *Feeney, Supra* at 273.

Our cases dealing with gender discrimination also require that the proffered purpose for the challenged law be the actual purpose. *See Ante*, at 15, 18. It is on this ground that the Court rejects the first of two justifications Virginia offers for VMI's single-sex admissions policy, namely, the goal of diversity among its public educational institutions. While I ultimately agree that the State has not carried the day with this justification, I disagree with the Court's method of analyzing the issue.

.....

Even if diversity in educational opportunity were the State's actual objective, the State's position would still be problematic. The difficulty with its position is that the diversity benefited only one sex; there was single-sex public education available for men at VMI, but no corresponding single-sex public education available for women. When Hogan placed Virginia on notice that VMI's admissions policy possibly was unconstitutional, VMI could have dealt with the problem by admitting women; but its governing body felt strongly that the admission of women would have seriously harmed the institution's educational approach. Was there something else the State could have done to avoid an equal protection violation? Since the State did nothing, we do not have to definitively answer that question.

.....

If a state decides to create single-sex programs, the state would, I expect, consider the public's interest and demand in designing curricula. And rightfully so. But the state should avoid assuming demand based on stereotypes; it must not assume a priori, without evidence, that there would be no interest in a women's school of civil engineering, or in a men's school of nursing.

In the end, the women's institution Virginia proposes, VWIL, fails as a remedy, because it is distinctly inferior to the existing men's institution and will continue to be for the foreseeable future. VWIL simply is not, in any sense, the institution that VMI is. In particular, VWIL is a program appended to a private college, not a self-standing institution; and VWIL is substantially under funded as compared to VMI. I therefore ultimately agree with the Court that Virginia has not provided an adequate remedy.

MISSISSIPPI UNIVERSITY FOR WOMEN v. HOGAN
458 U.S. 718 (1982)

OPINION: JUSTICE O'CONNOR delivered the opinion of the Court.

This case presents the narrow issue of whether a state statute that excludes males from enrolling in a state-supported professional nursing school violates the Equal Protection Clause of the Fourteenth Amendment.

I

The facts are not in dispute. In 1884, the Mississippi Legislature created the Mississippi Industrial Institute and College for the Education of White Girls of the State of Mississippi, now the oldest state-supported all-female college in the United States. 1884 Miss. Gen. Laws, Ch. 30, § 6. The school, known today as Mississippi University for Women (MUW), has from its inception limited its enrollment to women.

In 1971, MUW established a School of Nursing, initially offering a 2-year associate degree. Three years later, the school instituted a 4-year baccalaureate program in nursing and today also offers a graduate program. The School of Nursing has its own faculty and administrative officers and establishes its own criteria for admission.

Respondent, Joe Hogan, is a registered nurse but does not hold a baccalaureate degree in nursing. Since 1974, he has worked as a nursing supervisor in a medical center in Columbus, the city in which MUW is located. In 1979, Hogan applied for admission to the MUW School of Nursing's baccalaureate program.[3] Although he was otherwise qualified, he was denied admission to the

---

[3] With a baccalaureate degree, Hogan would be able to earn a higher salary and would be eligible to obtain specialized training as an anesthetist.

School of Nursing solely because of his sex. School officials informed him that he could audit the courses in which he was interested, but could not enroll for credit.[4]

Hogan filed an action in the United States District Court for the Northern District of Mississippi, claiming the single-sex admissions policy of MUW's School of Nursing violated the Equal Protection Clause of the Fourteenth Amendment. Hogan sought injunctive and declaratory relief, as well as compensatory damages.

****

II

We begin our analysis aided by several firmly established principles. Because the challenged policy expressly discriminates among applicants on the basis of gender, it is subject to scrutiny under the Equal Protection Clause of the Fourteenth Amendment.

That this statutory policy discriminates against males rather than against females does not exempt it from scrutiny or reduce the standard of review.[8] Our decisions also establish that the party seeking to uphold a statute that classifies individuals on the basis of their gender must carry the burden of showing an "exceedingly persuasive justification" for the classification. The burden is met only by showing at least that the classification serves "important governmental objectives and that the discriminatory means employed" are "substantially related to the achievement of those objectives." *Wengler v. Druggists Mutual Ins. Co.*, 446 U.S. 142, 150 (1980).

Although the test for determining the validity of a gender-based classification is straightforward, it must be applied free of fixed notions concerning the roles and abilities of males and females. Care must be taken in ascertaining whether the statutory objective itself reflects archaic and stereotypic notions. Thus, if the statutory objective is to exclude or "protect" members of one gender because they are presumed to suffer from an inherent handicap or to be innately inferior, the objective itself is illegitimate. *See Frontiero v. Richardson*, 411 U.S. 677, 684-85 (1973) (plurality opinion).

If the State's objective is legitimate and important, we next determine whether the requisite direct, substantial relationship between objective and means is present. The purpose of requiring that close relationship is to assure that the validity of a classification is determined through reasoned analysis rather than through the mechanical application of traditional, often inaccurate, assumptions about the proper roles of men and women. The need for the requirement is amply revealed by reference

---

[4] Dr. James Strobel, President of MUW, verified that men could audit the equivalent of a full class load in either night or daytime classes

[8] Without question, MUW's admissions policy worked to Hogan's disadvantage. Although Hogan could have attended classes and received credit in one of Mississippi's state-supported coeducational nursing programs, none of which was located in Columbus, he could attend only by driving a considerable distance from his home.. A similarly situated female would not have been required to choose between forgoing credit and bearing that inconvenience. Moreover, since many students enrolled in the School of Nursing hold full-time jobs, Hogan's female colleagues had available an opportunity, not open to Hogan, to obtain credit for additional training. The policy of denying males the right to obtain credit toward a baccalaureate degree thus imposed upon Hogan "a burden he would not bear were he female." *Orr v. Orr*, 440 U.S. 268, 273 (1979).

to the broad range of statutes already invalidated by this Court, statutes that relied upon the simplistic, outdated assumption that gender could be used as a "proxy for other, more germane bases of classification," *Craig v. Boren*, 429 U.S. 190, 198 (1976), to establish a link between objective and classification.

Applying this framework, we now analyze the arguments advanced by the State to justify its refusal to allow males to enroll for credit in MUW's School of Nursing.

III

A

The State's primary justification for maintaining the single-sex admissions policy of MUW's School of Nursing is that it compensates for discrimination against women and, therefore, constitutes educational affirmative action. As applied to the School of Nursing, we find the State's argument unpersuasive.

In limited circumstances, a gender-based classification favoring one sex can be justified if it intentionally and directly assists members of the sex that is disproportionately burdened. *See Schlesinger v. Ballard*, 419 U.S. 498 (1975). However, we consistently have emphasized that "the mere recitation of a benign, compensatory purpose is not an automatic shield which protects against any inquiry into the actual purposes underlying a statutory scheme." *Weinberger v. Wiesenfeld*, 420 U.S. 636, 648 (1975). The same searching analysis must be made, regardless of whether the State's objective is to eliminate family controversy, *Reed v. Reed*, 404 U.S. 71 (1971), to achieve administrative efficiency, *Frontiero v. Richardson*, 411 U.S. 677 (1973), or to balance the burdens borne by males and females.

It is readily apparent that a State can evoke a compensatory purpose to justify an otherwise discriminatory classification only if members of the gender benefited by the classification actually suffer a disadvantage related to the classification.

****

In sharp contrast, Mississippi has made no showing that women lacked opportunities to obtain training in the field of nursing or to attain positions of leadership in that field when the MUW School of Nursing opened its door or that women currently are deprived of such opportunities. In fact, in 1970, the year before the School of Nursing's first class enrolled, women earned 94 percent of the nursing baccalaureate degrees conferred in Mississippi and 98.6 percent of the degrees earned nationwide. U.S. Dept. of Health, Education, and Welfare, Earned Degrees Conferred: 1969-1970, Institutional Data 388 (1972). That year was not an aberration; one decade earlier, women had earned all the nursing degrees conferred in Mississippi and 98.9 percent of the degrees conferred nationwide. U.S. Dept. of Health, Education, and Welfare, Earned Degrees Conferred, 1959-1960: Bachelor's and Higher Degrees 135 (1960). As one would expect, the labor force reflects the same predominance of women in nursing. When MUW's School of Nursing began operation, nearly 98 percent of all employed registered nurses were female. United States Bureau of Census, 1981 Statistical Abstract of the United States 402 (1981).

Rather than compensate for discriminatory barriers faced by women, MUW's policy of excluding males from admission to the School of Nursing tends to perpetuate the stereotyped view of nursing as an exclusively woman's job. By assuring that Mississippi allots more openings in its state-supported nursing schools to women than it does to men, MUW's admissions policy lends credibility to the old view that women, not men, should become nurses, and makes the assumption that nursing is a field for women a self-fulfilling prophecy. *See Stanton v. Stanton*, 421 U.S. 7 (1975). Thus, we conclude that, although the State recited a "benign, compensatory purpose," it failed to establish that the alleged objective is the actual purpose underlying the discriminatory classification.

The policy is invalid also because it fails the second part of the equal protection test, for the State has made no showing that the gender-based classification is substantially and directly related to its proposed compensatory objective. To the contrary, MUW's policy of permitting men to attend classes as auditors fatally undermines its claim that women, at least those in the School of Nursing, are adversely affected by the presence of men.

MUW permits men who audit to participate fully in classes. Additionally, both men and women take part in continuing education courses offered by the School of Nursing, in which regular nursing students also can enroll. The uncontroverted record reveals that admitting men to nursing classes does not affect teaching style, that the presence of men in the classroom would not affect the performance of the female nursing students and that men in coeducational nursing schools do not dominate the classroom. In sum, the record in this case is flatly inconsistent with the claim that excluding men from the School of Nursing is necessary to reach any of MUW's educational goals.

Thus, considering both the asserted interest and the relationship between the interest and the methods used by the State, we conclude that the State has fallen far short of establishing the "exceedingly persuasive justification" needed to sustain the gender-based classification. Accordingly, we hold that MUW's policy of denying males the right to enroll for credit in its School of Nursing violates the Equal Protection Clause of the Fourteenth Amendment.

.....

Because we conclude that the State's policy of excluding males from MUW's School of Nursing violates the Equal Protection Clause of the Fourteenth Amendment, we affirm the judgment of the Court of Appeals.

It is so ordered.

DISSENT: CHIEF JUSTICE BURGER, dissenting.

I agree generally with JUSTICE POWELL's dissenting opinion. I write separately, however, to emphasize that the Court's holding today is limited to the context of a professional nursing school. Since the Court's opinion relies heavily on its finding that women have traditionally dominated the nursing profession, *see ante*, at 729-731, it suggests that a State might well be justified in maintaining, for example, the option of an all-women's business school or liberal arts program.

JUSTICE BLACKMUN, dissenting.

Unless Mississippi University for Women wished to preserve a historical anachronism, one only states the obvious when he observes that the University long ago should have replaced its original statement of purpose and brought its corporate papers into the 20th century. It failed to do so and, perhaps in partial consequence, finds itself in this litigation, with the Court's opinion, *ante*, at 719-720, and n. 1, now taking full advantage of that failure, to MUW's embarrassment and discomfiture.

Despite that failure, times have changed in the intervening 98 years. What was once an "Institute and College" is now a genuine university, with a 2-year School of Nursing established 11 years ago and then expanded to a 4-year baccalaureate program in 1974. But respondent Hogan "wants in" at this particular location in his home city of Columbus. It is not enough that his State of Mississippi offers baccalaureate programs in nursing open to males at Jackson and at Hattiesburg. Mississippi thus has not closed the doors of its educational system to males like Hogan. Assuming that he is qualified—and I have no reason whatsoever to doubt his qualifications—those doors are open and his maleness alone does not prevent his gaining the additional education he professes to seek.

JUSTICE POWELL, with whom JUSTICE REHNQUIST joins, dissenting.

The Court's opinion bows deeply to conformity. Left without honor—indeed, held unconstitutional—is an element of diversity that has characterized much of American education and enriched much of American life. The Court in effect holds today that no State now may provide even a single institution of higher learning open only to women students. It gives no heed to the efforts of the State of Mississippi to provide abundant opportunities for young men and young women to attend coeducational institutions, and none to the preferences of the more than 40,000 young women who over the years have evidenced their approval of an all-women's college by choosing Mississippi University for Women (MUW) over seven coeducational universities within the State. The Court decides today that the Equal Protection Clause makes it unlawful for the State to provide women with a traditionally popular and respected choice of educational environment. It does so in a case instituted by one man, who represents no class, and whose primary concern is personal convenience.

It is undisputed that women enjoy complete equality of opportunity in Mississippi's public system of higher education. Of the State's 8 universities and 16 junior colleges, all except MUW are coeducational. At least two other Mississippi universities would have provided respondent with the nursing curriculum that he wishes to pursue.[1] No other male has joined in his complaint. The only groups with any personal acquaintance with MUW to file amicus briefs are female students and

---

[1] "[Two] other Mississippi universities offered coeducational programs leading to a Bachelor of Science in Nursing—the University of Southern Mississippi in Hattiesburg, 178 miles from Columbus; and the University of Mississippi in Jackson, 147 miles from Columbus . . . ." Brief for Respondent 3. *See also* Tr. of Oral Arg. 8.

alumnae of MUW. And they have emphatically rejected respondent's arguments, urging that the State of Mississippi be allowed to continue offering the choice from which they have benefited.

Nor is respondent significantly disadvantaged by MUW's all-female tradition. His constitutional complaint is based upon a single asserted harm: that he must travel to attend the state-supported nursing schools that concededly are available to him. The Court characterizes this injury as one of "inconvenience." *Ante*, at 724, n. 8. This description is fair and accurate, though somewhat embarrassed by the fact that there is, of course, no constitutional right to attend a state-supported university in one's home town. Thus the Court, to redress respondent's injury of inconvenience, must rest its invalidation of MUW's single-sex program on a mode of "sexual stereotype" reasoning that has no application whatever to the respondent or to the "wrong" of which he complains. At best this is anomalous. And ultimately the anomaly reveals legal error—that of applying a heightened equal protection standard, developed in cases of genuine sexual stereotyping, to a narrowly utilized state classification that provides an additional choice for women. Moreover, I believe that Mississippi's educational system should be upheld in this case even if this inappropriate method of analysis is applied.

I

Coeducation, historically, is a novel educational theory. From grade school through high school, college, and graduate and professional training, much of the Nation's population during much of our history has been educated in sexually segregated classrooms.

.....

The arguable benefits of single-sex colleges also continue to be recognized by students of higher education. The Carnegie Commission on Higher Education has reported that it "[favors] the continuation of colleges for women. They provide an element of diversity . . . and [an environment in which women] generally . . . speak up more in their classes, . . . hold more positions of leadership on campus, . . . and . . . have more role models and mentors among women teachers and administrators." Carnegie Report, quoted in K. Davidson, R. Ginsburg, & H. Kay, Sex-Based Discrimination 814 (1975 ed.).

.....

In sum, the practice of voluntarily chosen single-sex education is an honored tradition in our country, even if it now rarely exists in state colleges and universities. Mississippi's accommodation of such student choices is legitimate because it is completely consensual and is important because it permits students to decide for themselves the type of college education they think will benefit them most. Finally, Mississippi's policy is substantially related to its long-respected objective.

A.N.A. EX REL. S.F.A. v. BRECKINRIDGE BD. OF EDUC.

833 F. Supp. 2d 673 (W.D. Ky. 2011)

OPINION BY: CHARLES R. SIMPSON III

This is an action brought under 42 U.S.C. § 1983 challenging the legality of a Breckinridge County Middle School ("BCMS") program offering students the option to participate in single-sex classes. This matter is presently before the court on the motions of the Breckinridge County Defendants to dismiss the class action representatives for lack of standing, DN 219) and for summary judgment on the claims of the individual plaintiffs for damages for the 2007–2008 school year.

I. Background

BCMS is a public school of approximately 600 students, both male and female, in grades six through eight, located in Harned, Kentucky. BCMS receives state and federal funding through the Breckinridge County School District, and is thus subject to the requirements of Title IX and other regulations. Plaintiffs filed this action against the Breckinridge County Defendants claiming that the single-sex education program utilized at BCMS in the 2007–2008 school year was in violation of both state and federal law. They seek damages for what they allege was unlawful sex discrimination during the 2007–2008 school year. Additionally, Plaintiffs claim that the single-sex program for the 2008–2009 and 2009–2010 school years also violated federal and state law. The plaintiffs seek only declaratory and injunctive relief for claims after the 2007–2008 school year.

The court certified four subclasses of plaintiffs challenging the 2008–2009 and 2009–2010 programs in which students were permitted to choose whether to participate in one or more single-sex classes offered at BCMS. The subclasses consist of those students enrolled in Breckinridge County Middle School who chose to participate in one or more single-sex classes for the 2008–2009 school year (Subclass 1) and the 2009–2010 school year (Subclass 3), and students who chose to participate solely in coeducational classes for the 2008–2009 school year (Subclass 2) and the 2009–2010 school year (Subclass 4). The defendants contend that the plaintiffs have failed to demonstrate (1) a redressable injury-in-fact suffered by designated subclass representatives J.J.N., K.A.S., and S.E.A., (2) causation or (3) gender discrimination. Thus, they urge that the requirements of standing have not been met and the class action claims must therefore be dismissed. The defendants also urge dismissal of Subclass 3, as subclass representative G.J. was voluntarily dismissed from this action on October 7, 2009 and no subclass representative has been named in his place.

S.E.A. is the Subclass 1 and 4 representative. She represents BCMS students who chose to participate in one or more single-sex classes in 2008–2009. She was assigned to a single-sex related arts class in 2007–2008.[37] Thereafter, she chose enrollment in a single-sex related arts class for

---

[37] "Related arts" at BCMS consists of four rotating topics (art, enrichment, music and PE) during one period for nine weeks each. S.E.A.'s claim for damages for the 2007–2008 school year is addressed later in this opinion.

2008–2009. She also represents Subclass 4 consisting of students who participated solely in coeducational classes in 2009–2010, as she enrolled in all coeducational classes for that year.

J.J.N. and K.A.S. are representatives for Subclass 2, representing all BCMS students who participated solely in coeducational classes in 2008–2009. In 2007–2008, J.J.N. chose to participate in a single-sex class for a short period of time. He requested and was transferred out of the class to a coeducational class after approximately one month. He chose to participate solely in coeducational classes in 2008–2009. K.A.S. was assigned to a single-sex related arts class in 2007–2008, but chose all coeducational classes for the 2009–2010 school year.

Three of the plaintiffs, A.N.A., Z.H.S. and S.L., were in eighth grade in 2007–2008 and thus were affected by the program during only one of the years in issue in this suit. The 2007–2008 school year was the only school year which began without parents being afforded the opportunity to make an election for their children not to participate in single-sex classes. A.N.A. and Z.H.S. were initially assigned to single-sex math classes for the 2007–2008 school year. When given the option to move to coeducational classes approximately three weeks later, they chose to remain in the single-sex class.

S.L. chose to enroll in coeducational classes for the 2007–2008 school year. Approximately three weeks later when given the option to move to single-sex classes, she chose to remain in coeducational classes.

The plaintiffs have alleged that the BCMS program, purportedly designed in accordance with the provisions of 34 C.F.R. § 106.34 (2007), violates Title IX, 20 U.S.C. § 1681(a); the Equal Education Opportunities Act, 20 U.S.C. § 1705; the Equal Protection Clause of the United States Constitution, and the Kentucky Sex Equity in Education Act, KRS 344.555.

II. 2008–2009 and 2009–2010 Class Claims

.....

In attempting to identify an injury in fact, the class representative plaintiffs (hereinafter "plaintiffs") urge that all BCMS students are injured by being required to attend a public middle school which engages in sex discrimination in education by offering a single-sex program. They urge that because, in their view, single-sex and coeducational classes can never offer substantially equal educational opportunities, the mere exposure to such alleged inequality is injurious to BCMS students.

The plaintiffs paint with too broad a brush. They do not identify specific facts demonstrating that the class representatives (and the students they represent) suffered any concrete and particularized harm to a legally protected interest as a result of the optional single-sex classes at BCMS. Instead, they spend substantial time arguing the general proposition that the coexistence of coed and single-sex classrooms in schools constitutes sex discrimination. This theory, however, finds no support either in law or in the record of this case.

No legal authority supports the conclusion that optional single-sex programs in public schools are *ipso facto* injurious to the schools' students. Unlike the separation of public school students by race, the separation of students by sex does not give rise to a finding of constitutional injury as a matter of law. Individuals are harmed when they attend schools in which students are separated on the basis of race because such separation "generates a feeling of inferiority ... that may affect [students'] hearts and minds in a way unlikely to ever be undone." *Brown v. Bd. of Educ. of Topeka,* 347 U.S. 483, 494, 74 S.Ct. 686, 98 L.Ed. 873 (1954). This is true even if all other "tangible" factors, such as the schools' physical facilities, are equal. *Id.* at 493, 74 S.Ct. 686. Moreover, because of the inherent harm that arises from educating students in racially separate schools, and because the intent of *Brown* and its progeny was to create "a unitary, nonracial system of public education," even "voluntary" racial segregation is prohibited. *See Green v. Cnty. Sch. Bd. for New Kent Cnty., Va.,* 391 U.S. 430, 88 S.Ct. 1689, 20 L.Ed.2d 716 (1968) (finding constitutionally deficient a "freedom of choice" plan that allowed parents to choose which schools their children would attend, with the result that a school district had an all-black school and an all-white school).

No such historically-grounded injury has been recognized as inherent in the separation of students by sex. The Supreme Court has never held that separating students by sex in a public school—unlike separating students by race—or offering a single-sex public institution is *per se* unconstitutional. *See United States v. Virginia,* 518 U.S. 515, 533 n. 7, 116 S.Ct. 2264, 135 L.Ed.2d 735 (1996) ("We do not question [Virginia's] prerogative evenhandedly to support diverse educational opportunities [such as single-sex schools]."); *Miss. Univ. for Women v. Hogan,* 458 U.S. 718, 720 n. 1, 102 S.Ct. 3331, 73 L.Ed.2d 1090 (1982) ("Mississippi maintains no other single-sex public university or college. Thus, we are not faced with the question of whether States can provide 'separate but equal' undergraduate institutions for male and females."). *See also Vorchheimer v. Sch. Dist. of Philadelphia,* 532 F.2d 880, 888 (3d Cir.1976), *aff'd by an equally divided Court,* 430 U.S. 703, 97 S.Ct. 1671, 51 L.Ed.2d 750 (1977) (holding that a school board's offering of an optional single-sex public school did not violate the Equal Protection Clause). Therefore, to the extent the plaintiffs attempt to rely on cases that prohibit the separation of students by race, their arguments in favor of an injury in fact fall short.

It is uncontested, of course, that barring students from educational opportunities based on their sex without an exceedingly persuasive justification constitutes an invasion of a legally protected interest. *See Virginia,* 518 U.S. at 534, 116 S.Ct. 2264 (holding unconstitutional Virginia's men-only admissions to the elite "citizen-soldier" corps at the publicly funded Virginia Military Institute); *Hogan,* 458 U.S. at 733, 102 S.Ct. 3331 (holding unconstitutional Mississippi's exclusion of men from a state-funded nursing school). However, the record does not support the conclusion that such a violation occurred because BCMS students were afforded the option of being educated in a single-sex environment.

The plaintiffs repeatedly refer to "exclusion" and "discrimination" in their briefs, but we have been shown no evidence of exclusion or discrimination in this case. The plaintiffs argue that students at BCMS were excluded from educational opportunities on the basis of sex because "boys [were] excluded from the all-girls classes, while girls [were] excluded from the (separate and distinct) all-boys classes." Pl.'s Resp. to Mot. to Dismiss (DN 234) at 19. The plaintiffs' assertion that girls were deprived of the opportunity to be in a "boys' class" or boys were deprived of an opportunity to be in a "girls' class" is simply incorrect. All BCMS students could choose to participate in coeducational classes. Therefore, girls could choose to be in a class with boys and boys could choose to be in a class with girls. What students could not do is choose to be in a certain class, be taught by a certain teacher, or learn with a certain group of other students of the opposite sex. However, BCMS is required only to provide students substantially equivalent single-sex and coed classes. It is not required to provide students the classes, teachers, or classmates of their choice.

Coeducational classes (and thus the opportunity to learn alongside students of both the same and opposite sex) were clearly available to all students at BCMS. Under the plaintiffs' theory, however, this is not sufficient. The plaintiffs postulate that a given student may aspire to participate in a class of students all of the opposite sex, but would be precluded from doing so under the BCMS program. For instance, the plaintiffs offer the example of class representative S.E.A., stating that she "can show that she was treated differently from the boys in her class with whom she was similarly situated but for their sex. To wit, she was barred from participation in the all-boys classes, because she is a girl, while the boys were not."

The plaintiffs call this result "sex discrimination" or "sex segregation." However, to rectify this problem as the plaintiffs have framed it, S.E.A. would have to be allowed to participate in a "boys' class" as the sole female in the classroom. This is so because the presence of students of *both* sexes would constitute a coeducational class, an option that was offered to S.E.A. but one that the plaintiffs apparently find objectionable. To allow S.E.A. to participate in a single-sex "boys' class," then, the plaintiffs would necessarily have BCMS exclude all female students other than S.E.A. Interestingly, this scenario smacks of the very "sex segregation" the plaintiffs decry. Moreover, the absurdity of the plaintiffs' argument becomes evident when taken to its logical conclusion. The presence of a student in a class of students all of the opposite sex—for instance, S.E.A.'s participation in an all-boys' class—would render the class a *coeducational* class. Thus, a student who desires to learn in such a setting need only select the coeducational offering to achieve the same goal. The plaintiffs' claims of "discrimination" and "exclusion" are not supported by law, fact, or logic, and provide no basis for a finding of injury.

Students may suffer concrete harm if they are not provided substantially equivalent coeducational classes when a single-sex program is offered in their school. This was the case in *Doe v. Vermilion Parish Sch. Bd.,* [421 Fed.Appx. 366 (5th Cir.2011)]. which was recently decided by the Fifth Circuit Court of Appeals. In *Vermilion Parish,* a mother (known by the pseudonym Jane Doe) brought an action on behalf of her daughters (Joan and Jill Doe) to challenge an optional single-sex program implemented at Rene A. Rost Middle School in Louisiana. *See id.* at 367–68. The defendants argued that Jill, who had attended only coeducational classes during her time at Rost, lacked standing to challenge the school's single-sex program because she had not participated in it. *Id.* at 372–73. The Fifth Circuit Court of Appeals held that Jill had provided sufficient evidence that the single-sex program was harmful to the overall educational environment at the school, and therefore gave rise to injury even to students who did not participate in the program. *Id.* at 373–74.

The Court of Appeals identified specific shortcomings in the Rost program that rendered coeducational classes substandard, thus depriving students of substantially equal educational opportunities. For instance, there was some evidence that due to efforts by the school district, students with learning difficulties almost always ended up in coeducational classrooms, while "talented and gifted" students ended up in the single-sex classes. *Id.* at 370–71. Jill testified that her coeducational class used different subject-matter tests than the single-sex class and that her teacher read tests aloud for students. *Id.* at 373–74. Jill also stated that she was taunted because other students considered the coeducational class a "special needs" class. *Id.* The Court of Appeals agreed with Jill's argument that Jill had sufficiently claimed injury:

> [B]oth the coed and the same-sex classes are inferior to what would be available were this program not in place. Girls are effectively denied the benefits of being in the same classroom with boys. Though there is a coed class in which those benefits would be available, the argument is that the same-sex classes prevent quality coed classes from being offered. [Jill] also argues that girls are subjected to an unfavorable education and teaching methods based on stereotypes. There is some evidence to support that. She further alleges that her own coed classroom has been modified unfavorably by the imposition of sex sorting. *Id.*

This case differs significantly from *Vermilion Parish.* While plaintiffs recite the mantra that single-sex offerings result in substandard coed education, there is simply no evidence in the record to support such an argument. Notably, the plaintiffs fail to identify any facts showing that any educational opportunity was offered exclusively to boys, exclusively to girls, or exclusively to coeducational classes. Further, experts for both the plaintiffs and the defendants found little difference in the way the single-sex and coeducational classes were conducted, and no disparity was found in the content taught. Although both expert reports noted variations among (1) classroom management styles, (2) teaching methods used, and (3) the pace of progress through materials, both experts concluded:

> While there were differences among teachers, during the periods I observed there were no differences in the ways the single-sex and coed classes were conducted. The teachers used the same classroom set-up, the same text books, the same instructional strategies, and the same behavior management techniques for their coed and single-sex classes. Campbell (plaintiffs' expert) Report, DN 234–17 at 4.
>
> Those teachers who teach both a co-ed class and a single sex class: offer the same curriculum to both classes; are using the same pacing (when and how long to teach a unit) for both types of classes; interact with their classes in the same demeanor; use the same instructional strategies for both; use the same formative (during the unit) and summative (the end of the unit) assessments. I saw no evidence in either type of single-sex classrooms that any stereotypical strategies are used for either girls or boys. Ronay (defendants' expert) Report, DN 219–15 at 16.

The plaintiffs' claims of substandard or unequal educational opportunities as a result of the single-sex offerings are unsubstantiated. Unlike in *Vermilion Parish,* there is no evidence of harm to any student as the result of the optional single-sex program at BCMS. At this stage in the litigation, the plaintiffs may no longer rest on mere allegations, but must set forth specific facts demonstrating that the elements of standing have been met. *See Lujan, supra.* While their brief is long on rhetoric, the plaintiffs simply have not met this burden here.

C.

The plaintiffs further urge that the single-sex classes program produced a disparity in class size at BCMS that disadvantaged students who chose to enroll in coeducational classes, which were in some cases larger than coeducational classes.[38] This does not, however, establish that any of the plaintiffs suffered an injury in fact to a legally protected interest as a result of the BCMS program.

Although plaintiff J.J.N. stated that it is "harder to learn," in a larger class than in a smaller class, and plaintiff K.A.S. claimed that she "lost educational opportunities because it's harder to learn when there are more kids in the classroom," the record does not reflect that either J.J.N. or K.A.S. suffered any concrete educational detriment as the result of being in a "larger" class during the 2008–2009 school year. J.J.N. received all "A's" (the highest letter grades possible) during the 2008–2009 school year, and K.A.S.' grades remained consistent throughout her middle school career, including during the 2008–2009 school year. Therefore, despite the allegation that it was "harder to learn" in a coeducational class, neither J.J.N. nor K.A.S. has shown a cognizable injury resulting from the BCMS single-sex program.

Equivalent educational opportunities do not mandate identical classroom experiences. Thus, the vague assertion that it was "harder to learn" is meaningless unless the plaintiffs have suffered the concrete and particularized injury that is necessary to confer standing.

Finally, we feel compelled to address the plaintiffs' haphazard wielding of certain emotionally charged terminology in their briefs. The plaintiffs contend that students were "classified" or "segregated" by sex. This contention is belied by the record. BCMS did not "classify" or "segregate" its students. Rather, BCMS afforded parents the option of selecting a single-sex or coeducational classroom environment for their children.

To "segregate," as that term has been used historically, means "to cause or force the separation of (as races or social classes) from the rest of society or from a larger group," WEBSTER'S THIRD NEW INTERNATIONAL DICTIONARY (2002). At BCMS, the single-sex or coeducational classrooms were not forced upon students. The choice was left to the discretion of parents, and participation in either classroom format was wholly voluntary. The plaintiffs' bald assertions of "classification" and "segregation" are nothing more than a vain attempt to cast a pall of unconstitutionality over the BCMS program.

In sum, the plaintiffs have failed to point to specific facts showing that they suffered a concrete and particularized injury to a legally protected interest as a result of BCMS' offering of optional single-sex classes. For the reasons stated above, the mere existence of an optional single-sex program in a public school does not establish an injury in fact. Further, to the extent the plaintiffs have attempted to allege specific facts regarding the effect of the BCMS program on their educational experience, they have failed. Nothing the plaintiffs point to demonstrates a concrete and particularized harm to any legally protected interest that was actual or imminent. *See Lujan, supra.*

---

[38] Plaintiffs cite evidence that the class sizes for eighth grade classes during the 2008–2009 school year ranged from 10–12 students in the all-boys classes, 24–28 students in the all-girls classes, and 20–31 students in the coeducational classes. DN 234 at 40–41.

Accordingly, the court concludes that the class plaintiffs have failed to make an adequate showing of standing on their own behalf and on behalf of the class members they represent. Their claims must be dismissed.

Notes and Comments

1. Is there an argument to be made in favor of the constitutionality of single-gender public schools? Some social scientists and education reformers advocate segregation of schools based upon gender as a way to improve the learning climate. Under what circumstances should courts defer to these policies?

2. How would the constitution apply to current experiments to segregate public school students based upon sexual preference? Would a separate public school for homosexual students be valid?

IV. Emerging Categories of Discrimination in Public Schools

ACEVEDO v. MONSIGNOR DONOVAN HIGH SCHOOL
420 F. Supp. 2d 337 (D.N.J. 2006)

COOPER, District Judge

Monsignor Donovan High School ("MDHS") employed Acevedo as a teacher during the 2003-2004 school year, which commenced on September 5, 2003. [Edward] Gere was the principal at MDHS during the school year. Acevedo alleges that Gere, on or about March 1, 2004, announced at a MDHS teachers' meeting that it was his goal to reduce the median age of the faculty at MDHS.

Acevedo claims that, on or about May 3, 2004, he was summoned to Gere's office and discharged from his teaching duties without cause and without benefit of the procedures set forth by the Diocese of Trenton, which oversees MDHS. Acevedo alleges that MDHS replaced him with a younger person. At the time of his discharge, Acevedo was fifty-five years old.

The plaintiffs brought this action against the defendants for, inter alia, violating the [Age Discrimination in Employment Act], on October 28, 2005. Acevedo contends that he was "performing his duties as a teacher [at MDHS] in an appropriate and satisfactory manner during the time of his employment at [MDHS] for many years and including the academic year 2003 to 2004." Therefore, Acevedo claims that MDHS willfully violated the ADEA by (1) terminating his employment "without cause," and (2) replacing him with a younger person.

Acevedo alleges that the defendants' actions (1) deprived him of "pension rights to which he would have otherwise been entitled if continued in the employ of [MDHS]," and (2) caused him "humiliation, anxiety, emotional distress, [and] pain and suffering." .....

II. Legal Sufficiency of G. Acevedo's ADEA Claim

The ADEA prohibits discrimination by employers on the basis of age. 29 U.S.C. § ("Section") 623(a)(1). To establish a prima facie case of age discrimination under the ADEA, Acevedo must demonstrate that (1) he was over forty years old at the time he was discharged; (2) he was qualified for the position from which he was discharged and performing same in a satisfactory manner; (3) his employment was discharged despite his qualifications and performance; and (4) his employer ultimately filled the position with a person sufficiently younger to permit an inference of age discrimination. *Narin v. Lower Merion Sch. Dist.*, 206 F.3d 323, 331 (3d Cir. 2000); *Healy v. N.Y. Life Ins. Co.*, 860 F.2d 1209, 1214 (3d Cir. 1988).

The defendants argue that—as indicated in the warnings MDHS allegedly provided to Acevedo—he was not performing his job duties in a satisfactory manner. Also, the defendants contend that MDHS did not discharge Acevedo; rather, they provided him with the opportunity to resign, and he did so. Moreover, the defendants allege that Acevedo's position was ultimately not filled with someone sufficiently younger. Therefore, the defendants assert that Acevedo has failed to state a viable cause of action under the ADEA.

Acevedo has set forth a prima facie case of age discrimination under the ADEA. In the amended complaint, Acevedo alleges that (1) MDHS employed him as a teacher, (2) he was "over the age of forty years having been born on December 2, 1948," (3) he was performing his duties as a teacher in an appropriate and satisfactory manner, (4) MDHS discharged him on May 3, 2004, and (5) his duties were taken over by a younger person. Taking all of the above allegations as true for purposes of this motion, Acevedo has set forth a prima facie case under the ADEA.

Acevedo first alleges, and the defendants do not dispute, that he was in the protected class—over forty years old—at the time of his alleged discharge. Also, Acevedo claims that he was performing his job as a teacher at MDHS in "an appropriate and satisfactory manner" before MDHS discharged him. This allegation is sufficient to satisfy the second prima facie element. The defendants argue that the warnings Acevedo received demonstrate that he was not performing his job duties in a satisfactory manner. However, the Court has already excluded the warnings from consideration in deciding this motion because they are not relied upon by the plaintiffs, nor are they integral to the amended complaint. The defendants make no other arguments attacking the legal sufficiency of Acevedo's allegations concerning the second prima facie element.

Acevedo alleges further that the defendants discharged him on May 3, 2004. This allegation is sufficient to satisfy the third prima facie element. The defendants contend that Acevedo cannot establish this element because he allegedly resigned and was not discharged. The defendants support their argument with (1) a document which allegedly represents a resignation letter signed by Acevedo, and (2) Gere's statement that Acevedo resigned. However, the Court has already excluded these documents from consideration, and the Court need not resolve the factual issue of whether Acevedo resigned or the defendants discharged him in deciding this motion. Instead, the

Court need only examine the sufficiency of Acevedo's allegations, which, as explained above, are sufficient to satisfy the third prima facie element.

Acevedo alleges that he was replaced by someone younger. Also, he contends that his replacement was not qualified and related to someone in MDHS's administration. (*Id.*) The Court finds that G. Acevedo's allegations are sufficient to satisfy the fourth prima facie element.

The defendants argue that Acevedo cannot demonstrate that they replaced him with someone "sufficiently younger" by pointing out that they temporarily replaced him—until the close of the school year—with "Assistant Principal Eileen McCullion's college age son, [Tim McCullion], who was majoring in Spanish and was substitute teaching at MDHS." The defendants state further that they hired Barbara Cedeno, forty-six years old, to replace Acevedo for the 2004-2005 school year.

The defendants also apparently argue that Acevedo cannot establish the "sufficiently younger" element because his permanent replacement was forty-six years old—nine years younger than Acevedo—at the time of her hire. Even if the Court had accepted, and therefore considered, the defendants' submissions regarding the circumstances involving MDHS finding a replacement for Acevedo and the ages of his apparent replacement(s), their argument is deficient on its face to support their motion.

A plaintiff—to satisfy the "sufficiently younger" standard—does not have to show a "particular age difference." *Showalter v. Univ. of Pitt. Med. Ctr.*, 190 F.3d 231, 236 (3d Cir. 1999) Also, although "different courts have held . . . that a five year difference can be sufficient… a one year difference cannot." *Sempier v. Johnson & Higgins*, 45 F.3d 724, 729 (3d Cir. 1995) (holding that "sufficiently younger" standard satisfied where plaintiff was replaced by two individuals—one who was four years younger than plaintiff and the other who was ten years younger); *see Showalter*, 190 F.3d at 236 (concluding that plaintiff satisfied "sufficiently younger" standard by showing replacements were eight years younger and sixteen years younger than plaintiff).[7] In other words, "there is no magical formula to measure a particular age gap and determine if it is sufficiently wide to give rise to an inference of discrimination." *Barber v. CSX Distribution Servs.*, 68 F.3d 694, 699 (3d Cir. 1995).

III. Gere's Individual Liability

---

[7] *See also Kehres v. Kline*, 132 Fed. Appx. 992, 994 (3d Cir. 2005) (finding one to two year age difference between replacement and plaintiff insufficient to create inference of age discrimination); *Coffman v. Abington Mem'l Hosp.*, 2003 U.S. Dist. LEXIS 10770, (E.D. Pa. June 24, 2003) (concluding six year age difference insufficient as matter of law to permit inference of age discrimination); *Martin v. Healthcare Bus. Res.*, 2002 U.S. Dist. LEXIS 5117 (E.D. Pa. Mar. 26, 2002) ("For purposes of a prima facie ADEA case, the fourth element contemplates an age difference of at least five years."); *Gutknecht v. SmithKline Beecham Clinical Lab.*, 950 F. Supp. 667, 672 (E.D. Pa. 1996) ("Although no uniform rule exists, it is generally accepted that when the difference in age between the fired employee and his or her replacement is fewer than five or six years, the replacement is not considered 'sufficiently younger,' and thus no prima facie case is made.").

Acevedo has also asserted an ADEA claim against Gere. …The ADEA makes it unlawful for an "employer" to discriminate on the basis of age. 29 U.S.C. § 623(a). The ADEA defines an "employer" as "a person engaged in an industry affecting commerce who has twenty or more employees for each working day in each of twenty or more calendar weeks in the current or preceding calendar year . . . [or] any agent of such a person . . ...." 29 U.S.C. § 630(b). Unless an individual qualifies as a plaintiff's "employer" as defined above, the ADEA does not provide for individual liability.

Acevedo apparently does not dispute that Gere cannot be held liable under the ADEA in his individual capacity. Rather, he claims that, as a "participant in the decision making process that formed the basis for the discrimination," Gere could be held liable in his "official capacity" as principal of MDHS. ….The ADEA does not permit official-capacity claims against non-employer individuals. *See Seres v. Liberty Chevrolet*, 1999 U.S. Dist. LEXIS 128 (S.D.N.Y. Jan. 12, 1999).

…..

[D]ecisions by district courts in this circuit have found "no basis for [distinguishing] between 'official' and 'individual' suits in the statutory language of Title VII." *Schanzer v. Rutgers Univ.*, 934 F. Supp. 669, 678 n.12 (D.N.J. 1996); *Cardoza v. Merion Cricket Club*, 1996 U.S. Dist. LEXIS 22537 (E.D. Pa. May 2, 1996); *Behrens v. Rutgers Univ.*, 1996 U.S. Dist. LEXIS 22311 (D.N.J. Mar. 29, 1996)….These courts, in rejecting the individual capacity/official capacity dichotomy, explained that "[a] suit against a supervisory employee in her official capacity is a suit against the individual in name only; it operates in all respects as a suit against the employer." *E.g.*, *Schanzer*, 934 F.Supp. at 678 n.12; "If the defendant is not [the] plaintiff's employer, . . . it is irrelevant whether that person was acting in an official or individual capacity, for a Title VII suit may not be properly maintained against the individual." *Schanzer*, 934 F. Supp. at 678 n.12. As such, "the relevant threshold question is not whether the defendant acted in an official capacity, but whether the defendant is the plaintiff's employer under the statute." *Id.*…Gere is not Acevedo's "employer" under the ADEA, Thus, the Court will not allow Acevedo's claim against Gere in his official capacity to continue.

…..

The Court, for the reasons discussed herein, finds that Acevedo has alleged a prima facie case of age discrimination under the ADEA against MDHS.

NATIONAL LAW CENTER ON HOMELESSNESS AND POVERTY v. NEW YORK

224 F.R.D. 314 (E.D.N.Y. 2004)

JUDGES: ARTHUR D. SPATT, United States District Judge.

This action, commenced by parents of homeless children that are residing in Suffolk County, New York, seeks enforcement of the McKinney-Vento Act, 42 U.S.C. §§ 11431-35, and the Equal

Protection Clause of the United States Constitution. Presently before the Court are two motions: (1) a motion by the defendants to dismiss the action; and (2) a motion by the plaintiffs, pursuant to Rule 23 of the Federal Rules of Civil Procedure ("Fed. R. Civ. P."), for class certification.

I. BACKGROUND

The plaintiffs in this action are homeless children and their parents living in Suffolk County, New York. They seek declaratory and injunctive relief against the State of New York...for alleged violations of the McKinney-Vento Act ("McKinney Act") and the Equal Protection Clause of the Fourteenth Amendment of the United States Constitution. Plaintiffs seek to invoke the provisions of 42 U.S.C. § 1983 to enforce the terms of the McKinney Act and the Constitution.

The Plaintiffs allege that the Defendants are responsible for a systematic failure to provide homeless children in Suffolk County, New York, access to education by failing to: (1) locate and ensure enrollment of homeless children; (2) provide uninterrupted transportation to enable homeless children to attend school; (3) provide immediate enrollment to homeless children upon becoming homeless; and (4) provide education services that are comparable to the services that nonhomeless children receive. The Plaintiffs allege that homeless children are entitled to these educational services through the provisions of the McKinney Act and the Constitution.

The proposed class representatives are six homeless families with school-age children in Suffolk County who all allege that they have faced obstacles in maintaining enrollment in school. From the allegations in the complaint, a common theme emerges. All of the children at some time became homeless and, as a consequence of their parents' misfortune, missed weeks and sometimes months of school due to failures in transportation or enrollment. For example, the W. family has four school-age children and one pre-school age child who was denied access to Head Start. After becoming homeless, the family moved from shelter to shelter, and with each move, transportation to and from school stopped, thus causing the children to miss school for weeks at a time. Another plaintiff, S.P., was out of school for more than two months while various agencies tried to determine who should provide transportation for the child. In another example, A.B., was attending school in the Middle Country Central School District until her family was placed in emergency housing in Copaigue. Both school districts refused to admit the child—Middle Country insisted she attend the Copaigue School District while Copaigue declined to admit A.B. without the proper paperwork. As a result, A.B. missed months of school.

.....

1. The McKinney-Vento Act

The McKinney-Vento Act was enacted in 1987 "to provide urgently needed assistance to protect and improve the lives and safety of the homeless . . . ." Pub. L. No. 100-77, 101 Stat. 525 (codified at 42 U.S.C. § 11431 (1988)). The Act required states to assure that each child of a homeless individual and each homeless youth had access to a free and appropriate public education. 42 U.S.C.

§ 11431. Under the Act, Congress authorized the Secretary of Education to grant funds to the States that comply with the provisions of the Act. *Id.*§ 11432.

In 2002, the McKinney Act was reauthorized as part of the No Child Left Behind Act (NCLBA). Pub. L. No. 107-10, 115 Stat. 1989. As part of the reauthorization, the McKinney Act underwent a general revision, but the purpose of the Act remained to "ensure that each child of a homeless individual and each homeless youth has equal access to the same free, appropriate public education, including a public preschool education, as provided to other children and youths." 42 U.S.C. § 11431 (2004). Congress stated that "homelessness alone is not sufficient reason to separate students from the mainstream school environment." *Id.* Thus, "homeless children and youths should have access to the education and other services" that are needed to meet "student academic achievement standards to which all students are held." *Id.*

A court's role in determining whether personal rights exist in the section 1983 context is to initially determine whether Congress intended to confer individual rights upon a class of persons. *Gonzaga University v. Doe*, 536 U.S. 273 (2002). "For a statute to create such private rights, its text must be 'phrased in terms of the persons benefitted.'" *Id.* at 284. In addition, a court must "determine if Congress foreclosed a § 1983 remedy either expressly or impliedly through the creation of a comprehensive administrative enforcement scheme." *Taylor v. Vermont Dep't of Educ.*, 313 F.3d 768, 783 (2d Cir. 2002) (citing *Blessing*, 520 U.S. at 342).

In light of these guidelines, it is clear that Congress intended that the McKinney Act confer individually enforceable rights. Indeed, the Court of Appeals for the District of Columbia has held that the McKinney Act confers enforceable rights on homeless children. *Lampkin v. District of Columbia*, 307 U.S. App. D.C. 155, 27 F.3d 605, 611 (D.C. Cir. 1994).

.....

...The Act provides mandatory entitlements to homeless children by clear and precise direction to state and local officials. The statute obligates State and local agencies to perform in a specific way to ensure that homeless children are provided an education on par with that of nonhomeless children. Finally, the lack of an enforcement scheme indicates that Congress intended to confer rights on a particular class of persons. Consequently, the Plaintiffs can maintain an action under section 1983 to enforce provisions of the McKinney Act.

2. The Equal Protection Clause

The Fourteenth Amendment of the United States Constitution guarantees that no state shall "deny to any person within its jurisdiction the equal protection of the laws." This is "essentially a direction that all persons similarly situated should be treated alike." *City of Cleburne v. Cleburne Living Ctr.*, 473 U.S. 432, 439, 105 S. Ct. 3249, 87 L. Ed. 2d 313 (1985). Plaintiffs in this case claim that homeless children in Suffolk County are not receiving the same access to public school education enjoyed by nonhomeless children.

Discriminatory treatment by the government is sufficient to trigger assessment under the Equal Protection Clause. *See Lewis v. Thompson*, 252 F.3d 567, 590 (2d Cir. 2001). If government action interferes with a "fundamental right" or discriminates against a "suspect class," it must be reviewed using the strict scrutiny analysis. Absent these circumstances, government action will ordinarily survive an equal protection challenge so long as the action is rationally related to a legitimate governmental purpose. *Plyler v. Doe*, 457 U.S. 202, 216-17 (1982). Further, in *Plyler*, the Supreme Court acknowledged that although public education is not a fundamental right granted to individuals by the Constitution, neither is it "merely some governmental 'benefit' indistinguishable from other forms of social welfare legislation." *Id.* at 221. The Court reasoned that education was so important to the American way of life and to the function of state and local governments that any denial of education must be justified by some "substantial goal" of the State. *Id.* at 223-24. This analysis amounts to a "heightened" or "intermediate scrutiny" with respect to government action that results in deprivation.

Since *Plyler*, the Supreme Court has declined to extend heightened scrutiny in regard to education beyond the "unique circumstances" of *Plyler*. *See Kadrmas v. Dickinson Public Schools*, 487 U.S. 450, 108 S. Ct. 2481, 101 L. Ed. 2d 399 (1988) (holding that a public school district's charging of a user fee for bus transportation to school did not violate the Equal Protection Clause). However, the Supreme Court implied that statutes which create circumstances that involve the penalization of children for the "illegal conduct of their parents" and risk significant and enduring adverse consequences to children should be reviewed using the *Plyler* rationale. *Id.* Indeed, the Second Circuit applied the rationale of *Plyler* when it ruled that the denial of eligibility for welfare benefits to children solely because of their mothers' alien status violated the Equal Protection Clause. *Lewis v. Thompson*, 252 F.3d 567, 591 (2d Cir. 2001). In determining the whether to apply heightened scrutiny, the court stated that the denial of public education would present an even more compelling case for heightened scrutiny than the postponement of welfare benefits.

In the instant case, the circumstances are significantly similar to those in *Plyler*. The Plaintiffs' contend that homeless children in Suffolk Country are not receiving the same access to public school education enjoyed by other children. Thus, taking the Plaintiffs' factual allegations as true, the Defendants appear to be penalizing these homeless children because of the misfortunes or misdeeds of their parents. Further, in exacting the penalty, the State Defendants are risking significant and enduring adverse consequences to the children by denying them access to a public education. On its face, the Plaintiffs' warrants the "heightened scrutiny" standard set forth in *Plyler*.

Under heightened scrutiny review, the Plaintiffs are not required to negate any reasonable conceivable set of facts that could provide any rational basis for the classification of the children, as required when utilizing rational basis review. In fact, the Defendants failed to assert even one rational basis for the homeless children transportation procedures currently in place in Suffolk County. Therefore, Plaintiffs have met their burden of stating a claim under the Equal Protection Clause, which may be enforced under section 1983. As such, the Defendants' motion to dismiss Plaintiffs' cause of action for failing to assert a federal right under section 1983 is denied.

B. Class Certification

Because the plaintiff has successfully fulfilled the requirements of Rule 23(a) and Rule 23(b)(2), the Court holds that certification of the putative class is proper.

Caroline Larsen: Balancing the Books: The Stewart B. McKinney Homeless Assistance Act and Separate Schools for Homeless Children in Arizona, 34 Ariz. St. L.J. 705 (2002)*

Arizona, along with each of the other forty-nine states, the District of Columbia, and the Commonwealth of Puerto Rico, receives annual federal funding under the Stewart B. McKinney Homeless Assistance Act ("McKinney Act" or "the Act") to support a variety of services for the homeless, including schools and educational programs.

Prior to the Act, many homeless individuals with children found it difficult, or even impossible, to enroll their children in public schools. In 1990, estimates indicated that more than fifty percent of homeless children did not attend school. One goal of the McKinney Act was to tackle the barriers that were preventing homeless children from accessing educational services, such as transportation issues, enrollment delays caused by a lack of student immunization records or birth certificates, guardianship concerns, and the inability to meet school district residency requirements. The Act orders states to provide services that help homeless children "enroll in, attend, and succeed in school," and requires a state plan that describes how recipient states will ensure that homeless children receive the same opportunity to meet state academic performance standards as other children.

Supporters of segregated homeless schools… argue that these schools recognize and cope with the unique educational needs and problems encountered by homeless children, and without such schools, these children might not attend school at all. In fact, eighty-eight percent of homeless children are enrolled in school, most in mainstream public schools. As the national homelessness crisis grows, public schools across the country are creating innovative solutions to help homeless students succeed….Proponents of segregated schools wonder whether homeless children can keep up with the academic pace of mainstream public schools. This view treats homelessness as an "educational condition," rather than the result of extreme poverty.

…..

Segregated homeless schools often provide sub-standard educational opportunities, and draw away money that could support specialized programs for homeless children in public schools. Many indicators show that homeless children can learn and succeed just like other students. Their failure to do so in many cases may be the result of their educational opportunities, not their abilities. Separate schools are plagued with a variety of problems not often encountered in mainstream public schools. Because students from different grade levels are taught together, teachers are often not certified to teach all of their students. Additionally, many of these schools do not conform to state curriculum standards.

In addition to serious concerns about the quality of education provided by separate schools, the idea of segregating students from the mainstream based on their socio-economic status is also cause for alarm. Proponents argue that homeless students are more comfortable in a school with their peers; they fear other children will ostracize homeless students in mainstream schools. This argument is based on a premise that has been defeated in the past; if society continued to support the concept that segregation "protects" students from discrimination in the 1950s, we would still have separate schools for blacks and whites. Providing clothing and hygiene and school supplies may eliminate some of the indicators that could automatically identify homeless students to their peers. In Austin, Texas, a homeless education program ensures that homeless students receive caps and gowns for their graduation ceremonies. Homeless students can successfully interact with their non-homeless classmates; not every homeless student in an integrated program is a pariah, with a scarlet "H" emblazoned on their chest. In reality, segregated schools draw more attention to the housing status of their students.

Finally, there are significant concerns about the de facto racial and ethnic segregation that often occurs at separate schools. Because homelessness typically results from extreme poverty, it is more likely to afflict those who are at the highest risk for poverty. Currently, in the United States, these high-risk individuals are more often minorities. As a result, separate homeless schools by default often isolate students not only by economic and housing status, but on the basis of their race or ethnicity as well. Separate schools have long been used to isolate segments of the population from the majority—due to gender, race, disability, etc. Homeless schools are no exception.... The McKinney Act [directs] states to conduct research into the problems that homeless children encounter in gaining access to public schools, define plans for resolving such problems, and train school personnel in how to recognize and address some of the specific issues that their homeless students may have. Perhaps with a greater focus on mainstream integration, additional funding, and no separate homeless school options available, mainstream public schools would have more incentive to adhere to these statutory guidelines.

RACINE CHARTER ONE, INC. v. RACINE UNIFIED SCHOOL DISTRICT

424 F.3d 677 (7th Cir. 2005)

[This case appears in Chapter Two on page 124]

Kristina Brittenham: Equal Protection Theory and the Harvey Milk High School: Why Anti-Subordination Alone Is Not Enough, 45 B.C. L. Rev 869 (2004)*

After decades of fighting for integration and watching racial desegregation efforts falter, attitudes toward equality in public schools have begun to change in recent years. Some advocates argue that the formal equal treatment sought in. These advocates are less concerned with different treatment on the basis of classifications like race or sex than with the disadvantages resulting from such classifications. Their approach focuses on repairing the negative impact discrimination has on members of disadvantaged groups. Advocates believe that this method, called anti-subordination, provides a better way to achieve equality than does formal equality, the method of treating everyone alike.

The anti-subordination movement contends that it is perfectly acceptable, even desirable, to treat children differently on the basis of their group membership if it will help them overcome the special obstacles they face. Discrimination on the basis of group classifications is therefore positive if it serves the ultimate purpose of achieving equality. Anti-subordination and formal equality advocates thus interpret the U.S. Constitution's guarantee of equal protection, which is rooted in the Fourteenth Amendment, from distinct perspectives. The anti-subordination movement has sought voluntary segregation as a solution to a public school system that is failing its female and minority students, preferring to target the immediate educational needs of these children rather than insist on integrated education—an ideal that has not lived up to its promise.

Voluntary school segregation has become increasingly popular over the last decade, particularly with regard to single-sex schools. Although some single-sex schools have existed for years, a new crop has appeared across the United States from New York to California. These schools are based on several different models. There are, for example, single-sex schools that are targeted at empowering young women; school districts have experimented with paired single-sex academies that educate boys and girls separately as well. Advocates have also pushed for all-male black schools, although this idea has appeared to be too controversial to sustain support.

The Harvey Milk High School ("HMHS") in New York City, the first public school designed to meet the needs of lesbian, gay, bisexual, transgender, and questioning ("LGBTQ") students, adds a new dimension to this trend. HMHS has existed since 1985 as a special program for LGBTQ students. The program operates as a partnership between the New York City Department of Education and the Hetrick-Martin Institute, a nonprofit organization dedicated to advocating for and supporting LGBTQ youths. Originally a small off-site program, HMHS is now a full-fledged, four-year institution. HMHS does not discriminate on the basis of sexual orientation in admissions; rather, it is open to all applicants and aims to admit students who have been the victims of verbal or physical abuse.

HMHS is a creative response to the unique problems LGBTQ youths face in public schools. Recent studies reflect that 69% of LGBTQ students reported experiencing harassment or violence at school. A wealth of statistics demonstrates the extent of the discrimination these students face. Over 40% of these students do not feel safe at their schools. Ultimately, 28% of LGBTQ students drop out of school altogether. In seeking to eliminate these problems, HMHS provides a fresh opportunity to examine voluntary school segregation through the lens of the anti-subordination versus formal equality debate underscoring it.

.....

In the context of public education, anti-subordination advocates argue that treating members of disadvantaged classifications differently may be necessary to achieve equality of educational opportunity. These advocates support an idea articulated by black activist and intellectual W.E.B. DuBois: children need education, not integrated education or segregated education. These advocates maintain that a fear of classifications must become secondary to a desire to meet each child's immediate educational needs, and therefore society should choose voluntary segregation over formal equality.

Anti-subordination advocates argue that public school teachers may be biased against members of certain disadvantaged classifications, such as girls or black boys. Alternatively, these teachers may simply lack the skills to deal with the specific issues these children face. As a result, these children suffer disparate treatment, including a lack of attention and lower academic expectations for girls and increased levels of punishment and special or remedial education tracking for black boys. Children also may face obstacles that other students create; for example, girls experience sexual harassment as early as junior high school. Treatment from teachers, students, or both may result in lower levels of personal confidence.

The problems that members of these classifications face may even be institutional. The scarcity of information in public education about black achievements, for instance, may prevent black children from obtaining a full sense of self-worth. This problem extends beyond one teacher or set of students to the entire educational system. Children who, as a result of their group membership, experience disadvantages with respect to teachers, other students, and the educational system as a whole may be less successful academically.

Anti-subordination advocates argue that voluntary school segregation can be an effective tool for remedying the problems these children encounter. For example, girls in single-sex schools have an opportunity to learn in an environment that challenges traditional sex roles. Similarly, black youths in black schools have a chance to learn in an environment free from racism. Students who have had a chance to take advantage of these opportunities have demonstrated, according to some research, increased academic achievement. From an anti-subordination perspective, voluntary school segregation thus functions as a form of affirmative action for children who have been disadvantaged in past educational experiences. It provides a compensatory function—an opportunity for these students to reach a level of achievement that they would have reached absent societal discrimination or disadvantage.

Anti-subordination advocates address some of the criticisms of voluntarily segregated schools by emphasizing the positive experiences of students who attend them. Rather than stigmatizing the students who attend or reinforcing negative stereotypes, these schools provide an opportunity for students to learn in a modern, alternative environment that helps them fight stereotypes. The true stigma exists in the disparate treatment these children face at their integrated public schools. Furthermore, students elect to attend voluntarily segregated schools. Unlike traditionally segregated schools, which enforce a discriminatory state agenda, these schools simply provide an opportunity and a choice. Ultimately, anti-subordination advocates urge society to prioritize the real educational needs of real children who face obstacles in public schools over any perceived abstract need to treat them the same as everyone else.

. . . . .

Formal equality advocates also maintain that the practice of segregation stigmatizes the children who are segregated, and they cite a wealth of social science data in the context of state-mandated segregation as support. According to this research, segregation unfairly burdens members of segregated groups because they alone must experience the dissonance between the ideals of democracy and the reality' of state-mandated segregation. Segregation is a particular source of difficulty' for those in the minority. Segregated minorities often experience disturbing feelings, such as a sense of inferiority, internal conflict regarding self-worth, aggressiveness, martyrdom, submissiveness, and a tendency to withdraw. Segregation results in a distorted perception of reality and perpetuates a vicious cycle in which disparate treatment begets negative effects which serve as a basis for more disparate treatment. Furthermore, those in the majority (that is not segregated) experience negative feelings ranging from increased hostility to internal conflict. Although the social science data indicating these effects is specific to state-mandated segregation, formal equality advocates believe it is unlikely that state-supported segregation in the form of voluntary school segregation would produce significantly different results.

. . . . .

HMHS would probably survive an equal protection challenge because the school's admissions policy lacks discriminatory intent based on sexual orientation. The policy does not discriminate on this basis, but rather targets students who are in crisis. Although the program is aimed towards LGBTQ students, heterosexual students are welcome to apply and to be considered for admission. HMHS simply seeks to provide a safe, hate-free learning environment for at-risk students. An equal protection challenge to HMHS, claiming that the school discriminates based on sexual orientation, probably would fail because heterosexual students are not excluded.

The basis for discrimination against a potential HMHS student is thus not sexual orientation but the extent to which that student is at risk, for any reason. That the school may attract a disproportionate number of LGBTQ students is a discriminatory impact problem requiring only rational basis scrutiny. Under a rational basis analysis, it appears that prioritizing admittance for at-risk youth bears a rational relationship to the legitimate state interest in providing safe educational opportunities for all students. Thus, HMHS is unlikely to violate equal protection.

Even if a court found that HMHS discriminates based on sexual orientation, the school is still likely to survive a constitutional challenge. Under this scenario, it is possible to imagine a court finding that HMHS's facially neutral policy is applied in a discriminatory manner, systematically excluding heterosexual students. Like in *Yick Wo v. Hopkins*, in which a facially neutral building ordinance was applied selectively to Chinese-Americans, this kind of activity may trigger a higher level of scrutiny than mere rational basis. In this case, the higher level of scrutiny available for discrimination based on sexual orientation would be something more than rational basis, which the U.S. Supreme Court has potentially applied but not officially acknowledged. And even if a court applied this slightly higher standard, discriminating based on sexual orientation in admissions appears to be rationally related to the legitimate state interest in providing safe educational opportunities to members of a disadvantaged group.

.....

The case for HMHS is strong. The statistics on discrimination against LGBTQ youths paint a disturbing picture of harassment and academic failure. Yet hostility against these students should not justify segregating them. In *Cooper v. Aaron*, the U.S. Supreme Court found that even violence against black students could not justify segregation; the public schools were required to fix the problem rather than avoid it. Advocates should adopt this theory in fighting discrimination against LGBTQ students as well.

HMHS admittedly can be distinguished from the circumstances in Cooper on two grounds. First, the motive behind voluntary segregation is positive. Anti-subordination advocates, not opponents of LGBTQ interests, are behind the development of the school. This justification is unlike the post hoc rationalization displayed by the Arkansas school system in *Cooper*, in which government officials attempted to cloak racist motives in false concern for the students in question. Furthermore, the segregation at issue is voluntary. The state is not mandating it, only tolerating it; no student will be forced to attend.

The resulting message, however, remains the same in either circumstance. Hostility against LGBTQ students justifies segregating them. Society therefore avoids dealing with the root of the problem, allowing discrimination to continue in public schools despite good intentions to the contrary. This message, therefore, is not mere ideology—it has a concrete, negative result. Even if society simultaneously works to overcome discrimination within integrated schools, as advocated by the Hetrick-Martin Institute (which helps to run HMHS), it is clear that removal itself functions as the immediate solution. It is unclear, however, how students and teachers who exacerbate the problem will truly learn to overcome bias when the targets of bias are removed. Supporting voluntary segregation thus endorses the message that hostility justifies segregation, a message that frees public schools from taking their duty to overcome discrimination against LGBTQ students seriously.

Chapter Eight
Title IX of the Educational Amendments of 1972

> No person in the United States shall, on the basis of sex, be excluded from participation in, be denied the benefits of, or be subjected to discrimination under any education program or activity receiving Federal financial assistance.
> Section 901 of Title IX, 86 Stat. 374 in 20 U. S. C. § 1682

> Congress enacted Title IX in 1972 with two principal objectives in mind: to avoid the use of federal resources to support discriminatory practices and to provide individual citizens effective protection against those practices.
> Gebser v. Lago Vista Independent School District, 524 U.S. 274 (1998)

Perhaps the greatest misunderstanding regarding Title IX centers around the belief that Title IX is intended solely to eradicate gender discrimination in athletics. Yet, in reality, Title IX has always focused primarily on non-discrimination in educational opportunities, of which athletics comprise merely a subset. Historically, employment issues—not athletic opportunities—were the impetus for Title IX. But such issues have long since faded from memory and often receive the least amount of attention surrounding Title IX's many protective measures.

As U. S. Supreme Court jurisprudence confirms, Title IX has repeatedly been invoked to challenge discriminatory practices in employment, admissions, sexual harassment, testing practices, pregnancy issues and, most recently, retaliation for speaking out against such discrimination. These protections are afforded to both genders—male and female. Only two of the major Supreme Court cases even address athletic opportunities. And, one of these decisions deals more specifically with retaliation for speaking out against gender discrimination under Title IX than with athletic participation per se.

Title IX, modeled after Title VI's racial equality legislation, has evolved greatly since its passage in 1972. And, as the following article and cases demonstrate, Title IX has developed into a significant enforcement mechanism for gender equity in education.

Bernice R. Sandler: "Too Strong for a Woman" – The Five Words That Created Title IX, About Women on Campus (1997)*

The year was 1969, I had been teaching part-time at the University of Maryland for several years during the time I worked on my doctorate and shortly after I finished it. There were seven openings in the department and I had just asked a faculty member, a friend of mine, why I was not even

* Bernice R. Sandler is a Senior Scholar at the Women's Research and Education Institute. Her web site is www.bernicesandler.com and she can be contacted at sandler@bernicesandler.com. Reprinted with permission.

considered for any of the openings. It was not my qualifications; they were excellent. "But let's face it," he said, "You come on too strong for a woman."

My reaction? I went home and cried. I had no idea that this rejection would not only change my life but would change the lives of millions of women and girls because it would lead ultimately to passage of Title IX, the law that prohibits sex discrimination in educational institutions receiving federal dollars. Instead, I bemoaned the fact that I had spoken out at staff meetings with suggestions for improving procedures. I lamented the times that I had discussed teaching and professional issues with faculty members. I regretted my participation in classes as a graduate student. In short, I accepted the assessment that I was "too strong for a woman."

It was my then husband who helped me understand what the words "too strong for a woman" meant. He labeled the department's behavior as "sex discrimination"—a label that started me thinking. Was this really a question of my being "too strong"? After all there were many strong men in the department. Yet the label of "sex discrimination" was a new one for me and initially I was not ready to apply it to my not getting the position at Maryland. Like many women at that time, I was somewhat ambivalent about the women's movement and halfway believed the press descriptions of its supporters as "abrasive," "man-hating," "radical," and "unfeminine." Surely I was not like that.

In the next few months I had two more similar rejections. A research executive who interviewed me for a position spent nearly an hour explaining to me why he wouldn't hire women because they stayed at home when their children were sick. (That my children were in high school was deemed irrelevant.) Then an employment agency counselor looked at my resume and told me that I was "not really a professional" but "just a housewife who went back to school."

Although later, in retrospect, I would discover other instances of sex discrimination in my life, at that point I had not consciously noticed it. Yet, here were three incidents within a short period which I could not rationalize away. . . .

But this was 1969. Although sex discrimination was indeed illegal in certain circumstances, I quickly discovered that none of the laws prohibiting discrimination covered sex discrimination in education. Title VII of the Civil Rights Act which prohibited discrimination in employment on the basis of race, color, religion, national origin and sex, excluded "educational institutions in their educational activities," meaning faculty and administrators were exempt. Title VI of the same act prohibited discrimination on the basis of race, color and national origin in federally assisted programs, but did not cover sex discrimination. Thus students were not protected against sex discrimination. The Equal Pay Act prohibited discrimination in salaries on the basis of sex but exempted all professional and administrative employees, including faculty. The Fourteenth Amendment to the Constitution assures all persons "equal protection of the laws," but at that time no case concerning discrimination against women in education had ever been decided in favor of women by the Supreme Court.

I began to read more about the civil rights movement to see what African Americans had done to break down segregated school systems and employment discrimination, with the hope of learning what might be applicable to women's issues. The breakthrough occurred when I was reading a report of the U.S. Commission on Civil Rights which examined the impact of antidiscrimination laws on race discrimination. The report described a presidential Executive Order prohibiting federal contractors from discrimination in employment on the basis of race, color, religion and national origin. There was a footnote, and being an academic, I quickly turned to the back of the report and read it. It stated that Executive Order 11246 had been amended by President Johnson, effective October 13, 1968, to include discrimination based on sex.

Even though I was alone, I shrieked aloud with my discovery: I had made the connection that since most universities and colleges had federal contracts they were forbidden from discriminating in employment on the basis of sex. . . .

I called the Office of Federal Contract Compliance at the Department of Labor to be certain that sex discrimination was covered by the Executive Order. I was immediately connected to the Director, Vincent Macaluso who had been waiting for someone to sue the Executive Order in regard to sex discrimination. We met, and together we planned the first complaint against universities and colleges, and the strategies to bring about enforcement of the Executive Order.

Two months later under the auspices of the Women's Equity Action League (WEAL) I began what was soon to become a national campaign to end discrimination in education and which eventually culminated in the passage of Title IX. On January 31, 1970, WEAL filed a historic class action complaint against all universities and colleges in the country with specific charges against the University of Maryland. The charges were filed with the U.S. Department of Labor under Executive Order 11246, as amended, and asked for an immediate compliance review of all institutions holding federal contracts. Because these were administrative charges filed with a federal agency rather than a lawsuit filed in court, it was not necessary for me to be an attorney. There were no special forms to fill out. Individuals did not need to be named; the charges were filed on behalf of all women in higher education. Thus, the complaint did not name me or describe the incident in which I was involved.

Until that time the Executive Order had been used almost exclusively in cases concerning blue-collar workers, and although the Order had covered sex discrimination since October 1968, there had been virtually no enforcement by the government until WEAL began its campaign.

The WEAL complaint charged "an industry-wide pattern" of discrimination against women in the academic community and asked for an investigation in the following areas: admission quotas to undergraduate and graduate schools, financial assistance, hiring practices, promotions and salary differentials. . . .

The result was striking: many departments had no women at all, even though women often obtained as many as 25 percent of the doctorates in all fields. The pattern was clear: the higher the rank, the fewer the women. The more prestigious the field, the department, or institution, the fewer the women. At the administrative ranks, women were a rarity; at that time even many women's colleges were headed by men. . . .

On March 9, 1970, Rep. Martha Griffiths (MI) who was on WEAL's national advisory board, gave the first speech in the U.S. Congress on discrimination against women in education. . . . Rep. Edith Green (OR) (also a member of WEAL's national advisory board) had long been aware of sex discrimination in higher education, and the lack of coverage by civil rights laws. As chair of the subcommittee that dealt with higher education, she was in a unique position to shape new legislation. . . .

The first Congressional hearings on the education and employment of women were held by Rep. Green in June and July of 1970. This was the official beginning of the bill that eventually became Title IX. The original bill, part of a larger measure on higher education, proposed to amend Title VII of the Civil Rights Act to cover employees in educational institutions, Title VI to cover sex discrimination in federally assisted programs, and the Equal Pay Act to cover executives, administrators and professionals. . . .

At some point after the hearings, higher education began to recognize that the bill might affect their institutions. Officials from Harvard, Princeton, Yale and Dartmouth were concerned that they might have to admit women in equal numbers. (The first three institutions had recently admitted women but had strict quota restricting their numbers to about 30 percent; Dartmouth was planning to admit women in the near future). These institutions lobbied successfully for an exemption in the bill for private undergraduate admissions, claiming that different sex ratios were best for learning and that individual institutions knew what the best ratios were. Of course there was no data to support these allegations but these institutions and their alumni in the Congress were powerful. The amendment stood, but Rep. Green made sure that once students of both sexes were admitted to an institution there could be no discrimination against them. The amendment also meant private men's and women's colleges would not be prohibited from remaining a[s] single-sex institutions. There was no opposition to this provision. The service academies were also exempted. An exemption for admission to publically-supported [sic] single-sex undergraduate institutions was also added to the bill.

The bill was ably managed in the Senate by Senator Birch Bayh (IN) who was also a member of WEAL's national advisory board. A few people (very few) noticed that athletics might be affected by the bill, and so there was a discussion on the floor of the Senate about whether the bill required educational institutions to allow women to play on football teams. Having inserted that notion into the legislative history, higher education retreated, apparently unaware that Title IX would have a profound impact on athletics even if women were kept off football teams.

Because colleges and universities had only a rudimentary understanding of the problem of discrimination at the time, the higher education community apparently believed it had taken care of what they saw as the major impacts of the bill—admissions and football. Higher education did not lobby for or against the bill, and because it was attached to a higher education measure, the elementary and secondary education community was largely unaware of the bill. . . .

In the spring of 1972, two years after the hearings, a portion of Rep. Green's original bill became law when Title VII of the Civil Rights Amendment was amended by Congress in a separate action to cover all employees in educational institutions. Initially, Rep. Green had also initially sought to amend Title VI of the Civil Rights Act (prohibiting discrimination on the basis of race, color and national origin in all federally-funded activities) to include sex discrimination. However, at the urging of African-American leaders and others, who were worried that opening Title VI for amendment could weaken its coverage, she proposed a separate and new title, which became Title XI. In its final form, Title IX was identical to that of Title VI, except that it was restricted to educational activities, contained additional exemptions and included the amendment to the Equal Pay Act. On June 23, 1972, Title IX of the Educational Amendments of 1972, was passed by the Congress and on July 1, was signed into law by President Richard Nixon.

I. Private Remedies under Title IX

The first cases interpreting Title IX challenged whether Congress, in passing Title IX, intended to create a private legally enforceable remedy. Many Congressional legislative schemes provide administrative rights, but few provide individuals the personal right to sue the offending party. Because Title IX itself was silent on the issue, several U. S. Supreme Court cases have had to address the issue.

CANNON v. UNIVERSITY OF CHICAGO
441 U.S. 677 (1979)

MR. JUSTICE STEVENS delivered the opinion of the Court.

Petitioner's complaints allege that her applications for admission to medical school were denied by the respondents because she is a woman. Accepting the truth of those allegations for the purpose of its decision, the Court of Appeals held that petitioner has no right of action against respondents that may be asserted in a federal court. We granted certiorari to review that holding.

Only two facts alleged in the complaints are relevant to our decision. First, petitioner was excluded from participation in the respondents' medical education programs because of her sex. Second, these education programs were receiving federal financial assistance at the time of her exclusion. These facts, admitted arguendo by respondents' motion to dismiss the complaints, establish a violation of § 901 (a) of Title IX of the Education Amendments of 1972 (hereinafter Title IX).

That section, in relevant part, provides:

> No person in the United States shall, on the basis of sex, be excluded from participation in, be denied the benefits of, or be subjected to discrimination under any education program or activity receiving Federal financial assistance . . . .

The statute does not, however, expressly authorize a private right of action by a person injured by a violation of § 901. For that reason, and because it concluded that no private remedy should be inferred, the District court granted the respondents' motions to dismiss. .....The Court of Appeals agreed that the statute did not contain an implied private remedy. Noting that § 902 of Title IX establishes a procedure for the termination of federal financial support for institutions violating § 901, the Court of Appeals concluded that Congress intended that remedy to be the exclusive means of enforcement. It recognized that the statute was patterned after Title VI of the Civil Rights Act of 1964 (hereinafter Title VI), but rejected petitioner's argument that Title VI included an implied private cause of action.

.....

The Court of Appeals quite properly devoted careful attention to this question of statutory construction. As our recent cases—particularly *Cort v. Ash*, 422 U.S. 66—demonstrate, the fact that a federal statute has been violated and some person harmed does not automatically give rise to a private cause of action in favor of that person. Instead, before concluding that Congress intended to make a remedy available to a special class of litigants, a court must carefully analyze the four factors that *Cort* identifies as indicative of such an intent.[9] Our review of those factors persuades us, however, that the Court of Appeals reached the wrong conclusion and that petitioner does have a statutory right to pursue her claim that respondents rejected her application on the basis of her sex. After commenting on each of the four factors, we shall explain why they are not overcome by respondents' countervailing arguments.

I

First, the threshold question under *Cort* is whether the statute was enacted for the benefit of a special class of which the plaintiff is a member. That question is answered by looking to the language of the statute itself. ...Unquestionably, therefore, the first of the four factors identified in *Cort* favors the implication of a private cause of action. Title IX explicitly confers a benefit on persons discriminated against on the basis of sex, and petitioner is clearly a member of that class for whose special benefit the statute was enacted.

Second, the *Cort* analysis requires consideration of legislative history. We must recognize, however, that the legislative history of a statute that does not expressly create or deny a private remedy will typically be equally silent or ambiguous on the question. Therefore, in situations such as the present one "in which it is clear that federal law has granted a class of persons certain rights, it is not necessary to show an intention to create a private cause of action, although an explicit purpose to deny such cause of action would be controlling." *Cort*, 422 U.S., at 82 (emphasis in original). But this is not the typical case. Far from evidencing any purpose to deny a private cause of action, the history of Title IX rather plainly indicates that Congress intended to create such a remedy.

Title IX was patterned after Title VI of the Civil Rights Act of 1964. Except for the substitution of the word "sex" in Title IX to replace the words "race, color, or national origin" in Title VI, the two statutes use identical language to describe the benefited class. Both statutes provide the same

---

[9] In determining whether a private remedy is implicit in a statute not expressly providing one, several factors are relevant. First, is the plaintiff 'one of the class for whose especial benefit the statute was enacted,'—that is, does the statute create a federal right in favor of the plaintiff? Second, is there any indication of legislative intent, explicit or implicit, either to create such a remedy or to deny one? Third, is it consistent with the underlying purposes of the legislative scheme to imply such a remedy for the plaintiff? And finally, is the cause of action one traditionally relegated to state law, in an area basically the concern of the States, so that it would be inappropriate to infer a cause of action based solely on federal law?

administrative mechanism for terminating federal financial support for institutions engaged in prohibited discrimination. Neither statute expressly mentions a private remedy for the person excluded from participation in a federally funded program. The drafters of Title IX explicitly assumed that it would be interpreted and applied as Title VI had been during the preceding eight years.

.....

In 1972 when Title IX was enacted, the critical language in Title VI had already been construed as creating a private remedy. Most particularly, in 1967, a distinguished panel of the Court of Appeals for the Fifth Circuit squarely decided this issue in an opinion that was repeatedly cited with approval and never questioned during the ensuing five years. In addition, at least a dozen other federal courts reached similar conclusions in the same or related contexts during those years. It is always appropriate to assume that our elected representatives, like other citizens, know the law; in this case, because of their repeated references to Title VI and its modes of enforcement, we are especially justified in presuming both that those representatives were aware of the prior interpretation of Title VI and that that interpretation reflects their intent with respect to Title IX.

.....

Third, under *Cort*, a private remedy should not be implied if it would frustrate the underlying purpose of the legislative scheme. On the other hand, when that remedy is necessary or at least helpful to the accomplishment of the statutory purpose, the Court is decidedly receptive to its implication under the statute.

Title IX, like its model Title VI, sought to accomplish two related, but nevertheless somewhat different, objectives. First, Congress wanted to avoid the use of federal resources to support discriminatory practices; second, it wanted to provide individual citizens effective protection against those practices. Both of these purposes were repeatedly identified in the debates on the two statutes.

.....

The first purpose is generally served by the statutory procedure for the termination of federal financial support for institutions engaged in discriminatory practices. That remedy is, however, severe and often may not provide an appropriate means of accomplishing the second purpose if merely an isolated violation has occurred. In that situation, the violation might be remedied more efficiently by an order requiring an institution to accept an applicant who had been improperly excluded. Moreover, in that kind of situation it makes little sense to impose on an individual, whose only interest is in obtaining a benefit for herself, or on HEW, the burden of demonstrating that an institution's practices are so pervasively discriminatory that a complete cutoff of federal funding is appropriate. The award of individual relief to a private litigant who has prosecuted her own suit is not only sensible but is also fully consistent with—and in some cases even necessary to—the orderly enforcement of the statute.

.....

True, this Court has sometimes refused to imply private rights of action where administrative or like remedies are expressly available. But it has never withheld a private remedy where the statute explicitly confers a benefit on a class of persons and where it does not assure those persons the ability to activate and participate in the administrative process contemplated by the statute. *See Rosado v. Wyman*, 397 U.S. 397, 406 n. 8; cf. *Cort v. Ash, supra*, at 74-75; *Calhoon v. Harvey*, 379 U.S. 134. As the Government itself points out in this case, Title IX not only does not provide such a mechanism, but the complaint procedure adopted by HEW does not allow the complainant to participate in the investigation or subsequent enforcement proceedings. Moreover, even if those proceedings result in a finding of a violation, a resulting voluntary compliance agreement need not include relief for the complainant. Furthermore, the agency may simply decide not to investigate—a decision that often will be based on a lack of enforcement resources, rather than on any conclusion on the merits of the complaint. In that case, if no private remedy exists, the complainant is relegated to a suit under the Administrative Procedure Act to compel the agency to investigate and cut off funds. E.g., *Adams v. Richardson*, 156 U. S. App. D. C. 267, 480 F.2d 1159 (1973). But surely this alternative is far more disruptive of HEW's efforts efficiently to allocate its enforcement resources under Title IX than a private suit against the recipient of federal aid could ever be.

.....

Fourth, the final inquiry suggested by *Cort* is whether implying a federal remedy is inappropriate because the subject matter involves an area basically of concern to the States. No such problem is raised by a prohibition against invidious discrimination of any sort, including that on the basis of sex. ...Moreover, it is the expenditure of federal funds that provides the justification for this particular statutory prohibition. There can be no question but that this aspect of the *Cort* analysis supports the implication of a private federal remedy.

In sum, there is no need in this case to weigh the four *Cort* factors; all of them support the same result. Not only the words and history of Title IX, but also its subject matter and underlying purposes, counsel implication of a cause of action in favor of private victims of discrimination.

.....

When Congress intends private litigants to have a cause of action to support their statutory rights, the far better course is for it to specify as much when it creates those rights. But the Court has long recognized that, under certain limited circumstances, the failure of Congress to do so is not inconsistent with an intent on its part to have such a remedy available to the persons benefited by its legislation. Title IX presents the atypical situation in which all of the circumstances that the Court has previously identified as supportive of an implied remedy are present. We therefore conclude that petitioner may maintain her lawsuit despite the absence of any express authorization for it in the statute.

FRANKLIN v. GWINNETT COUNTY PUBLIC SCHOOLS
503 U.S. 60 (1992)

WHITE, J.

This case presents the question whether the implied right of action under Title IX of the Education Amendments of 1972, 20 U.S.C. §§ 1681-88 (Title IX), which this Court recognized in *Cannon v. University of Chicago*, 441 U.S. 677, supports a claim for monetary damages.

Petitioner Christine Franklin was a student at North Gwinnett High School in Gwinnett County, Georgia, between September, 1985, and August, 1989. Respondent Gwinnett County School District operates the high school and receives federal funds. Accordingly to the complaint filed on December 29, 1988, in the United States District Court for the Northern District of Georgia, Franklin was subjected to continual sexual harassment beginning in the autumn of her tenth grade year (1986) from Andrew Hill, a sports coach and teacher employed by the district. Among other allegations, Franklin avers that Hill engaged her in sexually-oriented conversations in which he asked about her sexual experiences with her boyfriend and whether she would consider having sexual intercourse with an older man, that Hill forcibly kissed her on the mouth in the school parking lot, that he telephoned her at her home and asked if she would meet him socially, and that, on three occasions in her junior year, Hill interrupted a class, requested that the teacher excuse Franklin, and took her to a private office where he subjected her to coercive intercourse. The complaint further alleges that, though they became aware of and investigated Hill's sexual harassment of Franklin and other female students, teachers and administrators took no action to halt it, and discouraged Franklin from pressing charges against Hill. Hill resigned on the condition that all matters pending against him be dropped. The school thereupon closed its investigation.

In this action, the District Court dismissed the complaint on the ground that Title IX does not authorize an award of damages. The Court of Appeals affirmed.

II.

In *Cannon v. University of Chicago*, 441 U.S. 677 (1979), the Court held that Title IX is enforceable through an implied right of action. We have no occasion here to reconsider that decision. Rather, in this case we must decide what remedies are available in a suit brought pursuant to this implied right. As we have often stated, the question of what remedies are available under a statute that provides a private right of action is "analytically distinct" from the issue of whether such a right exists in the first place. *Davis v. Passman*, 442 U.S. 228 (1979). Thus, although we examine the text and history of a statute to determine whether Congress intended to create a right of action, *Touche Ross & Co. v. Redington*, 442 U.S. 560, 575-76 (1979), we presume the availability of all appropriate remedies unless Congress has expressly indicated otherwise. *Davis, Supra*, 442 U.S. at 246-47. This principle has deep roots in our jurisprudence.

A.

[W]here legal rights have been invaded, and a federal statute provides for a general right to sue for such invasion, federal courts may use any available remedy to make good the wrong done.

Bell v. Hood, 327 U.S. 678, 684 (1946). The Court explained this longstanding rule as jurisdictional, and upheld the exercise of the federal court's power to award appropriate relief so long as a cause of action existed under the Constitution or laws of the United States. *Ibid.*

.....

III.

We now address whether Congress intended to limit application of this general principle in the enforcement of Title IX. *See Bush v. Lucas*, 462 U.S. 367, 378 (1983); *Wyandotte Transp. Co. v. United States*, 389 U.S. 191, 200 (1967). Because the cause of action was inferred by the Court in *Cannon*, the usual recourse to statutory text and legislative history in the period prior to that decision necessarily will not enlighten our analysis. . . .

During the period prior to the decision in *Cannon*, the inquiry, in any event, is not "basically a matter of statutory construction," as the United States asserts. Brief for United States as *Amicus Curiae* 8 (quoting *Transamerica Mortgage Advisors, Inc. v. Lewis*, 444 U.S. 11, 15 (1979)). Rather, in determining Congress's intent to limit application of the traditional presumption in favor of all appropriate relief, we evaluate the state of the law when the legislature passed Title IX.

In the years *after* the announcement of *Cannon*, on the other hand, a more traditional method of statutory analysis is possible, because Congress was legislating with full cognizance of that decision. Our reading of the two amendments to Title IX enacted after *Cannon* leads us to conclude that Congress did not intent to limit the remedies available in a suit brought under Title IX. In the Civil Rights Remedies Equalization Amendment of 1986, 42 U.S.C. § 2000d-7, Congress abrogated the State's Eleventh Amendment immunity under Title IX, Title VI, § 504 of the Rehabilitation Act of 1973, and the Age Discrimination Act of 1975. This statute cannot be read except as a validation of *Cannon*'s holding. A subsection of the 1986 law provides that in a suit against a State,

> remedies (including remedies both at law and in equity) are available for such a violation to the same extent as such remedies are available for such a violation in the suit against any public or private entity other than a State.

42 U.S.C. § 2000-d7(a)(2). While it is true that this savings clause says nothing about the nature of those other available remedies, *cf. Milwaukee v. Illinois*, 451 U.S. 304, 329 n.22 (1981), absent any contrary indication in the text or history of the statute, we presume Congress enacted this statute with the prevailing traditional rule in mind.

In addition to the Civil Rights Remedies Equalization Amendment of 1986, Congress also enacted the Civil Rights Restoration Act of 1987, Pub. L. 100-259, 102 Stat. 28 (1988). Without in any way altering the existing rights of action and the corresponding remedies permissible under Title IX,

Title VI, § 504 of the Rehabilitation Act, and the Age Discrimination Act, Congress broadened the coverage of these antidiscrimination provisions in this legislation. In seeking to correct what it considered to be an unacceptable decision on our part in *Grove City College v. Bell*, 465 U.S. 555 (1984), Congress made no effort to restrict the right of action recognized in *Cannon* and ratified in the 1986 Act or to alter the traditional presumption in favor of any appropriate relief for violation of a federal right. We cannot say, therefore, that Congress has limited the remedies available to a complainant in a suit brought under Title IX.

. . .

In sum, we conclude that a damages remedy is available for an action brought to enforce Title IX. The judgment of the Court of Appeals, therefore, is reversed, and the case is remanded for further proceedings consistent with this opinion.

Notes and Comments

1. Title IX Claims versus Title VII Claims

Is Title IX now the best remedy for employment discrimination in education? Title VII is obviously the more comprehensive tool for employment discrimination. It provides that an employer cannot, "fail or refuse to hire or to discharge any individual, or otherwise to discriminate against any individual . . . because of such individual's race, color, religion, sex or national origin." 42 U.S.C. § 2000e-2(a)(1).

However, Title VII comes with a more rigorous set of administrative requirements that plaintiffs must satisfy before invoking its protection. Victims seeking a Title VII remedy must meet filing deadlines and must participate in administrative attempts to resolve the claim through negotiation or mediation. 42 U.S.C. § 2000e-5 and 2000e-6. *See Mohasco Corp. v. Silver*, 447 U.S. 807 (1980) (religious discrimination claims dismissed for failure to file on time). Title IX suits are unencumbered of these administrative exhaustion requirements. Plaintiffs who file lawsuits under Title IX avoid all of the Title VII administrative hurdles. *See* Matthew C. Stephenson: Public Regulation Of Private Enforcement: The Case for Expanding the Role Of Administrative Agencies, 91 Va. L. Rev. 93 (2005); Douglas P. Ruth: Title Vii & Title Ix = ?: Is Title IX The Exclusive Remedy for Employment Discrimination in the Educational Sector? 5 Cornell J. L. & Pub. Pol'y 185 (1996).

2. Title IX Claims versus Discrimination Claims under the Equal Protection Clause

Is Title IX the sole means of vindicating the constitutional right to be free from gender discrimination by educational institutions? In other words, if a plaintiff files suit under Title IX, does Title IX preclude an action under 42 U.S.C. § 1983, alleging gender discrimination in schools based on the Equal Protection Clause?

Section 1983 represents the primary basis for enforcement of a federal civil rights, created either by statute or by the Constitution of the U.S., by plaintiffs seeking money damages. Congress has the power when creating a statutory right to limit remedies available in a suit brought under section 1983. In *Fitzgerald v. Barnstable School Committee*; __ U.S. __; 129 S. Ct. 788 (2009), the Court ruled that Title IX was not meant to be an exclusive mechanism for addressing gender discrimination in schools. After *Fitzgerald*, suits based on the Equal Protection Clause remain available to plaintiffs alleging unconstitutional gender discrimination in schools.

> A comparison of the substantive rights and protections guaranteed under Title IX and under the Equal Protection Clause lends further support to the conclusion that Congress did not intend Title IX to preclude § 1983 constitutional suits. Title IX's protections are narrower in some respects and broader in others. ...Title IX reaches institutions and programs that receive federal funds, 20 U.S.C. § 1681(a), which may include nonpublic institutions, § 1681(c), but it has consistently been interpreted as not authorizing suit against school officials, teachers, and other individuals. The Equal Protection Clause reaches only state actors, but § 1983 equal protection claims may be brought against individuals as well as municipalities and certain other state entities. ...Title IX exempts from its restrictions several activities that may be challenged on constitutional grounds. For example, Title IX exempts elementary and secondary schools from its prohibition against discrimination in admissions, § 1681(a)(1); it exempts military service schools and traditionally single-sex public colleges from all of its provisions, §§ 1681(a)(4)-(5). Some exempted activities may form the basis of equal protection claims.... [A] Title IX plaintiff can establish school district liability by showing that a single school administrator with authority to take corrective action responded to harassment with deliberate indifference. A plaintiff stating a similar claim via § 1983 for violation of the Equal Protection Clause by a school district or other municipal entity must show that the harassment was the result of municipal custom, policy, or practice. 129 S. Ct. at 795-96.

3. *See* Kelly S. Terry: *Franklin v. Gwinnett County Public Schools*: Reviving the Presumption of Remedies Under Implied Rights of Action, 46 Ark. L. Rev. 715 (1993); and Richard J. Pierce, Jr.: The Role of The Judiciary In Implementing an Agency Theory Of Government, 64 N.Y.U. L. Rev. 1239 (1989).

II. Sexual Assaults and Harassment under Title IX

A common complaint under Title IX has involved either teacher/student sexual harassment or student/student sexual harassment. What responsibility should a school bear for such misbehavior? Did Title the drafters of Title IX intend to protect participation in education against sexual harassment? The United States Supreme Court provided significant insight into these questions in back to back years, 1998 and 1999. In both cases, Justice O'Connor, one of two female justices sitting on the Supreme Court at the time, authored the majority opinion for the Court.

GEBSER v. LAGO VISTA INDEPENDENT SCHOOL DISTRICT
524 U.S. 274 (1998)

O'CONNOR, J.

The question in this case is when a school district may be held liable in damages in an implied right of action under Title IX of the Education Amendments of 1972, 86 Stat. 373, as amended, 20 U.S.C. § 1681 *et seq.* (Title IX), for the sexual harassment of a student by one of the district's teachers. We conclude that damages may not be recovered in those circumstances unless an official of the school district who at a minimum has authority to institute corrective measures on the district's behalf has actual notice of, and is deliberately indifferent to, the teacher's misconduct.

I.

In the spring of 1991, when petitioner Alida Star Gebser was an eighth-grade student at a middle school in respondent Lago Vista Independent School District (Lago Vista), she joined a high school book discussion group led by Frank Waldrop, a teacher at Lago Vista's high school. Lago Vista received federal funds at all pertinent times. During the book discussion sessions, Waldrop often made sexually suggestive comments to the students. Gebser entered high school in the fall and was assigned to classes taught by Waldrop in both semesters. Waldrop continued to make inappropriate remarks to the students, and he began to direct more of his suggestive comments toward Gebser, including during the substantial amount of time that the two were alone in his classroom. He initiated sexual contact with Gebser in the spring, when, while visiting her home ostensibly to give her a book, he kissed and fondled her. The two had sexual intercourse on a number of occasions during the remainder of the school year. Their relationship continued through the summer and into the following school year, and they often had intercourse during class time, although never on school property.

Gebser did not report the relationship to school officials, testifying that while she realized Waldrop's conduct was improper, she was uncertain how to react and she wanted to continue having him as a teacher. In October 1992, the parents of two other students complained to the high school principal about Waldrop's comments in class. The principal arranged a meeting, at which, according to the principal, Waldrop indicated that he did not believe he had made offensive remarks but apologized to the parents and said it would not happen again. The principal also advised Waldrop to be careful about his classroom comments and told the school guidance counselor about the meeting, but he did not report the parents' complaint to Lago Vista's superintendent, who was the district's Title IX coordinator. A couple of months later, in January 1993, a police officer discovered Waldrop and Gebser engaging in sexual intercourse and arrested Waldrop. Lago Vista terminated his employment, and subsequently, the Texas Education Agency revoked his teaching license. During this time, the district had not promulgated or distributed an official grievance procedure for lodging sexual harassment complaints; nor had it issued a formal anti-harassment policy.

Gebser and her mother filed suit against Lago Vista and Waldrop in state court in November 1993, raising claims against the school district under Title IX, Rev. Stat. § 1979, 42 U.S.C. § 1983, and state negligence law, and claims against Waldrop primarily under state law. They sought compensatory and punitive damages from both defendants. After the case was removed [to federal court], the United States District Court for the Western District of Texas granted summary judgment in favor of Lago Vista on all claims, and remanded the allegations against Waldrop to state court. In rejecting the Title IX claim against the school district, the court reasoned that the statute "was enacted to counter *policies* of discrimination . . . in federally funded education programs," and that "[o]nly if school administrators have some type of notice of the gender discrimination and fail to respond in good faith can the discrimination be interpreted as a *policy* of the school district." Here, the court determined, the parents' complaint to the principal concerning Waldrop's comments in class was the only one Lago Vista had received about Waldrop, and that evidence was inadequate to raise a genuine issue on whether the school district had actual or constructive notice that Waldrop was involved in a sexual relationship with a student.

Petitioners appealed only on the Title IX claim. The Court of Appeals for the Fifth Circuit affirmed. . . .

II.

. . .

In this case, moreover, petitioners seek not just to establish a Title IX violation but to recover *damages* based on theories of *respondeat superior* and constructive notice. It is that aspect of their action, in our view, which is most critical to resolving the case. Unlike Title IX, Title VII contains an express cause of action, § 2000e-5(f), and specifically provides for relief in the form of monetary damages, § 1981a. Congress therefore has directly addressed the subject of damages relief under Title VII and has set out the particular situations in which damages are available as well as the maximum amounts recoverable. § 1981a(b). With respect to Title IX, however, the private right of action is judicially implied, *See Cannon*, 441 U.S., at 717, and there is thus no legislative expression of the scope of available remedies, including when it is appropriate to award monetary damages. . . . We made no effort in *Franklin* to delimit the circumstances in which a damages remedy should lie.

III.

Because the private right of action under Title IX is judicially implied, we have a measure of latitude to shape a sensible remedial scheme that best comports with the statute. That endeavor inherently entails a degree of speculation since it addresses an issue on which Congress has not specifically spoken. To guide the analysis, we generally examine the relevant statute to ensure that we do not fashion the parameters of an implied right in a manner at odds with the statutory structure and purpose. . . .

Those considerations, we think, are pertinent not only to the scope of the implied right, but also to the scope of available remedies. *See Transamerica Mortgage Advisors, Inc. v. Lewis*, 444 U.S. 11 (1979); *See also Franklin, supra,* at 77-78 (Scalia, J., concurring in judgment). We suggested as much in *Franklin*, where we recognized "the general rule that all appropriate relief is available in an action brought to vindicate a federal right," but indicated that the rule must be reconciled with congressional purpose. 503 U.S., at 68. The "general rule," that is, "yields where necessary to carry out the intent of Congress or to avoid frustrating the purposes of the statute involved." *Guardians Assn. v. Civil Serv. Comm'n of New York City*, 463 U.S. 582, 595 (1983) (opinion of White, J.); *cf.*, *Cannon*, 441 U.S., at 703 ("[A] private remedy should not be implied if it would frustrate the underlying purpose of the legislative scheme").

Applying those principles here, we conclude that it would "frustrate the purposes" of Title IX to permit a damages recovery against a school district for a teacher's sexual harassment of a student based on principles of *respondent superior* or constructive notice, i.e., without actual notice to a school district official. Because Congress did not expressly create a private right of action under Title IX, the statutory text does not shed light on Congress' intent with respect to the scope of available remedies. *Franklin*, 503 U.S., at 71; *Id.*, at 76 (Scalia, J., concurring in judgment). Instead, "we attempt to infer how the [1972] Congress would have addressed the issue had the . . . action been included as an express provision in the" statute. *Central Bank of Denver, N.A., v. First Interstate Bank of Denver, N.A.*, 511 U.S. 164, 178 (1994).

As a general matter, it does not appear that Congress contemplated unlimited recovery in damages against a funding recipient where the recipient is unaware of discrimination in its programs. When Title IX was enacted in 1972, the principal civil rights statutes containing an express right of action did not provide for recovery of monetary damages at all, instead allowing only injunctive and equitable relief. *See* 42 U.S.C. § 2000a-3(a) (1970 ed.); § 2000e-5(e), (g) (1970 ed., Supp. II). It was not until 1991 that Congress made damages available under Title VII, and even then, Congress carefully limited the amount recoverable in any individual case, calibrating the maximum recovery to the size of the employer. *See* 42 U.S.C. § 1981a(b)(3). Adopting petitioners' position would amount, then, to allowing unlimited recovery of damages under Title IX where Congress has not spoken on the subject of either the right or the remedy, and in the face of evidence that when Congress expressly considered both in Title VII it restricted the amount of damages recoverable.

Congress enacted Title IX in 1972 with two principal objectives in mind: "to avoid the use of federal resources to support discriminatory practices" and "to provide individual citizens effective protection against those practices." *Cannon*, *Supra*, at 704. The statute was modeled after Title VI of the Civil Rights Act of 1964, *See* 441 U.S., at 694-96; *Grove City College v. Bell*, 465 U.S. 555, 566 (1984), which is parallel to Title IX except that it prohibits race discrimination, not sex discrimination, and applies in all programs receiving federal funds, not only in education programs. *See* 42 U.S.C. § 2000d *et seq.* The two statutes operate in the same manner, conditioning an offer of federal funding on a promise by the recipient not to discriminate, in what amounts essentially to a contract between the Government and the recipient of funds. . . .

That contractual framework distinguishes Title IX from Title VII, which is framed in terms not of a condition but of an outright prohibition. Title VII applies to all employers without regard to federal funding and aims broadly to "eradicat[e] discrimination throughout the economy. *Lndgraf v. USI Film Products*, 511 U.S. 244, 254 (1994) (internal quotation marks omitted). Title VII, moreover, seeks to "make persons whole for injuries suffered through past discrimination." *Ibid* (internal quotation marks omitted). Thus, whereas Title VII aims centrally to compensate victims of discrimination, Title IX focuses more on "protecting" individuals from discriminatory practices carried out by recipients of federal funds. . . .

Title IX's contractual nature has implications for our construction of the scope of available remedies. When Congress attaches conditions to the award of federal funds under its spending power, U.S. Const., Art. I, § 8, cl. 1, as it has in Title IX and Title VI, we examine closely the propriety of private actions holding the recipient liable in monetary damages for noncompliance with the condition. *See Franklin*, 463 U.S., at 74-75; *Guardians, supra*, at 596-603 (White, J.); *see generally Pennhurst, supra*, at 28-29. Our central concern in that regard is with ensuring "that the receiving entity of federal funds [has] notice that it will be liable for a monetary award." . . . .

Most significantly, Title IX contains important clues that Congress did not intend to allow recovery in damages where the liability rests solely on principles of vicarious liability or constructive notice. Title IX's express means of enforcement—by administrative agencies—operates on an assumption of actual notice to officials of the funding recipient. The statute entitles agencies who disburse education funding to enforce their rules implementing the non-discrimination mandate through proceedings to suspend or terminate funding or through "other means authorized by law." 20 U.S.C. § 1682. Significantly, however, an agency may not initiate enforcement proceedings until it "has advised the appropriate person or persons of the failure to comply with the requirement and has determined that compliance cannot be secured by voluntary means." *Ibid.* The administrative regulations implement that obligation, requiring resolution of compliance issues "by informal means whenever possible," 34 CFR § 100.7(d) (1997), and prohibiting commencement of enforcement proceedings until the agency has determined that voluntary compliance is unobtainable and "the recipient . . . has been notified of its failure to comply and of the action to be taken to effect compliance." § 100.8(d); *See* § 100.8(c). . . .

IV.

Because the express remedial scheme under Title IX is predicated upon notice to an "appropriate person" and an opportunity to rectify any violation, 20 U.S.C. § 1682, we conclude, in the absence of further direction from Congress, that the implied damages remedy should be fashioned along the same lines. An "appropriate person" under § 1682 is, at a minimum, an official of the recipient entity with authority to take corrective action to end the discrimination. Consequently, in cases like this one that do not involve official policy of the recipient entity, we hold that a damages remedy will not lie under Title IX unless an official who at a minimum has authority to address the alleged discrimination and to institute corrective measures on the recipient's behalf has actual knowledge of discrimination in the recipient's programs and fails adequately to respond.

We think, moreover, that the response must amount to deliberate indifference to discrimination. The administrative enforcement scheme presupposes that an official who is advised of a Title IX violation refuses to take action to bring the recipient into compliance. The premise, in other words, is an official decision by the recipient not to remedy the violation. That framework finds a rough parallel in the standard of deliberate indifference. Under a lower standard, there would be a risk that the recipient would be liable in damages not for its own official decision but instead for its employees' independent actions. Comparable considerations led to our adoption of a deliberate indifference standard for claims under § 1983 alleging that a municipality's actions in failing to prevent a deprivation of federal rights was the cause of the violation. *See Board of Comm'rs of Bryan Cty. v. Brown,* 520 U.S. 397 (1997); *Canton v. Harris,* 489 U.S. 378 (1989); *see also Collins v. Harker Heights,* 503 U.S. 115, 123-124 (1992).

Applying the framework to this case is fairly straightforward, as petitioners do not contend they can prevail under an actual notice standard. The only official alleged to have had information about Waldrop's misconduct is the high school principal. That information, however, consisted of a complaint from parents of other students charging only that Waldrop had made inappropriate comments during class, which was plainly insufficient to alert the principal to the possibility that Waldrop was involved in a sexual relationship with a student. Lago Vista, moreover, terminated Waldrop's employment upon learning of his relationship with Gebser. Justice Stevens points out in his dissenting opinion that Waldrop of course had knowledge of his own actions. Where a school district's liability rests on actual notice principles, however, the knowledge of the wrongdoer himself is not pertinent to the analysis. *See* Restatement § 280.

V

The number of reported cases involving sexual harassment of students in schools confirms that harassment unfortunately is an all too common aspect of the educational experience. No one questions that a student suffers extraordinary harm when subjected to sexual harassment and abuse by a teacher, and that the teacher's conduct is reprehensible and undermines the basic purposes of the educational system. The issue in this case, however, is whether the independent misconduct of a teacher is attributable to the school district that employs him under a specific federal statute designed primarily to prevent recipients of federal financial assistance from using the funds in a discriminatory manner. Our decision does not affect any right of recovery that an individual may have against a school district as a matter of state law or against the teacher in his individual capacity under state law or under 42 U.S.C. § 1983. Until Congress speaks directly on the subject, however, we will not hold a school district liable in damages under Title IX for a teacher's sexual harassment of a student absent actual notice and deliberate indifference. We therefore affirm the judgment of the Court of Appeals.

DAVIS EX REL. LASHONDA D. v. MONROE COUNTY BOARDOF EDUCATION
526 U.S. 629 (1999)

O'CONNOR, J.

We consider here whether a private damages action may lie against the school board in cases of student-on-student harassment. We conclude that it may, but only where the funding recipient acts with deliberate indifference to known acts of harassment in its programs or activities. Moreover, we conclude that such an action will lie only for harassment that is so severe, pervasive, and objectively offensive that it is effectively bars the victim's access to an educational opportunity or benefit.

I.

A

Petitioner's minor daughter, LaShonda, was allegedly the victim of a prolonged pattern of sexual harassment by one of her fifth-grade classmates at Hubbard Elementary School, a public school in Monroe County, Georgia. According to petitioner's complaint, the harassment began in December 1992, when the classmate, G.F., attempted to touch LaShonda's breasts and genital area and made vulgar statements such as "'I want to get in bed with you'" and "'I want to feel your boobs.'" Similar conduct allegedly occurred on or about January 4 and January 20, 1993. LaShonda reported each of these incidents to her mother and to her classroom teacher, Diane Fort. Petitioner, in turn, also contacted Fort, who allegedly assured petitioner that the school principal, Bill Querry, had been informed of the incidents. Petitioner contends that, notwithstanding these reports, no disciplinary action was taken against G.F.

G.F.'s conduct allegedly continued for many months. In early February, G.F. purportedly placed a door stop in his pants and proceeded to act in a sexually suggestive manner toward LaShonda during physical education class. LaShonda reported G.F.'s behavior to her physical education teacher, Whit Maples. Approximately one week later, G.F. again allegedly engaged in harassing behavior, this time while under the supervision of another classroom teacher, Joyce Pippin. Again, LaShonda allegedly reported the incident to the teacher, and again petitioner contacted the teacher to follow up.

Petitioner alleges that G.F. once more directed sexually harassing conduct toward LaShonda in physical education class in early March, and that LaShonda reported the incident to both Maples and Pippen. In mid-April 1993, G.F. allegedly rubbed his body against LaShonda in the school hallway in what LaShonda considered a sexually suggestive manner, and LaShonda again reported the matter to Fort.

The string of incidents finally ended in mid-May, when G.F. was charged with, and pleaded guilty to, sexual battery for his misconduct. The complaint alleges that LaShonda had suffered during the months of harassment, however; specifically, her previously high grades allegedly dropped as she became unable to concentrate on her studies, and, in April 1993, her father discovered that she had written a suicide note, *ibid.* The complaint further alleges that, at one point, LaShonda told petitioner that she "'didn't know how much longer she could keep [G.F.] off her.'"

Nor was LaShonda G.F.'s only victim; it is alleged that other girls in the class fell prey to G.F.'s conduct. At one point, in fact, a group composed of LaShonda and other female students tried to speak with Principal Querry about G.F.'s behavior. According to the complaint, however, a teacher denied the students' request with the statement, "'If [Querry] wants you, he'll call you.'"

Petitioner alleges that no disciplinary action was taken in response to G.F.'s behavior toward LaShonda. In addition to her conversations with Fort and Pippen, petitioner alleges that she spoke with Principal Querry in mid-May 1993. When petitioner inquired as to what action the school intended to take against G.F., Querry simply stated, "'I guess I'll have to threaten him a little bit harder.'" Yet, petitioner alleges, at no point during the many months of his reported misconduct was G.F. disciplined for harassment. Indeed, Querry allegedly asked petitioner why LaShonda "'was the only one complaining.'"

Nor, according to the complaint, was any effort made to separate G.F. and LaShonda. On the contrary, notwithstanding LaShonda's frequent complaints, only after more than three months of reported harassment was she even permitted to change her classroom seat so that she was no longer seated next to G.F. Moreover, petitioner alleges that, at the time of the events in question, the Monroe County Board of Education (Board) had not instructed its personnel on how to respond to peer sexual harassment and had not established a policy on the issue.

II

Title IX provides, with certain exceptions not at issue here, that

> [n]o person in the United States shall, on the basis of sex, be excluded from participation in, be denied the benefits of, or be subjected to discrimination under any education program or activity receiving Federal financial assistance. 20 U.S.C. § 1681(a).

Congress authorized an administrative enforcement scheme for Title IX. Federal departments or agencies with the authority to provide financial assistance are entrusted to promulgate rules, regulations, and orders to enforce the objectives of § 1681, *See* § 1682, and these departments or agencies may rely on "any ... means authorized by law," including the termination of funding, *Ibid.*, to give effect to the statute's restrictions.

There is no dispute here that the Board is a recipient of federal education funding for Title IX purposes. 74 F.3d, at 1189. Nor do respondents support an argument that student-on-student harassment cannot rise to the level of "discrimination" for purposes of Title IX. Rather, at issue here is the question whether a recipient of federal education funding may be liable for damages under Title IX under any circumstances for discrimination in the form of student-on-student sexual harassment.

A

Petitioner urges that Title IX's plain language compels the conclusion that the statute is intended to bar recipients of federal funding from permitting this form of discrimination in their programs or activities. She emphasizes that the statute prohibits a student from being "*subjected to discrimination* under any education program or activity receiving Federal financial assistance." 20 U.S.C. § 1681(a) (emphasis added). It is Title IX's "unmistakable focus on the benefited class," *Cannon v. University of Chicago,* 441 U.S. 677, 691 (1979), rather than the perpetrator, that, in petitioner's view, compels the conclusion that the statute works to protect students from the discriminatory misconduct of their peers.

Here, however, we are asked to do more than define the scope of the behavior that Title IX proscribes. We must determine whether a district's failure to respond to student-on-student harassment in its schools can support a private suit for money damages. … This Court has indeed recognized an implied private right of action under Title IX …and we have held that money damages are available in such suits. Because we have repeatedly treated Title IX as legislation enacted pursuant to Congress' authority under the Spending Clause … private damages actions are available only where recipients of federal funding had adequate notice that they could be liable for the conduct at issue.

We agree with respondents that a recipient of federal funds may be liable in damages under Title IX only for its own misconduct. The recipient itself must "exclud[e] [persons] from participation in ... den[y] [persons] the benefits of, or ... subjec[t] [persons] to discrimination under" its "program[s] or activit[ies]" in order to be liable under Title IX. The Government's enforcement power may only be exercised against the funding recipient, see § 1682, and we have not extended damages liability under Title IX to parties outside the scope of this power.

We disagree with respondents' assertion, however, that petitioner seeks to hold the Board liable for *G. F.*'s actions instead of its own. Here, petitioner attempts to hold the Board liable for its *own* decision to remain idle in the face of known student-on-student harassment in its schools. In *Gebser,* we concluded that a recipient of federal education funds may be liable in damages under Title IX where it is deliberately indifferent to known acts of sexual harassment by a teacher. In that case, a teacher had entered into a sexual relationship with an eighth-grade student, and the student sought damages under Title IX for the teacher's misconduct. [I]n *Gebser* we once again required "that 'the receiving entity of federal funds [have] notice that it will be liable for a monetary award'" before subjecting it to damages liability. 524 U.S., at 287, 118 S.Ct. 1989 (quoting *Franklin v. Gwinnett County Public Schools,* 503 U.S., at 74, 112 S.Ct. 1028). We also recognized, however, that this limitation on private damages actions is not a bar to liability where a funding recipient intentionally violates the statute.

…..

Gebser … established that a recipient intentionally violates Title IX, and is subject to a private damages action, where the recipient is deliberately indifferent to known acts of teacher-student discrimination. Indeed, whether viewed as "discrimination" or "subject[ing]" students to discrimination, Title IX "[u]nquestionably ... placed on [the Board] the duty not" to permit teacher-student harassment in its schools, *Franklin v. Gwinnett County Public Schools, Supra,* at 75, 112 S. Ct. 1028, and recipients violate Title IX's plain terms when they remain deliberately indifferent to this form of misconduct.

We consider here whether the misconduct identified in *Gebser*—deliberate indifference to known acts of harassment—amounts to an intentional violation of Title IX, capable of supporting a private damages action, when the harasser is a student rather than a teacher. We conclude that, in certain limited circumstances, it does. [T]he regulatory scheme surrounding Title IX has long provided funding recipients with notice that they may be liable for their failure to respond to the discriminatory acts of certain nonagents. The Department of Education requires recipients to monitor third parties for discrimination in specified circumstances and to refrain from particular forms of interaction with outside entities that are known to discriminate. *See, e.g.,* 34 CFR §§ 106.31(b)(6), 106.31(d), 106.37(a)(2), 106.38(a), 106.51(a)(3) (1998).

The common law, too, has put schools on notice that they may be held responsible under state law for their failure to protect students from the tortious acts of third parties. *See* Restatement (Second) of Torts § 320, and Comment *a* (1965). In fact, state courts routinely uphold claims alleging that schools have been negligent in failing to protect their students from the torts of their peers. *See, e.g., Rupp v. Bryant,* 417 So.2d 658, 666-67 (Fla.1982); *Brahatcek v. Millard School Dist.,* 202 Neb. 86, 99-100, 273 N.W.2d 680, 688 (1979); *McLeod v. Grant County School Dist. No. 128,* 42 Wash.2d 316, 320, 255 P.2d 360, 362-363 (1953).

The language of Title IX itself—particularly when viewed in conjunction with the requirement that the recipient have notice of Title IX's prohibitions to be liable for damages—also cabins the range of misconduct that the statute proscribes. The statute's plain language confines the scope of prohibited conduct based on the recipient's degree of control over the harasser and the environment in which the harassment occurs. .....These factors combine to limit a recipient's damages liability to circumstances wherein the recipient exercises substantial control over both the harasser and the context in which the known harassment occurs. Only then can the recipient be said to "expose" its students to harassment or "cause" them to undergo it "under" the recipient's programs.

Where, as here, the misconduct occurs during school hours and on school grounds—the bulk of G.F.'s misconduct, in fact, took place in the classroom—the misconduct is taking place "under" an "operation" of the funding recipient. *See Doe v. University of Illinois,* 138 F.3d, at 661 (finding liability where school fails to respond properly to "student-on-student sexual harassment that takes place while the students are involved in school activities or otherwise under the supervision of school employees"). In these circumstances, the recipient retains substantial control over the context in which the harassment occurs. More importantly, however, in this setting the Board exercises significant control over the harasser. We have observed, for example, "that the nature of [the State's] power [over public schoolchildren] is custodial and tutelary, permitting a degree of supervision and control that could not be exercised over free adults." *Vernonia School Dist. 47J v. Acton,* 515 U.S. 646, 655 (1995). On more than one occasion, this Court has recognized the importance of school officials' "comprehensive authority ..., consistent with fundamental constitutional safeguards, to prescribe and control conduct in the schools." *Tinker v. Des Moines Independent Community School Dist.,* 393 U.S. 503, 507, 89 S. Ct. 733, 21 L.Ed.2d 731 (1969); *See also New Jersey v. T.L.O.,* 469 U.S. 325, 342, n. 9 (1985) ("The maintenance of discipline in the schools requires not only that students be restrained from assaulting one another, abusing drugs and alcohol, and committing other crimes, but also that students conform themselves to the standards of conduct prescribed by school authorities"); 74 F.3d, at 1193 ("The ability to control and influence behavior exists to an even greater extent in the classroom than in the workplace ..."). The common law, too, recognizes the school's disciplinary authority. See Restatement (Second) of Torts § 152 (1965). We thus conclude that recipients of federal funding may be liable for "subject[ing]" their students to discrimination where the recipient is deliberately indifferent to known acts of student-on-student sexual harassment and the harasser is under the school's disciplinary authority.

We stress that our conclusion here—that recipients may be liable for their deliberate indifference to known acts of peer sexual harassment—does not mean that recipients can avoid liability only by purging their schools of actionable peer harassment or that administrators must engage in particular disciplinary action. We thus disagree with respondents' contention that, if Title IX provides a cause of action for student-on-student harassment, "nothing short of expulsion of every student accused of misconduct involving sexual overtones would protect school systems from liability or damages." *See* Brief for Respondents 16; *See also* 120 F.3d, at 1402 (Tjoflat, J.) ("[A] school must immediately suspend or expel a student accused of sexual harassment"). Likewise, the dissent erroneously imagines that victims of peer harassment now have a Title IX right to make particular remedial demands. *See post,* at 1691 (contemplating that victim could demand new desk assignment). In fact, as we have previously noted, courts should refrain from second-guessing the disciplinary decisions made by school administrators. *New Jersey v. T.L.O., Supra,* at 342-43, n. 9, 105 S. Ct. 733.

School administrators will continue to enjoy the flexibility they require so long as funding recipients are deemed "deliberately indifferent" to acts of student-on-student harassment only where the recipient's response to the harassment or lack thereof is clearly unreasonable in light of the known circumstances. ..[S]chool administrators shoulder substantial burdens as a result of legal constraints on their disciplinary authority. To the extent that these restrictions arise from federal statutes, Congress can review these burdens with attention to the difficult position in which such legislation may place our Nation's schools. We believe, however, that the standard set out here is sufficiently flexible to account both for the level of disciplinary authority available to the school and for the potential liability arising from certain forms of disciplinary action. A university might not, for example, be expected to exercise the same degree of control over its students that a grade school would enjoy and it would be entirely reasonable for a school to refrain from a form of disciplinary action that would expose it to constitutional or statutory claims.

While it remains to be seen whether petitioner can show that the Board's response to reports of G.F.'s misconduct was clearly unreasonable in light of the known circumstances, petitioner may be able to show that the Board "subject [ed]" LaShonda to discrimination by failing to respond in any way over a period of five months to complaints of G.F.'s in-school misconduct from LaShonda and other female students.

B

The requirement that recipients receive adequate notice of Title IX's proscriptions also bears on the proper definition of "discrimination" in the context of a private damages action. We have elsewhere concluded that sexual harassment is a form of discrimination for Title IX purposes and that Title IX proscribes harassment with sufficient clarity to satisfy *Pennhurst's* notice requirement and serve as a basis for a damages action. *See Gebser v. Lago Vista Independent School Dist.,* 524 U.S., at 281, 118 S. Ct. 1989; *Franklin v. Gwinnett County Public Schools,* 503 U.S., at 74-75, 112 S. Ct. 1028. Having previously determined that "sexual harassment" is "discrimination" in the school context under Title IX, we are constrained to conclude that student-on-student sexual harassment, if sufficiently severe, can likewise rise to the level of discrimination actionable under the statute. *See Bennett v. Kentucky Dept. of Ed.,* 470 U.S. 656, 665-66, 105 S. Ct. 1544, 84 L.Ed.2d 590 (1985) (rejecting claim of insufficient notice under *Pennhurst* where statute made clear that there were some conditions placed on receipt of federal funds, and noting that Congress need not "specifically identif[y] and proscrib[e]" each condition in the legislation). The statute's other prohibitions, moreover, help give content to the term "discrimination" in this context. Students are not only protected from discrimination, but also specifically shielded from being "excluded from participation in" or "denied the benefits of" any "education program or activity receiving Federal financial assistance." § 1681(a). The statute makes clear that, whatever else it prohibits, students must not be denied access to educational benefits and opportunities on the basis of gender. We thus conclude that funding recipients are properly held liable in damages only where they are deliberately indifferent to sexual harassment, of which they have actual knowledge that is so severe, pervasive, and objectively offensive that it can be said to deprive the victims of access to the educational opportunities or benefits provided by the school.

The most obvious example of student-on-student sexual harassment capable of triggering a damages claim would thus involve the overt, physical deprivation of access to school resources. Consider, for example, a case in which male students physically threaten their female peers every day, successfully preventing the female students from using a particular school resource—an athletic field or a computer lab, for instance. District administrators are well aware of the daily ritual, yet they deliberately ignore requests for aid from the female students wishing to use the resource. The district's knowing refusal to take any action in response to such behavior would fly in the face of Title IX's core principles, and such deliberate indifference may appropriately be subject to claims for monetary damages. It is not necessary, however, to show physical exclusion to demonstrate that students have been deprived by the actions of another student or students of an educational opportunity on the basis of sex. Rather, a plaintiff must establish sexual harassment of students that is so severe, pervasive, and objectively offensive, and that so undermines and detracts from the victims' educational experience, that the victim-students are effectively denied equal access to an institution's resources and opportunities. *Cf. Meritor Savings Bank, FSB v. Vinson,* 477 U.S., at 67, 106 S. Ct. 2399.

. . . . .

The fact that it was a teacher who engaged in harassment in *Franklin* and *Gebser* is relevant. The relationship between the harasser and the victim necessarily affects the extent to which the misconduct can be said to breach Title IX's guarantee of equal access to educational benefits and to have a systemic effect on a program or activity. Peer harassment, in particular, is less likely to satisfy these requirements than is teacher-student harassment.

C

Applying this standard to the facts at issue here, we conclude that the Eleventh Circuit erred in dismissing petitioner's complaint. Petitioner alleges that her daughter was the victim of repeated acts of sexual harassment by G.F. over a 5-month period, and there are allegations in support of the conclusion that G.F.'s misconduct was severe, pervasive, and objectively offensive. The harassment was not only verbal; it included numerous acts of objectively offensive touching, and, indeed, G.F. ultimately pleaded guilty to criminal sexual misconduct. Moreover, the complaint alleges that there were multiple victims who were sufficiently disturbed by G.F.'s misconduct to seek an audience with the school principal. Further, petitioner contends that the harassment had a concrete, negative effect on her daughter's ability to receive an education. The complaint also suggests that petitioner may be able to show both actual knowledge and deliberate indifference on the part of the Board, which made no effort whatsoever either to investigate or to put an end to the harassment.

On this complaint, we cannot say "beyond doubt that [petitioner] can prove no set of facts in support of [her] claim which would entitle [her] to relief." *Conley v. Gibson,* 355 U.S. 41, 45-46 (1957). *See also Scheuer v. Rhodes,* 416 U.S. 232, 236 (1974) ("The issue is not whether a plaintiff will ultimately prevail but whether the claimant is entitled to offer evidence to support the claims"). Accordingly, the judgment of the United States Court of Appeals for the Eleventh Circuit is reversed, and the case is remanded for further proceedings consistent with this opinion.

MURRELL v. SCHOOL DISTRICT NO. 1
186 F.3d 1238 (10th Cir. 1999)

SEYMOUR, Chief Judge.

Penelope Jones began attending classes at GWHS on or about October 25, 1993. Ms. Jones was born with spastic cerebral palsy, which severely impairs her ability to use and control the right side of her body. She is also deaf in her left ear. Testing conducted by the School District established that Ms. Jones was also developmentally disabled. According to an Educational Assessment performed in December 1993, Ms. Jones functioned intellectually and developmentally at the level of a first-grader.

Upon enrolling Ms. Jones at GWHS, Ms. Murrell informed the principal of GWHS, Vivian Johnston, and special education teachers Kathleen Brady and Nelia Hicks, that Ms. Jones had been sexually assaulted at her previous school. Ms. Murrell expressed her fear that her daughter's mental and physical disabilities would place her at continued risk. Ms. Murrell asserts that the principal and the teachers assured her Ms. Jones would be properly supervised. The complaint also alleges that these officials had a duty to supervise and ensure the safety of all GWHS students.

GWHS assigned Ms. Jones to the special education program taught by teachers Brady and Hicks. There Ms. Jones encountered another special education student, "John Doe," who was known to have significant disciplinary and behavioral problems which included engaging in sexually inappropriate conduct. According to the allegations in the complaint, the School District was well aware of Mr. Doe's history. Indeed, Mr. Doe's mother had specifically cautioned the teachers and the principal of the need to keep a watchful eye on him and had informed them that Doe was receiving professional treatment for his problems. Despite Mr. Doe's known behavioral problems, the School District appointed him to a position as a "janitor's assistant," through which he gained access to certain unsupervised areas of the school.

In early November 1993, the teachers became aware that Mr. Doe was engaging in aggressive, sexually inappropriate conduct toward Ms. Jones. At about that same time, Ms. Murrell informed the teachers that Mr. Doe had been making harassing phone calls to Ms. Jones at her home. According to the complaint, it was also during this time that Mr. Doe sexually assaulted Ms. Jones on multiple occasions. Sometime in November, Mr. Doe took Ms. Jones to a secluded area and sexually assaulted her. Ms. Jones, who was menstruating at the time, bled and vomited during the course of the assault and battery. Upon discovering Mr. Doe and Ms. Jones, a janitor told them to clean up the mess, returned them to class, and advised the teachers where he had found them. Although the teachers allegedly knew that Mr. Doe had sexually assaulted Ms. Jones on this occasion, they did not so inform Ms. Murrell. Ms. Murrell learned that Ms. Jones had gotten menstrual blood on her clothing and that the teachers had tied other clothing around her waist to hide it, but Ms. Murrell was never told that the janitor had found Mr. Doe and Ms. Jones in a secluded, unsupervised area, nor was Ms. Murrell informed of any of the circumstances leading to the soiling of Ms. Jones' clothing. On at least one of the occasions on which Mr. Doe battered and sexually assaulted her, Ms. Jones informed the teachers of Mr. Doe's conduct. The teachers told Ms. Jones not to tell her mother about the incident and encouraged her to forget it had happened at all. On or about November 24, 1993, Mr. Doe again took Ms. Jones to a secluded area of the school and battered and sexually assaulted her. Although the teachers knew she had been battered and may have known she was sexually assaulted, they informed Ms. Jones' mother only about the non-sexual battery.

Because of these incidents and because she had begun to engage in self-destructive and suicidal behavior, Ms. Jones left school and entered a psychiatric hospital. Only then did Ms. Murrell learn about the sexual assaults and the batteries of her daughter by Mr. Doe. Although Ms. Murrell immediately contacted the teachers to advise them of what she had learned from Ms. Jones, the teachers denied the incidents could have occurred, told Ms. Murrell to send Ms. Jones back to school, and refused to discuss the matter further. Ms. Murrell asked that the information be provided to Principal Johnston in order that she might investigate Ms. Jones' allegations. Ms. Murrell then telephoned the principal herself and left a message on her answering machine. The principal neither returned Ms. Murrell's call nor undertook any investigation of the alleged incidents.

Following her release from the hospital, Ms. Jones attempted to return to school on December 6, 1993, but stayed for only one day because she was once again battered by Mr. Doe and ridiculed by other students for Mr. Doe's earlier sexual attacks on her. After making several unsuccessful attempts to contact the principal, Ms. Murrell eventually learned from the teachers and Mr. Doe's mother that a meeting had been scheduled to discuss Mr. Doe's sexual conduct with Ms. Jones. That meeting took place on December 10 at GWHS and was attended by the principal, Mr. Doe's mother, the teachers, Ms. Murrell and her husband, and Ms. Jones. The teachers and the principal were hostile towards Ms. Jones and Ms. Murrell. Indeed, the principal allegedly suggested that the sexual contact between Mr. Doe and Ms. Jones might have been consensual, although she knew Ms. Jones was legally incapable of consenting and that Mr. Doe had admitted assaulting Ms. Jones after she had resisted his advances. The principal declined to investigate the incident, and when Ms. Murrell suggested that both students be suspended pending an investigation, the principal responded by suspending only Ms. Jones for "behavior which is detrimental to the welfare, safety, or morals of other pupils or school personnel." Aplt. App. at 14.

In the meantime, the School District neither notified appropriate law enforcement officials of the alleged sexual assaults by Mr. Doe nor disciplined him in any way. Not only did Mr. Doe continue to attend GWHS after the December 1993 meeting, he retained his job as a janitor's assistant with the same access to all parts of the school he had previously enjoyed.

II.

A.

After oral argument on appeal, we abated this case pending the Supreme Court's review of *Davis v. Monroe County Bd. of Educ.*, 120 F.3d 1390 (11th Cir. 1997), *cert. granted*, 119 S. Ct. 29 (1998). The Court has now handed down an opinion in that case addressing "whether a recipient of federal education funding may be liable for damages under Title IX under any circumstances for discrimination in the form of student-on-student sexual harassment." *Davis v. Monroe County Bd. of Educ.*, 526 U.S. 629, 143 L. Ed. 2d 839, 119 S. Ct. 1661, 1669 (1999). Specifically, the Court considered whether a district's failure to respond to [such] harassment can support a private suit for money damages." *Id.* The Court decided that it could, holding:

> funding recipients are properly held liable in damages only where they are deliberately indifferent to sexual harassment, of which they have actual knowledge, that is so severe, pervasive, and objectively offensive that it can be said to deprive the victims of access to the educational opportunities or benefits provided by the school.

119 S. Ct. at 1675. Because *Davis* directly addresses many of the issues here, we analyze Ms. Murrell's claim in light of this recent precedent, having received supplemental briefing from the parties on the effect of *Davis*.

.....

In sum, a plaintiff must allege four factors to state a claim of school district liability under Title IX. She must allege that the district (1) had actual knowledge of, and (2) was deliberately indifferent to (3) harassment that was so severe, pervasive and objectively offensive that it (4) deprived the victim of access to the educational benefits or opportunities provided by the school. *Id.* at 1671-72. This limited rule imposes liability only on those school districts that choose to ignore Title IX's mandate for equal educational opportunities.

We now consider Ms. Murrell's claim in light of *Davis* and other relevant authority. The School District's argument and the district court's order dismissing the case both rest on the premise that an educational institution cannot be held liable under Title IX for conduct not attributable to the institution itself. The School District frames the question before us as whether Title IX imposes an affirmative duty on educational institutions receiving federal financial assistance to prevent students from sexually harassing or assaulting one another, and asserts that the plain language of the statute and the dictates of the Spending Clause preclude holding a grant recipient liable for the acts of its students. This argument misconstrues the nature of the liability Ms. Murrell seeks to impose. Like the plaintiff in *Davis*, Ms. Murrell asserts that school officials had actual knowledge of the repeated sexual assault of her daughter and yet decided to remain idle. Ms. Murrell thus seeks to hold the School District liable for its own "intentional conduct that violates the clear terms of [Title IX]." *Davis*, 119 S. Ct. at 1671.

The Court in *Davis* did not expressly set out the standard for determining when a school board has sufficient notice that harassment is taking place to be liable for failing to respond appropriately. Nonetheless, in contrasting a school district's liability for its own failure to act with liability improperly based on agency principles, the Court held that liability properly attaches when the misconduct "takes place while the students are involved in school activities or otherwise under the supervision of school employees." *Id.* at 1672-73. In so doing, the Court cited with approval *Doe v. University of Ill.*, 138 F.3d 653, 661 (7th Cir. 1998). *Doe* in turn held that a school district is liable if "a school official who had actual knowledge of the abuse was invested by the school board with the duty to supervise the [harasser] and the power to take action that would end such abuse and failed to do so." *Id.* at 668 (internal quotation omitted); *See also Rosa H. v. San Elizario Indep. Sch. Dist.*, 106 F.3d 648, 660 (5th Cir. 1997). Accordingly, we believe the first two prongs of the *Davis* analysis require that a school official who possessed the requisite control over the situation had actual knowledge of, and was deliberately indifferent to, the alleged harassment.

We decline simply to name job titles that would or would not adequately satisfy this requirement. "School districts contain a number of layers below the school board: superintendents, principals, vice-principals, and teachers and coaches, not to mention specialized counselors such as Title IX coordinators. Different school districts may assign different duties to these positions or even reject the traditional hierarchical structure altogether." *Rosa H.*, 106 F.3d at 660. Because officials' roles vary among school districts, deciding who exercises substantial control for the purposes of Title IX liability is necessarily a fact-based inquiry. Davis makes clear, however, that a school official who has the authority to halt known abuse, perhaps by measures such as transferring the harassing student to a different class, suspending him, curtailing his privileges, or providing additional supervision, would meet this definition.

Turning to Ms. Murrell's complaint, we conclude she has sufficiently alleged actual knowledge and deliberate indifference. Ms. Murrell alleged that she telephoned Principal Johnston to discuss Mr. Doe's harassing conduct, and therefore that the principal had actual knowledge of the assaults at least as of the time Ms. Jones was in the hospital. Nevertheless, Principal Johnston failed to take any action to remedy the situation when Ms. Jones returned to school. Indeed Principal Johnston allegedly refused to investigate the matter or discipline Mr. Doe, and instead suspended Ms. Jones and suggested that the sexual conduct was consensual.

We find little room for doubt that the highest-ranking administrator at GWHS exercised substantial control of Mr. Doe and the GWHS school environment during school hours, and so her knowledge may be charged to the School District. *See Davis*, 526 U.S. 629 (finding a basis for Title IX liability when principal allegedly had actual knowledge of sexual harassment and failed to respond to ameliorate the situation). The Denver Public Schools' sexual harassment policy, which prohibits peer sexual harassment, provides that "grievances would routinely be filed" with the principal. Principal Johnston had the authority to suspend students "for 'behavior which is detrimental to the welfare, safety, or morals of other pupils,'"; indeed, she allegedly enforced this policy against Ms. Jones, although not against Mr. Doe. According to the complaint, the principal and teachers "never appropriately disciplined Doe," *Id.*, and he continued to enjoy access to unsupervised parts of the GWHS facility. Principal Johnston's alleged "response to the harassment or lack thereof was clearly unreasonable in light of the known circumstances." *Davis*, 119 S. Ct. at 1674. Her complete refusal to investigate known claims of the nature advanced by Ms. Murrell, if true, amounts to deliberate indifference. As Ms. Murrell has adequately alleged actual knowledge and deliberate indifference on the part of Principal Johnston, she has satisfied the first two elements of the *Davis* inquiry.

Ms. Murrell also asserts that the teachers had a duty to supervise and ensure the safety of all GWHS students including Ms. Jones. They allegedly had actual knowledge of Mr. Doe's conduct toward Ms. Jones from almost the moment it began to occur, and not only refused to remedy the harassment but actively participated in concealing it, including telling Ms. Jones not to inform her mother of Mr. Doe's actions and refusing to inform her mother themselves when presented with myriad opportunities to do so. It is possible that these teachers would also meet the definition of "appropriate persons" for the purposes of Title IX liability if they exercised control over the harasser and the context in which the harassment occurred. Where the victim is complaining about a fellow student's action "during school hours and on school grounds," 119 S. Ct. at 1672, teachers may well possess the requisite control necessary to take corrective action to end the discrimination. *See Gebser*, 118 S. Ct. at 2004 n.8 (Stevens, J., dissenting) ("If petitioner had been the victim of sexually harassing conduct by other students during those classes, surely the teacher would have had ample authority to take corrective measures."). At this stage in the proceedings we must accept as true the allegation that Ms. Jones's teachers were invested with the authority to halt Mr. Doe's known sexually assaultive behavior. If they were, their alleged response quite plainly amounts to deliberate indifference.

We next consider whether the harassment inflicted upon Ms. Jones was sufficiently "severe, pervasive, and objectively offensive" to satisfy *Davis*, 119 S. Ct. at 1676. Ms. Murrell has alleged that over the course of about a month, Mr. Doe repeatedly took Ms. Jones to a secluded area and battered, undressed, and sexually assaulted her. Although Mr. Doe's behavior did not last as long as the harassment in *Davis*, we easily conclude that Ms. Murrell has alleged wrongdoing "sufficiently severe, pervasive and objectively offensive" to state a claim.

Our final consideration under *Davis* is whether the school officials' deliberate indifference deprived Ms. Jones of access to the educational opportunities or benefits provided by GWHS. Again, we have little difficulty concluding that it did under the allegations set forth here. After the assaults, Ms. Jones became a danger to herself and had to leave school to be hospitalized. Moreover, Principal Johnston suspended Ms. Jones when Ms. Murrell suggested the School District should investigate the claim. Ms. Jones is now home bound as a result of her experience at GWHS. The School District's deliberate indifference to her claims totally deprived Ms. Jones of its educational benefits.

Ms. Murrell's complaint satisfies the four factors necessary to impose Title IX liability on school districts for student-on-student harassment and she has therefore stated a claim on which relief can be granted. We reverse the district court's order dismissing Ms. Murrell's Title IX claim.

FITZGERALD v. BARNSTABLE SCHOOL COMMITTEE

504 F.3d 165 (1st Cir. 2007)

SELYA, Senior Circuit Judge.

This appeal grows out of allegations that paint a grotesque picture of peer-on-peer sexual harassment at the elementary school level. The district court, acting initially on a motion to dismiss and thereafter on a motion for summary judgment, resolved the case in favor of the defendants (a school committee and school superintendent). Although we in no way condone harassment such as is alleged here, we are mindful that school districts and school officials have limited ability to guard against such incidents. The defendants in this case responded reasonably to the reported harassment—and that is all that the law requires. Accordingly, even though we disagree with one portion of the district court's decisional calculus, we affirm the judgment below.

I. BACKGROUND

On the morning of February 14, 2001, Jacqueline Fitzgerald, a kindergarten student, informed her parents, Lisa Ryan and Robert Fitzgerald, that each time she wore a dress to school—typically, two to three times a week—an older student on her school bus would bully her into lifting her skirt. Lisa Ryan Fitzgerald believed that these incidents accounted for recent changes in Jacqueline's behavior. She immediately called the principal of Jacqueline's school, Frederick Scully, to report the allegations.

The school system employed a prevention specialist, Lynda Day, whose responsibilities included responding to reports of inappropriate student behavior and instituting warranted disciplinary measures. Scully and Day met with Jacqueline and her parents later that morning. Because school officials were unable to identify the alleged perpetrator from Jacqueline's sketchy account, they arranged for her to observe students disembarking from the school bus.....This surveillance took place over the next two days. Jacqueline identified the perpetrator as Briton Oleson, a third-grader. That same day, Scully and Day questioned Briton, who steadfastly denied the allegations. Day then interviewed the bus driver and a majority of the students who regularly rode the bus. Despite these efforts, she was unable to corroborate Jacqueline's version of the relevant events.

Shortly thereafter, the Fitzgeralds told Scully that Jacqueline had furnished additional details about her ordeal. She now said that, in addition to pressing her to lift her dress, Briton had bullied her into pulling down her underpants and spreading her legs. Scully immediately scheduled a meeting with the Fitzgeralds in order to discuss this new information. He also re-interrogated Briton and followed up on some of the interviews that Day had conducted....By this time, the local police department had launched a concurrent investigation. This probe was handled by a detective specializing in juvenile matters, Reid Hall, who among other things questioned both Jacqueline and Briton. Hall found Briton credible, and the police department ultimately decided that there was insufficient evidence to proceed criminally against him. Relying in part on this decision and in part on the results of the school's own investigation, Scully reached a similar conclusion as to disciplinary measures.

During the currency of these probes, the Fitzgeralds had been driving Jacqueline to and from school. In late February, the school offered to place her on a different bus or, alternatively, to leave rows of empty seats between the kindergarten students and the older pupils on the original bus. The Fitzgeralds rejected these suggestions. The school's primary suggestion—switching buses—attracted special indignation; in the Fitzgeralds' eyes, the school was punishing Jacqueline rather than Briton (who would continue to ride the original bus).

The Fitzgeralds countered with a series of other alternatives, such as placing a monitor on the bus or transferring Briton to a different bus. The superintendent of the school system, Russell Dever, declined to implement any of these proposals.

Although her parents' actions ensured that there were no further incidents aboard the school bus, Jacqueline asserted that she had several unsettling interactions with Briton as the school year progressed. Some were casual encounters in the hallways. The most notable interaction, however, occurred during a mixed-grade gym class. This was an episode in which a gym teacher randomly required Jacqueline to give Briton a "high five."

Each incident was acknowledged by Scully as soon as it was reported, and there is no claim that Scully failed to address these incidents. In any event, Jacqueline stopped participating in gym class and began to miss school with increasing frequency.

....

II. THE TITLE IX CLAIM

A school should be a haven for a youngster, and sexual harassment in an elementary school is never to be condoned. But schools and school officials face a daunting challenge in maintaining a safe, orderly, and well-disciplined environment. Where peer-on-peer sexual harassment is alleged, the Title IX framework, as authoritatively interpreted, imposes a distinct set of legal rules. Within that framework, an educational institution—and for present purposes we treat the School Committee, which stands in the shoes of Jacqueline's elementary school, as an educational institution—may be liable for student-on-student sexual harassment in certain limited circumstances. *See Davis v. Monroe County Bd. of Educ.*, 526 U.S. 629, 643 (1999). To prevail on such a claim, a student first must show that the educational institution is covered by Title IX, that is, that the institution is a recipient of federal funding. *See* 20 U.S.C. § 1681(a). Then, the student must prove that severe, pervasive, and objectively offensive harassment occurred; that the harassment deprived her of educational opportunities or benefits; that the educational institution had actual knowledge of the harassment; and, finally, that the institution's deliberate indifference caused the student to be subjected to the harassment.

Some comment is in order with respect to this final requirement. Title IX does not make an educational institution the insurer either of a student's safety or of a parent's peace of mind. Understandably, then, "deliberate indifference" requires more than a showing that the institution's response to harassment was less than ideal. In this context, the term requires a showing that the institution's response was "clearly unreasonable in light of the known circumstances." *Davis*, 526 U.S. at 648. Relatedly, to "subject" a student to harassment, the institution's deliberate indifference must, at a minimum, have caused the student to undergo harassment, made her more vulnerable to it, or made her more likely to experience it. See *Id.* at 645.

In this instance, three basic points are not in dispute. First, it is uncontradicted that the elementary school is a creature of the School Committee; that the School Committee is a recipient of federal funds; and that, therefore, the School Committee is legally bound to comply with the strictures of Title IX. Second, the parties agree that the School Committee acquired actual knowledge of the school-bus harassment on February 14, 2001 (when Lisa Ryan Fitzgerald reported what Jacqueline had told her). Third, it cannot be gainsaid that, if true, Jacqueline's allegation—that she was forced to pull up her skirt, drop her underpants, and spread her legs—constituted severe, pervasive, and objectively offensive harassment.

The waters are murkier beyond this frontier. In the district court's view, the plaintiffs' claim turned on a point of law: that a Title IX defendant could not be found deliberately indifferent as long as the plaintiff was not subjected to any acts of severe, pervasive, and objectively offensive harassment after the defendant first acquired actual knowledge of the offending conduct. *Hunter*, 456 F. Supp. 2d at 263-64. This ruling dictated the outcome because the court found that the later interactions between Jacqueline and Briton—even when viewed in light of the allegations about Briton's previous conduct—did not constitute continued sexual harassment. *Id.* at 265-66. Title IX liability, the court reasoned, therefore could not attach. *Id.*

The plaintiffs and the amici assail this statement of the law. They note that other courts have found (or countenanced the possibility of finding) Title IX liability, even though the plaintiff alleged only a single incident of pre-notice harassment. *See, e.g., Vance v. Spencer County Pub. Sch. Dist.*, 231 F.3d 253, 259 (6th Cir. 2000). Along these lines. the Eleventh Circuit has held that Title IX discrimination can occur even after a student has withdrawn from school and left the campus. *See Williams v. Bd. of Regents*, 477 F.3d 1282, 1297 (11th Cir. 2007). Though removed from the vicinity of her harassers, the victim in Williams could still be subject to the university's discrimination, which in that case took the form of a failure "to take any precautions that would prevent future attacks." *Id.*

Given this well-reasoned line of authority, we conclude that the district court's rationale is flawed. According to its statement of the law, Title IX liability only attaches after an institution receives actual notice of harassment and the institution subsequently "causes" the victim to be subjected to additional harassment. *Hunter*, 456 F. Supp. 2d at 255-56. To the extent that it held that harassment cannot be "caused" if that harassment never occurs, the district court was on sound footing. Withal, its formulation of the law overly distills the rule set forth by the *Davis* Court. There, the Court stated that funding recipients may run afoul of Title IX not merely by "caus[ing]" students to undergo harassment but also by "mak[ing] them liable or vulnerable" to it. *Davis*, 526 U.S. at 645 (quoting The Random House Dictionary of the English Language 1415 (1966)) (internal quotation marks omitted).

This broader formulation clearly sweeps more situations than the district court acknowledged within the zone of potential Title IX liability. *See, e.g., Wills v. Brown Univ.*, 184 F.3d 20, 27 (1st Cir. 1999) ("On some cases, merely to maintain a harasser in a position of authority over the victim, after notice of prior harassment, could create new liability."). Under it, a single instance of peer-on-peer harassment theoretically might form a basis for Title IX liability if that incident were vile enough and the institution's response, after learning of it, unreasonable enough to have the combined systemic effect of denying access to a scholastic program or activity. *A fortiori*, a case such as the one before us theoretically could form a basis for Title IX liability, given that post-notice interactions between the victim and the harasser have been alleged. The district court therefore erred in truncating its analysis and declining to conduct a broader deliberate indifference inquiry.

Despite this error, we may affirm the district court's entry of summary judgment if that result is supportable on some alternative ground made manifest by the record. *See Houlton Citizens' Coal.*, 175 F.3d at 184. That is the situation here.......The plaintiffs admit that Scully met with them on the very morning that they notified the school of Jacqueline's plight. They also acknowledge that Scully immediately launched an investigation. This investigation consisted of multiple interviews of both Jacqueline and Briton, an interview of the bus driver, and individual interviews of between 35 and 50 children who regularly rode the bus. A number of follow-up interviews were then conducted, including re-interviews of two students who were alleged to have witnessed the critical events. Furthermore, the school cooperated fully in an investigation undertaken by the local police and took the results of that investigation into account in considering disciplinary options.

Within two weeks after the initial report of harassment (and despite its inability to confirm that the harassment had in fact occurred), the school offered to change Jacqueline's transit assignment so that she could continue to ride a bus to and from school without being forced to interact with Briton. The school also suggested, as an alternative, separating kindergarten students from older students by leaving empty a row or two of seats on the bus.

These actions may not have constituted an ideal response to the complaint of harassment. In hindsight, there may be other and better avenues that the School Committee could have explored or other and better questions that could have been asked during the interviews. But Title IX does not require educational institutions to take heroic measures, to perform flawless investigations, to craft perfect solutions, or to adopt strategies advocated by parents. The test is objective—whether the institution's response, evaluated in light of the known circumstances, is so deficient as to be clearly unreasonable. The response here cannot plausibly be characterized in that derogatory manner......Title IX was not intended either to pretermit thoughtful consideration of students' rights or to demand a gadarene rush to judgment. After all, in situations involving charges of peer-on-peer harassment, a public school has obligations not only to the accuser but also to the accused.

The school's prompt commencement of an extensive investigation and its offer of suitable remedial measures distinguish this case from cases in which courts have glimpsed the potential for a finding of deliberate indifference. *See, e.g., Vance*, 231 F.3d at 262 (concluding that a school could be found deliberately indifferent in the absence of evidence that it "took any other action whatsoever" besides talking with the supposed perpetrator); *Murrell v. Sch. Dist. No. 1*, 186 F.3d 1238, 1244, 1247 (10th Cir. 1999) (recognizing potential Title IX liability when school principal "refused to investigate" an allegation of peer-on-peer sexual harassment and neglected to return parent's telephone calls).

The plaintiffs suggest that the adequacy of the School Committee's response is undermined by its offer of unsuitable remedial alternatives. They point out that they proposed other remedial measures, such as the placement of a monitor on Jacqueline's school bus, which the school rejected. They insist that an educational institution, acting in good faith, would have embraced these proposals. The problem, however, is that this line of argument misconstrues the nature of Title IX liability for peer-on-peer sexual harassment. As we have said, the statute does not require an educational institution either to assuage a victim's parents or to acquiesce in their demands. *See Davis*, 526 U.S. at 648; *See also Porto*, 488 F.3d at 73 ("[A] claim that the school system could or should have done more is insufficient to establish deliberate indifference.").

The plaintiffs have a fallback position. They say that the school's investigation, though promptly commenced, was clumsily executed and that, therefore, its response was clearly unreasonable. The plaintiffs' premise is correct; an institutional response to harassment may be carried out so inartfully as to render it clearly unreasonable. *See, e.g., Doe v. Sch. Admin. Dist. No. 19*, 66 F. Supp. 2d 57, 64-65 (D. Me. 1999). But the plaintiffs' conclusion does not follow. There is no competent evidence here that the school's investigation was bungled......

The fact that subsequent interactions between Jacqueline and Briton occurred does not render the School Committee deliberately indifferent. To avoid Title IX liability, an educational institution must act reasonably to prevent future harassment; it need not succeed in doing so. *See Davis*, 526 U.S. at 648 (explaining that a school need not purge itself of peer-on-peer harassment entirely in order to avoid Title IX liability). That ends this aspect of the matter. Given the facts and the law, no rational factfinder could supportably conclude that the School Committee acted with deliberate indifference in this case. It follows that the district court appropriately granted summary judgment in favor of the School Committee on the Title IX claim.

Notes and Comments

1. Consensual Relationships in Higher Education involving Faculty, Staff and Students
In light of the tone of the courts in applying Title IX to sexual harassment cases, would you advise institutions of higher education to have a consensual relationship policy that bans relationships between faculty members and students? Does the power of a faculty member preclude valid consent by a student to a sexual relationship?

The National Education Association rule of good practice on the issue sates that, "sexual relationships between a faculty member and a student currently enrolled in the faculty member's course, or under the supervision or direction of the faculty member, are unprofessional." National Education Association, Policies on Sexual Harassment and Personal Relationships in Higher Education, reprinted in The Educator's Guide, app. V at 129. *See Naragon v. Wharton*, 572 F. Supp. 1117 (M.D. La. 1983), *aff'd*, 737 F.2d 1403 (5th Cir. 1984) (Dismissal of a female instructor who had a relationship with a female student). For articles on the subject, see Jerome W.D. Stokes & D. Frank Vinik, Consensual Sexual Relations Between Faculty and Students in Higher Education, 96 Educ. Law Rep. 899 (1995). *See also*, Sherry Young: Getting to Yes: The Case Against Banning Consensual Relationships in Higher Education, 4 Am. U. J. Gender & Law 269 (1996).

2. Title IX and Same-Sex Harassment

In *Gebser*, the Court announced, "Congress enacted Title IX in 1972 with two principal objectives in mind: to avoid the use of federal resources to support discriminatory practices and to provide individual citizens effective protection against those practices." 524 U.S. 274, 301. (1998). Should remedies under Title IX be available to litigants who claim to be victims of same-sex sexual harassment?

The Title IX is silent on this question. However, the courts have decided that Title IX does cover allegations of same-sex sexual harassment. To do so, the courts have continued to borrow from Title VII discrimination case law. In the leading case, *Oncale v. Sundowner Offshore Servs.*, 523 U.S. 75 (1998), the Supreme Court of said of Title VII,

> [A] trier of fact might reasonably find such discrimination, for example, if a female victim is harassed in such sex-specific and derogatory terms by another woman as to make it clear that the harasser is motivated by general hostility to the presence of women in the workplace. A same-sex harassment plaintiff may also, of course, offer direct comparative evidence about how the alleged harasser treated members of both sexes in a mixed-sex workplace. ... Common sense, and an appropriate sensitivity to social context, will enable courts and juries to distinguish between simple teasing or roughhousing among members of the same sex, and conduct which a reasonable person in the plaintiff's position would find severely hostile or abusive. *Id.*, at 80-82.

Lower courts have found the reasoning of *Oncale* fully transferable to Title IX cases. *See Frazier v. Fairhaven Sch. Comm.*, 276 F.3d 52 (1st Cir. 2002) (Same-sex stalking at a high school when one female staff member alleged that she was relieving herself in a bathroom stall with the door closed when another female staff member peered into the stall through a crack between the door and the wall). *See, Doe v. D'Agostino*, 367 F. Supp. 2d 157 (D. Mass. 2005) (Same-sex harassment by teacher toward a student in class), and *Doe v. E. Haven Bd. of Educ.*, 430 F. Supp. 2d 54 (D. Conn. 2006) (group harassment from students of both genders). Professors Lewis and Fogerty have published a thorough review of same-sex harassment cases that includes the following observation:

> The act of sexual harassment itself creates an inference that the harasser harbors a sexually discriminatory animus towards the plaintiff. When a person "sexually harasses" another, i.e., makes comments or advances of an erotic or sexual nature,

> we infer that "the harasser [is making] advances towards the victim because the victim is a member of the gender the harasser prefers." Unless there is evidence to the contrary, therefore, we also infer that the harasser treats members of the "non-preferred" gender differently—and thus that the harasser harbors an impermissible discriminatory animus towards persons of the preferred gender. . . . This inference can be drawn regardless of the sexual orientation of the harasser, so long as the harassed victim is of the harasser's "preferred" gender.

Lewis and Fogerty, An Exemplar of Unintended Consequences: The Expanding View of "Sex" Protections In Post-Oncale Title VII Cases 36 U. Mem. L. Rev. 145, 179 (2005) (quoting from *Llampallas v. Mini-Circuits, Lab, Inc.* 163 F.3d 1236, 1246 (11th Cir. 1998).

3. Retaliation under Title IX

The enforcement of civil rights laws requires that those asserting complaints of discrimination be protected against retaliation for the assertion of such rights. Without access to a remedy, the right becomes elusive. Claims of retaliation under Title VII, the federal employment antidiscrimination law, are expressly protected in the statute (*See* § 704(a) of Title VII of the Civil Rights Act of 1964, 42 U.S.C.S. § 2000e-3(a); (providing that it is an "unlawful employment practice" for an employer to retaliate against an employee). This was confirmed by the United States Supreme Court in *Robinson v. Shell Oil Co.*, 519 U.S. 337 (1997). But, would a similar protection be extended to claims involving educational antidiscrimination laws? The answer was not provided for nearly 35 years.

In *Jackson v. Birmingham Board of Education*, 544 U.S. 167 (2005), the Court held that retaliation against a person because that person has complained of sex discrimination was another form of intentional sex discrimination encompassed by Title IX's private cause of action. The plaintiff in Johnson complained that his girl's basketball team was not receiving equal funding and equal access to athletic equipment and facilities. The response by school officials was to remove him as coach (which resulted in a reduction of pay). The lower courts had dismissed plaintiff's suit, finding that Title IX did not include claims of retaliation. The Supreme Court reversed,

> Congress certainly could have mentioned retaliation in Title IX expressly, as it did in § 704 of Title VII of the Civil Rights Act of 1964, 78 Stat. 257, as amended, 86 Stat. 109, 42 U.S.C. § 2000e-3(a). …... the Board should have been put on notice by the fact that our cases since *Cannon,* such as *Gebser* and *Davis,* have consistently interpreted Title IX's private cause of action broadly to encompass diverse forms of intentional sex discrimination. Indeed, retaliation presents an even easier case than deliberate indifference. ..... The regulations implementing Title IX clearly prohibit retaliation and have been on the books for nearly 30 years. More importantly, the Courts of Appeals that had considered the question at the time of the conduct at issue in this case all had already interpreted Title IX to cover retaliation. A reasonable school board would realize that institutions covered by Title IX cannot cover up violations of that law by means of discriminatory retaliation. 544 U.S. at 183-184.

The Court ruled that in order for the coach to prevail on the merits, "*Jackson* will have to prove that the Board retaliated against him because he complained of sex discrimination." 544 U.S. at 184.

After *Jackson*, it remains vital that the retaliation be directly linked to the assertion of Title IX charges. Otherwise, courts will simply rely on other employment laws, such as Title VII, to assess demotion or termination claims based on retaliation. *See Vandiver v. Little Rock Sch. Dist.*, 2007 WL 2973463 (E.D. Ark. Oct. 9, 2007) (reminding that Title IX does not "expand private rights of action . . . to include claims of employment discrimination which have no connection to the rights of students"). Post-*Jackson*, plaintiffs alleging retaliation under Title IX must demonstrate some linkage to a Title IX claim or assertion of rights.

Since *Jackson*, retaliation claims have been brought by plaintiffs in a variety of scenarios. *See Bastian v. New York City Dep't of Educ.*, 104 Fair Empl. Prac. Cas. (BNA) 614 (S.D.N.Y.2008) (dismissed for complaining about compensation as compared to female coaches); *Moore v. Greenwood Sch. Dist. No. 52*, 195 Fed. Appx. 140 (4th Cir. 2006) (same allegation); *Atkinson v. Lafayette College*, 460 F.3d 447 (3d Cir. 2006) (Director of Athletics dismissed for raising issues of gender equality in the athletic program); *Dawn L. v. Greater Johnstown Sch. Dist.*, 2008 U.S. Dist. LEXIS 51411 (W.D. Pa. July 2, 2008) (parents allege retaliation by school officials after reporting sexual harassment of their daughter by a teacher).

III. Expanded Scope of Title IX: Discrimination in Athletics

When enacted in 1972, Title IX was silent on its application to athletics. During debate of its provisions, colleges and universities succeeded in keeping its focus away from football and by necessary implication other school-sponsored sports. However, in 1974, Congress decided to expand the reach of Title IX into athletics. The Education Amendments of 1974, included provisions directing the Secretary of Health, Education, and Welfare to address discrimination in athletics, "which shall include with respect to intercollegiate athletic activities reasonable provisions considering the nature of particular sports." Pub. L. No. 93-380, § 844, 88 Stat. 484, 612 (1974)). The regulations that followed have been a constant source of interpretation and litigation. 45 CFR 86.41 provides:

> (a) General. No person shall, on the basis of sex, be excluded from participation in, be denied the benefits of, be treated differently from another person or otherwise be discriminated against in any interscholastic, intercollegiate, club or intramural athletics offered by a recipient, and no recipient shall provide any such athletics separately on such basis.
>
> (b) Separate teams. Notwithstanding the requirements of paragraph (a) of this section, a recipient may operate or sponsor separate teams for members of each sex where selection for such teams is based upon competitive skill or the activity involved is a contact sport. However, where a recipient operates or sponsors a team in a particular sport for members of one sex but operates or sponsors no such team for members of the other sex, and athletic opportunities for members of that sex have previously been limited, members of the excluded sex must be allowed to try-out for the team offered unless the sport involved is a

contact sport. For the purposes of this part, contact sports include boxing, wrestling, rugby, ice hockey, football, basketball and other sports the purpose of major activity of which involves bodily contact.

(c) Equal opportunity. A recipient, who operates or sponsors interscholastic, intercollegiate, club or intramural athletics shall provide equal athletic opportunity for members of both sexes. In determining whether equal opportunities are available, the Director will consider, among other factors:

(1) Whether the selection of sports and levels of competition effectively accommodate the interests and abilities of members of both sexes;

(2) The provision of equipment and supplies;

(3) Scheduling of games and practice time;

(4) Travel and per diem allowance;

(5) Opportunity to receive coaching and academic tutoring;

(6) Assignment and compensation of coaches and tutors;

(7) Provision of locker rooms, practice and competitive facilities;

(8) Provision of medical and training facilities and services;

(9) Provision of housing and dining facilities and services;

(10) Publicity.

Unequal aggregate expenditures for members of each sex or unequal expenditures for male and female teams if a recipient operates or sponsors separate teams will not constitute noncompliance with this section, but the Director may consider the failure to provide necessary funds for teams for one sex in assessing equality of opportunity for members of each sex. 45 CFR 86.41 (1975).

MCCORMICK EX REL. MCCORMICK v. SCHOOL DISTRICT OF MAMARONECK

370 F.3d 275 (2d Cir. 2004)

STRAUB, Circuit Judge:

Plaintiffs-Appellees Barry McCormick, on behalf of his minor daughter Katherine, a student at Pelham high school, and Josef Geldwert, on behalf of his minor daughter Emily, a student at Mamaroneck high school ("plaintiffs"), filed this action in April 2002 alleging that the decisions by the School Districts to schedule girls' high school soccer in the spring of the academic year violated Title IX and its governing regulations, and seeking an injunction requiring the School Districts to move girls' soccer to the fall.

The parties have stipulated to the following facts, unless otherwise indicated. The New York State Public High School Athletic Association ("NYSPHSAA") has approximately 750 members across the state, including the Pelham and Mamaroneck high schools. The NYSPHSAA divides its members into eleven sections and leaves the decision regarding which sports are played in which season to the individual sections. Section I, to which Pelham and Mamaroneck belong, leaves those season scheduling decisions to individual school districts.

Seven hundred fourteen public schools in New York offer girls' soccer, 649 of which offer it in the fall. The Regional and State Championships are scheduled at the end of the fall season. Prior to plaintiffs and others complaining to their schools about the scheduling of girls' soccer in the spring, 643 schools offered soccer in the fall. After complaints were made, six schools agreed to move girls' soccer to the fall.

The parties have stipulated that some girls' soccer teams at Section I schools began playing in the spring 15 years ago because of the popularity of girls' field hockey in the region. The girls' soccer teams in Pelham and Mamaroneck have an opportunity to compete in the Section I spring league championships. However, even if they win the sectional championship, they cannot compete at the Regional or State Championships, as those games are in the fall. Because the School Districts schedule boys' soccer in the fall, the boys have a chance to compete in the Regional and State Championships for boys' soccer which are held at the end of the fall season. Girls' soccer is the only sport at the Pelham and Mamaroneck high schools that is scheduled out of the State Championship game season.

Both girls are soccer players. Both McCormick and Geldwert qualified in 2003 for the Olympic Development Program ("ODP"), a program for girls with exceptional ability in soccer. ODP schedules practices and tournaments in the spring based on the assumption that there will be no conflicts with high school soccer, which is typically scheduled in the fall. ODP tryouts are in the fall, but practices do not begin until the winter. In the spring, ODP practices are on Monday evenings in Albany, which is two and a half hours from Pelham. Boys in Pelham and Mamaroneck who qualify for ODP do not face the same conflicts between ODP and high school soccer, because they play high school soccer in the fall.

Both McCormick and Geldwert also play soccer for the Eastchester Patriots club team, a private soccer team that competes in various high-level soccer tournaments. Club soccer has practices and tournaments throughout the year. Neither McCormick nor Geldwert planned to play on their high school teams in the spring of 2003 because neither wanted to play high school, club, and ODP soccer at the same time. In the spring of 2002, Geldwert's participation on the club team caused her to miss some Mamaroneck high school games. As a result of missing games for her high school team, Geldwert was docked playing time by the high school coach. McCormick and Geldwert would play for their high school soccer teams if girls' soccer were moved to the fall season. The parties informed us at oral argument that McCormick is currently playing for the Pelham team—during the spring 2004 season.

Both McCormick and Geldwert have expressed that they want a chance to compete in the Regional and State Championships. Both McCormick and Geldwert point out that the boys at their schools do not have to juggle ODP soccer and high school soccer because they get to play high school soccer in the fall.

There are some college coaches who recruit during the fall high school season, particularly during the regional and state championships. They need to see players perform before they recruit them, with or without the offer of scholarships. The Westchester girls who play high school soccer in the spring are disadvantaged, because they do not have the opportunity to compete in the regional and state championships. Additionally, they will not be seen in their senior year until the spring, when college application deadlines have expired, and recruiting classes have been filled and scholarships already have been awarded.

The School Districts submitted affidavits from coaches of women's teams at Cornell University, Old Dominion University, and Dominican College, which state that the coaches do not see any disadvantage to girls playing high school soccer in the spring. The Cornell and Old Dominion coaches say that they recruit at the club level in the spring. The parties have stipulated that Section I girls' soccer players are recruited just as much as girls from the other ten sections in the state. Mamaroneck currently offers in the fall: swimming, volleyball, cross-country, tennis, field hockey, and cheerleading for girls, and football, soccer, and cross-country for boys. In the spring in Mamaroneck, girls are offered soccer, lacrosse, softball, track, and golf, and boys are offered baseball, golf, lacrosse, tennis, and track. Pelham offers the same sports to boys and girls in each season as Mamaroneck—except Pelham does not offer golf to girls in the spring (only boys are offered golf). The Mamaroneck and Pelham School Districts offer three teams—varsity, junior varsity, and modified—for each sport. "Modified" teams are for students in seventh and eighth grade. The parties do not indicate in their stipulated facts which sports are offered at each school in the winter.

In Mamaroneck, there are currently nine teams that share five fields in the fall. Renovation of Mamaroneck's baseball diamond began in June 2002, which limited field practice space in the fall season because the football teams used the outfield of the baseball diamond for practices. However, the renovation was expected to be done by spring 2004. In Pelham, there are three fields currently shared by seven teams in the fall. Pelham has one varsity soccer coach and one assistant coach, who coach both the girls' and the boys' soccer teams. Mamaroneck has only one coach for soccer.

Plaintiffs initially moved for a preliminary injunction ordering the School Districts to move girls' soccer to the fall. The District Court denied that motion but held, after a trial on stipulated facts, that the School Districts' decision to schedule girls' but not boys' soccer in the spring season violated Title IX and that plaintiffs were entitled to declaratory and injunctive relief. The court ordered each School District to develop a plan "pursuant to which it shall offer soccer to men and women in the same season," and further ordered that "each such plan shall take effect in the academic year following appellate finality of this action." The court stayed the judgment pending "appellate finality of this action or the further order or direction of the Court of Appeals."

II. TITLE IX

"Congress enacted Title IX in 1972 with two principal objectives in mind: 'To avoid the use of federal resources to support discriminatory practices' and 'to provide individual citizens effective protection against those practices.'" *Gebser v. Lago Vista Indep. Sch. Dist.*, 524 U.S. 274, 296 (1998) (quoting *Cannon v. Univ. of Chicago*, 441 U.S. 677, 704 (1979)). .....In 1974, HEW proposed regulations which contained provisions specifically addressing Title IX's requirements in the athletics programs of educational institutions. In 1979, Congress split HEW into the Department of Health and Human Services ("HHS") and the Department of Education ("ED"). The HEW regulations in effect at that time were left with HHS, and ED duplicated them. All educational functions were transferred to ED, *See* 20 U.S.C. § 3441(a)(1), and thus we treat ED as the administrative agency charged with administrating Title IX.

B. The Regulations and the Policy Interpretation

The Department of Education's athletics regulations, *See* 34 C.F.R. § 106.41, set forth the standards for assessing an athletics program's compliance with section 901 of Title IX. We defer to the interpretation of Title IX that these regulations provide. The Title IX athletics regulations provide that "no person shall, on the basis of sex, be excluded from participation in, be denied the benefits of, be treated differently from another person or otherwise be discriminated against in any interscholastic, intercollegiate, club or intramural athletics offered by a recipient, and no recipient shall provide any such athletics separately on such basis." 34 C.F.R. § 106.41(a).

Particularly relevant for purposes of this case, the regulations state that "[a] recipient which operates or sponsors interscholastic, intercollegiate, club or intramural athletics shall provide equal athletic opportunity for members of both sexes." *Id.* § 106.41(c). In determining whether equal opportunities exist, the Department of Education's Office for Civil Rights ("OCR") considers, among other factors:

(1) Whether the selection of sports and levels of competition effectively accommodate the interests and abilities of members of both sexes;

(2) The provision of equipment and supplies;

(3) Scheduling of games and practice time;

(4) Travel and per diem allowance;

(5) Opportunity to receive coaching and academic tutoring;

(6) Assignment and compensation of coaches and tutors;

(7) Provision of locker rooms, practice and competitive facilities;

(8) Provision of medical and training facilities and services;

(9) Provision of housing and dining facilities and services;

(10) Publicity. *Id.* § 106.41(c) (emphasis added).

Plaintiffs in this case assert that the School Districts do not provide equal opportunities to girls and boys under factor three, "scheduling of games and practice time."…..A Policy Interpretation issued by HEW's Office for Civil Rights and used by ED's Office for Civil Rights explains that compliance under factor three of the regulations, "scheduling of games and practice time," is assessed by examining, among other factors, the equivalence for men and women of:

(1) The number of competitive events per sport;

(2) The number and length of practice opportunities;

(3) The time of day competitive events are scheduled;

(4) The time of day practice opportunities are scheduled; and

(5) The opportunities to engage in available pre-season and post-season competition.
Title IX of the Education Amendments of 1972, A Policy Interpretation, Title IX and Intercollegiate Athletics, 44 Fed. Reg. 71,413, 71,416 (Dec. 11, 1979).

Plaintiffs assert that the girls in Pelham and Mamaroneck do not have the same opportunities as the boys to engage in available post-season competition. The parties agree that we should defer to the Policy Interpretation; its applicability in this case is undisputed. Other circuits have deferred to the Policy Interpretation in determining whether a school has violated Title IX. …..Although the Policy Interpretation specifically addresses the requirements of Title IX in the context of intercollegiate athletics rather than interscholastic athletics, the parties agree that the Policy Interpretation should govern our inquiry in this case.

The Policy Interpretation divides Title IX coverage into three areas: 1) compliance in financial assistance based on athletic ability; 2) compliance in other program areas; and 3) compliance in meeting the interests and abilities of male and female students. Policy Interpretation, 44 Fed. Reg. at 71,414.

Most circuit court opinions in Title IX cases have addressed "accommodation" claims rather than "equal treatment" claims. *See, e.g., Pederson v. La. State Univ.*, 213 F.3d 858, 877-82 (5th Cir. 2000) (holding that university violated Title IX by failing to effectively accommodate interests and abilities of female athletes); *Cohen v. Brown Univ.*, 101 F.3d 155, 173-80 (1st Cir. 1996) (holding that university violated Title IX when it demoted from university-funded varsity status to donor-funded varsity status several women's and men's teams), *cert. denied*, 520 U.S. 1186, (1997); *Kelley v. Board of Trustees, Univ. of Ill.*, 35 F.3d 265, 269-70 (7th Cir. 1994) (holding that university's decision to terminate men's swimming program while retaining women's swimming program did not violate Title IX), *cert. denied*, 513 U.S. 1128 1995); *Roberts*, 998 F.2d at 831-32 (holding that university violated Title IX when it discontinued women's varsity fast pitch softball team).

Several district courts have considered "equal treatment" claims. *See, e.g., Cmtys. for Equity v. Mich. High Sch. Ath. Ass'n*, 178 F. Supp. 2d 805, 855-57 (W.D. Mich. 2001) (holding that high school athletic association violated Title IX by scheduling athletic seasons and tournaments for girls' sports during nontraditional and less advantageous times of the academic year than boys' athletic seasons and tournaments); *Landow v. Sch. Bd. of Brevard County*, 132 F. Supp. 2d 958, 962-66 (M.D. Fla. 2000) (holding that disparities between boys' baseball and girls' softball programs at two high schools in Brevard County violated Title IX); *Alston v. Virginia High Sch. League, Inc.*, 144 F. Supp. 2d 526, 535-36 (W.D. Va. 1999) (denying summary judgment to state high school athletic association on claim by female athletes that system under which girls' teams had to switch seasons whenever their school was reclassified to a new division, which could occur as frequently as every two years, and boys' teams remained in the same season, violated Title IX); *Daniels v. Sch. Bd. of Brevard County*, 985 F. Supp. 1458, 1460-63 (M.D. Fla. 1997) (holding that female varsity softball players were entitled to a preliminary injunction on their claim that their high school denied them the benefits given to the boys' varsity baseball team); *Cook v. Colgate Univ.*, 802 F. Supp. 737 (N.D.N.Y. 1992) (holding that university's unequal treatment of men's and women's ice hockey teams violated Title IX), vacated as moot, 992 F.2d 17 (2d Cir. 1993).

The Policy Interpretation describes factors two through ten of the regulations as "general athletic program components." The Policy Interpretation provides:

> The Department will assess compliance with . . . the general athletic program requirements of the regulation by comparing the availability, quality and kinds of benefits, opportunities, and treatment afforded members of both sexes. Institutions will be in compliance if the compared program components are equivalent, that is, equal or equal in effect. Under this standard, identical benefits, opportunities, or treatment are not required, provided the overall effects of any differences is negligible. Policy Interpretation, 44 Fed. Reg. at 71,415.

"If comparisons of program components reveal that treatment, benefits, or opportunities are not equivalent in kind, quality or availability, a finding of compliance may still be justified if the differences are the result of nondiscriminatory factors." *Id.* The Policy Interpretation provides a list of factors that may justify differences in treatment. *Id.* at 71,415-16.

For each program component, the Policy Interpretation lists the factors that should be examined to determine compliance. *See id.* at 71,416-17. As mentioned, with regard to the "scheduling of games and practice time" program component, the Policy Interpretation states that compliance will be assessed by examining, among other factors, the "equivalence of men and women of . . . the opportunities to engage in available pre-season and post-season competition." *Id.* at 71,416.

The section of the Policy Interpretation covering compliance in "other program areas" concludes by stating:

> Overall Determination of Compliance. The Department will base its compliance determination under § 86.41(c) of the regulation upon an examination of the following:
>
> a. Whether the policies of an institution are discriminatory in language or effect; or
>
> b. Whether disparities of a substantial and unjustified nature exist in the benefits, treatment, services, or opportunities afforded male and female athletes in the institution's program as a whole; or
>
> c. Whether disparities in benefits, treatment, services, or opportunities in individual segments of the program are substantial enough in and of themselves to deny equality of athletic opportunity.
> *Id.* at 71,417.

C. The Disparity in Athletic Opportunity

Thus, under the Policy Interpretation, a disparity in one program component (i.e., scheduling of games and practice time) can alone constitute a Title IX violation if it is substantial enough in and of itself to deny equality of athletic opportunity to students of one sex at a school. Under the Policy Interpretation, a disparity is a difference, on the basis of sex, in benefits, treatment, services, or opportunities that has a negative impact on athletes of one sex when compared with benefits, treatment, services, or opportunities available to athletes of the other sex. A disparity does not mean that benefits, treatment, services, or opportunities are merely different.

[T]he Policy Interpretation makes clear that identical scheduling for boys and girls is not required. Rather, compliance is assessed by first determining whether a difference in scheduling has a negative impact on one sex, and then determining whether that disparity is substantial enough to deny members of that sex equality of athletic opportunity.

Schools thus have considerable flexibility in complying with Title IX. For example, a school that provides better equipment to the men's basketball team than to the women's basketball team would be in compliance with Title IX if it provided comparably better equipment to the women's soccer team than to the men's soccer team. *See id.* at 71,422 ("There is no provision for the requirement of identical programs for men and women . . . ."); *see also* Investigator's Manual at 38 ("An institution is not required to schedule the same number of games or practices for men's and women's teams of the same or similar sport. However, any differences favoring, for example, men's teams, should be offset by differences favoring women's teams in other sports.").

In the present case, scheduling girls' soccer in the spring clearly creates a disparity—boys can strive to compete in the Regional and State Championships in soccer and girls cannot. Without a doubt, this difference has a negative impact on girls. The School Districts have not pointed to—in their submissions to the District Court or to us—any areas in which female athletes receive comparably better treatment than male athletes at their schools. Thus, the disadvantage that girls face in the scheduling of soccer has not been offset by any advantages given to girls as compared to boys in the Mamaroneck and Pelham athletics programs. Moreover, girls' soccer is the only sport at these schools scheduled in a season that precludes championship game play. Male athletes do not suffer from any comparable disadvantage.

D. The Significance of the Disparity

Because the School Districts have not come forth with evidence that the disparity in this case has been offset by some comparable advantage to girls or disadvantage to boys, we must determine whether the disparity is "substantial enough" by itself to deny girls at the Mamaroneck and Pelham schools equality of athletic opportunity. We conclude that the disparity meets that threshold.

The scheduling of soccer in the spring…places a ceiling on the possible achievement of the female soccer players that they cannot break through no matter how hard they strive. The boys are subject to no such ceiling. Treating girls differently regarding a matter so fundamental to the experience of sports—the chance to be champions—is inconsistent with Title IX's mandate of equal opportunity for both sexes. Scheduling the girls' soccer season out of the championship game season sends a message to the girls on the teams that they are not expected to succeed and that the school does not value their athletic abilities as much as it values the abilities of the boys.

E. Justification for Disparity

The Policy Interpretation states that "if comparisons of program components reveal that treatment, benefits, or opportunities are not equivalent in kind, quality or availability, a finding of compliance may still be justified if the differences are the result of nondiscriminatory factors." Policy Interpretation, 44 Fed. Reg. at 71,415. The Policy Interpretation lists "some of the factors that may justify these differences." 20 *Id.* Although none of the particular factors listed in the Policy Interpretation are relevant in this case, the list does not purport to be exhaustive. However, we conclude that the School Districts have not adequately justified the scheduling of girls' soccer in the spring.

The School Districts offer several reasons for why girls' soccer is scheduled in the spring and why moving it to the fall would be a problem. First, the schools assert that if girls' soccer is moved, there will not be enough field space, they will have to hire another coach, and there might be a shortage of officials. These reasons are not the kind of nondiscriminatory factors that can justify inferior treatment of female athletes. Hiring a new coach and finding more officials may cost money, but the fact that money needs to be spent to comply with Title IX is obviously not a defense to the statute. The schools will have to make some adjustments in order to provide field space to the girls' soccer teams for practices and games. However, the schools have not demonstrated that finding field space for practices will be impossible or will result in significantly shorter or more infrequent practices. In any event, all of these administrative problems could be avoided by moving boys' soccer to the spring. There is no reason that the boys' soccer teams should be entitled to the fields, coaches, and officials in the fall simply because they were in the fall first. The School Districts could comply with Title IX by offering soccer to boys and girls in the fall in alternating years (or every two years)—as long as the girls, who have been thus far denied the fall season, are scheduled in the upcoming 2004 fall season. Because the School Districts could avoid the administrative problems they complain about by alternating boys' and girls' soccer in the fall season, this case does not require us to decide the availability of an "administrative hardship defense," if any, or the threshold that would suffice to justify a significant disparity in equal athletic opportunity on the basis of such a defense.

It may well be that an alternating schedule is an undesirable outcome for both male and female athletes as it would mean a student's participation in soccer throughout high school would preclude consistent participation in another spring or fall sport throughout high school. In addition, it seems that the annual administrative difficulties with an alternating schedule would likely exceed those involved with a permanent switch of girls' soccer to the fall.

.....

Thus, we conclude that none of the reasons offered by the School Districts justify their decisions to schedule girls' soccer in the spring thereby denying the girls' soccer teams the opportunity to compete in the Regional and State Championships. We do not intend to foreclose the possibility that scheduling a sport outside the season of championship game play, may, under certain circumstances, be permissible under Title IX. As mentioned, a school that denied comparable championship opportunities to boys and girls in equal numbers would not be in violation of Title IX. In addition, off-season scheduling that disadvantaged members of only one sex might be permissible if supported by greater justification than that advanced here. We conclude in this case, however, that the School Districts have not adequately justified the unequal provision of competitive opportunities to girls and boys. The denial of equality of athletic opportunity therefore violates Title IX.

F. Effective Accommodation

One other matter must be addressed. The School Districts attempt to avoid a conclusion that they have violated Title IX by arguing that their survey data indicates that they are effectively accommodating the interests and abilities of the girls at their schools and therefore they fall within the "safe harbor" provisions of the Policy Interpretation. [T]his argument fails.

The first factor of the Title IX regulations states that OCR considers "whether the selection of sports and levels of competition effectively accommodate the interests and abilities of members of both sexes." 34 C.F.R. § 106.41(c)(1). The School Districts argue that plaintiffs' complaint about their inability to compete in the Regional and State Championships relates not only to factor three of the regulations, "scheduling of games and practice time," but may be analyzed under factor one of the regulations—because the complaint relates to "levels of competition."

The Policy Interpretation includes a separate discussion of factor one of the regulations. Claims relating to factor one are generally called "accommodation" claims. *See Boucher v. Syracuse University*, 164 F.3d 113, 115 n.1 (2d Cir. 1999). The Policy Interpretation states that the "regulation requires institutions to accommodate effectively the interests and abilities of students to the extent necessary to provide equal opportunity in the selection of sports and levels of competition available to members of both sexes." Policy Interpretation, 44 Fed. Reg. at 71,417. Compliance with factor one of the regulations is to be assessed by examining 1) the school's determination of athletic interests and abilities; 2) the selection of sports offered by the school; and 3) the levels of competition available including the opportunity for team competition. *Id.* Regarding the "levels of competition" assessment, the Policy Interpretation states:

In effectively accommodating the interests and abilities of male and female athletes, institutions must provide both the opportunity for individuals of each sex to participate in intercollegiate competition, and for athletes of each sex to have competitive team schedules which equally reflect their abilities.

a. Compliance will be assessed in any one of the following ways:

(1) Whether intercollegiate level participation opportunities for male and female students are provided in numbers substantially proportionate to their respective enrollments; or

(2) Where the members of one sex have been and are underrepresented among intercollegiate athletes, whether the institution can show a history and continuing practice of program expansion which is demonstrably responsive to the developing interest and abilities of the members of that sex; or

(3) Where the members of one sex are underrepresented among intercollegiate athletes, and the institution cannot show a continuing practice of program expansion such as that cited above, whether it can be demonstrated that the interests and abilities of the members of that sex have been fully and effectively accommodated by the present program. Policy Interpretation, 44 Fed. Reg. at 71,418.

This portion of the Policy Interpretation is generally referred to as the "three-part test," and most Title IX litigation has centered around application of this test. For example, courts have applied this test when female athletes have brought claims against schools that have cut women's varsity sports and therefore decreased the intercollegiate participation opportunities for women. The test is applied to assess whether an institution is providing nondiscriminatory participation opportunities to individuals of both sexes, and an institution is in compliance if it meets any one of the three prongs of the test.

The School Districts argue that survey data indicates that they are "fully and effectively" accommodating the interests and abilities of the girls at their schools and thus they satisfy the third prong of the three-part test. What the School Districts fail to recognize, however, is that the three-part test relates to whether a school is providing sufficient opportunities for participation in intercollegiate level sports. After providing the three-part test for participation opportunities, the Policy Interpretation states:

> b. Compliance with this provision of the regulation will also be assessed by examining the following:
>
> > (1) Whether the competitive schedules for men's and women's teams, on a program-wide basis, afford proportionally similar numbers of male and female athletes equivalently advanced competitive opportunities; or
> >
> > (2) Whether the institution can demonstrate a history and continuing practice of upgrading the competitive opportunities available to the historically disadvantaged sex as warranted by developing abilities among the athletes of that sex. Policy Interpretation, 44 Fed. Reg. at 71,418.

Thus, the three-part test relates to participation opportunities, and a second, two-part test relates to the competitive schedules and opportunities for men's and women's teams. .....To the extent that plaintiffs' claim regarding the inability to compete in the championship games falls under the "levels of competition" portion of factor one of the regulations, their claim relates to competitive schedules/opportunities (the two-part test)—not to participation opportunities (the three-part test). Assuming that the Policy Interpretation's reference to competitive schedules/opportunities includes whether a team has the ability to compete in championship games, as the School Districts suggest, the School Districts have not demonstrated either that "the competitive schedules for men's and women's teams, on a program-wide basis, afford proportionally similar numbers of male and female athletes equivalently advanced competitive opportunities" or that the schools have "a history and continuing practice of upgrading the competitive opportunities available to the historically disadvantaged sex as warranted by developing abilities among the athletes of that sex." Policy Interpretation, 44 Fed. Reg. at 71,418. Thus, the attempt by the School Districts to couch plaintiffs' claim as falling under factor one does not help them.

G. Compliance Plan

The District Court properly determined that plaintiffs are entitled to injunctive relief and ordered the School Districts to submit plans for compliance with Title IX. 25 However, the requirements for the compliance plans must be modified slightly. The District Court directed each School District to develop "a plan pursuant to which it shall offer soccer to men and women in the same season." Moving girls' soccer permanently to the fall, the same season as boys' soccer, would seem to be the easiest way for the School Districts to comply with Title IX. However, as discussed, the School Districts would be in compliance with Title IX if they offered soccer to girls and boys on a rational alternating basis—as long as girls are scheduled in the upcoming fall 2004 season. The relevant inquiry is whether girls and boys are given equal opportunities for post-season competition—not whether the sports are scheduled in the same season.

We are aware of, and have noted, the problems with the option of alternating the fall season between boys' and girls' soccer. Nonetheless, the School Districts may pursue this option if they wish. On remand the District Court should oversee the submission by the School Districts of compliance plans which are consistent with the requirements set forth here, and which shall take effect in the 2004-2005 school year. Regardless of which plan the School Districts adopt—a permanent move of girls' soccer to the fall, or a plan that alternates seasons—the girls' soccer teams must play in the fall of 2004.

CONCLUSION

To summarize, we affirm the District Court's holding that the decisions by the School Districts of Mamaroneck and Pelham to schedule girls' high school soccer in the spring and boys' high school soccer in the fall, which deprives girls but not boys of the opportunity to compete in the New York Regional and State Championships in soccer, violates Title IX of the Education Amendments of 1972, 20 U.S.C. § 1681, et seq., and its governing regulations. However, we modify the District Court's injunction to allow the School Districts to submit a plan that either alternates the fall soccer season between the girls and the boys or moves girls' soccer permanently to the fall. Whatever the plan, the School Districts must schedule girls' soccer in the fall of 2004. We remand to the District Court to oversee the submission and approval of the plans. Costs are awarded to the plaintiffs-appellees. The mandate shall issue forthwith.

EQUITY IN ATHLETICS, INC. v. U. S. DEPTARTMENT OF EDUCATION

291 F. App'x 517 (4th Cir. 2008)

HANSEN, Senior Circuit Judge:

Equity in Athletics, Inc. ("EIA") sought a preliminary injunction to prevent James Madison University ("JMU") from eliminating seven men's sports and three women's sports from its intercollegiate athletic program. EIA claimed that JMU intentionally discriminated against male athletes in violation of the United States Constitution and in violation of Title IX of the Education

Amendments of 1972. Because the district court did not abuse its discretion ...we affirm the district court's denial of EIA's motion for a preliminary injunction.

I.

Title IX provides that "[n]o person in the United States shall, on the basis of sex, be excluded from participation in, be denied the benefits of, or be subjected to discrimination under any education program or activity receiving Federal financial assistance." 20 U.S.C. § 1681(a). Title IX did not specifically address its application to athletics, and in 1974, Congress directed the Secretary of Health, Education, and Welfare ("HEW") to promulgate regulations, "which shall include with respect to intercollegiate athletic activities reasonable provisions considering the nature of particular sports." *McCormick v. Sch. Dist. of Mamaroneck*, 370 F.3d 275, 287 (2d Cir. 2004) (quoting Education Amendments of 1974, Pub. L. No. 93-380, § 844, 88 Stat. 484, 612 (1974)). HEW followed the rulemaking procedures in promulgating 45 C.F.R. § 86.41 in 1975, which provides that "[a] recipient which operates or sponsors interscholastic, intercollegiate, club or intramural athletics shall provide equal athletic opportunity for members of both sexes." § 86.41(c). One of the ten factors listed as assisting in that determination is "[w]hether the selection of sports and levels of competition effectively accommodate the interests and abilities of members of both sexes." § 86.41(c)(1).

EIA does not contest the validity of 45 C.F.R. § 86.41. Rather, at issue here is a Policy Interpretation issued by HEW in 1979 intended to provide further guidance for the 1975 regulation and subsequent clarifications of the Policy Interpretation. The Policy Interpretation provides, in part, that:

> [I]nstitutions must provide both the opportunity for individuals of each sex to participate in intercollegiate competition, and for athletes of each sex to have competitive team schedules which equally reflect their abilities.
>
> (a) Compliance will be assessed in any one of the following ways:
>
> (1) Whether intercollegiate level participation opportunities for male and female students are provided in numbers substantially proportionate to their respective enrollments. . . .44 Fed. Reg. 71,413, 71,418 (Dec. 11, 1979) ("1979 Policy Interpretation").

This provision, which also lists two other methods of compliance not at issue here, has come to be known as the "Three-Part Test." The DOE issued a Clarification to the 1979 Policy Interpretation in 1996, indicating that institutions needed to comply with only one part of the Three-Part Test; DOE issued a Further Clarification in 2003, expressing that the 1979 Policy Interpretation did not require reductions to men's teams or the use of quotas; and it issued an Additional Clarification in 2005, reiterating that each part of the Three-Part Test was an equally sufficient and separate method of complying with Title IX.

James Madison University (JMU) is a state-sponsored university in Virginia and receives federal funds. In an effort to comply with Title IX with respect to its athletic program, JMU's Board of Visitors voted on September 29, 2006, to eliminate seven men's sports (archery, cross country, gymnastics, indoor and outdoor track, swimming, and wrestling) and three women's sports (archery, fencing, and gymnastics) to obtain proportionality between the gender makeup of its athletic programs and its undergraduate enrollment. At the time, JMU's undergraduate population was divided 61% female and 39% male, while its student athletes were 51% female and 49% male. The proposed cuts relied on the first part of the Three-Part Test and were designed to put JMU's student-athlete population in a similar male/female ratio as its general student population. The Board issued a press release explaining its decision the same day. It also issued a "Title IX Statement" on February 8, 2007, further addressing the reasoning behind the cuts, which were to be effective as of July 1, 2007.

Athletes, coaches, and fans formed EIA, a not-for-profit organization, to fight the proposed cuts. EIA challenged the Title IX interpretive guidelines, specifically the Three-Part Test and its subsequent clarifications, as violating the Constitution, Title IX, and the Administrative Procedures Act and as permitting colleges to engage in the kind of gender-conscious decision-making that Title IX was intended to prohibit.

II.

****

Courts have consistently rejected EIA's underlying claim that equal opportunity under § 86.41 should be tied to expressed interest rather than actual participation. *See Neal v. Board of Trustees*, 198 F.3d 763, 767 (9th Cir. 1999) (reversing grant of preliminary injunction, noting that "Appellees' argument that equal opportunity is achieved when each gender's athletic participation roughly matches its interest in participating is hardly novel," and that "[s]everal courts of appeals have considered and rejected Appellees' approach as fundamentally inconsistent with the purpose of Title IX"); *Boulahanis v. Bd. of Regents*, 198 F.3d 633, 638-39 (7th Cir. 1999) ("[T]he elimination of men's athletic programs is not a violation of Title IX as long as men's participation in athletics continues to be 'substantially proportionate' to their enrollment."), *cert. denied*, 530 U.S. 1284, 120 S. Ct. 2762, 147 L. Ed. 2d 1022 (2000); *Cohen v. Brown Univ.*, 101 F.3d 155, 174 (1st Cir. 1996) (*Cohen II*) ("Brown's relative interests approach cannot withstand scrutiny on either legal or policy grounds, because it disadvantages women and undermines the remedial purposes of Title IX by limiting required program expansion for the underrepresented sex to the status quo level of relative interests." (internal citations and marks omitted)), *cert. denied*, 520 U.S. 1186, 117 S. Ct. 1469, 137 L. Ed. 2d 682 (1997). Courts have also rejected Equal Protection claims similar to EIA's constitutional claims against JMU. *See Neal*, 198 F.3d at 773 ("Title IX does not bar universities from taking steps to ensure that women are approximately as well represented in sports programs as they are in student bodies."); *Boulahanis*, 198 F.3d at 639 (rejecting equal protection challenge and holding that "[t]he elimination of sex-based discrimination in federally-funded educational institutions is an important government objective, and the actions of Illinois State University in eliminating the men's soccer and men's wrestling programs were substantially related to that objective"); *Kelley v. Board of Trustees, Univ. of Ill.*, 35 F.3d 265, 272 (7th Cir. 1994) ("To the extent that plaintiffs' argument is that Title IX and the applicable regulation . . . are unconstitutional, it is without merit."), *cert. denied*, 513 U.S. 1128 (1995).

. . . . .

Even if the promulgation of the 1979 Policy Interpretation involved procedural irregularities as EIA argues, the cases discussed above raise a serious doubt about whether EIA will be successful on the merits of its claims against JMU that JMU violated Title IX or the Constitution in using gender to select which athletic programs to cut. *See Kelley*, 35 F.3d at 272 ("[I]nsofar as the University actions were taken in an attempt to comply with the requirements of Title IX, plaintiffs' attack on those actions is merely a collateral attack on the statute and regulations and is therefore impermissible."). While EIA's claims against the federal defendants concerning the procedural validity of the 1979 Policy Interpretation raise novel issues, EIA offers no case directly on point that supports its challenge to the procedural validity of the 1979 Policy Interpretation. In the end, there are no cases directly supporting EIA's procedural challenges to the 1979 Policy Interpretations, and yet nearly every circuit in the country has rejected challenges similar to EIA's underlying complaint against JMU, i.e., that JMU violated Title IX and the Constitution when it used gender to determine which athletic programs to cut. We agree with the district court that EIA has failed to establish a likelihood of success on its claims against JMU sufficient to entitle it to a preliminary injunction.

Jennifer R. Capasso: Structure Versus Effect: Revealing the Unconstitutional Operation of Title IX's Athletics Provisions, 46 B.C. L. Rev. 825 (2005)*

Guided by the Policy Interpretation, universities attempt to comply with Title IX, but these attempts at compliance [create] a new set of concerns among institutions, athletes, and members of Congress. In June 1995, after holding a hearing on Title IX and the three-part test outlined above, 142 members of Congress wrote to the DOE expressing concern over the fact that educational institutions were satisfying prong one of the three-part test—substantial proportionality of opportunity—by eliminating men's athletic opportunities. In response to this request for more guidance about the existing standards governing the enforcement of Title IX, the DOE in 1996 issued a Policy Clarification.

The Policy Clarification provides specific factors intended to guide an analysis under each part of the three-part test and includes examples to demonstrate how these factors should be analyzed in practice. It underscores the fact that the requirement addressed by the three-part test—the effective accommodation of interests and abilities of both sexes—is only one of many factors considered under the Regulation to determine if an institution is in compliance with Title IX. Further, the letter accompanying the Policy Clarification describes the first prong as a "safe harbor" for establishing

---

compliance with the equal opportunity requirement. Finally, the Policy Clarification emphasizes that the three-part test provides an institution with three different avenues of compliance, that institutions have flexibility in deciding how to provide nondiscriminatory participation opportunities for their students, and that the OCR does not require quotas.

.....

In contrast to the typical early challenges to Title IX brought by female athletes, currently the more frequent challenges to the statute come from male athletes, who contend that the actions educational institutions undertake in an effort to comply with Title IX in fact violate Title IX and equal protection principles by impermissibly discriminating against men. Thus, in trying to avoid one type of lawsuit—a claim of a violation of Title IX because of the elimination of women's teams—educational institutions instead are finding themselves in another uncertain legal position: that of defending the elimination of men's teams to achieve compliance.

The practice of cutting teams has become prevalent because intercollegiate athletic departments are facing ever-increasing financial pressure to reduce budgets. In making the required cuts, however, institutions run the risk of violating Title IX if such cuts reduce the opportunities for women at an institution that does not maintain substantial proportionality between its female student-athletes and its female student population. The *Cohen* court's initial judicial and statutory interpretation has resulted in a situation where an institution that must impose budget cuts by cutting teams must comply with prong one or be deemed in violation of Title IX. As a result of this difficulty in compliance, female athletes largely have been successful in suing institutions when their programs are cut and getting their respective athletic programs reinstated. This trend in case law and Title IX interpretation, coupled with the intense pressures to reduce athletic budgets, has caused institutions to resort to cutting only men's teams in order to remain compliant with Title IX.

In an attempt to fight the elimination of their respective programs, male athletes first have attempted to claim that the elimination of their teams, motivated by a concern for achieving gender parity under Title IX, is itself a clear example of sex discrimination, which Title IX and its implementing regulations expressly forbid. In particular, male athletes argue that by eliminating their programs because of the sex of the participants, the institutions are discriminating against the male athletes on the basis of their sex, excluding them from participation in educational programs because of their sex, and denying them the benefits of educational programs because of their sex, all in violation of Title IX. Additionally, male athletes argue that allowing universities to make such cuts on the basis of sex, in an attempt to equalize the rates of participation and allocation of resources, is analogous to implementing a quota system based on sex. Such a quota system, they argue, is also contrary to Title IX's purpose of encouraging, rather than reducing, athletic opportunities for all students. .....Thus far, these arguments by male athletes have never succeeded in court.

.....

In addition to the Title IX claim, the second of the male athletes' key claims is that an institution's action in eliminating men's but not women's teams creates an illegal gender classification that violates the Equal Protection Clause of the Fourteenth Amendment. .....Male athletes frequently argue that the elimination of men's teams because of their gender does not satisfy this intermediate scrutiny standard because such actions are not substantially related to the purported goal of Title

IX. …… The basis of such a claim would be that the effect of the Policy Interpretation and Clarification is to cause Title IX to act as an impermissibly inflexible quota system, because there exists, in effect, only one way to comply.

…..

The key to unmasking the true problems with Title IX's current regulatory framework is in examining the *effects* of the regulatory framework's interpretation rather than its structure. … Such an analysis would reveal that the framework, in fact, operates as an inflexible quota system that forces education institutions to cut men's teams if they are to remain in compliance with Title IX. Such an inflexible system is of the type that the U.S. Supreme Court expressly rejected in its relevant affirmative action decisions, and as such, courts should reject it here as a violation of the Equal Protection Clause of the Fourteenth Amendment.

…..

The U.S. Supreme Court's recent rulings on affirmative action in higher education admissions provide insight to the Title IX discussion. First, in these cases, the Court has held that student body diversity is a compelling state interest and thus that the narrowly tailored use of race to achieve this compelling state interest is justified. Second, and more importantly, an institution that wishes to use race as a criterion in its decision-making process must do so in a "flexible, non-mechanical" way; only this flexibility allows such a policy to remain narrowly tailored enough to be constitutional. Indeed, in upholding the Law School's admission policy in *Grutter v. Bollinger*, the Court emphasized the flexibility of the Law School's approach, in which race and ethnic background were considered a "plus" factor in the admissions process, but each decision remained highly individual. Likewise, the Court emphasized the *non*-flexibility of the schools' approaches when it rejected the admissions policies used in both *Regents of the University of California v. Bakke* and *Gratz v. Bollinger*. In *Bakke*, the institution used a racial set-aside program whereby a certain number of seats were reserved for members of minority groups; in *Gratz*, the institution automatically granted extra points that counted toward automatic admission to applicants of particular racial and ethnic backgrounds. In both decisions, the Court emphasized that such broad, inflexible standards were not narrowly tailored, and as such the institutions had violated the Equal Protection Clause of the Fourteenth Amendment.

The Court's analysis in each of these three cases is instructive as to how courts should view the current operation of the Title IX statute. Title IX's operation is analogous to that of affirmative action programs in that, as currently interpreted, it forces universities to make decisions based on an individual's membership in a particular group—gender. Thus, it should follow that the key to withstanding constitutional scrutiny of such decisions is to emphasize the flexibility of the system, which can demonstrate that individual rights are not being curtailed. As discussed above, however, any flexibility that had been built into the Title IX statute now, in effect, has been interpreted out of it, such that an institution facing budget constraints has no choice but to cut men's teams or be in violation of Title IX. Though gender-based decisions are subject to the lesser standard of intermediate scrutiny (as opposed to the strict scrutiny of race-based decisions), it does not follow that the emphasis on flexibility in the process should be correspondingly lessened. The appropriate degree of flexibility remains to be determined, but the current lack of any flexibility at all is certainly not preferable. The decisions being made under Title IX to cut men's teams would not pass constitutional muster if they were based on race, and the current scheme also should not pass constitutional muster when the decisions are based on gender.

Notes and Comments

1. Does Title IX go too far in its application to athletics? Can you suggest an alternative approach to resolving disputes between men's' and women's' sports within a school?

2. *See* Karen Falduto: Can The Concept of "Good Coaching" Be Quantified for the Purposes of Title IX Sex Discrimination Claims?, 3 DePaul J. Sports L. Contemp. Probs. 220 (2006); and Jane Hefferan: Changing Seasons, Changing Times: The Validity of Nontraditional Sports Seasons Under Title IX and the Equal Protection Clause, 9 Vand. J. Ent. & Tech. L. 861 (2007).

Chapter Nine
Special Needs Education

> [T]he basic purpose of § 504, ... is to ensure that handicapped individuals are not denied jobs or other benefits because of the prejudiced attitudes or the ignorance of others.... The Act is carefully structured to replace such reflexive reactions to actual or perceived handicaps with actions based on reasoned and medically sound judgments: the definition of "handicapped individual" is broad, but only those individuals who are both handicapped *and* otherwise qualified are eligible for relief. *School Bd. of Nassau County v. Arline*, 480 U.S. 273 (1987)

> [The Individuals with Disabilities Education Act (IDEA)] grants parents independent, enforceable rights. These rights, which are not limited to certain procedural and reimbursement-related matters, encompass the entitlement to a free appropriate public education for the parents' child. *Winkelman ex rel. Winkelman v. Parma City School Dist.*, 550 U.S. 516 (2007)

Special education is an extraordinary component of American education law. The Individuals with Disabilities in Education Act (IDEA), Section 504 of the Rehabilitation Act of 1973, and the Americans with Disabilities Act of 1990 (ADA), provide disabled individuals with the opportunity to receive a "free appropriate public education." These laws also protect the disabled from discrimination in the pursuit of education or employment in education. Prior to the passage of federal legislation in this area, educators were allowed to promote a bias against the handicapped, openly excluding disabled individuals from educational opportunities and employment. Court opinions often upheld this right to exclude. The federal laws, enacted as conditions to the receipt of federal educational funding, create procedural and substantive structure for the new norm: the right to reasonable accommodation and fair treatment.

Section 504 of the Rehabilitation Act of 1973 provides:

> No otherwise qualified individual with a disability in the United States shall, solely by reason of her or his disability, be excluded from the participation in, be denied the benefits of, or be subjected to discrimination under any program or activity receiving Federal financial assistance or under any program or activity conducted by any Executive agency or by the United States Postal Service. 29 U.S.C. § 794.

The ADA compliments and expands this protection:

> Subject to the provisions of this subchapter, no qualified individual with a disability shall, by reason of such disability, be excluded from participation in or be denied the benefits of the services, programs, or activities of a public entity, or be subjected to discrimination by any such entity. 42 U.S.C. §§12132.

The Individuals with Disabilities Education Act was enacted on the belief of Congress that, "[d]isability is a natural part of the human experience and in no way diminishes the right of individuals to participate in or contribute to society. Improving educational results for children with disabilities is an essential element of our national policy of ensuring equality of opportunity, full participation, independent living, and economic self-sufficiency for individuals with disabilities." 20 U.S.C.S. § 1400(c). IDEA guarantees a disabled student, "a free appropriate public education that emphasizes special education and related services designed to meet their unique needs." 20 U.S.C.S. § 1400(d).

The materials below provide a survey of the decisions that define the scope of the rights and remedies of individuals with disabilities. It is important at the outset to note that individuals with disabilities may pursue remedies under each of the statutes. For example, a student who is denied an appropriate education may receive both an IDEA remedy and a Section 504 remedy for the same official misconduct. 20 U.S.C.S. § 1415(l). Moreover, the teeth of the remedies under Section 504 were fashioned after the framework of Title VI of the Civil Rights Act of 1964. The rigor of this framework animates the range of remedies for each of the federal laws. As a result, remedies for violating the rights of the disabled include the termination of federal funding when a school receiving federal funding fails to comply with the law and a private right of action so that individuals may sue to enforce the laws.

I. Historical Exclusion of the Disabled

PENNSYLVANIA ASS'N v. PENNSYLVANIA
334 F. Supp. 1257 (E.D. Pa. 1971)

PER CURIAM.

[F]or the reasons set out below it is ordered that defendants the Commonwealth of Pennsylvania, the Secretary of the Department of Education, the State Board of Education, the Secretary of the Department of Public Welfare, the named defendant school districts and intermediate units and each of the School Districts and Intermediate Units in the Commonwealth of Pennsylvania, their officers, employees, agents and successors be and they hereby are enjoined as follows:

> (a) from applying Section 1304 of the Public School Code of 1949, 24 Purd. Stat. Sec. 13-1304, so as to postpone or in any way to deny to any mentally retarded child access to a free public program of education and training;
>
> (b) from applying Section 1326 or Section 1330(2) of the School Code of 1949, 24 Purd.Stat. Secs. 13-1326, 13-1330(2) so as to postpone, to terminate or in any way to deny to any mentally retarded child access to a free public program of education and training;
>
> (c) from applying Section 1371(1) of the School Code of 1949, 24 Purd.Stat. Sec. 13-1371(1) so as to deny to any mentally retarded child access to a free public program of education and training;

(d) from applying Section 1376 of the School Code of 1949, 24 Purd.Stat. Sec. 13-1376, so as to deny tuition or tuition and maintenance to any mentally retarded person except on the same terms as may be applied to other exceptional children, including brain damaged children generally;

(e) from denying homebound instruction under Section 1372(3) of the School Code of 1949, 24 Purd.Stat. Sec. 13-1372(3) to any mentally retarded child merely because no physical disability accompanies the retardation or because retardation is not a short-term disability.

(f) from applying Section 1375 of the School Code of 1949, 24 Purd.Stat. Sec. 13-1375, so as to deny to any mentally retarded child access to a free public program of education and training;

(g) to immediately re-evaluate the named plaintiffs, and to accord to each of them, as soon as possible but in no event later than October 13, 1971, access to a free public program of education and training appropriate to his learning capacities;

(h) to provide, as soon as possible but in no event later than September 1, 1972, to every retarded person between the ages of six and twenty-one years as of the date of this Order and thereafter, access to a free public program of education and training appropriate to his learning capacities;

(i) to provide, as soon as possible but in no event later than September 1, 1972, wherever defendants provide a pre-school program of education and training for children aged less than six years of age, access to a free public program of education and training appropriate to his learning capacities to every mentally retarded child of the same age.

CONSENT AGREEMENT

The Complaint in this action having been filed on January 7, 1971, alleging the unconstitutionality of certain Pennsylvania statutes and practices under the Equal Protection Clause of the Fourteenth Amendment and certain pendent claims; a three-judge court having been constituted, after motion, briefing and argument thereon, on May 26, 1971; an Order and Stipulation having been entered on June 18, 1971, requiring notice and a due process hearing before the educational assignment of any retarded child may be changed; and evidence having been received at preliminary hearing on August 12, 1971;

Now, therefore, this 7th of October 1971, the parties being desirous of effecting an amicable settlement of this action, the parties by their counsel agree, subject to the approval and Order of this Court, as follows:

.....

II.

4. Expert testimony in this action indicates that all mentally retarded persons are capable of benefiting from a program of education and training; that the greatest number of retarded persons, given such education and training, are capable of achieving self-sufficiency, and the remaining few, with such education and training, are capable of achieving some degree of self-care; that the earlier such education and training begins, the more thoroughly and the more efficiently a mentally retarded person will benefit from it; and, whether begun early or not, that a mentally retarded person can benefit at any point in his life and development from a program of education and training.

5. The Commonwealth of Pennsylvania has undertaken to provide a free public education to all of its children between the ages of six and twenty-one years, and, even more specifically, has undertaken to provide education and training for all of its exceptional children.

6. Having undertaken to provide a free public education to all of its children, including its exceptional children, the Commonwealth of Pennsylvania may not deny any mentally retarded child access to a free public program of education and training.

7. It is the Commonwealth's obligation to place each mentally retarded child in a free, public program of education and training appropriate to the child's capacity, within the context of a presumption that, among the alternative programs of education and training required by statute to be available, placement in a regular public school class is preferable to placement in a special public school class and placement in a special public school class is preferable to placement in any other type of program of education and training.

II. Section 504 of the Rehabilitation Act and the ADA

Section 504 of the Rehabilitation Act of 1973, is a non-discrimination law that overlaps a bit with the rights given handicapped citizens in the ADA. Specifically, Section 504 protects students in institutions that receive federal funding. The ADA compliments this protection and expands it to include employees in matters of hiring, placement, or advancement. The ADA requires institutions to make reasonable accommodation for employees who suffer from a disability.

Be prepared to adjust to the habit of judges to use Section 504 and the ADA as interchangeable components in resolving lawsuits brought against institutions. Section 504 utilizes the interpretive decisions from ADA cases to apply to Section 504 cases. The two statutes overlap most often as courts set out to decide whether or not an institution is discriminating against an “otherwise qualified individual.” Thus, the two primary issues arising in the cases are: (1) whether an individual qualifies as a person with a disability, or a person perceived as having a disability; and, (2) whether the institution discriminated against an “otherwise qualified individual.”

SCHOOL BD. OF NASSAU COUNTY V. ARLINE
480 U.S. 273 (1987)

Justice BRENNAN delivered the opinion of the Court.

Section 504 of the Rehabilitation Act of 1973, 87 Stat. 394, as amended, 29 U.S.C. § 794 (Act), prohibits a federally funded state program from discriminating against a handicapped individual solely by reason of his or her handicap. This case presents the questions whether a person afflicted with tuberculosis, a contagious disease, may be considered a "handicapped individual" within the meaning of § 504 of the Act, and, if so, whether such an individual is "otherwise qualified" to teach elementary school.

I

From 1966 until 1979, respondent Gene Arline taught elementary school in Nassau County, Florida. She was discharged in 1979 after suffering a third relapse of tuberculosis within two years. After she was denied relief in state administrative proceedings, she brought suit in federal court, alleging that the school board's decision to dismiss her because of her tuberculosis violated § 504 of the Act.

A trial was held in the District Court, at which the principal medical evidence was provided by Marianne McEuen, M.D., an assistant director of the Community Tuberculosis Control Service of the Florida Department of Health and Rehabilitative Services. According to the medical records reviewed by Dr. McEuen, Arline was hospitalized for tuberculosis in 1957. For the next 20 years, Arline's disease was in remission. Then, in 1977, a culture revealed that tuberculosis was again active in her system; cultures taken in March 1978 and in November 1978 were also positive.

.....

The superintendent of schools for Nassau County, Craig Marsh, then testified as to the school board's response to Arline's medical reports. After both her second relapse, in the spring of 1978, and her third relapse in November 1978, the school board suspended Arline with pay for the remainder of the school year. At the end of the 1978-1979 school year, the school board held a hearing, after which it discharged Arline, "not because she had done anything wrong," but because of the "continued reoccurence [*sic*] of tuberculosis."

In her trial memorandum, Arline argued that it was "not disputed that the [school board dismissed her] solely on the basis of her illness. Since the illness in this case qualifies the Plaintiff as a 'handicapped person' it is clear that she was dismissed solely as a result of her handicap in violation of Section 504." The District Court held, however, that although there was "[n]o question that she suffers a handicap," Arline was nevertheless not "a handicapped person under the terms of that statute." The court found it "difficult ... to conceive that Congress intended contagious diseases to be included within the definition of a handicapped person." The court then went on to state that, "even assuming" that a person with a contagious disease could be deemed a handicapped person, Arline was not "qualified" to teach elementary school.

The Court of Appeals reversed, holding that "persons with contagious diseases are within the coverage of section 504," and that Arline's condition "falls ... neatly within the statutory and regulatory framework" of the Act. 772 F.2d 759, 764 (CA11 1985). The court remanded the case "for further findings as to whether the risks of infection precluded Mrs. Arline from being 'otherwise qualified' for her job and, if so, whether it was possible to make some reasonable accommodation for her in that teaching position" or in some other position. *Id.,* at 765 (footnote omitted). We granted certiorari, and now affirm.

II

In enacting and amending the Act, Congress enlisted all programs receiving federal funds in an effort "to share with handicapped Americans the opportunities for an education, transportation, housing, health care, and jobs that other Americans take for granted." 123 Cong.Rec. 13515 (1977) (statement of Sen. Humphrey). To that end, Congress not only increased federal support for vocational rehabilitation, but also addressed the broader problem of discrimination against the handicapped by including § 504, an antidiscrimination provision patterned after Title VI of the Civil Rights Act of 1964. Section 504 of the Rehabilitation Act reads in pertinent part:

> No otherwise qualified handicapped individual in the United States, as defined in section 706(7) of this title, shall, solely by reason of his handicap, be excluded from participation in, be denied the benefits of, or be subjected to discrimination under any program or activity receiving Federal financial assistance.... 29 U.S.C. § 794.

In 1974 Congress expanded the definition of "handicapped individual" for use in § 504 to read as follows:

> [A]ny person who (i) has a physical or mental impairment which substantially limits one or more of such person's major life activities, (ii) has a record of such an impairment, or (iii) is regarded as having such an impairment. 29 U.S.C. § 706(7)(B).

The amended definition reflected Congress' concern with protecting the handicapped against discrimination stemming not only from simple prejudice, but also from "archaic attitudes and laws" and from "the fact that the American people are simply unfamiliar with and insensitive to the difficulties confront [ing] individuals with handicaps." S. Rep. No. 93-1297, p. 50 (1974), U.S.Code Cong. & Admin.News 1974, p. 6400. To combat the effects of erroneous but nevertheless prevalent perceptions about the handicapped, Congress expanded the definition of "handicapped individual" so as to preclude discrimination against "[a] person who has a record of, or is regarded as having, an impairment [but who] may at present have no actual incapacity at all. *Southeastern Community College v. Davis,* 442 U.S. 397, 405-06 (1979)

In determining whether a particular individual is handicapped as defined by the Act, the regulations promulgated by the Department of Health and Human Services are of significant assistance. As we have previously recognized, these regulations were drafted with the oversight and approval of Congress, see *Consolidated Rail Corporation v. Darrone,* 465 U.S. 624, 634-35 (1984); they provide "an important source of guidance on the meaning of § 504." *Alexander v. Choate,* 469 U.S. 287, 304 (1985). The regulations are particularly significant here because they define two critical terms used in the statutory definition of handicapped individual. "Physical impairment" is defined as follows:

> [A]ny physiological disorder or condition, cosmetic disfigurement, or anatomical loss affecting one or more of the following body systems: neurological; musculoskeletal; special sense organs; respiratory, including speech organs; cardiovascular; reproductive, digestive, genito-urinary; hemic and lymphatic; skin; and endocrine. 45 CFR § 84.3(j)(2)(i) (1985).

In addition, the regulations define "major life activities" as

> functions such as caring for one's self, performing manual tasks, walking, seeing, hearing, speaking, breathing, learning, and working. § 84.3(j)(2)(ii).

III

Within this statutory and regulatory framework, then, we must consider whether Arline can be considered a handicapped individual. According to the testimony of Dr. McEuen, Arline suffered tuberculosis "in an acute form in such a degree that it affected her respiratory system," and was hospitalized for this condition. App. 11. Arline thus had a physical impairment as that term is defined by the regulations, since she had a "physiological disorder or condition ... affecting [her] ... respiratory [system]." 45 CFR § 84.3(j)(2)(i) (1985). This impairment was serious enough to require hospitalization, a fact more than sufficient to establish that one or more of her major life activities were substantially limited by her impairment. Thus, Arline's hospitalization for tuberculosis in 1957 suffices to establish that she has a "record of ... impairment" within the meaning of 29 U.S.C. § 706(7)(B)(ii), and is therefore a handicapped individual.

Petitioners concede that a contagious disease may constitute a handicapping condition to the extent that it leaves a person with "diminished physical or mental capabilities," Brief for Petitioners 15, and concede that Arline's hospitalization for tuberculosis in 1957 demonstrates that she has a record of a physical impairment, see Tr. of Oral Arg. 52-53. Petitioners maintain, however, that Arline's record of impairment is irrelevant in this case, since the school board dismissed Arline not because of her diminished physical capabilities, but because of the threat that her relapses of tuberculosis posed to the health of others.

We do not agree with petitioners that, in defining a handicapped individual under § 504, the contagious effects of a disease can be meaningfully distinguished from the disease's physical effects on a claimant in a case such as this. Arline's contagiousness and her physical impairment each resulted from the same underlying condition, tuberculosis. It would be unfair to allow an employer to seize upon the distinction between the effects of a disease on others and the effects of a disease on a patient and use that distinction to justify discriminatory treatment.

Nothing in the legislative history of § 504 suggests that Congress intended such a result. That history demonstrates that Congress was as concerned about the effect of an impairment on others as it was about its effect on the individual. Congress extended coverage, in 29 U.S.C. § 706(7)(B)(iii), to those individuals who are simply "regarded as having" a physical or mental impairment. The Senate Report provides as an example of a person who would be covered under this subsection "a person with some kind of visible physical impairment which in fact does not substantially limit that person's functioning." S. Rep. No. 93-1297, at 64. Such impairment might not diminish a person's physical or mental capabilities, but could nevertheless substantially limit that person's ability to work as a result of the negative reactions of others to the impairment.

Allowing discrimination based on the contagious effects of a physical impairment would be inconsistent with the basic purpose of § 504, which is to ensure that handicapped individuals are not denied jobs or other benefits because of the prejudiced attitudes or the ignorance of others. By amending the definition of "handicapped individual" to include not only those who are actually physically impaired, but also those who are regarded as impaired and who, as a result, are substantially limited in a major life activity, Congress acknowledged that society's accumulated myths and fears about disability and disease are as handicapping as are the physical limitations that flow from actual impairment. Few aspects of a handicap give rise to the same level of public fear and misapprehension as contagiousness. Even those who suffer or have recovered from such noninfectious diseases as epilepsy or cancer have faced discrimination based on the irrational fear that they might be contagious.

The Act is carefully structured to replace such reflexive reactions to actual or perceived handicaps with actions based on reasoned and medically sound judgments: the definition of "handicapped individual" is broad, but only those individuals who are both handicapped *and* otherwise qualified are eligible for relief. The fact that *some* persons who have contagious diseases may pose a serious health threat to others under certain circumstances does not justify excluding from the coverage of the Act *all* persons with actual or perceived contagious diseases. Such exclusion would mean that those accused of being contagious would never have the opportunity to have their condition evaluated in light of medical evidence and a determination made as to whether they were "otherwise qualified." Rather, they would be vulnerable to discrimination on the basis of mythology-precisely the type of injury Congress sought to prevent. We conclude that the fact that a person with a record of a physical impairment is also contagious does not suffice to remove that person from coverage under § 504.

IV

The remaining question is whether Arline is otherwise qualified for the job of elementary schoolteacher. To answer this question in most cases, the district court will need to conduct an individualized inquiry and make appropriate findings of fact. Such an inquiry is essential if § 504 is to achieve its goal of protecting handicapped individuals from deprivations based on prejudice, stereotypes, or unfounded fear, while giving appropriate weight to such legitimate concerns of grantees as avoiding exposing others to significant health and safety risks. The basic factors to be considered in conducting this inquiry are well established. In the context of the employment of a person handicapped with a contagious disease, we agree with *amicus* American Medical Association that this inquiry should include

> [findings of] facts, based on reasonable medical judgments given the state of medical knowledge, about (a) the nature of the risk (how the disease is transmitted), (b) the duration of the risk (how long is the carrier infectious), (c) the severity of the risk (what is the potential harm to third parties) and (d) the probabilities the disease will be transmitted and will cause varying degrees of harm. Brief for American Medical Association as *Amicus Curiae* 19.

In making these findings, courts normally should defer to the reasonable medical judgments of public health officials. The next step in the "otherwise-qualified" inquiry is for the court to evaluate, in light of these medical findings, whether the employer could reasonably accommodate the employee under the established standards for that inquiry.

Because of the paucity of factual findings by the District Court, we, like the Court of Appeals, are unable at this stage of the proceedings to resolve whether Arline is "otherwise qualified" for her job. The District Court made no findings as to the duration and severity of Arline's condition, nor as to the probability that she would transmit the disease. Nor did the court determine whether Arline was contagious at the time she was discharged, or whether the School Board could have reasonably accommodated her. Accordingly, the resolution of whether Arline was otherwise qualified requires further findings of fact.

V

We hold that a person suffering from the contagious disease of tuberculosis can be a handicapped person within the meaning of § 504 of the Rehabilitation Act of 1973, and that respondent Arline is such a person. We remand the case to the District Court to determine whether Arline is otherwise qualified for her position. The judgment of the Court of Appeals is *Affirmed.*

KNAPP v. NORTHWESTERN UNIVERSITY
101 F.3d 473 (7th Cir. 1996)

EVANS, Circuit Judge.

Nicholas Knapp wants to play NCAA basketball for Northwestern University--so badly that he is willing to face an increased risk of death to do so. Knapp is a competent, intelligent adult capable of assessing whether playing intercollegiate basketball is worth the risk to his heart and possible death, and to him the risk is acceptable. Usually, competent, intelligent adults are allowed to make such decisions. This is especially true when, as here, the individual's family approves of the decision and the individual and his parents are willing to sign liability waivers regarding the worst-case scenario should it occur.

Northwestern, however, refuses to allow Knapp to play on or even practice with its men's basketball team. Knapp, currently a sophomore at Northwestern, has the basketball skills to play at the intercollegiate level, but he has never taken the court for his team. Although Northwestern does not restrict him from playing pick-up basketball games, using recreational facilities on campus, or exerting himself physically on his own, the university disqualified Knapp from playing on its intercollegiate basketball team. The issue in this case boils down to whether the school--because of ß 504 of the Rehabilitation Act of 1973, as amended, 29 U.S.C. § 794--will be forced to let Knapp don a purple uniform and take the floor as a member of Northwestern's basketball team.

Prior to his senior year of high school Knapp was rated among the best basketball players in Illinois. He was recruited by numerous universities, including Northwestern. At the end of Knapp's junior year at Peoria's Woodruff High School, Northwestern orally offered him an athletic scholarship to play basketball. Knapp orally accepted the offer.

A few weeks into his senior year, Knapp suffered sudden cardiac death--meaning his heart stopped--during a pick-up basketball game. Paramedics used cardiopulmonary resuscitation, defibrillation (i.e., electric shocks), and injections of drugs to bring Knapp back to life. A few weeks later, doctors implanted an internal cardioverter-defibrillator in Knapp's abdomen. The device detects heart arrhythmia and delivers a shock to convert the abnormal heart rhythm back to normal. In other words, if Knapp's heart stops again the device is supposed to restart it.

On the day following his sudden cardiac death, Northwestern informed Knapp and his family that whatever the ultimate medical decision, Northwestern would honor its commitment for a scholarship. Seven weeks after his collapse Knapp signed a national letter of intent to attend Northwestern.

Knapp did not play basketball during his senior year in high school, but he was always a superb student, and in June 1995 he graduated as the valedictorian of his class. In September 1995 he enrolled as a Northwestern student.

On November 7, 1995, Dr. Howard Sweeney, Northwestern's head team physician, declared Knapp ineligible to participate on Northwestern's men's basketball team.

.....

The Rehabilitation Act, which is the sole basis for Knapp's claim, ensures that

> no otherwise qualified individual with a disability in the United States, as defined in section 7(8) [29 USCS § 706(8)], shall, solely by reason of her or his disability, be excluded from the participation in, be denied the benefits of, or be subjected to discrimination under any program or activity receiving Federal financial assistance . . . .

29 U.S.C. § 794(a). To prevail on his claim for discrimination under the Act, Knapp must prove that: (1) he is disabled as defined by the Act; (2) he is otherwise qualified for the position sought; (3) he has been excluded from the position solely because of his disability; and (4) the position exists as part of a program or activity receiving federal financial assistance. *Byrne v. Board of Educ., School of West Allis-West Milwaukee,* 979 F.2d 560, 563 (7th Cir. 1992). Northwestern does not dispute that it receives federal financial assistance and that it has excluded Knapp from its intercollegiate basketball program solely because of his cardiac condition, so our focus is on whether Knapp is an "otherwise qualified individual with a disability."

To show that he is disabled under the terms of the Act, Knapp must prove that he

> (i) has a physical . . . impairment which substantially limits one or more of [his] major life activities, (ii) has a record of such an impairment, or (iii) is regarded as having such an impairment.

29 U.S.C. § 706(8)(B). Knapp satisfies the first element of part (i) of this definition. A cardiovascular problem constitutes a physical impairment under § 706(8)(B). 34 C.F.R. ß 104.3(j)(2)(i)(A); 45 C.F.R. § 84.3(j)(2)(i)(A). Northwestern does not dispute this fact, but it instead zeros in on the second element of the disability definition: whether playing intercollegiate basketball is part of a major life activity and, if so, whether its diagnosis of Knapp's cardiac condition substantially limits Knapp in that activity.

.....

The regulations promulgated pursuant to the Rehabilitation Act do not define "substantial limitation," and this is not an oversight. In commentary following the regulations, both the Department of Education and the Department of Health and Human Services acknowledge "the lack of any definition in the proposed regulation of the phrase 'substantially limits.' The Department does not believe that a definition of this term is possible at this time." 34 C.F.R. pt. 104, app. A, subpt. A(3); 45 C.F.R. pt. 84, app. A, subpt. A(3). "The court must ask 'whether the particular impairment constitutes for the particular person a significant barrier to [a major life activity].' " *Byrne*, 979 F.2d at 565 (quoting *Forrisi v. Bowen,* 794 F.2d 931, 933 (4th Cir. 1986)).

This case is difficult because it does not fit neatly under the Rehabilitation Act. The "disability" *Knapp* claims is the basis for discrimination against him is not a continuing one like blindness or deafness. At any given moment in time when Knapp's heart is functioning properly his disability does not affect him. He is truly disabled only when his heart stops, which may or may not happen to him again. The disability regarding which Northwestern allegedly discriminates, therefore, actually is the greater risk of harm for Knapp than the risk faced by other male college basketball players. In addition, other impairments usually do not have as severe a result as is possible in this case. A person who is deaf, for instance, will not suddenly die on the basketball court because of that disability. Here, Knapp's disability is all or nothing. Finally, because Knapp's disability affects one of the most central organs of the body, his disability to some extent affects all major life activities--if his heart stops, he will not breathe, see, speak, walk, learn, or work. Once again it is all or nothing--either his heart is functioning and no major life activities are limited at that moment, or it has stopped and the most major life activity of all--living-- has been affected.

.....

If playing NCAA basketball reaches a major life activity, then it is likely that deprivation of that activity would, for the individual basketball player, be a substantial limitation. Likewise, if playing intercollegiate basketball does not reach the status of major life activity, then it is most likely that deprivation will not be a substantial limitation.

We do not think that the definition of "major life activity" can be as particularized as Knapp wants it to be. Playing intercollegiate basketball obviously is not in and of itself a major life activity, as it is not a basic function of life on the same level as walking, breathing, and speaking. Not everyone gets to go to college, let alone play intercollegiate sports. We acknowledge that intercollegiate sports can be an important part of the college learning experience for both athletes and many cheering students--especially at a Big Ten school. Knapp has indicated that such is the case for him. But not every student thinks so. Numerous college students graduate each year having neither participated in nor attended an intercollegiate sporting event. Their sheepskins are no less valuable because of the lack of intercollegiate sports in their lives. Not playing intercollegiate sports does not mean they have not learned. Playing or enjoying intercollegiate sports therefore cannot be held out as a necessary part of learning for *all* students.

A few cases, none of them binding on us, have considered school team sports a major life activity in and of themselves. *See Pahulu v. University of Kansas,* 897 F. Supp. 1387 (D. Kan. 1995) (intercollegiate football may be a major life activity); see also *Sandison v. Michigan High School Athletic Ass'n, Inc.,* 863 F. Supp. 483, 489 (E.D. Mich. 1994) (participation on the cross-country and track teams an important and integral part of education and a major life activity), *rev'd on other grounds*, 64 F.3d 1026 (6th Cir. 1995). In other cases involving school athletics, whether they constituted part of the major life activity of learning is not even discussed. *See Grube v. Bethlehem Area Sch. Dist.,* 550 F. Supp. 418 (E.D. Pa. 1982) (disability assumed, so major life activity not discussed); *see also Wright v. Columbia Univ.,* 520 F. Supp. 789 (E.D. Pa. 1981) (parties did not dispute that player was disabled).

Because intercollegiate athletics may be one part of the major life activity of learning for certain students, the parties here have framed the analysis of what constitutes a major life activity into a choice between a subjective test or an objective test--whether we look at what constitutes learning for Nick Knapp or what constitutes learning in general for the average person. The Rehabilitation Act and the regulations promulgated under it give little guidance regarding whether the determination of what constitutes a major life activity turns on an objective or subjective standard. [4] And while we have previously said that whether a person is disabled is "an individualized inquiry, best suited to a case-by-case determination," we have also indicated that "the definition of 'major life activity' in the regulations 'cannot be interpreted to include working at the specific job of one's choice,'" *Byrne*, 979 F.2d at 565. Other courts have been across the board on whether the test is objective or subjective. *Compare Pahulu*, 897 F. Supp. at 1393 ("for *Pahulu*, intercollegiate football may be a major life activity, i.e., learning"), *and Sandison,* 863 F. Supp. at 489 (participation on high school teams is "as to them a major life activity"), with *Welsh v. City of Tulsa, Okla.*, 977 F.2d 1415, 1417 (10th Cir. 1992) (major life activity of working does not necessarily mean working at the job of one's choice).

We decline to define the major life activity of learning in such a way that the Act applies whenever someone wants to play intercollegiate athletics. A "major life activity," as defined in the regulations, is a basic function of life "such as caring for one's self, performing manual tasks, walking, seeing, hearing, speaking, breathing, learning, and working." 34 C.F.R. § 104.3(j)(2)(ii); 45 C.F.R. ß 84.3(j)(2)(ii). These are basic functions, not more specific ones such as being an astronaut, working as a firefighter, driving a race car, or learning by playing Big Ten basketball.

. . . . .

Because learning through playing intercollegiate basketball is only one part of the education available to Knapp at Northwestern, even under a subjective standard, Knapp's ability to learn is not substantially limited. Knapp's scholarship continues, allowing him access to all academic and-- except for intercollegiate basketball--all nonacademic services and activities available to other Northwestern students, in addition to all other services available to scholarship athletes. Although perhaps not as great a learning experience as actually playing, it is even possible that Knapp may "learn" through the basketball team in a role other than as a player. [5] Knapp is an intelligent student and athlete, and the inability to play intercollegiate basketball at Northwestern [6] forecloses only a small portion of his collegiate opportunities. Like the firefighter in *Welsh*, who did not show that his education and training limited him to being a firefighter, *Welsh*, 977 F.2d at 1419, Knapp has not shown that his education and training limit him to do nothing but play basketball. The fact that Knapp's goal of playing intercollegiate basketball is frustrated does not substantially limit his education. The Rehabilitation Act does not guarantee an individual the exact educational experience that he may desire, just a fair one. Consequently, we hold that Knapp as a matter of law is not disabled within the meaning of the Rehabilitation Act.

MARTINEZ v. HILLSBOROUGH COUNTY
711 F. Supp. 1066 (M.D. Fla. 1989)

ELIZABETH A. KOVACHEVICH, UNITED STATES DISTRICT JUDGE

This cause of action is before the Court on remand from the Eleventh Circuit Court of Appeals. The matter previously came before the Court for trial, without jury, on July 13 and 14, 1988. The Court issued its memorandum opinion in the case on August 8, 1988. The Court made the following relevant conclusions of law:

> 1. The Rehabilitation Act of 1973 does not add to the rights available to Plaintiff under the EHCA. *Smith v. Robinson*, 468 U.S. 992, 104 S. Ct. 3457, 82 L. Ed. 2d 746 (1984). As in that case, the claims under the constitution are identical to those under the EHCA and the legal and factual questions are thus the same. The *Smith* decision has been amended by Congress insofar as recovery of attorney's fees under the EHCA has been added to the statute. The Supreme Court's conclusions with respect to identity of relief available under the two statutes and the constitution are still valid. Therefore, this cause may be decided using the legal test developed under the EHCA.
>
> 2. Under the Education for All Handicapped Children Act (hereafter EHCA), 20 U.S.C. §§ 1401, *et seq*., Plaintiff is entitled to a free, appropriate public education in the least restrictive appropriate environment.
>
> 3. The EHCA does not require the State provide services sufficient to maximize each child's potential "commensurate with the opportunity provided other children." *Hendrick Hudson District Board of Education v. Rowley*, 458 U.S. 176, 102 S. Ct. 3034, 73 L. Ed. 2d 690 (1982). Implicit in the congressional purpose of providing access to a "free appropriate public education" is the requirement that the education to which access is provided be sufficient to confer some educational benefit upon the handicapped child. *Id.* at 200.
>
> 4. The parties agree that the appropriate standard for placement of Eliana Martinez (hereinafter Eliana) is a "free appropriate public education" in the "least restrictive environment" appropriate to the circumstances of the case. The parties, however, do not agree what the appropriate least restrictive environment is in this case.
>
> 5. Plaintiff asserts that the appropriate placement is in a TMH classroom, without further modification. Plaintiff has proposed some restrictions to that access, if the Court does not agree to unrestricted access, such as placement in a non-ambulatory TMH class or provision for a full-time aide for Eliana; these are acceptable to Plaintiff in order to change Eliana's placement.
>
> 6. Defendant asserts, on the other hand, that the appropriate placement for Eliana remains homebound education, due to the facts that Eliana has AIDS, is not potty trained, and therefore poses a potential danger to the students of the TMH class

which she desires to attend. Defendant additionally alleges that the EHCA does not require the School Board to provide one-on-one education within the context of the integrated classroom.

7. The homebound program which is now being provided to Eliana clearly deprives her of certain benefits of a classroom education, including socialization and modeling processes. The question the Court must address is whether or not other factors outweigh this clear deprivation of educational benefits so as to prevent the placement of Eliana in a TMH classroom.

8. The parties have offered the Court two divergent views on what is the most appropriate and least restrictive educational placement for Eliana Martinez: homebound education, and, placement in an integrated TMH classroom, with or without special accommodations. The Court believes the appropriate educational placement lies somewhere between these two positions.

9. The Court, once again, is faced with the challenge of making a medical judgment based on divergent medical testimony and opinion. The Court must balance the right of Eliana Martinez to get the most appropriate education available, against the danger, if any, posed to the specific population, the TMH students, who will be exposed to Eliana. The children in this TMH classroom are there because of their right to an appropriate and free public education and as required by the laws of the state for school attendance. As this Court said in *Ray v. The School District of DeSoto County*, 666 F. Supp. 1524, 1535 (M.D.Fla. 1987):

The public at large has several interests to be considered here. First, is the concern of the public to provide adequate, non-discriminatory education to all the children of the state. The children of this state include children like the Ray boys, who, through no fault of their own, have contracted this disease; it clearly provokes in many, fear and a desperate desire to segregate them from mainstream life. However, there is an equally important public interest in protecting the health and safety of the public at large, and here, specifically, the school population which would be in contact with the Ray boys, if they are returned to an integrated classroom.

10. The Court's inquiry should focus on the following factors, based upon reasonable medical judgment and the state of medical knowledge: the nature of the risk, the duration of the risk, the severity of the harm, and the probability of transmission which will cause varying degrees of harm. *See, School Board of Nassau County v. Arline*, 480 U.S. 273, 107 S. Ct. 1123, 94 L. Ed. 2d 307 (1987).

11. These factors have been addressed by this Court in the findings of fact. The severity of the harm if transmission occurs is clear; it is most likely fatal.

At this time, the only time transmission would not be fatal is if the transmission resulted in seroconversion which never became symptomatic; otherwise, medical opinion is that all persons infected and symptomatic will die at some future time, perhaps as little as six (6) months from the onset of becoming symptomatic.

12. To the best of medical knowledge, at this time, the duration of the risk of transmission is perpetual; there is no evidence that transmissibility changes during the course of the disease.

13. The last two factors are essential to the consideration of this cause of action: the nature of the risk (How is the disease transmitted?) and the probabilities of transmission. AIDS has been proven to be transmitted in various ways: sexual intercourse, homosexual or heterosexual; intravenous drug use, sharing of needles and other equipment; perinatally; through breast milk; and through the transfusion of blood and blood products.

14. The virus has been isolated in other body secretions, including tears, saliva, and urine; but it has not been proven that transmission has occurred through any of these secretions. The possibility of transmission is generally conceded to be a "remote theoretical possibility." However, the CDC has not changed its recommendation that children without control of their bodily secretions might require a more restricted educational placement. It has added to its educational recommendations for schools, as of January 29, 1988, the statement that deep, open-mouthed kissing could theoretically transmit the HIV virus through the exposure of mucous membranes to infected blood and saliva.

15. Eliana Martinez is a neurologically handicapped child who has a case of AIDS, in the last stages of that disease, who is incontinent and who mouths her thumb and forefinger on a continuous basis. These bodily secretions, urine and saliva, have a remote possibility of being a route of transmission to the children of the TMH classroom that she desires to attend. For these reasons, the Court cannot find that the appropriate placement for Eliana is the totally unrestricted placement into the TMH classroom at Manhattan Elementary School; nor, on the other hand, can the Court agree that the proper placement for this child is in a homebound program. The Court finds that a restricted placement, as explained below, into the TMH classroom of Manhattan Elementary School is the appropriate least restrictive environment for Eliana Martinez, at this time, in the present circumstances.

16. As the Court noted earlier Eliana Martinez is free to enjoy the public and private areas of this city, this county, and this country in other respects. The only concern of this Court, in this opinion, is to balance the factors in this cause and devise an appropriate, free educational placement for Eliana Martinez, in the least restricted appropriate educational setting.

.....

The appellate court's opinion vacating and remanding the cause was issued December 1, 1988, 861 F.2d 1502. That court found that, in determining a case pursuant to the Education of the Handicapped Act (EHA) in conjunction with Section 504 of the Rehabilitation Act of 1973 (Section 504), the Court must first determine the most appropriate educational placement for the handicapped child that has an infectious disease under the EHA. Then, the question is whether the child is otherwise qualified pursuant to Section 504 to be educated in that setting despite the communicable disease. If the child is not otherwise qualified, the final question for the court is whether reasonable accommodations could reduce the risk of transmission so as to make the child otherwise qualified to be educated in that setting.

.....

Based on the remand from the appellate court, this Court, on January 10, 1989, reopened the case and ordered that the parties submit, by affidavit, deposition or otherwise, such additional evidence as they deem necessary to the Court's consideration of the effect of any contemplated accommodation.... The Court finds that the following findings of fact are relevant to the decision of the educational placement of Eliana Martinez:

> 1. The American Academy of Pediatrics' Redbook contained the following recommendation at the time of the trial and previous order in this cause: "Some infected students may pose an increased risk to others in school. Students *who lack control of their body secretions*, who display behavior such as biting, or who have open skin sores which cannot be covered require a more restricted school environment until more is known about the transmission of the virus in these circumstances. Arrangements for special education should be made for children who are unable to attend regular classes."
>
> 2. The revised AAP Redbook, the 1988 edition, has amended that recommendation as follows: "Some infected students may pose an increased risk to others in school. Students who display biting behavior or who have exudative, weeping skin sores that cannot be covered require a more restricted school environment until more is known about the transmission of the virus in these circumstances."

The American Academy of Pediatrics has thereby *eliminated* the recommendation that children who cannot control their bodily secretions should be placed in a more restricted environment.

> 3. The Center for Disease Control (hereinafter CDC)'s June 24, 1988, update states: Universal precautions do not apply to feces, nasal secretion, sputum, sweat, tears, urine and vomitus unless they contain visible blood. The risk of transmission of HIV and HBV from these fluids and materials is extremely low or non existent.
>
> 4. *At trial* Dr. Russell, one of Eliana's treating physicians at the University of South Florida, stated he felt Eliana should be set apart from other children by six (6) to

eight (8) feet and there would have to be a *guarantee* that there would be no contact between children and no contact between bodily secretions.

5. In his most *recent testimony, Dr. Russell* has *receded* from that position. Dr. Russell stated that his testimony about the separation of the children was probably more for his comfort than for the degree of risk involved. The doctor now states that the risk is so low statistically that he *doesn't feel* the *risk warrants* such *precautions*. Dr. Russell would still feel better if an aide was assigned to Eliana, as he feels the *risk* is *greater* that *Eliana will contract something from another child that will kill her than any risk to another child from her*. (Dr. Russell deposition of January 13, 1989).

6. At the time of the trial and first order, Eliana was fairly continuously *sucking on her fingers*. That behavior is *now controllable*. The testimony and evidence now reveals that Eliana can be instructed to refrain from placing her fingers in her mouth, that she will obey those instructions, that she has learned to sign a request to place her fingers in her mouth and wait for permission to do so, and that the finger sucking is primarily evident when Eliana is tired, bored or not involved in the surrounding events. When participating in activities which are interesting, Eliana does not tend to put her fingers in her mouth. (Depositions and affidavits of Rosa Martinez, Dr. McClowrey, and Peggy Kelly).

7. *Previously, Eliana* had not been and was *not being potty trained. Since* the *August, 1988*, order there has toilet training has been commenced with some success. Eliana has become an active participant in the training since about November or December of last year. Eliana is no longer content with wearing a soiled or wet diaper. *She has started to sign "toilet" when the procedure is necessary*, she may be in the process of the act but she has connected the act with the appropriate response of needing the toilet. (Deposition and affidavits of Rosa Martinez, Dr. McClowrey, and Peggy Kelly).

8. *Eliana's thrush* will typically follow only a regimen of broad spectrum antibiotics and is only intermittent. (Dr. Russell deposition). There has been *no report of visible blood in Eliana's mouth* during an onset of active thrush. (Affidavit of Rosa Martinez).

9. Although she does not believe them necessary, Rosa Martinez states she is willing to accept a one-on-one aide for Eliana and is willing to submit Eliana to a daily nurse's examination to ascertain that school attendance is advisable that day.

10. Plaintiff requests that the Court require the school system to undertake an aggressive and extensive education program to educate all adults and children involved with Eliana about AIDS.

The Court in this case, as in any case involving such a potentially lethal disease, must be cautious, considerate, and deliberate regarding any decision. The medical testimony in this cause is polarized; unfortunately, judicial decisions must be made before medical science has definitive answers.

..... The evidence reveals that Eliana is capable of being instructed not to suck or mouth her fingers and that she is well on her way to being fully toilet trained. This evidence, in conjunction with the previously stated changes in the testimony of Dr. Russell, whose testimony was a major factor in the Court's previous decision, *and*, the *changes* in Pediatric Redbook is the basis of the following conclusions of law:

1. The appropriate educational placement for Eliana Martinez under the Education for All Handicapped Children would be the regular Trainable Mentally Handicapped classroom if she did not suffer from AIDS.

2. The possibility of transmission with respect to tears, saliva, and urine is remote and theoretical and does not rise to the "significant" risk level that is required to bar Eliana Martinez from the regular Trainable Mentally Handicapped classroom.

3. The evidence does not support a finding that the overall risk of transmission from all bodily substances, including blood in the saliva, rises to the "significant" risk level of requiring this child's exclusion from the classroom. The Court finds that the previously defined conditions precedent to integration into the Trainable Mentally Handicapped have been substantially complied with by Plaintiff.

4. The Court finds that Eliana Martinez is "otherwise qualified" to attend the Trainable Mentally Handicapped classroom at Manhattan Elementary School, which is the most appropriate educational setting for this child pursuant to the EHA.

5. Since the Court finds Eliana Martinez "otherwise qualified" to attend this classroom, it is unnecessary for the Court to consider the effect of any accommodation.

6. The Court readopts its previous conclusion of law stating that if there is a question of the advisability of Eliana being in the classroom on a certain day, the school nurse should be consulted for an evaluation of either Eliana, or another child, if the danger may be an infection from another child to Eliana. It is not necessary for Eliana, nor the rest of the TMH students, to be seen by the nurse or other health practitioner on a daily basis to determine if Eliana should be in the integrated classroom that day.

7. The Court will require that the Hillsborough County School Board provide educational programs to the school parent population, and, student population as far as is practicable, that will be associated with Eliana Martinez in the classroom, with the aim of educating and informing them regarding the realities of AIDS, and, the proper procedures in order to deal with the situation and minimize the risk of transmission to others. In addition a copy of this Order is to be made available to the public at the Office of Manhattan Elementary School. Accordingly, it is

ORDERED that Defendant The School Board of Hillsborough County, Florida admit Plaintiff Eliana Martinez to the Trainable Mentally Handicapped classroom of Manhattan Elementary School within the parameters of this order.

Notes and Comments

1. The "Otherwise Qualified" Plaintiff

The United States Supreme Court first addressed whether an individual was "otherwise qualified" in three cases: *Southeastern Comm. College v. Davis*, 442 U.S. 397 (1979); *Alexander v. Choate*, 469 U.S. 287 (1985); and, *School Bd. of Nassau County v. Arline*, 480 U.S. 273 (1987). In *Davis*, the Supreme Court's first interpretation of Section 504, the Court held that "[a]n otherwise qualified person is one who is able to meet all of the program's requirements in spite of his handicap." *Davis*, 442 U.S. at 406. The *Davis* Court found that a hearing impaired nursing school applicant could lawfully be precluded from admission to a graduate program. The applicant's exclusion from the program was justified because her dependence on lip reading limited her ability to participate in clinical training. This portion of the rationale in *Davis* focused on a strict interpretation of Section 504's statutory language:

> As previously noted, this is the first case in which this Court has been called upon to interpret § 504. It is elementary that "[t]he starting point in every case involving construction of a statute is the language itself." *Blue Chip Stamps v. Manor Drug Stores*, 421 U.S. 723, 756, 95 S.Ct. 1917, 1935, 44 L.Ed.2d 539 (1975) (POWELL, J., concurring); see *Greyhound Corp. v. Mt. Hood Stages, Inc.*, 437 U.S. 322, 330, 98 S.Ct. 2370, 2375, 57 L.Ed.2d 239 (1978); *Santa Fe Industries, Inc. v. Green*, 430 U.S. 462, 472, 97 S.Ct. 1292, 1300, 51 L.Ed.2d 480 (1977). Section 504 by its terms does not compel educational institutions to disregard the disabilities of handicapped individuals or to make substantial modifications in their programs to allow disabled persons to participate. Instead, it requires only that an "otherwise qualified handicapped individual" not be excluded from participation in a federally funded program "solely by reason of his handicap," indicating only that mere possession of a handicap is not a permissible ground for assuming an inability to function in a particular context.
>
> The court below, however, believed that the "otherwise qualified" persons protected by § 504 include those who would be able to meet the requirements of a particular program in every respect except as to limitations imposed by their handicap. *See* 574 F.2d, at 1160. Taken literally, this holding would prevent an institution from taking into account any limitation resulting from the handicap, however disabling. It assumes, in effect, that a person need not meet legitimate physical requirements in order to be "otherwise qualified." We think the understanding of the District Court is closer to the plain meaning of the statutory language. An otherwise qualified person is one who is able to meet all of a program's requirements in spite of his handicap.
>
> The regulations promulgated by the Department of HEW to interpret § 504 reinforce, rather than contradict, this conclusion. According to these regulations, a "[q]ualified handicapped

> person" is, "[w]ith respect to postsecondary and vocational education services, a handicapped person who meets the academic and technical standards requisite to admission or participation in the [school's] education program or activity . . . ." 45 CFR § 84.3(k)(3) (1978). An explanatory note states:
>
>> The term 'technical standards' refers to *all* nonacademic admissions criteria that are essential to participation in the program in question. 45 CFR pt. 84, App. A, p. 405 (1978) (emphasis supplied).
>
> A further note emphasizes that legitimate physical qualifications may be essential to participation in particular programs. We think it clear, therefore, that HEW interprets the "other" qualifications which a handicapped person may be required to meet as including necessary physical qualifications.

Davis, 442 U.S. at 406.

2. Section 504 and "Reasonable Accommodations"

The issue of reasonable accommodations to ensure that an individual is not denied meaningful access to education arises frequently in Section 504 challenges. In most cases, however, courts remain deferential toward educators' determination of what accommodations are necessary. Provided the accommodations directly meet the disability, a student's or employee's desired accommodations need not be implemented. Reasonable accommodation decisions from the Sixth and Eighth Circuit provide excellent illustrations.

In the Sixth Circuit, the Court determined that a podiatry student's dismissal from the Ohio College of Podiatric Medicine did not violate Section 504. *Kaltenberge v. Ohio College of Podiatric Medicine*, 162 F.3d 432 (6th Cir. 1998). Ms. Kaltenberger, ultimately diagnosed with Attention Deficit-Hyperactivity Disorder (ADHD), was unable to meet the program's academic standards and was dismissed from the program. Her dismissal followed a list of accommodations including: (1) individualized tutoring in each class; (2) a place to sit in the front of each class; (3) permission to tape lectures; (4) extra time on tests; and, (5) the opportunity to take tests in room separated from other students. *Id.* at 434-35. The Court upheld the trial court's grant of summary judgment because it found that "[a] handicapped or disabled person is 'otherwise qualified' to participate in a program [only] if she can meet its necessary requirements with reasonable accommodations." *Id.* at 435. Granting Kaltenberger numerous accommodations, she was still not able to succeed in the program and, thus, was not an "otherwise qualified" handicapped individual.

The Eighth Circuit, in a case involving a dyslexic student, upheld a grant of summary judgment for the university because the student "failed to show why the school's administration of multiple-choice tests by an oral tape did not fully accommodate his dyslexia." *Kern v. Univ. of Osteopathic Medicine and Health Sciences*, 220 F.3d 906, 907 (8th Cir. 2000). Mr. Stern requested that he be permitted "to supplement his answers on any multiple-choice tests required, either with an essay or with responses to oral questioning." *Id.* at 907. The school, however, opted to: (1) have someone read the questions on an audiotape; (2) provide Kern a private room for testing purposes; and, (3) grant Kern additional time to complete the tests. *Id.* The district court granted the university's motion for summary judgment because Kern had not demonstrated how the school's reasonable accommodations failed to account for his dyslexia.

The Court, in affirming the trial court's decision, reminded that "reasonable accommodations are required when a disabled student would otherwise be denied meaningful access to a university." *Id.* at 908. However, the court also explained that "[i]n order to be a reasonable accommodation, any modifications requested in a program must be related to the disability." *Id.* Because Kern was unable to prove that the testing modifications did not fully address his disability, his claim failed.

3. Reasonable Accommodations in Admissions and Readmissions

As appears from Note 1 above, Section 504 challenges are common in admission and re-admission cases. In *Anderson v. Univ. of Wisconsin*, 841 F.2d 737 (7th Cir. 1988), the Seventh Circuit Court of Appeals, provides a notable case study. The plaintiff, sued the University of Wisconsin after being informed he would not be readmitted to the law school due to poor academic performance. The law school had twice admitted him back into the program notwithstanding a drinking problem, poor academic performance, and threatening behavior toward another student while drunk.

In ruling against the former student, the Court explained that "[n]othing in the record suggests that the University's decision was based on stereotypes about alcoholism [a recognized handicap under Section 504] as opposed to honest judgments about how Anderson had performed in fact and could be expected to perform. The Law School allowed Anderson to reenter the program twice, knowing that he is an alcoholic; the law School also allowed Anderson to take courses. In none of his four stints at the University did Anderson perform up to standard." *Id.* at 741.

Emphasizing the role of educators in assessing a student's ability to succeed academically, the Court reminded that Section 504 "does not designate a jury, rather than the faculty of the Law School, as the body to decide whether a would-be student is up to snuff. . . . The Supreme Court has repeatedly admonished courts to respect the academic judgment of university faculties." *Id.* See also, *Wynne v. Tufts University School of Medicine*, 932 F.2d 19, 26 (4th Cir. 1991) ("[i]f the institution submits undisputed facts demonstrating that the relevant officials within the institution considered alternative means, their feasibility, cost and effect on the academic program, and came to a rationally justifiable conclusion that the available alternatives would result either in lowering academic standards or requiring substantial program alteration, the court could rule as a matter of law that the institution had met its duty of seeking reasonable accommodation.").

4. The ADA Amendments Act of 2008

The ADA Amendments Act of 2008 (ADAA) is relevant to education and educators because Section 504 utilizes the interpretive decisions from ADA cases to apply to Section 504 cases. Thus, with the significant overlap between Section 504 and the ADA, changes to the ADA will undoubtedly affect Section 504 determinations and practices. The major changes are as follows:

a) LOWER STANDARD FOR ELIGIBILITY:

In legislatively overturning several United States Supreme Court decisions, the ADAA has lowered the standard imposed by courts in determining whether an individual is disabled. The ADAA requires courts to take use a "broad standard" in deciding which individuals are covered by the Act as disabled. The ADAA further explains that conditions that are episodic or in remission still qualify for protection if the conditions would be considered a disability if active. This amended standard for eligibility will likely lead to more students being covered under Section 504.

b) MITIGATING MEASURES

The ADAA prohibits the consideration of "mitigating measures" when determining whether an individual's disability "substantially limits" a major life activity under the statute. For example, use of medications, hearing aids or prosthetic devices cannot be used to circumvent eligibility determinations under the ADAA. Much like the eligibility determinations for disability, the new mitigating measures language should result in a greater number of students qualifying for protection under Section 504.

c) ADDED MAJOR LIFE ACTIVITIES:

The ADAA added several major life activities to the previous ADA definition. Included in the new classification are eating, sleeping, standing, lifting, bending, reading, concentrating, thinking and communicating. These later categories, namely, reading, concentrating and thinking will most affect students with learning disabilities not previously covered.

See generally 42 U.S.C. § 12101.

For a discussion of readmission issues under both Section 504 and IDEA, see Lynn Daggett, *Doing the Right Thing: Disability Discrimination and Readmission of Academically Dismissed Law Students,* 32 College & Univ. Law 505 (2006).

5. Collateral Estoppel, Res Judicata and Special Education Lawsuits

The difficulty of weaving together Section 504, the ADA, and IDEA is difficult to overstate. For example, should a violation of the provisions of one statute conclusively establish a violation of another? Does an institution that violates a provision of IDEA also violate the provisions of Section 504? See below, the *Indiana Area School District v. H.H.* decision.

INDIANA AREA SCHOOL DISTRICT v. H.H.
428 F. Supp. 2d 361 (W.D. Pa. 2006)

Pending before the Court is Defendants', H.H.'s and his parents', Motion for Partial Summary Judgment (Docket No. 50). After careful consideration of the submissions of the parties and for the reasons set forth below, I find that Defendants' Motion (Docket No. 50) is granted.

.....

The main issue for determination in the pending Motion is whether a finding of a denial of FAPE under the IDEA is discrimination *per se* under § 504 of the Rehabilitation Act and the ADA. *See,* Docket No. 50, P6. Specifically, Defendants urge this Court that its finding of a denial of FAPE for the 2003-2004 school year under the IDEA is *per se* discrimination under § 504 and the ADA, such that they are entitled to summary judgment as to those counts. *See,* Docket No. 50, P8. In response, Plaintiff argues that a finding of a FAPE violation under the IDEA does not equate to a *per se* violation under § 504 or the ADA. *See,* Docket No. 53.

Section 504 prohibits disability discrimination by, *inter alia,* programs and activities receiving federal funds. 29 U.S.C. § 794(a). Title II of the ADA "extends section 504's anti-discrimination principles to public entities" generally. *Helen L. v. DiDario,* 46 F.3d 325, 332 (3d Cir. 1995); 42 U.S.C. § 12132. To establish a *prima facie* case of disability discrimination under § 504, a plaintiff must prove that (1) he is "disabled" as defined by the Act; (2) he is "otherwise qualified" to participate in school activities; (3) the school or the board of education receives federal financial assistance; (4) he was excluded from participation in, denied the benefits of, or subject to discrimination at the school; and (5) the school or the board of education knew or should be reasonably expected to know of his disability.[39] *W.B. v. Matula,* 67 F.3d 484, 492 (3d Cir. 1995); *Ridgewood Bd. of Educ. v. N.E.,* 172 F.3d 238, 253 (3d Cir. 1999). All of the same elements, except the third element relating to federal funds, are required to establish a *prima facie* case of discrimination under the ADA. 42 U.S.C. § 12132.

It is true that the Third Circuit has held that "there are few differences, if any, between IDEA's affirmative duty and § 504's negative prohibition and [has] noted that the regulations implementing § 504 require school districts 'provide a free appropriate education to each qualified handicapped person in [its] jurisdiction.'" *Ridgewood,* 172 F.3d at 253, *quoting W.B.,* 67 F.3d at 492-93. This does not mean, however, that the failure to provide a FAPE is *per se* discrimination under § 504 or the ADA. To the contrary, as the Third Circuit stated later in its opinion, "the failure to provide a free appropriate public education violates IDEA and therefore *could* violate § 504." *Id,* (emphasis

---

[39] Plaintiff argues that there is an additional requirement to prove intentional discrimination via bad faith or gross misjudgment. *See,* Docket No. 53, pp. 8-10. The Third Circuit has clearly held, however, that "a plaintiff need not prove that defendants' discrimination was intentional." *Ridgewood Bd. of Educ.,* 172 F.3d at 253, *citing W.B. v. Matula,* 67 F.3d at 492. While I recognize that *Ridgewood* dealt only with § 504, the Third Circuit generally has held that the same analysis under § 504 applies in determining whether a defendant's actions violate the ADA. *Jeremy H. v. Mount Lebanon Sch. Dist.,* 95 F.3d 272, 279 (3d Cir.1996). Consequently, I find that Plaintiff need not prove the additional requirement of intentional discrimination to prove its case under the ADA. Therefore, I need not discuss whether Defendants can establish bad faith or gross misjudgment.

added). Thus, there is no *per se* finding. To recover under § 504 or the ADA, a plaintiff must still meet all of the elements of a *prima facie* case under said statutes. *Id.*

In this case, ...[t]he record contains direct and substantial evidence that the District did not discriminate against H.H. Special Education and related services were provided to H.H. at no cost, and he obtained benefit from the educational programs and placements in his IEP despite the District's failure to provide a behavioral intervention plan which resulted in an award of tuition reimbursement." Docket No. 53, pp. 7-8. ...I find there is no genuine issue of material fact that H.H. was excluded from participation in or denied the benefits of the school. Consequently, summary judgment in favor of Defendants on their § 504 and ADA claims is warranted.

B. DAMAGE

Under their IDEA claim, Defendants sought damages for H.H. only in the form of compensatory education.[40] *See,* Defendants' Brief in Support of Motion for Summary Judgment, pp. 19-20. (Docket No. 8). Defendants now seek a trial on damages for H.H. under § 504 and the ADA in the form of compensatory damages. (Docket No. 50-3, pp. 14-18). In response, Plaintiff argues that Defendants cannot receive two remedies for the same denial of FAPE. (Docket No. 53, pp. 3-4.) I note, however, that the remaining issue relates to damages for a violation of § 504 and the ADA. Moreover, compensatory damages under § 504 and the ADA can include monetary damages, which were not sought by H.H. under his IDEA claim and not discussed as an option in my Opinion and Order of Court dated July 25, 2005. *See, W.B. v. Matula,* 67 F.3d 484 (3d Cir. 1995)("plaintiffs may seek monetary damages directly under § 504...."). While I have already determined that H.H. cannot recover compensatory education as a remedy for the 2003-2004 school year, after a review of the evidence, I find there remains a genuine issue of material fact as to other compensatory damages available under § 504 and the ADA, such as pain and suffering. Thus, this case will proceed to trial only to determine compensatory damages as to H.H. for the violations of § 504 and the ADA for the 2003-2004 school year.

---

[40] In my opinion dated July 25, 2005, I found H.H. was not entitled to compensatory education. (Docket No. 34). Compensatory education may be an appropriate award where a school district knows or should know that a child has an inappropriate IEP or is not receiving more than a *de minimis* educational benefit and does not correct the situation. *M.C. on Behalf of J.C. v. Central Regional School Dist.,* 81 F.3d 389, 397 (3d Cir. 1996). Compensatory education is appropriate "for a period equal to the period of deprivation, but excluding the time reasonably required for the school district to rectify the problem." *Id.* Based on the fact that H.H. only attended Plaintiff's school district for 9 days before his parent unilaterally placed H.H. at Milestones (where H.H. received an appropriate education for the 2003-2004 school year), and that the parents did not give Plaintiff 10 days prior notice, I did not find compensatory education to be warranted in this case. *See,* Docket No. 34.

III. The Individuals with Disabilities Education Act: Affirmative Duties and an "Appropriate Education"

This Section explores the defining issue for a student with special needs: what is an "appropriate education" in light of the provisions of the Individuals with Disabilities Education Act? IDEA imposes an affirmative duty upon educators to provide "special education and related services" to disabled students. Two questions surface repeatedly in litigation over the scope of this duty. First, who is a disabled student entitled to the customized services that are not offered to the larger, nondisabled student body? Second, what standard is used to measure the success of the efforts of educators?

The answer to the first question is contained in the statute itself. A disabled student is one, "who by reason of" some physical or mental handicap "needs special education and related services." See 20 U.S.C. §1401. Because of the breadth of this definition, the answer to the second question is often hard to come by. The courts all agree that IDEA requires that schools educate a disabled student with students who are not disabled "to the maximum extent possible." See 20 U.S.C. §1412. The courts also agree that IDEA places a duty on educators to deliver individualized educational services at public expense to provide a meaningful benefit to the student. Beyond this, nothing is clear.

As you read these cases, be sensitive to the relationship between the efforts of educators to comply with IDEA and the severity of the handicap of the student. Is a school required, at all cost, to pay for special education services?

BOARD OF EDUCATION v. ROWLEY
458 U.S. 176 (1982)

Justice REHNQUIST delivered the opinion of the Court.

This case presents a question of statutory interpretation. Petitioners contend that the Court of Appeals and the District Court misconstrued the requirements imposed by Congress upon States which receive federal funds under the Education of the Handicapped Act. We agree and reverse the judgment of the Court of Appeals.

I

The Education of the Handicapped Act (Act), 84 Stat. 175, as amended, 20 U.S.C. § 1401 *et seq.* (1976 ed. and Supp. IV), provides federal money to assist state and local agencies in educating handicapped children, and conditions such funding upon a State's compliance with extensive goals and procedures. The Act represents an ambitious federal effort to promote the education of handicapped children, and was passed in response to Congress' perception that a majority of handicapped children in the United States "were either totally excluded from schools or [were] sitting idly in regular classrooms awaiting the time when they were old enough to 'drop out.'"

Congress first addressed the problem of educating the handicapped in 1966 when it amended the Elementary and Secondary Education Act of 1965 to establish a grant program "for the purpose of assisting the States in the initiation, expansion, and improvement of programs and projects ... for the education of handicapped children." Pub.L. 89-750, § 161, 80 Stat. 1204. That program was repealed in 1970 by the Education of the Handicapped Act, Pub.L. 91-230, 84 Stat. 175, Part B of which established a grant program similar in purpose to the repealed legislation. Neither the 1966 nor the 1970 legislation contained specific guidelines for state use of the grant money; both were aimed primarily at stimulating the States to develop educational resources and to train personnel for educating the handicapped.

Dissatisfied with the progress being made under these earlier enactments, and spurred by two District Court decisions holding that handicapped children should be given access to a public education, Congress in 1974 greatly increased federal funding for education of the handicapped and for the first time required recipient States to adopt "a goal of providing full educational opportunities to all handicapped children." Pub.L. 93-380, 88 Stat. 579, 583 (1974 statute). The 1974 statute was recognized as an interim measure only, adopted "in order to give the Congress an additional year in which to study what if any additional Federal assistance [was] required to enable the States to meet the needs of handicapped children." H.R. Rep., at 4. The ensuing year of study produced the Education for All Handicapped Children Act of 1975.

In order to qualify for federal financial assistance under the Act, a State must demonstrate that it "has in effect a policy that assures all handicapped children the right to a free appropriate public education." 20 U.S.C. § 1412(1). That policy must be reflected in a state plan submitted to and approved by the Secretary of Education, § 1413, which describes in detail the goals, programs, and timetables under which the State intends to educate handicapped children within its borders. §§ 1412, 1413. States receiving money under the Act must provide education to the handicapped by priority, first "to handicapped children who are not receiving an education" and second "to handicapped children ... with the most severe handicaps who are receiving an inadequate education," § 1412(3), and "to the maximum extent appropriate" must educate handicapped children "with children who are not handicapped." § 1412(5). The Act broadly defines "handicapped children" to include "mentally retarded, hard of hearing, deaf, speech impaired, visually handicapped, seriously emotionally disturbed, orthopedically impaired, [and] other health impaired children, [and] children with specific learning disabilities." § 1401(1).

The "free appropriate public education" required by the Act is tailored to the unique needs of the handicapped child by means of an "individualized educational program" (IEP). § 1401(18). The IEP, which is prepared at a meeting between a qualified representative of the local educational agency, the child's teacher, the child's parents or guardian, and, where appropriate, the child, consists of a written document containing

> (A) a statement of the present levels of educational performance of such child, (B) a statement of annual goals, including short-term instructional objectives, (C) a statement of the specific educational services to be provided to such child, and the extent to which such child will be able to participate in regular educational

> programs, (D) the projected date for initiation and anticipated duration of such services, and (E) appropriate objective criteria and evaluation procedures and schedules for determining, on at least an annual basis, whether instructional objectives are being achieved. § 1401(19).
>
> Local or regional educational agencies must review, and where appropriate revise, each child's IEP at least annually. § 1414(a)(5). *See also* § 1413(a)(11).

In addition to the state plan and the IEP already described, the Act imposes extensive procedural requirements upon States receiving federal funds under its provisions. Parents or guardians of handicapped children must be notified of any proposed change in "the identification, evaluation, or educational placement of the child or the provision of a free appropriate public education to such child," and must be permitted to bring a complaint about "any matter relating to" such evaluation and education. §§ 1415(b)(1)(D) and (E). Complaints brought by parents or guardians must be resolved at "an impartial due process hearing," and appeal to the state educational agency must be provided if the initial hearing is held at the local or regional level. §§ 1415(b)(2) and (c). Thereafter, "[a]ny party aggrieved by the findings and decision" of the state administrative hearing has "the right to bring a civil action with respect to the complaint ... in any State court of competent jurisdiction or in a district court of the United States without regard to the amount in controversy." § 1415(e)(2).

II

This case arose in connection with the education of Amy Rowley, a deaf student at the Furnace Woods School in the Hendrick Hudson Central School District, Peekskill, N.Y. Amy has minimal residual hearing and is an excellent lip reader. During the year before she began attending Furnace Woods, a meeting between her parents and school administrators resulted in a decision to place her in a regular kindergarten class in order to determine what supplemental services would be necessary to her education. Several members of the school administration prepared for Amy's arrival by attending a course in sign-language interpretation, and a teletype machine was installed in the principal's office to facilitate communication with her parents who are also deaf. At the end of the trial period it was determined that Amy should remain in the kindergarten class, but that she should be provided with an FM hearing aid which would amplify words spoken into a wireless receiver by the teacher or fellow students during certain classroom activities. Amy successfully completed her kindergarten year.

As required by the Act, an IEP was prepared for Amy during the fall of her first-grade year. The IEP provided that Amy should be educated in a regular classroom at Furnace Woods, should continue to use the FM hearing aid, and should receive instruction from a tutor for the deaf for one hour each day and from a speech therapist for three hours each week. The Rowleys agreed with parts of the IEP, but insisted that Amy also be provided a qualified sign-language interpreter in all her academic classes in lieu of the assistance proposed in other parts of the IEP. Such an interpreter had been placed in Amy's kindergarten class for a 2-week experimental period, but the interpreter had reported that Amy did not need his services at that time. The school administrators likewise concluded that Amy did not need such an interpreter in her first-grade classroom. They reached this conclusion after consulting the school district's Committee on the Handicapped, which had received expert evidence from Amy's parents on the importance of a sign-language interpreter, received testimony from Amy's teacher and other persons familiar with her academic and social progress, and visited a class for the deaf.

When their request for an interpreter was denied, the Rowleys demanded and received a hearing before an independent examiner. After receiving evidence from both sides, the examiner agreed with the administrators' determination that an interpreter was not necessary because "Amy was achieving educationally, academically, and socially" without such assistance. App. to Pet. for Cert. F-22. The examiner's decision was affirmed on appeal by the New York Commissioner of Education on the basis of substantial evidence in the record. *Id.*, at E-4. Pursuant to the Act's provision for judicial review, the Rowleys then brought an action in the United States District Court for the Southern District of New York, claiming that the administrators' denial of the sign-language interpreter constituted a denial of the "free appropriate public education" guaranteed by the Act.

The District Court found that Amy "is a remarkably well-adjusted child" who interacts and communicates well with her classmates and has "developed an extraordinary rapport" with her teachers. 483 F. Supp. 528, 531 (1980). It also found that "she performs better than the average child in her class and is advancing easily from grade to grade," *id.* at 534, but "that she understands considerably less of what goes on in class than she could if she were not deaf" and thus "is not learning as much, or performing as well academically, as she would without her handicap," *id.* at 532. This disparity between Amy's achievement and her potential led the court to decide that she was not receiving a "free appropriate public education," which the court defined as "an opportunity to achieve [her] full potential commensurate with the opportunity provided to other children." *Id.* at 534. According to the District Court, such a standard "requires that the potential of the handicapped child be measured and compared to his or her performance, and that the resulting differential or 'shortfall' be compared to the shortfall experienced by nonhandicapped children." *Ibid.* The District Court's definition arose from its assumption that the responsibility for "giv [ing] content to the requirement of an 'appropriate education'" had "been left entirely to the [federal] courts and the hearing officers." *Id.*, at 533.

A divided panel of the United States Court of Appeals for the Second Circuit affirmed.

III

A

This is the first case in which this Court has been called upon to interpret any provision of the Act.

We are loath to conclude that Congress failed to offer any assistance in defining the meaning of the principal substantive phrase used in the Act. It is beyond dispute that, contrary to the conclusions of the courts below, the Act does expressly define "free appropriate public education":

> The term 'free appropriate public education' means *special education* and *related services* which (A) have been provided at public expense, under public supervision

> and direction, and without charge, (B) meet the standards of the State educational agency, (C) include an appropriate preschool, elementary, or secondary school education in the State involved, and (D) are provided in conformity with the individualized education program required under section 1414(a)(5) of this title. § 1401(18) (emphasis added).

"Special education," as referred to in this definition, means "specially designed instruction, at no cost to parents or guardians, to meet the unique needs of a handicapped child, including classroom instruction, instruction in physical education, home instruction, and instruction in hospitals and institutions." § 1401(16). "Related services" are defined as "transportation, and such developmental, corrective, and other supportive services ... as may be required to assist a handicapped child to benefit from special education." § 1401(17).[10]

Like many statutory definitions, this one tends toward the cryptic rather than the comprehensive, but that is scarcely a reason for abandoning the quest for legislative intent. Whether or not the definition is a "functional" one, as respondents contend it is not, it is the principal tool which Congress has given us for parsing the critical phrase of the Act. We think more must be made of it than either respondents or the United States seems willing to admit.

According to the definitions contained in the Act, a "free appropriate public education" consists of educational instruction specially designed to meet the unique needs of the handicapped child, supported by such services as are necessary to permit the child "to benefit" from the instruction. Almost as a checklist for adequacy under the Act, the definition also requires that such instruction and services be provided at public expense and under public supervision, meet the State's educational standards, approximate the grade levels used in the State's regular education, and comport with the child's IEP. Thus, if personalized instruction is being provided with sufficient supportive services to permit the child to benefit from the instruction, and the other items on the definitional checklist are satisfied, the child is receiving a "free appropriate public education" as defined by the Act.

.....

B

(i)

.....

By passing the Act, Congress sought primarily to make public education available to handicapped children. But in seeking to provide such access to public education, Congress did not impose upon the States any greater substantive educational standard than would be necessary to make such access meaningful. Indeed, Congress expressly "recognize[d] that in many instances the process of

---

[10] Examples of "related services" identified in the Act are "speech pathology and audiology, psychological services, physical and occupational therapy, recreation, and medical and counseling services, except that such medical services shall be for diagnostic and evaluation purposes only." § 1401(17).

providing special education and related services to handicapped children is not guaranteed to produce any particular outcome." S. Rep., at 11, U.S.Code Cong. & Admin.News 1975, p. 1435. Thus, the intent of the Act was more to open the door of public education to handicapped children on appropriate terms than to guarantee any particular level of education once inside.

.....

Whatever Congress meant by an "appropriate" education, it is clear that it did not mean a potential-maximizing education.

The use of "appropriate" in the language of the Act, although by no means definitive, suggests that Congress used the word as much to describe the settings in which handicapped children should be educated as to prescribe the substantive content or supportive services of their education. For example, § 1412(5) requires that handicapped children be educated in classrooms with nonhandicapped children "to the maximum extent appropriate." Similarly, § 1401(19) provides that, "whenever appropriate," handicapped children should attend and participate in the meeting at which their IEP is drafted. In addition, the definition of "free appropriate public education" itself states that instruction given handicapped children should be at an "appropriate preschool, elementary, or secondary school" level. § 1401(18)(C). The Act's use of the word "appropriate" thus seems to reflect Congress' recognition that some settings simply are not suitable environments for the participation of some handicapped children. At the very least, these statutory uses of the word refute the contention that Congress used "appropriate" as a term of art which concisely expresses the standard found by the lower courts.

(ii)

Respondents contend that "the goal of the Act is to provide each handicapped child with an equal educational opportunity." Brief for Respondents 35. We think, however, that the requirement that a State provide specialized educational services to handicapped children generates no additional requirement that the services so provided be sufficient to maximize each child's potential "commensurate with the opportunity provided other children." Respondents and the United States correctly note that Congress sought "to provide assistance to the States in carrying out their responsibilities under ... the Constitution of the United States to provide equal protection of the laws." S. Rep., at 13, U.S. Code Cong. & Admin.News 1975, p. 1437. But we do not think that such statements imply a congressional intent to achieve strict equality of opportunity or services.

The educational opportunities provided by our public school systems undoubtedly differ from student to student, depending upon a myriad of factors that might affect a particular student's ability to assimilate information presented in the classroom. The requirement that States provide "equal" educational opportunities would thus seem to present an entirely unworkable standard requiring impossible measurements and comparisons.

.....

The District Court and the Court of Appeals thus erred when they held that the Act requires New York to maximize the potential of each handicapped child commensurate with the opportunity provided nonhandicapped children. Desirable though that goal might be, it is not the standard that Congress imposed upon States which receive funding under the Act. Rather, Congress sought primarily to identify and evaluate handicapped children, and to provide them with access to a free public education.

(iii)

Implicit in the congressional purpose of providing access to a "free appropriate public education" is the requirement that the education to which access is provided be sufficient to confer some educational benefit upon the handicapped child. It would do little good for Congress to spend millions of dollars in providing access to a public education only to have the handicapped child receive no benefit from that education. The statutory definition of "free appropriate public education," in addition to requiring that States provide each child with "specially designed instruction," expressly requires the provision of "such ... supportive services ... as may be required to assist a handicapped child *to benefit* from special education." § 1401(17) (emphasis added). We therefore conclude that the "basic floor of opportunity" provided by the Act consists of access to specialized instruction and related services which are individually designed to provide educational benefit to the handicapped child.

.....

The Act requires participating States to educate handicapped children with nonhandicapped children whenever possible. When that "mainstreaming" preference of the Act has been met and a child is being educated in the regular classrooms of a public school system, the system itself monitors the educational progress of the child. Regular examinations are administered, grades are awarded, and yearly advancement to higher grade levels is permitted for those children who attain an adequate knowledge of the course material. The grading and advancement system thus constitutes an important factor in determining educational benefit. Children who graduate from our public school systems are considered by our society to have been "educated" at least to the grade level they have completed, and access to an "education" for handicapped children is precisely what Congress sought to provide in the Act.

.....

C

When the language of the Act and its legislative history are considered together, the requirements imposed by Congress become tolerably clear. Insofar as a State is required to provide a handicapped child with a "free appropriate public education," we hold that it satisfies this requirement by providing personalized instruction with sufficient support services to permit the child to benefit educationally from that instruction. Such instruction and services must be provided at public expense, must meet the State's educational standards, must approximate the grade levels used in the State's regular education, and must comport with the child's IEP. In addition, the IEP, and therefore the personalized instruction, should be formulated in accordance with the requirements of the Act and, if the child is being educated in the regular classrooms of the public education system, should be reasonably calculated to enable the child to achieve passing marks and advance from grade to grade.

ENDREW F. v. DOUGLAS COUNTY SCHOOL DISTRICT
580 U. S. ____ (2017)

Chief Justice ROBERTS delivered the opinion of the Court.

Thirty-five years ago, this Court held that the Individuals with Disabilities Education Act establishes a substantive right to a "free appropriate public education" for certain children with disabilities. We declined, however, to endorse any one standard for determining when handicapped children are receiving sufficient educational benefits to satisfy the requirements of the Act. That more difficult problem is before us today.

……

Petitioner Endrew F. was diagnosed with autism at age two. Autism is a neurodevelopmental disorder generally marked by impaired social and communicative skills, "engagement in repetitive activities and stereotyped movements, resistance to environmental change or change in daily routines, and unusual responses to sensory experiences." 34 C.F.R. § 300.8(c)(1)(i) (2016); see Brief for Petitioner 8. A child with autism qualifies as a "[c]hild with a disability" under the IDEA, and Colorado (where Endrew resides) accepts IDEA funding. § 1401(3)(A). Endrew is therefore entitled to the benefits of the Act, including a FAPE provided by the State.

Endrew attended school in respondent Douglas County School District from preschool through fourth grade. Each year, his IEP Team drafted an IEP addressed to his educational and functional needs. By Endrew's fourth grade year, however, his parents had become dissatisfied with his progress. Although Endrew displayed a number of strengths—his teachers described him as a humorous child with a "sweet disposition" who "showed concern for friends"—he still "exhibited multiple behaviors that inhibited his ability to access learning in the classroom." Supp. App. 182a; 798 F.3d 1329, 1336 (C.A.10 2015). Endrew would scream in class, climb over furniture and other students, and occasionally run away from school. Id., at 1336. He was afflicted by severe fears of commonplace things like flies, spills, and public restrooms. As Endrew's parents saw it, his academic and functional progress had essentially stalled: Endrew's IEPs largely carried over the same basic goals and objectives from one year to the next, indicating that he was failing to make meaningful progress toward his aims. His parents believed that only a thorough overhaul of the school district's approach to Endrew's behavioral problems could reverse the trend. But in April 2010, the school district presented Endrew's parents with a proposed fifth grade IEP that was, in their view, pretty much the same as his past ones. So his parents removed Endrew from public school and enrolled him at Firefly Autism House, a private school that specializes in educating children with autism.

Endrew did much better at Firefly. The school developed a "behavioral intervention plan" that identified Endrew's most problematic behaviors and set out particular strategies for addressing them. Firefly also added heft to Endrew's academic goals. Within months, Endrew's behavior improved significantly, permitting him to make a degree of academic progress that had eluded him in public school.

In November 2010, some six months after Endrew started classes at Firefly, his parents again met with representatives of the Douglas County School District. The district presented a new IEP. Endrew's parents considered the IEP no more adequate than the one proposed in April, and rejected it. They were particularly concerned that the stated plan for addressing Endrew's behavior did not differ meaningfully from the plan in his fourth grade IEP, despite the fact that his experience at Firefly suggested that he would benefit from a different approach.

In February 2012, Endrew's parents filed a complaint with the Colorado Department of Education seeking reimbursement for Endrew's tuition at Firefly. To qualify for such relief, they were required to show that the school district had not provided Endrew a FAPE in a timely manner prior to his enrollment at the private school. See § 1412(a)(10)(C)(ii). Endrew's parents contended that the final IEP proposed by the school district was not "reasonably calculated to enable Endrew to receive educational benefits" and that Endrew had therefore been denied a FAPE. An Administrative Law Judge (ALJ) disagreed and denied relief.

Endrew's parents sought review in Federal District Court. Giving "due weight" to the decision of the ALJ, the District Court affirmed. …The Tenth Circuit affirmed. The Court of Appeals recited language from Rowley stating that the instruction and services furnished to children with disabilities must be calculated to confer "some educational benefit." (quoting Rowley, 458 U.S., at 200, 102 S.Ct. 3034). The court noted that it had long interpreted this language to mean that a child's IEP is adequate as long as it is calculated to confer an "educational benefit [that is] merely ... more than de minimis. " 798 F.3d, at 1338 (internal quotation marks omitted). Applying this standard, the Tenth Circuit held that Endrew's IEP had been "reasonably calculated to enable [him] to make some progress." Id., at 1342 (internal quotation marks omitted). Accordingly, he had not been denied a FAPE.

…….

II

A

Our statement that the face of the IDEA imposed no explicit substantive standard must be evaluated alongside our statement that a substantive standard was "implicit in the Act. " Rowley, 458 U.S., at 193, n. 15, 102 S.Ct. 3034. Similarly, we find little significance in the Court's language concerning the requirement that States provide instruction calculated to "confer some educational benefit." Id., at 200, 102 S.Ct. 3034. The Court had no need to say anything more particular, since the case before it involved a child whose progress plainly demonstrated that her IEP was designed to deliver more than adequate educational benefits. See id., at 202, 209–210, 102 S.Ct. 3034. The Court's principal concern was to correct what it viewed as the surprising rulings below: that the IDEA effectively empowers judges to elaborate a federal common law of public education, and that a child performing better than most in her class had been denied a FAPE. The Court was not concerned with precisely articulating a governing standard for closer cases. ... We cannot accept the school district's reading of Rowley.

B

While Rowley declined to articulate an overarching standard to evaluate the adequacy of the education provided under the Act, the decision and the statutory language point to a general approach: To meet its substantive obligation under the IDEA, a school must offer an IEP reasonably calculated to enable a child to make progress appropriate in light of the child's circumstances.

The "reasonably calculated" qualification reflects a recognition that crafting an appropriate program of education requires a prospective judgment by school officials. The Act contemplates that this fact-intensive exercise will be informed not only by the expertise of school officials, but also by the input of the child's parents or guardians. Any review of an IEP must appreciate that the question is whether the IEP is reasonable, not whether the court regards it as ideal.

The IEP must aim to enable the child to make progress. After all, the essential function of an IEP is to set out a plan for pursuing academic and functional advancement. See §§ 1414(d)(1)(A)(i)(I)–(IV). This reflects the broad purpose of the IDEA, an "ambitious" piece of legislation enacted "in response to Congress' perception that a majority of handicapped children in the United States 'were either totally excluded from schools or [were] sitting idly in regular classrooms awaiting the time when they were old enough to "drop out." ' " Rowley, 458 U.S., at 179, 102 S.Ct. 3034 (quoting H.R.Rep. No. 94–332, p. 2 (1975)). A substantive standard not focused on student progress would do little to remedy the pervasive and tragic academic stagnation that prompted Congress to act.

That the progress contemplated by the IEP must be appropriate in light of the child's circumstances should come as no surprise. A focus on the particular child is at the core of the IDEA. The instruction offered must be "specially designed" to meet a child's "unique needs" through an "[i]ndividualized education program." §§ 1401(29), (14) (emphasis added). An IEP is not a form document. It is constructed only after careful consideration of the child's present levels of achievement, disability, and potential for growth. §§ 1414(d)(1)(A)(i)(I)-(IV), (d)(3)(A)(i)-(iv). As we observed in Rowley, the IDEA "requires participating States to educate a wide spectrum of handicapped children," and "the benefits obtainable by children at one end of the spectrum will differ dramatically from those obtainable by children at the other end, with infinite variations in between." 458 U.S., at 202, 102 S.Ct. 3034.

Rowley sheds light on what appropriate progress will look like in many cases. There, the Court recognized that the IDEA requires that children with disabilities receive education in the regular classroom "whenever possible." (citing § 1412(a)(5)). When this preference is met, "the system itself monitors the educational progress of the child." "Regular examinations are administered, grades are awarded, and yearly advancement to higher grade levels is permitted for those children who attain an adequate knowledge of the course material." Progress through this system is what our society generally means by an "education." And access to an "education" is what the IDEA promises. Accordingly, for a child fully integrated in the regular classroom, an IEP typically should, as Rowley put it, be "reasonably calculated to enable the child to achieve passing marks and advance from grade to grade." Id., at 203–204, 102 S.Ct. 3034.

This guidance is grounded in the statutory definition of a FAPE. One of the components of a FAPE is "special education," defined as "specially designed instruction ... to meet the unique needs of a child with a disability." §§ 1401(9), (29). In determining what it means to "meet the unique needs" of a child with a disability, the provisions governing the IEP development process are a natural source of guidance: It is through the IEP that "[t]he 'free appropriate public education' required by the Act is tailored to the unique needs of" a particular child. Id., at 181, 102 S.Ct. 3034.

The IEP provisions reflect Rowley 's expectation that, for most children, a FAPE will involve integration in the regular classroom and individualized special education calculated to achieve advancement from grade to grade. Every IEP begins by describing a child's present level of achievement, including explaining "how the child's disability affects the child's involvement and progress in the general education curriculum." § 1414(d)(1)(A)(i)(I)(aa). It then sets out "a statement of measurable annual goals ... designed to ... enable the child to be involved in and make progress in the general education curriculum," along with a description of specialized instruction and services that the child will receive. §§ 1414(d)(1)(A)(i)(II), (IV). The instruction and services must likewise be provided with an eye toward "progress in the general education curriculum." § 1414(d)(1)(A)(i)(IV)(bb). Similar IEP requirements have been in place since the time the States began accepting funding under the IDEA.

The school district protests that these provisions impose only procedural requirements—a checklist of items the IEP must address—not a substantive standard enforceable in court. But the procedures are there for a reason, and their focus provides insight into what it means, for purposes of the FAPE definition, to "meet the unique needs" of a child with a disability. §§ 1401(9), (29). When a child is fully integrated in the regular classroom, as the Act prefers, what that typically means is providing a level of instruction reasonably calculated to permit advancement through the general curriculum.[2]

[2] This guidance should not be interpreted as an inflexible rule. We declined to hold in Rowley, and do not hold today, that "every handicapped child who is advancing from grade to grade ... is automatically receiving a [FAPE]." Board of Ed. of Hendrick Hudson Central School Dist., Westchester Cty. v. Rowley, 458 U.S. 176, 203, n. 25, 102 S.Ct. 3034, 73 L.Ed.2d 690 (1982).

Rowley had no need to provide concrete guidance with respect to a child who is not fully integrated in the regular classroom and not able to achieve on grade level. That case concerned a young girl who was progressing smoothly through the regular curriculum. If that is not a reasonable prospect for a child, his IEP need not aim for grade-level advancement. But his educational program must be appropriately ambitious in light of his circumstances, just as advancement from grade to grade is appropriately ambitious for most children in the regular classroom. The goals may differ, but every child should have the chance to meet challenging objectives.

Of course this describes a general standard, not a formula. But whatever else can be said about it, this standard is markedly more demanding than the "merely more than de minimis " test applied by the Tenth Circuit. It cannot be the case that the Act typically aims for grade-level advancement for children with disabilities who can be educated in the regular classroom, but is satisfied with barely more than de minimis progress for those who cannot.

When all is said and done, a student offered an educational program providing "merely more than de minimis " progress from year to year can hardly be said to have been offered an education at all. For children with disabilities, receiving instruction that aims so low would be tantamount to "sitting idly ... awaiting the time when they were old enough to 'drop out.' " Rowley, 458 U.S., at 179, 102 S.Ct. 3034 (some internal quotation marks omitted). The IDEA demands more. It requires an educational program reasonably calculated to enable a child to make progress appropriate in light of the child's circumstances.

……..

D

We will not attempt to elaborate on what "appropriate" progress will look like from case to case. It is in the nature of the Act and the standard we adopt to resist such an effort: The adequacy of a given IEP turns on the unique circumstances of the child for whom it was created. This absence of a bright-line rule, however, should not be mistaken for "an invitation to the courts to substitute their own notions of sound educational policy for those of the school authorities which they review." Rowley, 458 U.S., at 206, 102 S.Ct. 3034.

At the same time, deference is based on the application of expertise and the exercise of judgment by school authorities. The Act vests these officials with responsibility for decisions of critical importance to the life of a disabled child. The nature of the IEP process, from the initial consultation through state administrative proceedings, ensures that parents and school representatives will fully air their respective opinions on the degree of progress a child's IEP should pursue. See §§ 1414, 1415; id., at 208–209, 102 S.Ct. 3034. By the time any dispute reaches court, school authorities will have had a complete opportunity to bring their expertise and judgment to bear on areas of disagreement. A reviewing court may fairly expect those authorities to be able to offer a cogent and responsive explanation for their decisions that shows the IEP is reasonably calculated to enable the child to make progress appropriate in light of his circumstances.

The judgment of the United States Court of Appeals for the Tenth Circuit is vacated, and the case is remanded for further proceedings consistent with this opinion.

CEDAR RAPIDS COMMUNITY SCHOOL DISTRICT v. GARRET F.
526 U.S. 66 (1999)

Justice STEVENS delivered the opinion of the Court.

The Individuals with Disabilities Education Act (IDEA), 84 Stat. 175, as amended, was enacted, in part, "to assure that all children with disabilities have available to them ... a free appropriate public education which emphasizes special education and related services designed to meet their unique needs." 20 U.S.C. § 1400(c). Consistent with this purpose, the IDEA authorizes federal financial assistance to States that agree to provide disabled children with special education and "related services." See §§ 1401(a)(18), 1412(1). The question presented in this case is whether the definition of "related services" in § 1401(a)(17)1 requires a public school district in a participating State to provide a ventilator-dependent student with certain nursing services during school hours.

Originally, the statute was enacted without a definition of "related services." See Education of the Handicapped Act, 84 Stat. 175. In 1975, Congress added the definition at issue in this case. Education for All Handicapped Children Act of 1975, § 4(a)(4), 89 Stat. 775. Aside from nonsubstantive changes and added examples of included services, see, e.g., Individuals with Disabilities Education Act Amendments of 1997, § 101, 111 Stat. 45; Individuals with Disabilities Education Act Amendments of 1991, § 25(a)(1)(B), 105 Stat. 605; Education of the Handicapped Act Amendments of 1990, § 101(c), 104 Stat. 1103, the relevant language in § 1401(a)(17) has not been amended since 1975. All references to the IDEA herein are to the 1994 version as codified in Title 20 of the United States Code-the version of the statute in effect when this dispute arose.

I

Respondent Garret F. is a friendly, creative, and intelligent young man. When Garret was four years old, his spinal column was severed in a motorcycle accident. Though paralyzed from the neck down, his mental capacities were unaffected. He is able to speak, to control his motorized wheelchair through use of a puff and suck straw, and to operate a computer with a device that responds to head movements. Garret is currently a student in the Cedar Rapids Community School District (District), he attends regular classes in a typical school program, and his academic

---

[1] "The term 'related services' means transportation, and such developmental, corrective, and other supportive services (including speech pathology and audiology, psychological services, physical and occupational therapy, recreation, including therapeutic recreation, social work services, counseling services, including rehabilitation counseling, and medical services, except that such medical services shall be for diagnostic and evaluation purposes only) as may be required to assist a child with a disability to benefit from special education, and includes the early identification and assessment of disabling conditions in children." 20 U.S.C. § 1401(a)(17).

performance has been a success. Garret is, however, ventilator dependent,2 and therefore requires a responsible individual nearby to attend to certain physical needs while he is in school. 3

During Garret's early years at school his family provided for his physical care during the school day. When he was in kindergarten, his 18-year-old aunt attended him; in the next four years, his family used settlement proceeds they received after the accident, their insurance, and other resources to employ a licensed practical nurse. In 1993, Garret's mother requested the District to accept financial responsibility for the health care services that Garret requires during the school day. The District denied the request, believing that it was not legally obligated to provide continuous one-on-one nursing services.

Relying on both the IDEA and Iowa law, Garret's mother requested a hearing before the Iowa Department of Education. An Administrative Law Judge (ALJ) received extensive evidence concerning Garret's special needs, the District's treatment of other disabled students, and the assistance provided to other ventilator-dependent children in other parts of the country. In his 47-page report, the ALJ found that the District has about 17,500 students, of whom approximately 2,200 need some form of special education or special services. Although Garret is the only ventilator-dependent student in the District, most of the health care services that he needs are already provided for some other students. "The primary difference between Garret's situation and that of other students is his dependency on his ventilator for life support." App. to Pet. for Cert. 28a. The ALJ noted that the parties disagreed over the training or licensure required for the care and supervision of such students, and that those providing such care in other parts of the country ranged from non-licensed personnel to registered nurses. However, the District did not contend that only a licensed physician could provide the services in question.

The ALJ explained that federal law requires that children with a variety of health impairments be provided with "special education and related services" when their disabilities adversely affect their academic performance, and that such children should be educated to the maximum extent appropriate with children who are not disabled. In addition, the ALJ explained that applicable federal regulations distinguish between "school health services," which are provided by a "qualified

---

[2] In his report in this case, the Administrative Law Judge explained: "Being ventilator dependent means that [Garret] breathes only with external aids, usually an electric ventilator, and occasionally by someone else's manual pumping of an air bag attached to his tracheotomy tube when the ventilator is being maintained. This later procedure is called ambu bagging." App. to Pet. for Cert. 19a.

[3] "He needs assistance with urinary bladder catheterization once a day, the suctioning of his tracheotomy tube as needed, but at least once every six hours, with food and drink at lunchtime, in getting into a reclining position for five minutes of each hour, and ambu bagging occasionally as needed when the ventilator is checked for proper functioning. He also needs assistance from someone familiar with his ventilator in the event there is a malfunction or electrical problem, and someone who can perform emergency procedures in the event he experiences autonomic hyperreflexia. Autonomic hyperreflexia is an uncontrolled visceral reaction to anxiety or a full bladder. Blood pressure increases, heart rate increases, and flushing and sweating may occur. Garret has not experienced autonomic hyperreflexia frequently in recent years, and it has usually been alleviated by catheterization. He has not ever experienced autonomic hyperreflexia at school. Garret is capable of communicating his needs orally or in another fashion so long as he has not been rendered unable to do so by an extended lack of oxygen." *Id.*, at 20a.

school nurse or other qualified person," and "medical services," which are provided by a licensed physician. See 34 C.F.R. §§ 300.16(a), (b)(4), (b)(11) (1998). The District must provide the former, but need not provide the latter (except, of course, those "medical services" that are for diagnostic or evaluation purposes, 20 U.S.C. § 1401(a)(17)). According to the ALJ, the distinction in the regulations does not just depend on "the title of the person providing the service"; instead, the "medical services" exclusion is limited to services that are "in the special training, knowledge, and judgment of a physician to carry out." App. to Pet. for Cert. 51a. The ALJ thus concluded that the IDEA required the District to bear financial responsibility for all of the services in dispute, including continuous nursing services.

The District challenged the ALJ's decision in Federal District Court, but that court approved the ALJ's IDEA ruling and granted summary judgment against the District. Id. at 9a, 15a. The Court of Appeals affirmed. 106 F.3d 822 (C.A.8 1997). It noted that, as a recipient of federal funds under the IDEA, Iowa has a statutory duty to provide all disabled children a "free appropriate public education," which includes "related services." See id. at 824. The Court of Appeals read our opinion in Irving Independent School Dist. v. Tatro, 468 U.S. 883 (1984), to provide a two-step analysis of the "related services" definition in § 1401(a)(17)-asking first, whether the requested services are included within the phrase "supportive services"; and second, whether the services are excluded as "medical services." 106 F.3d, at 824-25. The Court of Appeals succinctly answered both questions in Garret's favor. The Court found the first step plainly satisfied, since Garret cannot attend school unless the requested services are available during the school day. Id. at 825. As to the second step, the court reasoned that Tatro "established a bright-line test: the services of a physician (other than for diagnostic and evaluation purposes) are subject to the medical services exclusion, but services that can be provided in the school setting by a nurse or qualified layperson are not." 106 F.3d, at 825.

In its petition for certiorari, the District challenged only the second step of the Court of Appeals' analysis. The District pointed out that some federal courts have not asked whether the requested health services must be delivered by a physician, but instead have applied a multifactor test that considers, generally speaking, the nature and extent of the services at issue. We granted the District's petition to resolve this conflict.

II

The District contends that § 1401(a)(17) does not require it to provide Garret with "continuous one-on-one nursing services" during the school day, even though Garret cannot remain in school without such care. Brief for Petitioner 10. However, the IDEA's definition of "related services," our decision in Irving Indept. Sch. Dist. v. Tatro, 468 U.S. 883 (1984), and the overall statutory scheme all support the decision of the Court of Appeals.

The text of the "related services" definition, see n. 1, supra, broadly encompasses those supportive services that "may be required to assist a child with a disability to benefit from special education." As we have already noted, the District does not challenge the Court of Appeals' conclusion that the in-school services at issue are within the covered category of "supportive services." As a general matter, services that enable a disabled child to remain in school during the day provide the student with "the meaningful access to education that Congress envisioned." Tatro, 468 U.S., at

891("'Congress sought primarily to make public education available to handicapped children' and 'to make such access meaningful'" (quoting Bd. of Ed. of Hendrick Hudson Central Sch. Dist., Westchester Cty. v. Rowley, 458 U.S. 176, 192, (1982))).

.....

The scope of the "medical services" exclusion is not a matter of first impression in this Court. In Tatro we concluded that the Secretary of Education had reasonably determined that the term "medical services" referred only to services that must be performed by a physician, and not to school health services. 468 U.S., at 892-94, 104 S. Ct. 3371. Accordingly, we held that a specific form of health care (clean intermittent catheterization) that is often, though not always, performed by a nurse is not an excluded medical service. We referenced the likely cost of the services and the competence of school staff as justifications for drawing a line between physician and other services, ibid., but our endorsement of that line was unmistakable. It is thus settled that the phrase "medical services" in § 1401(a)(17) does not embrace all forms of care that might loosely be described as "medical" in other contexts, such as a claim for an income tax deduction. See 26 U.S.C. § 213(d)(1) (1994 ed. and Supp. II) (defining "medical care").

....

The District does not ask us to define the term so broadly. Indeed, the District does not argue that any of the items of care that Garret needs, considered individually, could be excluded from the scope of 20 U.S.C. § 1401(a)(17). It could not make such an argument, considering that one of the services Garret needs (catheterization) was at issue in Tatro, and the others may be provided competently by a school nurse or other trained personnel. See App. to Pet. for Cert. 15a, 52a. As the ALJ concluded, most of the requested services are already provided by the District to other students, and the in-school care necessitated by Garret's ventilator dependency does not demand the training, knowledge, and judgment of a licensed physician. Id. at 51a-52a. While more extensive, the in-school services Garret needs are no more "medical" than was the care sought in Tatro.

Instead, the District points to the combined and continuous character of the required care, and proposes a test under which the outcome in any particular case would "depend upon a series of factors, such as [1] whether the care is continuous or intermittent, [2] whether existing school health personnel can provide the service, [3] the cost of the service, and [4] the potential consequences if the service is not properly performed." Brief for Petitioner 11; see also id. at 34-35.

The District's multifactor test is not supported by any recognized source of legal authority. The proposed factors can be found in neither the text of the statute nor the regulations that we upheld in Tatro. Moreover, the District offers no explanation why these characteristics make one service any more "medical" than another. The continuous character of certain services associated with Garret's ventilator dependency has no apparent relationship to "medical" services, much less a relationship of equivalence. Continuous services may be more costly and may require additional school personnel, but they are not thereby more "medical." Whatever its imperfections, a rule that limits the medical services exemption to physician services is unquestionably a reasonable and generally workable interpretation of the statute. Absent an elaboration of the statutory terms plainly more convincing than that which we reviewed in Tatro, there is no good reason to depart from settled law.

Finally, the District raises broader concerns about the financial burden that it must bear to provide the services that Garret needs to stay in school. The problem for the District in providing these services is not that its staff cannot be trained to deliver them; the problem, the District contends, is that the existing school health staff cannot meet all of their responsibilities and provide for Garret at the same time. Through its multifactor test, the District seeks to establish a kind of undue-burden exemption primarily based on the cost of the requested services. The first two factors can be seen as examples of cost-based distinctions: Intermittent care is often less expensive than continuous care, and the use of existing personnel is cheaper than hiring additional employees. The third factor—the cost of the service—would then encompass the first two. The relevance of the fourth factor is likewise related to cost because extra care may be necessary if potential consequences are especially serious.

The District may have legitimate financial concerns, but our role in this dispute is to interpret existing law. Defining "related services" in a manner that accommodates the cost concerns Congress may have had, cf. Tatro, 468 U.S., at 892, 104 S. Ct. 3371, is altogether different from using cost itself as the definition. Given that § 1401(a)(17) does not employ cost in its definition of "related services" or excluded "medical services," accepting the District's cost-based standard as the sole test for determining the scope of the provision would require us to engage in judicial lawmaking without any guidance from Congress. It would also create some tension with the purposes of the IDEA. The statute may not require public schools to maximize the potential of disabled students commensurate with the opportunities provided to other children, see Rowley, 458 U.S., at 200, 102 S. Ct. 3034; and the potential financial burdens imposed on participating States may be relevant to arriving at a sensible construction of the IDEA, see Tatro, 468 U.S., at 892, 104 S. Ct. 3371. But Congress intended "to open the door of public education" to all qualified children and "require[d] participating States to educate handicapped children with nonhandicapped children whenever possible." Rowley, 458 U.S., at 192, 202, 102 S. Ct. 3034; see id., at 179-81, 102 S. Ct. 3034; see also Honig v. Doe, 484 U.S. 305, 310-11, 324, 108 S. Ct. 592, 98 L. Ed. 2d 686 (1988); §§ 1412(1), (2)(C), (5)(B).

This case is about whether meaningful access to the public schools will be assured, not the level of education that a school must finance once access is attained. It is undisputed that the services at issue must be provided if Garret is to remain in school. Under the statute, our precedent, and the purposes of the IDEA, the District must fund such "related services" in order to help guarantee that students like Garret are integrated into the public schools.

INDEPENDENT SCHOOL DISTRICT NO. 283 v. E.M.D.H.
___ F3d ___; 2020 WL 2892238 (8th Cir, 2020)

ERICKSON, Circuit Judge.

E.M.D.H., a student in St. Louis Park, Minnesota, Independent School District No. 283 (the "District"), is plagued with various psychological disorders. E.M.D.H. and her parents, L.H. and S.D., filed a complaint with the Minnesota Department of Education, asserting the District's failure to classify E.M.D.H. as disabled denied her the right to a "free appropriate public education ("FAPE") under the Individuals with Disabilities Act ("IDEA"), 20 U.S.C. § 1400 et seq. After a seven-day evidentiary hearing, a state administrative law judge ("ALJ") concluded that the District's treatment of E.M.D.H. violated the IDEA and related state special-education laws. The District filed this action in federal court for judicial review of the ALJ's decision, as the IDEA authorizes. See 20 U.S.C. § 1415(i)(2). The district court denied the District's motion for judgment on the administrative record and granted, in part, E.M.D.H.'s motion for judgment on the record, modifying the award of compensatory education. We affirm, in part, and reverse, in part, reinstating the ALJ's award for compensatory education.

I. Background

E.M.D.H. ("Student") carries a plethora of diagnoses: generalized anxiety disorder, school phobia, autism spectrum disorder (with unspecified obsessive-compulsive disorder traits), panic disorder with associated agoraphobia, attention deficit hyperactivity disorder ("ADHD"), and severe recurrent major depressive disorder. The Student's problems became manifest early in her life. By age four she was prone to tantrums and outbursts. By the second grade she was in therapy. Even though the Student had some attendance issues, she progressed through and excelled in elementary school.

Middle school proved more challenging. By the fall of her eighth-grade year, in 2014, the Student began to be more frequently absent from school, telling her mother that she was afraid to go. By the last quarter of eighth grade, the Student was consistently absent from school and was placed in a psychiatric day-treatment facility. The Student's teachers were aware that her absences were due to her mental-health issues and noted her schoolwork as incomplete rather than entering failing grades. The District dis-enrolled the Student in the spring of her eighth grade year.

Before the Student entered the ninth grade in the fall of 2015, her parents alerted the ninth-grade guidance counselor that the Student had not been present for the latter part of eighth grade due to anxiety and school phobia. Notwithstanding these past difficulties, the Student was enrolled in the ninth grade. The Student's attendance was inconsistent and then she quit going to school altogether and was admitted to a psychiatric facility for treatment. By November the District dis-enrolled her again.

In the spring of 2016, the District discussed evaluating the Student as a candidate for special education. The ninth-grade guidance counselor spoke to the Student's parents about an evaluation, leaving them with the impression that decisions related to special education were theirs to make, but noting that if the Student availed herself of special-education opportunities she would not be allowed to remain in her honors classes. The parents did not request the evaluation and one was not undertaken by the District. The student was once again dis-enrolled that spring.

The Student spent most of the summer in 2016 at a treatment facility receiving therapy for her anxiety, depression, and ADHD. The staff at the facility noticed that while the Student struggled with increased sensory awareness she was able to manage her symptoms with assistance well enough to be gradually reintroduced to her academic work and daily routine. When the Student entered her tenth-grade year, the District developed a plan that allowed her extra time on assignments, adjustments in workload, breaks from class to visit the counseling office, and the use of a fidget spinner. However, even with these accommodations, the Student was unable to maintain consistent attendance. After the first six weeks, the Student attended almost no classes, resulting in another dis-enrollment by the District.

In January 2017 school staff met with the parents to reexamine the possibility of providing special education. Once again, the parents were told that if the Student was placed in special education, she would be removed from her honors classes, effectively placing her in course work that would not challenge or stimulate her intellectually. At the end of the first semester, the District had yet to perform a special-education evaluation. The Student attended only one day during the second semester. The District dis-enrolled her again in February.

In April 2017, the parents requested that the District evaluate the Student's eligibility for special education. The request came three days after the Student had been readmitted to a psychiatric facility. While at the facility, Dr. Denise K. Reese performed a comprehensive psychological evaluation of the Student, diagnosing her with major depressive disorder, autism spectrum disorder, ADHD, generalized anxiety disorder with panic and obsessive-compulsive-disorder features, and symptoms of borderline-personality disorder. Dr. Reese concluded that the Student's spate of mental illnesses had "resulted in an inability to attend school, increasing social isolation, and continued need for intensive therapeutic treatment."

The Student's problems continued unabated into her junior year. She attended three partial days of the eleventh grade in the District's PAUSE program, which is designed for students with emotional and behavioral disorders. She ceased attending school after September 11, 2017. At this point, the Student had earned far less than half of the 46 credits necessary to graduate. Most of the Student's credits were from instruction she received at treatment facilities, with only two credits coming from regular District coursework.

It was not until November 2017 that the District provided the parents with a report evaluating the Student's eligibility for special education. The report concluded that the Student did not qualify. The District's conclusion prompted the parents to hire a team of doctors and other professionals to conduct an independent educational evaluation of the Student. The evaluation confirmed the Student's diagnoses and included a recommendation that she receive special education that would allow her to complete rigorous coursework while managing the symptoms that had made doing so difficult, if not impossible, in the past. The District rejected the recommendations, persisting in its initial assessment, which led to the parents filing a due-process complaint with the Minnesota Department of Education.

The complaint alleged that the District violated the IDEA and state law when it failed to identify the Student as eligible for special education services and did not provide her with such services. During the due-process hearing, testimony was taken from 20 witnesses, and almost 80 exhibits were received. The ALJ concluded the District acted unlawfully when it failed to: (1) identify the student as a child with a disability, (2) conduct an appropriate special-education evaluation, (3) find the Student qualified for special education, and (4) provide the Student a FAPE. The ALJ ordered:

(1) the Student eligible for special education and related services;

(2) the District to develop an Individualized Education Plan ("IEP") providing the Student with a FAPE;

(3) the District to conduct quarterly meetings to consider changes to the IEP;

(4) the District to reimburse the parents in an amount over $25,000 for past diagnostic and educational expenses they incurred; and

(5) the District to pay for compensatory services in the form of private tutoring and the cost of attendance of the Student's psychiatrist and private tutor at IEP meetings.

In its appeal to the district court, the District requested leave to supplement the administrative record. The court denied the motion to supplement and affirmed the ALJ's decision, except for the order to pay for future private-tutoring services, which the district court reversed. The parties cross-appeal.

II. Discussion

This case raises issues under both the IDEA and related state laws, which exist "to ensure that all children with disabilities have available to them a free and appropriate public education that emphasizes special education and related services designed to meet their unique needs." 20 U.S.C. § 1400(d)(1)(A). On appeal, the District asserts that the court abused its discretion by denying its request to supplement the administrative record. The District also asserts that the court and ALJ erred when they concluded that the District's special-education evaluation, eligibility determination, and child-find activities were flawed and inadequate. Both the District and the Student contest the court's remedial award. The District, on the one side, contends the Student is owed neither reimbursement of her expenses nor compensatory services while, on the other side, the Student contends that the court erred when it reversed the ALJ's award of compensatory private tutoring.

……

B. IDEA Issues

We review the IDEA issues de novo, bearing in mind that under the Act the courts "render an independent decision based on a preponderance of the evidence in the administrative record." C.B. ex rel. B.B. v. Special Sch. Dist. No. 1, 636 F.3d 981, 988 (8th Cir. 2011). We give " 'due weight' to the results of the administrative proceedings and [do] not substitute [our] 'own notions of sound educational policy for those of the school authorities which [we] review.' " Id. at 989 (quoting Bd. of Educ. of Hendrick Hudson Cent. Sch. Dist. v. Rowley, 458 U.S. 176, 205–06, 102 S.Ct. 3034, 73 L.Ed.2d 690 (1982)).

1. Eligibility Evaluation

Notably, Minnesota regulations require school districts to provide the student regular and special-education services, whether or not the student is disabled, when a student spends extended time at home or in a medical facility being treated for illness. Minn. Stat. § 125A.515; see also id. §§ 125A.15 and 125A.51. Nevertheless, once the parents requested the District evaluate the Student for a disability, the applicable regulations under the IDEA required the District to "conduct a full and individual evaluation ... to determine if [she] is a child with a disability." 34 C.F.R. § 300.301(a)–(b). The District was also required to "ensure that ... the evaluation [was] sufficiently comprehensive to identify all of the child's special education and related services needs." Id. § 300.304(c)(6).

……

The District admits that it did not conduct either a functional behavioral assessment or make systematic observations of the Student. The District argues that it should be absolved of this duty because the Student was chronically absent, especially in the eleventh grade when the District's evaluation took place. We acknowledge that while the Student's absences might have made a comprehensive evaluation more difficult, the evidence does not support the conclusion that task was impossible to undertake. A functional behavioral assessment, which "identifies the antecedents, consequences, and reinforcers that maintain the behavior," does not depend on the Student's presence in the classroom. Minn. R. 3525.0210 subp. 22. And Minnesota's regulations make plain that "systematic observations" can be made both "in the classroom," and in "other learning environment[s]" as well. Id. at 3525.1329 subp. 3.

The record reflects that the District made no effort to assess the Student in her virtual classroom, at home, or in any one of the psychiatric facilities from which she earned school credits. The District's failure to avail itself of these possibilities or develop another way of gathering the necessary data is virtually conclusive evidence that the District's evaluation of the Student was insufficiently informed and legally deficient.

2. Eligibility Determination

The District's evaluation, resting as it did on incomplete data, concluded that the Student is not eligible for special education. On appeal, the District stands by that conclusion and asserts that the determinations of the ALJ and district court to the contrary are erroneous. To be eligible for a FAPE that includes special education and related services, a student must be a "child with a disability."

20 U.S.C. §§ 1401(3), (9), 1414(d), 34 C.F.R. § 300.500(a), (c); see Endrew F. ex rel. Joseph F. v. Douglas Cty. Sch. Dist. RE-1, — U.S. ——, 137 S. Ct. 988, 993–94, 197 L.Ed.2d 335 (2017). The IDEA defines a child with a disability as "a child ... with," among other ailments, a "serious emotional disturbance" or "other health impairments ... who, by reason thereof, needs special education and related services."[1] 20 U.S.C. § 1401(3).

[1] "Serious emotional disturbance" and "other health impairments" are the federal analogs of Minnesota regulations denominating "emotional or behavioral disorders" and "other health disabilities," respectively. Compare 34 C.F.R. § 300.8(c)(4)(i) (serious emotional disturbance), and id. § 300.8(c)(9) (other health impairment), with Minn. R. 3525.1329 (emotional behavioral disorders), and id. Minn. R. 3525.1335 (other health disabilities).

A "serious emotional disturbance" is:

[A] condition exhibiting one or more of the following characteristics over a long period of time and to a marked degree that adversely affects a child's educational performance:

(A) An inability to learn that cannot be explained by intellectual, sensory, or health factors.

(B) An inability to build or maintain satisfactory interpersonal relationships with peers and teachers.

(C) Inappropriate types of behavior or feelings under normal circumstances.

(D) A general pervasive mood of unhappiness or depression.

(E) A tendency to develop physical symptoms or fears associated with personal or school problems.

34 C.F.R. § 300.8(c)(4)(i). An "other health impairment" means:

having limited strength, vitality, or alertness, including a heightened alertness to environmental stimuli, that results in limited alertness with respect to the educational environment, that—

(i) Is due to chronic or acute health problems such as asthma, attention deficit disorder or attention deficit hyperactivity disorder, diabetes, epilepsy, a heart condition, hemophilia, lead poisoning, leukemia, nephritis, rheumatic fever, sickle cell anemia, and Tourette syndrome; and

(ii) Adversely affects a child's educational performance.

Id. § 300.8(c)(9).

Under the District's analysis the Student's symptoms are simply insufficient to constitute a "serious emotional disturbance" or "other health impairments." However, the preponderance of the evidence in the administrative record indicates the Student has both conditions. For years the Student has suffered from a panoply of mental-health issues that have kept her in her bedroom, socially isolated, and terrified to attend school...The administrative record demonstrates the Student has a serious emotional disturbance as she is unable "to build or maintain satisfactory interpersonal relationships with peers and teachers." 34 C.F.R. § 300.8(c)(4)(i)(B). The Student also displayed "[i]nappropriate types of behavior or feelings under normal circumstances" and has been living with a "general pervasive mood of unhappiness or depression." Id. § 300.8(c)(4)(i)(C), (D). The evidence in the record also shows that the Student suffers from "limited ... vitality" and "a heightened alertness to environmental stimuli" that are "due to chronic or acute health problems," including ADHD, all of which are symptoms of "other health impairments." Id. § 300.8(c)(9). The Student's absences from the classroom has put her well behind her peers in, among other things, earning the number of credits needed to graduate, and has therefore adversely affect[ed] her educational performance." Id. at 300.08(c)(9)(ii); see id. § 300.320(a)(2)(i)(A) (requiring special education be "designed to ... enable the child to be involved in and make progress in the general education curriculum").

Despite this evidence, the District maintains that the Student is simply too intellectually gifted to qualify for special education. The District suggests the Student's high standardized test scores and her exceptional performance on the rare occasions she made it to class are strong indicators that there are no services it can provide that would improve her educational situation. The District confuses intellect for an education. See Florence Cty. Sch. Dist. Four v. Carter ex rel. Carter, 510 U.S. 7, 13, 114 S.Ct. 361, 126 L.Ed.2d 284 (1993) ("IDEA was intended to ensure that children with disabilities receive an education that is both appropriate and free."). The IDEA guarantees disabled students access to the latter, no matter their innate intelligence. More practically, the positive results of the private tutoring and online learning indicate that the nearly three years where the Student foundered were not inevitable but the direct result of insufficient individualized attention under an appropriate IEP. The record demonstrates that the Student's intellect alone was insufficient for her to progress academically and that she was in need of special education and related services.

This Student may not present the paradigmatic case of a special-education student, but her situation does not vitiate the District's duty under the IDEA to provide her with a FAPE. "The IDEA requires public school districts to educate 'a wide spectrum of handicapped children,' " C.B. ex rel. B.B, 636 F.3d at 989 (quoting Rowley, 458 U.S. at 202, 102 S.Ct. 3034), including those whose handicap is not cognitive. See Indep. Sch. Dist. No. 284, 258 F.3d at 777 ("If the problem prevents a disabled child from receiving educational benefit, then it should not matter that the problem is not cognitive in nature or that it causes the child even more trouble outside the classroom than within it."). In Independent School District No. 284, for example, the court held that an educational placement in a residential facility pursuant to the IDEA was necessary for a student whose psychological infirmities contributed to her truancy and consequent lack of academic credit, even though she "ha[d] no learning disability" and "tests reveal[ed] [her] to be a shrewd problem solver." 258 F.3d at 777–78.

The Student is eligible for special education and a state-funded FAPE like every other "child with a disability." 20 U.S.C. § 1401(3). This "specially designed instruction," whether "conducted in the classroom, in the home, in hospitals and institutions, [or] in other settings," id. § 1401(29), must be "reasonably calculated to enable [her] to make progress" and "appropriately ambitious in light of [her] circumstances," Endrew F. ex rel. Joseph F., 137 S. Ct. at 999–1000.

3. Child-Find Obligation

The ALJ and district court determined that the District breached its obligation to identify the Student by the spring of her eighth-grade year as a child eligible for special education. In addition to a FAPE, an essential aspect of the IDEA is the requirement that "children with disabilities ... who are in need of special education and related services, are identified, located, and evaluated" by states. 20 U.S.C. § 1412(a)(3)(A); see Forest Grove Sch. Dist. v. T.A., 557 U.S. 230, 245, 129 S.Ct. 2484, 174 L.Ed.2d 168 (2009) (describing this requirement as one of "paramount importance"). The District contends it had no duty to identify the Student as eligible for special education, at least not until the parents requested an evaluation in the spring of the Student's junior year. The District also contends that if such a duty existed the Student's claim is barred by the IDEA's two-year statute of limitations. We are not persuaded by the District's arguments...Despite their knowledge that the Student was suffering from mental-health issues that impacted her ability to attend school, District staff did not refer the Student for a special-education evaluation because she had above-average intellectual ability. The District continued to embrace this decision until the parents requested an evaluation near the end of the Student's sophomore year. Even if the District was confronted with an unusual case marked by some confusion, in just the same way that the Student's eligibility for special education was not foreclosed by her intellect, the District's child-find obligation was not suspended because of her innate intelligence. The preponderance of the evidence supports the conclusion that the District breached its child-find obligation.

......

4. Relief

Having found violations of the IDEA, we turn to the parties' dispute regarding the appropriate relief. The IDEA confers "broad discretion" upon hearing officers and courts to order remedies that are " 'appropriate' in light of the purpose of the Act." Sch. Comm. v. Dep't of Educ., 471 U.S. 359, 369, 105 S.Ct. 1996, 85 L.Ed.2d 385 (1985); see also 20 U.S.C. § 1415(i)(2)(C)(3) ("[T]he court ... basing its decision on the preponderance of the evidence, shall grant such relief as the court determines is appropriate."). The District asserts the court improperly ordered it to reimburse the parents the amount expended on: (1) Dr. Reese's comprehensive psychological evaluation, (2) the independent educational evaluation, and (3) and private educational services. The District also asserts the court erred when it ordered quarterly IEP meetings to take place until the Student graduates.

A review of the record demonstrates that the costs incurred as a result of Dr. Reese's work and that of other professionals hired by the parents would have been unnecessary but for the District's failure to timely identify and properly evaluate the Student as a child in need of special education. We conclude the award of these costs was within the broad discretion of the ALJ and district court.

......

The Student challenges the district court's conclusion that the ALJ's award of compensatory education in the form of private tutoring was inappropriate. Although compensatory damages are unavailable through the IDEA, compensatory education is allowed. J.B. ex rel. Bailey v. Avilla R-XIII Sch. Dist., 721 F.3d 588, 593 (8th Cir. 2013)…[T]he purpose of any compensatory-education award is restorative–and the damages are strictly limited to expenses necessarily incurred to put the Student in the education position she would have been had the District appropriately provided a FAPE. … We therefore reinstate the ALJ's award of these services, to be provided only so long as the Student suffers from a credit deficiency caused from the years she spent without a FAPE.

Cynthia L. Kelly, Individuals with Disabilities Education Act—The Right 'IDEA' for All Children's Education, 75 J. Kan. B. Ass'n (2006)

The Individuals with Disabilities Education Act (IDEA), the federal law mandating special education programs in public schools, has ensured educational opportunities for children with disabilities for 30 years. In providing rights to children with disabilities and their parents, the law places a myriad of responsibilities on public school districts and their employees. The complex laws and regulations, at both the state and federal level, have resulted in a multitude of administrative proceedings and court cases that continue to refine the contours of the law.

I. A Brief Legislative History

Since the passage of the original legislation, the Education of All Handicapped Children Act of 1975 (EAHCA), access to education for children with disabilities has increased dramatically. Today more than 6 million children with disabilities are served in the nation's public schools under IDEA's provisions; more than 65,000 students are served in Kansas alone.

Legislation to assist individuals with disabilities was not prevalent prior to the 1960s. In 1970 public schools in the United States educated only 20 percent of children with disabilities. Many states had laws that specifically excluded certain students from school, including those who were deaf, blind, emotionally disturbed, or mentally retarded. For some children, although access was not totally blocked, opportunities to receive an appropriate education were limited.

Following the U.S. Supreme Court decision in *Brown v. Board of Education*, advocates for children with disabilities brought equal educational opportunity arguments to the courts. *Pennsylvania Association for Retarded Children (PARC) v. Commonwealth of Pennsylvania* and *Mills v. Board of Education* were two influential cases. Premised on equal protection and due process theories, each of these class action cases ultimately resulted in settlement agreements that recognized the state's obligation to provide appropriate educational opportunities for children with disabilities. Both settlement agreements provided for parental participation in determining an appropriate educational program and placement and provided the resolution mechanisms for any disputes that the parents might raise.

These cases, and others pending in the early 1970s, provided the impetus for the passage of the EAHCA. States joined advocates for children with disabilities in seeking federal legislation that would provide consistency in educational programming and subsidize the costs of providing special education. The settlement agreements in *PARC* and *Mills*, particularly the parts requiring parental participation in educational programming and administrative due process procedures for resolving disputes, provided the rudimentary elements of the EAHCA. In 1990 the law was renamed the Individuals with Disabilities Education Act.

Although many of the provisions of the law are discretionary and require reauthorization by Congress on a regular basis, Part B of EAHCA, the portion of the law that provides funding for special education programs in public schools, is permanent legislation. The primary purpose of this legislation is to assist states and local school districts in providing appropriate educational opportunities for children with disabilities. Additionally, the law protects the rights of children with disabilities and their parents through mandated participation in decision making and a myriad of procedural safeguards. Amendments to IDEA have expanded procedural and substantive rights under the law, but they have remained in line with IDEA's general purposes.

In response to the Supreme Court decision in *Smith v. Robinson*, the Handicapped Children's Protection Act of 1986 strengthened parental and student protections by allowing for recovery of attorney fees under IDEA and statutorily preventing pre-emption of Section 504 and constitutional claims. The 1986 amendments mandated services for children ages 3 to 5 and established a separate program for infants and toddlers. The 1990 amendments expanded the categories of disability by adding autism and traumatic brain injury. These amendments also attempted to improve the quality of services by adding assistive technology devices and assistive technology services to the law. Finally, the amendments helped facilitate a student's ultimate departure from school by requiring transition services - a coordinated set of activities designed to help a student prepare for employment, independent living, or postsecondary education after leaving high school—for each student.

The most sweeping amendments to IDEA came in 1997. For the first time, amendments to IDEA attempted to address the education of children with disabilities within the context of education reform. Focus shifted from access to educational opportunities to improvement of performance and educational achievement. Access to the general curriculum and participation in assessments were key components of the 1997 legislation and remained central in the 2004 amendments. In addition, the law strengthened the role of parents in educational decision making for their child by encouraging the use of mediation for dispute resolution and by including measures to prevent misidentification and mislabeling of students. Finally, the amendments attempted to balance safety and learning concerns for all students with the rights of children with disabilities through codification of comprehensive disciplinary procedures.

The amendments of 2004 shift the focus of IDEA from bureaucratic compliance with procedures to student outcomes and student achievement. The amendments attempt, at times imperfectly, to dovetail the IDEA requirements with student performance standards and teacher quality requirements set forth by Congress in the No Child Left Behind legislation. One of the most troublesome aspects of the law for schools is the lack of adequate funding for special education programs at both the state and federal levels. Recognizing there are costs above those involved in educating a regular education child, the federal law originally authorized federal funding to cover 40 percent of this excess cost. Current law calculates this amount based on 40 percent of the average per pupil expenditure in public elementary and secondary schools in the United States. However, appropriations have never approached the authorized expenditure level. For many years, federal appropriations did not cover even 10 percent of the excess cost. Although federal appropriations have increased substantially over the past decade, they still cover less than 20 percent of the cost involved in providing these programs, and they have declined precipitously since resources have been diverted to the war on terror.

Notes and Comments

1. FAPE and the Individualized Education Program

In *A.K. ex rel. J.K. v. Alexandria City Sch. Bd.*, 484 F.3d 672 (4th Cir. 2007), the Fourth Circuit set forth the FAPE procedural protections well:

> A school provides a FAPE by creating an "individualized education program" ("IEP") for each child. Before creating the IEP, the school district must conduct an initial evaluation to determine the student's eligibility and to identify his educational needs. If the child is deemed eligible, an IEP is created by an "IEP Team" comprised of the child's parents, at least one of his regular teachers, at least one of his special education teachers, a school board representative, an individual who can interpret evaluation results (who may be either of the teachers or the school board representative), and, if appropriate, the child himself. The IEP must outline the student's then-current educational status, establish annual goals, and detail the special educational services and other aids that the child will be provided. It also must provide, among other things, "the projected date for the beginning of the services and modifications ..., and the anticipated frequency, location, and duration of those services and modifications." An IEP is substantively satisfactory if it is "reasonably calculated to enable the child to receive educational benefits." *Bd. of Educ. v. Rowley,* 458 U.S. 176, 207 (1982).
>
> The IDEA also provides "procedural safeguards to insure the full participation of the parents and proper resolution of substantive disagreements." *Sch. Comm. of Burlington v. Dep't of Educ. of Mass.,* 471 U.S. 359, 368 (1985) (internal quotation marks omitted). As is relevant here, those safeguards include the right to present a complaint "with respect to any matter relating to the identification, evaluation, or educational placement of the child, or the provision of a free appropriate public education to such child." 20 U.S.C.A. § 1415(b)(6)(A). The IDEA also authorizes a party aggrieved by the state administrative proceeding intended to resolve the complaint to challenge the decision in a federal court action. Such an action is an independent civil action in which the district court considers the state administrative hearing record, as well as any new evidence that the parties offer, and makes findings by a preponderance of the evidence. Although the federal court

action is an independent action, the court must give "due weight" to the state administrative proceeding.
A.K. ex rel. J.K., 484 F.3d at 675-76.

2. State Policies on Special Education

States have enacted various pieces of legislation to help administer IDEA's provisions. The Second Circuit succinctly set forth New York's two-tiered approach in *Mackey ex rel. Thomas M. v. Bd. of Educ. for Arlington Central Sch. Dist.*, 386 F.3d 158 (2d Cir. 2004):

> The IDEA offers federal funds to states that demonstrate, *inter alia,* that they have developed plans to assure "all children with disabilities residing in the state" a "free appropriate public education" ("FAPE"). 20 U.S.C. § 1412(a)(1)(A) (2000); *see Bd. of Educ. v. Rowley,* 458 U.S. 176, 180-81 (1982) To meet the IDEA requirements, a school district must provide each child who has a disability with "special education and related services," 20 U.S.C. § 1401(8), that are "reasonably calculated to enable the child to receive educational benefits." *Rowley,* 458 U.S. at 203-04. "The centerpiece of the IDEA's education delivery system is the individualized education program, or IEP," *Murphy v. Arlington Cent. Sch. Dist. Bd. of Educ.,* 297 F.3d 195, 197 (2d Cir.2002) (internal quotations marks omitted), a document in which "[t]he particular educational needs of a disabled child and the services required to meet those needs" are "set forth at least annually," *Walczak v. Fla. Union Free Sch. Dist.,* 142 F.3d 119, 122 (2d Cir.1998). New York State has "assigned responsibility for developing appropriate IEPs to local Committees on Special Education ('CSE')." *Id.* at 123.
>
> The IDEA provides a variety of "procedural safeguards with respect to the provision of free appropriate public education" by school districts. 20 U.S.C. § 1415(a). In compliance with these requirements, New York State has implemented a "two-tier system of administrative review." *Murphy,* 297 F.3d at 197. The first tier entitles parents dissatisfied with a proposed IEP to have it reviewed before an impartial hearing officer ("IHO") appointed by the board of education. N.Y. Educ. Law § 4404(1) (McKinney 2001); *see generally* 20 U.S.C. § 1415(f). The IHO is required to render a decision "not later than 45 days after the receipt by the board of education of a request for a hearing." N.Y. Comp. Codes R. & Regs. tit. 8, § 200.5(i)(4) (2004). "[P]arties aggrieved by the outcome of the due process hearing may" proceed to the second tier, "an appeal before a state review officer ('SRO')." *Murphy,* 297 F.3d at 197; *see* N.Y. Educ. Law § 4404(2); *see generally* 20 U.S.C. § 1415(g). The SRO is required to reach a decision and mail it to the parties "not later than 30 days after the receipt of a request for a review." N.Y. Comp. Codes R. & Regs. tit. 8, § 200.5(j)(2) (2004). Any party still aggrieved may sue in state or federal court. *See* 20 U.S.C. § 1415(i)(2). *Mackey ex rel. Thomas M.*, 386 F.3d at 160.

3. Substantive Differences between Section 504, IDEA, and ADA

There are important differences between the statutes that merit discussion here:

A. Age and Eligibility Requirements: Section 504 does not contain age restrictions, as such. In contrast, IDEA only provides protections to children ranging in age from three to twenty-one enrolled in kindergarten through twelfth grade. When students transition from high school to college, it is incumbent upon the student to recognize that colleges and universities do not fall under IDEA. Instead, college and graduate students are covered by Section 504 and the ADA.

B. Covered Individuals: IDEA only covers students and seeks to provide a free appropriate education to handicapped students. Section 504 protects a broader ranger of persons, including coverage for students, teachers, *see Arline*, *supra*, and employees.

C. Anti-Discrimination v. Affirmative Action: Perhaps the biggest distinction between Section 504 and IDEA is that IDEA requires affirmative steps to be taken by schools to provide a free appropriate public education, including Individual Education Plans ("IEP") and parental involvement in certain education decisions. IDEA requires school boards to identify, locate and evaluate all children with disabilities. Thus, IDEA is proactive and requires local educational agencies and schools to take affirmative steps to comply with their statutory mandates. In contrast, Section 504 is simply a non-discrimination statute that may require certain reasonable accommodations be made, but educators need not include the students or parents to the same degree as IDEA requires.

D. Non-Discrimination vs. Funding Laws: Section 504 and the ADA are classic civil rights laws that prohibit discrimination against disabled individuals. They are simply non-discrimination laws. Section 504 applies only to those educational institutions that receive federal financial assistance. In other words, schools and institutions that receive federal assistance for any program, including grants, monies, books or free lunch programs, must comply with Section 504's provisions. IDEA, on the other hand, is a funding program whereby schools actually receive federal money specifically to assist them in the provision of a free appropriate public education.

E. Individual Education Plans: IDEA mandates that students qualifying under IDEA receive an Individual Education Plan. Because Section 504 and the ADA are non-discrimination laws, they contain only anti-discrimination protections and do not require an IEP. Section 504 accommodations may appear similar to IEPs as the modifications provided must be individualized to address a particular disability, but a standing IEP is not required under 504.

F. Defenses: There are no defenses under IDEA. All students, under IDEA, are entitled to a free appropriate public education in the least restrictive environment. However, under Section 504, schools may raise certain defenses. As the Supreme Court explained in *Davis*, any accommodation that would result in a fundamental alteration of a program is not considered a "reasonable accommodation" under Section 504. Similarly, *Davis* instructed that any accommodation that would result in an "undue financial burden" on an institution is not a "reasonable accommodation." Finally, students, teachers or other school employees may be excluded from classroom if their presence involves a serious risk of injury or illness to themselves or others. *See Arline, supra.*

G. Procedural Protections: Students and their parents have much greater procedural protections under IDEA than under Section 504. Parents have the right to be part of the IEP process and any subsequent change in an IDEA student's placement. Parents that are dissatisfied with their child's IDEA regime can request, at school expense, an impartial due process hearing. Schools that fail to provide a free appropriate public education will be monetarily liable to parents who must place their children in private school. The remainder of this chapter is dedicated to describing the procedural protections and requirements under IDEA.

IV. Special Education and Procedural Safeguards: Manifestation Hearings, "Staying-Put," and Mainstreaming

The rights of special education students are protected in a variety of ways. The provisions of IDEA create a series of protocols with specific, built-in expectations. The procedural requirements and service delivery standards combine to act as safeguards

against irregular placement and counterproductive outcomes. They also serve as due process barometers for the judiciary when a dispute over services arises.

As presented above in Section III, IDEA does not require school districts to maximize the potential of handicapped children *vis-a-vis* nonhandicapped children. Nevertheless, IDEA does require that a disabled student be "mainstreamed" – educated with children who are not disabled – to the maximum extent possible. Segregation of a special needs student is appropriate only when the nature or severity of the disability of a child is such that education in regular classes with the use of supplementary aids and services cannot be achieved. 20 U.S.C.S. § 1412(a)(5)(A). This so-called "least restrictive environment" has become an important right for parents and students.

Complimenting this safeguard is the "stay put" provision. When changes in the education plan or related services are being considered, IDEA states:

> Except as provided in subsection 20 U.S.C. § 1415(k)(7), during the pendency of any proceedings conducted pursuant to this section, unless the State or local educational agency and the parents or guardians otherwise agree, the child shall remain in the then-current educational placement of such child, or if applying for initial admission to a public school, shall, with the consent of the parents, be placed

in the public school program until all such proceedings have been completed. 20 U.S.C. § 1415(j).

Finally, linked closely to the safeguards above is the manifestation hearing. Educators are required to conduct a manifestation hearing to determine whether any conduct for which a disabled child is being disciplined was a result of the student's disability. If school authorities decide to remove a child from the classroom, the IEP team must conduct a manifestation determination review within ten days of that decision. 20 U.S.C. § 1415 (k) (4). If the school determines that the behavior was not a manifestation of the child's disability, then the school may proceed to discipline the child as it would any other non-disabled student. 20 U.S.C. § 1415(k)(5). If the school determines that the behavior was connected to the child's disability, then the discipline imposed must comply with other IDEA rules and regulations. 20 U.S.C. § 1415(k)(1)-(2).

The cases below illustrate the relationship between these safeguards and the right of a disabled student to an appropriate education. How would you characterize the attitude of the judges as they apply the safeguards to a dispute? In whose favor should a judge resolve doubts about decisions involving placement of a student?

HONIG v. DOE

484 U.S. 305 (1988)

Justice BRENNAN delivered the opinion of the Court.

As a condition of federal financial assistance, the Education of the Handicapped Act requires States to ensure a "free appropriate public education" for all disabled children within their jurisdictions. In aid of this goal, the Act establishes a comprehensive system of procedural safeguards designed to ensure parental participation in decisions concerning the education of their disabled children and to provide administrative and judicial review of any decisions with which those parents disagree. Among these safeguards is the so-called "stay-put" provision, which directs that a disabled child "shall remain in [his or her] then current educational placement" pending completion of any review proceedings, unless the parents and state or local educational agencies otherwise agree. 20 U.S.C. § 1415(e)(3). Today we must decide whether, in the face of this statutory proscription, state or local school authorities may nevertheless unilaterally exclude disabled children from the classroom for dangerous or disruptive conduct growing out of their disabilities. In addition, we are called upon to decide whether a district court may, in the exercise of its equitable powers, order a State to provide educational services directly to a disabled child when the local agency fails to do so.

I

In the Education of the Handicapped Act (EHA or the Act), 84 Stat. 175, as amended, 20 U.S.C. § 1400 *et seq.*, Congress sought "to assure that all handicapped children have available to them ... a free appropriate public education which emphasizes special education and related services designed to meet their unique needs, [and] to assure that the rights of handicapped children and their parents or guardians are protected." § 1400(c). When the law was passed in 1975, Congress had before it ample evidence that such legislative assurances were sorely needed: 21 years after this Court declared education to be "perhaps the most important function of state and local governments," *Brown v. Bd. of Educ.*, 347 U.S. 483, 493, 74 S. Ct. 686, 691, 98 L. Ed. 873 (1954), congressional studies revealed that better than half of the Nation's 8 million disabled children were not receiving appropriate educational services. § 1400(b)(3). Indeed, one out of every eight of these children was excluded from the public school system altogether, § 1400(b)(4); many others were simply "warehoused" in special classes or were neglectfully shepherded through the system until they were old enough to drop out. *See* H.R. Rep. No. 94-332, p. 2 (1975). Among the most poorly served of disabled students were emotionally disturbed children: Congressional statistics revealed that for the school year immediately preceding passage of the Act, the educational needs of 82 percent of all children with emotional disabilities went unmet. *See* S. Rep. No. 94-168, p. 8 (1975), U.S. Code Cong. & Admin. News 1975, p. 1425 (hereinafter S. Rep.).

Although these educational failings resulted in part from funding constraints, Congress recognized that the problem reflected more than a lack of financial resources at the state and local levels. Two federal-court decisions, which the Senate Report characterized as "landmark," *see id.*, at 6, U.S. Code Cong. & Admin. News 1430, demonstrated that many disabled children were excluded pursuant to state statutes or local rules and policies, typically without any consultation with, or even notice to, their parents. *See Mills v. Bd. of Ed. of Dist. of Columbia,* 348 F. Supp. 866 (DC 1972); *Pennsylvania Assn. for Retarded Children v. Pennsylvania,* 334 F. Supp. 1257 (ED Pa. 1971), and 343 F. Supp. 279 (1972) (*PARC*). Indeed, by the time of the EHA's enactment, parents had brought legal challenges to similar exclusionary practices in 27 other States. *See* S. Rep., at 6.

In responding to these problems, Congress did not content itself with passage of a simple funding statute. Rather, the EHA confers upon disabled students an enforceable substantive right to public education in participating States, see *Bd. of Educ. of Hendrick Hudson Central Sch. Dist. v. Rowley,* 458 U.S. 176, 102 S. Ct. 3034, 73 L. Ed. 2d 690 (1982),[1] and conditions federal financial assistance upon a State's compliance with the substantive and procedural goals of the Act. Accordingly, States seeking to qualify for federal funds must develop policies assuring all disabled children the "right to a free appropriate public education," and must file with the Secretary of Education formal plans mapping out in detail the programs, procedures, and timetables under which they will effectuate

[1] Congress' earlier efforts to ensure that disabled students received adequate public education had failed in part because the measures it adopted were largely hortatory. In the 1966 amendments to the Elementary and Secondary Education Act of 1965, Congress established a grant program "for the purpose of assisting the States in the initiation, expansion, and improvement of programs and projects ... for the education of handicapped children." Pub. L. 89-750, § 161, 80 Stat. 1204. It repealed that program four years later and replaced it with the original version of the Education of the Handicapped Act, Pub. L. 91-230, 84 Stat. 175, Part B of which contained a similar grant program. Neither statute, however, provided specific guidance as to how States were to use the funds, nor did they condition the availability of the grants on compliance with any procedural or substantive safeguards. In amending the EHA to its present form, Congress rejected its earlier policy of "merely establish[ing] an unenforceable goal requiring all children to be in school." 121 Cong. Rec. 37417 (1975) (remarks of Sen. Schweiker). Today, all 50 States and the District of Columbia receive funding assistance under the EHA. U.S. Dept. of Education, Ninth Annual Report to Congress on Implementation of Education of the Handicapped Act (1987).

these policies. 20 U.S.C. §§ 1412(1), 1413(a). Such plans must assure that, "to the maximum extent appropriate," States will "mainstream" disabled children, *i.e.*, that they will educate them with children who are not disabled, and that they will segregate or otherwise remove such children from the regular classroom setting "only when the nature or severity of the handicap is such that education in regular classes ... cannot be achieved satisfactorily." § 1412(5).

The primary vehicle for implementing these congressional goals is the "individualized educational program" (IEP), which the EHA mandates for each disabled child. Prepared at meetings between a representative of the local school district, the child's teacher, the parents or guardians, and, whenever appropriate, the disabled child, the IEP sets out the child's present educational performance, establishes annual and short-term objectives for improvements in that performance, and describes the specially designed instruction and services that will enable the child to meet those objectives. § 1401(19). The IEP must be reviewed and, where necessary, revised at least once a year in order to ensure that local agencies tailor the statutorily required "free appropriate public education" to each child's unique needs. § 1414(a)(5).

Envisioning the IEP as the centerpiece of the statute's education delivery system for disabled children, and aware that schools had all too often denied such children appropriate educations without in any way consulting their parents, Congress repeatedly emphasized throughout the Act the importance and indeed the necessity of parental participation in both the development of the IEP and any subsequent assessments of its effectiveness. *See* §§ 1400(c), 1401(19), 1412(7), 1415(b)(1)(A), (C), (D), (E), and 1415(b)(2). Accordingly, the Act establishes various procedural safeguards that guarantee parents both an opportunity for meaningful input into all decisions affecting their child's education and the right to seek review of any decisions they think inappropriate. These safeguards include the right to examine all relevant records pertaining to the identification, evaluation, and educational placement of their child; prior written notice whenever the responsible educational agency proposes (or refuses) to change the child's placement or program; an opportunity to present complaints concerning any aspect of the local agency's provision of a free appropriate public education; and an opportunity for "an impartial due process hearing" with respect to any such complaints. §§ 1415(b)(1), (2).

At the conclusion of any such hearing, both the parents and the local educational agency may seek further administrative review and, where that proves unsatisfactory, may file a civil action in any state or federal court. §§ 1415(c), (e)(2). In addition to reviewing the administrative record, courts are empowered to take additional evidence at the request of either party and to "grant such relief as [they] determine is appropriate." § 1415(e)(2). The "stay-put" provision at issue in this case governs the placement of a child while these often lengthy review procedures run their course. It directs that:

> During the pendency of any proceedings conducted pursuant to [§ 1415], unless the State or local educational agency and the parents or guardian otherwise agree, the child shall remain in the then current educational placement of such child....

§ 1415(e)(3).

The present dispute grows out of the efforts of certain officials of the San Francisco Unified School District (SFUSD) to expel two emotionally disturbed children from school indefinitely for violent and disruptive conduct related to their disabilities. In November 1980, respondent John Doe assaulted another student at the Louise Lombard School, a developmental center for disabled children. Doe's April 1980 IEP identified him as a socially and physically awkward 17-year-old who experienced considerable difficulty controlling his impulses and anger. Among the goals set out in his IEP was "[i]mprovement in [his] ability to relate to [his] peers [and to] cope with frustrating situations without resorting to aggressive acts." App. 17. Frustrating situations, however, were an unfortunately prominent feature of Doe's school career: physical abnormalities, speech difficulties, and poor grooming habits had made him the target of teasing and ridicule as early as the first grade, *id.,* at 23; his 1980 IEP reflected his continuing difficulties with peers, noting that his social skills had deteriorated and that he could tolerate only minor frustration before exploding. *Id.,* at 15-16.

On November 6, 1980, Doe responded to the taunts of a fellow student in precisely the explosive manner anticipated by his IEP: he choked the student with sufficient force to leave abrasions on the child's neck, and kicked out a school window while being escorted to the principal's office afterwards. *Id.,* at 208. Doe admitted his misconduct and the school subsequently suspended him for five days. Thereafter, his principal referred the matter to the SFUSD Student Placement Committee (SPC or Committee) with the recommendation that Doe be expelled. On the day the suspension was to end, the SPC notified Doe's mother that it was proposing to exclude her child permanently from SFUSD and was therefore extending his suspension until such time as the expulsion proceedings were completed. The Committee further advised her that she was entitled to attend the November 25 hearing at which it planned to discuss the proposed expulsion.

After unsuccessfully protesting these actions by letter, Doe brought this suit against a host of local school officials and the State Superintendent of Public Instructions. Alleging that the suspension and proposed expulsion violated the EHA, he sought a temporary restraining order canceling the SPC hearing and requiring school officials to convene an IEP meeting. The District Judge granted the requested injunctive relief and further ordered defendants to provide home tutoring for Doe on an interim basis; shortly thereafter, she issued a preliminary injunction directing defendants to return Doe to his then current educational placement at Louise Lombard School pending completion of the IEP review process. Doe reentered school on December 15, 5 1/2 weeks, and 24 school-days, after his initial suspension.

Respondent Jack Smith was identified as an emotionally disturbed child by the time he entered the second grade in 1976. School records prepared that year indicated that he was unable "to control verbal or physical outburst[s]" and exhibited a "[s]evere disturbance in relationships with peers and adults." *Id.* at 123. Further evaluations subsequently revealed that he had been physically and emotionally abused as an infant and young child and that, despite above average intelligence, he experienced academic and social difficulties as a result of extreme hyperactivity and low self-esteem. *Id.* at 136, 139, 155, 176. Of particular concern was Smith's propensity for verbal hostility; one evaluator noted that the child reacted to stress by "attempt [ing] to cover his feelings of low self worth through aggressive behavior [,] ... primarily verbal provocations." *Id.* at 136.

Based on these evaluations, SFUSD placed Smith in a learning center for emotionally disturbed children. His grandparents, however, believed that his needs would be better served in the public school setting and, in September 1979, the school district acceded to their requests and enrolled him at A.P. Giannini Middle School. His February 1980 IEP recommended placement in a Learning Disability Group, stressing the need for close supervision and a highly structured environment. *Id.* at 111. Like earlier evaluations, the February 1980 IEP noted that Smith was easily distracted, impulsive, and anxious; it therefore proposed a half-day schedule and suggested that the placement be undertaken on a trial basis. *Id.* at 112, 115.

At the beginning of the next school year, Smith was assigned to a full-day program; almost immediately thereafter he began misbehaving. School officials met twice with his grandparents in October 1980 to discuss returning him to a half-day program; although the grandparents agreed to the reduction, they apparently were never apprised of their right to challenge the decision through EHA procedures. The school officials also warned them that if the child continued his disruptive behavior-which included stealing, extorting money from fellow students, and making sexual comments to female classmates-they would seek to expel him. On November 14, they made good on this threat, suspending Smith for five days after he made further lewd comments. His principal referred the matter to the SPC, which recommended exclusion from SFUSD. As it did in John Doe's case, the Committee scheduled a hearing and extended the suspension indefinitely pending a final disposition in the matter. On November 28, Smith's counsel protested these actions on grounds essentially identical to those raised by Doe, and the SPC agreed to cancel the hearing and to return Smith to a half-day program at A.P. Giannini or to provide home tutoring. Smith's grandparents chose the latter option and the school began home instruction on December 10; on January 6, 1981, an IEP team convened to discuss alternative placements.

After learning of Doe's action, Smith sought and obtained leave to intervene in the suit. The District Court subsequently entered summary judgment in favor of respondents on their EHA claims and issued a permanent injunction. In a series of decisions, the District Judge found that the proposed expulsions and indefinite suspensions of respondents for conduct attributable to their disabilities deprived them of their congressionally mandated right to a free appropriate public education, as well as their right to have that education provided in accordance with the procedures set out in the EHA. The District Judge therefore permanently enjoined the school district from taking any disciplinary action other than a 2- or 5-day suspension against any disabled child for disability-related misconduct, or from effecting any other change in the educational placement of any such child without parental consent pending completion of any EHA proceedings. In addition, the judge barred the State from authorizing unilateral placement changes and directed it to establish an EHA compliance-monitoring system or, alternatively, to enact guidelines governing local school responses to disability-related misconduct. Finally, the judge ordered the State to provide services directly to disabled children when, in any individual case, the State determined that the local educational agency was unable or unwilling to do so.

On appeal, the Court of Appeals for the Ninth Circuit affirmed the orders with slight modifications. *Doe v. Maher,* 793 F.2d 1470 (1986).

Petitioner Bill Honig, California Superintendent of Public Instruction, sought review in this Court, claiming that the Court of Appeals' construction of the stay-put provision conflicted with that of several other Courts of Appeals which had recognized a dangerousness exception, compare Doe v. Maher, supra, (case below), with Jackson v. Franklin County Sch. Bd., 765 F.2d 535, 538 (CA5 1985); Victoria L. v. Dist. Sch. Bd. of Lee County, Fla., 741 F.2d 369, 374 (CA11 1984); S-1 v. Turlington, 635 F.2d 342, 348, n. 9 (CA5), cert. denied, 454 U.S. 1030, 102 S. Ct. 566, 70 L. Ed. 2d 473 (1981), and that the direct services ruling placed an intolerable burden on the State. We granted certiorari to resolve these questions, 479 U.S. 1084, 107 S. Ct. 1284, 94 L. Ed. 2d 142 (1987), and now affirm.

……

III

The language of § 1415(e)(3) is unequivocal. It states plainly that during the pendency of any proceedings initiated under the Act, unless the state or local educational agency and the parents or guardian of a disabled child otherwise agree, "the child shall remain in the then current educational placement." § 1415(e)(3) (emphasis added). Faced with this clear directive, petitioner asks us to read a "dangerousness" exception into the stay-put provision on the basis of either of two essentially inconsistent assumptions: first, that Congress thought the residual authority of school officials to exclude dangerous students from the classroom too obvious for comment; or second, that Congress inadvertently failed to provide such authority and this Court must therefore remedy the oversight. Because we cannot accept either premise, we decline petitioner's invitation to rewrite the statute.

Petitioner's arguments proceed, he suggests, from a simple, commonsense proposition: Congress could not have intended the stay-put provision to be read literally, for such a construction leads to the clearly unintended, and untenable, result that school districts must return violent or dangerous students to school while the often lengthy EHA proceedings run their course. We think it clear, however, that Congress very much meant to strip schools of the *unilateral* authority they had traditionally employed to exclude disabled students, particularly emotionally disturbed students, from school. In so doing, Congress did not leave school administrators powerless to deal with dangerous students; it did, however, deny school officials their former right to "self-help," and directed that in the future the removal of disabled students could be accomplished only with the permission of the parents or, as a last resort, the courts.

As noted above, Congress passed the EHA after finding that school systems across the country had excluded one out of every eight disabled children from classes. In drafting the law, Congress was largely guided by the recent decisions in *Mills v. Bd. of Educ. of District of Columbia,* 348 F. Supp. 866 (1972), and *PARC,* 343 F. Supp. 279 (1972), both of which involved the exclusion of hard-to-handle disabled students. *Mills* in particular demonstrated the extent to which schools used disciplinary measures to bar children from the classroom. There, school officials had labeled four of the seven minor plaintiffs "behavioral problems," and had excluded them from classes without providing any alternative education to them or any notice to their parents. 348 F. Supp., at 869-70. After finding that this practice was not limited to the named plaintiffs but affected in one way or another an estimated class of 12,000 to 18,000 disabled students, *id.* at 868-69, 875, the District Court enjoined future exclusions, suspensions, or expulsions "on grounds of discipline." *Id.* at 880.

Congress attacked such exclusionary practices in a variety of ways. It required participating States to educate *all* disabled children, regardless of the severity of their disabilities, 20 U.S.C. § 1412(2)(C), and included within the definition of "handicapped" those children with serious emotional disturbances. § 1401(1). It further provided for meaningful parental participation in all aspects of a child's educational placement, and barred schools, through the stay-put provision, from changing that placement over the parent's objection until all review proceedings were completed. Recognizing that those proceedings might prove long and tedious, the Act's drafters did not intend § 1415(e)(3) to operate inflexibly, *see* 121 Cong. Rec. 37412 (1975) (remarks of Sen. Stafford), and they therefore allowed for interim placements where parents and school officials are able to agree on one. Conspicuously absent from § 1415(e)(3), however, is any emergency exception for dangerous students. This absence is all the more telling in light of the injunctive decree issued in *PARC,* which permitted school officials unilaterally to remove students in "'extraordinary circumstances.'" 343 F. Supp., at 301. Given the lack of any similar exception in *Mills,* and the close attention Congress devoted to these "landmark" decisions, *see* S. Rep., at 6, U.S. Code Cong. & Admin. News p. 1430, we can only conclude that the omission was intentional; we are therefore not at liberty to engraft onto the statute an exception Congress chose not to create.

Our conclusion that § 1415(e)(3) means what it says does not leave educators hamstrung. The Department of Education has observed that, "[w]hile the [child's] placement may not be changed [during any complaint proceeding], this does not preclude the agency from using its normal procedures for dealing with children who are endangering themselves or others." Comment following 34 CFR § 300. 513 (1987). Such procedures may include the use of study carrels, timeouts, detention, or the restriction of privileges. More drastically, where a student poses an immediate threat to the safety of others, officials may temporarily suspend him or her for up to 10 schooldays. This authority, which respondent in no way disputes, not only ensures that school administrators can protect the safety of others by promptly removing the most dangerous of students, it also provides a "cooling down" period during which officials can initiate IEP review and seek to persuade the child's parents to agree to an interim placement. And in those cases in which the parents of a truly dangerous child adamantly refuse to permit any change in placement, the 10-day respite gives school officials an opportunity to invoke the aid of the courts under § 1415(e)(2), which empowers courts to grant any appropriate relief.

. . . .

In short, then, we believe that school officials are entitled to seek injunctive relief under § 1415(e)(2) in appropriate cases. In any such action, § 1415(e)(3) effectively creates a presumption in favor of the child's current educational placement which school officials can overcome only by showing that maintaining the child in his or her current placement is substantially likely to result in injury either to himself or herself, or to others. In the present case, we are satisfied that the District Court, in enjoining the state and local defendants from indefinitely suspending respondent or otherwise unilaterally altering his then current placement, properly balanced respondent's interest in receiving a free appropriate public education in accordance with the procedures and requirements of the EHA against the interests of the state and local school officials in maintaining a safe learning environment for all their students.

IV

We believe the courts below properly construed and applied § 1415(e)(3), except insofar as the Court of Appeals held that a suspension in excess of 10 schooldays does not constitute a "change in placement." We therefore affirm the Court of Appeals' judgment on this issue as modified herein. Because we are equally divided on the question whether a court may order a State to provide services directly to a disabled child where the local agency has failed to do so, we affirm the Court of Appeals' judgment on this issue as well.

M.C. v. ANTELOPE VALLEY UNION HIGH SCHOOL

858 F.3d 1189 (9th Cir. 2017)

KOZINSKI, Circuit Judge:

The Individuals with Disabilities Education Act ("IDEA") guarantees children with disabilities a free appropriate public education ("FAPE"). 20 U.S.C. § 1400(d)(1)(A). We consider the interplay between the IDEA's procedural and substantive safeguards.

BACKGROUND

M.C. suffers from Norrie Disease, a genetic disorder that renders him blind. He also has a host of other deficits that cause him developmental delays in all academic areas. M.C.'s mother, M.N., met with several school administrators and instructors to discuss M.C.'s educational challenges and draft an individualized educational program ("IEP"). At the conclusion of this meeting, she signed an IEP document and "authorize[d] the goals and services but [did] not agree it provides a FAPE."

M.N. then filed a due process complaint alleging that the Antelope Valley Union High School District (the "District") committed procedural and substantive violations of the IDEA. The due process hearing took place before an Administrative Law Judge who denied all of M.C.'s claims and the district court affirmed.

……

I. STANDARD OF REVIEW

Judicial review in IDEA cases "differs substantially from judicial review of other agency actions, in which courts are generally confined to the administrative record and are held to a highly deferential standard of review." Ojai Unified Sch. Dist. v. Jackson, 4 F.3d 1467, 1471 (9th Cir. 1993). We review whether the state has provided a FAPE de novo. Union Sch. Dist. v. Smith, 15 F.3d 1519, 1524 (9th Cir. 1994). We can accord some deference to the ALJ's factual findings, but only where they are "thorough and careful," and "the extent of deference to be given is within our discretion." Id. (citations omitted).

The district court accorded the ALJ's findings substantial deference because the ALJ "questioned witnesses during a three-day hearing" and "wrote a 21-page opinion that reviewed the qualifications of witnesses and culled relevant details from the record." But neither the duration of the hearing, nor the ALJ's active involvement, nor the length of the ALJ's opinion can ensure that the ALJ was "thorough and careful."[1] J.W. ex rel. J.E.W. v. Fresno Unified Sch. Dist., 626 F.3d 431, 440 (9th Cir. 2010). And, in this case, the ALJ was neither thorough nor careful. As plaintiffs point out, the ALJ didn't address all issues and disregarded some of the evidence presented at the hearing. Even the district court recognized that the ALJ's analysis "is not entirely satisfying." Accordingly, the district court erred in deferring to the ALJ's findings.

[1] In Timothy O. v. Paso Robles Unified Sch. Dist., for example, we reversed a lengthy ALJ opinion with detailed findings that were unsupported by the record. 822 F.3d 1105, 1117, 1123 (9th Cir. 2016). The district court nevertheless had deferred to the ALJ's findings, apparently impressed by the length and superficial plausibility of the ALJ's opinion. Id. at Dist. Ct. Dkt. No. 78. Such blind deference is not appropriate. Rather, the district judge must actually examine the record to determine whether it supports the ALJ's opinion. See, e.g., J.G. ex rel. Jimenez v. Baldwin Park Unified Sch. Dist., 78 F.Supp.3d 1268, 1281–82 (C.D. Cal. 2015) (Olguin, J.) (according "substantially less deference" where "the ALJ's decision ignore[d] and mischaracterize[d] key evidence").

II. PROCEDURAL VIOLATIONS

The IDEA contains numerous procedural safeguards that are designed to protect the rights of disabled children and their parents. See 20 U.S.C. § 1415. These safeguards are a central feature of the IDEA process, not a mere afterthought: "Congress placed every bit as much emphasis upon compliance with procedures giving parents and guardians a large measure of participation at every stage of the administrative process as it did upon the measurement of the resulting IEP against a substantive standard." Rowley, 458 U.S. at 205, 102 S.Ct. 3034. Because disabled children and their parents are generally not represented by counsel during the IEP process, procedural errors at that stage are particularly likely to be prejudicial and cause the loss of educational benefits.

Therefore, compliance with the IDEA's procedural safeguards "is essential to ensuring that every eligible child receives a FAPE, and those procedures which provide for meaningful parent participation are particularly important." Amanda J. v. Clark Cty. Sch. Dist., 267 F.3d 877, 891 (9th Cir. 2001). "Procedural violations that interfere with parental participation in the IEP formulation process undermine the very essence of the IDEA." Id. at 892.

Plaintiffs allege that the District violated the IDEA by (1) failing to adequately document the services provided by a teacher of the visually impaired ("TVI"), (2) failing to specify the assistive technology ("AT") devices provided and (3) failing to file a response to the due process complaint.

A. Failure to Adequately Document TVI Services

Plaintiffs claim that the District didn't provide a " 'written record of reasonable expectations' to hold the District accountable for the provision of vision services to M.C." (quoting Amanda J., 267 F.3d at 891). A brief history of the District's shifting offer of TVI services is necessary: The IEP document signed by M.N. and the District included an offer of 240 minutes of TVI services per month. According to the District, it realized a week later this was a mistake. But the District did nothing to notify M.N. More than a month later, the District purported to unilaterally amend the IEP by changing the offer of TVI services to 240 minutes per week. The District didn't send M.N. a copy of the revised IEP or otherwise notify her of this change. In fact, she didn't learn of it until the first day of the due process hearing, a month later. Moreover, at the hearing, District witnesses testified that the District offered M.C. 300 minutes of TVI services per week.

Plaintiffs claim that the District's failure to accurately document the offer of TVI services denied M.C. a FAPE by precluding M.N. from meaningfully participating in the IEP process.

……

2. The IEP is a "formal, written offer [that] creates a clear record that will do much to eliminate troublesome factual disputes ... about when placements were offered, what placements were offered, and what additional education assistance was offered to supplement a placement, if any." Union Sch. Dist., 15 F.3d at 1526. The IEP must specify "the anticipated frequency, location, and duration of [education] services." 20 U.S.C § 1414(d)(1)(A)(i)(VII). Such "a formal, specific offer from a school district will greatly assist parents in 'present[ing] complaints with respect to any matter relating to the ... educational placement of the child.' " Union Sch. Dist., 15 F.3d at 1526 (quoting 20 U.S.C. § 1415(b)(1)(E)).

The district judge agreed with the ALJ's finding "that the September 17, 2012 Amendment merely corrected an unintentional error in the August 2, 2012 IEP." We fail to see how this can be so. An IEP, like a contract, may not be changed unilaterally. It embodies a binding commitment and provides notice to both parties as to what services will be provided to the student during the period covered by the IEP. If the District discovered that the IEP did not reflect its understanding of the parties' agreement, it was required to notify M.N. and seek her consent for any amendment. See 20 U.S.C. § 1414(d)(3)(D), (F) (discussing amendments to the IEP). Absent such consent, the District was bound by the IEP as written unless it sought to re-open the IEP process and proposed a different IEP.

Because the District did neither of these things, the IEP actually in force at the time of the hearing was that signed by the parties, not that presented by the District as the amended IEP. Allowing the District to change the IEP unilaterally undermines its function of giving notice of the services the school district has agreed to provide and measuring the student's progress toward the goals outlined in the IEP. Moreover, any such unilateral amendment is a per se procedural violation of the IDEA because it vitiates the parents' right to participate at every step of the IEP drafting process.[4]

[4] The District's purported amendment was also improper for a separate reason: The District presented no evidence supporting its claim that the parties agreed to 240 minutes of TVI services per week when the IEP was drafted. Indeed, it is unclear how the District came up with this figure given that its witnesses at the hearing testified that M.C. was actually provided 300 minutes of TVI services per week. Nevertheless, the ALJ and the district court accepted this as true. However, a party's mere allegations are not proof.

……

Because the District denied M.N. an opportunity to participate in the IEP drafting process by unilaterally revising the IEP, and because the IEP as initially drafted didn't provide M.N. with an accurate offer of the TVI services provided to M.C., the District committed two procedural violations of the IDEA. Union Sch. Dist., 15 F.3d at 1526. The district court nevertheless found that M.C. wasn't denied a FAPE, reasoning that "[a] procedural violation denies a child a FAPE when the violation seriously infringe[s] the parents' opportunity to participate in the IEP formation process." (emphasis in original) (internal quotation and citation omitted). But, as explained above, M.N. was denied an opportunity to participate in the IEP drafting process. Moreover, in enacting the IDEA, Congress was as concerned with parental participation in the enforcement of the IEP as it was in its formation. See Rowley, 458 U.S. at 205, 102 S.Ct. 3034 (discussing Congress's intent to "giv[e] parents and guardians a large measure of participation at every stage of the administrative process" (emphasis added)). Under the IDEA, parental participation doesn't end when the parent signs the IEP. Parents must be able to use the IEP to monitor and enforce the services that their child is to receive. When a parent is unaware of the services offered to the student—and, therefore, can't monitor how these services are provided—a FAPE has been denied, whether or not the parent had ample opportunity to participate in the formulation of the IEP.

Whether, and to what extent, M.C. was prejudiced by these procedural improprieties is a more difficult question. Assuming that M.C. was receiving 300 minutes of TVI services per week, as the District apparently intended to offer, M.C. may not have suffered any substantive harm. M.N. nevertheless suffered procedural harm by not being apprised of the actual status of the services being provided, causing her to incur legal fees in attempting to protect that right. Because any TVI services provided beyond what was specified in the written IEP would have been gratuitous, M.N. could not be sure that the District would continue to provide them. With only 240 minutes per month (about an hour a week) specified in the IEP, the District was entitled to cut back these services to that level. M.N. was amply justified in seeking the aid of counsel to clarify the amount of services provided. Incurring unnecessary legal fees is, of course, a form of prejudice that denies a student and his parents an educational benefit. See Parents on Behalf of Student v. Julian Charter Sch., OAH No. 2012100933, at 2 (Jan. 17, 2013) (order denying motion to dismiss). The fact that the District could have avoided the harm by promptly notifying M.N. that it was agreeing to provide far more services than specified in the IEP only makes matters worse.

B. Failure to Identify the AT Devices Provided

When a student requires "a particular device or service" California requires that the IEP "include a statement to that effect." Cal. Educ. Code § 56341.1(b)(5), (c). M.C.'s IEP initially indicated that M.C. didn't require AT devices or services. The District conceded that this was erroneous and issued an amendment that changed the checkbox for AT devices from "no" to "yes." But neither the IEP nor the amendment specified the devices that M.C. required.

The district judge recognized that "the language of [section 56341.1] requires the District to identify the particular types of AT devices and services to be provided to M.C." But the judge found that this procedural violation didn't "seriously infringe[ ] M.N.'s opportunity to participate in the IEP formulation process." As we've made clear, however, parents must be able to participate in both the formulation and enforcement of the IEP. See supra at 1197–98. Even if M.N. was able to participate in the IEP's formulation, the District's failure to identify the AT devices that M.C. required rendered the IEP useless as a blueprint for enforcement.

The district judge noted that the IEP team discussed "at least some of the AT services and equipment to be provided to M.C." at the IEP meeting. But a discussion does not amount to an offer. M.N. could force the District to provide only those services and devices listed in the IEP, not those discussed at the IEP meeting but left out of the IEP document. See Union Sch. Dist., 15 F.3d at 1526 (requiring a "formal, written offer"). Indeed, items discussed at the IEP meeting but not included in the IEP document could be deemed to have been omitted on purpose.

Nor was this a case where "everyone involved in the individualized education team—including [the student's] parents—knew of the amounts [of services]" that were offered. J.L., 592 F.3d at 953. M.N. testified at the due process hearing that she didn't know which AT devices were offered to M.C. M.C.'s TVI services provider testified that M.C. received a laptop, a Book Port, software developed for the visually impaired, a screen reading program, a talking calculator and an Eye-Pal Solo. But M.N. was only aware that M.C. received a laptop, braille machine, braille calendar and a Book Port. M.N. also testified that the laptop didn't have the software that M.C. needed, but she didn't know which software was missing. Because the IEP didn't specify which AT devices were being offered, M.N. had no way of confirming whether they were actually being provided to M.C. The District's failure to specify the AT devices that were provided to M.C. thus infringed M.N.'s opportunity to participate in the IEP process and denied M.C. a FAPE. Id. at 953.

C. Failure to Respond to the Complaint

The IDEA requires a school district to respond to a parent's due process complaint within 10 days. 20 U.S.C. §§ 1415(c)(2)(B)(i)(I) & 1415(c)(2)(B)(ii). The District failed to do this and plaintiffs argue that this violated the IDEA. To be clear, the District didn't just miss a deadline: It failed to ever respond to the complaint. The district court found that the failure to respond didn't infringe M.N.'s opportunity to participate in the IEP formulation process and, therefore, wasn't a denial of a FAPE. But this misses the mark. The District's failure to respond may not have denied plaintiffs a FAPE but it still violated the IDEA and due process.

Like an answer to a complaint, a response serves an important dual purpose: It gives notice of the issues in dispute and binds the answering party to a position. See, e.g., United States v. All Assets Held at Bank Julius Baer & Co., 959 F.Supp.2d 81, 116 n.21 (D.D.C. 2013) (noting that "one function of an answer" is to identify "points of disagreement"); Lopez v. U.S. Fidelity & Guaranty Co., 18 F.R.D. 59, 61 (D. Alaska 1955) (explaining that the purpose of rules governing answers to a complaint "is to prevent surprise"). Failure to file a response puts the opposing party at a serious disadvantage in preparing for the hearing, as it must guess what defenses the opposing party will raise. The problem is particularly severe in IDEA cases because there is no discovery.

When a school district fails to file a timely response, the ALJ must not go forward with the hearing. Rather, it must order a response and shift the cost of the delay to the school district, regardless of who is ultimately the prevailing party. We remand for a determination of the prejudice M.N. suffered as a result of the District's failure to respond and the award of appropriate compensation therefor.

III. SUBSTANTIVE VIOLATIONS

In order for M.C. to have received a FAPE, the IEP must have "(1) addresse[d] [his] unique needs, (2) provide[d] adequate support services so [M.C.] can take advantage of the educational opportunities, and (3) [been] in accord with the individualized education program." Capistrano Unified Sch. Dist. v. Wartenberg, 59 F.3d 884, 893 (9th Cir. 1995) (citing Rowley, 458 U.S. at 188–89, 102 S.Ct. 3034).

……

1. We remand so the District can have an opportunity to make such a showing before the district court.

2. Plaintiffs also claim that the District denied M.C. a FAPE by failing to develop measurable goals in all areas of need, including "the areas of life skills, residential travel, and business travel." Additionally, plaintiffs argue that the District failed to provide adequate orientation and mobility services, as well as adequate social skills instruction. The district court found that plaintiffs failed to meet their burden of showing that the IEP wasn't "reasonably calculated to confer [M.C.] with a meaningful benefit." J.W., 626 F.3d at 439. In doing so, it relied on the Supreme Court's comment in Rowley that, by "an 'appropriate' education, it is clear that [Congress] did not mean a potential-maximizing education." 458 U.S. at 197 n.21, 102 S.Ct. 3034. But Rowley "d[id] not attempt to establish any one test for determining the adequacy of educational benefits." Id. at 202, 102 S.Ct. 3034. Recently, the Supreme Court clarified Rowley and provided a more precise standard for evaluating whether a school district has complied substantively with the IDEA: "To meet its substantive obligation under the IDEA, a school must offer an IEP reasonably calculated to enable a child to make progress appropriate in light of the child's circumstances." Endrew F., at ——, 137 S.Ct. 988. In other words, the school must implement an IEP that is reasonably calculated to remediate and, if appropriate, accommodate the child's disabilities so that the child can "make progress in the general education curriculum," id. at ——, 137 S.Ct. 988 (citation omitted), taking into account the progress of his non-disabled peers, and the child's potential. We remand so the district court can consider plaintiffs' claims in light of this new guidance from the Supreme Court.

REVERSED and REMANDED.

Notes and Comments

1. Special Education Students, Discipline and School Safety

When a special education student commits an act on campus that is disruptive, the misconduct may violate both the campus code of conduct and state law. A range of acts (assaults, threats, thefts, truancy, possession, sale and use of drugs, etc.) may create the need to quickly address the behavior through both the IEP and the juvenile justice system. When the juvenile justice system is focused on a special education student, the requirements of IDEA may not apply at all. The provisions of IDEA apply only to school districts that take federal education funding. Other state and local agencies that exist to provide services to juveniles with special needs are beyond the reach of IDEA. However, many of these agencies collaborate with educators in serving the same children.

In 1997, Congress amended the special education laws to clarify the role of the juvenile justice system and to give educators a school safety exception to the stay-put rules. The changes provide that:

> 1. Educators may, without triggering a change in a child's educational placement, suspend a child with a disability for up to ten days without having to provide for an alternative educational setting. 20 U.S.C. § 1415 (k)(1)(A).
>
> 2. Educators are not exempt from reporting criminal conduct by a child with a disability to the appropriate authorities. 20 U.S.C. § 1415(k)(9)(A).
>
>> Nothing in this subchapter shall be construed to prohibit an agency from reporting a crime committed by a child with a disability to appropriate authorities or to prevent State law enforcement and judicial authorities from exercising their responsibilities with regard to the application of Federal and State law to crimes committed by a child with a disability 20 U.S.C. § 1415(k)(9)(A). *See also* 34 C.F.R. § 300.529.

2. Stay-Put Discipline Quiz

Test your "Stay-Put IQ" on the following scenarios.

> a. A teacher at a high school approaches the principal to report what the teacher thought was a drug transaction. The teacher identifies two participants, one of whom is a special education student. The students are taken to the principal, who determines through questioning that the special education student was attempting to sell drugs. The principal then calls the SRO. Once the SRO arrives, the principal questions and searches the students. The special education student is found with two homemade pipes and two small packages of marijuana. The SRO arrests him and files a petition of delinquency for possession of marijuana in school. The Parents file a lawsuit claiming that the Juvenile Court proceedings constitute an illegal change in educational placement under the special education laws. Are the parents correct? *See Commonwealth vs. Nathaniel N.*, 764 N.E. 2d 883, 886-87 (Mass. App. Ct. 2002)
>
> b. A 14-year-old special education student, with an Individualized Education Plan ("IEP"), approaches a teacher's desk, and searches through papers on the desk. The teacher tells the student to stop. The student picks up a student desk and moves

toward the teacher, as if to strike her. Other educators intervene. School officials call the police and have the student arrested. The student is placed in a holding cell, where he remains for over twenty hours while juvenile proceedings begin. Do the special education laws allow this? *See Valentino C. v. School District of Philadelphia*, 2004 U.S. Dist. LEXIS 2114 (E.D. PA. 2004)

c. A high school student is diagnosed with Attention Deficit Hyperactivity Disorder (ADHS) and begins taking medication. Educators are told of the student's condition. Unfortunately, the student is often disruptive on campus. The SRO begins arresting the student after each incident. On one occasion, the student was charged with disorderly conduct for tapping his feet and fingers and being disruptive in class. On other occasion, he was charged with disorderly conduct for hitting another student with a rubber band, leaving a welt. In yet another incident, the student was charged with assault after throwing a bottle that struck another student. The parents file a lawsuit claiming that by assisting the school officials the police interfered with the student's educational rights in violation of federal law. Are the parents correct? *See S.A.S. v. Hibbing Public Schools*, 2005 U.S. Dist. LEXIS 46649 (D. Minn. 2005)

d. A special education student at a public high school started a small fire in the school cafeteria. The school notified the police, who arrest the student and a delinquency petition is filed. The student is incarcerated at a juvenile detention facility because of the incident. The student's IEP is based on an evaluation which concludes that the he has a "significant history of aggressive behavior with peers and is prone to starting fires." His parents file a lawsuit claiming that the arrest violated special education laws. The Parents claim that educators must conduct a manifestation determination review before notifying the authorities where a disabled child commits a crime. Are the parents correct? *See Joseph M. v. Southeast Delco School District*, 2001 U.S. Dist. 2994, 2001 WL 283154 (E.D.PA. 2001)

3. IDEA Discipline Checklist

Terry Jean Seligmann, has devised an eight step checklist for determining appropriate discipline for special education students.

Step 1. Is This a "Child with a Disability"?

If yes, continue to Step 2. If no, does the school have prior knowledge of a disability? The school may have prior knowledge from a parent's written concern, the student's behavior or performance, a request for an evaluation, or school personnel's expressions of concern. However, if the child has been evaluated as not having a disability, or a decision was made not to evaluate, these facts are not viewed as creating prior knowledge. If no, is the parent requesting an evaluation? If so, conduct an expedited evaluation, with the child remaining in school-authority determined placement. If the evaluation shows a child with a disability, continue to Step 2.

Step 2. Is Removal the Appropriate Disciplinary Action?
Steps such as study carrels, time outs, privilege restrictions, and in-school suspensions may be used, if not contrary to the child's IEP.

Step 3. Is the Disciplinary Action a Removal of Less than Ten Days?
If the action is a removal of less than ten days, and the child has not been removed from school for more than ten days cumulatively in the school year, school authorities may remove the child without providing services. If the removal is for less than ten days, but the student will have been removed from school for a cumulative total of ten school days in the year, school authorities and the special education teacher decide on the services t be provided during the removal. In addition, the IEP team should prepare a behavioral plan (Step 6). If the removal is less than ten days, but the child was previously removed for more than ten days and has a behavioral plan, IEP team members should review it (no meeting required). A removal of less than ten days is not considered a change in placement unless it is part of a pattern of suspensions which cumulatively exceed ten days in a school year and amount to a change in placement. If the action is removal for more than ten days, it is considered a change in placement.

Step 4. Is the Conduct a Weapon or Drug Offense?
If so, school authorities may place the child in an interim alternative placement, determined by the IEP team, for up to forty-five days. School authorities may immediately remove the child for less than ten days, followed by an IEP-determined alternative placement.

Step 5. Is the Child Dangerous to Himself or Others in His Current Placement?
If school authorities can demonstrate that it is substantially likely the child will injure himself or others if he stays in his current placement, they may seek an expedited hearing and an order from a hearing officer for an alternative educational placement of forty-five days, and may repeat the process as necessary. The United States district court also has authority in cases of dangerousness. School authorities may immediately remove the child for less than ten days and seek an order for an alternative educational placement.

Step 6. Does the Child Need a Behavioral Assessment and Plan?
For a child whose discipline is a change in placement (i.e., removal for more than ten days, a forty-five day alternative placement for weapon/drug offense, or an order for a forty-five day alternative placement based on dangerousness) or who has been removed from school for more than ten days in the school year, the IEP team should convene within ten days of the action to create or review a behavioral assessment and plan. The IEP team conducts a behavioral assessment, develops appropriate behavioral interventions, and implements the plan. If the child already has such a plan, the IEP team should review and modify it as necessary.

> Step 7. Is the Child's Conduct Related to His Disability?
> For a child whose discipline is a change in placement, the school must notify the parents of the decision on the date the action is taken and, within ten days, the IEP team must conduct a review, the manifestation determination, of the relationship between the child's disability and the behavior subject to disciplinary action. To find that the behavior is not related to the child's disability, the IEP team must determine that the IEP was appropriate and was being followed and that the child's disability did not prevent him from understanding or controlling his behavior. If the IEP team determines that the behavior was not related to the child's disability, the child may be disciplined as a non-disabled child, but with continuation of services which the IEP team determines will enable him to progress in the general curriculum and toward the goals of his IEP. If the child's behavior is determined to be related to his disability, the usual IEP and IDEA requirements apply to any proposed change in placement, with stay put provisions as set out in Step 8.
>
> Step 8. Does the Parent Contest the Placement or Manifestation Determination?
> If the child is in an interim alternative educational placement triggered by a weapon or drug offense, or ordered by the hearing officer based on dangerousness, this placement will be the stay put placement until the end of the prescribed period or the hearing officer's decision, whichever is sooner. After that, the last placement before the interim alternative educational placement will be the stay put placement, unless the expedited procedure for an order based on dangerousness is used. For other changes in placement, the usual stay put provisions apply, i.e., the last placement in effect before the contested change.

Terry Jean Seligmann, Not as Simple as ABC: Disciplining Children with Disabilities Under the 1997 IDEA Amendments, 42 Ariz. L. Rev. 77, 123-25 (2000). (Footnotes omitted).

4. Issues relating to the discipline of special education students are dynamic. For a good overview of the issue, see Perry A. Zirkel,, *Discipline of Students with Disabilities*, 235 Ed. Law Rprt. 1 (2008).

Part IV
Free Speech, Religion and the Right of Association

Chapter Ten
The First Amendment and Freedom of Speech

> First Amendment rights, applied in light of the special characteristics of the school environment, are available to teachers and students. It can hardly be argued that either students or teachers shed their constitutional rights to freedom of speech or expression at the schoolhouse gate. *Tinker v. Des Moines Independent Community School Dist.*, 393 U.S. 503 (1968).

The First Amendment protects expressive rights in a variety of context. Its provisions include protection for free speech, assembly, free exercise of religion, and prohibitions on establishment of religion. The decisions by the U.S. Supreme Court on First Amendment matters represent the vibrant core of American Constitutional Law. The expressive civil rights are essential to a working democracy such that they would be implied in the absence of a Bill of Rights. The quote above from the *Tinker* decision reflects a judicial commitment to apply these safeguards in the educational setting. As you read, the materials below you will be a judge of how well the courts have succeeded in doing so.

The outcomes of disputes over speech and expression vary widely with the context. If there is a common thread in free speech jurisprudence, it comes from *Tinker v. Des Moines Independent Community School Dist.*, 393 U.S. 503 (1968). The victorious, armband-wearing students in *Tinker* win the battle over that specific campus protest, but lose the war over a doctrine that protects students in other expressive contexts. After *Tinker*, a list of sorts emerges. First, modern doctrine is anchored to the authority of school officials to respond to disruptions in a manner that preserves the campus environment for learning. Second is the power of the education mission - the general authority of public educators to regulate expression consistent with legitimate pedagogical goals. Third, current free speech rules are tied to the public forum doctrine. The public-school campus is a nonpublic forum, giving school officials more control over the time, place, and manner of on-campus speech than off-campus expression.

As you read, each section, look for how the courts balance the desire for judicial deference against the search for abuse, bad faith, content discrimination and censorship unrelated to legitimate educational goals.

I. The Origins of Student Free Speech Rights

WEST VIRGINIA BOARD OF EDUCATION v. BARNETTE
319 U.S. 624 (1943)

MR. JUSTICE JACKSON delivered the opinion of the Court.

Following the decision by this Court on June 3, 1940, in *Minersville School District v. Gobitis*, 310 U.S. 586, the West Virginia legislature amended its statutes to require all schools therein to conduct courses of instruction in history, civics, and in the Constitutions of the United States and of the State "for the purpose of teaching, fostering and perpetuating the ideals, principles and spirit of Americanism, and increasing the knowledge of the organization and machinery of the government."

The Board of Education on January 9, 1942, adopted a resolution containing recitals taken largely from the Court's Gobitis opinion and ordering that the salute to the flag become "a regular part of the program of activities in the public schools," that all teachers and pupils "shall be required to participate in the salute honoring the Nation represented by the Flag; provided, however, that refusal to salute the Flag be regarded as an act of insubordination, and shall be dealt with accordingly." ...What is now required is the "stiff-arm" salute, the saluter to keep the right hand raised with palm turned up while the following is repeated:

> I pledge allegiance to the Flag of the United States of America and to the Republic for which it stands; one Nation, indivisible, with liberty and justice for all.

Failure to conform is "insubordination" dealt with by expulsion. Readmission is denied by statute until compliance. Meanwhile the expelled child is "unlawfully absent" and may be proceeded against as a delinquent. His parents or guardians are liable to prosecution, and if convicted are subject to fine not exceeding $50 and jail term not exceeding thirty days.

Appellees, citizens of the United States and of West Virginia, brought suit in the United States District Court for themselves and others similarly situated asking its injunction to restrain enforcement of these laws and regulations against Jehovah's Witnesses. ...Their religious beliefs include a literal version of Exodus, Chapter 20, verses 4 and 5, which says: "Thou shalt not make unto thee any graven image, or any likeness of anything that is in heaven above, or that is in the earth beneath, or that is in the water under the earth; thou shalt not bow down thyself to them nor serve them." They consider that the flag is an "image" within this command. For this reason they refuse to salute it.

.....

There is no doubt that, in connection with the pledges, the flag salute is a form of utterance. ... It is also to be noted that the compulsory flag salute and pledge requires affirmation of a belief and an attitude of mind.... It would seem that involuntary affirmation could be commanded only on even more immediate and urgent grounds than silence. But here the power of compulsion is invoked without any allegation that remaining passive during a flag salute ritual creates a clear and present danger that would justify an effort even to muffle expression. To sustain the compulsory flag salute we are required to say that a Bill of Rights which guards the individual's right to speak his own mind, left it open to public authorities to compel him to utter what is not in his mind.

Whether the First Amendment to the Constitution will permit officials to order observance of ritual of this nature does not depend upon whether as a voluntary exercise we would think it to be good, bad or merely innocuous. Any credo of nationalism is likely to include what some disapprove or to omit what others think essential, and to give off different overtones as it takes on different accents or interpretations. If official power exists to coerce acceptance of any patriotic creed, what it shall contain cannot be decided by courts, but must be largely discretionary with the ordaining authority, whose power to prescribe would no doubt include power to amend. Hence validity of the asserted power to force an American citizen publicly to profess any statement of belief or to engage in any ceremony of assent to one, presents questions of power that must be considered independently of any idea we may have as to the utility of the ceremony in question.

Nor does the issue as we see it turn on one's possession of particular religious views or the sincerity with which they are held. While religion supplies appellees' motive for enduring the discomforts of making the issue in this case, many citizens who do not share these religious views hold such a compulsory rite to infringe constitutional liberty of the individual. It is not necessary to inquire whether non-conformist beliefs will exempt from the duty to salute unless we first find power to make the salute a legal duty.

.....

The very purpose of a Bill of Rights was to withdraw certain subjects from the vicissitudes of political controversy, to place them beyond the reach of majorities and officials and to establish them as legal principles to be applied by the courts. One's right to life, liberty, and property, to free speech, a free press, freedom of worship and assembly, and other fundamental rights may not be submitted to vote; they depend on the outcome of no elections.

.....

National unity as an end which officials may foster by persuasion and example is not in question. The problem is whether under our Constitution compulsion as here employed is a permissible means for its achievement.

.....

The case is made difficult not because the principles of its decision are obscure but because the flag involved is our own. Nevertheless, we apply the limitations of the Constitution with no fear that freedom to be intellectually and spiritually diverse or even contrary will disintegrate the social organization. To believe that patriotism will not flourish if patriotic ceremonies are voluntary and spontaneous instead of a compulsory routine is to make an unflattering estimate of the appeal of our institutions to free minds.

If there is any fixed star in our constitutional constellation, it is that no official, high or petty, can prescribe what shall be orthodox in politics, nationalism, religion, or other matters of opinion or force citizens to confess by word or act their faith therein. If there are any circumstances which permit an exception, they do not now occur to us…We think the action of the local authorities in compelling the flag salute and pledge transcends constitutional limitations on their power and invades the sphere of intellect and spirit which it is the purpose of the First Amendment to our Constitution to reserve from all official control.

DISSENT: MR. JUSTICE FRANKFURTER, dissenting:

One who belongs to the most vilified and persecuted minority in history is not likely to be insensible to the freedoms guaranteed by our Constitution. Were my purely personal attitude relevant I should wholeheartedly associate myself with the general libertarian views in the Court's opinion, representing as they do the thought and action of a lifetime. …….. As a member of this Court I am not justified in writing my private notions of policy into the Constitution, no matter how deeply I may cherish them or how mischievous I may deem their disregard. ……. I cannot bring my mind to believe that the "liberty" secured by the Due Process Clause gives this Court authority to deny to the State of West Virginia the attainment of that which we all recognize as a legitimate legislative end, namely, the promotion of good citizenship, by employment of the means here chosen.

TINKER v. DES MOINES INDEPENDENT COMMUNITY SCHOOL DISTRICT

393 U.S. 503 (1968)

OPINION: MR. JUSTICE FORTAS delivered the opinion of the Court.

Petitioner John F. Tinker, 15 years old, and petitioner Christopher Eckhardt, 16 years old, attended high schools in Des Moines, Iowa. Petitioner Mary Beth Tinker, John's sister, was a 13-year-old student in junior high school.

In December 1965, a group of adults and students in Des Moines held a meeting at the Eckhardt home. The group determined to publicize their objections to the hostilities in Vietnam and their support for a truce by wearing black armbands during the holiday season and by fasting on December 16 and New Year's Eve. Petitioners and their parents had previously engaged in similar activities, and they decided to participate in the program.

The principals of the Des Moines schools became aware of the plan to wear armbands. On December 14, 1965, they met and adopted a policy that any student wearing an armband to school would be asked to remove it, and if he refused he would be suspended until he returned without the armband. Petitioners were aware of the regulation that the school authorities adopted.

On December 16, Mary Beth and Christopher wore black armbands to their schools. John Tinker wore his armband the next day. They were all sent home and suspended from school until they would come back without their armbands. They did not return to school until after the planned period for wearing armbands had expired—that is, until after New Year's Day.

I.

The District Court recognized that the wearing of an armband for the purpose of expressing certain views is the type of symbolic act that is within the Free Speech Clause of the First Amendment. As we shall discuss, the wearing of armbands in the circumstances of this case was entirely divorced from actually or potentially disruptive conduct by those participating in it. It was closely akin to "pure speech" which, we have repeatedly held, is entitled to comprehensive protection under the First Amendment.

First Amendment rights, applied in light of the special characteristics of the school environment, are available to teachers and students. It can hardly be argued that either students or teachers shed their constitutional rights to freedom of speech or expression at the schoolhouse gate. This has been the unmistakable holding of this Court for almost 50 years. In *Meyer v. Nebraska*, 262 U.S. 390 (1923), and *Bartels v. Iowa*, 262 U.S. 404 (1923), this Court, in opinions by Mr. Justice McReynolds, held that the Due Process Clause of the Fourteenth Amendment prevents States from forbidding the teaching of a foreign language to young students.

In *West Virginia v. Barnette*, *supra*, this Court held that under the First Amendment, the student in public school may not be compelled to salute the flag. Speaking through Mr. Justice Jackson, the Court said:

> The Fourteenth Amendment, as now applied to the States, protects the citizen against the State itself and all of its creatures—Boards of Education not excepted. These have, of course, important, delicate, and highly discretionary functions, but none that they may not perform within the limits of the Bill of Rights. That they are educating the young for citizenship is reason for scrupulous protection of Constitutional freedoms of the individual, if we are not to strangle the free mind at its source and teach youth to discount important principles of our government as mere platitudes. 319 U.S. at 637.

On the other hand, the Court has repeatedly emphasized the need for affirming the comprehensive authority of the States and of school officials, consistent with fundamental constitutional safeguards, to prescribe and control conduct in the schools. Our problem lies in the area where students in the exercise of First Amendment rights collide with the rules of the school authorities.

II.

The school officials banned and sought to punish petitioners for a silent, passive expression of opinion, unaccompanied by any disorder or disturbance on the part of petitioners. There is here no evidence whatever of petitioners' interference, actual or nascent, with the schools' work or of collision with the rights of other students to be secure and to be let alone. Accordingly, this case does not concern speech or action that intrudes upon the work of the schools or the rights of other students.

Only a few of the 18,000 students in the school system wore the black armbands. Only five students were suspended for wearing them. There is no indication that the work of the schools or any class was disrupted. Outside the classrooms, a few students made hostile remarks to the children wearing armbands, but there were no threats or acts of violence on school premises.

[I]n our system, undifferentiated fear or apprehension of disturbance is not enough to overcome the right to freedom of expression. Any departure from absolute regimentation may cause trouble. Any variation from the majority's opinion may inspire fear. Any word spoken, in class, in the lunchroom, or on the campus, that deviates from the views of another person may start an argument or cause a disturbance. But our Constitution says we must take this risk, and our history says that it is this sort of hazardous freedom—this kind of openness—that is the basis of our national strength and of the independence and vigor of Americans who grow up and live in this relatively permissive, often disputatious, society.

In order for the State in the person of school officials to justify prohibition of a particular expression of opinion, it must be able to show that its action was caused by something more than a mere desire to avoid the discomfort and unpleasantness that always accompany an unpopular viewpoint. Certainly where there is no finding and no showing that engaging in the forbidden conduct would "materially and substantially interfere with the requirements of appropriate discipline in the operation of the school," the prohibition cannot be sustained.

In the present case, the District Court made no such finding, and our independent examination of the record fails to yield evidence that the school authorities had reason to anticipate that the wearing of the armbands would substantially interfere with the work of the school or impinge upon the rights of other students. Even an official memorandum prepared after the suspension that listed the reasons for the ban on wearing the armbands made no reference to the anticipation of such disruption.[3]

On the contrary, the action of the school authorities appears to have been based upon an urgent wish to avoid the controversy which might result from the expression, even by the silent symbol of armbands, of opposition to this Nation's part in the conflagration in Vietnam. .... Clearly, the prohibition of expression of one particular opinion, at least without evidence that it is necessary to avoid material and substantial interference with schoolwork or discipline, is not constitutionally permissible.

In our system, state-operated schools may not be enclaves of totalitarianism. School officials do not possess absolute authority over their students. Students in school as well as out of school are "persons" under our Constitution. They are possessed of fundamental rights which the State must respect, just as they themselves must respect their obligations to the State. In our system, students may not be regarded

---

[3] The only suggestions of fear of disorder in the report are these:
"A former student of one of our high schools was killed in Viet Nam. Some of his friends are still in school and it was felt that if any kind of a demonstration existed, it might evolve into something which would be difficult to control."
"Students at one of the high schools were heard to say they would wear arm bands of other colors if the black bands prevailed."
Moreover, the testimony of school authorities at trial indicates that it was not fear of disruption that motivated the regulation prohibiting the armbands; the regulation was directed against "the principle of the demonstration" itself. School authorities simply felt that "the schools are no place for demonstrations," and if the students "didn't like the way our elected officials were handling things, it should be handled with the ballot box and not in the halls of our public schools."

as closed-circuit recipients of only that which the State chooses to communicate. They … cannot suppress "expressions of feelings with which they do not wish to contend."

A student's rights, therefore, do not embrace merely the classroom hours. When he is in the cafeteria, or on the playing field, or on the campus during the authorized hours, he may express his opinions, even on controversial subjects like the conflict in Vietnam, if he does so without "materially and substantially interfer[ing] with the requirements of appropriate discipline in the operation of the school" and without colliding with the rights of others. But conduct by the student, in class or out of it, which for any reason—whether it stems from time, place, or type of behavior—materially disrupts class work or involves substantial disorder or invasion of the rights of others is, of course, not immunized by the constitutional guarantee of freedom of speech.

…..

As we have discussed, the record does not demonstrate any facts which might reasonably have led school authorities to forecast substantial disruption of or material interference with school activities, and no disturbances or disorders on the school premises in fact occurred. These petitioners merely went about their ordained rounds in school. Their deviation consisted only in wearing on their sleeve a band of black cloth, not more than two inches wide. They wore it to exhibit their disapproval of the Vietnam hostilities and their advocacy of a truce, to make their views known, and, by their example, to influence others to adopt them. They neither interrupted school activities nor sought to intrude in the school affairs or the lives of others. They caused discussion outside of the classrooms, but no interference with work and no disorder. In the circumstances, our Constitution does not permit officials of the State to deny their form of expression.

Reversed and remanded.

CONCUR: MR. JUSTICE STEWART, concurring.

Although I agree with much of what is said in the Court's opinion, and with its judgment in this case, I cannot share the Court's uncritical assumption that, school discipline aside, the First Amendment rights of children are co-extensive with those of adults. Indeed, I had thought the Court decided otherwise just last Term in *Ginsberg v. New York*, 390 U.S. 629. I continue to hold the view I expressed in that case: "[A] State may permissibly determine that, at least in some precisely delineated areas, a child—like someone in a captive audience—is not possessed of that full capacity for individual choice which is the presupposition of First Amendment guarantees."

DISSENT: MR. JUSTICE BLACK, dissenting.

The Court's holding in this case ushers in what I deem to be an entirely new era in which the power to control pupils by the elected "officials of state supported public schools . . ." in the United States is in ultimate effect transferred to the Supreme Court. Here the constitutional right to "political expression" asserted was a right to wear black armbands during school hours and at classes in order to demonstrate to the other students that the petitioners were mourning because of the death of United States soldiers in Vietnam and to protest that war which they were against. Ordered to refrain from wearing the armbands in school by the elected school officials and the teachers vested with state authority to do so, apparently only seven out of the school system's 18,000 pupils deliberately refused to obey the order.

Even a casual reading of the record shows that this armband did divert students' minds from their regular lessons, and that talk, comments, etc., made John Tinker "self-conscious" in attending school with his armband. I think the record overwhelmingly shows that the armbands did exactly what the elected school officials and principals foresaw they would, that is, took the students' minds off their class work and diverted them to thoughts about the highly emotional subject of the Vietnam War. And I repeat that if the time has come when pupils of state-supported schools, kindergartens, grammar schools, or high schools, can defy and flout orders of school officials to keep their minds on their own schoolwork, it is the beginning of a new revolutionary era of permissiveness in this country fostered by the judiciary.

Notes and Comments

1. In *Barnette*, the Supreme Court overruled its decision in *Minersville School District v. Gobitis*, 310 U.S. 586 (1940). Factually, *Gobitis* is almost identical to *Barnette*. The *Gobitis* Court ruled that a state law that requiring pupils in the public schools, to salute the flag, and recite the pledge of allegiance was a valid exercise of legislative power. The *Gobitis* Court stated that "[r]eligious convictions do not relieve the individual from obedience to an otherwise valid general law not aimed at the promotion or restriction of religious beliefs."

2. The parents and students in *Barnette* raised a religious objection to the flag salute and the pledge of allegiance. Based on *Barnette*, could parents today use a religious objection to state compulsory attendance laws? For example, could a family whose religious beliefs forbid "associating with sinners" successfully obtain an exemption from compulsory education laws?

3. In *Tinker*, while the Court upheld "the students' right to engage in a nondisruptive, passive expression of a political viewpoint," it confirmed the educators' interest to respond to "speech or action that intrudes upon the work of the schools or the rights of other students." After *Tinker*, the rationale of decisions began to focus on this link. Educators discovered that their good-faith concerns could, with proper documentation, meet the standard with little difficulty.

For example, in *Jeglin v. San Jacinto Unified School District*, 827 F. Supp. 1459, 1461 (C.D. Cal. 1993), which involved a challenge to a school district dress code prohibiting clothing bearing any writing or pictures which identified any professional or college sports team, the court held that;

> [T]he First Amendment does not require school officials to wait until disruption actually occurs before they may act to curtail exercise of the right of free speech but that they have a duty to prevent the occurrence of disturbances.

See also West v. Derby Unified School District, 206 F.3d 1358 (10th Cir. 2000) (dress code upheld when existing racial tensions made it reasonable to ban confederate flag clothing and symbols). But *see also Castorina v. Madison County School Board*, 246 F.3d 536 (6th Cir. 2001) (dress code prohibiting confederate flag invalidated because educators were held to be acting on "fear or apprehension of disturbance" alone because there was no evidence of racial problems supporting the district's ban on confederate-flag clothing). Is the rule of *Tinker* too subjective to be truly useful to students? Can you think of an objective approach to *Tinker* that would bring draw a brighter line?

4. How would you advise a school district wishing to ban clothing and symbols that reflect membership in, or recognition of, a juvenile street gang? Try to draft a valid code of conduct provision. What advice would you give the educators as to the process of implementing such a ban? *See Olesen v. Board of Education*, 676 F. Supp. 820 (N.D. Ill. 1987). *See also* Comment: *Bloods, Crips, and Christians: Fighting Gangs or Fighting the First Amendment*?, 51 Baylor L. Rev. 389 (1999).

II. Current Doctrine on Protection of Student Expression

BETHEL SCHOOL DISTRICT NO. 403 v. FRASER
478 U.S. 675 (1986)

CHIEF JUSTICE BURGER delivered the opinion of the Court.

We granted certiorari to decide whether the First Amendment prevents a school district from disciplining a high school student for giving a lewd speech at a school assembly.

Matthew N. Fraser, a student at Bethel High School in Pierce County, Washington, delivered a speech nominating a fellow student for student elective office. Approximately 600 high school students, many of whom were 14-year-olds, attended the assembly. Students were required to attend the assembly or to report to the study hall. The assembly was part of a school-sponsored educational program in self-government. Students who elected not to attend the assembly were required to report to study hall. During the entire speech, Fraser referred to his candidate in terms of an elaborate, graphic, and explicit sexual metaphor.

Two of Fraser's teachers, with whom he discussed the contents of his speech in advance, informed him that the speech was "inappropriate and that he probably should not deliver it," and that his delivery of the speech might have "severe consequences."

During Fraser's delivery of the speech, a school counselor observed the reaction of students to the speech. Some students hooted and yelled; some by gestures graphically simulated the sexual activities pointedly alluded to in respondent's speech. Other students appeared to be bewildered and embarrassed by the speech. One teacher reported that on the day following the speech, she found it necessary to forgo a portion of the scheduled class lesson in order to discuss the speech with the class.

A Bethel High School disciplinary rule prohibiting the use of obscene language in the school provides:

> Conduct which materially and substantially interferes with the educational process is prohibited, including the use of obscene, profane language or gestures.

The morning after the assembly, the Assistant Principal called Fraser into her office and notified him that the school considered his speech to have been a violation of this rule. ... Fraser was then informed that he would be suspended for three days, and that his name would be removed from the list of candidates for graduation speaker at the school's commencement exercises..... Fraser sought review of this disciplinary action through the School District's grievance procedures. The hearing officer determined that the speech given by respondent was "indecent, lewd, and offensive to the modesty and decency of many of the students and faculty in attendance at the assembly." Fraser served two days of his suspension, and was allowed to return to school on the third day.

The District Court held that the school's sanctions violated respondent's right to freedom of speech under the First Amendment to the United States Constitution....The Court of Appeals for the Ninth Circuit affirmed the judgment of the District Court. .... We granted certiorari. We reverse.

This Court acknowledged in *Tinker v. Des Moines Ind. Comm. Sch. Dist.*, *supra*, that students do not "shed their constitutional rights to freedom of speech or expression at the schoolhouse gate." The Court of Appeals read that case as precluding any discipline of Fraser for indecent speech and lewd conduct in the school assembly. That court appears to have proceeded on the theory that the use of lewd and obscene speech in order to make what the speaker considered to be a point in a nominating speech for a fellow student was essentially the same as the wearing of an armband in Tinker as a form of protest or the expression of a political position.

The marked distinction between the political "message" of the armbands in *Tinker* and the sexual content of respondent's speech in this case seems to have been given little weight by the Court of Appeals. In upholding the students' right to engage in a nondisruptive, passive expression of a political viewpoint in *Tinker*, this Court was careful to note that the case did "not concern speech or action that intrudes upon the work of the schools or the rights of other students."

The role and purpose of the American public school system were well described by two historians, who stated: "[Public] education must prepare pupils for citizenship in the Republic. . . . It must inculcate the habits and manners of civility as values in themselves conducive to happiness and as indispensable to the practice of self-government in the community and the nation." C. Beard & M. Beard, New Basic History of the United States 228 (1968). In *Ambach v. Norwick*, 441 U.S. 68, 76-77 (1979), we echoed the essence of this statement of the objectives of public education as the "[inculcation of] fundamental values necessary to the maintenance of a democratic political system."

The undoubted freedom to advocate unpopular and controversial views in schools and classrooms must be balanced against the society's countervailing interest in teaching students the boundaries of socially appropriate behavior. Even the most heated political discourse in a democratic society requires consideration for the personal sensibilities of the other participants and audiences.

.....

Surely it is a highly appropriate function of public school education to prohibit the use of vulgar and offensive terms in public discourse. Indeed, the "fundamental values necessary to the maintenance of a democratic political system" disfavor the use of terms of debate highly offensive or highly threatening to others. .... The inculcation of these values is truly the "work of the schools." *Tinker*, 393 U.S. at 508..... The determination of what manner of speech in the classroom or in school assembly is inappropriate properly rests with the school board.

The process of educating our youth for citizenship in public schools is not confined to books, the curriculum, and the civics class; schools must teach by example the shared values of a civilized social order. Consciously or otherwise, teachers—and indeed the older students—demonstrate the appropriate form of civil discourse and political expression by their conduct and deportment in and out of class. Inescapably, like parents, they are role models. The schools, as instruments of the state, may determine that the essential lessons of civil, mature conduct cannot be conveyed in a school that tolerates lewd, indecent, or offensive speech and conduct such as that indulged in by this confused boy.

The pervasive sexual innuendo in Fraser's speech was plainly offensive to both teachers and students—indeed to any mature person. By glorifying male sexuality, and in its verbal content, the speech was acutely insulting to teenage girl students. The speech could well be seriously damaging to its less mature audience, many of whom were only 14 years old and on the threshold of awareness of human sexuality. Some students were reported as bewildered by the speech and the reaction of mimicry it provoked.

.....

We hold that petitioner School District acted entirely within its permissible authority in imposing sanctions upon Fraser in response to his offensively lewd and indecent speech. .... The First Amendment does not prevent the school officials from determining that to permit a vulgar and lewd speech such as respondent's would undermine the school's basic educational mission. A high school assembly or classroom is no place for a sexually explicit monologue directed towards an unsuspecting audience of teenage students. Accordingly, it was perfectly appropriate for the school to disassociate itself to make the point to the pupils that vulgar speech and lewd conduct is wholly inconsistent with the "fundamental values" of public school education. Justice Black, dissenting in Tinker, made a point that is especially relevant in this case:

> I wish therefore . . . to disclaim any purpose . . . to hold that the Federal Constitution compels the teachers, parents, and elected school officials to surrender control of the American public school system to public school students. 393 U.S. at 526.

.....

Reversed.

JUSTICE BRENNAN, concurring in the judgment.

Respondent gave the following speech at a high school assembly in support of a candidate for student government office:

"'I know a man who is firm—he's firm in his pants, he's firm in his shirt, his character is firm—but most . . . of all, his belief in you, the students of Bethel, is firm.

"'Jeff Kuhlman is a man who takes his point and pounds it in. If necessary, he'll take an issue and nail it to the wall. He doesn't attack things in spurts—he drives hard, pushing and pushing until finally—he succeeds.

"'Jeff is a man who will go to the very end—even the climax, for each and every one of you.

"'So vote for Jeff for A. S. B. vice-president—he'll never come between you and the best our high school can be.'"

To my mind, the most that can be said about respondent's speech—and all that need be said—is that in light of the discretion school officials have to teach high school students how to conduct civil and effective public discourse, and to prevent disruption of school educational activities, it was not unconstitutional for school officials to conclude, under the circumstances of this case, that respondent's remarks exceeded permissible limits.

HAZELWOOD SCHOOL DISTRICT. v. KUHLMEIER
484 U.S. 260 (1988)

JUSTICE WHITE delivered the opinion of the Court.

This case concerns the extent to which educators may exercise editorial control over the contents of a high school newspaper produced as part of the school's journalism curriculum.

Respondents are three former Hazelwood East students who were staff members of Spectrum, the school newspaper. They contend that school officials violated their First Amendment rights by deleting two pages of articles from the May 13, 1983, issue of Spectrum. ....On May 10, [one student] delivered the proofs of the May 13 edition to [the teacher], who objected to two of the articles scheduled to appear in that edition. One of the stories described three Hazelwood East students' experiences with pregnancy; the other discussed the impact of divorce on students at the school.

[The teacher] was concerned that, although the pregnancy story used false names "to keep the identity of these girls a secret," the pregnant students still might be identifiable from the text. He also believed that the article's references to sexual activity and birth control were inappropriate for some of the younger students at the school. In addition, [He] was concerned that a student identified by name in the divorce story had complained that her father "wasn't spending enough time with my mom, my sister and I" prior to the divorce, "was always out of town on business or out late playing cards with the guys," and "always argued about everything" with her mother. [He] believed that the student's parents should have been given an opportunity to respond to these remarks or to consent to their publication. He was unaware that [one of the student editors] had deleted the student's name from the final version of the article.

[The teacher] believed that there was no time to make the necessary changes in the stories before the scheduled press run and that the newspaper would not appear before the end of the school year if printing were delayed to any significant extent. He concluded that his only options under the circumstances were to publish a four-page newspaper instead of the planned six-page newspaper, eliminating the two pages on which the offending stories appeared, or to publish no newspaper at all.

....[T]he District Court denied an injunction, holding that no First Amendment violation had occurred. .....The Court of Appeals for the Eighth Circuit reversed.... [T]he court held that school officials had violated respondents' First Amendment rights by deleting the two pages of the newspaper.

We granted certiorari and we now reverse.

Students in the public schools do not "shed their constitutional rights to freedom of speech or expression at the schoolhouse gate." *Tinker, supra,* at 506. They cannot be punished merely for expressing their personal views on the school premises—whether "in the cafeteria, or on the playing field, or on the campus during the authorized hours,"—unless school authorities have reason to believe that such expression will "substantially interfere with the work of the school or impinge upon the rights of other students." *Id.* at 509.

We have nonetheless recognized that the First Amendment rights of students in the public schools "are not automatically coextensive with the rights of adults in other settings," *Bethel Sch. Dist. No. 403 v. Fraser*, 478 U.S. 675, 682 (1986), and must be "applied in light of the special characteristics of the school environment." *Tinker*, *supra*, at 506; *New Jersey v. T.L.O.*, 469 U.S. 325, 341-43 (1985). A school need not tolerate student speech that is inconsistent with its "basic educational mission," *Fraser*, *supra*, at 685, even though the government could not censor similar speech outside the school.

The public schools do not possess all of the attributes of streets, parks, and other traditional public forums that "time out of mind, have been used for purposes of assembly, communicating thoughts between citizens, and discussing public questions." *Hague v. CIO*, 307 U.S. 496, 515. Hence, school facilities may be deemed to be public forums only if school authorities have "by policy or by practice" opened those facilities "for indiscriminate use by the general public," Perry *Education Assn. v. Perry Local Educators' Assn.*, 460 U.S. 37, 47 (1983), or by some segment of the public, such as student organizations. *Id.* at 46. If the facilities have instead been reserved for other intended purposes, "communicative or otherwise," then no public forum has been created, and school officials may impose reasonable restrictions on the speech of students, teachers, and other members of the school community. 460 U.S. at 46. "The government does not create a public forum by inaction or by permitting limited discourse, but only by intentionally opening a nontraditional forum for public discourse." *Cornelius v. NAACP Legal Defense & Educational Fund, Inc.*, 473 U.S. 788, 802 (1985).

The policy of school officials toward Spectrum was reflected in Hazelwood School Board Policy 348.51 and the Hazelwood East Curriculum Guide. Board Policy 348.51 provided that "[s]chool sponsored publications are developed within the adopted curriculum and its educational implications in regular classroom activities." The Hazelwood East Curriculum Guide described the Journalism II course as a "laboratory situation in which the students publish the school newspaper applying skills they have learned in Journalism I." The lessons that were to be learned from the Journalism II course, according to the Curriculum Guide, included development of journalistic skills under deadline pressure, "the legal, moral, and ethical restrictions imposed upon journalists within the school community," and "responsibility and acceptance of criticism for articles of opinion." Journalism II was taught by a faculty member during regular class hours. Students received grades and academic credit for their performance in the course.

In sum, the evidence relied upon by the Court of Appeals fails to demonstrate the clear intent to create a public forum that existed in cases in which we found public forums to have been created. School officials did not evince either by policy or by practice any intent to open the pages of Spectrum to indiscriminate use by its student reporters and editors, or by the student body generally. Instead, they reserved the forum for its intended purpose as a supervised learning experience for journalism students. Accordingly, school officials were entitled to regulate the contents of Spectrum in any reasonable manner. It is this standard, rather than our decision in Tinker, that governs this case.

The question whether the First Amendment requires a school to tolerate particular student speech—the question that we addressed in *Tinker*—is different from the question whether the First Amendment requires a school affirmatively to promote particular student speech. The former question addresses educators' ability to silence a student's personal expression that happens to occur on the school premises. The latter question concerns educators' authority over school-sponsored publications, theatrical productions, and other expressive activities that students, parents, and members of the public might reasonably perceive to bear the imprimatur of the school. These activities may fairly be characterized as part of the school curriculum, whether or not they occur in a traditional classroom setting, so long as they are supervised by faculty members and designed to impart particular knowledge or skills to student participants and audiences.

Educators are entitled to exercise greater control over this second form of student expression to assure that participants learn whatever lessons the activity is designed to teach, that readers or listeners are not exposed to material that may be inappropriate for their level of maturity, and that the views of the individual speaker are not erroneously attributed to the school.... A school must also retain the authority to refuse to sponsor student speech that might reasonably be perceived to advocate drug or alcohol use, irresponsible sex, or conduct otherwise inconsistent with the shared values of a civilized social order or to associate the school with any position other than neutrality on matters of political controversy. Otherwise, the schools would be unduly constrained from fulfilling their role as a principal instrument in awakening the child to cultural values, in preparing him for later professional training, and in helping him to adjust normally to his environment.

This standard is consistent with our oft-expressed view that the education of the Nation's youth is primarily the responsibility of parents, teachers, and state and local school officials, and not of federal judges. It is only when the decision to censor a school-sponsored publication, theatrical production, or other vehicle of student expression has no valid educational purpose that the First Amendment is so "directly and sharply implicate[d]," *Ibid.* as to require judicial intervention to protect students' constitutional rights.

The judgment of the Court of Appeals for the Eighth Circuit is therefore reversed.

JUSTICE BRENNAN, with whom JUSTICE MARSHALL and JUSTICE BLACKMUN join, dissenting.

When the young men and women of Hazelwood East High School registered for Journalism II, they expected a civics lesson. Spectrum, the newspaper they were to publish, "was not just a class exercise in which students learned to prepare papers and hone writing skills, it was a . . . forum established to give students an opportunity to express their views while gaining an appreciation of their rights and responsibilities under the First Amendment to the United States Constitution . [A]t the beginning of each school year, the student journalists published a Statement of Policy—tacitly approved each year by school authorities—announcing their expectation that "Spectrum, as a student-press publication, accepts all rights implied by the First Amendment . . . . Only speech that materially and substantially interferes with the requirements of appropriate discipline' can be found unacceptable and therefore prohibited. The school board itself affirmatively guaranteed the students of Journalism II an atmosphere conducive to fostering such an appreciation and exercising the full panoply of rights associated with a free student press. "School sponsored student publications," it vowed, "will not restrict free expression or diverse viewpoints within the rules of responsible journalism."

In my view the principal broke more than just a promise. He violated the First Amendment's prohibitions against censorship of any student expression that neither disrupts class work nor invades the rights of others, and against any censorship that is not narrowly tailored to serve its purpose.

MORSE v. FREDERICK
551 U.S. 393 (2007)

CHIEF JUSTICE ROBERTS delivered the opinion of the Court.

On January 24, 2002, the Olympic Torch Relay passed through Juneau, Alaska, on its way to the winter games in Salt Lake City, Utah. The torchbearers were to proceed along a street in front of Juneau-Douglas High School (JDHS) while school was in session. Petitioner Deborah Morse, the school principal, decided to permit staff and students to participate in the Torch Relay as an approved social event or class trip. Students were allowed to leave class to observe the relay from either side of the street. Teachers and administrative officials monitored the students' actions.

Respondent Joseph Frederick, a JDHS senior, was late to school that day. When he arrived, he joined his friends (all but one of whom were JDHS students) across the street from the school to watch the event.... As the torchbearers and camera crews passed by, Frederick and his friends unfurled a 14-foot banner bearing the phrase: "BONG HITS 4 JESUS." The large banner was easily readable by the students on the other side of the street.

Principal Morse immediately crossed the street and demanded that the banner be taken down. Everyone but Frederick complied. Morse confiscated the banner and told Frederick to report to her office, where she suspended him for 10 days. Morse later explained that she told Frederick to take the banner down because she thought it encouraged illegal drug use, in violation of established school policy.

.....

We granted certiorari on two questions: whether Frederick had a First Amendment right to wield his banner, and, if so, whether that right was so clearly established that the principal may be held liable for damages. We resolve the first question against Frederick, and therefore have no occasion to reach the second.

II

At the outset, we reject Frederick's argument that this is not a school speech case—as has every other authority to address the question. The event occurred during normal school hours. It was sanctioned by Principal Morse "as an approved social event or class trip," and the school district's rules expressly provide that pupils in "approved social events and class trips are subject to district rules for student conduct." Teachers and administrators were interspersed among the students and charged with supervising them. The high school band and cheerleaders performed. Frederick, standing among other JDHS students across the street from the school, directed his banner toward the school, making it plainly visible to most students. Under these circumstances, we agree with the superintendent that Frederick cannot "stand in the midst of his fellow students, during school hours, at a school-sanctioned activity and claim he is not at school."

III

The message on Frederick's banner is cryptic. It is no doubt offensive to some, perhaps amusing to others. To still others, it probably means nothing at all. Frederick himself claimed "that the words were just nonsense meant to attract television cameras." But Principal Morse thought the banner would be interpreted by those viewing it as promoting illegal drug use, and that interpretation is plainly a reasonable one.

.....

The pro-drug interpretation of the banner gains further plausibility given the paucity of alternative meanings the banner might bear. The best Frederick can come up with is that the banner is "meaningless and funny." Gibberish is surely a possible interpretation of the words on the banner, but it is not the only one, and dismissing the banner as meaningless ignores its undeniable reference to illegal drugs.

IV

The question thus becomes whether a principal may, consistent with the First Amendment, restrict student speech at a school event, when that speech is reasonably viewed as promoting illegal drug use. We hold that she may.

Tinker held that student expression may not be suppressed unless school officials reasonably conclude that it will "materially and substantially disrupt the work and discipline of the school." ...The only interest the Court discerned underlying the school's actions was the "mere desire to avoid the discomfort and unpleasantness that always accompany an unpopular viewpoint," or "an urgent wish to avoid the controversy which might result from the expression." That interest was not enough to justify banning "a silent, passive expression of opinion, unaccompanied by any disorder or disturbance."

This Court's next student speech case was *Fraser*. [I]t is enough to distill from *Fraser* two basic principles. First, *Fraser's* holding demonstrates that "the constitutional rights of students in public school are not automatically coextensive with the rights of adults in other settings." Second, *Fraser* established that the mode of analysis set forth in *Tinker* is not absolute. Whatever approach *Fraser* employed, it certainly did not conduct the "substantial disruption" analysis prescribed by *Tinker*.

Drawing on the principles applied in our student speech cases, we have held in the Fourth Amendment context that "while children assuredly do not 'shed their constitutional rights . . . at the schoolhouse gate,' . . . the nature of those rights is what is appropriate for children in school." *Vernonia Sch. Dist. 47J v. Acton*, 515 U.S. 646, 655-56, (1995). In particular, "the school setting requires some easing of the restrictions to which searches by public authorities are ordinarily subject." *New Jersey v. T.L.O.*, 469 U.S. 325, 340 (1985). ("Fourth Amendment rights, no less than First and Fourteenth Amendment rights, are different in public schools than elsewhere . . ."); *Bd. of Educ. v. Earls*, 536 U.S. 822, 829-30 (2002) ("'special needs' inhere in the public school context"; "while schoolchildren do not shed their constitutional rights when they enter the schoolhouse, Fourth Amendment rights . . . are different in public schools than elsewhere; the 'reasonableness' inquiry cannot disregard the schools' custodial and tutelary responsibility for children". ...Even more to the point, these cases also recognize that deterring drug use by schoolchildren is an "important—indeed, perhaps compelling" interest.

.....

The "special characteristics of the school environment," and the governmental interest in stopping student drug abuse—reflected in the policies of Congress and myriad school boards, including JDHS—allow schools to restrict student expression that they reasonably regard as promoting illegal drug use.

.....

School principals have a difficult job, and a vitally important one. When Frederick suddenly and unexpectedly unfurled his banner, Morse had to decide to act—or not act—on the spot. It was reasonable for her to conclude that the banner promoted illegal drug use—in violation of established school policy—and that failing to act would send a powerful message to the students in her charge, including Frederick, about how serious the school was about the dangers of illegal drug use. The First Amendment does not require schools to tolerate at school events student expression that contributes to those dangers.

JUSTICE THOMAS, concurring.

I write separately to state my view that the standard set forth in *Tinker v. Des Moines Indep. Comm. Sch. Dist.* is without basis in the Constitution.

.....

During the colonial era, private schools and tutors offered the only educational opportunities for children, and teachers managed classrooms with an iron hand. ...Like their private counterparts, early public schools were not places for freewheeling debates or exploration of competing ideas. Rather, teachers instilled "a core of common values" in students and taught them self-control.

.....

In light of the history of American public education, it cannot seriously be suggested that the First Amendment "freedom of speech" encompasses a student's right to speak in public schools.

JUSTICE ALITO, with whom JUSTICE KENNEDY joins, concurring.

I join the opinion of the Court on the understanding that (a) it goes no further than to hold that a public school may restrict speech that a reasonable observer would interpret as advocating illegal drug use and (b) it provides no support for any restriction of speech that can plausibly be interpreted as commenting on any political or social issue, including speech on issues such as the wisdom of the war on drugs or of legalizing marijuana for medicinal use.

JUSTICE STEVENS, with whom JUSTICE SOUTER and JUSTICE GINSBURG join, dissenting.

In my judgment, the First Amendment protects student speech if the message itself neither violates a permissible rule nor expressly advocates conduct that is illegal and harmful to students. This nonsense banner does neither, and the Court does serious violence to the First Amendment in upholding—indeed, lauding—a school's decision to punish Frederick for expressing a view with which it disagreed.

GRIGGS EX REL. GRIGGS v. FT. WAYNE SCHOOL BOARD

359 F. Supp. 2d 731 (N.D. Ind. 2005)

JUDGES: Roger B. Cosbey, United States Magistrate Judge.

OPINION: MEMORANDUM OF DECISION AND ORDER

David Arnold Nelson Griggs is a student at Elmhurst High School and a strong supporter of the United States Marines. Wishing to publicly express his admiration for American troops overseas, he came to school wearing a T-shirt that reads:

> My Rifle
> The Creed of a United States Marine
> This is my rifle. There are many like it, but this one is
> mine. My rifle is my best friend. It is my life.
> I must master it as I must master my life.
> My rifle, without me, is useless. Without my rifle, I am
> useless. I must fire my rifle true. I must shoot
> straighter than my enemy who is trying to kill me. I
> must shoot him before he shoots me. I will . . .

A large picture of an M16 rifle (the standard weapon of the Marines) appears between the two stanzas of the creed, and the seal of the Marines is beneath the last line of text.

.....

While Griggs invokes several clauses of both the United States and Indiana Constitutions, the heart of this dispute concerns only the First Amendment, and thus we begin there. The two principal issues to be resolved are whether the First Amendment allows the Board to (1) generally proscribe clothing "depicting . . . symbols of violence"; and (2) forbid Griggs from wearing his Marine Creed shirt in school.

The boundaries of a student's free-speech rights in public school are particularly difficult to set. ...The [Supreme] Court has attempted to balance these competing values in a trilogy of school-speech cases. As we shall soon see, the proper interpretation of these cases is vigorously disputed by the parties and within and among the Circuit Courts of Appeals.

The first, *Tinker*, involved a group of students who were disciplined for wearing black armbands to protest the Vietnam War. ...*Tinker* stands for the proposition that a student's "pure speech" in school cannot be banned absent a reasonable forecast of "substantial disruption."

The second case in the trilogy is *Bethel Sch. Dist. v. Fraser*. In *Fraser*, the plaintiff made a speech at a school assembly nominating another student for an elected office. However, the plaintiff "referred to his candidate in terms of an elaborate, graphic, and explicit sexual metaphor," and thus the school punished him. The Court held that the school's interest in "teaching students the boundaries of socially appropriate behavior" gave it the right to determine "what manner of speech in the classroom or in school assembly is inappropriate." Thus, "it was perfectly appropriate for the school to . . . make the point to the pupils that vulgar speech and lewd conduct are wholly inconsistent with the fundamental values' of public school education."

The final chapter of the trilogy is *Hazelwood Sch. Dist. v. Kuhlmeier*. In *Hazelwood,* students sued when school officials refused to print two student-written articles in a school newspaper; the officials felt that the articles, which dealt with the effects of teenage pregnancy and divorce on the school's students, did not sufficiently protect the identity of the students referenced in them and contained material inappropriate for younger students. ...The Court then formulated a different test for school-sponsored speech: "educators do not offend the First Amendment by exercising editorial control over the style and content of student speech in school-sponsored expressive activities so long as their actions are reasonably related to legitimate pedagogical concerns." The Court determined that the school's actions satisfied this test and ruled in its favor.

The most common interpretation of these three cases, and the one that Griggs prefers, is that *Tinker* provides the default rule for suppression of student speech, and *Fraser* and *Hazelwood* create narrow exceptions to the rule. On this view, student speech generally cannot be banned unless the school presents facts that could reasonably lead it "to forecast substantial disruption of . . . school activities." *Tinker*, 393 U.S. at 514. However, this rule does not apply where the school objects to the "manner of speech" rather than its content; therefore, schools may ban offensive, lewd, or indecent speech regardless of its potential for disruption. *Fraser*, 478 U.S. at 683, 685. The *Tinker* rule also does not apply to speech that is (or reasonably appears to be) sponsored by the school; rather, educators may regulate school-sponsored speech "so long as their actions are reasonably related to legitimate pedagogical concerns," assuming that the speech was not in a public forum. *Hazelwood*, 484 U.S. at 271, 273.

Under such an analysis, the Board's ban on Griggs's Marine Creed shirt would fall under the ambit of *Tinker*. The shirt's message is not presented in an offensive, lewd or indecent manner, so Fraser would not apply, and shirt's message is not sponsored by the school (nor could it reasonably appear to be), so *Hazelwood* would not apply either. Rather, Griggs's shirt is speech that "happened to occur on the school premises," and thus it could not be banned unless the Board meets *Tinker*'s "substantial disruption" test. *Hazelwood*, 484 U.S. at 270-71 ("the question that we addressed in *Tinker* . . . involved educators' ability to silence a student's personal expression that happens to occur on the school premises.")

Griggs is not alone in viewing the *Tinker-Fraser-Hazelwood* trilogy this way eight Courts of Appeals have adopted identical or similar interpretations. *Saxe v. State Coll. Area Sch. Dist.*, 240 F.3d 200, 211-14 (3rd Cir. 2001); *Newsom v. Albemarle County Sch. Bd.*, 354 F.3d 249, 255-57 (4th Cir. 2003); *Porter v. Ascension Parish Sch. Bd.*, 393 F.3d 608 (5th Cir. 2004); *Castorina v. Madison County Sch. Bd.*, 246 F.3d 536 (6th Cir. 2001); *Henerey v. City of St. Charles*, 200 F.3d 1128 (8th Cir. 1999); *Chandler v. McMinnville Sch. Dist.*, 978 F.2d 524 (9th Cir. 1992); *Fleming v. Jefferson County Sch. Dist. R-1*, 298 F.3d 918 (10th Cir. 2002); *Bannon v. Sch. Dist. of Palm Beach County*, 387 F.3d 1208 (11th Cir. 2004). But the Seventh Circuit, whose opinions this Court is bound to apply, has charted a different course.

In *Muller v. Jefferson Lighthouse Sch.*, 98 F.3d 1530 (7th Cir. 1996), the Seventh Circuit considered whether the First Amendment allows a school to ban a student from distributing invitations to a religious gathering. The majority opinion began by identifying "two important but at times conflicting educational concepts" in the Supreme Court's jurisprudence: first, "the traditional view which holds that children are in the temporary custody of the state as 'schoolmaster,'" and second, the concept that "school children are autonomous individuals, treated as adults, entitled to free speech rights during school hours." *Id.* at 1535-36. The majority identified *Tinker* as an example of the second concept and *Fraser* and *Hazelwood* as examples of the first. *Id.* at 1536-37. The majority also put great emphasis on *Hazelwood*'s "initial determination of the type of forum at issue," and it seemed to imply that all student free-speech cases must now begin with such an analysis, regardless of whether the speech at issue is school-sponsored as in *Hazelwood*.

Having laid that foundation, the majority then announced that, absent a public forum, the Hazelwood test ("reasonably related to legitimate pedagogical concerns") applies to all student speech. The majority did not address *Hazelwood*'s explicit distinction between speech "that happens to occur on the school premises" and speech that one "might reasonably perceive to bear the imprimatur of the school." *Hazelwood*, 484 U.S. at 270-71. Rather, it focused only on the distinction between public and nonpublic forums, and held that all student speech in a nonpublic forum is governed by the *Hazelwood* test, regardless of whether the speech was (or could be seen as) school-sponsored. *Muller*, 98 F.3d at 1537-38. This interpretation of *Hazelwood* seems to restrict *Tinker*, but the majority avoided that question in an oblique footnote. *Id.* at 1538 ("Some might consider *Hazelwood* a narrowing of the free speech rights *Tinker* had granted public high school students. . . . We need not draw that conclusion; rather we can take *Hazelwood's* non-public forum analysis at face value.") Applying its new interpretation, the majority found that the school was not a public forum and that the administrators' actions met the *Hazelwood* test. ...As noted earlier, Griggs urges this Court to apply the *Tinker* test, and if this case was brought in the Third, Fourth, Fifth, Sixth, Eighth, Ninth, Tenth, or Eleventh Circuit, that analysis would prevail. However, *Muller* remains the law of this Circuit, and therefore this Court is bound to apply the *Muller/Hazelwood* standard instead.

.....

Obviously, if the school can ban speech for any reason related to a legitimate pedagogical concern, then it can ban many messages containing symbols of violence. The Board imagines two extreme examples: (1) a shirt depicting a woman being raped, with the legend "She Had It Coming"; and (2) a portrayal of the Columbine massacre, with the text "Trench Coat Mafia Victory Tour 2005." Clearly, Rule 3 would operate to ban these shirts, and that ban would be permissible under *Muller*.

Rule 3's prohibition on "symbols of violence" is constitutional, as it is "reasonably related" to the Board's "legitimate pedagogical concern" of preventing school violence. But this does not mean that every application of Rule 3 will pass constitutional muster; even a permissible regulation might occasionally be used to censor more speech than the First Amendment allows. As it turns out, the Board's ban on Griggs's Marine Creed shirt presents just such a case. Whether it is analyzed under the *Muller/Hazelwood* test as required by the Seventh Circuit, or under the *Tinker* test adopted by eight other circuits, the prohibition on Griggs's shirt reaches a bit too far.

Under *Muller*, the first question is whether Elmhurst High School, where Griggs's speech took place, is a "public forum." *Id.* at 1539. School facilities are public forums only if "school authorities have by policy or by practice' opened these facilities for indiscriminate use by the general public,' or by some segment of the public, such as student organizations." *Hazelwood*, 484 U.S. at 267. There is no evidence that Elmhurst has been opened for such "indiscriminate use," nor does Griggs claim that it has; to the contrary, Rule 3 of the Code puts many restrictions on the messages that can be displayed in the school. Accordingly, Elmhurst is not a public forum.

Since Griggs's speech occurred in a nonpublic forum, *Muller* requires this Court to uphold the Board's ban on the speech as long as it is "reasonably related to legitimate pedagogical concerns." *Muller*, 98 F.3d at 1540. But even under this "deferential approach," *Id.* at 1537, the Board fails to meet its burden.

The Board proffers several arguments in support of its actions, none of which are persuasive. ...Admittedly, the dominant feature of the shirt is the graphic of the M16—the gun is what first catches one's eye. ... But whatever one's instinctive reaction to the shirt is, it only takes a few seconds of study to realize that the gun is placed in the context of a relatively benign message of support for the military. As detailed below, this fundamental misconception by the Board fatally weakens each of its arguments.

The Board's principal argument is that, in the wake of tragic school shootings at Columbine High School and elsewhere, it has a "legitimate pedagogical interest" in discouraging a "culture of violence" in Elmhurst and other FWCS schools. But the Board fails to persuade that banning Griggs's shirt has any "reasonable relation" to that interest. The shirt, viewed in its obvious context, concerns only violence perpetrated by the Marines against America's enemies; no reasonable observer would think that it related to Columbine or other school shootings in any way.

The Board also makes a slippery-slope argument: if Griggs is allowed to wear this shirt, then what other shirts might Elmhurst have to permit? However, the shirts [feared] by the Board are not comparable to Griggs's shirt, as none of them have an explicit military context. Thus, they could reasonably be construed as a direct threat or approval of violence by the wearer, whereas the words on Griggs's shirt are put in the mouth of a U.S. Marine. In short, allowing Griggs to wear his shirt will not compel the Board to allow these other shirts, as the Board's arguments about preventing school violence would likely be more persuasive when applied to those shirts.

Finally, the Board implies that even if it cannot ban Griggs's shirt under the *Muller/Hazelwood* test, it might still be able to ban it under *Fraser*. In other words, the Board suggests that an image of a gun or other symbol of violence can transform otherwise acceptable speech into the sort of lewd, offensive, or indecent manner of speech that schools can ban under *Fraser*. This argument is rather disingenuous. The Board obviously does not have a blanket objection to depictions of guns or other symbols of violence in its schools; the very room where Griggs was sent as punishment has a poster of a Marine holding an identical rifle. Moreover, Elmhurst's mascot is the "Trojan," and the school accordingly features a statute of an ancient warrior, his hand resting on the hilt of a sword. Thus, the Board's suggestion that depiction of guns or other weapons are ipso facto lewd, offensive, or indecent does not hold water. *Fraser* has no application here.

. . . . .

In sum, the Board fails to meet the *Muller/Hazelwood* test, as it has not shown that banning Griggs's shirt is reasonably related to any legitimate pedagogical interest. While the Board certainly has an interest in preventing violence in its schools, it cannot merely incant "Columbine" or "Cheri Sue Hartman" like a magic spell allowing it to ban speech totally unrelated to those tragic incidents. Nor do the Board's other arguments provide any constitutional justification for censoring Griggs's speech. Therefore, Griggs is entitled to an injunction allowing him to wear his Marine Creed shirt to school.

. . . . .

Schools are under undeniable pressure to prevent student violence, and the commitment of the Board and administrators here in that regard is commendable. The Board's general prohibition of "apparel depicting . . . symbols of violence" is a reasonable, constitutional tool towards that end.

Yet, the discretion afforded to administrators to censor student speech cannot be limitless. As the Supreme Court eloquently stated," it can hardly be argued that either students or teachers shed their constitutional rights to freedom of speech or expression at the schoolhouse gate." *Tinker,* 393 U.S. at 506. Although this Court trusts that the Board and its administrators generally interpret Rule 3 within the confines of the First Amendment, in the case of Griggs's Marine Creed shirt, they have gone a bit too far. Griggs's shirt has no relation to the Board's legitimate concerns about school violence, nor is it likely to disrupt the educational process. Thus, the Board's ban on Griggs's shirt cannot stand.

Richard L. Roe: Valuing Student Speech: The Work of the Schools as Conceptual Development, 79 Cal. L. Rev. 1269 (1991)*

The Supreme Court currently views the work of the schools to be the inculcation of values. For example, in [*Hazelwood*] the Court implicitly relied on inculcative pedagogical notios when it ruled that the restriction of expression in school-sponsored activities by school authorities does not violate the first amendment provided the authorities' actions are "reasonably related to legitimate pedagogical concerns." The [*Hazelwood*] Court arguably expanded the notion of inculcation from a prescriptive sense, in which the school selectively offers knowledge and skills to students, to an exclusive sense, in which the school limits information that may contradict the ideas it prescribes—in other words, the Court broadened the school's authority to select ideas for the curriculum also to encompass the power to exclude ideas from the school. Thus, although the Court had proclaimed in an earlier opinion that students have an "undoubted freedom to advocate unpopular and controversial views in schools and classrooms," the practical effect of the judicial deference to school officials expressed in [*Hazelwood*] leaves little real protection for student expression not approved by school authorities.

The notion of the school as a marketplace of ideas has been largely unpersuasive in the area of student expression, and courts have generally limited its application to postsecondary education. The marketplace model allows students to exercise their constitutional freedoms, a practice that necessarily restrains the state from imposing its official dogma. But such restraint on the power of school authorities does not comport with the Court's current willingness to grant schools power to restrict student expression.

An inherent conflict between the authority of the state to instill knowledge and values it deems important and the speech interests of individual students characterizes Supreme Court jurisprudence in the area of school speech. This conflict has historically been reconciled in favor of the state's inculcative interests—courts, legal commentators, and educators alike agree that one of the functions of schools is to impart school-determined and school-endorsed knowledge, skills, and values to students. Recent Supreme Court jurisprudence in the area of school speech has echoed such inculcative views, recognizing the schools' authority to select and implement their curricula in furtherance of their educational mission.

Student speech rights are often viewed as weak despite the primacy of first amendment values. Freedom of speech for children simply has not been accorded the same weight as it has for adults. The rationale for this disparity is based on the supposed incompetence of children, arising from their physical, mental, and emotional immaturity....Furthermore, the immaturity of children is thought to make them more vulnerable to perceived negative influences that the state as well as parents may want to control through the curricular authority vested in the state as educator.

****

The mission of the schools should be based on the conceptual-development model because this theory explains what takes place at the core of the learning process better than the inculcation-of-values model. The difficulty with understanding education in inculcative terms is that inculcation does not adequately describe either the educational process or the principles on which schools are intended to function. An alternative view of education is based on principles and insights gleaned from a substantial body of literature in the fields of psychology, education, and cognitive science. The consensus of researchers and theorists in these fields is that the learning process is properly characterized as developing thinking skills.

Research in the cognitive sciences into the way we gain knowledge and formulate ideas views the functioning of the mind in terms of information processing. The learning process involves not only the recall of information but also, and most importantly, the building of cognitive structures—intellectual frameworks for conceptualization that hold information in some comprehensible form. As well as adding new information to one's cognitive structures, the learning process involves reformulation of the cognitive structures themselves to account for new, different, and more complex information. An increase in knowledge, for example, is a function not only of acquiring but also of developing the mental tools sufficient to organize new information. In addition to the recitation of information, knowledge requires the comprehension and association of ideas. Most significantly, research suggests that the learner constructs rather than simply receives knowledge. The quality of the knowledge one acquires, then, is a function of active intellectual inquiry.

Three general principles of cognitive and conceptual development reveal both that the inculcative model has limits and that the learning process is essential to effective education. First, students are not "empty vessels" waiting passively to be filled by the school's lessons. Rather, they come to the learning process with a base of knowledge and values as well as some cognitive structures already in place. Second, the building of cognitive structures, although greatly influenced by schooling, is ultimately a function of the learner, not the school. Knowledge is not simply inculcated or instilled directly by instruction but is assimilated or accommodated by the learner, who should not be viewed as merely a recipient of information but rather as a "constructor of meaning." Third, both the building and reformulation of cognitive structures are substantially enhanced by the learner's expression of ideas.

Understanding the work of the schools as conceptual development significantly affects the amount of deference courts should give to school-authority determinations that student speech disrupts the schools' work. Under the conceptual-development model, student speech that conflicts with the school's message may nevertheless have educational value. However, current court deference standards, based on the inculcative model of education, are insufficient to provide adequate protection to speech that is educationally valuable although distinct from the school's message. For example, the notion of judicial deference adhered to in cases such as [*Hazelwood*] permits school authorities to exercise broad discretionary judgment in restricting and punishing student speech. The [*Hazelwood*] standard permitting judicial intervention only when the restrictive action of school authorities "has no valid educational purpose" does not provide sufficient first amendment protection to expression that has legitimate educational value and is consistent with the work of the schools.

In addition to its tendency to exclude educationally valuable student speech, the inculcative model of teaching also contradicts first amendment values underlying democratic education for two reasons. First, the failure of a school to act in accordance with its espoused first amendment values when it suppresses student speech creates a dissonance between the school's declared doctrine and its actual educational practice.

[C]ourts should consider avoiding broad deference to the decisions of school authorities because school boards may not be as democratically sound as they may appear. Local school boards have often been criticized as unrepresentative of the community. At the other extreme, school boards may be overly sensitive to community pressures, responding either to strong but narrow interests or to majorities. Consequently, the counter majoritarian protections of the Bill of Rights may not be adequately safeguarded if the actions of school boards are not subject to judicial scrutiny.

Notes and Comments

1. The Current State of *Tinker*

How would you summarize the state of the law on the free speech rights of students after these cases? What has happened to *Tinker*?

In *Morse v. Frederick*, Justice Clarence Thomas says of the Courts treatment of *Tinker*;

> Today, the Court creates another exception [to *Tinker*]. In doing so, we continue to distance ourselves from *Tinker*, but we neither overrule it nor offer an explanation of when it operates and when it does not. I am afraid that our jurisprudence now says that students have a right to speak in schools except when they don't—a standard continuously developed through litigation against local schools and their administrators. In my view, petitioners could prevail for a much simpler reason: As originally understood, the Constitution does not afford students a right to free speech in public schools. (127 S. Ct. at 2634 Thomas, J., concurring).

Do you agree with Justice Thomas? Can the decisions in *Hazelwood* and *Morse* be reconciled with *Tinker*? Should *Tinker* be overruled?

2. The Public School and Public Forum Doctrine

Under this branch of free speech analysis, government officials may properly regulate expression based on the nature of the government property on which it takes place. A sliding scale of empowerment in favor of speech has been developed with streets, parks and sidewalks at one end (the so-called traditional public forum). On the other end of the scale is the closed forum, public property dedicated for a specific purpose that may be protected against general access for expressive purposes. The traditional public forum is said to be held in trust by government for expressive purposes. The non-traditional forum cases were forged out of the public protests and demonstrations of the 1960s and 1970s that took place on public property, begging the question over that type of limitations government officials could impose on speech other than streets, parks and public sidewalks. *See Greer v. Spock*, 424 U.S. 828 (1976) (restrictions on public demonstration upheld as to military base); *Adderley v.*

Florida, 385 U.S. 39 (1966) (reasonable restrictions on speech upheld as to County jail). The presumption in favor of censorship is strong.

These so-called time, place, and manner cases provide an additional basis for regulation of student speech on campus that is not linked to the disruption theory of *Tinker*. Public forum doctrine is grounded on the assumption that "school officials may impose reasonable restrictions on the speech of students, teachers, and other members of the school community… [when the restrictions are] related to legitimate pedagogical concerns." *Hazelwood School District v. Kuhlmeier*, 484 U.S. 260, 267 (1988). The *Hazelwood* Court ruled that the public-school campus is a nonpublic forum, giving school officials more control over speech than if it was a public forum. Schools are deemed a nonpublic forum until educators intentionally take steps (by policy or by practice) to open the campus for general public discourse. Unless this occurs, school facilities are reserved for expression that is compatible with its intended purposes.

> [S]chool facilities may be deemed to be public forums only if school authorities have by policy or by practice' opened those facilities for indiscriminate use by the general public, or by some segment of the public, such as student organizations. A public forum is not created by default, only by design: 'The government does not create a public forum by inaction or by permitting limited discourse, but only by intentionally opening a nontraditional forum for public discourse…. [and] school officials may impose reasonable restrictions on the speech of students, teachers, and other members of the school community. 484 U.S. at 267.

See also Perry Educ. Ass'n v. Perry Local Educators' Ass'n, 460 U.S. 37 (1983) (The inter-school mail system deemed the be a closed forum). For lower court application of this rule, *see Muller by Muller v. Jefferson Lighthouse Sch.*, 98 F.3d 1530 (7th Cir. Wis. 1996), *cert. denied,* 520 U.S. 1156 (1997) (code of conduct regulating distribution of religious flyers upheld). *Walz v. Egg Harbor Township Bd. of Educ.*, 187 F. Supp. 2d. 232 (D.N.J. 2002) (pupil could not distribute holiday gifts with religious messages, because no other pupils were allowed to do so making for a closed forum).

Courts do bring a suspicious attitude to evaluating claims by school officials that the campus is maintained as a closed forum. When the matter is in dispute, courts conduct a factual inquiry, examining both what school official declare to be the policy and what actually takes place as matter of daily practice on campus. For some examples of this inquiry, *see Good News Club v. Milford Cent. Schools*, 533 U.S. 98 (2001). (In practice educators created an open forum in elementary school after hours); *Bd. of Educ. of Westside Comm. Schs. v. Mergens*, 496 U.S. 226 (1990) (same outcome, "A public secondary school cannot simply declare that it maintains a closed forum and then discriminate against a particular … group on the basis of the content of the speech of the group"); *Bender v. Williamsport Area Sch. Dist.*, 741 F.2d 538, 547-49 (3d Cir. 1984), vacated on other grounds, 475 U.S. 534, 89 L. Ed. 2d 501, 106 S. Ct. 1326 (1986) (school district did establish a public forum for student groups to meet during school day); *Gregoire v. Centennial School Dist.*, 907 F.2d 1366 (3d Cir. Pa. 1990) (same for student groups meeting after school hours).

Is *Tinker* effectively overruled whenever the school is deemed to be a closed forum? Can an argument be made that all student speech in a nonpublic forum is governed by the *Hazelwood* test of reasonableness? Remember, this is the position taken by the Seventh Circuit in *Griggs* above. If this is true, then why does the court in *Griggs* rule against the school board? *Griggs* was decided before

Morse. In light of *Morse*, can one argue that *Griggs* is bad law? What type of forum is assumed by the court in the *Saxe* case?

3. Hate Speech, Threats and Disruptive Student Expression

Does the First Amendment allow educators to regulate hate speech and bullying? One scholar makes a compelling case for the validity of such regulations.

Tawnya Brady was in 8th grade when several boys began repeatedly mocking her in the halls and on the bus. She alleged that they yelled "Moo moo" and made vulgar references to her breasts and other parts of her body. She gave it a few weeks to die down, but it only got worse and spread into the classrooms. Tawnya and her mother sued, and the school district paid $20,000 to settle the claim.

Katy Lyle brought a complaint with the state Human Rights Commission after a friend told her about a bathroom stall at her high school filled with obscene graffiti about her. "The mild ones were 'Katy Lyle is a slut' or 'Katy Lyle is a whore,'" she said. Despite more than a dozen complaints, the graffiti remained for 18 months until her brother finally scrubbed everything away except the words chipped into the paint. The Human Rights Commission found in her favor and the school settled the suit for $15,000.

Cheltzie Hentz told her mother that she was troubled by the foul language and lewd behavior of a group of rowdy boys on her school bus. The boys allegedly repeatedly used profanity, called her obscene names, referred to her genitalia, and suggested that she perform oral sex on her father. Both the U.S. Department of Education's Office for Civil Rights and the Minnesota Department of Human Rights ruled that her school district had failed to take appropriate action to stop this behavior. Cheltzie Hentz was 6 years old.

Isolated incidents? Unfortunately not. A survey of 1,600 8-11th graders commissioned by the American Association of University Women and conducted in 79 classrooms across the country in February and March, 1993, found that four out of every five teenagers suffer sexual harassment in school. Overall, 76% of the girls and 56% of the boys reported that they had been the targets of sexual comments, jokes, gestures or looks, and 53% of the students-2/3rds of the girls and 42% of the boys-said they had been touched, grabbed or pinched in a sexual way.

What can—and should—schools do about the harassment which their students are suffering?

The Supreme Court has developed several tests in determining what speech is protected—and not protected—by the First Amendment.

.....

No matter what test is used, it is clear that public grade and high schools have a greater power to limit speech than do colleges or society in general. ... [H]ate messages and their stigmatization can cause long-term psychological harm and that the Supreme Court has restricted children's free speech rights in other contexts to protect them from these harms. [Moreover, by] applying *Tinker* certain expressive symbols, school songs, and team names (such as the Confederate flag, the song "Dixie," and the name "Rebels") may be proscribed because their racially charged history may have a potentially disruptive presence in the educational setting. In light of these cases and the discussion in *Tinker*, *Fraser*, and *Hazelwood* on the role of public schools …hate speech codes are not only constitutional but necessary for the well-being of children. … [S]chool districts should adopt rules directed against fighting words generally so that the regulations apply to all students. Milani: *Harassing Speech In The Public Schools: The Validity Of Schools' Regulation Of Fighting Words And The Consequences If They Do Not*, 28 Akron L. Rev. 187 (1995).

Here is a summary of recent court decisions involving threats.

T.V. ex rel. B.V. v. Smith-Green Community School Corp., 807 F. Supp. 2d 767 (N.D. Ind. 2011).

Two high school students brought action against their school district and school principle, alleging that their First Amendment rights were violated the school suspended them from competing in six volleyball games along with other extracurricular activities for posting provocative photographs on the internet. Although the photographs featured the students posing in a number of sexual suggestive photos, the court held that the students' speech was not obscene but protected speech, and thus, the school violated the students' First Amendment rights. Id. at 781. Further, the court held that Student Handbook that allowed students to be punished for activities occurring off campus outside a school activity was too vague and overly broad as to violate the Constitution, so the school should not have been allowed to punish the students for violating the Handbook.

J.R. v. Penns Manor Area School Disrict, 373 F. Supp. 3d 550 (W.D. Pa. 2019).

The United States District Court held that a 12-year-old student's constitutional rights were not violated when school officials expelled him for promoting school violence by telling fellow classmates he would shoot a teacher, and telling the guidance counselor he would "carry out the activity" using a pistol. The court ruled that language reasonably perceived as threatening school violence is not constitutionally protected. The court also held that school officials must have significant discretionary decision-making ability to maintain a safe environment.

Pillault v. United States, 371 F. Supp. 3d 325 (N.D. Miss. 2019)

In Mississippi, the United States District Court held that a former student's threatened acts of violence against a high school were not protected speech under First Amendment. The threats were made on the "RuneScape" game. The game developer forwarded the threats to authorities and reached out to the high school. The court ruled that his statements were not political speech or words that could be dismissed as mere hyperbole.

People v. D.N., No. D074293, 2019 WL 5091605 (Cal. Ct. App. Oct. 11, 2019)
The California Court of Appeal ruled that a student was properly adjudicated for making a criminal threat when he used a black "sharpie" marker to write the following statement on the wall of a bathroom stall: "Don't come!!! Skool Shooting after Spring Break [smiley face] Blood kidz." The court reasoned that officials could reasonably could infer that the graffiti was an actual threat written with the intention to instill fear of a school shooting in those who saw or heard about it. The state law focuses on attempting to instill fear in others and the evidence did not need to show that the student intended to carry out the threat.

In re A.N., No. E072495, 2020 WL 1061066 (Cal. Ct. App. Mar. 5, 2020)
The California Court of Appeal upheld the adjudication of a student who told fellow student during class, "I'm going to shoot up the school tomorrow." The court ruled that the California law prohibiting the making of criminal threats does not require intent to actually carry out the threatened crime. The court ruled that instead, the speaker must intend for the victim to receive and understand the threat, and the threat must be such that it would cause a reasonable person to fear for his or her safety. Given the frequency of school shootings in America, the court reasoned that the student knew his threat would be taken seriously even if he did not take it seriously himself.

4. What Makes for a Valid Regulation on Student Speech?

Draft a school regulation that addresses hate speech, bullying, or inappropriate behavior (or all three) that you believe would pass muster under current law. Pay particular attention to the *Saxe* opinion above to the wording of your policy.

5. Student Rights, School Discipline and "Off-Campus" Expression
An emerging area of controversy for both educators and the courts are lawsuits that challenge suspensions and expulsions for student misconduct that takes place off-campus. The majority of these case are easily decided without reference to the First Amendment because they do not involve speech, but involve misconduct that either violate school conditions for participation or that constitute criminally delinquent behavior (See page 199 in Chapter Four).

The First Amendment raises serious questions about the authority of educators to discipline students for expression that takes place beyond the schoolhouse gate. Student off-campus use of cell phones, text messengers, beepers, and the Internet may result in school discipline if the use raises legitimate educational concerns. The *Tinker* decision controls the legal analysis. Students are not protected when their transmissions, broadcasts and Internet postings are directed at the campus and disrupt the work and discipline of the school. Educational codes of conduct may properly punish use of these devices when they pose a reasonable risk that it would materially and substantially disrupt the work and discipline of the school. *See Doninger v. Niehoff*, 527 F.3d 41 (2nd Cir. 2008) (suspension of student upheld after she posted a vulgar and misleading message about the supposed cancellation of an upcoming school event on an independently operated, publicly accessible web log); *J.S. v. Bethlehem Area Sch. Dist.* 569 Pa. 638; 807 A.2d 847 (2002) (suspension and expulsion upheld for publishing internet site soliciting funds to hire a hitman to kill educators); *Requa v. Kent Sch. Dist. No. 415*, 492 F. Supp. 2d 1272 (W.D. Wa. 2007) (Suspension upheld for posting video of teacher that was secretly filmed during class). *Layshock ex rel. Layshock v. Hermitage Sch. Dist.*, 496 F. Supp. 2d 587, 602 (W.D. Pa. 2007) (suspension overturned for posting parody of principal on a website because school could not establish a sufficient nexus between the student's off-campus conduct and any substantial disruption of the school environment); *Emmett v. Kent Sch. Dist. No. 415*, 92 F. Supp. 2d 1088, 1089 (W.D. Wa. 2000) (suspension overturned for creating website with fake student obituaries of school students and staff when no nexus to actual threat or disruption); *Beussink, ex. Rel. Beussink v. Woodland R-IV Sch. Dist.*, 30 F. Supp. 2d 1175 (E.D. Mo. 1998). (suspension overturned, no nexus to creation of web site that contained remarks critical of the school).

Do you disagree with any of the following court decisions?

T.V. ex rel. B.V. v. Smith-Green Community School Corp., 807 F. Supp. 2d 767 (N.D. Ind. 2011).

Two high school students brought action against their school district and school principle, alleging that their First Amendment rights were violated the school suspended them from competing in six volleyball games along with other extracurricular activities for posting provocative photographs on the internet. Although the photographs featured the students posing in a number of sexual suggestive photos, the court held that the students' speech was not obscene but protected speech, and thus, the school violated the students' First Amendment rights. *Id.* at 781. Further, the court held that Student Handbook that allowed students to be punished for activities occurring off campus outside a school activity was too vague and overly broad as to violate the Constitution, so the school should not have been allowed to punish the students for violating the Handbook.

J.S. ex rel. Snyder v. Blue Mountain School Dist., 650 F.3d 915 (3d Cir. 2011).

The parents of a middle school student brought action against the school district, claiming a violation of the student's free speech rights, due process rights, and state law when the student was suspended for creating from her home computer a the school principal's MySpace profile containing his photograph and including statements that insinuated he was a sex addict and pedophile. Because the student's actions did not cause "substantial disruption in school and that could not reasonably have led school officials to forecast substantial disruption in school," the suspension violated the student's First Amendment free speech rights. However, because the School District's policies were not "overbroad or void-for vagueness," the District did not violate the student's substantive due process rights.

Wynar v. Douglas County School Dist., 2011 WL 3512534 (D. Nev. 2011).

A high school student was brought an action against the school district for due process and First Amendment violations after he was suspended ten days when the school was forwarded the student's instant message conversation discussing shooting multiple students at the school. The court found no due process violation as the student was provided sufficient notice of his suspension and opportunity to be heard and that his instant message conversation qualified as a written threat. Further, because the student stated that he had access to guns and ammunition and picked out a particular date to carry out his threats, the school district had a reasonable basis to forecast a disruption of school activities, and thus the school did not improperly suppress the student's speech.

A.S. by & through Schaefer v. Lincoln Cty. R-III Sch. Dist., 429 F. Supp. 3d 659 (E.D. Mo. 2019)

The United States District Court upheld the suspension of a student for the off-campus Internet posting of a fellow student in a coffin with information on the funeral. The student created a post on the social media platform Snapchat that included a doctored photograph depicting fellow student in a casket, words referring to a funeral and visitation at a funeral home, and 'crying' and 'praying hands' emojis. He shared this post with a limited group of classmates on Snapchat and encouraged them to post the meme to their own Snapchat stories, which they did. The court ruled that it was reasonably foreseeable that student's speech would cause a substantial disruption to the educational setting. The court focused on the reasonableness of the response of the school, not on the intent of the student. The court ruled that administrators that failing to enforce school rules against bullying or punishments for bullying could expose the school to liability.

Shen v. Albany Unified Sch. Dist., 2018 WL 4053482 (N.D. Cal. Aug. 24, 2018)

The United States District Court upheld a decision by school officials to discipline students for racist and derogatory content posted on an Instagram account that was directed at the school. The posts depicted a "Ku klux starter pack," an article on "Things The World Wouldn't Have If Black People Didn't Exist," a KKK hood, and multiple comparisons of African-American women and students to gorillas. The court held that although the speech originated off-campus, it was reasonably foreseeable that it would reach the school and create a risk of a substantial disruption.

Dunkley v. Board of Ed. of Egg Harbor High School District, 216 F. Supp. 3d 485 (D.N.J. 2016)

The federal district court ruled that educators did not violate a student's First Amendment rights when it suspended him for his out-of-school postings on social media that contained derogatory and demeaning comments about fellow students motivated by race, gender, and other distinguishing characteristics of those students. The court held that the student speech triggered school's obligations under New Jersey's Anti-Bullying Act to investigate, respond, and take remedial action.

III. Student Expression in Higher Education

CHRISTIAN LEGAL SOCIETY v. MARTINEZ
130 S. Ct. 2971 (2010)

JUSTICE GINSBURG delivered the opinion of the Court.

This case concerns a novel question regarding student activities at public universities: May a public law school condition its official recognition of a student group -- and the attendant use of school funds and facilities -- on the organization's agreement to open eligibility for membership and leadership to all students?

In the view of petitioner Christian Legal Society (CLS), an accept-all-comers policy impairs its First Amendment rights to free speech, expressive association, and free exercise of religion by prompting it, on pain of relinquishing the advantages of recognition, to accept members who do not share the organization's core beliefs about religion and sexual orientation. From the perspective of respondent Hastings College of the Law (Hastings or the Law School), CLS seeks special dispensation from an across-the-board open-access requirement designed to further the reasonable educational purposes underpinning the school's student-organization program.

In accord with the District Court and the Court of Appeals, we reject CLS's First Amendment challenge. Compliance with Hastings' all-comers policy, we conclude, is a reasonable, viewpoint-neutral condition on access to the student-organization forum. In requiring CLS -- in common with all other student organizations -- to choose between welcoming all students and forgoing the benefits of official recognition, we hold, Hastings did not transgress constitutional limitations. CLS, it bears emphasis, seeks not parity with other organizations, but a preferential exemption from Hastings' policy. The First Amendment shields CLS against state prohibition of the organization's expressive activity, however exclusionary that activity may be. But CLS enjoys no constitutional right to state subvention of its selectivity.

I

.....

At the beginning of the academic year, the leaders of a predecessor Christian organization -- which had been an RSO at Hastings for a decade -- formed CLS by affiliating with the national Christian Legal Society (CLS-National). CLS-National, an association of Christian lawyers and law students, charters student chapters at law schools throughout the country. CLS chapters must adopt bylaws that, *inter alia*, require members and officers to sign a "Statement of Faith" and to conduct their lives in accord with prescribed principles.[41] Among those tenets is the belief that sexual activity should not occur outside of marriage between a man and a woman; CLS thus interprets its bylaws to exclude from affiliation anyone who engages in "unrepentant homosexual conduct." CLS also excludes students who hold religious convictions different from those in the Statement of Faith.

On September 17, 2004, CLS submitted to Hastings an application for RSO status. [T]he Law School rejected the application; CLS's bylaws, Hastings explained, did not comply with the Nondiscrimination Policy because CLS barred students based on religion and sexual orientation.

CLS formally requested an exemption from the Nondiscrimination Policy, but Hastings declined to grant one. "[T]o be one of our student-recognized organizations," Hastings reiterated, "CLS must open its membership to all students irrespective of their religious beliefs or sexual orientation." If CLS instead chose to operate outside the RSO program, Hastings stated, the school "would be pleased to provide [CLS] the use of Hastings facilities for its meetings and activities." CLS would also have access to chalkboards and generally available campus bulletin boards to announce its events. In other

---

[41] The Statement of Faith provides:
"Trusting in Jesus Christ as my Savior, I believe in:
One God, eternally existent in three persons, Father, Son and Holy Spirit.
God the Father Almighty, Maker of heaven and earth.
The Deity of our Lord, Jesus Christ, God's only Son conceived of the Holy Spirit, born of the virgin Mary; His vicarious death for our sins through which we receive eternal life; His bodily resurrection and personal return.
The presence and power of the Holy Spirit in the work of regeneration.
The Bible as the inspired Word of God." App. 226.

words, Hastings would do nothing to suppress CLS's endeavors, but neither would it lend RSO-level support for them. ...

III

A

CLS draws on two lines of decisions. First, in a progression of cases, this Court has employed forum analysis to determine when a governmental entity, in regulating property in its charge, may place limitations on speech. Recognizing a State's right "to preserve the property under its control for the use to which it is lawfully dedicated, *Cornelius* v. *NAACP Legal Defense & Ed. Fund, Inc.*, 473 U.S. 788, 800 (1985) (internal quotation marks omitted), the Court has permitted restrictions on access to a limited public forum, like the RSO program here, with this key caveat: Any access barrier must be reasonable and viewpoint neutral, *e.g., Rosenberger*, 515 U.S., at 829. See also, *e.g., Good News Club* v. *Milford Central School*, 533 U.S. 98, 106-107 (2001); *Lamb's Chapel* v. *Center Moriches Union Free School Dist.*, 508 U.S. 384, 392-393 (1993); *Perry Ed. Assn.* v. *Perry Local Educators' Assn.*, 460 U.S. 37, 46 (1983).[42]

Second, as evidenced by another set of decisions, this Court has rigorously reviewed laws and regulations that constrain associational freedom. In the context of public accommodations, we have subjected restrictions on that freedom to close scrutiny; such restrictions are permitted only if they serve "compelling state interests" that are "unrelated to the suppression of ideas" -- interests that cannot be advanced "through . . . significantly less restrictive [means]. *Roberts* v. *United States Jaycees*, 468 U.S. 609, 623 (1984). See also, *e.g., Boy Scouts of America* v. *Dale*, 530 U.S. 640, 648, (2000). "Freedom of association," we have recognized, "plainly presupposes a freedom not to associate." *Roberts*, 468 U.S., at 623. Insisting that an organization embrace unwelcome members, we have therefore concluded, "directly and immediately affects associational rights." *Dale*, 530 U.S., at 659.

CLS would have us engage each line of cases independently, but its expressive-association and free-speech arguments merge: *Who* speaks on its behalf, CLS reasons, colors *what* concept is conveyed. Instead, three observations lead us to conclude that our limited-public-forum precedents supply the appropriate framework for assessing both CLS's speech and association rights.

First, the same considerations that have led us to apply a less restrictive level of scrutiny to speech in limited public forums as compared to other environments apply with equal force to expressive association occurring in limited public forums. As just noted, speech and expressive-association rights are closely linked. When these intertwined rights arise in exactly the same context, it would be anomalous for a restriction on speech to survive constitutional review under our limited-public-forum test only to be invalidated as an impermissible infringement of expressive association. That result

---

[42] Our decisions make clear, and the parties agree, that Hastings, through its RSO program, established a limited public forum. *See Rosenberger* v. *Rector and Visitors of Univ. of Va.*, 515 U.S. 819, 829, 115 S. Ct. 2510, 132 L. Ed. 2d 700 (1995); Tr. of Oral Arg. 24 (counsel for CLS); Brief for Petitioner 25-26; Brief for Hastings 27-28; Brief for Hastings Outlaw 27.

would be all the more anomalous in this case, for CLS suggests that its expressive-association claim plays a part auxiliary to speech's starring role.

Second, and closely related, the strict scrutiny we have applied in some settings to laws that burden expressive association would, in practical effect, invalidate a defining characteristic of limited public forums -- the State may "reserv[e] [them] for certain groups." *Rosenberger*, 515 U.S., at 829. See also *Perry Ed. Assn.*, 460 U.S., at 49. ("Implicit in the concept" of a limited public forum is the State's "right to make distinctions in access on the basis of . . . speaker identity."); *Cornelius*, 473 U.S., at 806 ("[A] speaker may be excluded from" a limited public forum "if he is not a member of the class of speakers for whose especial benefit the forum was created.").

An example sharpens the tip of this point: Schools, including Hastings, ordinarily, and without controversy, limit official student-group recognition to organizations comprising only students -- even if those groups wish to associate with nonstudents. The same ground rules must govern both speech and association challenges in the limited-public-forum context, lest strict scrutiny trump a public university's ability to "confin[e] a [speech] forum to the limited and legitimate purposes for which it was created." *Rosenberger*, 515 U.S., at 829. See also *Healy*, 408 U.S., at 189 ("Associational activities need not be tolerated where they infringe reasonable campus rules.").

Third, this case fits comfortably within the limited-public-forum category, for CLS, in seeking what is effectively a state subsidy, faces only indirect pressure to modify its membership policies; CLS may exclude any person for any reason if it forgoes the benefits of official recognition. The expressive-association precedents on which CLS relies, in contrast, involved regulations that *compelled* a group to include unwanted members, with no choice to opt out. See, *e.g., Dale*, 530 U.S., at 648. (regulation "forc[ed] [the Boy Scouts] to accept members it [did] not desire" (internal quotation marks omitted)); *Roberts*, 468 U.S., at 623. ("There can be no clearer example of an intrusion into the internal structure or affairs of an association than" forced inclusion of unwelcome participants.).

.....

In sum, we are persuaded that our limited-public-forum precedents adequately respect both CLS's speech and expressive-association rights, and fairly balance those rights against Hastings' interests as property owner and educational institution. We turn to the merits of the instant dispute, therefore, with the limited-public-forum decisions as our guide.

B

We have three times before considered clashes between public universities and student groups seeking official recognition or its attendant benefits. First, in *Healy*, a state college denied school affiliation to a student group that wished to form a local chapter of Students for a Democratic Society (SDS). 408 U.S., at 170. Characterizing SDS's mission as violent and disruptive, and finding the organization's philosophy repugnant, the college completely banned the SDS chapter from campus; in its effort to sever all channels of communication between students and the group, university officials went so far as to disband a meeting of SDS members in a campus coffee shop. *Id.,* at 174-176. The college, we noted, could require "that a group seeking official recognition affirm in advance its willingness to adhere to reasonable campus law," including "reasonable standards respecting conduct." *Id.,* at 193. But a public educational institution exceeds constitutional bounds, we held, when it "restrict[s] speech or association simply because it finds the views expressed by [a] group to be abhorrent." *Id.,* at 187-188.

We later relied on *Healy* in *Widmar*. In that case, a public university, in an effort to avoid state support for religion, had closed its facilities to a registered student group that sought to use university space for religious worship and discussion. 454 U.S., at 264-265. "A university's mission is education," we observed, "and decisions of this Court have never denied a university's authority to impose reasonable regulations compatible with that mission upon the use of its campus and facilities." *Id.,* at 268, n. 5. But because the university singled out religious organizations for disadvantageous treatment, we subjected the university's regulation to strict scrutiny. *Id.,* at 269-270. The school's interest "in maintaining strict separation of church and State," we held, was not "sufficiently compelling to justify . . . [viewpoint] discrimination against . . . religious speech." *Id.,* at 270, 276.

Most recently and comprehensively, in *Rosenberger*, we reiterated that a university generally may not with hold benefits from student groups because of their religious outlook. The officially recognized student group in *Rosenberger* was denied student-activity-fee funding to distribute a newspaper because the publication discussed issues from a Christian perspective. 515 U.S., at 825-827. By "select[ing] for disfavored treatment those student journalistic efforts with religious editorial viewpoints," we held, the university had engaged in "viewpoint discrimination, which is presumed impermissible when directed against speech otherwise within the forum's limitations." *Id.,* at 831, 830.

In all three cases, we ruled that student groups had been unconstitutionally singled out because of their points of view. "Once it has opened a limited [public] forum," we emphasized, "the State must respect the lawful boundaries it has itself set." *Id.,* at 829. The constitutional constraints on the boundaries the State may set bear repetition here: "The State may not exclude speech where its distinction is not reasonable in light of the purpose served by the forum, . . . nor may it discriminate against speech on the basis of . . . viewpoint." *Ibid.* (internal quotation marks omitted).

C

We first consider whether Hastings' policy is reasonable taking into account the RSO forum's function and "all the surrounding circumstances." *Cornelius*, 473 U.S., at 809.

1

Our inquiry is shaped by the educational context in which it arises: "First Amendment rights," we have observed, "must be analyzed in light of the special characteristics of the school environment." *Widmar*, 454 U.S., at 268, n. 5. (internal quotation marks omitted). This Court is the final arbiter of the question whether a public university has exceeded constitutional constraints, and we owe no deference to universities when we consider that question. Cf. *Pell* v. *Procunier*, 417 U.S. 817, 827 (1974) ("Courts cannot, of course, abdicate their constitutional responsibility to delineate and protect fundamental liberties."). Cognizant that judges lack the on-the-ground expertise and experience of school administrators, however, we have cautioned courts in various contexts to resist "substitut[ing] their own notions of sound educational policy for those of the school authorities which they review." *Board of Ed. of Hendrick Hudson Central School Dist., Westchester Cty.* v. *Rowley*, 458 U.S. 176, 206 (1982). See also, *e.g., Hazelwood School Dist.* v. *Kuhlmeier*, 484 U.S. 260, 273 (1988) (noting our "oft-expressed view that the education of the Nation's youth is primarily the responsibility of parents, teachers, and state and local school officials, and not of federal judges"); *Healy*, 408 U.S., at 180 ("[T]his Court has long recognized 'the need for affirming the comprehensive authority of the States and of school officials, consistent with fundamental constitutional safeguards, to prescribe and control conduct in the schools.'" (quoting *Tinker* v. *Des Moines Independent Community School Dist.*, 393 U.S. 503, 507 (1969))).

A college's commission -- and its concomitant license to choose among pedagogical approaches -- is not confined to the classroom, for extracurricular programs are, today, essential parts of the educational process. See *Board of Ed. of Independent School Dist. No. 92 of Pottawatomie Cty.* v. *Earls*, 536 U.S. 822, 831, n. 4 (2002) (involvement in student groups is "a significant contributor to the breadth and quality of the educational experience" (internal quotation marks omitted)). Schools, we have emphasized, enjoy "a significant measure of authority over the type of officially recognized activities in which their students participate." *Board of Ed. of Westside Community Schools (Dist. 66)* v. *Mergens*, 496 U.S. 226, 240 (1990). We therefore "approach our task with special caution," *Healy*, 408 U.S., at 171, mindful that Hastings' decisions about the character of its student-group program are due decent respect.

2

With appropriate regard for school administrators' judgment, we review the justifications Hastings offers in defense of its all-comers requirement. First, the open-access policy "ensures that the leadership, educational, and social opportunities afforded by [RSOs] are available to all students." Brief for Hastings 32; see Brief for American Civil Liberties Union et al. as *Amici Curiae* 11. Just as "Hastings does not allow its professors to host classes open only to those students with a certain status or belief," so the Law School may decide, reasonably in our view, "that the . . . educational experience is best promoted when all participants in the forum must provide equal access to all students." Brief for Hastings 32. RSOs, we count it significant, are eligible for financial assistance drawn from mandatory student-activity fees, see *supra*, at 3; the all-comers policy ensures that no Hastings student is forced to fund a group that would reject her as a member.

Second, the all-comers requirement helps Hastings police the written terms of its Nondiscrimination Policy without inquiring into an RSO's motivation for membership restrictions. To bring the RSO program within CLS's view of the Constitution's limits, CLS proposes that Hastings permit exclusion because of *belief* but forbid discrimination due to *status*. See Tr. of Oral Arg. 18. But that proposal would impose on Hastings a daunting labor. How should the Law School go about determining whether a student organization cloaked prohibited status exclusion in belief-based garb? If a hypothetical Male-Superiority Club barred a female student from running for its presidency, for example, how could the Law School tell whether the group rejected her bid because of her sex or because, by seeking to lead the club, she manifested a lack of belief in its fundamental philosophy?

This case itself is instructive in this regard. CLS contends that it does not exclude individuals because of sexual orientation, but rather "on the basis of a conjunction of conduct and the belief that the conduct is not wrong." Brief for Petitioner 35-36 (emphasis deleted). Our decisions have declined to distinguish between status and conduct in this context. See *Lawrence* v. *Texas*, 539 U.S. 558, 575 (2003) ("When homosexual *conduct* is made criminal by the law of the State, that declaration in and of itself is an invitation to subject homosexual *persons* to discrimination." (emphasis added)); *id.,* at 583 (O'Connor, J., concurring in judgment) ("While it is true that the law applies only to conduct, the conduct targeted by this law is conduct that is closely correlated with being homosexual. Under such circumstances, [the] law is targeted at more than conduct. It is instead directed toward gay persons as a class."); cf. *Bray* v. *Alexandria Women's Health Clinic*, 506 U.S. 263, 270 (1993) ("A tax on wearing yarmulkes is a tax on Jews."). See also Brief for Lambda Legal Defense and Education Fund, Inc., et al. as *Amici Curiae* 7-20.

Third, the Law School reasonably adheres to the view that an all-comers policy, to the extent it brings together individuals with diverse backgrounds and beliefs, "encourages tolerance, cooperation, and learning among students." App. 349.[43] And if the policy sometimes produces discord, Hastings can rationally rank among RSO-program goals development of conflict-resolution skills, toleration, and readiness to find common ground.

Fourth, Hastings' policy, which incorporates -- in fact, subsumes -- state-law proscriptions on discrimination, conveys the Law School's decision "to decline to subsidize with public monies and benefits conduct of which the people of California disapprove." Brief for Hastings 35; *id.,* at 33-34 (citing Cal. Educ. Code § 66270 (prohibiting discrimination on various bases)). State law, of course, may not *command* that public universities take action impermissible under the First Amendment. But so long as a public university does not contravene constitutional limits, its choice to advance state-law goals through the school's educational endeavors stands on firm footing.

In sum, the several justifications Hastings asserts in support of its all-comers requirement are surely reasonable in light of the RSO forum's purposes.

3

The Law School's policy is all the more creditworthy in view of the "substantial alternative channels that remain open for [CLS-student] communication to take place." *Perry Ed. Assn.*, 460 U.S., at 53. If restrictions on access to a limited public forum are viewpoint discriminatory, the ability of a group to exist outside the forum would not cure the constitutional shortcoming. But when access barriers are viewpoint neutral, our decisions have counted it significant that other available avenues for the group to exercise its First Amendment rights lessen the burden created by those barriers. See *ibid.*; *Cornelius*, 473 U.S., at 809 ; *Greer* v. *Spock*, 424 U.S. 828 (1976); *Pell*, 417 U.S., at 827-828.

In this case, Hastings offered CLS access to school facilities to conduct meetings and the use of chalkboards and generally available bulletin boards to advertise events. App. 232-233. Although CLS could not take advantage of RSO-specific methods of communication, see *supra*, at 3, the advent of electronic media and social-networking sites reduces the importance of those channels. See App. 114-

---

[43] CLS's predecessor organization, the Hastings Christian Fellowship (HCF), experienced these benefits first-hand when it welcomed an openly gay student as a member during the 2003-2004 academic year. That student, testified another HCF member, "was a joy to have" in the group and brought a unique perspective to Bible-study discussions. See App. 325, 327.

115 (CLS maintained a Yahoo! message group to disseminate information to students.); *Christian Legal Society* v. *Walker*, 453 F.3d 853, 874 (CA7 2006) (Wood, J., dissenting) ("Most universities and colleges, and most college-aged students, communicate through email, websites, and hosts like MySpace . . . . If CLS had its own website, any student at the school with access to Google -- that is, all of them -- could easily have found it."). See also Brief for Associated Students of the University of California, Hastings College of Law as *Amicus Curiae* 14-18 (describing host of ways CLS could communicate with Hastings' students outside official channels).

Private groups, from fraternities and sororities to social clubs and secret societies, commonly maintain a presence at universities without official school affiliation. Based on the record before us, CLS was similarly situated: It hosted a variety of activities the year after Hastings denied it recognition, and the number of students attending those meetings and events doubled. App. 224, 229-230. "The variety and type of alternative modes of access present here," in short, "compare favorably with those in other [limited public] forum cases where we have upheld restrictions on access." *Perry Ed. Assn.*, 460 U.S., at 53-54. ……

D

We next consider whether Hastings' all-comers policy is viewpoint neutral.

Although this aspect of limited-public-forum analysis has been the constitutional sticking point in our prior decisions, as earlier recounted, *supra*, at 17-19, we need not dwell on it here. It is, after all, hard to imagine a more viewpoint-neutral policy than one requiring *all* student groups to accept *all* comers. In contrast to *Healy*, *Widmar*, and *Rosenberger*, in which universities singled out organizations for disfavored treatment because of their points of view, Hastings' all-comers requirement draws no distinction between groups based on their message or perspective. An all-comers condition on access to RSO status, in short, is textbook viewpoint neutral.

For the foregoing reasons, we affirm the Court of Appeals' ruling that the all-comers policy is constitutional and remand the case for further proceedings consistent with this opinion.

JUSTICE STEVENS, concurring.

The Hastings College of Law's (Hastings) Nondiscrimination Policy contains boilerplate language used by institutions and workplaces across the country: It prohibits "unlawfu[l]" discrimination "on the basis of race, color, religion, national origin, ancestry, disability, age, sex or sexual orientation." …..As written, the Nondiscrimination Policy is content and viewpoint neutral.

JUSTICE KENNEDY, concurring.

To be effective, a limited forum often will exclude some speakers based on their affiliation (*e.g.*, student versus nonstudent) or based on the content of their speech, interests, and expertise (*e.g.*, art professor not chosen as speaker for conference on public transit). When the government does exclude from a limited forum, however, other content-based judgments may be impermissible. …Law students come from many backgrounds and have but three years to meet each other and develop their skills. They do so by participating in a community that teaches them how to create arguments in a convincing, rational, and respectful manner and to express doubt and disagreement in a professional way. A law school furthers these objectives by allowing broad diversity in registered student organizations. But these objectives may be better achieved if students can act cooperatively to learn from and teach each other through interactions in social and intellectual contexts. A vibrant dialogue is not possible if students wall themselves off from opposing points of view……A school quite properly may conclude that allowing an oath or belief-affirming requirement, or an outside conduct requirement, could be divisive for student relations and inconsistent with the basic concept that a view's validity should be tested through free and open discussion. The school's policy therefore represents a permissible effort to preserve the value of its forum.

JUSTICE ALITO, with whom THE CHIEF JUSTICE, JUSTICE SCALIA, and JUSTICE THOMAS join, dissenting.

The Court's treatment of this case is deeply disappointing. …..Brushing aside inconvenient precedent, the Court arms public educational institutions with a handy weapon for suppressing the speech of unpopular groups -- groups to which, as Hastings candidly puts it, these institutions "do not wish to . . . lend their name[s]." Brief for Respondent Hastings College of Law 11; see also *id.*, at 35……

To appreciate how far the Court has strayed, it is instructive to compare this case with *Healy* v. *James*, 408 U.S. 169 (1972), our only First Amendment precedent involving a public college's refusal to recognize a student group. The group in *Healy* was a local chapter of the Students for a Democratic Society (SDS). When the students who applied for recognition of the chapter were asked by a college committee whether they would "'respond to issues of violence as other S.D.S. chapters have,'" their answer was that their "'action would have to be dependent upon each issue.'" *Id.*, at 172-173. They similarly refused to provide a definitive answer when asked whether they would be willing to "use any means possible" to achieve their aims. *Id.*, at 173. The president of the college refused to allow the group to be recognized, concluding that the philosophy of the SDS was "antithetical to the school's policies" and that it was doubtful that the local chapter was independent of the national organization, the "'published aims and philosophy'" of which included "'disruption and violence.'" *Id.*, at 174-175 and n. 4. The effects of nonrecognition in *Healy* were largely the same as those present here. The Court held that the denial of recognition substantially burdened the students' right to freedom of association. …..

It is striking that all of these same burdens are now borne by CLS. CLS is prevented from using campus facilities -- unless at some future time Hastings chooses to provide a timely response to a CLS request and allow the group, as a favor or perhaps in exchange for a fee, to set up a table on the patio or to use a room that would otherwise be unoccupied. And CLS, like the SDS in *Healy*, has been cut off from "the customary media for communicating with the administration, faculty members, and other students." *Id.*, at 181-182. …

In the end, the Court refuses to acknowledge the consequences of its holding. A true accept-all-comers policy permits small unpopular groups to be taken over by students who wish to change the views that the group expresses. Rules requiring that members attend meetings, pay dues, and behave politely, see *ante*, at 27, would not eliminate this threat…..I do not think it is an exaggeration to say that today's decision is a serious setback for freedom of expression in this country. … I can only hope that this decision will turn out to be an aberration.

CHRISTIAN LEGAL SOCIETY v. WALKER
453 F.3d 853 (7th Cir. 2006)

SYKES, Circuit Judge.

Southern Illinois University at Carbondale and its School of Law, a public university and law school, encourage and support a wide variety of student organizations and invite them to apply for official recognition. The benefits of recognition are several. If an organization is officially recognized by the law school, benefits include access to the law school List-Serve (the law school's database of e-mail addresses), permission to post information on law school bulletin boards, an appearance on lists of official student organizations in law school publications and on its website, the ability to reserve conference rooms and meeting and storage space, a faculty advisor, and law school money. During the 2004-2005 school year, SIU School of Law recognized seventeen student organizations-among them, the Black Law Student Association, the Federalist Society, the Hispanic Law Student Association, Law School Democrats, Lesbian and Gay Law Students and Supporters, SIU Law School Republicans, the Student Animal Legal Defense Fund, Women's Law Forum, and CLS. Recognition by the law school does not automatically bestow upon an organization recognition by the larger university, however. For that, organizations must make separate application to SIU; the upside is even more benefits. Groups that register with the university also get university money (it is not clear how much) and access to meeting space at the SIU student center. In June 2005 SIU had 404 registered student organizations.

CLS is a nationwide association of legal professionals and law students who share (broadly speaking) a common faith-Christianity. Members are expected to subscribe to a statement of faith and agree to live by certain moral principles. One of those principles, the one that has caused the dispute in this case, is that sexual activity outside of a traditional (one man, one woman) marriage is forbidden. That means, in addition to fornication and adultery, CLS disapproves active homosexuality. CLS welcomes anyone to its meetings, but voting members and officers of the organization must subscribe to the statement of faith, meaning, among other things, that they must not engage in or approve of fornication, adultery, or homosexual conduct; or, having done so, must repent of that conduct.

In February 2005 someone complained to SIU about CLS's membership and leadership requirements that preclude active homosexuals from becoming voting members or officers. SIU informed CLS of the complaint and asked to see a statement of CLS's membership and leadership policies. CLS obliged. It explained that while "[a]ny student is welcome to participate in CLS chapter meetings and other activities," voting members and officers must subscribe to certain basic principles and beliefs contained in CLS's statement of faith, "including the Bible's prohibition of sexual conduct between persons of the same sex." CLS also told SIU that a person "who may have engaged in homosexual conduct in the past but has repented of that conduct, or who has homosexual inclinations but does not engage in or affirm homosexual conduct, would not be prevented from serving as an officer or member."

In response, the law school dean revoked CLS's registered student organization status, telling CLS that the "tenets of the national CLS" violated two university policies. The first is SIU's Affirmative Action/Equal Employment Opportunity Policy. In pertinent part, the policy states that SIU will "provide equal employment and education opportunities for all qualified persons without regard to race, color, religion, sex, national origin, age, disability, status as a disabled veteran of the Vietnam era, sexual orientation, or marital status." The second is a policy of the SIU Board of Trustees which provides that "[n]o student constituency body or recognized student organization shall be authorized unless it adheres to all appropriate federal or state laws concerning nondiscrimination and equal opportunity." As a result of derecognition, CLS was no longer able to reserve law school rooms for private meetings. CLS could use law school classrooms to meet, but not privately—other students and faculty were free to come and go from the room. CLS also was denied access to law school bulletin boards, representation on the law school's website or in its publications, and the liberty to refer to itself as the "SIU Chapter of" the Christian Legal Society. Finally, CLS was stripped of an official faculty advisor, free use of the SIU School of Law auditorium, access to the law school's List-Serve, and any funds provided to registered student organizations.

II. Discussion

To win a preliminary injunction, a party must show that it is reasonably likely to succeed on the merits, it is suffering irreparable harm that outweighs any harm the nonmoving party will suffer if the injunction is granted, there is no adequate remedy at law, and an injunction would not harm the public interest. ...In a First Amendment case, we are required to make an independent review of the record because "the reaches of the First Amendment are ultimately defined by the facts it is held to embrace," and the reviewing court must decide independently whether "a given course of conduct falls on the near or far side of the line of constitutional protection." *Hurley v. Irish-American Gay, Lesbian & Bisexual Group of Boston*, 515 U.S. 557, 567 (1995 *see also BSA v. Dale,* 530 U.S. 640, 648-49 (2000).

A. Likelihood of Success on the Merits

The district court concluded that because derecognition did not preclude CLS from meeting and expressing itself (it just had to do so without the benefits that official student organization status brings), CLS had not shown a likelihood of success on the merits. We disagree. There are three reasons CLS is reasonably likely to succeed on the merits, and any one of them is enough to carry CLS's burden. First, it is not clear CLS actually violated any SIU policy, which was the justification offered for revoking its recognized student organization status. Second, CLS has shown a likelihood that SIU impermissibly infringed on CLS's right of expressive association. Finally, CLS has shown a likelihood that SIU violated CLS's free speech rights by ejecting it from a speech forum in which it had a right to remain.

****

3. Free Speech

The government violates the Free Speech Clause of the First Amendment when it excludes a speaker from a speech forum the speaker is entitled to enter. *See Rosenberger*, 515 U.S. at 829-30; *Hosty v. Carter*, 412 F.3d 731, 737 (7th Cir. 2005). SIU has created a speech forum for student organizations and has bestowed certain benefits on those who are qualified to enter the forum. CLS alleges that SIU violated its free speech rights by ejecting it from that speech forum without a compelling reason.

The level of scrutiny applicable to the government's actions in this type of free speech case differs depending on the nature of forum from which the speaker has been excluded. *Good News Club v. Milford Cent. Sch.*, 533 U.S. 98, 106 (2001); *see also Anderson v. Milwaukee County*, 433 F.3d 975, 979 (7th Cir. 2006). The Supreme Court has identified three different types of speech for a for purposes of First Amendment analysis. In an open or traditional public forum, state restrictions on speech get strict scrutiny. *Good News Club*, 533 U.S. at 106; *Lamb's Chapel v. Ctr. Moriches Union Free Sch. Dist.*, 508 U.S. 384, 391 (1993); *Widmar v. Vincent*, 454 U.S. 263, 269-79 (1981); *Hosty*, 412 F.3d at 736-37. The government may "exclude a speaker from a traditional public forum 'only when the exclusion is necessary to serve a compelling state interest and the exclusion is narrowly drawn to achieve that interest.'" *Ark. Educ. Television Comm'n v. Forbes*, 523 U.S. 666, 677 (1998) (quoting *Cornelius v. NAACP Legal Def. & Educ. Fund., Inc.*, 473 U.S. 788, 800 (1985)). The same standard applies to a "designated public forum," which is created when the government opens a nontraditional public forum for public discourse. *Forbes*, 523 U.S. at 677; *DeBoer v. Vill. of Oak Park*, 267 F.3d 558, 565-66 (7th Cir. 2001).

Finally, a nonpublic forum—public property that "is not by tradition or designation a forum for public communication"—is subject to less rigorous scrutiny than a traditional open or designated public forum. *Perry Educ. Ass'n v. Perry Local Educators' Ass'n*, 460 U.S. 37, 46 (1983); *Good News Club*, 533 U.S. at 106. Speech restrictions in a nonpublic forum must not discriminate on the basis of viewpoint and "must be 'reasonable in light of the purpose served by the forum.'"[2] *Good News Club*, 533 U.S. at 106-07 (quoting *Cornelius*, 473 U.S. at 806); *Forbes*, 523 U.S. at 682; *Rosenberger*, 515 U.S. at 829; *Lamb's Chapel*, 508 U.S. at 392-93.

Once the government has set the boundaries of its forum, it may not renege; it must respect its own self-imposed boundaries. *Rosenberger*, 515 U.S. at 829; *Hosty*, 412 F.3d at 737 (noting that when a forum is "declared open to speech ex ante, [participants] may not be censored ex post" when government decides the speech is not welcome). Though recognized student organization status is a

---

[2] The forum nomenclature is not without confusion. Court decisions also speak of "limited public" fora; most recently this phrase has been used interchangeably with "nonpublic" fora, which means both are subject to a lower level of scrutiny. *See, e.g., Good News Club v. Milford Cent. Sch.*, 533 U.S. 98, 106 (2001) (identifying limited public fora as subject to the same test as nonpublic fora described in, for example, *Lamb's Chapel v. Ctr. Moriches Union Free Sch. Dist.*, 508 U.S. 384, 392 (1993)). But "limited public forum" has also been used to describe a subcategory of "designated public forum," meaning that it would be subject to the strict scrutiny test. *See, e.g., R.A.V. v. City of St. Paul, Minn.*, 505 U.S. 377, 427 (1992) (Stevens, J. concurring); *Cornelius v. NAACP Legal Def. & Educ. Fund., Inc.*, 473 U.S. 788, 796 (1985) (noting that appellate court did not decide whether forum in question was a limited public forum or nonpublic forum); *DeBoer v. Vill. of Oak Park*, 267 F.3d 558, 566 (7th Cir. 2001).
That confusion has infected this litigation. At oral argument both parties described the student organization forum at SIU as a "limited public forum," but we think they meant different things. CLS noted the diverse array of groups that have recognized student organization status at SIU and maintained that, like those other groups, CLS is entitled to presence in that forum. CLS went on: "[W]hat the law says is that when a public university sets up such a forum and excludes a group that is otherwise eligible for that forum[,] that it can only do so with reference to a compelling state interest." Given the reference to the strict scrutiny test (compelling state interest), CLS was probably thinking of "limited public forum" as "designated public forum." *See Cornelius*, 473 U.S. at 800 ("[W]hen the government has intentionally designated a place or means of communication as a public forum[,] speakers cannot be excluded without a compelling governmental interest."). SIU, on the other hand, focuses on the "limited public forum" test articulated by Good News Club: viewpoint neutrality and reasonableness. Accordingly, while the parties appeared to agree at oral argument that we are probably dealing with a "limited public forum," we will not hold them to that agreement because they were plainly arguing for different levels of scrutiny and the "forum" terminology has not always been clear.

forum of the theoretical rather than the physical kind—a street corner or public square is the physical kind—the same rules apply. *See Rosenberger*, 515 U.S. at 830.

Whether SIU's student organization forum is a public, designated public, or nonpublic forum is an inquiry that will require further factual development, and that is a task properly left for the district court. But even assuming at this stage of the litigation that SIU's student organization forum is a nonpublic forum—making the lowest level of scrutiny applicable—we believe CLS has the better of the argument.

There can be little doubt that SIU's Affirmative Action/EEO policy is viewpoint neutral on its face, but as the record stands, there is strong evidence that the policy has not been applied in a viewpoint neutral way. According to the present record evidence, CLS is the only student group that has been stripped of its recognized status on the basis that it discriminates on a ground prohibited by SIU's Affirmative Action/EEO policy. CLS presented evidence that other recognized student organizations discriminate in their membership requirements on grounds prohibited by SIU's policy. The Muslim Students' Association, for example, limits membership to Muslims. Similarly, membership in the Adventist Campus Ministries is limited to those "professing the Seventh Day Adventist Faith, and all other students who are interested in studying the Holy Bible and applying its principles." Membership in the Young Women's Coalition is for women only, though regardless of their race, color, creed, religion, ethnicity, sexual orientation, or physical ability. There are other examples, but we need not cite them all.

For whatever reason, SIU has applied its antidiscrimination policy to CLS alone, even though other student groups discriminate in their membership requirements on grounds that are prohibited by the policy. SIU contends there is no evidence that other groups would continue to discriminate if threatened with nonrecognition, but that argument is a nonstarter. SIU's Affirmative Action/EEO policy, which SIU insists applies to all student organizations, is a standing threat of nonrecognition; assuming it applies, that is the whole point of the policy.

Whether the policy is reasonable in light of the purposes the forum serves cannot be determined on this record because we do not know precisely what those purposes are (we could speculate, but that would be inappropriate). We need not reach this aspect of the inquiry, however, given our conclusion that CLS has demonstrated a likelihood of success on its claim that SIU is applying its policy in a viewpoint discriminatory fashion. SIU has singled out CLS for derecognition. The record may be spartan, but every part of it right now points to success for CLS.

YOUNG AMERICA'S FOUNDATION v. KALER
370 F.Supp.3d 967 (D. Minn. 2019)

Susan Richard Nelson, United States District Judge

This case arises at the intersection of two competing freedoms: the freedom of public university student groups, and their invited guest speakers, to exercise their First Amendment rights, and the freedom of public universities to manage their facilities in the manner that best advances the University's educational mission.

Plaintiffs – a University of Minnesota student group, Students for a Conservative Voice, as well as an outside organization dedicated to promoting conservative speech on campus, Young America's Foundation, and a conservative political commentator, Mr. Ben Shapiro – have brought "as-applied" and "facial" challenges to the University of Minnesota's policy for handling "large-scale events," under both the First and Fourteenth Amendments. In their "as-applied" challenge, Plaintiffs focus on the manner in which Defendants applied the University's "large-scale events" policy to a speech given by Mr. Shapiro on February 26, 2018. Defendants have moved to dismiss the complaint in its entirety.

The Court grants Defendants' motion in part and denies it in part. The Court grants Defendants' motion with respect to Plaintiffs' "facial" First Amendment challenge, but denies Defendants' motion with respect to Plaintiffs' "as-applied" First Amendment challenge. Further, the Court grants Defendants' motion with respect to Plaintiffs' Fourteenth Amendment Due Process and Fourteenth Amendment Equal Protection claims. The Court explains its reasoning at greater length below.

This litigation centers around a University of Minnesota student affairs policy called the "Large-Scale Events Process" ("LSEP")...The LSEP sets forth a process to be followed "by any registered student group proposing to host a large-scale event on the University of Minnesota campus." The LSEP first defines "large scale event" as a "student group sponsored event taking place in a large campus venue or outdoor space that will draw a significant amount of the campus population, a large off-campus crowd, or represents a significant security concern (i.e., public figure, celebrity, etc)." The LSEP then states that, although a student group has a right to reserve a "large campus venue" for such an event, "the reservation will only be confirmed upon approval by the Large-Scale Events Committee ("LSEC")." The LSEC includes representatives from various campus departments, such as "the University of Minnesota Police Department, University Services, Parking and Transportation, [and] Student Unions and Activities." To secure approval from the LSEC for a venue reservation, the student group must put together a "Large Scale Event Proposal," containing a variety of relevant logistical details, and then must meet with the LSEC, if asked. Ultimately, the LSEC's "determination of whether the campus can support the [student group proposed] event" will be based on factors such as "other events happening on campus, human resources needed to support the event, the impact of the event on the campus community, and the impact of the event on the community surrounding campus."

Plaintiffs allege that the LSEP is unconstitutional, on its face, under either the First Amendment or the Fourteenth Amendment's Due Process Clause. This is largely because the LSEP purportedly "does not provide any objective, non-content-based and non-viewpoint-based criteria for [University officials] to use when deciding to impose restrictions on a proposed event," and, further, "does not limit the discretion of [University officials] when deciding whether to apply the policy to student organizations' events."

Sometime in fall of 2017, SCV decided that it wanted to bring Mr. Shapiro to campus for a lecture. This was so because, although SCV found Mr. Shapiro "to be an incredibly articulate, consistent, and academically accomplished leader in conservative thought," SCV "believed that Mr. Shapiro's viewpoints [were] treated unfairly on campus by University of Minnesota faculty and administrators alike." With the assistance of YAF, SCV reached out to Mr. Shapiro, and Mr. Shapiro, in turn, agreed to come speak to University of Minnesota students (and members of the surrounding community) on February 26, 2018. (noting that YAF provided "assistance and financial support to bring Mr. Shapiro to the University of Minnesota's campus").)

In October 2017, several months before Mr. Shapiro's speech, SCV informed the University that it intended to bring Mr. Shapiro to campus the following February. According to Plaintiffs, "[b]efore any specific details were provided by SCV, Defendant Dussault [the Assistant Director of Student Unions & Activities] explicitly informed SCV that the Shapiro event would be subject to [the LSEP] and stated that he would schedule follow up meetings to discuss details." Nonetheless, because Defendants had allegedly used the LSEP to relocate one of SCV's prior events (a speech by conservative commentator Lauren Southern) "on three occasions without obtaining SCV's prior permission," Plaintiffs allege that SCV immediately took the initiative of reserving "multiple potential rooms" on the centrally-located Minneapolis campus "to avoid being forced to host the Shapiro event in an undesirable location and to make sure that at least one room was available." Because SCV's goal was to hold Mr. Shapiro's speech "in the largest venue available on the Minneapolis campus," the student group "placed reservation requests both verbally and via e-mail for several locations," with seating capacities ranging from 450 to 4,000. Plaintiffs allege that, as of December 6, 2018, at least two of the three rooms SCV reserved were open and available for use on the evening of February 26, 2018 – Mayo Hall, which seats 455 attendees, and Willey Hall, which seats 1,056 attendees. Consequently, on that date, SCV "formally requested use of Willey Hall."

Although the University of Minnesota-Twin Cities has a St. Paul campus that is, by Plaintiffs' admission, only a bus ride away from the Minneapolis campus, Plaintiffs allege that "they always intended to host the Shapiro lecture on the Minneapolis campus" because that campus is "more convenient for the majority of students," and because hosting the lecture on the St. Paul campus "would inhibit attendance" and "burden the effectiveness of the speech." ...However, in late December 2017, Defendants, acting pursuant to the LSEP, determined that the Shapiro speech would be held in a venue on the St. Paul campus that could accommodate a maximum of 500 attendees. Specifically, Plaintiffs allege that Chief of Police Clark sent an e-mail, which was later forwarded to SCV, stating that "the admin has asked that we try to move this visit to the St. Paul campus. It's going to be a security issue with past lectures at other universities." (alleging that, "upon information and belief," President Kaler and Vice President Berthelsen participated in this decision). Lieutenant Buhta and Mr. Dussault allegedly concurred with this assessment, and further asserted, in e-mails to SCV, that Willey Hall's "access to the [West Bank] Skyway" rendered the location unsafe to host Mr. Shapiro.

……

In response, SCV decided to reserve the North Star Ballroom, a 400-person venue on the St. Paul campus. According to Plaintiffs, "[t]ickets for the event sold out in only a few short hours after they were made available," with SCV receiving "725 inquiries within the first 24 hours of offering the tickets." Mr. Shapiro ultimately spoke to a crowd of around 450 people in the North Star Ballroom on February 26, 2018. However, Plaintiffs contend, Defendants' actions prevented Plaintiffs from "deliver[ing] their message to hundreds of students that wanted to attend the event," which "deprived" those students "the opportunity to ... participate in an important dialogue on matters of public concern."

Because of this experience, Plaintiffs' complaint concludes, SCV has "modified, self-censored and suppressed its speech ... by choosing not to invite certain speakers to campus whose content and viewpoint Defendants or other members of the campus community will consider to be more objectionable or controversial than other speakers."

C. The First Amendment Claim

As the Court noted at the outset, Plaintiffs' complaint is best understood as a "facial" challenge to the LSEP, on the one hand, and an "as-applied" challenge to the manner in which Defendants "applied" the LSEP to the Shapiro speech, on the other hand. See Village of Hoffman Estates v. Flipside, Hoffman Estates, Inc., 455 U.S. 489, 494 n.5, 102 S.Ct. 1186, 71 L.Ed.2d 362 (1982) (noting that, in contrast to an as-applied challenge, a "facial challenge means a claim that a law [or policy] is invalid in toto, and therefore incapable of any valid application"). The Court will accordingly analyze Plaintiffs' First Amendment claim on those terms.

……

The Applicable First Amendment Standard

In relevant part, the First Amendment provides that state actors "shall make no law ... abridging the freedom of speech." U.S. Const. amend. I; amend. XIV. Virtually all non-violent political speech is protected by the First Amendment, even when "hurtful," "offensive," or "disagreeable." Snyder v. Phelps, 562 U.S. 443, 458, 131 S.Ct. 1207, 179 L.Ed.2d 172 (2011) (citing Texas v. Johnson, 491 U.S. 397, 414, 109 S.Ct. 2533, 105 L.Ed.2d 342 (1989)). Moreover, because public universities are creatures of state government, the First Amendment's dictates unquestionably apply on their campuses. See Rosenberger v. Rector & Visitors of Univ. of Va., 515 U.S. 819, 115 S.Ct. 2510, 132 L.Ed.2d 700 (1995); Bowman v. White, 444 F.3d 967 (8th Cir. 2006). Indeed, the Supreme Court has noted, the "danger" of "chilling individual thought and expression" is "especially real in the University setting, where the State acts against a background and tradition of thought and experiment that is at the center of our intellectual and philosophic tradition." Rosenberger, 515 U.S. at 835, 115 S.Ct. 2510; accord Bowman, 444 F.3d at 979.

That said, it is equally unquestionable that public universities, just like any governmental entity, "may legally preserve the property under its control for the use to which it is dedicated." Rosenberger, 515 U.S. at 829, 115 S.Ct. 2510 (quoting Lamb's Chapel v. Center Moriches Sch. Dist., 508 U.S. 384, 390, 113 S.Ct. 2141, 124 L.Ed.2d 352 (1993)); see also Victory Found., 640 F.3d at 333 ("[I]t is well-established that the government need not permit all forms of speech on property that it owns and controls."). Because "[a] university's mission is education," federal courts have "never denied a university's *983 authority to impose reasonable regulations compatible with that mission upon the use of its campus and facilities," nor required that a university either "make all of its facilities equally available to students and nonstudents alike," or "grant free access to all of its grounds or buildings." Widmar v. Vincent, 454 U.S. 263, 267 n.5, 102 S.Ct. 269, 70 L.Ed.2d 440 (1981).

In recognition of this delicate balance between the First Amendment rights of individual speakers and the property rights of university proprietors, the Supreme Court and Eighth Circuit have generally held that both university property (like lecture halls) and university programming (like student activity funds) are "limited public forums." See Christian Legal Soc. v. Martinez, 561 U.S. 661, 679, 130 S.Ct. 2971, 177 L.Ed.2d 838 (2010); Rosenberger, 515 U.S. at 828-29, 115 S.Ct. 2510; Gerlich, 861 F.3d at 704-05; Bowman, 444 F.3d at 977-80. This is so because, for the most part, universities "open [their nonpublic] property, limited to use by certain groups," e.g., students, faculty, employees, or "dedicated solely to the discussion of certain subjects," e.g., student-or-university-sponsored lectures. Christian Legal Soc., 561 U.S. at 679 n.11, 130 S.Ct. 2971 (emphasis added). In a limited public forum, the states may place restrictions on First Amendment-protected speech so long as those restrictions are "reasonable in light of the purpose served by the forum," and do not "discriminate against speech on the basis of its viewpoint." Rosenberger, 515 U.S. at 829, 115 S.Ct. 2510; accord Powell v. Noble, 798 F.3d 690, 700 (8th Cir. 2015); Victory Found., 640 F.3d at 334-35.

However, the Eighth Circuit has enunciated a narrow exception to this general rule. That is, if a university "intentionally opens" a portion of its campus "for expressive conduct ... but not limited to a particular type of speech or speaker," that portion of campus is deemed a "designated public forum." Bowman, 444 F.3d at 976. Restrictions on speech in "designated public forums" are evaluated under the "traditional public forum" framework, which is the exacting standard courts apply when reviewing attempts to restrict speech occurring on streets, sidewalks, and public parks. See Ball v. City of Lincoln, Neb., 870 F.3d 722, 730 (8th Cir. 2017) (explaining that, in a "traditional public forum," the "government's ability to permissively restrict expressive conduct is very limited," and any "content-based restriction on speech" will be subject to "strict scrutiny"); but cf. Ward v. Rock Against Racism, 491 U.S. 781, 790, 109 S.Ct. 2746, 105 L.Ed.2d 661 (1989) (noting that, even in a traditional public forum, "content-neutral time, place, and manner requirements," such as noise ordinances or parade permit requirements, are generally permissible).

……

Here, Defendants argue that "limited public forum" analysis should govern the Court's treatment of the LSEP, because the LSEP primarily involves access to places like "classrooms" and "concert halls." (See Defs.' Br. at 15-16.) Plaintiffs, by contrast, argue that a stricter form of scrutiny should apply, such as that applied to "designated public forums," because venues subject to the LSEP, like Willey Hall, are purportedly "public forum[s] for speech and expressive activity by registered student groups at the University." (Pls.' Br. at 11.)

The Court agrees with Defendants, and will accordingly evaluate Plaintiffs' First Amendment claim under the "limited public forum" standard of review. The Court reaches this conclusion for a few reasons. First, every case cited by Plaintiffs in support of applying strict scrutiny involves government regulating access to traditional public forums (outside the university context), or is otherwise readily distinguishable. By contrast, virtually every recent case involving a First Amendment speech challenge to a university policy, regulation, or action has been analyzed under the "limited public forum" framework.

Second, although Plaintiffs could argue that "designated public forum" analysis applies because the LSEP, by its own terms, applies to both "indoor and outdoor areas," the latter of which the public may generally access, that argument is misplaced. [T]here is no plausible allegation here that Defendants have opened their outdoor facilities, with respect to hosting large-scale events, for indiscriminate use by the general public. Indeed, the whole point of the LSEP is to prevent even student groups from hosting such "large-scale" events, anywhere on campus, without first securing the university's permission. This is important because, in the forum analysis, the state's intention controls over all else.

Finally, although Plaintiffs' counsel argued at the motion hearing that strict scrutiny should at least apply with respect to the student plaintiffs (SCV), because, unlike Mr. Shapiro or YAF, they were the ones "the [limited] forum [of Willey Hall] was created for," the Eighth Circuit rejected an analogous argument only a few years ago See Powell, 798 F.3d at 700 n.2 (concluding that First Amendment "case law" does not distinguish between plaintiffs "completely exclude[d] from a forum," and plaintiffs "inside a forum"). Moreover,...the Supreme Court's most recent precedent on the matter effectively holds that "limited public forum" analysis applies to student group plaintiffs, even when those plaintiffs are the ones the "limited forum was created for." See generally Martinez, 561 U.S. at 679-85, 130 S.Ct. 2971.

For these reasons, the Court will review Plaintiffs' First Amendment claim under the standard applicable to "limited public forums."

Plaintiffs' Facial Challenge to the LSEP

As Plaintiffs' Complaint makes clear, Plaintiffs are waging a "facial" First Amendment challenge to the entire LSEP, and are accordingly seeking "injunctive relief" preventing the University from enforcing the LSEP writ large. The Court will review the plausibility of this aspect of Plaintiffs' First Amendment claim first.

As an initial note, it is well-established that, in the First Amendment context, "[f]acial challenges ... are disfavored." Phelps-Roper v. City of Manchester, Mo., 697 F.3d 678, 685 (8th Cir. 2012); accord Nat'l Endowment for the Arts v. Finley, 524 U.S. 569, 580, 118 S.Ct. 2168, 141 L.Ed.2d 500 (1998) (describing "facial invalidation" of a statute or regulation as "strong medicine," best employed "sparingly and only as a last resort"). This is especially so in the educational setting, where "neither [the Eighth Circuit] nor the Supreme Court has ever applied a stringent, facial standard of judicial supervision to the discretionary decisions of schools officials administering a [limited] educational forum." Victory Found., 640 F.3d at 337...With that background principle in mind, the relevant inquiry is whether the Complaint plausibly alleges that the LSEP, on its face, either (1) is not "reasonable in light of the purpose served by the [university] forum," or (2) "discriminate[s] against speech on the basis of its viewpoint." Rosenberger, 515 U.S. at 829, 115 S.Ct. 2510.

Reasonableness

As to the first criteria, the Supreme Court has "repeatedly stressed that a State's restriction on access to a limited public forum 'need not be the most reasonable or the only reasonable limitation.' " Martinez, 561 U.S. at 692, 130 S.Ct. 2971. Indeed, "control over access to a [limited public] forum may be based on the subject matter of the speech, on the identity or status of the speaker, or on the practical need to restrict access for reasons of manageability or the lack of resources to meet total demand." Victory Found., 640 F.3d at 335 (emphasis added). In the university context, the Supreme

Court has also "cautioned courts ... to resist substitut[ing] their own notions of sound educational policy for those of the school authorities which they review," and to give "decent respect" to officials' decisions about how best to manage their student programs. Martinez, 561 U.S. at 686-87, 130 S.Ct. 2971.

Even viewing the allegations in the light most favorable to Plaintiffs, the Complaint fails to plausibly allege that the LSEP, on its face, constitutes an unreasonable restraint on campus speech. The LSEP merely states that a registered student group must "have [the] support of the [LSEC] before a large campus venue reservation can be confirmed," and that, in determining whether the campus can support a large-scale event, the LSEC may consider "other events happening on campus, human resources needed to support the event, [the] impact of the event to the campus community, [and the] impact of [the] event on [the] community surrounding campus." (LSEP.) In other words, the LSEP functions as a kind of permit requirement for students wishing to hold "large-scale events" on campus property, i.e., limited public forums.

Given the "significant public safety interest[s]" universities have in "accommodating crowds," "minimizing the disruption of the educational setting," and "coordinating the use of limited space by multiple entities," this kind of requirement is imminently reasonable.

Viewpoint Discrimination

……

That said, a university policy may also discriminate on the basis of viewpoint if the policy vests unbridled discretion in a government official to control speech. This is so because, "without standards governing the exercise of discretion, a government official may decide who may speak and who may not based upon the content of the speech or viewpoint of the speaker." id. (quoting Lakewood, 486 U.S. at 763-64, 108 S.Ct. 2138)…Because there is no dispute that the LSEP is viewpoint-neutral on its face, Plaintiffs primarily rely on an "unbridled discretion" argument…The Court disagrees. First, almost all of the "unbridled discretion" cases cited by Plaintiffs involved state government regulations in "traditional public fora," and hence provide little guidance in this situation.

[T]he LSEP provides sufficient criteria by which to guide the discretion of the LSEC. The policy is only limited to "student group sponsored large-scale events," not to "any" event, as Plaintiffs suggest, and it provides specific examples of those kinds of events. Moreover, although the LSEP vests the LSEC with significant discretion to approve, deny, or alter a venue request for a "student sponsored large-scale event," the Policy provides sufficient criteria by which to guide this discretion: the LSEC must consider "other events happening on campus," "human resources needed to support the event," "the impact of the event on the campus community," and "the impact of the event on the surrounding community." …The (admittedly scant) on-point case law further buttresses this conclusion. As best the Court can tell, virtually every recent "unbridled discretion" challenge to a written university policy or procedure has been rejected, even when the policy uses similarly broad verbiage. Compare, e.g., Southworth v. Bd. of Regents of Univ. of Wis., 307 F.3d 566, 590-92 (7th Cir. 2002) (upholding university policy for allocating student group funds, even though policy gave university committee discretion to determine if a "substantially equivalent service" was already being provided to students, or if a student group was offering the campus an "identifiable educational service"); Collegians for a Constructive Tomorrow v. Bd. of Regents of Univ. of Wis., 820 F.Supp.2d 932, 942-46 (W.D. Wis. 2011) (same) with Ray, 699 F.3d at 1065 (upholding challenge to university policy because it was "not written or otherwise established by practice"); Southworth, 307 F.3d at 592 (upholding challenge to university "travel grant" policy because, unlike all other student funding decisions, the "Finance Committee did not provide any criteria governing the award of travel grants") (emphasis added).

......

For these reasons, the Court grants Defendants' motion with respect to Plaintiffs' facial First Amendment challenge.

Plaintiffs' As-Applied Challenge to the LSEP

The Court now turns to Plaintiffs' "as-applied" First Amendment challenge. Plaintiffs argue that, when the allegations recited in Section I.C, supra, are taken as true and viewed in the light most favorable to Plaintiffs, it is plausible to infer that Defendants "banished" Mr. Shapiro's speech to the St. Paul campus, not because of genuine "security concerns," but because his conservative message was seen as "controversial" on a liberal university campus. (See Pls.' Br. at 15-17.) What is more, Plaintiffs point out, even if Defendants did not themselves find Mr. Shapiro's speech disagreeable, viewpoint discrimination may still have occurred if Defendants moved Mr. Shapiro's speech simply to appease liberal students, faculty, or community members, without a genuine security concern to justify that appeasement. (See Id. at 18; accord Seattle Mideast Awareness Campaign v. King Cty., 781 F.3d 489, 502-03 (9th Cir. 2015) (noting that, even in a limited public forum, a "heckler's veto" may be a form of "viewpoint discrimination" if "asserted fears of hostile audience reaction are speculative and lack substance, or where speech on only one side of a contentious debate is suppressed"); Burnham v. Ianni, 119 F.3d 668, 676 (8th Cir. 1997) (en banc) (similarly holding that it is not "constitutionally valid" to curtail speech in a limited public forum simply because "other persons on the [ ] campus object[ ] to [the speaker's] viewpoint").)

In response, Defendants argue that it is implausible that viewpoint discrimination occurred here because "the allegations in the complaint make it clear that the University acted only on the basis ... of providing for the security of members of the campus community, as well as maintaining the education environment of the University." Moreover, Defendants contend, "Plaintiffs have not alleged facts giving rise to the inference of the existence of a nexus between the views of potential protestors and Defendants' actions."

On this point, the Court agrees with Plaintiffs. Taken together, and viewed in the light most favorable to Plaintiffs, the allegations in the Complaint plausibly allege that Plaintiffs' "controversial" viewpoint may have motivated Defendants' decisions with respect to the Shapiro speech. For instance, contrary to Defendants' argument that the Complaint "makes clear" that the University acted "only on the basis" of security concerns, the Complaint alleges that "Defendants decided to move the event to the St. Paul campus two months before the event and in the absence of any specific information regarding the event at the University." This allegation matters because, "in the absence of any specific information" about planned protests in response to Mr. Shapiro, or other potentially disruptive behavior, it is plausible that Defendants' decision to move the speech to the St. Paul campus may have been based merely on concerns that some persons on the campus objected to Mr. Shapiro's viewpoint," which, the Eighth Circuit has held, is not a constitutionally valid reason to prohibit someone from speaking in an otherwise-available limited public forum like Willey Hall. See Burnham, 119 F.3d at 676 (finding that University of Minnesota-Duluth officials violated history professors' First Amendment rights when it required them to remove photographs of themselves holding firearms from a departmental display case, simply because some campus members found the photographs "insensitive" and "inappropriate").

Further, the Complaint alleges that numerous well-known liberal speakers were allowed to speak in centrally-located University spaces connected to the skyway (all of whom had some need for security by virtue of their celebrity), while Mr. Shapiro, a well-known conservative speaker, was barred from doing so, based in large part on the purported "security concerns" raised by Willey Hall's access to the skyway. Taken as true, this kind of "unique scrutiny" raises a plausible allegation of viewpoint discrimination, given the Eighth Circuit's recent holding that "imposing" "unique scrutiny" on a campus speaker with a particular viewpoint, as compared to other speakers who do not share that viewpoint, potentially suggests that impermissible viewpoint discrimination is afoot.

For these reasons, the Court denies Defendants' motion with respect to Plaintiffs' as-applied First Amendment challenge.

……

IV. Faculty, Staff and Free Speech

MT. HEALTHY CITY SCHOOL DISTRICT BOARD OF EDUCATION v. DOYLE

429 U.S. 274 (1977)

MR. JUSTICE REHNQUIST delivered the opinion of the Court.

Respondent Doyle sued petitioner Mt. Healthy Board of Education in the United States District Court for the Southern District of Ohio. Doyle claimed that the Board's refusal to renew his contract in 1971 violated his rights under the First and Fourteenth Amendments to the United States Constitution. After a bench trial the District Court held that Doyle was entitled to reinstatement with backpay. The Court of Appeals for the Sixth Circuit affirmed the judgment, 529 F. 2d 524, and we granted the Board's petition for *certiorari*, 425 U.S. 933, to consider an admixture of jurisdictional and constitutional claims.

…..

Doyle was first employed by the Board in 1966. He worked under one-year contracts for the first three years, and under a two-year contract from 1969 to 1971. In 1969 he was elected president of the Teachers' Association, in which position he worked to expand the subjects of direct negotiation between the Association and the Board of Education. During Doyle's one-year term as president of the Association, and during the succeeding year when he served on its executive committee, there was apparently some tension in relations between the Board and the Association.

Beginning early in 1970, Doyle was involved in several incidents not directly connected with his role in the Teachers' Association. In one instance, he engaged in an argument with another teacher which culminated in the other teacher's slapping him. Doyle subsequently refused to accept an apology and insisted upon some punishment for the other teacher. His persistence in the matter resulted in the suspension of both teachers for one day, which was followed by a walkout by a number of other teachers, which in turn resulted in the lifting of the suspensions.

On other occasions, Doyle got into an argument with employees of the school cafeteria over the amount of spaghetti which had been served him; referred to students, in connection with a disciplinary complaint, as "sons of bitches"; and made an obscene gesture to two girls in connection with their failure to obey commands made in his capacity as cafeteria supervisor. Chronologically the last in the series of incidents which respondent was involved in during his employment by the Board was a telephone call by him to a local radio station. It was the Board's consideration of this incident which the court below found to be a violation of the First and Fourteenth Amendments.

In February 1971, the principal circulated to various teachers a memorandum relating to teacher dress and appearance, which was apparently prompted by the view of some in the administration that there was a relationship between teacher appearance and public support for bond issues. Doyle's response to the receipt of the memorandum—on a subject which he apparently understood was to be settled by joint teacher-administration action—was to convey the substance of the memorandum to a disc jockey at WSAI, a Cincinnati radio station, who promptly announced the adoption of the dress code as a news item. Doyle subsequently apologized to the principal, conceding that he should have made some prior communication of his criticism to the school administration.

Approximately one month later the superintendent made his customary annual recommendations to the Board as to the rehiring of nontenured teachers. He recommended that Doyle not be rehired. The same recommendation was made with respect to nine other teachers in the district, and in all instances, including Doyle's, the recommendation was adopted by the Board. Shortly after being notified of this decision, respondent requested a statement of reasons for the Board's actions. He received a statement citing "a notable lack of tact in handling professional matters which leaves much doubt as to your sincerity in establishing good school relationships." That general statement was followed by references to the radio station incident and to the obscene-gesture incident.

The District Court found that all of these incidents had in fact occurred. It concluded that respondent Doyle's telephone call to the radio station was "clearly protected by the First Amendment," and that because it had played a "substantial part" in the decision of the Board not to renew Doyle's employment, he was entitled to reinstatement with backpay. App. to Pet. for Cert. 12a-13a. The District Court did not expressly state what test it was applying in determining that the incident in question involved conduct protected by the First Amendment, but simply held that the communication to the radio station was such conduct. The Court of Appeals affirmed in a brief per curiam opinion. 529 F. 2d 524.

Doyle's claims under the First and Fourteenth Amendments are not defeated by the fact that he did not have tenure. Even though he could have been discharged for no reason whatever, and had no constitutional right to a hearing prior to the decision not to rehire him, Board of Regents v. *Roth*, 408 U.S. 564 (1972), he may nonetheless establish a claim to reinstatement if the decision not to rehire him was made by reason of his exercise of constitutionally protected First Amendment freedoms. *Perry v. Sindermann*, 408 U.S. 593 (1972).

That question of whether speech of a government employee is constitutionally protected expression necessarily entails striking "a balance between the interests of the teacher, as a citizen, in commenting upon matters of public concern and the interest of the State, as an employer, in promoting the efficiency of the public services it performs through its employees." *Pickering v. Board of Education*, 391 U.S. 563, 568 (1968). There is no suggestion by the Board that Doyle violated any established policy, or that its reaction to his communication to the radio station was anything more than an ad hoc response to Doyle's action in making the memorandum public. We therefore accept the District Court's finding that the communication was protected by the First and Fourteenth Amendments. We are not, however, entirely in agreement with that court's manner of reasoning from this finding to the conclusion that Doyle is entitled to reinstatement with backpay.

The District Court made the following "conclusions" on this aspect of the case:

> 1) If a non-permissible reason, e.g., exercise of First Amendment rights, played a substantial part in the decision not to renew—even in the face of other permissible grounds—the decision may not stand (citations omitted).
>
> 2) A non-permissible reason did play a substantial part. That is clear from the letter of the Superintendent immediately following the Board's decision, which stated two reasons—the one, the conversation with the radio station clearly protected by the First Amendment. A court may not engage in any limitation of First Amendment rights based on 'tact'—that is not to say that the 'tactfulness' is irrelevant to other issues in this case.

At the same time, though, it stated that

> [i]n fact, as this Court sees it and finds, both the Board and the Superintendent were faced with a situation in which there did exist in fact reason… independent of any First Amendment rights or exercise thereof, to not extend tenure. *Id.* at 12a.

Since respondent Doyle had no tenure, and there was therefore not even a state-law requirement of "cause" or "reason" before a decision could be made not to renew his employment, it is not clear what the District Court meant by this latter statement. Clearly the Board legally could have dismissed respondent had the radio station incident never come to its attention. One plausible meaning of the court's statement is that the Board and the Superintendent not only could, but in fact would have reached that decision had not the constitutionally protected incident of the telephone call to the radio station occurred. We are thus brought to the issue whether, even if that were the case, the fact that the protected conduct played a "substantial part" in the actual decision not to renew would necessarily amount to a constitutional violation justifying remedial action. We think that it would not.

A rule of causation which focuses solely on whether protected conduct played a part, "substantial" or otherwise, in a decision not to rehire, could place an employee in a better position as a result of the exercise of constitutionally protected conduct than he would have occupied had he done nothing. The difficulty with the rule enunciated by the District Court is that it would require reinstatement in cases where a dramatic and perhaps abrasive incident is inevitably on the minds of those responsible for the decision to rehire, and does indeed play a part in that decision—even if the same decision would have been reached had the incident not occurred. The constitutional principle at stake is sufficiently vindicated if such an employee is placed in no worse a position than if he had not engaged in the conduct. A borderline or marginal candidate should not have the employment question resolved against him because of constitutionally protected conduct. But that same candidate ought not to be able, by engaging in such conduct; to prevent his employer from assessing his performance record and reaching a decision not to rehire on the basis of that record, simply because the protected conduct makes the employer more certain of the correctness of its decision.

This is especially true where, as the District Court observed was the case here, the current decision to rehire will accord "tenure." The long-term consequences of an award of tenure are of great moment both to the employee and to the employer. They are too significant for us to hold that the Board in this case would be precluded, because it considered constitutionally protected conduct in deciding not to rehire Doyle, from attempting to prove to a trier of fact that quite apart from such conduct Doyle's record was such that he would not have been rehired in any event.

In other areas of constitutional law, this Court has found it necessary to formulate a test of causation which distinguishes between a result caused by a constitutional violation and one not so caused. We think those are instructive in formulating the test to be applied here.

In *Lyons v. Oklahoma*, 322 U.S. 596 (1944), the Court held that even though the first confession given by a defendant had been involuntary, the Fourteenth Amendment did not prevent the State from using a second confession obtained 12 hours later if the coercion surrounding the first confession had been sufficiently dissipated as to make the second confession voluntary. In *Wong Sun v. United States*, 371 U.S. 471, 491 (1963), the Court was willing to assume that a defendant's arrest had been unlawful, but held that "the connection between the arrest and the statement [given several days later] had 'become so attenuated as to dissipate the taint.' *Nardone v. United States*, 308 U.S. 338, 341." *Parker v. North Carolina*, 397 U.S. 790, 796 (1970), held that even though a confession be assumed to have been involuntary in the constitutional sense of the word, a guilty plea entered over a month later met the test for the voluntariness of such a plea. The Court in *Parker* relied on the same quoted language from *Nardone, supra*, as did the Court in *Wong Sun, supra*. While the type of causation on which the taint cases turn may differ somewhat from that which we apply here, those cases do suggest that the proper test to apply in the present context is one which likewise protects against the invasion of constitutional rights without commanding undesirable consequences not necessary to the assurance of those rights.

Initially, in this case, the burden was properly placed upon respondent to show that his conduct was constitutionally protected, and that this conduct was a "substantial factor"—or, to put it in other words, that it was a "motivating factor" in the Board's decision not to rehire him. Respondent having carried that burden, however, the District Court should have gone on to determine whether the Board had shown by a preponderance of the evidence that it would have reached the same decision as to respondent's re-employment even in the absence of the protected conduct.

We cannot tell from the District Court opinion and conclusions, nor from the opinion of the Court of Appeals affirming the judgment of the District Court, what conclusion those courts would have reached had they applied this test. The judgment of the Court of Appeals is therefore vacated, and the case remanded for further proceedings consistent with this opinion.

GIVHAN v. WESTERN LINE CONSOLIDATED SCHOOL DISTRICT

439 U.S. 410 (1979)

MR. JUSTICE REHNQUIST delivered the opinion of the Court.

Petitioner Bessie Givhan was dismissed from her employment as a junior high English teacher at the end of the 1970-1971 school year. ... [Because she believed that she was the victim of racial discrimination, she] filed a complaint... seeking reinstatement on the ... grounds that nonrenewal of her contract ... infringed her right of free speech secured by the First and Fourteenth Amendments of the United States Constitution. In an effort to show that its decision was justified, respondent School District introduced evidence of, among other things, a series of private encounters between petitioner and the school principal in which petitioner allegedly made "petty and unreasonable demands" in a manner variously described by the principal as "insulting," "hostile," "loud," and "arrogant." After a two-day bench trial, the District Court held that petitioner's termination had violated the First Amendment. Finding that petitioner had made "demands" on but two occasions and that those demands "were neither 'petty' nor 'unreasonable,' insomuch as all the complaints in question involved employment policies and practices at [the] school which [petitioner] conceived to be racially discriminatory in purpose or effect," the District Court concluded that "the primary reason for the school district's failure to renew [petitioner's] contract was her criticism of the policies and practices of the school district, especially the school to which she was assigned to teach."

****

The Court of Appeals for the Fifth Circuit reversed. *Ayers v. Western Line Consol. Sch. Dist.*, 555 F.2d 1309 (1977). Although it found the District Court's findings not clearly erroneous, the Court of Appeals concluded that because petitioner had privately expressed her complaints and opinions to the principal, her expression was not protected under the First Amendment. .... The Court of Appeals also concluded that there is no constitutional right to "press even 'good' ideas on an unwilling recipient," saying that to afford public employees the right to such private expression "would in effect force school principals to be ombudsmen, for damnable as well as laudable expressions." We are unable to agree that private expression of one's views is beyond constitutional protection, and therefore reverse the Court of Appeals' judgment and remand the case so that it may consider the contentions of the parties freed from this erroneous view of the First Amendment.

This Court's decisions in *Pickering*, *Perry*, and *Mt. Healthy* do not support the conclusion that a public employee forfeits his protection against governmental abridgment of freedom of speech if he decides to express his views privately rather than publicly. While those cases each arose in the context of a public employee's public expression, the rule to be derived from them is not dependent on that largely coincidental fact.

In *Pickering* a teacher was discharged for publicly criticizing, in a letter published in a local newspaper, the school board's handling of prior bond issue proposals and its subsequent allocation of financial resources between the schools' educational and athletic programs. Noting that the free speech rights of public employees are not absolute, the Court held that in determining whether a government employee's speech is constitutionally protected, "the interests of the [employee], as a citizen, in commenting upon matters of public concern" must be balanced against "the interests of the State, as an employer, in promoting the efficiency of the public services it performs through its employees." 391 U.S., at 568. The Court concluded that under the circumstances of that case "the interest of the school administration in limiting teachers' opportunities to contribute to public debate [was] not significantly greater than its interest in limiting a similar contribution by any member of the general public." *Id.* at 573. Here the opinion of the Court of Appeals may be read to turn in part on its view that the working relationship between principal and teacher is significantly different from the relationship between the parties in *Pickering*, as is evidenced by its reference to its own opinion in *Abbott v. Thetford*, 534 F.2d 1101 (1976) (en banc), *cert. denied,* 430 U.S. 954 (1977). But we do not feel confident that the Court of Appeals' decision would have been placed on that ground notwithstanding its view that the First Amendment does not require the same sort of *Pickering* balancing for the private expression of a public employee as it does for public expression.

Although the First Amendment's protection of government employees extends to private as well as public expression, striking the *Pickering* balance in each context may involve different considerations. When a teacher speaks publicly, it is generally the content of his statements that must be assessed to determine whether they "in any way either impeded the teacher's proper performance of his daily duties in the classroom or . . . interfered with the regular operation of the schools generally." *Id.* at 572-573. Private expression, however, may in some situations bring additional factors to the *Pickering* calculus. When a government employee personally confronts his immediate superior, the employing agency's institutional efficiency may be threatened not only by the content of the employee's message but also by the manner, time, and place in which it is delivered.

. . . . .

The First Amendment forbids abridgment of the "freedom of speech." Neither the Amendment itself nor our decisions indicate that this freedom is lost to the public employee who arranges to communicate privately with his employer rather than to spread his views before the public. We decline to adopt such a view of the First Amendment.

While this case was pending on appeal to the Court of Appeals, *Mt. Healthy City Bd. of Ed. v. Doyle*, [*Mt. Healthy City Sch. Dist. Bd. of Educ. v. Doyle*, 429 U.S. 274 (1977)] was decided. In that case this Court rejected the view that a public employee must be reinstated whenever constitutionally protected conduct plays a "substantial" part in the employer's decision to terminate. Such a rule would require reinstatement of employees that the public employer would have dismissed even if the constitutionally protected conduct had not occurred and, consequently, "could place an employee in a better position as a result of the exercise of constitutionally protected conduct than he would have occupied had he done nothing." 429 U.S., at 285. Thus, the Court held once the employee has shown that his constitutionally protected conduct played a "substantial" role in the employer's decision not to rehire him, the employer is entitled to show "by a preponderance of the evidence that it would have reached the same decision as to [the employee's] re-employment even in the absence of the protected conduct." *Id.* at 287.

.....

Since this case was tried before *Mt. Healthy* was decided, it is not surprising that respondents did not attempt to prove in the District Court that the decision not to rehire petitioner would have been made even absent consideration of her "demands." Thus, the case came to the Court of Appeals in very much the same posture as *Mt. Healthy* was presented to this Court. And while the District Court found that petitioner's "criticism" was the "primary" reason for the School District's failure to rehire her, it did not find that she would have been rehired but for her criticism. Respondents' *Mt. Healthy* claim called for a factual determination which could not, on this record, be resolved by the Court of Appeals.

Accordingly, the judgment of the Court of Appeals is vacated insofar as it relates to petitioner, and the case is remanded for further proceedings consistent with this opinion.

MAYER v. MONROE COUNTY COMMUNITY SCHOOL CORP.

474 F.3d 477 (7th Cir. 2007)

EASTERBROOK, Chief Judge.

Deborah Mayer worked for one year as a probationary elementary-school teacher in Monroe County, Indiana. When the school district did not renew her contract for a second year, Mayer filed this suit under 42 U.S.C. § 1983, maintaining that the school system let her go because she took a political stance during a current-events session in her class, thus violating the first amendment. The district court granted summary judgment to the defendants, so we must accept Mayer's version of events—which is that she answered a pupil's question about whether she participated in political demonstrations by saying that, when she passed a demonstration against this nation's military operations in Iraq and saw a placard saying "Honk for Peace", she honked her car's horn to show support for the demonstrators. Some parents complained, and the school's principal told all teachers not to take sides in any political controversy. Mayer believes that this incident led the school system to dismiss her; we must assume that this is so.

The district court concluded that because military intervention in Iraq is an issue of public importance, Mayer had a right to express her views on the subject, but that the right is qualified in the workplace by the requirement that expression not disrupt an employer's business unduly. This is the method of *Pickering v. Board of Education*, 391 U.S. 563 (1968). After concluding that the employer's interests predominate, the district court gave judgment for the defendants. Mayer contends on appeal that the balance under *Pickering* weighs in her favor. For their part, defendants contend that interest balancing plays no role when the speech in question is part of the employee's official duties. *See Garcetti v. Ceballos*, 126 S. Ct. 1951, 1960 (2006) ("[W]hen public employees make statements pursuant to their official duties, the employees are not speaking as citizens for First Amendment purposes, and the Constitution does not insulate their communications from employer discipline."); *Mills v. Evansville*, 452 F.3d 646 (7th Cir. 2006). Mayer concedes that the current-events session, conducted during class hours, was part of her official duties; if *Garcetti* supplies the rule of decision, then the school district prevails without further ado. Mayer insists, however, that principles of academic freedom supersede *Garcetti* in classrooms, and she relies on a statement in *Piggee v. Carl Sandburg College*, 464 F.3d 667, 672 (7th Cir. 2006), that *Garcetti* was "not directly relevant" to the college instructor's speech in that case.

Whether teachers in primary and secondary schools have a constitutional right to determine what they say in class is not a novel question in this circuit. We held in *Webster v. New Lenox School District No. 122*, 917 F.2d 1004 (7th Cir. 1990), that public-school teachers must hew to the approach prescribed by principals (and others higher up in the chain of authority). Ray Webster wanted to teach his social-studies class that the world is much younger than the four-billion-year age given in the textbook the class was using; he proposed that the pupils consider the possibility of divine creation as an alternative to the scientific understanding. We held that Webster did not have a constitutional right to introduce his own views on the subject but must stick to the prescribed curriculum—not only the prescribed subject matter, but also the prescribed perspective on that subject matter. Following *Palmer v. Board of Education*, 603 F.2d 1271 (7th Cir. 1979), we held in *Webster* that "those authorities charged by state law with curriculum development [may] require the obedience of subordinate employees, including the classroom teacher." 917 F.2d at 1007. *See also Boring v. Buncombe County Board of Education*, 136 F.3d 364 (4th Cir. 1998).

This is so in part because the school system does not "regulate" teachers' speech as much as it hires that speech. Expression is a teacher's stock in trade, the commodity she sells to her employer in exchange for a salary. A teacher hired to lead a social-studies class can't use it as a platform for a revisionist perspective that Benedict Arnold wasn't really a traitor, when the approved program calls him one; a high-school teacher hired to explicate Moby-Dick in a literature class can't use Cry, The Beloved Country instead, even if Paton's book better suits the instructor's style and point of view; a math teacher can't decide that calculus is more important than trigonometry and decide to let Hipparchus and Ptolemy slide in favor of Newton and Leibniz.

Beyond the fact that teachers hire out their own speech and must provide the service for which employers are willing to pay—which makes this an easier case for the employer than *Garcetti*, where speech was not what the employee was being paid to create—is the fact that the pupils are a captive audience. [If] indoctrination is likely, the power should be reposed in someone the people can vote out of office, rather than tenured teachers. At least the board's views can be debated openly, and the people may choose to elect persons committed to neutrality on contentious issues. That is the path Monroe County has chosen; Mayer was told that she could teach the controversy about policy toward Iraq, drawing out arguments from all perspectives, as long as she kept her opinions to herself. The Constitution does not entitle teachers to present personal views to captive audiences against the instructions of elected officials.

Piggee supports the school district rather than Mayer. An instructor at a community college, Piggee had argued that the first amendment allowed her to promote a religious perspective on homosexuality to students in a cosmetology class. We held, to the contrary, that a college may demand that instructors limit their speech to topics germane to the educational mission. A germaneness rule does not entail balancing under *Pickering*; Piggee could not conduct "just a little" proselytizing on the theory that it did not do "very much" harm to the educational mission. Our remark that *Garcetti* was "not directly relevant" did not reflect doubt about the rule that employers are entitled to control speech from an instructor to a student on college grounds during working hours; it reflected, rather, the fact that Piggee had not been hired to buttonhole cosmetology students in the corridors and hand out tracts proclaiming that homosexuality is a mortal sin. The speech to which the student (and the college) objected was not part of Piggee's teaching duties. By contrast, Mayer's current-events lesson was part of her assigned tasks in the classroom; *Garcetti* applies directly. How much room is left for constitutional protection of scholarly viewpoints in post-secondary education was left open in *Garcetti* and *Piggee* and need not be resolved today. Nor need we consider what rules apply to publications (scholarly or otherwise) by primary and secondary school teachers or the statements they make outside of class. It is enough to hold that the first amendment does not entitle primary and secondary teachers, when conducting the education of captive audiences, to cover topics, or advocate viewpoints, that depart from the curriculum adopted by the school system.

Kluge v. Brownsburg Community Schools
432 F. Supp. 3d 823 (S.D. Ind. 2020)

Hon. Jane Magnus-Stinson, Chief Judge

John M. Kluge, a former music and orchestra teacher at Brownsburg High School ("BHS"), filed this action against Brownsburg Community School Corporation ("BCSC") and several of its employees, alleging that he was discriminated against and ultimately forced to resign because his sincerely-held religious beliefs prevented him from following a school policy that required him to address transgender students by their preferred names and pronouns.

……

Mr. Kluge became employed by BCSC as a music and orchestra teacher at BHS in August of 2014, and throughout his employment has received positive performance evaluations and met and exceeded BCSC's legitimate expectations. His students have received multiple awards for their musical performances. Mr. Kluge "is a professing evangelical Christian who strives to live by his faith on a daily basis," and has practiced that faith since before he was employed by BCSC…Mr. Kluge also believes he cannot affirm as true ideas and concepts that he deems untrue and sinful, as this would violate Biblical injunctions against dishonesty, lying, and effeminacy.

During the summer of 2017, BCSC began to allow transgender students and students experiencing gender dysphoria1 to use the restroom of their choice and to change their names and genders in the

BCSC database known as PowerSchool. Name changes in the PowerSchool database required a letter from the student's parent(s) and a letter from a healthcare professional. Two BCSC employees, including Mr. Kluge, were instructed to refer to students using the names and genders listed in the PowerSchool database, which Mr. Kluge believes constitute preferred names "based upon the students' gender dysphoria."[1]

> [1] "Gender dysphoria" is "an acute form of mental distress stemming from strong feelings of incongruity between one's anatomy and one's gender identity." Campbell v. Kallas, 936 F.3d 536, 538 (7th Cir. 2019) (citing Am. Psychiatric Ass'n, Diagnostic & Statistical Manual of Mental Disorders 451 (5th ed. 2013)).

In July 2017, Mr. Kluge informed BCSC Superintendent Dr. James Snapp that the requirement that he use the students' names as listed in PowerSchool ("the Policy") conflicted with his religious beliefs against affirming gender dysphoria, and Dr. Snapp responded that Mr. Kluge could either use the transgender names, say he was forced to resign from BCSC, or be terminated without pay. Because Mr. Kluge refused to use the names listed in PowerSchool, Dr. Snapp initiated an administrative leave of absence for Mr. Kluge and Dr. Bret Daghe, the principal of BHS, issued Mr. Kluge an ultimatum...mandating the use of transgender preferred names, and giving Mr. Kluge three days to decide if he would comply. Mr. Kluge then requested "an accommodation for his religious beliefs," and proposed the solution of "addressing all students by their last names only, similar to a sports coach." Dr. Snapp and Jodi Gordon, the BCSC Human Resources Director, agreed in writing to allow Mr. Kluge to address all students by their last names only ("the last-names-only arrangement") and assigned someone to distribute gender-specific uniforms to students so Mr. Kluge would not have to. Despite this agreement, the school board retroactively administered a two-day suspension in response to Dr. Snapp's previous action.

On December 13, 2017, Mr. Kluge met with Dr. Daghe, at which time Dr. Daghe informed Mr. Kluge that the last-names-only arrangement had created "tension" and that Mr. Kluge should resign by the end of the school year...According to Mr. Kluge, "Defendants simply decided not to accommodate or tolerate [his] sincerely-held religious beliefs any longer," and Ms. Gordon informed him that the last-names-only arrangement was being withdrawn because "students were offended at the use of last names." Mr. Kluge asserts that Ms. Gordon provided no evidence that students were offended and maintains that he "never told his students why he was referring to them by their last names." Mr. Kluge again attempted to explain "that he believes encouraging students to present themselves as the opposite sex by calling them an opposite-sex first name is sinful and potentially harmful to the students," but Ms. Gordon advised him that he could either resign by May 1, 2018 and be paid over the summer or be fired without pay.

……

1. First Amendment Speech Claims

Mr. Kluge asserts three separate claims for violations of his right to freedom of speech under the First Amendment. First, in Count 4, Mr. Kluge alleges that, by punishing and threatening to punish him "for expressing his views regarding gender dysphoria," BCSC retaliated against him for engaging in protected speech. Second, in Count 5, Mr. Kluge asserts that BCSC discriminated against him by disciplining him due to the content and viewpoint of his speech. Finally, in Count 6, he alleges that, by punishing or threatening to punish him "for refusing to communicate a school corporation-mandated ideological message regarding gender dysphoria," BCSC compelled him to communicate messages about gender dysphoria with which he disagreed.

In relevant part, BCSC argues that all of Mr. Kluge's First Amendment speech claims fail because his refusal to address students by the names and genders listed in PowerSchool is not protected speech under the First Amendment. Specifically, it argues that, as a matter of law, Mr. Kluge was speaking in his capacity as a public-school teacher—not as a private citizen—when addressing students. Furthermore, according to BCSC, addressing students in the classroom does not constitute a matter of public concern.

Mr. Kluge responds that his speech is indeed protected under the First Amendment. Specifically, he argues that "[i]n speaking and refusing to speak on the mental disorder known as gender dysphoria, [he] spoke as a citizen on a matter of public concern." He asserts that "gender identity" is a matter of great public importance, and his official teaching duties did not include the use of "transgender names" or "a school-mandated message approving 'affirmance therapy' by the use of transgender names which were not students' legal names." He further asserts that neither his ability to teach music and orchestra nor his method of teaching hinged on the use of students' first or last names, pronouns, or honorifics. Mr. Kluge also argues that BCSC cannot now claim that using the first names listed in PowerSchool was part of his official duties, because it agreed to allow him to address students by last names only for a period of time...In reply, BCSC reiterates the arguments raised in its initial brief, and asserts in relevant part that requiring faculty to address students in a consistent manner is "plainly related to [BCSC's] pedagogical interest in having classroom instruction proceed efficiently."

"When a citizen enters government service, the citizen by necessity must accept certain limitations on his or her freedom." Garcetti v. Ceballos, 547 U.S. 410, 418, 126 S.Ct. 1951, 164 L.Ed.2d 689 (2006) (citation omitted). Nevertheless, "[t]he [Supreme] Court has made clear that public employees do not surrender all their First Amendment rights by reason of their employment." Id. at 417, 126 S.Ct. 1951 (collecting cases). "Rather, the First Amendment protects a public employee's right, in certain circumstances, to speak as a citizen addressing matters of public concern." Id. The determination of whether a public employee's speech is constitutionally protected is a question of law. E.g., Kubiak v. City of Chicago, 810 F.3d 476, 481 (7th Cir. 2016).

In Pickering, the Supreme Court considered whether the termination of a public-school teacher based on a letter he wrote to a local newspaper violated the First Amendment. Pickering v. Bd. of Ed. of Twp. High Sch. Dist. 205, Will Cty., Illinois, 391 U.S. 563, 565-66, 88 S.Ct. 1731, 20 L.Ed.2d 811 (1968). In doing so, the Court sought to balance "the interests of the teacher, as a citizen, in commenting upon matters of public concern and the interest of the State, as an employer, in promoting the efficiency of the public services it performs through its employees." Id. at 568, 88 S.Ct. 1731. The Court characterized the statements contained in the teacher's letter as concerning issues "currently the subject of public attention," which were critical of his employer but were "neither shown nor ... presumed to have in any way either impeded the teacher's proper performance ... or to have interfered with the regular operation of the schools," and, therefore, "the interest of the school administration in limiting teachers' opportunities to contribute to public debate [was] not significantly greater than its interest in limiting a similar contribution by any member of the general public." Id. at 572-73, 88 S.Ct. 1731. Accordingly, firing the teacher based on the contents of his letter violated the First Amendment.

From Pickering and its progeny, the Supreme Court has distilled a two-part inquiry to analyze the constitutional protection accorded to public employee speech. Garcetti, 547 U.S. at 418, 126 S.Ct. 1951. The first step is to determine whether the employee spoke as a citizen on a matter of public concern. Id. (citation omitted). If the answer is "no," the employee has no First Amendment cause of action based on the employer's reaction to the speech. Id. (citation omitted). If the answer is "yes," then the possibility of a First Amendment claim arises, and the second step is to determine whether the government entity had an adequate justification for treating the employee differently from any other member of the general public. Id. (citation omitted).

When considering whether an employee spoke as a private citizen, the fact that the employee spoke inside his workplace, rather than publicly, is not dispositive. Neither is the fact that the speech "concerned the subject matter of [his] employment." Id. at 421, 126 S.Ct. 1951. However, "when public employees make statements pursuant to their official duties, the employees are not speaking as citizens for First Amendment purposes, and the Constitution does not insulate their communications from employer discipline." Id. Determining the official duties of an employee requires "a practical inquiry into what duties the employee is expected to perform." Houskins v. Sheahan, 549 F.3d 480, 490 (7th Cir. 2008) (citation omitted).

……

In assessing whether speech addresses a matter of public concern, courts look to the "content, form, and context" of a given statement. Though none of these factors is singularly dispositive, content is the most important of the three. Furthermore, when examining the context of speech, the employee's motive for speaking is a relevant consideration. To that end, motive matters to the extent that even speech on a subject that would otherwise be of interest to the public will not be protected if the expression addresses only the personal effect upon the employee, or if the only point of the speech was to further some purely private interest.

Here, Mr. Kluge has failed to state any claim under the First Amendment because, as a matter of law, the speech at issue is not constitutionally protected. Importantly, he is not asserting that he was disciplined for criticizing or opposing the Policy, but that he was disciplined for refusing to follow it in his classroom by refusing to call students by the first names listed in PowerSchool. Mr. Kluge's own allegations establish that the way in which he addresses students is part of his official duties as a teacher. Mr. Kluge expressly alleges that BCSC sought to regulate his interactions with students inside school and in the context of the school day or school activities. While addressing students by name may not be part of the music or orchestra curriculum, it is difficult to imagine how a teacher could perform his teaching duties on any subject without a method by which to address individual students.

Indeed, addressing students is necessary to communicate with them and teach them the material—as the Seventh Circuit has stated, how teachers relate to students is part of their jobs, and running a classroom is a core academic duty. Thus, the speech at issue was part of Mr. Kluge's official duties, and this alone is sufficient to preclude any free speech claim under the First Amendment.

However, the Court also concludes that Mr. Kluge's choice as to how to address a given student did not involve a matter of public concern. To be sure, issues relating to the treatment of individuals based on their gender identity are of great public importance. However, Mr. Kluge was not conveying a message concerning such matters when he refused to call students by their names as listed in PowerSchool or referred to students by last name only, because the act of referring to a particular student by a particular name does not contribute to the broader public debate on transgender issues. Instead, choosing the name to call a student constituted a private interaction with that individual student and a private statement about Mr. Kluge's subjective perception of that student. In addition, according to Mr. Kluge's own allegations, the only point of his speech was to address students. He did not tell students that he had opinions about using transgender students' preferred names or explain why he was using last names only. Thus, Mr. Kluge's speech—merely stating (or refusing to state) names and pronouns without explaining that his opposition to "affirming" transgender students was the reason for doing so— adds little to the public discourse on gender identity issues, and therefore is not the kind of speech that is valuable to the public debate. Cf. Garcetti, 547 U.S. at 420, 126 S.Ct. 1951 (acknowledging that underlying the public concern inquiry is "the importance of promoting the public's interest in receiving the well-informed views of government employees engaging in civic discussion").

Because the speech at issue was pursuant to Mr. Kluge's official duties as a public employee and did not involve a matter of public concern, he cannot maintain a cause of action for his employer's regulation of or reaction to his speech. Accordingly, BCSC's Motion to Dismiss is GRANTED as to Mr. Kluge's claims for retaliation, content and viewpoint discrimination, and compelled speech under the First Amendment, and those claims are DISMISSED.

2. First Amendment Free Exercise Claim

Mr. Kluge asserts in his Amended Complaint that his "views and expression related to gender dysphoria are motivated by his sincerely-held religious beliefs, are avenues through which he exercises his religious faith, and constitute a central component of his sincerely-held religious beliefs." Accordingly, he alleges, expressing BCSC's "mandated message regarding gender dysphoria" by using the names listed in PowerSchool would require him to violate his sincerely-held religious beliefs.

……

"[N]o Free Exercise Clause violation results where a burden on religious exercise is the incidental effect of a neutral, generally applicable, and otherwise valid regulation, in which case such regulation need not be justified by a compelling governmental interest." Vision Church v. Vill. of Long Grove, 468 F.3d 975, 998 (7th Cir. 2006) (quoting Civil Liberties for Urban Believers v. City of Chicago, 342 F.3d 752, 763 (7th Cir. 2003)) (internal quotations omitted); see also Employment Div., Dep't of

Human Res. of Oregon v. Smith, 494 U.S. 872, 879, 110 S.Ct. 1595, 108 L.Ed.2d 876 (1990) ("[T]he right of free exercise does not relieve an individual of the obligation to comply with a 'valid and neutral law of general applicability on the ground that the law proscribes (or prescribes) conduct that his religion prescribes (or proscribes).' ")...However, the Supreme Court has "been careful to distinguish such [neutral and generally applicable] laws from those that single out the religious for disfavored treatment." Lutheran Church of Columbia, Inc. v. Comer, —— U.S. ——, 137 S. Ct. 2012, 2020, 198 L.Ed.2d 551 (2017).

......

Here, Mr. Kluge's allegations and supporting documentation demonstrate that the Policy was neutral and generally applicable: every teacher, regardless of religious belief, was required to address every student by the name listed in PowerSchool, regardless of what that name was or why...Because the Policy is neutral and generally applicable and Mr. Kluge has not alleged facts showing that it targeted or otherwise was motivated by an animus toward any particular religion or religious belief, he has not stated a claim for violation of the Free Exercise Clause.

Notes and Comments

1. Free Speech and Public Employment

How would you characterize the free speech rights of public educators? Does the *Garcetti* ruling (described in the *Piggee* case) differ all that much from the *Pickering* test that it purports to replace? To what disputes would the *Pickering* test still apply? When would the *Garcetti* test apply?

How do the rights of teachers compare with student rights of expression? Can you identify the line that separates protected speech from unprotected speech for teachers, administrators and staff? In other words, when is it clear beyond quibble that a teacher can speak freely without fear of punishment?

Even before *Garcetti*, some scholars voiced dissatisfaction with the *Pickering* test. One writer criticizes *Pickering* as a test that stifles speech and forces homogeneity among teachers.

> Diversity within the public teacher workforce helps to ensure that students receive the benefit of "wide exposure" to a "robust exchange of ideas," which, in turn, prepares them to become productive members of society. Applying the *Pickering* balancing test to associational rights, however, effectively homogenizes the class of individuals who become public school teachers. [Application of *Pickering*], which permit the government to retaliate against public employees for their associational activities outside the workplace, may preclude an entire subculture of individuals from becoming public educators. If the government may satisfy its *Pickering* burden merely by showing that the prospective teacher's associational activities will likely upset the students, parents, or other faculty members, individuals with ties to minority political groups or who engage in "alternative" lifestyles (or even those who attend midnight showings of the Rocky Horror Picture Show) need not apply. As a result, the individuals who do become teachers will most likely share substantially similar

> backgrounds, and public education will lose the benefit it derives from a diverse teacher force.
>
> Note: The *Pickering* Paper Shield: The Erosion of Public School Teachers' First Amendment Rights Jeopardizes the Quality of Public Education, 16 B.U. Pub. Int. L.J. 313 (2007).

Compare *Kluge v. Brownsburg Community School Corporation* with Professor Namod's criticism on *Garcetti* in the excerpt below that follows these notes.

2. *Givhan*, Mixed Motives and Free Speech Rights of Teachers

On remand from the Supreme Court, Bessie Givhan was reinstated. The trial court and the appellate court agreed that, "that but for Ms. Givhan's exercise of her First Amendment rights she would have been rehired." *Ayers v. Western Line Consol. School Dist.*, 691 F.2d 766, (5th Cir. Miss. 1982). The gist of *Givhan* is that a teacher's private conversation about racial discrimination in the school district with her direct supervisor, on school premises is protected speech.

Givhan may be more significant for its application of the new standards on so-called "mixed-motives" cases announced by the Court in *Mt. Healthy City Board of Education v. Doyle*, 429 U.S. 274 (1977). Under *Mt. Healthy*, Givhan's employers had the burden of establishing that the school board would not have rehired Givhan for reasons other than her free speech. The courts below rejected the evidence of the school district.

> [T]he principal had testified that he had recommended non-renewal of Ms. Givhan's teaching contract because of her hostile attitude and her making of unreasonable demands. These critical suggestions are treated at more length in our opinion on original hearing, We there affirmed the district court's conclusions that Ms. Givhan's "demands" were not constant and in fact were based on but two occasions; that the criticisms were not unreasonable but were of a substantial nature with regard to employment policies and practices perceived to be racially discriminatory; and that the school district's primary motivation in failing to renew her teaching contract was to rid itself of a vocal critic of the district's policies and practices that were capable of interpretation as embodying racial discrimination. *Ayers v. Western Line Consol. School Dist.*, 691 F.2d at 769 (5th Cir. Miss. 1982).

What practical rule on "mixed-motives" emerges from this case? What would you tell an administrator who wishes to dismiss a teacher?

3. Mayer v. Monroe County Community School: The Probationary Teacher

Deborah Mayer appealed her case to the U.S. Supreme Court. The Court refused to review the case. *Mayer v. Monroe County Community School*, 128 S. Ct. 160 (2007). Mayer's case was beset by two complicating factors. First, Mayer was not a teacher with tenure. As an employee who could be dismissed at the will of her employer during her probationary period, the free speech claim was weakened. *See* Second. the Court applied what was then the new rule of *Mt. Healthy City Sch. Dist. Bd. of Educ. v. Doyle*, 429 U.S. 274 (1977).

Sheldon Nahmod: Public Employee Speech, Categorical Balancing and § 1983: A Critique of *Garcetti v. Ceballos*, 42 U. Rich. L. Rev. 561 (2008)*

The Supreme Court's 2006 decision in *Garcetti v. Ceballos* is striking. In the course of limiting an important and respected thirty-eight-year-old First Amendment precedent, *Garcetti* effectively conferred absolute immunity on public employers by excluding employer discipline based on job-required public employee speech from First Amendment scrutiny. It also analogized job-required public employee speech to government speech. It may have thus called into question First Amendment protection for academic freedom because a teacher's classroom speech is job-required.

I conclude that *Garcetti* is unsound as a matter of First Amendment policy because it under-protects public employee speech that is vital to self-government. In addition, it creates perverse incentives for public employees to go public and for their employers to broaden job descriptions to capture as much employee speech as possible. Moreover, it is cause for concern that *Garcetti* calls into question the First Amendment grounding of academic freedom.

.....

In ruling that the job-required speech of public employees is not protected from employer discipline by the First Amendment, the Court used what has evolved into a conventional approach: categorical balancing. Categorical balancing, as distinct from the ad hoc balancing of the Pickering-Connick test, has been used by the Court to deny First Amendment protection to certain categories of speech, e.g., fighting words, obscenity, and child pornography, all of which are considered outside the scope of the First Amendment. On the other hand, categorical balancing has also been used to expand the protection of the First Amendment to include speech previously considered to be outside its scope, e.g., subversive advocacy, defamation, and commercial speech. In addition, categorical balancing was used in *Elrod v. Burns* to provide First Amendment protection to public employees from employer discipline based on their political affiliation, where party affiliation is not an appropriate requirement for the effective performance of job duties.

What the Court does when it balances categorically is weigh what it considers to be the relevant interests, social and individual, at a fairly high level of generality, and then by balancing those interests, arrive at a generally applicable rule to be applied in later cases without further balancing. Categorical balancing is thought to have the advantages of predictability (through rules), as well as the flexibility inherent in the balancing process.

The recent trend in the Court, with the unique exception of child pornography, has been to use categorical balancing to expand First Amendment-protected speech. *Garcetti* is an obvious departure from this trend, but it is also a departure in another way. When the Supreme Court determines that

---

certain categories of speech are unprotected by the First Amendment, a crucial aspect of its categorical balancing is its determination that the affected speech has little or no intrinsic First Amendment value. In marked contrast, *Garcetti* did not question the First Amendment value of job-required public employee speech because the speech was highly valuable and relevant to self-government. The *Garcetti* Court did, however, assert that the First Amendment value of job-related speech is trumped because of the government's overwhelming interest in workplace efficiency as employer. To put this another way, even job-required speech that is clearly a matter of public concern and that is required professionally—perhaps constitutionally—is not protected from employer discipline by the First Amendment because it is not considered the speech of a citizen.

.....

After *Garcetti*, however, the subject matter of the speech, the promotion of self-government, and the value of the speech are not relevant to the threshold inquiry. Now the function of the speech is determinative in deciding the public employee's First Amendment status. If the speech is required by the job, the public employee loses his status as a citizen with First Amendment protection against employer discipline, and he is exclusively an employee. Only where the speech is not job-required, such as when that employee goes public with his speech, does the *Pickering-Connick* test potentially become applicable because the public employee retains his status as a citizen.

D. Some Preliminary Observations on Government Speech and Academic Freedom

[I]t is impossible to ignore a potentially significant case citation in *Garcetti* at the point where Justice Kennedy finished explaining that job-required speech is not protected by the First Amendment because it is not the speech of a citizen. He then states: "Restricting speech that owes its existence to a public employee's professional responsibilities does not infringe any liberties the employee might have enjoyed as a private citizen. It simply reflects the exercise of employer control over what the employer itself has commissioned or created." This statement is immediately followed by a reference to *Rosenberger v. Rector & Visitors of University of Virginia*, and a parenthetical quote from that case: "When the government appropriates public funds to promote a particular policy of its own it is entitled to say what it wishes."

What may be significant about this reference to *Rosenberger* is that government speech is currently considered to be outside of the scope of the First Amendment. In government speech situations, the government is a kind of market participant in the marketplace of ideas, rather than a regulator of that marketplace—a role that insulates government speech from any meaningful First Amendment scrutiny. This exception for government speech suggests *Garcetti's* rationale to be that government employees who engage in job-required speech are never protected by the First Amendment from employer discipline, regardless of the content or context of their speech, because the government has bought the speech.

This possibility of an overbroad application of the government speech doctrine in the public employee speech setting is intimately connected to the issue of academic freedom. Because public elementary, secondary, and higher education teachers are public employees who are paid to speak, *Garcetti* could be read for the proposition that little if any speech uttered in the classroom by a public school teacher or professor is protected from employer discipline by the First Amendment. This reading, however, calls into question prior statements by the Supreme Court that academic freedom is protected by the First Amendment, particularly at the university level.

The Court's unsurprising response to this possible reading is to avoid the subject, because as it correctly observes, the facts in *Garcetti* do not expressly raise the issue of academic freedom. The Court says only the following: "There is some argument that expression related to academic scholarship or classroom instruction implicates additional constitutional interests that are not fully accounted for by this Court's customary employee-speech jurisprudence." However, the very difficult open question, which cannot be avoided by the Court for very long, is how to square *Garcetti*'s categorical balancing approach insulating job-required public employee speech with First Amendment protection of academic freedom.

Perhaps one possibility after *Garcetti* is to focus on the job in a particular educational setting. At the elementary and secondary levels, for example, the primary, albeit not sole, purpose as determined by government is the transmission of basic knowledge and values. Because the students in these environments are a captive audience (and the government typically determines the curriculum), a teacher assigned to teach mathematics should not be protected by the First Amendment from employer discipline if he or she instead teaches a different subject. This appears to be a relatively easy case in which to affirm that the government is hiring the teacher to engage in specified government speech. Also, the government may choose to provide considerable direction to teachers at the elementary and secondary levels to cover, or not cover, a particular topic or sub-topic or to teach by using a specific pedagogical approach. In such cases, if the teacher deviates from that direction, employer discipline for the deviation may be immune from First Amendment scrutiny, although it may be subject to procedural due process protection if inadequate notice was given to the teacher about such a requirement. Insulation from First Amendment scrutiny in such cases makes sense, because government should have the discretion to choose the educational and classroom approach it prefers, just as it should have the discretion to choose the kind of workplace it prefers, regardless of the wisdom of its decision.

In contrast, First Amendment protection may apply more broadly in the university setting than in elementary and secondary public schools, even after *Garcetti.* The purpose of a university, as determined by government, is not exclusively the transmission of knowledge and values but also the development of critical intellectual faculties. Further, the students are older and not a captive audience. Accordingly, the university classroom could be characterized as a kind of designated educational public forum where both faculty and students have a great deal of speech autonomy. Such autonomy is subject to two uncontroversial educational requirements: first, discussion in the classroom must be related, even if loosely, to the subject matter, and second, the educational process must not be impeded by disruptive tactics. In other words, by analogy to *Rosenberger* and its use of forum analysis, university classrooms could be viewed as government creations for the enabling of professorial and student speech, with government viewpoint discrimination prohibited by the First Amendment. Moreover, *Rosenberger* and forum analysis could be used to confer First Amendment protection on the publications of university professors who are required by their jobs to publish; the theory is that universities are in the business of promoting and enhancing the scholarship opportunities of their professors.

Finally, it may be worth noting that, as a practical matter, few public (or private) universities could realistically survive an attempt to treat university professors and their students like elementary and secondary teachers and their students. Not many would choose to teach at or attend institutions of higher education that eliminated academic freedom in teaching and scholarship.

Chapter Eleven
The First Amendment and the Right of Association

> There can be no clearer example of an intrusion into the internal structure or affairs of an association than a regulation that forces the group to accept members it does not desire. Freedom to associate plainly presupposes a freedom not to associate. When the government forces a group to accept for membership someone the group does not welcome and the presence of the unwelcome person affects in a significant way the group's ability to advocate" its viewpoint, the government has infringed on the group's freedom of expressive association. However, the freedom of expressive association, like many freedoms, is not absolute. *Christian Legal Society v. Walker*, 453 F.3d 853 (7th Cir. 2006)

The First Amendment protects the freedom to associate. The scope of the right includes the choice of associating with others as well withholding association with others. In public education, associational rights can be difficult to assert, and litigation by student groups provide an interesting insight into this difficulty. Below you will see cases involving, fraternities, sororities, religious clubs and other student organizations attempting to assert their associational rights.

Compulsory education laws bring students together for the primary purpose of implementing the education mission. Educational policies that further this significant interest cast a shadow over the associational rights of students. Conflicts often arise because of discrimination by student groups who limit their membership to those who share their beliefs. This discrimination may violate school policy, and educators may attempt to coerce the group by withholding official recognition, funding or other benefits.

A unique branch of the right of association involves students who individually object to mandatory fees they pay which then go to support student groups whose messages they find offensive. These students claim that because "money talks" they are being compelled to associate with the objectionable student groups. The courts accept such claims and try to apply a rule that balances the interests of educators and the objecting students.

As you read these cases, try to appreciate the degree of difficulty school officials encounter when managing student groups on campus. Consider how you might advise administrators who are attempting to draft campus rules for recognition, funding and supervision of student groups.

I. Intimate Association

CHI IOTA COLONY OF ALPHA EPSILON PI FRATERNITY v. CUNY
502 F.3d 136 (2d Cir. 2007)

LEVAL, J.:

The College of Staten Island is a public college within the City University of New York system. CSI is committed to pluralism and diversity. The school's mission statement says that it hopes to instill in its students "a sensitivity to pluralism and diversity," and that it views "[e]fforts to promote diversity and to combat bigotry [as] an inextricable part of [its] educational mission." The school requires all students to fulfill a "Pluralism and Diversity" requirement by taking at least one course on that topic. CSI also has a policy of "provid[ing] services for students without regard to . . . sex."

In order for a student group to gain recognition, it must comply with CSI's non-discrimination policy:

> [M]embership and participation in it must be available to all eligible students of the College. In addition, in order to be recognized, each organization must agree not to discriminate on the basis of . . . gender . . . .

A group that is recognized is entitled to the following benefits and privileges:

- The use of CSI facilities and services;
- Eligibility for insurance through the CSI Association;
- The right to use the College of Staten Island name in conjunction with the name of your group;
- The right to solicit contributions, underwriting and advertising outside the College;
- The use of all CSI approved bulletin boards to publicize events;
- Inclusion of events in monthly calendars . . . upon approval by the Office of Student Life;
- To arrange news coverage for events of public interest through the Office of Student Life;
- The opportunity to request a desk, or workspace in the Campus Center, or weekly meeting space in one of the academic buildings;
- The opportunity to apply for special funding through the CSI Student Government; and
- The exclusive use of a centralized mailbox located in Campus Center.

A group which fails to gain recognition is not banned or forbidden to meet or function; it is, however, not accorded the privileges listed above.

The Fraternity

Chi Iota Colony is a male, social fraternity, which draws its members primarily from the CSI student body. The Fraternity identifies itself as a Jewish organization devoted to "the inculcation of the traditional values of men's college social fraternities . . ., community service, and the expression of Jewish culture." Its charter states that the group aims "[t]o foster and promote brotherly love, to inaugurate a spirit of cooperation and helpfulness . . . [and] to encourage vigorous participation in university, college and general activities in [the] community . . . ." Though most Fraternity members are non-practicing Jews, the group welcomes non-Jewish members, and several current members are not Jewish.

The Fraternity does not admit women. According to its president, "The selective, single-sex, all-male nature of the Fraternity is essential to achieving and maintaining the congeniality, cohesion and stability that enable it to function as a surrogate family and to meet [the] social, emotional and cultural needs of its members." He explained that admitting women might lead to romantic relationships between members, causing "inevitable jealousies and other conflicts." Even admitting lesbians might disrupt the special bonds between Fraternity members, because "[h]aving a female in the fraternity is an issue itself."

[M]any of the Fraternity's activities involve non-members. It participates in weekly meetings arranged by JAM with a rabbi. The meetings, which are frequented by about half of the Fraternity's membership, are open to any student who wishes to attend. The Fraternity also participates "in other JAM activities, including building a sukkah for the Jewish celebration of Sukkot." The Fraternity uses the contacts that its members make at JAM meetings to recruit new members. The Fraternity also holds parties and social events once or twice a month that are open to non-members. The Fraternity advertises for these events, charges for admission, and often turns a profit on them. Women are not only allowed to attend these events but are actively encouraged to do so.

On or about March 3, 2004, the Fraternity applied to become a chartered and officially recognized CSI student group. On March 29, Carol Brower, CSI's Director of the Office of Student Life, denied the Fraternity's application. One reason given was the group's failure to comply with CSI's non-discrimination policy.

.....

The right to intimate association protects the close ties between individuals from inappropriate interference by the power of the state. *See Roberts v. U.S. Jaycees*, 468 U.S. 609, 619, 104 S. Ct. 3244, 82 L. Ed. 2d 462 (1984). To determine whether a governmental rule unconstitutionally infringes on an associational freedom, courts balance the strength of the associational interest in resisting governmental interference with the state 's justification for the interference. This will require an assessment of: (1) the strength of the associational interests asserted and their importance to the plaintiff; (2) the degree to which the rule interferes with those interests; (3) the public interests or policies served by the rule imposed; and (4) the tailoring of the rule to effectuate those interests or policies. The more important the associational interest asserted, and the more the challenged governmental rule burdens the associational freedom, the more persuasive must be the state's reasons for the intrusion, and the more precisely tailored the state's policy must be.

Where a policy interferes with core associational liberties, "it cannot be upheld unless it is supported by sufficiently important state interests and is closely tailored to effectuate only those interests." *Zablocki v. Redhail*, 434 U.S. 374 (1978). For instance, where a governmental regulation substantially interferes with close familial relationships, the most exigent level of inquiry—strict scrutiny—is applied.

Rather than balancing CSI's interests in its non-discrimination policy against the Fraternity's interests in opposing the policy, the district court adopted a categorical approach: Either the policy affected a constitutionally protected liberty or it did not. The court reasoned that, if CSI's policy affected a constitutionally protected interest, the "[i]ntrusion on [the] group's freedom of association [wa]s subject to strict scrutiny." In other words, the district court made no distinction between association claims that are strongly protected by the First Amendment and those that are weakly protected; as long as some First Amendment interest was implicated by the policy, the policy would be subjected to the rigors of strict scrutiny.

This categorical approach is inappropriate for dealing with association-rights cases. It fails to account for the "broad range of human relationships that may make greater or lesser claims to constitutional protection from particular incursions by the State." *Roberts*, 468 U.S. at 620. ... [G]overnment regulations may burden associational freedoms substantially, or minimally, or somewhere in between. Thus, the appropriate question in evaluating an associational-interest claim is not—as the district court asked—whether the associational interest claimed receives constitutional protection. Rather, the question is: Upon a balancing of all pertinent factors, do the state's interests, and its means of achieving them, justify the state's intrusion on the particular associational freedom?

The right to intimate association "reflects the realization that individuals draw much of their emotional enrichment from close ties with others," ties that allow for the cultivation and transmittal of shared beliefs. [T]he Court has declined to restrict the right to intimate association to the family context. Instead of adopting a categorical approach, the Court has instructed that relationships must be "locate[d] . . . on a spectrum from the most intimate to the most attenuated of personal attachments." *Rotary Int 'l v. Rotary Club of Duarte*, 481 U.S. 537 (1987). Criteria used to measure the strength of an association's interest in intimacy include "size, purpose, selectivity, and whether others are excluded from critical aspects of the relationship." *Id.* We examine these particulars in the context of the Fraternity's claim.

A. Strength of the Associational Interest

Size: The Fraternity currently has nineteen members, eighteen of whom are CSI students and one of whom is not. It aspires to one day have about fifty pledges per semester. But the Fraternity places no limit on membership size. The fact that the membership roll is not larger is due to the fact that CSI is primarily a commuter campus. Thus, the size limitation is the product of circumstances, not a desire to maintain intimacy. These characteristics render the Fraternity similar to other groups whose intimate-association interests were held to be weak. *See, e.g., Id.* ("The size of local Rotary Clubs ranges from fewer than 20 to more than 900." (emphasis added)); *Id.* ("There is no upper limit on the membership of any local Rotary Club.").

Selectivity: The Fraternity employs some care in selecting recruits in order to ensure that all its members are compatible. Every prospective member goes through a screening interview that involves personal questions, and decisions about whom to invite are made in consultation with all current members.

However, upon each year's graduation, the Fraternity presumably ceases to associate regularly with a quarter of its members and seeks to replace them with new members. Like the Rotary Clubs in Duarte, the Fraternity must "keep a flow of prospects coming to make up for . . . attrition and gradually to enlarge the membership." *Id.* at 546 (quotation marks omitted). The Fraternity thus aggressively recruits new members from the CSI student body. Fraternity members invite approximately one out of ten men they meet on campus—and about a third of the men they know through Jewish groups—to rush events. Most of those who attend a first rush event are invited back for later events, and the majority of those who attend multiple events are asked to pledge. The degree of selectivity displayed by the Fraternity in choosing new members thus compares unfavorably with that employed in creating the strongest of associational interests, as in the cases of marriage or adoption.

Purpose: The Fraternity's purposes are generally inclusive. The Fraternity aims to "foster and promote brotherly love, to inaugurate a spirit of cooperation and helpfulness . . . [and] to encourage vigorous participation in university, college and general activities in [the] community . . . ." The Fraternity hopes to promote in its members a respect for "the traditional values of men's college social fraternities . . ., community service, and the expression of Jewish culture." These are broad, public-minded goals that do not depend for their promotion on close-knit bonds. *See Duarte*, 481 U.S. at 546-47 (Rotary Club's goal, "an inclusive fellowship for service based on diversity of interest, . . . does not suggest the kind of private or personal relationship to which we have accorded protection under the First Amendment." (quotation marks and citation omitted)).

To be sure, the Fraternity also seeks to foster personal, intimate relationships between its members. According to its president, Fraternity brothers form "deep attachments and commitments" and share "a community of thoughts, experiences, beliefs and distinctly personal aspects of their lives." But the same can be said of nearly any student group in which members become close friends. As the Supreme Court explained in rejecting a facial challenge to an anti-discrimination law that affected clubs with more than 400 members:

It may well be that a considerable amount of private or intimate association occurs in such a setting, as is also true in many restaurants and other places of public accommodation, but that fact alone does not afford the entity as a whole any constitutional immunity to practice discrimination when the government has barred it from doing so. *N.Y. State Club Ass'n, Inc. v. City of N.Y.*, 487 U.S. 1, 12 (1988).

Exclusion of Non-Members: It is true that some Fraternity activities take place only among its members. ...Nonetheless, the Fraternity involves non-members in several crucial aspects of its existence. Many rush events are held in public places such as local cafes or pool halls. The Fraternity gives parties, sometimes at a profit, at which non-members—including women—are encouraged to attend. *See N.Y. State Club Ass'n,* 487 U.S. at 12 (regular receipt of payments from non-members is "at least as significant in defining the nonprivate nature of these associations, because of the kind of role that strangers play in their ordinary existence, as is the regular participation of strangers at meetings"). Social events involving non-members occur "perhaps once or twice a month."

.....

Based on its size, level of selectivity, purpose, and inclusion of non-members, the Fraternity lacks the characteristics that typify groups with strong claims to intimate association.

B. The Degree of State Interference

Also important is the fact that CSI's non-discrimination policy interferes only to a limited extent with the Fraternity's associational rights. CSI's policy does not prevent the Fraternity from continuing to exist, to hold intimate meetings, to exclude women, or to exercise selectivity in choosing new members. Denial of recognition has consequences primarily for the Fraternity's non-intimate aspects. CSI's denial of use of school facilities interferes more with the Fraternity's ability to solicit strangers from future classes to become new members than it interferes with the ability of its existing members to gather and share intimate associations. The Fraternity has not shown that the unavailability of school facilities makes it impossible, or even difficult, to find suitable places for meetings. CSI's refusal to subsidize the Fraternity's activities does not constitute a substantial imposition on the group's associational freedom.

C. The State's Interest

CSI's interests in applying its non-discrimination policy are substantial. As the district court acknowledged, "[t]here is undoubtedly a compelling interest in eradicating discrimination based on gender." *See Bd. of Dirs. of Rotary Int'l v. Rotary Club of Duarte*, 481 U.S. 537, 549 (1987) ("[P]ublic accommodations laws 'plainly serv[e] compelling state interests of the highest order.'" (quoting *Roberts*, 468 U.S. at 624) (second alteration in original)). The school's mission statement declares that "[e]fforts to promote diversity and to combat bigotry . . . are an inextricable part of the educational mission of the University." CSI encourages students to form clubs in order to support the school's goals. To gain recognition, a club must "exhibit a clear relationship with the educational mission" of CSI. By denying recognition to student groups that reject members based on gender, CSI's anti-discrimination policy directly promotes the significant, consistent commitment the school has made to oppose discrimination.

Moreover, CSI has a substantial interest in making sure that its resources are available to all its students. When a student group is officially recognized by CSI, it becomes entitled to a range of benefits, including use of CSI facilities and services, eligibility for insurance through the school, the right to use the CSI name in conjunction with the group, and the opportunity to apply for funding from the student government. These benefits are funded in part by tuition paid by CSI's students; CSI's non-discrimination policy ensures that all its students have access to the organizations that enjoy these benefits. *See Roberts*, 468 U.S. at 624 (state has a compelling interest in "assuring its citizens equal access to publicly available goods and services").

.....

In sum, the Fraternity's interests in intimate association are relatively weak; CSI's non-discrimination policy imposes no great burden on the plaintiffs' enjoyment of those interests; the policy serves several important state interests; and the policy is well tailored to effectuate those interests. Given this balance of the pertinent factors, we believe the district court erred in granting a preliminary injunction barring CSI from enforcing its policy of denial of recognition to a group that categorically excludes members on the basis of gender.

Notes and Comments

1. The Right of Intimate Association and Student Groups

The seminal cases on the right of association are Roberts v. United States Jaycees, 468 U.S. 609 (1984); Board of Directors of Rotary International v. Rotary Club of Duarte, 481 U.S. 537 (1987); and Boy Scouts of America v. Dale, 530 U.S. 640 (2000). In both Roberts and Duarte, the Court found that the Jaycees and the Rotary Club were not protected intimate associations because they were not small in size (ranging from fewer than 20 to 900 members), they actively recruited members from the public, they were not sufficiently selective in their admission policies, and the clubs performed many of their activities in public or invited members of the public to attend. See Duarte, 481 U.S. at 546-47; Roberts, 468 U.S. at 621.

In *Pi Lambda Phi Fraternity, Inc. v. University of Pittsburgh*, 229 F.3d 435 (3d Cir. Pa. 2000), a case relied upon for the decision in *Chi Iota Fraternity* above, the court applies *Roberts* and *Duarte* in manner that suggest that no student group can ever invoke protection as an intimate association:

> Similarly, the University chapter of Pi Lambda Phi is not a particularly small association. While the number of students in the Chapter was reduced to 22 after certain members had been expelled and the University had prohibited the Chapter from recruiting new members for a year, the chapter had inducted 20 new members during the fall of 1995, before the drug raid. At all events, a range of 20 to 80 members would put the Chapter within the same size range as the local Rotary Clubs that the Court held did not engage in intimate association in *Duarte*......Furthermore, the Chapter actively recruits new members from the University population at large and it is not particularly selective in whom it admits. The international organization of Pi Lambda Phi strongly encourages its chapters to recruit new members aggressively so as to continue the growth of the organization... We thus find the claim that the Chapter and its members enjoy a constitutional right to intimate association to be without merit.

Under what circumstances would a student group be able to claim associational protection as an intimate group?

2. The Right of Intimate Association and *Boy Scouts of America v. Dale*

In *Boy Scouts of America v. Dale*, 530 U.S. 640 (2000), the U.S. Supreme Court upheld an associational rights claim by the Boy Scouts of American to justify excluding homosexual members from its organization. The Court noted that the forced inclusion of an unwanted person is an infringement upon the group's right to expressive association if the presence of that person affects in a significant way the group's ability to advocate public or private viewpoints.

Professor Snyder contends that policymakers should be careful of the implications of *Dale* when regulating private group membership.

> [T]he State's power over other associations should be strongest in areas where the law is not fundamentally contested. Where there is general agreement among the associations in the community on the legitimacy of a law the State is unlikely to infringe on the sovereignty of a group by applying those laws to it. But where the law is fundamentally contested, as where significant associations in society reject the legitimacy of the rule, the State must tread carefully. In such cases there may be a legitimate reason to impose a contested meaning by force, but such situations should be relatively rare.....Where the meaning is fundamentally contested, it is generally illegitimate for the State to impose its meaning on other associations and compel their acquiescence. The origins of the objection, whether religious or secular, are unimportant." Franklin G. Snyder: Sharing Sovereignty: Non-State Associations and the Limits of State Power, 54 Am. U.L. Rev. 365 (2004).

Could an antidiscrimination law be enforced against a university that believes in racial discrimination? For example, could a State decide that a religious university must permit interracial dating to qualify for a tax exemption? *See Bob Jones Univ. v. United States*, 461 U.S. 574, 595 (1983) (holding that schools that discriminate based on race cannot be deemed to be conferring a public benefit such as to qualify for charitable tax-exemption status).

II. Expressive Association

CHRISTIAN LEGAL SOCIETY v. WALKER
453 F.3d 853 (7th Cir. 2006)

[The primary report of this case appears in Chapter Ten on page 710. The ruling on the expressive association claim by CLS appears below].

.....

The district court concluded that because derecognition did not preclude CLS from meeting and expressing itself (it just had to do so without the benefits that official student organization status brings); CLS had not shown a likelihood of success on the merits. We disagree. There are three reasons CLS is reasonably likely to succeed on the merits, and any one of them is enough to carry CLS's burden. First, it is not clear CLS actually violated any SIU policy, which was the justification offered for revoking its recognized student organization status. Second, CLS has shown a likelihood that SIU impermissibly infringed on CLS's right of expressive association. Finally, CLS has shown a likelihood that SIU violated CLS's free speech rights by ejecting it from a speech forum in which it had a right to remain.

.....

2. Expressive Association

Implicit in the First Amendment freedoms of speech, assembly, and petition is the freedom to gather together to express ideas—the freedom to associate. *Rumsfeld v. Forum for Academic & Institutional Rights, Inc.*, 126 S. Ct. 1297, 1311-12 (2006) ("FAIR"); *Dale*, 530 U.S. at 647-48; *Roberts v. United States Jaycees*, 468 U.S. 609, 622 (1984); *Healy v. James*, 408 U.S. 169, 181 (1972). The freedom to associate assures that the majority (or a powerful or vocal minority) cannot force its views on groups that choose to express unpopular ideas. Government action may impermissibly burden the freedom to associate in a variety of ways; two of them are "impos[ing] penalties or withold[ing] benefits from individuals because of their membership in a disfavored group" and "interfer[ing] with the internal organization or affairs of the group." *Roberts*, 468 U.S. at 623.

The Supreme Court has held that "[t]here can be no clearer example of an intrusion into the internal structure or affairs of an association than a regulation that forces the group to accept members it does not desire." *Id.* Freedom to associate "plainly presupposes a freedom not to associate." *Dale*, 530 U.S. at 648 (quoting *Roberts*, 468 U.S. at 623). When the government forces a group to accept for membership someone the group does not welcome and the presence of the unwelcome person "affects in a significant way the group's ability to advocate" its viewpoint, the government has infringed on the group's freedom of expressive association. *Dale*, 530 U.S. at 648. However, "the freedom of expressive association, like many freedoms, is not absolute." *Id.; see also Roberts*, 468 U.S. at 623. Infringements on expressive association are subject to strict scrutiny; the right of expressive association "may be overridden 'by regulations adopted to serve compelling state interests, unrelated to the suppression of ideas that cannot be achieved through means significantly less restrictive of associational freedoms.'" *Dale*, 530 U.S. at 648 (quoting *Roberts*, 468 U.S. at 623).

Dale and *Hurley* were "forced inclusion" expressive association cases. The Supreme Court held in *Dale* that a New Jersey law prohibiting discrimination in public accommodations could not be constitutionally applied to the Boy Scouts to force the Scouts to accept an openly gay scoutmaster. The Court held that the presence of an openly gay scoutmaster "would significantly burden the organization's right to oppose or disfavor homosexual conduct" and "[t]he state interests embodied in New Jersey's public accommodations law do not justify such a severe intrusion on the Boy Scouts' rights to freedom of expressive association." *Dale*, 530 U.S. at 659. Similarly, in *Hurley*, the Court held that Massachusetts 'public accommodations law could not be constitutionally applied to force a Boston St. Patrick's Day parade organization to accept a parade unit marching under the banner of an Irish gay and lesbian group. The Court held that "[w]hen the law is applied to expressive activity in the way it was done here, its apparent object is simply to require speakers to modify the content of their expression to whatever extent beneficiaries of the law choose to alter it with a message of their own." *Hurley*, 515 U.S. at 578. This, the Court said, "is a decidedly fatal objective." *Id.* at 579.

CLS alleges that SIU's application of its antidiscrimination policy as a justification for revocation of CLS's student organization status unconstitutionally intrudes upon its right of expressive association. The likelihood of success on this claim turns on three questions: (1) Is CLS an expressive association? (2) Would the forced inclusion of active homosexuals significantly affect CLS's ability to express its disapproval of homosexual activity? and (3) Does CLS's interest in expressive association outweigh the university 's interest in eradicating discrimination against homosexuals? *See Dale*, 530 U.S. at 648-59.

It goes without saying that a group must engage in expressive association in order to avail itself of the First Amendment's protections for expressive association. *Id.* at 648. CLS is a group of people bound together by their shared Christian faith and a commitment to "[s]howing the love of Christ to the campus community and the community at large by proclaiming the gospel in word and deed" and "[a]ddressing the question, 'What does it mean to be a Christian in law?'" Members must dedicate themselves to the moral principles embodied in CLS's statement of faith; one of those principles is affirmance of "certain Biblical standards for sexual morality." CLS interprets the Bible to prohibit sexual conduct outside of a traditional marriage between one man and one woman. As such, CLS disapproves of fornication, adultery, and homosexual conduct, and believes that participation in or affirmation of such sexual activity is inconsistent with its statement of beliefs. It would be hard to argue—and no one does—that CLS is not an expressive association.

Our next question is whether application of SIU's antidiscrimination policy to force inclusion of those who engage in or affirm homosexual conduct would significantly affect CLS's ability to express its disapproval of homosexual activity. *Dale*, 530 U.S. at 648. To ask this question is very nearly to answer it. As we have noted, while voting members and officers of CLS must affirm and abide by the standards of sexual conduct contained in its statement of faith, CLS meetings are open to all. SIU's enforcement of its antidiscrimination policy upon penalty of derecognition can only be understood as intended to induce CLS to alter its membership standards—not merely to allow attendance by nonmembers—in order to maintain recognition. There can be little doubt that requiring CLS to make this change would impair its ability to express disapproval of active homosexuality.

CLS is a faith-based organization. One of its beliefs is that sexual conduct outside of a traditional marriage is immoral. It would be difficult for CLS to sincerely and effectively convey a message of disapproval of certain types of conduct if, at the same time, it must accept members who engage in that conduct. CLS's beliefs about sexual morality are among its defining values; forcing it to accept as members those who engage in or approve of homosexual conduct would cause the group as it currently identifies itself to cease to exist. We have no difficulty concluding that SIU's application of its nondiscrimination policies in this way burdens CLS's ability to express its ideas. *See Roberts*, 468 U.S. at 623; *see also Dale*, 530 U.S. at 659; *Hurley*, 515 U.S. at 576 ("[W]hen dissemination of a view contrary to one 's own is forced upon a speaker[,] . . . the speaker's right to autonomy over the message is compromised."); *cf.* FAIR, 126 S. Ct. at 1312 (holding that law school's associational rights are not burdened by law requiring that military recruiters be allowed the same campus access other recruiters are given because military recruiters do not become "members of the school 's expressive association").

Our final question is this: Does SIU's interest in preventing discrimination against homosexuals outweigh CLS's interest in expressing its disapproval of homosexual activity? *Dale*, 530 U.S. at 658-59. In order to justify interfering with CLS's freedom of expressive association, SIU's policy must serve a compelling state interest that is not related to the suppression of ideas and that cannot be achieved through a less restrictive means. *Id.* at 648. Certainly the state has an interest in eliminating discriminatory conduct and providing for equal access to opportunities. *See, e.g., Roberts*, 468 U.S. at 624. But the Supreme Court has made it clear that antidiscrimination regulations may not be applied to expressive conduct with the purpose of either suppressing or promoting a particular viewpoint. *Dale*, 530 U.S. at 659-61; *Hurley*, 515 U.S. at 578-79.

> While the law is free to promote all sorts of conduct in place of harmful behavior, it is not free to interfere with speech for no better reason than promoting an approved message or discouraging a disfavored one, however enlightened either purpose may strike the government." *Hurley*, 515 U.S. at 579; *see also Dale*, 530 U.S. at 661.

What interest does SIU have in forcing CLS to accept members whose activities violate its creed other than eradicating or neutralizing particular beliefs contained in that creed? SIU has identified none. The only apparent point of applying the policy to an organization like CLS is to induce CLS to modify the content of its expression or suffer the penalty of derecognition.

On the other side of the scale, CLS's interest in exercising its First Amendment freedoms is unquestionably substantial. "The First Amendment protects expression, be it of the popular variety or not," *Dale*, 530 U.S. at 660, and "public or judicial disapproval of a tenet of an organization's expression does not justify the State's effort to compel the organization to accept members where such acceptance would derogate from the organization's expressive message." *Id.* at 661. CLS has carried its burden of proving a likelihood of success on its claim for violation of its right of expressive association.

.....

... SIU may not do indirectly what it is constitutionally prohibited from doing directly. Read together, the Supreme Court's holdings in *Dale*, *Hurley*, and *Healy* provide substantial support for CLS's expressive association claim. CLS has demonstrated a reasonable likelihood of success on its claim for violation of its right of expressive association.

CHRISTIAN LEGAL SOCIETY v. MARTINEZ

130 S. Ct. 2971 (2010)

[This Case appears in Chapter Ten, on page 701.]

Notes and Comments

1. The Right of Association and other Student Activities
Do the associational rights of students in college extend beyond their membership in clubs and student groups? Evaluate the following policies:

- a regulation that prohibits visitation by persons of the opposite sex, "in any residence hall, or dormitory maintained by the University, except when moving into the residence halls and during annual homecoming celebrations." *See Futrell v. Ahrens*, 88 N.M. 284, 540 P. 2d 214 (1975).

- a city zoning ordinance valid that restricts the number of homes in which students may live and the number of individuals allowed to reside in each home. *See Farley v. Zoning Hearing Bd.*, 161 Pa. Commw. 229, 636 A. 2d 1232 (1994).

- a campus policy that prohibits door-to-door solicitation in a dormitory if a majority of the students agree that canvassing should be prohibited. *See Brush v. Pennsylvania State University Board of Trustees*, 249 Pa. Super. 164, 375 A. 2d 810 (1977).

2. *See* Martha Minow: Should Religious Groups Be Exempt From Civil Rights Laws?, 48 B.C. L. Rev. 781 (2007); Anne K. Knight: Striking The Balance Between Anti-Discrimination Laws and First Amendment Freedoms: An Alternative Proposal to Preserve Diversity, 30 T. Jefferson L. Rev. 249 (2007); Kenneth L. Marcus: The Most Important Right We Think We Have But Don't: Freedom From Religious Discrimination In Education, 7 Nev. L.J. 171 (2006).

III. Compelled Association

BOARD OF REGENTS v. SOUTHWORTH
529 U.S. 217 (2000)

JUSTICE KENNEDY delivered the opinion of the Court.

Respondents are a group of students at the University of Wisconsin. They brought a First Amendment challenge to a mandatory student activity fee imposed by petitioner Board of Regents of the University of Wisconsin and used in part by the University to support student organizations engaging in political or ideological speech. Respondents object to the speech and expression of some of the student organizations. Relying upon our precedents which protect members of unions and bar associations from being required to pay fees used for speech the members find objectionable, both the District Court and the Court of Appeals invalidated the University's student fee program. The University contends that its mandatory student activity fee and the speech which it supports are appropriate to further its educational mission.

The First Amendment permits a public university to charge its students an activity fee used to fund a program to facilitate extracurricular student speech if the program is viewpoint neutral. We do not sustain, however, the student referendum mechanism of the University's program, which appears to permit the exaction of fees in violation of the viewpoint neutrality principle. As to that aspect of the program, we remand for further proceedings.

I

It seems that since its founding the University has required full-time students enrolled at its Madison campus to pay a nonrefundable activity fee. For the 1995-1996 academic year, when this suit was commenced, the activity fee amounted to $331.50 per year. The fee is segregated from the University's tuition charge. Once collected, the activity fees are deposited by the University into the accounts of the State of Wisconsin. The fees are drawn upon by the University to support various campus services and extracurricular student activities. In the University's view, the activity fees "enhance the educational experience" of its students by "promoting extracurricular activities," "stimulating advocacy and debate on diverse points of view," enabling "participation in political activity," "promoting student participation in campus administrative activity," and providing "opportunities to develop social skills," all consistent with the University 's mission. The allocable portion of the fee supports extracurricular endeavors pursued by the University's registered student organizations or RSO's. To qualify for RSO status students must organize as a not-for-profit group, limit membership primarily to students, and agree to undertake activities related to student life on campus. During the 1995-1996 school year, 623 groups had RSO status on the Madison campus.

.....

RSO's may obtain a portion of the allocable fees in one of three ways. Most do so by seeking funding from the Student Government Activity Fund (SGAF), administered by the ASM. As an alternative, an RSO can apply for funding from the General Student Services Fund (GSSF), administered through the ASM's finance committee. During the 1995-1996 academic year, RSO's received GSSF funding. These RSO's included a campus tutoring center, the student radio station, a student environmental group, a gay and bisexual student center, a community legal office, an AIDS support network, a campus women's center, and the Wisconsin Student Public Interest Research Group (WISPIRG). The University acknowledges that, in addition to providing campus services (e.g., tutoring and counseling); the GSSF-funded RSO's engage in political and ideological expression.

A student referendum provides a third means for an RSO to obtain funding. While the record is sparse on this feature of the University's program, the parties inform us that the student body can vote either to approve or to disapprove an assessment for a particular RSO. One referendum resulted in an allocation of $45,000 to WISPIRG during the 1995-1996 academic year. At oral argument, counsel for the University acknowledged that a referendum could also operate to defund an RSO or to veto a funding decision of the ASM. In October 1996, for example, the student body voted to terminate funding to a national student organization to which the University belonged. Both parties confirmed at oral argument that their stipulation regarding the program's viewpoint neutrality does not extend to the referendum process.

.....

In March 1996, respondents, each of whom attended or still attend the University's Madison campus, filed suit in the United States District Court for the Western District of Wisconsin against members of the board of regents. Respondents alleged, inter alia, that imposition of the segregated fee violated their rights of free speech, free association, and free exercise under the First Amendment. They contended the University must grant them the choice not to fund those RSO's that engage in political and ideological expression offensive to their personal beliefs.

II

The University of Wisconsin exacts the fee at issue for the sole purpose of facilitating the free and open exchange of ideas by, and among, its students. We conclude the objecting students may insist upon certain safeguards with respect to the expressive activities which they are required to support. Our public forum cases are instructive here by close analogy. This is true even though the student activities fund is not a public forum in the traditional sense of the term and despite the circumstance that those cases most often involve a demand for access, not a claim to be exempt from supporting speech. *See, e.g., Lamb's Chapel v. Center Moriches Union Free School Dist.*, 508 U.S. 384 (1993); *Widmar v. Vincent*, 454 U.S. 263 (1981). The standard of viewpoint neutrality found in the public forum cases provides the standard we find controlling. We decide that the viewpoint neutrality requirement of the University program is in general sufficient to protect the rights of the objecting students. The student referendum aspect of the program for funding speech and expressive activities, however, appears to be inconsistent with the viewpoint neutrality requirement.

We must begin by recognizing that the complaining students are being required to pay fees which are subsidies for speech they find objectionable, even offensive. The *Abood* and *Keller* cases, then, provide the beginning point for our analysis. *Abood v. Detroit Bd. of Ed.*, 431 U.S. 209 (1977); *Keller v. State Bar of Cal.*, 496 U.S. 1 (1990). While those precedents identify the interests of the protesting students, the means of implementing First Amendment protections adopted in those decisions are neither applicable nor workable in the context of extracurricular student speech at a university.

In *Abood*, some nonunion public school teachers challenged an agreement requiring them, as a condition of their employment, to pay a service fee equal in amount to union dues. The objecting teachers alleged that the union's use of their fees to engage in political speech violated their freedom of association guaranteed by the First and Fourteenth Amendments. The Court agreed and held that any objecting teacher could "prevent the Union's spending a part of their required service fees to contribute to political candidates and to express political views unrelated to its duties as exclusive bargaining representative." 431 U.S. at 234. The principles outlined in *Abood* provided the foundation for our later decision in *Keller*. There we held that lawyers admitted to practice in California could be required to join a state bar association and to fund activities "germane" to the association's mission of "regulating the legal profession and improving the quality of legal services." 496 U.S. at 13-14. The lawyers could not, however, be required to fund the bar association's own political expression.

The proposition that students who attend the University cannot be required to pay subsidies for the speech of other students without some First Amendment protection follows from the *Abood* and *Keller* cases. Students enroll in public universities to seek fulfillment of their personal aspirations and of their own potential. If the University conditions the opportunity to receive a college education, an opportunity comparable in importance to joining a labor union or bar association, on an agreement to support objectionable, extracurricular expression by other students, the rights acknowledged in *Abood* and *Keller* become implicated. It infringes on the speech and beliefs of the individual to be required, by this mandatory student activity fee program, to pay subsidies for the objectionable speech of others without any recognition of the State's corresponding duty to him or her. Yet recognition must be given as well to the important and substantial purposes of the University, which seeks to facilitate a wide range of speech.

****

The speech the University seeks to encourage in the program before us is distinguished not by discernable limits but by its vast, unexplored bounds. To insist upon asking what speech is germane would be contrary to the very goal the University seeks to pursue. It is not for the Court to say what is or is not germane to the ideas to be pursued in an institution of higher learning.

Just as the vast extent of permitted expression makes the test of germane speech inappropriate for intervention, so too does it underscore the high potential for intrusion on the First Amendment rights of the objecting students. It is all but inevitable that the fees will result in subsidies to speech which some students find objectionable and offensive to their personal beliefs. If the standard of germane speech is inapplicable, then, it might be argued the remedy is to allow each student to list those causes which he or she will or will not support. If a university decided that its students' First Amendment interests were better protected by some type of optional or refund system it would be free to do so. We decline to impose a system of that sort as a constitutional requirement, however. The restriction could be so disruptive and expensive that the program to support extracurricular speech would be ineffective. The First Amendment does not require the University to put the program at risk.

The University may determine that its mission is well served if students have the means to engage in dynamic discussions of philosophical, religious, scientific, social, and political subjects in their extracurricular campus life outside the lecture hall. If the University reaches this conclusion, it is entitled to impose a mandatory fee to sustain an open dialogue to these ends.

The University must provide some protection to its students' First Amendment interests, however. The proper measure, and the principal standard of protection for objecting students, we conclude, is the requirement of viewpoint neutrality in the allocation of funding support. Viewpoint neutrality was the obligation to which we gave substance in *Rosenberger v. Rector* and *Visitors of Univ. of Va.*, 515 U.S. 819 (1995). There the University of Virginia feared that any association with a student newspaper advancing religious viewpoints would violate the Establishment Clause. We rejected the argument, holding that the school's adherence to a rule of viewpoint neutrality in administering its student fee program would prevent "any mistaken impression that the student newspapers speak for the University." *Id.* at 841. While *Rosenberger* was concerned with the rights a student has to use an extracurricular speech program already in place, today's case considers the antecedent question, acknowledged but unresolved in *Rosenberger*: whether a public university may require its students to pay a fee which creates the mechanism for the extracurricular speech in the first instance. When a university requires its students to pay fees to support the extracurricular speech of other students, all in the interest of open discussion, it may not prefer some viewpoints to others. There is symmetry then in our holding here and in *Rosenberger*: Viewpoint neutrality is the justification for requiring the student to pay the fee in the first instance and for ensuring the integrity of the program's operation once the funds have been collected. We conclude that the University of Wisconsin may sustain the extracurricular dimensions of its programs by using mandatory student fees with viewpoint neutrality as the operational principle.

.....

Our decision ought not to be taken to imply that in other instances the University, its agents or employees, or—of particular importance—its faculty, are subject to the First Amendment analysis which controls in this case. Where the University speaks, either in its own name through its regents or officers, or in myriad other ways through its diverse faculties, the analysis likely would be altogether different. *See Rust v. Sullivan*, 500 U.S. 173 (1991); *Regan v. Taxation With Representation of Wash.*, 461 U.S. 540 (1983).The Court has not held, or suggested, that when the government speaks the rules we have discussed come into play.

When the government speaks, for instance to promote its own policies or to advance a particular idea, it is, in the end, accountable to the electorate and the political process for its advocacy. If the citizenry objects, newly elected officials later could espouse some different or contrary position. In the instant case, the speech is not that of the University or its agents. It is not, furthermore, speech by an instructor or a professor in the academic context, where principles applicable to government speech would have to be considered.

III

It remains to discuss the referendum aspect of the University's program. While the record is not well developed on the point, it appears that by majority vote of the student body a given RSO may be funded or defunded. It is unclear to us what protection, if any, there is for viewpoint neutrality in this part of the process. To the extent the referendum substitutes majority determinations for viewpoint neutrality it would undermine the constitutional protection the program requires. The whole theory of viewpoint neutrality is that minority views are treated with the same respect as are majority views. Access to a public forum, for instance, does not depend upon majoritarian consent. That principle is controlling here. A remand is necessary and appropriate to resolve this point; and the case in all events must be reexamined in light of the principles we have discussed.

SOUTHWORTH v. BOARD OF REGENTS

307 F.3d 566 (7th Cir. 2002)

Six years ago, several students at the University of Wisconsin-Madison ("the University") sued the University challenging its mandatory student activity fee system on First Amendment grounds. Following appeals to this court and to the United States Supreme Court, on remand to the district court, the sole issue remaining was whether the mandatory fee system unconstitutionally granted the student government unbridled discretion for deciding which student organizations to fund.

The district court agreed with the students and held that the University of Wisconsin-Madison's mandatory student activity fee system violated the First Amendment. We reverse the district court's decision that the mandatory fee system unconstitutionally grants the student government unfettered discretion, except as to the funding of travel grants for which the student government has yet to adopt specific funding criteria.....

****

To determine whether the unbridled discretion standard is a component of viewpoint neutrality, we turn to several Supreme Court cases for guidance, beginning with *Freedman v. Maryland*, 380 U.S. 51 (1965). In *Freedman*, the Supreme Court considered the constitutionality of a state law requiring movies to be approved by a Board of Censors before being shown anywhere in the state. The Board had the authority to reject films considered "obscene" or that "tended in the judgment of the Board, to debase or corrupt morals or incite to crimes," terms that were broadly defined by the statute. The Court in *Freedman* held that the state law constituted a prior restraint on speech and established a censorship system, and thus was constitutional only if it satisfied certain procedural safeguards. ... While Freedman focused on the procedural requirements for a prior restraint and censorship system, as opposed to the unbridled discretion standard, it is important to begin with *Freedman*. ...

More directly discussing the question of unbridled discretion is the Supreme Court's decision in *Shuttlesworth v. City of Birmingham*, 394 U.S. 147 (1969). In *Shuttlesworth*, the appellant challenged the constitutionality of a city ordinance making it an offense to participate in a parade, procession or other public demonstration without first obtaining a permit from the city commissioner. The ordinance granted the commissioner absolute power to deny a permit to protect "public welfare, peace, safety, health, decency, good order, morals or convenience." The Court began its analysis by reiterating its consistent condemnation of "'licensing systems which vest in an administrative official discretion to grant or withhold a permit upon broad criteria unrelated to proper regulation of public places.'" The Court then concluded that the city's ordinance, as written, was unconstitutional because it conferred upon the city commission "virtually unbridled and absolute power to prohibit any 'parade,' 'procession,' or 'demonstration' on the city's streets or public ways."

.....

From this line of cases there is much to be garnered, but we begin with the initial question of whether the unbridled discretion standard is part of the constitutional requirement of viewpoint neutrality. While the Supreme Court has never expressly held that the prohibition on unbridled discretion is an element of viewpoint neutrality, we believe that conclusion inevitably flows from the Court's unbridled discretion cases. [T]he Supreme Court has made clear that when a decision maker has unbridled discretion there are two risks: First, the risk of self-censorship, where the plaintiff may edit his own viewpoint or the content of his speech to avoid governmental censorship; and second, the risk that the decision maker will use its unduly broad discretion to favor or disfavor speech based on its viewpoint or content, and that without standards to guide the official's decision an as-applied challenge will be ineffective to ferret out viewpoint discrimination. Both of these risks threaten viewpoint neutrality. Given that the risks which the Supreme Court sought to protect against in adopting the unbridled discretion standard are risks to the constitutional mandate of viewpoint neutrality, we conclude that the prohibition against unbridled discretion is a component of the viewpoint-neutrality requirement.

****

Back before the district court, the University moved to dismiss the constitutional challenge to the referendum method of funding student groups. The University maintained that the plaintiffs' challenge to the referendum was moot because, following the Supreme Court's decision in *Southworth*, the University had amended its student activity fee policy, eliminating the referendum method of funding student organizations.

Following trial, the district court issued an oral ruling, holding that the University's mandatory fee system violated the plaintiffs' First Amendment rights by granting the student government too much discretion for determining which student organizations to fund. ... Specifically, the district court explained that "some degree of discretion may be both necessary and constitutionally permissible in the segregated fee program." But the court went on to note that the student government's "discretion not limited by express objective standards is insufficient to adequately safeguard the principle of viewpoint neutrality."

.....

We agree with the University. First, the University has an expressed policy prohibiting viewpoint discrimination and requiring conformity with the constitutional requirements set forth in *Southworth*. The University seeks to assure compliance with this policy by requiring ASM officials to take an oath that they will abide by the principle of viewpoint neutrality. [T]he Funding Standards provide for the removal of any ASM official who violates this constitutional mandate. As detailed above, the Funding Standards also set forth specific, narrowly drawn and clear criteria to guide the student government in their funding decisions as to GSSF grants and SGAF operations and event grants. Together, these Funding Standards greatly limit the student government's discretion.... Additionally, the University adopted specific deadlines for funding decisions, created a very comprehensive appeals process, and established prompt deadlines for the appeals.

Ann K. Knight: Striking the Balance Between Anti-Discrimination Laws and First Amendment Freedoms: An Alternative Proposal to Preserve Diversity, 30 T. Jefferson L. Rev. 249 (2007)[*]

Two major policy and legal concerns are at issue in these disputes. First is the responsibility of the State and the university to protect the student body from discrimination. Courts must balance these anti-discrimination goals against the second set of concerns, the First Amendment freedoms of student groups, namely: freedom of speech, freedom of association, and free exercise of religion. Because these competing interests are both vital to maintain diversity and freedom, the courts must be cognizant of the future implications of their decisions. Those battling First Amendment infringements today may face discrimination tomorrow. And today's victims of discrimination may one day find themselves fighting for their right to speak. The courts must strike an appropriate balance so that First Amendment freedoms do not weaken protections against discrimination and anti-discrimination laws do not chill First Amendment rights.

.....

A. Freedom of Speech

Under the appropriate tests, the universities' derecognition of discriminating student groups does not necessarily infringe on the groups' First Amendment freedoms..... Exclusion of discriminatory student groups from the university's limited public forum is viewpoint neutral regulation of conduct and therefore constitutional. When a university derecognizes a student group, it essentially ejects that group from the limited public forum it has created for student groups to communicate with the student body. Any benefits the derecognized group is still able to take advantage of are purely at the discretion of the university. Since the university can constitutionally regulate content in the limited public forum it creates, the issue is whether the school's decision to eject the student group from the forum based on their discriminatory conduct constitutes viewpoint discrimination, which would be unconstitutional.

The act of derecognizing discriminatory student groups is not unconstitutional viewpoint discrimination for two reasons. First, the university does not enforce the anti-discrimination policy based upon the group's speech, as discussed above, but rather upon its discriminatory conduct. Therefore, the group is able to express any opinion it likes within the forum as long as it does not discriminate in choosing its members and leaders. Second, the non-discrimination policy, on its face, applies equally to all student groups. Thus, the university will derecognize and deny access to the limited public forum any student group that acts discriminatorily regardless of the viewpoint they wish to express. Such derecognition is a constitutional viewpoint neutral limitation on speech within a limited public forum.

B. Freedom of Expressive Association

When a university enforces its anti-discrimination policy it does not violate a derecognized student group's freedom of expressive association. Derecognition does not significantly burden discriminating groups' ability to advocate a specific point of view.... First, derecognition does involve withholding some benefits, but it does not rise to the level of creating an unconstitutional burden on the freedom of expressive association. Removal from the university's limited public forum, which often includes loss of financial support, faculty advisors, office or storage space, among other advantages, arguably is "withholding benefits." But ... [w]hen a university simply refuses to recognize a student group, without making further efforts to prevent it from meeting on campus, there is no infringement on the group's freedom of expressive association. Second, university enforcement of anti-discrimination policies does not interfere in student groups' internal affairs sufficiently to constitute a burden on their freedom of expressive association. ...[T]he universities in the CLS cases are not forcing the discriminating groups to accept certain "undesirable" members, but simply denying the groups affirmative university support if they continue to discriminate against these individuals.... Denying a student group recognized status, therefore, is not a sufficient invasion into the group's internal affairs to constitute a freedom of association violation because derecognition does not force the group to accept certain members. And, even if the group feels pressure to accept the undesired members, they are not required to accept individuals who openly, actively, and publicly espouse views contrary to the goals of the organization.

****

D. The Equal Access Act as a Model

The Equal Access Act (20 U.S.C. §§ 4071-74 (2000)), provides an excellent framework for protecting all the rights involved. The Equal Access Act states:

It shall be unlawful for any public secondary school which receives Federal financial assistance and which has a limited open forum to deny equal access or a fair opportunity to, or discriminate against, any students who wish to conduct a meeting within that limited open forum on the basis of the religious, political, philosophical, or other content of the speech at such meetings.

This statute discusses several key aspects necessary to ensure the forum functions properly and in accordance with the law. First, the statute defines a "limited open forum" as a forum that allows one or more groups of students to use school facilities during non-instructional times for a purpose unrelated to school curriculum. Second, it identifies a "fair opportunity" as one that requires the meeting to be voluntary and initiated by students without sponsorship by the school or government (these entities may only be present in a non-participatory fashion). The meetings cannot substantially interfere with the school's ability to orderly conduct its educational activities. Also, they cannot be directed, controlled, or regularly attended by individuals who are not students or employees of the school.

The statute also lists important restrictions on school and government involvement. These restrictions establish that neither the government nor any political subdivision shall: influence the form or content or require anyone to participate in any religious activity; spend funds in support beyond those incidental to providing the space; require any school employees to attend; sanction unlawful meetings; limit the rights of the group based on its size; or abridge any constitutional rights of the individuals involved. Finally, the statute states that the Act must not limit the school's authority to "maintain order and discipline on school premises, to protect the well-being of students and faculty, and to assure that attendance of students at meetings is voluntary."

The obvious problem with this statute, as far as its applicability to the issue at hand, is that it applies to secondary schools as opposed to higher education. There are two ways to remedy this dilemma at the university level: (1) a virtually identical statute could be enacted as applied to public institutions of higher education simply by replacing the words "public secondary school" with "public institution of higher education;" or (2) the Equal Access Act could be amended to include the words "or public institution of higher education" immediately following the words "public secondary school" in section 4071(a). Following either of these paths of regulatory action would allow diverse thought to flourish on the university campus while still permitting the university to further its compelling interest in prohibiting discrimination in school-sponsored programs.

Chapter Twelve
The First Amendment and Religious Expression

> Neutral rules of general applicability ordinarily do not raise free exercise concerns even if they incidentally burden a particular religious practice or belief. When it comes to the enforcement of such rules, the Free Exercise Clause offers no protection. [A] law that burdens a religious practice or belief [that] is not neutral or generally applicable is subject to strict scrutiny, and the burden on religious conduct violates the Free Exercise Clause.
> *Axson-Flynn v. Johnson*, 356 F.3d 1277 (10th Cir. 2004).

> The "establishment of religion" clause of the First Amendment means at least this: Neither a state nor the Federal Government can set up a church. Neither can pass laws which aid one religion, aid all religions, or prefer one religion over another. Neither can force nor influence a person to go to or to remain away from church against his will or force him to profess a belief or disbelief in any religion. No person can be punished for entertaining or professing religious beliefs or disbeliefs... Neither a state nor the Federal Government can, openly or secretly, participate in the affairs of any religious organizations or groups and vice versa.
> *Everson v. Board of Education*, 330 U.S. 1 (1947).

"Congress shall make no law respecting an establishment of religion, or prohibiting the free exercise thereof." U.S. Const. Amend. I. Longstanding uncertainty over the role of religion in public education has spawned over a score of decisions on student rights. At present, no single philosophy unifies the interpretation of the Establishment Clause with the Free Exercise Clause. Moreover, the Establishment Clause comes laden with an array of approaches, each competing for dominance with each new decision. The Court, to its credit, has acknowledged the difficulty of deciding cases arising out of the Religion Clauses and has not shirked from the challenge of weaving a doctrine from the text. The education cases reflect a unique balancing of legitimate, competing interests.

As you read these materials consider the following questions: What has religion to do with the education mission? How should school policies accommodate religion without running afoul the Religion Clauses? When does a student's right to expression her religious beliefs on campus outweigh an educator's disapproval?

I. The Free Exercise Clause

CHALIFOUX v. NEW CANEY SCHOOL DISTRICT
976 F. Supp. 659 (S.D. Tex. 1997)

HITTNER, District Judge

Plaintiffs David Chalifoux and Jerry Robertson, students enrolled at New Caney High School in New Caney, Montgomery County, Texas, filed the instant lawsuit pursuant to 42 U.S.C. § 1983, alleging that defendant New Caney Independent School District ("NCISD") violated their First Amendment rights to free speech and religious expression by prohibiting them, pursuant to the District's ban on "gang-related" apparel, from wearing rosaries outside their clothing while on school premises.

FINDINGS OF FACT

During early 1997, Plaintiffs began wearing white plastic rosaries[44] on the outside of their shirts as a means of displaying their religious faith. Plaintiffs wore rosaries for several weeks on the New Caney High School campus without comment from school administrators. Plaintiffs are not members of any criminal gang operating in the NCISD. Moreover, during the period they wore the rosaries, they were never approached by gang members because of the rosaries. Nor did Plaintiffs' display of their rosaries cause any disruptions or altercations at New Caney High School.

On or about March 6, 1997, NCISD police officers Eddie Gampher and Troy Wootten approached Plaintiffs on campus and advised them that they could not continue wearing their rosaries outside their clothing, but that they could wear them inside their shirts where they could not be seen by others. Wootten told Plaintiffs that the school had identified rosaries as "gang-related apparel," and, therefore, their display on campus had been prohibited. Wootten did not accuse Plaintiffs of being gang members or wearing rosaries to identify themselves as gang members. Indeed, Defendants do not dispute that Chalifoux and Robertson are not members of any gang. Rather, Wootten told Plaintiffs that by prohibiting them from displaying their rosaries, he was acting out of concern for their safety.

The NCISD dress code prohibits the wearing of "gang-related apparel . . . in school or at any school-related function." The dress code is outlined in a Student Handbook. To inform students of the parameters of the prohibition on gang-related apparel, the Handbook states, "A sample list of specific items that law enforcement agencies consider gang-related is available in the principal's office." However, the evidence at trial indicated that the New Caney High School principal's office does not maintain a list of gang-related apparel. The only list of prohibited apparel published by NCISD, which is found in the Student Handbook, does not include rosaries. The Handbook states, inter alia:

> The following gang-related apparel has been prohibited in school or at any school-related function:
>
> > 1. Oversized apparel, including baggy pants which are worn low on the waist; overalls with one strap unfastened; pants that are cut off below the knees and worn with knee socks. (Pants should fit at the waist and have properly sewn hems).
> >
> > 2. Any attire which identifies students as a group (gang-related) may not be worn to school or school-related activities.

---

[44] Webster's Dictionary defines "rosary" as:

> [A] string of beads used in counting prayers; *specif.*: a string of beads by which the prayers of the Roman Catholic rosary are counted.

Webster's Third New International Dictionary 1974 (3d ed. 1986).

3. Baseball caps, hair nets, bandanas, sweatbands.

Charles York, the principal of New Caney High School, testified that because gangs frequently change their identifying symbols, the list of prohibited gang-related items in the Student Handbook only is meant to be a representative list. York also testified that his office has available for distribution to students and parents various materials prepared by NCISD's police department which contain information on gangs and gang-related apparel. However, none of the materials contain a list of specific items the school prohibits as gang-related, and none mention rosaries.

Wootten is the "Gang Liaison Officer" for the NCISD Police Department. In his position, he investigates gang activity in the school district and is responsible for determining what is and is not "gang-related apparel." Once Wootten determines, based on his investigation, that a particular item is "gang-related," Wootten informs York who then decides whether to prohibit the item. While the evidence showed that the NCISD Police Department, and Wootten in particular, heavily influences the administration's determination of what should be classified as "gang-related apparel," the Police Department does not have the authority to enforce the school's dress code. Despite the fact that NCISD police officers are not charged with enforcing the dress code, it was Wootten who approached Chalifoux and Robertson on March 6, 1997, and stopped them from wearing their rosaries outside their shirts.

Wootten testified that he classified rosaries as gang-related apparel after receiving information that members of the "United Homies," a gang operating within NCISD, were wearing rosaries as identifying symbols. The information upon which Wootten acted included a statement in February 1997, from an admitted member of the United Homies who told him that he was wearing rosaries as a gang symbol. Later in February 1997, Wootten stopped a vehicle off campus containing five members of the United Homies for violating traffic laws. Two of the individuals in the car were wearing rosaries. On one occasion, York observed three students known to be gang members wearing rosaries on campus and asked them to stop wearing the beads outside their clothing. Based upon these incidents, Wootten, and subsequently York, determined that wearing rosaries as a necklace outside the shirt should be prohibited under the District's ban on gang-related apparel. Pursuant to that policy, Wootten and York prohibited, and continue to prohibit, Plaintiffs from wearing their rosaries outside their shirts on school premises.

.....

I. FREE SPEECH CLAIM

A. Is Plaintiff's Speech Protected?

The First Amendment protects private, religious speech. Moreover, it is well-settled that the First Amendment protects not only verbal and written expression, but also symbols and conduct that constitute "symbolic speech." See Tinker v. DesMoines Indep. Community Sch. Dist., 393 U.S. 503 (1969). Symbolic speech is protectible under the First Amendment if the person displaying the symbol intends to convey a particularized message and there is a "great likelihood" that the message will be understood by those observing it. Spence v. Washington, 418 U.S. 405, 410-11, (1974).

The uncontested evidence at trial demonstrated that Plaintiffs wore their rosaries with the intent to communicate their Catholic faith to others. ...Even assuming that some persons are not familiar with the rosary, undoubtedly they are familiar with the crucifix attached to the center of the rosary, which is recognized universally as a symbol of Christianity. ... Therefore, the Court finds that the symbolic speech at issue in this case is a form of religious expression protected under the First Amendment.

B. What Analysis Applies?

The parties' legal arguments at trial and in their post-trial briefing reflect a fundamental disagreement over the standard this Court should apply in analyzing Plaintiffs' free speech claim. Plaintiffs contend that Tinker v. DesMoines Ind. Community Sch. Dist., 393 U.S. 503 (1969), provides the proper level of scrutiny. [T]he Court set out a stringent standard requiring the school to show that the prohibited speech would "materially and substantially interfere" with appropriate discipline in the operation of the school before the prohibition could be sustained. The Court justified its broad protection of the student's symbolic speech, noting that the use of the armband to convey a message was "closely akin to pure speech." Id. at 505.

Plaintiffs in this case contend that their wearing of rosaries was "pure speech" to which Tinker's requirement of a "material and substantial interference" applies. Defendants, on the other hand, point to United States v. O'Brien, 391 U.S. 367 (1968) as support for their contention that a less stringent test applies to NCISD's regulation of Plaintiffs' speech. In O'Brien, the plaintiff had been convicted under a Massachusetts statute for burning his draft card during a public demonstration. The plaintiff then challenged the statute as an unconstitutional restriction of symbolic speech protected by the First Amendment. In upholding the restriction, the Court stated:

When "speech" and "non-speech" elements are combined in the same course of conduct, a sufficiently important governmental interest in regulating the nonspeech element can justify incidental limitations on First Amendment freedoms.

Id. at 376. The Court held that a governmental regulation on "speech-plus-conduct" expression is constitutional if: (1) it is within the constitutional power of the Government; (2) it furthers an important government interest; (3) the governmental interest is unrelated to the suppression of free expression; and (4) the incidental restriction on First Amendment freedoms is not greater than is essential to the furtherance of that interest. Id. Applying this standard, the Supreme Court held that the state's interest in preventing the destruction of draft cards was sufficient to justify the incidental restriction on the plaintiff's anti-war message.

In this case, Defendant contends that because NCISD's ban on wearing rosaries outside the shirt is not intended to suppress the specific religious content of Plaintiffs' message, but is intended to restrict gang activity on school premises, the less stringent test set out in O'Brien applies.[45]

---

[45] Defendants have also urged this Court to apply the forum-based analysis used by the Supreme Court in Hazelwood Sch. Dist. v. Kuhlmeier, 484 U.S. 260, 98 L. Ed. 2d 592, 108 S. Ct. 562 (1988). There, the Supreme Court distinguished Tinker by differentiating between "personal expression that happens to occur on the school premises" and expressive activities that are "sponsored" by the school and "may fairly be characterized as part of the school curriculum . . . ." Id. at 271. An infringement of "school-sponsored speech" will be upheld as long as the actions of educators are "reasonably related to

...Like the flag and other religious symbols referenced in Goguen and the armband in Tinker, Plaintiffs' rosaries are "akin to pure speech." Accordingly, the Court will apply Tinker.

Pursuant to the standard in Tinker, Defendants must show that Plaintiffs' religious speech caused a substantial disruption of or material interference with school activities. Tinker, 393 U.S. at 513. Moreover, even in the school setting, more than mere speculation about disruption and interference is required: "Undifferentiated fear or apprehension of disturbance is not enough to overcome the right to freedom of expression." Id. at 508.

In this case, although Plaintiffs wore their rosaries outside their shirts for several months, they were never misidentified as gang members nor approached by gang members. There also was no evidence that they attracted the attention of other students because of their rosaries. In Tinker, even though several students made hostile remarks to the Plaintiffs because of their armbands, the Court found that there was no disruption sufficient to uphold the school's prohibition. Here too, Defendants have failed to show any evidence of hostility from students at New Caney High School or any other threat of interference with school safety. Moreover, the only evidence presented by Defendants of gang members wearing rosaries on campus was one incident over a span of several months in which three students, all siblings, wore rosaries on campus as an alleged gang identifier. The remaining two incidents in which alleged gang members were seen wearing rosaries occurred off campus. Accordingly, the Court finds that there was insufficient evidence of actual disruption at New Caney High School, or that there was substantial reason for NCISD to anticipate a disruption, to justify the infringement on Plaintiffs' religiously-motivated speech.[46] ...

IV. FREE EXERCISE OF RELIGION CLAIM

Plaintiffs also assert a claim under the free exercise clause of the First Amendment. ...Precedent supports a finding that Plaintiffs' form of religious practice is entitled to First Amendment protection. In Church of the Lukumi Babalu Aye v. Hialeah, 508 U.S. 520, 531 (1993), the plaintiff challenged a state ordinance restricting their right to practice animal sacrifice as a method of religious observance. In considering the threshold question of whether the practice was entitled to protection under the First Amendment, the Supreme Court stated that "although the practice of animal sacrifice may seem abhorrent to some, 'religious beliefs need not be acceptable, logical, consistent, or comprehensible to

---

legitimate pedagogical concerns." Id. Because this case involves speech that happened to occur on the school campus, and was not school-sponsored, the Court finds Tinker, not Hazelwood, provides the proper standard.

[46] Alternatively, even if the Court applies the test in O'Brien, NCISD's prohibition on wearing rosaries fails. Under the fourth requirement of the O'Brien test, the Court must determine whether the restriction on the Plaintiffs' First Amendment freedoms is greater than is essential to the furtherance of the school's important interest. O'Brien, 391 U.S. at 376. As noted *infra* in the analysis of Plaintiffs' free exercise of religion claims, the minimal evidence of gang members wearing rosaries on the New Caney High School campus causes this Court to question the effectiveness of the ban on rosaries in reducing gang activity. Moreover, although Defendants insist that they have not acted with the intent to burden Plaintiffs' message, but only their method, here "the medium is the message and to suppress the medium is to censor the message." Goguen v. Smith, 471 F.2d at 104 (citation omitted). Thus, while the burden on Plaintiffs' symbolic speech is considerable, the ban on rosaries does not appear to this Court to be an essential or effective means of furthering the school's interest in reducing gang activity.

others to merit First Amendment protection.'" Id., quoting Thomas v. Review Bd. of Indiana Employment Security Div., 450 U.S. 707, 714 (1981). Noting that there was no factual dispute that the Plaintiffs chose to perform animal sacrifices for "religious reasons," the Court held that the practice was entitled to First Amendment protection.

In this case, the facts clearly showed, and Defendants do not dispute, that Plaintiffs wore their rosaries for religious reasons. Moreover, the rosary is deeply rooted in orthodox Catholic beliefs. Its use by Catholics is unique among all Christian denominations. ...

In Employment Div. Dept. of Human Resources of Ore. v. Smith, the Supreme Court rejected a free exercise challenge by a Native American to a law criminalizing peyote use, holding that "the right of free exercise does not relieve an individual of the obligation to comply with a 'valid and neutral law of general applicability on the ground that the law proscribes (or prescribes) conduct that his religion prescribes (or proscribes).'" 494 U.S. 872, 878, (1990)). In arriving at its ruling, the Court applied a rational basis test and stated that a law of general applicability need not be justified by a compelling governmental interest, even if the law incidentally burdens a particular religious practice. However, the Court also stated that, where a free exercise claim is combined with "other guarantees, such as freedom of speech," a more rigorous standard of review applies. Id. In such "hybrid" religion-plus-speech cases, the government must demonstrate more than merely a reasonable relation to a substantial state interest to sustain the infringement on First Amendment expression. See Wisconsin v. Yoder, 406 U.S. 205, 233, 32 L. Ed. 2d 15, 92 S. Ct. 1526 (1972); Society of Separationists, Inc. v. Herman, 939 F.2d 1207, 1216 (5th Cir. 1991); Alabama & Coushatta Tribes v. Big Sandy Sch. Dist., 817 F. Supp. at 1332.

Plaintiffs' causes of action combine free exercise of religion and free speech claims; accordingly, the heightened level of scrutiny used in hybrid cases applies. Therefore, pursuant to the holding in Yoder, this Court must perform a balancing test to determine whether the school's regulation places an "undue burden" on Plaintiffs' religious exercise and whether the regulation bears more than a "reasonable relation" to NCISD's stated objective. See Yoder, 406 U.S. at 220-21; Alabama & Coushatta, 817 F. Supp. at 1333.

After considering the burden placed on Plaintiffs' religious exercise and NCISD's stated objective of regulating gang activity on campus, the Court finds that the prohibition on wearing rosaries violates Plaintiffs' First Amendment rights. This Court does not doubt that a dress code can be one means of restricting gang activity on campus. However, while this Court will not endeavor to make a comprehensive list, surely there are a number of more effective means available to NCISD, other than a blanket ban on wearing rosaries, to control gang activity and ensure the safety of its schools. This is particularly true where, as here, the evidence showed only three instances of alleged gang members wearing rosaries as gang identifiers, with only one of those incidents occurring on campus. Therefore, the Court finds that NCISD's restriction on rosaries does not "bear more than a reasonable relation" to regulating gang activity in the District. Yoder, 406 U.S. at 233. Moreover, the regulation places an undue burden on Plaintiffs, who seek to display the rosary not to identify themselves with a gang, but as a sincere expression of their religious beliefs.

LITTLEFIELD v. FORNEY INDEPENDENT SCHOOL DISTRICT
268 F.3d 275 (5th Cir. 2001)

KING, Chief Judge:

Appellants are students and parents of students who attend schools situated in the Forney Independent School District ("Forney") in Forney, Texas. [They] assert several constitutional challenges to the mandatory school uniform policy ("Uniform Policy" or "Policy") adopted by Forney.

The disputed Uniform Policy requires students to wear solid color polo-type shirts with collars, oxford-type shirts, or blouses with collars in one of four colors (white, yellow, red, or navy blue). The shirts may be either short or long-sleeved but must be tucked in at all times. Students must also wear either blue or khaki colored pants, shorts, skirts, or jumpers. The shorts and skirts must be of appropriate size and length (no shorter than three inches above the knee). The Policy prohibits the wearing of, inter alia, denim, leather, suede, or vinyl, or any clothing that suggests gang affiliation, could conceal contraband, or could create a distraction. Certain other clothing items are also banned, such as open-heeled sandals, flip-flops, military boots, overalls, athletic pants, spandex, baggy clothing, and sleeveless shirts. The Uniform Policy also regulates the sizes of manufacturer logos permitted on clothing. Prior to the adoption of the Policy, Forney had a dress code that prohibited certain types of clothing deemed unsafe, immodest, or otherwise inimical to the educational process.

[The school district] asserts that the Uniform Policy was adopted to promote school spirit and school values, and "to promote decorum (and thereby the notion that school is a place of order and work), to promote respect for authority, to decrease socioeconomic tensions, to increase attendance, and to reduce drop out rates." Forney also asserts that it intended the Policy "to increase student safety by reducing gang and drug related activity as well as the likelihood of students bringing weapons to school undetected and by allowing teachers to more readily distinguish Forney students from outsiders."

. . . . .

Failure to comply with the Uniform Policy results in disciplinary action, which could lead to expulsion.

. . . . .

In compliance with the requirement of Texas Education Code § 11.162(c), the Uniform Policy includes an "opt-out" provision whereby parents and students with "bona fide" religious or philosophical objections to the wearing of a uniform can apply for an exemption to the Policy. The opt-out provision requires parents to request an Application for Exemption and fill out a questionnaire designed to gauge the sincerity of the beliefs of those parents who assert objections. This questionnaire asks whether the student has ever participated in any of a number of activities that would have required him or her to wear a uniform. Families granted exemptions from the Uniform Policy must reapply each school year. A three-step grievance system was created to address issues arising from the opt-out procedure.

The district court found that the parents of seventy-two students sought exemptions from compliance with the Uniform Policy, of which twelve exemptions were granted. A few of the Plaintiffs-Appellants were within the group of students who were granted exemptions from the Policy. Most students who had based their objections on philosophical or religious grounds were denied exemptions because they had worn some type of uniform in the past.

.....

V. FREE EXERCISE CLAUSE AND ESTABLISHMENT CLAUSE CLAIMS

We find no merit in the family-Plaintiffs-Appellants' claims under the Free Exercise and the Establishment Clauses of the First Amendment. On appeal, the Families do not challenge the constitutionality of Texas Education Code § 11.162(c), focusing instead on the application of the "opt-out" procedures by the Defendants. The district court properly dismissed these First Amendment challenges in its well-reasoned opinion. We agree with the district court that the Forney opt-out policy neither infringes on the families' free exercise of religion nor violates the Establishment Clause.

A. Free Exercise Claim

The Free Exercise Clause of the First Amendment, which has been made applicable to the states by incorporation into the Fourteenth Amendment, provides that "Congress shall make no law respecting an establishment of religion, or prohibiting the free exercise thereof." In *Employment Division v. Smith*, the Supreme Court held that a neutral, generally applicable governmental regulation will withstand a free exercise challenge when the regulation is reasonably related to a legitimate state interest. *See* 494 U.S. 872 (1990).

On its face, the opt-out policy enacted by Forney is neutral and of general application, in that it applies to all persons who might wish to attend Forney and choose to opt-out of the Uniform Policy. All parties also agree that the opt-out policy was not enacted to inhibit religion and, in fact, recognize that the statutory provision was enacted to protect the reasonable state interest of fostering the free exercise of religion. As a threshold matter, then, the opt-out policy survives constitutional scrutiny under Smith.

The Families' specific complaint, however, is that in the process of legitimately inquiring about the religious beliefs of families seeking exemption from the Uniform Policy, Defendants have "crossed the line between the legitimate inquiry into the sincerity of Plaintiffs' religious beliefs and prohibited inquiry into the substance of those beliefs." The Families argue that, because there was no established school policy for determining who would be granted an exception, Defendants have become arbiters of the substance of religions in a manner that infringes the Families' free exercise of their beliefs.

The difficulty for the Families is twofold. First, the Families concede that it is permissible for Forney to examine the "sincerity" of their beliefs. Second, on this record there exists an established district policy that Defendants have followed in a consistent manner. We address these issues together.

Section 11.162(c) of the Texas Education Code provides that parents may exempt their children from the Uniform Policy if they can provide a bona fide religious or philosophical objection to

the wearing of the uniform. In an effort to provide an objective means of determining the sincerity of the "bona fides" of a religious belief, *Forney* established a process of requiring written objection, the completion of a questionnaire that requests information regarding whether students had worn uniforms in the past and personal meetings with the parents. This process to determine the sincerity of a religious objection, while fraught with difficulty, is necessary to separate sincere beliefs from fraudulent beliefs.

Because the opt-out procedures are a neutral and rational means to determine sincerity, as a legal matter under *Smith*, they do not interfere with the free exercise of religion. *See* 494 U.S. at 877. Further, in practice, "opt-outs" have been granted to parents who have demonstrated a sincere and consistent objection to the wearing of uniforms. Therefore, we conclude that the Families have not created a genuine issue of material fact that the application of Forney's opt-out policy violates their free exercise rights under the First Amendment.

B. Establishment Clause Claim

In the instant case, the Families have alleged that the application of the opt-out policy appears to favor certain organized religions to which the Families do not belong. This direct exposure to the policy satisfies the "intangible injury" requirement to bring an Establishment Clause challenge.

The Families' Establishment Clause argument is equally without merit. The Families assert that Defendants will grant exemption requests only upon proof that the applicant strictly adhered to an organized religion, thus manifesting a preference for only those religions in which adherents could provide written proof of the tenets of their beliefs. The Families argue that, in granting exemptions only to religions for which a prohibition on uniforms was clearly stated in the tenets of that religion, Defendants were establishing some religions as favored over others, in violation of the Establishment Clause.

To withstand an Establishment Clause challenge, a statute must have a secular legislative purpose, the statute's primary purpose must neither advance nor inhibit religion, and the statute must not foster an excessive entanglement with religion. *See Lemon v. Kurtzman*, 403 U.S. 602 (1971). As the district court found:

> The uniform policy unquestionably has a secular purpose. Next, the principal effect neither advances nor inhibits religion. Its purpose is to enhance the learning environment in the Forney schools, irrespective of the religious faith of a particular student. Finally, the policy does not unnecessarily entangle the School Board with religion....

We agree with the district court's conclusion. None of the families raising the Establishment Clause challenge can point to any religious purpose behind the implementation of the opt-out policy. Nor can these families point to any "primary effect" of the opt-out policy that advances a particular religion or that inhibits a religion. On this record, it appears that those families that could demonstrate sincere and consistent rejection of mandatory uniforms were granted exemptions regardless of the particular tenets of their faith. Finally, we do not perceive an intolerable risk of excessive government entanglement in the requirement that parents demonstrate their consistency and sincerity by explaining the basis of their religious objections to Defendants. We therefore affirm the district court's grant of summary judgment on these claims.

AXSON-FLYNN v. JOHNSON
356 F.3d 1277 (10th Cir. 2004)

EBEL, Circuit Judge.

In 1998, Plaintiff-Appellant Christina Axson-Flynn ("Axson-Flynn"), a member of the Church of Jesus Christ of Latter-day Saints ("Mormon church"), applied to the University of Utah's Actor Training Program (ATP). As part of the application process, she attended an audition conducted by ATP instructors Barbara Smith, Sandy Shotwell, Jerry Gardner, and Sarah Shippobotham (hereinafter "Defendants"). During her audition, Sandy Shotwell asked Axson-Flynn if there was anything she would feel uncomfortable doing or saying as an actor. Axson-Flynn replied that she would not remove her clothing, "take the name of God in vain," "take the name of Christ in vain" or "say the four-letter expletive beginning with the letter F." Although the record is unclear as to whether Axson-Flynn explained at the time why she had those objections, the district court summarized her reasons as follows:

Her refusal to use the words "God" or "Christ" as profanity is based on one of the Ten Commandments, which prohibits believers from taking "the name of the Lord thy God in vain . . . ." Exodus 20:8. Plaintiff has also explained that her refusal to say the word "fuck" is due to the fact that it is religiously offensive to her because she finds that it vulgarizes what Plaintiff, as a Mormon, believes is a sacred act, appropriate only within the bounds of marriage. *Axson-Flynn v. Johnson*, 151 F. Supp. 2d 1326, 1328 (D. Utah 2001).

Axson-Flynn was admitted to the ATP, and she matriculated in the fall of 1998. As part of a class exercise that fall, she was asked to perform a monologue called "Friday" that included two instances of the word "goddamn" and one instance of the word "shit."[2] Without informing her instructor (Defendant Barbara Smith), Axson-Flynn substituted other words for the two "goddamn"s but otherwise performed the monologue as written. Smith did not notice, and Axson-Flynn received an "A" grade for her performance.

A few weeks later, as part of another class exercise, Smith asked Axson-Flynn to perform a scene from the play "The Quadrangle." Axson-Flynn was to play the part of an unmarried girl who had recently had an abortion. She expressed no concerns about the role itself. She did, however, object to some of the words that she would be required to say, which included "goddamn" and "fucking." Axson-Flynn mentioned her concerns to Smith, who asked why Axson-Flynn was raising these concerns now, when she apparently had no language concerns with respect to the "Friday" monologue. Axson-Flynn replied that she had omitted the offensive words from the "Friday" monologue and that no one had noticed. Smith became angry, told Axson-Flynn her behavior was unacceptable, and said that Axson-Flynn would have to "get over" her language concerns. She told Axson-Flynn that she could "still be a good Mormon and say these words." Axson-Flynn offered to perform a different scene if she were not allowed to change or omit the offensive words, but Smith refused to allow that, saying that Axson-Flynn would either perform the "Quadrangle" scene as written or receive a grade of zero on the

---

[2] Axson-Flynn had no religious objections to saying the word "shit." Her objections appear to be limited to the word "fuck" and to the words "goddamn" and its variants.

exercise. If Axson-Flynn received a zero, the highest grade she would have been able to receive in the class would have been a "C." Axson-Flynn said that she would take a zero on that and any other assignment she could not complete due to her language concerns. Smith suggested that before making such a decision, Axson-Flynn should take the weekend and think about it, which Axson-Flynn agreed to do.

Shortly thereafter (the record is not clear as to when), Smith asked Axson-Flynn if she had changed her mind. Axson-Flynn replied that she had not, and that she would accept a zero. Smith then relented, telling Axson-Flynn that she "admired [her] character" and that she would be allowed "to omit the language that was offensive" to her. Axson-Flynn performed the scene from "The Quadrangle" without the offensive language and received a high grade on her performance. For the rest of the semester, Axson-Flynn was allowed to omit any language she found offensive during class exercises.

At the end of the fall semester, Axson-Flynn attended her semester review. Defendants confronted Axson-Flynn about her language concerns and said that her request for an accommodation was "unacceptable behavior." They recommended that she "talk to some other Mormon girls who are good Mormons, who don't have a problem with this." Finally, they told her, "You can choose to continue in the program if you modify your values. If you don't, you can leave. That's your choice."

Axson-Flynn decided to withdraw from the ATP and leave the University of Utah. While she had never been asked to leave, she nonetheless apparently believed that it was only a matter of time before that would happen. After Axson-Flynn left the University of Utah, she enrolled in the acting program at Utah Valley State College. At Utah Valley State, Axson-Flynn was allowed to omit the language she found offensive. ...Axson-Flynn filed suit against Defendants pursuant to 42 U.S.C. § 1983 for violating her free speech and free exercise rights under the First Amendment.

DISCUSSION

I. FREEDOM OF SPEECH

Axson-Flynn argues that Defendants' insistence that she speak her lines as written, without omitting the words she found offensive, violated her First Amendment right to refrain from speaking. The district court rejected this argument and granted summary judgment to Defendants, finding that what Axson-Flynn was being asked to do fell outside the bounds of the Supreme Court precedents that prohibit compelled speech.

.....

[B]ecause the speech was to take place in the classroom context as part of a mandated school curriculum, it clearly bore the school's "imprimatur" and "involved pedagogical interests." As such, it is school-sponsored speech. Thus, we will uphold the ATP's decision to restrict (or compel) that speech as long as the ATP's decision was "'reasonably related to legitimate pedagogical concerns. We give substantial deference to "educators' stated pedagogical concerns."

In the instant case, Defendants justified their restriction on speech—the requirement that students, including Axson-Flynn, perform the acting exercises as written—as a methodology for preparing students for careers in professional acting. Requiring an acting student, in the context of a classroom exercise, to speak the words of a script as written is no different than requiring that a law or history student argue a position with which he disagrees. Both types of restriction on student speech, if not pretextual, can meet the *Hazelwood* standard, which does not require that the [restrictions] be the most reasonable or the only reasonable limitations, only that they be reasonable. The school's methodology may not be necessary to the achievement of its goals and it may not even be the most effective means of teaching, but it can still be "reasonably related" to pedagogical concerns. A more stringent standard would effectively give each student veto power over curricular requirements, subjecting the curricular decisions of teachers to the whims of what a particular student does or does not feel like learning on a given day. This we decline to do.

.....

In her amended complaint, Axson-Flynn posits that Defendants forced her to adhere strictly to the script not because of their educational goals as described above, but rather because of "anti-Mormon sentiment." Additionally, the program's insistence that Axson-Flynn speak with other "good Mormon girls" and that she could "still be a good Mormon" and say these words certainly raises concern that hostility to her faith rather than a pedagogical interest in her growth as an actress was at stake in Defendants' behavior in this case. Viewing the evidence in a light most favorable to Axson-Flynn, we find that there is a genuine issue of material fact as to whether Defendants' justification for the script adherence requirement was truly pedagogical or whether it was a pretext for religious discrimination. Therefore, summary judgment was improper.

II. FREE EXERCISE

Axson-Flynn also argues that by attempting to force her to say words whose utterance would violate her religious beliefs, Defendants violated the free exercise clause of the First Amendment. The district court rejected this argument and granted summary judgment to Defendants. We review that decision de novo, *see Phelan* and reverse the decision of the district court.

Neutral rules of general applicability ordinarily do not raise free exercise concerns even if they incidentally burden a particular religious practice or belief. *Church of Lukumi Babalu Aye, Inc. v. City of Hialeah*, 508 U.S. 520 (1993); *Employment Div. v. Smith*, 494 U.S. 872 (1990). When it comes to the enforcement of such rules, the Free Exercise Clause offers no protection. By contrast, if a law that burdens a religious practice or belief is not neutral or generally applicable, it is subject to strict scrutiny, and the burden on religious conduct violates the Free Exercise Clause unless it is narrowly tailored to advance a compelling government interest.

A rule that is discriminatorily motivated and applied is not a neutral rule of general applicability. As discussed in the free speech section above, we find a genuine issue of fact in the record as to whether Defendants' requirement of script adherence was pretextual. Therefore, we remand for further proceedings on whether the script adherence requirement was discriminatorily applied to religious conduct (and thus was not generally applicable). Unless Defendants succeed in showing that the script requirement was a neutral rule of general applicability, they will face the daunting task of establishing that the requirement was narrowly tailored to advance a compelling governmental interest.

If Defendants succeed on remand in showing their requirement was not pretextual but rather was a neutral and generally applicable requirement, *Axson-Flynn* argues that the two exceptions to the *Smith* rule apply, and if she were to be successful in establishing an exemption, Defendants' conduct would not be sheltered by the rational basis test of *Smith*. The first exception, following *Wisconsin v. Yoder*, 406 U.S. 205 (1972), has come to be called the "hybrid rights" exception: when a free exercise claim is coupled with some other constitutional claim (such a free speech claim), heightened scrutiny may be appropriate. *Smith*, 494 U.S. at 881-82. The second exception, following *Sherbert v. Verner*, 374 U.S. 398 (1963), is the "individualized exemption" exception: where a state's facially neutral rule contains a system of individualized exemptions, a state "may not refuse to extend that system to cases of 'religious hardship' without compelling reason." *Smith*, 494 U.S. at 884. The district court held that *Axson-Flynn*'s case fit within neither *Smith* exception. *Axson-Flynn*, 151 F. Supp. 2d at 1334, 1341. For the reasons that follow, we disagree and find that *Axson-Flynn* has raised a genuine issue of material fact as to both exceptions.

A. Hybrid rights

In *Swanson v. Guthrie Indep. Sch. Dist. No. I-L*, 135 F.3d 694, 699 (10th Cir. 1998), we recognized the hybrid-rights free exercise theory discussed in Smith, but declined to apply that theory to a claim by a home-schooled student that she should be allowed to attend public school on a part-time basis. We acknowledged in Swanson that "it is difficult to delineate the exact contours of the hybrid-rights theory discussed in Smith." *Id.* We stated that the hybrid-rights theory "at least requires a colorable showing" of infringement of a companion constitutional right, which left open for later development the definition of "colorable" in this context.

In defining "colorability" for purposes of hybrid-rights claims, the Ninth Circuit has required the companion claim to have a "fair probability or a likelihood, but not a certitude, of success on the merits." We find these analogies helpful, and will only apply the hybrid-rights exception to Smith where the plaintiff establishes a "fair probability, or a likelihood," of success on the companion claim. ... The adoption of a "non-frivolous" standard would open the floodgates for hybrid-rights claims, as nearly every plaintiff with a free exercise claim would be able to assert an additional non-frivolous constitutional claim. We decline to allow such a result, given the fact that the hybrid-rights theory has been roundly criticized from every quarter and many have pointed out the danger of interpreting such hybrid-rights claims broadly. As then-Professor McConnell has pointed out, the *Smith* Court itself did not have an expansive standard in mind for a separate hybrid-rights cause of action or it would have found a hybrid-rights claim on the facts before it. *See Michael W. McConnell*, Free Exercise Revisionism and the Smith Decision, 57 U. CHI. L. REV. 1109, 1122.

****

B. The individualized-exemption exception

The Court has never explained with specificity what constitutes a "system" of individualized exceptions, and as with the hybrid rights exception, courts and commentators are divided on the question.

Our Circuit has held that a system of individualized exemptions is one that gives rise to the application of a subjective test. Such a system is one in which case-by-case inquiries are routinely made, such that there is an "individualized governmental assessment of the reasons for the relevant conduct" that "invites considerations of the particular circumstances" involved in the particular case. *Smith*, 494 U.S. at 884.

Perhaps the best example of such a system, and indeed the one in which this exception originated, is a system of unemployment benefits which requires claimants to show "good cause" as to why they are unable to find work. In *Sherbert v. Verner*, 374 U.S. 398 (1963), a Seventh Day Adventist was fired by her employer because she refused to work on Saturdays, which her faith did not permit. ...In *Sherbert*, then, the "good cause" exemption required an official to examine an applicant's specific, personal circumstances.

Smith's "individualized exemption" exception is limited, then, to systems that are designed to make case-by-case determinations. ...With this understanding of the "individualized exemption" exception, we now address whether *Axson-Flynn*'s case falls within the exception. We conclude that there is an issue of fact as to this point and thus we remand.

The syllabus for First-Year Acting (the ATP class that Axson-Flynn was taking in the fall of 1998) contained a curricular requirement to do improvisational work. However, a Jewish student named Jeremy Rische asked for and received permission to avoid doing an improvisational exercise on Yom Kippur without suffering adverse consequences. ...When this evidence is coupled with the fact that Defendants sometimes granted Axson-Flynn herself an exemption from their script adherence requirement, we find that the record raises a material fact issue as to whether Defendants maintained a discretionary system of making individualized case-by-case determinations regarding who should receive exemptions from curricular requirements.

.....

CONCLUSION

For the foregoing reasons, we REVERSE the district court's grant of summary judgment to Defendants on *Axson-Flynn*'s free speech and free exercise claims and REMAND for further proceedings.

Michael E. Lechliter: The Free Exercise of Religion and Public Schools: The Implications of Hybrid Rights on the Religious Upbringing of Children, 103 Mich. L. Rev. 2209 (2005)*

[L]ower courts have failed to universally embrace hybrid rights, and the courts that have accepted the idea have struggled to set forth a consistent understanding of when and how the constitutional right should apply. The circuit courts have offered three very different general schools of thought on how to address a hybrid claim. Some circuits do not accept hybrid rights at all. Even in those circuits that do accept hybrid rights, two distinct modes of analysis have developed. As a result, claimants, attorneys, and judges all appear deeply confused about how exactly to frame a free exercise hybrid rights challenge. Complicating matters, the Supreme Court has offered no further guidance on who is right or wrong.

....

By distinguishing *Yoder*, *Smith* confirmed that the Court's 1972 decision remained good law. Furthermore, the Court made the means for distinguishing Yoder abundantly clear—in *Yoder*, the Free Exercise Clause was acting in conjunction with the "right of parents ... to direct the education of their children," while in *Smith* the free exercise claim stood alone. The longstanding ambiguity of the decision comes not from what the Court said in *Smith*, but from what the opinion did not say—the Court offered no support for why it should matter that the two rights were acting "in conjunction." This seemingly illogical conclusion coupled with a lack of support has been the reason that hybrid rights have received the ire of lower courts and commentators alike.

.....

Perhaps part of the confusion is that the word "hybrid" or the phrase "in conjunction with" are not precise descriptions of the Court's thinking. Instead of viewing individual constitutional rights as completely set off from one another in individual boxes—as the word "hybrid" and the phrase "in conjunction with" may suggest—it is more precise to think of the rights as interconnected spheres. Thinking of a kind of constitutional Venn diagram allows one to visualize a more powerful First Amendment free exercise case when the sphere is interconnected with parental rights. It appears more accurate to claim that the Free Exercise Clause incorporates parental rights in this instance, as opposed to acting in conjunction with them. Regardless of how one characterizes it, Smith stands as a recognition that individual rights do not exist in a vacuum, but instead interplay and work together as well as against each other.

B. Mere Dicta: Circuit Courts Denying the Existence of Hybrid Rights

Furthermore, there is in fact more to Justice Scalia's hybrid language than a simple means to distinguish *Yoder*. First, *Yoder*'s proclamation that higher scrutiny was needed when "the interests of parenthood

---

are combined with a free exercise claim" closely mirrors *Smith*'s "in conjunction with" language. This certainly weakens claims that Justice Scalia plucked hybrid rights out of thin air. ... It is certainly possible to classify the Court's hybrid language as dicta, although it is questionable that Justice Scalia would.

.....

C. Independently Viable Claims: Circuit Courts Recognizing Hybrid Rights While Eviscerating Their Power

Only the Second and Sixth Circuits have gone so far as to proclaim that a hybrid right can never exist. ... The independently viable approach to hybrid rights claims presents many of the same problems that are inherent in the Sixth and Second Circuits' approach of simply denying the right's existence. Although courts that follow the independently viable approach are making a good faith attempt to adhere to *Smith*, the approach will typically lead to the evisceration of all hybrid rights. If the independently viable claim on its own can raise the level of scrutiny, there is no need to invoke the Free Exercise Clause at all, let alone in conjunction with the independent right. This point is best summed up in *Justice Souter's Church of Lukumi Babalu v. City of Hialeah* concurrence:

> But if a hybrid claim is one in which a litigant would actually obtain an exemption from a formally neutral, generally applicable law under another constitutional provision, then there would have been no reason for the Court in what Smith calls the hybrid cases to have mentioned the Free Exercise Clause at all.

.....

D. Colorable Claims: Circuit Courts Searching for Meaningful Hybrid Rights Ground

In an attempt to add more clarity and substance to *Smith*'s hybrid rights language, the Tenth and Ninth Circuits adopted a third approach to examining free exercise claims made in conjunction with another constitutional right. This approach requires something less than an independently viable claim: a colorable claim. Again, this approach shows the difficulty in interpreting and implementing a coherent hybrid rights standard.

In 1999, the Ninth Circuit also entered the fray. ...The court agreed with Justice Souter that the right could not rest on an independently viable claim standard or be triggered every time some other right was implicated. ...In an attempt to work around these two extremes, the court decided to use a "colorable claim" standard as a type of middle ground. Under the court's theory, the companion claim must be colorable, or "seemingly valid and genuine," meaning that it must have a fair probability or likelihood of success on the merits. ...Although this colorable claim standard is the best attempt so far made by courts to legitimately interpret *Smith*'s hybrid exception, the approach is far from substantively perfect and also presents procedural challenges. ....The main problem with the colorable claim approach is that it will often be impossible to distinguish it from the independently viable claim approach because there is no standard for what amounts to a "genuine" or colorable claim. The difference between an "independently viable" claim and a "genuine" claim might often prove hard to recognize and it is easy to see the two seemingly distinct standards joining together to form one blurry, malleable standard. Because of this danger, all of the problems inherent in the independently viable claim approach are also potentially present in the colorable claim approach.

II. The Vigor of the Free Exercise Clause Acting in Conjunction with Parental Rights

The very nature of parents' right to direct the religious education of their children requires special scrutiny. Few would dispute that religious liberty and a commitment to public education are two of the most important goals of America's democracy. Our devotion to education is evident in mandatory schooling laws, but it is because of this unwavering determination to educate American children that religious values are at stake. The ultimate catch-22 is to tell a parent that of course her child will be educated, but her religion must suffer at the whims of school administrators. If a parent cannot pay for private education, the government effectively makes the decision between education and religion for the parent via mandatory schooling laws. Although schools typically are sensitive to religious convictions, especially majority religions, a hybrid right is especially important to safeguard minority religions. The need for a more stringent Free Exercise Clause—or at least a closer examination by courts of the conflicting interests at stake—is essential when minority religious faiths are threatened.

Consider the recent ordeal of Nashala Hern, an eleven-year-old, sixth-grade girl in Oklahoma. Nashala is Muslim, and her religion requires her to wear a headscarf known as a hijab. Initially, her school seemed to have no complaints with the hijab, but on September 11, 2003, she was summoned to the principal's office and her parents were called and told that Nashala must remove her headscarf. Her parents refused and Nashala was suspended. The school district's attorney then informed her parents that she would not be allowed back at school as long as she continued to wear the hijab because the school, in order to reduce gang activity, had implemented a ban on headwear. …

[W]ithout a hybrid parental right, *Smith*'s general ruling would prohibit any redress from this generally applicable law. Placing aside the constitutional infirmity that would result in such a misreading of *Smith* and *Yoder*, this seems completely illogical. The best solution leaves both the school's policy and Nashala's religion completely intact—simply recognize that the policy remains in place while simultaneously recognizing that Nashala must be given a religious exemption.

Hopefully, the Supreme Court will revisit its somewhat infamous *Smith* language and give lower courts further guidance in how to address this difficult question. …The true fear is that minority religions will not receive the same protections afforded to the more traditional "American" religions.

Notes and Comments

1. Free Exercise Claims and Student Rights after *Smith*

Under what circumstances can a student invoke the protection of the Free Exercise Clause after *Smith*? Would you rule in favor of the students in any of the following cases?

- a school dress code that in order to reduce gang activity, bans the wearing of all headwear. It is enforced against an eleven-year-old, sixth-grade girl, whose Muslim beliefs require her to wear a headscarf known as a hijab. *See Cheema v. Thompson*, 67 F.3d 883 (9th Cir. 1995).

- a dress code restricting hair length of all male students to no longer than the top of a standard dress collar. It is applied to four boys who wore their hair long as a spiritual Native American belief that the hair, similar to other body parts, was sacred, and a hair cut was considered the equivalent of dismemberment of a body part. Under this belief system, hair was to be cut only as a sign of mourning a close family member's death. *See Alabama & Coushatta Tribes v. Trustees of Big Sandy Indep. Sch. Dist.*, 817 F. Supp. 1319 (E.D. Tex. 1993). Compare with *Lansdale v. Tyler Junior College*, 470 F.2d 659, 662-63 (5th Cir. 1972).

- a dress code that prohibits the wearing of gang-related apparel. It is enforced against three students wearing white plastic rosaries on the outside of their shirts as a means of displaying their religious faith. Rosaries are a string of beads by which the prayers of the Roman Catholic rosary are counted. *See Chalifoux v. New Caney*, 976 F.Supp. 659, 665-66 (S.D. Tex. 1997).

2. *See Renah R. Holmes*: First Amendment Rights: May a School Ban Religious Symbols That Are Arguably Gang-Related?, 27 J.L. & Educ. 511 (1998). Symposium: Religious Freedom and The Interscholastic Athlete, 12 Marq. Sports L. Rev. 295 (2001). Thomas C. Berg: State Religious Freedom Statutes in Private and Public Education, 32 U.C. Davis L. Rev. 531 (1999).

II. The Establishment Clause

Most attempts to analyze Establishment Clause doctrine are diverted by expressions of annoyance over the failure of the Court to organize its decision-making around a unifying theme. The reluctance of the Court to simplify Establishment Clause analysis, at least in the area of public education, underscores a reality about judicial review of educational policies that is discussed in Chapter One. The *Lemon* Test, the endorsement test, the coercion test, the neutrality principle, and the free-speech analysis each acknowledge, in varying degree, the importance of uncovering bad faith in policy-making. In this regard, the education cases below provide a clearer set of guidelines on improper purposes and permissible effects than some would care to acknowledge.

EVERSON v. BOARD OF EDUCATION
330 U.S. 1 (1947)

MR. JUSTICE BLACK delivered the opinion of the Court.

A New Jersey statute authorizes its local school districts to make rules and contracts for the transportation of children to and from schools. The appellee, a township board of education, acting pursuant to this statute, authorized reimbursement to parents of money expended by them for the bus transportation of their children on regular busses operated by the public transportation system. Part of this money was for the payment of transportation of some children in the community to Catholic parochial schools. These church schools give their students, in addition to secular education, regular religious instruction conforming to the religious tenets and modes of worship of the Catholic Faith. The superintendent of these schools is a Catholic priest.

The only contention here is that the state statute and the resolution, insofar as they authorized reimbursement to parents of children attending parochial schools, violate the Federal Constitution in these two respects, which to some extent overlap. First. They authorize the State to take by taxation the private property of some and bestow it upon others, to be used for their own private purposes. This, it is alleged, violates the due process clause of the Fourteenth Amendment. Second. The statute and the resolution forced inhabitants to pay taxes to help support and maintain schools which are dedicated to, and which regularly teach, the Catholic Faith. This is alleged to be a use of state power to support church schools contrary to the prohibition of the First Amendment which the Fourteenth Amendment made applicable to the states.

First. … [i]t is much too late to argue that legislation intended to facilitate the opportunity of children to get a secular education serves no public purpose. … The same thing is no less true of legislation to reimburse needy parents, or all parents, for payment of the fares of their children so that they can ride in public busses to and from schools rather than run the risk of traffic and other hazards incident to walking or "hitchhiking."

Second. The New Jersey statute is challenged as a "law respecting an establishment of religion." …

A large proportion of the early settlers of this country came here from Europe to escape the bondage of laws which compelled them to support and attend government-favored churches. …

These practices of the old world were transplanted to and began to thrive in the soil of the new America. The very charters granted by the English Crown to the individuals and companies designated to make the laws which would control the destinies of the colonials authorized these individuals and companies to erect religious establishments which all, whether believers or non-believers, would be required to support and attend. …

These practices became so commonplace as to shock the freedom-loving colonials into a feeling of abhorrence. The imposition of taxes to pay ministers' salaries and to build and maintain churches and church property aroused their indignation. It was these feelings which found expression in the First Amendment. No one locality and no one group throughout the Colonies can rightly be given entire credit for having aroused the sentiment that culminated in adoption of the Bill of Rights' provisions embracing religious liberty. But Virginia, where the established church had achieved a dominant influence in political affairs and where many excesses attracted wide public attention, provided a great stimulus and able leadership for the movement. The people there, as elsewhere, reached the conviction that individual religious liberty could be achieved best under a government which was stripped of all power to tax, to support, or otherwise to assist any or all religions, or to interfere with the beliefs of any religious individual or group.

The movement toward this end reached its dramatic climax in Virginia in 1785-86 when the Virginia legislative body was about to renew Virginia's tax levy for the support of the established church. Thomas Jefferson and James Madison led the fight against this tax. Madison wrote his great Memorial and Remonstrance against the law. In it, he eloquently argued that a true religion did not need the support of law; that no person, either believer or non-believer, should be taxed to support a religious institution of any kind; that the best interest of a society required that the minds of men always be wholly free; and that cruel persecutions were the inevitable result of government-established religions. Madison's Remonstrance received strong support throughout Virginia, and the Assembly postponed consideration of the proposed tax measure until its next session. When the proposal came up for consideration at that session, it not only died in committee, but the Assembly enacted the famous "Virginia Bill for Religious Liberty" originally written by Thomas Jefferson. The preamble to that Bill stated among other things that

> Almighty God hath created the mind free; that all attempts to influence it by temporal punishments or burthens, or by civil incapacitations, tend only to beget habits of hypocrisy and meanness, and are a departure from the plan of the Holy author of our religion, who being Lord both of body and mind, yet chose not to propagate it by coercions on either . . .; that to compel a man to furnish contributions of money for the propagation of opinions which he disbelieves, is sinful and tyrannical; that even the forcing him to support this or that teacher of his own religious persuasion, is depriving him of the comfortable liberty of giving his contributions to the particular pastor, whose morals he would make his pattern . . . .

And the statute itself enacted

> That no man shall be compelled to frequent or support any religious worship, place, or ministry whatsoever, nor shall be enforced, restrained, molested, or burthened in his body or goods, nor shall otherwise suffer on account of his religious opinions or belief . . . .

This Court has previously recognized that the provisions of the First Amendment, in the drafting and adoption of which Madison and Jefferson played such leading roles, had the same objective and were intended to provide the same protection against governmental intrusion on religious liberty as the Virginia statute. ...Prior to the adoption of the Fourteenth Amendment, the First Amendment did not apply as a restraint against the states. Most of them did soon provide similar constitutional protections for religious liberty. But some states persisted for about half a century in imposing restraints upon the free exercise of religion and in discriminating against particular religious groups.

The meaning and scope of the First Amendment, preventing establishment of religion or prohibiting the free exercise thereof, in the light of its history and the evils it was designed forever to suppress, have been several times elaborated by the decisions of this Court prior to the application of the First Amendment to the states by the Fourteenth. The broad meaning given the Amendment by these earlier cases has been accepted by this Court in its decisions concerning an individual's religious freedom rendered since the Fourteenth Amendment was interpreted to make the prohibitions of the First applicable to state action abridging religious freedom. There is every reason to give the same application and broad interpretation to the "establishment of religion" clause.

The "establishment of religion" clause of the First Amendment means at least this: Neither a state nor the Federal Government can set up a church. Neither can pass laws which aid one religion, aid all religions, or prefer one religion over another. Neither can force nor influence a person to go to or to remain away from church against his will or force him to profess a belief or disbelief in any religion.

No person can be punished for entertaining or professing religious beliefs or disbeliefs, for church attendance or non-attendance. No tax in any amount, large or small, can be levied to support any religious activities or institutions, whatever they may be called, or whatever form they may adopt to teach or practice religion. Neither a state nor the Federal Government can, openly or secretly, participate in the affairs of any religious organizations or groups and vice versa. In the words of Jefferson, the clause against establishment of religion by law was intended to erect "a wall of separation between church and State." ...

New Jersey cannot consistently with the "establishment of religion" clause of the First Amendment contribute tax-raised funds to the support of an institution which teaches the tenets and faith of any church. On the other hand, other language of the amendment commands that New Jersey cannot hamper its citizens in the free exercise of their own religion. Consequently, it cannot exclude individual Catholics, Lutherans, Mohammedans, Baptists, Jews, Methodists, Non-believers, Presbyterians, or the members of any other faith, because of their faith, or lack of it, from receiving the benefits of public welfare legislation. While we do not mean to intimate that a state could not provide transportation only to children attending public schools, we must be careful, in protecting the citizens of New Jersey against state-established churches, to be sure that we do not inadvertently prohibit New Jersey from extending its general state law benefits to all its citizens without regard to their religious belief.

Measured by these standards, we cannot say that the First Amendment prohibits New Jersey from spending tax-raised funds to pay the bus fares of parochial school pupils as a part of a general program under which it pays the fares of pupils attending public and other schools. It is undoubtedly true that children are helped to get to church schools. There is even a possibility that some of the children might not be sent to the church schools if the parents were compelled to pay their children's bus fares out of their own pockets when transportation to a public school would have been paid for by the State. The same possibility exists where the state requires a local transit company to provide reduced fares to school children including those attending parochial schools, or where a municipally owned transportation system undertakes to carry all school children free of charge. Moreover, state-paid policemen, detailed to protect children going to and from church schools from the very real hazards of traffic, would serve much the same purpose and accomplish much the same result as state provisions intended to guarantee free transportation of a kind which the state deems to be best for the school children's welfare. And parents might refuse to risk their children to the serious danger of traffic accidents going to and from parochial schools, the approaches to which were not protected by policemen. Similarly, parents might be reluctant to permit their children to attend schools which the state had cut off from such general government services as ordinary police and fire protection, connections for sewage disposal, public highways and sidewalks. Of course, cutting off church schools from these services, so separate and so indisputably marked off from the religious function, would make it far more difficult for the schools to operate. But such is obviously not the purpose of the First Amendment. That Amendment requires the state to be a neutral in its relations with groups of religious believers and non-believers; it does not require the state to be their adversary. State power is no more to be used so as to handicap religions than it is to favor them.

[New Jersey's law], as applied, does no more than provide a general program to help parents get their children, regardless of their religion, safely and expeditiously to and from accredited schools.

The First Amendment has erected a wall between church and state. That wall must be kept high and impregnable. We could not approve the slightest breach. New Jersey has not breached it here.

Affirmed.

ZORACH v. CLAUSON
343 U.S. 306 (1952)

MR. JUSTICE DOUGLAS delivered the opinion of the Court.

New York City has a program which permits its public schools to release students during the school day so that they may leave the school buildings and school grounds and go to religious centers for religious instruction or devotional exercises. A student is released on written request of his parents. Those not released stay in the classrooms. The churches make weekly reports to the schools, sending a list of children who have been released from public school but who have not reported for religious instruction.

This "released time" program involves neither religious instruction in public school classrooms nor the expenditure of public funds. All costs, including the application blanks, are paid by the religious organizations. The case is therefore unlike *McCollum v. Board of Education*, 333 U.S. 203, which involved a "released time" program from Illinois. In that case the classrooms were turned over to religious instructors. We accordingly held that the program violated the First Amendment which (by reason of the Fourteenth Amendment) prohibits the states from establishing religion or prohibiting its free exercise.

Appellants, who are taxpayers and residents of New York City and whose children attend its public schools, challenge the present law, contending it is in essence not different from the one involved in the *McCollum* case. Their argument, stated elaborately in various ways, reduces itself to this: the weight and influence of the school is put behind a program for religious instruction; public school teachers police it, keeping tab on students who are released; the classroom activities come to a halt while the students who are released for religious instruction are on leave; the school is a crutch on which the churches are leaning for support in their religious training; without the cooperation of the schools this "released time" program, like the one in the *McCollum* case, would be futile and ineffective. The New York Court of Appeals sustained the law against this claim of unconstitutionality.

The briefs and arguments are replete with data bearing on the merits of this type of "released time" program. ... Those matters are of no concern here, since our problem reduces itself to whether New York by this system has either prohibited the "free exercise" of religion or has made a law "respecting an establishment of religion" within the meaning of the First Amendment.

It takes obtuse reasoning to inject any issue of the "free exercise" of religion into the present case. No one is forced to go to the religious classroom and no religious exercise or instruction is brought to the classrooms of the public schools. A student need not take religious instruction. He is left to his own desires as to the manner or time of his religious devotions, if any.

There is a suggestion that the system involves the use of coercion to get public school students into religious classrooms. There is no evidence in the record before us that supports that conclusion. The present record indeed tells us that the school authorities are neutral in this regard and do no more than release students whose parents so request. If in fact coercion were used, if it were established that any one or more teachers were using their office to persuade or force students to take the religious instruction, a wholly different case would be presented. Hence we put aside that claim of coercion both as respects the "free exercise" of religion and "an establishment of religion" within the meaning of the First Amendment.

Moreover, apart from that claim of coercion, we do not see how New York by this type of "released time" program has made a law respecting an establishment of religion within the meaning of the First Amendment. ....There cannot be the slightest doubt that the First Amendment reflects the philosophy that Church and State should be separated. And so far as interference with the "free exercise" of religion and an "establishment" of religion are concerned, the separation must be complete and unequivocal. The First Amendment within the scope of its coverage permits no exception; the prohibition is absolute. The First Amendment, however, does not say that in every and all respects there shall be a separation of Church and State. Rather, it studiously defines the manner, the specific ways, in which there shall be no concern or union or dependency one on the other. That is the common sense of the matter. Otherwise the state and religion would be aliens to each other—hostile, suspicious, and even unfriendly. Churches could not be required to pay even property taxes. Municipalities would not be permitted to render police or fire protection to religious groups. Policemen who helped parishioners into their places of worship would violate the Constitution. Prayers in our legislative halls; the appeals to the Almighty in the messages of the Chief Executive; the proclamations making Thanksgiving Day a holiday; "so help me God" in our courtroom oaths—these and all other references to the Almighty that run through our laws, our public rituals, our ceremonies would be flouting the First Amendment. A fastidious atheist or agnostic could even object to the supplication with which the Court opens each session: "God save the United States and this Honorable Court."

We would have to press the concept of separation of Church and State to these extremes to condemn the present law on constitutional grounds. The nullification of this law would have wide and profound effects. A Catholic student applies to his teacher for permission to leave the school during hours on a Holy Day of Obligation to attend a mass. A Jewish student asks his teacher for permission to be excused for Yom Kippur. A Protestant wants the afternoon off for a family baptismal ceremony. In each case the teacher requires parental consent in writing. In each case the teacher, in order to make sure the student is not a truant, goes further and requires a report from the priest, the rabbi, or the minister. The teacher in other words cooperates in a religious program to the extent of making it possible for her students to participate in it. Whether she does it occasionally for a few students, regularly for one, or pursuant to a systematized program designed to further the religious needs of all the students does not alter the character of the act.

We are a religious people whose institutions presuppose a Supreme Being. We guarantee the freedom to worship as one chooses. We make room for as wide a variety of beliefs and creeds as the spiritual needs of man deem necessary. We sponsor an attitude on the part of government that shows no partiality to any one group and that lets each flourish according to the zeal of its adherents and the appeal of its dogma. When the state encourages religious instruction or cooperates with religious authorities by adjusting the schedule of public events to sectarian needs, it follows the best of our traditions. For it then respects the religious nature of our people and accommodates the public service to their spiritual needs. To hold that it may not would be to find in the Constitution a requirement that the government show a callous indifference to religious groups. That would be preferring those who believe in no religion over those who do believe. Government may not finance religious groups nor undertake religious instruction nor blend secular and sectarian education nor use secular institutions to force one or some religion on any person. But we find no constitutional requirement which makes it necessary for government to be hostile to religion and to throw its weight against efforts to widen the effective scope of religious influence. The government must be neutral when it comes to competition between sects. It may not thrust any sect on any person. It may not make a religious observance compulsory. It may not coerce anyone to attend church, to observe a religious holiday, or to take religious instruction. But it can close its doors or suspend its operations as to those who want to repair to their religious sanctuary for worship or instruction. No more than that is undertaken here.

In the *McCollum* case the classrooms were used for religious instruction and the force of the public school was used to promote that instruction. Here, as we have said, the public schools do no more than accommodate their schedules to a program of outside religious instruction. We follow the *McCollum* case. But we cannot expand it to cover the present released time program unless separation of Church and State means that public institutions can make no adjustments of their schedules to accommodate the religious needs of the people. We cannot read into the Bill of Rights such a philosophy of hostility to religion.

Affirmed.

EDWARDS v. AGUILLARD
482 U.S. 578 (1987)

JUSTICE BRENNAN delivered the opinion of the Court.

The question for decision is whether Louisiana's "Balanced Treatment for Creation-Science and Evolution-Science in Public School Instruction" Act (Creationism Act), is facially invalid as violative of the Establishment Clause of the First Amendment.

I

The Creationism Act forbids the teaching of the theory of evolution in public schools unless accompanied by instruction in "creation science." § 17:286.4A. No school is required to teach evolution or creation science. If either is taught, however, the other must also be taught. *Ibid.* The theories of evolution and creation science are statutorily defined as "the scientific evidences for [creation or evolution] and inferences from those scientific evidences."

II

The Establishment Clause forbids the enactment of any law "respecting an establishment of religion." The Court has applied a three-pronged test to determine whether legislation comports with the Establishment Clause. First, the legislature must have adopted the law with a secular purpose. Second, the statute's principal or primary effect must be one that neither advances nor inhibits religion. Third, the statute must not result in an excessive entanglement of government with religion. *Lemon v. Kurtzman*, 403 U.S. 602, 612-13 (1971). State action violates the Establishment Clause if it fails to satisfy any of these prongs.

The Court has been particularly vigilant in monitoring compliance with the Establishment Clause in elementary and secondary schools. Families entrust public schools with the education of their children, but condition their trust on the understanding that the classroom will not purposely be used to advance religious views that may conflict with the private beliefs of the student and his or her family. Students in such institutions are impressionable and their attendance is involuntary. ... The State exerts great authority and coercive power through mandatory attendance requirements and because of the students' emulation of teachers as role models and the children's susceptibility to peer pressure.

III

Lemon's first prong focuses on the purpose that animated adoption of the Act. "The purpose prong of the *Lemon* test asks whether government's actual purpose is to endorse or disapprove of religion." *Lynch v. Donnelly*, 465 U.S. 668, 690 (1984) (O'CONNOR, J., concurring). If the law was enacted for the purpose of endorsing religion, "no consideration of the second or third criteria [of *Lemon*] is necessary." In this case, appellants have identified no clear secular purpose for the Louisiana Act.

While the Court is normally deferential to a State's articulation of a secular purpose, it is required that the statement of such purpose be sincere and not a sham. ...

It is clear from the legislative history that the purpose of the legislative sponsor, Senator Bill Keith, was to narrow the science curriculum. During the legislative hearings, Senator Keith stated: "My preference would be that neither [creationism nor evolution] be taught." Such a ban on teaching does not promote—indeed, it undermines—the provision of a comprehensive scientific education.

.....

We do not imply that a legislature could never require that scientific critiques of prevailing scientific theories be taught. Indeed, the Court acknowledged in Stone that its decision forbidding the posting of the Ten Commandments did not mean that no use could ever be made of the Ten Commandments, or that the Ten Commandments played an exclusively religious role in the history of Western Civilization. In a similar way, teaching a variety of scientific theories about the origins of humankind to schoolchildren might be validly done with the clear secular intent of enhancing the effectiveness of science instruction. But because the primary purpose of the Creationism Act is to endorse a particular religious doctrine, the Act furthers religion in violation of the Establishment Clause.

****

V

The Louisiana Creationism Act advances a religious doctrine by requiring either the banishment of the theory of evolution from public school classrooms or the presentation of a religious viewpoint that rejects evolution in its entirety. The Act violates the Establishment Clause of the First Amendment because it seeks to employ the symbolic and financial support of government to achieve a religious purpose. The judgment of the Court of Appeals therefore is

Affirmed.

ZELMAN v. SIMMONS-HARRIS
536 U.S. 639 (2002)

[This case appears in Chapter Two on page 133].

Ralph D. Mawdsley: Access to Public School Facilities for Religious Expression by Students, Student Groups and Community Organizations: Extending the Reach of the Free Speech Clause, 2004 BYU Educ. & L. J. 269 (2004)*

Both individuals and groups can make religious claims on public schools. Individual claims by students can involve a wide range of issues, such as religious meetings during non-instructional time, wearing religious clothing or symbols, making speeches, or distributing literature. Students can make claims through their religious organizations as well. Those claims most frequently involve meeting space in school facilities, availability of resources, and distribution of religious materials. Community religious organizations also make demands of school officials, but their demands have been limited to asking for meeting space on school premises and requesting distribution of religious materials.

Religious claims concerning public schools raise three legal issues. These three issues represent the precarious balance between the Free Speech (and, occasionally, the Free Exercise) Clause and the

Establishment Clause. First, what religious practices should be allowed under free speech? Under [Good News], a school that permits subject matter expression from a non-religious perspective during non-school hours cannot refuse a religious organization's viewpoint on the same subject. In other words, unless the school wants to prohibit all expression on a particular subject, it is required by free speech to allow a religious viewpoint where other viewpoints have been permitted.

Second, what religious practices are prohibited by the Establishment Clause? Some religious expression, such as school-organized or sponsored prayer at graduations or football games, are not permissible because, under the Establishment Clause's endorsement and psychological coercion tests, a school would be perceived as sponsoring religion and coercing participation in a religious activity.

Third, what religious practices, even if not required under the free speech clause, are permissible because they do not violate the Establishment Clause? School graduations are controlled by school boards and school officials and are, essentially, non-public fora. However, school boards could choose to give control over the content of graduation speeches to the students. To the extent that school officials are willing to create what would be a limited public forum for student speeches during an otherwise school-controlled graduation, case law suggests that a student's speech with religious content might be permissible.

Community groups and individual students/student groups have convergent, yet separable, free speech issues regarding access to public schools. Whether the resistance of some public schools to religious expression belies an attitude that "bristles with hostility to all things religious" may never be clear. What is more important, though, is that the free speech rights forged by the Supreme Court in *Lamb's Chapel* and *Good News* have served to level the playing field for religious claimants.

By merging the Free Speech Clause's concept of the limited public forum with the Establishment Clause's concept of neutrality, federal courts have infused free expression with the notion of evenhandedness. Access by religious claimants to public schools can still be restricted, and in some cases even prohibited, but the rules for governing access will now be defined under Free Speech, not under the misplaced Establishment Clause aphorism of a "wall of separation of church and state."

Religious expression, as any other kind of expression, can be restricted and even prohibited if it becomes disruptive to the school environment, but only to the extent that the alleged disruption is, pursuant to *Tinker*, material and substantial and not the product of a school official's personal opinion. In addition, school districts are free to make educational choices about the district's mission and curriculum, but these choices, if *Hazelwood* is to apply, must be those of the school board and school officials. Once school officials look beyond the school and have the school district's choices championed by persons outside the school or by students selected for their points of view, the school runs the risk of violating free speech.

Religious groups afford unique challenges for school boards because such groups invariably have a viewpoint to present. To the extent that school districts want to prevent access by religious community groups to their schools, their options are somewhat limited. They can choose to prohibit all community groups from their schools, with whatever public relations impact that decision might have in the community. School boards also have the option, as boards did in *Stafford* and *Goulart*, of designating the uses of the forum; but as *Good News* and *Bronx II* suggest, boards cannot prohibit all religious uses while permitting non-religious ones. What remains, then, is the delicate dance between viewpoint discrimination, which is prohibited, and subject matter exclusions, which arguably may still be permissible under *Good News*.

Similarly, if school districts want to ban religious student organizations from their schools, they can close their schools under EAA to all but student organizations that are curriculum-related. Such a decision might not be popular with parents and students, but it invokes no free speech rights for non-curriculum-related groups. However, once a school permits a non-curriculum-related student group to meet on school premises, a cognizable argument can be made that the creation of a limited open forum under EAA automatically invokes a limited public forum under free speech. Once a school has passed over to a limited public forum, the school arguably has lost the force of *Hazelwood* to control the educational process, and is essentially left with only the disruptive restrictions from *Tinker* to limit the expression of religious content.

The expressive rights of individual students are more complicated by the limited public forum difference between classrooms and non-classroom areas. However, even here, school officials can close these non-classroom areas to student expression, in effect eliminating these areas as limited public fora. In the alternative, school officials can maintain these non-classroom areas as limited public fora, subject to the *Tinker* test for disruption. Free speech does not deprive school districts of their right to control their schools, but it does assure that this control will occur in a fair and evenhanded manner

---

GOOD NEWS CLUB v. MILFORD CENTRAL SCHOOL
533 U.S. 98 (2001)

JUSTICE THOMAS delivered the opinion of the Court.

This case presents two questions. The first question is whether Milford Central School violated the free speech rights of the Good News Club when it excluded the Club from meeting after hours at the school. The second question is whether any such violation is justified by Milford's concern that permitting the Club's activities would violate the Establishment Clause. We conclude that Milford's restriction violates the Club's free speech rights and that no Establishment Clause concern justifies that violation.

I

In 1992, respondent Milford Central School (Milford) enacted a community use policy adopting seven of …purposes for which its building could be used after school. Two of the stated purposes are relevant here. First, district residents may use the school for "instruction in any branch of education, learning or the arts." Second, the school is available for "social, civic and recreational meetings and entertainment events, and other uses pertaining to the welfare of the community, provided that such uses shall be nonexclusive and shall be opened to the general public."

Stephen and Darleen Fournier reside within Milford's district and therefore are eligible to use the school's facilities as long as their proposed use is approved by the school. Together they are sponsors of the local Good News Club, a private Christian organization for children ages 6 to 12. Pursuant to Milford's policy, the Fourniers submitted a request to Dr. Robert McGruder, interim superintendent of the district, in which they sought permission to hold the Club's weekly after school meetings in the school cafeteria. The next month, McGruder formally denied the Fourniers' request on the ground that the proposed use—to have "a fun time of singing songs, hearing a Bible lesson and memorizing scripture," *Ibid.*—was "the equivalent of religious worship." According to McGruder, the community use policy, which prohibits use "by any individual or organization for religious purposes," foreclosed the Club's activities.

****

II

The standards that we apply to determine whether a State has unconstitutionally excluded a private speaker from use of a public forum depend on the nature of the forum. *See Perry Ed. Assn. v. Perry Local Educators' Assn.*, 460 U.S. 37, 44 (1983). If the forum is a traditional or open public forum, the State's restrictions on speech are subject to stricter scrutiny than are restrictions in a limited public forum.. Because the parties have agreed that Milford created a limited public forum when it opened its facilities in 1992, see we need not resolve the issue here. Instead, we simply will assume that Milford operates a limited public forum.

III

Applying this test, we first address whether the exclusion constituted viewpoint discrimination. We are guided in our analysis by two of our prior opinions, *Lamb's Chapel* and *Rosenberger*. In *Lamb's Chapel*, we held that a school district violated the Free Speech Clause of the First Amendment when it excluded a private group from presenting films at the school based solely on the films' discussions of family values from a religious perspective. Likewise, in *Rosenberger*, we held that a university's refusal to fund a student publication because the publication addressed issues from a religious perspective violated the Free Speech Clause. Concluding that Milford's exclusion of the Good News Club based on its religious nature is indistinguishable from the exclusions in these cases; we hold that the exclusion constitutes viewpoint discrimination. Because the restriction is viewpoint discriminatory, we need not decide whether it is unreasonable in light of the purposes served by the forum.

****

Applying *Lamb's Chapel*, we find it quite clear that Milford engaged in viewpoint discrimination when it excluded the Club from the afterschool forum. In *Lamb's Chapel*, the local New York school district similarly had adopted … "social, civic or recreational use" category as a permitted use in its limited public forum. The district also prohibited use "by any group for religious purposes." … Citing this prohibition, the school district excluded a church that wanted to present films teaching family values from a Christian perspective. We held that, because the films "no doubt dealt with a subject otherwise permissible" under the rule, the teaching of family values, the district's exclusion of the church was unconstitutional viewpoint discrimination.

IV

Milford argues that, even if its restriction constitutes viewpoint discrimination, its interest in not violating the Establishment Clause outweighs the Club's interest in gaining equal access to the school's facilities. In other words, according to Milford, its restriction was required to avoid violating the Establishment Clause. We disagree.

We have said that a state interest in avoiding an Establishment Clause violation "may be characterized as compelling," and therefore may justify content-based discrimination... However, it is not clear whether a State's interest in avoiding an Establishment Clause violation would justify viewpoint discrimination. ... We need not, however, confront the issue in this case, because we conclude that the school has no valid Establishment Clause interest.

We rejected Establishment Clause defenses similar to Milford's in two previous free speech cases, *Lamb's Chapel* and *Widmar*. In particular, in *Lamb's Chapel*, we explained that "the showing of the film series would not have been during school hours, would not have been sponsored by the school, and would have been open to the public, not just to church members." Accordingly, we found that "there would have been no realistic danger that the community would think that the District was endorsing religion or any particular creed." ... Likewise, in *Widmar*, where the university's forum was already available to other groups, this Court concluded that there was no Establishment Clause problem.

V

When Milford denied the Good News Club access to the school's limited public forum on the ground that the Club was religious in nature, it discriminated against the Club because of its religious viewpoint in violation of the Free Speech Clause of the First Amendment. Because Milford has not raised a valid Establishment Clause claim, we do not address the question whether such a claim could excuse Milford's viewpoint discrimination.

SANTA FE INDEPENDENT SCHOOL DISTRICT v. DOE
530 U.S. 290 (2000)

JUSTICE STEVENS delivered the opinion of the Court.

Prior to 1995, the Santa Fe High School student who occupied the school's elective office of student council chaplain delivered a prayer over the public address system before each varsity football game for the entire season. This practice...was challenged in District Court....While these proceedings were pending in the District Court, the school district adopted a different policy that permits, but does not require, prayer initiated and led by a student at all home games. The District Court entered an order modifying that policy to permit only nonsectarian, nonproselytizing prayer. The Court of Appeals held that, even as modified by the District Court, the football prayer policy was invalid.

****

Respondents commenced this action in April 1995 and moved for a temporary restraining order to prevent the District from violating the Establishment Clause at the imminent graduation exercises. In their complaint the Does alleged that the District had engaged in several proselytizing practices, such as promoting attendance at a Baptist revival meeting, encouraging membership in religious clubs, chastising children who held minority religious beliefs, and distributing Gideon Bibles on school premises. They also alleged that the District allowed students to read Christian invocations and benedictions from the stage at graduation ceremonies, and to deliver overtly Christian prayers over the public address system at home football games.

The policy, which was titled "Prayer at Football Games," was similar to the policy for graduations. [T]he district's high school students voted to determine whether a student would deliver prayer at varsity football games . . . . The students chose to allow a student to say a prayer at football games." A week later, in a separate election, they selected a student "to deliver the prayer at varsity football games."

II

The first Clause in the First Amendment to the Federal Constitution provides that "Congress shall make no law respecting an establishment of religion, or prohibiting the free exercise thereof." ...In *Lee v. Weisman*, 505 U.S. 577 (1992), we held that a prayer delivered by a rabbi at a middle school graduation ceremony violated that Clause. Although this case involves student prayer at a different type of school function, our analysis is properly guided by the principles that we endorsed in Lee.

As we held in that case:

> The principle that government may accommodate the free exercise of religion does not supersede the fundamental limitations imposed by the Establishment Clause. It is beyond dispute that, at a minimum, the Constitution guarantees that government may not coerce anyone to support or participate in religion or its exercise, or otherwise act in a way which 'establishes a [state] religion or religious faith, or tends to do fso.'"

In this case the District first argues that this principle is inapplicable to its October policy because the messages are private student speech, not public speech. It reminds us that "there is a crucial difference between government speech endorsing religion, which the Establishment Clause forbids, and private speech endorsing religion, which the Free Speech and Free Exercise Clauses protect." We certainly agree with that distinction, but we are not persuaded that the pregame invocations should be regarded as "private speech."

These invocations are authorized by a government policy and take place on government property at government-sponsored school-related events. Of course, not every message delivered under such circumstances is the government's own. We have held, for example, that an individual's contribution to a government-created forum was not government speech. *See Rosenberger v. Rector and Visitors of Univ. of Va.*, 515 U.S. 819 (1995). Although the District relies heavily on *Rosenberger* and similar cases involving such forums, it is clear that the pregame ceremony is not the type of forum discussed in those cases. The Santa Fe school officials simply do not "evince either 'by policy or by practice,' any intent to open the [pregame ceremony] to 'indiscriminate use,' . . . by the student body generally." Rather, the school allows only one student, the same student for the entire season, to give the invocation. The statement or invocation, moreover, is subject to particular regulations that confine the content and topic of the student's message.

Granting only one student access to the stage at a time does not, of course, necessarily preclude a finding that a school has created a limited public forum. Here, however, Santa Fe's student election system ensures that only those messages deemed "appropriate" under the District's policy may be delivered. That is, the majoritarian process implemented by the District guarantees, by definition, that minority candidates will never prevail and that their views will be effectively silenced.

Recently, in *Board of Regents of Univ. of Wis. System v. Southworth,* 529 U.S. 217 (2000), we explained why student elections that determine, by majority vote, which expressive activities shall receive or not receive school benefits are constitutionally problematic:

> To the extent the referendum substitutes majority determinations for viewpoint neutrality it would undermine the constitutional protection the program requires. The whole theory of viewpoint neutrality is that minority views are treated with the same respect as are majority views. Access to a public forum, for instance, does not depend upon majoritarian consent. That principle is controlling here.

Like the student referendum for funding in *Southworth,* this student election does nothing to protect minority views but rather places the students who hold such views at the mercy of the majority.

In *Lee*, the school district made the related argument that its policy of endorsing only "civic or nonsectarian" prayer was acceptable because it minimized the intrusion on the audience as a whole. We rejected that claim by explaining that such a majoritarian policy "does not lessen the offense or isolation to the objectors. At best it narrows their number, at worst increases their sense of isolation and affront." Similarly, while Santa Fe's majoritarian election might ensure that most of the students are represented, it does nothing to protect the minority; indeed, it likely serves to intensify their offense.

Moreover, the District has failed to divorce itself from the religious content in the invocations. It has not succeeded in doing so, either by claiming that its policy is "'one of neutrality rather than endorsement'" or by characterizing the individual student as the "circuit-breaker" in the process. Contrary to the District's repeated assertions that it has adopted a "hands-off" approach to the pregame invocation, the realities of the situation plainly reveal that its policy involves both perceived and actual endorsement of religion. In this case, as we found in Lee, the "degree of school involvement" makes it clear that the pregame prayers bear "the imprint of the State and thus put school-age children who objected in an untenable position."

The District has attempted to disentangle itself from the religious messages by developing the two-step student election process. The text of the October policy, however, exposes the extent of the school's entanglement. The elections take place at all only because the school "board has chosen to permit students to deliver a brief invocation and/or message." The elections thus "shall" be conducted "by the high school student council" and "upon advice and direction of the high school principal." *Id.* at 104-05. The decision whether to deliver a message is first made by majority vote of the entire student body, followed by a choice of the speaker in a separate, similar majority election. Even though the particular words used by the speaker are not determined by those votes, the policy mandates that the "statement or invocation" be "consistent with the goals and purposes of this policy," which are "to solemnize the event, to promote good sportsmanship and student safety, and to establish the appropriate environment for the competition."

In addition to involving the school in the selection of the speaker, the policy, by its terms, invites and encourages religious messages. The policy itself states that the purpose of the message is "to solemnize the event." A religious message is the most obvious method of solemnizing an event. Moreover, the requirements that the message "promote good citizenship" and "establish the appropriate environment for competition" further narrow the types of message deemed appropriate, suggesting that a solemn, yet nonreligious, message, such as commentary on United States foreign policy, would be prohibited. Thus, the expressed purposes of the policy encourage the selection of a religious message, and that is precisely how the students understand the policy. We recognize the important role that public worship plays in many communities, as well as the sincere desire to include public prayer as a part of various occasions so as to mark those occasions' significance. But such religious activity in public schools, as elsewhere, must comport with the First Amendment.

The actual or perceived endorsement of the message, moreover, is established by factors beyond just the text of the policy. Once the student speaker is selected and the message composed, the invocation is then delivered to a large audience assembled as part of a regularly scheduled, school-sponsored function conducted on school property. The message is broadcast over the school's public address system, which remains subject to the control of school officials. It is fair to assume that the pregame ceremony is clothed in the traditional indicia of school sporting events, which generally include not just the team, but also cheerleaders and band members dressed in uniforms sporting the school name and mascot. The school's name is likely written in large print across the field and on banners and flags. The crowd will certainly include many who display the school colors and insignia on their school T-shirts, jackets, or hats and who may also be waving signs displaying the school name. It is in a setting such as this that "the board has chosen to permit" the elected student to rise and give the "statement or invocation."

In this context the members of the listening audience must perceive the pregame message as a public expression of the views of the majority of the student body delivered with the approval of the school administration.

.....

Most striking to us is the evolution of the current policy from the long-sanctioned office of "Student Chaplain" to the candidly titled "Prayer at Football Games" regulation. This history indicates that the District intended to preserve the practice of prayer before football games. The conclusion that the District viewed the October policy simply as a continuation of the previous policies is dramatically illustrated by the fact that the school did not conduct a new election, pursuant to the current policy, to replace the results of the previous election, which occurred under the former policy. Given these observations, and in light of the school's history of regular delivery of a student-led prayer at athletic events, it is reasonable to infer that the specific purpose of the policy was to preserve a popular "state-sponsored religious practice."

School sponsorship of a religious message is impermissible because it sends the ancillary message to members of the audience who are nonadherants "that they are outsiders, not full members of the political community, and an accompanying message to adherants that they are insiders, favored members of the political community." The delivery of such a message—over the school's public address system, by a speaker representing the student body, under the supervision of school faculty, and pursuant to a school policy that explicitly and implicitly encourages public prayer—is not properly characterized as "private" speech.

III

One of the purposes served by the Establishment Clause is to remove debate over this kind of issue from governmental supervision or control. We explained in *Lee* that the "preservation and transmission of religious beliefs and worship is a responsibility and a choice committed to the private sphere." The two student elections authorized by the policy, coupled with the debates that presumably must precede each, impermissibly invade that private sphere. The election mechanism, when considered in light of the history in which the policy in question evolved, reflects a device the District put in place that determines whether religious messages will be delivered at home football games. The mechanism encourages divisiveness along religious lines in a public school setting, a result at odds with the Establishment Clause. Although it is true that the ultimate choice of student speaker is "attributable to the students," the District's decision to hold the constitutionally problematic election is clearly "a choice attributable to the State," …

The District further argues that attendance at the commencement ceremonies at issue in *Lee* "differs dramatically" from attendance at high school football games, which it contends "are of no more than passing interest to many students" and are "decidedly extracurricular," thus dissipating any coercion. Attendance at a high school football game, unlike showing up for class, is certainly not required in order to receive a diploma. Moreover, we may assume that the District is correct in arguing that the informal pressure to attend an athletic event is not as strong as a senior's desire to attend her own graduation ceremony.

There are some students, however, such as cheerleaders, members of the band, and, of course, the team members themselves, for whom seasonal commitments mandate their attendance, sometimes for class credit. The District also minimizes the importance to many students of attending and participating in extracurricular activities as part of a complete educational experience. As we noted in *Lee*, "law reaches past formalism." To assert that high school students do not feel immense social pressure, or have a truly genuine desire, to be involved in the extracurricular event that is American high school football is "formalistic in the extreme." We stressed in *Lee* the obvious observation that "adolescents are often susceptible to pressure from their peers towards conformity, and that the influence is strongest in matters of social convention." High school home football games are traditional gatherings of a school community; they bring together students and faculty as well as friends and family from years present and past to root for a common cause. Undoubtedly, the games are not important to some students, and they voluntarily choose not to attend. For many others, however, the choice between whether to attend these games or to risk facing a personally offensive religious ritual is in no practical sense an easy one. The Constitution, moreover, demands that the school may not force this difficult choice upon these students for "it is a tenet of the First Amendment that the State cannot require one of its citizens to forfeit his or her rights and benefits as the price of resisting conformance to state-sponsored religious practice."

Even if we regard every high school student's decision to attend a home football game as purely voluntary, we are nevertheless persuaded that the delivery of a pregame prayer has the improper effect of coercing those present to participate in an act of religious worship. For "the government may no more use social pressure to enforce orthodoxy than it may use more direct means." As in *Lee*, "what to most believers may seem nothing more than a reasonable request that the nonbeliever respect their religious practices, in a school context may appear to the nonbeliever or dissenter to be an attempt to employ the machinery of the State to enforce a religious orthodoxy." The constitutional command will not permit the District "to exact religious conformity from a student as the price" of joining her classmates at a varsity football game.

[Nothing] in the Constitution as interpreted by this Court prohibits any public school student from voluntarily praying at any time before, during, or after the school day. But the religious liberty protected by the Constitution is abridged when the State affirmatively sponsors the particular religious practice of prayer.

IV

This policy… empowers the student body majority with the authority to subject students of minority views to constitutionally improper messages. The award of that power alone, regardless of the students' ultimate use of it, is not acceptable. Like the referendum in *Board of Regents of Univ. of Wis. System v. Southworth*, 529 U.S. 217 (2000), the election mechanism established by the District undermines the essential protection of minority viewpoints. No further injury is required for the policy to fail a facial challenge.

The judgment of the Court of Appeals is, accordingly, affirmed.

NEWDOW v. RIO LINDA UNION SCHOOL DISTRICT
597 F.3d 1007 (9th Cir. 2010)

BEA, Circuit Judge

I. Introduction

We are called upon to decide whether the teacher-led recitation of the Pledge of Allegiance to the Flag of the United States of America, and to the Republic for which it stands, by students in public schools constitutes an establishment of religion prohibited by the United States Constitution. We hold it does not; the Pledge is constitutional.

The Pledge of Allegiance serves to unite our vast nation through the proud recitation of some of the ideals upon which our Republic was founded and for which we continue to strive: *one Nation under God*-the Founding Fathers' belief that the people of this nation are endowed by their Creator with certain inalienable rights; *indivisible*-although we have individual states, they are united in one Republic; *with liberty*-the government cannot take away the people's inalienable rights; *and justice for all*-everyone in America is entitled to "equal justice under the law" (as is inscribed above the main entrance to our Supreme Court). Millions of people daily recite these words when pledging allegiance to the United States of America:

> I pledge allegiance to the Flag of the United States of America, and to the Republic for which it stands, one Nation under God, indivisible, with liberty and justice for all. 4 U.S.C. § 4 (2002).

Pursuant to California Education Code § 52720, the Rio Linda Union School District in California ("the School District") has a practice that every morning, willing students, led by their teachers, face the American Flag, place their right hands over their hearts, and recite the Pledge of Allegiance.

Plaintiff Jan Roe is a self-proclaimed atheist whose child, RoeChild-2, attends elementary school in the School District. Roe filed suit alleging that the words "under God" in the Pledge offend her belief that there is no God, interfere with her right to direct her child's upbringing, and indoctrinate her child with the belief that God exists. The parties have stipulated that RoeChild-2 has never recited the Pledge, but Roe nevertheless asks us to prohibit the recitation of the Pledge by *other* students. Thus, this case presents a familiar dilemma in our pluralistic society-how to balance conflicting interests when one group wants to do something for patriotic reasons that another groups finds offensive to its religious (or atheistic) beliefs. In other words, does Roe have the right to prevent teachers from leading other students from reciting the Pledge of Allegiance-something we all agree is a patriotic exercise-because the mention of God in the Pledge offends her as an atheist?

Plaintiffs challenge the School District's policy as constituting a violation of the Establishment Clause: "Congress shall make no law respecting an establishment of religion." U.S. Const. amend. I.

The Pledge reflects many beliefs held by the Founding Fathers of this country-the same men who authored the Establishment Clause-including the belief that it is the people who should and do hold the power, not the government. They believed that the people derive their most important rights, not from the government, but from God:

> We hold these truths to be self-evident, that all men are created equal, that *they are endowed by their Creator with certain unalienable Rights,* that among these are Life, Liberty and the pursuit of Happiness.

The Declaration of Independence, 1 U.S.C. § XLIII (1776) (emphasis added). The Founders did not see these two ideas-that individuals possessed certain God-given rights which no government can take away, and that we do not want our nation to establish a religion-as being in conflict.

Not every mention of God or religion by our government or at the government's direction is a violation of the Establishment Clause. *See Lynch v. Donnelly,* 465 U.S. 668, 673, 104 S.Ct. 1355, 79 L.Ed.2d 604 (1984) ("Nor does the Constitution require complete separation of church and state; it affirmatively mandates accommodation, not merely tolerance, of all religions, and forbids hostility toward any."). The Supreme Court has upheld several government actions that contained a religious element against Establishment Clause claims: a display of the Ten Commandments on the Texas State Capitol grounds;[47] the display of a Chanukah menorah outside a City-County Building;[48] the display of a Nativity scene in a public Christmas display;[49] a state legislature's practice of opening each day with a prayer led by a chaplain paid with state funds;[50] a state's property tax exemption for religious organizations;[51] and a township's program for reimbursing parents for the cost of transporting their children to parochial schools.[52] Each of these cases involved religion. But taken in context, none of the government actions violated the Establishment Clause.

The plaintiffs and the dissent focus solely on the words "under God" in isolation, stripped of all context and history. Plaintiffs and the dissent even go so far as to disregard the plain text of the preamble to 4 U.S.C. § 4 which sets forth that Congress had two primary purposes in including the phrase "one nation under God" in the Pledge: (1) to underscore the political philosophy of the Founding Fathers that God granted certain inalienable rights to the people which the government cannot take away; and (2) to add the note of importance which a Pledge to our Nation ought to have and which ceremonial references to God invoke. The Supreme Court has instructed us to do otherwise: "Focus exclusively on the religious component of any [governmental] activity would inevitably lead to its invalidation under the Establishment Clause." *Lynch,* 465 U.S. at 678, 104 S.Ct. 1355. Were the correct focus as the dissent suggests, all of the above examples would have been found to violate the Establishment Clause, for all contain religious symbols or words. On the contrary, under Supreme Court law we are instructed to examine the history and context in which the phrase "one Nation under God" is used so that we may

---

[47] *Van Orden v. Perry,* 545 U.S. 677, 681, 125 S.Ct. 2854, 162 L.Ed.2d 607 (2005).

[48] *County of Allegheny v. ACLU,* 492 U.S. 573, 578-79, 109 S.Ct. 3086, 106 L.Ed.2d 472 (1989).

[49] *Lynch v. Donnelly,* 465 U.S. 668, 670-71, 104 S.Ct. 1355, 79 L.Ed.2d 604 (1984).

[50] *Marsh v. Chambers,* 463 U.S. 783, 784-86, 103 S.Ct. 3330, 77 L.Ed.2d 1019 (1983).

[51] *Walz v. Tax Comm'n,* 397 U.S. 664, 667, 90 S.Ct. 1409, 25 L.Ed.2d 697 (1970).

[52] *Everson v. Bd. of Educ.,* 330 U.S. 1, 8-11, 67 S.Ct. 504, 91 L.Ed. 711 (1947).

discern Congress' "ostensible and predominant" purpose when it enacted the Pledge. *See McCreary County v. ACLU,* 545 U.S. 844, 867-68, 125 S.Ct. 2722, 162 L.Ed.2d 729 (2005). Because California Education Code § 52720 as implemented by the School District's Policy requires the recitation of the Pledge as a whole, we must examine the Pledge as a whole, not just the two words the Plaintiffs find offensive. In doing so, we find the Pledge is one of allegiance to our Republic, not of allegiance to the God or to any religion. Furthermore, Congress' ostensible and predominant purpose when it enacted and amended the Pledge over time was patriotic, not religious.

. . .

We hold that the Pledge of Allegiance does not violate the Establishment Clause because Congress' ostensible and predominant purpose was to inspire patriotism and that the context of the Pledge-its wording as a whole, the preamble to the statute, and this nation's history-demonstrate that it is a predominantly patriotic exercise. For these reasons, the phrase "one Nation under God" does not turn this patriotic exercise into a religious activity.

Accordingly, we hold that California's statute requiring school districts to begin the school day with an "appropriate patriotic exercise" does not violate the Establishment Clause even though it permits teachers to lead students in recitation of the Pledge. California Education Code § 52720. In doing so we join our sister circuits who have held similar school policies do not violate the Establishment Clause. *See Myers v. Loudoun County Pub. Schs.,* 418 F.3d 395, 409 (4th Cir.2005) (upholding a Virginia statute requiring the daily recitation of the Pledge of Allegiance by students, but allowing students to sit or stand quietly if they object); *Sherman v. Cmty. Consol. Sch. Dist. 21 of Wheeling Twp.,* 980 F.2d 437, 447 (7th Cir.1992), *cert. denied,* 508 U.S. 950, 113 S.Ct. 2439, 124 L.Ed.2d 658 (1993) (same as to an Illinois statute).[53] Therefore, we reverse the district court's judgment and vacate the permanent injunction prohibiting the daily recitation of the Pledge in the School District.

...

V. The Lemon Test

There are three possible tests for determining whether a statute violates the Establishment Clause-the *Lemon* test, the Endorsement test and the Coercion Test. We examine each in turn.

Plaintiffs contend the School District's policy violates the Establishment Clause test announced in *Lemon v. Kurtzman,* 403 U.S. 602, 91 S.Ct. 2105, 29 L.Ed.2d 745 (1971), commonly known as the "*Lemon* test." ...Under the *Lemon* test, to be constitutional (1) the challenged governmental action must have a secular purpose; (2) "its principal or primary effect must be one that neither advances nor inhibits religion"; and (3) it "must not foster an excessive government entanglement with religion." *Lemon,* 403 U.S. at 612-13, 91 S.Ct. 2105 (citations and internal quotation marks omitted). The School District's Policy must satisfy all three prongs of the *Lemon* test.

---

[53] Contrary to the dissent's assertion, *Myers* and *Sherman* are not based solely on Supreme Court dicta. We encourage the reader to read these cases for himself for we find them to be not only well-written, but also elegantly reasoned.

All parties agree that the "ostensible and predominant" purpose of both California Education Code § 52720 and the School District's Policy is patriotic. We agree. ...*Lemon*'s second prong is also met. The effect of California Education Code § 52720 and the School District's Policy is stated quite clearly in each: each school shall conduct "appropriate patriotic exercises" daily. There is no mention of anything religious in either. ...Plaintiffs also concede that *Lemon*'s third prong, "excessive [governmental] entanglement" with religion, is not violated by California Education Code § 52720 or the School District's Policy, and we agree. Neither involves any entanglement with religion at all, let alone excessive entanglement.

...

The Supreme Court has held prayers, invocations and other overtly religious activities in public school violate the Establishment Clause. A student-led prayer before high school football games;[54] a prayer delivered by a clergyman in a high school graduation ceremony;[55] a period of silence in a public school for "meditation or voluntary prayer;"[56] a required Bible reading before each school day;[57] and a daily prayer[58] all have been invalidated by the Supreme Court as unconstitutional school-sponsored religious exercises.

All of the religious exercises invalidated in those cases shared a fundamental characteristic absent from the recitation of the Pledge: the exercise, observance, classroom lecture, or activity was predominantly religious in nature-a prayer, invocation, petition, or a lecture about "creation science."[59]

---

[54] *Santa Fe Indep. Sch. Dist. v. Doe,* 530 U.S. 290, 120 S.Ct. 2266, 147 L.Ed.2d 295 (2000).

[55] *Lee v. Weisman,* 505 U.S. 577, 112 S.Ct. 2649, 120 L.Ed.2d 467 (1992). In *Lee,* the Court found that a prayer led by a Rabbi specifically made reference to the Judeo-Christian tradition, because it was taken from Micah 6:8. *See id.* at 603 n. 5, 112 S.Ct. 2649. In the Pledge, the phrase "one Nation under God" does not make reference to any text, doctrine, or the practice of any particular religion in a manner that might be taken as suggestive, let alone coercive. The most likely provenance of the words is from either George Washington's address to boost his troops' morale, the Declaration of Independence, or President's Lincoln's tribute to the dead at Gettysburg. George Washington, General Orders (July 2, 1776); Abraham Lincoln, The Gettysburg Address (Nov. 19, 1863). *See* pages 3903 to 3908 *infra.*
Much as Justice Brennan explained, the "references to God contained in the Pledge of Allegiance" are "uniquely suited to serve such wholly secular purposes as solemnizing public occasions, or inspiring commitment to meet some national challenge in a manner that simply could not be fully served in our culture if government were limited to purely non-religious phrases." *Lynch,* 465 U.S. at 716-17, 104 S.Ct. 1355.

[56] *Wallace v. Jaffree,* 472 U.S. 38, 105 S.Ct. 2479, 86 L.Ed.2d 29 (1985)

[57] *Sch. Dist. of Abington Twp., Pa. v. Schempp,* 374 U.S. 203, 83 S.Ct. 1560, 10 L.Ed.2d 844 (1963).

[58] *Engel v. Vitale,* 370 U.S. 421, 82 S.Ct. 1261, 8 L.Ed.2d 601 (1962).

[59] *See e.g. Santa Fe,* 530 U.S. at 306-07, 120 S.Ct. 2266 ("[T]he only type of message that is expressly endorsed in the text [of the school policy] is an 'invocation'-a term that primarily describes an appeal for divine assistance."); *Lee,* 505 U.S. at 581-82, 598, 112 S.Ct. 2649 ("[T]he State has ... compelled attendance and participation in an explicit religious exercise [involving repeated thanks to God and requests for blessings] at an event of singular importance to every student."); *Wallace,*

The purpose of public prayer is always active-to invite divine intercession, to express personal gratitude, to ask forgiveness, etc. On the other hand, the recitation of "one Nation under God" is a description of the Republic rather than an expression of the speaker's particular theological beliefs, a recognition of the historical principles of governance, affected by religious belief, embedded in the Pledge. "[Our] institutions presuppose a Supreme Being." *Zorach v. Clauson,* 343 U.S. 306, 313, 72 S.Ct. 679, 96 L.Ed. 954 (1952).

...

Where the very same religious symbols are displayed for traditional cultural purposes and in a context evoking themes and values other than religion, they have been found not to violate the Establishment Clause. *See Van Orden v. Perry,* 545 U.S. 677, 681, 125 S.Ct. 2854, 162 L.Ed.2d 607 (2005) (upholding a Ten Commandments display on state capitol grounds among other historical monuments); *Lynch,* 465 U.S. at 670-71, 680, 687, 104 S.Ct. 1355 (upholding a crèche displayed as just one part of a city's annual Christmas display because the crèche depicted the "historical origins of this traditional event long recognized as a National Holiday").

The Supreme Court's most recent pronouncements on the Establishment Clause, *Van Orden* and *McCreary County,* are instructive on the importance of context. *Van Orden* and *McCreary County* were decided on the same day in 2005. Although a display containing the Ten Commandments was at issue in both cases, the Court upheld the display in *Van Orden,* but invalidated it in *McCreary County.* The words displayed were the same, but the context made all the difference:

> On the one hand, the Commandments' text undeniably has a religious message, invoking, indeed emphasizing, the Deity. On the other hand, focusing on the text of the Commandments alone cannot conclusively resolve this case. Rather, to determine the message that the text here conveys, we must examine how the text is *used.* And that inquiry requires us to consider the context of the display.

Van Orden, 545 U.S. at 700-01, 125 S.Ct. 2854 (Breyer, J., concurring) (emphasis in original).

...

In the context of the Pledge, the phrase "one Nation under God" constitutes a powerful admission by the government of its own limitations.[60] Although the phrase also has religious connotations, "one

---

472 U.S. at 58, 105 S.Ct. 2479 ("The wholly religious character of the later enactment [of the Alabama statute] is plainly evident from its text."); *Edwards,* 482 U.S. at 589, 107 S.Ct. 2573 (striking down a Louisiana statute that had the "purpose of discrediting 'evolution by counter-balancing its teaching at every turn with the teaching of creationism' "); *Schempp,* 374 U.S. at 210, 83 S.Ct. 1560 ("The reading of the[Bible] verses, even without comment, possesses a devotional and religious character and constitutes in effect a religious observance." (citation and internal quotation marks omitted)); *Engel,* 370 U.S. at 424, 82 S.Ct. 1261 ("There can, of course, be no doubt that New York's program of daily classroom invocation of God's blessings as prescribed in the Regents' prayer is a religious activity. It is a solemn avowal of divine faith and supplication for the blessings of the Almighty.").

[60] Whether Congress could have represented sufficiently the historical and political foundations of our nation with a wholly secular phrase instead of "one Nation under God" is not for us to say. The Establishment Clause does not require the government to show it has adopted the most narrow means of accomplishing its objectives by avoiding reference to religion or God wherever possible. In upholding the display of a crèche as part of a City's annual Christmas display, the *Lynch* Court stated that "Justice [Brennan in dissent] argues that the City's objectives could have been achieved without including the

Nation under God" in the Pledge is a reference to the historical and political underpinnings of our nation. As Justice Brennan noted, "[T]he revised pledge of allegiance, for example, may merely recognize the historical fact that our Nation was believed to have been founded 'under God.' Thus reciting the pledge may be no more of a religious exercise than the reading aloud of Lincoln's Gettysburg Address, which contains an allusion to the same historical fact." *Schempp,* 374 U.S. at 304, 83 S.Ct. 1560 (Brennan, J., concurring).

In light of the patriotic context in which the phrase "under God" is recited and the historical context in which that phrase has been enacted into law, we hold its voluntary recitation as part of the Pledge by school children, as practiced by the Rio Linda Union School District, does not violate the Establishment Clause.

.....

VIII. The Endorsement Test: The Pledge has neither the purpose nor the effect of endorsing religion.

For the same reasons we find the Pledge does not violate the *Lemon* test, we similarly find the Pledge does not violate the Endorsement Test, first articulated by Justice O'Connor in her *Lynch* concurrence and subsequently adopted by a majority of the Court in *County of Allegheny,* 492 U.S. at 578-79, 109 S.Ct. 3086. Under the Endorsement Test, we look to see whether the challenged governmental action has the purpose or effect of endorsing, favoring, or promoting religion, particularly if it has the effect of endorsing one religion over another. ...

Here, in contrast, as analyzed in detail above, both the purpose and effect of the Pledge are that of a predominantly patriotic, not a religious, exercise. The phrase "under God" is a recognition of our Founder's political philosophy that a power greater than the government gives the people their inalienable rights. Thus, the Pledge is an endorsement of our form of government, not of religion or any particular sect.

...

IX. The Coercion Test: The Pledge does not coerce students to support or participate in religion or in a religious exercise.

This brings us to plaintiffs' next contention, that the recitation of the Pledge in a public school classroom unconstitutionally coerces objecting students into affirming a belief in God. Even though the students in the school are not compelled[61] to recite the Pledge by threat of penalty, are they nonetheless coerced into participating in a religious exercise?

---

crèche in the display. True or not, that is irrelevant. The question is whether the display of the crèche violates the Establishment Clause." *Lynch,* 465 U.S. at 681 n. 7, 104 S.Ct. 1355 (citation omitted).

[61] Under the School District's policy, the recitation of the Pledge is purely voluntary. Students can choose not to recite the Pledge for any personal reason and to keep that reason to themselves. No student is required to recite or even to hear the recitation of the Pledge, nor can any student be disciplined for refusing to participate. Students can also participate in the

...

We agree that the students in elementary schools are being coerced to listen to the other students recite the Pledge. They may even feel induced to recite the Pledge themselves. Although the School District's Policy does not compel them to recite the Pledge, or even to listen to others reciting the Pledge, we recognize that elementary school children are unlikely to walk out of the classroom in protest. But the main distinction is this: Here, the students are being coerced to participate in a patriotic exercise, not a religious exercise. The Pledge is not a prayer and its recitation is not a religious exercise. The students are not being forced to become involuntary congregants listening to a prayer, as they were in *Lee*.... In *Lee v. Weisman,* the Supreme Court addressed the constitutionality of an invocation and benediction prayer delivered by a rabbi during a high school graduation ceremony. 505 U.S. at 580, 112 S.Ct. 2649. The prayer contained repeated references and thanks to God and, throughout its opinion, the Court described the prayer as a "religious exercise." *See e.g., id.* at 580-82, 588, 589, 598, 112 S.Ct. 2649. In analyzing the constitutionality of the prayer, the *Lee* Court adopted and applied what is now known as the coercion test: "[A]t a minimum, the Constitution guarantees that government may not coerce anyone to support or participate in religion or its exercise." *Id.* at 587, 112 S.Ct. 2649.[62]

...

Limiting *Lee*'s indirect coercion analysis to religious exercises is consistent with the purposes of the Establishment Clause. Where, as here, compulsion to recite is absent, government action respects an establishment of religion only if the government coerces students to engage in a religious exercise. Coercion to engage in a patriotic activity, like the Pledge of Allegiance, does not run afoul of the Establishment Clause.

REINHARDT, Circuit Judge, dissenting:

To put it bluntly, no judge familiar with the history of the Pledge could in good conscience believe, as today's majority purports to do, that the words "under God" were inserted into the Pledge for any purpose other than an explicitly and predominantly religious one: "to recognize the power and the universality of God in our pledge of allegiance;" to "acknowledge the dependence of our people, and our Government upon the moral direction and the restraints of religion," 100 Cong. Rec. 7590-91 (1954); and to indoctrinate schoolchildren in the belief that God exists, *id.* at 5915, 6919. Nor could any judge familiar with controlling Supreme Court precedent seriously deny that carrying out such an indoctrination in a public school classroom unconstitutionally forces many young children either to profess a religious belief antithetical to their personal views or to declare themselves through their

---

recitation of the Pledge and simply omit the words "under God" without fear of discipline. Thus, the free speech claim that was involved in *Barnette,* where the students were forced to say the Pledge, is not at issue in this case. 319 U.S. at 630, 63 S.Ct. 1178. We note that even though the *Barnette* Court held students who considered it to be against their religion could not be forced to recite the Pledge, the Court nonetheless did not hold that those students could also prevent *other* students who had no such religious objection from reciting the Pledge, which is what plaintiffs seek here.

[62] Although plaintiffs do not raise the argument RoeChild-2 is required to "support or participate" in religion, the dissent calls attention to these words in *Lee.* It is difficult to see how RoeChild-2 supports or participates in religion when she is neither required to recite nor even to listen to the Pledge, and when it is stipulated by her attorneys that she has never said the Pledge.

silence or nonparticipation to be protesting nonbelievers, thereby subjecting themselves to hostility and ridicule.

The undeniably religious purpose of the "under God" [1954] amendment to the Pledge and the inherently coercive nature of its teacher-led daily recitation in public schools ought to be sufficient under any Establishment Clause analysis to vindicate Jan Roe and her child's constitutional claim, and to require that the Pledge of Allegiance, when recited as part of a daily state-directed, teacher-led program, be performed in its original, pre-amendment secular incarnation that served us so well for generations. Surely, our original Pledge, without the McCarthy-era effort to indoctrinate our nation's children with a state-held religious belief, was no less patriotic. For purposes of this case, the only difference between the original secular Pledge and the amended religious version is that the former did not subject, and was not designed to subject, our children to an attempt by their government to impose on them a religious belief regarding the existence of God.

Notes and Comments

1. Establishment Clause Jurisprudence
The Establishment Clause has been used to address a wide range of public-school policies. Some disputes have centered on state programs that provide aid or special benefits to religious schools or their students. *See Bd. of Educ. v. Grumet*, 512 U.S. 687 (1994) (invalidating a state policy that formed a separate school district composed entirely of members of one religious sect); *Everson v. Bd. of Educ.*, 330 U.S. 1 (1947) (upholding state program that provided transportation services for students attending public and private schools); *Bd. of Educ. v. Allen*, 392 U.S. 236 (1968) (upholding state program of providing textbooks to students attending religious schools); *Grand Rapids v. Ball*, 473 U.S. 373 (1985); *Aguilar v. Felton*, 473 U.S. 402 (1985) (disallowing public school programs that provided remedial assistance to students attending religious schools), *overruled by Agostini v. Felton*, 521 U.S. 203 (1997) (upholding remedial programs as applied to public school that provided services to students attending religious schools); *Zobrest v. Catalina Foothills*, 509 U.S. 1 (1993) (upholding government program that provided a sign language interpreter for a student attending a religious school); *Meuller v. Allen*, 463 U.S. 388 (1983) (upholding a state tax policy of permitting deductions for private educational expenses); *Witters v. Wash. Dep't of Servs.*, 474 U.S. 481 91986) (upholding vocational scholarship program that provided tuition assistance to students attending religious school); *Zelman v. Simmons-Harris*, 536 U.S. 639 (2002) (upholding state school voucher program).

Other challenges have focused on local school policies that serve to encourage or require acts of religious observance. *See Lee v. Weisman*, 403 U.S. 602 (1971) (invalidating school prayer at graduation ceremony); *Santa Fe Indep. Sch. Dist. v. Doe*, 530 U.S. 290 (2000) (invalidating school prayer over public address system before football games); *Wallace v. Jefferies*, 472 U.S. 38 (1985) (invalidating moment of silence statute); *Engel v. Vitale*, 370 U.S. 421 (1962) (invalidating school prayer); *Sch. Dist. v. Schempp*, 374 U.S. 203 (1963) (invalidating bible reading).

A third category of decisions addresses the degree to which school officials may introduce religious materials and doctrine into the classroom. *See Stone v. Graham*, 449 U.S. 39 (1980) (invalidating practice of posting the Ten Commandments on the wall of each classroom); *Epperson v. Arkansas*, 393 U.S. 97 (1968) (invalidating state statute forbidding the teaching of human evolution); *Edwards v. Aguillard*, 482 U.S. 578 (1987) (invalidating state statute requiring the teaching of "creation science"). *See* Alan E. Brownstein, Harmonizing the Heavenly and Earthly Spheres: The Fragmentation and Synthesis of Religion, Equality, and Speech in the Constitution, 51 Ohio St. L.J. 89 (1990). Michael W. McConnell, Religious Participation In Public Programs: Religious Freedom at a Crossroads, 59 U. Chi. L. Rev. 115 117, (1993).

2. Untangling the Establishment Clause and the *Lemon* Test

Is there a unifying theme for applying the Establishment Clause to disputes in public education? Can you state the basics of the approach that the courts in the case above appear to be applying?

Several Commentators have addressed the issue of the confusion that currently exists over Establishment Clause doctrine. Why does it appear that it is so difficult for educators to comply with the basic notion of Separation of Church and State? Professor Douglas W. Kmiec notes that, "[There are] some unique American confusions over the meaning of the religion clauses in Constitutional text. There is a profound difference between the separation of church and state and the constitutional freedom of religion. The difference was of immense importance to the founders, yet, as a comprehensive recent history reveals, for many Americans, the difference between these ideals has become difficult to discern." *Symposium on Religion in the Public Square: Foreword: Oh God! Can I Say That In Public?* 17 ND J. L. Ethics & Pub Pol'y 307, 309 (2003). Professor Alan E. Brownstein opines, "Maybe we—academics, lawyers, and judges—who deal with these issues are not very bright people. More probably, this incoherence and doctrinal instability suggests that these constitutional clauses raise very difficult problems that cannot be easily resolved. Acknowledging the difficulty of the problems and the futility of searching for simple doctrinal formulas to solve them may be the necessary first step in determining the constitutional relationship between church and state." Alan E. Brownstein: *Panel Three: Constitutional Questions About Vouchers*, 57 N.Y.U. Ann. Surv. Am. L. 119, 124 (2000).

At the core of the Establishment Clause, analysis of public-school policies is the mandate to prevent school officials from using their authority and influence to give direct support to religion. Loosely phrased against the rationale of the *McCollum* decision (which is distinguished by the Court in *Zorach*), where the Court invalidated a policy of bringing sectarian teachers into public schools to provide religious instruction, this framework tries to determine "whether classrooms are used for religious instruction and/or whether the force of the public school is used to promote religious instruction or worship. *Illinois ex rel. McCollum v. Bd. of Educ.*, 333 U.S. 203, 212 (1948).

The *Lemon* Test, the endorsement test, the history exception, the neutrality principle, and the free-speech analysis each acknowledge, in varying degree, the importance of uncovering bad faith in policy-making. In this regard, the public-education cases provide a clearer set of guidelines on improper purposes and permissible effects than some would care to acknowledge.

When the Establishment Clause is looked at in this manner, the *Lemon* Test does not always fare well. Should *Lemon* be overruled? Justice Scalia says of the *Lemon* Test:

> As to the Court's invocation of the *Lemon* test: Like some ghoul in a late-night horror movie that repeatedly sits up in its grave and shuffles abroad, after being repeatedly killed and buried, *Lemon* stalks our Establishment Clause jurisprudence once again, frightening the little children and school attorneys...The secret of the *Lemon* test's survival, I think, is that it is so easy to kill. It is there to scare us (and our audience) when we wish it to do so, but we can command it to return to the tomb at will. When we wish to strike down a practice it forbids, we invoke it, when we wish to uphold a practice it forbids, we ignore it entirely. Sometimes, we take a middle course, calling its three prongs no more than helpful signposts. Such a docile and useful monster is worth keeping around, at least in a somnolent state; one never knows when one might need him.
> *Lamb's Chapel v. Center Moriches Union Free School Dist.*, 508 U.S. 384, 398-99 (1993).

If one abandons the *Lemon* Test, then with what is it replaced?

3. The Establishment Clause and the Pledge of Allegiance
You will recall a discussion of the flag pledge in *West Virginia v. Barnette* in Chapter Ten. Can the Pledge of Allegiance survive scrutiny under the Establishment Clause? Professor Russo says that such a challenge is certain to make its way to the U.S. Supreme Court. Of the possible outcomes, he notes:

> [T]he Justices must consider whether the Pledge is, in fact, an unconstitutional establishment of religion or whether it is a form of ceremonial deism—an expression of America's deeply, long held belief in God. In reaching its conclusion, the Court is likely to consider the various Establishment Clause tests that it has enunciated over the years. However, insofar as the Lemon test has fallen increasingly out of favor, the Court is likely to turn to either Justice O'Connor's endorsement standard and/or to Justice Kennedy's coercion test. Under either of these tests, as discussed above, a majority, or at least a plurality, of the Justices can place their ideological biases aside and permit the Pledge to withstand constitutional muster.
>
> The Justices must also examine the impact that striking down the Pledge might have on American public schools and society as a whole. Put another way, it is possible that the public would lose respect for the Court as an institution if it were to vitiate the Pledge. Further, if judicial ideologues who find an impermissible governmental establishment of religion in such matters as the words "under God" in the Pledge, continue to impose their wills on the American people, then perhaps Congressional leaders will make good on their promise to restrict the authority of the federal courts in matters of religion, thereby setting off a potentially divisive constitutional crisis, not only over the words "under God," but also over the scope congressional authority to act.

Charles J. Russo: The Supreme Court and Pledge of Allegiance: Does God Still Have a Place in American Schools?, 2004 BYU Educ. & L. J. 301, 327-28 (2004).

Part V
Liability, Affirmative Duties and Educational Accountability

Chapter Thirteen
Constitutional Liability and Substantive Due Process

> The Due Process Clause ...was intended to give Americans at least the protection against governmental power that they had enjoyed as Englishmen against the power of the Crown. The liberty preserved from deprivation without due process included the right "generally to enjoy those privileges long recognized at common law as essential to the orderly pursuit of happiness by free men. Among the historic liberties so protected was a right to be free from, and to obtain judicial relief for, unjustified intrusions on personal security. *Ingraham v. Wright,* 430 U.S. 651 (1977).

> Although the liberty protected by the Due Process Clause affords protection against unwarranted government interference . . ., it does not confer an entitlement to such [governmental aid] as may be necessary to realize all the advantages of that freedom. If the Due Process Clause does not require the State to provide its citizens with particular protective services, it follows that the State cannot be held liable under the Clause for injuries that could have been averted had it chosen to provide them. *DeShaney v. Winnebago County, 489 U.S. (1989).*

Despite the ruling in *San Antonio v. Rodriguez*, that education is not a fundamental right under the Federal Constitution, the U.S. Supreme Court interprets the Due Process Clause to create fundamental rights that apply to public education. The Due Process Clause provides that "[N]or shall any State deprive any person of life, liberty, or property without due process of law." The Due Process Clause imposes substantive and procedural limits on educators, the latter based largely on the seminal case of *Goss v. Lopez*, discussed in Chapter Four. You will recall that procedural due process applies when students or faculty are faced with the deprivation of a "property interest." Procedural due process creates, at best, a methodology for documenting unfairness and uncovering policies that violate other rights. Substantive due process acts as an independent source of liability, compensating victims when the actions of school officials violate "liberty" or "property" interests."

In public education most substantive due process, claims involve claims for damages against educators for misconduct that results in harm to students, faculty or staff. The materials below highlight the goal of these claims: eliminating policies that are arbitrary, capricious, danger creating, or that are wholly unrelated to the legitimate goal of maintaining an atmosphere conducive to learning.

Injury claims against public school officials brought under substantive due process must either be based on a deprivation of a specifically identified liberty or property interest protected under the notion of due process, or be based upon gross misconduct by school officials that "shocks the conscience." A suit may be based on misconduct by a school official or a third party. Substantive due process cases "sound in tort" but, because of their constitutional origins, are not limited by tort immunity laws. Together with the Equal Protection Clause, the substantive aspects of the Due Process Clause provide the most rigorous protection against campus policies that infringe on fundamental rights.

I. Substantive Due Process and Intentionally or Maliciously Inflicted Injuries

INGRAHAM v. WRIGHT
430 U.S. 651 (1977)

OPINION: JUSTICE POWELL delivered the opinion of the Court.

This case presents questions concerning the use of corporal punishment in public schools: First, whether the paddling of students as a means of maintaining school discipline constitutes cruel and unusual punishment in violation of the Eighth Amendment; and, second, to the extent that paddling is constitutionally permissible, whether the Due Process Clause of the Fourteenth Amendment requires prior notice and an opportunity to be heard.

I

Petitioners James Ingraham and Roosevelt Andrews filed the complaint in this case on January 7, 1971, in the United States District Court for the Southern District of Florida. At the time both were enrolled in the Charles R. Drew Junior High School in Dade County, Fla., Ingraham in the eighth grade and Andrews in the ninth. The complaint contained three counts, each alleging a separate cause of action for deprivation of constitutional rights, under 42 U.S.C. §§ 1981-1988. Counts one and two were individual actions for damages by Ingraham and Andrews based on paddling incidents that allegedly occurred in October 1970 at Drew Junior High School. Count three was a class action for declaratory and injunctive relief filed on behalf of all students in the Dade County schools. Named as defendants in all counts were respondents Willie J. Wright (principal at Drew Junior High School), Lemmie Deliford (an assistant principal), Solomon Barnes (an assistant to the principal), and Edward L. Whigham (superintendent of the Dade County School System).

****

Petitioners' evidence may be summarized briefly. In the 1970-1971 school year many of the 237 schools in Dade County used corporal punishment as a means of maintaining discipline pursuant to Florida legislation and a local School Board regulation. The statute then in effect authorized limited corporal punishment by negative inference, proscribing punishment which was "degrading or unduly severe" or which was inflicted without prior consultation with the principal or the teacher in charge of the school. *Fla. Stat. Ann.* § 232.27 (1961). The regulation, Dade County School Board Policy 5144, contained explicit directions and limitations. The authorized punishment consisted of paddling the recalcitrant student on the buttocks with a flat wooden paddle measuring less than two feet long, three to four inches wide, and about one-half inch thick. The normal punishment was limited to one to five "licks" or blows with the paddle and resulted in no apparent physical injury to the student. School authorities viewed corporal punishment as a less drastic means of discipline than suspension or expulsion. Contrary to the procedural requirements of the statute and regulation, teachers often paddled students on their own authority without first consulting the principal.

Petitioners focused on Drew Junior High School, the school in which both Ingraham and Andrews were enrolled in the fall of 1970. ..... The testimony of Ingraham and Andrews, in support of their individual claims for damages, is illustrative. Because he was slow to respond to his teacher's instructions, Ingraham was subjected to more than 20 licks with a paddle while being held over a table in the principal's office. The paddling was so severe that he suffered a hematoma requiring medical attention and keeping him out of school for several days. Andrews was paddled several times for minor infractions. On two occasions he was struck on his arms, once depriving him of the full use of his arm for a week.

The District Court made no findings on the credibility of the students' testimony. Rather, assuming their testimony to be credible, the court found no constitutional basis for relief. A panel of the Court of Appeals voted to reverse. The panel concluded that the punishment was so severe and oppressive as to violate the Eighth and Fourteenth Amendments, and that the procedures outlined in Policy 5144 failed to satisfy the requirements of the Due Process Clause. Upon rehearing, the en banc court rejected these conclusions and affirmed the judgment of the District Court. The Eighth Amendment, in the court's view, was simply inapplicable to corporal punishment in public schools.

II

The use of corporal punishment in this country as a means of disciplining school children dates back to the colonial period. It has survived the transformation of primary and secondary education from the colonials' reliance on optional private arrangements to our present system of compulsory education and dependence on public schools. Despite the general abandonment of corporal punishment as a means of punishing criminal offenders, the practice continues to play a role in the public education of schoolchildren in most parts of the country. Professional and public opinion is sharply divided on the practice, and has been for more than a century. Yet we can discern no trend toward its elimination.

At common law a single principle has governed the use of corporal punishment since before the American Revolution: Teachers may impose reasonable but not excessive force to discipline a child. The basic doctrine has not changed. The prevalent rule in this country today privileges such force as a teacher or administrator "reasonably believes to be necessary for [the child's] proper control, training, or education." Restatement (Second) of Torts § 147 (2) (1965); *see id.*, § 153 (2). To the extent that the force is excessive or unreasonable, the educator in virtually all States is subject to possible civil and criminal liability.

Of the 23 States that have addressed the problem through legislation, 21 have authorized the moderate use of corporal punishment in public schools. Of these States only a few have elaborated on the common-law test of reasonableness, typically providing for approval or notification of the child's parents, or for infliction of punishment only by the principal or in the presence of an adult witness. Only two States, Massachusetts and New Jersey, have prohibited all corporal punishment in their public schools. Where the legislatures have not acted, the state courts have uniformly preserved the common-law rule permitting teachers to use reasonable force in disciplining children in their charge.

Against this background of historical and contemporary approval of reasonable corporal punishment, we turn to the constitutional questions before us.

III

The Eighth Amendment provides: "Excessive bail shall not be required, nor excessive fines imposed, nor cruel and unusual punishments inflicted." Bail, fines, and punishment traditionally have been associated with the criminal process, and by subjecting the three to parallel limitations the text of the Amendment suggests an intention to limit the power of those entrusted with the criminal-law function of government. An examination of the history of the Amendment and the decisions of this Court construing the proscription against cruel and unusual punishment confirms that it was designed to protect those convicted of crimes. We adhere to this longstanding limitation and hold that the Eighth Amendment does not apply to the paddling of children as a means of maintaining discipline in public schools.

.....

In light of this history, it is not surprising to find that every decision of this Court considering whether a punishment is "cruel and unusual" within the meaning of the Eighth and Fourteenth Amendments has dealt with a criminal punishment.

.....

Petitioners acknowledge that the original design of the Cruel and Unusual Punishments Clause was to limit criminal punishments, but urge nonetheless that the prohibition should be extended to ban the paddling of schoolchildren. Observing that the Framers of the Eighth Amendment could not have envisioned our present system of public and compulsory education, with its opportunities for noncriminal punishments, petitioners contend that extension of the prohibition against cruel punishments is necessary lest we afford greater protection to criminals than to school children. It would be anomalous, they say, if schoolchildren could be beaten without constitutional redress, while hardened criminals suffering the same beatings at the hands of their jailers might have a valid claim under the Eighth Amendment. *See Jackson v. Bishop*, 404 F. 2d 571 (CA8 1968); *cf. Estelle v. Gamble*, *supra*. Whatever force this logic may have in other settings, we find it an inadequate basis for wrenching the Eighth Amendment from its historical context and extending it to traditional disciplinary practices in the public schools.

.....

The schoolchild has little need for the protection of the Eighth Amendment. Though attendance may not always be voluntary, the public school remains an open institution. Except perhaps when very young, the child is not physically restrained from leaving school during school hours; and at the end of the school day, the child is invariably free to return home. Even while at school, the child brings with him the support of family and friends and is rarely apart from teachers and other pupils who may witness and protest any instances of mistreatment.

The openness of the public school and its supervision by the community afford significant safeguards against the kinds of abuses from which the Eighth Amendment protects the prisoner. In virtually every community where corporal punishment is permitted in the schools, these safeguards are reinforced by the legal constraints of the common law. As long as the schools are open to public scrutiny, there is no reason to believe that the common-law constraints will not effectively remedy and deter excesses such as those alleged in this case.

We conclude that when public school teachers or administrators impose disciplinary corporal punishment, the Eighth Amendment is inapplicable. The pertinent constitutional question is whether the imposition is consonant with the requirements of due process.

. . . . .

The Fourteenth Amendment prohibits any state deprivation of life, liberty, or property without due process of law. Application of this prohibition requires the familiar two-stage analysis: We must first ask whether the asserted individual interests are encompassed within the Fourteenth Amendment's protection of "life, liberty or property"; if protected interests are implicated, we then must decide what procedures constitute "due process of law." *Morrissey v. Brewer*, 408 U.S., at 481; *Board of Regents v. Roth*, 408 U.S. 564, 569-72 (1972). Following that analysis here, we find that corporal punishment in public schools implicates a constitutionally protected liberty interest, but we hold that the traditional common-law remedies are fully adequate to afford due process.

****

The Due Process Clause of the Fifth Amendment, later incorporated into the Fourteenth, was intended to give Americans at least the protection against governmental power that they had enjoyed as Englishmen against the power of the Crown. The liberty preserved from deprivation without due process included the right "generally to enjoy those privileges long recognized at common law as essential to the orderly pursuit of happiness by free men." *Meyer v. Nebraska*, 262 U.S. 390, 399 (1923); *see Dent v. West Virginia*, 129 U.S. 114, 123-24 (1889). Among the historic liberties so protected was a right to be free from, and to obtain judicial relief for, unjustified intrusions on personal security.

While the contours of this historic liberty interest in the context of our federal system of government have not been defined precisely, they always have been thought to encompass freedom from bodily restraint and punishment. *See Rochin v. California*, 342 U.S. 165 (1952). It is fundamental that the state cannot hold and physically punish an individual except in accordance with due process of law.

This constitutionally protected liberty interest is at stake in this case. There is, of course, a de minimis level of imposition with which the Constitution is not concerned. But at least where school authorities, acting under color of state law, deliberately decide to punish a child for misconduct by restraining the child and inflicting appreciable physical pain, we hold that Fourteenth Amendment liberty interests are implicated.

. . . . .

The concept that reasonable corporal punishment in school is justifiable continues to be recognized in the laws of most States. *See* Part II, *supra*. It represents "the balance struck by this country," *Poe v. Ullman*, 367 U.S. 497, 542 (1961) (Harlan, J., dissenting), between the child's interest in personal security and the traditional view that some limited corporal punishment may be necessary in the course of a child's education. Under that longstanding accommodation of interests, there can be no deprivation of substantive rights as long as disciplinary corporal punishment is within the limits of the common-law privilege.

.....

Petitioners cannot prevail on either of the theories before us in this case. The Eighth Amendment's prohibition against cruel and unusual punishment is inapplicable to school paddlings, and the Fourteenth Amendment's requirement of procedural due process is satisfied by Florida's preservation of common-law constraints and remedies. We therefore agree with the Court of Appeals that petitioners' evidence affords no basis for injunctive relief, and that petitioners cannot recover damages on the basis of any Eighth Amendment or procedural due process violation.

Affirmed.

DISSENT: MR. JUSTICE WHITE, with whom MR. JUSTICE BRENNAN, MR. JUSTICE MARSHALL, and MR. JUSTICE STEVENS join, dissenting.

Today the Court holds that corporal punishment in public schools, no matter how severe, can never be the subject of the protections afforded by the Eighth Amendment. It also holds that students in the public school systems are not constitutionally entitled to a hearing of any sort before beatings can be inflicted on them. Because I believe that these holdings are inconsistent with the prior decisions of this Court and are contrary to a reasoned analysis of the constitutional provisions involved, I respectfully dissent.

The Eighth Amendment places a flat prohibition against the infliction of "cruel and unusual punishments." This reflects a societal judgment that there are some punishments that are so barbaric and inhumane that we will not permit them to be imposed on anyone, no matter how opprobrious the offense. *See Robinson v. California*, 370 U.S. 660, 676 (1962) (Douglas, J., concurring). If there are some punishments that are so barbaric that they may not be imposed for the commission of crimes, designated by our social system as the most thoroughly reprehensible acts an individual can commit, then, a fortiori, similar punishments may not be imposed on persons for less culpable acts, such as breaches of school discipline. Thus, if it is constitutionally impermissible to cut off someone's ear for the commission of murder, it must be unconstitutional to cut off a child's ear for being late to class.

SAYLOR v. BOARD OF EDUCATION
118 F.3d 507 (6th Cir. 1997)

SUBSEQUENT HISTORY: Certiorari Denied 522 U.S. 1029 (1997)

DAVID A. NELSON, Circuit Judge.

A fourteen-year-old schoolboy, Randy Saylor, Jr., got into a wild fight with a classmate in a public school in Harlan County, Kentucky. Their teacher, Sam Saylor, punished each of them by administering five licks with a paddle. The paddling left the boys with bruised buttocks.

Young Saylor and his parents brought a federal civil rights action alleging, among other things, a violation of substantive due process rights guaranteed by the United States Constitution. The defendants (who include the teacher and the school's principal and assistant principal) ultimately asserted qualified immunity and other defenses in a motion for summary judgment. The district court denied the request for qualified immunity, and this interlocutory appeal followed.

Upon de novo review of the record, and treating all genuine issues of fact as having been resolved in favor of the plaintiffs, we conclude that judgment ought to have been entered in favor of the individual defendants on the basis of qualified immunity. The denial of such immunity will be reversed.

I

Randy Saylor, Jr., was born at Harlan Appalachian Hospital on September 11, 1976. He attended Wallins Elementary School, in Harlan County, from kindergarten through the eighth grade. A younger sister followed him in school.

Resort to corporal punishment was not unknown at Wallins, and a number of the teachers kept paddles in their rooms. Prior to the incident out of which this lawsuit arose, according to the boy's deposition testimony, Randy had been spanked by five different teachers (but never by defendant Saylor) beginning as early as the fourth grade.

When Randy was in the seventh grade, a teacher named Henry Howard paddled him on the back of the legs hard enough to leave bruises. Upset at this, Randy's parents told the principal, defendant William Lee, that henceforth they did not want the school to administer corporal punishment to either of their children. (A "Code of Conduct" for the Harlan County schools provided that parents who objected to corporal punishment could so notify the proper school official upon enrollment of the student.) Mr. Lee subsequently testified at his deposition that he told all the teachers they were not to spank Randy Saylor.

When Randy entered the eighth grade in the fall of 1990, his mother testified, defendant Jim Roark, the assistant principal, was told that the Saylors didn't want their kids whipped in school. Randy's father, similarly, testified that he told both Roark and Lee at the beginning of the school year that he did not want corporal punishment used on his kids at Wallins. Neither Mr. Saylor nor Mrs. Saylor had occasion to convey this message directly to defendant Sam Saylor, Randy's eighth grade mathematics and history teacher. Sam Saylor had been told by Mr. Lee during the prior school year, however, that Randy's parents did not want him spanked at school.

A few weeks after Randy started the eighth grade, as the testimony of several witnesses established, Sam Saylor telephoned one of Randy's parents to report a problem with the boy's classroom behavior. Randy and his father met with Sam Saylor at the school the following day. In the course of the meeting, Sam Saylor testified, Randy's father told the teacher, in haec verba, "that if he [young Randy] gives you any more problem . . . I'm telling you to bust his ass." The father added, Sam Saylor said, that "if that don't do any good . . . you call me and [looking at the boy] I'll take you in front of that class and take my damned belt off and wear your ass out in front of that class." This conversation was reported to Assistant Principal Roark the next day, according to Sam Saylor, and Principal Lee testified that Sam Saylor likewise told him in October that Randy's father had given Sam permission to spank the boy.

Randy Saylor, Sr., testified that when his son misbehaved at home, he (the father) would whip him with a belt or a switch. In response to a general question by counsel for the defendants, however, Mr. Saylor denied ever having told Sam Saylor that it was all right for the latter to administer corporal punishment. The father subsequently volunteered that

> I have told them people, all of them, if you have any problems with my kids whatsoever in this school, you are to contact me or their mother. If I'm not here that day, I'll miss work the next day to be here. If they need whipped, I'll whip them in front of you.

Young Randy testified that he remembered his father telling Sam Saylor, "Well, if he gives you any more problems, call me and I'll take care of him." The boy was not directly asked if he remembered his father telling the teacher to "bust his ass" if young Randy gave the teacher any more problems—nor was this question posed by counsel for either side during the father's deposition.

On December 12, 1990, as young Randy later told it, Randy was challenged to fight by a classmate, Brian Turner. Randy was big for his age—much bigger than Brian—but this seems to have been no deterrent as far as Brian was concerned.

The trouble started in Mr. Howard's science class, according to Randy's testimony, when Randy felt something on his shoulder. He thought it was a paper wad thrown by Brian Turner, who was sitting a few seats behind him. Randy threw a paper wad at Brian, whereupon the latter, "cussing and carrying on," said he wanted to fight. Randy asked him to name the time, and Brian proposed the next break. (As both boys presumably knew, the Code of Conduct expressly prohibited fighting on school property. In this connection the Code said that "any student who finds himself/herself the victim of harassment should notify a teacher or principal.")

When the bell rang at the end of the period, the boys went on to Mr. Saylor's room for their mathematics class. The class was scheduled to begin at 12:45 p.m., but Mr. Saylor was late in getting back from a sixth grade class he had volunteered to teach several days a week during his lunch hour. The sixth grade class was on another floor of the building.

When Randy arrived at Mr. Saylor's room, according to Randy's testimony, Brian proposed getting the fight over with then and there. Randy, unfortunately, agreed. Brian swung first, hitting Randy in the face with his fist hard enough to leave a bruise. The boys fought for a time standing up, and Randy then wrestled Brian to the floor. Suggesting that they needed to stop fighting before Mr. Saylor arrived, Randy let Brian up. The latter came at him again, however, so Randy hit him with a plastic garbage can, scattering garbage everywhere. Then Randy hit Brian in the face with a small plastic water bucket, after which Randy started throwing yardsticks. Brian still wanted to fight, so Randy—"getting mad," in his words—picked up a folding metal chair with which he intended to hit the smaller boy. Other students got the chair away, whereupon Randy picked up a second chair. He testified that he was going at Brian with the chair when the assistant principal, Mr. Roark, came to the door and screamed at the combatants to get to his office. Randy threw the chair down and left the classroom.

When the boys got to the office, Randy testified, Mr. Roark told them that Mr. Saylor was going to be very angry and would expect them to be paddled; that fighting was against the rules; and that the boys had to apologize to one another. Sam Saylor arrived at the office at about this point and was filled in on the fight.

Mr. Saylor may or may not have been angry—Randy testified that "he was kind of angry acting"—but the prediction as to paddling proved accurate. Mr. Saylor told the boys that each of them would get five licks (the maximum permitted under school policy), and he asked Mr. Roark for the latter's paddle.

In Roark's presence, but with Randy waiting outside the office, Saylor paddled Brian five times. Asked whether they were "easy licks or hard licks," Mr. Roark said they were "good licks," licks that Roark thought were "appropriate." Brian was not required to lower his trousers during or after the punishment, but school officials learned the next day that the boy's buttocks had been bruised.

As for Randy, he initially told Roark and Saylor that he did not want to be paddled. Mr. Saylor responded that the boy would not be allowed back in the classroom unless he took his discipline. Randy again said that he wasn't getting paddled, and Mr. Saylor suggested to him that he speak with his mother on the telephone. Randy attempted to do so, but was unable to reach her.

Mr. Saylor returned to his classroom with Brian, but Mr. Roark continued to talk with Randy, urging him to take the paddling. (Roark testified that although Randy's parents had never told him directly they were lifting their prohibition against Randy's being spanked at school, he had understood from Sam Saylor that the boy's father had lifted the prohibition in October. In speaking with Roark, Lee and Sam Saylor after the fight and before the paddling, Randy himself does not appear to have said a word about his parents' current stance on corporal punishment.)

Randy still refused the paddling, so Mr. Roark gave him a standard-form letter of suspension. Where the words "Dates of Suspension" were printed on the form, Roark wrote "Parents to school." Mr. Roark explained at his deposition that this meant Randy was to bring his parents to school and would be suspended unless the problem was resolved with the parents.

Sam Saylor came back to the office at some point and told Randy that the other students in the math class were being given a test; that Randy's absence was unexcused; and that he would receive a zero if he missed the test. Randy testified that he was also told he would have to repeat the eighth grade;

Sam Saylor denied having made the latter statement, and Mr. Roark testified that he did not recall anything of the sort having been said.

After returning again to his classroom, Mr. Saylor was summoned to the office to take a phone call. Mr. Roark had left on other business by this time, but Randy was still at the office. On seeing Mr. Saylor, Randy asked if it were too late for him to take the paddling. It wasn't, and Mr. Saylor told Randy to find Mr. Lee or Mr. Roark. (The Code of Conduct provided that "[a] teacher or principal must administer corporal punishment in the presence of a second school official.")

Randy went into Mr. Lee's office and informed the principal that he had decided to take the spanking. After finishing a report he was working on, Mr. Lee went to talk with Mr. Saylor.

When Lee found Saylor, according to the latter's testimony, Saylor asked him "do you want to watch me bust Randy's butt." After correcting his language, Lee inquired if Saylor wanted him (Lee) to take care of it. Saylor's response, according to Lee, was, "no . . . I spanked the other boy and it wouldn't be fair if I don't spank him." Randy testified that Saylor responded, "No, this one's mine . . . ." Randy and both his parents further testified that they did not have any reason to believe that the spanking was for anything other than fighting in the classroom.

Randy, Mr. Lee and Mr. Saylor went into Mr. Roark's office, where the paddle was again taken out of the desk. Randy testified that it was an older paddle, perhaps two and a half or three inches wide and fourteen or fifteen inches long. Randy kept his trousers on, as Brian had done, and Mr. Saylor paddled him three times before being interrupted by the ringing of a telephone. The third blow was so hard, Randy testified, "it's just like it knocked the breath out of me."

The telephone call was for Mr. Lee, who took it in an adjoining office. Mr. Lee had thought the boy was to receive only three licks, he testified, so when he got back from the call he said something to Randy indicating that the punishment was over. Mr. Saylor, however, explained that there were to be five licks in all. Although Randy said that he didn't want to take any more, according to his testimony, Mr. Saylor then administered the final two licks. The first three had been "fairly hard," in Mr. Lee's opinion, but Lee thought that the last ones were "easy." Mr. Lee further testified that Mr. Saylor's attitude was "normal" at the time of the spanking, that Saylor did not seem upset, and that he did not show any hostility.

Randy had started to cry during the spanking, but he composed himself afterwards and went back to class with Mr. Saylor to take the test. The boy wrote only a little, and then told Mr. Saylor that he had forgotten to study the night before and was still shaken up about the paddling. Mr. Saylor told him he could study at home that evening and take the test the next day.

Randy attended the final class of the day and then rode home on the school bus, reaching home around 3:10 in the afternoon. He told his mother about the spanking and showed her his bottom, which was bruised and swollen. (A photograph taken that evening shows a large red area on the right haunch. A smaller and somewhat fainter bruise is visible on the left side.) Mrs. Saylor took Randy to a hospital emergency room, where he was examined but not treated. In retrospect (a phrase we suppose preferable to the more obvious one) the defendants acknowledge that the force used in administering the paddling was excessive.

Randy's father, when he arrived home after work and saw the bruises, got "real mad," as he later testified. Taking out his 12-gauge shotgun and some shells, he put them in his car and drove to the Wallins School with his family. A baseball game was in progress, and Mr. Saylor asked if anyone had seen Sam Saylor or Bill Lee. No one had, apparently, and neither man could be found at his residence. The Saylors returned home, and Mr. Saylor put up his gun.

Mr. and Mrs. Saylor went to the school the next day and made their displeasure known verbally. Randy's father told Lee, Roark and Sam Saylor that they all knew they were not to use corporal punishment on the boy. The father expressed outrage, moreover, that his son should have been punished for defending himself in a fight—something Randy had been taught at home that he should do.

It seems clear to us that the plaintiffs cannot show that either the principal of the school, Mr. Lee, or the assistant principal, Mr. Roark, violated anyone's constitutional rights. The record contains nothing to contradict the evidence that both men had been told by Sam Saylor in October that Randy's father had authorized the school to use corporal punishment—and there is no basis on which a jury could be permitted to find that the principal and assistant principal lacked a good faith belief that the parents' instructions not to paddle Randy had been withdrawn. Against this background, the case law leaves no room for doubt that Mr. Lee and Mr. Roark acted within the limits set by the Constitution when they allowed Randy's teacher to paddle him for fighting in the classroom.

As the district court correctly observed in dismissing the plaintiffs' cruel and unusual punishment claim, "the Supreme Court has unequivocally stated that the Eighth Amendment is inapplicable to situations where public school teachers or administrators impose disciplinary corporal punishment. *Ingraham v. Wright*, 430 U.S. 651, 671, 51 L. Ed. 2d 711, 97 S. Ct. 1401 (1977)." Because the grant of certiorari in *Ingraham v. Wright* was "limited to the questions of cruel and unusual punishment and procedural due process," *id.* at 659, the Supreme Court had "no occasion [in *Ingraham*] . . . to decide whether or under what circumstances corporal punishment of a public school child may give rise to an independent federal cause of action to vindicate substantive rights under the Due Process Clause." *Id.* at 679 n.47.[9] The courts of appeals are not of one mind on the substantive due process question, but we know of no circuit where the precedents indicate that the conduct of Principal Lee and Assistant Principal Roark could be held unconstitutional.

The Fifth Circuit, which issued the en banc decision reviewed by the Supreme Court in *Ingraham*, takes the view that where state law provides "adequate post-punishment remedies to deter unjustified or excessive punishment and to redress that which may nevertheless occur, the student receives all the process that is constitutionally due." *Woodard v. Los Fresnos Ind. Sch. Dis.*, 732 F.2d 1243, 1245 (5th

---

[9] In *Brown v. Johnson*, 710 F. Supp. 183 (E.D. Ky. 1989), a decision by the same district court that decided the case at bar, the court held that school officials did not violate the substantive due process rights of a nine-year-old schoolgirl by paddling her seven times with sufficient force to bruise her buttocks severely. In noting that the bruises did not "shock the conscience" of the court—a test sometimes used for resolving substantive due process questions—the court repeatedly suggested that in *Ingraham v. Wright* "the Supreme Court found that a severe beating [20 licks with a paddle] and the resulting hematoma [which required the plaintiff to miss 11 days of school] did not shock its conscience." *Brown*, 710 F. Supp. at 186. We believe that the result reached in *Brown* was correct, but the *Brown* court's reading of *Ingraham v. Wright* seems incorrect; the Supreme Court did not address the "conscience shocking" question in *Ingraham*.

Cir. 1984). Corporal punishment of a public school child, as the Fifth Circuit sees it, simply does not "give rise to an independent cause of action to vindicate substantive rights under the due process clause . . . ." *Id.*, citing *Ingraham v. Wright*, 525 F.2d 909, 916 (5th Cir. 1976) (en banc), *aff'd on other grounds*, 430 U.S. 651, 51 L. Ed. 2d 711, 97 S. Ct. 1401 (1977). As the Fifth Circuit said in *Ingraham,*

> We think it a misuse of our judicial power to determine, for example, whether a teacher has acted arbitrarily in paddling a particular child for certain behavior or whether in a particular instance of misconduct five licks would have been a more appropriate punishment than ten licks. We note again the possibility of a civil or criminal action in state court against a teacher who has excessively punished a child." *Id.* at 917 (footnote omitted).

The order of the district court denying qualified immunity is REVERSED, and the case is REMANDED with instructions to enter judgment in favor of each of the individual defendants.

Notes and Comments

1. Which argument do you find more persuasive in *Ingraham*? The dissenting opinion proposes an approach, which implies a bright-line test for measuring violations of student rights based on the long history of decisions on the Eight Amendment. Does the approach of the majority offer a clear test? How would you help a school district develop official policy on the subject of "touching a student" in light of the rationale in *Ingraham*?

2. *Saylor*, Parental Rights and Corporal Punishment
Randy Saylor's parents appear to have authorized educators to use corporal punishment ("I'm telling you to bust his ass."). Does the right of parents to direct the upbringing of their children include the right to authorize corporal punishment? In *In re Lunn*, 176 Ohio App. 3d 186, 891 N.E.2d 778 (2008), the Ohio courts held that the fundamental liberty interest that parents have in the care, custody, and management of their children includes, "the right of restraint over their children and the duty of correcting and punishing them for misbehavior." In *In re Lunn*, the appellate court overturned a trial court ruling that a parent committed child abuse by repeatedly whipping the child with a belt. The court held that parents "have the right to use reasonable physical discipline, or corporal punishment, to prevent and punish a child's misconduct." Does this mean that a parent can delegate this right to educators? Should such a delegation protect an educator from a liability claim based on Substantive Due Process?

3. Scope of Substantive Due Process Protection

Injury claims against public school officials brought under substantive due process must either be based on a deprivation of a specifically identified liberty or property interest protected under the notion of due process, or be based upon gross misconduct by school officials that "shocks the conscience." Most student-rights claims fall under the latter category because of the short list of rights deemed fundamental under substantive due process. As you will see below, claims based upon due process and complicated by the fact that current doctrine does not recognize a fundamental right to an education or a right to a safe learning environment as an interest that implicates life, liberty, or property.

The "shocks the conscience" approach to claims under the due process clause are more like ordinary tort cases and are thus easier to describe and prosecute. In most instances, the theory of recovery is that a school official is abusing his power, or employing it as an instrument of oppression. *See Metzger v. Osbeck*, 841 F.2d 518 (3d Cir. 1988) (broken arm by acts of teacher); *Johnson v. Newburgh Enlarged Sch. Dist.*, 239 F.3d 246 (2d Cir. 2001) (pattern of assaults by angry gym teacher); *Dockery v. Barnett*, 167 F. Supp. 2d 597 (S.D.N.Y. 2001) (pattern of physical violence against special-education students); *P.B. v. Koch*, 96 F.3d 1298 (9th Cir. 1996) (principal's hitting, grabbing, and pushing of several students).

4. Practical Aspects of Substantive Due Process Litigation

Most student-rights claims filed in federal court are framed as constitutional torts under the federal civil rights statute 42 U.S.C. § 1983, which states: "Every person who, under color of any statute, ordinance, regulation, custom, or usage, of any State or Territory or the District of Columbia, subjects, or causes to be subjected, any citizen of the United States or other person within the jurisdiction thereof to the deprivation of any rights, privileges, or immunities secured by the Constitution and laws, shall be liable to the party injured in an action at law, suit in equity, or other proper proceeding for redress…." This hundred-year-old civil-rights provision allows a person to sue government officials and entities for the violation of federal rights.

To state a claim under § 1983, a plaintiff must (1) allege a violation of rights secured by the Constitution or laws of the United States and (2) demonstrate that the alleged deprivation was committed by a person acting under color of state law. *See, e.g., West v. Atkins*, 487 U.S. 42, 48 (1988); *Resident Council of Allen Parkway Village v. United States Dep't of Hous. & Urban Dev.*, 980 F.2d 1043, 1050 (5th Cir. 1993).

A claim may also be brought against a local governmental agency or unit when the injury is alleged to have occurred because of an "official policy or custom." *Monell v. Dep't of Social Servs.*, 436 U.S. 658 (1978); *see also Webster v. City of Houston*, 735 F.2d 838, 841 (5th Cir.) (en banc) (adopting a definition of "official policy"), *modified on other grounds on reh'g*, 739 F.2d 993 (5th Cir. 1984) (en banc). Local governmental units may not be held liable under § 1983 under a theory of respondeat superior. *Monell*, 436 U.S. at 691; *Lankford v. Doe*, 513 U.S. 815 (1994); *Doe v. Taylor Indep. Sch. Dist.*, 15 F.3d 443, 452 (5th Cir. 1994).

In *Paul v. Davis*, the U.S. Supreme Court held that the Due Process Clause should not become a "font of tort law.... altering the basic relations between the States and the national government." 424 U.S. 693, 700-01 (1976). Later in *Collins v. City of Harker Heights*, the Court noted:

As a general matter the Court has always been reluctant to expand the concept of substantive due process because guideposts for responsible decision making in this unchartered area are scarce and open-ended....It is important, therefore, to focus on the allegations in the complaint to determine how [a plaintiff] describes the constitutional right at stake and what the [government] allegedly did to deprive [plaintiff] of that right.

Deana A. Pollard: Banning Corporal Punishment: A Constitutional Analysis, 52 Am. U.L. Rev. 447 (2002)*

American use of violence against children, including spanking and other forms of subabusive corporal punishment, is presently unparalleled among industrialized nations. America's rate of societal violence is also unparalleled among industrialized countries; our violence rate is nearly four times that of Canada and nearly eight times that of our Western European counterparts. American law supports and protects parental use of physical violence as a child-rearing method, with all fifty states recognizing some form of a privilege for parents and legal guardians to hit children in their custody. Ironically, the privilege to "discipline" children with physical force is based on the notion that physical discipline is efficacious, a notion that is not only undermined but contradicted by the most recent, most reliable research regarding the impact of child corporal punishment. The reality is that physical discipline is dangerous and contributes to many individual and societal problems.

American law in relation to corporal punishment of children is at odds with scientific research regarding the impact and efficacy of this child-rearing method. This Article argues that American law must change in accordance with current scientific knowledge about the individual and societal impact of child corporal punishment. The law could change in two ways. First, state legislatures could take the initiative to ban child spanking and other forms of subabusive corporal punishment. Second, state laws that exclude children from protection against assault based on a parental privilege should be declared unconstitutional as violating children's equal protection and liberty interests.

.....

If a state chose to ban child corporal punishment, the state would be in the position of defending its action against potential constitutional challenges, which would most likely be based on infringement of the fundamental right to control children's upbringing or interference with religious freedom. Particularly considering the current Court's "hands off" position in relation to state legislative decisions, state action banning corporal punishment could survive both of these constitutional challenges, based on its police power and/or parens patriae power.

.....

The administration of corporal punishment creates and exacerbates family discord per se. The interest in avoiding family discord through state interference is also substantially less where family discord already exists, as is the case with parental acts of corporal punishment. In addition, to the extent that prohibiting corporal punishment discourages its use, less child abuse prosecution—with the attendant likelihood of creating or exacerbating family discord—should be necessary, leading ultimately to less state interference with family relations. Therefore, the concerns expressed in Parham support banning corporal punishment.

Second, basic humanitarian concerns motivate the Court to protect children from poor parenting choices. In *Yoder*, the Court explained that compulsory education and child labor laws find their historical origin in common humanitarian instincts. Based on these basic humanitarian values, the Court has set a limit on parental choices that would leave their children wholly illiterate, or subject them to inappropriate labor conditions. From a purely humanitarian standpoint, it seems inhumane to cause physical pain to children simply because they are engaged in irritating or belligerent behavior that may be developmentally normal and age-appropriate, such as challenging authority and testing boundaries. Apart from the physical pain involved in spanking, humanitarian concerns justify banning corporal punishment based on its impact on the child's cognitive development and emotional/psychological well-being—the same concerns underlying the state's power to require that children be educated. It would be perverse to afford convicted felons greater protection from corporal punishment based on "humanitarian" concerns than relatively innocent (not to mention small) human beings. These concerns lend additional support for a state to render unconstitutional the practice of corporally punishing children under its police power authority.

State laws that specifically allow for corporal punishment of children, but no one else, constitute state action that denies children equal protection of the laws. In addition, these laws violate children's liberty interest in their bodily integrity. Although the current conservative Court generally may not be inclined to recognize new liberties, individual rights, or suspect classifications, the current research on child corporal punishment amply supports arguments that exempting children as a class from laws protecting them from assault and battery violates their constitutional rights. Thus, in the event that state legislatures fail to act in response to the research on child corporal punishment, current state laws exempting children from tort and criminal laws of general applicability should be challenged on constitutional grounds.

.....

The Supreme Court has articulated a number of factors to be used in determining whether a group of people should be considered a suspect or quasi-suspect class. In general, underlying all suspect classifications is the stigma of inferiority and second class citizenship. However, two fundamental concerns have motivated the Court to afford special protection for certain groups in society: fairness and the judicial system's responsibility to protect minorities from the majoritarian political process.

The specific factors courts look to in making a determination as to the proper level of scrutiny are: whether the class member has a choice in being a class member, i.e., whether the trait involved is "immutable"; whether class members suffer from unique disabilities based on stereotyped notions of abilities and characteristics; whether the class historically has suffered from discrimination; and whether the class is politically powerless, such as with "discreet and insular minorities." None of these factors per se determine the level of scrutiny; rather, they are considered together in assessing the judiciary's appropriate level of protection. In addition, when a classification is considered "suspect," it tends to be irrelevant to any proper legislative goal.

Children should be considered a suspect or quasi-suspect class. Regarding the first factor, childhood is an immutable trait during the period of minority status because children have no choice in being born and have no way out of minority status pending the passage of time. Immutability is important primarily because it relates to a class member's control over his class status, and it would be unfair to discriminate against him when he has no way out of class membership. Thus, in finding unconstitutional a Texas law that denied public education to minor children of illegal aliens, the Court in *Plyler* emphasized that minor illegal aliens have no control over their status, that they could "affect neither their parents' conduct nor their own status," and that "legislation directing the onus of a parent's misconduct against his children does not comport with fundamental conceptions of justice." In essence, legal burdens should bear some relationship to individual responsibility or wrongdoing, and because children have no control over their undocumented status, basic notions of fairness require that they not be singled out and discriminated against.

.....

Laws already protect children from numerous abuses, including corporal punishment that crosses the line into physical "abuse." To the extent that society believes corporal punishment is a form of abuse, or otherwise should be discouraged in the same way as domestic violence, the notion of "privacy" must be balanced against the need to protect victims of corporal punishment. Where corporal punishment is involved, privacy should give way in this context as it has in relation to spousal rape and other forms of domestic violence.

Children have a liberty interest in not being physically assaulted. Over a hundred years ago, the Court recognized the right of each person to possess and control his body and to be free from restraint and interference. The Court has already recognized that children have a constitutionally protected liberty interest in being free of bodily restraints or bodily harm. In *Ingraham v. Wright*, the Court upheld the use of school corporal punishment against constitutional challenges based on procedural due process and the Eighth Amendment right to be free from cruel and unusual punishment. The Court nonetheless acknowledged a child's substantive due process right in being "free from ... unjustified intrusions on personal security." A number of circuit courts have considered whether corporal punishment in the schools violates students' substantive due process rights. The Fifth Circuit has stated that "corporal punishment is a deprivation of substantive due process when it is arbitrary, capricious, or wholly unrelated to the legitimate state goal or maintaining an atmosphere conducive to learning." Children thus have a liberty interest in being free from corporal punishment.

Where state action is challenged on substantive due process grounds, such as where a state law infringes on a person's fundamental liberty interest, the state must demonstrate a sufficiently important purpose to justify its infringement of the right. Also, the means used must be sufficiently related to that purpose. If the state cannot show both a sufficiently important interest and a sufficient nexus between the purpose and the state action taken to advance that purpose, then its action is unconstitutional.

Government action that interferes with a fundamental right may be analyzed under the fundamental rights branch of equal protection, or under a substantive due process analysis. As a practical matter, under both equal protection and substantive due process analysis, the nature of the right affected, the state's interest in infringing on the right, and the efficacy of the state's method for advancing its interest should all be considered to determine constitutionality. Both analyses involve a balancing approach: only government interests of sufficient importance will justify interference with fundamental rights.

Realistically, the degree of protection or level of analysis afforded to fundamental rights should not depend upon whether the constitutional challenge is grounded in equal protection or substantive due process. While terminology may vary a bit, the analyses are essentially the same. State laws that single children out for physical punishment cannot withstand constitutional scrutiny under either equal protection or due process analysis because of the insufficient relationship between the state purpose and the action taken to advance the purpose. These laws therefore constitute an unconstitutional infringement on children's liberty interests.

MEEKER v. EDMUNDSON

415 F.3d 317 (4th Cir. 2005)

DIANA GRIBBON MOTZ, Circuit Judge:

This appeal arises from a claim that a public high school wrestling coach violated the constitutional rights of a member of his high school wrestling team by instituting and encouraging repeated beatings of the student by other members of the team. The coach appeals the district court's refusal to dismiss the complaint on the basis of qualified immunity. We affirm.

I.

The amended complaint alleges that in the fall of 2000, James Robert Meeker, a freshman at Rosewood High School in Wayne County, North Carolina, joined the school's wrestling team, which William Henderson Edmundson II coached. According to the complaint, from November 2000 through January 2001, Coach Edmundson frequently "initiated and encouraged" abuse of Meeker by other members of the wrestling team.

During these attacks, at least two team members restrained Meeker, who was only five feet, five inches tall and weighed 115 pounds, while additional teammates would pull up or remove his clothing and take turns "repeatedly beating [his] bare torso" until it turned red. Meeker received such beatings; referred to as "red bellies," at least twenty-five times during the few months he was a member of the team. Coach Edmundson allegedly "instituted, permitted, endorsed, encouraged, facilitated, and condoned" the abuse, using other students as his "instruments" to beat Meeker.

The complaint alleges that Coach Edmundson employed the beatings as "his sole means of discipline" and as a way to force an unwanted member to quit the team, which had a purported no-cut policy.

Edmundson assertedly told Meeker that the beatings would continue until Meeker "toughened up and stopped crying," and the coach prevented disclosure of the abuse by "intimidation and retaliation, including more . . . severe beatings." The beatings caused Meeker "excruciating physical pain, inflammation of the body, and severe emotional anguish and humiliation," requiring him to seek professional care and medical treatment for "among other conditions, traumatic stress disorders," which "may be permanent in nature." In January 2001, suffering from traumatic stress and reacting to the most recent beatings, Meeker brought a "multi-tool" to school, which led to his suspension and reassignment to another school in the district.

In August 2003, Meeker's parents, individually and as guardians ad litem for Meeker, filed this action for compensatory and punitive damages against Coach Edmundson, Principal Richard Gene Sauls, and Superintendent Steven D. Taylor, in their official and individual capacities; Chairman of the Wayne County Board of Education, George E. Moye, Jr., in his official capacity; and the Wayne County Board of Education. In addition to claiming that the defendants acted negligently in violation of state law, the amended complaint alleges violation of Meeker's and his parents' constitutional rights under 42 U.S.C. §§ 1983 and 1988 (2000) and civil rights conspiracy in violation of 42 U.S.C. §§ 1983 and 1985 (2000).

The district court refused to dismiss this claim against Coach Edmundson on the basis of qualified immunity, reasoning that "at the time of the alleged incidents, it was clearly established that a state actor could not arbitrarily commit violence against a student."

II.

In an appeal from the denial of qualified immunity, we first determine whether the facts alleged, "taken in the light most favorable to the party asserting the injury," show that the official's conduct violated a constitutional right. *Saucier v. Katz*, 533 U.S. 194, 201, 150 L. Ed. 2d 272, 121 S. Ct. 2151 (2001). If not, "the analysis ends; the plaintiff cannot prevail." *Clem v. Corbeau*, 284 F.3d 543, 549 (4th Cir. 2002). If, however, a plaintiff has alleged the violation of a constitutional right, we then "ask whether the right was clearly established" at the time of the asserted violation. *Saucier*, 533 U.S. at 201; *Clem*, 284 F.3d at 549. "If the right was not clearly established in the specific context of the case," then the official is entitled to immunity from suit. *Clem*, 284 F.3d at 549 (internal quotation marks and citation omitted). Only if a plaintiff alleges the violation of a clearly established constitutional right does his complaint survive a motion to dismiss on qualified immunity grounds.

A.

Our first task, then, is to resolve whether, "taken in the light most favorable" to *Meeker*, "the facts alleged show" that Coach Edmundson's conduct "violated a constitutional right." *Saucier*, 533 U.S. at 201. Meeker maintains that the facts show that Edmundson violated his substantive due process right to be free from the infliction of malicious corporal punishment by school officials.

Twenty-five years ago in *Hall v. Tawney*, 621 F.2d 607 (4th Cir. 1980), we considered whether a student could state a substantive due process claim by alleging malicious corporal punishment inflicted by school officials. There, a public school student and her parents asserted, in "admittedly . . . conclusory allegations," that, after a teacher had paddled the student without provocation, the school principal "supervised and approved" an additional paddling, which caused the student serious injury. *id.* at 614. We found that the complaint set forth a substantive due process claim against both the teacher and the principal.

In doing so, we relied on the fact that three years earlier, in *Ingraham v. Wright*, 430 U.S. 651, 672 (1977), the Supreme Court had expressly recognized that "corporal punishment in public schools implicates a constitutionally protected liberty interest . . . to be free from . . . unjustified intrusions on personal security." The *Ingraham* Court said such punishment did not infringe a student's Eighth Amendment or procedural due process rights, but it specifically left open the possibility that corporal punishment at a public school could give rise to a substantive due process claim. *See Id.* at 679 n.47. In Hall we concluded that "the Court's express reservation of the issue" in *Ingraham* "compelled" the conclusion "that substantive due process rights might be implicated in school disciplinary punishments even though procedural due process is afforded by adequate civil and criminal state remedies." *Hall*, 621 F.2d at 611 (emphasis omitted).

We then held that the proper "substantive due process inquiry" focuses on the force imposed by school authorities: whether the force was "disproportionate to the need presented," whether the force was "inspired by malice or sadism rather than a merely careless or unwise excess of zeal," and whether the force inflicted "severe" injury. *Id.* at 613 (citation omitted). If consideration of these factors leads to the conclusion that the force imposed "amounted to a brutal and inhumane abuse of official power literally shocking to the conscience," *Id.*, then the plaintiff has made out a substantive due process claim. Applying this test in Hall, we concluded that the district court erred in dismissing the student's substantive due process claim against the teacher who had paddled her and the principal who had authorized the paddling. *Id.* at 614-15; *see also P.B. v. Koch*, 96 F.3d 1298, 1302 (9th Cir. 1996) (collecting cases from several circuits that have adopted Hall's rationale and holding).

Meeker's complaint clearly alleges facts sufficient to state a substantive due process claim under the criteria set forth in *Hall*. The complaint alleges facts asserting a use of force—brutal, unprovoked beatings—"disproportionate to [any] need." *Hall*, 621 F.2d at 613. The complaint further alleges that Edmundson deliberately and intentionally instituted these unprovoked beatings on numerous occasions; a fact-finder certainly could determine that such beatings were "inspired by malice." *Id.* Finally, Meeker's allegations that Coach Edmundson repeatedly directed the unprovoked and malicious beatings, causing him to suffer "excruciating physical pain, inflammation of the body," and "traumatic stress disorders" which "may be permanent in nature," are adequate to allege the requisite injury to support a substantive due process claim. *See, e.g., P.B.*, 96 F.3d at 1304 (holding that "pain, bruising, and emotional injury" provide the basis for a substantive due process claim when a school official acts maliciously and without any disciplinary purpose); *Webb v. McCullough*, 828 F.2d 1151, 1159 (6th Cir. 1987) (holding that when "a trier of fact could find" a school official's "need to strike a student was "minimal or nonexistent" it could conclude that the "blows inflicted were a brutal and inhumane abuse of . . . official power literally shocking to the conscience"); *cf. Kirkland v. Greene County Bd. of Ed.*, 347 F.3d 903, 904-5 (11th Cir. 2003) (holding allegations that a principal repeatedly struck a thirteen-year-old student, causing a large knot on the student's head and continuing migraine headaches, provide an adequate basis for a substantive due process claim.)[2]

---

[2] In *Hall* itself we noted that "it is clear that the rights to bodily security protected by the Eighth Amendment and by substantive due process respectively are substantially congruent as far as content is concerned." *Id.* at 611. The "unnecessary and wanton infliction of pain" alone suffices to form an injury severe enough to be cognizable under the Eighth Amendment. *Hudson v.*

.....

Having concluded that Meeker has alleged the violation of a constitutional right, we turn to the second step of the Saucier qualified immunity analysis to determine whether Coach Edmundson is nonetheless entitled to immunity from suit. That is, we must ascertain "whether a reasonable [official] could have believed [the challenged conduct] to be lawful, in light of clearly established law" at the time of the beatings. *Anderson v. Creighton*, 483 U.S. 635, 641 (1987). The law is clearly established for qualified immunity purposes not only when "the very action in question has previously been held unlawful," but also when "pre-existing law" makes the "unlawfulness" of the act "apparent." *Id.* at 640. And so, here we ask whether in November 2000 a reasonable educator could have believed that repeatedly instituting the unprovoked and painful beatings of one of his students was lawful, in light of clearly established law.

By November 2000, the law provided clear guidance: No school official could, consistent with constitutional principles, cause a student to be subjected to such beatings. As the district court recognized, "the Fourteenth Amendment liberty interest in bodily integrity has been recognized since at least 1977" with the issuance of *Ingraham,* 430 U.S. at 673, and "in the Fourth Circuit, educators have been aware that arbitrary use of corporal punishment . . . [has been] prohibited by the Fourteenth Amendment since at least" the issuance of *Hall* in 1980. Not only has such conduct been unlawful in this circuit since our decision in *Hall*, but by November 2000, the Third, Sixth, Eighth, Ninth, and Tenth Circuits had adopted the *Hall* rationale and holding. *See P.B.*, 96 F.3d at 1302-03; *Wise v. Pea Ridge Sch. Dist.*, 855 F.2d 560, 564 (8th Cir. 1988); *Metzger v. Osbeck*, 841 F.2d 518, 520 (3d Cir. 1988); *Webb*, 828 F.2d at 1158; *Garcia v. Miera*, 817 F.2d 650, 653 (10th Cir. 1987).

For the foregoing reasons, the judgment of the district court is affirmed.

DOE EX REL. DOE v. HAWAII DEPARTMENT OF EDUCATION
334 F.3d 906 (9th Cir. 2003)

SCHROEDER, Chief Judge:

This is a 42 U.S.C. § 1983 case against an elementary school vice principal who taped a second grade student's head to a tree for disciplinary purposes. The district court correctly denied the vice principal's motion for summary judgment on the basis of qualified immunity. Indeed, our decision in *P.B. v. Koch*, 96 F.3d 1298 (9th Cir. 1996), compelled that result. We publish this opinion to clarify the issue that we left open in Koch regarding whether claims of excessive force by a school official generally should be decided under the Constitution's Fourth Amendment or under the Due Process Clause. *See Koch*, 96 F.3d at 1303 We now hold that Doe is entitled to proceed under the Fourth Amendment, in light of the Supreme Court's direction to analyze § 1983 claims under more specific constitutional provisions, when applicable, rather than generalized notions of due process. *See Graham v. Connor*, 490 U.S. 386, 395 (1989).

McMillian, 503 U.S. 1, 8 (1992) (internal quotation marks and citation omitted); *Norman v. Taylor*, 25 F.3d 1259, 1263 (4th Cir. 1994) (en banc) (recognizing that "pain itself" may constitute the requisite injury for Eighth Amendment purposes).

The facts are not complicated. In February 1998, Plaintiff John Doe was a second-grader at Pukalani Elementary School. Doe's teacher sent him to the defendant, Vice Principal David Keala, to be disciplined for fighting, but Doe then refused to stand still against a wall for his time-out punishment. Keala followed through on his threat to take Doe outside and tape him to a nearby tree if he did not stand still. The vice principal used masking tape to tape Doe's head to the tree. The record is unclear as to whether Doe's face was pressed against the bark. The tape remained for about five minutes until a fifth-grade girl told Keala that she did not think he should be doing that. He instructed the girl to remove the tape, which she did.

In January 2000, Doe filed this action in the district court. The complaint alleged both state and federal claims. Keala moved for summary judgment, arguing, among other things, that he was entitled to qualified immunity. Keala appeals the district court's order denying qualified immunity on the § 1983 claim. We have jurisdiction pursuant to *Mitchell v. Forsyth*, 472 U.S. 511, 530 (1985), and its progeny, and we affirm.

A public official is not entitled to qualified immunity if his conduct violates "'clearly established constitutional rights of which a reasonable person would have known.'" *Koch*, 96 F.3d at 1301 (quoting *Harlow v. Fitzgerald*, 457 U.S. 800, 818 (1982)). The Supreme Court's decision in *Saucier v. Katz*, 533 U.S. 194 (2001), dictates our qualified immunity analysis. We must first determine whether the defendant's alleged conduct constituted a constitutional violation. *Id.* at 201. If so, the defendant is entitled to qualified immunity only if the constitutional right that he allegedly violated was not clearly established. *Id.*

Doe argues that Keala's conduct in taping his head to the tree violated his rights under both the Fourth and Fourteenth Amendments. In Koch, we declined to resolve whether a student's claim of excessive force by a school official is more appropriately brought under the Fourth Amendment, rather than under substantive due process standards inherent in the Fourteenth Amendment. *See Koch*, 96 F.3d at 1303. We suggested in a footnote that we might agree with the Seventh Circuit's decision that the Fourth Amendment analysis generally applies in the school context. *See id.* (citing *Wallace v. Batavia Sch. Dist.*, 68 F.3d 1010, 1016 (7th Cir. 1995)). We do so now.

In *Graham v. Connor*, 490 U.S. 386, 395 (1989), the Supreme Court directed courts to analyze claims of excessive force under a more specific constitutional provision, if one applies, rather than the general notion of substantive due process. The Court concluded that in most cases, the appropriate constitutional provision will be either the Fourth Amendment's protection against unreasonable seizures or the Eighth Amendment's ban on cruel and unusual punishments. *Id.* at 394. The *Graham* rule is grounded in the notion that the specific constitutional provisions provide more guidance to judicial decision makers than the more open-ended concept of substantive due process. *See Armendariz v. Penman*, 75 F.3d 1311, 1319 (9th Cir. 1996) (en banc). Although *Graham* dealt with the criminal context, we have recognized the movement away from substantive due process and toward the Fourth Amendment outside the criminal context as well. *See id.* at 1320.

It is clear that the Fourth Amendment applies in the school environment. *See Vernonia Sch. Dist. 47J v. Acton*, 515 U.S. 646, 655-56 (1995); *New Jersey v. T.L.O.*, 469 U.S. 325, 333 (1985). Additionally, the Fifth, Seventh, and Tenth Circuits have all recognized that the Fourth Amendment governs a teacher's seizure of a student. *See Hassan v. Lubbock Indep. Sch. Dist.*, 55 F.3d 1075, 1079 (5th Cir. 1995); *Wallace*, 68 F.3d at 1012-15; *Edwards v. Rees*, 883 F.2d 882, 884-85 (10th Cir. 1989). We agree that Doe's Fourth Amendment right to be free from an unreasonable seizure "extends to seizures by or at the direction of school officials." *Hassan*, 55 F.3d at 1079. We hold that Doe's claim is appropriately brought under the Fourth Amendment, not the Due Process Clause.

Keala argues that the Fourth Amendment should not apply because this case does not involve a law enforcement official acting in an investigatory capacity. The Fourth Amendment applies, however, to government conduct motivated by "investigatory or administrative purposes." *See United States v. Attson*, 900 F.2d 1427, 1430-31 (9th Cir. 1990) (emphasis added). Keala was a school administrator performing an administrative function by disciplining Doe and maintaining order in the school. *See Wallace*, 68 F.3d at 1013. His conduct is therefore within the scope of the Fourth Amendment.

We recognize that it may be possible for a school official to use excessive force against a student without seizing or searching the student, and that the Fourth Amendment would not apply to such conduct. We therefore do not foreclose the possibility that under some circumstances, a student's excessive force claim against a school official might be more appropriately analyzed under the Due Process Clause of the Fourteenth Amendment than under the Fourth Amendment.

Having concluded that Doe's claim should proceed under the Fourth Amendment, we turn to whether Doe can establish that Keala's conduct constituted an unreasonable seizure. Viewing the facts and evidence in Doe's favor as the nonmoving party, *see Koch*, 96 F.3d at 1301, we hold that there is sufficient evidence to find a Fourth Amendment violation.

Doe has alleged a seizure here in the constitutional sense. Such a seizure occurs when there is a restraint on liberty to the degree that a reasonable person would not feel free to leave. *See United States v. Summers*, 268 F.3d 683, 686 (9th Cir. 2001). Being held to a tree with tape for five minutes was such a restraint on Doe's liberty, and constituted a seizure within the meaning of the Fourth Amendment's prohibition against unreasonable search and seizure.

A seizure violates the Fourth Amendment if it is objectively unreasonable under the circumstances. *See Santos v. Gates*, 287 F.3d 846, 853 (9th Cir. 2002). In applying the Fourth Amendment in the school context, the reasonableness of the seizure must be considered in light of the educational objectives Keala was trying to achieve. *See T.L.O.*, 469 U.S. 325, 341-42. In *New Jersey v. T.L.O.*, 469 U.S. 325, 342 (1985), the Supreme Court considered the reasonableness of a search in a school. The court stressed that the search must be reasonably related to its purpose, and must not be "excessively intrusive in light of the age and sex of the student and the nature of the infraction." *Id.*

At the time that Keala taped him to the tree, Doe's only offense had been "horsing around" and refusing to stand still. There is no indication that Doe was fighting or that he posed a danger to other students. Doe was eight years old. Taping his head to a tree for five minutes was so intrusive that a fifth grader observed it was inappropriate. There is sufficient evidence for a fact finder to conclude that Keala's conduct was objectively unreasonable in violation of the Fourth Amendment.

We now address an alleged violation of a student's right to be free of excessive physical punishment or restraint. We observed in *Koch* that the right of a student to be free from excessive force at the hands of teachers employed by the state was clearly established as early as 1990. *See Koch*, 96 F.3d at 1303

("Regardless of the appropriate 'home' for plaintiffs' right to be free from excessive force, there was a clearly established right to be free from such force in 1990 and 1991."). There need not be a case dealing with these particular facts to find Keala's conduct unreasonable. *See Headwaters Forest Def. v. County of Humboldt*, 276 F.3d 1125, 1131 (9th Cir. 2002). Indeed it is difficult to imagine this situation recurring with any frequency. The district court therefore properly concluded that Doe's right to be free from excessive forcible restraint was clearly established in 1998, when the events giving rise to this case occurred.

Robert E. Rains: Out on a Limb: *Doe v. State of Hawaii Department of Education* (with apologies to Joyce Kilmer) 82 Or. L. Rev. 933 (2003)*

We thought that we would never see
A student taped against a tree:
A kiddie from the second grade -
We hope that he was in the shade.
When little John got in a fight,
They tried to teach him wrong from right.
So to the principal he was sent
For tutelary punishment.
The principal said, "You must stand still
And have a time-out, or I will
Take you outside to yonder tree
And stick you there for all to see."
John squirmed, but he could not escape,
And soon was bound with masking tape.
The principal did just as he'd said
And wrapped John up around the head.
A fifth grade girl then came along
And told the grown-up it seemed wrong.

Although the principal must have pined,
He shortly had young John untwined

* * *

John's parents thought it not a lark
To use their son as extra bark.
They sued the principal at once
Asserting he had been the dunce.
The principal claimed there's no clear rule

Against hog-tying kids at school.
The circuit court said, "Yes, there is;
One need not be a legal whiz
To know there's no immunity
To tape a student to a tree."

II. Substantive Due Process, Affirmative Duties and Deliberate Indifference

JOHNSON v. DALLAS INDEPENDENT SCHOOL DISTRICT
38 F.3d 198 (5th Cir. 1994)

OPINION BY: EDITH H. JONES

Andrew Gaston's last moments on earth were passed in the hallway at A. Maceo Smith High School in Dallas, Texas. He was hit in the head by a stray bullet shot during a melee instigated by the killer, non-student Drumestic Contreal Brown. The question before this court is whether Gaston had either (1) a constitutional right not to be placed in danger of deadly violence while at school or (2) a more general constitutional right to some level of affirmative protection while at school. Despite our sympathy for Andrew's untimely death, we find no constitutional damage remedy available to his family.

The § 1983 case filed by Gaston's father against Dallas Independent School District and Donnie Breedlove, the principal of Smith High, was dismissed for failure to state a claim. Fed. R. Civ. P. 12(b)(6). The skeletal pleadings, our only guide to the facts, reveal few details of the incident in which Gaston died. They state that the assailant Brown somehow rode a school bus to Smith High on the morning of October 23, 1991. Brown went onto campus and into the high school building although he was not wearing a student ID badge required in some of DISD's schools. Further, Brown carried a concealed handgun, which was not discovered because the metal detectors placed by DISD at the school were not being used. Brown then created a disturbance, causing students—allegedly without the aid of school employees—to attempt to evict him. Gaston was tragically in the line of fire when Brown shot his gun.

The district court's conscientiously reasoned dismissal rested on three pivotal elements of a § 1983 claim. First, the court held, Gaston had no affirmative constitutional right to protection by DISD while he was at school. Second, because plaintiff had not pled that DISD's actions, custom, or policy caused Gaston's death, DISD could not be held constitutionally liable. Third, plaintiff had not pled facts sufficient to overcome principal Breedlove's assertion of qualified immunity. This court may affirm the dismissal for failure to state a claim only if "it appears 'beyond doubt that the plaintiff can prove no set of facts in support of his claim which would entitle him to relief.'" *Haines v. Kerner*, 404 U.S. 519, 520-21; 92 S. Ct. 594, 596, 30 L. Ed. 2d 652 (1972) (quoting *Conley v. Gibson*, 355 U.S. 41, 45-46, 78 S. Ct. 99, 102, 2 L. Ed. 2d 80 (1957)).

The epidemic of violence in American public schools is a relatively new phenomenon, but one which has already generated considerable case law. Whether that epidemic invokes constitutional consequences for the innocent, law-abiding students forced to attend those schools raises grave questions that must be carefully analyzed... [T]wo potential theories of constitutional liability have been proposed. First, it may be contended that DISD and Principal Breedlove

> "violated [Andrew's] constitutional rights by affirmatively creating the hazardous environment" in which he attended school. *Id.* at 530. Alternatively, Andrew's father asserts that the state bore Andrew an affirmative duty of care arising from the state's compulsory attendance laws. These theories will be discussed in turn.

1. State-Created Danger

When state actors knowingly place a person in danger, the due process clause of the constitution has been held to render them accountable for the foreseeable injuries that result from their conduct, whether or not the victim was in formal state "custody." This principle has been applied in a number of cases from other circuits. Three cases exemplify the state-created danger theory of liability. In *Wood v. Ostrander*, 879 F.2d 583 (9th Cir.1989), *cert. denied,* 498 U.S. 938 (1990), a police officer arrested a drunken driver and impounded his car, leaving the female passenger alone at night, without any means to go home, in a neighborhood known for criminal activity. She was raped by a stranger who offered her a lift. In *Cornelius v. Town of Highland Lake*, 880 F.2d 348 (11th Cir.1989), *cert. denied*, 494 U.S. 1066 (1990), the state permitted a prisoner with a violent criminal history to participate in a work program at a municipal town hall under the supervision of an untrained city employee. He gained access to a knife, abducted the plaintiff who worked for the city, and held her hostage for three days. Finally, in *K.H. ex rel. Murphy v. Morgan*, 914 F.2d 846 (7th Cir.1990), the state removed a sixteen-month-old child from her parents' custody and in the next four years shuttled her among eleven foster homes, in at least two of which she was molested or abused. The court held that, if the allegations of the child's complaint were correct, state officials could be guilty of knowingly subjecting her to serious psychological damage. *See also White v. Rochford*, 592 F.2d 381, 384-85 (7th Cir. 1979) (state liable for injuries to minor children left in car on side of busy highway after state officer arrested the driver). Although different facts underlie each of these cases, the courts uniformly held that state actors may be liable if they created the plaintiffs' peril, increased their risk of harm, or acted to render them more vulnerable to danger.

In contrast to these cases, but not in conflict, stands *D.R. v. Middle Bucks Area Vocational Technical School*, 972 F.2d 1364 (3rd Cir. 1992) (en banc), *cert. denied*, 506 U.S. 1079 (1993), in which the Third Circuit held en banc that a school could not be liable for a series of sexual assaults allegedly committed against two female students in the unisex class. The abuse allegedly occurred during class, virtually under the eye of a teacher trainee, two to four times weekly for an entire semester. Unlike the preceding state-created danger cases, however, the facts in *Middle Bucks* did not sufficiently demonstrate that the state placed the plaintiffs in danger, increased their risk of harm, or made them more vulnerable to danger. A classroom is not per se dangerous, nor can it ordinarily be expected that even an undertrained teacher will permit or be ignorant of sexual molestation going on in class. The risk that some students would sexually molest other students during a class was not found to be foreseeable to or known by school officials.

The key to the state-created danger cases, and the essence of their distinction from *Middle Bucks*, lies in the state actors' culpable knowledge and conduct in "affirmatively placing an individual in a position of danger, effectively stripping a person of her ability to defend herself, or cutting off potential sources of private aid." ......Thus the environment created by the state actors must be dangerous; they must know it is dangerous; and, to be liable, they must have used their authority to create an opportunity that would not otherwise have existed for the third party's crime to occur. Put otherwise, the defendants must have been at least deliberately indifferent to the plight of the plaintiff.

****

Even if the state-created danger theory is constitutionally sound, the pleadings in this case fall short of the demanding standard for constitutional liability. First, they posit the question whether the environment at Smith High School was "dangerous." If for no other reason, the presence of numerous trained adults would assure that a school cannot be as dangerous as the nocturnal condition of the high-crime neighborhood described in Wood or the prisoner release program gone awry in Cornelius. No inference of dangerousness arises simply from the presence of student ID badges or metal detectors; such devices could have been installed prophylactically, in the absence of any prior trespasses onto campus or incidents of criminal violence. Moreover, to infer the existence of a dangerous environment—the condition of § 1983 liability—solely from the presence of measures designed to avert violence would erect a serious disincentive to their use. The law cannot so turn against its purposes; the use of security devices should be encouraged, not discouraged. There would have to be allegations at least of previous criminal conduct at Smith High School from which a trier of fact could conclude it was tantamount to a "high-crime area."

Second, school officials must have actually known that Smith High was dangerous to students such as Andrew Gaston. Actual knowledge of a serious risk of physical danger to the plaintiff has been a common feature of the state-created danger cases. From the pleadings in this case, no legitimate inference can be drawn that school officials might have been actually aware of a high risk that an armed non-student invader would enter the campus and fire a pistol randomly during school hours.

Appellant's claim also fails the third element of the state-created danger cases. There is no pleading that school officials placed Gaston in a dangerous environment stripped of means to defend himself and cut off from sources of aid. There is no sufficiently culpable affirmative conduct. Andrew went to school. No state actor placed Andrew in a "unique, confrontational encounter" with a violent criminal. *Cornelius*, 880 F.2d at 359. No official in the performance of her duties abandoned him in a crack house or released a known criminal in front of his locker. There is no suggestion that the school district or principal fostered or tolerated anarchy at Smith High—the ID badges and metal detectors permit the opposite inference. Even if the deployment of such security measures was haphazard or negligent, it may not be inferred that the conduct of the defendants rose to the level of deliberate indifference. As in *Leffall*, the most that may be said of defendants' ultimately ineffective attempts to secure the environment is that they were negligent, but not that they were deliberately indifferent. *See also Graham v. Indep. Sch. Dist. No. I-89*, 22 F.3d 991, 995 (10th Cir.1994); compare *Salas v. Carpenter*,980 F.2d 299 (5th Cir. 1992). On the contrary, the facts here pleaded suggest only that Andrew was the tragic victim of random criminal conduct rather than of school officials' deliberate, callous decisions to interpose him in the midst of a criminally dangerous environment. Appellant's complaint, in short, does not suffice to plead that Andrew was the victim of state-created danger.

2. Constitutional "Special Relationship"

Although Gaston's death was not a result of an unconstitutional state-created danger, this does not necessarily preclude the broader theory of liability, premised on *DeShaney*, if a "special relationship" exists between the plaintiff and the state. In that case, the Supreme Court held that a minor could not maintain a § 1983 action against Winnebago County and its social services department or employees for serious injuries inflicted by his father after a county caseworker returned *DeShaney* to his father's custody and allegedly knew or should have known that the father would be violent. The Court concluded that "a State's failure to protect an individual against private violence simply does not constitute a violation of the Due Process Clause." *DeShaney*, 489 U.S. at 197, 109 S. Ct. at 1004. The Court rejected the contention that a "special relationship," carrying affirmative constitutional obligations toward the child, existed by virtue of the social welfare services the state provided. Such affirmative obligations of care and protection arise only when the state "takes a person into its custody and holds him there against his will." *Id.* at 199-200, 109 S. Ct. at 1005-06 (citing *Youngberg v. Romeo*, 457 U.S. 307, 317 (1982) (institutionalized mentally ill) and *Estelle v. Gamble*, 429 U.S. 97, 103-04 (1976) (prisoners)). The district court here concluded, as has every circuit court that has considered the issue, that *DeShaney* forecloses a constitutional claim on behalf of Andrew Gaston for affirmative protection while at school.

As in *Doe* and *Leffall*, we find it unnecessary to decide the "special relationship" issue in this case. We agree with the district court's conclusion on somewhat different grounds than it expressed. While a persuasive argument can be made for applying a *DeShaney* "special relationship" in some measure to public school students who are forced by compulsory education laws to attend school and have no choice among public schools, even under such a legal regime the appellant's claim would not succeed. Andrew Gaston's death is attributable to the fortuity that an armed, violent non-student trespassed on campus. There can be no liability of state actors for this random criminal act unless the fourteenth amendment were to make the schools virtual guarantors of student safety—a rule never yet adopted even for those in society, such as prisoners or the mentally ill or handicapped, who are the beneficiaries of a "special relationship" with the state. *See, e.g., Farmer v. Brennan*, 511 U.S. 825 (1994).

The fact is, however, that the state's custody of children in public schools is more comprehensive than is its intervention in family affairs via noncustodial welfare services. Such services often involve sporadic, intermittent contact with clients on a schedule that may not be predictable. Social workers provide valuable services to their un-institutionalized clients, but they cannot and do not tend to them continuously nor do they necessarily rely upon state-managed facilities as the locus of care. Schools, however, take care of children day after day for years in public facilities. Schools may be said to control children's environments to the same or even greater degree than state-sponsored foster care services, which have been held, post-*DeShaney*, to bear affirmative obligations to their client children.

The argument against holding that public schools have "custody," at least for some purposes of protecting their physical well-being, appears to derive less from logic than from a pragmatic desire to limit their legal liability. As has been shown, students must attend school and may not leave without permission. To say that student attendance is voluntary because parents may elect to home-school their children or send them to a private school is lamentably, for most parents, a myth. To intimate that parents retain effective responsibility for their children's well-being when the school alone makes critical decisions regarding student safety and discipline is inaccurate. To suggest that parents somehow are in a better position than the schools to protect their children from the ravages of weapons smuggled onto campus during the school day is cruelly irrational. To hope that students who are unarmed can protect themselves from the depredation of armed criminals in their midst is ridiculous. That parents yield so much of their children's care into the hands of public school officials may well be argued to place upon the officials an obligation to protect students at least from certain kinds of foreseeably dangerous harm during regular school hours.

The author of this opinion dissented in *Doe v. Taylor ISD*, 15 F.3d 443 (5th Cir.1994) (en banc). In suggesting that the "special relationship" theory of *DeShaney* may logically apply to public schools governed by compulsory attendance laws, I do not retreat from my reticence to expand the scope of constitutional claims, yet I feel compelled to observe the deficiencies of governing circuit case law.

For the foregoing reasons, the judgment of the district court is AFFIRMED.

Notes and Comments

1. Which argument do you find more persuasive in *Middle Bucks*? The dissenting opinion argues that school officials created a special relationship. How would you define a "special relationship" for purposes of substantive due process? In *Deshaney*, the Court reaffirms the case of *Youngberg v. Romeo*, 457 U.S. 307 (1982). In *Youngberg,* the Court held that a special relationship is created (the substantive component of the Fourteenth Amendment's Due Process Clause applies) for citizens who are involuntarily committed mental patients. As to these patients, there is a constitutional duty to ensure their "reasonable safety". Why would courts refuse to extend *Youngberg* to apply to students in public school?

2. *DeShaney* and "Danger-Creation"

The danger-creation exception precedes *DeShaney*. It has been recognized by the courts as a simple affirmance of the principle set forth in numerous rulings holding that "[i]f the state puts a man in a position of danger from private persons and then fails to protect him, it will not be heard to say that its role was merely passive; it is as much an active tortfeasor as if it had thrown him into the snake pit." *Bowers v. DeVito*, 686 F.2d 616, 618 (7th Cir. 1982); *see also Wells v. Walker*, 852 F.2d 368, 370-71 (8th Cir. 1988); *Escamilla v. City of Santa Ana*, 796 F.2d 266, 269 (9th Cir. 1986); *Estate of Gilmore v. Buckley*, 787 F.2d 714, 722 (1st Cir. 1986); *Jones v. Phyfer*, 761 F.2d 642, 646 (11th Cir. 1985); *Bowers v. DeVito*, 686 F.2d 616, 618 (7th Cir. 1982).

In a school context, its operation is straightforward. To make out a proper danger-creation claim, a student must demonstrate that (1) the school and the charged individual educators created the danger or increased the student's vulnerability to the danger in some way; (2) the student was a member of a limited and specifically definable group; (3) the school officials' conduct put the student at substantial risk of serious, immediate, and proximate harm; (4) the risk was obvious or known; (5) defendants acted recklessly in conscious disregard of that risk; and (6) such conduct, when viewed in total, is conscience shocking.

Finally, keep in mind that the state is liable when it affirmatively places a citizen in danger even though the person injured may not have been in custody. *See Wood v. Ostrander*, 879 F.2d 583 (9th Cir. 1989) (victim left in high-crime area after automobile impounded); *White v. Rochford*, 592 F.2d 381 (7th Cir. 1979) (children left by the side of the road after driver of car arrested); *see also Reed v. Gardner*, 986 F.2d 1122 (7th Cir. 1993) (auto collision proximate result of police leaving drunk driver in control of car after arresting initial driver who was sober). *See generally* "State-created danger," or similar theory, as basis for civil rights action under 42 U.S.C.A. § 1983, 159 A.L.R. Fed. 37.

Stephen Faberman: The Lessons of *Deshaney*: Special Relationships, Schools & the Fifth Circuit,

35 B.C. L. Rev 97 (1993)[*]

Poor Joshua! Victim of repeated attacks by an irresponsible, bullying, cowardly, and intemperate father, and abandoned by respondents, who placed him in a dangerous predicament, and who knew or learned what was going on and yet did essentially nothing.

In recent years, as this nation's school campuses have become increasingly dangerous, students who have been injured while at school, have invoked due process to attempt to hold their school district liable for failure to protect them from harm. The plaintiff students have filed damage suits under 42 U.S.C. § 1983 against the school officials and school districts involved, claiming that they have deprived the students of their Fourteenth Amendment liberty interests.

Until very recently, the federal circuit courts of appeals have almost universally held that school officials do not owe students, compelled by state law to attend school and entrusted to their care, an affirmative obligation to protect them from harm while in school. These courts have reached this conclusion based upon the Supreme Court's decision in *DeShaney v. Winnebago County Department of Social Services*, which held that a state owes its citizens an affirmative duty to protect them from harm only where the state has affirmatively acted to place limitations on an individual's ability to act on his or her behalf, through incarceration, institutionalization or other similar means of restraint. In October 1992, however, the United States Court of Appeals for the Fifth Circuit broke with the other circuits and created a conflict that, to date, the Supreme Court has declined to address.

****

Despite the Supreme Court's attempts to end the ambiguity that had existed, the *DeShaney* opinion, especially when read in the context of schools, has spawned much litigation. The goal of this litigation has been to determine the applicability, if any, of the Court's analysis to public schools. The insertion of the phrase ". . . or other similar restraint of personal liberty" has been interpreted by some courts to indicate that a special relationship may exist between school officials and students, who may in effect be in custody of the state because of compulsory attendance laws. Where a court finds that a special relationship does exist, an affirmative obligation to provide protective services may be imposed on the

---

school even to the extent of providing protection from private actors, such as a fellow student. Additionally, *DeShaney* raised the specter that where a special relationship exists, the court owes the individual an affirmative obligation to provide "undefined" protective services. Conversely, where a court finds that no special relationship exists, school officials are under an obligation only to refrain from acting "deliberately indifferent" to the misconduct of their employees.

COURTS' RESPONSES TO DESHANEY

After *DeShaney*, the federal courts were confronted with two kinds of section 1983 suits brought by students against school officials, alleging constitutional violations. The first involved instances where a school employee was accused of sexually assaulting or injuring a student. The second dealt with the issue of liability when a student alleges sexual assault or injury by a fellow student.

Supervisory Liability

In cases where a school official allegedly sexually assaulted a student, the circuit courts ruled that *DeShaney* did not affect liability where the offending actor was a state actor. Regardless of whether the court considered students to be in a special relationship with the school district, the circuit courts ruled that nothing in the Supreme Court's opinion altered the fact that school officials could be held liable for their deliberate indifference to actions taken by subordinates. Although *DeShaney* may have foreclosed the possibility of imposing liability where the offending actor was a private citizen, where it is the state, through one of its subordinates, which has deprived a citizen of life, liberty or property, the Due Process Clause of the Constitution has clearly been implicated. The first federal court to address the dilemma after the *DeShaney* decision was the United States Court of Appeals for the Third Circuit, which had been directed to re-consider its decision in *Stoneking I*, in light of *DeShaney*. In *Stoneking I*, the court had held that a special relationship did exist in the school context. The *Stoneking II court*, hearing the appeal again on direction of the Supreme Court, changed its holding. The court noted that the primary difference between *DeShaney* and the case before it was that in *Stoneking II*, a state actor, the teacher, was accused of the sexual assault, while in *DeShaney*, a private actor had committed the violence. This difference allowed the Third Circuit to hold that the school district could be liable upon sufficient proof that its deliberate indifference to the actions of one of its subordinates represented a custom, policy or practice in violation of the student's constitutional rights, regardless of whether a special relationship did in fact exist. Even though the court rested its decision on supervisory liability, it also addressed the special relationship question in post-*DeShaney* schools. Despite the statement that in light of *DeShaney* it could no longer rely on a theory imposing the affirmative obligation to protect students established in *Stoneking I*, the court, in dicta, stated that "[a]rguably, our earlier discussion noting that 'students are in what may be viewed as functional custody of the school authorities during their presence at school' . . . is not inconsistent with the *DeShaney* opinion." Other courts, confronted by the special relationship issue, have cited this statement.

Student Versus Student

When a student alleges that he or she was sexually assaulted by another student, the plaintiff may not plead supervisory liability since no state actor is involved. In this situation, courts are directly forced to address whether the special relationship exists in schools such that an affirmative duty to protect the students from harm arises. With very few exceptions, courts have, since *DeShaney* and *Stoneking II*, rejected the contention that students are in a special relationship with the state.

.....

The Fifth Circuit, in *Doe v. Taylor Independent School District*, although concluding that an affirmative obligation to protect students existed in the schools because of the special relationship undertaken between school officials and students, stated that its decision did not necessarily mean that school officials could be liable for injuries inflicted by other students. The court specifically declined to address this issue and because the offending individual in the case was a school employee, and a state actor, the court did not have to address this question. However, because of what it did do, the *Taylor* court has created a schism in the judicial opinion among the federal courts. At the very least, the decision will have profound consequences within the Fifth Circuit.

By declaring that schoolchildren are in a special relationship with the state, when read in light of *DeShaney* and its progeny, the Fifth Circuit has imposed similar obligations as are owed state institutionalized mental patients and prisoners. Further, within the Fifth Circuit, as well as other circuits, a finding of a special relationship carries with it obligations to children in foster care or under state supervision, to those in the "functional custody" of the state, and possibly to those whom the state has placed in a position of danger. In each of these cases, the state becomes obligated to protect the individual against harm from both state as well as private actors. Additionally, the state may be held liable for failing, under sufficiently culpable circumstances, to provide protective services and ensure the general welfare and safety of the students entrusted to its care. Equating special relationships and the necessary obligations attached to them to the nation's public schools has two flaws, one from a doctrinal legal perspective and another from a practical standpoint.

.....

Although public school students are compelled by law to attend school, it can hardly be said that this fact alone constitutes the kind of affirmative act by the state of taking an individual into custody that *DeShaney* contemplated. Schoolchildren, by statute, are required to attend school for only 180, six-hour days per year. Further, schoolchildren remain residents of their homes and are free to leave school after school hours. Unlike the custodial relationships that exist in the contexts of prisons and mental hospitals, schoolchildren have not become wards of the state, subject to continuous and full-time severe state restriction of liberty.

One commentator has suggested that "[a] proper analysis should look to the implications of custodial control, rather than only to the control itself, because it is the underlying dependency that actually obligates the state to act, not the state's legal status as custodian." Even if this is the proper interpretation to be given to the "legal" creation of special relationships under *DeShaney*, it seems equally clear that when examined closely, the state has not so restricted the liberty interests of students forced to attend public school as to completely deprive those students of the ability to provide for their own basic human needs. Thus, even under a non-custodial analysis, the state has not become so intertwined with one of its citizens' lives, that it has assumed responsibility for ensuring that citizen's welfare and protection.

As has been noted in the past, schoolchildren and prisoners stand in wholly different circumstances, as incarceration deprives prisoners of, "the freedom to be with family and friends and to form the other enduring attachments of normal life." In contrast, this is not the case with regard to students compelled by law to attend public school. The schoolchild is not left completely defenseless while at school, completely shut off from the outside world. As the Supreme Court stated:

> Though attendance may not always be voluntary, the public school remains an open institution . . . . The child is not physically restrained from leaving school during school hours; and at the end of the school day, the child is invariably free to return home. Even while at school, the child brings with him the support of family and friends, and is rarely apart from teachers and other pupils who may witness and protest any instances of mistreatment.

Additionally, compulsory school attendance laws do not prevent students from seeking outside help. Further, the state has not assumed responsibility for the child's entire personal life, as it has when it imprisons or institutionalizes a citizen. In sum, while school officials have been judicially and statutorily granted much control over their students' lives, they do not exercise the kind or degree of control that *DeShaney* contemplated.

Parents, Not the State, Owe the Child Primary Care Duties

Not only has the state not adversely affected the parents' ability to perform their primary caretaker responsibilities while their children are in school, but the state, by both statute and judicial precedent, lacks the power to fill that void. By statute, state school officials are allowed to develop only those reasonable regulations necessary to governing student conduct. School officials are vested with only such control and authority as is reasonably necessary to prevent infractions of discipline and interference with the educational process. Finally, teachers are not among those persons responsible for a child's welfare under typical statutes designed to provide child protective services.

One of the justifications used for claiming that a special relationship exists in schools is that teachers and school officials act in loco parentis in their dealings with students: their authority is that of the parent and not of the state. The Supreme Court has since rejected this doctrine, arguing that today's public school officials do not merely exercise authority voluntarily conferred on them by parents, but rather, they act in furtherance of publicly-mandated educational and disciplinary policies. As a result, the Supreme Court has held that school officials are subject to the commands and restrictions of the First and Fourth Amendments, the Due Process Clause of the Fourteenth Amendment, and possibly the Fifth Amendment.

This rejection of the in loco parentis doctrine has a tremendous detrimental effect on the major tenet of the special relationship argument which provides that by removing the child from his or her home, the state has assumed the role and obligations of the parent in ensuring the safety and welfare of the child. The Supreme Court has recognized that school officials are ill-suited for the in loco parentis task because they are compelled to act in the best interests of the state, a goal often mutually exclusive and even at odds with the interests of individual students. As one commentator stated, "[w]hen the school official takes a child in hand, searches him, and turns him over to the police, the school official acts as a representative of government and not as a representative of the parent."

In sum, although those advocating special relationship application to schools would continue to regard school officials as surrogate parents of students, the Supreme Court has destroyed any validity to this argument by rejecting it in the context of school disciplinary procedures. Conversely, what authority has been taken away from the school officials has been given, in the form of constitutional liberty rights, to students. To that effect, students are entitled to freedom of expression while in school. Further, students are to be protected from unreasonable searches and seizures, and in some school circumstances may have the same Fourth Amendment rights as adults. Finally, students are entitled to procedural safeguards that minimize the risk of wrongful punishment in the name of school discipline and may be entitled to the Fifth Amendment's protection against self-incrimination. Even in denying Eighth Amendment applicability to corporal punishment in schools, the Supreme Court in effect emancipated students by contrasting them with prisoners and declaring that for the purposes of the Eighth Amendment, students need little protection because the school is an open institution where students are not to be considered in custody of the state.

If students are not in the custody of the state while attending public school for purposes of the First, Fourth, Fifth and Eighth Amendments to the Constitution, it is inconceivable how they can be for another part of the Constitution. *DeShaney* stands for the proposition that when the state has affirmatively acted to deprive a citizen of his or her constitutionally-protected liberty interests, the Constitution demands that the state fill the void left by its own action. Because the Supreme Court has found that students have not been deprived of their basic constitutional liberty interests while in school, the first part of the special relationship analysis fails: the state has not affirmatively acted to suppress students' constitutional rights. *DeShaney* clearly dictates that, in this situation, the state has not assumed an obligation to fill a void that it has not created, and that, in fact, does not exist.

Impracticability of Special Relationships to Schools

Not only is it difficult to justify the existence of special relationships because of the lack of coercion exercised by the state in schools on a "legal basis," but it is also difficult to justify imposing affirmative duties on school officials on a "practical basis." Must the state, through its school officials, ensure the safety of school-children from injuries inflicted by other students, from injuries as a result of typical childhood accidents, and from injuries as a result of extracurricular activities, such as school sports? Is the state required to protect the child after school hours and on off-school grounds? Perhaps more significantly, must the state provide the kind of necessary services that are required for others involved in special relationships with the state, like prisoners and mental patients, such as food, clothing, shelter and medical care, where the parents fail to provide these essentials?

School officials would be constitutionally obligated to assume the roles of police-officers or even prison guards to ensure the safety of every student in today's more dangerous schools. In addition, "school officials who are too restrictive would likely be charged under the same Due Process Clause with violating student's [sic] rights not to be treated like incarcerated prisoners," rights that the Supreme Court has only within the last twenty-five years proclaimed. Further, much of the change in the legal status of children was rendered by the growing violence in today's schools, violence that altered the status of school officials to "quasi-police officers" rather than teachers. Finally, the change in the environment of schools themselves has made it unrealistic and nearly impossible to require and to expect that school officials can be responsive to all student needs and threats. With schools already terribly overburdened, imposing more constitutional duties and liability for failure to fulfill impossible obligations will exacerbate an already desperate situation.

CONCLUSION

Not every tort committed by a state actor can be remedied by the Constitution. To impose constitutional duties on school officials, the likes of which exist only in prisons and mental hospitals, would overburden, both legally and practicably, the special relationship analysis outlined by the *DeShaney* Supreme Court. School officials would be forced to ensure the protection of students from teachers, other employees, other students, and even from their own youthful antics. School officials, already overburdened, would be forced to provide the kind of services reserved for only those in full-time custody of the state to students who spend only half the year and one-quarter of the day in the classroom.

In its search for a bright-line standard to determine when, if ever, the state owes a citizen an affirmative duty to protect, the Supreme Court had created a conflict that, until recently, appeared to be resolving itself. The Fifth Circuit, however, has thrown new logs onto the fire, and it appears likely that the conflict will grow more heated. Additionally, by refusing to hear the *Doe* and *Middle Bucks* cases, the Supreme Court has apparently given its assurance that it intends to allow the fire to continue burning.

DOE v. HILLSBORO INDEPENDENT SCHOOL DISTRICT

113 F.3d 1412 (5th Cir. 1997)

OPINION BY: PATRICK E. HIGGINBOTHAM

The custodian of the Hillsboro Independent School District raped a 14-year-old eighth grade student in an empty classroom. The student through her parents filed this lawsuit under 42 U.S.C. § 1983 asserting deprivations of constitutional rights and seeking money damages for this assault from the Hillsboro Independent School District, as well as its trustees and present and past superintendents in their individual capacities. The district court denied motions to dismiss filed by the individual defendants under Rule 12(b)(6). This appeal of the district court's denial of qualified immunity followed. A divided panel of this court affirmed. We took the case en banc and now reverse.

We conclude that no claim was stated under 42 U.S.C. § 1983 against the individual defendants and that their motions to dismiss should have been granted.

The motions to dismiss targeted the amended complaint. It read in relevant part:

> 5. Jane Doe is a minor child who was, at the time of the events described, thirteen (13) years old. 6. Near the end of the 1992-1993 School Year (sometime in May of 1993), Jane Doe was kept after school to do special work on her studies . . . . 7. Jane Doe stayed after school . . . . 8. Jane Doe did her studies for a while, but was asked, by a teacher, to go upstairs in the school building to retrieve some supplies for the teacher. Jane Doe did. 9. When she went upstairs, a black male school district employee, then acting as a custodian, trapped Jane Doe in an empty classroom, and raped her. The school employee also physically assaulted Jane Doe in the course of the rape causing her bodily injury different from the sexual assault. 10. Jane Doe did not tell anyone what had happened to her until the following Christmas holidays—when it became apparent that Jane Doe was pregnant. Jane Doe then told her mother and father what had happened. 11. The rapist was arrested, and pleaded guilty. 12. Jane Doe had a healthy baby boy in March of 1994 at fourteen (14) years of age . . . . 19. Other members of the maintenance staff have, on information and belief, convictions for murder, armed robbery, cruelty to animals, failure to ID-Fugitive, unlawful weapons possession, multiple DWI, and drug offenses . ... 21. The Hillsboro Independent School District . . . warned new employees to "stay away from the little girls."

Plaintiffs contend that the individuals sued here are liable under two distinct theories. First, plaintiffs urge that "the amended complaint states a claim for liability based on the custody of Jane Doe, whereby she was owed some minimum degree of protection," matching "the contours of liability" that were outlined in *DeShaney v. Winnebago County Dept. of Social Services*, 489 U.S. 189 (1989). Second, plaintiffs would bring themselves within our decision in *Doe v. Taylor Indep. School Dist.*, 15 F.3d 443 (5th Cir.) (en banc), *cert. denied*, 513 U.S. 815 (1994). As we will explain, these theories offer plaintiffs no comfort.

II

In *DeShaney v. Winnebago County Dept. of Social Services*, the Supreme Court rejected the contention that government owes a constitutional duty to protect people from the misdeeds of other private actors, in the absence of a special relationship. We have not accepted the argument that school compulsory attendance laws create such a special relationship between student and school. In *Walton v. Alexander*, 44 F.3d 1297 (5th Cir. 1995) (en banc), we refused to find a special relationship between a state school for deaf children and its students who were residents in the school where they slept and took their meals. It is true that attendance at the school was not required by state law, and we emphasized the absence of this legal compulsion. It is equally true that poor students may have had no real alternatives. The year before Walton we held that, whatever the effect of compulsory attendance, it ended when compulsory attendance ended. *Leffall v. Dallas Indep. School Dist.*, 28 F.3d 521, 529 (5th Cir. 1994) ("Even though Steadham may have been compelled to attend school during the day, any special relationship that may have existed lapsed when compulsory attendance ended."). *See also Johnson v. Dallas Indep. School Dist.*, 38 F.3d 198 (5th Cir. 1994), *cert. denied*, 131 L. Ed. 2d 218 (1995).

We decline to hold that compulsory attendance laws alone create a special relationship giving rise to a constitutionally rooted duty of school officials to protect students from private actors. Much has been written about this issue, and we will not pause to rehearse fully the arguments again. *See Seamons v. Snow*, 84 F.3d 1226, 1236 (10th Cir. 1996); *Sargi v. Kent City Bd. of Educ.*, 70 F.3d 907, 911 (6th Cir. 1995); *Dorothy J. v. Little Rock School Dist.*, 7 F.3d 729, 732 (8th Cir. 1993); *D.R. by L.R. v. Middle Bucks Area Vo. Tech. School*, 972 F.2d 1364, 1368-73 (3d Cir. 1992) (en banc), *cert. denied*, 506 U.S. 1079 (1993); *J.O. Alton Community Unit School Dist. 11*, 909 F.2d 267, 272 (7th Cir. 1990). We join every circuit court that has considered the issue in holding that compulsory school attendance, in Texas to attend seven hours of programmed education on each school day, does not create the custodial relationship envisioned by *DeShaney*. The restrictions imposed by attendance laws upon students and their parents are not analogous to the restraints of prisons and mental institutions. The custody is intermittent and the student returns home each day. Parents remain the primary source for the basic needs of their children. Finally, we find helpful the rationale of the Supreme Court's decision in *Ingraham* to deny school children the protections of the Eighth Amendment:

> The school child has little need for the protection of the Eighth Amendment. Though attendance may not always be voluntary, the public school remains an open institution. Except perhaps when very young, the child is not physically restrained from leaving school during school hours; and at the end of the school day, the child is invariably free to return home. Even while at school, the child brings with him the support of family and friends and is rarely apart from teachers and other pupils who may witness and protest any instances of mistreatment.
> *Ingraham v. Wright*, 430 U.S. 651, 670 (1977).

Refusing to create a whole new class of constitutional rights does not leave the student without legal protection. A review of our recent decisions alone makes that clear. There are concerns pointing in a different direction. *See Johnson*, 38 F.3d 198, 203 (5th Cir. 1994). To say that compulsory attendance laws restrict the freedom of students and parents in significant ways, however, is not to say that this status of students is sufficiently akin to that of prisoners and persons committed to mental institutions to trigger a constitutionally rooted duty.

Nor does a state-created-danger theory save plaintiffs' claims. Its narrow compass is reflected by the reality that we have never sustained liability on this ground. In Johnson we observed that "the environment created by the state actors must be dangerous; they must know it is dangerous; and, to be liable, they must have used their authority to create an opportunity that would not otherwise have existed for the third party's crime to occur." 38 F.3d at 201. *See also L.W. v. Grubbs*, 974 F.2d 119 (9th Cir. 1992) (assault of nurse working with known sex offender under directive of state supervisor), *cert. denied*, 508 660 (1993); *Wood v. Ostrander*, 879 F.2d 583 (9th Cir. 1989) (woman raped when police impounded car of drunk driver leaving her in high crime area), *cert. denied*, 498 U.S. 938 (1990); *White v. Rochford*, 592 F.2d 381 (7th Cir. 1979) (children left by police officers alone in car after arresting driver). Viewed in the light most favorable to the plaintiffs, the school district placed the student in the same area as a school custodian who had no known criminal record, sexual or otherwise, with school teachers in the same building but not in the immediate area. This we were to adopt such a theory. Such post hoc attribution of known danger would turn inside out this limited exception to the principle of no duty.

……

Plaintiffs have stated no claim against these individuals. The denial of the motions to dismiss is reversed. The case is remanded with instructions to enter judgments for the defendants in their individual capacities and for further proceedings consistent with this opinion.

REVERSED and REMANDED.

L.R. v. SCHOOL DISTRICT OF PHILADELPHIA
836 F.3d 235 (3rd Cir. 2016)

FUENTES, Circuit Judge.

Teachers not only educate our children, but also provide them with sources of care and comfort outside the home. Recognizing that the threat of civil liability might discourage teachers and other public servants from taking on such significant roles, courts have developed a doctrine of qualified immunity that, in many instances, shields them from civil lawsuits. But there are exceptions and this is one of those cases.

In January 2013, a teacher in the Philadelphia School District allowed a kindergarten student to leave his classroom with an adult who failed to identify herself. The adult sexually assaulted the child later that day. In the early hours of the next morning, a sanitation worker found the child in a playground after hearing her cries. The child's parent sued the teacher, who claims he is immune from suit.

We hold that the parent's allegations sufficiently state a constitutional violation of the young child's clearly established right to be free from exposure by her teacher to an obvious danger. In short, we conclude that it is shocking to the conscience that a kindergarten teacher would allow a child in his care to leave his classroom with a complete stranger. Accordingly, we will affirm the District Court's denial of qualified immunity.

I. BACKGROUND

A. Factual Background

Because this case comes to us on a motion to dismiss, the allegations are taken from the complaint and are assumed true for purposes of this appeal. On an ordinary school day in January 2013, Christina Regusters entered W.C. Bryant Elementary School in Philadelphia, Pennsylvania, where Jane was enrolled as a kindergarten student. Regusters proceeded directly to Jane's classroom, where she encountered Defendant Reginald Littlejohn, Jane's teacher. Per Philadelphia School District policy,[2] Littlejohn asked Regusters to produce identification and verification that Jane had permission to leave school. Regusters failed to do so. Despite this failure, Littlejohn allowed Jane to leave his classroom with Regusters. Later that day, Regusters sexually assaulted Jane off school premises, causing her significant physical and emotional injuries.

[2] The complaint states that Philadelphia School District policy provides that only the principal or his/her designee, the assistant principal, or the teacher-in-charge may grant a release of students during the school day. The policy also states that (i) under no circumstances may a pre-kindergarten through eighth grade student be released without a properly identified adult, (ii) the adult's identification must be checked against school records, and (iii) the release must take place in the school office. Compl. (J.A. Vol. II 58–67) ¶¶ 15–16.

……

A. Substantive Due Process Claim under the State–Created Danger Theory

The threshold question in any § 1983 lawsuit is whether the plaintiff has sufficiently alleged a deprivation of a constitutional right. L.R.'s claim invokes the substantive component of the Due Process Clause of the Fourteenth Amendment, which "protects individual liberty against certain government actions regardless of the fairness of the procedures used to implement them."[15] In DeShaney v. Winnebago County Department of Social Services,[16] the Supreme Court explained that "nothing in the language of the Due Process Clause itself requires the State to protect the life, liberty, and property of its citizens against invasion by private actors."[17] Rather, the purpose of the Clause is "to protect the people from the State, not to ensure that the State protect[s] [the people] from each other."[18] Applying this principle, the Court held that state social workers did not deprive four-year-old Joshua DeShaney of substantive due process when they failed to remove him from a physically abusive household, despite their ongoing knowledge of suspected abuse by his father.[19] The Court held that, "[a]s a general matter ... a State's failure to protect an individual against private violence simply does not constitute a violation of the Due Process Clause."[20] It suggested, however, that the result may have been different had the State played a role in creating or enhancing the danger to which Joshua was exposed.[21]

[15] Collins v. City of Harker Heights, 503 U.S. 115, 125, 112 S.Ct. 1061, 117 L.Ed.2d 261 (1992) (internal quotation marks omitted).

[16] 489 U.S. 189, 109 S.Ct. 998, 103 L.Ed.2d 249 (1989).

[17] Id. at 195, 109 S.Ct. 998.

[18] Id. at 196, 109 S.Ct. 998 (emphasis added).

[19] Id. at 201–02, 109 S.Ct. 998.

[20] Id. at 197, 109 S.Ct. 998.

[21] See id. at 201, 109 S.Ct. 998 ("While the State may have been aware of the dangers that Joshua faced in the free world, it played no part in their creation, nor did it do anything to render him any more vulnerable to them.").

Building off that concept, we and other circuits have adopted a "state-created danger" exception to the general rule that the Due Process Clause imposes no duty on states to protect their citizens from private harm.[22] In Bright v. Westmoreland County,[23] we clarified the elements necessary to successfully plead a state-created danger claim:

1. the harm ultimately caused was foreseeable and fairly direct;

2. a state actor acted with a degree of culpability that shocks the conscience;

3. a relationship between the state and the plaintiff existed such that the plaintiff was a foreseeable victim of the defendant's acts, or a member of a discrete class of persons subjected to the potential harm brought about by the state's actions, as opposed to a member of the public in general; and

4. a state actor affirmatively used his or her authority in a way that created a danger to the citizen or that rendered the citizen more vulnerable to danger than had the state not acted at all.[24]

[22] See Kneipp v. Tedder, 95 F.3d 1199, 1211 (3d Cir. 1996) ("[W]e hold that the state-created danger theory is a viable mechanism for establishing a constitutional claim under 42 U.S.C. § 1983.").

[23] 443 F.3d 276 (3d Cir. 2006).

[24] Id. at 281 (citations and internal quotation marks omitted).

For the reasons set forth below, we hold that L.R. has sufficiently alleged all four of these elements and has therefore sufficiently pled a substantive due process violation.

i. Affirmative Use of Authority Creating or Increasing Danger

We begin with the fourth element, as it is typically the most contested. This element asks whether the state's conduct created or increased the risk of danger to the plaintiff. As we noted in Bright, "[i]t is misuse of state authority, rather than a failure to use it, that can violate the Due Process Clause."

This element is often contested because of the inherent difficulty in drawing a line between an affirmative act and a failure to act. Often times there is no clear line to draw; virtually any action may be characterized as a failure to take some alternative action. For example, Defendants attempt to reframe Littlejohn's alleged actions as inactions, or failures. They argue that Littlejohn's failure to follow School District policy, failure to obtain proper identification from Regusters, and failure to obtain verification from Regusters that Jane had been permitted to leave school are not affirmative acts. This strategy is unavailing.

Rather than approach this inquiry as a choice between an act and an omission, we find it useful to first evaluate the setting or the "status quo" of the environment before the alleged act or omission occurred, and then to ask whether the state actor's exercise of authority resulted in a departure from that status quo. This approach, which is not a new rule or concept but rather a way to think about how to determine whether this element has been satisfied, helps to clarify whether the state actor's conduct created a danger" or "rendered the citizen more vulnerable to danger than had the state not acted at all.

The setting here is a typical kindergarten classroom. Children in this setting are closely supervised by their teacher. Their freedom of movement is restricted. Indeed, they are not likely to use the bathroom without permission, much less wander unattended from the classroom. In the classroom, the teacher acts as the gatekeeper for very young children who are unable to make reasoned decisions about when and with whom to leave the classroom. Viewed in this light, Jane was safe in her classroom unless and until her teacher, Littlejohn, permitted her to leave.

We can therefore easily distinguish Littlejohn's conduct from the state actors' conduct in DeShaney. The Supreme Court's focus in DeShaney was on the State's failure to remove Joshua a second time from a situation it had reason to believe was dangerous, meaning the State's decision to leave Joshua with his father was a maintenance of the status quo. Moreover, in responding to the argument that the State's action in previously intervening and then returning Joshua to his father gave rise to an affirmative duty to protect and remove him again, the Court further observed: "That the State once took temporary custody of Joshua does not alter the analysis, for when it returned him to his father's custody, it placed him in no worse position than that in which he would have been had it not acted at all." In other words, had the State done nothing, Joshua would have been in the same dangerous position. The setting here, by contrast, was a kindergarten classroom where students presumably were safe from outside dangers. When Littlejohn allowed Jane to leave the classroom with an adult who failed to produce proper identification or verification, he exposed Jane to a danger she would not have otherwise encountered.

We can also distinguish this case from our decision in Morrow v. Balaski,[30] where we declined to find a state-created danger in a school setting. In Morrow, two high school students sued their school for failing to protect them from another student who was bullying them persistently. The school at one point temporarily suspended the bully but then allowed her to return to school, contrary to a school policy requiring expulsion of students adjudicated "guilty of a crime." We held that the school's failure to enforce its own disciplinary policy was not equivalent to an "affirmative act." Thus, Morrow paralleled DeShaney in that maintenance of the status quo was insufficient to create liability.

[30] 719 F.3d 160.

This case is different. Littlejohn's actions resulted in a drastic change to the classroom status quo, not a maintenance of a situation that was already dangerous. And unlike in Morrow, the presence or absence of a school policy is largely irrelevant to L.R.'s claim. Littlejohn's actions in asking Regusters for proper identification and verification, and then permitting Jane to leave with Regusters despite her failure to produce either, amounted to an affirmative misuse of his authority as Jane's teacher and "gatekeeper."

Defendants contend that there is no constitutional right to have a school official intervene to prevent an unauthorized person from removing a child from school. But this was not just a failure to intervene. Under the facts as pled, Littlejohn had the authority to release Jane from his classroom and used it. By allowing Jane to leave his classroom with an unidentified adult, Littlejohn "created or increased the risk [of harm] itself."

We find clear parallels between this case and our seminal state-created danger case, Kneipp v. Tedder.[34] There, police officers stopped a couple walking home from a tavern, released the husband first to relieve the babysitter, and then left the visibly intoxicated wife to walk home alone in the cold. Police later discovered the wife unconscious at the bottom of an embankment near her home. She suffered permanent brain damage as a result of her exposure to the cold. We concluded that the officers created a dangerous situation or at least made the intoxicated woman more vulnerable to danger. This was because the officers chose to displace the caretaker of someone who was clearly unable to care for herself. Having taken on responsibility for the woman's wellbeing, the officers thereafter abandoned it and, in so doing, subjected a vulnerable individual to an obvious risk of harm—walking home alone in the cold while highly intoxicated.

[34] 95 F.3d 1199.

The dynamic of a kindergarten classroom is similar. The state is responsible for the safety of very young children unable to care for themselves. Indeed, it is a responsibility the state undertakes when young children are left in its care. When Littlejohn surrendered that responsibility by releasing Jane to an unidentified adult, thereby terminating her access to the school's care, he affirmatively misused his authority just as culpably as the officers in Kneipp misused theirs.

Our decision in Horton v. Flenory35 is similarly instructive. In that case, a police officer intervened in a dispute between a night club owner and a crime suspect, then allowed the night club owner to interrogate the suspect, leading to the suspect's death. We explained that the officer's action in delegating his authority to the night club owner was "anything but passive," as he "used his official status to confirm that [the night club owner] was free to continue the custodial interrogation" despite signs of physical mistreatment. In both Horton and this case, the particular responsibilities that were relinquished—interrogating suspects and protecting the safety of kindergarteners—were an integral part of the state actor's job functions. In both cases, the state actor handed over their responsibility to a private actor who, under the circumstances, posed an obvious risk of harm to the plaintiff. Such actions are an affirmative misuse of state authority.

[35] 889 F.2d 454 (3d Cir. 1989).

ii. Foreseeable and Fairly Direct Harm

Next, we ask whether "the harm ultimately caused was a foreseeable and a fairly direct result of the state's actions." L.R. alleges that Littlejohn "w[as] aware that releasing pupils to unidentified and otherwise unverified adults would result in harm to those pupils, including but not limited to sexual assault." Defendants counter that the complaint is devoid of any facts that support the inference that Littlejohn could have known of Regusters' intent to harm Jane. That is not the appropriate inquiry. Rather, the plaintiff must only "allege an awareness on the part of the state actors that rises to the level of actual knowledge or an awareness of risk that is sufficiently concrete to put the actors on notice of the harm." We think the risk of harm in releasing a five-year-old child to a complete stranger was obvious.

A comparison of Kneipp with our decision in Morse v. Lower Merion School District40 illustrates this concept. In Kneipp, we explained that a highly intoxicated woman was "more likely to fall and injure herself if left unescorted than someone who was not inebriated,"[41] and we indicated that the police officers' "ordinary common sense and experience" sufficiently informed them of this risk.[42] By contrast, we held in Morse that school officials could not have foreseen that allowing construction workers to leave the school's rear entrance unlocked would result in the fatal shooting of a teacher by a trespasser. We explained that there was no allegation that the school was aware of the assailant or anyone else posing a credible threat of violence to persons inside the school. Rather, the only facts alleged that would have alerted school officials to any danger were that there had been "previous 'security breaches' by unnamed persons" and the assailant had been seen loitering in the school area the week before the shooting.[43] This, we held, was not enough to warn officials that a person "would enter the school in search of a victim."[44]

[40] 132 F.3d 902.

[41] Kneipp, 95 F.3d at 1208.

[42] Phillips, 515 F.3d at 237 (citing Kneipp, 95 F.3d at 1208); cf. Wood v. Ostrander, 879 F.2d 583, 590 (9th Cir. 1989) (noting the "inherent danger facing a woman left alone at night in an unsafe area is a matter of common sense").

[43] Morse, 132 F.3d at 908.

[44] Id.

Here, it was foreseeable that releasing a young child to a stranger could result in harm to the child. This inherent risk is not only a matter of experience as a teacher in charge of a kindergarten classroom, but, as in Kneipp, it is also a matter of common sense. Regardless of which of the many apparent risks of harm—whether kidnapping, child pornography, human trafficking, sexual assault or some other violation—came to pass, Littlejohn knew, or should have known, about the risk of his actions.

We also conclude that the harm ultimately caused to Jane was a fairly direct result of Littlejohn's conduct. We have explained that, although this inquiry is fact-specific, "a distinction exists between harm that occurs to an identifiable or discrete individual ... and harm that occurs to a 'random' individual with no connection to the harm-causing party." In Morse, we declined to find the school's decision to allow the back door to remain open to be the "catalyst for the attack" on the teacher because "[t]he causation, if any, [was] too attenuated." Here, randomness and attenuation are not in play. Littlejohn released Jane directly to the unidentified adult who sexually assaulted her the same day. On the facts as pled, Littlejohn's actions were indeed the "catalyst for the attack."

iii. Conscience–Shocking Conduct

We next consider whether Littlejohn's actions "shock the conscience." The Supreme Court has emphasized that the "touchstone of due process" is protection against arbitrary government action.[47] Government action is "arbitrary in the constitutional sense"48 when it is "so egregious, so outrageous, that it may fairly be said to shock the contemporary conscience."[49]

[47] Cty. of Sacramento v. Lewis, 523 U.S. 833, 845, 118 S.Ct. 1708, 140 L.Ed.2d 1043 (1998) (internal quotation marks omitted).

[48] Id. at 846, 118 S.Ct. 1708 (quoting Collins, 503 U.S. at 129, 112 S.Ct. 1061).

[49] Id. at 847 n.8, 118 S.Ct. 1708.

The level of culpability required for behavior to shock the conscience largely depends on the context in which the action takes place. In a "hyperpressurized environment," such as a high-speed police chase, intent to harm is required. But in situations "where deliberation is possible and officials have the time to make 'unhurried judgments,' deliberate indifference is sufficient."51 On the facts as pled, the appropriate culpability standard here is deliberate indifference, since there is nothing to indicate that Littlejohn faced circumstances requiring him to make a quick decision. We have defined deliberate indifference as requiring a "conscious disregard of a substantial risk of serious harm." That is, "deliberate indifference might exist without actual knowledge of a risk of harm when the risk is so obvious that it should be known."

As we have already explained, the risk of harm in releasing a five-year-old child to an unidentified, unverified adult is "so obvious" as to rise to the level of deliberate indifference. The fact that there was a school policy in place prohibiting the release of pre-kindergarten through eighth grade students to an adult without proper documentation tends to show that school officials were aware that releasing a young child to a stranger is inherently dangerous. What is more, whether or not that policy existed, the fact that Littlejohn asked Regusters for her identification illustrates that Littlejohn himself was indeed aware of the risk of harm in releasing Jane to a stranger, even if he was unaware of Regusters' specific criminal intent. That he still allowed Jane to leave despite Regusters' failure to produce identification or verification, we think, rises to conscience-shocking behavior.

……

IV. Foreseeable Victim

The "foreseeable victim" element requires that some sort of relationship exist between the state actor and the plaintiff such that the plaintiff was a foreseeable victim of the state actor's conduct.[57] This element is satisfied easily here. Jane was a member of the discrete class of kindergarten children for whose benefit the School District's release policy had been instituted. In this sense, Jane was a foreseeable victim of Littlejohn's actions.

[57] A "special relationship" is not required. Indeed, this is an entirely separate theory on which to base a substantive due process claim, applicable when "the State takes a person into its custody and holds him there against his will." Morrow, 719 F.3d at 167 (quoting DeShaney, 489 U.S. at 199–200, 109 S.Ct. 998). In the public high school context, we have explained that compulsory attendance laws and in loco parentis authority do not give rise to a special relationship between schools and their students. Id. at 171–72; Middle Bucks, 972 F.2d at 1371–72. In Morrow, however, we left open the possibility that a special relationship between a school and its students could arise under certain "unique and narrow circumstances," 719 F.3d at 171, as when a school locks classroom doors or otherwise imposes limitations on a student's "freedom to act on his own behalf." Id. at 181 (quoting DeShaney, 489 U.S. at 200, 109 S.Ct. 998). We have never addressed the special relationship theory in the context of a school's youngest and most vulnerable students. Although we decline to do so here, as L.R. does not raise this claim, we note that, at some point, the age and/or dependency of certain students in combination with restraints a school may place on its students may indeed forge a "special relationship." See, e.g., Ingraham v. Wright, 430 U.S. 651, 670, 97 S.Ct. 1401, 51 L.Ed.2d 711 (1977) ("Except perhaps when very young, the child is not physically restrained from leaving school during

school hours ...." (emphasis added))... For these reasons, we conclude that L.R. has sufficiently alleged all the elements of a state-created danger claim.

......

IV. CONCLUSION

State-created danger cases often involve unsettling facts and this case is no different. Even so, our resolution of the legal issues is straightforward. Exposing a young child to an obvious danger is the quintessential example of when qualified immunity should not shield a public official from suit. Accordingly, the order of the District Court is affirmed.

Alison Bethel: Keeping Schools Safe: Why Schools Should Have an Affirmative Duty to Protect Students from Harm by Other Students 2 Pierce L. Rev. 183 (2004)*

The Due Process Clause does not impose an affirmative duty of protection on the states, unless a state actor causes the harm. Consequently, section 1983 is generally not available to individuals who are injured by private actors, even when the state has notice of the potential for harm, or has notice that an actual harm is occurring. ....When a special relationship exists the state has an affirmative duty to protect individuals from harm, even if the individual causing the harm is a private actor. Thus far, courts have held that a special relationship exists only in certain situations, including in prisons, state-operated residential schools, and where patients have been committed involuntarily. [M]ost courts have declined to hold that compulsory education laws create the type of special relationship that, under *DeShaney,* would require the states to protect citizens from harm by private actors.

......

Post-*DeShaney*, the majority of courts, reasoning that compulsory education laws do not render students or their parents unable to care for the child's basic needs, have held that schools have no affirmative duty to protect students from harm by other students. [H]owever, a few courts have held that compulsory education laws do impose on schools a limited duty to protect students from harm by other students. The limited duty imposed by these courts requires schools to protect students from "foreseeable risks of injury or loss of life" and from behavior that shocks the conscience.

A few courts have imposed a limited duty on schools, requiring school officials to protect students from harm inflicted by other students.[78] These courts reasoned that although parents remain the primary caretakers, schools should protect students who, because of compulsory education laws, are in the care and supervision of school officials during school-hours. These courts have not made the duty absolute, but they recognized that compulsory education laws do restrain the freedom of students and parents, and consequently mandate limited protection for students during school-hours.

---

[78] *See Hasenfus*, 175 F.3d 68; *Lichtler*, 813 F.Supp. 1054; *Pagano*, 714 F.Supp. 641.

.....

V. OTHER REMEDIES

Section 320 of the Second Restatement of Torts states:

320 of the Reststement

> One who is required by law to take . . . custody of another under circumstances such as to deprive the other of his normal power of self-protection or to subject him to association with persons likely to harm him, is under a duty to exercise reasonable care so to control the conduct of third persons as to prevent them from intentionally harming the other or so conducting themselves as to create an unreasonable risk of harm to him, if the actor (a) knows or has reason to know that he has the ability to control the conduct of the third persons, and (b) knows or should know of the necessity and opportunity for exercising such control. Restatement (Second) of Torts § 320 (2000).

[S]ection 320 applies to "teachers or other persons in charge of a public school" because students are "deprived of the protection of [their] parents or guardians." Comment (d) to section 320 also requires people with custody of others to give them effective protection should the need arise. 118 Comment (d) states:

> A schoolmaster who knows that a group of older boys are in the habit of bullying the younger pupils to an extent likely to do them actual harm, is not only required to interfere when he sees the bullying going on, but also to be reasonably vigilant in his supervision of his pupils so as to ascertain when such conduct is about to occur. This is true whether the actor is or is not under a duty to take custody of the other.

Thus, tort law requires teachers to protect students from harm by other students. Tort law also requires teachers to anticipate harms and intervene to prevent them from occurring. Courts have recognized this duty drawn from the Restatements when confronted with cases involving injured students who sue their school for negligence. Courts recognize that children must attend school and while there, the protection that they receive from their parents is "mandatorily substituted" with the protection that they should receive from their teachers.... A few courts have held that even colleges have a duty to protect students from harm by third parties.[125] This duty exists even though compulsory education laws do not require individuals to attend college. In *Peterson v. San Francisco Community College District*, the

[125] *Kleinknecht v. Gettysburg College*, 989 F.2d 1360 (3d Cir. 1993); *Peterson v. S.F. Community College*, 685 P.2d 1193, 1201 (Ca. 1984).

Supreme Court of California held that a community college had to exercise due care to protect students from foreseeable harm.

> In the closed environment of a school campus where students pay tuition . . ., where they spend a significant portion of their time and may in fact live, they can reasonably expect that the premises will be free from physical defects and that school authorities will also exercise reasonable care to keep the campus free from conditions which increase the risk of crime.[127]

As these cases indicate, courts have been willing to impose tort-law duties on school officials to anticipate and protect students from harm inflicted by third parties. These tort-law duties, however, do not create constitutional protections, and lack the benefits that section 1983 provides for plaintiffs. In addition, in states that recognize a defense of sovereign immunity from tort action, injured students would be precluded from suing a school district for negligence. Thus, imposing section 1983 liability on school officials would be more beneficial to injured students than tort law remedies.

State laws attempting to create safe school environments similarly fall short of benefits of section 1983. Some state legislatures, in trying to create a safer school environment, have responded to incidents of school violence by passing bullying laws. These statutes recognize the importance of safe schools and they generally require

> Any school employee, or employee of a company under contract with a school or school district, who has witnessed or has reliable information that a pupil has been subjected to insults, taunts, or challenges, whether verbal or physical in nature, which are likely to intimidate or provoke a violent or disorderly response to report the incident to the principal.[134] School employees who report violations are then immune from any cause of action that might arise from a failure to remedy the incident.[135]

.....

Although there are some remedies available to students who are harmed by other students, they are not as adequate as a constitutional remedy would be. Unlike section 1983, tort law and the bullying statutes do not statutorily permit the prevailing party to recover attorney's fees. In addition, not all states have passed bullying statutes, and tort law remedies vary from state to state. A limited Fourteenth Amendment duty, enforceable through section 1983, would benefit injured students, as well as non-injured students, by requiring school officials to protect students from harm that they know, or should know, is occurring. Unlike tort law remedies and state bullying laws, this federal constitutional

---

[127] 685 P.2d at 1201

[134] N.H. Rev. Stat. Ann. § 193-F:3(II).

[135] N.H. Rev. Stat. Ann. § 193-F:3(IV).

requirement would be imposed on every school, in every state, creating safer learning environments for all students.

VI. ARGUMENT IN FAVOR OF A LIMITED DUTY

.....

The special relationship exception to the Due Process Clause should encompass students who are compelled to attend school. Although compulsory education laws do not render parents unable to care for their children's basic needs, they do restrain students' freedom to act on their own behalf by requiring students to attend school. The "nature [of the State's power over schoolchildren] is custodial and tutelary, permitting a degree of supervision and control that could not be exercised over free adults."[150] Because compulsory education laws mandate attendance, "for a portion of the day, students are entrusted by their parents to the control and supervision of teachers."[151] School officials, therefore should be required to protect students whom they know, or should know, are being harmed by other students.

This duty should not be absolute. As under the bullying laws, students would have no recourse against school officials who were not aware, or could not reasonably have become aware, of the harm. Nor should school officials who made a reasonable attempt to protect the student-victim be held liable for their inability to adequately protect the student, unless the teacher's behavior is conscience shocking. Courts should only hold liable the school officials who are aware, or should reasonably be aware, that students are harming other students, as it is these officials who have failed to adequately protect students from danger.

.....

A limited Fourteenth Amendment duty would permit victimized students to recover damages under section 1983 when the student could show that the school officials were aware of the harm and did nothing to prevent it, or when students could show that the school officials' behavior was conscience shocking. Teachers must "'protect the very safety of students and school personnel'"[166] because "government has a heightened obligation to safeguard students whom it compels to attend school."[167] This variation of the *DeShaney* special relationship exception would require school officials to act to protect students from harm and would therefore assist in ensuring that all children have the opportunity to receive the best education possible, in the safest environment possible.

---

[150] *Vernonia Sch. Dist. v. Acton*, 515 U.S. 646, 655 (1995). The Court also states, in dicta, that it is not suggesting "that public schools as a general matter have such a degree of control over children as to give rise to a constitutional duty to protect." *Id.*

[151] *Hasenfus*, 175 F.3d at 72.

[166] *T.L.O.*, 469 U.S. at 357 (Brennan & Marshall, JJ., concurring in part and dissenting in part).

[167] *Id.* at 353 (Blackmun, J., concurring).

Notes and Comments

1. Professor Bethel argues in her article for a constitutional right to safe schools based on a limited affirmative duty educators should have to protect students whom they know, or should know, are being harmed by other students. Would the right, defined in this fashion, bring about substantive changes in the school/student relationship? How might educators get around such a constitutional duty?

2. The level of accountability imposed on educators by traditional tort law is presented in Chapter 14. In her article, Professor Bethel presents tort law through the lens of the Second Restatement of Torts. Section 320 of the Restatement imposes a duty to "exercise reasonable care so to control the conduct of third persons as to prevent them from intentionally harming the other or so conducting themselves as to create an unreasonable risk of harm." Is this standard substantively different from the limited constitutional right Professor Bethel proposes? Is it clear to you why a constitutional remedy is better than one imposed by the common law of torts?

3. See Richard Salgado, Protecting Student Speech Rights While Increasing School Safety: School Jurisdiction and the Search for Warning Signs in a Post-Columbine/Red Lake Environment, 2005 BYU L. Rev. 1371 (2005). Also see, Note: A Right to Learn?: Improving Educational Outcomes through Substantive Due Process, 120 Harv. L. Rev. 1323 (2007). See also Kathleen Hart: Sticks and Stones and Shotguns at School: The Ineffectiveness of Constitutional Antibullying Legislation as A Response to School Violence, 39 Ga. L. Rev. 1109 (2005).

Chapter Fourteen
Common Law Torts and Statutory Approaches to Liability

> [S]chool districts can be held liable for failure to take reasonable steps to provide security for their students.... [A school] district has a duty to take reasonable steps for the protection of its students. ... [The] failure to take reasonable safety precautions is not within the common law immunity for failure to prevent crime. *King v. School District of Washington Township*, 790 N.E.2d 474 (Ind. 2003)

> The university-student relationship is certainly unique. [T]he institution is involved in all aspects of student life. Through it's providing of food, housing, security, and a range of extracurricular activities the modern university provides a setting in which every aspect of student life is, to some degree, university guided. ...Despite the recognition of adulthood, universities continue to make an effort to regulate student life and the courts have utilized diverse theories in attempting to fix the extent of the university's [liability]. *Furek v. University of Delaware*, 594 A.2d 506 (Del. 1991)

I. Liability in K-12 Institutions

A. Common Law Torts

1. Negligence

BROWARD COUNTY SCHOOL BOARD v. RUIZ
493 So. 2d 474 (Fla. Dist. Ct. App. 1986)

OPINION BY: ANSTEAD

This is an appeal from a final judgment entered upon a jury verdict holding school officials liable for injuries inflicted upon appellee Jose Ruiz by fellow students. The case was tried in January, 1985 and the jury returned a verdict of $30,000.00 in favor of Ruiz. The trial court denied motions to set aside the verdict. We affirm the actions of the trial court.

Ruiz sued the School Board as a result of injuries he suffered in an assault at Hallandale High School on November 13, 1980. Ruiz, then a sophomore and a member of the school's junior varsity football team, had stayed briefly after school to have his picture taken with the rest of the team. The coach of the team had arranged for some of his players to practice with the varsity team that day, as the JV season had ended. However, Ruiz did not join this practice and instead, after the picture session, went to the cafeteria area to call his father for a ride home. Ruiz testified that his normal routine after practice had been to go to the cafeteria area to call his father and wait for a ride. The coach remained with the rest of the JV team at the varsity practice.

The cafeteria was located in the center of the main campus building. The precise location of the incident was across from the cafeteria door, in an area containing benches and pay phones. While waiting there for his father, Ruiz was attacked and beaten by three other students: Anthony Wilson, Jimmy Wright, and Ray Sands. According to Ruiz's testimony, he was sitting on a bench and looking at a book when he heard someone say "Hey." After that he lost consciousness and woke up in a hospital room. The only other witness to testify was a female student, Lateasea Fredericks. Fredericks and two other friends were in the area waiting for a bus. Fredericks knew the boys who beat Ruiz, but she had not seen Ruiz before. Fredericks stated that Wilson first said something to Ruiz, after which the two got into an "argument." Ruiz then turned around and started walking backwards away from Wilson in the direction of the office, when he was attacked from behind by Wright and severely beaten by all three students. Two custodians who had been in the cafeteria testified that they had been tricked into leaving the area by another group of students who told them that a custodian in another part of the building was in trouble. When they returned some thirty minutes later they found Ruiz on the floor. No direct connection was established between the two incidents.

School principal Linda Brown testified that responsibility to provide adequate supervision and security for students was delegated to teachers, administrators, and security personnel. However, these employees were not required to remain at the school for more than fifteen to twenty minutes after the last classes ended at 2:45 p.m. Significantly, no one was specifically instructed to watch the small group of students who regularly congregated in the cafeteria area after school to wait for the bus or for rides. Although one custodian testified that he sometimes took this responsibility upon himself, Brown stated that the custodians' responsibilities were limited to cleaning the building. In the case of after school extra-curricular activities, the coach or club sponsor would have supervisory responsibility. Coaches were instructed to remain on campus until the students had secured rides home. However, until practice was over, the coach's responsibility was over the students at the practice. The JV coach testified that it was not his duty to patrol the cafeteria or common areas after practice.

To prevail on a theory of negligent supervision by a teacher, a plaintiff must establish (1) the existence of a teacher-student relationship giving rise to a legal duty to supervise; (2) the negligent breach of that duty by the teacher; and (3) the proximate causation of the student's injury by the teacher's negligence. *Collins v. School Board of Broward County*, 471 So.2d 560 (Fla. 4th DCA 1985). In *Collins*, this court found a duty of supervision to exist where a substitute teacher was conducting a shop class in which a student was sexually assaulted. 471 So. 2d at 564. One of the controlling factors identified in *Collins* was the fact that class was in session and the school had an absolute right to control the students' behavior at that time. *Id.* In contrast is *Benton v. School Board of Broward County*, 386 So.2d 831 (Fla. 4th DCA 1980), in which the court found no duty to exist where a kindergarten student left the class unaccompanied to go to the bathroom, and another student closed the bathroom door on her finger. 386 So.2d at 834. The court in *Benton* viewed the imposition of a duty in that case to be "demonstrably unreasonable," for it would require the teacher to abandon her co-existing responsibility to the remainder of the class. *Id. see also Rupp v. Bryant*, 417 So.2d 658, 668 (Fla. 1982) (duty will not be imposed where inconsistent with duty to supervise generally). With respect to the responsibility of the JV coach, we think *Benton* is more closely analogous to the present facts. If a kindergarten teacher is held not to have a duty to leave her class behind and accompany one student to the bathroom, then surely it cannot be said that a football coach has a duty to leave an ongoing practice to accompany a sixteen year old student to the telephone.

Although we agree with the School Board's contention that an inadequate case has been made as to any breach of supervision by the JV coach, we believe there was sufficient evidence for the jury to find a breach of the duty to provide adequate security to its students. While a school board is not an insurer against a student being injured, the school board is entrusted with the care of the students and has a legal duty to properly supervise student activity. The question is whether the absence of any supervisory personnel in the cafeteria area at the time of the beating constituted actionable negligence.[1] In other words, did the school have a duty to provide some form of security in this area to prevent incidents from occurring? The School Board argues that this duty is foreclosed by *Relyea v. State*, 385 So.2d 1378 (Fla. 4th DCA 1980). *Relyea* held that the decisions of a university regarding "whether to provide security guards, parking attendants, security gates, and the numbers thereof" are discretionary and protected by sovereign immunity. 385 So. 2d at 1382. We cannot agree that *Relyea* controls.

Initially we would note that there are obvious differences between the supervisory and security responsibilities at a state university, like the one involved in *Relyea*, and a public high school. The age of the children and the authority of the school over them are significant factors. In both *Benton* and *Collins* we confirmed the existence of a duty to provide supervision and protection to minor students on the school premises. In our view, this duty includes responsibility for a centrally located part of the school building which students regularly occupy with the school's consent and knowledge during the hours immediately after the end of classes. The school's duty to provide supervision does not end when the bell rings. If anything, the time period immediately after the end of school presents the greatest danger of misconduct by students who have been restrained all day in a disciplined setting. In addition, while there was testimony that no one was specifically assigned to patrol the cafeteria area after school, the school itself recognized the need for supervision by adopting a comprehensive system of supervision and patrols designed to prevent students from being left alone on the campus either during the school day or during after-school activities. Accordingly, we conclude that there was evidence on the issue of duty to provide supervision at the time and place in question.[2]

We also reject the contention advanced by the School Board "that under no circumstance it is [sic] foreseeable that fighting will occur when no more than a handful of students are in an area waiting to be picked up from school."[3] The Florida Supreme Court's opinion in *Rupp* directly refutes this position:

---

[1] Again, we note that the School Board did not contend at trial, nor does it argue on appeal, that the custodians in the cafeteria area had supervisory responsibilities.

[2] For the same reasons we reject the School Board's contention that the instruction given to the jury on the issue of the duty of the school to reasonably provide for the supervision of its students, was an inaccurate statement of law. The instruction given was derived from this court's decision in *Benton*, and in no way implied that the school had a duty to allocate its security resources in a way not required by *Relyea*.

[3] The appellee also maintains that the incident was foreseeable because numerous previous incidents of violence were documented at the school. The court below was presented with the difficult evidentiary issue of whether these prior incidents were sufficiently similar in nature and location to the attack on Ruiz to admit as evidence on foreseeability. This court need not resolve the issue, as the finding of foreseeability is sustainable on other grounds. However, in our view prior acts of violence between students on the school grounds, even though occurring during school hours would be relevant to the issue of whether acts of violence may be expected immediately after school hours while students are still on the grounds. While

Whether a principal's or teacher's failure to supervise a student was the proximate cause of injuries suffered by a student is the issue most consistently litigated in negligent school supervision cases. The issue is usually complicated by the simultaneous tortious conduct of fellow students, so that the question becomes one of whether the fellow students' negligence was the intervening cause of the harm. Two distinct standards have developed. The first holds that a teacher's absence leading to an injury to one student by another can be the proximate cause of the injury only if the injury could not happen while the teacher was present. These cases generally find student misbehavior is the proximate and superceding cause of the harm. See *Ohman v. Board of Education*, 300 N.Y. 306, 90 N.E. 2d 474 (1949). The second, and more reasonably supported, holds that certain student misbehavior is itself foreseeable and therefore is not an intervening cause which will relieve principals or teachers from liability for failure to supervise:

> "We should not close our eyes to the fact that . . . boys of seventeen and eighteen years of age, particularly in groups where the herd instinct and competitive spirit tend naturally to relax vigilance, are not accustomed to exercise the same amount of care for their own safety as persons of more mature years." Recognizing that a principal task of supervisors is to anticipate and curb rash student behavior, our courts have often held that a failure to prevent injuries caused by the intentional or reckless conduct of the victim or a fellow student may constitute negligence.

Dailey v. Los Angeles Unified School District, 2 Cal. 3d 741, 748-49 (1970). Courts following this standard find that a lack of deportment in unsupervised students is to be expected. Thus rough-housing or hazing at a high school club initiation is behavior which is not so extraordinary as to break the chain of causation between the school's failure to supervise and the injury to the student. *See, e.g., Sheehan v. St. Peter's Catholic School*, 291 Minn. 1, 188 N.W.2d 868 (1971); *Titus v. Lindberg*, 49 N.J. 66, 228 A.2d 65 (1967); *Cirillo v. City of Milwaukee*, 34 Wis. 2d 705, 150 N.W. 2d 460 (1967).

We perceive that the *Dailey* standard more nearly comports with Florida negligence law which recognizes that .the intervening negligence of a third party does not relieve the original tortfeasor of his negligence if the intervening negligence is foreseeable. *See Gibson v. Avis Rent-A-Car System*, Inc., 386 So. 2d 520 (Fla.1980); Vining. A standard which recognizes that certain student misconduct will foreseeably occur when students are left unsupervised fulfills the definition in *Gibson* which finds an intervening cause foreseeable when "'in the field of human experience' the same type of result may be expected again." *Id.* at 522-23.

---

the circumstances may not be as compelling, such acts demonstrate that misconduct may be anticipated to take place spontaneously if the students are left unsupervised.

417 So. 2d at 668-69 (footnotes omitted) (emphasis in original). A breach of the school's duty would be established by a failure to exercise reasonable care in discharging the duty of supervision. In this case the jury was entitled to find under the evidence presented that no supervision was provided at the time and place of the assault and that such supervision, if provided, would have prevented the assault from occurring. In summary, we find that the lower court did not err in refusing to set aside the jury's verdict, as there was sufficient evidence for the jury to find for *Ruiz* on his negligent supervision claim. While we are concerned that a public school should have to bear the cost of injuries intentionally inflicted by its students, we believe that the circumstances involved herein were such that a jury question was presented on the school's responsibilities to its students, and we have no authority to second-guess the jury's decision.

....

Accordingly, the judgment based upon the jury verdict is affirmed.

GIBBONS v. ORLEANS PARISH SCHOOL BOARD

391 So. 2d 976 (La. Ct. App. 1980)

OPINION BY: BARRY

Plaintiff, Pamela Gibbons, filed suit individually and on behalf of her minor child Sasha, against the Orleans Parish School Board because of injuries sustained by the minor child while playing in defendant's school yard. The defendant was found negligent and appeals denying its negligence and also seeks a reduction in the award. The appeal was answered by the mother asking that she be awarded damages for mental anguish as a result of her daughter's injury.

Sasha, a six year old, was a first grade student at Lakeview School in New Orleans at the time of the accident. The child arrived in the school yard at approximately 8:30 a. m. and began swinging on "monkey bars". Located adjacent to the bars was a "tether ball pole" about ten feet in height. When Sasha reached the end of the bars she grabbed onto the pole and attempted to slide down to the ground. Attached to the center area of the pole was a screw that protruded approximately 11/2 inches and which caused a laceration on the inside of the child's left thigh when she slid over it.

The District Court held the defendant negligent in failing to provide adequate supervision in the school yard and found the tether ball pole to be an "attractive nuisance" because of its close proximity to the bars. The Court awarded $7,500.00 for pain, disfigurement, and future cosmetic surgery expenses and denied recovery to the mother for her mental anguish.

At the time of the accident approximately 150-180 children were in the school yard under the supervision of one teacher. Her duties that morning included supervision in unloading school buses, patrolling the "T" shaped playground area, and overseeing students in the school basement. It is apparent that one teacher attempting to effectively perform these various supervisory functions over so many students in several locations is totally inadequate and virtually impossible. Even the presence of sufficient supervisory personnel may not have prevented this accident.

There is no explanation why the pole was located next to the bars. The fact that it was situated in such close proximity provided a natural inclination or impulse for a young child to switch from the bars to the pole and slide to the ground. The pole, in proper use and without the protruding screw, is not per se dangerous; however, when situated next to the bars with its protruding screw the pole becomes a dangerous instrumentality. In fact, it was foreseeable that a child using the bars would be tempted to swing over to the pole.

The lack of adequate supervision, the location of the pole next to the bars, and the protruding screw clearly constituted negligence on the part of the defendant.

The laceration to Sasha's thigh required nine inside and twenty outside stitches to close the wound. The scar is "v" shaped about 1 X 11/2 in length. The child remained home approximately one week convalescing and was later seen by a psychiatrist, psychologist and a social worker. Their testimony showed a nominal degree of traumatic neurosis without a definitive prognosis of difficulty.

Considering the circumstances of the trauma, the type of injury and its effect upon the child, we feel the award of $7,500 is neither excessive nor insufficient and within the sound discretion of the trial judge following the guidelines of *Reck v. Stevens*, 373 So.2d 498 (LA.1979).

....

The judgment of the District Court is affirmed with costs of this appeal to be paid by appellant.

SIMONETTI EX REL. SIMONETTI v. SCHOOL DISTRICT OF PHILADELPHIA

454 A. 2d 1038 (Pa. Super. Ct. 1982)

OPINION BY: WIEAND

Richard Simonetti, a fifth grade student, returned to the classroom from recess and was struck in the left eye by a pencil which had been propelled from the hand of a classmate when he tripped. The teacher, an employee of the School District of Philadelphia, was outside the classroom, standing at the door, when Simonetti was injured. There she was engaged in monitoring the return of her students from recess and talking with another teacher. The student who dropped or threw the pencil and two other students had been required to remain in the classroom during recess as punishment for misbehavior at breakfast. They had been talking with the teacher during the recess period and were instructed to take their seats when the teacher stepped outside the classroom to supervise the return of the students from recess.

In an action against the School District, it was contended by Simonetti that the teacher had been negligent in failing to provide adequate classroom supervision. The case was tried without a jury, and damages of $15,000 were awarded to the minor plaintiff and his mother. After the School District's exceptions had been dismissed and judgment entered on the verdict, this appeal followed.

. . . .

In *Bottorf v. Waltz*, 245 PA. Super. 139, 369 A.2d 332 (1976), a case in which a student had been burned when melted wax was spilled on his back, this Court defined the standard of care required of a teacher by quoting from 38 A.L.R.3d 830, 843-46, in part, as follows:

> What constitutes proper supervision depends largely upon the circumstances attending the event. Thus, the fact that supervisory personnel present when an accident occurs could conceivably have prevented its occurrence does not necessarily render the school agency liable if the supervisory personnel was competent and acted reasonably under all the circumstances.
>
> . . .
>
> There is no liability predicated on lack or insufficiency of supervision where the event in connection with which the injury occurred was not reasonably foreseeable . . . . The courts frequently state that a teacher is not required to anticipate the myriad of unexpected acts which occur daily in and about school, to guard against all dangers inherent in the rashness of children, or to watch all movements of children.
>
> Where injury results from an unforeseen, sudden, impulsive, or spontaneous act of another pupil, such act has been held the intervening proximate cause of the injury notwithstanding lack, or possible inadequacy, of supervision. Thus, it has been said that failure of supervision is not that proximate cause of an accident where injury results from an unanticipated act of a fellow pupil, since the teacher cannot be expected to watch all movement of pupils in the absence of anything to place the teacher on notice to guard against the occurrence.

Id. 245 Pa. Super. Ct. at 143, 369 A. 2d at 334.

Although there is a paucity of Pennsylvania decisions, cases from other jurisdictions illustrate the application of these principles. In *Ohman v. Board of Education of City of New York*, 300 N.Y. 306, 90 N.E. 2d 474 (1949), the facts were remarkably similar to those of the instant case. There, a thirteen year old student sustained injury when struck in the eye by a pencil. The pencil had been thrown by one student to another, and when the boy for whom it was intended ducked, the pencil hit the minor plaintiff. The accident occurred while the teacher in charge of the classroom was temporarily absent for the purpose of sorting and storing supplies in a corridor closet. The court held that the teacher's absence from the room was insufficient to impose liability upon the Board of Education, saying:

> [A] teacher may be charged only with reasonable care such as a parent of ordinary prudence would exercise under comparable circumstances. Proper supervision

> depends largely on the circumstances attending the event but so far as the cases indicate there has been no departure from the usual rules of negligence. *Id.* at 309, 90 N.E. 2d at 475.

In *Swaitkowski v. Board of Education of the City of Buffalo*, 36 A.D. 2d 685, 319 N.Y.S. 2d 783 (1971), the Court held that the Board of Education was not liable for injuries sustained by a student who, upon returning to his seat, sat on the point of a pencil placed on the seat by another student while the teacher was absent from the classroom for a short period to assist another teacher locate books in a bookroom 10 1/2 feet away with the doors open. The Court said:

> Nor can respondents prevail on their claim of inadequate supervision by the teacher in leaving the classroom unattended for the short space of time she was required to be absent. As in *Ohman v. Board of Educ. of City of N.Y.*, 300 N.Y. 306, 90 N.E. 2d 474, the injury resulted from "the act of an intervening third party which under the circumstances could hardly have been anticipated in the reasonable exercise of the teacher's legal duty toward the plaintiff" (p. 309, 90 N.E. 2d p. 475) and which act was "one of those events which could occur equally as well in the presence of the teacher as during her absence" (p. 310, 90 N.E.2d p. 475). We are, of course, mindful of the proposition that a school board is not the insurer of the safety of students (*Ohman v. Board of Educ. of City of N.Y.*, supra; *Cambareri v. Board of Educ. of City of Albany*, 246 App. Div. 127, 284 N.Y.S. 892, *affd.* 283 N.Y. 741, 28 N.E. 2d 968) and that a school or teacher may be charged only with reasonable care such as a parent of ordinary prudence would exercise under comparable circumstances [*560] (Lawes *v. Board of Educ. of City of N.Y.*, 16 N.Y. 2d 302, 305, 266 N.Y.S. 2d 364, 366, 213 N.E. 2d 667, 668). *Id. at* 686, 319 N.Y.S. 2d at 784.

In *Morris v. Ortiz, 103 Ariz.* 119, 437 P. 2d 652, 35 A.L.R. 3d 747 (1968), a student in an auto mechanics class was injured when another student jumped on a car top which the former student was holding. The trial court directed a verdict in favor of the teacher and school district. In affirming, the Arizona Supreme Court said:

> To hold that [the teacher] had to anticipate [the student's] act and somehow circumvent it is to say that it is the responsibility of a school teacher to anticipate the myriad of unexpected acts which occur daily in and about schools and school premises, the penalty for failure of which would be financial responsibility in negligence. We do not think that either the teacher or the district should be subject to such harassment nor is there an invocable legal doctrine or principle which can lead to such an absurd result. *Id. at* 121, 437 P. 2d at 654, 35 A.L.R. 3d at 752.

In *Butler v. District of Columbia*, 417 F. 2d 1150 (D.C. Cir. 1969), a seventh grade student was struck in the left eye by a sharp piece of metal when he entered a printing classroom. The teacher was then absent because he had been assigned as a hall or cafeteria supervisor. The plaintiff's case was based on alleged negligent supervision of the classroom after the teacher and principal had prior knowledge that "horseplay" and throwing had occurred in the classroom. In holding that there could be no recovery, the Court took note of the district's dilemma of balancing "the need for a teacher to supervise several hundred students milling about the corridors and the cafeteria against the need to supervise fourteen students in a certain classroom for a period of time." *Id. at* 1153.

From these decisions it can safely be concluded that momentary absence from a classroom is not negligence. This is particularly true where, as in the instant case, the absence was for the authorized and compelling reason of monitoring the return of about thirty students from recess. The teacher, it may confidently be observed, could not have been at two places at the same time. With equal confidence, it can be said that it was not negligence for the teacher to give priority to an entire class of approximately thirty students returning from recess rather than to remain in the classroom to supervise three students who had been required to stay in the classroom during the recess period.

It is common knowledge that children may indulge in horseplay. They may throw a pencil, shoot a paper clip or snap a rubber band when a teacher is absent or turns his or her back. In the instant case, the teacher attempted to guard against any horseplay by instructing the three students who were in the classroom to return to their seats and remain there. While these students were capable of free spirits and were even being punished for unrelated misconduct at breakfast, there is no evidence that they were hellions who required constant custody.[2]

To require the teacher to anticipate the events which occurred while she was outside the classroom door would be to hold that a teacher is required to anticipate the myriad of unexpected acts which occur daily in classrooms in every school in the land. This is not the law, and we perceive no good reason for imposing such an absolute standard on teachers and school districts.

The judgment is reversed and is now entered for the appellant.

CIRILLO, Judge, dissenting:

I respectfully dissent. The majority begins its discussion by pointing out the proper standard of review for this Court as follows:

> Appellate review of the record of a trial before a judge without a jury is limited to a determination of whether the findings of fact of the court below are supported by competent evidence and whether or not the lower court committed error of law. In reviewing the sufficiency of the evidence, we are required to view the evidence in the light most favorable to the verdict winners.

---

[2] The dissenting opinion contends that the teacher was negligent because she positioned herself so that she could neither see nor hear what was transpiring in the classroom. This is not in accord with the facts found by the trial judge and recited in his opinion. Even the minor plaintiff testified that the teacher was but a few feet from the classroom door. Despite her position outside the door, she heard nothing to suggest a "ruckus." The trial court also made no finding that there had been "yelling" or "hollering" in the classroom. This is understandable. The minor plaintiff, who at one point in his testimony used those words, immediately changed his testimony to "talking loudly." The trial judge did find that the boy with the pencil had been running in the classroom. Specifically, he was running up the aisle at the time the minor plaintiff was struck in the eye with the pencil.

Rather than applying this standard though, the majority takes a neutral view of the evidence and begins comparing the instant case with similar cases in other jurisdictions and reaches the overly simplistic conclusion that momentary absence from a classroom by a teacher is not negligence. Since I do not believe that the majority presented the evidence in the light most favorable to the verdict winner, as required, I will begin by stating the facts as I feel they should be viewed in this appeal.

The teacher, Mrs. Powell, remained in the classroom with three children during recess period while the other children were outside playing. The three children were not at recess because they were being punished by the teacher for their misbehavior earlier in the day. At least one of the three children had been a persistent behavior problem since he began school. Mrs. Powell went outside the classroom, following the recess period, to monitor the other thirty children who were returning. Mrs. Powell positioned herself in the hall in such a way that she could not see the classroom, which was filling up with children returning from recess and in which the three discipline-problem children were sitting. Because she could not see into the classroom from where she stood, she was not aware that there were children running around with sharp pencils in their hands. She also could not hear the "hollering" or "yelling" going on inside the classroom. Not only was Mrs. Powell not in a position to see or hear what was happening in the classroom during this ru[c]kus, but she was busy talking to another teacher. In fact, she was so engulfed in conversation that following the incident in question, the minor plaintiff, who was crying, had to go into the hall and interrupt the two teachers to get Mrs. Powell's attention. Based on these facts, we must determine whether there is evidence in the record to justify the trial court's findings of negligence.

Besides failing to apply the proper standard of review, the majority attempts to find support for their position by citing non-Pennsylvania cases, all of which are factually distinguishable from the instant case. All of those cases involved a teacher who left the classroom unattended to do another assigned task. While the teacher was absent, a student was injured through some mishap. The majority concludes that these cases support the conclusion that "momentary absence from a classroom is not negligence." While I agree that momentary absence alone is not sufficient to support a finding of negligence, I do believe that additional factors coupled with momentary absence could support a finding of negligence. The majority does not consider questions such as why the teacher left the room, how long she was gone, and what she did while she was out, as being important in determining negligence. I believe these facts are essential in distinguishing our case from those cited by the majority.

In the case at bar, while Mrs. Powell may have been authorized to stand outside the classroom to monitor those coming in from recess, this did not relieve her of the duty to supervise the children as they entered the classroom, especially when she knew the behavior-problem children were in the room; nor did it free her to strike up conversations with fellow teachers in the hallway. Unlike the cases cited by the majority, the teacher could have done both tasks, i.e., monitor those in the hallway and watch those in the classroom at the same time by positioning herself in the doorway so she had a view of the inside of the classroom and that of the hallway. Moreover, the distraction of talking to other teachers when she was supposed to be supervising her thirty students is another factor which should be considered in determining whether there was sufficient evidence for the trial court to find negligence. These additional facts, which are absent in the cases relied upon by the majority, are sufficient to qualify the "momentary absence" of the teacher and support a finding of negligence. Therefore, I would affirm the finding of negligence by the lower court because it was supported by competent evidence.

Notes and Comments

1. Liability for the Failure to Supervise

In each of the decisions above the courts appear to apply the same principles for establishing liability for the failure to supervise students. Generally, educators are at risk of liability for injuries sustained by students when (a) it occurs in the context of a school sponsored activity (b) arises in a setting in which educators are in control (more or less) of the actions of the individuals involved; and (c) the incident out of with the injury arises is foreseeable. Which of the decisions apply the elements correctly?

What recommendations for school policies on supervision emerge from these cases?

> -- In West Virginia, the Supreme Court of Appeals of West Virginia held that educators were not liable for injuries to a student. The student, who injured his arm while wrestling with a classmate on the school soccer field, had left the high school building without authorization. The court ruled that under the in loco parentis doctrine, schools have a special relationship with students entrusted to their care, which imposes upon them certain duties of reasonable supervision. But, school officials did not owe a duty of supervision to the student once he left school building without authorization. (*Goodwin v. Bd. of Educ. of Fayette Cty.*, 242 W. Va. 322, 835 S.E.2d 566 (2019).
>
> -- In Connecticut, the Superior Court of Connecticut ruled that school officials should have done more to prevent a 16-year-old student from stabbing to death a high school classmate. The court refused to dismiss the wrongful death lawsuit because notice given to administrators by the victim should have triggered mandatory school intervention procedures. The court held that educators have a duty to protect school children from reasonably anticipated dangers. (*Cimarelli-Sanchez v. City of Milford Bd. of Educ.*, No. CV166020436S, 2019 WL 413587 (Conn. Super. Ct. Jan. 4, 2019), reconsideration denied, (Conn. Super. Ct. 2019).
>
> -- In Illinois, the Appellate Court of Illinois ruled that school officials owed a student no duty for injuries she sustained when, after school was let out, a fellow student accidentally ran into her in a crosswalk, about half a block from the school. The court declined to impose portal-to-portal liability on the school district. Instead the court limited this concept to risks that occur while the student is at school or otherwise engaged in school activities. (*Stephens v. Bd. of Educ. of Sch. Dist. 172 Adams Cty. Illinois*, 2019 IL App (4th) 190156-U.
>
> -- In Connecticut, the Supreme Court of Connecticut remanded for retrial a lawsuit brought against educators for the failure to properly supervise students. An elementary school student was assaulted by other students while they were on the playground during the lunchtime recess. The court ruled that persons who were assigned to monitor the students on the playground during recess were not properly

trained. The court also held that one student intern and three or four staff members were not enough to exercise control over as many as 400 students on the playground and that expert testimony was not required to establish this fact. *Osborn v. City of Waterbury*, 333 Conn. 816, 220 A.3d 1 (2019)

2. Liability Standards for School-Sponsored Field Trips
Should a school policy for supervision be any different for off-campus school sponsored events?

> -- In Washington State, the Court of Appeals of Washington refused to dismiss a lawsuit brought by parents of a student who was killed during a field trip consisting of a teacher taking his class on a short walk alongside a busy road in violation of school policy. The court ruled that a trial was necessary to determine whether the accident, caused when a driver fell asleep behind the wheel and drove his vehicle onto the sidewalk, was foreseeable. *Meyers v. Ferndale Sch. Dist.*, 457 P.3d 483 (Wash. Ct. App. 2020)

Compare Rhea v. Grandview School District, 39 Wn. App. 557; 694 P. 2d 666 (1985) (no liability for injuries during off-campus party on "release day" for all graduating seniors at which alcohol was consumed), and *Rhodes v. Guarricino*, 54 F. Supp. 2d 186 (S.D.N.Y. 1999) (class field trip that required sleep over in a hotel. The court held that it was reasonable for school principal-chaperone to ask hotel security to open the students' rooms for searches). How would you recommend that school personnel other than teachers be used to help maintain safer schools?

3. Gibbons v. Orleans Parish School Board and "Negligence Per Se"
The court in *Gibbons* declares with great conviction that, "[t]he lack of adequate supervision, the location of the pole next to the bars, and the protruding screw *clearly constituted negligence* on the part of the defendant." This language is an application of the rule of "negligence per se" that applies a higher duty of careful supervision on educators for the benefit of students engaged in certain high risk activities that are known to occur on campus. In "negligence per se" cases the risk of injury is so high that educators are expected to take steps to diminish the risk or avoid the high-risk activity altogether. Health and safety laws often regulate these high-risk activities. In any event, the failure to act when the need to supervise is obvious is treated as an automatic failure of the duty. *See Scott v. Ind. Sch. Dist. No. 709*, Duluth, 256 N.W. 2d 485 (Minn. 1977) (negligence per se when student was injured when drill bit broke and lodged in his eye while he was unprotected by goggles. State statute required students in industrial arts class to wear eye protective devices of industrial quality). *Mueller v. Cmty. Consol. Sch. Dist. 54*, 678 N.E. 2d 660, 667 (1997) (negligence per se when school wrestling coach sexually assaulted student while driving him home after practice. Educators had a statutory duty to conduct a background check on the wrestling coach). *Gattavara v. Lundin*, 166 Wash. 548, 554, 7 P. 2d 958 (1932) (negligence per se for allowing cars to drive across school grounds during school hours).

4. Broward County School Board v. Ruiz and Role of Forseeability

A school district's duty requires that it exercise reasonable care to protect students from physical hazards in the school building or on school grounds. The court in *Broward County* notes that, "a failure to prevent injuries caused by the intentional or reckless conduct of [students] may constitute negligence... [A] lack of deportment in unsupervised students is to be expected." This statement suggests that forseeability plays a critical role in determining liability in public education. School officials are not liable merely because injuries occur. Instead, educators will be liable if the incident is foreseeable.

Foreseeability in education law focuses solely on whether or not educators knew or (in the exercise of reasonable care) should have known of the risk that results in an incident. The evolution of standards of forseeability is now codified in the Restatement of the Law, Second, Torts, § 320.

> § 320 Duty of Person Having Custody of Another to Control Conduct of Third Persons
>
> One who is required by law to take or who voluntarily takes the custody of another under circumstances such as to deprive the other of his normal power of self-protection or to subject him to association with persons likely to harm him, is under a duty to exercise reasonable care so to control the conduct of third persons as to prevent them from intentionally harming the other or so conducting themselves as to create an unreasonable risk of harm to him, if the actor
>
> (a) knows or has reason to know that he has the ability to control the conduct of the third persons, and
>
> (b) knows or should know of the necessity and opportunity for exercising such control.

Comment (D) to section 320 of the Restatement directly addresses the role that the element of forseeability should play in determining the scope of the duty to protect students.

> d. Duty to anticipate danger. One who has taken custody of another may not only be required to exercise reasonable care for the other's protection when he knows or has reason to know that the other is in immediate need of it, but also to make careful preparations to enable him to give effective protection when the need arises, and to exercise reasonable vigilance to ascertain the need of giving it. Thus if a sheriff or peace officer knows that public opinion is so violently incensed against his prisoner that there is danger of mob violence, he may be required not only himself to defend the prisoner, but also to exercise reasonable care to secure assistance which will enable him to do so effectively. So too, a schoolmaster who knows that a group of older boys are in the habit of bullying the younger pupils to an extent likely to do them actual harm, is not only required to interfere when he sees the bullying going on, but also to be reasonably vigilant in his supervision of

> his pupils so as to ascertain when such conduct is about to occur. This is true whether the actor is or is not under a duty to take custody of the other.

A majority of States has adopted the Restatement of Torts on these matters or has codified its rules into its statutory laws. The remaining States apply a variation of the same principles. *See Ferreira v. Sanchez*, 79 N.M. 768, 449 P. 2d 784 (N.M. 1969) (A high school student placed a live bullet in a gun that was used in a play and discharged it. The gun was for use as a prop in a school play. The court dismissed the claims against the teacher and the principal. The discharge of the weapon with a live bullet was not foreseeable). Compare with *Wesley v. Page*, 514 S.W. 2d 697 (KY. 1974) (Theatre teacher found liable for failing to properly supervise students who used live ammunition in a prop gun during a school play. The court ruled that the teacher was "required to foresee the events" which resulted in the injury.). *See also* Donald L. Beci: School Violence: Protecting Our Children and the Fourth Amendment., 41 Cath. U.L. Rev. 817 (1992); Ashley Smith: Students Hurting Students: Who Will Pay? 34 Hous. L. Rev. 579 (1997).

5. Torts and Teachers: The Absence of a Remedy for Injuries at School

All states have unique rules to resolve disputes between schools and teachers who are injured while acting in the scope of their professional duties. The prevailing law is summarized by Noel M. Johnston in a critical analysis of the laws. Noel M. Johnston, *The Chicago Public Schools and Its Violent Students: How Can the Law Protect Teachers*?, 48 DePaul L. Rev. 907 (1999).

> To the extent that the school district is an employer of teachers and other personnel, the main remedy available to its staff for work-related injury is the Illinois Workers' Compensation statute. Under this statute, the school district must compensate its employees who are victims of assaults while on the job. The Chicago school district's unique role as a municipality does nothing to limit the responsibilities the school district has to its employees as an employer. The Workers' Compensation Act is remedial in nature; it is intended to provide financial protection for the injured worker as the costs are borne by the employer. Through the Workers' Compensation Act, the employee may receive an award of compensation without having to show negligence on the part of the employer, and he need not show he was free from any contributory negligence. Significantly, the employee forfeits a great deal in exchange for this certain recovery. The employee cannot invoke common law tort remedies against the employer. In fact, recovery under the Workers' Compensation Act expressly precludes an employee from obtaining any other common law or statutory remedies for a work-related injury.

Other courts concur:

> -- In Minnesota, the United States Court of Appeals, Eighth Circuit held that a school was not liable to a teacher who was injured when he attempted to stop a lunchroom fight. The court reasoned that his lawsuit was preempted by the Minnesota Workers' Compensation Act because it was an injury sustained while on the job. *Ekblad v. Indep. Sch. Dist. No. 625*, 744 F. App'x 325 (8th Cir. 2018).
>
> -- In New York, the Supreme Court, Appellate Division, ruled that a school district was not liable to a Middle school assistant principal for injuries sustained when

she attempted to stop a fight between two students. The court reasoned that the school did not assume a special duty to the assistant principal, and that the administrator could not sue the school based on promises to improve security. *Morgan-Word v. New York City Dep't of Educ.*, 161 A.D.3d 1065, 77 N.Y.S.3d 709 (N.Y. App. Div. 2018).

-- In Louisiana, the State Court of Appeals rejected personal injury claims against the school board brought by a high school teacher who was assaulted by a student when she was six weeks pregnant. The court ruled that she could not pursue tort recovery for injuries and was limited to workers' compensation, even though the student had an extensive history of disciplinary issues. *Field v. Lafayette Par. Sch. Bd.*, 2016-495 (La. App. 3 Cir. 11/9/16), 205 So. 3d 986, writ denied, 2016-2141 (La. 1/13/17), 215 So. 3d 256.

---

2. Strict Liability

FALLON v. INDIAN TRAIL SCHOOL
500 N.E. 2d 101 (Ill. App. Ct. 1986)

JUSTICE STROUSE delivered the opinion of the court

The plaintiff, Mary Jane Fallon, appeals from the order of the circuit court which dismissed counts I, II, and III of her four-count amended complaint against the defendants, Indian Trail School (school), Addison Township School District No. 4 (school district), Maureen Roach and Louise Roynan-Leo (teachers). For the reasons set forth below, we affirm the decision of the circuit court.

The plaintiff's amended complaint sought to recover damages for spinal injuries suffered as a result of a trampoline accident which occurred on February 23, 1975. At that time the plaintiff was a sixth-grade student at the school and the defendants, Roach and Roynan-Leo, were physical education teachers. The incident occurred when the plaintiff attempted a "front drop" maneuver on the trampoline during her physical education class. In her attempt to perform the maneuver, the plaintiff sustained spinal injuries.

The plaintiff's amended complaint contained four counts. Count I alleged that the school and school district were strictly liable for the consequences of exposing pupils to an "abnormally dangerous instrumentality," a trampoline, during the physical education program. Count II alleged that the school and school district were negligent in the selection and use of an "abnormally dangerous" apparatus, a trampoline. Count III alleged the school and school district were negligent in the hiring and supervising of their teachers. Count IV alleged the willful and wanton misconduct of all of the defendants with regard to the method in which they conducted the physical education class. The trial court dismissed counts I, II, and III, but left pending count IV. The plaintiff then filed a notice of appeal from the dismissal of counts I through III.

On appeal, the plaintiff contends that the trial court erroneously granted the motion to dismiss counts I and II, thereby preventing her from introducing evidence which would demonstrate that trampoline usage is an "abnormally dangerous" activity. The plaintiff also contends that the trial court erroneously granted the motion to dismiss count III, as it properly included the elements of a negligent hiring and supervision claim.

As this case comes before us on the granting of a motion to dismiss, we note that, in considering this matter, all well-pleaded facts must be taken as true, as well as all reasonable inferences which may be drawn there from. (*Morrow v. L. A. Goldschmidt Associates, Inc.* (1984), 126 Ill. App. 3d 1089, 1096, *rev'd* other grounds (1986), 112 Ill. 2d 87.) Moreover, in ruling on a motion to dismiss, the allegations of the complaint are to be interpreted in the light most favorable to the plaintiff. *Denkewalter v. Wolberg* (1980), 82 Ill. App. 3d 569, 572.

In count I, the plaintiff alleged that the trampoline was an abnormally dangerous instrumentality, and the school district should, therefore, be held accountable under strict tort liability for any injuries due to its use. In count II, the plaintiff charged the school and school district with negligence as a result of a violation of section 10—20.8 of the School Code (Ill. Rev. Stat. 1985, ch. 122, par. 10—20.8) because the trampoline was an abnormally dangerous instrumentality. We must, therefore, decide whether the plaintiff has alleged sufficient facts to support the contention that the trampoline is an abnormally dangerous instrumentality and trampoline usage is an abnormally dangerous activity.

Illinois recognizes strict liability under two theories: unreasonably dangerous defective products (*Suvada v. White Motor Co.* (1965), 32 Ill. 2d 612, 621), and the theory which plaintiff alleges is applicable to this case, ultra hazardous activities (*City of Joliet v. Harwood* (1877), 86 Ill. 110). Sections 519 and 520 of the Restatement (Second) of Torts (1981) (Restatement) have formulated a definition of ultra hazardous activities. Under section 519(1) of the Restatement, "[o]ne who carries on an abnormally dangerous activity is subject to liability for harm to the person, land or chattels of another resulting from the activity, although he has exercised the utmost care to prevent the harm." (Restatement (Second) of Torts sec. 519(1) (1981).) Section 520 of the Restatement lists the elements of an ultra hazardous activity as follows: "existence of a high degree of risk of some harm * * *; likelihood that the harm that results from it will be great; inability to eliminate the risk by the exercise of reasonable care; [and] extent to which the activity is not a matter of common usage * * *." Restatement (Second) of Torts sec. 520 (1981).

Illinois has long recognized strict liability for damages caused by engaging in an ultra hazardous activity, although it has never explicitly relied upon the Restatement factors in determining whether a given activity is abnormally dangerous. In *City of Joliet v. Harwood* (1877), 86 Ill. 110, the Illinois Supreme Court held that blasting dynamite in a residential area was intrinsically dangerous and gave rise to strict liability for the blaster. A similar result was reached in *FitzSimons & Connell Co. v. Braun & Fitts* (1902), 199 Ill. 390, 394-97, and *Opal v. Material Service Corp.* (1956), 9 Ill. App. 2d 433, 451-61. Finally, a Federal district court held that shipping acrylonitrile, a hazardous and toxic substance, was an ultra hazardous activity that subjected the shipper to strict liability under Illinois law. (*Indiana Harbor Belt R.R. Co. v. American Cyanamid Co.* (N.D. Ill. 1981), 517 F. Supp. 314.) In so holding, the court relied upon the Restatement formulation of abnormally dangerous activities. 517 F. Supp. 314, 318-20.

The plaintiff concedes that there is no Illinois authority discussing either whether (1) trampoline usage of this sort is an ultra hazardous activity, or (2) the trampoline is an abnormally dangerous instrumentality. Indeed, the trial court, in its written disposition dismissing counts I and II, noted that most of the discussion which related to this subject had to do with such obviously dangerous instrumentalities and activities as blasting, transport of explosives, maintenance of high electrical current, large animals, and maintenance of water reservoirs. In support of her argument, the plaintiff attached Exhibit A, "Trampoline-Related Quadriplegia: Review of the Literature and Reflections on the American Academy of Pediatrics' Position Statement," a review documenting cervical spine injuries resulting from trampoline-related accidents.

After reviewing Exhibit A, the trial court's disposition, as well as the plaintiff's amended complaint, we believe the trial court was correct in finding that trampoline usage, as alleged in the present case, does not fall within the parameter of an abnormally dangerous activity. We also agree that the trampoline, as a matter of law, is not an abnormally dangerous instrumentality.

Trampolines are widely used in the school systems as well as other centers of gymnastic activity. The injuries that may be caused result not from the trampoline itself but rather from the manner of its use. The terms "ultra hazardous," "abnormally dangerous," or "intrinsically dangerous," as traditionally used, refer to that type of danger which is inherent in the instrumentality itself at all times and do not mean danger which arises from mere casual or collateral negligence of others with respect to it under the particular circumstances. More concisely, it means dangerous in its normal or nondefective state. (*Clark v. City of Chicago* (1980), 88 Ill. App. 3d 760, 763.) We conclude that although it's negligent use can be the basis for liability, neither the trampoline itself nor its ordinary use is abnormally dangerous or ultra hazardous. Therefore, counts I and II were properly dismissed.

Levie v. Orleans Parish School Board

537 So. 2d 351 (La. Ct. App. 1988) writ denied 538 So. 2d 616 (La. 1989)

KLEES, Judge.

On May 24, 1983, twelve-year-old Jennifer Levie fell and hurt her ankle in the school yard of Hynes Elementary, where she was waiting to meet her cousins, who were Hynes students. The fall occurred when, while walking toward the monkey bars, Jennifer stepped in a hole in the ground and her foot became trapped by the Y-shaped root of a tree which surrounded the hole. Both the hole and the root were covered with grass.

Jennifer was immediately diagnosed as having either strained ligaments or a displaced fracture, and her leg was placed in a cast to her knee. The cast was removed by Dr. Bruce Razza, her orthopedic surgeon, on June 21, 1983, and Jennifer was released. On May 16, 1984, she again consulted Dr. Razza concerning pain in her ankle which had begun about one month after the cast was removed. She also complained of swelling and pain in her knee and occasions when her knee would "lock," causing her to fall. At this point, Dr. Razza determined that Jennifer had a probable torn medial meniscus (torn cartilage) in her right knee, as well as post-traumatic arthritis in her right ankle and knee, all of which were likely to have been caused by her fall in the school yard. Dr. Razza has not recommended surgery, but has treated these problems with medication and heat therapy. As a result of these injuries, Jennifer has had to severely restrict her participation in physical activities, such as sports, dancing, and physical education classes.

Jennifer's parents sued the Orleans Parish School Board claiming it was strictly liable under Civil Code article 2317 for the defective condition of the playground. The case was tried in the district court on December 10, 1987, and the trial judge found in favor of plaintiffs, awarding them $176,000 ($1,000 medical expenses plus $175,000 general damages) for their daughter's injuries. On appeal, the school board contends that the trial judge committed manifest error by finding that the condition of the school yard posed an unreasonable danger to Jennifer Levie and thus holding the board strictly liable. Alternatively, defendant argues that the trial court erred in awarding an excessive amount of damages. After reviewing the evidence, we affirm the trial court's judgment of liability but find that the damages awarded were excessive.

I. Liability

In order to make out a case under Civil Code article 2317, the injured party must show: (1) that the thing he complains of was in the care or custody of the defendant; (2) the existence of a vice or defect in the thing; and (3) that his injury was caused by the vice or defect. Loescher v. Parr, 324 So.2d 441, 449 (La.1975). The school board does not dispute that it had custody of the Hynes school yard nor that Jennifer's injury was caused by a condition of the yard; the issue is whether the school yard was defective.

For a thing to be defective so as to trigger strict liability, it must pose "an unreasonable risk of harm to persons." Entrevia v. Hood, 427 So.2d 1146, 1149 (La.1983). Regarding this criterion, the Supreme Court in Entrevia stated:

> The unreasonable risk of harm criterion, however is not a simple rule of law which may be applied mechanically to the facts of a case. It is a concept employed by this court to symbolize the judicial process required by the civil code. Since Article 2317 and 2322 state general precepts and not detailed rules for all concrete cases, it becomes the interpreter's duty to decide which risks are encompassed by the codal obligations from the standpoint of justice and social utility.
> Id. at 1149 (Citation omitted.).

Defendant first argues that the hole in the Hynes school yard did not pose an unreasonable risk of harm because it was not visible, and because "[s]tudents had played ... around this tree for years without any reports of injury." In essence, defendant's argument is that the hole did not constitute a defect because it was not discoverable. Unfortunately, under the law as it existed at the time of Jennifer's accident, whether or not the defect is discovered or discoverable is not relevant in determining the existence of strict liability.[1] As the Court stated in Entrevia v. Hood, "The owner is absolved from his strict liability neither by his ignorance of the [defective] condition ... nor by circumstances that the defect could not easily be detected." 427 So.2d at 1148. Thus, the inability of the defendant to know or prevent the risk is not a defense in a strict liability case. Id. at 1150.

[1] The legislature has recently changed the law of strict liability by providing that a public entity (such as the school board) cannot be held liable for damages caused by the condition of things within its care and custody unless the public entity had "actual or constructive notice of the particular vice or defect which caused the damage prior to the occurrence, and the public entity has had a reasonable opportunity to remedy the defect and has failed to do so." R.S. 9:2800. This statute, which became effective on July 12, 1985, changes substantive law and therefore is not to be applied retroactively. Landry v. State, 495 So.2d 1284 (La.1986).

Defendant also argues that the condition of the yard did not pose an unreasonable risk of harm because it was caused by a natural phenomenon, the tree, which has aesthetic value and is a desirable thing to have on a school playground. This argument is partially based upon the assumption that the hole had formed naturally, which was not proven or even addressed at trial. Moreover, while we recognize that the determination of what constitutes an unreasonable risk of harm involves a balancing of interests (see Langlois v. Allied Chemical Corp., 258 La. 1067, 249 So.2d 133, 140 (1971)), we believe that the risk of injury to a child such as Jennifer Levie greatly outweighs the aesthetic value of this particular tree. Furthermore, it was never shown that the only appropriate remedial measure would be removal of the tree, rather than merely cutting back the offensive root and/or filling in the hole.

In Landry v. State, 495 So.2d 1284 (La.1986), the Supreme court found that a hole immediately adjacent to the Lake Pontchatrain seawall presented an unreasonable risk of harm to the plaintiff, a recreational fisherman who was injured when he tried to avoid stepping in the hole, which was partially obscured by grass. Although the hole was a natural consequence of wave action and erosion, the Court found that the risk of harm it created in this heavily used recreational area outweighed the cost of prevention. The Court stated:

Our review of the record disclosed no evidence was presented to confirm the argument that the costs of repair or frequent inspections would be an undue burden on the Levee Board. On the contrary, there was evidence of the Levee Board's existing efforts to clean up after severe weather and to keep the lakefront and seawall in good repair. The Levee Board presented a log which showed a seven-month period of periodic clean-up or grading and filling along the seawall in the aftermath of severe weather. Given the board's existing maintenance efforts, the cost of filling holes such as the one which injured plaintiff does not seem a burden when weighed against the risk of harm presented by holes in an area where recreational use occurs daily, and the number of people present is large and their activities varied.

495 So.2d at 1288.

The facts of Landry are similar to those of the instant case in several key ways. Like the lakefront, a school playground is a heavily used recreational area. As in Landry, there was no showing at trial that the cost of repair would be prohibitive; in fact, the supervisor of grounds for the Orleans Parish school system testified that he inspected the Hynes playground more frequently than most other schools, about three to five times per year, because of the special hazards posed by the large number of trees. He also stated that the employees who mow the grass three times per month are instructed to check for holes and other potentially dangerous conditions so that these may be corrected.

Jennifer Levie testified that the hole into which she stepped was deep enough that the ground came to one inch above her ankle. We find that the hole combined with the tree root posed an unreasonable risk of harm to Jennifer. Under the law, the fact that this condition was not easily discoverable does not absolve the school board. Therefore, the trial court did not commit manifest error by holding defendant strictly liable for Jennifer's injuries.

II. Damages

……

In awarding $175,000 in general damages, the trial judge emphasized Jennifer's tender age and the fact that her physical activity would be restricted for the rest of her life. He also noted that Jennifer had apparently gained a good deal of weight since the accident, which her mother had attributed to her inability to exercise as before.

……

Our review of the record in this case leaves no doubt that the trial judge abused his discretion in awarding an excessive amount of damages, and an examination of prior awards merely confirms this point. Although the trial judge relied heavily on Jennifer's young age in determining quantum, past awards to youthful plaintiffs with similar injuries have been significantly lower. See, e.g.: Johnson v. Allstate Ins. Co., 410 So.2d 777 (La.App. 4th Cir.1982), writ denied, 414 So.2d 378 (La.1982) (Confirming award of $18,775 to minor who suffered a fractured tibia of the right leg, was hospitalized briefly, wore a cast for two months, and was left with residual pain and a 5% permanent disability of the leg); Vega v. St. Bernard Water District No. 1, 398 So.2d 1248 (La.App. 4th Cir.1981), writ denied, 401 So.2d 986 (La.1981) (Confirming award of $30,000 to thirteen-year-old boy who suffered amputation of a portion of his big toe, causing impairment of his athletic ability, which had been above average); Buckley v. Exxon Corp., 399 So.2d 1225 (La.App. 3d Cir.1981) (Confirming award of $40,000 to seven-year-old boy whose legs were run over by a tractor trailer and who had residual pain and a slight permanent diability of his left knee); *355 Bickford v. Reliance Ins. Co., 415 So.2d 405 (La.App. 1st Cir.1982), writ denied, 420 So.2d 442 (La.1982) (Confirming award of $45,000 to sixteen-year-old plaintiff with severe fractures of right knee and ankle as well as other injuries causing a permanent partial disability of 40% to his right leg); Fleischmann v. Hanover Ins. Co., 470 So.2d 216 (La.App. 4th Cir.1985) (Confirming award of $100,000 reduced to $72,000 to account for plaintiff's fault, to bicyclist with injured knee who had been a high school track star with aspirations of obtaining an athletic scholarship to a major university, and whose residual knee damage prevented him from running at his previous level).

Similarly, a look at past damage awards to adult plaintiffs with comparable injuries shows the trial court's award to be out of proportion. See, e.g.: Bergeron v. Firestone Tire & Rubber Co., 482 So.2d 54 (La.App. 5th Cir.1986), writ denied, 484 So.2d 136 (La.1986) (Confirming award of $30,000 for pain and suffering to plaintiff with multiple muscle strains in her right foot and leg which would continue to cause her pain indefinitely and which prevented her from doing such pre-accident activities as bowling, dancing, walking and domestic chores); Wallace v. State Farm Mutual Auto Ins. Co., 509 So.2d 466 (La.App. 3d Cir.1987), writ denied, 510 So.2d 377 (La.1987) (Confirming award of $50,000 to plaintiff with a 20% impairment of his left knee which prevented him from engaging in jogging, basketball, racketball and bicycling, activities in which he had previously participated).

Considering the facts of the instant case and using the cited prior decisions as a guideline only, we find $75,000 to be the highest amount that was reasonably within the discretion of the trial court to award for the present and future pain and suffering of Jennifer Levie. See Reck v. Stevens, supra, at 500. Accordingly, the judgment of the trial court is hereby modified to reduce the amount awarded plaintiffs to $75,000 in general damages plus $1,000 in medical expenses, or a total of $76,000. In all other respects, the judgment is affirmed.

Cory v. Stroudsburg Area School Authority

13 Pa. D. & C.4th 27 (Com. Pl. 1991)

O'BRIEN, J.

On February 28, 1991, plaintiffs filed a complaint seeking damages for personal injuries sustained by Jean Cory as the result of a fall in the bleachers at the Stroudsburg High School football stadium on September 8, 1989.

……

Plaintiffs' complaint sets forth three different theories of liability. Count I alleges negligence as a result of an unsafe condition of the bleachers. Count II alleges strict liability and Count III alleges a breach of implied warranty. The school district has filed a demurrer to all three counts asserting that it is immune from suit by virtue of the Political Subdivision Tort Claims Act. Therefore, we must determine whether the immunity provided by that Act protects the defendant school district from liability with respect to each theory of liability asserted by the plaintiffs in their complaint.

The grant of governmental immunity to local agencies such as the defendant school district is set forth in 42 Pa.C.S. §8541 which provides: "Except as otherwise provided in this subchapter, no local agency shall be liable for any damages on account of any injury to a person or property caused by any act of the local agency or an employee thereof or any other person." The Act specifically provides exceptions to the grant of governmental immunity in 42 Pa.C.S. §8542 which provides in pertinent part:

"(a) Liability imposed

A local agency shall be liable for damages on account of an injury to a person or property within the limits set forth in this subchapter if both of the following conditions are satisfied and the injury occurs as a result of one of the acts set forth in subsection (b):

(1) The damages would be recoverable under common law or a statute creating a cause of action if the injury were caused by a person not having available defense under section 8541 (relating to defense of official immunity); and

(2) The injury was caused by the negligent acts of the local agency or an employee thereof acting within the scope of his office or duties with respect to one of the categories listed in subsection (b). As used in this paragraph, 'negligent acts' shall not include acts or conduct which constitutes a crime, actual fraud, actual malice or willful misconduct.

(b) Acts which may impose liability

The following acts by a local agency or any of its employees may result in the imposition of liability on a local agency:

……

(3) Real property--the care, custody or control of real property in the possession of the local agency, except that the local agency shall not be liable for damages on account of any injury sustained by a person intentionally trespassing on real property in the possession of the local agency. As used in this paragraph, 'real property' shall not include:

> (i) trees, traffic signs, lights and other traffic controls, street lights and street lighting systems;
>
> (ii) facilities of steam, sewer, water, gas and electric systems owned by the local agency and located within rights-of-way;
>
> (iii) streets; or
>
> (iv) sidewalks."

While defendant school district asserts that it is immune from liability for the allegations of negligence set forth in Count I of plaintiffs' complaint, plaintiffs argues that the allegations of Count I fall within the real property exception set forth in 42 Pa.C.S. 8542 (b)(3). Applying the standards for evaluating a demurrer as set forth by our Supreme Court in Firing v. Kephart, 466 Pa. 560, 353 A.2d 833 (1976) and the holding of our Commonwealth Court in Lowman v. Indiana School District, 96 Pa. Commw. 389, 507 A.2d 1270 (1986) interpreting the real property exception to the facts at the case at bar, we conclude that defendant school district's demurrer to Count I of the complaint must be dismissed.

Count II of plaintiffs' complaint seeks damages against the defendant school district on a theory of strict liability. The doctrine of strict liability has been expressly recognized in Pennsylvania case law. Schriner v. Pa. Power and Light Co., 348 Pa. Super. 177, 501 A.2d 1128 (1985). This theory of liability is premised upon the following provision of the Restatement of Torts (Second):

§402A. Special Liability of Seller of Product for Physical Harm to User or Consumer

(1) One who sells any product in a defective condition unreasonably dangerous to the user or consumer or to his property is subject to liability for physical harm thereby caused to the ultimate user or consumer, or to his property, if:

> (a) the seller is engaged in the business of selling such a product; and
>
> (b) it is expected to and does reach the user or consumer without substantial change in the condition in which it is sold.

(2) The rule stated in subsection (1) applies although:

> (a) the seller has exercised all possible care in the preparation and sale of his product; and
>
> (b) the user or consumer has not bought the product from or entered into any contractual relation with the seller.'

When we distill §402A into its constituent elements, we find that the following are necessary to an appropriate application of this section:

(1) a product;

(2) a sale of that product;

(3) a user or consumer;

(4) a defective condition, unreasonably dangerous; and

(5) causation--that the product caused physical harm to the ultimate user or consumer, or to his property."

A common sense reading of the foregoing provision as well as the decisions by our appellate courts make it apparent that this theory of liability is not applicable to school districts. It is apparent that the defendant school district is not a seller as defined in Berkibile v. Brantly Helicopter Corporation, 462 Pa. 83, 337 A.2d 893 (1975) nor do the allegations of Count II meet the threshold determination delineated in Ellis v. Chicago Bridge and Iron Co., 376 Pa. Super. 220, 545 A.2d 906 (1988). Further the exceptions to governmental immunity hereinabove enumerated only apply to negligent acts by a local agency. Our Superior Court held in Carrecter v. Colson Equipment Co., 346 Pa. Super. 177, 499 A.2d 362 (1985) that negligence is not an element of proof in establishing a strict liability claim. Thus strict liability is not included within the exceptions to governmental immunity enumerated in 42 Pa.C.S. §8542. Therefore, we conclude that the demurrer by the defendant school district to Count II of plaintiffs' complaint must be sustained.

Seal v. Carlsbad Independent School District
116 N.M. 101, 860 P.2d 743 (1993)

RANSOM, Chief Justice.

This is a wrongful death action brought by Judy Seal as personal representative of the estate of her deceased son, Kevin. Seal appeals from a summary judgment holding that the operation of a swimming pool is an inherently dangerous activity giving rise to strict liability, from which a school district and its employees enjoy statutory sovereign immunity under Section 41–4–4(A) of the Tort Claims Act, NMSA 1978, §§ 41–4–1 to –27 (Repl.Pamp.1989). See also Saiz v. Belen Sch. Dist., 113 N.M. 387, 391, 827 P.2d 102, 106 (1992) (school districts immune under Tort Claims Act from strict liability for inherently dangerous activity). Holding that operation of a swimming pool is not an inherently dangerous activity and that neither of the alternative holdings of the trial court is dispositive, we reverse.

Kevin Seal was a physically and mentally disabled eighteen-year-old member of a Boy Scout troop for the handicapped. He could not swim and had a history of multiple seizure disorder. In 1988, Kevin went swimming with his troop as part of an aquatic camp that was planned, provided, and supervised by the Boy Scouts of America. The camp was held at the Carlsbad Natatorium, which is owned and operated by the Carlsbad Independent School District. While participating in the program, Kevin drowned, unnoticed by the Scout staff.

The trial court granted immunity from liability to the school district and its employees on two theories. The first was that the operation of a swimming area is an inherently dangerous activity under the definition in Saiz and, therefore, any duty to provide adequate safety measures is nondelegable. This results in a strict liability claim for which there is no waiver of immunity under the Tort Claims Act. Alternatively, the court ruled that if operation of a natatorium is not an inherently dangerous activity and the duty is delegable, either the duty was delegated to and accepted by the Boy Scouts as an independent contractor or the Scouts were an agent of the school district and no claim against the school district would have survived an earlier settlement that Seal made with the Scouts. In arriving at the independent contractor alternative, the trial court found as undisputed the facts that an agreement was reached between the school district and the Scouts that the school district would not have the responsibility of furnishing lifeguards and that the responsibility would be assumed solely by the Scouts. The trial court determined that even if Martin Fleming, a seventeen-year-old Scout who entered into the agreement on behalf of the Scouts, did not have actual authority to contract for the organization, either he had apparent authority or the transaction was ratified by Sheldon Johnson (the district executive for the Boy Scouts) on the first day of the aquatic camp. The court also found undisputed that the Scouts took responsibility for furnishing the lifeguards and did furnish them.

……

In Saiz, we discussed at length what activities are inherently dangerous. We stated that an "activity is inherently dangerous because it involves a 'peculiar risk' in the absence of special precautions, or because it involves a 'special danger' inherent in the work." Saiz, 113 N.M. at 394 n. 6, 827 P.2d at 109 n. 6. The school district argues that the activity of swimming by handicapped individuals in need of special attention involves "peculiar risks" of the type referred to in the opinion.

The school district misapplies the definition to the activity of swimming by handicapped individuals. In Saiz, if reasonable precautions were not taken, it was relatively certain that injury would occur at some point because of the public location of a high-voltage light post. While the operator of a public swimming pool must provide a lifeguard as a reasonable precaution against the possibility of drowning, see Regulations Governing Public Swimming Pools & Private Baths, E.I.B. Reg. 76–1(2–101)(I)(1) (Mar. 25, 1976), the activity of swimming itself is not highly likely to result in injury if that precaution is not taken, as is the touching of an uninsulated high-voltage line.

In Saiz, we cited to the seminal English case on strict liability, Bower v. Peate, 1 Q.B.D. 321 (1876), which states:

> [A] man who orders a work to be executed, from which, in the natural course of things, injurious consequences to his neighbour must be expected to arise, unless means are adopted by which such consequences may be prevented, is bound to ... do what is necessary to prevent the act he has ordered to be done from becoming wrongful.
> Id. at 326.

There are three elements to liability for inherently dangerous activity: the owner or occupier of the premises must instigate or tolerate the activity; injury must be a relatively certain consequence of the activity unless reasonable precautions are taken; and the absence of the necessary precaution must cause injury. We are aware of no case of "inherently dangerous activity" in which liability was based on harm that should have been anticipated to an especially susceptible victim. The doctrine of inherently dangerous activity pertains to creation or maintenance of a condition that is universally dangerous, not one that gives rise to a high risk of harm because of the special circumstances involving the persons coming in contact with the instrumentality. Danger in a swimming pool is not a peculiar risk.

Primary negligence. We harbor significant uncertainty as to whether the trial court addressed the question of genuine issues of material fact regarding primary negligence of the school district, although we acknowledge that any allegations of such negligence may have been poorly presented in response to the motion for summary judgment. Yet the question was presented, and we believe the trial court was diverted from giving that claim of negligence any consideration because of its misconception concerning the law of inherently dangerous activity. ......

Because we hold that the operation of a swimming pool is not an inherently dangerous activity, we reverse the summary judgment based on that rationale. Further, we believe that when the trial court said that the Boy Scouts were either an independent contractor or an agent of the school district, the court may have been diverted from considering any genuine issue of material fact of primary negligence. While we do not preclude the trial court from again granting summary judgment if raised by appropriate motion on remand, we cannot assume, on this record, that the court properly has considered issues of primary negligence.

While we do not preclude the trial court from again granting summary judgment if raised by appropriate motion on remand, we cannot assume, on this record, that the court properly has considered issues of primary negligence.

The grant of summary judgment is reversed except for that portion of the judgment in favor of the school district employees in their individual capacities, and the cause is remanded for further proceedings consistent with this opinion.

Notes and Comments

1. Educators and Strict Liability
Courts have refused to hold school districts responsible for injuries on a strict liability theory. See *Dibortolo v. Metropolitan School Dist. of Washington Township*, 440 N.E.2d 506 (Ind.App.1982) (physical education class not inherently dangerous setting.) But see *Kingsley v. Independent School Dist., Hill City*, 312 Minn. 572, 251 N.W.2d 634 (1977) (liability of school district for ¼ inch protuberance on top of student locker over six feet high approaches strict liability.)

Is this a defensible position?

Professor Ralph D. Mawdsley argues that the standard of care for supervision of disabled students should be relaxed to a version of strict liability, appropriately fitted to the unique circumstances of children with special needs.

> Where the standard of care is clearly understood as a part of the provision of services to disabled students, liability seems fairly easy to determine. In *Guidry v. Rapides Parish School Board* [60 So.2d 125 (La.App.1990)], a nineteen year old female student who functioned at the level of a five or six year old had been placed in a coeducational residential training school. When the employees supervising the students gathered in a room adjacent to the room in which the students were located, and with a glass window furnishing a partial view of the students, a male student sexually assaulted the plaintiff in a part of the classroom the employees could not see. In this case, a duty of supervision was established because the employees understood that the students required "constant supervision." The assault against plaintiff was included within the scope of the duty because the protection afforded by the duty not to leave students alone encompasses the risk of sexual behavior by students whose bodies have developed beyond their mental abilities to understand or control their urges.
>
> *Guidry* seems to stand for the principle that school liability will be premised on what supervisory personnel understand to be the standard of care for disabled students, whether or not the specific misconduct was foreseeable. Whether or not an IEP actually requires "constant supervision," *Guidry* suggests not only that liability will flow from an understood standard, but that the actual misconduct need not have been foreseeable when the standard was formulated. In the regular student

world of tort liability, such separation of a standard from foreseeability of the specific conduct that resulted in injury comes very close to strict liability."

Ralph D. Mawdsley, Supervisory Standard of Care for Students with Disabilities, 80 Ed. Law Rep. 779, 786-787 (1993)

Do you agree?

2. Educators Defenses to Liability: The Public Duty Doctrine

Educators often assert a range of defenses in liability lawsuits. The following defenses, when properly asserted provide school officials with a complete defense to a negligence claim.

Under the public duty doctrine, no governmental agency have a duty to protect particular individuals from harm by third parties, thus no claim may be brought against them for negligence. The doctrine was originally devised to prevent suits for negligence against police officers in their attempts to exercise discretion in protecting the public from crime. The doctrine recognizes the limited resources of law enforcement and refuses to judicially impose an overwhelming burden of liability for failure to prevent every criminal act. Thus, the phrase often used is that "a duty owed to all is a duty owed to none."

There are well-established exceptions to the public duty doctrine. These are:

(1) an assumption through promises or actions, of an affirmative duty to act on behalf of the party who was injured;
(2) knowledge on the part of the public official that inaction could lead to harm;
(3) some form of direct contact between the agency's agents and the injured party; and
(4) that party's justifiable reliance on the agency's affirmative undertaking.

The public duty doctrine has not been applied to the school setting with much success. Some courts have expressly held that "the public duty doctrine . . . does not apply outside the police protection context." *Hamilton v. Cannon*, 267 Ga. 655, 656; 482 S.E.2d 370 (1997). *See Dollar v. Dalton Public Schools*, 233 Ga. App. 827, 828; 505 S.E.2d 789 (1998), and *Doe v. McKenna*, 1998 R.I. Super. LEXIS 34 (1998). Other courts have found that a special relationship between an educator, as the parent-on-campus, and students places most lawsuits outside the parameters of the public duty doctrine. North Carolina courts have found a special relationship between students and a school crossing guard and a school resource officer. *See Isenhour v. Hutto*, 350 N.C. 601, 517 S.E.2d 121 (1999); *Smith v. Jackson County Bd. of Educ.*, 168 N.C. App. 452, 608 S.E.2d 399 (2005); and *Stoddard v. District of Columbia*, 623 A.2d 1152, 1993 D.C. App. LEXIS 91 (D.C. 1993). However, the doctrine has been successfully applied in a few cases. The public duty doctrine did apply to defeat a lawsuit by a student who was severely injured after school when he jumped over a stonewall in front of the school and landed on a snow bank. *Kuhl v. Perri*, 706 A.2d 1328, 1998 R.I. LEXIS 32 (R.I. 1998). And the public-duty doctrine was held to apply to the design of school-bus routes. *Houle v. Galloway Sch. Lines*, 643 A.2d 822, 1994 R.I. LEXIS 199 (R.I. 1994) (However, the court ruled that the doctrine did not insulate the school district from liability for the negligent operation of school buses.).

The public duty doctrine has been abrogated by a number of jurisdictions. *See, Adams v. State*, 555 P. 2d 235, 241-42 (Alaska 1976); *Ryan v. State*, 134 Ariz. 308, 310, 656 P. 2d 597 (1982); *Leake v. Cain*, 720 P. 2d 152, 158 (Colo. 1986); *Wilson v. Nepstad*, 282 N.W. 2d 664 (Iowa 1979); *Brennan v. Eugene*, 285 Or. 401, 409, 591 P.2d 719 (1979); *Petersen v. State*, 100 Wash. 2d 421, 432-33, 671 P. 2d 230 (1983). In these States the prevailing view is that the underlying purposes of the public duty doctrine are better served by the application of conventional tort principles and the protection afforded by statutes governing sovereign immunity than by a rule that precludes a finding of a duty based on a defendant's status as a public entity.

3. Educators Defenses to Liability: Immunity for Discretionary Acts

All public officials are liable for torts committed when acting in a ministerial capacity. However, under the official immunity doctrine, certain public officials acting within the scope of their policymaking authority are not liable for injuries arising from their discretionary acts or omissions.

An act is discretionary if,

> - that act necessarily requires the exercise of reason in the adaption of means to an end, and discretion in determining how or whether an act should be done or a course pursued.

An act is ministerial if the act is,

> - of a clerical nature which a public official is required to perform upon a given state of facts, in a prescribed manner, in obedience to the mandate of legal authority, without regard to his own judgment or opinion concerning the propriety of the act to be performed.

The United States Supreme Court has simplified the analysis of determining which acts are entitled to immunity by distinguishing acts performed at the planning level from acts performed at the operational level. *Dalehite v. United States*, 346 U.S. 15, 42, (1953). The Court in *Dalehite* reasoned that, "the "discretionary function or duty" that cannot form a basis for suit … includes more than the initiation of programs and activities. It also includes determinations made by executives or administrators in establishing plans, specifications or schedules. Where there is room for policy judgment and decision there is discretion." 346 U.S. at 42. A growing number of States have adopted this refinement to immunity for discretionary acts.

> The test for discretionary function immunity is a "planning-operational test." Under that test, a governmental entity is not liable for negligence arising from decisions, which are made at a planning level, as opposed to an operational level. Under the planning-operational test, if the decision of the governmental entity is a planning activity, that is a function involving the formulation of basic policy characterized by official judgment, discretion, weighing of alternatives, and public policy choices, then the decision is discretionary and immune. Government decisions about policy formation which involve assessment of competing priorities, a weighing of budgetary considerations, or the allocation of scarce resources are also planning activities. On the other hand, if the function is operational, for example, decisions regarding only the execution or implementation of already formulated policy, the function is not discretionary

> under the statute and no immunity attaches. *Madden v. Ind. DOT*, 832 N.E.2d 1122 (Ind. Ct. App. 2005)

For a range of cases involving this defense to liability, *see Santiago v. Cooper*, 2004 Tenn. App. LEXIS 329 (Tenn. Ct. App. 2004) (Teachers' decisions regarding the use of a plastic toy hammer at kindergarten recess and their care of an injured student were operational acts rather than discretionary functions). *Staack v. Indep. Sch. Dist.* No. 118, 2005 Minn. App. Unpub. LEXIS 484 (Minn. Ct. App. Unpub. 2005) (A student was punched by a fellow classmate in a hallway after class. School policy required teachers to be in the hallway observing students during changeovers. The court ruled that the negligent supervision arose from operational conduct). *Babb v. Hamilton County Bd. of Educ.*, 2004 Tenn. App. LEXIS 615 (Tenn. Ct. App., 2004) (A school principal's decision to place a student back in a teacher's classroom, despite a previous assault, was an exercise of discretion). *Orlando v. Broward County*, 920 So. 2d 54 (Fla. 4th DCA 2005) (School Board decision as to when to begin and end the school day was a discretionary, planning-level decision that defeated a lawsuit brought by a student injured while traveling to school).

4. Educators Defenses to Liability: Assumption of the Risk

The defense of assumption of the risk acts as a complete bar to a plaintiff's recovery due to a defendant's negligent act. This defense is particularly useful to educators in the context of school-sponsored activities such as sports because of the inherent risks of injury in such activities. The student who voluntarily participates in these sponsored activities is said to consent possibility of an injury.

In the education context, assumption of the risk works when school officials establish to things:

> (1) that the student had knowledge of the danger involved, and an appreciation for the magnitude of the danger. A subjective standard is used to prove this.
>
> (2) that the student voluntarily participated in the activity, despite the presence of the danger.

The doctrine of express assumption of risk is often present in school injury cases when a student signs a release of liability form before engaging in a school-sponsored activity. Such an express waiver acts as a complete bar to recovery by the student as long as the language of the waiver is sufficient and, therefore, valid as per the principles of contract law. However, many courts will not honor these releases when school officials are found to have engaged in reckless, grossly negligent, or intentionally tortious conduct. For example, if a coach knows or should have reason to know that a student athlete is injured and unable to compete, but, nonetheless, requires the student to compete, then courts may refuse to allow the coach and the school to utilize the defense of assumption of the risk.

For a set of interesting cases that involve the defense of assumption of the risk, *see, Perry v. Seattle School Dist.*, 66 Wn.2d 800, 405 P.2d 589, 1965 Wash. LEXIS 933 (1965) (A spectator's claim against the school district was properly dismissed because the school district was not negligent, and the spectator was contributorily negligent and assumed the risk while standing on the sidelines of a football game). *Aaris v. Las Virgenes Unified School Dist.*, 64 Cal. App. 4th 1112, 75 Cal. Rptr. 2d 801 (Cal. App. 2d Dist. 1998) (A high school cheerleader's injury claim was barred by assumption of the risk because the student's parents signed a waiver of liability). *Wagenblast v. Odessa School District*, 110 Wash.2d 845, 758 P.2d 968 (1988) (Public schools may not condition participation in interscholastic athletics on students releasing school district from all potential negligence claims). *Lilley v. Elk Grove Unified School Dist.*, 68 Cal. App. 4th 939, 80 Cal. Rptr. 2d 638 (Cal. App. 3d Dist. 1998) (A student wrestler's injury claim was barred by assumption of the risk).

For articles discussing the assumption of risk, *see* Symposium: Risk Management Issues in Sports: Effectiveness of Parental Waivers, Parental Indemnification Agreements, and Parental Arbitration Agreements as Risk Management Tools, 17 J. Legal Aspects of Sport 53 (2007). *See also*, Keya Denner: Taking One for the Team: The Role of Assumption of the Risk in Sports Torts Cases, 14 Seton Hall J. Sports & Ent. L. 209 (2004).

B. Statutory Remedies for Injuries

1. Federal Statutory Liability

FITZGERALD v. BARNSTABLE SCHOOL COMMITTEE
504 F. 3d 165 (1st Cir. 2007)

[This case appears in Chapter Eight on page 573]

STEVENSON EX REL. STEVENSON v. MARTIN COUNTY BOARD OF EDUCATION

3 F. App'x 25 (4th Cir. 2001)

PER CURIAM:

The complaint sets forth a disturbing set of facts, which we take as true. In August 1998 ten-year-old Alex Stevenson began the sixth grade at Williamston Middle School in Martin County, North Carolina. He did not finish the year there, however. In November his father had to remove him from Williamston Middle School and enroll him in a private school because of the repeated assaults Alex suffered at the hands of several of his classmates.

The abuse started as soon as the school year began. On August 7, 1998, the second day of school, Alex's sixth-grade classmates Charles McEachern and Kemadrick Terrell Sherrod robbed and assaulted Alex in the lunch yard. Several days later on August 10 Sherrod threw books at Alex, and Sherrod was subsequently suspended. On August 20 McEachern picked a fight with Alex in retaliation for Sherrod's suspension. The school suspended both McEachern and Alex because of this fight.

On August 20 Alex's father, Elmer William Stevenson ("Stevenson"), met with the principal of Williamston Middle School, Harry Respass. At this meeting Stevenson told Respass that McEachern was threatening Alex, and he (Stevenson) expressed his concern that McEachern and his friends would seek revenge on Alex. Stevenson then requested that the school remove Alex from McEachern's classes. Although Respass assured Stevenson that the boys would be placed in separate classes, this was not done.

For the next month (from mid-August to mid-September) McEachern continued to harass and intimidate Alex. As he walked past Alex's locker, McEachern would hit and kick Alex in the head, chest, and back. Alex and his father complained to Principal Respass and school counselor Babbie Mills about these assaults, but McEachern was neither disciplined nor removed from Alex's classes.

The situation reached a new low on September 18. Alex and McEachern were in Swanola Chance's first-period art class, and McEachern wrongly accused Alex of breaking his glasses. When Alex denied it, McEachern began to punch Alex in the head. Alex temporarily escaped from the attack and asked Chance for help, but she responded, "There isn't anything I can do." She added, "You probably deserved it anyway." Because he was receiving no help from Chance, Alex told her that he was going to the principal's office. McEachern and a friend, Broderick Jones, followed Alex out of the classroom and chased him down the hallway. They knocked Alex to the floor, and for about ten minutes proceeded to punch and kick him in the head, throat, chest, arms, and legs. Adele Dees, a teacher in a nearby classroom, tried to stop McEachern and Jones, but they assaulted her as well. Several students eventually restrained the two attackers.

McEachern and Jones were suspended, and for several weeks they attended a school for students with disciplinary problems. Principal Respass did not, however, report the assaults to the juvenile authorities. On September 21 Stevenson filed juvenile petitions against McEachern and Jones, alleging assault with infliction of serious bodily injury. In January 1999 McEachern and Jones admitted the charges and received sentences of twelve-month probation and community service.

While the juvenile proceedings were pending, the assaults on Alex continued. On September 22 three of McEachern's friends threatened Alex during his first-period class. Alex promptly reported the threats to Principal Respass, but that did not prevent McEachern and his friends from assaulting Alex later in the day during lunch. One of the lunchtime attackers was suspended from school. On September 25 McEachern and several of his friends harassed Alex and his father while they were at a music festival in Williamston. The police intervened and escorted McEachern from the scene. Stevenson finally decided that because of the assaults and harassment, Alex would have to transfer to private school.

Alex suffered physical and emotional problems because of the repeated assaults and harassment. After the September 18 assault a doctor treated him for contusions, lacerations, and temporary eye dysfunction. A psychologist diagnosed Alex with major depression and attention deficit/hyperactivity disorder, and Alex began taking medication. He continues to receive counseling for his psychological problems.

****

III.

Alex ... argues that the defendants violated the Safe and Drug-Free Schools and Communities Act of 1994 (Safe Schools Act), 20 U.S.C. §§ 7101-04, 7111-43, by failing to develop an appropriate school safety plan that would help control student-on-student violence. The Safe Schools Act is a federal grant program that aims to prevent violence and drug abuse in schools. These goals are accomplished through federal assistance to states so that they can make grants to local educational agencies and community organizations. Federal money also goes to fund private, non-profit organizations and colleges and universities that develop anti-violence and anti-drug initiatives. *See* 20 U.S.C. § 7103. The Act does not expressly create a private right of action. Therefore, we must determine whether Alex has an implied right to maintain a Safe Schools Act claim.

In answering this question, we must first decide if the Act grants Alex any substantive rights. For a person to bring a claim under conditional spending legislation, the statute must confer substantive rights in favor of the class to which the person belongs. *See Pennhurst State Sch. & Hosp. v. Halderman*, 451 U.S. 1 (1981). Substantive rights are created only if Congress provided the recipients of federal funding clear notice that by accepting funds, they have chosen to participate in a statutory scheme under which private individuals gain enforceable rights. *See id.* at 24-25. Because the Safe Schools Act was enacted pursuant to the Spending Clause, Alex's claim will be allowed only if the statute puts funding recipients on notice of a private right of action.

.....

Unlike Title IX, the Safe Schools Act does not put schools on notice that they can be sued for failing to implement anti-violence programs. Alex has not pointed to anything in the language or purpose of the Act that would suggest otherwise. The Department of Education has not promulgated any regulations pursuant to the Act. Furthermore, no court has held that the Safe Schools Act creates a private right of action in any situation, whereas for Title IX, it had already been established before Davis that Title IX creates a cause of action for damages when the school officials themselves engage in the discriminatory conduct. *See Franklin v. Gwinnett County Pub. Schs.*, 503 U.S. 60 1992); *Cannon v. University of Chicago*, 441 U.S. 677 (1979).

The fact that the common law might allow suits against schools for student-on-student violence does not help Stevenson either. The Court in Davis placed little, if any, emphasis on the common law in reaching the conclusion that Title IX gave schools notice of a private right of action for student-on-student harassment. It only mentioned the common law after discussing the language, purpose, and regulations of Title IX. There is nothing in *Davis* to suggest that the common law alone could put the recipient of federal funds on notice that a Spending Clause statute creates a private right of action. We hold that because the Safe Schools Act does not put schools on notice of the creation of an enforceable substantive right, Alex cannot bring a Safe Schools Act claim.

S.S. v. EASTERN KENTUCKY UNIVERSITY
532 F. 3d 445 (6th Cir. 2008)

RONALD LEE GILMAN, Circuit Judge.

From 2000 to 2003, S.S. was a student at the Model Laboratory Middle School (Model), which is operated by Eastern Kentucky University (EKU) to train student teachers under the supervision of certified teachers. S.S. has various disabilities, including cerebral palsy, attention deficit/hyperactivity disorder, dyslexia, pervasive developmental disorder, and post-traumatic stress disorder. During his attendance at Model, S.S. was involved in numerous physical and verbal altercations with other students, leading S.S. to complain that he was being bullied and harassed. Model investigated the incidents as they occurred, determining that some were initiated by S.S. and some were initiated by other students. In response, Model took various steps as the school administration deemed appropriate, including interviewing S.S. and his classmates, disciplining the students that it found to be culpable, monitoring S.S., and at times separating S.S. from his harassers.

S.S. left Model after successfully completing the sixth, seventh, and eighth grades. He subsequently filed suit against EKU, Model's director Jacqueline Vance, and Model's psychologist Ellen Rini, alleging that the defendants had discriminated against him on the basis of his disability, in violation of both federal and state law.

A. Factual background

The district court summarized this case as arising "out of a long and unfortunate string of incidents that occurred during Plaintiff's time at Model. . . . [T]he core of all of Plaintiff's allegations is the failure of Model and its administrators, particularly Vance and Rini, to adequately respond to those incidents and maintain a safe educational environment for Plaintiff." *S.S. v. E. Ky. Univ.*, 431 F. Supp. 2d 718, 722-23 (E.D. Ky. 2006). Because the district court's 32-page opinion and order granting summary judgment in favor of the defendants sets forth an accurate description of the numerous incidents that underlie S.S.'s claims, we need not repeat them here. As will be discussed in Part II below, the key issue in this case is not the specific details of each confrontation between S.S. and his peers, but rather the overall adequacy of Model's response to those confrontations.

B. Procedural background

S.S. filed suit in the district court in January of 2003, alleging numerous claims under federal and state law against EKU as an entity and against Vance and Rini in both their individual and official capacities. (The defendants will henceforth be collectively referred to as "Model.") S.S. contended that Model's conduct in disciplining and monitoring him, its failure to respond to and adequately investigate his complaints of discrimination and harassment, and its failure to discipline and monitor the students who harassed him constituted discrimination on the basis of his disability, in violation of both Title II of the Americans with Disabilities Act of 1990 (the ADA), 42 U.S.C. § 12132, and Section 504 of the Rehabilitation Act of 1973 (§ 504), 29 U.S.C. § 794.

****

C. Claims under the ADA and § 504

S.S. framed his ADA and § 504 claims as asserting two types of violations. First, he claimed that Model's actions in responding to and investigating his complaints of discrimination and harassment, as well as in monitoring and disciplining him and his alleged harassers, were discriminatory. Second, he claimed that the peer-on-peer harassment he experienced created a hostile learning environment, and that Model failed to adequately protect him from it. The district court analyzed the ADA and § 504 claims accordingly, but ultimately concluded that, under a bad-faith and gross-misjudgment standard of conduct, Model was entitled to summary judgment.

Title II of the ADA provides that "no qualified individual with a disability shall, by reason of such disability, be excluded from participation in or be denied the benefits of the services, programs, or activities of a public entity, or be subjected to discrimination by any such entity." 42 U.S.C. § 12132. Section 504 of the Rehabilitation Act likewise provides that "[n]o otherwise qualified individual with a disability in the United States …shall, solely by reason of her or his disability, be excluded from the participation in, be denied the benefits of, or be subjected to discrimination under any program or activity receiving Federal financial assistance." 29 U.S.C. § 794(a).

"Apart from [§ 504's] limitation to denials of benefits 'solely' by reason of disability and its reach of only federally funded—as opposed to 'public'—entities, the reach and requirements of both statutes are precisely the same." *Weixel v. Bd. of Educ. of N.Y.*, 287 F.3d 138, 146 n.6 (2d Cir. 2002). Neither of these differences between the ADA and § 504 is at issue in S.S.'s case. We will therefore analyze S.S.'s ADA and § 504 claims together. *See Thompson v. Williamson County*, 219 F.3d 555, 557 n.3 (6th Cir. 2000) (noting that the plaintiff's ADA and § 504 claims may be analyzed together because the statutes provide the same remedies, procedures, and rights); *see also Maddox v. Univ. of Tenn.*, 62 F.3d 843, 846 n.2 (6th Cir. 1995) (concluding that the protections under the ADA parallel the protections available under the Rehabilitation Act, so that the court's reasoning with respect to the Rehabilitation Act "applied with equal force to the ADA claim").

Accordingly, a plaintiff seeking to state a claim under either the ADA or § 504 against a school receiving federal financial assistance must show that he or she is (1) disabled under the statute, (2) "otherwise qualified" for participation in the program, and (3) being excluded from participation in, denied the benefits of, or subjected to discrimination under the program by reason of his or her disability. *Maddox*, 62 F.3d at 846. The discrimination requirement

> is rooted in two parts of the statute's text: plaintiffs must prove that they have either been subjected to discrimination or excluded from a program or denied benefits solely by reason of their disability. To prove discrimination in the education context, something more than a mere failure to provide the free appropriate education required by [the IDEA] must be shown.
>
> *Sellers v. Sch. Bd. of Manassas*, 141 F.3d 524, 528-29 (4th Cir. 1998) (internal quotation marks omitted).

Although S.S. framed his ADA and § 504 allegations as raising two different types of claims—discriminatory responses to the harassment and, separately, a failure to respond to the harassment—all of his claims arise from the same allegations of peer-on-peer harassment. We therefore analyze them as asserting a disability-based peer-on-peer harassment claim.

****

The Supreme Court in *Davis* determined that schools "are properly held liable in damages only where they are deliberately indifferent to sexual harassment, of which they have actual knowledge that is so severe, pervasive, and objectively offensive that it can be said to deprive the victims of access to the educational opportunities or benefits provided by the school." *Davis*, 526 U.S. at 650. Title IX provides that "[n]o person in the United States shall, on the basis of sex, be excluded from participation in, be denied the benefits of, or be subjected to discrimination under any education program or activity receiving Federal financial assistance." 20 U.S.C. § 1681(a). A school district that is sued for peer-on-peer harassment, the Supreme Court explained, is not held liable for the actions of the harassing students, but instead is held liable for its own "deliberate indifference" to the students' harassing acts. *Id.* at 641-42.

The facts alleged in *Davis* showed that the school district was aware that a male high-school student had engaged in repeated acts of sexual harassment toward a female classmate over a five-month period, including verbal harassment and "numerous acts of objectively offensive touching," but that the school had "made no effort whatsoever either to investigate or to put an end to the harassment." *Id.* at 653-54. The Court held that the plaintiff's allegations survived the school's motion to dismiss because "[t]he district's knowing refusal to take any action in response to such behavior would fly in the face of Title IX's core principles, and such deliberate indifference may appropriately be subject to claims for monetary damages." *Id.* at 651.

The most recent federal court to apply *Davis* to a disability-based peer-on-peer harassment claim articulated the following five-part test that must be met to impose liability:

> (1) the plaintiff is an individual with a disability, (2) he or she was harassed based on that disability, (3) the harassment was sufficiently severe or pervasive that it altered the condition of his or her education and created an abusive educational environment, (4) the defendant knew about the harassment, and (5) the defendant was deliberately indifferent to the harassment.

Werth, 472 F. Supp. 2d at 1127 (citing *K.M.*, 381 F. Supp. 2d at 359 (articulating the same five-part test), and *Biggs*, 229 F. Supp. 2d 437 (same)). Applying this test to the present case, S.S. must show that (1) he was an individual with a disability, (2) he was harassed based on his disability, (3) the harassment was sufficiently severe or pervasive that it altered the condition of his education and created an abusive educational environment, (4) Model knew about the harassment, and (5) Model was deliberately indifferent to the harassment. *See Biggs*, 229 F. Supp. 2d at 445 (citing *Davis*, 526 U.S. at 650).

The parties do not dispute that the first and fourth prongs are satisfied. And although questions of fact exist regarding the second and third prongs, we need not address them because, as the following analysis bears out, we conclude that Model was not deliberately indifferent (under the fifth prong) to the peer-on-peer harassment at issue here.

S.S. alleges that Vance and Rini denied that a bullying problem existed and that they failed to consider the possibility that he was not the source of the problem. These allegations, however, are not only unsupported by the record, but are squarely contradicted by it. The record shows that Model responded to all of the alleged incidents involving S.S. of which it was made aware, and that its responses included conducting individual and group interviews with S.S.'s classmates in an attempt to determine who was at fault, instructing S.S.'s classmates not to taunt him, arranging for outside speakers to talk to the students about name-calling, identifying related topics for discussion at school assemblies and in small groups, monitoring S.S., at times separating S.S. from other students who had been involved in the altercations, holding a mediation session between S.S. and another student, disciplining both S.S. and the other students who were found to be at fault, calling the police, having the police talk to an offending student, and calling the other students' and S.S.'s parents to discuss the disciplinary problems. Indeed, S.S. does not dispute that Model responded by taking the foregoing actions—although he argues that such actions were discriminatory.

The cases of *K.M.* and *Biggs* are instructive in determining whether Model's actions evinced a deliberate indifference to S.S.'s situation. In *K.M.*, a disabled child had repeatedly been subjected to verbal abuse and physical attacks over the course of two middle-school years, including disability-related slurs. The student and his mother reported each incident to the school, but school officials initially took no action to protect him from further harassment. After the student was beaten up on a school bus, the school advised his mother to keep him out of school for an indeterminate period of time, but provided no educational services for him. Furthermore, no one was disciplined in connection with the incidents, which caused the student to become suicidal. He subsequently sued the school under the ADA and § 504 for inadequately responding to the peer-on-peer disability-based harassment. The district court denied the school's motion for summary judgment, concluding that triable issues of fact existed with respect to the school district's lack of response to the student's repeated complaints. 381 F. Supp. 2d at 348-51, 360-61; *see also Davis*, 526 U.S. at 653-54 (reversing the district court's grant of the school's motion to dismiss where the harassment was reported to school authorities, but no disciplinary action was taken in response and no effort was made to separate the harasser from the plaintiff).

Biggs similarly involved a disabled student and her mother who reported incidents of harassment to school administrators. But in *Biggs* the school took action each time, including counseling the child, meeting with the offending students, sending letters to parents, threatening the offenders with suspension, and alerting teachers to the problem. Concluding that such responses established that the school was not deliberately indifferent to the harassment, the court granted the school's motion for summary judgment. 229 F. Supp. 2d at 445.

Model, unlike the schools in *K.M.* and *Davis*, took the affirmative steps described above to address the incidents of harassment involving S.S. And Model's actions closely mirrored those of the school in *Biggs*—specifically, meeting with the students, communicating with parents, and disciplining the offending students. In sum, this case is easily distinguishable from *Davis* and *K.M.* Even viewing the record in the light most favorable to S. S., proof is lacking as to what Model could have or should have done differently in order to bring the peer-on-peer harassment to a stop. The record in this case does not give rise to an inference that Model was deliberately indifferent to S. S.'s situation or that it had an attitude of permissiveness that amounted to discrimination.

As for S.S.'s claim that Model's responses to the harassment—including the investigation, discipline, and monitoring of S.S.—were discriminatory, the district court aptly observed that S.S.'s allegations suffer from a fundamental flaw: "According to Plaintiff, virtually everything Defendants did in response to incidents was discriminatory, including the actions Defendants took that were the opposite of other actions that Plaintiff also claims were discriminatory." The district court further explained that the incidents that S.S. raised as examples of purportedly disparate treatment of himself as compared to other students who also complained of harassment do not support a finding that Vance and Rini discriminated against S. S. by reason of his disability. After Model investigated the various complaints lodged by S. S. and by other students, it concluded that the circumstances of each incident were different with respect to the level and type of harassment and who was involved, thus warranting different responses. We find no fault with the district court's reasoning on this issue and therefore affirm its grant of summary judgment to Model on all of S.S.'s ADA and § 504 claims.........

---

2. State Statutory Liability

CLAUSING v. SAN FRANCISCO UNIFIED SCHOOL DISTRICT

271 Cal. Rptr. 72 (Ct. App. 1990)

OPINION BY: MERRILL

Robert Clausing, Brian Clausing as guardian ad litem for Robert Clausing, and Betty Simmerman (the mother of Robert) appeal from an order sustaining a [dismissal] without leave to amend to the class action allegations and to the cause of action for breach of mandatory duty under Government Code section 815.6 ...against respondents San Francisco Unified School District (the District), San Francisco Board of Education, Louise Lombard School, Joan Michaels, and Henry A. Caruso.

I. Procedural Background

The complaint alleged, inter alia, that from September through November 1986, appellant Robert Clausing was a 20-year-old physically handicapped and mentally retarded student at a special school for the handicapped in a class taught by respondent Joan Michaels at respondent Louise Lombard School; that during that time, respondent Michaels repeatedly subjected appellant Robert Clausing to physical, psychological, and verbal abuse, beatings, and public humiliation; that as a result appellant Robert Clausing suffered severe physical, mental, emotional, and psychological injury and damages; and that the respondent District authorized or failed to prevent the physical, mental, emotional, and psychological abuse inflicted by teachers and other employees on appellant Robert Clausing and other students similarly situated. The complaint sought damages and "such equitable, legal or injunctive relief as the court may deem appropriate" on behalf of appellants and of a purported class of "all persons similarly situated" under various causes of action for assault and battery, intentional and negligent infliction of emotional distress, and negligence.

.....

III. Demurrer to Action for Breach of Mandatory Duty

.....

In "Count One" of their [lawsuit], appellants allege that respondents breached their "duty to secure to the [appellants] their inalienable right to attend campuses which are safe, secure and peaceful as mandated by Article I, Section 28 of the California Constitution." Appellants are relying on a broad interpretation of the safe schools provision of the California Constitution, adopted by initiative as part of "The Victims' Bill of Rights." This provision states:

> Right to Safe Schools. All students and staff of public primary, elementary, junior high and senior high schools have the inalienable right to attend campuses which are safe, secure and peaceful. (Cal. Const., art. I, § 28, subd. (c) (hereafter section 28, subdivision (c)).)

...Under article I, section 26, of the California Constitution, all provisions of the state Constitution "are mandatory and prohibitory, unless by express words they are declared to be otherwise."

Unquestionably, section 28, subdivision (c), is mandatory. Thus, all agencies of government are required to comply with it, and are prohibited from taking official actions which violate it or contravene its provisions. ...However, it is an entirely different matter to conclude that section 28, subdivision (c), is self-executing in the sense that it establishes an affirmative duty to act on the part of school districts, provides remedies for its violation, or creates a private cause of action for damages. "The following rule has been consistently applied in California to determine whether a constitutional provision is self-executing in the sense of providing a specific method for its enforcement:

> '"A constitutional provision may be said to be self-executing if it supplies a sufficient rule by means of which the right given may be enjoyed and protected, or the duty imposed may be enforced; and it is not self-executing when it merely indicates principles, without laying down rules by means of which those principles may be given the force of law."' "[Citations.]" (*Leger v. Stockton Unified School Dist., supra,* 202 Cal.App. 3d at p. 1455.)

As stated in the recent opinion of the Court of Appeal, Third Appellate District, in Leger v. Stockton Unified School Dist., supra, 202 Cal.App.3d 1448, with which we are in agreement, "section 28(c) declares a general right without specifying any rules for its enforcement. It imposes no express duty on anyone to make schools safe. It is wholly devoid of guidelines, mechanisms, or procedures from which a damages remedy could be inferred. Rather, '"it merely indicates principles, without laying down rules by means of which those principles may be given the force of law."' "[Citation.]" (*Id.*, at p. 1455, fn. omitted.) There is nothing in the legislative history of section 28, subdivision (c), to suggest that it was intended to create a civil action for damages or an affirmative duty to insure that schools are free from all risk of crime and violence. The right proclaimed in section 28, subdivision (c), although inalienable and mandatory, simply establishes the parameters of the principle enunciated; the specific means by which it is to be achieved for the people of California are left to the Legislature.

Thus, we conclude that section 28, subdivision (c), is not self-executing, in the sense that it does not provide an independent basis for a private right of action for damages. Neither does it impose an express affirmative duty on any government agency to guarantee the safety of schools. (*Leger v. Stockton Unified School Dist., supra,* 202 Cal. App. 3d at pp. 1453-57; *Halliman v. Los Angeles Unified School Dist.* (1984) 163 Cal. App. 3d 46, 52 [209 Cal. Rptr. 175].)

SNETHEN v. BOARD OF EDUCATION

No. 406CV259, 2007 U.S. Dist. LEXIS 59784 (S.D. Ga. 2007)

OPINION BY: B. AVANT EDENFIELD

I. BACKGROUND

This case arises from an 11/15/03 attack on Tamatha Snethen by a fellow student at Jenkins High School in Savannah, Georgia. Tamatha originally brought this action through her mother, Brenda Snethen, against The Board of Public Education for the City of Savannah and the County of Chatham ("Board"), alleging a violation of Title IX of the Education Amendments Act of 1972, 20 U.S.C. § 1681-88. She also pursues members of the Board in their individual capacities, alleging violations of Georgia law.

Boiled down, Tamatha complains that the defendants failed to protect her from sexual and other harassment. The defendants, she says, also maintained a hostile learning environment. ... [she was] violently assaulted [and] sexually molested.

B. Snethen's State Law Claims

She alleges that the individual defendants were negligent in their failure to prepare a school safety plan as required by Georgia law. O.C.G.A. § 20-2-1185 ("Every public school shall prepare a school safety plan...."). The defendants argued that there can be no negligence because they had no individual duty to enact a school safety plan.

This Court noted that in *Leake v. Murphy*, 274 Ga. App. 219, 617 S.E. 2d 575 (2005), like here, a student was attacked and injured at school, and her parents brought an action against the individual members of the relevant board of education and the Superintendent of the area schools. *Id.* at 219. But the *Leake* plaintiffs, unlike here, also sued the school principal and staff on duty at the time of the attack. *Id.* at 220. The trial court dismissed the case against all defendants on official immunity grounds. *Id.*

Reversing, the Georgia Court of Appeals ruled that the legislature conferred an absolute, ministerial duty to prepare a school safety on the Superintendent and on the individual board members. *Id.* at 222. The board members and Superintendent therefore were not entitled to immunity because "official immunity does not apply to the performance of ministerial duties." *Id.* at 221. Thus, while the case could not proceed against the principal and staff, it could proceed against the individual board members and Superintendent. *Id.* at 224.

Leake, however, has since been overruled by *Murphy v. Bajjani*, 282 Ga. 197, 647 S.E. 2d 54 (6/25/07). There a high-school student's parents brought an action against a county school district, board of education, board members, superintendent, and school officials, seeking award of damages for injuries suffered by their son, who had been assaulted by fellow student. 282 Ga. 197; 647 S.E. 2d 54.

Overruling Leake, the Murphy court ruled that the very same action mandated by O.C.G.A. § 20-2-1185—requiring the school board and superintendent to prepare a school safety plan—in fact is a discretionary, not ministerial duty, for purposes of official immunity. 282 Ga. 197; 647 S.E. 2d 54. Leave therefore is granted to the defendants to again challenge *Snethen*'s § 20-2-1185-based claim, via summary disposition. Should there be no opposition; the Court would welcome a Consent Dismissal Order.

KING v. NORTHEAST SECURITY, INC.
790 N.E. 2d 474 (Ind. 2003)

RUCKER, Justice

In this appeal, we hold that a school district is not immune from a claim that the district failed to take reasonable steps to provide security for persons on its premises. We further hold that a security service employed by a school district may be liable for negligence in carrying out its contractually assumed obligations.

After some incidents of criminal mischief during the previous two years, the Assistant Superintendent for the Metropolitan School District of Washington Township ("the District") entered into a contract with Northeast Security, Inc. ("Northeast") for security services at North Central High School in the 1995-1996 school year. Specifically, Northeast was to provide three uniformed Special Deputies positioned outside the school in marked white security vehicles from 7:00 a.m. to 3:30 p.m. The Special Deputies were to perform the following duties:

> Provide exterior patrols at checkpoints for all North Central High School buildings by the means of three vehicle patrols occupied by three Marion County Special Deputies provided and employed by Northeast Security. These officers are trained personnel and understand the procedures of patrol. They will also be responsible for insuring all personnel that enter the premises are possessing the proper identification. They are to be observant of any criminal activity which may occur in the parking lots and to the exterior of the building..... Northeast was to be paid $6,375 every two weeks for these services.

On April 18, 1996, the Northeast employee posted in the parking lot was inside the school building making a personal telephone call when classes were dismissed at 3:00 p.m. As Nicholas King stood in the school parking lot waiting for a ride home with another student, a large crowd approached. After a verbal exchange, the crowd increased and some began yelling and screaming. Ultimately a student struck King, and then others joined in. Finally, someone yelled that the police were coming and the crowd of students quickly dispersed. One eyewitness stated he was one of the last students to leave and never saw the police. As a result of the beating, King suffered two fractures to his jaw as well as several lacerations and bruises to his head and body.

King sued both Northeast and the District.

.....

The Court of Appeals reversed the trial court's grant of summary judgment in favor of the District, finding the District owed a duty to exercise reasonable care for the safety of students under its authority. The District concedes that it had this general duty, but contends that the District is protected by governmental immunity under the Tort Claims Act and a common law doctrine that there is no duty to protect against criminal activity of others. In the alternative, the District argues that even if it is not immune, there is no breach of duty because the District took reasonable steps for the safety of its students.

Indiana, like many jurisdictions, over the years found the doctrine [of sovereign immunity] increasingly unsatisfactory. In 1972, in Campbell v. State, 259 Ind. 55, 284 N.E.2d 733, 736-37 (1972), this Court concluded that the doctrine of sovereign immunity was an outmoded concept in today's society, and suggested that the proper forum for any debate over governmental immunity was the legislature. Accordingly, Campbell held that governmental units would generally no longer be shielded by sovereign immunity. Id. However, Campbell cited three situations where a governmental unit would remain immune from liability for acts or omissions that result in personal injuries. These were: (1) where a city or state fails to provide adequate police protection to prevent crime; (2) where a state official makes an appointment of an individual whose incompetent performance gives rise to a suit alleging negligence on the part of the state official for making such an appointment; and (3) where judicial decision-making is challenged. Id. at 737.

In response to Campbell, in 1974 the Indiana legislature enacted the Indiana Tort Claims Act ("ITCA") which identified a list of governmental activities, now twenty-two in number, that are immunized from tort liability. See Ind. Code § 34-13-3-3. After a number of detours since that time, Campbell was largely reaffirmed in Benton v. City of Oakland City, 721 N.E.2d 224 (Ind. 1999). Thus, some common law immunity doctrines remain despite the ITCA's codification of much of Indiana's governmental immunity law.

Benton spoke in terms of duty rather than immunity:

> We hold that Campbell is properly applied by presuming that a governmental unit is bound by the same duty of care as a non-governmental unit except where the duty alleged to have been breached is so closely akin to one of the limited exceptions (prevent crime, appoint competent officials, or make correct judicial decisions) that it should be treated as one as well. Id. at 230.

Benton held that under common law, governmental units have "the same duty of care as non-governmental entities," with the exception of the three Campbell areas. In immunity terms, the governmental unit is immune under the common law only if it is engaged in an activity closely related to one of the three areas identified in Campbell.

.....

We have held repeatedly that school districts can be held liable for failure to take reasonable steps to provide security for their students. *Mangold v. Ind. Dep't of Natural Res.*, 756 N.E. 2d 970, 974 (Ind. 2001); *Beckett v. Clinton Prairie Sch. Corp.*, 504 N.E. 2d 552, 553 (Ind. 1987); *Norman v. Turkey Run*

Cmty. Sch. Corp., 274 Ind. 310, 411 N.E.2d 614, 617 (1980); *Miller v. Griesel*, 261 Ind. 604, 308 N.E. 2d 701, 706 (1974). In *Benton* duty terms, the school district has a duty to take reasonable steps for the protection of its students. In immunity terms, failure to take reasonable safety precautions is not within the common law immunity for failure to prevent crime.

.....

It is a matter for the legislature to the extent that school districts or other governmental agencies whose mission is not law enforcement are exposed to undesired liability. To the extent the District asserts common law immunity, we think the school's activities here are more "closely akin" to those of landowners or businesses generally that must provide reasonable security for their patrons and guests. *See Delta Tau Delta, Beta Alpha Chapter v. Johnson*, 712 N.E. 2d 968, 974 (Ind. 1999). Indeed, there is specific precedent on this point. *See Miller*, 308 N.E. 2d at 706 (recognizing that school authorities must exercise reasonable care and supervision for the safety of the children under their control).

In sum, we do not think the common law confers blanket immunity for every school and every other governmental entity that fails to take reasonable precautions for the safety of persons or their facilities. If the Campbell exception extended as far as the District proposes, it would grant immunity to any and all governmental units that fail to arrange reasonable security. Like many governmental units ... the District's principal mission is not to prevent crime. Indeed, Campbell itself appears to limit its law enforcement immunity to "cities and states" that understand their role as providing general police protection throughout the jurisdiction. *Campbell*, 284 N.E.2d at 737.

.....

The [School] District is a governmental entity within the meaning of the ITCA 3 and therefore enjoys the immunity conferred by the statute pursuant to Indiana Code section 34-6-2-49. Section 3(9) provides, "A governmental entity or an employee acting within the scope of the employee's employment is not liable if a loss results from . . . the act or omission of anyone other than the governmental entity or the governmental entity's employee."

Section 9 immunity applies in "actions seeking to impose vicarious liability by reason of conduct of third parties" other than governmental employees acting within the scope of their employment. *Hinshaw v. Bd. of Comm'rs of Jay County*, 611 N.E. 2d 637, 640-41 (Ind. 1993). "Under such circumstances, the alleged basis of governmental entity liability is the act or omission of a third person not within the scope of employment as a government employee." *Id.* at 641.

The District is correct that "a principal is not liable for the negligence of an independent contractor." *Bagley v. Insight Communications Co., L.P.*, 658 N.E. 2d 584, 586 (Ind. 1995). And the District is also correct that the statute does more for governmental entities than the common law does for others. Thus, the District contends that it is immune to the extent liability is predicated on the act or omission of Northeast or Northeast's employees. However, there is a dispute of fact over whether the injuries King suffered were caused by an act or omission of Northeast or by the District itself. One of King's allegations is that the District was negligent because the Assistant Vice Principal Bart Austin, who normally stayed outside the school building to personally monitor the students' departure, was absent the day of King's incident and did not find a replacement. The District has not shown as a matter of law that its conduct comes within the Act. Accordingly, summary judgment for the District on the basis of section 3(9) is inappropriate.

The District also relies on section 3(7) of the ITCA for its claim of immunity. That section provides:

> A governmental entity or an employee acting within the scope of the employee's employment is not liable if a loss results from . . . the adoption and enforcement of or failure to adopt or enforce a law (including rules and regulations), unless the act of enforcement constitutes false arrest or false imprisonment. I.C. § 34-13-3-3(7).
>
> The District argues it is immune pursuant to section 3(7) because "the [District] failed to prevent an assault or battery, or failed to enforce a rule or regulation (student misconduct, substantial disobedience or unlawful activity)."

In *Quakenbush v. Lackey*, 622 N.E. 2d 1284, 1288-91 (Ind. 1993), this Court discussed at some length the meaning of "enforcement" as used in section 3(7). We concluded first that section 3(7) was intended to codify the common law of immunity in this area as that law existed at the time the ITCA was passed. Second, under that common law regime, governments and their employees were subject to liability for "the breach of private duties owed to individuals, but were immune from liability for the breach of public duties owed to the public at large." *Id.* at 1291. Subsequent Indiana decisions relied on this public/private duty test in applying section 3(7), but others have concluded *Benton* eliminated the test. As explained in Part I.A., *Benton* addressed only the common law presence or absence of duty of a governmental unit. It did not deal with statutory immunity under the ITCA. Indeed, *Benton* expressly observed, "In general, it is only after a determination is made that a governmental defendant is not immune under the ITCA that a court undertakes the analysis of whether a common law duty exists under the circumstances." *Benton*, 721 N.E. 2d at 232.

Although *Benton* did not expressly disavow *Quakenbush*'s public/private duty test under section 3(7), we believe it implicitly achieved this result. *Quakenbush* held that section 3(7) adopted the common law of immunity for law enforcement activities, and concluded that the public/private duty test was the common law approach to law enforcement immunity at the time the ITCA was enacted. We do not believe the public/private duty test was frozen by statutory adoption. It is a tool for applying the "adopting or enforcing of a law" language, but as *Benton* pointed out, this test is frequently not susceptible to ready application. *Id.* For that reason, *Benton* overruled the public/private duty test at common law. We think the courts remain free to interpret the statutory language without referring to the public/private duty analysis when appropriate.

We think the statute itself provides the key to resolution of the immunity issue in this case. Section 3(7) confers immunity on governmental units for "the adoption and enforcement of or failure to adopt or enforce a law." We think this language restricts the immunity to the adoption and enforcement of laws that are within the assignment of the governmental unit. First, it is clear that "laws" include "rules and regulations." Thus, a variety of administrative and executive functions engage in some immunized activities. But not all actions are immunized. The statute refers to immunity for the "adoption and enforcement" of a law. Only a unit charged with regulating the areas of law involved can "adopt" a law. Similarly, the "enforcement" of a law is an activity assigned to specific units of government: the police, the Board of Health, etc. The immunity for failure to "adopt" or "enforce" is similarly limited.

We think this interpretation is supported by the language of section 3(7) and is also consistent with other provisions of the ITCA and existing case law. An employee is protected under the terms of section 3 of the ITCA only if "acting within the scope of the employee's employment." I.C. § 34-13-3-3. Similarly, case law has held that the ITCA expresses a legislative policy to protect the State's finances and also to ensure "'that public employees can exercise their independent judgment necessary to carry out their duties without threat of hamade within the scope of their employment.'" *Celebration Fireworks, Inc. v. Smith*, 727 N.E. 2d 450, 452 (Ind. 2000) (quoting *Ind. Dep't of Corr. v. Stagg*, 556 N.E. 2d 1338, 1343 (Ind. Ct. App. 1990), trans. *denied*). *See also Martin v. Heffelfinger*, 744 N.E. 2d 555, 559 (Ind. Ct. App. 2001); *Ind. State Police Dep't v. Swaggerty*, 507 N.E. 2d 649, 651-52 (Ind. Ct. App. 1987), trans. *denied*; *Bd. of Comm'rs of Hendricks County v. King*, 481 N.E. 2d 1327, 1330 (Ind. Ct. App. 1985). An employee's scope of employment consists of activities involving the pursuit of the governmental entity's purpose. Similarly, we think the legislature intended that a governmental entity be immune only for failing to adopt or enforce a law that falls within the scope of the entity's purpose or operational power.

Case law supports the notion that section 3(7) is limited to those laws, rules, or regulations that fall within the realm of the governmental entity. *Stagg*, 556 N.E. 2d at 1342 ("The defendants were acting within the scope of their employment in enforcing laws, rules or regulations pertaining to the standards and procedures for the operation of the correctional facilities pursuant to [the Indiana statute]."); *City of Seymour v. Onyx Paving Co., Inc.*, 541 N.E. 2d 951, 958 (Ind. Ct. App. 1989) ("The zoning ordinance at issue here is part of the municipal code of Seymour [and] adopted in accordance with [the Indiana act] delegating to local legislative bodies the authority to enact zoning ordinances and amendments thereto."), trans. *denied*; *Ind. Dep't of Natural Res. v. Taylor*, 419 N.E. 2d 819, 823 (Ind. Ct. App. 1981) ("Insomuch as this action was undertaken by the Department pursuant to a duty entrusted to it by statute, it qualifies for immunity under [subsections (5), (6), or (7)].").

We do not think a school district is "enforcing" a law when it provides for school security, even if the action taken may deter or prevent acts that would violate a law "adopted" and "enforced" by other units of government. It is correct, as the District points out schools are authorized to promulgate rules for school discipline. But preventing crime is not an activity schools are expected to carry out pursuant to a school's operational purpose. Put another way, even though the school must reasonably supervise the students for safety reasons, it is not the mission of the school to prevent crime. Indeed, the statutes the Indiana legislature enacted on behalf of the elementary and secondary schools providing for student discipline authorize disciplinary rules "reasonably necessary to carry out the school purposes." I.C. § 20-8.1-5.1-7(c). Schools have the power to expel or suspend students for student misconduct or unlawful activity and can claim immunity for doing so or failing to do so. But we think a school has no immunity for failing to prevent an assault and battery. It has the obligation to ake reasonable steps to provide security on its premises, even if it has not adopted any rules or regulations prohibiting assaults. As the District stated in its brief, "Law enforcement is not a traditional responsibility of the School." Appellee's Br. in Supp. of Pet. to Trans. at 16. Accordingly, immunity for "enforcement" of laws prohibiting an assault and battery is reserved to governmental units with police powers—not schools.

The District relies on *Klobuchar v. Purdue Univ.*, 553 N.E. 2d 169 (Ind. Ct. App. 1990), in claiming it is immune under section 3(7). In *Klobuchar*, the plaintiff, a part-time student at Purdue University, was seriously injured when attacked by her estranged husband after class. When the plaintiff was attacked, she was parked in a campus parking lot that required vehicles to exhibit a school parking ticket. The campus police routinely checked vehicles in the lot for permits. The plaintiff claimed her injuries were proximately caused by the University's failure to provide adequate security for the school's parking lot. The University moved for summary judgment claiming it was immune under the ITCA. *Id.* at 170. The court found that the University was given the authority to provide campus security by statute, and the decision to provide security or to patrol the parking lot for permit violators is a decision on whether or not to enforce the law. *Id.* at 173. Relying in part on the public/private duty test, the court concluded that the police duty is one owed to the general public and does not give rise to an individual action. As a result, the University was immune from liability for failing to enforce the law. *Id.* Assuming *Klobuchar* was correctly decided, it does not extend immunity to the District in *King*'s case. Purdue University, pursuant to statute, provided campus security for the safety of the general public. I.C. § 20-12-3.5-1. Here, although the school must exercise reasonable care and supervision for the safety of the children under its control, it is not charged with general law enforcement on its premises. *See Miller*, 308 N.E. 2d at 706.

In order to prevail on a claim of negligence the plaintiff must show: (1) duty owed to plaintiff by defendant; (2) breach of duty by allowing conduct to fall below the applicable standard of care; and (3) compensable injury proximately caused by defendant's breach of duty. *Ashcraft v. N.E. Sullivan County Sch. Corp.*, 706 N.E. 2d 1101, 1103 (Ind. Ct. App. 1999). This jurisdiction has long recognized that school authorities owe a "duty . . . 'to exercise reasonable care and supervision for the safety of the children under their control.'" *Mangold*, 756 N.E. 2d at 974 (quoting *Miller*, 308 N.E. 2d at 706). Although the existence of duty is a matter of law for the courts to decide, a breach of duty is usually a matter left to the trier of fact. *Stephenson v. Ledbetter*, 596 N.E. 2d 1369, 1371-72 (Ind. 1992). Only where the facts are undisputed and lead to but a single inference or conclusion may the court as a matter of law determine whether a breach of duty has occurred. *Id.* at 1372.

King alleges the District failed to exercise reasonable care in part because Assistant Vice Principal Bart Austin, who normally stayed outside the school building to personally monitor the students' departure, was absent the day of King's incident and did not find a replacement. King contends that he would not have been injured if Austin had been present at his regular post to observe and deter criminal activity in the parking lot. The District essentially responds that it discharged any duty owed to students by entering into a contract with Northeast to provide services for North Central High School. Essentially, the District takes the position that it has breached no duty owed to its students.

Summary judgment is inappropriate in this case because there is a discrepancy in the evidence bearing on the extent of control retained by the District, and also how it was exercised. The contract between Northeast and the District required Northeast officers to be outside from 7:00 a.m. to 3:30 p.m. We also have the incomplete testimony that District officials were, on some occasions, present in the parking lot at 3:00 p.m., but at least Austin, the senior person among them, was absent on April 18. Further, whether merely entering a contract is all the District should have done or was required to do in discharging its duty of care and supervision for the safety of its students is a matter for the jury to decide and is not appropriate for summary disposition.

The trial court granted Northeast's motion for summary judgment on the grounds that a direct action against Northeast was not consistent with the terms of the contract entered into by the District and

Northeast and that King was not a third party beneficiary to the contract because King was unable to show the District owed a particularized obligation to any single student of the school.

.....

Status as a third party beneficiary has been held sufficient to create tort liability to the beneficiary on the part of a party to the contract. ..... The students, including King, are plainly among the persons who are properly on the premises and entitled to expect reasonable steps to be taken for their safety. The District in turn has an obligation to its students and others to take reasonable steps for their safety. We see no reason why negligent failure to carry out these assumed responsibilities should not give rise to liability to students who are injured as a result. There may be significant issues as to negligence and causation that remain in this case. But at this summary judgment stage, there is nothing inherent to the students' status or relationship to the District or Northeast that prevents recovery. Nor is the class of persons who are properly on school premises so remote that liability to them should be precluded as a mater of law for injuries resulting from negligent performance of assumed responsibilities.

The issue is not how, but whether, an obligation is undertaken. ... Accordingly, those specifically engaged in providing services undertaken for security services may well be found to have a higher standard of care than the public at large, whether or not they are on notice of specific activity at the site. *Rosh v. Cave Imaging Sys*., Inc., 26 Cal. App. 4th 1225, 32 Cal.Rptr. 2d 136, 139 (Cal. Ct. App. 1994) (establishing the requisite standard of care of a security guard company through expert testimony); *Erickson v. Curtis Inv. Co.*, 447 N.W. 2d 165, 170-71 (Minn. 1989) (noting that a security firm hired by a commercial parking ramp owner has a "duty to use that degree of care which a reasonably prudent professional security firm would use").

Having previously granted transfer, we reverse the trial court's grant of summary judgment in favor of the District and in favor of Northeast. This cause is remanded.

Notes and Comments

1. School Liability Quiz
In which of the following cases should school officials be liable?

> -- A case arising out of the misconduct of a teacher who gave drugs and alcohol to a high school student at a residential school for at-risk youth and then engaged in sexual acts with the student. *Doe v. Lawrence Hall Youth Services*, 2012 IL App (1st) 103758, 966 N.E.2d 52.
>
> -- A case arising out of the death of a student who collapsed and died after he and a group of junior high school students played a "game" called "body shots," which involved voluntarily punching each other with closed fists as hard as they could in the abdomen, chest, and ribs. *Brooks v. McLean Cty. Unit Dist. No. 5*, 20 N.E.3d 1251 (Ill. 2014).

-- A case arising out of injuries to a student who, while riding on the school bus, was grabbed by two older students who grabbed the student's neck and began to jerk his head back and forth causing a severe cervical strain and a concussion. *Robinson ex rel. C.R. v. Ignacio Sch. Dist.*, 11JT, 328 P.3d 297, 298 (Colo. App. 2014).

-- A case arising out of injuries to a student when a high school shop teacher removed the safety guard from a table saw, leading the student to amputate the fingers on his right hand. *Brown v. Fountain Hill Sch. Dist.*, 1 S.W.3d 27, 28 (Ark. Ct. App. 1999).

-- A case arising out of injuries to a student when school officials allowed its wrestling team to use the high school hallways for timed relay races, leading the student to smash his arm through a glass window. *Lightfoot v. Sch. Admin. Dist. No. 35*, 816 A.2d 63, 63 (Me. 2003).

2. Abrogation of Sovereign Immunity

State legislatures tacitly tinker with abrogation of sovereign immunity with the goal of providing accountability for student safety. The Illinois legislature has set aside common law sovereign immunity, replacing it with in a statutory definition of the standard of care that districts and district employees owe to the students they are supervising. See, 745 Ill. Comp. Stat. 10/3-108(a). Under Illinois law, neither a school district nor an employee is liable for injuries incurred by a student unless the injuries are the result of "willful and wanton conduct" on the part of the district or employee supervising that student. "Willful and wanton conduct" is defined in Illinois law as "a course of action which shows an actual or deliberate intention to cause harm or which, if not intentional, shows an utter indifference to or conscious disregard for the safety of others." 745 Ill. Comp. Stat. 10/1-210. In Colorado, the Claire Davis School Safety Act imposes a limited waiver of sovereign immunity for schools when educators fail to exercise "reasonable care" to protect all students, faculty and staff from "reasonably foreseeable" acts of violence that occurs at school or a school-sponsored activity. Colorado Revised Statutes 24-10-106.3. A district may be liable for up to $350,000 for an injury to one person in a single occurrence and up to $990,000 for an injury to two or more persons in a single occurrence. Individual capacity lawsuits may be brought against specific educators when the employee's actions or omissions are willful and wanton.

How would you assess the impact of this statutory tort reform? Does it make any substantive differences in the relationship between students and school officials? Are students better off with the common law remedies or the new statutory tools?

3. Faculty, Staff and Statutory Limits on Liability

One area where statutory tort reform is having a profound effect is the litigation brought by teachers, administrators and staff members who suffer injuries while in the job. When employees of the school are injured, statutory workers' compensation is considered an exclusive remedy that preempts a civil lawsuit for damages against the school district. All states impose this barrier on their civil servants, even those who wish to bring claims that the school district created an unsafe working environment.

See Halliman v. Los Angeles Unified School Dist., 163 Cal. App. 3d 46, 209 Cal. Rptr. 175 (Cal. App. 2d Dist. 1984) (Teacher injured by rock thrown by student during he school day.). Only intentional conduct is outside the scope of the exclusivity provision. *See Evans v. Bossier Parish Sch. Bd*., La. App. 39718, 903 So. 2d 600 (La.App. 2 Cir. May 11, 2005) (school bus driver's suit against the school board for injuries sustained when dealing with a mentally disabled student.).

4. For articles that critically examine state tort reform, see Daniel B. Weddle: *Bullying in Schools: The Disconnect Between Empirical Research And Constitutional, Statutory, And Tort Duties to Supervise*, 77 Temp. L. Rev. 641 (2004) ("[C]ourts and legislators stop short of requiring schools across the country to make the necessary changes. State and federal laws fail to create the incentives that will force reluctant school officials to move aggressively against a culture of bullying in their schools. Where states have enacted legislation to require schools to implement vigorous anti-bullying policies, the statutes fail to require the kinds of processes that make those policies effective."). See also, Scott R. Simpson: *Report Card: Grading the Country's Response to Columbine*, 53 Buff. L. Rev. 415 (2005) ("[I]t is not surprising that there have been few attempts at prosecuting parents or others under the statutes …, nor have there been many "contributing to the delinquency of a minor" statutes. Legislators have been hesitant to hold parents liable for their children's actions because of the generally accepted sentiment that it is possible for even responsible parents to be unaware of their child's criminal intentions.").

II. Liability in Higher Education: Colleges and Universities

MCCLURE v. FAIRFIELD UNIVERSITY
35 Conn. L. Rptr. 169 2003 WL 21524786 (Conn 2003)

OPINION BY: GALLAGHER, J.

On September 12, 1998, the plaintiff was a 19-year-old freshman at Fairfield University. He alleges that, on that date, he was walking on Reef Road at approximately 1:43 in the morning when he was struck by a car driven by Colleen Capuzzi, another student at Fairfield. Hours earlier, the plaintiff and a number of his friends had left the Fairfield University campus to attend private parties at various residences located on or near the Fairfield town beach. The driver had also been drinking, and was returning to the beach from campus when the accident occurred. The beach is located approximately 2 miles from the university campus, where about 15-20% of the undergraduate students live.

DISCUSSION

According to the defendant, summary judgment is appropriate because it had no duty to protect the plaintiff from injuries that occurred while the plaintiff was returning to campus after attending a private, off-campus party. The defendant argues that the residences at the beach were private residences and in no way related to any Fairfield University event or organization and that the University did not sponsor or sanction the parties. According to the defendant, because the University did not owe the plaintiff a duty, it cannot be liable in negligence for his injuries.

....

While the issue of what, if any, duty the University owed to the plaintiff to protect him from an accident that occurred while he was returning from an off campus party where underage students were drinking alcohol is one of first impression in the state of Connecticut, other jurisdictions have considered similar issues. The defendant cites *Bradshaw v. Rawlings*, 612 F. 2d 135 (3d Cir 1979), *cert. denied*, *Doylestown v. Bradshaw*, 446 U.S. 909, 100 S. Ct. 1836, 64 L. Ed. 2d 261 (1980), as the seminal case on the subject.

In *Bradshaw*, the Third Circuit Court of Appeals held that a college may not be subject to tort liability for injuries sustained by a student that was involved in an automobile accident where the driver of the car was another student who had become intoxicated at a university sponsored class picnic. *Id.*, 144. "[The plaintiff's] primary argument is that the college had knowledge that its students would drink beer at the picnic, that this conduct violated a school regulation and state law, that it created a known probability of harm to third persons, and that knowledge by the college of this probable harm imposed a duty on the college either to control [the driver's] conduct or to protect [the plaintiff] from possible harm." *Id.*, 141.

> "The competing interests of the student and of the institution of higher learning are much different today than they were in the past. At the risk of oversimplification,

> the change has occurred because society considers the modern college student an adult, not a child of tender years. It could be argued . . . that an educational institution possesses a different pattern of rights and responsibilities and retains more of the traditional custodial responsibilities when its students are all minors, as in an elementary school, or mostly minors, as in a high school . . . But here, because the circumstances show that the students have reached the age of majority and are capable of protecting their own self interests, we believe that the rule would be different." (Citations omitted.) *Id.,* 140. The court noted that while the legal drinking age in Pennsylvania was 21, that in the majority of U.S. states it was only 18, and stated that "it would be placing an impossible burden on the college to impose a duty in this case." *Id.,* 142. "We conclude that [the plaintiff] failed to establish a prima facie case against the college that it should be charged with a duty of custodial care as a matter of law . . ." *Id.,* 143.

The defendant also cites *Beach v. University of Utah*, 726 P. 2d 413 (Utah, 1986), in which the Supreme Court of Utah refused to impose a duty on a University where an intoxicated student sustained injuries after falling from a cliff during a university sponsored field trip. "The law imposes upon one party an affirmative duty to act only when certain special relationships exist between parties. These relationships generally arise when one assumes responsibility for another's safety or deprives another of his or her normal opportunities for self-protection . . . The essence of a special relationship is dependence by one party upon the other or mutual dependence between the parties." *Id.,* 415-16. The court relied on the reasoning set out in *Bradshaw*, and concluded that "no special relationship existed between the parties requiring the university to protect [the plaintiff] from the consequences of her voluntary intoxication." *Id.*, 414.

In addition, the defendant cites *Rabel v. Illinois Wesleyan University*, 161 Ill. App. 3d 348, 514 N.E. 2d 552 (Ill.App.Ct. 4th Dist. 1987), *appeal denied*, 520 N.E. 2d 392 (Ill. 1998), in which the plaintiff sued her university in negligence after she was physically taken from her dorm and injured by a drunken fraternity member. She claimed that the university had a duty to protect her from the misconduct of fellow students due to a "special relationship." *Id.*, 555-58. The court, relying on *Bradshaw* and *Beach*, held that the "university's responsibility to its students, as an institution of higher education, is to properly educate them. It would be unrealistic to impose upon a university the additional role of custodian over its adult students and to charge it with the responsibility for assuring their safety and the safety of others. Imposing such a duty of protection would place the university in the position of an insurer of the safety of its students." *Id.*, 560-61.

The plaintiff in the present case argues that a duty should be imposed based on traditional tort law principles, because the accident was foreseeable. In support of his argument, the plaintiff has provided evidence that a substantial number of Fairfield University students lived in the beach area and that while the beach area housing was not part of the Fairfield University campus, the school made information about such housing available to students in the student housing binder. The plaintiff has also provided evidence that students frequently attended parties at the beach where alcohol was served; and that the university administration was aware of this and monitored such activities at the beach by receiving weekly police blotters. In addition, while the university had an alcohol policy, which applied to all students, both on and off campus; it did not attempt to enforce its rules against students at the beach area. Finally, since before 1998, the student government has provided a "Safe Rides" program using university-owned vans to transport students from the beach area to campus late at night on

Thursday, Friday and Saturday nights, in response to concern about student safety. This service, however, was limited only to those times when student volunteers were available to drive the vans.

The plaintiff argues that the university knew that students frequently attended parties at the beach area where they would drink alcohol, that some students would walk to and from the beach area after drinking, and that some students would drive home from the beach area after drinking. In addition, the plaintiff argues that the University's strict enforcement of the drinking age on campus but not at the beach actually encouraged underage students to go to there to drink alcohol. The plaintiff further argues that the University recognized the need for transportation between the campus and the beach area, but that such transportation was not adequately provided. For these reasons, the plaintiff argues that it was foreseeable that a student would be injured by another student who was driving between the campus and the beach area while intoxicated, and that it therefore had a duty to protect him. Additionally, the plaintiff argues that even if no duty originally existed, the University by its conduct had assumed a duty to provide transportation to and from the beach area.

In support of its argument, the plaintiff relies on Furek v. University of Delaware, 594 A.2d 506 (Del. 1991). In that case, a student who was injured in a fraternity-hazing incident sued the university alleging that it had negligently failed to control the fraternity and its members. *Id.,* 511. In its motion for summary judgment, the University claimed that it had no duty to protect the plaintiff and that he had assumed the risk of injury by engaging in hazing. *Id.* "The Superior Court, relying upon § 315 of the Restatement of Torts, determined that the University had a duty to protect Furek through its control of the fraternity. In view of its knowledge of the dangers of hazing on its campus, Furek's claim against the University stated a cause of action as a matter of law." *Id.,* 511-12. Following trial, the University moved for a judgment n.o.v., arguing that based on the evidence, no duty could be imposed on it, and the court agreed. On appeal from the lower court's granting of judgment n.o.v., the defendant argued that it had no duty to protect the plaintiff, but the Supreme Court of Delaware did not agree. "While we agree that the University's duty is a limited one, we are not persuaded that none exists." *Id.,* 517.

The *Furek* court considered and rejected the *Bradshaw* and *Beach* decisions along with other cases that rejected a duty to supervise, stating that they "provide no empirical support for the proposition that supervision is inversely related to the maturation of college students. Aside from the opinion in *Bradshaw*, no legal or other authority is cited for the assertion that supervision of potentially dangerous student activities would create an inhospitable environment or would be largely inconsistent with the objectives of college education. It seems equally reasonable to conclude that university supervision of potentially dangerous student activities is not fundamentally at odds with the nature of the parties' relationship, particularly if such supervision advances the health and safety of at least some students." *Id.*, 518. "*Beach* and *Bradshaw* may also be faulted on the logic of their analysis. In both cases, it was asserted that the major reason for the rejection of a university duty to supervise was that the students were responsible adults. In both cases, the injuries were alcohol-related. However in the area of activity that was the subject matter of the dispute, alcohol consumption, the students were unquestionably not deemed adults under the law since most, if not all, participants were below the drinking age." *Id.*

> "In earlier times of strict university control, the institution was viewed as acting in loco parentis, i.e., the university exercised delegated parental authority with a

> concomitant duty of broad protection . . . The concept of university control based on the doctrine of in loco parentis has all but disappeared in the face of the realities of modern college life where students are now regarded as adults in almost every phase of community life . . . To the extent that the doctrine of in loco parentis is still viable, its application is limited to claims against high school authorities for injuries to students arising out of a failure to supervise." (Citations omitted; internal quotation marks omitted.) *Id.,* 516-17. "The university contends that the demise of the doctrine of in loco parentis has dispelled the notion that any special relationship exists between the university and its student body upon which to posit any duty to protect students from activities of their fellow students. It is argued that the student and the university operate at arms-length, with the student responsible for dealing with other students or student groups . . . While we agree that the university's duty is a limited one, we are not persuaded that none exists." *Id.,* 517.
>
> "A number of courts have examined whether a university's failure to supervise student activities could be deemed a breach of a duty arising from the student-university relationship. Some courts have been unwilling to impose liability because the university is not an insurer of its students safety, and the students are legally responsible adults who are able to take care of themselves. Thus, these courts have rejected both a duty under the in loco parentis doctrine and a duty of supervision . . . when one assumes responsibility for another's safety or deprives another of a normal opportunity for self-protection." Id. "Cases subsequent to Bradshaw which rejected a duty to supervise seem to rely on the policy analysis set out in Bradshaw without considering the factual validity of its premises or the accuracy and consistency of its logic. [Another] court stated that taking away student's control over private recreational and personal safety choices would deprive students of their recently recognized authority in these areas. [That] court concluded that taking away this responsibility would produce a repressive and inhospitable environment, largely inconsistent with the objectives of modern college education." *Id.*, 518.

The court reasoned that, based on Restatement § 323, "if one takes charge and control of [a] situation, he is regarded as entering into a relation which is attenuated with responsibility." *Id.*, 520. "The evidence in this record . . . strongly suggests that the University not only was knowledgeable of the dangers of hazing but, in repeated communications to students in general and fraternities in particular, emphasized the University policy of discipline for hazing infractions. The University's policy against hazing, like its overall commitment to provide security on its campus, thus constituted an assumed duty which became an indispensable part of the bundle of services which colleges . . . afford their students." (Internal quotation marks omitted.) *Id.*

The university-student relationship is certainly unique. While its primary function is to foster intellectual development through an academic curriculum, the institution is involved in all aspects of student life. Through it's providing of food, housing, security, and a range of extracurricular activities the modern university provides a setting in which every aspect of student life is, to some degree, university guided. This attempt at control, however, is directed toward a group whose members are adults in the contemplation of law and thus free agents in many aspects of their lives and life styles . .

. Despite the recognition of adulthood, universities continue to make an effort to regulate student life and the courts have utilized diverse theories in attempting to fix the extent of the university's residential duty. *Id.*, 516.

The *Furek* court ultimately held that "although the University no longer stands in loco parentis to its students, the relationship is sufficiently close and direct to impose a duty . . . The university is not an insurer of the safety of its students nor a policeman of student morality; nonetheless, it has a duty to regulate and supervise foreseeable dangerous activities occurring on its property. That duty extends to the negligent or intentional activities of third persons." *Id.*, 522. "Even though the policy analysis of *Bradshaw* has been followed by numerous courts, the justification for following that decision has seriously eroded by changing societal attitudes toward alcohol use and hazing. The likelihood of injury during fraternity activities occurring on university campuses is greater than the utility of the university inaction. The magnitude of the burden placed on the university is no greater than to require compliance with self imposed standards." *Id.*, 522-23.

The plaintiff also cites *Mullins v. Pine Manor College*, 389 Mass. 47, 449 N.E. 2d 331 (Mass. 1983), in which the Supreme Judicial Court of Massachusetts held that a college owed a duty of care to a student who was raped on campus. While the defendant argued that it did not have any duty to protect the plaintiff from the criminal acts of a third party, the court disagreed. "The duty of care owed to the plaintiff by the defendants in the present case can be grounded on either of two well established principles of law. First, we have said that a duty finds its source in existing social values and customs . . . We think it can be said with confidence that colleges of ordinary prudence customarily exercise care to protect the well-being of their resident students, including seeking to protect them against the criminal acts of third parties . . . Of course, changes in college life, reflected in the general decline of the theory that a college stands in loco parentis to its students, arguably cut against this view. The fact that a college need not police the morals of its resident students, however, does not entitle it to abandon any effort to ensure their physical safety." (Citations omitted; internal quotation marks omitted.) *Id.*, 50-52. In addition, "it is an established principal that a duty voluntarily assumed must be performed with due care . . . Restatement (Second) of Torts § 323 (1965), states: 'One who undertakes gratuitously or for consideration, to render services to another which he should recognize as necessary for the protection of the other's person or things, is subject to liability to the other for physical harm resulting from his failure to exercise reasonable care to perform his undertaking, if (a) his failure to exercise such care increases the risk of such harm, or (b) the harm is suffered because of the other's reliance upon the undertaking.'" *Id.*, 52-53. The court reasoned that because the university provided security to the students due to foreseeable risks associated with its urban location, and because students relied on this service, the university could be required "to use reasonable care to prevent injury to their students by third persons whether their acts were accidental, negligent, or intentional." *Id.*, 54.

Both *Furek* and *Mullins* are distinguishable from the present case in that the events in those cases occurred on campus. However, while the events in the present case occurred off campus, the university's providing information about the beach area housing in the student binder was an imprimatur. It was well known that students would attend parties at the beach residences where they would consume alcohol. When *Bradshaw* and *Beach* were decided, the legal drinking age in a majority of jurisdictions was 18 years of age. In Connecticut, the legal drinking age is presently 21 years of age, as it was at the time of the accident. A large percentage of university students are therefore below the age of majority with respect to the usage of alcohol. Student alcohol use has become an increasingly serious problem in recent years. The university has acknowledged this in that it has an anti-alcohol policy that applies to all underage students. While the university had knowledge that underage drinking frequently occurred at the beach area, it did nothing to enforce the policy there, which indirectly encouraged students to go to the beach area in order to drink alcohol.

The Safe-Rides program in which student volunteers used university-owned vans to provide rides to students traveling between the campus and the beach area on Thursday, Friday and Saturday nights was provided because of the concern for student safety. "[Restatement] § 323 addresses the duty owed by one who assumes direct responsibility for the safety of another through the rendering of services in the area of protection. As the Restatement makes clear, this section applies to any undertakings to render service to another which the defendant should recognize as necessary for the protection of the other person and the harm to be protected against results from negligence in performance of the undertaking or from failure to exercise reasonable care to complete it or to protect the other when he discontinues it. If one takes charge and control of [a] situation, he is regarded as entering into a relation which is attenuated with responsibility." *Furek v. University of Delaware*, supra, 594 A. 2d 520. The shuttle service was limited to times when student volunteers were available to drive the vans, and was therefore not always available to students who attended parties at the beach area. Based on Restatement § 323, the university, by offering the shuttle service, had assumed a responsibility for the safety of students while traveling between the beach area and the university campus. Under the circumstances, the university had a duty to protect students who traveled to and from parties at the beach area.

CONCLUSION

For the reasons stated above, the motion for summary judgment is denied.

Theodore C. Stamatakos: The Doctrine of In Loco Parentis, Tort Liability and the Student-College Relationship, 65 Ind. L.J. 471 (1990)

The doctrine of in loco parentis—literally "in the place of a parent"—was formally recognized in the educational context as early as the late eighteenth-century in England. ....The doctrine of in loco parentis was rendered inoperative in a series of cases decided in the 1960s. These early decisions concerned college disciplinary actions—including rules of conduct and student searches—not institutional tort liability. Nevertheless, the demise of in loco parentis altered all facets of the student-college relationship. ... Thus, the doctrine of in loco parentis was invalidated. Courts, scholars and college administrators had to look elsewhere for an explanation of the legal relationship between college and student. Consequently, several alternative models of the student-college relationship have been developed.

The Contract Model

The student-college relationship has been defined under contract principles. The contractual method, however, is also seriously flawed. Students and colleges do not engage in an "arm's length" agreement. Without such bargaining, quasi-contracts, unconscionable contracts, and contracts of adhesion all emerge as impairments to contractual analysis. Contract law does not adequately capture the underlying dynamics of tort law. For example, contractual analysis does not permit the proper operation of the compensatory, deterrent and cost-spreading objectives so fundamental to tort law. Accordingly, the contract model is not appropriate for tort analysis because the goals and principles of contract law and tort law are too disparate.

The Fiduciary Model

The legal relationship between college and student has also been described as a fiduciary relationship. …The fiduciary model recognizes the trust a student places in the institution she attends. In response to this trust, a legally stringent standard of conduct is imposed upon the university….However, the fiduciary model is not practical. Whenever the student-college relationship is implicated, an institution must justify all actions affecting the relationship with fully-defensible explanations. Further, placing a fiduciary responsibility on institutions reduces students' responsibilities. This state of affairs compromises the institution's ability to foster responsible student decision-making and mature behavior. More damaging to the fiduciary model, however, is judicial resistance towards its adoption. To date, no court has characterized an educational institution as owing a fiduciary duty to its students.

The "Unitary Theory"

The "unitary theory," … describes the legal relationship between college and student as a relationship that is both dynamic and unique. [A] court reviewing institutional behavior implicating the legal relationship between college and student, should focus its inquiry on the particular goals of the educational institution and its students. After identifying the parties' educational objectives, the court must next relate the problem to the goals and apply a standard test: Whether or not the act or acts complained of injure, obstruct, or adversely affect the educational goals of the school or student. The approach is "unitary" because it links the method by which courts assess student-college litigation with the reasons behind the parties' relationship.

The "unitary" theory suffers from at least three deficiencies. First, the "unitary" theory's goal-oriented analysis is not effective for resolving student personal injury suits against colleges and universities. A "test based on the goals of each party" could never properly determine the point at which liability should obtain…The "unitary" theory also fails to facilitate tort law's deterrent function. Deterrence cannot be accommodated by a theory that espouses judicial inquiry into the "particular goals of the educational institution and its students....Finally, the "unitary" theory fails because it has not been viable. The literature of higher education tort law and court holdings have yet to address the "unitary" theory.

……..

The courts of the 1980s have invariably adhered to the Third Circuit's statement of the student-college relationship in *Bradshaw v. Rawlings*:

> There was a time when college administrators and faculties assumed a role in loco parentis. Students were committed to their charge because the students were

> considered minors. A special relationship was created between college and student that imposed a duty on the college to exercise control over student conduct and, reciprocally, gave the students certain rights of protection by the college . . . . [But with the campus revolutions, legislation, and case law, a] dramatic reapportionment of responsibilities and social interests of general security took place . . . . [T]oday students vigorously claim the right to define and regulate their own lives. Especially, have they demanded and received satisfaction of their interest in self-assertion in both physical and mental activities, and have vindicated what may be called the interest in freedom of the individual will. [*Bradshaw v. Rawlings*, 612 F. 2d 135 (3d Cir. 1979), *cert. denied*, 446 U.S. 909 (1980)].

The court in *Bradshaw* articulated two fundamental policy considerations that underpin many student-college tort cases: (1) a recognition "that the modern American college is not an insurer of the safety of its students," and (2) "society considers the modern college student an adult, not a child of tender years."

The courts of the 1980s have shaped institutional tort liability under the direction of *Bradshaw*'s policies and traditional tort principles, not a revived and reshaped in loco parentis doctrine. ... While courts are holding colleges liable for injuries sustained by students, the duty to protect students arises from the college's status as landlord, supervisor and controller of third persons. Courts, as ever, are assessing liability within the confines of traditional tort principles. Further, in loco parentis has never served as a basis for institutional duty to protect students' physical well-being; when viable, the doctrine operated only in the context of student discipline and moral welfare.

It is thus a mistake to signal the coming of a "new" in loco parentis, both as a matter of analysis, and because of the possible effects of such a warning. Although the cancer of institutional liability is not benign, college administrators need to know where to look in order to design and implement the appropriate treatment, and courts need to know where to look to resolve liability issues. Accordingly, the doctrine of in loco parentis does not provide relief.

FREEMAN v. BUSCH

349 F.3d 582 (8th Cir. 2003)

Smith, Circuit Judge.

Carolyn Freeman attended a party at the invitation of Scott Busch, Gene Hildreth, and John Hatfield in Busch's and Hildreth's dorm room at Simpson College. At the party, Freeman became inebriated, passed out, and was allegedly sexually assaulted. Later, Freeman filed tort claims against Simpson College, Busch, Hildreth, and Hatfield. Simpson College and Busch filed motions for summary judgment. After a jury trial on the remaining issues, the jury found for Freeman. Freeman appeals the district court's grants of summary judgment and dismissal of a claim for punitive damages. Busch cross-appeals.

I.

Busch invited his ex-girlfriend Freeman-who was nineteen at the time-and her friends Anne Huffman and Ricci Kowalski to his Simpson College dorm room for a party. All three women accepted Busch's invitation with the expectation that there would be alcohol served at the party. A friend of Busch's purchased the alcohol-a bottle of vodka and a bottle of rum-for the party. Busch and Hildreth contributed money to the alcohol and other party supplies.

After consuming an unknown quantity of alcohol, Freeman became visibly intoxicated. Busch, with the assistance of Huffman and Kowalski, carried Freeman to his bedroom to lie down. Freeman became ill, vomited on her clothes and passed out. Busch and others helped her to change her clothes. Eventually the others left to attend a fraternity party, leaving Freeman and Busch alone in Busch's bedroom. At some point later, Busch left his fourth floor room and went downstairs to the third floor of his dormitory. While there, he had a conversation with the on-duty resident assistant ("R.A."), Brian Huggins. Busch informed Huggins that Freeman was his visitor; that she had consumed alcohol; and that after consuming it, she had vomited and passed out. Huggins told Busch-who knew Busch because both served as Simpson College security officers-to monitor Freeman's condition and, if the condition worsened, to report back to him.

Later that evening, Busch and Freeman had sexual intercourse. Busch claims that they had consensual sex after Freeman awoke. Freeman, who cannot remember what happened after she became inebriated, alleged that Busch sexually assaulted her. After Busch and Freeman's sexual encounter, the others returned from the fraternity party to Busch's dorm room. When Hatfield was getting ready to leave, Busch called him into the bedroom. Busch directed Hatfield's attention to a then-unconscious Freeman and permitted him to fondle her breasts. Busch later also admitted that he permitted Hildreth to do the same.

The next morning Freeman awoke on Busch's couch, unable to remember what had happened the previous evening. She first became suspicious that something may have happened when she went to the bathroom, discovered that her underwear was on backwards, and realized that her tampon was crushed.

As a result of these events, Freeman sued Simpson College, Busch, Hildreth, and Hatfield. Freeman alleged counts of negligence against Busch for failure to summon medical assistance and against Simpson College for the acts of its employees-Busch and Huggins. The district court dismissed the claims, however, on Simpson College's and Busch's motions for summary judgment. ...The case went to trial on claims of sexual battery and of negligence based upon delivery of alcohol to a minor. Prior to and during trial, the district court made a number of evidentiary rulings to which either Freeman or Busch objected. In addition, Busch objected to one of the trial court's jury instructions and also argued for a mistrial. After finding for Freeman on both counts and against Busch on his one count, the jury awarded Freeman $81,396.27 in damages ($66,947.64 against Busch, $14,447.63 against Hildreth, and $1.00 against Hatfield). Both Freeman and Busch appeal.

II.

....

First, Freeman alleged a claim of negligence against Simpson College. In this claim, Freeman alleged in part that Simpson College should be liable for the negligence of its employees-Busch and Huggins-under the doctrine of respondeat superior. However, the doctrine of respondeat superior provides that an employer is liable for the negligent acts of its employees, only if the employees' acts were within the scope of their employment. *Godar v. Edwards*, 588 N.W. 2d 701, 705 (Iowa 1999). In this case, it is undisputed that neither Busch nor Huggins was on duty as a university security guard. As a result, Simpson College cannot be responsible for any negligent acts that their employees may perform while off duty. Restatement (Second) of Agency § 219 cmt. d (1958) ("The master's liability for the servant's tortious conduct ordinarily exists only during . . . such times and in such places as he is authorized to perform service, or at times and places reasonably close to them."); *see also* Restatement (Second) of Agency § 228 (1958). Nevertheless, Simpson College concedes that Huggins was acting within the scope of his duties as an R.A. Thus, if Huggins was negligent as an R.A., then Simpson College could be liable for any of his negligent acts.

In order to prove a case of negligence against Huggins, Freeman must establish: that Huggins owed her a legal duty; that he breached that duty; and that the breach of the duty caused her damages. Freeman argues that Huggins owed her legal duties based upon §§ 314A and 324 of the Restatement (Second) of Torts.

Freeman first argues that Huggins owed her a legal duty based upon Restatement § 314A. In essence, she argues that a special relationship existed between Freeman and Huggins, which imposed such a duty on Huggins to act for Freeman's protection. *See* Restatement (Second) of Torts § 314A. Usually the law recognizes that a special relationship exists between persons in a relationship of "dependence or of mutual dependence." *Id.* cmt. b. Commonly recognized "special relations" under Restatement § 314A "include common carrier/passenger, innkeeper/guest, landlord/invitee, and peace officer/arrestee." *Garofalo v. Lambda Chi Alpha Fraternity*, 616 N.W.2d 647, 652 (Iowa 2000) (citing Restatement (Second) of Torts § 314A, at 118 (1968)). Freeman urges us to recognize a new "special relationship"-one between a college and a guest of a student attending that college. Freeman does not cite, and we can find no cases that so hold.

In fact, since the late 1970s, the general rule is that no special relationship exists between a college and its own students because a college is not an insurer of the safety of its students. *See,* e.g., *Bradshaw v. Rawlings*, 612 F. 2d 135, 138-40 (3d Cir. 1979) (holding that the time in which colleges and universities "assumed a role In loco parentis" no longer exists and as a result no special "custodial duty" between a college and its students exists)...[6]

---

[6] However, the rule is not absolute, and in very limited circumstances, courts have found such a relationship. *See Kleinknecht v. Gettysburg College*, 989 F. 2d 1360, 1368 (3d Cir. 1993) (holding that there is a distinction between the relationship of a college and its students and the relationship of a college and its student-athletes); *Schieszler v. Ferrum College*, 236 F. Supp. 2d 602, 609 (E.D. Va. 2002) (finding in general that no university/student relationship exists, but in this specific case in which a college had repeated warnings that a student had emotional problems, had made threats of suicide, and had required the student to sign a statement that "he would no longer hurt himself," a special relationship did exist); *see also Furek v. Univ. of Delaware*, 594 A. 2d 506, 521-22 (Del. 1991) (finding a duty in the context of fraternity hazing); *McClure v. Fairfield Univ.*, 35 Conn. L. Rptr. 169, *available at* 2003 Conn. Super. LEXIS 1778, 2003 WL 21524786 (Conn. Super. 2003) (holding that the rule of *Bradshaw* and *Beach* is not absolute and that a university had a duty to its students under Restatement § 322).

In this case Freeman asks us to overlook this precedent. We decline to do so. Creation of a special relationship between a college and a student's guest would result in a broad and unprecedented expansion of duty under Restatement § 314A. As a result, we conclude that no "special relationship" existed between Huggins and Freeman which would impose a legal duty on Huggins, as an R.A., to act for Freeman's protection.

Freeman also argues that Huggins assumed a legal duty to come to her aid under Restatement § 324. *See also Garofalo*, 616 N.W. 2d at 654-55. (Restatement § 324 applicable in Iowa). Restatement § 324 provides that Huggins may assume a duty to act reasonably if he, being under no duty to do so, "took charge of" Freeman. Restatement (Second) of Torts § 324 (1965). However, a finding that Huggins "took charge of" Freeman requires that he took specific action to exercise control or custody over her. See Restatement (Second) of Torts § 324.

....

In this case, there is much less evidence that Huggins took control of Freeman. Busch informed Huggins that Freeman was his visitor; that she had consumed a substantial quantity of alcohol; and that after consuming it, she had thrown up and passed out. Huggins did nothing to take charge. Instead, he left Freeman's welfare to Busch; he told Busch to monitor Freeman's condition and, if her condition worsened, then to report back to him. Thus, because Huggins took no specific action to exercise control or custody over Freeman, Huggins had no legal duty to come to her aid.

Consequently, because Freeman cannot establish that Huggins had a legal duty to her under either Restatement § 314A or Restatement § 324, Freeman's claims of negligence against Simpson College, based upon the doctrine of respondeat superior, also fail.

Notes and Comments

1. How would you assess the current state of the law on the duty of colleges and universities to their students? How is this law different from the rules that govern liability in the K-12 setting? What are the rights of parents who send their children to college?

2. Liability in Higher Education: IQ Test
A college has a general obligation to its students to maintain a campus environment free of foreseeable harm. However, courts are not always consistent in resolving liability disputes. In which scenario below should liability be found?

> a. Lawsuit brought by a student for injuries received when an intoxicated student harmed a classmate following a class picnic for which the college furnished alcoholic beverages. *See Bradshaw v. Rawlings*, 612 F. 2d 135 (3d Cir. 1979), cert. denied, 446 U.S. 909 (1980)

b. Lawsuit brought by a student for injuries sustained in an automobile speed contest which occurred after drinking on university premises. *See Baldwin v. Zoradi*, 123 Cal. App. 3d 275, 287, 176 Cal. Rptr. 809, 816 (1981)

c. Lawsuit brought by parents alleging that a university "permitted" their seventeen year-old daughter, a student, "to become associated with criminals, to be seduced, to become a drug user and further allowed her to be absent from her dormitory and failed to return her to her parents' custody on demand." *See Hegel v. Langsam*, 29 Ohio Misc. 147, 148 (1971)

d. Lawsuit brought by a student for injuries sustained when abducted from her campus dormitory and assaulted in another campus building. *See Miller v. Pine Manor College*, 449 N.E. 2d 331 (Mass. 1983).

e. Lawsuit brought by a student for injured sustained in a drunken fall from the second floor of a fraternity house, brought suit against school alleging that the university had breached its duty to control or supervise the conduct of students in fraternity houses. *See Rothbard v. Colgate University*, 235 A.D. 2d 675, 652 N.Y.S. 2d 146 (N.Y. App. Div. 1997).

3. For a discussion of how court view liability in higher education, *see* Tia Miyamoto: Liability of Colleges and Universities for Injuries During Extracurricular Activities, 15 J.C. & U.L. 149, 152 (1988) **("**[C]ourts have been reluctant to impose liability on institutions for injuries sustained by students while participating in extracurricular activities. The two broad policy considerations underlying this reluctance are "a recognition that the modern American college is not an insurer of the safety of its students," and awareness that students are adults who are able to take care of themselves.").

III. Educational Malpractice

MILLER v. LOYOLA UNIVERSITY
829 So. 2d 1057 (La. Ct. App. 2002)

OPINION BY: Terri F. Love

Leonce Jennings Miller, III ("Miller") …is a part-time student in the evening division of Loyola University of New Orleans School of Law. In the fall semester of 2000, he enrolled in a course entitled "The Legal Profession." The purpose of the course was to teach professional and ethical issues related to the legal profession.

Professor Cynthia Lepow, a tenured professor, was selected to instruct this course. Professor Lepow's specialty is tax law, and this was the first time that she had been called upon to instruct this course.

Miller alleges several deficiencies in Professor Lepow's instruction. Miller complains that Professor Lepow did not timely order materials for class, that she changed the course time without permission from the law school, Professor Lepow had the students perform class presentations on subjects she was obligated to teach, Professor Lepow only covered approximately 60% of the Model Rules of Professional Conduct with her lectures and all of the student presentations combined, and finally, Professor Lepow gave a final examination consisting of materials from the National Conference of Bar Examiners and her original questions, which contained serious errors.

.....

[T]he Dean of the Law School, convened a special ad hoc committee to review this case, which consisted of former Deans and Associate Deans of the law school. The committee found: 1) that Professor Lepow violated the faculty handbook by making an arbitrary and unauthorized change in the time that the course was scheduled; 2) that Professor Lepow failed to timely request books for the course; 3) that Professor Lepow gave a final examination that contained errors and copied questions from the National Conference of Bar Examiners materials; 4) that the overall effectiveness of the professor was below satisfactory; 5) that the professor's responses to questions asked were below satisfactory; 6) that the professor excused one student from half of the regularly scheduled classes and this presented a problem with the Socratic method of teaching; and 7) that the professor had difficulty in communicating the course material to the students. The Dean adopted all of the committee recommendations and Professor Lepow was sanctioned with the procedures set out on the faculty handbook.

Miller filed this action to recover the cost of the course and other damages including reimbursement for taking the course a second time at his own expense. His amended petition asserts the following theories of liability against Loyola: 1) Loyola was negligent for failing to provide a qualified professor to teach the legal profession course; 2) Loyola was negligent for failing to have the requisite number of professors required to teach their course offerings as was outlined in the School of Law course listing for the Fall 2000 semester; 3) Loyola breached "[its] conventional obligation" by accepting payment for the course, then not giving complete instruction in the subjects as stated in the law bulletin; 4) Loyola breached its obligation to provide the course of instruction reasonably expected for a recognized accredited institution of higher education; 5) Loyola was monetarily unjustly enriched; 6) Loyola breached its obligation to provide the course at the time it was listed in the course schedule; 7) Loyola breached its obligation to supply the course instruction necessary to pass the MPRE examination and to practice in the profession of law; 8) Loyola was negligent for falsely representing the course of instruction, the details of the course of instruction and the time the course was offered; 9) Miller detrimentally relied on Loyola's promise to provide a specific course of instruction as outlined in the catalog, at the time published, and to provide the necessary course of instruction required to practice in the legal profession, which Loyola failed to keep; Loyola knew plaintiff would rely on its promises; and, Miller is irreparably harmed by Loyola's refusal to remove the course from his official transcript and Miller's lost time and effort toward the pursuit for his Juris Doctor degree, including additional time required to retake the course and the delay in graduation and his ability to practice law.

Loyola asserts that Miller, along with the other students of Professor Lepow's class, were given the opportunity to audit the course the following semester at no charge. However, Miller refused this opportunity, enrolling in the course in the fall semester of 2001 at his own expense.

DISCUSSION

.....

The great weight of authority generally holds that the law recognizes no cause of action for "educational malpractice", either in tort or contract, by a student against a private educational institution asserting inadequate or improper instruction. *Bittle v. Oklahoma City University*, 2000 OK CIV APP 66, 6 P. 3d 509, 514 (Ct. App. Div. 3 4/21/00). The courts uniformly reason that such a claim runs afoul of established public policy with both accords educational institutions broad discretion in matters purely academic...and directs judicial non-interference in the decisions with that discretion. *Id.* ...We are persuaded by the overwhelming weight of authority from other jurisdictions that, absent a specific, identifiable agreement for the provision of particular services, the public policy...militates against recognition of a claim by a student against a private educational institution arising from the institution's alleged improper or inadequate instruction however denominated—either in tort or contract—for "educational malpractice."

In *Ross v. Creighton University*, 957 F.2d 410 (7th Cir. 1992), the Court of Appeals discussed the issue as follows:

> Courts have identified several policy concerns that counsel against allowing claims for educational malpractice. First, there is a lack of a satisfactory standard of care by which to evaluate an educator. Theories of education are not uniform, and "different but acceptable scientific methods of academic training[make] it unfeasible to formulate a standard by which to judge the conduct of those delivering the services." Second, inherent uncertainties exist in this type of case about the cause and nature if damages. "Factors such as the student's attitude, motivation, temperament, past experience and home environment may all play an essential and immeasurable role in learning." Consequently, it may be a "practical impossibility [to] prove that the alleged malpractice of the teacher proximately caused the learning deficiency of the plaintiff student." A third reason for denying this cause of action is the potential it presents for a flood of litigation against schools. ... "education is a service rendered on an immensely greater scale than other professional services." The sheer number of claims that could arise if this cause of action were allowed might overburden schools. The final reason courts have cited for denying this cause of action is that it threatens to embroil the courts into overseeing the day-to-day operations of school. This oversight might be particularly troubling in the university setting where it necessarily implicated considerations of academic freedom and autonomy. To state a claim for breach of contract, the plaintiff must do more than simply allege that the education was not good enough. Instead he must point to an identifiable contractual promise that the defendant failed to honor. ...If the defendant took tuition money and then provided no education, or alternatively, promised a set number of hours of instruction and then failed to deliver, a breach of contract action may be available. In these, cases, the essence of the plaintiffs complaint would not be that the institution failed to perform adequately a promised educational service, but rather that it failed to perform that service at all. Ruling on this issue would not require an inquiry in to the nuances of educational processes and theories, but rather an objective

> assessment of whether the institution made a good faith effort to perform on its promise. (Internal citations omitted). *Ross*, 957 F.2d at 414-15, 416-17.

The New Jersey Superior Court stated in *Swidryk v. St. Michael's Medical Ctr.*, 201 N.J. Super. 601, 493 A. 2d 641, 643 (1985):

> To entertain a cause of action for "educational malpractice" would require the courts not merely to make judgments as to the validity of broad educational policies-a course we have unfalteringly eschewed in the past- but, more importantly to sit in review of the day-to-day implementations of those policies. Recognition in the courts of this cause of action would constitute blatant interference with the responsibility for the administration of the...school system... (Internal citations omitted).

Louisiana law does not recognize a cause of action for educational malpractice under contract or tort law. Miller cites to many contract provisions in the Civil Code, none of which apply to a situation such as this one, where a student complains that the content and quality of instruction in a particular class was insufficient, and that an instructor improperly changed the time of the course. While there are instances where a contractual breach has been found between a university and a student, it has been based on the university's failure to provide a guaranteed service. This is not the case here. The same conclusions may be drawn about tort claims of educational malpractice. Miller asserts that Loyola was negligent in not having enough professors available to teach courses, thus resulting in the negligent quality of instruction. However there is no legal basis to allow such a claim. This Court looked to other jurisdictions and found that there is a persuasive public policy argument against findings a cause of action for educational malpractice that is endorsed by most states. We are inclined to follow these other jurisdictions and do not recognize a claim for educational malpractice either in contract or tort. Universities must be allowed the flexibility to manage themselves and correct their own mistakes. In the instant case, Loyola did have a procedure in place to deal with a situation as the one before use. It is not the place of the court system to micro-manage the adequacy of instruction or management at institutions of higher learning, even if it were feasible, which we feel it is not. This is a task best handled by the universities themselves.

Since the law does not provide for a cause of action under contract or tort for Miller's various claims, we find that Miller does not state a cause of action against Loyola.

.....

In his final assignment of error, Miller asserts that the trial court incorrectly held that he failed to state a cause of action against Loyola for his detrimental reliance on the Loyola's promises, made in the course description for "The Legal Profession."

La. C.C. art. 1967 defines detrimental reliance as follows:

> A party may be obligated by a promise when he knew or should have known that the promise would induce the other party to rely on it to his detriment and the other

> part was reasonable in so relying. Recovery may be limited to the expenses incurred or the damages suffered as a result of the promisee's reliance on the promise. Reliance on a gratuitous promise made without required formalities is not reasonable.

In order for Miller to successfully assert a claim of detrimental reliance he must show that Loyola wrote the course descriptions knowing that he would rely on the statements made and whether or not Miller reasonably relied upon the promises and was damaged by his reliance. We find that Miller's reliance on the course description was unreasonable. Course descriptions are given to inform the student of what is generally covered in the course; they are not contractual provisions that bind the school to teach exactly what is written in the description. There are many reasons why a particular course might not live up to its description. For instance, perhaps the students need extra instruction on a particular subject, which precludes every topic from being covered in a given semester. Current events may dictate that the course structure be changed to address more pertinent topics. Perhaps a teacher does not manage the course time optimally, and some subjects are not taught. Education must be flexible to accommodate changing circumstances; therefore the course bulletin cannot be looked upon as contractual provision that gives students opportunity to sue the school if they feel that their expectations are not met or if the course does not fit the description exactly.

Not only do we find Miller's reliance on the course description unreasonable but also Louisiana law does not recognize that course descriptions are binding contract. Despite Miller's attempt to apply traditional contract law to the instant claim, there is no law either by the legislature or jurisprudence that supports his argument. A claim of detrimental reliance cannot be based on a contractual claim that is not provided for by law.

.....

AFFIRMED.

DISSENT BY: PLOTKIN, J.

I must respectfully dissent from the majority's conclusion that Louisiana law does not recognize a cause of action for educational malpractice under contract or tort law. The majority does not cite any prior case law in order to support this notion. Because I have concluded that in some narrow and specific instances a cause of action for educational malpractice should be recognized, I must dissent.

The Appellant's cause of action represents a case of first impression in this jurisdiction. The majority of courts have rejected a claim of educational malpractice on the basis of public policy concerns outlined within the majority opinion. Only Montana allows these claims to go forward, and its decision was based on state statutes that place a duty of care on educators, a circumstance not present here. *B.M v. State*, 200 Mont. 58, 649 P.2d 425, 427-28 (1982). Courts in at least eleven states have considered and rejected claims for educational malpractice: Alabama, Alaska, California, Florida, Idaho, Iowa, Kentucky, Maryland, New Jersey, New York, and Wisconsin.

.....

1. Educational Malpractice: A Mix of Tort and Contract Law Claims.

The educational malpractice cause of action stems from both tort and contract law. There is an important distinction between the two, which the *Ross* decision illustrates. There are a number of public policy concerns cited in *Ross* and reiterated in the majority opinion against allowing a educational malpractice cause of action as a general tort law claim. I support the majority opinion's rejection of a general negligence cause of action, which simply attacks the general quality of an education. Judicial oversight as to the reasonableness and quality of education would be an immense effort without ascertainable or clearly definable standards. Much in the same way the business judgment rule exists to keep judges from substituting their judgment for that of the executive or the board member, here too the courts should defer to the expertise of educators and administrators when it comes to negligence claims by students. Therefore, I would bar a claim of educational malpractice under traditional tort law theory because the judiciary should continue to defer to the expertise of the educators regarding the overall quality of an education.

The educational malpractice cause of action is much stronger when it evolves directly from a breach of contract claim. When the cause of action results from a breach of contract by the university, I believe there are certain remedies, which a court can fashion for the wronged student. The breach of contract claim cannot result from a general lack of a quality education. Rather a narrow cause of action can exist which results from the principles of good faith and fair dealing. The traditional remedies employed by the courts can be used to ensure that if the contract existing between students and universities is breached, the plaintiff can be compensated. In this day and age, with the ever increasing price of higher education, universities now aggressively market themselves to would be consumers. Students should have some form of remedy available to them when they are specifically promised something, which is not delivered. With the use of marketing tactics by universities, comes added responsibility and accountability to the consuming public. Therefore, public policy and sentiments of equity and justice require Louisiana law to allow for a limited cause of action for educational malpractice involving breach of contract claims.

Traditionally the courts have been very reluctant to rigidly apply contract law in adjudicating student claims against colleges due to the necessity of allowing schools significant leeway in educating their students. This general reluctance and deference allows for student claims against universities to be largely ignored, resulting in a continued and prolonged lack of oversight and accountability. Students can use contract law's implied obligations of good faith and fair dealing in some cases in order to receive what was promised to them. Inherent within the contract between students and universities are a number of implied promises and an imbalance of bargaining power. Courts cannot and should not attempt to be the forum to litigate all potential implied promises between the educating institution and the student. Courts can, however, use good faith and fair dealing as a framework to protect institutional autonomy, accord substantial deference to educators and administrators, while protecting student rights and providing some accountability to higher education.

.....

In the present matter, the record is incomplete, as the defendant has filed a peremptory exception of no cause of action. The plaintiff/appellant has sued claiming breach of contract, unjust enrichment and detrimental reliance. I would remand this case to the trial court in order to give the Appellant an opportunity to further develop the facts supporting his assertion that the Appellee breached the contract existing between the two parties. I would limit the plaintiff's available cause of action to whether or not the Appellee upheld the standards of good faith and fair dealing.

HUNTER v. BOARD OF EDUCATION
439 A. 2d 582 (Md. 1982)

[Ross Hunter attended the Montgomery County Public School until he reached his sixteenth birthday. Hunter's parents sued the school board alleging that since the first grade educators negligently assessed his learning abilities and misplaced him in his classes. For example, Ross was promoted to second grade, but while there was retaught the curriculum of the first grade. Because of the misplacement, Hunter's parents argued that his entire education was ruined, causing Ross "to 'feel embarrassment', to develop 'learning deficiencies', and to experience 'depletion of ego strength'". Hunter's parents also alleged that individual educators intentionally engaged in a cover up of their actions which prevented the parents from discovering the damage being done. The court affirmed the dismissal of the negligence action, but allowed the intentional harm claim to go forward.]

"It is clear, however, that the gravamen of petitioners' claim in this case sounds in negligence, asserting damages for the alleged failure of the school system to properly educate young Hunter, and we first focus our attention on this aspect of it. In so doing, we note that these so-called "educational malpractice" claims have been unanimously rejected by those few jurisdictions considering the topic. These decisions generally hold that a cause of action seeking damages for acts of negligence in the educational process is precluded by considerations of public policy, among them being the absence of a workable rule of care against which the defendant's conduct may be measured, the inherent uncertainty in determining the cause and nature of any damages, and the extreme burden which would be imposed on the already strained resources of the public school system to say nothing of those of the judiciary. .....We find ourselves in substantial agreement with the reasoning employed by the courts.

"Count II represents the parents' somewhat amorphous claim that the respondents intentionally and maliciously acted to injure their child. Research reveals that none of the prior cases discussing educational malpractice have squarely confronted the question of whether public educators may be held responsible for their intentional torts arising in the educational context. In declining to entertain the educational negligence and breach of contract actions, we in no way intend to shield individual educators from liability for their intentional torts. It is our view that where an individual engaged in the educational process is shown to have willfully and maliciously injured a child entrusted to his educational care, such outrageous conduct greatly outweighs any public policy considerations which would otherwise preclude liability so as to authorize recovery. It may well be true that a claimant will usually face a formidable burden in attempting to produce adequate evidence to establish the intent requirement of the tort, but that factor alone cannot prevent a plaintiff from instituting the action.[8] Thus, the petitioners are entitled to make such an attempt here."

DONOHUE v. COPIAGUE UNION FREE SCHOOL DISTRICT
391 N.E. 2d 1352 (N.Y. 1979)

[Donohue graduated from Copiague Senior High School in June, 1976. He filed suit against the school district alleging that he lacked even the rudimentary ability to comprehend written English on a level sufficient to enable him to complete applications for employment. His complaint presented two causes of action, one of educational malpractice, and the second alleging the negligent of breach of a duty to educate. The court affirmed the dismissal of the suit].

> "To entertain a cause of action for "educational malpractice" would require the courts not merely to make judgments as to the validity of broad educational policies—a course we have unalteringly eschewed in the past—but, more importantly, to sit in review of the day-to-day implementation of these policies. Recognition in the courts of this cause of action would constitute blatant interference with the responsibility for the administration of the public school system lodged by Constitution and statute in school administrative agencies. Of course, "[this] is not to say that there may never be gross violations of defined public policy which the courts would be obliged to recognize and correct."

[Judge Wachtler concurred with the following observations]:

> There is, however, another even more fundamental objection to entertaining plaintiff's cause of action alleging educational malpractice. It is a basic principle that the law does not provide a remedy for every injury. As the majority notes, the decision of whether a new cause of action should be recognized at law is largely a question of policy. The practical problems raised by a cause of action sounding in educational malpractice are so formidable that I would conclude that such a legal theory should not be cognizable in our courts. These problems... include the practical impossibility of proving that the alleged malpractice of the teacher proximately caused the learning deficiency of the plaintiff student. Factors such as

[8] We note that petitioners do not allege that any individual members of the school board acted intentionally and maliciously toward young Hunter. Under the doctrine of respondeat superior, the Board can only be held liable for the intentional torts of its employees committed while acting within the scope of their employment. ... An intentional tort is within the scope of employment where it is carried out in furtherance of the master's business or is intended in part for the master's benefit. ...Where, as here, it is alleged that the individual educators have wi[l]lfully and maliciously acted to injure a student enrolled in a public school, such actions can never be considered to have been done in furtherance of the beneficent purposes of the educational system. Since such alleged intentional torts constitute an abandonment of employment, the Board is absolved of liability for these purported acts of its individual employees. Consequently, we are not called upon here to consider whether or to what extent the board has another defense available to it under the doctrine of governmental immunity.

> the student's attitude, motivation, temperament, past experience and home environment may all play an essential and immeasurable role in learning. Indeed as the majority observes proximate cause might "be difficult, if not impossible, to prove.

Jenna Watts: Educational Malpractice: If Our Children Aren't Learning Who Should be Held Responsible?, 34 J.L. & Educ. 167 (2005)

[T]here have been no cases where the student has been successful in claiming negligent educational malpractice. …Most states already have an accountability system in place to help ensure a student's education. This system holds students and schools accountable. The problem is that educators, unlike other professionals, such as doctors and accountants, are not held personally accountable for their work.

II. Public Policy

Why would claims for educational malpractice contravene the public policy? The public policy should be to educate all children. If children are not being educated then they should not advance to the next grade level or receive a diploma. In the past, courts have been unwilling to find for the plaintiff in negligent educational malpractice claims on policy reasons. Some of the public policy reasons cited are that there is not a "workable rule of care" to measure the defendant's conduct and another being the "inherent uncertainty" in determining the cause and nature of any injury. The courts have also stated that ruling in favor of the student would overstep boundaries and interfere with the responsibilities of school administrative agencies.

The courts have feared that finding a cause of action for negligent educational malpractice would force a court to substitute its judgment for that of professional public school educators and administrators. While it may not be the court's duty or responsibility to substitute its judgment for that of a professional educator, on a regular basis, there are times when the courts do substitute their judgment for that of others. There are prime examples in the corporate world. In the corporate world, the courts substitute their judgment for that of a board of directors when it can be proven that a board of directors has breached its duty to the company with gross negligence. The courts should be able to set up a checks and balances system with regards to the education of children, as they did with regards to integration. If the courts can be asked to protect people's money, the courts should be asked to protect people's right to an adequate education.

The courts also fear a flood of new cases if negligent educational malpractice was allowed to proceed as a viable cause of action. Courts have stated that, if the states allow suits for negligent educational malpractice, there would be an influx of cases that would burden the courts, the public and the school system in defending the cases. The courts feared that an award of money damages where there is "inherent immeasurability" of damages might also add to the burden. While fears of a large increase in new cases may be valid, that would indicate a serious problem in our schools that must be addressed. There may be many policy reasons behind the courts' decisions not to allow negligent educational malpractice claims to proceed, however, the courts have recognized intentional educational malpractice as a viable cause of action.

III. Intentional Educational Malpractice

While negligent educational malpractice has always failed in the courts, a student may be able to bring the action as intentional educational malpractice. The court in *Hunter v. Board of Education* allowed a case for educational malpractice when it is based on intentional and malicious conduct of the school officials stating that:

Where an individual engaged in the educational process is shown to have willfully and maliciously injured a child entrusted to his educational care, such outrageous conduct greatly outweighs any public policy considerations which would otherwise preclude liability so as to authorize recovery.

There must still be proof that there was injury and that the injury was caused by the defendant but there is no duty question, because the allegation is that the teacher or school official acted intentionally and the teacher or school official has a recognized duty not to intentionally harm a student, physically, emotionally or intellectually.

A case for intentional educational malpractice is still very difficult for the student because of the significant burden of proving that a school official intentionally made it impossible for the student to gain an education while in the system. While the *Hunter* court did warn that the plaintiff would have an arduous burden of proof, it does give hope that a court is willing to recognize intentional educational malpractice as a viable claim, which would open the doors for other plaintiffs and may convince the courts or the state legislatures to recognize negligent educational malpractice as a viable cause of action.

NEWARK PARENTS ASS'N v. NEWARK SCHOOLS
547 F. 3d 199 (3d Cir. 2008)

BARRY, Circuit Judge

Appellants are a putative class of parents of children enrolled in the public elementary and middle schools of Newark, New Jersey, and an organization that represents them. They brought suit against appellees, Newark's public school system and various school administrators, under the No Child Left Behind Act ("NCLBA" or the "Act"), 20 U.S.C. § 6301 et seq., and 42 U.S.C. § 1983. The complaint alleges that because the Newark public school system has failed to live up to its obligations under certain provisions of the Act, appellants are entitled to privately enforce those provisions. Appellees moved to dismiss and the District Court granted the motion, concluding that Congress did not confer on individuals an enforceable right of action under the Act. Deciding what is an issue of first impression in the federal courts of appeals, we will affirm.

I. The No Child Left Behind Act

A. The Act's Purpose and Its Funding Provisions

Congress enacted the Act pursuant to its spending power. *See* U.S. Const. art. I, § 8, cl. 1. The Act, at its outset, states that its purpose is "to ensure that all children have a fair, equal, and significant opportunity to obtain a high-quality education and reach, at a minimum, proficiency on challenging State academic achievement standards and state academic assessments." 20 U.S.C. § 6301 (footnote omitted). This eminently laudatory purpose is to be accomplished by, among other things,

> holding schools, local educational agencies, and States accountable for improving the academic achievement of all students, and identifying and turning around low-performing schools that have failed to provide a high-quality education to their students, while providing alternatives to students in such schools to enable the students to receive a high-quality education. *Id.* § 6301(4).

As with other legislation enacted under Congress's spending power, the Act offers a simple quid pro quo: Congress shall appropriate funds to a State educational agency if it agrees to take certain specific actions. The State, in turn, appropriates those funds to its local educational agencies (referred to alternatively as "LEAs") for the purpose of helping schools to improve in accordance with the Act. *See id.* §§ 6302(i), 6303(g), 6311(a)(1), 6316(a)(1). To become eligible for federal funding, the State educational agency must first submit to the U.S. Secretary of Education a plan demonstrating that "the State has adopted challenging academic content standards and challenging student academic achievement standards that will be used by the State, its local educational agencies, and its schools." *Id.* § 6311(b)(1)(A). The State plan shall, among other things, "demonstrate that the State has developed and is implementing a single, statewide State accountability system that will be effective in ensuring that all local educational agencies, public elementary schools, and public secondary schools make adequate yearly progress." *Id.* § 6311(b)(2)(A). The State is tasked with defining "adequate yearly progress" in a "statistically valid and reliable" manner that uniformly applies "the same high standards of academic achievement" to all of its schools. *Id.* § 6311(b)(2)(C)(i)-(ii).

Every local educational agency receiving funds under the Act is obligated to "use the State academic assessments and other indicators described in the State plan to review annually the progress of each school served under this part to determine whether the school is making adequate yearly progress." *Id.* § 6316(a)(1)(A). If a local educational agency determines that a school has failed to make "adequate yearly progress" for two consecutive years, the agency shall identify the school for "school improvement." *Id.* § 6316(b)(1)(A). If, for two years after being identified as requiring "school improvement," a school continues to fail to achieve "adequate yearly progress," the agency shall identify the school for "corrective action." *Id.* § 6316(b)(7)(C). If, after one full school year of "corrective action," the school continues to fail to achieve "adequate yearly progress," the agency shall identify the school for "restructuring." *Id.* § 6316(b)(8)(A)-(B).

B. The Act's Notification and Supplemental Educational Services Provisions

If a school is identified for "improvement," "corrective action," or "restructuring," the local educational agency

> shall promptly provide to a parent or parents . . . an explanation of what the identification means, . . . the reasons for the identification[,] . . . an explanation of what the school identified for school improvement is doing to address the problem of low achievement[,] . . . an explanation of what the local educational agency or

> State educational agency is doing to help the school address the achievement problem[, and] . . . an explanation of how the parents can become involved in addressing the academic issues that caused the school to be identified for school improvement.

Id. § 6316(b)(6)(A)-(E). Importantly, this written explanation must also provide "an explanation of the parents' option to transfer their child to another public school . . . or to obtain supplemental educational services for the child." *Id.* § 6316(b)(6)(F); *See also id.* §§ (b)(1)(E), (b)(5)(A), (b)(7)(C)(i), (c)(10)(C)(vii). As for supplemental educational services (referred to alternatively as "SES"),

> the local educational agency serving such school shall. . . arrange for the provision of supplemental educational services to eligible children in the school from a provider with a demonstrated record of effectiveness, that is selected by the parents and approved for that purpose by the State educational agency in accordance with reasonable criteria.

Id. § 6316(e)(1).

A parent's right to obtain supplemental educational services for his or her child, however, is qualified in that children from low-income families and children with the lowest achievement levels are prioritized. The Act provides that the local educational agency is obligated to arrange for the provision of supplemental educational services to "eligible children," *id.* § 6316(e)(1), with "eligible child" defined to mean "a child from a low-income family, as determined by the local educational agency," *id.* § 6316(e)(12)(A). If the amount of funds allocated to a local educational agency to provide supplemental educational services is insufficient to provide those services to every eligible child, the local educational agency is directed to give priority to the lowest-achieving children. *Id.* § 6316(b)(10)(C). The State may, at the request of a local educational agency, waive the obligation of the local educational agency to provide supplemental educational services if the State determines that no eligible supplemental educational services provider is located close enough to the local educational agency, and the agency demonstrates that it cannot provide the services. *Id.* § 6316(e)(10)(A).

Students' parents are also entitled to be notified, on an annual basis and regardless of the status of the child's school, of their right to request and receive information concerning their children's teachers' qualifications. More specifically,

> [a]t the beginning of each school year, a local educational agency that receives funds under this part shall notify the parents of each student attending any school receiving funds under this part that the parents may request, and the agency will provide the parents on request (and in a timely manner), information regarding the professional qualifications of the student's classroom teachers.

Id. § 6311(h)(6)(A).

C. The Act's Enforcement Provision

The Act includes a "Penalties" section, which provides as follows: "If a State fails to meet any of the requirements of this section . . . then the Secretary may withhold funds for State administration under this part until the Secretary determines that the State has fulfilled those requirements." *Id.* § 6311(g)(2). The provision does not offer any remedy to parents in the event of noncompliance by a State or a local educational agency with any of the Act's terms.

. . . . .

The Act's introductory statement states that its purpose is "to ensure that all children have a fair, equal, and significant opportunity to obtain a high-quality education." 20 U.S.C. § 6301. While the reference to "all children" could ostensibly be read as a proclamation that each and every child shall have certain rights, Congress did not refer to the individual rights of each and every child. ...The NCLBA's general appropriations and enforcement provisions also evince an agreement between Congress and the States, rather than the creation of individual rights. The appropriations provision makes no mention of individuals; it simply states that for purposes of carrying out parts of the Act, Congress shall appropriate to State agencies certain amounts of money in each subsequent fiscal year. 20 U.S.C. § 6302(a).

Read in concert with the less-than rights-creating language used in the notice and supplemental educational services provisions, the overall structure of the Act supports the conclusion that Congress did not intend to confer enforceable individual rights under those provisions.

. . . . .

IV. Conclusion

We hold that Congress did not intend to give individuals a right to enforce the notice and supplemental educational services provisions of the Act. We will affirm the Order of the District Court.

Benjamin Michael Superfine: Using the Courts to Influence the Implementation of No Child Left Behind, NCLB, 28 Cardozo L. Rev. 779 (2006)

In the lawsuits that have been brought to influence NCLB, the courts have not constituted an effective venue for addressing implementation problems or for enforcing salient NCLB provisions. An array of procedural hurdles and hurdles stemming from NCLB's statutory language has prevented courts from having the power to address these problems effectively. Moreover, even in the absence of these hurdles, it appears that courts still would not be in a position to address effectively many NCLB implementation problems. Plaintiffs' claims regarding these problems are naturally shaped by the statutory language of NCLB. In cases where NCLB does not include detailed language regarding the capacities that various entities need to implement NCLB, the law may simply fail to support claims that target the primary roots of the implementation problems....The ineffective use of the courts thus far to address NCLB implementation problems accordingly raises the question of whether there is any useful role for the courts to play in regard to NCLB.

On January 8, 2002, President George W. Bush signed into law NCLB. While the underlying logic of NCLB is grounded in earlier statutes, such as Goals 2000 and the IASA, NCLB entails more stringent demands on states than its predecessors regarding testing and accountability. According to its statutory text, NCLB is designed to strengthen "accountability, teaching, and learning by using State assessment systems designed to ensure that students are meeting challenging State academic achievement and content standards and increasing achievement overall." In order to achieve this goal, NCLB specifies in great detail the specific means that must be used. NCLB requires states to have submitted plans specifying how they will comply with the requirements of NCLB. Moreover, NCLB requires states to adopt their own "challenging academic standards" in reading, mathematics, and science. These standards must "specify what children are expected to know and be able to do" in the appropriate subject areas. Furthermore, these standards must describe at least three levels of achievement—basic, proficient, and advanced.

In addition, NCLB requires each state to adopt a system of assessments to monitor the progress of student achievement in relation to state standards. These assessments must be aligned with a state's standards and must measure proficiency in mathematics, reading, and science. Through the 2004-2005 school year, reading and mathematics tests must be administered at least once annually in three different grades. Beginning in the 2005-2006 school year, these tests must be administered at least once annually to students in grades three through eight. States must begin to administer science tests in the 2007-2008 school year. Having developed academic standards and constructed an assessment to measure student achievement in relation to these standards, states also must ensure that schools receiving Title I funds make "adequate yearly progress" (AYP). In order to comply with this requirement, states must define for themselves what constitutes an acceptable annual increase of student proficiency on state assessments in schools. This annual increase must include separate objectives for economically disadvantaged students, students from major racial and ethnic groups, students with disabilities, and students with limited English proficiency. Under the AYP provisions of NCLB, states must ensure that each of these student subgroups reaches proficiency by 2014.

If a school fails to make AYP on state assessments, the school becomes subject to a variety of accountability measures. The sanctions that flow from failure to make AYP are markedly more demanding than any type of accountability sanctions that have previously been prescribed by a federal law. A school that fails to make AYP for two consecutive years is to be identified for school improvement. When a school district contains a school labeled for school improvement, the local educational agency must provide all students enrolled in the school with the option to transfer to another public school within the district. A school identified for school improvement must also develop and implement a plan to strengthen the school's core academic subjects and to address the reasons why the school is identified for school improvement. If a school fails to make AYP after its first year of identification for school improvement, "supplemental educational services" must be made available to all of its students. The school's local educational agency must arrange for provision of these services to eligible children from a provider with a demonstrated record of effectiveness that is selected by parents and approved by the proper state educational agency.

If a school fails to make AYP after its second year of identification for school improvement status, that school is identified for corrective action. Once a school is identified for corrective action, the appropriate local educational agency must implement at least one out of several demanding actions, such as replacing the school's staff. If a school fails to make AYP after its first year of identification for corrective action, the local educational agency must implement one out of another set of even more demanding actions, including turning the operation of the school over to the state.

In addition to these requirements governing standards, testing, and accountability, NCLB requires states to ensure that there is a "highly qualified teacher" (HQT) in every public school classroom by the end of the 2005-06 school year. While the definition of what constitutes "highly qualified" varies for different types of teachers, NCLB generally requires teachers to have received a bachelor's degree, be fully certified, and to have demonstrated their knowledge and skills.

In order to accomplish all these goals, Congress has provided for large increases in education funding. Upon NCLB's passage, the discretionary budget of the U.S. Department of Education (ED) was increased to $48.9 billion. This figure represented an increase of 15.9 percent—the largest in the history of ED. NCLB funds were also authorized at higher levels than ever before in ESEA history. For its first year of implementation, NCLB was authorized at $26.4 billion by Congress. In its second year, it was authorized at $29.2 billion, and in its third year, it was authorized at $32 billion. Notably, these authorization levels were the outcome of much congressional debate regarding the funding that states need to implement effectively the new requirements of NCLB. Indeed, the final text of NCLB contains the "Unfunded Mandates Provision," which prohibits federal officers or employees from mandating states and localities to spend funds for costs not paid for by NCLB. This provision has become particularly important in the debates that surround NCLB and cases launched to influence the implementation of NCLB.

****

II. Lawsuits Aimed At No Child Left Behind

In the short time since NCLB was enacted, it has come under legal attack from a variety of plaintiffs. Entities such as private individuals, non-profit organizations, teachers' unions, and school districts have brought suit to influence NCLB's implementation. In these cases, plaintiffs focused on an array of NCLB implementation problems and employed several different legal strategies. Thus far, these strategies have generally proven ineffective at enabling courts to remedy targeted implementation problems.

.....

B. Major Hurdles Faced by NCLB Plaintiffs

[P]laintiffs have employed several different legal strategies. These legal strategies have generally proven ineffective.

1. Section 1983

In almost all of the cases brought to affect NCLB's implementation, plaintiffs claimed that NCLB was not being implemented in accordance with its statutory requirements. Thus, many of these plaintiffs attempted to use the courts to enforce NCLB's statutory language against a governmental entity. Private plaintiffs, however, cannot bring a successful claim against a governmental entity by simply proving that an entity has failed to comply with the requirements of a federal statute. Private plaintiffs also need to establish a cause of action that allows them to bring such a claim. Generally, private plaintiffs can find a cause of action to enforce the provisions of a federal statute from three primary sources: an express private cause of action, an implied private cause of action, and a "Section 1983" action. Because NCLB does not appear to include an express private cause of action, and the requirements regarding an implied private cause of action have largely collapsed with those regarding Section 1983 actions, bringing a Section 1983 action appears at first glance to be a logical move for plaintiffs wishing to enforce NCLB requirements….[However], [i]n the absence of an express private cause of action, Section 1983 [is not] one of the primary tools that [NCLB] plaintiffs can employ to enforce the provisions of a federal statute in the courts. [E]ven in cases where it clearly appears that a governmental entity has failed to comply with NCLB requirements, using Section 1983 does not constitute a viable option for plaintiffs who wish to address such problems. If the courts are to constitute an effective venue for addressing NCLB implementation problems, it appears that plaintiffs must employ another legal strategy.

2. Appealing Administrative Decisions

Although the unavailability of Section 1983 actions has made it more difficult for plaintiffs to influence NCLB's implementation, plaintiffs still have other strategies available to them. In particular, plaintiffs can appeal the determinations of administrative agencies that have ruled in regard to NCLB. As both federal and state education departments implement and make decisions regarding NCLB, plaintiffs have already questioned decisions made by both types of education departments. However, even where plaintiffs have employed this strategy, the courts have still failed to constitute an effective venue to address NCLB's implementation problems.

In order to appeal successfully the decision of an administrative agency, plaintiffs must fulfill certain procedural requirements. Generally, plaintiffs must exhaust all administrative remedies available to them before going to a court to appeal the decision of an administrative agency. .....Even where plaintiffs have exhausted all their administrative remedies, it still has proven difficult for such plaintiffs to overturn an agency decision in court. …In particular, [Plaintiffs] face a standard of review that [is] already somewhat deferential to [agency] determinations. As the substantial evidence standard is inherently deferential to administrative agencies, it is somewhat difficult for a court to find that such an agency has improperly implemented NCLB—in comparison to the deference that would be employed in the case of a successful Section 1983 action, the deference employed in the case of an administrative appeal favors governmental entities to a greater extent. Thus, appeals of administrative decisions inherently make it difficult for a court to find that administrative agencies have acted improperly when implementing NCLB.

…..

C. The NCLB Adequacy Approach

This section details the new approach that courts could use to address NCLB implementation problems. This new approach, hereinafter referred to as the "NCLB Adequacy Approach," would allow courts to examine NCLB implementation problems directly through the lens of educational adequacy.

The legal basis for this new approach directly grows out of the reasoning employed by courts that have decided recent school finance cases. In order for a court to employ this approach, a plaintiff would first bring a claim in the proper state court by arguing that a state is not implementing NCLB effectively and is thereby failing to provide its students with an adequate education. Because the mandate to provide students with an adequate education is vague, a court would have to define with specificity what constitutes educational adequacy in the state. Following the reasoning of the recent school finance cases discussed above, a court would use state standards to define educational adequacy.

The use of state standards to define adequacy in this context makes sense for several reasons. This use of standards would relieve courts of the difficult decision about how to define adequacy, a decision that many courts have expressed their lack of competency to make. Indeed, the use of standards in this manner could remedy the judicial concerns that led to the dismissal of plaintiffs' claims under the non-justiciable political question doctrine—by using legislatively mandated standards to define adequacy, a court could overcome the concern that the standard for educational adequacy is neither judicially discoverable nor manageable.

.....

A court using the NCLB Adequacy Approach would then proceed to the next step of actually determining whether a state is failing to provide students with a constitutionally adequate education. In order to determine whether students are receiving a constitutionally adequate education, a court would follow the lead of the other courts that have heard recent school finance cases and examine different performance indicators. Disaggregated student performance data on NCLB assessments certainly constitutes one useful indicator for courts to examine. The extent to which schools in a state make AYP can potentially constitute another useful indicator—as AYP is meant to represent how well a school is performing and improving, the extent to which schools in a state make AYP can serve as a window into how well schools are providing students with an adequate education. To be sure, the measurement of organizational performance and AYP is far from perfect. However, AYP or other similar measures of school or district performance at least focuses on organizational entities instead of individuals. In this respect, measures like AYP (if validly constructed) can arguably provide courts with useful information about the quality of education being provided by different state-level organizational entities to students. As states, districts, and schools have generally had a difficult time boosting student performance levels to proficient under state standards and ensuring that schools make AYP; these indicators would probably suggest in most cases that a state is failing to provide students with an adequate education as defined by state standards.

Assuming that the performance of students and schools within a state does not indicate that a state is providing students with an adequate education, a court then is well positioned to examine the extent to which NCLB is being effectively implemented within a state. In some of the school finance cases discussed above, the effective implementation of a state accountability system was construed as central to a state's ability to provide students with an adequate education. Courts employing the NCLB

Adequacy Approach would follow the lead of these courts and construe the implementation of the NCLB mandated standards-based accountability system as necessary to comply with the state constitution. As NCLB requires states receiving Title I funds to administer a single accountability system for the entire state, the accountability system used to fulfill NCLB mandates must also fulfill the requirements of the state education clause. Moreover, as NCLB mandated accountability systems are policies directly tied to increasing student performance in specific relation to state standards, it would make sense for a court to order states to implement these accountability systems effectively under a state education clause. As opposed to other possible state policies, such as a class size reduction policy, NCLB accountability systems are built to ensure that students receive the level of education specifically defined by state standards. Such an accountability system would also relieve a court from delving too deeply into technical matters of education policy by increasing the flow of information about student and school performance, and automatically triggering responses for insufficient performance. Finally, ordering a state to implement NCLB effectively would relieve the court from crafting a new solution to the problems plaguing a state's education system. In this case, a court would simply order a state to implement effectively a comprehensive education policy that the state had adopted but failed to implement effectively thus far.

Accordingly, a court using the NCLB Adequacy Approach could order a state to remedy specific problems that have plagued NCLB's implementation. While there are several types of problems that a court could potentially examine, a few major types of problems stand out. A court could examine the extent to which NCLB mandates regarding standards and accountability are underfunded and order a state to ensure that these mandates are sufficiently funded. Without such funding, it would be difficult to claim that a state's accountability mechanisms are fulfilling the constitutional goal of providing students with an adequate education. Moreover, a court could order a state to provide districts with more technical assistance to implement testing and accountability provisions if such assistance is needed. Without technical assistance, many districts (such as Reading) are having trouble implementing NCLB testing and accountability provisions. If more technical assistance could help districts implement NCLB more effectively, the order to provide more assistance would constitute a well-targeted remedy to the problems that states face implementing NCLB.

Following similar reasoning, a court could examine the extent to which a state's testing practices are valid. ...Similarly, a court could order a state to use criterion-referenced tests in situations where psychometric standards indicate that such use would result in more valid interpretations of data. Without the use of such tests, NCLB accountability systems also may not yield justifiable results. This list of problems that courts could address in regard to the validity of NCLB testing practices is certainly not exhaustive, and a court would have to consider in each case which problems apply and need to be addressed. Without such consideration, there would be little assurance that NCLB accountability measures flow from unacceptable student and school performance, and fulfill their purpose of providing students with an adequate education.

By using the NCLB Adequacy Approach to address NCLB implementation problems, courts would be well positioned to avoid the major hurdles that have thus far emerged in the cases that have targeted NCLB. ...Moreover, the specific language of somewhat deferential provisions would not prevent a court from ordering changes in NCLB's implementation. In order to ensure that NCLB testing practices are valid and are hence aimed at providing students with an adequate education as defined by state standards, a court could rule that such tests are required under the state education clause instead of under the native language testing provision. Without such tests, a state may not be able to fulfill its goal of implementing an effective testing and accountability system and thereby providing all students with an adequate education. Similarly, courts could avoid the Unfunded Mandates Provision and instead rule that the education clause requires states to fund NCLB testing and accountability mandates more fully. Without sufficient funds, a state also cannot implement an effective testing and accountability system to fulfill the requirements of the state education clause. Indeed, as the basic logic of adequacy has traditionally allowed courts to address educational entities' capacities to provide students with an adequate education, the approach taken in third wave school finance cases appears to constitute a natural legal response to the underlying capacity problems NCLB has experienced.

Notes and Comments

1. NCLB and Special Education Students

What responsibilities does NCLB impose on state educators as to special education students? In *State of Connecticut v. Spellings*, 549 F. Supp. 2d 161 (D. CT. 2008) State education officials sought to exempt learning disabled and special education students from the testing requirements of NCLB. Under their proposal, testing under NCLB would assess some special education students at instructional, rather than grade, level and exempt entirely recently arrived learning disabled students from testing for three years. The U.S. Department of Education did not allow the change and the court upheld the decision:

> The very clear message of Congress in the text of the Act was that States should apply the same academic standards to all students—including special education students, who were a particular focus of congressional interest. The Act could not be clearer and nothing about the structure of its provisions suggests otherwise.

549 F. Supp. 2d, at 174.

2. NCLB, Federal Funding and the "Unfunded Mandates Provision"

Soon after its passage, state and local school officials began to complain that NCLB did not adequately fund its requirements. The controversy on this issue is fueled, in part, by the provisions of NCLB. 20 U.S.C. § 6321(b)(1) provides that States may use federal funds made available under NCLB "only to supplement the funds that would, in the absence of such Federal funds, be made available from non-Federal sources for the education of pupils participating in programs assisted under this part, and not to supplant such funds." However, 20 U.S.C. § 7907(a) also provides that, "[n]othing in this Act shall be construed to . . . mandate a State or any subdivision thereof to spend any funds or incur any costs not paid for under this Act."

In *City of Pontiac v. U. S. Department of Education*, 512 F. 3d 252 (6th Cir. 2006), state and local officials from the State of Michigan filed suit to argue that NCLB should not require school districts to comply with NCLB educational requirements if doing so would require the expenditure of state and local funds to cover the additional costs of compliance. The Sixth Circuit agreed,

> [S]tatutes enacted under the Spending Clause of the United States Constitution must provide clear notice to the States of their liabilities should they decide to accept federal funding under those statutes... [A] State official deciding to participate in NCLB could reasonably read § 7907(a) to mean that her State need not comply with requirements that are "not paid for under the Act" through federal funds. Thus, Congress has not spoken so clearly that we can fairly say that the State[s] could make an informed choice to participate in the Act with the knowledge that they would have to comply with the Act's requirements regardless of federal funding. 512 F. 3d at 255, 272.

The Sixth Circuit later vacated the decision and agreed to rehear the appeal en banc. (*City of Pontiac v. U. S. Department of Education*, 2008 U.S. App. LEXIS 12121 (6th Cir. May 1, 2008)).

3. NCLB and Teacher Certification Standards
States receiving funding under NCLB are required to enforce newer and tougher standards upon teachers. In *Forte v. Hughes*, 2009 U.S. Dist. LEXIS 7854 (CT. 2008), Connecticut public school teachers filed suit to challenge the enforcement of tougher standards in math and science classes. The court dismissed the case, noting, "The Court cannot say, though, that it was unreasonable for the DOE to impose newer, more rigorous standards for the attainment of a 029 endorsement, especially considering that the federal government had imposed more stringent standards upon state school systems." 2009 U.S. Dist. LEXIS 7854 at *20.

4. NCLB and Scholarly Criticism
See Thomas Rentschler: *No Child Left Behind: Admirable Goals, Disastrous Outcomes*, 12 Widener L. Rev. 637 (2006) ("NCLB ignores many facets in education that make the mandated goal of having virtually all children being rated as "proficient" and at their grade level by the 2013-2014 school year virtually impossible."). *See also* Michael Heise: *The Unintended Legal and Policy Consequences of the No Child Left Behind Act*, 86 Neb. L. Rev. 119 (2007) ("[S]chool finance activists increasingly rely on NCLB-generated evidence to support lawsuits demanding increased school spending. [And] some states have diluted their student performance requirements to blunt the threat of NCLB-related sanctions.").

Table of Cases

A

A.K. *ex rel.* J.K. v. Alexandria City Sch. Bd 650
Acevedo v. Monsignor Donovan High School 531
Ambach v. Norwick 509
Axson-Flynn v. Johnson 770

B

Bethel School District No. 403 v. Fraser 7, 679
Board of Ed of Hendrick Hudson Central School District v. Rowley 626
Board of Education v. Earls 307
Board of Education v. Pico 1
Board of Regents v. Roth .... 263, passim
Board. of Education v. Rowley 4, 624
Board of Regents v. Southworth 752
Bradshaw v. Rawlings 909
Broward County Sch Bd v. Ruiz 855
Brown v. Bd. of Education .... 46, passim
BRV, Inc. v. Superior Court 365

C

Cain v. Horne 138
Cannon v. University of Chicago 549
Catapult Learning, L.L.C. v. Board of Education 122
Cedar Rapids Community School District v. Garret F. *ex rel.* Charlene F 636
Chalifoux v. New Caney 761
Chi Iota Colony of Alpha Epsilon Pi Fraternity v. CUNY 742
Christian Legal Society v. Martinez 701
Christian Legal Society v. Walker 710
City of Pontiac v. U. S. Department of Education 932
Clausing v. San Francisco Unified School District 891
Cleveland Bd of Education v. Loudermill 267
Cobb v. O'Connell 35
Collins v. City of Harker Heights 820
Ct. Office of Protection and Advocacy for Persons with Disabilities v. Hartford Bd. of Ed 373

D

D.R. *ex rel.* L.R. v. Middle Bucks Area Vocational Technical School 831
Davis *ex rel.* Lashonda D. v. Monroe County Board of Education 561
Doe *ex rel.* Doe v. Hawaii Department of Education 826
Doe v. Hillsboro Independent School District 840
Doe v. Superintendent of Schools of Stoughton 245
Doe v. Taylor Indep. Sch. Dist 837
Doninger v. Niehoff 256
Donohue v. Copiague Union Free School District 921

E

Edwards v. Aguillard 784
Endrew F. v. Douglas County School District 631
Epperson v. Arkansas 2
Equity in Athletics, Inc. v. U.S. Department of Education 592
Everson v. Board of Education 778

F

Fallon v. Indian Trail School 869
Fields v. Palmdale School District 57
Fitzgerald v. Barnstable School Committee 573
Forte v. Hughes 933
Franklin v. Gwinnett County Public Schools 553
Freeman v. Busch 910

Freeman v. Pitts 471
Fuller *ex rel.* Fuller v. Decatur Public School Board 218

G

Gebser v. Lago Vista Independent School District 557
Gibbons v. Orleans Parish School Board 859
Givhan v. Western Line Consolidated School District 725
Gonzaga University v. Doe 357
Good News Club v. Milford Cent. Schools 788
Goss v. Lopez ..... 212, passim
Griggs *ex rel.* Griggs v. Ft. Wayne School Board 688
Grutter v. Bollinger 492

H

Hazelwood School District v. Kuhlmeier 682
Hearn v. Board of Public Education 337
Honig v. Doe 654
Hootch v. Alaska State-Operated School System 195
Hunter v. Board of Education 920

I

In re F.B 413
In re Lunn 818
Ingraham v. Wright ..... 808, pasim

J

J.C. v. Beverly Hills Sch. Dist. 252
J.D.B. v. North Carolina ..... 419, passim
J.S. v. Bethlehem Area Sch. Dist. 256
Jackson v. Birmingham Board of Education 579
James v. Alabama Coalition for Equity, Inc 198
Jeglin v. San Jacinto Unified School District 678
Jensen v. Reeves 375
Johnson v. Dallas Independent School District 830
Justice v. Peachtree City 302

K

Kadrmas v. Dickinson Public Schools 170
Kaltenberge v. Ohio College of Podiatric Medicine 619
Kern v. Univ. of Osteopathic Medicine and Health Sciences 619
King v. Northeast Security, Inc 894
Knox County Education Association v Knox County Board of Education 355
Kukor v. Grover 180

L

L.R. v. School District of Philadelphia 843
Lake View Sch. Dist. No. 25 v. Huckabee 200
Lamb's Chapel v. Center Moriches Union Free School Dist ..... 805, passim
Lee v. University of Michigan 243
Lee v. Weisman 791
Littlefield v. Forney Independent School District 767

M

Mackey *ex rel.* Thomas M. v. Bd. of Educ. for Arlington Central Sch Dist. 651
Madden v. Ind. DOT 883
Martinez v. Bynum 507
Mayer v. Monroe County Community School Corp 727
McClure v. Fairfield University 903
McCormick *ex rel.* McCormick v. School District of Mamaroneck 582
Meeker v. Edmundson 823
Mendoza v. State 30
Miller v. Loyola University 914
Milliken v. Bradley ..... 481, passim
Mississippi University for Women v. Hogan 519
Morse v. Frederick ..... 685, passim

Mt. Healthy City School District Board of Education v. Doyle 721
Murrell v. School District No. 1 568

N

National Law Center on Homelessness and Poverty v. New York 534
New Jersey v. T. L. O. .... 282, passim
Newark Parents Assn v. Newark Schools..923

O

Owasso Independent School District No.I-011 v. Falvo .... 361, passim

P

Parents Involved in Community Schools v.Seattle School District No. 1 498
People v. Bennett...101
Pi Lambda Phi Fraternity, Inc. v. University of Pittsburgh 747
Pierce v. Society of Sisters ....60, passim
Plyler v. Doe .... 164, passim
Protection & Advocacy System, Inc. v. Freudenthal 383

R

Racine Charter One, Inc. v. Racine Unified School District.................................... 124
Rogers v. Helena-West Helena School District 24
Rose v. Council for Better Education, Inc... 188
Rumsfeld v. Forum for Academic & Institutional Rights, Inc 52

S

S.S. v. Eastern Kentucky University 887
Safford Unified School District v. Redding ....286, passim
San Antonio Independent School District v. Rodriguez ....148, passim
Santa Fe Independent School District v.Doe 790
Saylor v. Board of Education 813
School Bd. of Nassau County v. Arline.. 603
Segal v. City of New York 271
Serrano v. Priest (1971).................................. 174
Serrano v. Priest (1976).................................. 177
Simonetti *ex rel.* Simonetti v. School District of Philadelphia..............................860
Snethen v. Board of Education 893
Southworth v. Board of Regents.......................756
Stevenson *ex rel.* Stevenson v. Martin County Board of Education 902

T

T.S. v. State 296
The Trustees of Schools v. People *ex rel.* Van Allen 58
Theodore v. Del. Valley Sch. Dist. 322
Tinker v. Des Moines Indep. Cmty. Sch. Dist .... 674, passim

U

United States v. Lopez...................................... 48
University of Colorado v. Derdeyn 332
U. S. v. Virginia... 511
Utah School Boards Association v. Utah State Board of Education.............................37

V

Vernonia School District 47J v. James Acton .... 304, passim
Villanueva v. Carere...482

W

West Virginia Board of Education v. Hechler 26
West Virginia State Board of Education v. Barnette 672
Whalen v. Roe 361
Wilson v. Cahokia Sch. Dist. # 187..................300
Wisconsin v. Yoder .... 63, passim

Z

Zelman v. Simmons-Harris...............................133
Zorach v. Clauson 782

INDEX

[References are to Pages.]

A

Academic Freedom
Generally 17
Educational Malpractice 914
Free Speech
.... 721-736
Faculty Speech 721
Judicial Deference in light of 2
Affirmative Action
K thru 12 498
Higher education 492
Affirmative Duties
Substantive Due Process 830
Common Law Torts 855
Alternative Schools
Parental Rights 101
Property Interest 211
Discretion of Educator to assign 225
Alienage Discrimination
Generally 504
Students 504
Faculty and Staff 509
At-will Employees 212; 263; 721
Athletics
Title IX 545
Americans with Disabilities Act (ADA)
Generally 599
Compared with IDEA 603; 650

B

Bullying 234; 240; 403; 701; 835

C

Charter Schools 121
Colleges and Universities
Affirmative Action 492
Gender Discrimination 511; 545
Military Recruiting 52
Faculty Rights 263; 721
Searches and Seizures 332
Privacy, FERPA 332; 357
HIPAA 383
Student Speech 701; 742; 770
Religion 638; 640
Liability 767
Commerce Clause
As a basis for Federal Law 48
Compelled Association 752
Corporal Punishment 807
Curriculum
and Home Schools 101
and Parents' Rights 77; 133
Columbine
.... 377; 402; 688; 854

D

Defenses to Liability
Substantive Due Process 807
Common Law 855
Deference to Educators
.... 2; 14; 17; 276; 316
Deliberate Indifference 556; 830
Discipline
Students 211; 245; 282; 311; 679
Faculty and 263; 721
Restorative Justice 232
Discrimination
Generally 471
Class of One 124
Race 471
Alienage 504
Gender 511
Age 531
Homeless 534
Title IX 545
Sexual Preference 81; 540
Drug Testing
Students 304
Faculty 337

E

Expressive Association 748
Expulsion
.... 211; 218; 220; 232; 260; 444; 699
Extracurricular Activities
.... .76; 241; 304; 307; 323; 699; 752
Education Malpractice 914
Education Record
FERPA 357
HIPAA 383

F

Faculty Rights
Generally 263
Privacy 337
Free Speech 721
Family Educational Rights and Privacy Act (FERPA) 357
Federal Funding
Affecting Free Speech 52
FERPA 357
HIPAA 383
Safe and Drug Free 407
Federal Laws
Generally 43
School Safety 407
Military Recruiting 52
Fourth Amendment 281
Fifth Amendment 419
First Amendment
.... 671; 679; 701; 721; 741; 761
Fourteenth Amendment
Due Process .... .211; 807
Equal Protection of the Laws 471
Fraternities and Sororities
Right of Association 742
Religion 748
Freedom of Association
Intimate Association 742
Expressive Association 748
Compelled Association 752
Free Exercise of Religion 761
Fundamental Rights
Freedom of Association 741
Free Speech 671
Religion 761
Privacy 281
Interrogations 418
Education as a 147
Federal Constitution 148
State Constitutions 173

G

Gangs and Drugs 218; 417; 679; 763
Gender Discrimination 511; 545
Guns on Campus 48; 282; 401

H

Harassment
.... 557; 697; 840; 884; 887
Health Insurance Portability and Accountability Act (HIPAA) 383
Higher Education. See Colleges and Universities
Home Schooling 101
Homeless Students 534
Hybrid Rights 775

I

Immunity 282; 303; 448; 460; 736
In loco Parentis 10; 57; 99; 908
Interrogations 419
Intimate Association 742
Individuals with Disabilities Education Act (IDEA)
Generally 599
Compared with ADA 652
Stay 654
Related 648
Burden of Proof 654

J

Judicial System
Deference to 2

L

Legislative Authority 19
Liability
Generally 807
Substantive Due Process 808
Common Law 855
Deliberate 823
Bullying 403

Strict Liability 869; 875; 878; 880
Federal Statutory 884
State Statutory 891
Colleges and Universities 903
Educational Malpractice 914
No Child Left Behind 926
Negligence 855
Local Government and Education 24

M

Migrant Students 534
Miranda Warnings 419

N

Negligence 855
No Child Left Behind 926

P

Parental Rights
Generally 58
Home Schools 101
Charter Schools 121
Voucher Programs 133
Private Schools
Generally 58
Home Schools 101
Religion 60; 133
Privacy
Generally 281
FERPA 357
HIPAA 383
Students 282; 311
Faculty and Staff 337
Procedural Due Process 211; 245; 263
Public Forum Doctrine 682

R

Race Discrimination 471
Religion
Free Exercise 761
Establishment 778
Voucher Programs 786
Right to an Education 147; 173

S

Sexual Harassment 557; 697; 840; 889
Section 504 of the Rehabilitation Act
.... 603; 620; 622; 652; 887
Secret Service Report on Columbine 402
Separation of Powers 24
Sex Education 77
Sexual Orientation 52; 81; 540; 701
School Finance Litigation
Generally 161
Federal Litigation 148
State Litigation 174
School Safety
Generally 401
Statutory Reform 407
Bullying 403
Drug Testing 304
Interrogations 419
School Resource Officers
.... 410; 427; 442; 447
Searches and Seizures 237
State Laws 2
School Vouchers 133; 145; 804
Searches and Seizures
Generally 281
Students 282
Faculty and Staff 337
Solomon Amendment 45
State Constitutions
Education as a Fundamental Right 147
State Statutes
Arkansas Statutes 2
California Statutes 16; 353
Colorado Statutes 20
District of Columbia Ordinances
.... 115; 409; 538
Florida Statutes 179; 341; 380; 410
Nevada Statutes 21
West Virginia Statutes 22
Stayput Provisions 653; 670
Strict Liability 869; 875; 878; 880
Strip Searches 286; 291; 302

Student Fees 38; 61; 139; 141; 505; 706; 741
Student Organizations.................... 701; 710; 714
Substantive Due Process 830
Suicide.. 240; 402; 403
Suspensions 211

T

Teachers Rights
Due Process.. 263
Free Speech.. 721
Privacy 337
Title IX.. 549
Title IX
Generally... 545
Remedies... 549
Harassment.. 556
Athletics 580

Z

Zero Tolerance........................... 51; 220; 232; 260

CPSIA information can be obtained
at www.ICGtesting.com
Printed in the USA
BVHW092357060522
636276BV00008B/131